HILTON | HERAUF

EDITION

MODERN ADVANCED
ACCOUNTING
IN CANADA

Murray W. Hilton
Darrell Herauf

McGraw-Hill
Ryerson
Connect. Learn. Succeed.

Modern Advanced Accounting in Canada
Sixth Edition

ISBN-13: 978-0-07-000153-4
ISBN-10: 0-07-000153-7

6 7 8 9 0 DOW 1 9 8 7 6 5 4 3 2

Printed and bound in the United States

Vice-President and Editor-in-Chief: Joanna Cotton
Executive Editor: Rhondda McNabb
Executive Marketing Manager: Joy Armitage Taylor
Developmental Editor: Rachel Horner
Permissions Editor: Amy Rydzanicz
Editorial Associate: Jennifer Clark
Copy Editor: Julia Cochrane
Proofreader: Deborah Cooper-Bullock
Production Coordinator: Sharon Stefanowicz
Supervising Editor: Kara Stahl
Cover Design: Greg Devitt Design
Cover Image Credit: ©Rob Little Photography
Interior Design: Michelle Losier
Page Layout: Aptara, Inc.®
Printer: RR Donnelley

Library and Archives Canada Cataloguing in Publication

Hilton, Murray W.
        Modern advanced accounting in Canada / Murray W. Hilton, Darrell Herauf. — 6th ed.

Includes index.
ISBN 978-0-07-000153-4

        1. Accounting—Canada—Textbooks. I. Herauf, Darrell II. Title.

HF5635.H486 2010   657'.046   C2009-906964-4

Murray W. Hilton, FCA

Murray Hilton holds the rank of Senior Scholar at the University of Manitoba where he has continued to teach in the MBA programs since his retirement in 2002. For thirty-five years he was Professor of Accounting at the university's Asper School of Business, teaching graduate and undergraduate courses in financial accounting. A Chartered Accountant with business degrees from the University of Saskatchewan and Oregon State University, he has published five advanced accounting books. In addition, he has been active in university and faculty administration, having previously served as Head of the Department of Accounting and Finance and as Director of the Master of Accountancy Program. He is currently the Director of the Centre for Accounting Research and Education. Murray has also been very involved in the accounting profession, teaching CA and CMA courses for many years, and serving on numerous national and provincial committees of both accounting bodies. He has on two separate occasions been a member of the National Examination Board of the Society of Management Accountants of Canada. In 1991, he received the FCA designation from the Institute of Chartered Accountants of Manitoba, and in 1994 he was made an honorary member of the Society of Management Accountants of Manitoba. For relaxation, he enjoys reading, golfing, and fishing.

Darrell Herauf, CA, CGA

Darrell Herauf teaches graduate and undergraduate courses in financial and managerial accounting at the Eric Sprott School of Business, Carleton University. A Chartered Accountant and a Certified General Accountant with a business degree from the University of Saskatchewan, this co-author of *Modern Advanced Accounting in Canada* is also the author of testbanks for several financial accounting textbooks. He is the recipient of numerous teaching awards, and participates on many committees at the university. Darrell has been involved in professional accounting education at the Institute of Chartered Accountants of Ontario for over 20 years in a variety of roles, including teaching, developing case/program material, and serving as a member of the Examinations subcommittee. For more than 15 years, he has been involved with the Certified General Accountants Association of Canada as national examiner, course author, and consultant. For relaxation, he enjoys cycling and skating.

Contents in Brief

Preface   xii

Prologue   xix

CHAPTER 1   A Survey of International Accounting   1

CHAPTER 2   Investments in Equity Securities   39

CHAPTER 3   Business Combinations   71

CHAPTER 4   Consolidated Statements on Date of Acquisition   120

CHAPTER 5   Consolidation Subsequent to Acquisition Date   170

CHAPTER 6   Intercompany Inventory and Land Profits   248

CHAPTER 7   (A) Intercompany Profits in Depreciable Assets

(B) Intercompany Bondholdings   308

CHAPTER 8   Consolidated Cash Flows and Ownership Issues   382

CHAPTER 9   Other Consolidation Reporting Issues   449

CHAPTER 10   Foreign-currency Transactions   516

CHAPTER 11   Translation and Consolidation of the Financial Statements of Foreign Operations   568

CHAPTER 12   Accounting for Not-for-profit Organizations and Governments   635

Credits   711

Index   713

Contents

Preface xii
Prologue xix

CHAPTER 1   A Survey of International Accounting   1
Learning Objectives   1
Introduction   1
A Survey of International Accounting   2
Factors that Can Influence a Country's Accounting Standards   3
Toward Accounting Harmonization and Convergence   5
Recent Initiatives from the European Union and Australia and
New Zealand   10
IFRSs versus U.S. GAAP   11
Where Is Canada Going?   15
A Unique Example that Presents a Comparison between Canadian GAAP
and IFRSs   21
Summary   22
Significant Changes in the Last Two Years   22
Changes Expected in the Next Three Years   22
Self-study Problem   23
Review Questions   26
Multiple-choice Questions   27
Cases   30
Problems   36
Web-based Problems   37

CHAPTER 2   Investments in Equity Securities   39
Learning Objectives   39
Introduction   39
Equity Investments — The Big Picture   40
Directly Related IFRSs   42
Other Related IFRSs   43
Investments Valued at Fair Value   45
Investments Not Valued at Fair Value   46
Cost Method of Reporting on Equity Investment   46
Equity Method of Reporting on Equity Investment   47
Illustration of Equity Method Basics   48
Additional Features Associated with the Equity Method   49
GAAP for Private Enterprises   54
U.S. GAAP Differences   56
Summary   56
Significant Changes in the Last Two Years   57
Changes Expected in the Next Three Years   57
Self-study Problem   57

Review Questions 59
Multiple-choice Questions 60
Cases 63
Problems 67
Web-based Problems 70

CHAPTER 3   Business Combinations 71
Learning Objectives 71
Introduction 71
Forms of Business Combinations 73
Methods of Accounting for Business Combinations 74
    Provisions of IFRS 3 76
Illustrations of Business Combination Accounting 79
    Purchase of Assets 80
Control and Consolidated Financial Statements 82
    GAAP for Private Enterprises 92
    U.S. GAAP Differences 93
Summary 93
    Significant Changes in the Last Two Years 93
    Changes Expected in the Next Three Years 94
Self-study Problem 94
Appendix 3A: Reverse Takeovers 95
Review Questions 100
Multiple-choice Questions 100
Cases 104
Problems 109
Web-based Problems 118

CHAPTER 4   Consolidated Statements on Date of Acquisition 120
Learning Objectives 120
Introduction 120
Consolidation of Wholly Owned Subsidiaries 121
    100-Percent Ownership 121
Consolidation of Non-wholly Owned Subsidiaries 131
Introduction to Consolidation Theories 132
    Proprietary Theory 133
    Entity Theory 133
    Parent Company Theory 139
    Parent Company Extension Theory 140
Contingent Consideration 140
    GAAP for Private Enterprises 144
    U.S. GAAP Differences 144
Summary 146
    Significant Changes in the Last Two Years 146
    Changes Expected in the Next Three Years 146
Self-study Problem 147
Review Questions 148
Multiple-choice Questions 149

Cases   152
Problems   160
Web-based Problems   169

CHAPTER 5   Consolidation Subsequent to Acquisition Date   170
Learning Objectives   170
Introduction   170
Methods of Accounting for an Investment in a Subsidiary   171
Consolidated Income and Retained Earnings Statements   173
Testing Goodwill and Other Intangibles for Impairment   175
    Intangible Assets with Definite Useful Lives   176
    Intangible Assets with Indefinite Useful Lives   177
    Cash-generating Units and Goodwill   177
    Reversing an Impairment Loss   179
    Disclosure Requirements   180
Consolidation of a 100-Percent-Owned Subsidiary   183
    Consolidated Statements, End of Year 1   184
    Consolidated Statements, End of Year 2   187
Consolidation of an 80-Percent-Owned Subsidiary — Direct Approach   191
    Consolidated Statements, End of Year 1   192
    Consolidated Statements, End of Year 2   195
Acquisition Differential Assigned to Liabilities   198
Intercompany Receivables and Payables   201
Subsidiary Acquired during the Year   201
Equity Method of Recording   202
    GAAP for Private Enterprises   204
    U.S. GAAP Differences   204
Summary   205
    Significant Changes in the Last Two Years   206
    Changes Expected in the Next Three Years   206
Self-study Problem   206
Appendix 5A: Preparing Consolidated Financial Statements Using the
    Working Paper Approach   211
Review Questions   220
Multiple-choice Questions   221
Cases   226
Problems   233
Web-based Problems   247

CHAPTER 6   Intercompany Inventory and Land Profits   248
Learning Objectives   248
Introduction   248
Intercompany Revenue and Expenses   249
    Intercompany Sales and Purchases   249
    Other Examples of Intercompany Revenue and Expenses   251
Intercompany Profits in Assets   252
    Intercompany Inventory Profits: Subsidiary Selling (Upstream Transactions)   253
    Intercompany Inventory Profits: Parent Selling (Downstream Transactions)   263

Losses on Intercompany Transactions 266
Intercompany Land Profit Holdback 267
Realization of Intercompany Land Profits 268
Intercompany Transfer Pricing 271
GAAP for Private Enterprises 272
U.S. GAAP Differences 272
Summary 272
Significant Changes in the Last Two Years 273
Changes Expected in the Next Three Years 273
Self-study Problem 274
Review Questions 279
Multiple-choice Questions 280
Cases 285
Problems 292
Web-based Problems 306

CHAPTER 7   (A) Intercompany Profits in Depreciable Assets
(B) Intercompany Bondholdings 308
Learning Objectives 308
Introduction 308
(A) Intercompany Profits in Depreciable Assets 309
Holdback and Realization — Year 1 309
Realization of Remaining Gain — Year 2 314
Comparison of Realization of Inventory and Equipment Profits over a
Two-year Period 319
(B) Intercompany Bondholdings 320
Intercompany Bondholdings — No Gain or Loss 321
Intercompany Bondholdings — With Gain or Loss 322
Calculation of the Portion of the Gain Allocated to the Affiliates 324
Accounting for Gain in Subsequent Years 329
Less Than 100 Percent Purchase of Affiliate's Bonds 336
Intercompany Purchases during the Fiscal Year 336
Gains (Losses) Not Allocated to the Two Equities 337
Gains (Losses) Allocated to Two Equities — Loss to One, Gain to the
Other 337
Effective-Yield Method of Amortization 338
GAAP for Private Enterprises 340
U.S. GAAP Differences 340
Summary 340
Significant Changes in the Last Two Years 341
Changes Expected in the Next Three Years 341
Self-study Problem 1 341
Self-study Problem 2 345
Appendix 7A: Depreciable Assets under Revaluation Model 350
Review Questions 351
Multiple-choice Questions 353
Cases 357

Problems   363
Web-based Problems   380

CHAPTER 8   Consolidated Cash Flows and Ownership Issues   382
                Learning Objectives   382
                Introduction   382
                Consolidated Cash Flow Statement   383
                    Preparing the Consolidated Cash Flow Statement   385
                Changes in Parent's Ownership Interest   387
                    Block Acquisitions of Subsidiary (Step Purchases)   387
                    Parent Sells Some of Its Holdings in Subsidiary   398
                    Income Statement Analysis   399
                Subsidiary Issues Additional Shares to Public   401
                Subsidiary with Preferred Shares Outstanding   404
                    Illustration — Preferred Shareholdings   404
                    Other Types of Preferred Shares   406
                    Subsidiary Preferred Shares Owned by Parent   407
                Indirect Shareholdings   408
                    GAAP for Private Enterprises   412
                    U.S. GAAP Differences   413
                Summary   414
                    Significant Changes in the Last Two Years   414
                    Changes Expected in the Next Three Years   414
                Self-study Problem   415
                Review Questions   417
                Multiple-choice Questions   418
                Cases   423
                Problems   429
                Web-based Problems   447

CHAPTER 9   Other Consolidation Reporting Issues   449
                Learning Objectives   449
                Introduction   449
                Special-purpose Entities   450
                Joint Arrangements   460
                    Accounting for Joint Operations   462
                    Accounting for an Interest in a Joint Venture   464
                    Contributions to the Joint Venture   466
                Deferred Income Taxes and Business Combinations   471
                    Deferred Income Tax Concepts   471
                    Business Combination Illustrations   473
                    Operating Loss Carry-forwards   475
                Segment Disclosures   476
                    IFRS 8: Operating Segments   477
                    Identification of Reportable Operating Segments   477
                    GAAP for Private Enterprises   483
                    U.S. GAAP Differences   483

Summary   484
   Significant Changes in the Last Two Years   484
   Changes Expected in the Next Three Years   485
Self-study Problem   485
Appendix 9A: Reporting an Interest in a Joint Venture Using Proportionate
   Consolidation   490
Review Questions   493
Multiple-choice Questions   494
Cases   498
Problems   504
Web-based Problems   514

CHAPTER 10   Foreign-currency Transactions   516
Learning Objectives   516
Introduction   516
Currency Exchange Rates   517
Accounting for Foreign-currency Transactions   519
   Import/Export Transactions Denominated in Foreign Currency   523
   Transaction Gains and Losses from Non-current Monetary Items   526
Speculative Forward Exchange Contracts   527
Hedges   530
   Hedging a Recognized Monetary Item   532
   Hedging an Unrecognized Firm Commitment   535
   Hedging a Forecasted Transaction   539
   GAAP for Private Enterprises   546
   U.S. GAAP Differences   547
Summary   547
   Significant Changes in the Last Two Years   547
   Changes Expected in the Next Three Years   548
Self-study Problem 1   548
Self-study Problem 2   550
Appendix 10A: Determining the Fair Value of Forward Exchange Contracts   551
Review Questions   552
Multiple-choice Questions   553
Cases   557
Problems   560
Web-based Problems   567

CHAPTER 11   Translation and Consolidation of the Financial Statements of Foreign
   Operations   568
Learning Objectives   568
Introduction   568
Accounting Exposure versus Economic Exposure   569
Translation Methods   571
   The Temporal Method   571
   The Current Rate Method   572
Translation under IAS 21   573
   Unit of Measure   577

Illustration of Translation and Consolidation 577
    Translation and Consolidation Subsequent to Acquisition 579
    Comparative Observations of the Two Translation Methods 588
    Complications with an Acquisition Differential 588
    Other Considerations 595
    GAAP for Private Enterprises 599
    U.S. GAAP Differences 599
Summary 599
    Significant Changes in the Last Two Years 600
    Changes Expected in the Next Three Years 600
Self-study Problem 600
Review Questions 605
Multiple-choice Questions 606
Cases 611
Problems 618
Web-based Problems 634

CHAPTER 12   Accounting for Not-for-profit Organizations and Governments 635
Learning Objectives 635
Introduction 635
The Basics of Fund Accounting 636
Not-for-profit Reporting Today 639
    Financial Statements 647
Accounting for Contributions 649
    The Deferral Method 649
    The Restricted Fund Method 650
Net Assets Invested in Capital Assets 651
    The Restricted Fund Method 652
    The Deferral Method 654
Donated Capital Assets, Materials, and Services 656
Budgetary Control and Encumbrances 658
Illustration of the Restricted Fund Method 660
Illustration of the Deferral Method 667
Summary 675
    Significant Changes in the Last Two Years 675
    Changes Expected in the Next Three Years 676
Self-study Problem 676
Appendix 12A: Sample Financial Statements 678
Appendix 12B: Accounting for Governments 680
Summary 684
Review Questions 684
Multiple-choice Questions 685
Cases 691
Problems 697
Web-based Problems 709

Credits 711

Index 713

Preface

Welcome to the sixth edition of *Modern Advanced Accounting in Canada*. This book's well-deserved reputation for being the most current, concise, and technically accurate advanced accounting text on the market has not only been maintained but has been improved upon in this new edition. This edition is 100 percent compliant with International Financial Reporting Standards (IFRSs), not only with regard to the typical advanced accounting topics of business combinations and foreign currency transactions, but also in terms of intermediate accounting topics. It also contains the reporting requirements for private enterprises and not-for-profit organizations.

The book reflects standards that are expected to be in effect as of January 1, 2011, the date that publicly accountable enterprises in Canada must start using IFRSs and private companies must start using the new standards for private enterprises. We have made every effort to illustrate and explain the requirements of the current standards at the time of publication, anticipating how these might change, what the effects of the changes will be, and what they will mean to the industry, professionals, and students.

We have also continued the presentation of advanced accounting topics that has been so well received by such a large number of instructors and students. Emphasis on the direct approach of preparing consolidated financial statements along with the "building block" development of the basics of consolidations has been maintained and strengthened. The working-paper approach is illustrated in Chapters 3 through 5, either in the body of the chapter or in the appendices.

Finally, as requested by instructors on behalf of their students, the following enhancements to problem material have been made in this edition:

- At least one new case has been added to each chapter to encourage critical thinking and classroom discussion. There are now four to six cases in each chapter.

- Two web-based problems have been added to each chapter. These problems involve the analysis and interpretation of the published financial statements of public companies and not-for-profit organizations.

- One new self-study problem has been added to three chapters, such that each chapter now has one or two self-study problems.

- The questions and/or solutions have been revised for approximately 40 percent of the end-of-chapter material.

- Finally, even more problems and questions can be found online for additional study at www.mcgrawhillconnect.ca.

New Features

- Much more attention is given to financial statement disclosure in the body of each chapter. The IFRS disclosure requirements are summarized, followed by a real-life example from a public company or a not-for-profit organization.

- Chapter 2 no longer contains detailed examples involving amortization of the acquisition differential and unrealized profits from intercompany transactions.

Accounting for these items under the equity method is explained in later chapters, after the consolidation adjustments have been explained in detail.

- Chapters 5 and 6 from the fifth edition have been combined into one chapter to emphasize that consolidated financial statements are the same regardless of whether the parent uses the cost method or equity method to account for its investment in its internal records. Detailed illustrations are provided under the cost method. Journal entries under the equity method are provided once the consolidation adjustments have been thoroughly explained.

- Non-controlling interest is now presented as a component of shareholders' equity in the consolidated balance sheet, and consolidated net income is now defined to include both the controlling and non-controlling shareholders' share of this net income.

- Although the titles and format of financial statements as recommended by the IASB are used throughout the text, it is not the only format used. The titles and format used by Canadian companies prior to the adoption of IFRSs are used in approximately half of the problems and illustrations on the assumption that many Canadian companies will continue to use the same titles and format that they have used in the past.

- The term "purchase discrepancy" has been replaced with "acquisition differential" to better reflect the principles involved with the acquisition method. In calculating the acquisition differential, most illustrations now use the net book value of identifiable net assets (i.e., assets less liabilities), rather than shareholders' equity of the subsidiary.

- Major reorganization and rewriting has been done for the materials in Chapters 1, 2, 5, and 9.

The following sections are provided at the end of all relevant chapters:

- *GAAP for Private Enterprises.* This section highlights the differences in GAAP between private enterprises and publicly accountable enterprises. There are sufficient illustrations throughout the text for the user of the text to know and apply both sets of GAAP.

- *U.S. GAAP Differences.* This section highlights the differences in GAAP between IFRS and U.S. GAAP. Since the IASB and the FASB are working to converge their standards over the next few years, it is important to know where the differences lie so that we can anticipate where changes in IFRSs are likely to be made.

- *Significant Changes in the Last Two Years.* This section lists the IFRSs covered in the chapter along with their counterparts from the former sections of the *CICA Handbook*. It also summarizes the major changes in GAAP since the publication of the fifth edition of the text.

- *Changes Expected in the Next Three Years.* This section summarizes the changes expected in IFRSs in the next few years based on the projects currently on the IASB's work plan.

Organization

Chapter 1 is a survey of international accounting practices. It now includes a listing of countries requiring or permitting the use of IFRSs for listed companies. Some of the major differences between IFRSs and U.S. GAAP are identified, and the convergence project between the FASB and the IASB to harmonize their accounting standards is described. The transition of accounting standards for private enterprises is also discussed. A new self-study problem on U.S. GAAP differences has been added.

Chapter 2 commences with an overview of the CICA pronouncements that make up the "big picture." Readers are encouraged to revisit this "big picture" many times as consolidation topics are developed in later chapters so that they do not lose sight of the forest as they examine the myriad of details that make up the trees. The chapter continues with a comprehensive example to illustrate the fair value, cost, and equity methods of reporting investments in equity securities and concludes with a self-study problem. Coverage of the comprehensive example could be postponed until after Chapter 4 without breaking continuity or could be omitted altogether if it is felt that adequate coverage has occurred in previous intermediate accounting courses.

Chapter 3 discusses two forms of business combinations and four methods that have been proposed or used to account for business combinations in past years. The acquisition of assets and the acquisition of voting shares are used to illustrate the acquisition method of accounting for a business combination. The concept of control is discussed and used as the criterion for preparation of consolidated financial statements. Reverse takeovers are covered in an appendix.

Chapter 4 examines the preparation of consolidated financial statements as at the date a parent obtains control over a subsidiary. The direct and working-paper methods are both illustrated for 100-percent-owned subsidiaries, as well as for those that are less than 100-percent-owned. Four theories of consolidation are discussed and illustrated. All four theories are currently or have recently been required under Canadian GAAP. Accounting for contingent consideration is also illustrated.

Chapter 5 covers the preparation of consolidated financial statements subsequent to the date of acquisition when the parent uses the cost method in its internal records. The amortization and impairment of the acquisition differential is explained and illustrated including an application of the effective interest method. The parent's journal entries under the equity method are summarized. Ten basic steps in the preparation of consolidated statements are introduced, which form the foundation for the consolidation topics in the chapters that follow. The chapter concludes with a self-study problem using the direct approach. The appendix illustrates the working-paper approach for the same examples used throughout the chapter.

Chapter 6 deals with the elimination of intercompany revenues and expenses, as well as intercompany unrealized profits or losses in inventory and land. The income tax matching associated with the holdback and realization of intercompany profits forms an integral part of the discussions and illustrations. The consolidation adjustments when the entities use the revaluation model for reporting land are described. The chapter concludes with a comprehensive self-study problem using the direct approach.

Chapter 7 discusses the elimination of intercompany profits in depreciable assets, the recognition of gains or losses resulting from the elimination of intercompany bond-holdings, and the related income tax adjustments that are required. Two self-study problems are presented using the direct approach.

Chapter 8 discusses the preparation of the consolidated cash flow statement and such ownership issues as subsidiaries with preferred shares, step purchases, reduction of parent's interest, and indirect holdings. In all situations, the direct approach is used. The chapter concludes with a self-study problem involving preferred shares using the direct approach.

Chapter 9 examines other consolidation reporting issues, including special-purpose entities, deferred income taxes and business combinations, and segment disclosures. The accounting for joint arrangements is illustrated under both the equity method in the body of the chapter and under proportionate consolidation in the appendix. A new self-study problem on joint ventures has been added.

Chapter 10 introduces the topic of foreign currency and four different perspectives in which currencies can be viewed. Foreign currency transactions are discussed, as are the concepts of hedging and hedge accounting. The handling of foreign currency gains and losses is illustrated, as are the accounting for fair value and cash flow hedges. The appendix describes how discounting can be applied when determining the fair value of a forward contract.

Chapter 11 concludes the foreign currency portion of the text by examining and illustrating the translation and subsequent consolidation of subsidiaries whose functional currency is the same as the parent's (i.e., integrated subsidiary) and whose functional currency is not the same as the parent's (self-sustaining subsidiary). The reporting of exchange gains and losses from the translation of self-sustaining subsidiaries in other comprehensive income is also illustrated. The chapter concludes with a self-study problem to illustrate both the temporal and current-rate methods.

Chapter 12 discusses in depth the eight not-for-profit sections in the *CICA Handbook*. The chapter concludes with a comprehensive illustration of the required journal entries and the preparation of financial statements using both the deferral method and the restricted fund method. A new self-study problem involving the deferral method has been added. Appendix 13A provides a real-life example of the deferral method by reproducing the financial statements of the United Way/Centraide Ottawa. Appendix 13B provides a comprehensive outline of the PSAB reporting requirements for federal, provincial, and local governments.

McGraw-Hill Connect™

McGraw-Hill Connect™ (www.mcgrawhillconnect.ca): Developed in partnership with Youthography, a Canadian youth research company, and hundreds of students from across Canada, McGraw-Hill Connect™ embraces diverse study behaviours and preferences to maximize active learning and engagement.

With McGraw-Hill Connect™, students complete pre- and post-diagnostic assessments that identify knowledge gaps and point them to concepts they need to learn. McGraw-Hill Connect™ provides students the option to work through recommended learning exercises and create their own personalized study plan using multiple sources of content, including a searchable e-book, multiple-choice and true/false quizzes, chapter-by-chapter learning goals, personal notes, and more. Using the copy, paste, highlight and sticky note features, students collect, organize and customize their study plan content to optimize learning outcomes.

Instructor Resources: McGraw-Hill Connect™ assessment activities don't stop with students! There is material for instructors to leverage as well, including a personalized teaching plan where instructors can choose from a variety of quizzes to use in class, assign as homework, or add to exams. They can edit existing questions and add new ones; track individual student performance — by question, assignment, or in relation to the class overall — with detailed grade reports; integrate grade reports easily with Learning Management Systems such as WebCT and Blackboard; and much more.

Instructors can also browse or search teaching resources and text specific supplements and organize them into customizable categories. All the teaching resources are now located in one convenient place. These include:

- **Solutions Manual:** containing thorough, up-to-date solutions to the book's end-of-chapter material.
- **Testbank:** containing over 1,000 multiple-choice, true/false, and problem questions.
- **Microsoft® PowerPoint® Presentations:** to help support and organize lectures.

McGraw-Hill Connect™ — helping instructors and students **Connect, Learn, Succeed!**

Superior Service

McGraw-Hill's Create Online gives you the most abundant resource at your fingertips — literally. With a few mouse clicks, you can create customized learning tools simply and affordably. McGraw-Hill Ryerson has included many of our market-leading textbooks within Create Online for e-book and print customization as well as many licensed readings and cases.

CourseSmart brings together thousands of textbooks across hundreds of courses in an eTextbook format providing unique benefits to students and faculty. By purchasing an eTextbook, students can save up to 50 percent off the cost of a print textbook, reduce their impact on the environment, and gain access to powerful Web tools for learning including full text search, notes and highlighting, and e-mail tools for sharing notes between classmates. For faculty, CourseSmart provides instant access to review and compare textbooks and course materials in their discipline area without the time, cost, and environmental impact of mailing print examination copies. For further details contact your iLearning Sales Specialist or go to www.coursesmart.com.

*i***Learning Sales Specialist:** Your Integrated Learning Sales Specialist is a McGraw-Hill Ryerson representative who has the experience, product knowledge, training, and support to help you assess and integrate any of the above-noted products, technology, and services into your course for optimum teaching and learning performance. Whether it's how to use our test bank software, helping your students improve their grades, or how to put your entire course online, your *i*Learning Sales Specialist is there to help. Contact your local *i*Learning Sales Specialist today to learning how to maximize all McGraw-Hill Ryerson resources!

*i***Learning Services Program:** McGraw-Hill Ryerson offers a unique *i*Services package designed for Canadian faculty. Our mission is to equip providers of higher education with superior tolls and resources required for excellence in teaching. For additional information, visit www.mcgrawhill.ca/highereducation/iservices/.

Acknowledgements

This text includes the thoughts and contributions of many individuals, and we wish to express our sincere appreciation to them. First and foremost, we thank all the students in our advanced accounting classes, from whom we have learned so much. In many respects, this text is an outcome of the learning experiences we have shared with our students. Second, we wish to thank the technical checkers, Jake Chazan, Sean Homuth, and Shari Mann. The accuracy of the text is due in large part to their efforts. We also wish to thank the following colleagues for their invaluable advice:

Bill Dawson, University of Western Ontario
Robert Ducharme, University of Waterloo
Chuck Campbell, University of British Columbia
Allan Foerster, University of Waterloo
Patrice Gelinas, York University
David Hiscock, McMaster University
Paul Hurley, Durham College
Bibi John, Seneca College
Stuart H. Jones, University of Calgary
Valorie Leonard, Laurentian University
Yue Li, University of Toronto
Don Lockwood, University of British Columbia
Christine Maher, Conestoga College
Chima Mbagwu, Wilfrid Laurier University
James Moore, Brock University
James Myers, University of Toronto
Joe Nemi, University of Guelph Humber
Morina Rennie, University of Regina
Julia Scott, McGill University
Sandra Scott, York University
Deirdre Taylor, Ryerson University
John Western, Kwantlen University College
Barbara Wyntjes, Kwantlen Polytechnic University

Thanks also to the Canadian Institute of Chartered Accountants for granting permission to reproduce material from the *CICA Handbook* as well as questions from the Uniform Final Examinations (UFEs) and to the Certified General Accountants of Canada and the Certified Management Accountants for their permission to reproduce questions adapted from past examinations. Thank you to Peter Secord of St. Mary's University for all of his case contributions.

We are very grateful to the staff at McGraw-Hill Ryerson: Executive Editor Rhondda McNabb, Developmental Editor Rachel Horner, and Supervising Editor Kara Stahl, who applied pressure in a gentle but persistent manner when we strayed from the project's schedule. Thanks also to Copy Editor Julia Cochrane and Proofreader Deborah Cooper-Bullock, whose technical expertise was necessary to carry the project to its end.

And finally, we are grateful to our families for all of their support and encouragement.

Murray Hilton
Asper School of Business
University of Manitoba

Darrell Herauf
Eric Sprott School of Business
Carleton University

Prologue

Welcome to *Modern Advanced Accounting in Canada*. We wish you a prosperous learning experience. We will study three major accounting topics: consolidations, foreign currency transactions and operations, and not-for-profit and government organizations. You may have had some exposure to these topics in your previous accounting courses. We will build on this prior knowledge and the conceptual framework studied in Intermediate Accounting while we develop a thorough understanding of these selected topics. Before embarking on the study of these topics, we should review the role of accountants and the objectives of reporting.

Objectives of Reporting

Professional accountants provide a variety of services ranging from accounting to tax planning to assurance to business consulting. In this course, we will focus on financial accounting, i.e., providing financial information to present and potential capital providers such as investors and creditors. These users usually have limited financial resources to invest in an entity. They wish to invest where they can earn the highest return with the lowest amount of risk. The general-purpose financial reports (statement of financial position, statement of comprehensive income, cash flow statement, statement of changes in equity, and notes to the financial statements) will be used by the external users to help them make their resource allocation decisions and to assess the stewardship of management. The general-purpose reports are not the only source of information but are a good starting point.

In most cases, users want to receive the general-purpose financial reports prepared in accordance with generally accepted accounting principles (GAAP) because when these principles are followed the information is understandable, comparable, and reliable. However, there are times when users may want or require special-purpose financial reports that do not follow GAAP. For example, entities may need to prepare non-GAAP-based statements for legislative or regulatory purposes, or for contract compliance. Or, a prospective lender may want to receive a balance sheet with assets reported at fair value rather than historical cost. As accountants, we should be able to provide financial information in a variety of formats or using a variety of accounting policies because we have the skills and abilities to produce this information. If we do provide fair-value-based financial statements, we cannot say that the statements were prepared in accordance with GAAP. We must simply state that the statements were prepared in accordance with the policies described in the notes to the financial statements.

In some cases, the users of the financial statements have access to information about the entity in addition to that provided in the financial statements. For example, the owner of a private company may also be the manager of the company and have intimate knowledge of the company. In such cases, the owner may rely less on the financial statements than investors in public companies do. In other situations, the owner may not understand the financial reporting for complex transactions such as business combinations. In both of these situations, the owners may feel that the costs of complying with some of the complex sections of the *Handbook* are not worth the benefit. They may prefer to issue more simplified statements. The CICA recognized this difference in users' needs and, in 2002, issued a new *Handbook* section on differential reporting. With the introduction of this section, qualifying enterprises can choose to apply differential reporting options and still be in compliance with GAAP. Late in 2009, the CICA approved a completely new set of GAAP for private enterprises, which will be contained in Part II of the *CICA Handbook*. Commencing in 2011, private enterprises can opt to follow GAAP for public companies, i.e., IFRSs or GAAP for private enterprises. The method adopted must be followed as a whole package. A private enterprise can adopt Part II of the *Handbook* early, starting with its 2009 financial statements.

GAAP encompass broad principles and conventions of general application as well as rules and procedures that determine accepted accounting practices at a particular time. The process of developing GAAP is political. Both preparers and users of financial statements have an opportunity to comment on a proposal for a new accounting standard before it becomes generally accepted. If a new rule is preferred by the preparers but not accepted by users, it is unlikely to become part of GAAP. Therefore, as we study existing accounting practices and proposed changes, we need to continually evaluate whether information provided by a reporting entity will satisfy users' needs.

The *CICA Handbook* is an authoritative document because many legal statutes require its use. For example, companies incorporated under the Canada Business Corporations Act and certain provincial Corporations Acts are required to prepare financial statements in accordance with the *CICA Handbook*. Publicly traded companies are required to submit financial statements that comply with GAAP to the securities commissions under which they are registered.

The *CICA Handbook* provides the financial statement accounting and reporting requirements as well as explanations and guidance for most transactions and events encountered by an entity. When an entity encounters transactions or events that are not explicitly addressed by one of the *Handbook* sections, the publicly accountable entity should adopt accounting practices that are consistent with the spirit of the *Handbook* and consistent with the financial statement concepts described in the "Framework for the Preparation of Financial Statements," which is a document found just prior to the IFRSs in Part I of the *CICA Handbook*. The private enterprise should adopt accounting practices that are consistent with Section 1000: Financial Statement Concepts, in Part II of the *Handbook*.

Framework for the Preparation and Presentation of Financial Statements

The Framework for the Preparation and Presentation of Financial Statements describes the concepts underlying the accounting principles used in general-purpose financial statements. It is a very important component of the *Handbook* because it provides the conceptual framework for the development and issuance of other financial accounting standards. The main items included in this section are as follows:

- The objective of financial statements;
- Underlying assumptions;
- Qualitative characteristics of financial statements;

- The recognition and measure of the elements of financial statements;
- Concepts of capital and capital maintenance.

You will probably recognize most of the concepts and remember studying them in your intermediate accounting courses. If you can explain the accounting practices learned there in terms of these basic concepts, you should have no trouble applying these concepts in the new situations we will encounter in this course. If you do not understand or cannot explain accounting rules in terms of these basic concepts, it is never too late to start. As you study the accounting rules in this course, try to understand them in terms of the basic concepts and principles that the *Handbook* describes.

By gaining a broad understanding of the logic and basic principles behind the accounting rules, you will develop confidence in being able to apply these basic principles in a wide variety of situations. Rather than simply accepting accounting practices or memorizing specific rules in the *Handbook*, you will begin to understand the logic of the rules and evaluate whether the rules are consistent with the basic financial statement concepts. You will soon realize that most of the rules in accounting can be understood, developed, and derived from these basic principles and concepts. Then, in turn, you will be able to use professional judgment to apply these basic principles to whatever situation you may encounter.

Professional Judgment

Judgment is the ability to make a decision in situations where the answer is not clear-cut. Professional judgment is the ability to make decisions for issues encountered by professionals in carrying out their day-to-day responsibilities. Judgment is a skill developed over many years of study and learning from one's experiences. Professional judgment is derived from knowledge and experience in the profession. It is not something that is learned from rote or memorization of rules or answers to certain problems. It often involves making decisions after considering meaningful alternatives and the ability to understand the consequences of one's actions.

In the preparation of financial statements, there are three main areas where decisions must be made. First, accounting policies such as when to recognize revenue, how to report an interest in a joint venture, and whether or not to consolidate a special-purpose entity involve making a decision after considering various methods. The method adopted for a particular company must be appropriate for that company based on its existing situation. For example, if Company A is selling to customers with poor credit history and without obtaining any security for the receivables from these customers, it would be appropriate to recognize revenue when cash is received even though most of its competitors may be recognizing revenue when the goods are delivered. If the competitors are selling to customers with very high credit ratings, it would be appropriate for them to recognize revenue on delivery. An accountant will use his or her professional judgment, taking these factors into account and recognizing that although one method is appropriate for the competitors, another may be more appropriate for Company A.

Secondly, judgment is involved in making accounting estimates of many kinds. What is the estimated useful life of property, plant, and equipment? What is the recoverable amount for goodwill? Will a forward contract be effective as a hedge of expected sales for the next three years? The answers to these questions are not clear-cut. In the classroom, we are usually provided with this information. In the real world, we must gather data and make our own assessment. Whether we feel that the company can continue as a going concern or not could have a material difference on the valuation of goodwill and the bottom line on the income statement.

Thirdly, judgment is involved in deciding what to disclose and how to disclose it in the notes to the financial statements. For example, in disclosing a contingent liability resulting from a lawsuit, the company could simply say that it has been sued but no provision is made in the financial statements because it feels that the lawsuit has no merit. Or, it could provide details of the lawsuit and give some probabilities of different outcomes.

Is there too much latitude in accounting? Do the financial statements ever portray the complete facts? One could argue that there is no latitude because accountants are not free to randomly select any reporting method. They must represent faithfully what really happened and what really exists using the reporting framework. If the revenue has been earned, then the revenue should be recognized. If the cost will provide a probable future benefit, then the cost should be capitalized as an asset. Latitude is necessary so that the accountant can choose the methods to reflect the real situation. If the rules are written too rigidly, companies may be forced to use methods that do not reflect their own situation.

If accountants take their jobs seriously and have high ethical standards, they will present the financial statements as reliably as possible by using appropriate accounting policies, by making the best estimates possible, and by making honest and forthright statements in the notes to the financial statements. They will use judgment to fairly present the financial position and results of operations. Otherwise, the individual accountants and the entire accounting profession will lose credibility.

In this course, we will have an opportunity to develop our judgment skills and to exercise judgment through the use of cases. The cases provide realistic scenarios where conflicts exist and choices must be made. The answers are usually not clear-cut. In fact, different answers can be defended. For these cases, it is how you support your recommendation that is important as opposed to what your final recommendation is. You will need to apply basic principles and use judgment to come up with an answer that "tells it how it is" as accurately as possible. In so doing, you will be developing the skills required of a professional accountant.

Chapter 1 — A Survey of International Accounting

LEARNING OBJECTIVES

After studying this chapter, you should be able to do the following:

1. Identify factors that can influence a country's accounting standards.
2. Describe areas where Canada's accounting standards differ from those used in other countries.
3. Identify the role the IASB intends to play in the establishment of uniform worldwide accounting standards.
4. Identify the direction that the CICA intends to follow for public and private companies.
5. Identify the direction that the FASB intends to follow for public companies.

INTRODUCTION

Canadian companies are now able to raise capital resources on the world's marketplace.

This book covers a number of topics that are often presented in the final course of the financial accounting sequence. The topics are presented and illustrated in accordance with the generally accepted accounting principles (GAAP) that are expected to be in effect in Canada as of January 1, 2011. Prior to the 1990s, the study of accounting principles as set out in the *CICA Handbook* was all that was necessary as preparation for students intending to pursue professional accounting as a career in Canada. But since then rapid changes have taken place throughout the world, and even more drastic changes are coming. Canadian companies now view the entire world as their marketplace; not only are they exporting their products to more countries than ever before, but they are also establishing factories and offices in foreign locations. Companies that used to raise capital resources strictly in their home countries are now finding that capital markets are available to them around the world. Because their shares trade on stock exchanges, they are often required to prepare financial reports using accounting principles of countries other than Canada. Many accounting firms have offices throughout the world, and there are abundant opportunities for their Canadian staff members to transfer to these offices. With all these changes taking place, an accounting education that takes a narrow, parochial view is clearly inadequate. Canadian students of accounting need to be fully aware of what is happening in the rapid movement toward worldwide accounting standards, and it is imperative that the textbooks of today address this topic.

A large portion of this book covers the preparation of consolidated financial statements and other directly related topics. Before we begin considering this very broad topic, we first survey the accounting principles and practices used in a sample of other countries. It is hoped that this exposure to international accounting will inspire readers to continue studying this exciting and fast-growing area.

1

A Survey of International Accounting

In past years, the variety of accounting principles being used throughout the world was large.

GAAP have varied in the past from country to country around the world. If a detailed study had been made of the accounting practices used by every country in the world, it would probably have concluded that very few countries used exactly the same standards for external financial reporting purposes. Some comparisons would have yielded minor differences; others would have shown substantial ones. Differences existed in terminology and style of presentation, as well as in methods of measurement and disclosure.

Differences in measurement ranged from departures from historical cost to varying standards within the historical cost model. A variety of methods existed worldwide for measuring and reporting inventories, research and development costs, fixed assets, leases, computer software, and deferred income taxes. Income-smoothing devices varied from country to country. In Canada and the United States, GAAP allowed little opportunity to smooth income, while in other countries income-smoothing devices were allowed under GAAP or were encouraged by government regulation. This was often accomplished by setting up reserves, which are special equity accounts, and using them to transfer amounts to and from the income statement as needed. Inadequate disclosures often masked the real effect on yearly income measurements.

Asset revaluations have been a common practice in many countries.

Asset revaluations have been acceptable in many countries. These circumstances range from price-level-adjusted historical costs, used to counteract distortions resulting from very high inflation rates, to the regular or periodic adjustment of asset measurements to current replacement costs. Even under historical costs, great variations have existed in yearly measurements. The accounting for the asset of goodwill, which arises as a result of one company buying another, is a prime example. Practices included the immediate write-off of purchased goodwill to equity, capitalization with amortization over greatly varying periods, capitalization without amortization (thus leaving it on the balance sheet forever), and capitalization and write-off to income only when there is evidence of impairment.

Many countries have different descriptions and presentations of financial statement elements than those used in Canada.

Not only were there differences in measurement, but there were often also differences in the presentation and description of elements in financial statements. For example, in many countries, long-term assets were and continue to be presented before current assets on the balance sheet, and shareholders' equity appears before liabilities.

Examples of areas where disclosure differences still exist are segment reporting, reporting financial forecasts, shareholder and environmental disclosures, and value-added reporting. While many foreign multinational companies disclose the lines of business they are in and the geographic area in which they operate, there is still inconsistency in the level of detail provided. While the provision of financial forecasts is not common in North America, some companies in Europe do provide this information. Foreign companies often provide voluminous disclosures about their shares, shareholders' rights, and changes in shareholders' equity. Finally, while this is not required by accounting standards, multinational companies are increasingly providing information about environmental safety and protection issues and the ways in which they have added value to society by their distributions to owners, creditors, employees, and governments.

Information disclosed is often more voluminous in other countries than that required in Canada.

Differences in accounting standards have always existed, but they have been receiving greater attention in recent years because of the many changes taking place in the world economy. For example, the dismantling of the former Soviet empire has been accompanied by a shift from controlled to market-driven economies, and most of the countries in Europe have joined together to form the European Union (E.U.). The North American Free Trade Agreement allows the free flow of goods and services among Canada, the United States, and Mexico, and this agreement may soon be expanded to include some countries in South America.

Technology has improved the global flow of information.

In the midst of all this, there have been major advances in computer and communication technology that are dramatically improving the global flow of information and changing how business activities are conducted. As a result, foreign currencies now trade 24 hours a day in the world's financial centres. Accompanying this shift toward a global marketplace has been substantial growth in the size and number of multinational corporations. This growth has been achieved to a great extent by takeovers and mergers, often financed through the capital markets of *many* countries. Not only has there been a shift to a global marketplace for goods and services, but there has also been a shift toward a global capital market. Many of the world's stock exchanges now list foreign companies.

With such a global capital market comes the need to provide the suppliers of capital with useful accounting information. Fragmented accounting principles seriously compromise comparability, which is one of the key concepts associated with information usefulness. To counter this, securities regulators in foreign countries often require foreign companies listed on their stock exchanges either to prepare financial statements in accordance with their domestic accounting standards or to prepare reconciliations from foreign to domestic standards. For example, Canadian companies listed on U.S. stock exchanges are required by the Securities and Exchange Commission (SEC) to prepare reconciliations of net income measured in accordance with Canadian GAAP to net income in accordance with U.S. GAAP unless they use the IFRSs.[1] These requirements substantially increase a company's costs of preparing financial statements. Investment analysts and other users then incur further additional costs when interpreting financial statements prepared under different standards. Because of these problems, the world's securities regulators have been increasing their demands for some sort of accounting harmonization. It is not yet clear exactly when this will take place, but as we shall see later, a great deal of effort has been made to change the situation. However, in order to fully understand the issues and how changes may occur in the future, we must first examine the major causes of differences in GAAP.

The SEC requires Canadian companies to reconcile their earnings to U.S. GAAP unless they use IFRSs.

Factors that Can Influence a Country's Accounting Standards

Many factors can influence a country's accounting standards. Usually there is not one dominant factor. The following five factors can affect standards.

The Role of Taxation   In some countries, income tax has a minimal effect on how net income is measured for financial reporting. For example, in Canada and the United States, companies often report net incomes on their operating statements that are substantially different from the taxable incomes they report on their tax returns. This has led to the GAAP concept of interperiod tax allocation, although in some countries where such differences exist, differences between net income and taxable income have not always resulted in full tax allocation being used.

---

[1] If a Canadian or non-U.S. company uses IFRSs, a reconciliation to U.S. GAAP is not required.

Accounting income and taxable income are virtually the same in some countries.

In other countries, taxation has a profound effect on how accounting income is measured. Accounting income will not differ much from taxable income if a country's tax statutes state that expenses must be recorded on the income statement if they are to be allowed as a deduction on the tax return. In countries where this is the case, the result is often the use of extreme conservatism in accounting measurements on the part of companies trying to keep their incomes as low as possible within the law. Germany and Japan are examples of countries whose tax laws have strongly influenced GAAP. In the United States, while taxable income and accounting income are different numbers, one area where consistency is required is the costing of inventory. If LIFO (last in, first out) is to be used for tax purposes, it must also be used for financial reporting.

The Level of Development of Capital Markets In countries where publicly traded debt and equity securities play a substantial role in the financing of business activities, accounting and disclosure standards tend to be much more extensive than in countries where this is not the case. This is because highly developed public capital markets tend to have fairly sophisticated investors who demand current and useful information from those who have received their capital. Canada, the United Kingdom, and the United States all have highly developed capital markets

Highly developed capital markets often result in the development of quality accounting standards.

and strong accounting and disclosure standards. In countries where business financing tends to be private rather than public, there is less reliance on extensive accounting standards, because the private suppliers of capital can demand and receive the information they need directly from the "consumers" of such capital. Japan is a prime example; there, corporate capital needs have been supplied by very large private suppliers such as banks. However, it should be noted that when Japan's economy took a severe dive in the 1990s, many of Japan's major banks incurred massive loan losses that nearly bankrupted them; this was cited as a major contributor to the Japanese recession. Germany and Switzerland also have very large banks that satisfy much of the capital needs of business. Historically, a large number of businesses in Mexico were state owned, but in the 1990s a change to private ownership resulted in a shift to financing through private and public capital markets.

Differing Legal Systems Two different kinds of legal system are in existence today: code law systems and common law systems. Code law systems, which originated with the Roman Empire, contain very detailed statutes that govern a wide range of human activities. In general, they specify what individuals and corporations *can* do.

Code law systems specify what individuals and corporations can do, while common law systems specify what cannot be done.

Common law systems have less detailed statutes and rely on the court system to interpret statutes and thus establish precedents through case law. In general, they specify what individuals and corporations *cannot* do (i.e., what is illegal).

In many common law countries, governments tend to take a hands-off approach to the setting of accounting standards. While there may be statutes requiring that companies make information available to the providers of capital, the *type* of information required is left to the private sector. In the United States, the SEC, which administers securities legislation, has given the right to develop accounting standards to a private group, the Financial Accounting Standards Board (FASB). In Canada, the *CICA Handbook* pronouncements constitute the accounting standards required by the provincial and federal Companies Acts and the Ontario Securities Commission. The United Kingdom also uses a private standard-setting body.

In Germany, France, and Japan, accounting standards are set by legal statutes.

In code law countries such as Germany, France, and Japan, the private sector is involved only in an advisory capacity, and accounting standards are reflected in legal statutes, often as protection for creditors and other capital suppliers. It should not be surprising to note that tax law also heavily influences accounting standards in these countries.

Ties between Countries   Political and economic ties between countries have historically had some effect on accounting standards. For example, the accounting standards and professional accounting organizations of countries that were once colonies are often patterned after those of the "home" country. There have been strong similarities between the standards of India, South Africa, Australia, New Zealand, and Malaysia and those of Great Britain. During their early development, Canadian accounting standards were influenced by Great Britain's, but in later years this influence shifted away from Britain to the United States due to the very strong economic ties that developed between those two countries. The formation of the European Union has certainly had an effect on the accounting standards used by its member countries. We will see more of this later.

Canadian standards have been influenced by those of the United States.

High inflation rates often result in departures from historical cost measurements.

Inflation Levels   The historical cost model, which implicitly assumes a relatively stable unit of measure, is used by many countries. However, the model is not useful when inflation rates are very high. Countries that have experienced high inflation rates often make financial reporting adjustments to counteract the effects of inflation. These adjustments involve price-level-adjusted statements, or a shift from historical costs to current-value accounting, or both. Many countries in South America that experienced inflation rates of 1,000 percent or more per annum in the 1980s and 1990s adopted inflation-based accounting.[2] Inflation in most of these South American countries is now more reasonable and inflation accounting has also been discontinued. Mexico used price level accounting because of previous high inflation rates from 1983 to 2007. Canada, the United States, and the United Kingdom all experimented with the supplemental reporting of price level and current-value information in the 1970s when the inflation rate approached 20 percent. The experiment was not successful because of the high cost of providing such information and the general lack of comprehension on the part of financial statement users. All three countries abandoned the experiment when inflation declined.

Toward Accounting Harmonization and Convergence

A truly global economy will require some sort of harmonized accounting standards if it is to function properly. Three organizations that have been working toward accomplishing this objective are the European Union, the International Accounting Standards Board (IASB), and the FASB. The role of these three organizations is discussed next.

The European Union, the International Accounting Standards Board (IASB), and the FASB have been working toward accounting harmonization.

The European Union   In 1957, six European countries signed the Treaty of Rome, thereby establishing a common market for goods and services and common institutions for economic development. Originally called the European Economic Community, the

---

[2] For example, Brazil's inflation rate was more than 2,000 percent in 1993.

agreement is now called the European Union (E.U.) and had 27 members at the end of 2009.[3] A major goal of the European Union is the promotion of the free flow of goods, labour, and capital among member countries. In 1998, in order to establish a common economic policy for the area, a European central bank was established, which subsequently issued a common currency called the euro.

The intent was that the currencies of the member nations would be gradually phased out with full adoption of this common currency. As of January 1, 2010, only 17 members had complied.[4] Both Sweden and Denmark held referendums in which their citizens voted to reject the adoption of the euro. The government of the United Kingdom, sensing that a referendum would be defeated, decided to wait until such time that the public mood had changed. A major reason for rejection by these three countries was the fact that they did not wish to individually relinquish their ability to determine economic policy. It was also observed that each country's economy had performed much better than many of the other E.U. member countries that had switched their currencies, such as Germany, Italy, and France.

The European Union has also attempted to harmonize the accounting principles used by its member countries by issuing "directives." In order to minimize conflict with the legal reporting requirements of certain of its member nations, these directives often allowed many alternative reporting practices. This is particularly true with respect to the first accounting directive. The second directive, issued in 1983, requiring the presentation of consolidated financial statements, has had a major impact on the accounting of many countries where consolidation was not previously a common practice. While flexibility appears to be contrary to the concept of harmonization, the adoption of the directives has nevertheless caused major changes to the accounting practices of some of its members. In addition, former Soviet Bloc countries, including Hungary and Poland, established new accounting principles based on the E.U. directives in anticipation of some day being admitted to the union. (They were admitted in 2004.)

The IASB   The IASB became operational in 2001 as a result of a major restructuring of its former organization, which was called the International Accounting Standards Committee (IASC). This committee, based in London, was formed in 1973 by an agreement between the professional accounting bodies of 10 countries with the purpose of establishing worldwide accounting principles. The founding members came from Australia, Canada, France, Germany, Japan, Mexico, Netherlands, United Kingdom, Ireland, and United States. Over the years, the membership grew so that it represented more than 140 accounting organizations from over 100 countries. It should be pointed out, however, that membership in the organization did not translate into the adoption of its standards, and the number of countries actually using IASC standards was a much lower number. The IASC's operating costs

The use of the euro as a common currency in the European Union has not been a resounding success.

The E.U. has attempted to harmonize accounting standards used by its member countries.

---

[3] Austria, Belgium, Bulgaria, Cyprus, Czech Republic, Denmark, Estonia, Finland, France, Germany, Greece, Hungary, Ireland, Italy, Latvia, Lithuania, Luxembourg, Malta, Netherlands, Poland, Portugal, Romania, Slovakia, Slovenia, Spain, Sweden, and United Kingdom.

[4] The E.U. countries that have maintained their own currencies are Bulgaria, Czech Republic, Denmark, Estonia, Hungary, Latvia, Poland, Romania, Sweden, and United Kingdom. On January 1, 2011, Estonia is expected to convert to the euro. On the other hand, Andorra, Kosovo, Montenegro, Monaco, San Marino, and the Vatican City are not E.U. members but do officially use the euro as their currency.

of approximately £2 million a year were met by contributions from professional accounting bodies, accounting firms, and other organizations, and by the sale of IASC publications. It was governed by a board made up of representatives from 13 countries and 4 organizations. The committee met two or three times a year to release exposures of proposed standards, to examine public comments that resulted from them, and to issue International Accounting Standards (IASs). Initially, many of the standards issued by the IASC were characterized by the number of acceptable alternatives that were permitted, but in the early 1990s efforts were made to eliminate many of these alternatives. This initiative was partially successful, but it left a number of standards still allowing alternative treatments. Given that some of the board members came from countries whose accounting standards are reflected in legal statutes, it is understandable that the removal of alternatives can be a tricky political process requiring compromise. Notwithstanding this difficulty, achieving worldwide accounting uniformity will depend greatly on eliminating alternative accounting practices. To date, 49 standards have been issued and 38 are still in force. Exhibit 1.1 on page 8 provides a listing of the standards that were in force at the end of 2009. Where a standard has been superseded by a subsequent standard, it is not included in the list.

IASs often allow alternative accounting treatments.

Note that standards issued by the original IASC were issued in numerical order with the prefix IAS, while subsequent standards issued by the IASB were also issued numerically with the prefix IFRS. In future we will refer to the current collection of international financial reporting standards as IFRSs.

In March 2001, a major restructuring of the IASB was completed, and the board adopted the following major objectives:

The IASB hopes to develop a single set of high-quality, global accounting standards that will be adopted by countries around the world.

- To develop a single set of high-quality, global accounting standards that require transparent and comparable information in general-purpose financial statements.

- To cooperate with various national accounting standard-setters in order to achieve convergence in accounting standards around the world.

A dictionary meaning of the term *converge* is "to approach" or "to tend to meet." The hope of the board is that the appropriate national bodies will adjust their individual standards in such a way that the essence of the IASB standard is achieved even though the exact wording is not adopted.

The IASB is now located in London, England, and has 15 members from 9 countries. The members are chosen more for their expertise than for geographical representation. However, nine of the members are expected to have formal liaison responsibilities with major national standard-setting bodies but must not be actual members of such national bodies. These nine standard-setting bodies are located in Sweden, China, South Africa, Brazil, France, United States, Great Britain, Japan, and Australia–New Zealand. Presumably such a liaison will be instrumental in harmonizing the national standards of a very important group of countries with those of the IASB.

Shortly after being restructured, the IASB announced that previous standards issued by the IASC would continue in force and that it intended to issue new IFRSs in areas where no international standards existed. It also announced an improvement project whose purpose was to raise the quality and consistency of existing IASs. This project was completed in December 2003 when 13 standards were revised and one was withdrawn.

Exhibit 1.1

LIST OF CURRENT IASB STANDARDS AT THE END OF 2009

IFRS 1	First-time Adoption of International Financial Reporting Standards
IFRS 2	Share-based Payment
IFRS 3	Business Combinations
IFRS 4	Insurance Contracts
IFRS 5	Non-current Assets Held for Sale and Discontinued Operations
IFRS 6	Exploration for and Evaluation of Mineral Assets
IFRS 7	Financial Instrument Disclosures
IFRS 8	Operating Segments
IFRS 9	Financial Instruments — Classification and Measurement
IAS 1	Presentation of Financial Statements
IAS 2	Inventories
IAS 7	Cash Flow Statements
IAS 8	Accounting Policies, Changes in Accounting Estimates and Errors
IAS 10	Events After the Balance Sheet Date
IAS 11	Construction Contracts
IAS 12	Income Taxes
IAS 16	Property, Plant and Equipment
IAS 17	Leases
IAS 18	Revenue
IAS 19	Employee Benefits
IAS 20	Accounting for Government Grants and Disclosure of Government Assistance
IAS 21	The Effects of Changes in Foreign Exchange Rates
IAS 23	Borrowing Costs
IAS 24	Related Party Disclosures
IAS 26	Accounting and Reporting by Retirement Benefit Plans
IAS 27	Consolidated and Separate Financial Statements
IAS 28	Investments in Associates
IAS 29	Financial Reporting in Hyperinflationary Economies
IAS 31	Interests in Joint Ventures
IAS 32	Financial Instruments: Presentation
IAS 33	Earnings per Share
IAS 34	Interim Financial Reporting
IAS 36	Impairment of Assets
IAS 37	Provisions, Contingent Liabilities and Contingent Assets
IAS 38	Intangible Assets
IAS 39	Financial Instruments: Recognition and Measurement
IAS 40	Investment Property
IAS 41	Agriculture

Source: International Accounting Standards Board, www.iasb.org

Companies in over 100 countries are now using IFRSs.

The number of countries adopting international standards has rapidly increased in recent years. Some of the increase has come from the adoption by those countries that previously had no standards but, because of a shift to a market economy, required new forms of financial reporting. Most of the increase has come from initiatives of the European Union and the standard-setters from Australia and New Zealand. (These initiatives are fully discussed in the next section.) The result is that, as of December 2009, 93 countries required IFRSs for all publicly traded domestic companies, 5 countries required IFRSs for some companies, 23 countries permitted but did not require its use, and 30 countries did not permit the use of IFRSs. Notable among the countries not yet allowing international standards were China, Canada, and the United States. For a list of countries and the required, permitted, or lack of usage of IFRSs, see Exhibit 1.2.

Exhibit 1.2

USE OF IFRS BY COUNTRY — DECEMBER 2009

IFRSs Required for All Domestic Listed Companies

Anguilla	Estonia*	Kuwait	Peru
Antigua & Barbuda	Fiji	Kyrgyzstan	Poland*
Armenia	Finland*	Latvia*	Portugal*
Australia	France*	Lebanon	Qatar
Austria*	Germany*	Liechtenstein	Romania*
Bahamas	Georgia	Lithuania*	Serbia
Bahrain	Ghana	Luxembourg*	Singapore (begin 2012)
Barbados	Granada	Macedonia	Slovak Republic*
Belgium*	Greece*	Malawi	Slovenia*
Bosnia & Herzegovina	Guatamala	Malaysia (begin 2012)	South Africa
Botswana	Guyana	Malta*	South Korea (begin 2011)
Brazil (begin 2010)	Honduras	Mauritius	Spain*
Bulgaria*	Hong Kong	Mexico (begin 2012)	St. Kitts & Nevis
Canada (begin 2011)	Hungary*	Mongolia	Sweden*
Chile	Iceland	Montenegro	Tajikistan
Costa Rica	India (begin 2011)	Namibia	Tanzania
Croatia	Iraq	Nepal	Trinidad & Tobago
Cyprus*	Ireland*	Netherlands*	Turkey
Czech Republic*	Italy*	New Zealand	Ukraine
Denmark*	Jamaica	Nicaragua	United Arab Emirates
Dominican Republic	Jordan	Norway	United Kingdom*
Ecuador (phase-in 2010–2012)	Kazakhstan	Oman	Venezuela
Egypt	Kenya	Panama	West Bank/Gaza
		Papua New Guinea	

IFRSs Required for Some Domestic Listed Companies

Azerbaijan	Israel	Russia
Belarus	Morocco	

IFRSs Permitted for Domestic Listed Companies

Aruba	Gibraltar	Myanmar	Switzerland
Bermuda	Haiti	Netherlands Antilles	Uganda
Bolivia	Laos	Paraguay	Virgin Islands (British)
Cayman Islands	Lesotho	Sri Lanka	Zambia
Dominica	Maldives	Suriname	Zimbabwe
El Salvador	Mozambique	Swaziland	

IFRSs Not Permitted for Domestic Listed Companies

Argentina	Cuba	Nigeria	Togo¥
Bangladesh	Indonesia	Pakistan	Tunisia
Benin¥	Iran	Philippines	United States
Bhutan	Japan‡	Saudi Arabia	Uruguay
Burkina Faso¥	Libya	Senegal¥	Uzbekistan
China†	Mali¥	Syria	Vietnam
Cote d'Ivoire¥	Moldova	Taiwan	
Colombia	Niger¥	Thailand	

---

* Denotes E.U. membership. The E.U. has not adopted portions of IAS 39.

† Approximately 150 Chinese companies are listed on the Hong Kong Stock Exchange. They are permitted to use IFRSs or Hong Kong FRSs.

‡ In August 2007, the ASBJ and the IASB agreed on a process for converging Japanese GAAP and IFRSs. Major differences between Japanese GAAP and IFRSs will be eliminated by June 30, 2011. The target date of 2011 does not apply to any major new IFRSs now being developed that will become effective after 2011.

¥ These nations have adopted SYSCOA (La Système Comptable Ouest-Africain). Governments developed these accounting standards based on the needs of governmental users.

Source: Deloitte Touche Tohmatsu, "Use of IFRSs by Jurisdiction," http://www.iasplus.com/country/useias.htm, accessed December 2009

Recent Initiatives from the European Union and Australia and New Zealand

A major development toward the convergence/harmonization of accounting standards throughout the world occurred in 2002 when the European Union issued a directive stating that, effective January 1, 2005, all European companies whose shares trade on stock exchanges would be required to prepare their consolidated financial statements in accordance with IFRSs. Two other important developments occurred when Australia switched over to IFRSs in 2005, and New Zealand switched in 2007. It should be noted that while these developments brought 29 countries into the international standards arena, the methods used to do so were different.

The standards boards of both Australia and New Zealand issued new domestic standards that were "equivalent to" IFRSs. In Australia's case, it was announced in 2002 that the Australian Accounting Standards Board intended to issue new standards that would essentially be the same as IFRSs, effective for all Australian business entities (public or private and incorporated or unincorporated). The issue of new standards was essential because Australian corporate law requires financial reports to comply with Australian accounting standards. The standards issued were not identical to IFRSs. In some instances, the new Australian standards restricted the use of the optional provisions allowed in some international standards and in other cases required additional disclosures when international disclosure requirements did not match existing Australian ones. The standards board also indicated that it intends to issue additional standards to cover areas that are purely domestic and not covered by IFRSs.

In the E.U. situation, the directive did not require each of the 27 member countries to change their domestic accounting standards but rather required all publicly traded companies located in union countries to prepare their financial statements in accordance with IFRSs. The member states were not all required to issue new standards in such a short period of time but were expected to do so later. Keep in mind that the accounting standards of France and Germany are set by legislation, and changes to legislation are not made quickly.

The E.U. directive resulted in more than 8,000 listed companies implementing international standards in their 2005 financial reports. Ernst and Young has published "Observations on the Implementation of IFRS."[5] This document provided an overview of how some large multinationals reported their 2005 results using IFRSs. In general, the study concluded that the changeover was successful even though many companies found that they had to make significant changes in their measurement and disclosure practices.

Because IFRSs do not require uniform presentation of the financial statement elements and descriptions, many companies were able to maintain previous presentations that were unique to their particular country. While this helps comparability from a domestic point of view, consistency and comparability are compromised from an international point of view when terminology differences are not understood.

In many cases, it was noted the IFRS statements were far more complex than those based on national standards. Overall, the 2005 statements were 20 to 30 percent longer than the prior year's statements and contained far more notes than in

Public companies in the European Union as well as in Australia and New Zealand are required to use IFRSs.

The E.U. changeover affected more than 8,000 companies.

Significant changes to corporate reporting were the result of the switch to IFRSs.

[5] Ernst & Young, www.ey.com

prior years. The study questioned whether the overall usefulness of the financial information had been compromised as a result.

The study concluded that because IFRSs are broad based, extensive judgment is required in their application, and if judgment is not used on a consistent basis by the preparers of the financial statements in each of the union's countries, comparability could be, and probably is, severely compromised.

It should be noted that when IFRSs were adopted by the European Union, Australia, and New Zealand, some tailoring of the standards for local conditions was done. For example, the E.U. standards related to IAS 39: Financial Instruments — Recognition and Measurement are not the same as the IASB standards. As a result, companies must disclose in their financial statements whether they are following the IASB standards or some sort of modified standards. Unless otherwise stated, when we refer to IFRSs in this textbook, we will always be referring to the standards published by the IASB.

IFRSs versus U.S. GAAP

FASB's statements are considered to be rule based, while IFRSs are principle based.

Accounting principles in the United States are set by FASB, which is a private organization. FASB's pronouncements are rule based and are far more detailed than those of both the *CICA Handbook* and IFRSs, which are often described as principle-based standards requiring greater application of professional judgment by the preparers and auditors of financial statements. (U.S. public accounting firms have often indicated their support for the rule-based FASB over principle-based standards.)

Canadian/U.S. GAAP reconciliations often show substantial differences in reported earnings.

Canada's standards are closer to those of the United States than to those of any other country but, even so, the differences that do exist are so great that Canadian companies whose shares trade on U.S. stock exchanges are required to prepare reconciliations to U.S. GAAP. These reconciliations often show substantial differences in reported earnings. For example, the December 31, 2008, annual report of EnCana showed Canadian GAAP net earnings of $5,944 million and U.S. GAAP net earnings of $4,810 million. Both amounts are in U.S. dollars because EnCana reports using the U.S. dollar as its presentation currency. The reconciliation showed differences in seven items of which the major one was an impairment loss on oil and gas properties.

While FASB has often indicated its support for a single set of global accounting standards, it has also stated its belief that its standards are the best in the world and therefore should be used as a benchmark by the IASB. This argument somewhat lost its thrust with the accounting scandals associated with companies such as Enron and WorldCom. Despite this setback, FASB still carries a lot of clout, and its cooperation with the IASB is imperative if the goal of common worldwide standards is to be met.

The FASB and the IASB have undertaken a project to converge their standards.

In September 2002, the IASB and the FASB signed the Norwalk Agreement, in which they each acknowledged their commitment to the development of high-quality, compatible accounting standards that could be used for both domestic and cross-border financial reporting. They pledged to use their best efforts (a) to make their existing financial reporting standards fully compatible as soon as is practicable and (b) to coordinate their future work programs to ensure that once achieved, compatibility is maintained.

As part of the Norwalk Agreement, the two boards identified areas where differences could be eliminated in the short term by selecting existing standards from either the IASB or the FASB as the high-quality solution. This project was called the *Short Term Convergence Project.* By the end of 2009, the FASB issued new or amended standards to converge with IFRSs in the following areas:

The FASB has already revised a number of its standards to be fully consistent with IFRSs.

- *Inventory costs:* Recognize idle facilities costs, excessive spoilage, double freight, and rehandling costs as current-period expenses.
- *Asset exchanges:* A non-monetary exchange of similar assets must apply the general rules for asset exchange and does not receive special treatment.
- *Accounting changes:* Reporting the cumulative effect of a change in accounting principle in the current-period net income is no longer permissible; retrospective adjustment is now required.
- *Financial instruments:* Require the reporting entity to measure a wide range of financial assets and liabilities at fair value.
- *Business combination:* In-process research and development could be recognized as an asset at the date of acquisition and tested for impairment thereafter.
- *Subsequent events:* The period for subsequent events ends when the financial statements are "available to be issued."

In a reciprocal fashion, the IASB issued new or amended standards to converge with the FASB for borrowing costs and segment reporting and is expected to issue new standards on joint ventures and income taxes early in 2010. The projects on impairment and government grants have been deferred pending work on other more important projects.

In 2006, the FASB and the IASB issued a memorandum of understanding (MOU) setting out the milestones of the FASB-IASB joint work program to be reached by 2008. It specified the short-term convergence projects described above, joint projects that were already on the active agendas of the two boards and joint projects that were at the research stage but not yet on the active agendas on the boards. The joint projects deal with broader issues that are expected to take longer to resolve and will likely result in new common standards that significantly improve the financial information reported to investors.

After much deliberation, the IASB and the FASB issued new but slightly different standards on a joint project on business combinations.

The first joint project on business combinations has been completed, and both boards issued new standards in 2007/2008. Unfortunately, the standards issued by the two boards are not exactly the same even though the project was carried out jointly with the goal of convergence. This underlies a key aspect of convergence. The process of attempting to dissect and eliminate every possible difference that may be experienced in practice is very costly and time-consuming, if not impossible. A more effective approach focuses on aligning the general principles and overall methodologies. This is further illustrated in other converged standards such as operating segments and borrowing costs. Although the general principles and overall methodology of these standards are converged, there are a few differences in the detail. We may have been overly optimistic in expecting that convergence would eliminate all differences.

Given that companies from the European Union had to report under IFRSs and given that progress was being made on converging IFRSs and U.S. GAAP, there was increasing pressure from the European Union to allow its companies to use IFRSs when reporting on American exchanges. As a result, the SEC made a monumental decision to change the requirements for foreign registrants. Commencing

The SEC now allows foreign registrants to use IFRSs instead of U.S. GAAP for reporting on U.S. stock exchanges.

in November 2007, foreign registrants could use IFRSs in preparing their financial statements without reconciling them to U.S. GAAP. In order to qualify for this exemption, a foreign private issuer's financial statements must fully comply with the IASB's version of IFRSs, with one exception. The exception relates to foreign private issuers that use the version of IFRSs that includes the European Commission's special rules on financial instruments, which has been referred to as a "carve-out for IAS 39." The SEC has permitted such issuers to use that version in preparing their financial statements for a two-year period as long as reconciliation to the IASB's version of IFRSs is provided. After the two-year period, these issuers will have to either use the IASB's version of IFRSs or provide a reconciliation to U.S. GAAP.

Sample Company is a multinational corporation with a balanced business portfolio of activities predominantly in the field of electronics and electrical engineering. Prior to 2007, it prepared financial statements in accordance with U.S. GAAP for reporting to the SEC. For the year ended September 30, 2007, its primary financial statements were prepared in accordance with IFRSs. As required by the SEC at that time, the notes to the financial statements included a reconciliation of net income per IFRSs to net income per U.S. GAAP. Exhibit 1.3 is an extract from Note 40 of Sample Company's 2007 financial statements.

The reconciliation of net income from a foreign country's GAAP to U.S. GAAP is very costly to prepare.

It is important to note that net income under IFRSs was substantially different than net income under U.S. GAAP. The above extract is only a small portion of Note 40. The entire note is more than eight pages long. It provides narrative explanations of the main reasons for the difference in net income and shareholders' equity and provides a condensed income statement and condensed balance sheet under U.S. GAAP. With such a significant difference in net income and such extensive note

---

Exhibit 1.3

SAMPLE COMPANY
NOTES TO CONSOLIDATED FINANCIAL STATEMENTS
(in millions of €, except where otherwise stated and per share amounts)

	Explanatory note	Year ended September 30,		
		2007	2006	2005
Net income under IFRS		**4,038**	**3,345**	**2,576**
Capitalization of development costs	a	(74)	(17)	(13)
Investments accounted for using the equity method	b	(75)	(32)	(15)
Sale and leaseback transactions	c	(5)	(21)	22
Financial instruments	d	(1,436)	294	(64)
Pensions and other post-employment benefits	e	(719)	(613)	(552)
Termination benefits	f	(228)	231	(42)
Provisions	g	(63)	148	173
Other		16	110	60
Deferred taxes	h	1,194	(189)	177
Total adjustments		**(1,390)**	**(89)**	**(254)**
Net income under U.S. GAAP before reclassification of minority interest		**2,648**	**3,256**	**2,322**
Change in presentation of minority interest	i	(231)	(213)	(158)
Net income under U.S. GAAP		**2,417**	**3,043**	**2,164**

disclosure, it is little wonder that there is pressure to develop one high-quality world-wide accounting standard.

In September 2008, an updated MOU was published that sets out priorities and milestones to be achieved on major joint projects by 2011. The boards have acknowledged that, although considerable progress has been made on a number of designated projects, achievements on other projects have been limited for various reasons, including differences in views over issues of agenda size and project scope, over the most appropriate approach, and about whether and how similar issues in active projects should be resolved consistently. As a result, the scopes and objectives of many of the projects have been or are expected to be revised. In updating the MOU, the boards noted that the major joint projects will take account of the ongoing work to improve and converge their respective conceptual frameworks. The following major joint projects are part of the MOU:

Revised standards are imminent for consolidations, derecognition, and financial instruments.

- Consolidation;
- Leases;
- Liabilities and equity;
- Fair value measurement guidance;
- Post-employment benefits (including pensions);
- Financial statement presentation;
- Revenue recognition;
- Derecognition;
- Financial instruments.

IASB issued IFRS 9: Financial Instruments — Classification and Measurement in November 2009. The revised standards will be discussed in Chapter 2. The IASB has issued exposure drafts on consolidation and derecognition; revised standards are expected to be issued in 2010. Exposure drafts are expected to be issued for the other joint projects in 2010.

The SEC has announced its intention to require IFRSs for U.S. public companies by 2014 or soon thereafter.

With the resolution of the debate regarding foreign private issuers, the focus of attention has now switched to the potential for U.S. domestic issuers to submit IFRS financial statements to comply with the rules and regulations of the SEC. In a significant step toward that objective, in August 2008 the SEC issued proposals that, if accepted, could allow some U.S. issuers, based on specific criteria, an option to use IFRSs for fiscal years ending on or after December 15, 2009, and could lead to mandatory transition to IFRSs for domestic issuers starting with fiscal years ending on or after December 15, 2014.

A roadmap has been proposed by the SEC that acknowledges that IFRSs have the potential to become the global set of high-quality accounting standards and sets out the following seven milestones that, if achieved, could lead to mandatory adoption by 2014:

Milestones 1–4 (issues that need to be addressed before mandatory adoption of IFRSs):

1. Improvements in accounting standards (i.e., IFRSs);
2. Funding and accountability of the International Accounting Standards Committee Foundation;
3. Improvement in the ability to use interactive data (e.g., XBRL) for IFRS reporting;
4. Education and training on IFRSs in the United States.

Milestones 5–7 (the transition plan for the mandatory use of IFRSs):

5. Limited early use by eligible entities — this milestone would give a limited number of U.S. issuers the option of using IFRSs for fiscal years ending on or after December 15, 2009.

6. Anticipated timing of future rule-making by the SEC — on the basis of the progress of milestones 1–4 and the experience gained from milestone 5, the SEC will determine in 2011 whether to require mandatory adoption of IFRSs for all U.S. issuers. If so, the SEC will determine the date and approach for a mandatory transition to IFRSs. Potentially, the option to use IFRSs when filing could also be expanded to other issuers before 2014.

7. Potential implementation of mandatory use.

In December 2008, the European Commission proposed the European Union remove the requirement for U.S. companies with securities registered in European capital markets and reporting under U.S. GAAP to reconcile their accounts to IFRSs. This measure acknowledges that U.S., Japanese, Chinese, Canadian, South Korean, and Indian GAAP are fairly similar to the modified IFRSs adopted by the European Union. The European Commission will review the situation of some of these countries (China, Canada, South Korea, India) by 2011 at the latest. The measures will mean that many foreign companies listed on E.U. markets will continue to be able to file their financial statements prepared in accordance with those GAAPs (the transitional provisions allowing the use of these GAAPs in the European Union would otherwise have expired at the end of 2008).

In the light of these proposals for change, and the now very real prospect of all U.S. companies transitioning to IFRSs by 2014, there is a heightened interest in the differences between IFRSs and U.S. GAAP. Will U.S. GAAP become the international standard or will the rule-based approach of U.S. standards give way to the principle-based approach of IFRSs? We should know the answer in the next 5 to 10 years.

The Big Four accounting firms have all published documents comparing IFRSs and U.S. GAAP. Many of these documents are available on their Web sites. In Deloitte's *IFRSs and U.S. GAAP — A Pocket Comparison*, July 2008, more than 200 differences were noted. Exhibit 1.4 on page 16 summarizes some of these main differences. Other differences will be listed in the *U.S. GAAP Differences* section at the end of each chapter in this text. If all of these standards are to be converged over the next six years, we can expect many changes. By noting these differences, we can get a sense of what standards may change.

Where Is Canada Going?

GAAP for Public Companies   Public companies seemed to be moving toward American accounting standards when in 1998 the CICA announced that it would work with the FASB to harmonize the accounting standards of the United States and Canada while at the same time encouraging the IASB in its efforts to develop global accounting standards.

The concept of harmonization would probably have proven to be a fairly difficult one due to the fact that Canadian accounting standards tend to be broad based while American standards tend to be based on detailed rules. This problem was alleviated when the CICA's position changed in 2006 with the announcement of the adoption of a strategic plan that would see the harmonization of the *CICA*

Exhibit 1.4

SOME KEY DIFFERENCES BETWEEN IFRSs AND U.S. GAAP AT JULY 2008

Accounting Item	IFRSs	U.S. GAAP
Conceptual Framework	Transaction should be accounted for in accordance with its substance	No equivalent statement
Financial Statement Presentation	Expenses should be classified either by function or by nature	No equivalent statement
Inventory Lower of cost or market	Net realizable value is used for market value	Market value is midpoint of net realizable value, replacement cost, and net realizable value less normal profit margin
Property, plant, and equipment Major inspection or overhaul costs	Generally capitalized	May be added to cost, expensed as incurred, or capitalized and amortized over the period to the next overhaul
Asset impairment Indication of impairment	Asset's carrying value exceeds the higher of its (1) value in use (discounted expected future cash flows) and (2) fair value less costs to sell	Asset's carrying value exceeds the undiscounted expected future cash flows from the asset
Subsequent reversal of an impairment loss	Required if certain criteria are met	Not allowed
Construction contracts Method used when percentage of completion not appropriate	Cost recovery method	Completed contract method
Research and development costs Development costs	Capitalized if certain criteria are met	Expensed immediately (except computer software development)
Leases Recognition of gain on sale and leaseback on an operating lease	Recognized immediately	Amortized over the lease term
Pensions Recognition of past service costs related to benefits that have vested	Recognized immediately	Amortized over the remaining service period of life expectancy
Recognition of minimum liability	No minimum liability requirement	Unfunded accumulated benefit obligation must be recognized as a minimum
Income taxes Recognition of deferred tax assets	Recognized only if realization of tax benefit is probable	Always recognized but a valuation allowance is provided
Presentation of "extraordinary" items	Not allowed	Required when certain criteria are met
Definition of a "discontinued operation"	A reportable business or geographic segment	A reportable segment, operating segment, reporting unit, subsidiary, or asset group
Interim reporting	Interim period treated as discrete accounting period	Interim period treated as integral part of full year

Source: Deloitte Touche Tohmatsu, IFRSs and U.S. GAAP — A Pocket Comparison. July 2008. http://www.iasplus.com/dttpubs/0809ifrsusgaap.pdf

Canadian publicly accountable enterprises will need to report under IFRSs starting in 2011.

Handbook with IFRSs for publicly accountable enterprises. A publicly accountable enterprise (PAE) is defined as an entity other than a not-for-profit organization or a government or other entity in the public sector that

(i) has issued, or is in the process of issuing, debt or equity instruments that are, or will be, outstanding and traded in a public market (a domestic or foreign stock exchange or an over-the-counter market, including local and regional markets); or

(ii) holds assets in a fiduciary capacity for a broad group of outsiders as one of its primary businesses.

Banks, credit unions, insurance companies, securities brokers/dealers, mutual funds, and investment banks typically meet the second of these criteria. Other entities may also hold assets in a fiduciary capacity for a broad group of outsiders because they hold and manage financial resources entrusted to them by clients, customers, or members not involved in the management of the entity. However, if an entity does so for reasons incidental to one of its primary businesses (as, for example, may be the case for some travel or real estate agents, or cooperative enterprises requiring a nominal membership deposit), it is not considered to be publicly accountable.

Part 1 of the *CICA Handbook* will contain the IFRSs.

Harmonization was chosen instead of the simple adoption of the international standards because security regulations and federal and provincial Companies Acts require financial reporting to be in accordance with Canadian GAAP. Because of this requirement, after the usual public exposure, a separate part of the *CICA Handbook* will contain standards that are the same as IFRSs. All publicly accountable enterprises (essentially those trading on stock exchanges) will have to use the new standards effective for fiscal years beginning after January 1, 2011.

During the transitional period between 2006 and 2011, any converged standards issued by the FASB and the IASB as a result of their agreement to attempt to eliminate differences between U.S. GAAP and IFRSs will be adopted by the CICA. This should reduce the number of differences between Canadian GAAP and IFRSs on the changeover date. In the meantime, it is imperative that Canadian public companies begin to plan for this major change in financial reporting. Education and training will have to start early if the transition is to be a smooth one. Various Canadian organizations involved in education and training will be offering courses. The CICA has dedicated a significant portion of its Web site to IFRSs. It is called Canadian Standards in Transition.[6] The Web site contains CICA publications, publications from the Big Four CA firms, and publications from a variety of other sources. It provides guidance for people at all levels of knowledge of and preparation for IFRSs. The "CICA's Guide to IFRS in Canada" identifies the main differences between *CICA Handbook* sections and IFRSs as at July 31, 2008.

The CICA has published a document comparing current Canadian standards with IFRSs.

While the document states that, in general, the international standards are quite similar to Canadian standards because they are based on similar conceptual frameworks and reach similar conclusions, there are very few section by section comparisons where no differences are noted. Often the document states that "*Handbook* Section X and IFRS Y are converged except for," and in many cases the list of exceptions is fairly lengthy. IFRSs often allow for optional treatments and in some

---

[6] http://www.cica.ca/transition//index.aspx

IFRSs allow the use of fair values and optional treatments to a greater degree than the *CICA Handbook* does.

instances allow or require the use of fair values in financial statement measurements, whereas Canadian standards do not often allow optional treatments and tend to require more historical cost measurements.

While the changeover date is expected to be January 1, 2011, Canadian companies will have to plan for the implementation of the change in years prior to this date. In both their 2008 and 2009 financial statements they were required to disclose management's estimate of the effect that the subsequent changeover would have on their future financial statements.

In 2010, they will have to keep dual records in both Canadian GAAP and in IFRSs, because their 2011 statements will present both the current year and comparative amounts for the previous year under IFRSs. In addition, the 2011 financial statements must include a reconciliation of income under previous GAAP to income under IFRSs for 2010.

GAAP for Private Enterprises

In the 1970s, there was considerable discussion in Canada of Big GAAP versus Little GAAP. The question was as follows: Should there be different rules for big companies than for little companies?

The cost-benefit constraint is used when determining whether a private enterprise can use simpler reporting methods.

It was argued that accounting standards were becoming increasingly complex and that a small company's costs of preparing its financial statements in compliance with the standards were greater than the benefits received by the users of such statements. Hence, small companies should be granted some sort of relief from having to use complex and hard-to-understand standards. Counter-arguments suggested that the concept of fair presentation could not be achieved with different sets of standards and the dividing line between big and small would be too arbitrary to be useful. After much study and discussion the concept of Big GAAP/Little GAAP was abandoned.

In the meantime, the issuance of new complex financial reporting standards continued, and the last straw, so to speak, was the issuance of both the section on presentation and disclosure of financial instruments and the exposure draft on the related measurement issues in the early 1990s. The issue of different standards was revisited by a CICA task force, but this time in relation to public/non-public companies. The task force considered two basic approaches:

- A non-GAAP approach whereby non-public companies could use accounting policies completely separate from GAAP. An example is the use of cash-basis reporting instead of the required accrual basis. This approach was abandoned mainly because provincial and federal Companies Acts require companies to prepare financial statements in accordance with GAAP.

- A GAAP approach. This was looked at from two perspectives: full differentiation and partial differentiation. Full differentiation would encompass two distinct sets of GAAP somewhat similar to the accounting for non-profit organizations and governments (discussed in chapter 12). Partial differentiation encompasses one set of accounting standards with different treatments. This latter approach was adopted in 2002 when Section 1300 Differential Reporting was issued and certain sections of the *CICA Handbook* were amended to allow optional treatments.

Companies were following GAAP when they adopted differential reporting options.

Section 1300 allowed a qualifying enterprise to select which reporting options it would apply when it prepared its financial statements. The differential reporting options allowed were contained in individual *Handbook* sections, and only a few sections contained such options.

Section 1300 was a part of the *Handbook* and was considered a primary source of GAAP. When a company adopted one or more of the differential reporting options, it was still considered to be following GAAP.

A company could adopt some or all of the differential reporting options and had to disclose which options it had adopted.

A company had to disclose that differential reporting had been adopted, which options it had adopted, and that unanimous consent had been obtained from all owners. Each option selected had its own additional disclosure requirements, many of which were extensive.

In 2006, when the decision was made by the Accounting Standards Board (AcSB) to adopt IFRSs for publicly accountable enterprises commencing in 2011, a CICA task force was established to revisit the question of what standards should be applied to private companies. The task force considered three different approaches:

- A non-GAAP approach, whereby private companies could use a more simplified method of reporting than what was presently required under differential reporting.
- A GAAP approach based on requirements being developed by IASB for non-public companies.
- A GAAP approach by developing a separate part of the *CICA Handbook* dedicated solely to private enterprises.

Part 2 of the *CICA Handbook* will contain GAAP for private enterprises.

After much discussion and input from interested stakeholders, in 2009 the Canadian AcSB chose the third approach, which will take effect in 2011 with early adoption allowed in 2009. First of all, it defined a private enterprise (PE) as a profit-oriented enterprise that

(a) has not issued, and is not in the process of issuing, debt or equity instruments that are, or will be, outstanding and traded in a public market (a domestic or foreign stock exchange or an over-the-counter market, including local and regional markets), and

(b) does not hold assets in a fiduciary capacity for a broad group of outsiders as one of its primary businesses.

The proposed standards will be available to any private enterprise. No size threshold or other barriers, such as unanimous consent by shareholders or other users, will be imposed. The standards will stand alone (i.e., private enterprises applying them will not be required to refer to standards applicable to publicly accountable enterprises).

Private enterprises can either report under IFRSs or GAAP for private enterprises.

Private enterprises could follow either the stand-alone standards for private enterprises or IFRSs applicable to public companies. Whatever set of standards is adopted, it must be the whole package. It is not possible to apply certain standards from GAAP for private enterprises and others from GAAP for public companies.

Some private companies may choose to follow GAAP for public companies for the following reasons:

- The company may be of a similar size to certain public companies, and the users of its financial statements may insist on IFRSs so that the company can be compared to other public companies.
- The company may be planning to go public in the near future.

Prior to 2009, the IASB did not have any special standards for private enterprises. In response to strong international demand from both developed and emerging economies for a rigorous and common set of accounting standards for smaller and

The IASB has also developed a self-contained set of standards for small and medium-sized businesses.

medium-sized businesses, the IASB developed a separate set of standards for use by small and medium-sized entities (SMEs), which are estimated to represent more than 95 percent of all companies. The *IFRS for SMEs* is a self-contained standard of about 230 pages (about 10 percent the size of IFRSs for public companies) tailored to the needs and capabilities of smaller businesses. Many of the principles for recognizing and measuring assets, liabilities, income, and expenses for public-company IFRSs have been simplified, topics not relevant to SMEs have been omitted, and the number of required disclosures has been significantly reduced. To further reduce the reporting burden for SMEs, revisions to the IFRSs will be limited to once every three years.

The *IFRS for SMEs* will

- provide improved comparability for users of financial statements;
- enhance the overall confidence in the accounts of SMEs; and
- reduce the significant costs involved in maintaining standards on a national basis.

For now, Canada has decided to develop and maintain its own standards for private enterprises. It is possible that it could adopt *IFRS for SMEs* some time in the future.

GAAP for Not-for-profit Organizations   Prior to 2011, the *CICA Handbook* had a series of sections, the 4400 series, dedicated to not-for-profit organizations (NFPOs). Many of the other *Handbook* sections were also applicable to NFPOs. With the adoption of IFRSs for public companies and the simplification of *Handbook* sections for private companies, a decision had to be made as to how to service the NFPOs.

In December 2008, the AcSB and the Public Sector Accounting Board (PSAB) jointly issued an Invitation to Comment, *Financial Reporting by Not-For-Profit Organizations.* The exposure draft sets out options for the direction of accounting standards for both private and public sector NFPOs. Like their counterparts in private enterprises, NFPOs could use IFRSs for publicly accountable enterprises. IFRSs do not contain any specific standards for NFPOs. The other options were as follows:

NFPOs can choose between IFRSs or some other form of GAAP, which was not yet determined as of December 2009.

1. Use the newly developed standards for private enterprise supplemented by standards specific to NFPOs, i.e., the 4400 series.
2. Use the public-sector standards, i.e., the *Public Sector Accounting Handbook.*
3. Use the public-sector standards supplemented by standards specific to NFPOs, i.e., the 4400 series.

The CICA plans to make a decision on GAAP for NFPOs early in 2010 for reporting periods commencing after January 1, 2011. In the meantime, NFPOs must continue to apply the existing *Handbook* sections.

Reorganization of the *CICA Handbook*   To clearly differentiate the different sets of standards, in 2010 the *CICA Handbook* was broken down into five parts as follows:

- Part I — the IFRSs that apply to publicly accountable enterprises;
- Part II — the made-in-Canada standards that apply to private enterprises;
- Part III — the standards for not-for-profit organizations;

- Part IV — the standards that apply to pension plans; and
- Part V — the standards constituting Canadian GAAP before the mandatory effective date for the adoption of Parts I, II, III, or IV.

Unless otherwise stated, the standards described throughout the text are the IFRSs contained in Part 1 of the *CICA Handbook*.

This textbook will concentrate on IFRSs (i.e., Part I of the *CICA Handbook*) for public companies throughout the main body of each chapter. At the end of each chapter, we will summarize the main differences in the standards for private enterprises as compared to the standards for publicly accountable enterprises. To avoid information overload, we will not compare the Canadian standards for private enterprises to the IFRSs for SMEs. Unless otherwise stated, assume that IFRSs should be applied when answering end-of-chapter material.

A Unique Example that Presents a Comparison between Canadian GAAP and IFRSs

Homburg uses both Canadian standards and IFRSs.

Homburg Invest Inc. is a real estate investment and development company with its head office located in Halifax, Nova Scotia. The company owns office, retail, industrial, and residential apartment and townhouse properties in Canada, Netherlands, Germany, and the United States. The company's real estate portfolio has grown rapidly from approximately $89 million in the year 2000 to approximately $3.7 billion in 2008, at which time it derived 68 percent of its net operating income from Europe, 13 percent from Canada, and 19 percent from other countries. Its shares are listed on both the TSX in Canada and the Euronext in Amsterdam, Netherlands. What makes this company particularly unique is that it presents its shareholders with two sets of annual financial statements: one prepared under Canadian GAAP and the other in accordance with IFRSs.

The two sets of statements for 2008 can be viewed on the company's SEDAR Web site, www.sedar.com. The Canadian GAAP statements include a consolidated balance sheet, statement of earnings, statement of comprehensive income, statement of retained earnings, and statement of cash flows. The IFRS statements contain a consolidated balance sheet, statement of earnings, statement of comprehensive income, statement of changes in equity, and statement of cash flows.

A cursory examination of the two sets of financial statements shows a few minor descriptive differences. It also shows that the form of the two sets of statements is basically the same except for the retained earnings and changes in equity statements, which are quite different because of the greater disclosures required by the international standards.

The differences between reported earnings are very large.

It is when we examine the numbers presented in the statement that we can see some very large differences. Net (loss) is $(276.7) million under IFRSs, while it is $(96.1) million when measured under Canadian GAAP, a difference of almost 190 percent.

A comparison of the two balance sheets indicates the cause of the major differences. Under IAS 40, companies have the option of reporting investment and development properties at either their historical cost (after taking appropriate depreciation) or at fair value (with no depreciation taken). Homburg has chosen the second option. The unrealized gains and losses have been taken into income, and because they do not attract income tax, an appropriate deferred income tax liability has been created. While it was indicated earlier that the differences between the two sets of standards are not great, a comparison of the results presented by Homburg will allow readers to form their own conclusions.

SUMMARY

The diversity among the accounting principles in use throughout the world has long been viewed as a major stumbling block toward achieving the desired goal of a truly global capital market. The IASB has attempted to narrow this diversity by issuing a set of international standards, with the intent that they will be adopted worldwide. While a great deal of progress has been made, the goal of global harmonization and/or convergence has not yet been fully reached. Over 100 countries have adopted these standards, but the United States is still not on board. The United States is lobbying the IASB to incorporate some of the American standards in IFRSs as a condition for their adoption of IFRSs. However, there is often a clash between the rule-based standards used in the United States and the more principle-based approach used in IFRSs. Even if this problem is solved, absolute comparability of financial information on a worldwide basis is still going to be difficult to achieve. There is a problem of consistency in the interpretation of the standards by preparers of financial statements because these standards are broad based and require professional judgment. An additional problem is created by the fact that some countries are not adopting IFRSs, but rather are modifying their own standards so that they are essentially but not completely the same. Other countries are adding additional home-grown standards where it is felt that the international standards are inadequate. Readers of the financial statements of companies from countries such as have just been described will have to understand where the differences lie if they wish to make realistic comparisons with companies in other countries.

The CICA has announced that Canadian public companies will report using IFRSs in 2011. A simplified self-contained set of *Handbook* sections has been developed for private enterprises. The process of reviewing and developing new standards for NFPOs is underway. Needless to say, a great deal is changing. Lots of work will be required to change over to the new standards. Further changes can be expected over the next few years as IFRSs and U.S. GAAP are converged.

Significant Changes in the Last Two Years

1. In the *CICA Handbook*, accounting has been reorganized into four parts. Part I contains IFRSs that apply to publicly accountable enterprises. Part IV contains the standards constituting Canadian GAAP before the mandatory effective date for the adoption of IFRSs.

2. For publicly accountable enterprises, IFRSs have replaced the former sections of the *CICA Handbook*.

3. Differential reporting has been withdrawn and replaced by a self-contained set of standards for private enterprises.

4. FASB has announced that IFRSs may be required by U.S. companies by 2014.

Changes Expected in the Next Three Years

1. The format and structure of financial statements may change to present a cohesive relationship between the various statements. There would be separate sections for operating, investing, and financing activities in each

of the balance sheet, income statement, and cash flow statement. The classification of assets and liabilities in the balance sheet would determine the classification of any related income or expense in the income statement and any related cash flows in the cash flow statement. There may be further disaggregation of assets and liabilities into current and non-current and then according to the measurement basis used. There would be further disaggregation of expenses by function and then by nature. Discontinued operations and income taxes would be presented separately in each of the statements.

2. The Conceptual Framework will be revised to create a sound foundation for future accounting standards that are principles based, internally consistent, and internationally converged. Relevance and faithful representation will be the fundamental qualitative characteristics of financial information. The definitions of assets and liabilities may change to focus more on rights and obligations and to eliminate the reference to past events. When and how to use the various measurement bases may be clarified.

SELF-STUDY PROBLEM

Hyde Ltd. is an E.U.-based company that prepares its consolidated financial statements in accordance with IFRSs. Its profit in Year 3 was $1,000,000, and shareholders' equity at December 31, Year 3, was $8,000,000.

Hyde wishes to list its shares on a U.S. stock exchange. Although no longer required to do so, Hyde has decided to provide a U.S. GAAP reconciliation voluntarily and has engaged you to reconcile profit and shareholders' equity to a U.S. GAAP basis. You have identified the following five areas in which Hyde's accounting principles differ from U.S. GAAP:

1. Inventory — lower of cost or market;
2. Property, plant, and equipment — measurement subsequent to initial recognition;
3. Research and development costs — capitalization of development costs;
4. Sale and leaseback transaction — gain on sale;
5. Property, plant, and equipment — impairment.

Hyde provides the following information with respect to each of these accounting differences.

Inventory

At the end of Year 3, inventory had a historical cost of $20,000, a replacement cost of $18,000, and a net realizable value of $19,000, and the normal profit margin was 20 percent of cost.

Property, Plant, and Equipment

Hyde acquired equipment at the beginning of Year 2 at a cost of $250,000. The equipment has an estimated useful life of 10 years and an estimated residual value of $50,000 and is being depreciated on a straight-line basis. At the beginning of the current year, the equipment was appraised and determined to have a fair value of

$320,000; its estimated useful life and residual value did not change. The company uses the allowed alternative treatment in IAS 16 to periodically revalue the equipment at fair value subsequent to acquisition.

Research and Development Costs

Hyde incurred research and development costs of $100,000 in Year 3. Of this amount, 60 percent related to development activities subsequent to the point at which criteria indicating that the creation of an intangible asset had been met. As of year-end, development of the new product had not been completed.

Sale and Leaseback

In January Year 1, Hyde realized a $150,000 gain on the sale and leaseback of an office building. The lease is accounted for as an operating lease and the term of the lease is five years.

Property, Plant, and Equipment

Hyde owns machinery on December 31, Year 3, with a book value of $20,000, an estimated salvage value of $2,000, and an estimated remaining useful life of 10 years. On that date, the machinery is expected to generate future cash flows of $22,500 and has an estimated fair value, after deducting costs to sell, of $18,000. The present value of expected future cash flows is $18,600.

Required:

Prepare a schedule reconciling IFRS profit and IFRS shareholders' equity to a U.S. GAAP basis. Ignore income taxes.

Solution to Self-study Problem

Hyde Ltd. Reconciliation from IFRSs to U.S. GAAP

Profit under IFRSs	$1,000,000
Adjustments:	
Additional write-down of inventory to replacement cost	(1,000)
Additional depreciation on revaluation of equipment	10,000
Reversal of deferred development costs	(60,000)
Amortization of deferred gain on sale and leaseback	30,000
Reversal of impairment loss	1,400
Profit under U.S. GAAP	$ 980,400
Shareholders' equity under IFRSs	$8,000,000
Adjustments:	
Additional write-down of inventory to replacement cost	(1,000)
Reversal of revaluation surplus on equipment	(90,000)
Accumulated depreciation on revaluation of equipment	10,000
Reversal of deferred development costs	(60,000)
Reversal of gain on sale and leaseback in Year 1	(150,000)
Accumulated amortization of deferred gain on sale and leaseback (Year 1 – Year 3)	90,000
Reversal of impairment loss	1,400
Shareholders' equity under U.S. GAAP	$7,800,400

Explanation

Inventory   In accordance with IAS 2, the company reports inventory on the statement of financial position at the lower of cost ($20,000) and net realizable value ($19,000). As a result, it reported inventory on the December 31, Year 3, statement of financial position at its net realizable value of $19,000, and profit reflected a loss on write-down of inventory of $1,000.

Under U.S. GAAP, the company reports inventory at the lower of cost or market, with market defined as the midpoint of replacement cost ($18,000), net realizable value ($19,000), and net realizable value less a normal profit ($19,000 − 20% × $20,000 = $15,000). In this case, inventory would be written down to replacement cost. A $2,000 loss would be included in Year 3 profit.

U.S. GAAP profit is $1,000 less than IFRS profit. U.S. GAAP retained earnings are lower by the same amount.

Property, Plant, and Equipment   Under IAS 16's benchmark treatment, depreciation expense on equipment in Year 2 was $20,000 ([$250,000 − $50,000]/ 10 years), resulting in a book value of $230,000 at the end of Year 2. The equipment was then revalued upward to its fair value of $320,000 at the beginning of Year 3. The journal entry to record the revaluation was as follows:

Dr. Equipment — net	90,000	
Cr. Revaluation Surplus		90,000

Revaluation Surplus is a shareholders' equity account. In Year 3, depreciation expense was $30,000 ([$320,000 − $50,000]/9 years). Under U.S. GAAP, the company reported depreciation expense of $20,000 in both Year 2 and Year 3. The additional depreciation under IFRSs causes IFRS-based profit in Year 3 to be $10,000 lower than U.S. GAAP-based profit. The revaluation surplus caused IFRS-based shareholders' equity to be $90,000 higher than U.S. GAAP shareholders' equity. This is partially offset by the $10,000 additional depreciation in Year 3 under IFRSs, which resulted in retained earnings being $10,000 lower under IFRSs than under U.S. GAAP.

Research and Development Costs   Under IAS 38, $40,000 of research and development costs would be expensed in Year 3, and $60,000 of development costs would be capitalized as an intangible asset.

Under U.S. GAAP, research and development expense of $100,000 would be recognized in determining Year 3 profit.

IFRS-based profit and retained earnings in Year 3 would be $60,000 higher than U.S. GAAP-based profit. Because the new product had not yet been brought to market, there was no amortization of the deferred development costs under IFRSs in Year 3.

Sale and Leaseback   Under IAS 17, the entire gain of $150,000 on the sale and leaseback was recognized in profit in Year 1. This resulted in a $150,000 increase in retained earnings in that year.

Under U.S. GAAP, the gain on the sale and leaseback is recognized in profit over the life of the lease. With a lease term of five years, $30,000 of the gain would be recognized in Year 3, and $30,000 of the gain would have been recognized in each of Year 1 and Year 2, resulting in a cumulative amount of retained earnings of $90,000 at the end of Year 3.

In Year 3, U.S. GAAP profit was $30,000 higher than IFRS-based profit, and shareholders' equity under IFRS was $60,000 higher than under U.S. GAAP at December 31, Year 3.

Property, Plant, and Equipment   Under IAS 36, an asset is impaired when its carrying value exceeds its recoverable amount, which is the higher of (1) its value in use (present value of expected future cash flows) and (2) its fair value less costs to sell. The machinery had a carrying value of $20,000, and its value in use was $18,600, which is more than the fair value less cost to sell of $18,000. An impairment loss of $1,400 ($20,000 − $18,600) would have been recognized in determining Year 3 profit, with a corresponding reduction in retained earnings under IFRSs.

Under U.S. GAAP, an impairment occurs when an asset's carrying value exceeds its undiscounted expected future cash flows. In this case, the expected future cash flows are $22,500, which is higher than the machinery's carrying value, so no impairment occurred.

REVIEW QUESTIONS

1. Why is it important to supplement studies of Canadian accounting principles with studies of the accounting practices used in other countries?

2. In what manner has there been a shift toward a global capital market in recent years?

3. List the factors that have influenced the accounting standards used in a particular country.

4. What role does the stage of development of a country's capital markets have on the direction taken by the country's accounting standards?

5. In what way has the level of inflation influenced the accounting standards of a particular country?

6. In what manner does the balance-sheet format used by companies in other countries differ from the format used by Canadian companies?

7. Up until 2011, Canadian companies whose shares trade on U.S. stock exchanges are required to reconcile Canadian GAAP income to U.S. GAAP income. What are some of the causes of differences?

8. What is the goal of the IASB?

9. What does the FASB-IASB convergence project expect to achieve? How will it be carried out?

10. What evidence is there that IASB pronouncements are becoming acceptable throughout the world?

11. What direction does Canada plan to take with regard to the harmonization or convergence of accounting standards for publicly accountable enterprises?

12. Explain why complete comparability on a worldwide basis is going to be difficult to achieve despite a switch-over to IFRSs.

13. Briefly explain why the Canadian AcSB decided to create a separate section of the *CICA Handbook* for private enterprises.

14. Briefly explain why a Canadian private company may decide to follow IFRSs for public companies, even though it could follow GAAP for private companies.

15. Financial statements are now beyond the comprehension of the average person. Many of the accounting terms and methods of accounting used

are simply too complex to understand just from reading the financial statements. Additional explanations should be provided with, or in, the financial statements, to help investors understand the financial statements. Discuss.

(*CICA adapted*)

MULTIPLE-CHOICE QUESTIONS

1. Which of the following is not a reason for establishing international accounting standards?
   a. Some countries do not have the resources to develop accounting standards on their own.
   b. Comparability is needed between companies operating in different areas of the world.
   c. Some of the accounting principles allowed in various countries report markedly different results for similar transactions.
   d. Demand in Canada is heavy for an alternative to the principles found in the *CICA Handbook*.

2. A key factor necessary for the future realization of worldwide use of common accounting standards is the convergence of IASB standards with those of
   a. Canada.
   b. The European Union.
   c. China.
   d. The United States.

3. The IASB-FASB convergence project has as its goal
   a. Having IASB standards acceptable for reporting under SEC regulations.
   b. Focusing on the elimination of minor differences that currently exist between the standards of the two bodies.
   c. Working together on the issuance of future standards in areas where serious differences exist.
   d. All of the above.

4. According to critics, what is the major problem with the original standards produced by the IASB?
   a. Too many popular methods have been eliminated.
   b. Too many optional methods have remained.
   c. The IASB has failed to examine and report on key accounting issues.
   d. The pronouncements have tended to be too similar to Canadian GAAP.

5. Accounting and other types of technology are imported and exported, and countries have similar accounting for this reason. Which one of the following reasons has been most significant in increasing the influence that the United States has had on accounting in Canada?
   a. Canadian companies routinely sell shares of stock or borrow money in the United States.
   b. The countries have similar political systems.
   c. Both countries are involved in the European Community.
   d. The countries are close geographically.

6. By which of the following means has the IASB made efforts to improve its standards?
   a. By ensuring member countries reflect IASB standards in legal statutes.
   b. By reducing the number of acceptable alternatives permitted.
   c. By requiring all member countries to comply with IASB standards.
   d. By adopting U.S. accounting standards.

7. Which of the following is *not* a fundamental focus of the IASB?
   a. To achieve harmonization with Canadian GAAP.
   b. To achieve convergence with the FASB.
   c. To work with the FASB to agree on much-needed improvements to existing standards.
   d. To provide uniform accounting standards for multinational corporations.

8. Great strides have been made toward achieving international accounting harmonization over the last few years. Which of the following has helped to facilitate international accounting harmonization?
   a. Harmonization of the tax systems of many countries.
   b. The U.S. SEC.
   c. Adoption in 2003 of an enforcement mechanism to ensure correct application of IASB standards.
   d. A requirement that European companies report their results using IASB standards.

(*CGA-Canada adapted*)

Use the following data for Questions 9 and 10.

Lawland Co. owns 100 percent of the common shares of Minerva Co., a British company with a manufacturing plant in Oxford, England. Using IFRSs, British companies are allowed to revalue their fixed assets to current values with the revaluation adjustment recorded in a reserve account in shareholders' equity. Amortization expense is based on the current values of any revalued assets. The revaluation adjustment is transferred from the reserve account directly to retained earnings over the life of the revalued asset. At the end of Year 7, an appraisal of Minerva's manufacturing plant indicated that the current value was £500,000 greater than its net book value and indicated an estimated remaining life of 10 years.

9. If Minerva revalues its manufacturing plant, what impact will this revaluation have on its debt-to-equity ratio on the date of the revaluation?
   a. It will not change.
   b. It will decrease.
   c. It will increase.
   d. It cannot be determined.

10. If Minerva revalues its manufacturing plant, what impact will this revaluation have on Minerva's income in the first year after the revaluation?
   a. It will not change.
   b. It will increase.
   c. It will decrease.
   d. It cannot be determined.

(*CGA-Canada adapted*)

11. Which of the following best describes a difference in the application of Canadian and U.S. GAAP?
     a. Income under Canadian GAAP is typically lower than income under U.S. GAAP.
     b. American pronouncements tend to be more detailed than Canadian pronouncements.
     c. Both countries adopt accounting standards based on income tax laws.
     d. The level of inflation is a big factor in determining accounting standards in the United States but is not a big factor in Canada.

     (CGA-Canada adapted)

12. What is the Norwalk Agreement?
     a. An agreement between the FASB and the SEC to allow foreign companies to use IFRSs in their filing of financial statements with the SEC.
     b. An agreement between FASB and the U.K. AcSB to converge their respective accounting standards as soon as practicable.
     c. An agreement between the SEC chairman and the E.U. Internal Market commissioner to allow E.U. companies to list securities in the United States without providing a U.S. GAAP reconciliation.
     d. An agreement between the FASB and the IASB to make their existing standards compatible as soon as practicable and to work together to ensure compatibility in the future.

Use the following data for Questions 13 and 14.

ACC Communications Inc. is a Canadian public company with its head office located in Kanata, Ontario. Its common shares are listed on both the Toronto and Tokyo stock exchanges. ACC has a wholly owned subsidiary in Japan. The subsidiary uses accounting principles consistent with Canadian GAAP except for one item. It amortizes its capital assets using rates allowed for income tax purposes, which has the effect of amortizing the assets over a period much shorter than the useful lives of the assets.

13. Which of the following would best satisfy the various international users of ACC's financial statements?
     a. Issuing consolidated financial statements prepared in accordance with U.S. GAAP and using the Canadian dollar as the reporting currency.
     b. Issuing consolidated financial statements prepared in accordance with Canadian GAAP and using the U.S. dollar as the reporting currency.
     c. Issuing consolidated financial statements prepared in accordance with Japanese GAAP and using the Canadian dollar as the reporting currency.
     d. Issuing consolidated financial statements prepared in accordance with Japanese GAAP and using the U.S. dollar as the reporting currency.

14. What is the impact of converting the financial statements of the Japanese subsidiary to Canadian GAAP?
     a. Net income will increase.
     b. The debt-to-equity ratio will increase.
     c. The return on assets will decrease.
     d. The current ratio will decrease.

15. Which of the following is true for reporting by private enterprises in accordance with GAAP?
    a. They must use the stand-alone standards for private enterprises.
    b. They can choose to use some policies from GAAP for private enterprises and some policies from GAAP for publicly accountable enterprises.
    c. They can choose to report investments in associates under the cost method or the equity method.
    d. They would choose to use GAAP for publicly accountable enterprises if the cost of providing this information to the users is greater than the benefits provided.

CASES

Case 1 In this era of rapidly changing technology, research and development (R&D) expenditures represent one of the most important factors in the future success of many companies. Organizations that spend too little on R&D risk being left behind by the competition. Conversely, companies that spend too much may waste money or not be able to make efficient use of the results.

In the United States, all R&D expenditures are expensed as incurred. Mexico uses this same treatment. However, expensing all R&D costs is not an approach used in much of the world. Firms using IFRSs must capitalize development costs as an intangible asset when they can demonstrate

(a) the technical feasibility of completing the intangible asset so that it will be available for use or sale;
(b) its intention to complete the intangible asset and use or sell it;
(c) its ability to use or sell the intangible asset;
(d) how the intangible asset will generate probable future economic benefits — among other things, the entity can demonstrate the existence of a market for the output of the intangible asset or the intangible asset itself or, if it is to be used internally, the usefulness of the intangible asset;
(e) the availability of adequate technical, financial, and other resources to complete the development and to use or sell the intangible asset; and
(f) its ability to measure reliably the expenditure attributable to the intangible asset during its development.

Similarly, Canadian companies must capitalize development costs when certain criteria are met. Japanese accounting allows R&D costs to be capitalized if the research is directed toward new goods or techniques, development of markets, or exploitation of resources. Korean businesses capitalize their R&D costs when they are incurred in relation to a specific product or technology, when costs can be separately identified, and when the recovery of costs is reasonably expected. Brazil also allows R&D costs to be capitalized under certain conditions.

Required:
Provide your response and a brief explanation to each of the following questions:
(a) Should any portion of R&D costs be capitalized?
(b) Is expensing all R&D expenditures the best method of reporting these vital costs?

(c) Is the U.S. system necessarily the best approach?

(d) Which approach provides the best representation of the company's activities?

Case 2 You are examining the consolidated financial statements of a European company that have been prepared in accordance with IFRSs. You determine that property, plant, and equipment is revalued each year to its current replacement cost; income and equity are adjusted; and the notes to the financial statements include the following items as a part of the summary of significant accounting policies:

- Tangible fixed assets are valued at replacement cost, less accumulated depreciation. The replacement cost is based on valuations made by internal and external experts, taking technical and economic developments into account and supported by the experience gained in the construction of plant assets throughout the world.
- Valuation differences resulting from revaluation are credited or debited to equity, where it is applicable, after deduction of an amount for deferred tax liabilities.
- Depreciation based on replacement cost is applied on a straight-line basis in accordance with the estimated useful life of each asset.

The provisions of IFRSs permit the use of alternatives to historical cost in the valuation of assets. IAS 16 specifically notes that, as an allowed alternative treatment to historical cost:

> Subsequent to initial recognition as an asset, an item of property, plant and equipment should be carried at a revalued amount, being its fair value at the date of the revaluation less any subsequent accumulated depreciation and subsequent accumulated impairment losses. Revaluations should be made with sufficient regularity such that the carrying amount does not differ materially from that which would be determined using fair value at the balance sheet date.

The auditor of the company has expressed his opinion on the financial statements and concluded that they present a "true and fair view."

The use of replacement cost accounting is a departure from the historical cost principle and represents a fundamental difference in the approach to financial reporting in this country as compared to the United States. The debate as to the relative importance of relevance and reliability is one that surfaces often in the study of international accounting issues. Many countries are very strict as to the use of historical cost for all valuations and in the computation of income and often allow reductions from historical cost, but not increases (such as with the application of the lower of cost or market rule); others are very flexible in the choice of permissible approaches; still others are very strict in that particular alternatives to historical cost (such as replacement cost or general price-level-adjusted amounts) must be used.

Required:

(a) Can any alternative to historical cost provide for fair presentation in financial reports, or are the risks too great? Discuss.

(b) Discuss the relative merits of historical cost accounting and replacement cost accounting. Consider the question of the achievement of a balance between relevance and reliability and the provision of a "true and fair view" or "fair presentation" in financial reporting.

Case 3   John McCurdy has recently joined a consultant group that provides investment advice to the managers of a special investment fund. This investment fund was created by a group of NFPOs, all of which have endowment funds, and rather than investing their resources individually, they have instead chosen a pooled approach whereby a single fund invests their moneys and distributes the earnings back to them on an annual basis. The board of directors of the investment fund, made up of members from each of the NFPOs, meets periodically to review performance and to make investment decisions.

John has been following the fortunes of Ajax Communications Corporation for a number of years. Ajax is a Canadian company listed on the TSX. During the past year it made a major acquisition that has changed the basic parameters of the firm. It also obtained a listing on the New York Stock Exchange, and as a result, it has presented two sets of year-end financial statements, one based on Canadian GAAP and the other prepared in accordance with U.S. GAAP. John has been asked to prepare a report on Ajax that he will present to the board of the investment fund. He knows that the board will be interested in knowing why the two sets of financial statements show markedly different results. As a starting point John listed the following items taken from the year-end statements (in millions of dollars except for earnings per share):

	U.S. GAAP U.S. dollars	Canadian GAAP U.S. dollars
Extracts from the income statement		
Total revenue	$3,388.9	$2,611.9
Operating income	89.1	329.1
Income before extraordinary items	14.9	199.4
Net income	(66.2)	199.4
Extracts from the balance sheet		
Total current assets	$ 862.1	$1,360.7
Investments	233.1	59.2
Property, plant, and equipment, net	889.9	1,866.5
Deferred income taxes	50.3	47.6
Intangibles, net	1,016.4	5,473.0
Other assets	90.8	265.1
Total assets	$3,142.6	$9,072.1

Working with this list, John's next step will be to determine why there is such a difference in the numbers.

Required:

(a) As John McCurdy, outline the initial approach that you will take in order to determine the reasons for the differences in the numbers.
(b) List some of the obvious items that need resolution and indicate some of the possible causes of the discrepancies.

(adapted from a case developed by Peter Secord, St. Mary's University)

Case 4   A shareholder of Homburg Invest Inc. has approached you with a copy of the company's 2008 financial statements prepared under both IFRSs and Canadian GAAP. This person indicates that she would gain a better picture as to where the differences in net earnings come from if she could see a reconciliation of net income under IFRSs to net earnings under Canadian GAAP.

Required:

(a) Prepare such a reconciliation.
(b) Review the notes to the financial statements and write a brief note outlining why the differences shown in your reconciliation exist.

Case 5   Roman Systems Inc. (RSI) is a Canadian private company. It was incorporated in Year 1 by its sole common shareholder, Marge Roman. RSI manufactures, installs, and provides product support for its line of surveillance cameras.

Marge started the company with a small investment. For Years 7 through 9, the company grew rapidly. Most of the expansion was funded through debt financing. The rapid growth is attributable to several large contracts signed with banks for the installation of security camera systems at their branches.

RSI has a June 30 year-end. You, CA, are with the firm of Sylvain and Charest, Chartered Accountants (SC). Your firm has performed the audit of RSI since its incorporation and prepares RSI's corporate tax returns and those of Marge Roman and her family.

Marge Roman called you in April Year 12, just as you were about to start planning the audit. Marge informed you that she plans to take RSI public within the next year. Marge is negotiating with several underwriters, but no deal is in place yet.

During the telephone conversation, Marge asked you and the partner on the audit to meet with her some time in early June to discuss and resolve potential issues related to the June 30 audit of RSI. In prior years, financial statements were issued in September, but this year the deadline for finalizing the financial statements will likely be in early August. Marge agreed that you would perform your interim audit procedures based on RSI's results as at April 30, Year 12.

It is now June Year 12. The planning and interim work for the fiscal Year 12 audit has been completed. A summary of items noted in the April 30, Year 12, interim financial statements as a result of work done to date is included in Exhibit I.

You are about to leave for the day when the partner in charge of the account comes into your office and announces that he has just received a call from Marge and she would like to meet with him within the next few days. He asks you to prepare a memo discussing the financial reporting issues arising from the interim audit work and any other matters that he should raise at the meeting. Ignore, for now, any additional audit procedures that should be considered as a result of the issues raised during the interim audit.

Required:

Prepare the memo.

NOTES FROM THE INTERIM AUDIT

General

Pre-tax earnings for the period ended April 30, Year 12, were $1,375,000. For the fiscal years Year 11 and Year 10, RSI recorded pre-tax earnings of $435,000 and $325,000, respectively.

Marge Roman has received a valuation report valuing the company at $12 million. Shareholders' equity as at April 30, Year 12, consisted of:

100 common shares (voting)	$100
Retained earnings	$9,159,000

New Software

The company has been using a standard general ledger software package originally installed in Year 6 by a local computer consulting firm and upgraded annually.

In January Year 12, RSI hired BBC to oversee the implementation of a new third-party package. In March Year 12, RSI began converting its financial reporting system. The new general ledger software was installed in parallel with the old software and went live on April 1, Year 12.

The new general ledger software has been used to generate RSI's financial results since April 1, Year 12. Starting July 1, Year 12, the old system will no longer be used in parallel.

To date, RSI has been invoiced $720,000 by BBC. These costs have all been capitalized in the April 30, Year 12, financial statements. The invoices show the following services and costs:

Initial review and recommendations	$110,000
Cost of new software	200,000
Implementation work	120,000
Training work	225,000
Monthly support fee (April)	25,000
Other consulting (to April 30)	40,000
	$720,000

In addition, as at April 30, Year 12, RSI also capitalized $70,000 related to the salaries of four employees who have worked on the accounting software project since January 1, Year 12. As a result of these individuals being pulled out of their regular jobs to handle the problem, RSI had to hire two additional employees.

The costs will be amortized beginning on July 1, Year 12, on a straight-line basis over three years. RSI intends to treat approximately $135,000 of net book value for the old software as part of the cost of the new software by reallocating this balance.

Revenues

During fiscal Year 11, total product revenue was $18.2 million and maintenance contract revenue was $5.6 million. For the period ended April Year 12, product revenue was $13.2 million, and maintenance contract revenue was $5.2 million.

RSI recognizes product revenue when shipment and installation take place. It is RSI's standard practice to request a customer sign-off for any installation work. The installation crew normally gets sign-off on the day of installation. During interim work for fiscal Year 12, it was noted in the audit file that approximately $640,000 of revenue recognized in April Year 12 related to work installed and invoiced in April, but customer sign-off was obtained only in early May. Such situations have not caught anyone's attention in previous years. RSI explained that it had recently hired new service technicians who were unfamiliar with the policy of customer sign-off and, accordingly, had to send technicians back to the client days after the installation was completed to get the sign-offs.

In addition, there was a new product line in fiscal Year 12, called "Automated Bank Machine" (ABM), which generated transaction-fee revenue of $4.25 million. The company is planning to highlight its revenue growth in its annual press release publicizing its year-end results. Marge wants to show strong revenue growth to attract investors.

Maintenance contract revenues relate to one-year agreements that RSI signs with customers wanting product support. During the year, the company changed its revenue recognition policy on maintenance contracts to recognize revenue based on estimated costs incurred on the contract. Revenue is recognized as follows: 25 percent in each of the first two months of the contract and 5 percent in each subsequent month. This allocation is based on a study done by RSI in Year 10, which showed that the costs incurred on the contracts are mostly incurred in the first two months, during which RSI sends out a technician to perform preventive maintenance. The preventive maintenance reduces the number of future service calls and, therefore, overall costs.

ABM Business

As a result of RSI's strong relationship with its financial institution and Marge's desire to diversify RSI's product line, RSI began selling ABMs in fiscal Year 12. The machines are purchased from a large electronic equipment manufacturer that is responsible for ongoing maintenance of the ABMs. RSI sells the ABMs to restaurants, bars, and clubs at margins of 5 percent. The sales revenue is included as product revenue.

The standard ABM sales agreement states that, for a three-year period from the date of sale, RSI receives 40 percent of the transaction fee charged to customers using the machine in addition to the sales revenue. A further 40 percent of the fee is payable to the financial institution for managing the cash in the machines, and the remaining 20 percent is remitted to the machine owners. The transaction fee charged to customers using an ABM is normally $1.50. RSI is not responsible for stocking the ABM with cash or emptying the cash machine. The financial institution performs all cash management duties and remits to RSI, at month-end, a statement showing money owed to RSI for its share of the transaction fee. A day later, the funds are deposited directly into RSI's main bank account.

RSI has booked as an expense $2,547,000 related to the fees attributable to the financial institution and the machine owners.

Debentures

In January Year 12, RSI needed long-term financing and issued to a third-party venture capitalist $2,500,000 of debentures maturing in 10 years, with interest at 7.35 percent. The debentures are included as long-term debt in the accounts. The debentures are convertible at the option of the holder, at a rate of one voting common share for every $5 of debenture, if RSI issues shares to the public. If RSI does not issue shares to the public before June 30, Year 13, the debentures are repayable upon demand.

Accounts Receivable

Review of the aging of accounts receivable at April 30, Year 12, showed an amount of $835,000 in the over-120-day category. According to RSI's collection department, the balance relates to payments withheld by one of RSI's largest customers, Mountain Bank. RSI had contracted to install security cameras at all of its branches. The work was performed in August Year 11, a customer sign-off was received at each branch, and invoices were sent in early September. Mountain Bank refused to pay individual invoices. It wants to pay the total of all invoices in one payment.

In October Year 11, a few branches of Mountain Bank contacted their head office and requested that no payment be made to RSI until certain corrections were made to the angles at which the cameras were installed. Although not required to do so under its agreement with Mountain Bank, RSI fixed the problems, as Mountain Bank is one of its largest customers.

On June 1, Year 12, $450,000 was received. Mountain Bank asserts that some work remains to be done at 5 to 10 sites and is withholding final payment until it is completely satisfied. All amounts related to the contract are recorded as revenues. Internal reports reveal that it takes a service person approximately one hour to fix the problems at each branch. No significant materials costs have been incurred for the follow-up visits.

(CICA adapted)

PROBLEMS

Problem 1 IAS 16, "Property, Plant, and Equipment" requires assets to be initially measured at cost. Subsequently, assets may be carried at cost less accumulated amortization or they can be periodically revalued upward to current value and carried at the revalued amount less accumulated amortization. If revalued, the adjustment is recorded as a component of shareholders' equity. Subsequent amortization is based on the revalued amount. U.S. GAAP does not allow assets to be revalued at an amount exceeding historical cost less accumulated amortization.

ABC Ltd. lists its shares on an exchange that allows it to report either in accordance with U.S. GAAP or by using IFRSs. On January 1, Year 1, it acquired an asset at a cost of $10 million, which will be amortized on a straight-line basis over an estimated useful life of 20 years. On January 1, Year 3, the company hired an appraiser, who determined the fair value of the asset (net of accumulated amortization) to be $12 million.

Required:

(a) Determine the amortization expense recognized in Year 2, Year 3, and Year 4 under
   (i) the revaluation treatment allowed under IAS 16, and
   (ii) U.S. GAAP.
(b) Determine the book value of the asset under the two different sets of accounting rules at January 2, Year 3; December 31, Year 3; and December 31, Year 4.
(c) Summarize the differences in profit and shareholders' equity over the 20-year life of the asset using the two different sets of accounting rules.

Problem 2 Fast Ltd. is an E.U.-based company that prepares its consolidated financial statements in accordance with IFRSs. Its net income in Year 2 was $200,000, and shareholders' equity at December 31, Year 2, was $1,800,000.

Fast lists its shares on a U.S. stock exchange. Although no longer required to do so, Fast has decided to voluntarily provide a U.S. GAAP reconciliation. You have identified the following four areas in which Fast's accounting principles differ from U.S. GAAP.

1. Fast Company gathered the following information related to inventory that it owned on December 31, Year 2:

Historical cost	$100,000
Replacement cost	95,000
Net realizable value	98,000
Normal profit margin as percentage of cost	20%

2. Fast incurs research and development costs of $500,000 in Year 1, 30 percent of which relate to development activities subsequent to certain criteria having been met that suggest that an intangible asset has been created. The newly developed product is brought to market in January Year 2 and is expected to generate sales revenue for 10 years.

3. Fast sold a building to a bank at the beginning of Year 1 at a gain of $50,000 and immediately leased the building back for a period of five years. The lease is accounted for as an operating lease.

4. Fast acquired equipment at the beginning of Year 1 at a cost of $100,000. The equipment has a five-year life with no expected residual value and is depreciated on a straight-line basis. At December 31, Year 1, Fast compiled the following information related to this equipment:

Expected future cash flows from use of the equipment	$85,000
Present value of expected future cash flows from use of the equipment	75,000
Fair value (net selling price), less costs to dispose	72,000

Required:

(a) Determine the amount at which Fast should report each of the following on its balance sheet at December 31, Year 2, using (1) IFRSs and (2) U.S. GAAP. Ignore the possibility of any additional impairment or reversal of impairment loss at the end of Year 2.
 (i) Inventory.
 (ii) Research and development.
 (iii) Deferred gain on lease.
 (iv) Equipment.

(b) Prepare a reconciliation of net income for Year 2 and shareholders' equity at December 31, Year 2, under IFRSs to a U.S. GAAP basis.

WEB-BASED PROBLEMS

Note: The annual reports of companies listed on U.S. stock exchanges can be accessed through the SEC's EDGAR system at www.sec.gov/edgar.shtml. Under this system, one can search by company name, country, SIC code, etc. The annual report is labelled as Form 20-F or Form 40-F.

Problem 1   Access a recent annual report for a company incorporated in China and listed on a U.S. stock exchange. Answer the questions below. For each question, indicate where in the financial statements you found the answer and/or provide a brief explanation.

(a) In what currency are the financial statements presented?

(b) GAAP from what country or jurisdiction were used in preparing the financial statements? See the notes to the financial statements.

(c) Is there a reconciliation of net income as reported to net income under U.S. GAAP? If so, identify the three major differences. If not, explain why the reconciliation was not provided.

(d) Calculate the current ratio for each of the last two years. Did the liquidity position of the company improve or weaken during the year?

(e) Calculate the total debt-to-equity ratio for each of the last two years. Did the solvency position of the company improve or weaken during the year?

(f) Did income increase or decrease from the previous year? What item on the income statement had the biggest impact on the change in income?

Problem 2   Access a recent annual report for a company incorporated in India and listed on a U.S. stock exchange. Answer the same questions as in Problem 1. (Not all questions are necessarily applicable.)

Problem 3   Access a recent annual report for a company incorporated in Japan and listed on a U.S. stock exchange. Answer the same questions as in Problem 1. (Not all questions are necessarily applicable.)

Problem 4   Commencing in 2007, foreign companies that were using IFRSs did not have to reconcile their reported profit to profit under U.S. GAAP. Access the most recent annual report for Cadbury, a British chocolate manufacturer, and the 2006 annual report for Cadbury. Answer the questions below for each of the two years. For each question, indicate where in the financial statements you found the answer and/or provide a brief explanation.

(a) In what currency are the financial statements presented?

(b) GAAP from what country or jurisdiction were used in preparing the financial statements?

(c) What was the percentage difference in reported profit versus profit under U.S. GAAP?

(d) What three items caused the biggest change in profit between the two different GAAPs?

(e) If a reconciliation to U.S. GAAP were not provided, how would a financial analyst deal with this situation when comparing Cadbury to another company reporting under U.S. GAAP?

Problem 5   Commencing in 2007, foreign companies that were using IFRSs did not have to reconcile their reported shareholders' equity to shareholders' equity under U.S. GAAP. Access the most recent annual report for Philips Electronics, a Dutch company, and the 2006 annual report for Philips. Answer the questions below for each of the two years. For each question, indicate where in the financial statements you found the answer and/or provide a brief explanation.

(a) In what currency are the financial statements presented?

(b) GAAP from what country or jurisdiction were used in preparing the financial statements?

(c) What was the percentage difference between the reported shareholders' equity and shareholders' equity under U.S. GAAP?

(d) What three items caused the biggest change in shareholders' equity between the two different GAAPs?

(e) If a reconciliation to U.S. GAAP were not provided, how would a financial analyst deal with this situation when comparing Philips to another company reporting under U.S. GAAP?

Chapter ② Investments in Equity Securities

LEARNING OBJECTIVES

After studying this chapter, you should be able to do the following:

1. Describe the broad relationship between all the relevant standards from Part I of the *CICA Handbook* that comprise the "big picture."
2. Distinguish between the various types of equity investments.
3. Evaluate relevant factors to determine whether an investor has significant influence over an investee.
4. Prepare journal entries to account for investments under the cost and equity methods.
5. State the disclosure requirements related to an investment in associate.

INTRODUCTION

There are many different methods for reporting investments in equity securities.

Emera Inc. is an energy and services company with 600,000 customers and $5.3 billion in assets. Emera operates two wholly owned regulated utility subsidiaries, Nova Scotia Power Inc. and Bangor Hydro-Electric Company. Nova Scotia Power supplies over 95 percent of the electric generation, transmission, and distribution in Nova Scotia. Bangor Hydro provides electricity transmission and distribution service to 117,000 customers in eastern Maine. In addition to its electric utilities, Emera owns a 12.9 percent interest in the Maritimes & Northeast Pipeline that transports Sable natural gas to markets in Maritime Canada and the northeastern United States.

Such information is hardly uncommon in the business world; corporate as well as individual investors frequently acquire ownership shares of both domestic and foreign businesses. These investments can range from a few shares to the acquisition of 100 percent control. There are many different methods of reporting these investments, ranging from fair value approaches to cost-based approaches. Unrealized gains can be recognized in profit or in other comprehensive income.

Over the next eight chapters, we will examine various methods of reporting investments in equity securities. The focus is on investments where one firm possesses either significant influence or control over another through ownership of voting shares. Transactions between these non-arm's-length entities require special scrutiny and special accounting procedures. We will begin our journey by reviewing the rules for financial instruments and then spend considerable time in preparing consolidated financial statements in increasingly complicated situations.

Equity Investments — The Big Picture

Equity investments are investments in shares of another company.

This is the first of eight chapters that make up a single accounting topic. This topic can be described by the following question: How should a Canadian company report, in its financial statements, an investment in the shares of another company?

As of January 1, 2010, there are five different types of share investments:

- Significant influence.
- Control.
- Joint control.
- Fair value through profit and loss (FVTPL).
- Available-for-sale (AFS).

The first three types of investments are called strategic investments because the investor intends to establish or maintain a long-term operating relationship with the entity in which the investment is made. The last two types are nonstrategic investments. The method of reporting these investments is summarized in Exhibit 2.1. We will discuss and illustrate the accounting for these different types of investments later in this chapter and throughout the text.

In November 2009, the IASB approved IFRS 9: Financial Instruments — Classification and Measurement. It replaces and supercedes the classification and measurement standards that are in IAS 39: Financial Instruments — Recognition and Measurement. It will be mandatorily effective for fiscal period beginning on or after January 1, 2013, but early adoption is permitted starting in 2009.

Starting in 2013, nonstrategic investments in private companies must be reported at fair value.

IFRS 9 requires that all nonstrategic equity investments be valued at fair value, including investments in private companies. Under IAS 39, investments that did not have a quoted market price in an active market and whose fair value could not be reliably measured were reported at cost. This provision no longer exists under IFRS 9.

The IASB recognizes that measuring all investments in equity instruments at fair value would impose additional costs on preparers. In the IASB's view, these costs are justified by improved and useful decision-making information about equity investments for users of financial statements. Measuring all investments in equity

---

Exhibit 2.1

REPORTING METHODS FOR INVESTMENTS IN EQUITY SECURITIES

Type of Investment	Reporting Method	Reporting of Unrealized Gains
Strategic		
Significant influence	Equity method	Not applicable
Control	Full consolidation	Not applicable
Joint control	Proportionate consolidation	Not applicable
Nonstrategic	Fair value method	In net income
FVTPL		
Available-for-sale		
— Market value available	Fair value method	In other comprehensive income
— Market value not available	Cost method	Not applicable

instruments in the same way would also simplify the accounting requirements and improve comparability.

In limited circumstances, cost may be an appropriate estimate of fair value. The IASB has a fair value measurement project on its agenda and hopes to develop a standard for fair value measurement within the next few years.

Available-for-sale investments are being phased out as a separate category of investments.

IFRS 9 no longer refers to and does not have any specific provisions for available-for-sale investments; in effect, the available-for-sale investment disappears as a separate category of equity investments. However, an entity can elect on initial recognition to present the fair value changes on an equity investment that is not held for short-term trading in other comprehensive income (OCI). These are the same rules that were previously applied for available-for-sale investments. One significant change is that the gains or losses are cleared out of OCI and credited or charged directly to retained earnings when the investment is sold and are never recycled through net income.

A major subset of this large topic is the preparation of consolidated financial statements, which in itself is fraught with complexity. There is always a danger that, in attempting to absorb a large amount of new material, you will concentrate on the details to the point of losing sight of the big picture. It is very important that you don't lose sight of the forest when you study the trees.

Always try to understand the forest before looking at the trees.

Before proceeding with our examination of the "trees," it would be useful to look at this "forest." The question posed above provides a path into the forest. The accounting principles involved with this question are contained in numerous standards and interpretations issued by the IASB.

We will use a summarized balance sheet to illustrate the question, and then outline the possible answers that are contained in the IASB standards.

The balance sheet of J Company Ltd. is below.

J COMPANY LTD.
BALANCE SHEET

Miscellaneous assets	$ XXX	Liabilities	$ XXX
Investment in shares		Shareholders' equity	
of K Corporation	**XXX**	Common shares	XXX
		Retained earnings	XXX
	$ XXX		$ XXX

Dollar amounts have been omitted from the statement because our focus is on the amount that should be shown for "Investment in shares of K Corporation."

Four IFRSs are directly related to providing an answer to this question; eight other IFRSs and three interpretations must also be considered. A brief summary of the provisions contained in these sections is presented next.

A Cautionary Note   At the time of writing this sixth edition, there were a number of CICA and IASB exposure drafts outstanding on topics relevant to this course. This text has incorporated the proposals in any exposure drafts with an effective date of January 1, 2011, or earlier on the basis that all proposed changes will be approved and will be required as of January 1, 2011. We will use Connect (www.mcgrawhillconnect.ca) to keep you informed of any deviations from what was proposed to what finally ends up in the *CICA Handbook.*

Directly Related IFRSs

1. IAS 27: Consolidated and Separate Financial Statements

Consolidated financial
statements are prepared
when one company controls
another company.

If J Company controls K Corporation, then J Company is called a parent company and K Corporation is called a subsidiary, and GAAP require the preparation of consolidated financial statements by J Company. This involves removing the investment in K Corporation from J Company's balance sheet and replacing it with the assets and liabilities from the balance sheet of K Corporation. This process is illustrated in Chapter 3 and in the chapters that follow it.

Control is the power to direct
the activities of another
entity to generate returns.

Control exists if J Company has the power to direct the activities of K Company to generate returns for J Company. In other words, J Company can determine the key operating and financing policies of K Company. Control is generally presumed if J Company's investment consists of a majority of the voting shares of K Corporation; but as we will see in later discussions,[1] control can exist with smaller holdings and does not necessarily exist with majority holdings.

If the investment is not one that produces control, then IAS 28, IAS 31, and IAS 39 must be examined to determine the required financial reporting.

2. IAS 28: Investments in Associates

This standard describes the financial reporting required for investments in associates, i.e., investments where the investor has significant influence over the investee. Significant influence refers to an investment that does not convey control or joint control, but that does allow the investor to exercise significant influence over the strategic operating and financing policies of the investee. IAS 28 indicates that an investment of 20 percent or more of the voting shares of K Corporation, without control being present, would be presumed to be a significant influence investment, unless there is evidence to the contrary.

The equity method is used
when the investor has
significant influence over the
investee.

If J Company's investment is one of significant influence, it must be reported by the equity method. Thus the investment is initially recorded at cost and then adjusted thereafter to include J Company's pro rata share of the earnings or losses of K Corporation adjusted for the acquisition differential[2] and the elimination and subsequent recognition of all unrealized intercompany profits that occur as a result of transactions between the two companies. Dividends received from K Corporation are recorded as a reduction of the investment.

The accounting for significant influence investments will be illustrated fully in later sections of this chapter.

3. IAS 31: Joint Arrangements

If the investment is not one of the two just described, it may possibly be a joint arrangement if the following general provisions of this standard are satisfied.

For a joint arrangement to exist, the owners (the venturers) must have made a contractual arrangement that establishes joint control over the venture. Under such joint control, each venturer shares in some manner the power to determine strategic operating and financing policies, and no single venturer is able to unilaterally control the venture.

---

[1] The concept of control is discussed in greater detail in Chapter 3.
[2] The concept of an acquisition differential is discussed later.

Under this standard, J Company Ltd. (the "venturer") reports its investment in K Corporation Ltd. (the "venture") by using either proportionate consolidation or the equity method. These methods are illustrated in Chapter 9.

4. IFRS 9: Financial Instruments — Classification and Measurement

IFRS 9 requires that all nonstrategic equity investments be valued at fair value with the fair value changes reported in profit or loss. However, an entity can elect on initial recognition to present the fair value changes on an equity investment that is not held for short-term trading in OCI. The dividends on such investments must be recognized in profit and loss. When the investment is sold, the gains or losses are cleared out of OCI and credited or charged directly to retained earnings. Accounting for fair value investments will be illustrated later in this chapter.

Other Related IFRSs

The remaining eight important IFRSs and three interpretations are directly related to the four standards that were just outlined. They are discussed briefly below.

5. IAS 39: Financial Instruments — Recognition and Measurement

IAS 39 indicates when and how hedge accounting can be used to ensure that gains and losses on a hedged item are reported in income in the same period as the gains and losses on the hedging item. In Chapters 10 and 11, we will illustrate fair value hedges, cash flow hedges, and hedges of a net investment in a foreign operation whose functional currency is not Canadian dollars.

6. IFRS 3: Business Combinations

A business combination is a transaction or other event in which an acquirer obtains control of one or more businesses. J Company Ltd. usually obtains *control* over the net assets of K Corporation by either

(a) investing in the voting shares of K Corporation (a parent–subsidiary relationship), or

(b) purchasing the net assets of K Corporation (not a parent–subsidiary relationship).

Business combination accounting is explained in Chapter 3. On the date that a parent–subsidiary relationship is established, a business combination has occurred.

7. IFRS 8: Operating Segments

Consolidated financial statements often result in the aggregating of the statements of companies in diverse businesses located in countries throughout the world. Disaggregation into operating segments and disclosures about products, geographic areas, and major customers is required by this standard in order to improve the information content of the consolidated statements. Segment disclosures are discussed in Chapter 9.

8. IAS 1: Presentation of Financial Statements

This standard states that a complete set of financial statements comprises the following:

(a) A statement of financial position as at the end of the period;

(b) A statement of comprehensive income for the period;

The equity method or proportionate consolidation is required when the investor has joint control over a joint venture.

All nonstrategic investments must be valued at fair value at each reporting date.

The cost method is used when market value is not available for available-for-sale investments.

A business combination can occur indirectly by buying shares or directly by buying the net assets of another company.

Segment disclosures provide a breakdown of the aggregated information into various operating and geographical segments.

(c) A statement of changes in equity for the period;

(d) A statement of cash flows for the period.

The statement of comprehensive income comprises a section for profit or loss and a section for other comprehensive income.

Different titles and formats may be used for the financial statements under IAS 1.

A Cautionary Note   Although the titles stated above are recommended, they are not mandatory. Many Canadian companies now use and will likely continue to use the titles of *balance sheet* (rather than *statement of financial position*) and *income statement* (rather than *statement of profit or loss*). In this textbook, we will use both sets of titles. We will also vary the ordering of assets, liabilities, and shareholders' equity. In some cases, current assets will appear first and shareholders' equity will appear last. In other cases, long-term assets will be followed by current assets and shareholders' equity will precede liabilities on the credit side of the statement of financial position. Both formats are acceptable under IAS 1. In the problems and illustrations that do not involve OCI, we will focus only on the statement of profit or loss (i.e., the income statement), rather than on the statement of comprehensive income, and a statement of retained earnings, rather than on preparing a complete statement of changes in equity.

IAS 1 requires reporting enterprises to differentiate between profit as traditionally reported on the income statement and other comprehensive income. Other comprehensive income includes unrealized gains on certain equity investments and exchange gains and losses related to certain hedges of foreign currency transactions and types of foreign operations (illustrated in Chapters 10 and 11).

9. IFRS 12: Income Taxes

The provisions of this standard add some complications to the asset valuations associated with business combinations and consolidated financial statements. These provisions are discussed in Chapters 6 and 9.

10. IAS 21: The Effects of Changes in Foreign Exchange Rates

This standard deals with the translation of the financial statements of foreign investees, subsidiaries, and joint ventures, and with the translation of transactions denominated in foreign currencies.

Provisions of this section would apply if

Foreign transactions and foreign financial statements must be translated to the entity's presentation currency.

(a) K Corporation was located in a foreign country and/or prepared its financial statements in a foreign currency, or

(b) J Company Ltd. had borrowings or lendings and/or export/import activities denominated in foreign currencies.

Chapters 10 and 11 examine the accounting concepts involved here.

11. IAS 36: Impairment of Assets

This standard describes the impairment tests to be applied to all assets. We will primarily apply the standard to investments in associates, goodwill, and other intangible assets. This topic is discussed in Chapter 5.

12. IAS 38: Intangible Assets

IFRS 3: Business Combinations outlines the procedures for allocating the acquisition cost of a subsidiary company to identifiable net assets and goodwill. IAS 38 provides additional guidance regarding the allocation problem by detailing the various intangible assets that might have been acquired. This topic is discussed in Chapter 3.

13. IFRIC 16: Hedges of a Net Investment in a Foreign Operation

This interpretation provides guidance in applying IAS 21. We will discuss this topic further in Chapter 11.

14. SIC 12: Consolidation — Special-Purpose Entities

An SPE must be consolidated when the reporting entity has control of the SPE.

In the 1990s, many companies incorporated a special purpose entity (SPE) to carry out very specific and limited functions on behalf of the reporting entity. SIC 12 provides guidance in determining whether the reporting entity has control of the SPE and whether it should consolidate the SPE. We will discuss SPEs in Chapter 9.

15. SIC 13: Jointly Controlled Entities — Non-monetary Contributions by Venturers

This interpretation provides guidance in determining the amount of gain to be recognized when a venturer invests in a joint venture by contributing a non-monetary asset. This topic will be discussed in Chapter 9.

The big picture, the details of which are contained in a number of later chapters in this book, has been outlined in this overview. You will find it useful to refer to this overview and the "forest" described as you study the material that follows. We will now begin our examination of the "trees."

This chapter examines situations where a share investment does not constitute control or joint control. We will segregate our discussion of these investments on the basis of whether the investments are or are not valued at fair value on each reporting date.

Investments Valued at Fair Value

Unrealized gains/losses are reported in net income for FVTPL investments.

IAS 39 deals with two types of equity investments: fair value through profit or loss (FVTPL) and available for sale (AFS). FVTPL investments include investments held for short-term trading and any other investments the entity wishes to designate in this category. Investments held for short-term trading are classified as current assets on the basis that these investments are actively traded and intended by management to be sold within one year. FVPTL investments are initially reported at fair value and subsequently revalued at fair value at each reporting date. The unrealized gains and losses are reported in net income along with dividends received or receivable.

Unrealized gains/losses are reported in other comprehensive income for available-for-sale investments.

Available-for-sale investments are classified as current or noncurrent assets depending on how long company managers intend to hold on to these shares. These investments are initially reported at fair value and subsequently revalued at fair value at each reporting date, with one exception. If fair value cannot be reliably measured, these investments will be reported using the cost method. When these shares are valued at fair value, the unrealized gains and losses are reported in other comprehensive income. When the investment is sold, the previously reported unrealized gains and losses will be removed from other comprehensive income and realized gains and losses will be reported in net income. Dividends are recorded as income when they are declared.

There are two options for reporting other comprehensive income. Under the first option, all items of income and expense are reported in a single statement of comprehensive income; the other comprehensive income items are reported separately at the bottom of this statement after net income. Under the second option, two separate statements are prepared. The first statement, typically called the income statement, displays the components of net income. The second statement, typically called the statement of comprehensive income, starts with net income from the income statements and then displays the different components of other comprehensive income. Both options end up showing comprehensive income as the last line on the statement. In either case, net income is added to retained earnings as in the past and other comprehensive income is added to cumulative other comprehensive income. Retained earnings and each class of cumulative other comprehensive income must be reported as separate components of shareholders' equity. We will illustrate the presentation of other comprehensive income and the components of shareholders' equity in Chapters 10 and 11.

Other comprehensive income is not included in retained earnings but is included as a separate component of shareholders' equity.

Investments Not Valued at Fair Value

When investments are not reported at fair value, they are usually reported using the cost method or the equity method. The next two subsections describe when these methods are used and illustrate how to apply them.

Cost Method of Reporting on Equity Investment

The cost method is used for external and internal reporting purposes.

The cost method is used under IFRSs in the following situations:

- For available-for-sale investments when the market price in an active market is not available and fair value is not reliably measurable. This requirement is specified in IAS 39 and is available until 2013 if the reporting entity does not adopt IFRS 9 early.
- For investments in controlled entities. This is an option when the reporting entity prepares separate-entity financial statements in addition to consolidated financial statements. This situation will be discussed further in Chapter 5.
- For a parent company's internal accounting records prior to preparing consolidated financial statements. This situation will also be discussed further in Chapter 5.

The cost method is the main method of reporting nonstrategic investments by private enterprises when the market value of the investment is not readily available.

The investment must be written down when there is an impairment.

Under the cost method, the investment is initially recorded at cost. The investor's share of the dividends declared is reported in net income. The investment is reported at original cost at each reporting date unless the investment becomes impaired. Impairment losses are reported in net income.

Prior to 2009, a liquidating dividend was treated by the investor as a reduction in the investment account. A liquidating dividend occurred when the cumulative amount paid out as dividends since acquisition of the investment was greater than the total of the net incomes earned by the investee since acquisition. Since dividends are a company's method of distributing earnings to its owners, it follows that a company cannot distribute as income more than it has earned. When it does so, it is really returning part of the original investment to its owners.

A liquidating dividend is reported as dividend income under the cost method.

Even though it may be conceptually more appropriate to treat a liquidating dividend as a return of capital, the costs and complexities involved in determining whether or not the dividend is a liquidating dividend is often greater than the benefit. Accordingly, IAS 27 was changed in 2009 to require that all dividends be recognized in net income regardless of whether or not they were liquidating dividends.

Illustration On January 1, Year 1, Jenstar Corp. purchased 10 percent of the outstanding common shares of Safebuy Company at a cost of $95,000. Safebuy reported net income of $100,000 and paid dividends of $75,000 for the year ended December 31, Year 1.

Utilizing the cost method to account for its investment, Jenstar would make the following journal entries:

```
Jan. 1, Year 1
Investment in Safebuy                                    95,000
    Cash                                                          95,000
To record the acquisition of 10% of Safebuy's shares
```

Under the cost method, income is recognized when dividends are received/receivable.

```
Dec. 31, Year 1
Cash                                                      7,500
    Dividend income                                               7,500
Receipt of dividend from Safebuy
```

Equity Method of Reporting an Equity Investment

An investment in associate is an investment in the voting shares of a corporation that permits the investor to exercise significant influence over the strategic operating and financing policies of the investee; at the same time, however, it does not establish control or joint control over that investee. Note that the criteria for this type of investment require only the *ability* to exercise significant influence; there is no requirement to show that such influence is actually being exercised in a particular situation.

An associate is an entity over which the investor has significant influence.

The following conditions are possible indicators that significant influence is present and that the investee is an associate:

(a) Representation on the board of directors or equivalent governing body of the investee;

(b) Participation in policy-making processes, including participation in decisions about dividends or other distributions;

(c) Material transactions between the investor and the investee;

(d) Interchange of managerial personnel; or

(e) Provision of essential technical information.

A guideline (not a rigid rule) in determining whether there is significant influence is 20 to 50 percent of voting shares.

IAS 28 suggests that a holding between 20 and 50 percent may indicate the presence of significant influence, but it also states that a holding of this size does not necessarily mean that such influence exists. The following scenarios will illustrate this.

Given that A Company owns 60 percent of the voting shares of C Company (probably a control investment), does B Company's holding of 30 percent of C Company's shares indicate that B Company has a significant influence investment?

When one investor has control, other investors usually do not have significant influence.

Not necessarily. If B Company were unable to obtain membership on the board of directors of C Company or participate in its strategic policymaking because of A Company's control, it would be difficult to conclude that B Company has significant influence. In such a situation, B Company's holding would be considered a nonstrategic investment. Would this situation be different if B Company were allowed membership on C Company's board of directors?

IAS 28 indicates that a substantial or majority ownership by another investor would not necessarily preclude an investor from exercising significant influence. In other words, another company's control investment in C Company does not mean that B Company's 30 percent investment in C Company can never be considered to be significant influence. Determination of significant influence depends on the particular circumstances and the use of judgment.

On the other hand, is it possible to have significant influence with less than 20 percent? Normally, an investment of less than 20 percent would not allow the investor to elect any members to the board of directors of the investee corporation; because of this, it probably cannot exert any influence on the decision-making processes of that company. However, 20 percent is only a guideline, and an examination of the facts may suggest some other type of investment. For example, if the investee's shares are widely distributed, and all the other shareholders hold very small blocks of shares and display indifference as to the make-up of the board of directors, an investment of less than 20 percent may be considered a significant influence investment. This could certainly be the case if some of the remaining shareholders gave the investor proxies to vote their shares.

When an investor has less than 20 percent of the voting shares, it usually does not have significant influence.

From all these discussions and examples, it should be obvious that considerable professional judgment is required in determining whether an investor has significant influence. In later chapters, when we discuss the criteria used to determine whether a particular investment establishes control over an investee, we will also conclude that considerable professional judgment is required.

When an investor has significant influence, the investment should be reported by the equity method. The basic concept behind the equity method is that the investor records its proportionate share of the associate's income as its own income and reduces the investment account by its share of the associate's dividends declared.

Illustration of Equity Method Basics

We return to the example of the Jenstar and Safebuy companies. All the facts remain the same, including the 10 percent ownership, except that we assume this is a significant influence investment. Using the equity method, Jenstar's journal entries would be as follows:

Jan. 1, Year 1

Investment in Safebuy	95,000	
Cash		95,000

To record the acquisition of 10% of Safebuy's shares

Income is recognized based on the income reported by the associate, and dividends are reported as a reduction of the investment account.

Dec. 31, Year 1

Investment in Safebuy	10,000	
Investment income		10,000

10% of Safebuy's Year 1 net income

Cash	7,500	
Investment in Safebuy		7,500
Receipt of dividend from Safebuy		

The equity method picks up the investor's share of the changes in the associate's shareholders' equity.

Under the equity method, the investor's investment account changes in direct relation to the changes taking place in the investee's equity accounts. The accounting objective is to reflect in the investor's financial statements the financial results arising from the close relationship between the companies. The equity method is effective at achieving this. Because the investor is able to influence the associate's dividend policy, dividends could end up being paid in periods during which the investee was suffering considerable losses. The cost method of reporting would reflect investment income, whereas the equity method would report investment losses during these periods.

The equity method provides information on the potential for future cash flows.

The equity method reflects the accrual method of income measurement. As the investee earns income, the investor accrues its share of this income. The associate is not obligated to pay out this income as a dividend on an annual basis. The investor can expect to get the dividend at a later date or expect to sell its shares at a higher value if the income is not paid out as a dividend. Therefore, the equity method does provide useful information about the future cash flow potential from the investment.

Additional Features Associated with the Equity Method

The previous example illustrated the basic concepts of the equity method. Besides these fundamentals, the following features are relevant for this course:

- The accounting for other changes in associate's equity,
- Acquisition costs greater than book value,
- Unrealized intercompany profits,
- Changes to and from the equity method,
- Losses exceeding the balance in the investment account,
- Impairment losses,
- Gains or losses on sale of investment, and
- Disclosure requirements.

Other Changes in Associate's Equity   In accounting for an investment by the equity method, IAS 28 requires that the investor's proportionate share of the associate's discontinued operations, other comprehensive income, changes in accounting policy, corrections of errors relating to prior-period financial statements, and capital transactions should be presented and disclosed in the investor's financial statements according to their nature.

The investor's income statement should reflect its share of the investee's income according to the different categories of comprehensive income.

Companies report certain items separately on their statements of comprehensive income so that financial statement users can distinguish between the portion of comprehensive income that comes from continuing operations and the portion that comes from other sources, such as discontinued operations and other comprehensive income. Retrospective adjustments of prior-period results and capital transactions are shown as separate components of retained earnings, or are disclosed in the footnotes.

Example   A Company owns 30 percent of B Company. The statement of comprehensive income for B Company for the current year is as follows:

B COMPANY
STATEMENT OF COMPREHENSIVE INCOME
CURRENT YEAR

Sales	$500,000
Operating expenses	200,000
Operating income before income tax	300,000
Income tax	120,000
Net income from operations	180,000
Loss from discontinued operations (net of tax)	40,000
Net income	140,000
Other comprehensive income (net of tax)	10,000
Comprehensive income	$150,000

Upon receiving this income statement, A Company makes the following journal entry to apply the equity method:

The investor's shares of income from continuing operations, discontinued operations, and other comprehensive income are reported separately.

Investment in B Company (30% × 150,000)	45,000	
Investment loss, discontinued operations*	12,000	
Other comprehensive income**		3,000
Investment income (30% × 180,000)		54,000

   * 30% × 40,000
  ** 30% × 10,000

All three income items, which total $45,000, will appear on A Company's statement of comprehensive income. The investment loss from discontinued operations and the other comprehensive income items require the same presentation as would be made if A Company had discontinued operations or other comprehensive income of its own. Full footnote disclosure is required to indicate that these particular items arise from an investment in associate accounted for by the equity method. Materiality has to be considered because these items do not require special treatment in A Company's income statement if they are not material from A Company's point of view, even though they *are* material from B Company's perspective.

Many accounting procedures required for consolidated purposes are also required under the equity method.

Many of the accounting procedures for the application of the equity method are similar to the consolidation procedures for a parent and its subsidiary. Furthermore, the concepts underlying the procedures used in accounting for the acquisition of a subsidiary are also adopted in accounting for the acquisition of an investment in associate. The next two sections briefly describe procedures required in applying the equity method that are equally applicable under the consolidation process. In this chapter, we will describe the procedures very generally. We will discuss these procedures in more detail in later chapters when we illustrate the consolidation of a parent and its subsidiary.

Acquisition Costs Greater than Book Values   In the previous examples, we recorded Jenstar's initial investment at its cost, but we did not consider the implications of this cost with regard to Safebuy's book value at the time. We now add a new feature to equity method reporting by considering the difference between the amount paid for the investment and the investor's share of the book value of the associate's shareholders' equity.

Companies' shares often trade at prices that are different from their book values. There are many reasons for this. The share price presumably reflects the fair value of the company as a whole. In effect, it reflects the fair value of the assets and liabilities of the company as a whole. However, many of the company's assets are reported at historical cost or cost less accumulated amortization. For these assets, there will be a difference between the fair value and the carrying value. Some of the company's value may be attributed to assets that are not even reported on the company's books. For example, the company may have expensed its research and development costs in the past but is now close to patenting a new technology. This technology could have considerable value to a prospective purchaser even though there is no asset recorded in the company's books. Last but not least, the company's earnings potential may be so great that an investor is willing to pay an amount in excess of the fair value of the company's net assets.[3] This excess payment is referred to as goodwill.

The difference between the investor's cost and the investor's percentage of the book value of the associate's identifiable net assets is called the acquisition differential. The investor allocates this differential to specific assets and liabilities of the associate and then either depreciates the allocated components over their useful lives or writes down the allocated component when there has been an impairment in its value. This process of identifying, allocating, and amortizing the acquisition differential will be illustrated in later chapters.

The investor's cost is usually greater than its share of the book value of the associate's net assets.

Consolidated statements should reflect only the results of transactions with outsiders.

Profits from intercompany transactions must be eliminated until the assets are sold to outsiders or consumed by the purchaser.

Unrealized Profits   As we will see in later chapters, consolidated financial statements result from combining the financial statements of a parent company with the financial statements of its subsidiaries. The end result is the financial reporting of a single economic entity, made up of a number of separate legal entities. One of the major tasks in this process is to eliminate all intercompany transactions — especially intercompany "profits" — so that the consolidated statements reflect only transactions with outsiders. The basic premise behind the elimination is that from the point of view of this single accounting entity, "you can't make a profit selling to yourself." Any such "unrealized profits" from intercompany transfers of inventory (or other assets) must be held back until the specific assets involved are sold to outside entities.

In the case of a significant influence investment, any transactions between the investor and the associate (they are related parties) must be scrutinized so that incomes are not overstated through the back-and-forth transfer of assets. From an accounting perspective, any transfer is acceptable provided that both parties record the transfer at the value at which it is being carried in the records of the selling company. However, if the transfer involves a profit, a portion of that profit must be held back on an after-tax basis in the investor's equity method journal entries. When the asset in question is sold outside or consumed by the purchaser, the after-tax profit is realized through an equity method journal entry, again made by the investor. The entries under the equity method to account for unrealized and realized profit from intercompany transactions will be discussed and illustrated in detail in Chapters 6 and 7.

---

[3] Net assets are equal to total assets less total liabilities. Shareholders' equity is equal to net assets. In making this type of calculation, it is often easier to use the amount for shareholders' equity rather than compute the amount for net assets.

Changes in reporting methods are accounted for prospectively if they are changed because of a change in circumstance.

Changes to and from the Equity Method   The classification of long-term investments will change as the particular facts change. An investment may initially be FVTPL and subsequently change to one of significant influence. This could happen if additional shares were acquired. Once significant influence has been achieved, a switch from the previous way of reporting is made on a prospective basis. The fair value carrying amount on this date becomes its new cost. If circumstances change, significant influence may also be achieved without additional shares being acquired, in which case the equity method would commence. For example, the holdings of a large block of investee shares by another company could prevent an investor from exercising significant influence. But if that other company sells its block on the market, the investor's previous FVTPL investment may now amount to significant influence.

The carrying amount on the date of the change becomes the cost of the investment for future reporting.

When an investment changes from significant influence to FVTPL the equity method ceases to be appropriate and the fair value method takes its place, also on a prospective basis. On this date, the investor shall measure at fair value any investment the investor retains in the former associate. The investor shall recognize in profit or loss any difference between

(a) the fair value of any retained investment and any proceeds from disposing of the part interest in the associate; and

(b) the carrying amount of the investment at the date when significant influence is lost.

If an investor loses significant influence over an associate, the investor must account for all amounts recognized in other comprehensive income in relation to that associate on the same basis as would be required if the associate had directly disposed of the related assets or liabilities. When the investor sells its investment in the associate, it is, in effect, selling its proportionate share of the assets and liabilities of the associate. Therefore, if a gain or loss previously recognized in other comprehensive income by an associate would be reclassified to net income on the disposal of the related assets or liabilities, the investor reclassifies the gain or loss from cumulative other comprehensive income to net income (as a reclassification adjustment) when it loses significant influence over the associate. For example, if an associate had reported other comprehensive income on a cash flow hedge and the investor loses significant influence over the associate, the investor must reclassify to net income the gain or loss previously recognized in other comprehensive income in relation to that hedge. If an investor's ownership interest in an associate is reduced, but the investment continues to be an associate, the investor must reclassify to net income only a proportionate amount of the gain or loss previously recognized in other comprehensive income.

When an investment changes from significant influence to control, the preparation of consolidated statements commences, again on a prospective basis. The concepts relating to this particular situation will be discussed at length in later chapters.

If an investor guaranteed an investee's obligations, the investor could end up reporting its investment as a liability rather than an asset.

Losses Exceeding the Balance in the Investment Account   A question arises as to the appropriate accounting when an investor's share of associate's losses exceeds the carrying amount of the investment. There are two possible ways to treat this. The investor could reduce the investment account to zero and commence the use of the equity method when its share of associate's earnings exceeds its share of losses. Alternatively, the investor could continue to accrue losses even though they result in a negative balance in the investment account. IAS 28 provides some guidance on this issue. After the investor's interest in the associate is reduced to zero, additional losses are provided for, and a liability is recognized, *only* to the extent that the investor has incurred legal or constructive obligations or made payments on behalf of the associate. The investor would have an obligation if it guaranteed certain liabilities of the associate or if it committed to provide additional financial support to the associate. If a liability is not reported, the investor resumes recognizing its share of those profits only after its share of the profits equals the share of losses not recognized.

Other long-term interests in the associate may have to be written down when the associate is reporting losses.

If the investor has other long-term interests in the associate over and above its equity investment, these other assets may also have to be written down. Such items may include preference shares and long-term receivables or loans but do not include trade receivables, trade payables, or any long-term receivables for which adequate collateral exists. Losses recognized under the equity method in excess of the investor's investment in ordinary shares are applied to the other components of the investor's interest in an associate in the reverse order of their seniority (i.e., priority in liquidation). Accordingly, an investment in preferred shares should be written down before a long-term note receivable because the preferred share becomes worthless before a note receivable. In other words, the note receivable has priority over the investment in preferred shares in the event that the associate is liquidated.

Impairment Losses   After application of the equity method as described in the previous paragraphs, the investment is tested for impairment in accordance with IAS 36, as a single asset, by comparing its recoverable amount (higher of value in use and fair value less costs to sell) to its carrying amount. In determining the value in use of the investment, an entity estimates

(a) its share of the present value of the estimated future cash flows expected to be generated by the associate, including the cash flows from the operations of the associate and the proceeds on the ultimate disposal of the investment, or

(b) the present value of the estimated future cash flows expected to arise from dividends to be received from the investment and from its ultimate disposal.

If the recoverable amount is less than the carrying value, the investment is written down to the recoverable amount. The impairment loss is not allocated to goodwill or any other assets underlying the carrying amount of the investment because these underlying assets were not separately recognized. If the recoverable amount increases in subsequent periods, the impairment loss can be reversed.

Average cost should be used in determining any gain or loss when an investor sells part of its investment.

Gains and Losses on Sale of Investments   When all the shares that make up a long-term investment are sold, the gain (loss) is shown on the income statement and is calculated as the difference between the sale proceeds and the carrying amount of the investment. When only some of the shares are sold, the gain is calculated using the average carrying value of the investment. Formulas such as first in, first out (FIFO) or last in, last out (LIFO) or specific identification are not permitted. If a portion of a significant influence or a control investment is sold, a re-evaluation must be made to determine whether the previous classification is still valid.

Disclosure Requirements   Investments in associates shall be classified as non-current assets. The investor's share of the profit or loss of such associates, and the carrying amount of these investments, must be separately disclosed. In addition, the following summarizes the main disclosures required in IAS 28 for investments in associates:

The fair value of an investment in associate should be disclosed when it is readily available.

(a) The fair value of investments in associates for which there are published price quotations;

(b) Summarized financial information of associates, including the aggregated amounts of assets, liabilities, revenues, and profit or loss;

(c) The reasons the investor has significant influence even though it owns less than 20 percent of the voting or potential voting power of the investee;

(d) The reasons the investor does not have significant influence even though it owns 20 percent or more of the voting or potential voting power of the investee;

(e) The unrecognized share of losses of an associate, both for the period and cumulatively, if an investor has discontinued recognition of its share of losses of an associate; and

(f) Its share of the contingent liabilities of an associate incurred jointly with other investors and those contingent liabilities that arise because the investor is severally liable for all or part of the liabilities of the associate.

A Cautionary Note   Most of the examples of note disclosure in the text are taken from foreign countries where IFRSs have been used for a few years. This ensures that the illustrations capture IFRSs currently in use. Future editions of the text will use examples from Canadian companies once they have implemented IFRSs.

XYZ Company is a multinational corporation with a balanced business portfolio of activities predominantly in the field of electronics and electrical engineering. It reported numerous investments under the equity method in its 2008 financial statements. Excerpts from these statements are presented in Exhibit 2.2.

GAAP for Private Enterprises

As mentioned in Chapter 1 and as we have seen in this chapter, most of the discussion in this textbook deals with GAAP for publicly accountable enterprises. Starting in this chapter and in each subsequent chapter, we will have a section at the end of each chapter on GAAP for private enterprises, which we will refer to as *PE GAAP*. In this section, the differences in the reporting requirements for private entities for the topics discussed in the chapter will be summarized. Detailed illustrations will not be provided.

Section 3051: Investments is the first section we have discussed that provides different standards for a private enterprise than for a publicly accountable enterprise. The following excerpts from Section 3051 of Part II of the *CICA Handbook* outline the main requirements for significant influence investments:

Under PE GAAP, investments in associates can be reported at cost or a simplified version of the equity method.

• An investor that is able to exercise significant influence over an investee should make an accounting policy choice to account for the investment using either the equity method or the cost method. An investor should account for all investments within the scope of this Section using the same method.

Exhibit 2.2

EXTRACTS (IN PART) FROM XYZ COMPANY'S 2008 FINANCIAL STATEMENTS

Associated companies — Companies in which XYZ has the ability to exercise significant influence over operating and financial policies (generally through direct or indirect ownership of 20% to 50% of the voting rights) are recorded in the Consolidated Financial Statements using the equity method of accounting and are initially recognized at cost.... When XYZ's share of losses in an associated company equals or exceeds its interest in the associate, XYZ does not recognize further losses, unless it incurs obligations or makes payments on behalf of the associate. Material intercompany results arising from transactions between Siemens and its associated companies are eliminated to the extent of XYZ's interest in the associated company.

8. Income (loss) from investments accounted for using the equity method, net

	Year ended September 30,	
	2008	2007
Share of profit, net	259	75
Gains (losses) on sales, net	1	35
Impairment	–	(2)
	260	108

19. Investments accounted for using the equity method

Significant information on the income, assets, and liabilities of the associate must be disclosed.

As of September 30, 2008 LIM Limited, NOX Inc., and TAP Company, which are all unlisted, were the principal investments accounted for using the equity method. Summarized financial information for LIM, NOX, and TAP, not adjusted for the percentage of ownership held by XYZ is presented below.

	September 30,	
	2008	2007
Total assets*	27,300	26,457
Total liabilities*	18,642	17,355

* Balance sheet information for NOX and TAP as of June 30; for LIM as of September 30.

	Year ended, September 30,	
	2008	2007
Revenue**	27,871	18,631
Net income (loss)**	(24)	(628)

** Income statement information for LIM for the twelve months ended September 30, 2008 and the six months ended September 30, 2007; for NOX and TAP for the twelve months ended June 30, 2008 and 2007.

- When an investee's equity securities are traded in an active market, the cost method should not be used. Under such circumstances, the investment may be accounted for at fair value, with changes in fair value recorded in net income.
- Investment income as calculated by the equity method should be the investor's share of the income or losses of the investee. No adjustments are required for the amortization of the acquisition differential.
- The investments in and income from companies subject to significant influence and other investments accounted for at cost should be reported separately.

GAAP for private companies is also quite different for financial instruments. The following excerpts from Section 3856: Financial Instruments of Part II of the *CICA Handbook* outline the main requirements for nonstrategic investments:

Under PE GAAP, nonstrategic equity investments will be reported at cost unless the market value is readily available or the entity elects to report at fair value.

- Investments in equity instruments that are quoted in an active market should be reported at fair value and any changes in fair value should be reported in net income.

- Investments in equity instruments that are not quoted in an active market should be reported at cost less any reduction for impairment, and the impairment losses should be reported in net income.

- An entity may elect to measure any equity investment at fair value by designating that fair value measurement shall apply.

U.S. GAAP Differences

U.S. GAAP and IFRSs are essentially the same for investments in associates. The significant differences are summarized as follows:

There are some minor differences for reporting investments in associates under U.S. GAAP.

1. Whereas IFRSs require that the time between reporting dates of the investor and associate must not be more than three months apart and the reporting entity must adjust for any significant intervening transactions, U.S. GAAP states that the time between reporting dates generally should not be more than three months and the reporting entity must disclose the effects of (and may adjust for) any significant intervening transactions.

2. Whereas IFRSs require that the accounting policies of the investor and associate conform, the SEC staff does not require policies to conform provided that policies are in accordance with U.S. GAAP.

3. Losses in excess of the investor's interest in the associate should continue to be recognized when the associate is imminently expected to return to profitability.

A Cautionary Note When answering the end-of-chapter material for Chapters 2 through 11, assume that IFRSs are to be applied unless otherwise stated.

SUMMARY

FVTPL investments and most AFS investments are reported at fair value. Dividends from these investments are reported in income when they are declared. Unrealized gains and losses are reported in net income for FVTPL investments and in other comprehensive income for AFS investments. If a quoted market price in an active market is not available for the AFS investments, these investments are reported using the cost method. AFS investments will cease to exist as an investment category when IFRS 9 becomes mandatory on January 1, 2013, or when an reporting entity chooses to adopt IFRS 9 early.

An investment where the investor is able to significantly influence the operations of the investee is called an investment in associate and must be accounted for using the equity method, as described in IAS 28. This requires the investor to record its share of all increases in the shareholders' equity of the investee, adjusted for the amortization of the acquisition differential and the holdback and realization of profits from the intercompany sale of assets.

Significant Changes in the Last Two Years

1. For publicly accountable enterprises, IFRSs have replaced the former sections of the *CICA Handbook*. The following table shows the IFRSs covered in this chapter along with their counterparts from the former sections of the *CICA Handbook:*

IFRSs	CICA Handbook *Counterparts*
IFRS 9: Financial Instruments — Classification and Measurement IAS 39: Financial Instruments — Recognition and Measurement	Section 3855: Financial Instruments — Recognition and Measurement
IAS 1: Presentation of Financial Statements	Section 1530: Comprehensive Income Section 3251: Equity
IAS 28: Investments in Associates	Section 3051: Investments

2. IFRSs classify certain investments as fair-value-through-profit-or-loss, whereas the *CICA Handbook* called these investments held for trading.

3. IFRS 9 has been issued as a replacement for parts of IAS 39. It will become mandatorily effective on January 1, 2013, with early adoption permitted starting in 2009. All nonstrategic equity investments will have to be valued at fair value with changes in fair value reported in net income; however, an entity can elect on initial recognition to report the fair value changes on an equity investment that is not held for short-term trading in other comprehensive income.

4. A receipt of a liquidating dividend is reported in net income, whereas it used to be reported as a reduction in the investment account.

5. If the investor has other long-term interests in the associate over and above its equity investment, these other assets may have to be written down when the losses by the investee have wiped out any balance in the investment account.

6. The fair value of investments in associates for which there are published price quotations should be disclosed.

Changes Expected in the Next Three Years

1. Fair value measurement guidance contained in individual IFRSs may be replaced by a single, unified definition of fair value, which may be defined as the price that would be received to sell an asset or paid to transfer a liability in an orderly transaction between market participants at the measurement date (an exit price). It would reflect the highest and best use for the asset.

2. Authoritative guidance may be provided on the application of fair value measurement in inactive or illiquid markets.

SELF-STUDY PROBLEM

Part A   On January 1, Year 5, High Inc. purchased 10 percent of the outstanding common shares of Lowe Corp. for $192,000. From High's perspective, Lowe was a FVTPL investment. The fair value of High's investment was $200,000 at December 31, Year 5.

   On January 1, Year 6, High purchased an additional 25 percent of Lowe's shares for $500,000. This second purchase allowed High to exert significant influence over Lowe. There was no acquisition differential on the date of the 25 percent acquisition.

During the two years, Lowe reported the following:

	Profit	Dividends
Year 5	$200,000	$120,000
Year 6	270,000	130,000

Required:

With respect to this investment, prepare High's journal entries for both Year 5 and Year 6.

Part B   The following are summarized income statements for the two companies for Year 7:

	High Inc.	Lowe Corp.
Operating revenue	$900,000	$600,000
Expenses (including income tax)	450,000	400,000
Profit before discontinued operations	450,000	200,000
Discontinued operations (net of tax)	—	20,000
Profit	*$450,000	$180,000

* The net income of High does not include any investment income from its investment in Lowe Corp.

Lowe paid no dividends in Year 7.

Required:

(a) Prepare the journal entries that High should make at the end of Year 7 with respect to its investment in Lowe.
(b) Prepare the income statement of High, taking into consideration the journal entries in part (a).

Solution to Self-study Problem

Part A   The 10 percent purchase should be accounted for under the fair value method. High's journal entries during Year 5 are as follows:

Investment in Lowe	192,000	
Cash		192,000
Purchase of 10% of shares of Lowe		

Cash	12,000	
Dividend income		12,000
10% × 120,000		

Investment in Lowe	8,000	
Unrealized gain on FVTPL investment		8,000
200,000 − 192,000		

The 25 percent purchase in Year 6 changes the investment to one of significant influence, which is accounted for prospectively.

The journal entries under the equity method in Year 6 are as follows:

Investment in Lowe	500,000	
Cash		500,000
Purchase of 25% of shares of Lowe		
Investment in Lowe	94,500	
Investment income		94,500
35% × 270,000 profit		
Cash	45,500	
Investment in Lowe		45,500
35% × 130,000 dividends		

Part B (a) Applying the equity method, High makes the following journal entries in Year 7:

Investment in Love*	63,000	
Investment loss, discontinued operations**	7,000	
Investment Income***		70,000

      * 35% × 180,000
    ** 35% × 20,000
  *** 35% × 200,000

(b)

HIGH INC.
INCOME STATEMENT
year ended December 31, Year 7

Operating revenue	$900,000
Expenses (including income tax)	450,000
Profit from operations	450,000
Investment income*	70,000
Profit before discontinued operations	520,000
Investment loss — discontinued operations (net of tax)*	7,000
Profit	$513,000

* A footnote would disclose that these items came from a 35% investment in Lowe, accounted for using the equity method.

REVIEW QUESTIONS

1. How is the concept of a business combination related to the concept of a parent–subsidiary relationship?

2. Distinguish between the financial reporting for FVTPL investments and that for investments in associates.

3. What is the difference between a "control" investment and a "joint control" investment?

4. What is the purpose of IFRS 8 on Operating Segments?

5. What criteria would be used to determine whether the equity method should be used to account for a particular investment?

6. The equity method records dividends as a reduction in the investment account. Explain why.

7. What factors would be used as evidence that an investor had obtained significant influence over an investee?

8. The Ralston Company owns 35 percent of the outstanding voting shares of Purina Inc. Under what circumstances would Ralston determine that it is inappropriate to report this investment in its financial statements using the equity method?

9. Because of the acquisition of additional investee shares, an investor may need to change from the fair value method for a FVTPL investment to the equity method for a significant influence investment. What procedures are applied to effect this accounting change?

10. An investor uses the equity method to report its investment in an investee. During the current year, the investee reports other comprehensive income on its statement of comprehensive income. How should this item be reflected in the investor's financial statements?

11. Ashton Inc. acquired a 40 percent interest in Villa Corp. at a bargain price because Villa had suffered significant losses in past years. Ashton's cost was $200,000. In the first year after acquisition, Villa reported a loss of $700,000. Using the equity method, how should Ashton account for this loss?

12. Able Company holds a 40 percent interest in Baker Corp. During the year, Able sold a portion of this investment. How should this investment be reported after the sale?

13. Briefly describe the disclosure requirements related to an investment in an associated company.

14. How should a private company that has opted to not follow GAAP for publicly accountable enterprises report an investment in an associate?

15. How will the investment in a private company be reported under IFRS 9 and how does this differ from IAS 39?

MULTIPLE-CHOICE QUESTIONS

1. Which one of the following accounting methods is recommended by IAS 39 for reporting FVTPL investments?
   a. Cost method.
   b. Fair value method.
   c. Equity method.
   d. Consolidation.

2. Which one of the following would not be a factor to consider when determining whether an investment results in significant influence?
   a. Whether the investor held a position on the investee's board of directors.
   b. Whether the investor purchased a significant amount of the investee's production output.
   c. Whether the investor and the investee operated in the same country.
   d. Whether the investor and the investee exchanged technical expertise.

3. On January 1, Year 5, PORT acquired 100,000 common shares of SUN (a 10 percent voting interest) for $1,000,000. PORT designates this investment as FVTPL but shows it as a long-term investment. On December 31, Year 5, the shares of SUN were trading at $9.50 per share. On March 15, Year 6, when

PORT's financial statements were finalized, SUN's shares were trading at $11.00 per share. How should PORT report its investment in SUN on its balance sheet at December 31, Year 5?
  a. At $1,000,000, with the market value of the shares disclosed as additional information.
  b. At $1,100,000, with the cost of the purchase presented as additional information.
  c. At $950,000, with the unrealized loss reported in net income.
  d. At $950,000, with the unrealized loss reported in other comprehensive income.

Use the following data for Questions 4 and 5.

AB Company purchased 25 percent of the shares of KC Corporation on January 1, Year 5, for $100,000, which allows it to exercise significant influence. Both companies had December 31, Year 5, year-ends. During Year 5, KC had a net income of $120,000 and paid dividends of $80,000. At December 31, Year 5, the fair value of AB's investment was $115,000.

4. As at December 31, Year 5, how much would AB's investment in KC be on AB's balance sheet?
  a. $100,000
  b. $105,000
  c. $110,000
  d. $120,000

5. Assuming that AB does not exercise significant influence and classifies its investment as FVTPL, how much income would AB report from its investment in KC for the year ended December 31, Year 5?
  a. $20,000
  b. $30,000
  c. $35,000
  d. $45,000

6. On January 1, Year 5, X Company acquired 20 percent of Y Company for $4,800,000. From January 1, Year 5, to December 31, Year 7, Y Company earned profit of $3,600,000 and paid dividends of $1,200,000. What would be the balance in the Investment in Y Company account in the accounting records of X Company on December 31, Year 7?
  a. Assuming X Company uses the cost method, $4,800,000.
  b. Assuming X Company uses the cost method, $5,024,000.
  c. Assuming X Company uses the equity method, $4,800,000.
  d. Assuming X Company uses the equity method, $5,520,000.
  (CGA-Canada adapted)

7. RU Ltd. has invested in several domestic manufacturing corporations. Which of the following investments would most likely be accounted for under the equity method on the consolidated financial statements of RU?
  a. A holding of 2,000 of the 50,000 outstanding common shares of SU.
  b. A holding of 3,000 of the 10,000 outstanding preferred shares of TU.
  c. A holding of 15,000 of the 60,000 outstanding common shares of XU.
  d. A holding of 20,000 of the 25,000 outstanding common shares of VU.
  (CGA-Canada adapted)

8. On January 1, Year 5, Top Company purchased a 10 percent interest in the common shares of Bottom Ltd. for $60,000. Bottom reported profit and paid dividends as follows:

    Year 5 — profit $72,000; dividends paid $96,000.

    Year 6 — profit $126,000; dividends paid $96,000.

    Assume that Top uses the cost method to account for its investment in Bottom. Which of the following is the amount that a statement of financial position for Top would report as "Investment in Bottom" at December 31, Year 6?
    a. $57,600
    b. $59,400
    c. $60,000
    d. $60,600

Use the following data for Questions 9 and 10.

On January 1, Year 5, Xanadu Co. purchased a 20 percent interest in Zap Inc. for $4,000,000. In Year 5, Zap reported net income from continuing operations of $525,000 and a gain from discontinued operations of $83,000 (net of tax). Zap declared and paid dividends of $90,000 on December 31, Year 5.

9. Assume the investment is accounted for using the cost method. Which of the following amounts would be reported on Xanadu's Year 5 income statement relating to Zap?
    a. Investment income of $116,600.
    b. Dividend income of $90,000.
    c. Investment income of $105,000 and gain from discontinued operations of $16,600.
    d. Dividend income of $18,000.

10. Assume the above is an investment in associate. Which of the following amounts would be reported on Xanadu's Year 5 income statement relating to Zap?
    a. Investment income of $121,600 and gain from discontinued operations of $16,600.
    b. Investment income of $121,600.
    c. Investment income of $105,000 and gain from discontinued operations of $16,600.
    d. Dividend income of $18,000.

11. Price Co. has gradually been acquiring shares of Berry Co. and now owns 37 percent of the outstanding voting common shares. The remaining 63 percent of the shares are held by members of the family of the company founder. To date, the family has elected all members of the board of directors, and Price Co. has not been able to obtain a seat on the board. Price is hoping to eventually buy a block of shares from an elderly family member and thus one day own 60 percent. The shares of Berry Co. are not traded in an active market.

    How should the investment in Berry Co. be reported in the financial statements of Price Co., assuming that IFRS 9 is adopted early?
    a. Consolidation.
    b. Cost method.
    c. Equity method.
    d. Fair value method.

(CGA-Canada adapted)

12. DER Ltd. has owned 10 percent of LAS Company for several years but did not have significant influence over LAS. DER recently purchased an additional 20 percent of LAS and now has significant influence. How will this change be reported by DER?
    a. A cumulative effect of an accounting change is shown in the current income statement.
    b. A cumulative effect of an accounting change is shown in the statement of retained earnings.
    c. The equity method should be used starting from the date of the 20 percent acquisition.
    d. DER can use either the cost method or the equity method to account for the change in ownership.

13. Which of the following statements is false for accounting for or reporting of investments in associates?
    a. The fair value of investments in associates must be disclosed when there are published price quotations for the shares of the associates.
    b. The investor must own at least 20 percent of the voting shares of the company before it can be considered an associated company.
    c. An investment in associate could end up with a credit balance and be reported as a liability on the statement of financial position.
    d. An investment in associate should normally be reported as a non-current asset.

Use the following data for Questions 14 and 15.

TOR Ltd. purchased 2,000 common shares (20 percent) of JAP Inc. on January 1, Year 1, for $20,000. During Year 1, JAP reported profit of $12,000 and paid dividends of $9,000. At December 31, Year 1, the market value of JAP shares was $10.50 per share. TOR reported its investment in JAP as a FVTPL investment in its Year 1 financial statements. The ROI for Year 1 was 11 percent, where ROI is defined as net income/shareholders' equity.

14. What would be the impact on the ROI for Year 1 if the investment in JAP were classified as fair-value-through-OCI?
    a. ROI would increase.
    b. ROI would decrease.
    c. ROI would not change.
    d. The impact on ROI cannot be determined.

15. What would be the impact on ROI for Year 1 if the investment in JAP were reported using the equity method?
    a. ROI would increase.
    b. ROI would decrease.
    c. ROI would not change.
    d. The impact on ROI cannot be determined.

CASES

Case 1   Hil Company purchased 10,000 common shares (10 percent) of Ton Inc. on January 1, Year 4, for $345,000, when Ton's shareholders' equity was $2,600,000, and classified the investment as a FVTPL security. On January 1, Year 5, Hil acquired an additional 15,000 common shares (15 percent) of Ton for $525,000. On both dates, any difference between the purchase price and the book value of Ton's shareholders' equity is attributed to land. The market value of Ton's common shares was $35 per share on December 31, Year 4, and $37 per share on December 31, Year 5. Ton reported net income of $500,000 in Year 4 and $520,000 in Year 5 and paid dividends of $450,000 in both years.

The management of Hil is very excited about the increase in ownership interest in Ton because Ton has been very profitable. Hil pays a bonus to management based on its net income determined in accordance with GAAP.

The management of Hil is wondering how the increase in ownership will affect the reporting of the investment in Ton. Will Hil continue to classify the investment as FVTPL in Year 5? What factors will be considered in determining whether the equity method should now be used? If the equity method is now appropriate, will the change be made retroactively? They would like to see a comparison of income for Year 5 and the balance in the investment account at the end of Year 5 under the two options for reporting this investment. Last but not least, they would like to get your opinion on which method should be used to best reflect the performance of Hil for Year 5.

Required:

Respond to the questions raised and the requests made by management. Prepare schedules and/or financial statements to support your presentation.

Case 2   Floyd's Specialty Foods Inc. (FSFI) operates over 60 shops throughout Ontario. The company was founded by George Floyd when he opened a single shop in the city of Cornwall. This store sold prepared dinners and directed its products at customers who were too busy to prepare meals after a long day at work. The concept proved to be very successful and more stores were opened in Cornwall. Recently new stores were opened in five other Ontario cities. Up to the current year, the shares of FSFI have been owned entirely by Floyd. However, during this year, the company suffered severe cash flow problems, due to too-rapid expansion exacerbated by a major decline in economic activity. Profitability suffered and creditors threatened to take legal action for long-overdue accounts. To avoid bankruptcy, Floyd sought additional financing from his old friend James Connelly, who is a majority shareholder of Cornwall Autobody Inc. (CAI). Subsequently, CAI paid $950,000 cash to FSFI to acquire enough newly issued shares of common stock for a one-third interest.

At the end of this year, CAI's accountants are discussing how they should properly report this investment in the company's financial statements.

One argues for maintaining the asset at original cost, saying, "What we have done is to advance money to bail out these stores. Floyd will continue to run the organization with little or no attention to us, so in effect we have lent him money. After all, what does anyone in our company know about the specialty food business? My guess is that as soon as the stores become solvent, Floyd will want to buy back our shares."

Another accountant disagrees, stating that the equity method is appropriate. "I realize that our company is not capable of running a specialty food company. But the rules state that ownership of over 20 percent is evidence of significant influence."

A third accountant supports equity method reporting for a different reason. "If the investment gives us the ability to exert significant influence, that is all that is required. We don't have to actually exert it. One-third of the common shares certainly gives us that ability."

Required:

How should CAI report its investment? Your answer should include a discussion of all three accountants' positions.

Case 3   Magno Industries Ltd. is a major supplier to the automotive replacement parts market, selling parts to nearly every segment of the industry. Magno has a September 30 year-end.

During January Year 5, Magno acquired a 13 percent interest in the common shares of Grille-to-Bumper Automotive Stores and in June Year 5 it acquired an additional 15 percent. Grille-to-Bumper is a retail chain of company-owned automotive replacement parts stores operating in most Canadian provinces. Its shares are not traded in an active market. Grille-to-Bumper has a December 31 year-end and, despite being profitable each year for the last 10 years, has never paid a dividend. While Magno occasionally makes sales to Grille-to-Bumper, it has never been one of its major suppliers.

After the second acquisition of Grille-to-Bumper's shares, Magno Industries contacted Grille-to-Bumper to obtain certain financial information and to discuss mutual timing problems with respect to financial reporting. In the initial contact, Magno found Grille-to-Bumper to be uncooperative. In addition, Grille-to-Bumper accused Magno of attempting to take it over. Magno replied that it had no intention of attempting to gain control but rather was interested only in making a sound long-term investment. Grille-to-Bumper was not impressed with this explanation and refused to have any further discussions regarding future information exchanges and the problems created by a difference in year-ends.

At the year-end of September 30, Year 5, Magno's management expressed a desire to use the equity method to account for its investment.

Required:

(a) What method of accounting would you recommend Magno Industries use for its investment in Grille-to-Bumper Automotive common shares? As part of your answer, discuss the alternatives available.

(b) Why would the management of Magno want to use the equity method to account for the investment, as compared to other alternatives that you have discussed?

(c) Are there any circumstances under which the method you have recommended might have to be changed? If so, how would Magno Industries account for such a change?

Case 4   On January 1, Year 6, Progress Technologies Inc. acquired 40 percent (10,000 shares) of the voting shares of the Calgana Corp. Toward the end of Year 6, it seemed likely that Progress would have earnings for the year of approximately $10,000 (exclusive of earnings attributed to its investment in Calgana) and that Calgana would have earnings of approximately $50,000. The CEO of Progress was disappointed in the forecast earnings of both companies. Prior to Year 6, Progress had increased its earnings by 10 percent each year, and Progress would have to report total earnings in Year 6 of $45,000 if the trend was to continue.

Required:

(a) Suppose Progress Technologies Inc. reports its interest in Calgana Corp. using the equity method.

    (i)   If Calgana is to declare its usual dividend of $0.50 per share, what would be the total reported income of Progress?

    (ii) The CEO of Progress suggested that Calgana be directed to declare a special dividend of $3 per share. What impact would the additional dividend have on the reported earnings of Progress?

(b) Suppose that Progress Technologies Inc. reports its investment in Calgana Corp. using the cost method.

(i) What would be the total reported earnings of Progress if Calgana declared its regular dividend of $0.50 per share?

(ii) What impact would the additional dividend of $3 per share have on reported earnings of Progress?

(c) Explain fully why the equity method (rather than the cost method) is appropriate for firms that can exert significant influence over other companies in which they have an interest.

Case 5 "The thing you have to understand, CA, is how these stage plays work. You start out with just an idea, but generally no cash. That's where promoters like me come in. First, we set up a separate legal entity for each play. Then, we find ways of raising the money necessary to get the play written and the actors trained. If the play is a success, we hope to recover all those costs and a whole lot more, but cash flow is the problem. Since less than half of all plays make money, you cannot get very much money from banks.

"Take my current project, 'Penguins in Paradise.' You only have to look at the cash inflows (Exhibit I) to see how many sources I had to approach to get the cash. As you can see, most of the initial funding comes from the investors in the Penguins in Paradise Limited Partnership (PIP). They put up their money to buy a percentage of the future profits of the play. One main reason a partnership is used is to let them immediately write off, for tax purposes, the costs of producing the play.

"Some investors do not want to invest the amount required for a partnership unit. So, for them, we structure the deal a little differently. Instead of buying a unit in the partnership, they buy a right to a royalty — a percentage of future operating profits (i.e., gross revenue less true operating expenses). In this way, these investors get an interest in the play without being in the partnership. Since they do not have a vote at the partnership meetings, they are more concerned about their risks. However, we agreed that PIP would get term insurance on my life in case I get hit by a truck!

"Funding the play is not that easy. The money that the investors put up is not enough to fund all the start-up costs, so you have to be creative. Take reservation fees

Exhibit I

PENGUINS IN PARADISE (A LIMITED PARTNERSHIP)
SUMMARY OF CASH FLOWS
For the period ended December 31, Year 1
(in thousands of dollars)

Cash inflows	
Investor contributions to limited partnership	$5,000
Sale of royalty rights	1,000
Bank loan	2,000
Sale of movie rights	500
Government grant	50
Reservation fees	20
	8,570
Cash outflows	
Salaries and fees	3,500
Costumes and sets	1,000
Life insurance	10
Miscellaneous costs	1,250
	5,760
Net cash inflows	$2,810

for example. You know how tough it is to get good seats for a really hot play. Well, PIP sold the right to buy great seats to some dedicated theatre-goers this year for next year's performance. These amounts are non-refundable, and the great thing is that the buyers still have to pay full price for the tickets when they buy them.

"Consider the sale of movie rights. Lots of good plays get turned into movies. Once the stage play is a success, the movie rights are incredibly expensive. My idea was to sell the movie rights in advance. PIP got a lot less money, but at least we got it up front when we needed it.

"The other sources are much the same. We received the government grant by agreeing to have at least 50 percent Canadian content. We also negotiated a bank loan with an interest rate of 5 percent a year plus 1 percent of the gross revenue of the play, instead of the usual 20 percent interest a year. Even my fee for putting the deal together was taken as a percentage of the operating profits, so just about everybody has a strong interest in the play's performance.

"As you know, I know nothing about accounting, so I need you to put together a set of financial statements. I will need you to certify that they are in accordance with GAAP for enterprises such as Penguins in Paradise, because the investors and the bank require this. Since everybody else has taken an interest in the play in lieu of cash, I would like you to consider doing the same for your fees."

When you, CA, discussed this conversation with a partner in your office, he asked you to prepare a memo addressing the major accounting implications of the client's requests.

Required:

(a) Prepare the memo to the partner.
(b) Briefly discuss how the following three investor groups would classify and account for their investment:
    (i) Investor in Limited Partnership units.
    (ii) Investor in royalties.
    (iii) Investor in movie rights.

PROBLEMS

Problem 1   *PART A*

On January 1, Year 5, Anderson Corporation paid $650,000 for 20,000 (20 percent) of the outstanding shares of Carter Inc. The investment was considered to be one of significant influence. In Year 5, Carter reported profit of $95,000; in Year 6, its profit was $105,000. Dividends paid were $50,000 in each of the two years.

Required:

Calculate the balance in Anderson's investment account as at December 31, Year 6.

PART B

Now assume that on December 31, Year 6, Anderson lost its ability to significantly influence the operating, investing, and financing decisions for Carter when another party obtained sufficient shares in the open market to obtain control over Carter. Accordingly, the investment in Carter was reclassified as a FVTPL investment. The fair value of the Carter shares was $35 per share on this date.

In Year 7, Carter reported profit of $115,000 and paid dividends of $50,000. On December 31, Year 7, Anderson sold its investment in Carter for $37 per share.

Required:

(a) Prepare the journal entry at December 31, Year 6, to reclassify the investment from significant influence to FVTPL.

(b) Prepare all journal entries for Year 7 related to Anderson's investment in Carter.

Problem 2 Baskin purchased 20,000 common shares (20 percent) of Robbin on January 1, Year 5, for $275,000 and classified the investment as FVTPL. Robbin reported net income of $85,000 in Year 5 and $90,000 in Year 6 and paid dividends of $40,000 in each year. Robbin's shares were trading at $15 per share on December 31, Year 5, and January 1, Year 6. On January 1, Year 6, Baskin obtained significant influence over the operating, investing, and financing decisions of Robbin when the controlling shareholder sold some shares in the open market and lost control over Robbin. Accordingly, the investment in Robbin was reclassified to an investment in associate. On December 31, Year 6, Baskin sold its investment in Robbin for $16 per share.

Required:

Prepare all journal entries for Years 5 and 6 related to Baskin's investment in Robbin.

Problem 3 On January 1, Year 5, Blake Corporation purchased 30 percent of the outstanding common shares of Stergis Limited for $1,500,000.

The following relates to Stergis since the acquisition date:

Year	Net income	Other comprehensive income	Dividends paid
Year 5	$ 42,000	$10,000	$60,000
Year 6	120,000	25,000	60,000

Required:

(a) Assume that the number of shares held by Blake is enough to give it significant influence over Stergis. Prepare all the journal entries that Blake should make regarding this investment in Year 5 and Year 6.

(b) Assume that Blake uses the cost method to account for its investment. Prepare all the journal entries that Blake should make regarding this investment in Year 5 and Year 6.

Problem 4 Pender Corp. paid $234,000 for a 30 percent interest in Saltspring Limited on January 1, Year 6. During Year 6, Saltspring paid dividends of $100,000 and reported profit as follows:

Profit before discontinued operations	$290,000
Discontinued operations loss (net of tax)	30,000
Profit	$260,000

Pender's profit for Year 6 consisted of $900,000 in sales, expenses of $600,000, and its investment income from Saltspring.

Required

(a) Assume that Pender reports its investment using the equity method.
   (i) Prepare all journal entries necessary to account for Pender's investment for Year 6.
   (ii) Determine the correct balance in Pender's investment account at December 31, Year 6.
   (iii) Prepare an income statement for Pender for Year 6.

(b) Assume that Pender uses the cost method.
   (i) Prepare all journal entries necessary to account for Pender's investment for Year 6.
   (ii) Determine the correct balance in Pender's investment account at December 31, Year 6.
   (iii) Prepare an income statement for Pender for Year 6.
(c) Which reporting method would Pender want to use if its bias is to report the highest possible return on investment to users of its financial statements? Briefly explain and show supporting calculations.

Problem 5   Her Company purchased 20,000 common shares (20 percent) of Him Inc. on January 1, Year 4, for $340,000. Additional information on Him for the three years ending December 31, Year 6, is as follows:

Year	Net income	Dividends paid	Market value per share at December 31
Year 4	$200,000	$150,000	$18
Year 5	225,000	160,000	20
Year 6	240,000	175,000	23

On December 31, Year 6, Her sold its investment in Him for $460,000.

Required:

(a) Compute the balance in the investment account at the end of Year 5 assuming that the investment is classified as
   (i) FVTPL.
   (ii) Investment in associate.
   (iii) Fair-value-through-OCI.
(b) Calculate how much income will be reported in net income and other comprehensive income in each of Years 4, 5, and 6, and in total for the three years assuming that the investment is classified as
   (i) FVTPL.
   (ii) Investment in associate.
   (iii) Fair-value-through-OCI.
(c) What are the similarities and differences in your answers for the three parts of (b)?

Problem 6   COX Limited is a multinational telecommunication company owned by a Canadian businesswoman. It has numerous long-term investments in a wide variety of equity instruments.

Some investments have to be reported at fair value at each reporting date. In turn, the unrealized gains will be reported in either net income or other comprehensive income. Since COX has considerable external financing through a number of Canadian banks, it applies IFRSs for public companies in its general-purpose financial statements.

The CFO of COX has heard about the reporting standards for equity investments but has had limited time to study them in detail. He would like you to prepare a presentation on the reporting requirements. He wants to understand how equity investments should be reported. More specifically, he wants to know

• which investments must be reported at fair value and what is the main rationale for this change in reporting;

- how to determine whether the unrealized gains are to be reported in net income or other comprehensive income and what is the main rationale for the difference in reporting; and
- which investments, if any, will still be reported using the cost method, using the equity method, or on a consolidated basis.

Required:

Prepare the slides for the presentation. Limit your presentation to six slides. Ignore the section on Hedging. Your presentation should cover the reporting of (1) FVTPL, (2) fair-value-through-OCI, (3) cost method, (4) held-for-significant-influence, and (5) held-for-control investments.

(CGA-Canada adapted)

Problem 7   All facts are the same as in Problem 6 except that COX applies GAAP for private enterprises in its general-purpose financial statements. Follow the same instructions as those given in the Required section of Problem 6.

WEB-BASED PROBLEMS

Problem 1   Access the most recent consolidated financial statements of Vodafone, a British company. (Go to the investor relations section at www.vodafone.com) Answer the questions below. For each question, indicate where in the financial statements you found the answer and/or provide a brief explanation.

(a) What percentage of total assets at the end of the year is represented by investments in associates?

(b) What was the rate of return for the most recent year from the investments in associates?

(c) Assume that each year the associates have generated a return similar to the return in part (b) and have paid dividends equal to 75 percent of the income earned. If the company had used the cost method rather than the equity method since the date of acquisition of the investments, how would this change affect the following ratios for this year's financial statements:

(i) Current ratio.

(ii) Debt-to-equity ratio.

(iii) Return on equity.

(d) How much income was earned from available-for-sale investments?

(e) What percentage of shareholders' equity is represented by unrealized gains from available-for-sale investments?

(f) What accounts on the balance sheet would change and would they increase or decrease if the available-for-sale investments had always been classified as FVTPL investments?

Problem 2   Access the most recent consolidated financial statements for Siemens, a German company. (Go to the investor relations section at www.siemens.com.) Answer the same questions as in Problem 1. For each question, indicate where in the financial statements you found the answer and/or provide a brief explanation. (Some questions may not be applicable.)

Chapter ③ Business Combinations

LEARNING OBJECTIVES

After studying this chapter, you should be able to do the following:

1. Define a business combination, and describe the two basic forms for achieving a business combination.
2. Compare and contrast the acquisition and new entity methods.
3. Evaluate relevant factors to determine whether control exists in a business acquisition.
4. Compare the balance sheet of the acquirer after a purchase-of-net-assets business combination and the consolidated balance sheet after a purchase-of-shares business combination.
5. Explain a reverse takeover and its reporting implications.

INTRODUCTION

The parent is the controlling company and the subsidiary is the controlled company.

In Chapter 2 we illustrated the accounting for two types of long-term intercorporate investments: significant influence and neither control nor significant influence. The next six chapters are largely devoted to the accounting for a third type — long-term investments that enable the investor to control the investee. When one company obtains control of one or more businesses, a business combination has occurred. In such cases, GAAP requires that we prepare consolidated financial statements to combine the financial position and results of operations of the controlling company (the parent) and the controlled company (the subsidiary). A business combination also occurs when one enterprise acquires the net assets of another business. A business is defined as an integrated set of activities and assets that is capable of being conducted and managed for the purpose of providing a return in the form of dividends, lower costs, or other economic benefits directly to investors or other owners, members, or participants.

There are many types of business combinations. A *conglomerate business combination* involves economic units operating in widely different industries. A *horizontal business combination* involves economic units whose products are similar. A *vertical business combination* involves economic units where the output from one can be used as input for another.[1] Other terms that are often used synonymously with the term *business combination* are *takeover, amalgamation, acquisition,* and *merger.*

For a business combination to exist, one economic unit must control substantially all of the net assets of another economic unit. The purchase of some but

---

[1] *Terminology for Accountants,* 4th edition, Toronto: CICA, 1992, p. 35.

In a business combination, one company unites with or obtains control over another company.

not all of an entity's assets is not considered a business combination. While the units involved are usually incorporated, this is not a requirement for a business combination. Also, the units involved cannot have been under common control immediately before the combination. The transfer of assets or the exchange of shares between two subsidiaries of the same parent, or between a parent and its subsidiary, would not be considered a business combination.

Business combinations are frequent events in Canada and the United States and throughout the world. Hardly a week passes without some reference in the press to actual or proposed takeovers and mergers.

Many people think that the typical takeover involves an American multinational swallowing up a smaller Canadian firm. But that is not always the case. In fact, figures for Canadian M&A activity show that Canadian acquisitions of foreign companies outpaced foreign acquisitions of Canadian companies from 2002 to 2004. Between 2005 and 2007, many big-name Canadian companies were taken over by foreign entities, e.g., Falconbridge, Dofasco, ATI Technologies, Intrawest, Hudson's Bay Co., Sleeman Breweries, and Inco.

According to a study by KPMG, in 2008 there were nearly 2,000 mergers and acquisitions involving Canadian public companies.[2] Approximately 57 percent involved Canadian companies taking over other Canadian companies. The other 43 percent were fairly evenly split between Canadian companies being acquired versus being the acquirer. The six biggest deals in 2008 were as follows:

There were nearly 2,000 mergers and acquisitions involving Canadian public companies in 2008.

- Teck Cominco Ltd. of Canada acquired Fording Canadian Coal Trust of Canada for $13.6 billion.
- Toronto-Dominion Bank of Canada acquired Commerce Bancorp of the United States for $8.6 billion.
- Shell Canada Limited of Canada acquired Duvernay Oil Corp. of Canada for $5.4 billion.
- IBM Corp. of the United States acquired Cognos Inc. of Canada for $4.9 billion.
- Evraz Group SA of Russia acquired IPSCO Inc. of Canada for $4.0 billion.
- TAQA of the United Arab Emirates acquired PrimeWest Energy Trust of Canada for $4.0 billion.

Business combinations can be described as either friendly or hostile. Often a merger is initiated by one company submitting a formal tender offer to the shareholders of another company. In a friendly combination, the top management and the board of directors of the companies involved negotiate the terms of the combination and then submit the proposal to the shareholders of both companies along with a recommendation for approval. An unfriendly combination occurs when the board of directors of the target company recommends that its shareholders reject the tender offer. The management of the target company will often employ defences to resist the takeover. They include the following:

There are many tactics to resist takeover.

- *Poison pill.* This occurs when a company issues rights to its existing shareholders, exercisable only in the event of a potential takeover, to purchase additional shares at prices below market.

---

[2] http://www.kpmg.ca/en/news/pr20090112.html

- *Pac-man defence.* This involves the target company making an unfriendly countervailing takeover offer to the shareholders of the company that is attempting to take it over.
- *White knight.* In this case, the target company searches out another company that will come to its rescue with a more appealing offer for its shares.
- *Selling the crown jewels.* This involves selling certain desirable assets to other companies so the would-be acquirer loses interest.

In the next section of this chapter we discuss the two basic forms of business combinations. The discussion then proceeds to the accounting for business combinations and the acceptable methods that have been used. We will then focus on current GAAP in Canada.

Forms of Business Combinations

Essentially, there are only two forms of business combinations. One company can obtain control over the net assets of another company by (a) purchasing its net assets or (b) acquiring enough of its voting shares to control the use of its net assets. In examining these two forms of combinations, one must also consider closely the method of payment used. Payment can be cash, or promises to pay cash in the future, or the issuance of shares, or some combination of these. As we will see later, the method of payment has a direct bearing on the determination of which company is the acquirer.

When purchasing assets, the transaction is carried out with the selling company.

Purchase of Assets An obvious way to obtain control over another company's assets is to purchase them outright. The selling company is left only with the cash or other consideration received as payment from the purchaser, and the liabilities present before the sale. Often, the acquirer purchases all the assets of the acquiree and assumes all its liabilities and records these assets and liabilities in its accounting records. The shareholders of the selling company have to approve the sale, as well as decide whether their company should be wound up or should continue operations.

When purchasing shares, the transaction is consummated with the shareholders of the selling company.

Purchase of Shares An alternative to the purchase of assets is for the acquirer to purchase enough voting shares from the shareholders of the acquiree that it can determine the acquiree's strategic operating, investing, and financing policies. This is the most common form of combination, and it is often achieved through a tender offer made by the management of the acquirer to the shareholders of the acquiree. These shareholders are invited to exchange their shares for cash or for shares of the acquirer company.

The share purchase form of combination is usually the least costly to the acquirer because control can be achieved by purchasing less than 100 percent of the outstanding voting shares. In addition, in Canada there can be important tax advantages to the vendor if shares rather than assets are sold.

The acquired company makes no journal entries when the acquiring company purchases shares.

Because the transaction is between the acquirer and the acquiree's shareholders, the acquiree's accounting for its assets and liabilities is not affected,[3] and this company

---

[3] An exception to this occurs when the acquiree applies "push-down accounting." This topic is discussed in Chapter 4.

carries on as a subsidiary of the acquirer. The acquirer becomes a parent company and therefore must consolidate its subsidiary when it prepares its financial statements.

Both forms of business combination result in the assets and liabilities of the acquiree being combined with those of the acquirer. If control is achieved by purchasing net assets, the combining takes place in the accounting records of the acquirer. If control is achieved by purchasing shares, the combining takes place when the consolidated financial statements are prepared.

> **There are many different legal forms in which a business combination can be consummated.**

Variations   One variation from the two basic forms of business combinations occurs when the companies involved agree to create a new company, which either purchases the net assets of the combining companies or purchases enough shares from the shareholders of the combining companies to achieve control of these companies.

Another variation that can occur is a *statutory amalgamation*, whereby under the provisions of federal or provincial law, two or more companies incorporated under the same companies act can combine and continue as a single entity. The shareholders of the combining companies become shareholders of the surviving company, and the non-surviving companies are wound up. The substance of a statutory amalgamation indicates that it is simply a variation of one of the basic forms. If only one of the companies survives, it is essentially a purchase of assets, with the method of payment being shares of the surviving company.

Methods of Accounting for Business Combinations

There are four methods of accounting for business combinations that have either been used in practice or discussed in theory over the years:

- The purchase method;
- The acquisition method;
- The pooling-of-interests method; and
- The new entity method.

The following table indicates the current status and effective usage dates for these four methods:

Method	Status
Purchase method	Required GAAP prior to adoption of acquisition method, which must be adopted by January 1, 2011, but can be adopted earlier
Acquisition method	New method must be adopted by January 1, 2011, but can be adopted earlier
Pooling-of-interests method	Acceptable in limited situations prior to July 1, 2001, but no longer acceptable
New entity method	Never achieved status as an acceptable method but worthy of future consideration

We will now briefly discuss the merits of these four methods.

> **The net assets of the acquired company are reported at the amount paid by the acquiring company under the purchase method.**

Prior to 2011 (or sooner if IFRS 3 had been adopted earlier), the *purchase method* was used to account for the combination. Under this method, the acquiring company reported the net assets of the acquired company at the price that it paid. This price included any cash payment, the fair value of any shares issued, and the present value of any promises to pay cash in the future. Any excess of the price paid over the fair value of the acquired company's identifiable net assets was recorded as goodwill. The fair values of the identifiable net assets acquired were systematically charged against earnings in the normal manner of expense matching. In addition, any goodwill was regularly reviewed for impairment and any impairment loss was reflected as a charge against earnings. As a result, the price paid for the acquired company was reflected as a deduction from the revenues generated from that company over time. This method of accounting was consistent with the historical cost principle of accounting for any assets acquired by a company. Such assets were initially recorded at the price paid for them, and subsequently their cost was charged against earnings over their useful lives.

The identifiable net assets of the acquired company are reported at their fair value under the acquisition method.

After January 1, 2011 (or sooner if IFRS 3 had been adopted earlier), IFRS 3 requires that the *acquisition method* be used to account for the combination. Under this method, the acquiring company reports the *identifiable* net assets being acquired at the fair value of these net assets regardless of the amount paid for these net assets. When the purchase price is greater than the fair value of identifiable net assets, the excess is reported as goodwill similar to the purchase method. When the purchase price is less than the fair value of identifiable net assets, the identifiable net assets are still reported at fair value and the deficiency in purchase price is reported as a gain on purchase. This practice is not consistent with the historical cost principle, where assets are reported at the amount paid for the assets. However, it is consistent with the general trend in financial reporting to use fair value more and more often to report assets and liabilities. We will illustrate the acquisition method in detail later in this chapter. Unless otherwise noted, all of the illustrations throughout this text and in the end-of-chapter material will use the acquisition method.

The net assets of the acquired company are reported at their net book value under the pooling-of-interests method.

Prior to July 1, 2001, the *pooling-of-interests method* was used to account for those business combinations where an acquirer could not be identified. Pooling of interests could be used only when there was an exchange of shares between the combining companies, and the shares were distributed in such a manner that an acquirer could not be identified. The idea behind pooling came from the concept of "a merger of equals," whereby the shareholders of the companies involved agreed to combine their companies. Under pooling, there was no concept of an acquired company, and so the accounting for the combination involved simply adding together the book values of the combining companies. This was justified by the argument that because they were simply carrying on the business of two (or more) former entities as one company, with no major disruptions in operations or key personnel, there was no need to revalue the assets of any of the entities. A major problem with this concept was determining if the companies involved really were "equals."

The pooling method is not acceptable in Canada or the United States for business combinations occurring after July 1, 2001.

Despite the fact that the pooling of interests is no longer accepted as a method of accounting for business combinations occuring after July 1, 2001, its effects on the financial statements of many large corporations in the United States and Canada will be felt for many years to come. Assets acquired in a combination often have lives ranging up to 20 or 30 years. Differences in yearly reported earnings between the two methods will exist during these time periods because of the fair value amortizations that have to take place under the acquisition method. A large portion of the acquisition price of a purchase business combination is typically allocated to goodwill. Eventually, earnings will reflect goodwill write-offs if impairment occurs. Under pooling this does not take place. Even though pooling is no longer acceptable, financial statement analysts will need to understand its accounting and its affects on financial statements well into the future. For further discussion and illustration of the pooling-of-interests method, see Connect at www.mcgrawhillconnect.ca.

The fourth method, the *new entity method*, has been proposed in the past as an alternative to the pooling of interests. It has been suggested that a new entity has been created when two companies combine by the joining together of two owner-ship groups. As a result, the assets and liabilities contributed by the two combining companies should be reported by this new entity at their fair values. This method has received virtually no support because of the additional revaluation difficulties and costs that would result. Furthermore, it has been argued that if the owners were simply combining their interests, there would be no new invested capital and there-fore no new entity created.

The net assets of both the acquiring company and acquired company are reported at their fair value under the new entity method.

Provisions of IFRS 3

IFRS 3 outlines the accounting requirements for business combinations:

The acquisition method is required for all business combinations in Canada after January 1, 2011.

- All business combinations should be accounted for by applying the acquisition method.
- An acquirer should be identified for all business combinations.
- The acquisition date is the date the acquirer obtains control of the acquiree.
- The acquirer should attempt to measure the fair value of the acquiree, as a whole, as of the acquisition date. The fair value of the acquiree as a whole is usually determined by adding together the fair value of consideration trans-ferred by the acquirer (i.e., the acquisition cost) plus the value assigned to the non-controlling shareholders. The value of the non-controlling interest is measured as either the fair value of the shares owned by the non-controlling shareholders or as the non-controlling interest's proportionate share of the acquiree's identifiable net assets. Business valuation techniques would be used to measure the fair value of the business acquired if no consideration is trans-ferred, or if the consideration transferred does not represent the fair value of the business acquired. Certain business valuation techniques are referred to in IFRS 3 but are beyond the scope of this book.
- The acquirer should recognize and measure the identifiable assets acquired and the liabilities assumed at fair value and report them separately from goodwill.

An acquirer must be identified for all business combinations.

Identifying the Acquirer   IFRS 3 outlines the requirements for identifying the com-pany that is the acquirer in the business combination. This is important because it is the net assets of the acquiree that are reported at fair values. Considerations in determining which company is the acquirer are as follows:

- If the means of payment is cash or a promise to pay cash in the future, the acquirer is usually the company making the payment.
- If shares are issued as a means of payment, a key element would be the relative holdings of the voting shares of the combined company by shareholders as a group of the combining companies. In a combination involving two compa-nies, if one shareholder group holds more than 50 percent of the voting shares of the combined company, that company is the acquirer. If more than two companies are involved, the shareholder group that holds the largest number of voting shares identifies the company that is the acquirer.

- When an acquirer cannot seem to be determined by examining voting rights because each group of shareholders owns the same percentage, then the make-up of the board of directors and senior management is examined to see which company is dominant.
- When there has been a share exchange, the acquirer is often (but not always) the company that issues shares.
- The acquirer is often (but not always) the larger company.

After an acquirer has been identified, the acquisition cost has to be determined and then allocated to the assets and liabilities acquired.

Acquisition Cost   The acquisition cost is made up of

> **The acquisition cost is measured as the fair value of consideration given to acquire the business.**

- any cash paid;
- the fair value of assets transferred;
- the present value of any promises to pay cash in the future;
- the fair value of any shares issued — the value of shares is based on the market price of the shares on the acquisition date; and
- the fair value of contingent consideration, which is illustrated in Chapter 4.

> **The acquisition cost does not include costs such as professional fees or costs of issuing shares.**

The acquisition cost does not include costs such as fees for consultants, accountants, and lawyers. These costs do not increase the fair value of the acquired company and therefore should not be included in the values assigned to net assets acquired in the business combination. These costs should be expensed in the period of acquisition.

Costs incurred in issuing debt or shares are also not considered part of the acquisition cost. These costs should be deducted from the amount recorded for the proceeds received for the debt or share issue, e.g., deducted from loan payable or common shares. The deduction from loan payable would be treated like a discount on notes payable and would be amortized into income over the life of the loan using the effective interest method.

> **Identifiable assets and liabilities should be recorded separately from goodwill.**

Allocation of the Acquisition Cost   The acquisition cost is allocated to the acquirer's interest[4] in the fair value of the identifiable assets and liabilities of the acquired company. An identifiable asset is not necessarily one that is presently recorded in the records of the acquiree company. For example, the acquiree company may have patent rights that have a definite market value but are not shown on the balance sheet because they had been developed internally. Or the acquiree's balance sheet may show a pension asset, though an up-to-date actuarial valuation may indicate a net pension obligation.

IAS 38 defines an identifiable asset if it either

(a) is separable, i.e., is capable of being separated or divided from the entity and sold, transferred, licensed, rented, or exchanged, either individually or together with a related contract, identifiable asset, or liability, regardless of whether the entity intends to do so, or

(b) arises from contractual or other legal rights, regardless of whether those rights are transferable or separable from the entity or from other rights and obligations.

---

[4] This reference to the acquirer's interest applies only to the consolidation of a subsidiary that is less than 100 percent owned.

To qualify for recognition as part of applying the acquisition method, the identifiable assets acquired and liabilities assumed must meet the definitions of assets and liabilities in IASB's *Framework for the Preparation and Presentation of Financial Statements* at the acquisition date. For example, costs the acquirer expects but is not obliged to incur in the future to effect its plan to exit an activity of an acquiree or to terminate the employment of or to relocate an acquiree's employees are not liabilities at the acquisition date. Therefore, the acquirer does not recognize those costs as part of applying the acquisition method. Instead, the acquirer recognizes those costs in its post-combination financial statements in accordance with other IFRSs.

Appendix B to IFRS 3 provides guidance in identifying assets to be recognized separately as part of a business combination.

It has been implied in the past that a large portion of the acquisition cost in a business combination ends up as goodwill. This is because the amount recorded as goodwill is often made up of a mixture of goodwill itself plus intangible assets that were not identified and measured.

> **Most, but not all, of the acquiree's assets and liabilities are valued at fair value at the date of acquisition.**

Not all assets and liabilities on the balance sheet of the acquired entity are recognized or measured at fair value. For example, the acquirer must recognize a contingent liability if it is a present obligation that arises from past events and its fair value can be measured reliably. Normally, the contingent liability would only be recognized if it were probable that an outflow of resources would be required to settle the obligation. Special rules for recognition and measurement of financial statement items at the date of acquisition also apply to employee benefits, indemnification assets, reacquired rights, share-based payment awards, and assets held for sale. Deferred income tax assets and liabilities are not fair valued and carried forward. Instead, new amounts for deferred tax assets and liabilities become part of the allocation of the acquisition cost. Because of the added complexity that this brings, discussion and illustration of this topic is saved until a later chapter.

> **Goodwill is the excess of the purchase price over the fair value of identifiable assets and liabilities.**

If the acquisition cost is greater than the acquirer's interest in the fair value of identifiable assets and liabilities acquired, the excess is recorded in the acquirer's financial statements as goodwill. In theory, goodwill represents the amount paid for excess earning power; in practice, it represents the premium paid to achieve control.

> **Negative goodwill could result in the reporting of a gain on purchase by the acquiring company.**

If the acquisition cost is less than the fair value of the identifiable net assets acquired, we have what is sometimes described as a "negative goodwill" situation. This negative goodwill is accounted for by first reducing the amount of any goodwill presently being reported on the acquiree's own financial statements. Once the acquiree's existing goodwill is reduced to zero, any remaining excess is recognized as a gain attributable to the acquirer on the acquisition date. We will illustrate the accounting for negative goodwill in Chapter 4.

Financial Reporting after the Combination   The net income generated by the net assets of the acquired company is reported in the financial statements of the acquirer commencing with the date of acquisition. This net income must be adjusted to reflect the amortizations of the fair values of the assets and liabilities purchased and any goodwill losses due to impairment. Prior years' comparative financial statements are not retrospectively changed to reflect the combination.

Illustrations of Business Combination Accounting

To illustrate the accounting involved using the acquisition method, we will use the summarized balance sheets of two companies. Summarized statements are used here so that we can focus completely on the broad accounting concepts. In later examples, detailed statements will be used. Exhibit 3.1 presents the December 31, Year 1, balance sheets of the two companies that are party to a business combination.

Because the identification of an acquirer requires the analysis of shareholdings after the combination, Notes 1 and 2 are presented in the exhibit to identify the shareholders of each company as belonging to two distinct groups.

A Company Ltd. will initiate the takeover of B Corporation. The first two illustrations will involve the purchase of net assets with cash and the issuance of shares as the means of payment. Later illustrations will have A Company purchasing enough shares of B Corporation to obtain control over that company's net assets, and will introduce the preparation of consolidated statements.

Exhibit 3.1

A COMPANY LTD.
BALANCE SHEET
December 31, Year 1

Company A and Company B are separate legal entities.

Assets	$300,000
Liabilities	$120,000
Shareholders' equity	
Common shares (Note 1)	100,000
Retained earnings	80,000
	$300,000

Note 1
The shareholders of the 5,000 common shares issued and outstanding are identified as Group X.

B CORPORATION
BALANCE SHEET
December 31, Year 1

Assets	$ 88,000
Liabilities	$ 30,000
Shareholders' equity	
Common shares (Note 2)	25,000
Retained earnings	33,000
	$ 88,000

The fair values of B Corporation's identifiable assets and liabilities are as follows as at December 31, Year 1:

Fair value of assets	$109,000
Fair value of liabilities	29,000
Fair value of net assets	$ 80,000

Note 2
The shareholders of the common shares of B Corporation are identified as Group Y. The actual number of shares issued and outstanding has been purposely omitted because this number would have no bearing on the analysis required later.

Purchase of Assets

In the following independent illustrations, A Company offers to buy all assets and assume all liabilities of B Corporation. The management of B Corporation accepts the offer.

Illustration 1   Assume that on January 1, Year 2, A Company pays $95,000 in cash to B Corporation for all of the net assets of that company, and that no other direct costs are involved. Because cash is the means of payment, A Company is the acquirer. The acquisition cost is allocated in the following manner:

Purchase price	$95,000
Fair value of net assets acquired	80,000
Difference — goodwill	$15,000

A Company would make the following journal entry to record the acquisition of B Corporation's net assets:

The acquiring company records the assets purchased on its own books at fair value.

Assets (in detail)	109,000	
Goodwill	15,000	
Liabilities (in detail)		29,000
Cash		95,000

A Company's balance sheet after the business combination would be as shown at the bottom of this page.

Using the acquisition method to account for the business combination, the identifiable net assets acquired were recorded at fair values, with the purchase price difference recorded as goodwill. The balance sheet of A Company is not a consolidated balance sheet. But note that if A Company had paid $95,000 cash for 100 percent of the common shares of B Corporation, the consolidated balance prepared immediately after the business combination would be identical to the one shown below. (See Exhibit 3.3 on page 89.)

A COMPANY LTD.
BALANCE SHEET
January 1, Year 2

The acquiring company's own assets and liabilities are not revalued when it purchases the net assets of the acquired company.

Assets (300,000 − 95,000* + 109,000)	$314,000
Goodwill	15,000
	$329,000
Liabilities (120,000 + 29,000)	$149,000
Shareholders' equity	
Common shares	100,000
Retained earnings	80,000
	$329,000

* Cash paid by A Company to B Corporation

While this illustration focuses on the balance sheet of A Company immediately after the business combination, it is also useful to look at B Corporation in order to see the effect of this economic event on that company. The balance sheet of B Corporation immediately after the sale of all of its net assets follows.

The selling company records the sale of its net assets on its own books.

B CORPORATION LTD.
BALANCE SHEET
January 1, Year 2

Cash	$95,000
Shareholders' equity	
Common shares	$25,000
Retained earnings (33,000 + 37,000*)	70,000
	$95,000

* The gain on sale of the net assets amounts to $37,000 (95,000 − 58,000).

The management of B Corporation must now decide the future of their company. They could decide to invest the company's cash in productive assets and carry on in some other line of business. Alternatively, they could decide to wind up the company and distribute the sole asset (cash) to the shareholders.

Illustration 2   Assume that on January 1, Year 2, A Company issues 4,000 common shares, with a market value of $23.75 per share, to B Corporation as payment for the company's net assets. B Corporation will be wound up after the sale of its net assets. Because the method of payment is shares, the following analysis is made to determine which company is the acquirer.

	Shares of A Company
Group X now holds	5,000
Group Y will hold (when B Corporation is wound up)	4,000
	9,000

The acquirer is determined based on which shareholder group controls Company A after B Corporation is wound up.

Group X will hold 5/9 (56 percent) of the total shares of A Company after the combination, and Group Y will hold 4/9 (44 percent) of this total after the dissolution of B Corporation. Because one shareholder group holds more than 50 percent of the voting shares, an acquirer has been identified. The purchase price is allocated in the following manner:

Purchase price (4,000 shares @ 23.75)	$95,000
Fair value of net assets acquired	80,000
Difference — goodwill	$15,000

A Company would make the following journal entry to record the acquisition of B Corporation's net assets and the issuance of 4,000 common shares at fair value on January 1, Year 2:

Assets (in detail)	109,000	
Goodwill	15,000	
Liabilities (in detail)		29,000
Common shares		95,000

A Company's balance sheet after the business combination would be as follows:

A COMPANY LTD.
BALANCE SHEET
January 1, Year 2

The acquiring company's recently purchased assets are recorded at fair value and the old assets are retained at book value.

Assets (300,000 + 109,000)	$409,000
Goodwill	15,000
	$424,000
Liabilities (120,000 + 29,000)	$149,000
Shareholders' equity	
Common shares (100,000 + 95,000)	195,000
Retained earnings	80,000
	$424,000

This balance sheet was prepared by combining the book values of A Company's assets and liabilities with the fair values of those of B Corporation.

B Corporation's balance sheet immediately following the sale of its net assets is reproduced below:

B CORPORATION
BALANCE SHEET
January 1, Year 2

The selling company records the sale of its net assets in exchange for shares of the acquiring company.

Investment in shares of A Company	$95,000
Shareholders' equity	
Common shares	$25,000
Retained earnings (33,000 + 37,000)	70,000
	$95,000

B Corporation is wound up and distributes the investment, consisting of 4,000 shares of A Company, to its shareholders (Group Y). The reason for winding up B Corporation should be intuitively obvious. B Corporation's sole asset is 4,000 of the issued shares of A Company. This single block represents a voting threat to A Company's shareholders (Group X). A Company will likely insist that B Corporation be wound up and distribute these 4,000 shares to its shareholders (Group Y), who presumably will not get together to determine how to vote them.

Control and Consolidated Financial Statements

Distinguish between separate-entity financial statements and consolidated financial statements.

When a parent–subsidiary relationship is the result of a business combination, the two (or more) companies involved continue as separate legal entities, with each maintaining separate accounting records and producing separate financial statements. GAAP ignores this separate-company legal status and views the substance of the relationship as one that has created a single economic entity that should report as such.

The requirement for the preparation of consolidated financial statements is stated in IAS 27 as follows:

A parent shall present consolidated financial statements in which it consolidates its investments in subsidiaries in accordance with this Standard.

The following definitions are provided in IAS 27:

Consolidated financial statements combine the financial statements of the parent and its subsidiaries as if they were one entity.

(a) *Consolidated financial statements* are the financial statements of a group presented as those of a single economic entity.

(b) *Control* is the power to govern the financial and operating policies of an entity so as to obtain benefits from its activities.

(c) A *group* is a parent and all its subsidiaries.

(d) A *parent* is an entity that has one or more subsidiaries.

(e) A *subsidiary* is an entity, including an unincorporated entity such as a partnership, that is controlled by another entity (known as the parent).

When a parent company has control over one or more subsidiaries, it has the right to benefit economically from the subsidiaries' resources and at the same time is exposed to the related risks involved. Consolidated financial statements reflect a group of economic resources that are under the common control of the parent company even though these resources are owned separately by the parent and the subsidiary companies. Notice that the key concept is common control. This concept is reinforced in *Framework for the Preparation and Presentation of Financial Statements*, where the definition of an asset focuses on control rather than ownership.[5] When control over a subsidiary is present, the parent is required to consolidate its subsidiaries for external reporting purposes. In other words, the parent and subsidiary will each prepare their own financial statements (which we will refer to as separate-entity financial statements or financial statements for internal purposes). The consolidated financial statements are additional financial statements that combine the separate-entity financial statements of the parent and subsidiary under the hypothetical situation that these two legal entities were operating as one single entity. The consolidated financial statements are prepared by the parent company and are often referred to as the third set of financial statements.

All intercompany transactions are eliminated in the preparation of the consolidated statements. As a result, these statements reflect only transactions of this single entity with those outside the entity. (The process required to eliminate these intercompany transactions will be discussed thoroughly in later chapters.)

Consolidated financial statements are prepared primarily for the benefit of the shareholders and creditors of the parent company.

Consolidated statements are considered more useful to financial statement users than would be the separate financial statements of all of the companies that make up the group. Present and prospective shareholders of the parent company are interested in future profitability and cash flows. Creditors of the parent company have interests and information needs similar to those of the shareholders. The profitability and financial health of the parent are directly related to those of the companies it controls.

The minority shareholders and creditors of the subsidiary find the separate-entity statement of the subsidiary more useful than the consolidated statements.

While consolidated statements are considered the best vehicle to satisfy user needs, they also have limitations. A poor performance by certain subsidiaries can be hidden as a result of the aggregation process. In addition, many parent companies have subsidiaries in different industries in various countries throughout the world, and this can be hidden in a single set of statements. Footnote disclosures that present details about the companies' operating segments help to alleviate this problem. Finally, the information needs of minority shareholders and creditors of the subsidiary

---

[5] *Framework for the Preparation and Presentation of Financial Statements*, paragraph 49.

companies are not served by consolidated statements. This sector relies on the separate statements to determine the operating results and financial position of these companies.

A parent company does not have to issue consolidated financial statements if its parent issues consolidated financial statements.

IAS 27 states that a parent is not required to present consolidated financial statements for external reporting purposes if and only if

(a) the parent is itself a wholly owned subsidiary, or is a partially owned subsidiary, of another entity and its other owners, including those that are not otherwise entitled to vote, have been informed about, and do not object to, the parent not presenting consolidated financial statements;

(b) the parent's debt or equity instruments are not traded in a public market (a domestic or foreign stock exchange or an over-the-counter market, including local and regional markets);

(c) the parent did not file, nor is it in the process of filing, its financial statements with a securities commission or other regulatory organization for the purpose of issuing any class of instruments in a public market; and

(d) the ultimate or any intermediate parent of the parent produces consolidated financial statements available for public use that comply with IFRSs.

In the parent's *separate financial statements* for external users, the investment in subsidiary would be reported at cost or fair value.

If the parent meets these conditions, it *can* (but is not required to) present *separate financial statements* in accordance with GAAP as its only financial statements to external users. When an entity prepares *separate financial statements*, it shall account for investments in subsidiaries

(a) at cost, or

(b) in accordance with IAS 39: Financial Instruments — Recognition and Measurement.

If a parent does not issue either consolidated or separate financial statements in accordance with GAAP to external users, it may still prepare financial statements for internal record-keeping purposes and/or for special external users with special needs. The accounting policies used for these special-purpose financial statements should be disclosed. Unless otherwise noted, our illustrations throughout the text will comply with GAAP and will produce general-purpose financial statements for use by external users.

How Is Control Determined?   As we have seen from the *Handbook* definition, control is the power to direct the activities of the other entity. The ability to exercise this power is all that is required; it is not necessary to actually exercise it. Because the board of directors establishes the strategic policies of a corporation, the ability to elect a majority of the members of the board would generally be evidence of control. Therefore, control is presumed to exist if the parent owns directly or indirectly enough voting shares to elect the majority of the board of directors of a subsidiary. Indirect control would exist if, for example, B Company controls C Company and C Company controls D Company. B Company has direct control over C Company and indirectly controls D Company. Consolidation when control is achieved through indirect holdings is discussed in Chapter 8.

Owning more than 50 percent of the voting shares usually, but not always, indicates control.

In most situations, more than 50 percent of the voting shares are required to elect the majority of the board, and so control is presumed to exist if the percentage owned is over 50 percent. However, we have to look at all factors.

For example, if A Company owns 60 percent of the voting shares of B Company and C Company owns the other 40 percent, then we can presume that A Company controls B Company. But if C Company owns convertible bonds of B Company or options or warrants to purchase B Company shares, which if converted or exercised would give C Company 62 percent of the outstanding shares of B Company, then C Company, not A Company, controls B Company.

There is also a general presumption that a holding of less than 50 percent of the voting shares does not constitute control. This presumption can be overcome if other factors clearly indicate control. For example, an irrevocable agreement with other shareholders to convey voting rights to the parent would constitute control, even when the parent owned less than 50 percent of the voting shares. A parent may also have control despite owning less than 50 percent of the voting shares if its holdings of rights, warrants, convertible debt, or convertible preferred shares would give it enough voting power to control the board of directors of the subsidiary. Exercise or conversion would not be necessary, only the right to exercise or convert.

It is also possible for a parent to have control without a majority share ownership if it also has agreements in writing whose nature allow it to dictate subsidiary operating policies and result in it receiving fees, royalties, and profits from intercompany sales.

One parent could have control with less than 50 percent of the voting shares when contractual agreements give the parent control. In Chapter 10, we will discuss special-purpose entities where control exists through operating agreements. For these situations, the primary beneficiary makes the key decisions, receives the majority of the benefits and absorbs most of the risk even though he/she may own very few, if any, of the shares in the controlled company.

In another example, X Company owns 40 percent of Y Company, which is the largest single block of Y Company's outstanding shares. The other 60 percent is very widely held and only a very small proportion of the holders appear at the annual meeting of Y Company. As a result, X Company has had no trouble electing the majority of the board of directors. Under the Exposure Draft on Consolidated Financial Statements, which was issued by the IASB in 2008, X Company could be deemed to have control in this situation as long as the other shareholders are not organized in such a way that they actively cooperate when they exercise their votes so as to have more voting power than X Company. Under Canadian GAAP prior to IFRSs, X Company would be deemed to not have control because X Company required the cooperation of other shareholders to either not show up at the shareholders' meeting or to vote along with X Company.

Temporary control of an entity does not of itself change the fact that control exists. During the time that control is held and until such time as control ceases, the controlled assets are part of the group and should be recognized as such by preparing consolidated financial statements.

If control is present, a parent must consolidate a subsidiary; if control ceases, consolidation is discontinued. The seizure of the company's assets by a trustee in a receivership or bankruptcy situation would be evidence that control has probably ceased, as would the imposition of governmental restrictions over a foreign subsidiary's ability to pay dividends to its parent. However, when a receiver seizes a specific asset in satisfaction of a default under a loan agreement but permits the subsidiary to continue in business under the direction of the parent, this is not a loss of control.

A reporting entity can control another entity even though other parties have protective rights relating to the activities of that other entity. Protective rights are

A parent could have control with less than 50 percent of the voting shares when contractual agreements give the parent control.

Normal business restrictions do not preclude control by the parent.

designed to protect the interests of the party holding those rights without giving that party control of the entity to which they relate. They include, for example,

A parent can control a subsidiary even though other parties have protective rights relating to the subsidiary.

(a) approval or veto rights granted to other parties that do not affect the strategic operating and financing policies of the entity. Protective rights often apply to fundamental changes in the activities of an entity, or apply only in exceptional circumstances. For example,

    (i) a lender might have rights that protect the lender from the risk that the entity will change its activities to the detriment of the lender, such as selling important assets or undertaking activities that change the credit risk of the entity.

    (ii) non-controlling interests might have the right to approve capital expenditure greater than a particular amount, or the right to approve the issue of equity or debt instruments.

(b) the ability to remove the party that directs the activities of the entity in circumstances such as bankruptcy or on breach of contract by that party.

(c) limitations on the operating activities of an entity. For example, a franchise agreement for which the entity is the franchisee might restrict the pricing, advertising, or other operating activities of the entity but would not give the franchisor control of the franchisee. Such rights usually protect the brand of the franchisor.

While numerical guidelines are the starting point in determining whether or not control exists, professional judgment plays a major role because of all the relevant factors that must be taken into account. Appendix 3A describes the accounting for a Reverse Takeover, whereby Company A acquires Company B, but the accounting is done as if Company B controls Company A.

Item of Interest   The collapse of Enron Corporation has often been in the news since it occurred in 2001, and litigation against the company and criminal charges against management and auditors are still before the courts.

One of the many financial reporting problems involved with this debacle occurred because of the company's use of special-purpose entities (SPEs). SPEs were well known in the business world because they often allowed companies to employ "off-balance-sheet financing" by obtaining the use of borrowed money without showing the liability on its balance sheet. For example, an organization might create an SPE to borrow funds (guaranteed by the organization) that are then used to purchase assets. These assets are fully pledged against the borrowed funds and are then leased back to the organization with terms that make it an operating lease. Often the SPE has a very small equity, and the organization that created it does not own any of its shares.

The collapse of Enron caused the standard-setters to quickly introduce new standards for consolidation of special-purpose entities.

The accounting standards in existence at the time of the Enron collapse allowed the company to argue against the consolidation of its many SPEs and therefore leave billions of dollars of liabilities off its balance sheet. Its auditors, Arthur Andersen, accepted the argument. In the resulting investigation it appeared obvious that control was achieved even though no voting shares were held. In 2003, FASB strengthened its standards by issuing Interpretation No. 46, "Consolidation of Variable Interest Entities." Shortly after, the CICA issued an accounting guideline with the same title. Ironically, the IASB's Standing Interpretations Committee (SIC) had issued SIC-12 *Consolidation — Special Purpose Entities* (SPEs) in 1998. This Committee concluded that an SPE shall be consolidated when the substance of the relationship between an entity and the SPE indicates that the SPE is controlled by that entity. If a similar standard had been in effect in the United States, Enron would likely have had to consolidate its SPEs.

Now that we have a better understanding of the concept of control, we will turn our attention to the most common form of combination, the purchase of shares. We will continue to use the financial statements of the two companies in Exhibit 3.1 on page 79.

In the next two illustrations, A Company issues a tender offer to the shareholders of B Corporation (Group Y) for all of their shareholdings. Group Y accepts the offer.

Illustration 3 Assume that on January 1, Year 2, A Company pays $95,000 in cash to the shareholders of B Corporation for all of their shares, and that no other direct costs are involved. Because cash was the means of payment, A Company is the acquirer.

A Company's journal entry to record the acquisition of 100 percent of B Corporation's shares on January 1, Year 2, is as follows:

Investment in B Corporation	95,000	
Cash		95,000

With a purchase of shares, the transaction is with the shareholders of the acquired company, not with the acquired company itself.

The financial statements of B Corporation have not been affected by this transaction because the shareholders of B Corporation, not B Corporation itself, sold their shares. A Company is now a parent company and must prepare consolidated financial statements for external reporting purposes. We will now illustrate the preparation of the consolidated balance sheet as at January 1, Year 2, using a working paper approach.

Before preparing the working paper, it is useful to calculate and allocate the acquisition differential. The acquisition differential is defined as the difference between the amount paid by an acquiring company for shares and its proportionate interest in the net book value of the assets of the acquired limited company, at the date of acquisition. This concept was introduced in Chapter 2.

The required calculation and allocation is shown in Exhibit 3.2.

Exhibit 3.2

CALCULATION AND ALLOCATION
OF THE ACQUISITION DIFFERENTIAL

Cost of A Company's investment						$ 95,000
Net book value of B Corporation's net assets						
Assets					88,000	
Liabilities					30,000	
					58,000	
A Company's proportionate interest					100%	58,000
Acquisition differential						37,000

The acquisition differential comprises two components — a fair value excess (or deficiency) and goodwill.

Allocated as follows:

	Fair value	−	Book value	×	Ownership percentage			
Assets	109,000	−	88,000	×	100%	=	21,000	
Liabilities	29,000	−	30,000	×	100%	=	1,000	22,000
Balance — goodwill								$15,000

The $95,000 cost of the investment represents the total value of the subsidiary on the date of acquisition. The $95,000 value can be segregated into three components as indicated in the following bar chart:

The total value of the subsidiary can be segregated into three components.

Total Value of Subsidiary

Net book value of
identifiable assets and liabilities
$58,000

Excess of fair value over carrying amount
of identifiable assets and liabilities
$22,000

Goodwill
$15,000

Since assets minus liabilities equals shareholders' equity, the top component of the bar chart could be described as either net book value of identifiable assets and liabilities or net book value of shareholders' equity. The net book value component is the amount reflected on the subsidiary's separate-entity balance sheet.

The sum of the top two components is equal to the fair value of identifiable assets and liabilities. The bottom component, goodwill, is the extra amount paid by the acquirer over and above the fair value of the identifiable net assets. When the parent acquires 100 percent of the subsidiary, goodwill can be calculated as follows:

Goodwill is the difference between the acquisition cost and the fair value of identifiable net assets.

Cost of A Company's investment		$95,000
Fair value of B Corporation's identifiable net assets		
Assets	109,000	
Liabilities	29,000	
		80,000
Balance — goodwill		$15,000

The fair value excess is added to the book value of the subsidiary's assets on the consolidated balance; it is not added to the tax basis of the assets for income tax purposes. The fair value excess meets the definition of a temporary difference. Accordingly, deferred taxes should be set up for the tax effect on these temporary differences. We will ignore the deferred tax implications for now because they overly complicate the allocation of the acquisition differential. We will revisit this issue in Chapter 9.

Because consolidated working papers use the financial statements of the parent and its subsidiary, which do not contain fair values, the calculation and allocation of the acquisition differential is necessary because it provides the amounts needed to make the working paper eliminations and adjustments.

The working paper for the preparation of the consolidated balance sheet on the date of acquisition is shown in Exhibit 3.3.

Exhibit 3.3

A COMPANY LTD.
CONSOLIDATED BALANCE SHEET WORKING PAPER
January 1, Year 2

The consolidated balance sheet produces the same financial position as when A Company purchased the net assets directly.

	A Company	B Corp.	Adjustments and Eliminations Dr.	Adjustments and Eliminations Cr.	Consolidated balance sheet
Assets	$205,000	$88,000	**(2)** $ 21,000		$314,000
Investment in B Corporation	95,000			**(1)** $ 95,000	
Acquisition differential			**(1)** 37,000	**(2)** 37,000	
Goodwill			**(2)** 15,000		15,000
	$300,000	$88,000			$329,000
Liabilities	$120,000	$30,000	**(2)** 1,000		$149,000
Common shares	100,000				100,000
Retained earnings	80,000				80,000
Common shares		25,000	**(1)** 25,000		
Retained earnings		33,000	**(1)** 33,000		
	$300,000	$88,000	$132,000	$132,000	$329,000

The following points should be noted regarding the preparation of this working paper:

1. A Company's asset "Investment in B Corporation" and B Corporation's common shares and retained earnings do not appear on the consolidated balance sheet. These items are eliminated by a working paper elimination entry because they are reciprocal in nature. The entry labelled (1) eliminates the parent's ownership percentage of the shareholders' equity of the subsidiary against the parent's investment account. These shareholders' equity accounts are separately shown in the working paper to facilitate this. The acquisition differential that results is the portion of the investment account not eliminated.

2. The acquisition differential does not appear on the consolidated balance sheet. With reference to the calculations of Exhibit 3.2 on page 87 the acquisition differential is allocated to revalue the net assets of B Corporation for consolidation purposes. This is accomplished by the entry labelled (2).

The consolidated balance sheet reflects the acquiring company's net assets at book value and the acquired company's net assets at fair value.

3. When we add the book value of the net assets of B Corporation to 100 percent of the difference between its fair value and book value, the resulting amount used for the consolidation is the fair value of each individual asset and liability of B Corporation.

4. The elimination entries are made on the working paper only. They are not entered in the accounting records of the parent or the subsidiary.

The consolidation entries are made on the consolidated working papers and not in the accounting records of the combining companies.

5. The consolidated balance sheet is prepared from the amounts shown in the last column of the working paper.

6. Under the acquisition method of accounting, consolidated shareholders' equity on acquisition date is that of the parent.

Illustration 4   Assume that on January 1, Year 2, A Company issues 4,000 common shares, with a market value of $23.75 per share, to the shareholders of B Corporation (Group Y) for all of their shares, and that there are no direct costs involved. The analysis made in Illustration 2 indicates that A Company is the acquirer.

A Company's January 1, Year 2, journal entry to record the issuance of 4,000 shares at market value in payment for the acquisition of 100 percent of B Corporation's shares is as follows:

Investment in B Corporation (4,000 × 23.75)	95,000	
Common shares		95,000

The calculation and allocation of the acquisition differential is identical to the one used in the last illustration (see Exhibit 3.2 on page 87). The working paper for the preparation of the consolidated balance sheet as at January 1, Year 2, is shown in Exhibit 3.4.

The accounting for a business combination has been examined in four illustrations. The first two involved the acquisition of net assets, and the last two the acquisition of 100 percent of shareholdings. Because the amount paid was the same in each of these paired illustrations, the balance sheets prepared immediately after the combination are identical for each pair.

In the last two illustrations, it was quite clear who was the acquirer. In the appendix to this chapter, we consider a situation where the former shareholders of the acquired company have control over the acquiring company. This is a reverse takeover situation.

Disclosure Requirements   The acquirer must disclose information that enables users of its financial statements to evaluate the basis of control and how this affects the amounts included in the consolidated financial statements and the nature and financial effect of restrictions that are a consequence of assets and liabilities being

---

Exhibit 3.4

A COMPANY LTD.
CONSOLIDATED BALANCE SHEET WORKING PAPER
January 1, Year 2

	A Company	B Corp.	Adjustments and Eliminations Dr.	Adjustments and Eliminations Cr.	Consolidated balance sheet
Assets	$300,000	$88,000	**(2)** $ 21,000		$409,000
Investment in B Corporation	95,000			**(1)** $ 95,000	
Acquisition differential			**(1)** 37,000	**(2)** 37,000	
Goodwill			**(2)** 15,000		15,000
	$395,000	$88,000			$424,000
Liabilities	$120,000	$30,000	**(2)** 1,000		$149,000
Common shares	195,000				195,000
Retained earnings	80,000				80,000
Common shares		25,000	**(1)** 25,000		
Retained earnings		33,000	**(1)** 33,000		
	$395,000	$88,000	$132,000	$132,000	$424,000

The allocation of the acquisition differential is made on the consolidated worksheet and is not recorded in the accounting records of the combining companies.

The consolidated financial statements are a third set of financial statements supported by a working paper that combines the separate-entity financial statements of the parent and subsidiaries.

held by subsidiaries. To achieve these objectives, Appendix B of IFRS 3 provides an extensive list of what must be disclosed for each business combination. The more substantial items included in that list are as follows:

- The acquisition-date fair value of the total consideration given and the acquisition-date fair value of each major class of consideration given;
- The amounts recognized as of the acquisition date for each major class of assets acquired and liabilities assumed; and
- Legal, contractual, and regulatory restrictions and the carrying amount of the assets and liabilities to which those restrictions apply.

AkzoNobel, with headquaters in the Netherlands, is the world's largest global paints and coatings company. It reported the acquisition of several subsidiaries in 2008. Excerpts from its 2008 financial statements are presented in Exhibit 3.5.

Exhibit 3.5

EXTRACTS (IN PART) FROM AKZONOBEL 2008 FINANCIAL STATEMENTS

Note 2 Acquisitions and divestments

On January 2, 2008, we acquired 100 percent of the share capital of Imperial Chemical Industries plc (ICI). The total cost of the acquisition, paid mostly in cash, was €11.6 billion. ICI was one of the world's leading coatings, adhesives, starches and synthetic polymer businesses, with products and ingredients developed for a wide range of markets. It had operations in more than 50 countries around the world and its customers are spread across a diverse range of product sectors.

Additionally, in Performance Coatings we acquired Enviroline, a specialist supplier of corrosion-resistant linings, predominantly for the oil and gas industries. We acquired our floor coatings portfolio through an acquisition from Lord Corporation. In Specialty Chemicals we acquired Levasil, a silica sol business. These acquisitions in 2008, both individually and in total, were deemed immaterial in respect of the IFRS 3 disclosure requirements.

Acquisition of ICI

In € Millions	Pre-Acquisition Carrying Amounts	Recognized Values At Acquisition
Goodwill	413	4,465
Other intangible assets	61	3,763
Property, plant and equipment	1,135	1,382
Other non-current assets	545	513
Inventories	568	622
Trade and other receivables	977	979
Assets held for sale	1,200	4,413
Cash and cash equivalents	1,088	1,088
Provisions	(1,271)	(1,402)
Deferred tax liabilities	(21)	(884)
Long-term borrowings	(372)	(372)
Trade and other payables	(1,915)	(1,940)
Liabilities held for sale	(554)	(581)
Net identifiable assets and liabilities	**1,854**	**12,046**
Minority interests		(435)
Consideration paid		**11,611**

(continued)

Cash flows used for acquisitions

In € Millions

Consideration paid for ICI	11,611
Cash and cash equivalents acquired	(1,088)
Paid through loan notes	(142)
Paid in 2007	(349)
Other acquisitions	155
Cash flows used for acquisitions	**10,187**

The goodwill recognized is related to ICI's workforce and the synergies expected to be achieved from integrating ICI into Decorative Paints and Specialty Chemicals. The major intangibles recognized are acquired brands, the most significant being Dulux. Several brands are expected to have an indefinite useful life. As a result, they will not be amortized but tested for impairment annually.

Other intangible assets acquired in ICI at acquisition date

In € Millions	Amount	Amortization Period (In Years)
Brands and trade names with indefinite useful life	1,929	—
Brands and trade names with finite useful life	410	31
Customer relationships	1,146	15
Other intangibles	278	13
Intangibles acquired	**3,763**	

As the acquisition of ICI took place on January 2, 2008, our financial outcomes include the full year's results from ICI. Due to the immediate integration, we cannot determine the amount that the acquisition contributed to operating income in 2008 on a stand alone basis. All other acquisitions in 2008 have made a marginal contribution to net income, even if all acquisitions had occurred on January 1, 2008.

In connection with the acquisition of ICI, we sold all assets and liabilities comprising the businesses known within ICI as the Adhesives business and the Electronic Materials business to Henkel, for €3.6 billion in cash after a pension settlement and before final settlement adjustments. The transaction took place in April 2008.

In addition, in granting clearance, the EU and Canadian authorities accepted a commitment package from AkzoNobel involving the divestment of a number of AkzoNobel Decorative Paints businesses in the UK, Ireland, Belgium and Canada. These businesses were sold in the course of 2008.

Source: AkzoNobel 2008 Financial Statements. © AkzoNobel.

GAAP for Private Enterprises

The following paragraphs from Section 1590: Subsidiaries of Part II of the *CICA Handbook* outline the main accounting and reporting requirements for investments in subsidiaries:

- An enterprise shall make an accounting policy choice to either consolidate its subsidiaries or report for its subsidiaries using either the equity method, the cost method, or at fair value. All subsidiaries should be accounted for using the same method.

- When a subsidiary's equity securities are quoted in an active market, the investment should not be accounted for using the cost method. Under such circumstances, the investment may be accounted for at its quoted amount, with changes recorded in net income.

- The investments in and income from non-consolidated subsidiaries should be presented separately from other investments.

U.S. GAAP Differences

U.S. GAAP and IFRSs for business combination have many similarities. The significant differences are summarized as follows:

1. Whereas IFRSs define control as the power to direct the operating and financing activities of the other entity, U.S. GAAP generally looks for majority voting rights, except for variable interest entities, where it looks for control and other factors.

2. Whereas IFRSs define fair value in IFRS 3 as the amount for which an asset could be exchanged, or a liability settled, between knowledgeable, willing parties in an arm's-length transaction, U.S. GAAP uses a different definition and provides general valuation guidance for determining fair value.

3. Whereas IFRSs provide an exemption from the requirement to prepare consolidated financial statements if the reporting entity's parent prepares consolidated financial statements, U.S. GAAP does not provide an exemption.

4. Whereas IFRSs require that the accounting policies of the parent and subsidiary conform, the SEC staff does not require policies to conform provided that policies are in accordance with U.S. GAAP.

SUMMARY

A *business combination* takes place when one company gains control over the net assets of another company. Control can be achieved by the purchase of the net assets or by the purchase of enough voting shares to gain control over the use of the net assets. In the latter situation a parent–subsidiary relationship is created that requires the preparation of consolidated financial statements.

Prior to 2001, both the purchase method and the pooling-of-interests method were acceptable methods to account for a business combination. Pooling could be used only if there was a share exchange and even then only in exceptional circumstances. On July 1, 2001, pooling was disallowed in both Canada and the United States, leaving the purchase method as the only acceptable method to account for a business combination. Effective January 1, 2011, the *acquisition method* must be used to report a business combination, and an acquirer must be identified.

Under the acquisition method, the identifiable assets and liabilities acquired are recorded at fair values, with the acquisition cost excess recorded as goodwill.

Significant Changes in the Last Two Years

1. For publicly accountable enterprises, IFRSs have replaced the former sections of the *CICA Handbook*. The following table shows the IFRSs covered in this chapter along with their counterpart from the former sections of the *CICA Handbook:*

IFRSs	CICA Handbook *Counterparts*
IFRS 3: Business Combinations	Section 1582: Business Combinations
IAS 27: Consolidated and Separate Financial Statements	Section 1590: Subsidiaries Section 1601: Consolidated Financial Statements
IAS 38: Intangible Assets	Section 3064: Goodwill and Other Intangible Assets

2. The definition of control has changed. It now focuses on the power to direct the activities of another entity by determining that other entity's strategic operating and financing policies.

3. Exceptions are provided for a parent not having to prepare consolidated financial statements when consolidated financial statements are provided for the entity that directly or indirectly controls the parent. In this situation, the parent can prepare separate-entity financial statements for its external users.

4. We have changed terminology from *purchase discrepancy* to *acquisition differential*.

5. We now use subsidiary's net assets (i.e., assets minus liabilities) rather than shareholders' equity when calculating the acquisition differential.

Changes Expected in the Next Three Years

The definition of control may change again since the IASB and the FASB are working on a joint project related to consolidated financial statements. The new definition of control being considered by the IASB is as follows: *Control* is the power to direct the activities of that other entity to generate returns for the reporting entity.

SELF-STUDY PROBLEM

On December 31, Year 1, P Company wants to take control over the net assets of S Company by buying the net assets directly or by purchasing 100 percent of the common shares of S Company. In either case, P Company will pay for the purchase by issuing common shares with a fair value of $44,000. In addition, P Company paid $1,000 for professional fees to facilitate the transaction. The following information has been assembled:

	P Company		S Company	
	Book value	Fair value	Book value	Fair value
Goodwill	$ 0	$ 38,000	$ 0	$22,000
Plant assets	80,000	90,000	20,000	26,000
Current assets	50,000	55,000	15,000	14,000
	$130,000	$183,000	$35,000	$62,000
Shareholders' equity	$ 75,000		$18,000	
Long-term debt	25,000	$ 29,000	7,000	$ 8,000
Current liabilities	30,000	30,000	10,000	10,000
	$130,000		$35,000	

Required:

(a) Prepare P Company's statement of financial position immediately after the combination assuming that P acquires the net assets directly.

(b) Prepare a consolidated statement of financial position for P Company immediately after the combination under

(i) the acquisition method.

(ii) the new entity method.

(c) Describe the similarities in the statement of financial position for the purchase of net assets in part (a) as compared to the consolidated statement of financial position under the acquisition method in part (b) (i).

www.mcgrawhillconnect.ca

Solution to Self-study Problem

P COMPANY
Statement of Financial Position
At December 31, Year 1
(See notes)

	(a)	(b) (i)	(b) (ii)
Goodwill	$ 22,000	$ 22,000	$ 60,000
Plant assets	106,000	106,000	116,000
Current assets	63,000	63,000	68,000
	$191,000	$191,000	$244,000
Shareholders' equity	$118,000	$118,000	$167,000
Long-term debt	33,000	33,000	37,000
Current liabilities	40,000	40,000	40,000
	$191,000	$191,000	$244,000

(c) The consolidated financial position for the parent and subsidiary in part (b)(i) is exactly the same as the separate-entity balance sheet for P Company in part (a) when P Company acquired the net assets directly.

Notes:
1. The statement of financial position values for assets and liabilities are calculated as follows:
   (a) Book values for P plus fair values for S.
   (b) (i) Book values for P plus fair values for S.
       (ii) Fair values for P plus fair values for S.
2. The $1,000 paid for professional fees reduces cash (which is included in current assets) and increases expenses (which reduces shareholders' equity)
3. Shareholders' equity is the amount required to balance the statement of financial position.

APPENDIX 3A

Reverse Takeovers

For accounting purposes, the acquirer is identified based on which shareholder group has control over the combined entity.

A reverse takeover occurs when an enterprise obtains ownership of the shares of another enterprise but, as part of the transaction, issues enough voting shares as consideration that control of the combined enterprise passes to the shareholders of the acquired enterprise. Although legally the enterprise that issues the shares is regarded as the parent or continuing enterprise, the enterprise whose former shareholders now control the combined enterprise is treated as the acquirer. As a result, the issuing enterprise is deemed to be a continuation of the acquirer and the acquirer is deemed to have acquired control of the assets and business of the issuing enterprise in consideration for the issue of capital.

While not a common event, this form of business combination is often used by active non-public companies as a means to obtain a stock exchange listing without having to go through the listing procedures established by the exchange. A takeover of a public company that has a stock exchange listing is arranged in such a way that the public company emerges as the legal parent, but the former shareholders of the non-public company have control of the public company.

Exhibit 3A.1

BALANCE SHEETS

| | Reverse Ltd. | | Takeover Co. |
	Book value	Fair value	Book value
Current assets	$ 560	$ 700	$1,560
Plant assets	1,600	1,650	5,100
	$ 2,160		$6,660
Liabilities	$ 720	$ 720	$3,060
Common shares (160 shares)	500		
Retained earnings	940		
Common shares (96 shares)*			1,080
Retained earnings			2,520
	$ 2,160		$6,660

* The shares of Takeover Co. have a current market value of $30 per share.

Reverse Takeover Illustration   The balance sheets of Reverse Ltd. and Takeover Co. on the date of a reverse takeover business combination are shown in Exhibit 3A.1.

In a reverse takeover, the legal parent is deemed to be the subsidiary for accounting purposes and the legal subsidiary is deemed to be the parent.

Reverse is a small public company engaged in business activity with a listing on a major stock exchange. Takeover is an active company not listed on any exchange. A business combination is initiated by Takeover whereby Reverse issues 240 shares to the shareholders of Takeover for 100 percent of their shareholdings. By structuring the combination in this manner, Reverse becomes the legal parent and Takeover the legal subsidiary.

An examination of the shares held by the two shareholder groups in the following manner clearly indicates that Takeover is identified as the acquirer:

	Shares of Reverse Ltd.	%
Shareholders of Reverse Ltd.	160	40%
Shareholders of Takeover Co.	240	60%
	400	100%

Under the acquisition method of accounting for a business combination, the fair value of the net assets of the acquiree is combined with the book value of the net assets of the acquirer. Because Takeover is the acquirer, the acquisition cost is determined *as if* Takeover had issued shares to the shareholders of Reverse. A calculation has to be made to determine the number of shares that Takeover would have issued to achieve the same result (i.e., so that its shareholders would end up holding 60 percent of Takeover's outstanding shares). The number of shares can be determined as follows:

The acquisition cost for the deemed parent is determined based on a hypothetical situation that could have achieved the same percentage ownership in the combined entity.

1. Before the combination the shareholders of Takeover hold 96 shares in that company.
2. Takeover would have to issue X additional shares, such that the 96 shares will represent 60 percent of the total shares outstanding.
3. After the share issue, the total shares outstanding will be 96 + X shares.
4. $96 = 0.6(96 + X)$. Therefore, $X = 64$ shares.

If Takeover had issued 64 shares, the holdings of the two groups of shareholders would have been as follows:

	Shares of Takeover Co.	%
Shareholders of Takeover	96	60%
Shareholders of Reverse	64	40%
	160	100%

The acquisition cost is the number of shares that Takeover would have issued, valued at their fair market value, and is allocated in the following manner:

Goodwill of the deemed subsidiary is based on the hypothetical acquisition cost.

Acquisition cost — 64 shares @ $30	$1,920
Fair value of identifiable net assets of Reverse Co.	1,630
Goodwill	$ 290

The balance sheet of the combined company immediately after the business combination is prepared by combining the fair value of the net assets of Reverse, including the goodwill from the combination, with the book value of the net assets of Takeover. It should be noted that Takeover's shareholders' equity becomes the shareholders' equity of the combined company. The dollar amount shown for common shares is determined by summing the dollar amount of the common shares of Takeover before the combination and the deemed issue of 64 shares at market value.

Shareholders' equity should reflect the shareholders' equity of the deemed parent.

However, the number of shares shown as issued are the outstanding shares of the legal parent Reverse. The consolidated balance sheet of Reverse immediately after the reverse takeover takes place is shown in Exhibit 3A.2.

The financial statements of Reverse would contain the following footnote to describe this event:

> During the year, Reverse Ltd. entered into a share exchange agreement with the shareholders of Takeover Co. Under this agreement Reverse exchanged 240 common shares for 100% of the issued and outstanding shares of Takeover. As a result of the share exchange, Reverse obtained control over Takeover.
>
> Legally Reverse is the parent of Takeover; however, as a result of the share exchange, control of the combined companies passed to the shareholders of Takeover, which for accounting purposes is deemed to be the acquirer. For financial reporting purposes, this share exchange is considered to be a reverse takeover and Reverse is considered to be a continuation of Takeover. The net

Note disclosure is required to explain that the reporting follows the substance (rather than the legal form) of who has control.

Exhibit 3A.2

The legal parent/deemed subsidiary's assets are brought in at fair value while the legal subsidiary/deemed parent's assets are brought in at book value.

REVERSE LTD.
CONSOLIDATED BALANCE SHEET

Current assets (700 + 1,560)	$2,260
Plant assets (1,650 + 5,100)	6,750
Goodwill	290
	$9,300
Liabilities (720 + 3,060)	$3,780
Common shares* (1,080 + 1,920)	3,000
Retained earnings	2,520
	$9,300

* The number of shares issued and outstanding would be shown as 400 shares (160 + 240).

assets of Takeover are included in the balance sheet at book values, and the deemed acquisition of Reverse is accounted for by the acquisition method, with the net assets of Reverse recorded at fair values. The fair value of Reverse on the date of acquisition was as follows:

Current assets	$ 700
Plant assets	1,650
Goodwill	290
Liabilities	(720)
	$1,920

In this example the acquisition cost was determined by multiplying the number of shares that the legal subsidiary would have had to issue by the market price of that company's shares. However, because the legal subsidiary is often a private company, the market value of its shares may have to be determined using business valuation concepts. If a market price can not be determined for the shares of the legal subsidiary, the fair value of the net assets of the legal parent are used to determine acquisition cost.

The comparative amounts are those of the legal subsidiary/ deemed parent.

Comparative amounts presented in the consolidated financial statements of the legal parent are those of the legal subsidiary. In the year of the reverse takeover, consolidated net income is made up of the income of the legal subsidiary *before* the takeover and the income of the combined company *after* the takeover.

Because the outstanding shares shown on the consolidated balance sheet are those of the legal parent, the calculation of earnings per share is based on these shares; so is the calculation of the weighted average shares outstanding in the year of the takeover.

In the example of Reverse, assuming the combination date was July 31, the weighted average shares outstanding for the fiscal year December 31 is 307 shares, calculated as follows:

- 240 shares deemed outstanding for 7 months, *and*
- 400 shares outstanding for 5 months.

The consolidated financial statements use the name and shares outstanding of the legal parent.

This calculation is in contrast to the normal calculation of weighted average shares outstanding and requires further clarification. Remember that the consolidated statements of Reverse (the legal parent) are considered to be a continuation of those of Takeover (the legal subsidiary) and that the accounting assumes that the legal subsidiary acquired the legal parent. But the shares outstanding are those of the legal parent.

The consolidated financial statements use values consistent with who, in substance, is the parent and who, in substance, is the subsidiary.

Consolidated net income for the year *does not* contain the income of Reverse prior to the takeover date because this income is considered to be pre-acquisition earnings. Reverse picked up the first seven months' income of Takeover with the issue of 240 shares. The last five months' income is that of Takeover and Reverse, during which time 400 shares (160 + 240) were outstanding.

The consolidated balance sheet of Reverse Ltd. (Exhibit 3A.2 on page 97) was prepared using a non-working paper (or direct) approach. We will now illustrate the preparation of the consolidated balance sheet using a working paper (Exhibit 3A.3). On the date of the reverse takeover, Reverse (the legal parent) would make the following journal entry to record the acquisition of 100 percent of the outstanding shares of Takeover by the issuance of 240 common shares:

Investment in Takeover Co.	1,920	
Common shares (new)		1,920

These "new" shares are issued at the deemed acquisition cost and are shown separately on the working paper to simplify the consolidation process.

The calculation and allocation of the acquisition differential is as follows:

The purchase allocation uses the acquisition cost under the hypothetical situation.

Acquisition cost of Takeover Co.			$ 1,920
Book value of Reverse Ltd's net assets			
Assets		2,160	
Liabilities		720	1,440
Acquisition differential			480
Allocated:	(FV − BV)		
Current assets	140		
Plant assets	50		190
Goodwill			$ 290

Elimination entry **(1)** eliminates Reverse's investment in Takeover against *Reverse's precombination shareholders' equity,* with the acquisition differential the balancing amount.

Elimination **(2)** allocates the acquisition differential to revalue the net assets of Reverse.

The consolidated common shares are the common shares of Takeover (the legal subsidiary) before the takeover plus the new shares issued by Reverse, which are valued at Takeover's deemed acquisition cost of Reverse.

Exhibit 3A.3

REVERSE LTD.
CONSOLIDATED BALANCE SHEET WORKING PAPER
(immediately after the reverse takeover)

	Reverse Ltd.	Takeover Co.	Adjustments and Eliminations Dr.	Adjustments and Eliminations Cr.	Consolidated balance sheet
The assets reflect the fair values of the deemed subsidiary and the book values of the deemed parent. Current assets	$ 560	$1,560	**(2)** $ 140		$2,260
Plant assets	1,600	5,100	**(2)** 50		6,750
Investment in					
Takeover Co.	1,920			**(1)** $1,920	
Acquisition differential			**(1)** 480	**(2)** 480	
Goodwill			**(2)** 290		290
	$4,080	$6,660			$9,300
Retained earnings are the retained earnings of the deemed parent. Liabilities	$ 720	$3,060			$3,780
Common shares (old)	500		**(1)** 500		
Retained earnings	940		**(1)** 940		
Common shares		1,080			3,000
Common shares (new)	1,920				
Retained earnings		2,520			2,520
	$4,080	$6,660	$2,400	$2,400	$9,300

REVIEW QUESTIONS

Questions, cases, and problems that deal with the appendix material are denoted with an asterisk.

1. What key element must be present in a business combination?
2. Can a statutory amalgamation be considered a form of business combination? Explain.
3. Explain how an acquirer is determined in a business combination for a 100-percent-owned subsidiary.
4. Outline the accounting involved with the acquisition method for a 100-percent-owned subsidiary.
5. Briefly describe the accounting involved with the new entity method.
6. If one company issued shares as payment for the net assets of another company, it would probably insist that the other company be wound up after the sale. Explain why this condition would be part of the asset purchase agreement.
7. What criteria must be met for a subsidiary to be consolidated? Explain.
8. What part do irrevocable agreements, convertible securities, and warrants play in determining whether control exists? Explain.
9. What is an acquisition differential, and where does it appear on the consolidated balance sheet?
10. What are some reasons for the purchase price being in excess of the carrying value of the acquiree's assets and liabilities? What does this say about the accuracy of the values used in the financial statements of the acquiree?
11. How is goodwill determined at the date of acquisition? Describe the nature of goodwill.
12. When must an intangible asset be shown separately from goodwill? What are the criteria for reporting these intangible assets separately from goodwill?
13. Does the historical cost principle or fair value reporting take precedence when preparing consolidated financial statements at the date of acquisition under the acquisition method? Explain.
14. What are separate financial statements and when can they be presented to external users in accordance with GAAP?
15. What are protective rights and how do they affect the decision of whether one entity has control over another entity?
*16. What is a reverse takeover, and why is such a transaction entered into?
*17. Explain how the acquisition cost is determined for a reverse takeover.

MULTIPLE-CHOICE QUESTIONS

1. When a parent uses the acquisition method to consolidate a wholly owned subsidiary, what amount will appear as "common shares" in the equity section of the consolidated statement of financial position?
   a. The book value of the parent's common shares plus the book value of the subsidiary's common shares.
   b. The book value of the parent's common shares plus the fair value of the subsidiary's common shares.

c. The fair value of the parent's common shares on the date of the purchase of the subsidiary.

d. The book value of the parent's common shares at the date of acquisition.

2. P Company acquires 100 percent of the common shares of S Company by issuing non-voting preferred shares. For both P Company and S Company, the fair value of all assets is greater than the recorded book values. Which of the following approaches to consolidation will show the highest total asset value on the consolidated balance sheet on the date of acquisition?

a. Acquisition.

b. Purchase.

c. New entity.

d. Cannot be determined based on the information provided.

3. Which of the following characteristics is not associated with a business combination in Canada today?

a. A clearly identified acquisition cost is evident for the transaction.

b. Two subsidiaries of a single parent merge together as one.

c. Cash or debt or shares can be used as payment for the acquired company.

d. One company can always be identified as the acquirer.

4. Harper Corp. has only three assets constituting its business:

	Book value	Fair value
Inventory	$ 165,000	$ 225,000
Land	1,050,000	900,000
Buildings	1,050,000	1,350,000

Kandon Inc. purchases Harper's assets by issuing 100,000 common shares with a market value of $30 per share.

What is the amount of goodwill from this business combination?

a. $525,000

b. Negative $525,000

c. $735,000

d. Nil

5. During Year 5, XYZ Ltd. purchased all of the 100,000 outstanding Class B shares of Sub Limited. Each share carries one vote. The previous owner, Mr. Bill, retained all 80,000 outstanding Class A shares of Sub, each also carrying one vote. In order to avoid sudden changes, Mr. Bill stipulated in the sale agreement that he was to retain the right to veto management appointments for Sub and to approve any significant operating and financing transactions of Sub. How should XYZ report its investment in Sub?

a. Full consolidation.

b. Proportionate consolidation.

c. Equity method.

d. Fair value method.

(CICA adapted)

6. On January 1, Year 5, KL Corporation and XT Corporation entered into a business combination. On that date, the fair value of KL's depreciable assets was greater than the book value. Similarly, the fair value of XT's depreciable assets was greater than the book value. Both companies had been profitable every year from

Year 2 through Year 4. Which of the following is true regarding the earnings for the business combination on the Year 5 consolidated financial statements?

a. The acquisition method would produce higher earnings than the new entity method.

b. The new entity method would produce higher earnings than the acquisition method.

c. Earnings would be the same under the acquisition and new entity methods.

d. The relative earnings of the two methods cannot be determined based on the information provided.

(CGA-Canada adapted)

Use the following data for Questions 7 and 8.

On January 1, Year 6, Green Company acquired 100 percent of the outstanding common shares of Blue Inc. by issuing 10,000 common shares. The book values and the fair values of both companies immediately before the acquisition were as follows:

	Green Company		Blue Inc.	
	Book values	Fair values	Book values	Fair values
Assets	$2,175,000	$2,400,000	$900,000	$1,042,500
Liabilities	$1,155,000	1,132,000	$375,000	405,000
Common shares*	450,000		97,500	
Retained earnings	570,000		427,500	
	$2,175,000		$900,000	

* *Immediately before the acquisition transaction, Green Company had 20,000 common shares outstanding and Blue Inc. had 6,500 common shares outstanding. Green's shares were actively trading at $75 on the date of the acquisition.*

7. What amount would Green Company report on its consolidated financial statements for assets immediately after the acquisition transaction?
   a. $3,075,000
   b. $3,217,500
   c. $3,330,000
   d. $3,442,500

8. What amount would Green Company report on its consolidated financial statements for common shares immediately after the acquisition transaction?
   a. $450,000
   b. $547,500
   c. $1,200,000
   d. $1,297,500

9. Which of the following is the best theoretical justification for consolidated financial statements?
   a. In form, the companies are one entity; in substance, they are separate.
   b. In form, the companies are separate; in substance, they are one entity.
   c. In form and substance, the companies are one entity.
   d. In form and substance, the companies are separate.

10. What is the appropriate accounting treatment for the value assigned to in-process research and development acquired in a business combination?
    a. Always expense upon acquisition.
    b. Always capitalize as an asset with future economic benefit.

    c.   Expense if there is no alternative use for the assets used in the research and development and technological feasibility has yet to be reached.

    d.   Expense until future economic benefits become certain and then capitalize as an asset.

11. An acquired entity has a long-term operating lease for an office building used for central management. The terms of the lease are very favourable relative to current market rates. However, the lease prohibits subleasing or any other transfer of rights. How should the acquiring firm report the value assigned to the lease contract in its financial statements?

    a.   As an intangible asset under the contractual-legal criterion.

    b.   As a part of goodwill.

    c.   As an intangible asset under the separability criterion.

    d.   As a building.

12. When one company controls another company, IAS 27 recommends that the parent report the subsidiary on a consolidated basis. Which of the following best describes the primary reason for this recommendation?

    a.   To report the combined retained earnings of the two companies, allowing shareholders to better predict dividend payments.

    b.   To allow for taxation of the combined entity.

    c.   To report the total resources of the combined economic entity under the control of the parent's shareholders.

    d.   To meet the requirements of the federal and provincial securities commissions.

13. Which of the following is not a necessary condition for consolidating another enterprise in a reporting enterprise's financial statements?

    a.   The reporting enterprise has control over the other enterprise.

    b.   The reporting enterprise has the right and ability to obtain future economic benefits from the resources of the other enterprise.

    c.   The reporting enterprise can determine the other entity's strategic operating and financing policies.

    d.   The reporting enterprise owns, either directly or indirectly, more than 50 percent of the other enterprise's voting shares.

14. Which of the following is not an appropriate reason for leaving a subsidiary unconsolidated?

    a.   The subsidiary is being managed by a trustee under bankruptcy.

    b.   The subsidiary is in an industry that is significantly different from that of the parent.

    c.   A foreign government prevents the subsidiary from paying dividends.

    d.   The parent and subsidiary will be consolidated at a higher level in the corporate hierachy.

15. In which of the following situations would PUR have the ability to control the strategic operating and financing activities of SUR?

    a.   PUR owns 48 percent of the voting shares of SUR.

    b.   PUR owns 40,000 of the 100,000 voting shares of SUR and 80 percent of the non-voting shares of SUR.

c. PUR owns 60,000 of the 100,000 voting shares of SUR and 10,000 of the 50,000 convertible non-voting shares. Each of the non-voting shares is convertible into one voting share.

d. PUR owns 40,000 of the 100,000 voting shares of SUR and 44,000 of the 50,000 convertible non-voting shares. Each of the non-voting shares is convertible into one voting share.

(CGA-Canada adapted)

*16. At December 31, Year 5, Alpha Company had 20,000 common shares outstanding while Beta Inc. has 10,000 common shares outstanding. Alpha wishes to enter into a reverse takeover of Beta to gain its listing on the stock exchange. Which one of the following describes how many shares would have to be issued, and by which company, for this to occur?

a. Alpha would have to issue more than 10,000 shares.
b. Alpha would have to issue more than 20,000 shares.
c. Beta would have to issue more than 10,000 shares.
d. Beta would have to issue more than 20,000 shares.

*17. Refer to Question 16. Which company's name would appear on the financial statements of the combined company after the reverse takeover?

a. Alpha Company.
b. Beta Inc.
c. Both names would appear on the statements, by law.
d. A new name would have to be created to identify the new economic entity that has been created.

CASES

Case 1 On December 30, Year 7, Pepper Company agreed to form a business combination with Salt Limited. Pepper issued 2,320 of its common shares for all (2,900) of the outstanding common shares of Salt. This transaction increased the number of the outstanding Pepper shares from 3,800 to 6,120. The market value of the shares was $50 per share for Pepper and $40 for Salt. The balance sheets for the two companies just prior to the acquisition were as follows (in 000s):

	Pepper Book value	Pepper Fair value	Salt Book value	Salt Fair value
Identifiable assets	$200	$250	$100	$130
Goodwill	0	100	0	70
	$200	$350	$100	$200
Liabilities	$150	$160	$ 80	$ 84
Shareholders' equity	50	190	20	116
	$200	$350	$100	$200

Consolidated financial statements will be prepared to combine the financial statements for the two companies. The management of Pepper is concerned about not exceeding a debt-to-equity ratio of 3:1 because of a covenant in a borrowing agreement with its bank. It wants to see how these consolidated statements would differ under two different methods of reporting: acquisition and new entity. Management also has the following questions when reporting this business combination:

- Why, under the acquisition method, is one set of assets and liabilities adjusted to fair value whereas the other set is left at book value?
- Given that under the acquisition method we can measure and report the net assets at fair values at the date of acquisition, why would we not report fair values at each subsequent reporting date?
- Which balance sheet best reflects the economic reality of the business combination?

Required:

Prepare a consolidated balance sheet at the date of acquisition under the two methods and respond to the questions asked by management.

Case 2   The directors of Atlas Inc. and Beta Corp. have reached an agreement in principle to merge the two companies and create a new company called AB Ltd. The basics of the agreement confirmed so far are outlined below.

The new company will purchase all of the assets and assume all of the liabilities of Atlas and Beta by issuing shares. After the sale the two companies will be wound up. Some but not all members of the top management of each company will be retained.

The number of AB shares that will be issued has not yet been determined.

The founding shareholders of Atlas Corp., who owned 60 percent of the voting shares of Atlas prior to the merger, have rights to veto any sale of patents, which they developed and registered. Some of the other shareholders of Atlas also owned non-voting preferred shares of Atlas. These preferred shares were convertible into common shares of Atlas on a one-for-one basis.

The chair of the merger committee has asked you to provide him with advice as to the accounting implications that will result from this merger, even though many of the details have not yet been ironed out. He has requested that you submit to him a preliminary report.

Required:

Prepare an outline of your report.

Case 3   Manitoba Peat Moss (MPM) was the first Canadian company to provide a reliable supply of high-quality peat moss to be used for greenhouse operations. Owned by Paul Parker, the company's founder and president, MPM began operations approximately 30 years ago when demand for peat moss was high. It has shown consistently high profits and stable growth for over 20 years. Parker holds all of the 50,000 outstanding common shares in MPM.

Prairie Greenhouses (PG), a publicly traded company that purchases over 70 percent of MPM's output, provides tree seedlings to various government agencies and logging companies for reforestation projects. In Year 5, PG approached MPM with an offer to buy all of the company's outstanding shares in exchange for a part ownership in PG, with a view to vertically integrating. Parker was very interested in the offer, since he hoped to soon retire. PG currently has 100,000 shares outstanding and widely distributed. It would issue 100,000 new common shares in a two-for-one exchange for all of MPM's shares. PG's shares are currently trading on the TSX at $60 per share.

The board of directors of PG is uncertain as to the accounting implications of the proposed share exchange. They believe that since they are purchasing all of the outstanding common shares of MPM, it is similar to buying the company outright; as a result they want to report all of MPM's assets on PG's consolidated financial statements at fair value. This will be very advantageous to PG, because the land carried on MPM's books was purchased 30 years ago and has appreciated substantially in value over the years.

The board has asked you, its accounting adviser, to prepare a report explaining how PG's purchase of shares should be reported. They are particularly interested in how the increase in the value of the land will be shown on the consolidated statements.

The condensed balance sheets of the two companies at the time of the offer are shown below:

	PG	MPM
Current assets	$ 870,000	$ 450,000
Property, plant, and equipment	8,210,000	2,050,000
	$9,080,000	$2,500,000
Current liabilities	$ 525,000	$ 200,000
Long-term debt	2,325,000	1,300,000
Common shares	4,000,000	500,000
Retained earnings	2,230,000	500,000
	$9,080,000	$2,500,000

Note: Land held by MPM at a book value of $1,000,000 has a fair value of $6,000,000. All other assets of both companies have book values approximately equal to their fair values.

Required:

Prepare the report to the board of directors.

(adapted from a case prepared by J.C. (Jan) Thatcher, Lakehead University, and Margaret Forbes, University of Saskatchewan)

Case 4   When Conoco Inc. of Houston, Texas, announced the CDN$7 billion acquisition of Gulf Canada Resources Limited of Calgary, Alberta, a large segment of the press release was devoted to outlining all of the expected benefits to be received from the assets acquired. The acquisition price represented a 35 percent premium over Gulf's closing share price on the announcement date. Included in the assets of Gulf were the following:

- Proven reserves of over 1 billion barrels of oil;
- Probable reserves of approximately 1.2 billion barrels of oil;
- Proven reserves of 1.4 trillion cubic feet of natural gas;
- Probable reserves of 2.9 trillion cubic feet of natural gas;
- Four million acres of undeveloped land in western Canada;
- A 72 percent interest in Gulf Indonesia Resources Limited; included in this company's assets were reserves of 180 million barrels of oil and 1.5 trillion cubic feet of gas;
- A 9 percent interest in joint venture, Syncrude Canada Ltd., which is developing the heavy oil tar sands in northern Alberta;

- Long-term contracts to deliver 3 trillion cubic feet of natural gas to Southeast Asia;
- Recent exploration successes in Sumatra and offshore Java.

Required:

Many of the assets acquired in this business combination present particular valuation challenges. Provide guidance to the financial staff of Conoco as to how the aggregate purchase price should be allocated among the various tangible and intangible assets and liabilities included in the portfolio of Gulf Canada Resources Limited. Explain your answer in terms of the provisions of IFRSs.

(case prepared by Peter Secord, St. Mary's University)

Case 5   Smith & Stewart (Stewart) is a partnership of lawyers. It was recently formed from a merger of two predecessor partnerships: Becker and Brackman (Becker) and Copp and Copp (Copp). The merged firm has 38 partners, six from Becker and 32 from Copp, and a total of 75 employees. At the date of the merger, Stewart purchased land and an office building for $1.25 million and fully computerized the new offices. The partners have decided that the financial statements will be audited annually, although neither of the predecessor firms was audited.

The partnership agreement requires an annual valuation of the assets and liabilities of the firm. This valuation is to be used to determine the payment to be made by the partnership to a withdrawing partner and the contribution to be made to the partnership by a newly admitted partner. The partners are unsure of the accounting implications of this requirement.

The partners have been actively engaged in establishing and managing the practice and have paid little attention to the accounting policies.

Before the merger, Becker recorded revenue when it invoiced the client. Time reports were used to keep track of the number of hours worked for each client, although this information was not recorded in the accounting system. In general, its accounting records were not well maintained.

In contrast, work in progress was recorded for employees of Copp at their regular billing rate, on a client-by-client basis, based on the hours worked, even though the full amount was not always recoverable. At year-end, an adjustment was made to reduce work in progress to reflect the actual costs incurred by Copp. Copp recorded revenue for partner hours at the time that clients were invoiced.

The new partnership agreement requires a valuation of the work in progress at the merger date, with this amount to be recorded as goodwill. This amount has not yet been determined.

Stewart has arranged a line of credit with a bank that allows the partnership to borrow up to 75 percent of the carrying value of receivables and 40 percent of the carrying value of work in progress as recorded in the monthly financial statements. The bank has also provided mortgage financing of $750,000 on the recently acquired land and building. As well as annually audited financial statements, the bank requires unaudited financial statements monthly.

As of the date of the merger, property, plant, and equipment owned by the predecessor firms were transferred to the new partnership.

Each partner receives a monthly "draw" payment, which represents an advance on the partner's share of annual profit.

Although the individual partners cannot incorporate, the partnership is considering incorporating a company to provide management services to the partnership. If it proceeds with this idea, the land and building, and related mortgage, and equipment would be transferred to this company.

Your firm has been engaged by Stewart to prepare a report advising the partnership on financial accounting issues. The manager in charge of the Stewart engagement has asked you, CA, to prepare a draft report to the client addressing its concerns.

Required:

Prepare the draft report. *(CICA adapted)*

*Case 6   Uni-Invest Ltd. was traded on the TSX Venture Exchange under the symbol "UIL." The company holds commercial and residential real estate interests in Nova Scotia, New Brunswick, Prince Edward Island, Alberta, and British Columbia. On October 23, Year 10, Basic Realty Investment Corporation acquired 100 percent of the outstanding common shares of Uni-Invest Ltd. in exchange for 32,584,051 common shares of Basic.

At October 31, Year 9, Basic had 3,333,320 common shares and 6,000,001 Class C preferred shares issued and outstanding. Prior to the acquisition, the 6,000,001 Class C preferred shares were converted to common shares on a share-for-share basis. Then, on October 23, Year 10, the 9,333,321 common shares were consolidated five for one to yield 1,866,664 common shares, with a book value of $746 and a fair value of $2,024,845. Values for Basic's shareholders' equity are summarized as follows:

Capital shares issued	Number of shares	Amount
Balance prior to investment in Uni-Invest	1,866,664	$ 746
Issued to effect investment on October 23, Year 10, net of costs of $84,177	32,584,051	33,236,248
Balance December 31, Year 10	34,450,715	$33,236,994

Details of the fair value excess for the assets acquired and liabilities assumed on the transaction are as follows:

Assets acquired	
Property and equipment	$4,632,398
Other assets	271,436
	4,903,834
Liabilities assumed	
Long-term debt	2,707,504
Other liabilities	143,000
	2,850,504
Fair value excess for net assets acquired	$2,053,330

Required:

Based on this information, how should this investment be reported? More specifically, which company is the parent? Which is the subsidiary? Why? What earnings, and for what period, are reported in the consolidated financial statements for the year ended December 31, Year 10? Why?

(adapted from a case prepared by Peter Second, St. Mary's University)

PROBLEMS

Problem 1   G Company is considering the takeover of K Company, whereby it will issue 6,000 common shares for all of the outstanding shares of K Company. K Company will become a wholly owned subsidiary of G Company. Prior to the acquisition, G Company had 20,000 shares outstanding, which were trading at $4.90 per share. The following information has been assembled:

	G Company		K Company	
	Book value	Fair value	Book value	Fair value
Current assets	$ 40,000	$47,500	$10,000	$ 9,200
Plant assets	60,000	70,000	20,000	25,000
	$100,000		$30,000	
Current liabilities	$ 20,000	20,000	$ 5,000	5,000
Long-term debt	15,000	19,000	2,500	3,200
Common shares	30,000		10,000	
Retained earnings	35,000		12,500	
	$100,000		$30,000	

Required:

(a) Prepare G Company's consolidated balance sheet immediately after the combination using
   (i) the new entity method, and
   (ii) the acquisition method.
(b) Calculate the current ratio and debt-to-equity ratio for G Company under both methods. Explain which method shows the strongest liquidity and solvency position and which method best reflects the true financial condition of the company.

Problem 2   Three companies, A, L, and M, whose December 31, Year 5, balance sheets appear below, have agreed to combine as at January 1, Year 6.

Each of the companies has a very small proportion of an intensely competitive market dominated by four much larger companies. In order to survive, they have decided to merge into one company. The merger agreement states that Company A will buy the assets and liabilities of each of the other two companies by issuing 27,000 common shares to Company L and 25,000 common shares to Company M, after which the two companies will be wound up.

Company A's shares are currently trading at $5 per share.

Company A will incur the following costs:

Costs of issuing shares	$ 8,000
Professional fees	20,000
	$28,000

The following information has been assembled regarding the three companies:

COMPANY A

	Book value	Fair value
Current assets	$ 99,900	$102,000
Plant and equipment	147,600	160,000
	$247,500	
Liabilities	$ 80,000	75,000
Common shares (50,000 shares)	75,000	
Retained earnings	92,500	
	$247,500	

COMPANY L

	Book value	Fair value
Current assets	$ 60,000	$ 65,000
Plant and equipment	93,000	98,000
	$153,000	
Liabilities	$ 35,000	36,000
Common shares (24,000 shares)	48,000	
Retained earnings	70,000	
	$153,000	

COMPANY M

	Book value	Fair value
Current assets	$ 52,000	$ 68,000
Plant and equipment	115,000	120,000
	$167,000	
Liabilities	$ 72,000	70,000
Common shares (33,000 shares)	60,000	
Retained earnings	35,000	
	$167,000	

Required:

Prepare the balance sheet of Company A on January 2, Year 6, after Company L and Company M have been wound up.

Problem 3 The statement of financial position of Bagley Incorporated as at July 31, Year 4, is shown below:

BAGLEY INCORPORATED
STATEMENT OF FINANCIAL POSITION
at July 31, Year 4

	Book value	Fair value
Plant and equipment	$ 910,000	$1,053,000
Patents	—	78,000
Current assets	455,000	507,000
	$1,365,000	
Common shares	$ 182,000	
Retained earnings	520,000	
Long-term debt	390,000	416,000
Current liabilities	273,000	273,000
	$1,365,000	

On August 1, Year 4, the directors of Bagley were considering a takeover offer from Davis Inc. whereby the corporation would sell all of its assets and liabilities. Davis's costs of investigation and drawing up the merger agreement would amount to $19,500.

Required:

(a) Assume that Davis made a $1,040,000 cash payment to Bagley for its net assets. Prepare the journal entries in the accounting records of Davis to record the business combination.

(b) Assume that Davis issued 130,000 common shares, with market value of $8 per share, to Bagley for its net assets. Legal fees associated with issuing these shares amounted to $6,500 and were paid in cash. Davis had 150,000 shares outstanding prior to the takeover.

(i) Prepare the journal entries in the records of Davis to record the business combination.

(ii) Prepare the statement of financial position of Bagley immediately after the sale.

Problem 4 The shareholders of Prong Company and Horn Company agreed to a statutory amalgamation under which a share exchange took place. On September 1, Year 5, Prong Company issued 60,000 common shares for all of the common shares of Horn Company, after which Horn Company was dissolved. The common shares of Prong Company traded at $7 per share on this date.

After the amalgamation, Prong Company changed its name to Pronghorn Corporation.

The statements of financial position of the two companies on August 31, Year 5, were as follows:

	Prong Company	Horn Company
Plant and equipment (net)	$430,000	$300,000
Other assets	41,000	20,000
Current assets	135,000	170,000
	$606,000	$490,000
Common shares (note 1)	$ 70,000	$100,000
Retained earnings	260,000	200,000
Long-term debt	180,000	160,000
Current liabilities	96,000	30,000
	$606,000	$490,000

Note 1

Common shares outstanding	70,000 sh.	25,000 sh.

The book values of the net assets of both companies were equal to fair values except for plant and equipment. The fair values of plant and equipment were as follows:

| Prong Company | $ 500,000 |
| Horn Company | 280,000 |

Prong's other assets include patent registration costs with a carrying value of $25,000. An independent appraiser placed a value of $100,000 on this patent.

Required:

Prepare the statement of financial position of Pronghorn Corporation immediately after the statutory amalgamation.

Problem 5   The balance sheet of Drake Enterprises as at December 31, Year 5, is as follows:

Assets

Cash	$ 99,000
Accounts receivable	143,000
Inventory	191,400
Land	132,000
Plant and equipment (net)	660,000
	$1,225,400

Liabilities and Equity

Current liabilities	$ 242,000
Bonds payable	352,000
Common shares (100,000 shares)	220,000
Retained earnings	411,400
	$1,225,400

Effective January 1, Year 6, Drake proposes to issue 82,500 common shares (currently trading at $20 per share) for all of the assets and liabilities of Hanson Industries. In determining the acquisition price, the management of Drake noted that Hanson Industries has unrecorded customer service contracts and directed its accounting staff to reflect this when recording the acquisition. An independent appraiser placed a value of $150,000 on this unrecorded intangible asset. Costs of the acquisition are expected to be as follows:

Costs of issuing shares	$44,000
Professional fees	38,500
	$82,500

The balance sheet of Hanson Industries as at December 31, Year 5, is as follows:

	Book value	Fair value
Cash	$ 55,000	$ 55,000
Accounts receivable	275,000	280,500
Inventory	187,000	178,200
Land	99,000	126,500
Plant and equipment (net)	770,000	891,000
	$1,386,000	
Current liabilities	$ 137,500	137,500
Liability for warranties	99,000	129,800
Common shares	660,000	
Retained earnings	489,500	
	$1,386,000	

Hanson Industries is to be wound up after the sale.

Required:

Assume that Drake's offer is accepted by the shareholders of Hanson on the proposed date. Prepare Drake's January 2, Year 6, balance sheet.

Problem 6 D Ltd. and H Corporation are both engaged in the manufacture of computers. On July 1, Year 5, they agree to a merger whereby D will issue 300,000 shares with current market value of $8 each for the net assets of H.

Summarized balance sheets of the two companies prior to the merger are presented below:

BALANCE SHEET
June 30, Year 5

	D Ltd. Book value	H Corporation Book value	Fair value
Current assets	$ 450,000	$ 500,000	$ 510,000
Non-current assets (net)	4,950,000	3,200,000	3,500,000
	$5,400,000	$3,700,000	
Current liabilities	$ 600,000	$ 800,000	800,000
Long-term debt	1,100,000	900,000	920,000
Common shares	2,500,000	500,000	
Retained earnings	1,200,000	1,500,000	
	$5,400,000	$3,700,000	

In determining the purchase price, the management of D Ltd. noted that H Corporation leases a manufacturing facility under an operating lease that has terms that are favourable relative to market terms. However, the lease agreement explicitly prohibits transfer of the lease (through either sale or sublease). An independent appraiser placed a value of $60,000 on this favourable lease agreement.

Required:

Prepare the July 1, Year 5, balance sheet of D, after the merger.

Problem 7 The July 31, Year 3, balance sheets of two companies that are parties to a business combination are as follows:

	Red Corp. Book value	Sax Inc. Book value	Fair value
Current assets	$1,600,000	$ 420,000	$468,000
Plant and equipment	1,080,000	840,000	972,000
Patents	—	—	72,000
	$2,680,000	$1,260,000	
Current liabilities	$1,360,000	$ 252,000	252,000
Long-term debt	480,000	360,000	384,000
Common shares	720,000	168,000	
Retained earnings	120,000	480,000	
	$2,680,000	$1,260,000	

In addition to the capital assets identified above, Red Corp. attributed a value of $100,000 to Sax's assembled workforce. They have the knowledge and skill to operate Sax's manufacturing facility and are critical to the success of operation. Although the eight manufacturing employees are not under any employment contracts, management of Red was willing to pay $100,000 as part of the purchase price on the belief that most or all of these employees would continue to work for the company.

Effective on August 1, Year 3, the shareholders of Sax accepted an offer from Red Corporation to purchase all of their common shares. Red's costs for investigating and drawing up the share purchase agreement amounted to $18,000.

Required:

(a) Assume that Red made a $960,000 cash payment to the shareholders of Sax for 100 percent of their shares.

    (i) Prepare the journal entry in the records of Red to record the share acquisition.

    (ii) Prepare the consolidated balance sheet of Red Corp. as at August 1, Year 3.

(b) Assume that Red issued 120,000 common shares, with market value of $8 per share to the shareholders of Sax for 100 percent of their shares. Legal fees associated with issuing these shares amounted to $6,000 and were paid in cash. Red is identified as the acquirer.

    (i) Prepare the journal entries in the records of Red to record the share acquisition.

    (ii) Prepare the consolidated balance sheet of Red as at August 1, Year 3.

(c) Would the assumption in Part A result in higher future earnings to Red than those resulting from the assumption in Part B? Explain.

Problem 8   The following are summarized statements of financial position of three companies as at December 31, Year 3:

	Company X	Company Y	Company Z
Assets	$400,000	$300,000	$250,000
Common shares (note 1)	$ 75,000	$ 48,000	$ 60,000
Retained earnings	92,500	70,000	35,000
Liabilities	232,500	182,000	155,000
	$400,000	$300,000	$250,000
Note 1			
Shares outstanding	50,000 sh.	12,000 sh.	16,500 sh.

The fair values of the identifiable assets and liabilities of the three companies as at December 31, Year 3, were as follows:

	Company X	Company Y	Company Z
Assets	$420,000	$350,000	$265,000
Liabilities	233,000	180,000	162,000

On January 2, Year 4, Company X will purchase the assets and assume the liabilities of Company Y and Company Z. It has been agreed that Company X will issue common shares to each of the two companies as payment for their net assets as follows:

    to Company Y — 13,500 shares
    to Company Z — 12,000 shares

The shares of Company X traded at $14 on December 31, Year 3.
Company X will incur the following costs associated with this acquisition:

Costs of registering and issuing shares	$12,000
Other professional fees associated with the takeover	30,000
	$42,000

Company Y and Company Z will wind up after the sale.

Required:

(a) Prepare a summarized pro forma statement of financial position of Company X as at January 2, Year 4, after the purchase of net assets from Company Y and Company Z.

(b) Prepare the pro forma statements of financial position of Company Y and Company Z as at January 2, Year 4, after the sale of net assets to Company X and prior to being wound up.

Problem 9 Myers Company Ltd. was formed 10 years ago by the issuance of 22,000 common shares to three shareholders. Four years later the company went public and issued an additional 30,000 common shares.

The management of Myers is considering a takeover in which Myers would purchase all of the assets and assume all of the liabilities of Norris Inc. Other costs associated with the takeover would be as follows:

Legal, appraisal, and finders' fees	$ 5,000
Costs of issuing shares	7,000
	$12,000

Two alternative proposals are being considered:

PROPOSAL 1

Myers would offer to pay $300,000 cash for the Norris net assets, to be financed by a $300,000 bank loan due in five years.

PROPOSAL 2

Myers would issue 50,000 shares currently trading at $8 each for the Norris net assets. Norris shareholders would be offered five seats on the 10-member board of directors of Myers, and the management of Norris would be absorbed into the surviving company.

Balance sheet data for the two companies prior to the combination are as follows:

	Myers	Norris	
	Book value	Book value	Fair value
Cash	$ 140,000	$ 52,500	$ 52,500
Accounts receivable	167,200	61,450	56,200
Inventory	374,120	110,110	134,220
Land	425,000	75,000	210,000
Buildings (net)	250,505	21,020	24,020
Equipment (net)	78,945	17,705	15,945
	$1,435,770	$337,785	
Current liabilities	$ 133,335	$ 41,115	41,115
Non-current liabilities	—	150,000	155,000
Common shares	500,000	100,000	
Retained earnings	802,435	46,670	
	$1,435,770	$337,785	

Required:

(a) Prepare the journal entries of Myers for each of the two proposals being considered.

(b) Prepare the balance sheet of Myers after the takeover for each of the proposals being considered.

Problem 10 Refer to Problem 9. All of the facts and data are the same except that in the proposed takeover, Myers Company will purchase all of the outstanding common shares of Norris Inc.

Required:

(a) Prepare the journal entries of Myers for each of the two proposals being considered.

(b) Prepare the consolidated balance sheet of Myers after the takeover for each of the proposals being considered.

Problem 11 Baker Corporation has the following account balances at December 31, Year 4:

Receivables	$ 80,000
Inventory	200,000
Land	600,000
Building	500,000
Liabilities	400,000
Common shares	200,000
Retained earnings, 1/1/Year 4	700,000
Revenues	300,000
Expenses	220,000

Several of Baker's accounts have fair values that differ from book value: land — $400,000; building — $600,000; inventory — $280,000; and liabilities — $330,000. Home Inc. purchases all of the outstanding shares of Baker by issuing 20,000 common shares with a market value of $55 per share. Stock issuance costs amount to $10,000.

Required:

(a) What is the purchase price in this combination?

(b) What is the book value of Baker's net assets on the date of the takeover?

(c) How does the issuance of these shares affect the shareholders' equity accounts of Home, the parent?

(d) How are the stock issuance costs handled?

(e) What allocations are made of Home's purchase price to specific accounts and to goodwill for the consolidated financial statements?

(f) How do Baker's revenues and expenses affect consolidated totals? Why?

(g) How do Baker's common shares affect consolidated totals?

(h) If Home's shares had been worth only $40 per share rather than $55, how would the consolidation of Baker's assets and liabilities have been affected?

Problem 12 The financial statements for CAP Inc. and SAP Company for the year ended December 31, Year 5, follow:

	CAP	SAP
Revenues	$ 900,000	$ 300,000
Expenses	660,000	200,000
Profit	$ 240,000	$ 100,000
Retained earnings, 1/1/Year 5	$ 800,000	$ 200,000
Profit	240,000	100,000
Dividends paid	90,000	0
Retained earnings, 12/31/Year 5	$ 950,000	$ 300,000
Equipment (net)	$ 700,000	$ 600,000
Patented technology (net)	900,000	300,000
Receivables and inventory	400,000	170,000
Cash	80,000	110,000
Total assets	$2,080,000	$1,180,000
Common shares	$ 530,000	$ 470,000
Retained earnings	950,000	300,000
Liabilities	600,000	410,000
Total equities and liabilities	$2,080,000	$1,180,000

On December 31, Year 5, after the above figures were prepared, CAP issued $300,000 in debt and 15,000 new shares to the owners of SAP to purchase all of the outstanding shares of that company. CAP shares had a fair value of $40 per share.

CAP also paid $30,000 to a broker for arranging the transaction. In addition, CAP paid $40,000 in stock issuance costs. SAP's equipment was actually worth $710,000 but its patented technology was valued at only $270,000.

Required:

What are the balances on the Year 5 consolidated financial statements, for the following accounts?
(a) Profit.
(b) Retained earnings, 31/12/Year 5.
(c) Equipment.
(d) Patented technology.
(e) Goodwill.
(f) Common shares.
(g) Liabilities.

Problem 13 Z Ltd. is a public company with factories and distribution centres located throughout Canada. It has 100,000 common shares outstanding. In past years it has reported high earnings, but in Year 5 its earnings declined substantially due in part to a loss of markets as a result of the North American Free Trade Agreement. In Year 6 it closed a large number of its manufacturing and distribution facilities and reported a substantial loss for the year.

Prior to Year 6, 70,000 of Z Ltd.'s shares were held by C Ltd., with the remaining shares being widely distributed in the hands of individual investors in Canada and the United States. On January 1, Year 6, C Ltd. sold 40,000 of its shares in Z Ltd. to W Corporation.

Required:

(a) How should C Ltd. report its investment in Z Ltd., both before the sale of 40,000 shares and after the sale?

(b) How should W Corporation report its investment in Z Ltd.? Explain fully, and include in your answers a reference to Z Ltd.'s Year 6 loss.

*Problem 14   The balance sheets of X Ltd. and Y Ltd. on December 30, Year 7, are as follows:

	X Ltd. Book value	X Ltd. Fair value	Y Ltd. Book value	Y Ltd. Fair value
Current assets	$ 300	$ 300	$1,000	$1,000
Non-current assets	1,500	1,700	2,700	2,800
	$1,800		$3,700	
Current liabilities	$ 400	400	$ 900	900
Long-term debt	300	300	800	800
Common shares — issued 100 sh.	400			
Common shares — issued 60 sh.			600	
Retained earnings	700		1,400	
	$1,800		$3,700	

On December 31, Year 7, X issued 150 common shares for all 60 outstanding common shares of Y. The fair value of each of Y's common shares was $40 on this date.

Required:

(a) Explain why this share issue most likely occurred.

(b) Prepare the consolidated balance sheet of X Ltd. on December 31, Year 7.

(*CICA adapted*)

WEB-BASED PROBLEMS

Problem 1   Access the most recent consolidated financial statements for Vodafone, a British company, in which there was a business acquisition. (Go to the investor relations section at www.vodafone.com.) Answer the questions below. For each question, indicate where in the financial statements you found the answer and/or provide a brief explanation.

(a) What method is used to account for business combinations?

(b) Describe the most significant business acquisition during the year.

(c) How much cash was paid for all business acquisitions during the year?

(d) In the allocation of the purchase price for the most significant business acquisition, what amounts were allocated to (i) intangible assets and (ii) goodwill?

(e) What percentage of total assets at the end of the year is represented by (i) intangible assets and (ii) goodwill?

(f) Assume that the company had paid 10 percent more for its acquisitions of 100-percent-owned subsidiaries and that the extra amount was paid in cash. How would this have affected the (i) current ratio and (ii) debt-to-equity ratio at the date of acquisition?

(g) Assume that the market capitalization of the company's shares (i.e., number of shares outstanding times market value per share) was double the book value of shareholders' equity on the date when the business acquisitions occurred and that the company uses the new entity method to account for business combinations. How would this have affected the (i) debt-to-equity ratio at the date of acquisition and (ii) the return on equity for the first year after the date of acquisition?

Problem 2   Access the most recent consolidated financial statements for Siemens, a German company. (Go to the investor relations section at www.siemens.com.) Answer the same questions as in Problem 1. For each question, indicate where in the financial statements you found the answer and/or provide a brief explanation. (Some questions may not be applicable.)

Chapter ④ Consolidated Statements on Date of Acquisition

LEARNING OBJECTIVES

After studying this chapter, you should be able to do the following:

1. Calculate and allocate the acquisition differential.
2. Explain the concept of negative goodwill and describe how it should be treated when it arises in a business combination.
3. Prepare a consolidated balance sheet on acquisition date, using both the working paper and direct approaches.
4. Describe the concept of push-down accounting.
5. Explain the differences between the four consolidation theories, and apply these theories by preparing a consolidated balance sheet on acquisition date.
6. Account for contingent consideration based on its classification as a liability or equity.

INTRODUCTION

Consolidated financial statements report the combined results of the parent and all its subsidiaries.

Financial statements, published and distributed to owners, creditors, and other interested parties, appear to report the operations and financial position of a single company. In reality, these statements frequently represent a number of separate organizations tied together through common control (a *business combination*). Whenever financial statements represent more than one corporation, we refer to them as *consolidated financial statements*.

Consolidated financial statements are typical in today's business world. Most major organizations, and many smaller ones, hold control over an array of organizations. For example, between 2006 and 2009, Cisco Systems, Inc., acquired or established more than 60 subsidiaries that now are consolidated in its financial reports. PepsiCo, Inc., as another example, annually consolidates data from a multitude of companies into a single set of financial statements. By gaining control over these companies, which include among others Pepsi-Cola Company, Quaker Foods, and Frito-Lay, a single business combination and single reporting entity is formed by PepsiCo.

The consolidation of financial information as exemplified by Cisco Systems and PepsiCo is one of the most complex procedures in all of accounting. To comprehend this process completely, the theoretical logic that underlies the creation of a business combination must be understood. Furthermore, a variety of procedural steps must be mastered to ensure that proper accounting is achieved for this single reporting entity. In this chapter, we will continue our coverage of the consolidation process including the consolidation of non–wholly owned subsidiaries.

Consolidation of Wholly Owned Subsidiaries

The accounting principles involved in the preparation of consolidated financial statements are found in IAS 27. In the material that follows in this and later chapters, the preparation of consolidated statements will follow this standard's requirements unless the contrary is indicated. Consolidated statements consist of a balance sheet, a statement of comprehensive income, a statement of changes in equity, a cash flow statement, and the accompanying notes. In this chapter, we will illustrate the preparation of the consolidated balance sheet on the date that control is obtained by the parent company. Consolidation of other financial statements will be illustrated in later chapters.

The acquisition method is required by GAAP and will be used throughout the rest of this book.

In Chapter 3, we introduced the preparation of a consolidated balance sheet immediately after a business combination, using the acquisition method. Summarized financial statements were used to focus on the basic concepts involved. In this chapter, we elaborate on these concepts and use more detailed financial statements. The following example will form the basis of many of the illustrations that will be used in this chapter.

We will call the two companies to be consolidated P Ltd. and S Ltd. Both companies have a June 30 fiscal year-end. The balance sheets of the two companies on June 29, Year 1, are shown in Exhibit 4.1.

On June 30, Year 1, P Ltd. obtains control over S Ltd. by paying cash for a portion of that company's outstanding common shares to the shareholders of S Ltd. No additional transactions take place on this date. Immediately after the share acquisition, P Ltd. prepares a consolidated balance sheet.

100-Percent Ownership

Illustration 1 Assume that on June 30, Year 1, S Ltd. had 10,000 shares outstanding and P Ltd. purchases 100 percent of S Ltd. for a total cost of $90,000. Given that P Ltd. paid $90,000 for 100 percent of the shares of S Ltd., we will assume

Exhibit 4.1

BALANCE SHEET
At June 29, Year 1

	P Ltd. Book value	S Ltd. Book value	S Ltd. Fair value
Cash	$100,000	$ 12,000	$ 12,000
Accounts receivable	90,000	7,000	7,000
Inventory	130,000	20,000	22,000
Plant	280,000	50,000	59,000
Patent	—	11,000	10,000
	$600,000	$100,000	$110,000
Current liabilities	$ 60,000	$ 8,000	$ 8,000
Long-term debt	180,000	22,000	25,000
Total liabilities	240,000	30,000	$ 33,000
Common shares	200,000	40,000	
Retained earnings	160,000	30,000	
	$600,000	$100,000	

These balance sheets present the financial position just prior to the business combination.

(and it is logical to assume) that the fair value of S Ltd. as a whole was $90,000 on the date of acquisition. P Ltd.'s journal entry to record the acquisition is as follows:

The investment is recorded in the separate-entity records of the parent.

Investment in S Ltd.	90,000	
Cash		90,000

P Ltd.'s year-end is June 30, and the only consolidated statement prepared at this time would be the balance sheet. The income statement, statement of changes in equity, and cash flow statement present only the parent's income, changes in equity, and cash flows since the two entities were not operating as a combined entity prior to June 30.

The calculation and allocation of the acquisition differential is a useful first step in the preparation of the consolidated balance sheet. The information provided in this calculation forms the basis of the elimination and adjusting entries required. This calculation is shown in Exhibit 4.2.

The preparation of the consolidated balance sheet using a working paper approach is illustrated in Exhibit 4.3.

The consolidated balance sheet is the third balance sheet involving the two entities.

Note that the parent's cash has been reduced by the cost of the acquisition. Two elimination entries are used in the working paper. Entry **(1)** eliminates the parent's share of the shareholders' equity accounts of the subsidiary and the parent's investment account, with the difference established as the acquisition differential. Entry **(2)** allocates the acquisition differential to the identifiable assets and liabilities of the subsidiary, and establishes the goodwill resulting from the business combination. (It should be obvious that only one entry needs to be used if the acquisition differential is not established.) The amounts shown in the consolidated balance sheet column

---

Exhibit 4.2

CALCULATION AND ALLOCATION OF ACQUISITION DIFFERENTIAL
(100-percent-owned subsidiary)

The purchase price consists of two components — book value of subsidiary's net assets and acquisition differential.

Cost of 100 percent of S Ltd.			$ 90,000
Book value of S Ltd.'s net assets			
Assets		100,000	
Liabilities		(30,000)	
		70,000	
P Ltd.'s ownership		100%	70,000
Acquisition differential			20,000
Allocated:	*(FV − BV) × 100%		
Inventory	+ 2,000		
Plant	+ 9,000		
Patent	− 1,000		
	10,000		
Long-term debt	+ 3,000		7,000
Balance — goodwill			$ 13,000

* FV fair value
 BV book value

Exhibit 4.3

P LTD.
CONSOLIDATED BALANCE SHEET WORKING PAPER
At June 30, Year 1

	P Ltd.	S Ltd.	Adjustments and Eliminations Dr.	Adjustments and Eliminations Cr.	Consolidated balance sheet
Cash	$ 10,000	$ 12,000			$ 22,000
Accounts receivable	90,000	7,000			97,000
Inventory	130,000	20,000	**(2)** $ 2,000		152,000
Plant	280,000	50,000	**(2)** 9,000		339,000
Patent		11,000		**(2)** $ 1,000	10,000
Investment in S Ltd.	90,000			**(1)** 90,000	
Acquisition differential			**(1)** 20,000	**(2)** 20,000	
Goodwill			**(2)** 13,000		13,000
	$600,000	$100,000			$633,000
Current liabilities	$ 60,000	$ 8,000			$ 68,000
Long-term debt	180,000	22,000		**(2)** 3,000	205,000
Common shares	200,000				200,000
Retained earnings	160,000				160,000
Common shares		40,000	**(1)** 40,000		
Retained earnings		30,000	**(1)** 30,000		
	$600,000	$100,000	$114,000	$114,000	$633,000

The investment account now appears on P's separate-entity records.

When consolidating, S's assets and liabilities replace the investment account.

are used to prepare the consolidated balance sheet. The two working paper entries are summarized next:

These entries are made on the consolidated worksheet and not in the separate-entity records of the two companies.

(1) Common shares — S Ltd.	40,000	
Retained earnings — S Ltd.	30,000	
Acquisition differential	20,000	
Investment in S Ltd.		90,000
(2) Inventory — S Ltd.	2,000	
Plant — S Ltd.	9,000	
Goodwill	13,000	
Patent — S Ltd.		1,000
Long-term debt — S Ltd.		3,000
Acquisition differential		20,000

It must be emphasized that these entries[1] are made only in the working paper; they are *not* entered in the accounting records of either P Ltd. or S Ltd.

The Direct Approach   An alternative approach to the preparation of consolidated financial statements is to prepare the statements directly without the use of a working paper. It should be obvious from examining the working paper that the investment account, the acquisition differential, and the shareholders' equity accounts of the subsidiary do *not* appear on the consolidated balance sheet. The calculation of

---

[1] In later chapters, the working paper eliminations will be illustrated without the intermediate step of setting up the acquisition differential.

the acquisition differential in a sense eliminates the investment and shareholders' equity accounts. The allocation of the acquisition differential provides the amounts used to revalue the net assets of the subsidiary. Having made the necessary calculations, the preparer ignores these accounts (i.e., eliminates them) and prepares the consolidated balance sheet. This is done by combining, on an item-by-item basis, the balance sheets of the parent and the subsidiary while at the same time revaluing for consolidation purposes the balance sheet items of the subsidiary. The basic process involved in the direct approach is as follows:

$$\underset{\text{(parent)}}{\text{Book value}} + \underset{\text{(subsidiary)}}{\text{Book value}} +(-) \underset{\text{differential}}{\text{Acquisition}} = \underset{\text{amounts}}{\text{Consolidated}}$$

The preparation of the consolidated balance sheet using the direct approach is shown in Exhibit 4.4. The non-bolded amounts shown in brackets come from the balance sheets of P Ltd. and S Ltd. The bolded amounts in brackets are consolidation adjustments related to the allocation of the acquisition differential. It should be noted that under the acquisition method of accounting for a business combination, consolidated shareholders' equity on acquisition date is always that of the parent company.

Income Statement in Year of Acquisition   When a business combination is accounted for using the acquisition method, only the net income earned by the subsidiary after the date of acquisition is included in consolidated net income. For example, if the acquisition occurred halfway through the fiscal year, consolidated net income would consist of the net income of the parent for the full year plus the half-year net income earned by the subsidiary after the acquisition date.[2] In the example used here, both

Consolidated net income, retained earnings, and cash flows include the subsidiary's income and cash flows only subsequent to the date of acquisition.

Exhibit 4.4		

Illustration of the Direct Approach

P LTD.
CONSOLIDATED BALANCE SHEET
At June 30, Year 1

Cash (100,000 − 90,000* + 12,000)	$ 22,000
Accounts receivable (90,000 + 7,000)	97,000
Inventory (130,000 + 20,000 + **2,000**)	152,000
Plant (280,000 + 50,000 + **9,000**)	339,000
Patent (0 + 11,000 − **1,000**)	10,000
Goodwill (0 + 0 + **13,000**)	13,000
	$633,000
Current liabilities (60,000 + 8,000)	$ 68,000
Long-term debt (180,000 + 22,000 + **3,000**)	205,000
Common shares	200,000
Retained earning	160,000
	$633,000

On the date of acquisition, consolidated shareholders' equity = parent's shareholders' equity.

* Cash paid by P Ltd. to acquire S Ltd.

---

[2] The net income of the subsidiary earned after the acquisition date would be reduced by the amortization of the acquisition differential because the asset values in the accounting records of the subsidiary are not the values used for consolidation. This concept will be discussed in Chapter 5.

P Ltd. and S Ltd. have a June 30 year-end. P Ltd.'s consolidated financial statements for the year ended June 30, Year 1, would consist of a consolidated balance sheet and the net income, retained earnings, and cash flows from P Ltd.'s separate entity statements. This is consistent with what would be done if the parent had purchased the net assets directly from the subsidiary. When a company acquires assets, it records these assets on its own books; it does not record the profit earned by the assets when they belonged to the previous owner. The parent's income and retained earnings do not change on the date of acquisition. The consolidated statements will combine the results of the parent and subsidiary for transactions occurring on and subsequent to the date of acquisition.

Under push-down accounting, the subsidiary revalues its assets and liabilities based on the price paid by the parent to acquire these net assets.

Push-down Accounting   Under push-down accounting, on the date of acquisition the subsidiary revalues its assets and liabilities based on the parent's acquisition cost. The allocation of the acquisition differential is "pushed down" to the actual accounting records of the subsidiary. This practice became permissible under Canadian GAAP in 1992 with the issuance of Section 1625, "Comprehensive Revaluation of Assets and Liabilities." Push-down accounting is not presently allowed under IFRSs. Since it may be incorporated in IFRSs in the future, we will briefly describe how it works.

Push-down accounting is another example where GAAP allowed a departure from historical cost accounting and allowed the use of current values in financial reporting. Even though the subsidiary was not involved in the transaction with the parent (the transaction involved the parent and the shareholders of the subsidiary), the subsidiary was allowed to revalue its assets and liabilities based on the value paid by the parent to acquire these net assets. Since the parent and subsidiary were not related prior to the acquisition, the amount paid by the parent was probably equal to or fairly close to the fair value of these net assets. So, why not use these values to provide more relevant, yet very reliable, information to the users of the subsidiary's financial statements?

Section 1625 allowed push-down accounting only when a subsidiary was at least 90 percent owned by a parent, and so theoretically a parent could demand a 95-percent-owned subsidiary to use it. Practically, it probably would not, because when a non-controlling interest is present, the consolidation becomes very complex and the benefits from its use disappear. We will not provide a detailed illustration of push-down accounting in the textbook; however, for those readers that wish to pursue this further, a full discussion and illustration of comprehensive revaluations can be found on Connect at www.mcgrawhillconnect.ca.

When the parent establishes a new company as a subsidiary, there should be no acquisition differential.

Subsidiary Formed by Parent   In some situations a subsidiary is not acquired through a share purchase, but rather by the parent company forming the subsidiary company. The parent company purchases all of the initial share issue after the subsidiary is incorporated.[3] At this time, the book values and fair values of the subsidiary's net assets are obviously equal, and there is no goodwill. It should also be obvious that the subsidiary has no retained earnings at this time. The preparation of the consolidated balance sheet on the date of formation of the subsidiary is simplified, requiring only the elimination of the parent's investment account against the subsidiary's share capital.

---

[3] It is also possible for a parent to form a less than 100-percent-owned subsidiary, or for a 100-percent-owned subsidiary, to later issue shares that are not purchased by the parent. In either case, the observations made in this paragraph are basically the same.

Illustration 2 — Negative Goodwill   Assume that on June 30, Year 1, P Ltd. purchased 100 percent of the outstanding shares of S Ltd. at a total cost of $75,000. P Ltd.'s journal entry to record the acquisition is as follows:

Investment in S Ltd.	75,000	
Cash		75,000

The calculation and allocation of the acquisition differential on this date is shown in Exhibit 4.5.

Negative goodwill arises when the purchase price is less than the fair value of identifiable net assets.

The calculations for the acquisition differential and for its initial allocation are similar to what is shown in Exhibit 4.2 on page 122. However, in this situation the goodwill is negative because the acquisition cost is less than the fair value of identifiable net assets. A business combination that results in negative goodwill is often described as a "bargain purchase." This means that the parent gained control over the subsidiary's assets and liabilities at a price that was less than the fair values assigned to those assets and liabilities. This can occur when share prices are depressed or the subsidiary has a recent history of operating losses. Regardless of the cause, negative goodwill should be allocated to reduce the value of the subsidiary's goodwill to zero and to record any remaining amount as a gain. To record a gain on a purchase of an investment may seem very strange but it is required according to IFRS 3, paragraph 34.

Prior to the adoption of IFRSs, the purchase method of accounting was required, negative goodwill was assigned to certain non-monetary assets, and gains on purchases would have been very rare. With the adoption of IFRSs, the acquisition method is required, the identifiable net assets are valued at fair value regardless of the purchase price, and gains are recognized when the purchase price is less than the fair value of identifiable net assets. This change is consistent with the general trend of revaluing assets and liabilities at fair value and recognizing unrealized gains in income.

The negative goodwill is recognized as a gain on the date of acquisition.

Since there is no goodwill on the subsidiary's books, none of the negative goodwill can be used to reduce goodwill to zero. Therefore, the entire $2,000 of negative goodwill is recorded as a gain on the consolidated income statement and ends up

Exhibit 4.5

CALCULATION AND ALLOCATION OF ACQUISITION DIFFERENTIAL
(negative goodwill)

The purchase price (75,000) is less than the fair value of identifiable net assets (70,000 + 7,000).

Cost of investment in S Ltd.			$ 75,000
Book value of S Ltd.'s net assets			
Assets		100,000	
Liabilities		(30,000)	
		70,000	
P Ltd.'s ownership		100%	70,000
Acquisition differential			5,000
Allocated:	(FV − BV) × 100%		
Inventory	+ 2,000		
Plant	+ 9,000		
Patent	− 1,000		
	10,000		
Long-term debt	+ 3,000		7,000
Balance — "negative goodwill" (recognize as gain)			$−2,000

in consolidated retained earnings at the date of acquisition. The working paper to prepare the consolidated balance sheet is shown in Exhibit 4.6.

Entry (1) eliminates the parent's share of the subsidiary's shareholders' equity accounts and the parent's investment account, and establishes the difference as the acquisition differential. Entry (2) allocates the acquisition differential to revalue the net assets of the subsidiary, and to recognize the gain as shown in the summary at the bottom of Exhibit 4.5.

The two working paper elimination entries are shown next:

(1) Common shares — S Ltd.	40,000	
Retained earnings — S Ltd.	30,000	
Acquisition differential	5,000	
Investment in S Ltd.		75,000
(2) Inventory — S Ltd.	2,000	
Plant — S Ltd.	9,000	
Patent — S Ltd.		1,000
Long-term debt — S Ltd.		3,000
Acquisition differential		5,000
Retained earnings — P Ltd. (gain on purchase)		2,000

It must be emphasized again that these worksheet entries are made only in the working paper; they are *not* entered in the accounting records of either P Ltd. or S Ltd. If the parent company uses the equity method to account for its investment in the subsidiary, the following entry should be made in the parent's separate-entity records to record the $2,000 gain resulting from the bargain purchase:

Investment in S Ltd.	2,000	
Gain on purchase of S Ltd.		2,000

Exhibit 4.6

P LTD.
CONSOLIDATED BALANCE SHEET WORKING PAPER
At June 30, Year 1

		P Ltd.	S Ltd.	Adjustments and Eliminations Dr.	Adjustments and Eliminations Cr.	Consolidated balance sheet
The subsidiary's identifiable assets and liabilities are valued at fair value on the consolidated balance sheet.	Cash	$ 25,000	$ 12,000			$ 37,000
	Accounts receivable	90,000	7,000			97,000
	Inventory	130,000	20,000	(2) $ 2,000		152,000
	Plant	280,000	50,000	(2) 9,000		339,000
	Patent		11,000		(2) $ 1,000	10,000
	Investment in S Ltd.	75,000			(1) 75,000	
	Acquisition differential			(1) 5,000	(2) 5,000	
		$600,000	$100,000			$635,000
The gain from the bargain purchase is recorded in income and ends up in consolidated retained earnings on the date of acquisition.	Current liabilities	$ 60,000	$ 8,000			$ 68,000
	Long-term debt	180,000	22,000		(2) 3,000	205,000
	Common shares	200,000				200,000
	Retained earnings	160,000			2,000	162,000
	Common shares		40,000	(1) 40,000		
	Retained earnings		30,000	(1) 30,000		
		$600,000	$100,000	$86,000	$86,000	$635,000

The equity method makes the parent's separate-entity income equal to consolidated income.

This entry will result in the investment account being valued at the fair value of identifiable net assets of the subsidiary. Furthermore, the parent's separate-entity income under the equity method will now be equal to consolidated net income. As we learned in Chapter 2 and as we will study further in Chapter 5, the parent's income under the equity method should be equal to consolidated net income.

The Direct Approach   Exhibit 4.7 shows the preparation of the consolidated balance sheet on June 30, Year 1, using the direct approach. The summary of the allocation of the acquisition differential (see Exhibit 4.5 on page 126) provides all the information needed to avoid having to use a working paper.

A negative acquisition differential is not the same as negative goodwill.

Negative Acquisition Differential   It is possible for an acquisition differential to be negative. In this situation the parent's interest in the book values of the subsidiary's net assets exceeds the acquisition cost. A negative acquisition differential is not the same as negative goodwill, nor does it necessarily imply that there will be negative goodwill. If the fair values of the subsidiary's net assets are less than their book values, the amounts used to revalue the specific identifiable net assets of the subsidiary downward could be greater than the negative acquisition differential, resulting in positive goodwill.

Illustration 3 — Subsidiary with Goodwill   The goodwill appearing on the balance sheet of a subsidiary on the date of a business combination is not carried forward when the consolidated balance sheet is prepared. At some date in the past the subsidiary was the acquirer in a business combination and recorded the goodwill as the difference between the acquisition cost and the fair value of the identifiable net assets acquired. Now this company has itself become an acquiree. From the perspective of its new parent, the goodwill is not considered to be an identifiable asset at

The subsidiary's goodwill arose in a previous business combination.

the time of the business combination. The acquisition differential is calculated as if the goodwill had been written off by the subsidiary, even though in fact this is not the case. The acquisition differential is allocated first to the fair value excess for

---

Exhibit 4.7

Illustration of the Direct Approach
(negative goodwill)

P LTD.
CONSOLIDATED BALANCE SHEET
At June 30, Year 1

Under the direct approach, we add the parent's book value + subsidiary's book value + acquisition differential for each asset and liability.

Cash (100,000 − 75,000* + 12,000)	$ 37,000
Accounts receivable (90,000 + 7,000)	97,000
Inventory (130,000 + 20,000 + **2,000**)	152,000
Plant (280,000 + 50,000 + **9,000**)	339,000
Patent (0 + 11,000 − **1,000**)	10,000
	$635,000
Current liabilities (60,000 + 8,000)	$ 68,000
Long-term debt (180,000 + 22,000 + **3,000**)	205,000
Common shares	200,000
Retained earnings (160,000 + 0 + **2,000**)	162,000
	$635,000

* Cash paid by P Ltd. to acquire S Ltd.

identifiable net assets, and then the remaining balance goes to goodwill. In effect, the old goodwill is ignored and the purchase price determines the value, if any, of new goodwill at the date of acquisition. The following illustration will examine the consolidation process when the subsidiary has existing goodwill.

Assume that on June 30, Year 1, P Ltd. purchased 100 percent of the outstanding shares of S Ltd. for a total cost of $75,000, paid in cash. Exhibit 4.8 shows the balance sheets of the two companies at this time.

Notice that the goodwill (highlighted in boldface), in the amount of $11,000, was called a patent in Exhibit 4.1 on page 121. Notice also that the acquisition cost is the same as in Illustration 2, where the result turned out to be negative goodwill. When we calculate and allocate the acquisition differential in this illustration, the result is positive goodwill of $8,000, as shown in Exhibit 4.9.

Exhibit 4.8

BALANCE SHEET
At June 29, Year 1

		P Ltd.	S Ltd.	
		Book value	Book value	Fair value
The goodwill on the subsidiary's books (its old goodwill) will be revalued on the date of acquisition.	Cash	$100,000	$ 12,000	$12,000
	Accounts receivable	90,000	7,000	7,000
	Inventory	130,000	20,000	22,000
	Plant	280,000	50,000	59,000
	Goodwill	—	**11,000**	
		$600,000	$100,000	
	Current liabilities	$ 60,000	$ 8,000	8,000
	Long-term debt	180,000	22,000	25,000
	Common shares	200,000	40,000	
	Retained earnings	160,000	30,000	
		$600,000	$100,000	

Exhibit 4.9

CALCULATION AND ALLOCATION OF ACQUISITION DIFFERENTIAL
(subsidiary with goodwill)

The subsidiary's goodwill is currently worth $8,000 based on the price paid by the parent.	Cost of investment in S Ltd.			$75,000
	Book value of S Ltd.'s net assets			
	Assets		100,000	
	Liabilities		(30,000)	
			70,000	
	Deduct old goodwill of S Ltd.		11,000	
	Adjusted net assets		59,000	
	P Ltd.'s ownership		100%	59,000
	Acquisition differential			16,000
	Allocated:	(FV − BV) × 100%		
	Inventory	+ 2,000		
	Plant	+ 9,000		
		11,000		
	Long-term debt	+ 3,000		8,000
	Balance — goodwill			$ 8,000

The working papers for the preparation of the June 30, Year 1, consolidated balance sheet are presented in Exhibit 4.10.

Three working paper entries are required. Entry **(1)** writes off the previous goodwill (labelled "old" goodwill in the working paper) to S Ltd.'s retained earnings for purposes of consolidation. Entry **(2)** eliminates the parent's share of the subsidiary's common shares and adjusted retained earnings and the parent's investment account, and establishes the difference as the acquisition differential. Entry **(3)** allocates the acquisition differential to revalue the net assets of the subsidiary and establishes the new goodwill from the business combination.

The three working paper elimination entries are shown below:

(1)	Retained earnings — S Ltd.	11,000	
	Goodwill — old — S Ltd.		11,000
(2)	Common shares — S Ltd.	40,000	
	Retained earnings — S Ltd.	19,000	
	Acquisition differential	16,000	
	Investment in S Ltd.		75,000
(3)	Inventory — S Ltd.	2,000	
	Plant — S Ltd.	9,000	
	Goodwill	8,000	
	Long-term debt — S Ltd.		3,000
	Acquisition differential		16,000

These worksheet entries establish the appropriate account balances for the consolidated balance sheet.

Exhibit 4.10

P LTD.
CONSOLIDATED BALANCE SHEET WORKING PAPER
At June 30, Year 1

	P Ltd.	S Ltd.	Adjustments and Eliminations Dr.	Adjustments and Eliminations Cr.	Consolidated balance sheet
Cash	$ 25,000	$ 12,000			$ 37,000
Accounts receivable	90,000	7,000			97,000
Inventory	130,000	20,000	**(3)** $ 2,000		152,000
Plant	280,000	50,000	**(3)** 9,000		339,000
Goodwill — old		11,000		**(1)** $ 11,000	
Investment in S Ltd.	75,000			**(2)** 75,000	
Acquisition differential			**(2)** 16,000	**(3)** 16,000	
Goodwill			**(3)** 8,000		8,000
	$600,000	$100,000			$633,000
Current liabilities	$ 60,000	$ 8,000			$ 68,000
Long-term debt	180,000	22,000		**(3)** 3,000	205,000
Common shares	200,000				200,000
Retained earnings	160,000				160,000
Common shares		40,000	**(2)** 40,000		
Retained earnings		30,000	**(1)** 11,000		
			(2) 19,000		
	$600,000	$100,000	$105,000	$105,000	$633,000

The revalued goodwill appears on the consolidated balance sheet.

Exhibit 4.11		

Illustration of the Direct Approach
(subsidiary with goodwill)
P LTD.
CONSOLIDATED BALANCE SHEET
At June 30, Year 1

The direct approach produces the same results as the working paper approach but appears to be easier to perform.

Cash (100,000 − 75,000* + 12,000)		$ 37,000
Accounts receivable (90,000 + 7,000)		97,000
Inventory (130,000 + 20,000 + **2,000**)		152,000
Plant (280,000 + 50,000 + **9,000**)		339,000
Goodwill (0 + 11,000 − **11,000** + **8,000**)		8,000
		$633,000
Current liabilities (60,000 + 8,000)		$ 68,000
Long-term debt (180,000 + 22,000 + **3,000**)		205,000
Common shares		200,000
Retained earnings		160,000
		$633,000

* Cash paid by P Ltd. to acquire S Ltd.

Entry **(1)** was only a working paper entry and was not recorded in the records of S Ltd. If P Ltd. directs S Ltd. to actually write off its $11,000 goodwill as at June 30, Year 1, no further working paper entries will be required for this item in future years. However, if S Ltd. does not write off its recorded goodwill, the preparation of consolidated statements in Year 2 and all future years will require working paper entries to write off any goodwill that still exists in S Ltd.'s records and to reverse any goodwill impairment that has been recorded.

The Direct Approach   Using the calculations shown in Exhibit 4.9 on page 129, the consolidated balance sheet can easily be prepared without the use of a working paper, as Exhibit 4.11 shows.

Consolidation of Non–wholly Owned Subsidiaries

In the first three illustrations, the parent acquired 100 percent of the subsidiary. The subsidiary's assets and liabilities were brought onto the consolidated balance at fair value.[4] We will now consider situations where the parent acquires less than 100 percent of the shares. We will still prepare consolidated financial statements when the parent acquires sufficient shares to control the subsidiary.

The part of the subsidiary not owned by the parent is called non-controlling interest (NCI).

The shares not acquired by the parent are owned by other shareholders, which are referred to as the non-controlling shareholders. The value of the shares attributed to the non-controlling shareholders when presented on the consolidated financial statements is referred to as non-controlling interest, which is abbreviated as NCI.

---

[4] Book value + 100% × (FV − BV) = Fair value.

Three questions arise when preparing consolidated financial statements for less than 100-percent-owned subsidiaries:

1. How should the portion of the subsidiary's assets and liabilities, which was not acquired by the parent, be valued on the consolidated financial statements?
2. How should NCI be valued on the consolidated financial statements?
3. How should NCI be presented on the consolidated financial statements?

The following theories have developed over time and have been proposed as solutions to preparing consolidated financial statements for non–wholly owned subsidiaries:

- Proprietary theory.
- Parent company theory.
- Parent company extension theory.
- Entity theory.

Each of the theories has been or is currently required by GAAP. The following table indicates the current status and effective usage dates for these four theories:

Method	Status
Proprietary theory	Present GAAP when consolidating joint ventures but may be discontinued within the next few years when new standards for accounting for joint ventures are implemented by IASB.
Parent company theory	Was GAAP for consolidating subsidiaries prior to January 1, 2011, (or sooner if IFRS 3 was adopted earlier) but is not acceptable under GAAP after January 1, 2011.
Parent company extension theory	An acceptable method of consolidating subsidiaries after January 1, 2011 (or sooner if IFRS 3 was adopted earlier).
Entity theory	The preferred method for consolidating a subsidiary after January 1, 2011 (or sooner if IFRS 3 was adopted earlier).

The merits of these four theories are discussed in the following section.

Introduction to Consolidation Theories

These four theories differ in the valuation of the NCI and how much of the subsidiary's value pertaining to the NCI is brought onto the consolidated financial statements. The following chart highlights the differences between the four theories. The left side for each theory shows the portion of the subsidiary owned by the parent while the right side shows the portion owned by the NCI. The shaded area represents the values brought into the consolidated financial statements.

	Proprietary		Parent Company		Parent Company Extension		Entity	
	Parent	NCI	Parent	NCI	Parent	NCI	Parent	NCI
Book value of Sub's net assets								
Fair value excess								
Goodwill								

> The parent's portion of the subsidiary's value is fully represented under all theories. The NCI's share varies under the four theories.

We will illustrate the preparation of consolidated financial statements under these four theories using the following example. Assume that on June 30, Year 1, P Ltd. purchased 8,000 shares (80 percent) of S Ltd. at a total cost of $72,000. P Ltd.'s journal entry to record this purchase is as follows:

| Investment in S Ltd. | 72,000 | |
| Cash | | 72,000 |

We will use the balance sheets of the two companies on June 29, Year 1, as shown in Exhibit 4.1 on page 121. Note that the amount paid of $72,000 is 80 percent of $90,000 that was the amount paid in Illustration 1 when P Ltd. acquired 100 percent of S Ltd.

Proprietary Theory

> The proprietary theory focuses solely on the parent's percentage interest in the subsidiary.

Proprietary theory views the consolidated entity from the standpoint of the shareholders of the parent company. The consolidated statements do not acknowledge or show the equity of the non-controlling shareholders. The consolidated balance sheet on the date of acquisition reflects only the parent's share of the assets and liabilities of the subsidiary, based on their fair values, and the resultant goodwill from the combination. The allocation of the purchase price is shown in Exhibit 4.12 on page 134.

> Only the parent's share of the fair values of the subsidiary is brought onto the consolidated balance sheet.

Using the direct approach, the consolidated balance sheet is prepared by combining, on an item-by-item basis, the book values of the parent with the *parent's share* of the fair values of the subsidiary, which is derived by using the parent's share of the net book value of the subsidiary plus the acquisition differential. Goodwill is established based on the parent's acquisition cost. This process is shown in Exhibit 4.13 on page 134.

Proprietary theory is not used in practice to consolidate a parent and its subsidiaries. However, its use is required by the *Handbook* as a means of reporting an investment in a joint arrangement, and the consolidation process is described as "proportionate consolidation." This topic will be fully covered in Chapter 9.

Entity Theory

> The entity theory gives equal attention to the controlling and non-controlling shareholders.

The entity theory views the consolidated entity as having two distinct groups of shareholders — the controlling shareholders and the non-controlling shareholders. NCI is presented as a separate component of shareholders' equity on the consolidated balance sheet. This theory was described in an American Accounting Association

Exhibit 4.12

CALCULATION OF ACQUISITION DIFFERENTIAL
(proprietary theory)

Cost of 80 percent investment in S Ltd.			$72,000
Book value of S Ltd.'s net assets			
Assets		100,000	
Liabilities		(30,000)	
		70,000	
P Ltd.'s ownership		80%	56,000
Acquisition differential			16,000
Allocated:	(FV − BV) × 80%		
Inventory	+ 2,000 × 80% = + 1,600		
Plant	+ 9,000 × 80% = + 7,200		
Patent	− 1,000 × 80% = − 800		
		8,000	
Long-term debt	+ 3,000 × 80% = + 2,400	5,600	
Balance — goodwill			$10,400

The acquisition differential consists of 80 percent of the fair value excess plus the parent's share of the goodwill.

Exhibit 4.13

Illustration of the Direct Approach
(proprietary theory)

P LTD.
CONSOLIDATED BALANCE SHEET
At June 30, Year 1

NCI is not recognized under the proprietary theory.

Cash (100,000 − 72,000* + 80% × 12,000)	$ 37,600
Accounts receivable (90,000 + 80% × 7,000)	95,600
Inventory (130,000 + 80% × 20,000 + **1,600**)	147,600
Plant (280,000 + 80% × 50,000 + **7,200**)	327,200
Patent (0 + 80% × 11,000 − **800**)	8,000
Goodwill (0 + 0 + **10,400**)	10,400
	$626,400
Current liabilities (60,000 + 80% × 8,000)	$ 66,400
Long-term debt (180,000 + 80% × 22,000 + **2,400**)	200,000
Total liabilities	266,400
Shareholders' equity	
Common shares 200,000	
Retained earnings 160,000	360,000
	$626,400

* Cash paid by P Ltd. to acquire S Ltd.

publication, "The Entity Theory of Consolidated Statements," by Maurice Moonitz. Under this theory the consolidated balance sheet reflects the full fair values of the subsidiary's identifiable net assets plus an amount for goodwill.

The full fair value of the subsidiary is typically determined by combining the amount paid by the parent for its share and the fair value of the NCI. The fair value of the NCI can be determined in one of three ways. The first approach is to use the amount

Exhibit 4.14

The acquisition differential consists of 100 percent of the fair value excess plus the implied value of total goodwill.

CALCULATION OF ACQUISITION DIFFERENTIAL
(entity theory)

Cost of 80 percent investment in S Ltd.			$72,000
Implied cost of 100 percent investment in S Ltd. (72,000 ÷ 80%)			$90,000
Book value of S Ltd.'s net assets			
Assets		100,000	
Liabilities		(30,000)	
			70,000
Implied acquisition differential			20,000
Allocated:	(FV − BV) × 100%		
Inventory	+ 2,000 × 100% = + 2,000		
Plant	+ 9,000 × 100% = + 9,000		
Patent	− 1,000 × 100% = − 1,000		
	10,000		
Long-term debt	+ 3,000 × 100% = + 3,000		7,000
Balance — goodwill			$13,000

CALCULATION OF NCI

Implied value of 100 percent investment in S Ltd.	$90,000
NCI ownership	20%
	$18,000

NCI can be easily valued, if we assume a linear relationship between percentage ownership and value of that ownership.

paid by the parent for the portion of the subsidiary it did acquire and use this amount to extrapolate what the parent would have paid if it had acquired 100 percent of the subsidiary's shares. In our example, the parent paid $72,000 for 80 percent of the subsidiary's shares. Using basic math and assuming a linear relationship between percentage ownership and value of that interest, this would imply that the value for 100 percent of the shares would have been $90,000 (72,000/0.8). Under this approach, goodwill for the subsidiary as a whole would be valued at $13,000 and NCI would be valued at $18,000 as indicated in Exhibit 4.14.

Many people would argue against this approach on the basis that there is not a linear relationship between percentage ownership and value of that interest. Usually an investor will pay a premium just to obtain control of another company. The premium could range from 10 to 20 percent above the trading price for the shares and will often depend on the portion of the outstanding shares being acquired. If the investor acquires 51 percent of the shares the premium may be 20 percent whereas the premium would be much less if 90 percent is acquired. This approach also loses validity in situations where the parent's ownership percentage increases through a series of small purchases, and control is eventually achieved after more than 50 percent of the subsidiary's shares have been acquired.

The trading price of the subsidiary's shares in an active market is probably the most accurate reflection of the value of the NCI.

A second approach for valuing the NCI is to use the trading price of the subsidiary's shares at the date of acquisition. If the subsidiary is a public company and there is a high volume of trading activity, the trading price of the shares would reasonably reflect the fair value of the NCI. However, this approach would probably not be used if the subsidiary was a private company and the shares are not actively traded.

In our example, the parent acquired 8,000 shares of S Ltd. for $72,000 or $9 per share. If the trading price of S's shares was $8 per share at the date of the acquisition, the NCI would be valued at $16,000 (2,000 shares × $8 per share). This would imply that the total value of the subsidiary is $88,000, not $90,000 as calculated earlier. The implied goodwill for S Ltd. is $11,000 and can be attributed to the controlling and non-controlling shareholders as follows:

	Controlling 80%	NCI 20%	Total 100%
Value of investment	$72,000	$16,000	$88,000
Allocated to identifiable net assets	61,600*	15,400**	77,000
Goodwill	$10,400	$ 600	$11,000

* 80% × (fair value of assets − fair value of liabilities from Exhibit 4.1 on page 121)
** 20% × (fair value of assets − fair value of liabilities from Exhibit 4.1)

NCI could be valued using business valuation techniques, but this is a costly exercise.

A third approach for valuing the NCI is to perform an independent business valuation. This involves many assessments and assumptions relating to future cash flows, inflation rates, growth rates, discount rates, synergies between the parent and subsidiary, valuation of identifiable assets and liabilities, etc. Not only is a business valuation a very costly exercise, it also involves a lot of judgment. In some cases, the cost of determining the implied value of the subsidiary as a whole may not be worth the benefit of the information provided. If so, the reporting entity may be reluctant to use the entity theory.

We should note that the value assigned to the subsidiary as a whole will have a big impact on the value allocated to goodwill. The fair values of identifiable assets and liabilities are usually readily available because these items are traded quite often in the marketplace. However, goodwill is not traded in the marketplace by itself. Therefore, determining a value for goodwill is quite subjective and is directly tied to the overall value of the firm.

We will assume a linear relationship to calculate the value of NCI except when we are given the market price of the subsidiary's shares.

Throughout this text, when the market price of the subsidiary's shares at the date of acquisition is not given, the implied value of the subsidiary as a whole will be calculated by dividing the price paid for the shares purchased by the percentage acquired. We recognize that this is an oversimplication. However, the material in this text is complicated enough as is; by keeping it simple in some cases, we may be able to see the forest rather than the multitude of trees. When the market price of the subsidiary's shares at the date of acquisition is given, we will use this price to value the NCI and then calculate the goodwill attributable to each of the controlling and non-controlling interests. This latter approach is more complicated, but it is consistent with IFRS 3, paragraph 32, which states the following:

The acquirer shall recognize goodwill as of the acquisition date measured as the excess of (a) over (b) below:

Goodwill is the difference between the total value of the subsidiary and the amount assigned to identifiable assets and liabilities.

(a) the aggregate of:

(i)   the consideration given by the acquirer

(ii) the amount of any non-controlling interest in the acquiree and

(iii) in a business combination achieved in stages, the acquisition-date fair value of the acquirer's previously held equity interest in the acquiree.

(b) the net of the acquisition-date amounts of the identifiable assets acquired and the liabilities assumed measured in accordance with this IFRS.[5]

Item (a) (iii) will be discussed further in Chapter 8.

Using the direct approach and the implied value of $90,000, the consolidated balance sheet is prepared by combining, on an item-by-item basis, the book values of P Ltd. with the fair values[6] of S Ltd. The calculated goodwill is inserted on the asset side, and the calculated NCI is shown in shareholders' equity. Exhibit 4.15 illustrates the preparation of the consolidated balance sheet using the direct approach.

The working paper used to prepare the consolidated balance sheet is shown in Exhibit 4.16 on page 138.

Three working paper entries are used. Entry **(1)** eliminates the parent's share of the subsidiary's shareholders' equity accounts and the parent's investment account, with the difference established as the acquisition differential. Entry **(2)** eliminates the NCI's share of the subsidiary's shareholders' equity accounts and establishes the NCI on the consolidated balance sheet with the difference going to acquisition differential. Entry **(3)** allocates the acquisition differential to revalue the identifiable net assets of the subsidiary and establishes the resulting goodwill.

Exhibit 4.15		

Illustration of the Direct Approach
(entity theory)

P LTD.
CONSOLIDATED BALANCE SHEET
At June 30, Year 1

100 percent of the subsidiary's fair values are brought on to the consolidated balance sheet.	Cash (100,000 − 72,000* + 12,000)	$ 40,000
	Accounts receivable (90,000 + 7,000)	97,000
	Inventory (130,000 + 20,000 + **2,000**)	152,000
	Plant (280,000 + 50,000 + **9,000**)	339,000
	Patent (0 + 11,000 − **1,000**)	10,000
	Goodwill (0 + 0 + **13,000**)	13,000
		$651,000
	Current liabilities (60,000 + 8,000)	$ 68,000
	Long-term debt (180,000 + 22,000 + **3,000**)	205,000
	Total liabilities	273,000
	Shareholders' equity	

NCI is presented as a separate component in shareholders' equity.	Controlling interest		
	Common shares	200,000	
	Retained earnings	160,000	
		360,000	
	Non-controlling interest	18,000	378,000
			$651,000

---

* *Cash paid by P Ltd. to acquire S Ltd.*

---

[5] IFRS 3 requires that most identifiable assets and liabilities be measured at fair value.
[6] Book value + (FV − BV) × 100% = Fair value.

Exhibit 4.16

P LTD.
CONSOLIDATED BALANCE SHEET WORKING PAPER
(entity theory)

		P Ltd.	S Ltd.	Adjustments and Eliminations Dr.	Cr.	Consolidated balance sheet
The subsidiary's assets and liabilities are brought onto the consolidated balance sheet at 100 percent of their fair values.	Cash	$ 28,000	$ 12,000			$ 40,000
	Accounts receivable	90,000	7,000			97,000
	Inventory	130,000	20,000	(3) $ 2,000		152,000
	Plant	280,000	50,000	(3) 9,000		339,000
	Patent		11,000		(3) $ 1,000	10,000
	Investment in S Ltd.	72,000			(1) 72,000	
	Acquisition differential			(1) 16,000	(3) 20,000	
				(2) 4,000		
	Goodwill			(3) 13,000		13,000
		$600,000	$100,000			$651,000
	Current liabilities	$ 60,000	$ 8,000			$ 68,000
	Long-term debt	180,000	22,000		(3) 3,000	205,000
	Common shares	200,000				200,000
NCI is presented as a component of shareholders' equity on the consolidated balance sheet.	Retained earnings	160,000				160,000
	Common shares		40,000	(1) 32,000		
				(2) 8,000		
	Retained earnings		30,000	(1) 24,000		
				(2) 6,000		
	Non-controlling interest				(2) 18,000	18,000
		$600,000	$100,000	$114,000	$114,000	$651,000

The three working paper elimination entries are as follows:

<table>
<tr><td>The first two entries record the acquisition differential and the NCI on the consolidated balance sheet.</td><td>

(1) Common shares — S Ltd.   32,000
Retained earnings — S Ltd.   24,000
Acquisition differential   16,000
      Investment in S Ltd.   72,000

(2) Acquisition differential   4,000
Common shares   8,000
Retained earnings — S Ltd.   6,000
      Non-controlling interest   18,000

</td></tr>
<tr><td>The implied acquisition differential is allocated to identifiable assets and liabilities and goodwill.</td><td>

(3) Inventory — S Ltd.   2,000
Plant — S Ltd.   9,000
Goodwill   13,000
      Patent — S Ltd.   1,000
      Long-term debt — S Ltd.   3,000
      Acquisition differential   20,000

</td></tr>
</table>

Unless otherwise noted, all of the illustrations throughout this text and in the end-of-chapter material will use the entity theory. It is the IASB's preferred theory. It will likely be used when the total value of goodwill of the subsidiary can be reasonably measured at the date of acquisition.

Parent Company Theory

The parent company theory focuses on the parent company but gives some recognition to NCI.

The parent company theory is similar to the proprietary theory in that the focus of the consolidated statements is directed toward the shareholders of the parent company. However, NCI is recognized and reflected as a liability in the consolidated balance sheet; its amount is based on the book values of the net assets of the subsidiary.

NCI is calculated as follows:

Book value of S Ltd.'s net assets	
Assets	$100,000
Liabilities	(30,000)
	70,000
Non-controlling ownership percentage	20%
Non-controlling interest	$14,000

The consolidated balance sheet is prepared by combining, on an item-by-item basis, the book value of the parent with 100 percent of the book value of the subsidiary *plus* the parent's share of the acquisition differential.

Under this theory, the parent's share of the subsidiary is valued at fair value whereas the NCI's share is based on the subsidiary's book value on the consolidated balance sheet. This process is consistent with the historical cost principle because the parent's portion of the subsidiary's net asset is being acquired by the parent at the date of acquisition. Since the NCI's share of the subsidiary's net assets is not being purchased and is not changing hands, this portion is retained at book value. Exhibit 4.17 shows the preparation of the consolidated balance sheet under the parent company theory. This theory was required by GAAP prior to January 1, 2011, unless the entity adopted IFRS 3 early.

Exhibit 4.17	Illustration of the Direct Approach

(parent company theory)

P LTD.
CONSOLIDATED BALANCE SHEET
At June 30, Year 1

100 percent of the subsidiary's book values plus the parent's share of the fair value excess are brought onto the consolidated balance sheet.

Cash (100,000 − 72,000* + 12,000)	$ 40,000
Accounts receivable (90,000 + 7,000)	97,000
Inventory (130,000 + 20,000 + **1,600**)	151,600
Plant (280,000 + 50,000 + **7,200**)	337,200
Patent (0 + 11,000 − **800**)	10,200
Goodwill (0 + 0 + **10,400**)	10,400
	$646,400

NCI is presented as a liability.

Current liabilities (60,000 + 8,000)		$ 68,000
Long-term debt (180,000 + 22,000 + **2,400**)		204,400
Non-controlling interest		14,000
Total liabilities		286,400
Shareholders' equity		
Common shares	200,000	
Retained earnings	160,000	360,000
		$646,400

* Cash paid by P Ltd. to acquire S Ltd.

Parent Company Extension Theory

All of the subsidiary's value except for the NCI's share of goodwill is brought onto the consolidated balance sheet.

The parent company extension theory was invented to address the concerns about goodwill valuation under the entity theory. Given that many people feel that goodwill for the subsidiary, as a whole, is very difficult to measure when the parent does not purchase 100 percent of the subsidiary, they did not support the use of the entity theory. However, there is much support for valuing the subsidiary's identifiable assets and liabilities at their full fair value on the consolidated statements. The parent company extension theory does just that — it values both the parent's share and the NCI's share of identifiable net assets at fair value. Only the parent's share of the subsidiary's goodwill is brought onto the consolidated statements at the value paid by the parent. Since the total value of the subsidiary's goodwill is not reasonably measurable, the NCI's portion of the subsidiary's goodwill is not valued and not brought onto the consolidated statements.

NCI is based on the fair value of identifiable assets and liabilities.

Under the parent company extension theory, NCI is recognized in shareholders' equity in the consolidated balance sheet, similar to the entity theory. Its amount is based on the fair values of the identifiable net assets of the subsidiary; it excludes any value pertaining to the subsidiary's goodwill. NCI is calculated as follows:

Book value of S Ltd.'s net assets	
Assets	$100,000
Liabilities	(30,000)
	70,000
Excess of fair value over book value for identifiable net assets	
(see Exhibit 4.14 on page 135)	7,000
Fair value of identifiable net assets	77,000
Non-controlling ownership percentage	20%
Non-controlling interest	$15,400

The consolidated balance sheet is prepared by combining, on an item-by-item basis, the book value of the parent with the fair value of the subsidiary's identifiable assets plus the parent's share of the subsidiary's goodwill. Exhibit 4.18 shows the preparation of the consolidated balance sheet under the parent company extension theory. This theory can be used under IFRS 3 when the total value of the subsidiary's goodwill cannot be reasonably measured. However, IFRS 3 does not use the term *parent company extension theory*. It simply states the following in paragraph 19:

> For each business combination, the acquirer shall measure any non-controlling interest in the acquiree either at fair value or at the non-controlling interest's proportionate share of the acquiree's identifiable net assets.

In this text, we will refer to the different theories by the names introduced in this chapter.

Contingent Consideration

The terms of a business combination may require an additional cash payment, or an additional share issue contingent on some specified future event. The accounting for contingent consideration is contained in IFRS 3; the material that follows illustrates the concepts involved.

Contingent consideration should be recorded at the date of acquisition at its expected value.

Contingent consideration should be valued at fair value at the date of acquisition. To do so, the parent should assess the amount expected to be paid in the future

Exhibit 4.18

Illustration of the Direct Approach
(parent company extension theory)

P LTD.
CONSOLIDATED BALANCE SHEET
At June 30, Year 1

100 percent of the subsidiary's fair values of identifiable assets and liabilities plus the parent's share of the subsidiary's goodwill are brought onto the consolidated balance sheet.

Cash (100,000 − 72,000* + 12,000)	$ 40,000
Accounts receivable (90,000 + 7,000)	97,000
Inventory (130,000 + 20,000 + **2,000**)	152,000
Plant (280,000 + 50,000 + **9,000**)	339,000
Patent (0 + 11,000 − **1,000**)	10,000
Goodwill (0 + 0 + **10,400**)	10,400
	$648,400

Current liabilities (60,000 + 8,000)	$ 68,000
Long-term debt (180,000 + 22,000 + **3,000**)	205,000
Total liabilities	273,000

NCI is presented in shareholders' equity.

Shareholders' equity		
Common shares	200,000	
Retained earnings	160,000	
Non-controlling interest	15,400	375,400
		$648,400

* Cash paid by P Ltd. to acquire S Ltd.

under different scenarios, assign probabilities as to the likelihood of the scenarios occurring, derive an expected value of the likely amount to be paid, and use a discount rate to derive the value of the expected payment in today's dollars. This is all very subjective and involves a lot of judgment.

The contingent consideration will be classified as either a liability or equity depending on its nature. If the contingent consideration will be paid in the form of cash or another asset, it will be classified as a liability. If issuing additional shares will satisfy the contingent consideration, it will be classified as equity. After the initial recognition, the contingent consideration classified as equity will not be remeasured.

After the acquisition date, the fair value of a contingent consideration classified as a liability may change due to changes in circumstances such as meeting specified sales targets, fluctuations in share price, or subsequent events such as receiving government approval on an in-process research and development project. Changes in the fair value of a contingent consideration classified as a liability due to changes in circumstances since the acquisition date should be recognized in earnings. Changes in the fair value of a contingent consideration due to gathering of new information about facts and circumstances that existed at the acquisition date, however, would be considered measurement period adjustments and reflected in the purchase price.

Given the uncertainty involved, the following should be disclosed regarding contingent consideration:

The range of potential payment for contingent consideration should be disclosed.

- The amount of contingent consideration recognized on the acquisition date;
- A description of the arrangement and the basis for determining the amount of the payment; and

- An estimate of the range of outcomes (undiscounted) or, if a range cannot be estimated, that fact and the reasons why a range cannot be estimated. If the maximum amount of the payment is unlimited, the acquirer shall disclose that fact.

The following discussions illustrate the two types of contingent consideration discussed above.

Changes in contingent consideration classified as a liability are reported in net income.

Contingent Consideration Classified as a Liability   If the contingency is classified as a liability, any consideration issued at some future date is recorded at fair value and the change in fair value is recognized in net income. The following example will illustrate this situation.

Able Corporation issues 500,000 common shares for all of the outstanding common shares of Baker Company on January 1, Year 1. The shares issued have a fair value of $10 at that time. Able's journal entry on January 1, Year 1, is as follows:

Investment in Baker Company	5,000,000	
Common shares		5,000,000

The expected value incorporates the probability of payments being made.

The business combination agreement states that if the earnings of Baker Company exceed an average of $1.75 per share over the next two years, Able Corporation will make an additional cash payment of $600,000 to the former shareholders of Baker Company. Able predicts that there is a 30 percent probability that Baker's earnings will be less than $1.75 per share and a 70 percent probability that Baker's will be greater than $1.75 per share. The probability-adjusted expected payment is $420,000 (30% × 0 + 70% × 600,000). Using a discount rate of 15 percent, the fair value of the contingent consideration at January 1, Year 1, is $317,580 ($420,000/1.15^2$). The following additional journal entry would be made by Able on January 1, Year 1:

Investment in Baker Company	317,580	
Liability for contingent consideration		317,580

The likelihood of having to make an additional payment should be reassessed and the liability revalued, if necessary, at the end of each reporting period.

Because Able's fiscal year-end falls on December 31, Year 1, the consolidated financial statements are prepared using the $5,317,580 purchase price. This amount is allocated to the identifiable net assets of Baker Company in the usual manner and may result in goodwill, or "negative goodwill." If at the end of Year 1, the probability assessment has not changed, the undiscounted probability-adjusted expected payment remains at $420,000; but the present value is now $365,217 (420,000/1.15), an increase of $47,637 since the beginning of the year. Able's journal entry at December 31, Year 1, is as follows:

Contingency loss	47,637	
Liability for contingent consideration		47,637

If at the end of the two-year period it is determined that Baker's earnings exceeded the average of $1.75 per share, the required cash payment will be recorded by Able on December 31, Year 2, as follows:

Liability for contingent consideration	365,217	
Loss from contingent consideration	234,783	
Cash		600,000

If Baker did not exceed the earnings level and Able does not have to pay the contingent consideration, Able would make the following journal entry at December 31, Year 2:

Liability for contingent consideration	365,217	
Gain from contingent consideration		365,217

Item of Interest   West Fraser Timber Co. Ltd. is one of North America's leading forest product companies. With more than 6,900 employees, it produces lumber, kraft paper, and newsprint at more than 30 facilities in British Columbia, Alberta, and the southern United States. On December 31, 2004, the company acquired the only issued share of Weldwood of Canada Limited (Weldwood), an integrated forest products company, for net cash consideration of $1.1 billion. The terms of the transaction provided that the seller be entitled to the net after-tax value of any refunds of softwood lumber duties paid by Weldwood before December 31, 2004, and to further cash consideration, not to exceed $50 million in aggregate, if the average market price of NBSK pulp per tonne exceeds the greater of US$710 and Cdn $950 during any quarter ending on or before June 30, 2007.

Contingent Consideration Classified as Equity   If the contingency is classified as equity, any consideration issued at some future date will be recorded at fair value but will not be considered an additional cost of the purchase. Instead, the consideration issued will be treated as a reduction in the amount recorded for the original share issue. The following example illustrates this.

> *Changes in contingent consideration classified as equity are reported as adjustments to equity.*

Alpha Corporation issues 500,000 common shares for all the outstanding common shares of Beta Company on July 1, Year 1. If the shares issued have a fair market value of $5.00, Alpha's journal entry is as follows:

Investment in Beta Company	2,500,000	
Common shares		2,500,000

The combination agreement states that if the market price of Alpha's shares is below $5.00 one year from the date of the agreement, Alpha will issue additional shares to the former shareholders of Beta in an amount that will compensate them for their loss in value. On July 1, Year 2, the market price of Alpha's shares is $4.50. In accordance with the agreement, Alpha Corporation issues an additional 55,555.55 shares (2,500,000 ÷ 4.50 − 500,000) and records the transaction as follows:

> *The additional consideration compensates for the loss in value for shares originally issued as consideration for the purchase.*

Common shares — old shares (55,555.55 × 4.50)	250,000	
Common shares — new shares		250,000

Alternatively, Alpha could simply make a memorandum entry to indicate that 55,555 additional shares were issued for no consideration.

Footnote disclosure in the Year 2 statements will be made for the amount of and the reasons for the consideration and the accounting treatment used.

> *Companies must disclose their accounting policies for long-term investments.*

Disclosure Requirements   Companies should disclose their policies with regard to long-term investments. The following footnote is taken from the financial statements of Siemens and is fairly typical in content:

> **Basis of Consolidation**   The Consolidated Financial Statements include the accounts of Siemens AG and its subsidiaries which are directly or indirectly

controlled. Control is generally conveyed by ownership of the majority of voting rights. Additionally, the Company consolidates special purpose entities (SPE's) when, based on the evaluation of the substance of the relationship with Siemens, the Company concludes that it controls the SPE. Associated companies are recorded in the Consolidated Financial Statements using the equity method of accounting. Companies in which Siemens has joint control are also recorded using the equity method.

In Chapter 3, we discussed the general presumptions regarding the factors that establish a control investment and noted that these presumptions could be overcome in certain situations. IAS 27 requires that a reporting entity describe the basis for its assessment and any significant assumptions or judgments when the reporting entity has concluded that

(a) it controls an entity whose activities are directed through voting shares even though the reporting entity has less than half of that entity's voting shares, and

(b) it does not control an entity whose activities are directed through voting shares even though the reporting entity is the dominant shareholder with voting rights.

Companies must disclose the value for NCI at the date of acquisition and how it was measured.

IFRS 3 requires that a reporting entity disclose the following for each business combination in which the acquirer holds less than 100 percent of the equity interests in the acquiree at the acquisition date:

(a) The amount of the NCI in the acquiree recognized at the acquisition date and the measurement basis for that amount; and

(b) For each NCI in an acquiree measured at fair value, the valuation techniques and key model inputs used for determining that value.

At the time of writing this text, there were no examples from practice to illustrate the acquisition of a non–wholly owned subsidiary under the entity theory because the requirement to use the entity theory became effective only for fiscal years beginning on or after July 1, 2009. The extract in Exhibit 4.19 is taken from the Model Financial Statements 2009[7] published by Deloitte.

GAAP for Private Enterprises

- As mentioned in Chapter 3, private companies can either consolidate their subsidiaries or report their investments in subsidiaries under the cost method, the equity method, or at fair value.

- Private companies can apply push-down accounting but must disclose the amount of the change in each major class of assets, liabilities, and shareholders' equity in the year that push-down accounting is first applied.

U.S. GAAP Differences

There are some significant differences between U.S. GAAP and IFRSs with respect to consolidated financial statements.

U.S. GAAP and IFRSs for consolidated statements have many similarities. The significant differences are summarized as follows:

1. Whereas IFRSs do not allow push-down accounting, it is required for SEC registrants in some cases.

---

[7] http://www.iasplus.com/fs/2009modelfs.pdf

Exhibit 4.19

44.4 Non-controlling interests

The non-controlling interests (20%) in Subsix Limited recognized at the acquisition date was measured by reference to the fair value of the non-controlling interests and amounted to CU132,000. This fair value was estimated by applying an income approach. The following were the key model inputs used in determining the fair value:

- assumed discount rate range of 18% to 22%;
- assumed long-term sustainable growth rates of 3% to 5%; and
- assumed adjustments because of the lack of control or lack of marketability that market participants would consider when estimating the fair value of the non-controlling interests in Subsix Limited.

Source: Deloitte Touche Tohmatsu, www.iasplus.com.

2. Whereas IFRSs will allow the use of the parent company extension theory when the NCI's share of the subsidiary's goodwill is not reliably determinable, U.S. GAAP requires that 100 percent of the subsidiary's goodwill be valued at the date of acquisition.

3. Whereas IFRSs require that contingent payments be recognized at fair value using best estimates at the date of acquisition, U.S. GAAP requires that contingent payments be recognized only if the obligation is probable and the amount is reasonably estimated.

4. Whereas IFRSs use a broad definition of control to determine when consolidated statements are required, U.S. GAAP typically requires a reporting entity to have greater than 50 percent of the voting shares.

Item of Interest   On December 31, 2008, The Coca-Cola Company (the Company) owned approximately 35 percent of the voting shares of Coca-Cola Enterprises Inc. (CCE). Under agreements with the Company, CCE has exclusive rights to bottle and market the Company's products in specified territories throughout the world using containers authorized by the Company. The agreements also require CCE to use concentrates and syrups purchased from the Company in the products that it manufactures. The sale of Coca-Cola products makes up about 90 percent of CCE's revenues. On December 31, 2008, CCE showed the following in its financial statements:

Total assets	$16 billion
Total liabilities	$16 billion
Sales	$22 billion

The Coca-Cola Company reports its investment in CCE as a significant influence investment using the equity method, because U.S. GAAP requires a majority ownership in order to consolidate an investee company. If U.S. GAAP defined control in the same manner as IFRS 3 does, the Coca-Cola Company would probably have to consolidate CCE and bring its assets and liabilities onto its consolidated balance sheet and its sales revenues onto its consolidated income statement. Consolidated net income would not change but many financial ratios used by analysts to assess performance and position could be quite different.

SUMMARY

Consolidated financial statements present the financial position and operating results of a group of companies under common control as if they constitute a single entity. When one company gains control over another company, it becomes a parent company and GAAP requires it to present consolidated statements for external reporting purposes. The preparation involves eliminating the parent's investment account and the parent's share of the subsidiary's shareholders' equity accounts, revaluing the net assets of the subsidiary to fair value, and establishing the non-controlling interest (NCI) in the fair value of the subsidiary's net assets. Either the entity method or the parent company extension method must be used when consolidating non–wholly owned subsidiaries.

When the purchase price is less than the fair value of identifiable net assets, the negative goodwill is used to eliminate any goodwill reported on the subsidiaries' separate-entity financial statements. Any remaining negative goodwill is reported as a gain on purchase of the consolidated income statement.

A working paper can be used to prepare the consolidated statements, and is necessary if there are a large number of subsidiaries to consolidate. A computerized spreadsheet is particularly useful in this situation. When there are only one or two subsidiaries, the direct approach is by far the fastest way to arrive at the desired results.

Significant Changes in the Last Two Years

1. For publicly accountable enterprises, IFRSs have replaced the former sections of the *CICA Handbook*. The following table shows the IFRSs covered in this chapter along with their counterparts from the former sections of the *CICA Handbook:*

IFRSs	CICA Handbook *Counterparts*
IFRS 3: Business Combinations	Section 1582: Business Combinations
IAS 27: Consolidated and Separate Financial Statements	Section 1601: Consolidated Financial Statements Section 1602: Non-controlling Interests
No equivalent	Section 1625: Comprehensive Revaluation of Assets and Liabilities

2. Push-down accounting is not allowed under IFRSs.

Changes Expected in the Next Three Years

The definition of control may change again since the IASB and the FASB are working on a joint project related to consolidated financial statements.

SELF-STUDY PROBLEM

On December 31, Year 1, CAN Company takes control over the net assets of UKS Company by purchasing 80 percent of the common shares of UKS Company. CAN Company paid for the purchase by issuing common shares with a market value of $35,200. The following information has been assembled:

	CAN Company Book value	UKS Company Book value	UKS Company Fair value
Plant assets	$ 80,000	$ 20,000	$ 26,000
Goodwill	0	0	22,000
Current assets	50,000	15,000	14,000
	$130,000	$35,000	$62,000
Shareholders' equity	$ 75,000	$18,000	
Long-term debt	25,000	7,000	$ 8,000
Current liabilities	30,000	10,000	10,000
	$130,000	$35,000	

Required:

Prepare a consolidated statement of financial position for CAN Company immediately after the combination under the

(a) Proprietary theory.
(b) Parent company theory.
(c) Parent company extension theory.
(d) Entity theory.

Solution to Self-study Problem

CAN COMPANY
Balance Sheet
At December 31, Year 1
(See notes)

	(a)	(b)	(c)	(d)
Plant assets	$100,800	$104,800	$106,000	$106,000
Goodwill	17,600	17,600	17,600	22,000
Current assets	61,200	64,200	64,000	64,000
	$179,600	$186,600	$187,600	$192,000
Shareholders' equity				
CAN	$110,200	$110,200	$110,200	$110,200
Non-controlling interest				8,800
Non-controlling interest		3,600	4,400	
Long-term debt	31,400	32,800	33,000	33,000
Current liabilities	38,000	40,000	40,000	40,000
	$179,600	$186,600	$187,600	$192,000

Notes:

1. The assets and liabilities are calculated as follows:

   (a) Book values for CAN and 80 percent of fair values for UKS.
   (b) Book values for CAN and book values for UKS plus 80 percent of fair value excess for UKS's identifiable assets and liabilities plus 80 percent of the value of UKS's goodwill.

    (c) Book values for CAN and book values for UKS plus 100 percent of fair value excess for UKS's identifiable assets and liabilities plus 80 percent of the value of UKS's goodwill.

    (d) Book values for CAN and book values for UKS plus 100 percent of fair value excess for UKS's identifiable assets and liabilities plus 100 percent of the value of UKS's goodwill.

2. The non-controlling interest is calculated as follows:

    (b) 20 percent × book value of UKS's identifiable assets and liabilities.

    (c) 20 percent × fair value of UKS's identifiable assets and liabilities.

    (d) 20 percent × fair value of UKS's identifiable assets, identifiable liabilities, and goodwill.

REVIEW QUESTIONS

1. In the preparation of a consolidated balance sheet, the differences between the fair value and the book value of the subsidiary's net assets are used. Would these differences be used if the subsidiary applied push-down accounting? Explain.

2. Is a negative acquisition differential the same as negative goodwill? Explain.

3. With respect to the valuation of non-controlling interest, what are the major differences between the proprietary, parent, and entity theories?

4. How does the presentation of non-controlling interest on the consolidated balance sheet differ under the four theories of consolidating a non–wholly owned subsidiary?

5. How is the goodwill appearing on the statement of financial position of a subsidiary prior to a business combination treated in the subsequent preparation of consolidated statements? Explain.

6. Under the entity theory, consolidated goodwill is determined by inference. Describe how this is achieved and comment on its shortcomings.

7. What is non-controlling interest, and how is it reported in the consolidated balance sheet under IFRSs?

8. Explain how changes in the fair value of contingent consideration should be reported assuming that the contingent consideration will be paid in the form of cash.

9. What reporting options related to business combinations are available to private companies?

10. What is negative goodwill and how is it accounted for?

11. Explain whether or not the historical cost principle is applied when accounting for negative goodwill.

12. How is the net income earned by a subsidiary in the year of acquisition incorporated in the consolidated income statement?

13. In whose accounting records are the consolidation elimination entries recorded? Explain.

14. Don Ltd. purchased 80 percent of the outstanding shares of Gunn Ltd. Before the purchase, Gunn had a deferred charge of $10.5 million on its balance

sheet. This item consisted of organization costs that were being amortized over a 20-year period. What amount should be reported in Don's consolidated statements? Explain briefly.

MULTIPLE-CHOICE QUESTIONS

1. Non-controlling interest on a consolidated balance sheet prepared in accordance with IAS 27 represents which of the following?
   a. An equity interest in a subsidiary company that exists because the parent's interest in the subsidiary is less than 100 percent.
   b. A liability of the parent company.
   c. The net amount by which subsidiary assets and liabilities have been revalued following a business combination.
   d. An equity interest in the subsidiary's income earned for the year.

2. What is push-down accounting?
   a. The parent company revalues its shareholders' equity to reflect the market value of its shares on the date of acquisition of a wholly owned subsidiary.
   b. The parent company revalues its investment in a subsidiary at fair value at the date of acquisition and at each reporting date subsequent to the date of acquisition.
   c. The subsidiary company revalues its assets and liabilities at the date of acquisition based on the price paid by the parent to acquire the subsidiary.
   d. The subsidiary company revalues its assets and liabilities to fair value at each reporting date subsequent to the date of acquisition.

3. Which of the following does the proprietary theory require the parent to report when consolidating its subsidiary?
   a. The subsidiary's assets at 100 percent of book value plus the parent's share of fair value increments or decrements.
   b. The subsidiary's assets at the parent's share of fair values.
   c. The subsidiary's assets at the parent's share of book values.
   d. The subsidiary's assets at 100 percent of fair value.

Use the following data for Questions 4 and 5.

On January 1, Year 5, Poor Co. acquired 80 percent of the outstanding common shares of Standard Inc. by paying cash of $275,000. The book values and fair values of both companies immediately before the acquisition were as follows:

	Poor Co.		Standard Inc.	
	Book values	Fair values	Book values	Fair values
Current assets	$ 470,000	$ 485,000	$100,000	$120,000
Plant assets	2,879,000	3,200,000	175,000	250,000
Intangibles	45,000	50,000	50,000	75,000
	$3,394,000		$325,000	
Current liabilities	$ 367,000	355,000	$125,000	125,000
Long-term debt	1,462,000	1,460,000	50,000	40,000
Common shares	1,000,000		60,000	
Retained earnings	565,000		90,000	
	$3,394,000		$325,000	

4.   Assume that intangibles do not include goodwill. What amount would Poor Co. report for goodwill on its consolidated financial statements immediately after the acquisition transaction?
   a. $25,000
   b. $51,000
   c. $63,750
   d. $87,750

5.   What amount would Poor Co. report for plant assets on its consolidated financial statements immediately after the acquisition transaction?
   a. $3,129,000
   b. $3,114,000
   c. $3,079,000
   d. $3,054,000

The following scenario applies to Questions 6 and 7, although each question should be considered independently.

A parent company acquires 80 percent of the shares of a subsidiary for $400,000. The carrying amount of the subsidiary's net assets is $350,000. The fair value of the identifiable net assets of the subsidiary is $380,000.

6.   Which of the following represents the amount of goodwill that should be reported at the time of the acquisition?
   a. $16,000
   b. $20,000
   c. $96,000
   d. $120,000

(*CICA adapted*)

7.   Which of the following represents the non-controlling interest that should be reported when the acquisition takes place?
   a. $70,000
   b. $76,000
   c. $80,000
   d. $100,000

(*CICA adapted*)

8.   Albany Ltd. purchased all of the outstanding shares of Gerrad Inc. on January 1, Year 4, for $1,200,000. The price resulted in a $90,000 allocation to equipment and goodwill of $75,000. Because the subsidiary earned especially high profits, Albany was required to pay the previous owners of Gerrard an additional $200,000 on January 1, Year 6. How should this extra amount be reported, assuming that nothing had been previously recorded for contingent consideration?
   a.   The $200,000 additional payment is reflected as a reduction in consolidated retained earnings.
   b.   A retroactive adjustment is made to record the $200,000 as an additional expense for Year 4.
   c.   Consolidated goodwill is increased by $200,000 as at January 1, Year 6.
   d.   The $200,000 is recorded as an expense in Year 6.

9. XT follows IFRSs for consolidation of companies involved in a business combination. It owns 80 percent of the shares of its subsidiary, YB. Which of the following combinations of YB's net book value (NBV) and fair value increments (FVI) would be included in its consolidated asset values?
   a. 80 percent of NBV and 80 percent of FVI.
   b. 100 percent of NBV and 80 percent of FVI.
   c. 100 percent of NBV and 100 percent of FVI.
   d. 80 percent of NBV and 100 percent of FVI.

   (CGA-Canada adapted)

Use the following data for Questions 10 and 11.

On August 1, Year 5, Aluminum Company acquired 70 percent of the common shares of Copper Company for $700,000. On that date, the fair value of Copper's identifiable net assets was $600,000 and the book value of its shareholders' equity was $500,000.

10. Assume that the acquisition method, entity theory will be used to prepare consolidated financial statements. What amount of non-controlling interest should be reported on the consolidated balance sheet on the date of acquisition?
    a. $0
    b. $150,000
    c. $180,000
    d. $300,000

11. Assume that the acquisition method, parent company extension theory will be used to prepare consolidated financial statements. What amount of non-controlling interest should be reported on the consolidated balance sheet on the date of acquisition?
    a. $0
    b. $150,000
    c. $180,000
    d. $300,000

12. On January 1, Year 5, PEB acquired 100 percent of the common shares of SEB for $600,000. On that date, the fair value of SEB's identifiable net assets was $700,000. Which of the following is the appropriate treatment of the $100,000 acquisition differential?
    a. It should be recognized as a gain on purchase.
    b. It should be allocated to identifiable non-monetary assets.
    c. It should be allocated to non-current assets with any remaining balance reported as an extraordinary item.
    d. A deferred credit should be set up and amortized over a maximum of 40 years.

    (CGA-Canada adapted)

13. Under GAAP for private enterprises an enterprise may elect to
    a. Consolidate only those subsidiaries that are homogeneous.
    b. Account for some subsidiaries by the cost method and some subsidiaries by the equity method.
    c. Consolidate all subsidiaries using the proportionate consolidation method.
    d. Report its subsidiaries using either the cost method, the equity method, or at fair value.

Use the following data for Questions 14 and 15.

On August 1, Year 1, ALS Company acquired 70 percent of the common shares of NLS Company for $700,000 in cash. On that date, the fair value of ALS's identifiable net assets was $2,000,000 and the book value of its shareholders' equity was $800,000. On that date, the fair value of NLS's identifiable net assets was $600,000 and the book value of its shareholders' equity was $500,000. For both companies the fair value of all liabilities is equal to the book value.

14. What is the impact of the above-noted transaction on the debt-to-equity ratio on ALS's separate-entity financial statements at the date of acquisition?
   a. It would increase.
   b. It would decrease.
   c. It would not change.
   d. The impact cannot be determined based on the information provided.

15. Which of the following consolidation theories would show the lowest debt-to-equity ratio on ALS's consolidated financial statements at the date of acquisition?
   a. Proprietary.
   b. Parent company.
   c. Parent company extension.
   d. Entity.

CASES

Case 1 On December 31, Year 7, Maple Company issued preferred shares with a fair value of $600,000 to acquire 12,000 (60 percent) of the common shares of Leafs Limited. The Leafs shares were trading in the market at around $40 per share just days prior to and just after the purchase by Maple. Maple had to and was willing to pay a premium of $10 per share or $120,000 in total in order to gain control over Leafs. The balance sheets for the two companies just prior to acquisition were as follows (in 000s):

	Maple		Leafs	
	Book value	Fair value	Book value	Fair value
Identifiable assets	$2,000	$2,500	$1,000	$1,300
Goodwill	0	??	0	??
	$2,000		$1,000	
Liabilities	$1,500	1,600	$ 800	840
Shareholders' equity	500	??	200	??
	$2,000		$1,000	

Consolidated financial statements will be prepared to combine the financial statements for the two companies. The management of Maple is concerned about the valuation of goodwill on the consolidated financial statements. It was willing to pay a premium of $120,000 to gain control of Leafs. It maintains that it would have paid the same premium in total whether it acquired 60 percent or 100 percent of the shares of Leafs.

Given that the return on assets is a closely monitored ratio by the shareholders, the management of Maple would like to minimize the value assigned to goodwill on consolidation. Management wants to see how the consolidated balance sheet would differ under four different theories of reporting: proprietary, parent company, parent company extension, and entity. Management also has the following questions when reporting this business combination:

- How will we determine the value of the goodwill for the subsidiary?
- How will this affect the valuation of NCI?
- Will we have to revalue the subsidiary's assets and liabilities every year when we prepare the consolidated financial statements?
- Which consolidation theory best reflects the economic reality of the business combination?

Required:

Prepare a consolidated balance sheet at the date of acquisition under the four theories and respond to the questions asked by management.

Case 2   Eternal Rest Limited (ERL) is a public company; its shares are traded on a stock exchange in Canada. ERL operates both funeral homes and cemeteries in Canada. Funeral services (casket, flowers, cemetery stone, prayer service) are sold on an "as needed" basis and also "in advance" (prepaid). ERL recognizes revenue only as the funeral services are performed.

Cemetery land is purchased years in advance, and carrying costs (e.g., interest and property taxes) are capitalized. The company sells burial plots or gravesites in advance, or on an "as needed" basis. Revenues from plots sold in advance are recognized upon signing a contract, regardless of the timing of receipt of cash. The cost of maintenance for 100 years is recognized as an expense of earning revenue. By law, funds for maintenance are sent to a trustee, for investment. Funds are allowed to be withdrawn annually for current maintenance costs. The cost of the cemetery land and land improvements (including trees, fencing, and pathways) is allocated to cost of sales.

As a result of acquisitions, ERL tripled its assets in fiscal Year 5. Effective September 1, Year 4, ERL acquired the assets and liabilities of Tranquil Cemeteries Limited (Tranquil) by issuing common shares and debt. ERL also acquired, effective November 1, Year 4, 70 percent of the voting common shares of Peaceful Cemeteries Limited (Peaceful) in exchange for $1 million cash (borrowed from ERL's banker) plus common shares of ERL. Peaceful was privately owned by a single shareholder before the purchase of its shares by ERL. The common shares of ERL that were issued with respect to the acquisitions have been escrowed and may not be sold for one year from their issuance date.

You, CA, are a new manager with a CA firm. Your firm was appointed as the auditor of ERL in September Year 4, for the year ending June 30, Year 5. Your firm was also appointed as the auditor of Peaceful.

It is now September Year 5. Your firm has experienced severe staffing shortages. The partner has advised you that because of the recent departure of another manager, you have been assigned to the ERL and Peaceful engagements. The audit fieldwork has been completed, but the file review has not taken place. The partner has asked you to review the audit files and notes prepared by the senior in charge of the engagements and to prepare a memo that provides your analysis and disposition of the accounting issues.

The following information was assembled from your review of the working papers of ERL and Peaceful.

1. The acquisition of Tranquil's net assets resulted in the following additions to ERL's balance sheet as at September 1, Year 4 (in thousands of dollars):

Working capital	$ 850
Land	1,400
Buildings and equipment, net	3,700
Non-competition agreements	3,000
Goodwill	11,250
Total net assets of Tranquil	$20,200

The $20.2 million was paid as follows:	
5-year non-interest-bearing first mortgage bonds of ERL	$18,150
Common shares of ERL, escrowed for one year	2,050
	$20,200

The auditors read the purchase and sale agreement and noted that $820,000 of the working capital represented funds that were being held in trust for future maintenance of the cemetery lands. The new common shares issued by ERL were valued at the market price on the day prior to the signing of the agreement.

The $3 million paid for non-competition agreements represents a payment to the sellers of Tranquil in exchange for their commitment not to engage in the same type of business for five years. The $3 million represents the otherwise expected earnings of the sellers, discounted at the 9 percent market rate of interest that prevailed at the time. The $1.4 million and $3.7 million assigned to land and buildings and equipment represent management's estimates of the fair values of these assets and coincide with book values on Tranquil's books.

2. The shares of Peaceful were acquired primarily because the company had non–capital loss carry-forwards for income tax purposes. The purchase price for the acquisition was a $1 million cash payment by ERL plus the issuance of $24 million of ERL shares for the 70 percent ownership. The purchase price was allocated to assets and liabilities in a manner similar to the allocation for the Tranquil acquisition. The auditors did not request that the estimated value of the loss carry-forward be recorded. ERL attributed $4 million to non-competition agreements (to be amortized over five years) and $14 million to goodwill.

3. After the acquisition of Peaceful by ERL, sufficient business was directed to Peaceful to commence the process of utilizing the tax loss carry-forwards. During fiscal Year 5, the benefit realized from the utilization of the loss carry-forwards amounted to $2.36 million and was credited to extraordinary gain on the income statement.

4. Excess cemetery land (acquired in the purchase of Tranquil) was sold in December Year 4 at a gain of $1.2 million. The proceeds were reported as "other revenue."

5. One working paper entitled "Land" contains the following note: "Land recorded on the books at $2,305,600 and called 'Sunset Hill' is undeveloped and is not scheduled for use until Year 8 or Year 9. It is subject to a Year 5 government order requiring that ERL clear up environmental concerns on the site. I asked one employee what the cost would be and was told 'half a million dollars.' No amount was accrued, because of uncertainty."

6. A working paper entitled "Management Compensation" shows that senior management shares in what is called a "Bonus Pool." The bonus is 15 percent of income before income taxes.

Required:

Prepare the memo.

(CICA adapted)

Case 3 Factory Optical Distributors (FOD) is a publicly held manufacturer and distributor of high-quality eyeglass lenses located in Burnaby, British Columbia. For the past 10 years, the company has sold its lenses on a wholesale basis to optical shops across Canada. Beginning in Year 3, the company began to offer franchise opportunities to opticians wanting to sell only FOD lenses.

The franchise agreements contain the following stipulations:

- Each franchise must be a corporation. FOD (Burnaby) will purchase 35 percent of the corporation's outstanding common shares and the franchisee will hold the remaining 65 percent. No other equity instruments can be issued.
- Franchises can be established in new locations or in existing locations under the name Factory Optical Distributors. If a new building is required, FOD (Burnaby) will guarantee the mortgage to ensure that the best interest rates can be obtained. If an existing location is used, it must be renovated to meet company specifications, and again FOD (Burnaby) will guarantee any required financing.
- To qualify as a franchisee, an individual must be a licensed optician and must commit to 40 hours a week in the franchise location, managing the day-to-day activities.
- Franchisees are to be paid a salary that does not exceed 1.5 times the industry average for opticians with equivalent experience.
- The franchise agreement specifies that only FOD lenses can be sold in franchise locations. FOD lenses can be purchased by franchisees at 20 percent below normal selling price for the first $500,000 of purchases, and at 25 percent below normal selling price if purchases exceed $500,000.
- The agreement also requires that frames sold by the franchisee be purchased from designated suppliers, to ensure the best quality and fit to FOD lenses.
- All franchise advertising must be approved by FOD (Burnaby). Franchisees must allocate 1 percent of revenue to advertising each month.
- The franchisee is required to participate in special promotions and seasonal sales as determined by FOD (Burnaby).
- A franchise fee of 2 percent of sales is payable monthly to FOD (Burnaby).
- Other products and services can be sold from the franchise location provided that they do not negatively impact the sale of FOD lenses.

During Year 5, eight franchise agreements were signed in locations across Canada. At December 31, Year 5, the company's year-end, five of these locations were open for business.

It is now January Year 6. You are the senior auditor on the FOD (Burnaby) account. The company's corporate controller has come to you with the franchise agreement to discuss how FOD must report its share ownership in the five operating franchises. She has heard that the definition of control in IAS 27 encompasses some situations where 50 percent share ownership does not exist.

Required:

Examine the details of the franchise agreement. Do you think FOD controls the franchise operations? Would consolidation be required? Explain.

(adapted from a case prepared by J.C. Thatcher, Lakehead University, and Margaret Forbes, University of Saskatchewan)

Case 4   The following are a number of scenarios that show variations in the nature of long-term intercorporate investments.

1.   A Ltd. owns 45 percent of B Co. Typically, only about 70 percent of the outstanding shares are voted at the annual meetings of B Company. Because of this, A Ltd. always casts a majority of the votes on every ballot when it votes the shares it holds.

2.   A Ltd. holds no shares of B Co.; however, it holds convertible bonds issued by B Co. that, if A Ltd. converted them, would result in the ownership of 51 percent of the outstanding shares of B Co.

3.   A Ltd. owns 75 percent of B Co. Recently a receiver, acting on behalf of a bank, seized a portion of B Co.'s inventory when B Co. defaulted on a loan.

4.   Last year B Co. was a wholly owned subsidiary of C Inc. At the beginning of this year, B Co. was put up for sale and A Ltd. purchased all of its 100,000 voting shares from C Inc. by making a cash payment of 40 percent of the purchase price and by issuing a promissory note for the balance owing, due in equal instalments over the next two years.

   B Co. has a bond issue outstanding that can be converted at the option of the holder into 150,000 voting common shares of that company. At the time of the sale, C Inc. held 80 percent of these bonds; it has agreed to sell these bonds proportionately to A Ltd. as it receives the proceeds from the promissory note.

5.   A Ltd. owns 100 percent of B Co., which is insolvent. All of its assets have been seized by a licensed trustee in bankruptcy.

6.   B Co. is located in a foreign country. This country requires that a majority of the ownership of all businesses be held by its citizens. A Ltd. has the expertise and technical knowledge required to successfully operate B Co. In order to satisfy the country's foreign ownership requirements, B Co. has been structured as a partnership, with 50 partners each having a 2 percent equity interest. Forty-nine of the partners, who are all citizens of the foreign country, have signed an irrevocable agreement that establishes A Ltd. as the managing partner, with complete authority to determine the operating, financing, and investing policies of B Co.

Required:

For each scenario, discuss how A Ltd. should report its investment in B Co.

Case 5   Regina Communications Ltd. develops and manufactures equipment for technology and communications enterprises. Since its incorporation in Year 5, it has grown steadily through internal expansion. In mid Year 14, Arthur Lajord, the sole owner of Regina, met a couple of engineering students who were working on new technology to increase the efficiency of data transferred over cable lines. Arthur has provided moral support and some financial support to these students over the past few months. At a lunch with the students last Friday, the students told Arthur that they had been able to register a patent to protect their technology. Furthermore, they were interested in selling their business, Davin Technologies Inc., which owns the patent and some other assets used in the development of this technology. After a week of negotiation, Arthur and the students agreed to the following:

- Rather than buying the shares of Davin, Regina would buy the assets and assume the liabilities of Davin effective January 1, Year 15.
- The purchase price would be payable as follows:
  - $200,000 on January 1, Year 15
  - $100,000 a year for three years commencing January 1, Year 16
- The students would commit to work for Regina as consultants over the next three years and would be paid $40 per hour for their services.
- The students would get an additional $200,000 if the patent were sold by Regina for more than $1,000,000 or if Regina were to go public on or before January 1, Year 18.

The condensed statement of financial position for Davin at January 1, Year 15, was as follows:

	Net book value	Fair value
Computer equipment	$ 30,000	$35,000
Patent registration costs	25,000	?
Current assets	50,000	50,000
	$105,000	
Shareholders' equity	$ 95,000	?
Liabilities	10,000	10,000
	$105,000	

Arthur was pleased and excited about the acquisition. He felt that it was a fair deal for both parties given that the business had not yet earned any revenue. He was particularly pleased that the students agreed to be paid over three years because he otherwise would have had to arrange a bank loan with an interest rate of 8 percent.

Arthur is now worried about the accounting for this acquisition because it is the first time that his company has purchased another business. Although Regina has always followed IFRSs, he is wondering whether now is the time to opt for a simpler approach. In particular, he is wondering whether the entire acquisition differential can be allocated to goodwill. This would keep it simple and would also avoid a charge to income over the first few years since goodwill does not need to be amortized. If the acquisition differential is allocated to patent, then Arthur would like to write off the patent over the maximum period of 20 years.

Arthur has asked you, a CGA, to prepare a presentation on the accounting implications for the proposed acquisition. He wants to understand how to determine the purchase price, how the purchase price would be allocated to individual assets and liabilities, and how this allocation would affect profit in the first year after the date of acquisition.

Required:

Prepare the presentation slides and related speaker's notes for the presentation. Limit your presentation to five slides. Your presentation should provide recommendations related to the issues raised by Arthur. Use financial statement concepts to support your recommendations. Provide a detailed calculation to show the impact on profit for Year 15. State your assumptions.

(*CGA-Canada adapted*)

Case 6 Canadian Computer Systems Limited (CCS) is a public company engaged in the development of computer software and the manufacturing of computer hardware. CCS is listed on a Canadian stock exchange and has a 40 percent non-controlling interest in Sandra Investments Limited (SIL), a U.S. public company that was de-listed by an American stock exchange due to financial difficulties. In addition, CCS has three wholly owned subsidiaries.

CCS is audited by Roth & Minch, a large public accounting firm. You, CA, are the audit manager responsible for the engagement.

CCS has a September 30 fiscal year-end. It is now mid-November Year 11 and the year-end audit is nearing completion. CCS's draft financial statements are included in Exhibit I. While reviewing the audit working papers (see Exhibit II), you identify

---

Exhibit I

CANADIAN COMPUTER SYSTEMS LIMITED
EXTRACTS FROM CONSOLIDATED BALANCE SHEET
As at September 30
(in thousands of dollars)

	Year 11	Year 10
Assets		
Current assets		
Cash	$ 190	$ 170
Accounts receivable	2,540	1,600
Inventories, at the lower of cost and net realizable value	610	420
	3,340	2,190
Plant assets (net of accumulated depreciation)	33,930	34,970
Property held for resale	1,850	1,840
Other assets	410	420
	$39,530	$39,420
Liabilities		
Current liabilities		
Demand loans	$ 1,150	$ 3,080
Accrued interest payable	11,510	10,480
Accounts payable	2,500	2,100
Mortgages payable due currently because of loan defaults	21,600	21,600
Long-term debt due within one year	290	1,780
Debt obligation of Sandra Investments Limited	50,000	55,420
	87,050	94,460
Long-term debt	26,830	21,330
Other long-term liabilities	250	330
	114,130	116,120
Share Capital and Deficit		
Share capital		
Issued:		
261 9% cumulative, convertible, preferred shares	10	10
1,000,000 Class B preferred shares	250	250
10,243,019 Common shares	100,170	100,010
	100,430	100,270
Deficit	(175,030)	(176,970)
	(74,600)	(76,700)
	$39,530	$39,420

CANADIAN COMPUTER SYSTEMS LIMITED
EXTRACTS FROM CONSOLIDATED STATEMENT
OF OPERATIONS AND DEFICIT
For the years ended September 30
(in thousands of dollars)

	Year 11	Year 10
Sales		
Hardware	$ 12,430	$ 19,960
Software	3,070	3,890
	15,500	23,850
Other income	1,120	
	16,620	23,850
Expenses		
Operating	10,240	15,050
Interest	4,590	4,690
General and administrative	2,970	4,140
Depreciation	2,400	3,630
Provision for impairment in plant assets	–	2,220
	20,200	29,730
Loss before the undernoted items	(3,580)	(5,880)
Loss from Sandra Investments Limited	(2,830)	(55,420)
Gain (loss) from discontinued operations	8,350	(4,040)
Net income (loss)	1,940	(65,340)
Deficit, beginning of year	(176,970)	(111,630)
Deficit, end of year	$(175,030)	$(176,970)

several issues that raise doubts about CCS's ability to realize its assets and discharge its liabilities in the normal course of business.

After you have reviewed the situation with the engagement partner, he asks you to prepare a memo for his use in discussing the going-concern problem with the president of CCS and suggests that you look to IAS 1 for guidance. Your memo should include all factors necessary to assess CCS's ability to continue operations. You are also to comment on the accounting and disclosure implications.

Required:

Prepare the memo requested by the partner.

Exhibit II

EXTRACTS FROM AUDIT WORKING PAPERS

1. Cash receipts are collected by one of CCS's banks. This bank then releases funds to CCS based on operating budgets prepared by management. Demand loans bearing interest at 1 percent over the bank's prime rate are used to finance ongoing operations. The demand loans are secured by a general assignment of accounts receivable and a floating-charge debenture on all assets.

2. CCS accounts for its interest in SIL on the equity basis. As a result of SIL's recurring losses in prior years, the investment account was written off in Year 9. In Year 10, CCS recorded in its accounts the amount of SIL's bank loan and accrued interest, as CCS guaranteed this amount. During Year 11, CCS made debt payments of $5.42 million and interest payments of $1.8 million on behalf of SIL. In December Year 11, SIL issued preferred shares in the amount of US$40 million, used the proceeds to pay down the loan, and was re-listed on the

(continued)

stock exchange. Interest expense on the debt obligation in Year 11 totalled $2.83 million and has been included in the income statement under "Loss from Sandra Investments Limited."

3. Current liabilities include mortgages payable of $21.6 million due currently. They have been re-classified from long-term debt because of CCS's failure to comply with operating covenants and restrictions. The prior year's financial statements have been restated for comparative purposes.

4. Long-term debt is repayable over varying periods of time. However, the banks reserve the right to declare the loans due and payable upon demand. The loan agreements require CCS to obtain advance approval in writing from the bank if it wishes to exceed certain limits on borrowing and capital expenditures. The agreements also prohibit the sale of certain plant assets, payment of dividends, and transfer of funds among related companies without prior written approval. One loan of $15 million was in default at September 30, Year 11.

5. During the year, CCS issued common shares to the directors and officers to satisfy amounts owing to them totalling $160,000. New equity issues are being considered for this year.

6. On November 10, Year 11, a claim related to a breach of contract was filed against one of the company's subsidiaries in the amount of $3.7 million plus interest and costs of the action. Management believes that this claim is without merit. However, if any amounts do have to be paid as a result of this action, management believes that the amounts would be covered by liability insurance.

7. In Year 11, operating expenses include $1 million in development costs relating to a computer software program. Sales of this software are expected to commence in Year 12.

PROBLEMS

Problem 1   The statements of financial position of Pork Co. and Barrel Ltd. on December 31, Year 2, are shown next:

	Pork Co.	Barrel Ltd.
Plant and equipment (net)	$400,000	$270,000
Investment in Barrel Ltd.	294,000	—
Inventory	120,000	102,000
Accounts receivable	80,000	48,000
Cash	22,000	60,000
	$916,000	$480,000
Common shares	$260,000	$120,000
Retained earnings	200,000	180,000
Long-term debt	240,000	108,000
Current liabilities	216,000	72,000
	$916,000	$480,000

Pork acquired 70 percent of the outstanding shares of Barrel on December 30, Year 2, for $294,000. Direct costs of the acquisition amounted to $12,000. The book values of the net assets of Barrel approximated fair values except for plant and equipment, which had a fair value of $320,000.

Required:

(a) Prepare a consolidated statement of financial position at December 31, Year 2, under the entity theory.

(b) Calculate goodwill and non-controlling interest on the consolidated statement of financial position at December 31, Year 2, under the parent company extension theory.

Problem 2 The balance sheets of Par Ltd. and Sub Ltd. on December 31, Year 1, are as follows:

	Par Ltd.	Sub Ltd.
Cash	$100,000	$ 2,000
Accounts receivable	25,000	7,000
Inventory	30,000	21,000
Plant	175,000	51,000
Trademarks	—	7,000
	$330,000	$88,000
Current liabilities	$ 50,000	$10,000
Long-term debt	80,000	20,000
Common shares	110,000	30,000
Retained earnings	90,000	28,000
	$330,000	$88,000

The fair values of the identifiable net assets of Sub on December 31, Year 1, are as follows:

Cash		$ 2,000
Accounts receivable		7,000
Inventory		26,000
Plant		60,000
Trademarks		14,000
		109,000
Current liabilities	$10,000	
Long-term debt	19,000	29,000
Net assets		$ 80,000

Assume that the following took place on January 1, Year 2. (Par acquired the shares with a cash payment to the shareholders of Sub.)

Case 1. Par paid $95,000 to acquire all of the common shares of Sub.
Case 2. Par paid $76,000 to acquire 80 percent of the common shares of Sub.
Case 3. Par paid $80,000 to acquire all of the common shares of Sub.
Case 4. Par paid $70,000 to acquire all of the common shares of Sub.
Case 5. Par paid $63,000 to acquire 90 percent of the common shares of Sub.

Required:

For each of the five cases, prepare a consolidated balance sheet as at January 1, Year 2.

Problem 3 The balance sheets of Petron Co. and Seeview Co. on June 29, Year 2, were as follows:

	Petron	Seeview
Cash and receivables	$ 80,000	$ 16,250
Inventory	47,500	7,500
Plant assets (net)	190,000	58,750
Intangible assets	20,000	5,000
	$337,500	$ 87,500
Current liabilities	$ 52,500	$ 25,000
Long-term debt	81,250	37,500
Common shares	127,500	38,750
Retained earnings (deficit)	76,250	(13,750)
	$337,500	$ 87,500

On June 30, Year 2, Petron Co. purchased 90 percent of the outstanding shares of Seeview Co. for $40,500 cash. Legal fees involved with the acquisition were an additional $1,000. The book value of Seeview's net assets were equal to fair value except for the following:

	Fair value
Inventory	8,750
Plant assets	67,500
Intangible assets	7,500
Long-term debt	32,500

Seeview has a five-year agreement to supply goods to Customer. Both Petron and Seeview believe that Customer will renew the agreement at the end of the current contract. The agreement is between Seeview and Customer; it cannot be transferred to another company without Seeview's consent. Seeview does not report any value with respect to this contract on its balance sheet. However, an independent appraiser feels that this contract is worth $10,000.

Required:

Prepare the consolidated balance sheet of Petron Co. on June 30, Year 2. (Round all calculations to the nearest dollar.)

Problem 4 The balance sheets of Hill Corp. and McGraw Ltd. on December 31, Year 4, were as follows:

	Hill Corp.	McGraw Ltd.
Cash	$ 13,000	$ 6,500
Accounts receivable	181,300	45,500
Inventory	117,000	208,000
Land	91,000	52,000
Plant and equipment	468,000	377,000
Investment in McGraw Ltd.	288,000	—
Goodwill	117,000	39,000
	$1,275,300	$728,000
Current liabilities	$ 156,000	$104,000
Long-term debt	416,000	286,000
Common shares	520,000	390,000
Retained earnings	183,300	(52,000)
	$1,275,300	$728,000

On December 30, Year 4, Hill purchased 80 percent of the common shares of McGraw for $288,000. On this date the inventory of McGraw had a fair value of $214,500, its land had a fair value of $91,000, and its plant and equipment had a fair value of $364,000.

Required:

Prepare a consolidated balance sheet as at December 31, Year 4.

Problem 5 Following are the statements of financial position of Blue Ltd. and Joy Corp. on December 31, Year 2.

	Blue Ltd.	Joy Corp.
Plant and equipment	$ 440,000	$320,000
Investment in Joy Corp.	424,000	—
Inventory	105,000	220,000
Accounts receivable	78,000	35,000
Cash	17,000	5,000
	$1,064,000	$580,000
Common shares	$ 422,000	$300,000
Retained earnings	224,000	(40,000)
Long-term debt	250,000	240,000
Current liabilities	168,000	80,000
	$1,064,000	$580,000

On December 31, Year 2, Blue purchased a percentage of the outstanding common shares of Joy. On this date all but two categories of Joy's identifiable assets and liabilities had fair values equal to book values.

Below is the consolidated statement of financial position for Blue at December 31, Year 2.

BLUE LTD.
CONSOLIDATED STATEMENT OF FINANCIAL POSITION
December 31, Year 2

Plant and equipment	$ 860,000
Goodwill	150,000
Inventory	345,000
Accounts receivable	113,000
Cash	22,000
	$1,490,000
Common shares	$ 422,000
Retained earnings	224,000
Non-controlling interest	106,000
Long-term debt	490,000
Current liabilities	248,000
	$1,490,000

Required:

(a) From the information provided, determine the percentage of Joy's common shares purchased by Blue on December 31, Year 2.

(b) Which of Joy's assets or liabilities had fair values that were not equal to their book values at acquisition? Calculate the fair value of each of these assets at December 31, Year 2.

Problem 6   The balance sheets of E Ltd. and J Ltd. on December 30, Year 6, were as follows:

	E Ltd.	J Ltd.
Cash and receivables	$ 96,000	$ 19,500
Inventory	57,000	9,000
Plant assets (net)	228,000	70,500
Intangible assets	24,000	6,000
	$405,000	$105,000
Current liabilities	$ 63,000	$ 30,000
Long-term debt	97,500	45,000
Common shares	153,000	46,500
Retained earnings (deficit)	91,500	(16,500)
	$405,000	$105,000

On December 31, Year 6, E issued 350 shares, with a fair value of $40 each, for 70 percent of the outstanding shares of J. Costs involved in the acquisition, paid in cash, were as follows:

Costs of arranging the acquisition	$2,500
Costs of issuing shares	1,600
	$4,100

The book values of J's net assets were equal to fair values on this date except for the following:

	Fair value
Plant assets	$65,000
Long-term debt	40,000

E was identified as the acquirer in the combination.

Required:

(a) Prepare the consolidated balance sheet of E Ltd. on December 31, Year 6, under each of the following:
   (i) Proprietary theory.
   (ii) Parent company theory.
   (iii)Parent company extension theory.
   (iv) Entity theory.

(b) Calculate the current ratio and debt-to-equity ratio for E Ltd. under the four different theories. Explain which theory shows the strongest liquidity and solvency position and which method best reflects the true financial condition of the company.

Problem 7   On December 31, Year 1, P Company purchased 80 percent of the outstanding shares of S Company for $6,960 cash.

The statements of financial position of the two companies immediately after the acquisition transaction appear below.

	P Company Book value	S Company Book value	S Company Fair value
Plant and equipment (net)	$ 8,100	$ 6,900	$6,000
Investment in S Company	6,960	—	
Inventory	5,160	3,750	3,900
Accounts receivable	3,150	1,800	1,800
Cash	1,500	1,050	1,050
	$24,870	$13,500	
Common shares	$10,500	$ 3,000	
Retained earnings	8,370	6,000	
Long-term liabilities	4,200	2,000	2,000
Other current liabilities	1,200	1,800	1,800
Accounts payable	600	700	700
	$24,870	$13,500	

Required:

(a) Prepare a consolidated statement of financial position at the date of acquisition under each of the following:
   (i) Proprietary theory.
   (ii) Parent company theory.
   (iii) Parent company extension theory.
   (iv) Entity theory.
(b) Calculate the current ratio and debt-to-equity ratio for P Company under the four different theories. Explain which theory shows the strongest liquidity and solvency position and which method best reflects the true financial condition of the company.

Problem 8   On January 1, Year 5, Black Corp. purchased 90 percent of the common shares of Whyte Inc. On this date the following differences were observed with regard to specific net assets of Whyte:

	Fair value − book value differences
Land	+50,000
Buildings (net)	+20,000
Equipment (net)	−10,000
Notes payable	+ 5,000

The nonconsolidated and consolidated balance sheets of Black Corp. on January 1, Year 5, are presented below. Whyte's retained earnings were $140,000 on this date.

	Nonconsolidated	Consolidated
Cash	$ 36,000	$ 52,000
Accounts receivable	116,000	168,000
Inventory	144,000	234,000
Investment in Whyte	292,500	—
Land	210,000	280,000
Buildings (net)	640,000	720,000
Equipment (net)	308,000	338,000
Goodwill	—	50,000
	$1,746,500	$1,842,000
Accounts payable	$ 88,000	$ 96,000
Notes payable	507,500	562,500
Common shares	380,000	380,000
Retained earnings	771,000	771,000
Non-controlling interest	—	32,500
	$1,746,500	$1,842,000

Required:

Prepare the January 1, Year 5, balance sheet of Whyte Inc.

Problem 9 The balance sheets of Percy Corp. and Saltz Ltd. on December 31, Year 10, are shown below:

	Percy	Saltz
Cash	$200,000	$ 4,000
Accounts receivable	50,000	14,000
Inventory	60,000	42,000
Plant	350,000	102,000
Trademarks	—	14,000
	$660,000	$176,000
Current liabilities	$100,000	$ 20,000
Long-term debt	160,000	40,000
Common shares	220,000	60,000 ✓
Retained earnings	180,000	56,000 ✓
	$660,000	$176,000

The fair values of the identifiable net assets of Saltz Ltd. on December 31, Year 10, were as follows:

Cash		$ 4,000
Accounts receivable		14,000
Inventory		52,000
Plant		120,000
Trademarks		28,000
		218,000
Current liabilities	$20,000	
Long-term debt	38,000	58,000
Net assets		$160,000

On January 1, Year 11, Percy Corp paid $140,000 in cash to acquire 7,000 (70 percent) of the common shares of Saltz Ltd. Saltz's shares were trading for $16 per share just after the acquisition by Percy.

Required:

Prepare the consolidated balance sheet on January 1, Year 1.

Problem 10 The balance sheets of Prima Ltd. and Donna Corp. on December 31, Year 5, are shown below:

	Prima	Donna
Cash	$ 370,000	$ 6,400
Accounts receivable	80,000	22,400
Inventory	96,000	67,200
Plant	510,000	163,200
Patents	100,000	22,400
	$1,156,000	$281,600
Current liabilities	$ 160,000	$ 32,000
Long-term debt	256,000	64,000
Common shares	352,000	96,000
Retained earnings	388,000	89,600
	$1,156,000	$281,600

The fair values of the identifiable net assets of Donna Corp. on this date are as follows:

Cash	$ 6,400
Accounts receivable	20,000
Inventory	85,000
Plant	192,000
Trademarks	30,000
Patents	50,000
Current liabilities	32,000
Long-term debt	70,000

In addition to the assets identified above, Donna owned a significant number of Internet domain names, which are unique alphanumeric names that are used to identify a particular numeric Internet address. These domain names can be sold separately and are estimated to be worth $50,000.

On January 1, Year 6, Prima Ltd. paid $351,000 in cash to acquire 90 percent of the common shares of Donna Corp.

Required:

(a) Prepare the consolidated balance sheet on January 1, Year 6, under the entity theory.

(b) Calculate goodwill and non-controlling interest on the consolidated balance sheet on January 1, Year 6, under the parent company extension theory.

Problem 11 On January 1, Year 5, FLA Company issued 6,300 common shares from treasury to purchase 9,000 common shares of MES Company. Prior to the acquisition, FLA had 180,000 and MES had 10,000 common shares outstanding, which were trading at

$5 and $3 per share, respectively. The following information has been assembled for these two companies at the date of acquisition:

	FLA Company		MES Company	
	Book value	Fair value	Book value	Fair value
Plant assets	$ 60,000	$70,000	$20,000	$25,000
Current assets	40,000	47,500	10,000	11,200
	$100,000		$30,000	
Common shares	$ 30,000		$10,000	
Retained earnings	35,000		12,500	
Long-term debt	15,000	19,000	2,500	3,200
Current liabilities	20,000	20,000	5,000	5,000
	$100,000		$30,000	

Required:

(a) Prepare a consolidated statement of financial position for FLA Company and its non–wholly owned subsidiary at January 1, Year 5, under each of the following:
   (i) Proprietary theory.
   (ii) Parent company theory.
   (iii) Parent company extension theory.
   (iv) Entity theory.
(b) Which of the above theories is required under IFRS 3?

Problem 12   The condensed financial statements for OIL Inc. and ERS Company for the year ended December 31, Year 5, follow:

	OIL	ERS
Revenues	$ 900,000	$ 300,000
Expenses	660,000	200,000
Net income	$ 240,000	$ 100,000
Retained earnings, 1/1/Year 5	$ 800,000	$ 200,000
Net income	240,000	100,000
Dividends paid	90,000	0
Retained earnings, 31/12/Year 5	$ 950,000	$ 300,000
Cash	$ 80,000	$ 110,000
Receivables and inventory	400,000	170,000
Patented technology (net)	900,000	300,000
Equipment (net)	700,000	600,000
Total assets	$2,080,000	$1,180,000
Liabilities	$ 600,000	$ 410,000
Common shares	530,000	470,000
Retained earnings	950,000	300,000
Total liabilities and equities	$2,080,000	$1,180,000

On December 31, Year 5, after the above figures were prepared, OIL issued $240,000 in debt and 12,000 new shares to the owners of ERS for 80 percent of the outstanding shares of that company. OIL shares had a fair value of $40 per share.

OIL also paid $30,000 to a broker for arranging the transaction. In addition, OIL paid $32,000 in stock issuance costs. ERS's equipment was actually worth $690,000, but its patented technology was appraised at only $280,000.

Required:

What are the consolidated balances for the year ended/at December 31, Year 5, for the following accounts?

(a) Net income.
(b) Retained earnings, 1/1/Year 5.
(c) Equipment.
(d) Patented technology.
(e) Goodwill.
(f) Liabilities.
(g) Common shares.

WEB-BASED PROBLEMS

Problem 1   When accounting for the acquisition of a non–wholly owned subsidiary, the parent can use the entity theory or parent company extension theory to account for the business combination. Access the most recent consolidated financial statements for Vodafone, a British company. (Go to the investor relations section at www.vodafone.com.) Answer the questions below. For each question, indicate where in the financial statements you found the answer and/or provide a brief explanation.

(a) Which theory of consolidation did the parent use to account for the business combination?
(b) What portion of the additions to property, plant, and equipment during the year came from business combinations and what portion came from direct purchases?
(c) What percentage of shareholders' equity at the end of the year do non-controlling interests (sometimes referred to as minority interests) represent?
(d) How were costs directly attributable to the business combination accounted for?
(e) Were any of the subsidiaries controlled even though the percentage ownership was less than 50 percent? If so, what explanation was provided to explain how control was achieved with less than 50 percent ownership?
(f) Assume that the company used the other acceptable theory of accounting for its business combinations and that the fair value of the subsidiary as a whole was greater than the fair value of the identifiable net assets at the date of acquisition. How would this change in theory affect the debt-to-equity ratio at the date of acquisition?

Problem 2   Access the most recent consolidated financial statements for Siemens, a German company. (Go to the investor relations section at www.siemens.com.) Answer the same questions as in Problem 1. For each question, indicate where in the financial statements you found the answer and/or provide a brief explanation. (Some questions may not be applicable.)

Chapter (5) Consolidation Subsequent to Acquisition Date

LEARNING OBJECTIVES

After studying this chapter, you should be able to do the following:

1. Explain the basic differences between the cost and equity methods of recording investments.
2. Explain how impairment tests are performed on long-lived assets, other intangibles, and goodwill.
3. Calculate the amortization and/or impairment of acquisition differential on both an annual and a cumulative basis.
4. Calculate consolidated net income attributable to the parent's shareholders and consolidated retained earnings.
5. Explain how the matching principle is applied when amortizing or writing off the acquisition differential.
6. Prepare consolidated financial statements in years subsequent to acquisition.
7. Prepare journal entries under the equity method to report changes in the investment account during the year.

INTRODUCTION

In Chapters 3 and 4, we discussed and illustrated the preparation of a consolidated balance sheet immediately after a parent company gained control over a subsidiary. We saw that the acquisition differential was allocated to identifiable assets and liabilities when the fair values were different than book values and the excess was allocated to goodwill. In this chapter, we will see that the acquisition differential must be amortized and tested for impairment when preparing financial statements subsequent to the date of acquisition. The impairment testing can result in huge impairment losses when business slows down, as indicated in the following example for Nortel Networks Corporation, one of Canada's most famous hi-tech companies.

During the high-tech boom in the late 1990s, Nortel stock prices soared to over $120 a share, and the company used these high prices to embark on an acquisitions binge. In one year alone it acquired 11 companies for a total cost of $20.4 billion, with payment being made by the issuance of new shares in nearly all cases. Allocated to goodwill was $18.5 billion, which represented over 90 percent of the total acquisition cost. Shortly after Nortel made these acquisitions, the tech bubble burst, and the prolonged bear market that followed saw Nortel's share price drop to less than $1. With such a substantial decline in the fair value of the company, it came as no surprise when Nortel announced that it was going to write down its intangible assets (mostly goodwill) by $12.3 billion and, in addition, was going to take an $830 million restructuring charge as a result of closing plants and discontinuing operations. Many of these abandoned operations had just recently been purchased. All of this resulted in a second-quarter loss of $19.2 billion, the largest ever reported by a Canadian company.

In this chapter, we will prepare the consolidated income statement, retained earnings statement, and balance sheet at fiscal year-ends after the date of acquisition. The consolidated cash flow statement will be discussed in a later chapter. We will start by looking at how the parent accounts for its investment in its own internal records.

Methods of Accounting for an Investment in a Subsidiary

The cost and equity methods are methods of accounting in the parent's own internal records.

There are two methods available to a parent company to account for an investment in a subsidiary in its own internal accounting records in periods subsequent to the date of acquisition: the *cost method* and the *equity method*. The cost and equity methods of accounting were discussed in Chapter 2 for various types of equity investments. While this chapter is concerned with control investments (requiring consolidation), the accounting concepts involved with the cost and equity methods are identical to those presented in Chapter 2. These concepts will be outlined again in this chapter and in the ones that follow. The key difference is that here they are discussed in relation to the preparation of consolidated financial statements, whereas before, the emphasis was on the presentation in an investor's unconsolidated financial statements for external users.

The cost method records income when the investor's right to receive a dividend is established.

The cost method is a method of accounting for investments whereby the investment is initially recorded at cost; income from the subsidiary is recognized in net income when the investor's right to receive a dividend is established. This usually occurs when the dividend is declared.

IAS 28 defines the equity method as a method of accounting whereby the investment is initially recognized at cost and adjusted thereafter for the post-acquisition change in the investor's share of net assets of the investee. The profit or loss of the investor includes the investor's share of the profit or loss of the investee. Distributions received from an investee reduce the carrying amount of the investment. Adjustments to the carrying amount may also be necessary for changes in the investor's proportionate interest in the investee arising from changes in the investee's other comprehensive income. Such changes include those arising from the revaluation of property, plant, and equipment and from foreign-exchange translation differences. The investor's share of those changes is recognized in other comprehensive income of the investor.

The equity method captures the investor's share of any changes to the investee's shareholders' equity.

The cost method is the simplest of the two methods because typically the only entry made by the parent each year is to record, as revenue, its pro rata share of dividends declared by the subsidiary. Occasionally, there may be an entry to record an impairment loss on the investment.

IAS 28.20 states that the concepts underlying the procedures used in accounting for the acquisition of a subsidiary are also adopted in accounting for the acquisition of an investment in an associate, which is reported using the equity method. This means that the types of adjustments made for consolidation purposes will also be made under the equity method. For this reason, the equity method is often referred to as the "one-line consolidation." If used fully and correctly for an investment in a subsidiary, the equity method will produce the same net income and retained

The equity method captures the net effect of any adjustments that would be made on the consolidated financial statements.

earnings on the internal records of the parent as reported on the parent's consolidated financial statements. The only difference is that the consolidated financial statements incorporate the subsidiary's values on a line-by-line basis, whereas the equity method incorporates the net amount of the subsidiary's values on one line (investment in the subsidiary) on the balance sheet and typically on one line (investment income from the subsidiary) on the income statement.

As we will see later in this chapter, the acquisition differential must be amortized or written off over the useful lives of the related assets. The consolidated financial statements must be adjusted to reflect the amortization and/or impairment. In Chapters 6 and 7, we will make consolidation adjustments to eliminate unrealized profits from intercompany transactions. When the parent uses the equity method to account for its investment in the subsidiary, the net effect of the aforementioned consolidation adjustments must be processed through the investment and investment income accounts on the parent's internal records.

We must differentiate between accounting in the internal records and reporting in the external financial statements.

It is very important that we differentiate between the internal accounting records and the financial statements for external users. Each entity maintains its own internal accounting records, i.e., a general ledger supported by various subledgers. In the internal records for the parent, there will be an investment in subsidiary account, which will be accounted for using the cost, equity, or fair value method. Since the parent controls the subsidiary, it will prepare consolidated financial statements for distribution to its external users. The consolidated financial statements will be supported by a worksheet or set of working papers.

An entity could issue nonconsolidated financial statements to external users in addition to consolidated financial statements.

In addition to the consolidated financial statements, the parent could also prepare nonconsolidated financial statements for its external users. In this text, we will refer to these nonconsolidated financial statements as separate-entity financial statements, which may or may not be prepared in accordance with GAAP. Since income tax is assessed in Canada at a separate-entity level, a Canadian company must prepare nonconsolidated statements for the Canada Revenue Agency.[1] Since dividends received and investment income pertaining to a subsidiary are not usually taxable for income tax purposes, this income will have to be reversed when calculating taxable income. Accordingly, the income tax authorities are indifferent as to whether the parent uses the cost method or the equity method on its separate-entity financial statements. In fact, the statements given to the tax authorities may be prepared using tax laws rather than GAAP.

When a bank or other external user wants to receive nonconsolidated statements, it may insist that they be prepared in accordance with GAAP. If so, IAS 27 requires that the investment in subsidiary on the separate-entity financial statements be reported at cost or in accordance with IAS 39.

The following diagram shows the interrelationships between the various records and financial statements:

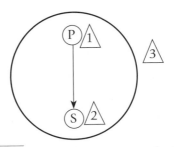

---

[1] Some foreign jurisdictions assess tax at the corporate group level.

Each circle represents a different set of records/financial statements. The triangle indicates the number given to the set of records/financial statements — the parent's separate records/financial statements is number 1, the subsidiary's separate records/ financial statements is number 2, and the consolidated set is number 3. In the first part of this chapter, the parent will be using the cost method on set number 1.

Consolidated net income will be the same regardless of whether the parent used the cost method or the equity method for its internal accounting records.

At the end of this chapter, we will show the entries if the parent had used the equity method in its internal records. The adjustments on consolidation will be different depending on whether the parent uses the cost method or the equity method on set 1. However, the consolidated financial statements will look exactly the same regardless of whether the parent used the cost method or the equity method in its internal records.

The parent can choose any method to account for its investment for internal purposes. In most cases, it will use the cost method because it is simple and involves little effort. However, if the entity wants to capture its share of the income earned by the subsidiary without having to prepare consolidated financial statements, the equity method should be used. Since net income under the equity method should be equal to consolidated net income attributable to the parent's shareholders, the results from the equity method should be compared to the consolidated financial statements to ensure that no errors have been made. In the end, it is a cost-benefit decision. The equity method should be used for internal purposes only if the benefits derived from the information provided exceed the extra cost involved in using this method.

Consolidated Income and Retained Earnings Statements

Before examining the details for preparing consolidated income and retained earnings statements,[2] it is useful to outline the overall consolidation process. Just as a consolidated balance sheet is prepared basically by combining, on an item-by-item basis, the assets and liabilities of the parent and the subsidiary, the consolidated income statement is prepared by combining, on an item-by-item basis, the revenues and expenses of the two companies. The parent's investment does not appear on the consolidated balance sheet, and some of the subsidiary's assets and liabilities are revalued to reflect the fair values used in the consolidation process. In a similar manner, the parent's investment income from its subsidiary does not appear on the consolidated income statement, and some of the expenses of the subsidiary are revalued to reflect the amortizations and impairments of the fair values being used in the consolidated balance sheet. Except for the eliminations and adjustments that are required, the whole consolidation process is basically one of combining the components of financial statements. No preparation is required for the consolidated retained earnings statement when the parent has used the equity method.

The investment income from subsidiary is replaced by the subsidiary's revenues and expenses on a line-by-line basis.

---

[2] IAS 1: Presentation of Financial Statements requires a Statement of Changes in Equity as part of the complete set of financial statements. It does not require a Statement of Retained Earnings. However, the Statement of Changes in Equity does provide a reconciliation between the carrying amount of each component of equity at the beginning and the end of the period. Retained earnings is one of those components. In this textbook, we will the use the Statement of Retained Earnings as a surrogate for the retained earnings component of the Statement of Changes in Equity.

We commence our discussion of the preparation of the consolidated income statement by describing the make-up of the bottom line: consolidated net income. Consolidated net income for any fiscal year is made up of the following:

The net income of the parent from its own operations		
(i.e., excluding any income resulting from its investment in the subsidiary)		$ XXX
plus:	**the net income of the subsidiary**	XXX
less:	**the amortization and impairment of the acquisition differential**	(XXX)
equals:	**consolidated net income**	$ XXX
Attributable to		
	Shareholders of parent company	$ XXX
	Non-controlling interest	XXX

The amortization of the acquisition differential is reflected on the consolidated financial statements — not on the subsidiary's financial statements.

Take, for example, a 100-percent-owned subsidiary that was purchased at book value (i.e., no acquisition differential and no fair value–book value differences). Consolidated net income will be made up of the sum of the parent's and the subsidiary's net incomes. If the subsidiary was purchased at a price greater than book value, the subsidiary's net income will not be correct from a consolidated-single-entity point of view because the subsidiary's expenses have not been measured using amortizations of the fair values being used in the consolidated balance sheet. Therefore, the third component — the amortization and impairment of the acquisition differential — must be deducted in determining consolidated net income.

The acquisition differential is amortized or written off on consolidation as if the parent had purchased these net assets directly.

The acquisition differential is allocated to revalue the assets and liabilities of the subsidiary for consolidated purposes. It must be amortized or written off for consolidation purposes to reflect the use, impairment, or sale of the underlying net assets. The amount amortized or written off is calculated in the same way as if these items were owned directly by the parent. The acquisition differential related to long-term assets with definite useful lives (such as buildings, equipment, and patents) is amortized over the useful lives of these assets. Inventory is not amortized, but is reflected on the income statement as cost of goods sold expense when it is sold. The amount allocated to land is not amortized and its cost is reflected as a charge on the income statement only when it is sold. Goodwill and certain other intangible assets are also not amortized, but instead a loss is reflected on the income statement when a test indicates that they are impaired. Testing for impairment is explained in more detail in the following section.

All of these charges against consolidated income will collectively be referred to as "the amortization of the acquisition differential," even though technically some of them are impairments and not really amortizations. In the same manner, the balances not yet written off for consolidation purposes will be referred to as the "unamortized acquisition differential."

The parent's separate-entity retained earnings accounted for under the equity method should always be equal to consolidated retained earnings.

Consolidated retained earnings on the date of acquisition is the parent's retained earnings only. The changes in consolidated retained earnings subsequent to acquisition consist of the yearly consolidated net incomes attributable to the parent less the yearly dividends declared by the parent. Dividends paid or declared by a subsidiary company do not appear on the consolidated statement of changes in equity. When dividends are paid by a 100-percent-owned subsidiary, the subsidiary's cash decreases and the parent's cash increases, but the single entity's cash remains unchanged, as does the shareholders' equity of the entity.

Testing Goodwill and Other Intangibles for Impairment

Starting in 2001, goodwill and certain intangible assets were no longer amortized but tested for impairment on an annual basis.

Prior to July 1, 2001, Canadian GAAP required that any goodwill recognized as a result of a business combination had to be amortized over its estimated useful life, which could not exceed 40 years. This resulted in substantial reductions to reported earnings due to yearly goodwill amortization. On July 1, 2001, new rules were introduced. They provided more workable guidelines for the recognition and measurement of intangibles other than goodwill and, in addition, replaced the annual amortization of goodwill with periodic reviews for impairment. In addition, extensive guidelines were provided for the impairment testing of all long-lived assets including intangibles.

An asset is impaired if its carrying amount exceeds its recoverable amount.

In 2011, the old *Handbook* sections will be replaced by *Handbook* — Part I, which contains IFRSs. IAS 36: Impairment of Assets applies to all assets unless they are specifically excluded because of special rules in another standard. It prescribes the procedures that an entity applies to ensure that its assets are carried at no more than their recoverable amount. It indicates that an asset, a group of assets, or a cash-generating unit should be written down if its carrying amount exceeds the amount to be recovered through use or sale of the asset. The write-down is called an impairment loss and is reported in net income unless the asset is carried at a revalued amount in accordance with another standard (e.g., in accordance with the revaluation model in IAS 16). Any impairment loss of a revalued asset must be treated as a revaluation decrease in accordance with that other standard.

Recoverable amount is the higher of fair value less cost to sell and value in use.

Recoverable amount is defined as the higher of fair value less costs to sell and value in use. *Fair value* is the amount obtainable from the sale in an arm's-length transaction between knowledgeable, willing parties. It can be determined by using quoted market prices, if available, or by making comparisons with the prices of other similar assets. *Value in use* is the present value of the future cash flows expected to be derived from the asset or group of assets.

It may not be necessary to measure both fair value less costs to sell and value in use when testing for impairment. If it is determined that one of these values is higher than the carrying amount, then the asset is not impaired and the other value need not be determined. Sometimes, it will not be possible to determine fair value less costs to sell because there is no basis for making a reliable estimate of the amount obtainable from the sale of the asset in an arm's-length transaction between knowledgeable, willing parties. In this case, the entity may use the asset's value in use as its recoverable amount. When an asset is being held for disposal, most of its value in use will consist of the net disposal proceeds to be received in the near term, and future cash flows from continuing use of the asset until its disposal are likely to be negligible. As a result, the fair value less costs to sell would be very similar to value in use and it would be unnecessary to explicitly determine a value in use.

Impairment testing requires the estimation of future net cash flows (cash inflows less cash outflows) associated with an individual asset. In many instances, it is impossible to associate cash flows with a single asset, and so the standard suggests that it should be accomplished with a cash-generating unit, which is defined as the smallest identifiable group of assets that generates cash inflows that are largely independent of the cash inflows from other assets or groups of assets. In the ensuing discussion on impairment testing, any reference to an individual asset is equally applicable to an individual asset or a cash-generating unit.

It is possible for an asset not to be impaired at the subsidiary level but to be impaired at the consolidated level.

In this chapter, we will discuss impairment at the level of the consolidated financial statements. Although the principles of impairment testing are the same whether it is applied at the consolidated level or at the separate-entity level, the results could be different. For example, a subsidiary could determine that there is no impairment of its assets based on the carrying amounts used in its separate-entity statements. Since the values used on the consolidated statements are often reported at a higher amount than the separate-entity statements because of the acquisition differential, there could be an impairment at the consolidated level.

IAS 36 has different rules and procedures for impairment testing for the following types of intangible assets:

- Intangible assets with definite useful lives
- Intangible assets with indefinite useful lives or not yet available for use
- Cash-generating units and goodwill

We will discuss these three different groups separately in the following sections.

Intangible Assets with Definite Useful Lives

The reporting requirements for intangible assets with definite useful lives are similar to what is required for tangible capital assets. These assets should be amortized over their useful lives. At the end of each reporting period, there is a two-step approach to determining whether an impairment loss should be reported. In step 1, the entity assesses whether there is any indication that an asset may be impaired. If any such indication exists, then step 2 must be performed and the recoverable amount must be determined. If no such indication exists, then it is not necessary to perform step 2.

The recoverable amount needs to be determined only if there is an indication that the asset may be impaired.

In step 2, the recoverable amount is determined and compared to carrying amount. If the recoverable amount is greater than the carrying amount, no impairment exists and the asset is reported at the carrying amount. If the recoverable amount is less than the carrying amount, an impairment exists and the asset is written down to its recoverable amount.

The following factors should be considered at a minimum when assessing whether there is an indication of impairment:

Internal and external factors are considered when assessing if there is an indication that the asset may be impaired.

External Factors	Internal Factors
An asset's market value has declined significantly.	There is evidence of obsolescence or physical damage of an asset.
Significant adverse changes in the technological, market, economic, or legal environment of the entity have occurred.	There have been significant adverse changes in how an asset is used or expected to be used.
A significant increase in market rates of return has occurred that will cause a reduction to value in use.	Evidence has arisen that the economic performance of an asset is, or will be, worse than expected.
The carrying amount of the net assets of the entity is more than its market capitalization.	The carrying amount of the investment in subsidiary in the separate-entity financial statements exceeds the carrying amounts in the consolidated financial statements of the investee's net assets, including associated goodwill.
	The dividend from the subsidiary exceeds the total comprehensive income of the subsidiary.

Intangible Assets with Indefinite Useful Lives

An intangible asset that is not subject to amortization is tested for impairment annually (step 2 above).

Intangible assets with indefinite[3] useful lives are not amortized but must be assessed for impairment on an annual basis regardless of whether there is any indication that it may be impaired. In other words, step 1 as mentioned in the previous section is ignored and step 2 must be performed. This same rule is applied to an intangible asset that is not yet available for use.

This impairment test may be performed at any time during an annual period, provided it is performed at the same time every year. Different intangible assets may be tested for impairment at different times. However, if such an intangible asset was initially recognized during the current annual period, that intangible asset must be tested for impairment before the end of the current annual period.

In exceptional circumstances, the entity can use the recoverable amount from a preceding period rather than determining a new recoverable amount this period. This cost-saving measure may be used provided all of the following criteria are met:

(a) If the intangible asset does not generate cash inflows from continuing use that are largely independent of those from other assets or groups of assets and is therefore tested for impairment as part of the cash-generating unit to which it belongs, the assets and liabilities making up that unit have not changed significantly since the most recent recoverable amount calculation.

(b) The most recent recoverable amount calculation resulted in an amount that exceeded the asset's carrying amount by a substantial margin.

(c) Based on an analysis of events that have occurred and circumstances that have changed since the most recent recoverable amount calculation, the likelihood that a current recoverable amount determination would be less than the asset's carrying amount is remote.

Cash-generating Units and Goodwill

Goodwill is tested for impairment annually at the cash-generating unit level.

Cash-generating units that have goodwill assigned to them must be assessed for impairment on an annual basis and whenever there is an indication that the unit may be impaired. In identifying individual cash-generating units, the entity must consider whether the cash inflows from an asset (or group of assets) are largely independent of the cash inflows from other assets (or groups of assets). Various factors should be considered, such as how management monitors the entity's operations, i.e., by product lines, businesses, individual locations, districts, or regional areas, or by how management makes decisions about continuing or disposing of the entity's assets and operations. The following example from IAS 36 illustrates the application of this requirement.

A bus company provides services under contract with a municipality that requires minimum service on each of five separate routes. Assets devoted to each route and the cash flows from each route can be identified separately. One of the routes operates at a significant loss. Because the entity does not have the option to curtail any one bus route, the lowest level of identifiable cash inflows that are largely independent of the cash inflows from other assets or groups of assets is the cash

---

[3] *Indefinite* does not necessarily mean an infinite life, but rather one that extends beyond the foreseeable future.

inflows generated by the five routes together. The cash-generating unit for each route is the bus company as a whole.

Goodwill is recorded only when it is purchased as part of a business combination. At the date of acquisition, goodwill should be allocated to each of the acquirer's cash-generating units or groups of cash-generating units that is expected to benefit from the synergies of the combination, regardless of whether other assets or liabilities of the acquiree are assigned to those units or groups of units. Each unit or group of units to which the goodwill is so allocated shall

(a) represent the lowest level within the entity at which the goodwill is monitored for internal management purposes; and

(b) not be larger than an operating segment determined in accordance with IFRS 8: Operating Segments.[4]

At the date of acquisition, the total value of the subsidiary is segregated by cash-generating units.

The process of allocating goodwill to the cash-generating units is as follows:

- The total value of the subsidiary is allocated to cash-generating units.
- The fair value of the subsidiary's individual net assets is also allocated to each cash-generating unit. This will become carrying amount (amortized) when impairment tests are performed later.
- For each cash-generating unit, the allocated value is compared with the parent's share of the fair value of the unit's identifiable net assets.
- The difference is the goodwill of the cash-generating unit.
- The sum of each cash-generating unit's goodwill equals the total acquisition goodwill.

Individual assets should be tested for impairment before each cash-generating unit is tested for impairment.

Each year, starting with the year of acquisition, goodwill is tested for impairment. At the time of impairment testing of a cash-generating unit to which goodwill has been allocated, there may be an indication of an impairment of an asset within the unit containing the goodwill. In such circumstances, the entity tests the individual asset for impairment first, and recognizes any impairment loss for that asset before testing for impairment of the cash-generating unit containing the goodwill. In other words, the impairment of procedures are applied at the single asset level first and the cash-generating unit levels last.

In some cases, the entity as a whole would be the lowest level at which goodwill is monitored. If so, goodwill would be assessed for impairment at the level of the entity as a whole. Unless otherwise noted, the examples used in the body of the text and in the end-of-chapter material will assume that goodwill is assessed for impairment at the level of the entity as a whole. When information is available to test for impairment at lower levels, then the tests should be performed at the lower level.

The recoverable amount is compared to the carrying amount of net assets for each cash-generating unit.

To test goodwill for impairment, the recoverable amount of each cash-generating unit is compared with its carrying amount, including goodwill. If the recoverable amount exceeds the carrying amount, goodwill is not impaired. If the recoverable amount is less than the carrying amount, an impairment loss should be recognized and should be allocated to reduce the carrying amount of the assets of the unit (group of units) in the following order:

---

[4] IFRS 8: Operating Segments is discussed in more detail in Chapter 9.

Any impairment loss is applied first to goodwill and then to other assets.

(a) First, to reduce the carrying amount of any goodwill allocated to the cash-generating unit; and

(b) Then, to the other assets of the unit pro rata on the basis of the carrying amount of each asset in the unit.

However, an entity shall not reduce the carrying amount of an individual asset below the higher of its recoverable amount and zero. The amount of the impairment loss that could not be allocated to an individual asset because of this limitation must be allocated pro rata to the other assets of the unit (group of units).

From now on in this textbook, we will assume, unless otherwise stated, that the recoverable amount for the entity as a whole is greater than the fair value of identifiable net assets at each reporting date. As such, any impairment loss for the entity as a whole would be allocated entirely to goodwill as per (a) above. This will avoid having to provide detailed information for each problem on recoverable amounts and fair value for individual assets, cash-generating units, and the entity as a whole. Instead, we will simply indicate the goodwill impairment loss or the recoverable amount for goodwill by itself.

The most recent detailed calculation made in a preceding period of the recoverable amount of a cash-generating unit to which goodwill has been allocated may be used in the impairment test of that unit in the current period provided that

(a) there is very little change in the make-up of the assets and liabilities of the cash-generating unit since the most recent recoverable amount determination, and

(b) the most recent recoverable amount determination yielded an amount that substantially exceeded the carrying amount of the unit, and

(c) based on analyzing events since the most recent recoverable amount determination, the likelihood that a current recoverable amount determination would be less than the carrying amount of the unit is remote.

The impairment tests are complex and often require considerable professional judgment.

The discontinuance of the amortization of goodwill, and the subsequent introduction of complex impairment-testing rules for goodwill and all other tangible and intangible assets, has added a new and complex valuation exercise to the consolidation process. The determination of recoverable amounts will be a costly one for many companies and their auditors, requiring the yearly services of business valuation specialists. The large auditing firms will no doubt have business valuators on board as part of their audit staff, but smaller audit firms will have to hire outside valuators if any of their clients prepare consolidated statements.

Reversing an Impairment Loss

Impairment losses on intangible assets other than goodwill can be reversed.

An impairment loss recognized in a prior period for an asset or a cash-generating unit other than goodwill can be reversed under certain conditions. A two-step process is followed, similar to the process followed for the initial recognition of impairment losses. In step 1, an entity assesses whether there is any indication that an impairment loss may no longer exist or may have decreased. If any such indication exists, then step 2 must be performed and the recoverable amount must be determined. If no such indication exists, then it is not necessary to perform step 2.

Indications of a potential decrease in an impairment loss are basically the same as the indications of a potential impairment loss, which were described earlier.

If there is an indication that an impairment loss may no longer exist or may have decreased, this may indicate that the remaining useful life, the depreciation method, or the residual value may need to be reviewed and adjusted in accordance with the IFRS applicable to the asset, even if no impairment loss is reversed for the asset.

An impairment loss shall be reversed if, and only if, there has been a change in the estimates used to determine the asset's recoverable amount. An impairment loss is not reversed when the recoverable amount increases due strictly to the passage of time; i.e., the present value of future cash inflows increases as they become closer to occurring.

The reversal of an impairment loss is reported in net income unless the asset is carried at a revalued amount in accordance with another standard (e.g., in accordance with the revaluation model in IAS 16). Any reversal of an impairment loss of a revalued asset shall be treated as a revaluation increase in accordance with that other standard. The assets should not be written up to an amount exceeding the carrying amount that would have been determined had no impairment loss been recognized for the asset in prior years.

> **The asset cannot be written up to an amount higher than it would have been if impairment losses had not been recognized.**

A reversal of an impairment loss for a cash-generating unit must be allocated to the assets of the unit pro rata with the carrying amount of those assets. An impairment loss relating to goodwill must not be reversed. Any increase in the recoverable amount of goodwill is likely to be an increase in internally generated goodwill, rather than a reversal of the impairment loss recognized for the acquired goodwill. IAS 38 prohibits the recognition of internally generated goodwill.

Disclosure Requirements

The disclosure requirements related to impairment of assets are quite extensive. The following summarizes the main requirements:

> **Substantial information relating to impairment losses and reversals of impairment losses must be disclosed.**

- For each class of assets, the amount of impairment losses and reversals of impairment losses segregated by what amounts are recognized in net income versus other comprehensive income;

- For each major impairment loss recognized or reversed related to individual assets, the events and circumstances that led to the recognition or reversal, whether the recoverable amount is its fair value less costs to sell or value in use; the basis used to determine fair value less costs to sell; and the discount rate(s) used in determining value in use; and

- For cash-generating units or intangible assets with indefinite lives, the carrying amount of goodwill and of intangible assets with indefinite useful lives allocated to the unit, the basis used in determining recoverable amount, a description of key assumptions on which management has based its cash flow projections, and the methodology used to determine fair value less costs to sell.

AkzoNobel N. V., with headquarters in the Netherlands, is the world's largest global paints and coatings company. It reported impairment losses on intangible assets of €1,296 million in its 2008 financial statements. Excerpts from these statements are presented in Exhibit 5.1.

Exhibit 5.1

EXTRACTS (IN PART) FROM AKZONOBEL'S 2008 FINANCIAL STATEMENTS

1. Summary of significant accounting policies

Impairment of intangible assets and property, plant and equipment (note 9)

Recoverable amounts are based on strategic plans and estimates of future cash flows.

We assess whether the carrying values of intangible assets and of property, plant and equipment are recoverable. In this assessment, we make significant judgments and estimates to determine if the future cash flows expected to be generated by those assets are less than their carrying value. The data necessary for the impairment tests are based on our strategic plans and our estimates of future cash flows, which require estimating revenue growth rates and profit margins. The estimated cash flows are discounted using a net present value technique with business-specific discount rates.

Impairments of intangible assets and property, plant and equipment (note 9)

We assess the carrying value of intangible assets and property, plant and equipment whenever events or changes in circumstances indicate that the carrying amount of an asset may not be recoverable. In addition, for goodwill and other intangible assets with an indefinite useful life, we review the carrying value annually in the fourth quarter.

Impairment tests are performed at the business unit level, which is one level below the segment level.

The recoverable amount of an asset or its cash-generating unit is the greater of its value in use and its fair value less costs to sell, whereby estimated future cash flows are discounted to their present value. The discount rate used reflects current market assessments of the time value of money and, if appropriate, the risks specific to the assets. If the carrying value of an asset or its cash-generating unit exceeds its estimated recoverable amount, an impairment loss is recognized in the statement of income. The assessment for impairment is performed at the lowest level of assets generating largely independent cash inflows which we have determined to be at business unit level (one level below segment). We allocate impairment losses in respect of cash-generating units first to goodwill and then to the carrying amount of the other assets on a pro rata basis.

Except for goodwill, we reverse impairment losses if and to the extent we have identified a change in estimates used to determine the recoverable amount. We only reverse to the extent that the carrying value of the asset does not exceed the carrying value that would have been determined, net of amortization or depreciation, if no impairment loss had been recognized. Reversals of impairment are recognized in the statement of income.

9. Intangible assets

IN € MILLIONS	TOTAL	GOODWILL	BRANDS	CUSTOMER LISTS	OTHER INTANGIBLES
Balance at January 1, 2008					
Cost of acquisition	784	502	104	110	68
Cost of internally developed intangibles	12	—	—	—	12
Accumulated amortization/impairment	(127)	(39)	(3)	(40)	(45)
Carrying value	**669**	**463**	**101**	**70**	**35**
Changes in carrying value					
Acquisitions through business combinations[1]	8,315	4,485	2,344	1,181	305
Other investments – including internally developed	55	10	—	2	43
Divestments	(12)	(3)	(6)	(3)	—
Amortization	(159)	—	(18)	(101)	(40)
Impairments	(1,296)	(1,215)	(79)	(2)	—
Changes in exchange rates	(400)	(176)	(195)	(33)	4
Total changes	**6,503**	**3,101**	**2,046**	**1,044**	**312**

[1] *Mainly ICI. Goodwill included €551 million due to hedge activities for the acquisition of ICI.*

(continued)

Balance at December 31, 2008

Cost of acquisitions	8,667	4,822	2,247	1,253	345
Cost of internally developed intangibles	32	—	—	—	32
Accumulated amortization/impairment	(1,527)	(1,258)	(100)	(139)	(30)
Carrying value	**7,172**	**3,564**	**2,147**	**1,114**	**347**

Other intangibles include licenses, know-how, intellectual property rights and development cost. Both at year-end 2008 and 2007, there were no purchase commitments for individual intangible assets. Neither were there any intangible assets registered as security for bank loans.

Impairment of ICI intangibles

Due to lower growth rates, the goodwill impairment loss was more than €1.2 billion in 2008.

Goodwill and other intangibles with indefinite useful lives are tested, per business unit (one level below segment level), for impairment in the fourth quarter or whenever an impairment trigger exists. As a consequence of the current market conditions and the continuing lack of visibility of future global demand, we have assessed the recoverable amount of our assets against lower growth rates which we now expect. This resulted in a non-cash impairment charge of €1.2 billion after tax, covering the value of ICI intangibles (mainly goodwill) related to the Decorative Paints (€0.8 billion) and National Starch businesses (€0.4 billion).

The impairment test is based on cash flow projections of the five-year operational plan as approved by the Board of Management. The key assumptions used in the projections are:

- Revenue growth: based on actual experience, an analysis of market growth and the expected development of market share
- Margin development: based on actual experience and management's long-term projections.

Revenue growth and margin development projections are extrapolated beyond this five-year explicit forecast period for another five years with reduced growth rates, except for the emerging markets. The average of the revenue growth rates used for the explicit forecast period, respectively the subsequent five-year period amount to:

Growth rates are expected to decrease in the last half of the decade.

Average revenue growth rates per forecast period per segment

	IN %/YEAR	
	2009–2013	2014–2018
Decorative Paints	4.1	3.6
Performance Coatings	6.1	3.2
Specialty Chemicals	3.5	2.4

For almost all business units, a terminal value was calculated using a long-term average market growth rate that did not exceed 2 percent.

The estimated post-tax cash flows are discounted to their present value using an adjusted post-tax weighted average cost of capital. The discount rates are determined for each business unit and range from 7.3 percent to 11.2 percent, with an average of 8.1 percent.

The outcome of a sensitivity analysis was that reasonably possible adverse changes in key assumptions of 100 basispoints (lower growth rates and higher discount rates respectively) would not result in significant other conclusions for the impairment test for businesses not affected by the current impairment charge.

Source: AkzoNobel 2008 Financial Statements. © AkzoNobel.

Now that we have seen how to test for impairment, we will illustrate the preparation of consolidated financial statements subsequent to the date of acquisition. The first illustrations assume that the subsidiary is 100 percent owned. Later illustrations will assume a less than 100-percent-owned subsidiary.

Consolidation of a 100-Percent-Owned Subsidiary

Company P purchased 100 percent of the outstanding common shares of Company S on January 1, Year 1, for $19,000. On that date Company S's common shares had a value of $10,000 and its retained earnings balance was $6,000. The inventory of Company S had a fair value that was $2,000 greater than book value, and the book values of all other assets and liabilities of Company S were equal to fair values. Any goodwill will be tested yearly for impairment. Both companies have a December 31 year-end. The journal entry made by Company P to record the acquisition of 100 percent of Company S was as follows:

Investment in S	19,000	
Cash		19,000

There is no compelling reason for Company P to prepare a consolidated balance sheet on acquisition date; however, it is useful to illustrate its preparation as the starting point for the preparation of consolidated statements in subsequent years. The calculation and allocation of the acquisition differential is shown in Exhibit 5.2.

Below are the individual balance sheets of Company P and Company S on January 1, Year 1, along with Company P's consolidated balance sheet prepared using the *direct approach*.

BALANCE SHEETS — January 1, Year 1

	Company P	Company S	Consolidated
Assets (miscellaneous)	$139,000	$17,000	$156,000
Inventory	22,000	10,000	34,000
Investment in S	19,000	—	—
Goodwill	—	—	1,000
	$180,000	$27,000	$191,000
Liabilities	$ 45,000	$11,000	$ 56,000
Common shares	50,000	10,000	50,000
Retained earnings	85,000	6,000	85,000
	$180,000	$27,000	$191,000

The investment account is replaced by the carrying value of the subsidiary's assets and liabilities plus the acquisition differential.

Exhibit 5.2

COMPANY P
CALCULATION OF ACQUISITION DIFFERENTIAL
January 1, Year 1

The purchase price comprises the carrying value of the subsidiary's assets and liabilities plus the acquisition differential.

Cost of 100 percent of Company S		$19,000
Book value of Company S's net assets		
Assets	$27,000	
Liabilities	(11,000)	
		16,000
Acquisition differential		3,000
Allocated:	FV – BV	
Inventory	2,000	2,000 **(a)**
Balance — goodwill		$ 1,000 **(b)**

The consolidated balance sheet was prepared by eliminating the shareholders' equity of Company S ($16,000) against Company P's investment account ($19,000) and then by allocating the resultant acquisition differential ($3,000) to the inventory of Company S ($2,000), with the unallocated balance recorded as goodwill ($1,000).

The consolidation process is becoming increasingly more complicated as we proceed from one chapter to the next. To make it easier to follow the consolidation adjustments, a referencing system will be adopted for subsequent illustrations in the book and starting with Exhibit 5.4. The references will be placed either after the account name or before the dollar figure to which they relate. The references will look something like this, (1b), which means that we are referring to item "b" in Exhibit 1 for this chapter.

Consolidated Statements, End of Year 1

On December 31, Year 1, Company S reported a net income of $7,300 for the year and paid a cash dividend of $2,500. Company P's net income for the year was $18,300 at this time (not including income from its investment in Company S). Using the cost method to account for its investment, Company P makes a single entry to record the dividend received from Company S on December 31, Year 1, as follows:

The cost method records income when dividends are received or receivable.

Cash	2,500	
Dividend income		2,500
Dividend received from Company S		

Company P adds the dividend income ($2,500) to its earnings from its own operations ($18,300) and reports a final net income for Year 1 of $20,800. An impairment test on goodwill conducted on December 31, Year 1, indicated that a $50 loss had occurred.

The financial statements of Company P and Company S as at December 31, Year 1, are presented in Exhibit 5.3.

Before beginning to prepare the consolidated financial statements, Company P prepares Exhibit 5.4, which shows the amortization of the acquisition differential for Year 1. This schedule and the financial statements of the two companies shown in Exhibit 5.3 form the basis for the preparation of Company P's Year 1 consolidated statements.

The details of the Year 1 amortizations are explained as follows:

The acquisition differential related to inventory is expensed when the inventory is sold.

1. The inventory of Company S was revalued for consolidated purposes on January 1, Year 1, to reflect its fair value. If we assume that Company S uses a FIFO cost-flow,[5] it would be safe to assume that this inventory was sold during Year 1. Since the cost of sales of Company S does not reflect the $2,000 additional cost, cost of sales on the Year 1 consolidated income statement will be increased by $2,000 to reflect all of this.

2. An impairment test on goodwill conducted on December 31, Year 1, indicated that a $50 loss had occurred.

3. The $1,000 goodwill is not reflected in the financial statements of Company S, nor is the impairment loss. The consolidated income statement will have to reflect this loss, and at December 31, Year 1, the consolidated balance sheet will have to show the balance not written off.

---

[5] Since LIFO is no longer acceptable under Canadian GAAP, we will assume a FIFO cost flow in all examples.

Exhibit 5.3

YEAR 1 INCOME STATEMENT

The parent's income from its own operations is $20,800 − $2,500 = $18,300.

	Company P	Company S
Sales	$ 50,000	$ 30,000
Dividend income	2,500	—
Total revenue	52,500	30,000
Cost of sales	26,500	14,700
Expenses (miscellaneous)	5,200	8,000
Total expenses	31,700	22,700
Net income	$ 20,800	$ 7,300

YEAR 1 RETAINED EARNINGS STATEMENTS

	Company P	Company S
Balance, January 1	$ 85,000	$ 6,000
Net income	20,800	7,300
	105,800	13,300
Dividends	6,000	2,500
Balance, December 31	$ 99,800	$ 10,800

BALANCE SHEETS — December 31, Year 1

The investment account remains at the original cost in the parent's separate-entity balance sheet.

	Company P	Company S
Assets (misc.)	$147,800	$ 18,300
Inventory	30,000	14,000
Investment in S (cost method)	19,000	—
	$196,800	$ 32,300
Liabilities	$ 47,000	$ 11,500
Common shares	50,000	10,000
Retained earnings	99,800	10,800
	$196,800	$ 32,300

Exhibit 5.4

ACQUISITION-DIFFERENTIAL AMORTIZATION AND IMPAIRMENT SCHEDULE

The amortization and impairment of the acquisition differential will be recorded on the consolidated financial statements.

	Balance Jan. 1, Year 1	Amortization and Impairment Year 1	Balance Dec. 31, Year 1
Inventory **(2a)**	$2,000	$2,000	$ — **(a)**
Goodwill **(2b)**	1,000	50	950 **(b)**
	$3,000	$2,050	$950 **(c)**

Using the schedule we introduced on page 174, we make the following calculation:

CALCULATION OF CONSOLIDATED NET INCOME — Year 1

This calculation starts with income under the cost method and converts it to consolidated net income.

Company P net income — cost method		$20,800
Less dividend income from Company S		2,500
Company P net income, own operations		18,300
Company S net income	7,300	
Acquisition-differential amortization and impairment **(4c)**	(2,050)	5,250
Consolidated net income		$23,550

Exhibit 5.5		

Year 1 Consolidated Financial Statements
(direct approach)

COMPANY P
CONSOLIDATED INCOME STATEMENT
for the Year Ended December 31, Year 1

Consolidated net income is the same regardless of whether the parent used the cost method or the equity method in its separate-entity records.	Sales (50,000 + 30,000)	$ 80,000
	Cost of sales (26,500 + 14,700 + **(4a) 2,000**)	43,200
	Goodwill impairment loss (0 + 0 + **(4b) 50**)	50
	Expenses (misc.) (5,200 + 8,000)	13,200
		56,450
	Net income	$ 23,550

COMPANY P
CONSOLIDATED STATEMENT OF RETAINED EARNINGS
for the Year Ended December 31, Year 1

Dividends on the consolidated statement of retained earnings are the dividends of the parent.	Balance, January 1	$ 85,000
	Net income	23,550
		108,550
	Dividends	6,000
	Balance, December 31	$102,550

COMPANY P
CONSOLIDATED BALANCE SHEET
December 31, Year 1

The consolidated balance sheet accounts are the same regardless of whether the parent used the cost method or the equity method in its separate-entity records.	Assets (misc.) (147,800 + 18,300)	$166,100
	Inventory (30,000 + 14,000)	44,000
	Goodwill (0 + 0 + **(4b) 950**)	950
		$211,050
	Liabilities (47,000 + 11,500)	$ 58,500
	Common shares	50,000
	Retained earnings	102,550
		$211,050

Note that dividend income from Company S is not included in consolidated net income. The consolidated income statement is prepared by excluding the dividend income and adding the revenues and expenses of the two companies.

The amortization/impairment of the various components of the acquisition differential are reflected on the consolidated financial statements.

The preparation of the Year 1 consolidated financial statements is shown in Exhibit 5.5. The consolidated amounts were determined by adding the amounts shown in brackets. These amounts came from the financial statements of Company P and Company S and from the acquisition-differential amortization and impairment schedule.

Note the bracketed amounts shown for goodwill impairment loss and for the goodwill on the balance sheet. The two zero amounts indicate that these items do not appear in the financial statements of Company P and Company S.

The Year 1 consolidated retained earnings statement is prepared using the January 1 retained earnings of Company P, consolidated net income attributable to Company P, and Company P's dividends. Only Company P's retained earnings is included on January 1 because, as we learned in Chapter 3, consolidated retained earnings at the date of acquisition consists only of the parent's retained earnings. Only the parent's dividends are included on the consolidated statement of retained earnings because only the parent's dividends were paid to shareholders outside of the consolidated entity. The subsidiary's dividends were received by the parent and were not paid to anyone outside of the consolidated entity and are therefore eliminated when preparing the consolidated financial statements.

The underlying assets and liabilities of the subsidiary plus the unamortized acquisition differential replace the investment account.

The parent's investment account does not appear on the consolidated balance sheet. Consolidated shareholders' equity contains the capital stock accounts of the parent and retained earnings from the consolidated retained earnings statement. The net assets of the parent are combined with the net assets of the subsidiary revalued with the unamortized acquisition differential.

Consolidated Statements, End of Year 2

On December 31, Year 2, Company S reported a net income of $10,000 for the year and paid a cash dividend of $3,000. Company P's net income for the year was $19,000 at this time (not including income from its investment in Company S). An impairment test conducted on December 31, Year 2, indicated that the goodwill had a recoverable amount of $870. As a result, a loss of $80 has occurred.

On December 31, Year 2, Company P makes the following cost-method journal entry:

Cash	3,000	
Dividend income		3,000
Dividend received by Company S		

The dividend income ($3,000) combined with the previous operating earnings ($19,000) gives Company P a final net income for Year 2 of $22,000.

The financial statements of the two companies as at December 31, Year 2, are presented in Exhibit 5.6 on page 188.

The acquisition-differential amortization and impairment schedule at the end of Year 2 is shown in Exhibit 5.7 on page 188.

Because Company P has used the cost method, it is necessary to make two preliminary calculations before preparing the consolidated income statement and retained earnings statement. We first calculate consolidated net income for Year 2, as follows:

Only the Year 2 amortization of the acquisition differential is deducted when calculating consolidated net income for Year 2.

Company P net income — cost method		$22,000
Less: dividend income from Company S		3,000
Company P net income, own operations		19,000
Company S net income	10,000	
Acquisition-differential amortization **(7c)**	(80)	9,920
Consolidated net income		$28,920
Attributable to		
Shareholders of Company P		$28,920
Non-controlling interest		0

Exhibit 5.6

YEAR 2 INCOME STATEMENTS

	Company P	Company S
Sales	$ 60,000	$40,000
Dividend income	3,000	—
Total revenue	63,000	40,000
Cost of sales	32,000	18,000
Expenses (misc.)	9,000	12,000
Total expenses	41,000	30,000
Net income	$ 22,000	$10,000

The parent's income includes dividend income from the subsidiary, which can be reconciled to dividends paid by the subsidiary.

YEAR 2 RETAINED EARNINGS STATEMENTS

	Company P	Company S
Balance, January 1	$ 99,800	$10,800
Net income	22,000	10,000
	121,800	20,800
Dividends	8,000	3,000
Balance, December 31	$113,800	$17,800

BALANCE SHEETS — December 31, Year 2

	Company P	Company S
Assets (misc.)	$131,800	$21,000
Inventory	35,000	16,000
Investment in S (cost method)	19,000	—
	$185,800	$37,000
Liabilities	$ 22,000	$ 9,200
Common shares	50,000	10,000
Retained earnings	113,800	17,800
	$185,800	$37,000

The investment account still remains at the original cost.

Exhibit 5.7

ACQUISITION-DIFFERENTIAL AMORTIZATION AND IMPAIRMENT SCHEDULE

The amortization of the acquisition differential is not reflected in the investment account when the parent uses the cost method.

	Balance Jan. 1, Year 1	Amort. & Impair. to end of Year 1	Balance Dec. 31, Year 1	Amort. & Impair. Year 2	Balance Dec. 31, Year 2
Inventory **(2a)**	$2,000	$2,000	$ —	$ —	$ — **(a)**
Goodwill **(2b)**	1,000	50	950	80	870 **(b)**
	$3,000	$2,050	$950	$80	$870 **(c)**

Because we are consolidating more than one year after the date of acquisition, an additional calculation is required. Company P's retained earnings on January 1, Year 2, are not equal to consolidated retained earnings. The calculation of consolidated retained earnings as at January 1, Year 2, is as follows:

Company P retained earnings, Jan. 1, Year 2 (cost method)			$ 99,800
Company S retained earnings, Jan. 1, Year 2		10,800	
Company S retained earnings, acquisition date		6,000	
Increase since acquisition		4,800	
Acquisition-differential amortization and impairment to end of Year 1 **(7c)**		(2,050)	
		2,750	
Company P ownership		100%	2,750
Consolidated retained earnings			$102,550

This calculation converts from the cost method to the equity method at a point in time.

Retained earnings reflects the cumulative effect of all adjustments to a point in time.

The points that follow are presented as further explanation of why a calculation of this nature adjusts a parent's retained earnings under the cost method to retained earnings under the equity method. These points require careful reading, because it is very important for you to understand fully why this particular process actually works.

1. Consolidated retained earnings at acquisition date consist only of the retained earnings of the parent company. Consolidated retained earnings subsequent to the date of acquisition represent only the parent's portion of retained earnings of the combined entities. The non-controlling interest's portion of retained earnings is incorporated in non-controlling interest, which is reported in a separate line in shareholders' equity.

2. Consolidated net income attributable to the parent company in any single year since the acquisition date consists of the net income of the parent company (from its own operations), plus the parent's share of the net income of the subsidiary, less the acquisition-differential amortization for that year.

3. It should logically follow that the consolidated retained earnings balance at any time subsequent to the acquisition date must contain the parent's share of the subsidiary's net incomes earned since the acquisition date less the total of the amortization of the acquisition differential to that date.

The parent's retained earnings under the cost method includes dividend income from the subsidiary since the date of acquisition.

4. Since the parent has used the cost method for internal record-keeping, the parent's retained earnings contain only the parent's share of the dividends that the subsidiary has declared since the acquisition date.

5. The sum of net incomes less the sum of dividends — both measured from the acquisition date — equals the change (increase or decrease) in retained earnings measured from the same date.

The change in retained earnings plus cumulative dividends paid is equal to cumulative net income.

6. When we add the parent's share of the change in the retained earnings of the subsidiary to the retained earnings of the parent (which contain the parent's share of the subsidiary's dividends under the cost method), the resulting calculated amount now contains the parent's share of the subsidiary's net income earned since the date of acquisition. By deducting the parent's share of the total amortization of the acquisition differential to date from this amount, we arrive at a retained earnings number that represents the retained earnings of the parent under the equity method, which of course is equal to consolidated retained earnings.

The consolidated income statement is prepared — using the income statements of the two companies (Exhibit 5.6), the Year 2 acquisition-differential amortization and impairment schedule, and the calculation of consolidated net income for

Year 2 — by adding the revenues and expenses of the two companies, adjusting the expenses for the Year 2 amortization, excluding the dividend income, and verifying that the net income on the statement equals the calculated net income.

The consolidated financial statements present the combined position of the parent and the subsidiary as if the parent had acquired the subsidiary's assets and liabilities directly.

The consolidated retained earnings statement for Year 2 is prepared using the calculated amount for consolidated retained earnings for January 1, by adding consolidated net income and deducting the dividends of Company P.

The consolidated balance sheet is prepared in the usual manner except that the amount for retained earnings is taken from the consolidated retained earnings statement.

Exhibit 5.8 shows the preparation of the Year 2 consolidated financial statements using the direct approach.

Exhibit 5.8	**Year 2 Consolidated Financial Statements**
	(direct approach)

COMPANY P
CONSOLIDATED INCOME STATEMENT
for the Year Ended December 31, Year 2

Consolidated net income is the same regardless of whether the parent used the cost method or the equity method in its internal records.

Sales (60,000 + 40,000)	$100,000
Cost of sales (32,000 + 18,000)	50,000
Goodwill impairment loss (0 + 0 + **(7b) 80**)	80
Expenses (misc.) (9,000 + 12,000)	21,000
	71,080
Net income	$ 28,920
Attributable to	
Shareholders of Company P	$ 28,920
Non-controlling interest	0

COMPANY P
CONSOLIDATED STATEMENT OF RETAINED EARNINGS
for the Year Ended December 31, Year 2

Consolidated retained earnings is the same regardless of whether the parent used the cost method or the equity method in its internal records.

Balance, January 1	$102,550
Net income	28,920
	131,470
Dividends	8,000
Balance, December 31	$123,470

COMPANY P
CONSOLIDATED BALANCE SHEET
December 31, Year 2

The unamortized acquisition differential related to goodwill is reported on the consolidated balance sheet and is the same amount regardless of whether the parent used the cost method or the equity method in its internal records.

Assets (misc.) (131,800 + 21,000)	$152,800
Inventory (35,000 + 16,000)	51,000
Goodwill (0 + 0 + **(7b) 870**)	870
	$204,670
Liabilities (22,000 + 9,200)	$ 31,200
Common shares	50,000
Retained earnings	123,470
	$204,670

Consolidation of an 80-Percent-Owned Subsidiary — Direct Approach

We now illustrate the consolidation of Company P and its 80-percent-owned subsidiary Company S over a two-year period when the cost method has been used to account for the investment.

Assume that on January 1, Year 1, instead of purchasing 100 percent of Company S for $19,000, Company P purchased 80 percent for $15,200. All other facts about the two companies are the same as in the previous example. The journal entry of Company P on January 1, Year 1, is as follows:

Investment in S	15,200	
Cash		15,200

The calculation and allocation of the acquisition differential and the calculation of the non-controlling interest on January 1, Year 1, are shown in Exhibit 5.9.

The following are the individual balance sheets of Company P and Company S, as well as Company P's consolidated balance sheet on January 1, Year 1, prepared using the direct approach.

BALANCE SHEETS — January 1, Year 1

	Company P	Company S	Consolidated
Assets (misc.)	$142,800	$17,000	$159,800
Inventory	22,000	10,000	34,000
Investment in S	15,200	—	—
Goodwill	—	—	1,000
	$180,000	$27,000	$194,800
Liabilities	$ 45,000	$11,000	$ 56,000
Common shares	50,000	10,000	50,000
Retained earnings	85,000	6,000	85,000
Non-controlling interest	—	—	3,800
	$180,000	$27,000	$194,800

The subsidiary's assets and liabilities are brought onto the consolidated financial statements at 100 percent of their fair values.

Exhibit 5.9

COMPANY P
CALCULATION OF ACQUISITION DIFFERENTIAL
January 1, Year 1

The implied value of the subsidiary is derived by taking the purchase price and dividing by the percentage ownership acquired by the parent.

Cost of 80 percent of Company S		$15,200
Implied value of 100 percent of Company S		$19,000
Book value of Company S's net assets		
Assets	$27,000	
Liabilities	(11,000)	
		16,000
Acquisition differential		3,000
Allocated:	(FV − BV)	
Inventory	2,000	2,000 **(a)**
Balance — goodwill		$ 1,000 **(b)**

CALCULATION OF NON-CONTROLLING INTEREST — January 1, Year 1

NCI is based on the imputed fair value of the subsidiary as a whole.

Implied shareholders' equity, Company S (above)	$19,000
Non-controlling interest's ownership	20%
Non-controlling interest	$ 3,800 **(c)**

The consolidated balance sheet was prepared as follows:

1. Eliminate the investment account and Company S's shareholders' equity.

2. Add the implied acquisition differential to Company S's assets and liabilities in order to use 100 percent of the fair values for Company S's assets and liabilities.

3. Report non-controlling interest as a component of shareholders' equity at a value representing the non-controlling interest's share of Company S's implied value.

Consolidated Statements, End of Year 1

On December 31, Year 1, Company S reported a net income of $7,300 for the year and paid a cash dividend of $2,500. Company P's net income for the year was $18,300 at this time (not including income from its investment in Company S).

The cost method journal entry of Company P on December 31, Year 1, is as follows:

Dividend income is 80 percent of dividends paid by subsidiary.

Cash	2,000	
Dividend income		2,000
80% of the dividend paid by Company S		

Company P's net income for Year 1 is reported as $20,300 after the receipt of the dividend from Company S. An impairment test on goodwill conducted on December 31, Year 1, indicated that a $50 loss had occurred. The financial statements of Company P and Company S as at December 31, Year 1, are shown in Exhibit 5.10.

The Year 1 amortizations of the acquisition differential and consolidated net income must be calculated before the consolidated financial statements can be prepared. These calculations are as shown in Exhibit 5.11.

These calculations form the basis for preparing the Year 1 consolidated financial statements for both the direct and the working paper approaches (see Appendix 5A for the latter).

Exhibit 5.10

YEAR 1 INCOME STATEMENTS

	Company P	Company S	
Sales	$50,000	$30,000	
Dividend income	2,000	—	(a)
Total revenue	52,000	30,000	
Cost of sales	26,500	14,700	
Expenses (miscellaneous)	5,200	8,000	
Total expenses	31,700	22,700	
Net income	$20,300	$ 7,300	(b)

The parent's income includes dividend income from the subsidiary, which can be reconciled to dividends paid by the subsidiary.

YEAR 1 RETAINED EARNINGS STATEMENTS

	Company P	Company S	
Balance, January 1	$85,000	$ 6,000	(c)
Net income	20,300	7,300	
	105,300	13,300	
Dividends	6,000	2,500	
Balance, December 31	$99,300	$10,800	

The parent's retained earnings include the parent's income under the cost method, which includes dividend income from the subsidiary.

BALANCE SHEETS — December 31, Year 1

	Company P	Company S	
Assets (misc.)	$151,100	$18,300	
Inventory	30,000	14,000	
Investment in S (cost method)	15,200	—	
	$196,300	$32,300	
Liabilities	$ 47,000	$11,500	
Common shares	50,000	10,000	**(d)**
Retained earnings	99,300	10,800	**(e)**
	$196,300	$32,300	

These are the separate-entity balance sheets of the two legal entities.

Exhibit 5.11

ACQUISITION-DIFFERENTIAL AMORTIZATION AND IMPAIRMENT SCHEDULE

	Balance Jan. 1, Year 1	Amortization and Impairment Year 1	Balance Dec. 31, Year 1	
Inventory **(9a)**	$2,000	$2,000	$ —	**(a)**
Goodwill **(9b)**	1,000	50	950	**(b)**
	$3,000	$2,050	$950	**(c)**

This schedule reflects 100 percent of the acquisition differential, which will be attributed to the shareholders of the parent and the non-controlling interest.

CALCULATION OF CONSOLIDATED NET INCOME — Year 1

Company P net income — cost method **(10b)**		$20,300
Less: dividend income from Company S **(10a)**		2,000
Company P net income, own operations		18,300
Company S net income **(10b)**	7,300	
Less: Acquisition-differential amortization and impairment	(2,050)	
		5,250 **(d)**
Consolidated net income		$23,550 **(e)**
Attributable to		
Shareholders of Company P		$22,500 **(f)**
Non-controlling interest (20% × **(d)** 5,250)		1,050 **(g)**

Exhibit 5.12 on page 194 shows the preparation of the consolidated financial statements when the direct approach is used.

The consolidated income statement combines the income statements of the separate legal entities and incorporates consolidation adjustments for the amortization of the acquisition differential.

The consolidated income statement is prepared by combining the revenues and expenses of the two companies, adjusted for the Year 1 amortization of the acquisition differential. Company P's dividend income is excluded. The bottom portion of the consolidated income statement attributes the consolidated net income between the shareholders of the parent company and the non-controlling interest. First, the portion attributable to the non-controlling interest is calculated by multiplying the non-controlling interest's percentage ownership times the subsidiary's net income less the amortization of the acquisition differential. The portion attributable to the parent is equal to consolidated net income less the portion attributable to the non-controlling interest.

Exhibit 5.12	Year 1 Consolidated Financial Statements

Year 1 Consolidated Financial Statements
(direct approach)

COMPANY P
CONSOLIDATED INCOME STATEMENTS
for the Year Ended December 31, Year 1

Consolidated net income is attributed to the controlling shareholders and non-controlling interest.

Sales (50,000 + 30,000)	$ 80,000
Cost of sales (26,500 + 14,700 + **(11a) 2,000**)	43,200
Goodwill impairment loss (0 + 0 + **(11b) 50**)	50
Expenses (miscellaneous) (5,200 + 8,000)	13,200
	56,450
Net income	$ 23,550
Attributable to	
Shareholders of Company P **(10f)**	$ 22,500
Non-controlling interest **(10g)**	1,050

COMPANY P
CONSOLIDATED STATEMENT OF RETAINED EARNINGS
for the Year Ended December 31, Year 1

Balance, January 1	$ 85,000
Net income	22,500
	107,500
Dividends	6,000
Balance, December 31	$101,500

COMPANY P
CONSOLIDATED BALANCE SHEET
December 31, Year 1

Assets (miscellaneous) (151,100 + 18,300)	$169,400
Inventory (30,000 + 14,000)	44,000
Goodwill (0 + 0 + **(11b) 950**)	950
	$214,350
Liabilities (47,000 + 11,500)	$ 58,500
Common shares	50,000
Retained earnings	101,500
Non-controlling interest (20% × [**(10d) 10,000** + **(10e) 10,800** + **(11c) 950**)]	4,350
	$214,350

Non-controlling interest is shown as a component of shareholders' equity.

The consolidated retained earnings statement contains the retained earnings of Company P at the beginning of the year, consolidated net income attributable to Company P, and the dividends of Company P.

The consolidated balance sheet is prepared by combining the assets and liabilities of the two companies, adjusted for the unamortized acquisition differential. The parent's investment account is excluded, and the non-controlling interest in the net assets of the subsidiary is shown as a component of shareholders' equity. This amount is 20 percent of the December 31 shareholders' equity of Company S plus 20 percent of the unamortized acquisition differential.

The changes in non-controlling interest would be presented, in the column for non-controlling interest in the statement of changes in equity, as follows:

CHANGES IN NON-CONTROLLING INTEREST

Non-controlling interest on the balance sheet increases when the subsidiary earns income and decreases when the subsidiary pays a dividend.

Balance, January 1 **(9c)**	$3,800
Allocated income of entity **(11g)**	1,050
	4,850
Dividends to non-controlling shareholders	500*
Balance, December 31	$4,350

* *$2,500 × 20% = $500*

It is often useful to prepare this reconciliation when preparing a solution to consolidation problems, because it helps show where the allocated income of this single entity and the dividends of the subsidiary end up in the consolidated financial statements. The consolidated retained earnings statement does not contain the dividends of the subsidiary. In this example, Company S paid $2,500 in dividends. Eighty percent of this amount ($2,000) was paid to Company P and therefore did not leave the consolidated entity. The other 20 percent ($500) was paid to the non-controlling shareholders and reduced the equity of that group, as shown in the statement.

The consolidation of the 80-percent-owned subsidiary for Year 1 financial statements using the working paper approach is illustrated in Appendix 5A.

Consolidated Statements, End of Year 2

On December 31, Year 2, Company S reported earnings of $10,000 for the year and paid a cash dividend of $3,000. Company P's earnings for the year were $19,000 at this time (excluding any income from its investment in Company S). Company P's journal entry to record the dividend received from Company S is as follows:

Under the cost method, investment income is reported when dividends are received or receivable from the investee company.

Cash	2,400	
Dividend income		2,400
80% of the dividend paid by Company S		

Company P reports earnings of $21,400 in Year 2. That amount includes this dividend income. An impairment test conducted on December 31, Year 2, indicated that the goodwill had a recoverable amount of $870, and therefore a $80 impairment loss had occurred. The financial statements of the two companies as at December 31, Year 2, are shown in Exhibit 5.13 on page 196.

Regardless of the approach to be used (direct or working paper), the four calculations shown in Exhibit 5.14 on page 196 must be made before the consolidated financial statements are prepared.

These four calculations are the starting point for the preparation of the consolidated financial statements whether the direct or the working paper approach is used.

Exhibit 5.15 on page 197 shows the consolidated financial statements prepared using the direct approach. The concepts involved are the same as were outlined earlier for a 100-percent-owned subsidiary. The only difference here is

Exhibit 5.13

YEAR 2 INCOME STATEMENTS

		Company P	Company S	
These statements are the separate-entity statements of the parent and the subsidiary.	Sales	$ 60,000	$40,000	
	Dividend income	2,400	—	(a)
	Total revenue	62,400	40,000	
	Cost of sales	32,000	18,000	
	Expenses (misc.)	9,000	12,000	
	Total expenses	41,000	30,000	
	Net income	$ 21,400	$10,000	(b)

YEAR 2 RETAINED EARNINGS STATEMENTS

		Company P	Company S	
The parent's retained earnings includes dividend income received from the subsidiary since the date of acquisition.	Balance, Jan. 1	$ 99,300	$10,800	(c)
	Net income	21,400	10,000	
		120,700	20,800	
	Dividends	8,000	3,000	
	Balance, Dec. 31	$112,700	$17,800	(d)

BALANCE SHEETS — December 31, Year 2

		Company P	Company S	
The parent has used the cost method on its separate-entity financial statements.	Assets (misc.)	$134,500	$21,000	
	Inventory	35,000	16,000	
	Investment in S (cost method)	15,200	—	
		$184,700	$37,000	
	Liabilities	$ 22,000	$ 9,200	
	Common shares	50,000	10,000	(e)
	Retained earnings	112,700	17,800	(f)
		$184,700	$37,000	

Exhibit 5.14

ACQUISITION-DIFFERENTIAL IMPAIRMENT SCHEDULE

		Balance Jan. 1, Year 2	Impairment Year 2	Balance Dec. 31, Year 2	
This schedule is used to support adjustments made when preparing consolidated financial statements.	Inventory **(11a)**	$ —	$ —	$ —	
	Goodwill **(11b)**	950	80	870	
		$950	$80	$870	(a)

CALCULATION OF CONSOLIDATED NET INCOME — Year 2

	Company P net income — cost method **(13b)**		$21,400
	Less dividend income from Company S **(13a)**		2,400
	Company P net income, own operations		19,000
	Company S net income **(13b)**	10,000	
This schedule calculates the bottom line for the consolidated income statement.	Less acquisition-differential impairment **(14a)**	(80)	
			9,920 (b)
	Consolidated net income		$28,920 (c)
	Attributable to		
	Shareholders of Company P		$26,936 (d)
	Non-controlling interest (20% × **(14b)** 9,920)		1,984 (e)

CALCULATION OF CONSOLIDATED RETAINED EARNINGS
as at January 1, Year 2

Company P retained earnings, Jan. 1, Year 2		
(cost method) **(13c)**		$ 99,300
Company S retained earnings, Jan. 1, Year 2 **(13c)**	10,800	
Company S retained earnings, acquisition date **(10c)**	6,000	
Increase since acquisition	4,800	
Less acquisition-differential amortization and impairment		
to end of Year 1 **(11c)**	(2,050)	
	2,750	
Company P's ownership	80%	
		2,200
Consolidated retained earnings		
(which is equal to retained earnings — equity method)		$101,500 **(f)**

This schedule incorporates cumulative adjustments to a point in time.

CALCULATION OF NON-CONTROLLING INTEREST
December 31, Year 2

Shareholders' equity — Company S	
Common shares **(13e)**	$10,000
Retained earnings **(13f)**	17,800
	27,800
Unamortized acquisition differential **(14a)**	870
	28,670
Non-controlling interest's ownership	20%
	$ 5,734 **(g)**

This schedule calculates non-controlling interest on the balance sheet at a point in time.

Exhibit 5.15	**Year 2 Consolidated Financial Statements**

(direct approach)

COMPANY P
CONSOLIDATED INCOME STATEMENT
for the Year Ended December 31, Year 2

Sales (60,000 + 40,000)	$100,000
Cost of sales (32,000 + 18,000)	50,000
Goodwill impairment loss (0 + 0 + **(14a) 80**)	80
Expenses (misc.) (9,000 + 12,000)	21,000
	71,080
Net income	$ 28,920
Attributable to	
Shareholders of Company P **(13d)**	$ 26,936
Non-controlling interest **(13e)**	1,984

The income statement includes adjustments for only one year and non-controlling interest's share of income for only one year.

COMPANY P
CONSOLIDATED STATEMENT OF RETAINED EARNINGS
for the Year Ended December 31, Year 2

Balance, January 1 **(14f)**	$101,500
Net income	26,936
	128,436
Dividends	8,000
Balance, December 31	$120,436

(continued)

COMPANY P
CONSOLIDATED BALANCE SHEET
December 31, Year 2

The balance sheet reflects adjustments at the end of the year and non-controlling interest's share of net assets at the end of the year.	Assets (misc.) (134,500 + 21,000)

Assets (misc.) (134,500 + 21,000)	$155,500
Inventory (35,000 + 16,000)	51,000
Goodwill (0 + 0 + **(14a) 870**)	870
	$207,370
Liabilities (22,000 + 9,200)	$ 31,200
Common shares	50,000
Retained earnings	120,436
Non-controlling interest **(14g)**	5,734
	$207,370

The balance sheet reflects adjustments at the end of the year and non-controlling interest's share of net assets at the end of the year.

that the non-controlling interest is reflected in the consolidated income statement and balance sheet.

The consolidation of the 80-percent-owned subsidiary for Year 2 financial statements using the working paper approach is illustrated in Appendix 5A.

Additional Calculations   The preparation of the consolidated financial statements of companies P and S for Year 2 has been illustrated. Because the parent, Company P, used the cost method, additional calculations had to be made to determine certain consolidated amounts. One more calculation can be made to verify the consolidated retained earnings shown on the balance sheet. This calculation is shown below.

CALCULATION OF CONSOLIDATED RETAINED EARNINGS
as at December 31, Year 2

This schedule incorporates cumulative adjustments to the end of Year 2 and is used to verify retained earnings at the end of Year 2.

Company P retained earnings, Dec. 31, Year 2 — cost method **(13d)**		$112,700
Company S retained earnings, Dec. 31, Year 2 **(13d)**	17,800	
Company S retained earnings, acquisition date **(10c)**	6,000	
Increase since acquisition	11,800	
Less acquisition-differential amortization and impairment to the end of Year 2 ((**11c) 2,050** + **(14a) 80**)	(2,130)	
	9,670	
Company P's ownership	80%	7,736
Consolidated retained earnings		$120,436

Acquisition Differential Assigned to Liabilities

With the considerable swings in interest rates over the past decade, companies often find that liabilities assumed in a business combination have fair values different from their carrying amounts. As with assets acquired, liabilities assumed in a business combination must be valued at their fair values. The difference between fair value and carrying amount for these liabilities is similar to a bond premium or discount that must be amortized over its remaining life.

The effective interest method should be used to account for financial assets and liabilities.

Prior to 2006, the *CICA Handbook* was silent on the amortization method to be used in amortizing any premium or discount on a bond payable or investment in bonds. Companies could use either the straight-line method or the effective interest method. Most companies used the straight-line method because it is simpler to use. IAS 39 requires the use of the effective interest method. Some companies may continue to use the straight-line method where the difference between the two methods is not material. In this text, we will use both the straight-line and the effective interest methods.

Bonds trade at a premium when the stated rate is greater than the market rate of interest.

For situation A, assume that Pubco acquires 100 percent of the common shares of Subco on December 31, Year 2. On that date, Pubco had no bonds payable outstanding and Subco had bonds payable with a carrying amount of $100,000 and a fair value of $105,154. These bonds were issued on January 1, Year 1, at their par value of $100,000, and mature on December 31, Year 5. The bonds pay interest on December 31 each year at a stated rate of 10 percent. The market rate of interest was 8 percent on December 31, Year 2. Given that the stated rate of interest was higher than the market rate, the bonds were trading at a premium. The fair value of the bonds can be determined by taking the present value of future cash flows using a discount rate of 8 percent as follows:

Principal $100,000 × (P/F, 8%, 3 years) (0.79383)	$ 79,383
Interest 10,000 × (P/A, 8%, 3 years) (2.57710)	25,771
	$105,154

The acquisition differential of $5,154 is considered a premium on the bonds from a consolidated viewpoint. On the date of acquisition, the entire $5,154 is assigned to the bonds payable, and bonds payable will be reported at $105,154 on the consolidated balance sheet. The following schedule shows the amortization of this premium using the effective interest method as if Pubco had actually issued these bonds at $105,154:

Period	Interest paid	Interest expense	Amortization of bond premium	Amortized cost of bonds
Year 2				$105,154
Year 3	$10,000[1]	$8,412[2]	$1,588[3]	103,566[4]
Year 4	10,000	8,285	1,715	101,851
Year 5	10,000	8,149	1,851	100,000

[1] $100,000 × 10% = $10,000   [2] $105,154 × 8% = $8,412
[3] $10,000 − $8,412 = $1,588   [4] $105,154 − $1,588 = $103,566

In preparing consolidated financial statements subsequent to the date of acquisition, interest expense and bonds payable must be adjusted as follows to obtain the same results as if the parent had issued the bonds itself:

The acquisition differential related to bonds payable should be amortized using the effective interest method.

Period	Subco's interest expense	Adjustment on consolidation	Consolidated interest expense	Subco's bond payable	Adjustment on consolidation	Consolidated bond payable
Year 2				$100,000	$5,154	$105,154
Year 3	$10,000	$1,588	$8,412	100,000	3,566	103,566
Year 4	10,000	1,715	8,285	100,000	1,851	101,851
Year 5	10,000	1,851	8,149	100,000	0	100,000

Subco's interest expense is equal to the interest paid because the bonds were issued at par; i.e., there is no premium or discount on the bonds.

For situation B, assume that Subco had issued the bonds on January 1, Year 1, at $92,791 when the market rate of interest was 12 percent and everything else was the same as in situation A. Given that the stated rate of interest was lower than the market rate, the bonds were issued at a discount. The following schedule shows how Subco would amortize this discount on its own financial statements:

Period	Interest paid	Interest expense	Amortization of bond discount	Amortized cost of bonds
Year 0				$ 92,791
Year 1	$10,000[1]	$11,135[2]	$1,135[3]	93,926[4]
Year 2	10,000	11,271	1,271	95,197
Year 3	10,000	11,424	1,424	96,621
Year 4	10,000	11,594	1,594	98,215
Year 5	10,000	11,785	1,785	100,000

The subsidiary amortizes the bond discount for its separate-entity financial statements.

[1] $100,000 × 10\% = \$10,000$ [2] $\$92,791 × 12\% = \$11,135$
[3] $\$10,000 - \$11,135 = -\$1,135$ [4] $\$92,791 + \$1,135 = \$93,926$

The acquisition differential on December 31, Year 2, the date of acquisition, would now be $9,957 ($105,154 − $95,197) and is considered a premium on the bonds from a consolidated viewpoint. The entire $9,957 is assigned to the bonds payable, and bonds payable will be reported at $105,154 (same amount as in situation A) on the consolidated balance sheet. In preparing consolidated financial statements subsequent to the date of acquisition, interest expense and bonds payable must be adjusted as follows to obtain the same results as in situation A:

Period	Subco's interest expense	Adjustment on consolidation	Consolidated interest expense	Subco's bond payable	Adjustment on consolidation	Consolidated bond payable
Year 2				$ 95,197	$9,957	$105,154
Year 3	$11,424	$3,012	$8,412	96,621	6,945	103,566
Year 4	11,594	3,309	8,285	98,215	3,636	101,851
Year 5	11,785	3,636	8,149	100,000	0	100,000

The straight-line and effective interest methods produce the same results in total over the life of the bond.

In both situations, the acquisition differential was amortized over the three-year term to maturity of the bonds. Under the effective interest method, the annual amortization changes over time. If the straight-line method were used, the annual amortization would be the same each year. The following schedule summarizes the amortization of the acquisition differential under the effective interest and straight-line methods:

	Acquisition differential at acquisition	Amortization of acquisition differential			
		Effective interest method			St-line
		Year 3	Year 4	Year 5	per year
A	$5,154	$1,588	$1,715	$1,851	$1,718
B	9,957	3,012	3,309	3,636	3,319

If Pubco acquired less than 100 percent of Subco, the non-controlling interest would absorb their share of the acquisition differential and amortization of the acquisition differential.

Intercompany Receivables and Payables

Consolidated financial statements are designed to reflect the results of transactions between the consolidated single entity and those outside the entity. All transactions between the parent and its subsidiaries, or between the subsidiaries of a parent, must be eliminated in the consolidation process to reflect this single-entity concept. While many of these intercompany eliminations are discussed in later chapters, we will introduce the topic now by discussing the elimination of intercompany receivables and payables. If the parent's accounts receivable contain a receivable of $5,000 from its subsidiary, then the accounts payable of the subsidiary must contain a $5,000 payable to the parent. If these intercompany receivables and payables were not eliminated in the consolidation process, both the accounts receivable and the accounts payable on the consolidated balance sheet would be overstated from a single-entity point of view. The entry to eliminate these intercompany balances on the consolidated worksheet or working papers is as follows:

> **The consolidated financial statements should reflect only the result of transactions with outsiders.**

Accounts payable — subsidiary	5,000	
Accounts receivable — parent		5,000

Because the net assets (assets less liabilities) are unchanged after this elimination, the equities of the non-controlling and controlling interests are not affected.

Subsidiary Acquired during the Year

In all of our examples to date, we have assumed that the parent acquired the subsidiary on the first day of the fiscal year. As a result, when we prepared the first consolidated income statement at the end of the first fiscal year it contained all of the subsidiary's revenue and expenses for that year. We will now describe the consolidation process if the acquisition took place *during* the year.

Assume that Parent Inc. (which has a December 31 year-end) acquired 80 percent of Subsidiary Ltd. on September 30, Year 2. The Year 2 operations of Subsidiary would impact the December 31, Year 2, consolidated income statement in the following manner:

Revenues: Subsidiary's revenues October 1 to December 31

Expenses: Subsidiary's expenses plus amortization and impairment of acquisition differential October 1 to December 31

Net impact on consolidated net income attributable to shareholders of Parent Inc.: Increased by 80 percent of Subsidiary's net income adjusted for amortization and impairment of acquisition differential for last three months.

> **The consolidated financial statements should include the subsidiary's income only from the date of acquisition.**

Net impact on consolidated net income attributable to non-controlling interest: 20 percent × Subsidiary's net income adjusted for amortization and impairment of acquisition differential for period October 1 to December 31

This form of presentation makes subsequent-year comparisons difficult for readers. To solve this problem, a pro forma consolidated income statement could be prepared as if the subsidiary had been acquired at the beginning of the fiscal year. This pro forma consolidated income statement could be presented in summary form in the notes to the financial statements.

Equity Method of Recording

The illustrations throughout this chapter have assumed that the parent used the cost method of recording its investment for its internal records. We will use the same example for an 80-percent-owned subsidiary to illustrate the use of the equity method. The key events of the example are repeated here for ease of use.

On January 1, Year 1, Company P purchased 80 percent of Company S for $15,200. On December 31, Year 1, Company S reported a net income of $7,300 for the year and paid a cash dividend of $2,500. Company P's net income for the year was $18,300 at this time (not including income from its investment in Company S).

Company P would make the following journal entries in Year 1 under the equity method:

> **Only the investor's share of the investee's income, dividends, and amortization of acquisition differential are recorded in the investor's records.**

Investment in S	15,200	
Cash		15,200
Purchased 80% of Company S		
Investment in S (7,300 × 80%)	5,840	
Investment income		5,840
80% of Company S Year 1 net income		
Cash (2,500 × 80%)	2,000	
Investment in S		2,000
80% of the dividend paid by Company S		
Investment income (2,050 × 80%)	1,640	
Investment in S		1,640
Acquisition-differential amortization and impairment— Year 1		

After these journal entries are posted, the two related accounts in the records of Company P will show the following changes and balances:

	Investment in S	Investment income
January 1, Year 1	$15,200	$ nil
December 31, Year 1		
Income from S	5,840	5,840
Dividends from S	(2,000)	—
Acquisition-differential amortization		
and impairment	(1,640)	(1,640)
Balance, December 31, Year 1	$17,400	$4,200

Company P's net income for Year 1 would now be $22,500 (18,300 + 4,200). It is not a coincidence that P's net income is now equal to P's share of consolidated net income. In fact, it should be equal to the consolidated net income attributable to the shareholders of Company P as reported on the consolidated income statement. That is why the equity method is sometimes referred to as the one-line consolidation. The one line on Company P's unconsolidated income statement, being investment income, captures the net effect of all entries related to the subsidiary such that net income from the separate-entity books for Company P equals the consolidated net income attributable to the shareholders of Company P.

> **The parent's separate-entity net income should be equal to consolidated net income attributable to shareholders of the parent.**

Even though Company P has used the equity method for its internal record-keeping, the amounts reported on the consolidated financial statements would be exactly the same as in our previous illustration when P used the cost method. What differs is what is recorded in Company P's general ledger. This does not change what is reported on the consolidated financial statements.

The investment account can be reconciled to the book value of the subsidiary's shareholders' equity and the unamortized acquisition differential.

At this point it is useful to discuss a further relationship that results from the use of the equity method of accounting. The balance in the investment account at any point in time can be broken down into two components — the book value of the subsidiary's shareholders' equity and the unamortized acquisition differential. The following illustrates this point at December 31, Year 1:

	Total 100%	P's share 80%	NCI's share 20%
Shareholders' equity, Company S			
Common shares	$10,000		
Retained earnings	10,800		
	20,800	$16,640	$4,160
Unamortized acquisition differential	950	760	190
	$21,750		
Balance in the investment account		$17,400	
Non-controlling interest			$4,350

Let's now look at what happens in Year 2.

On December 31, Year 2, Company S reported earnings of $10,000 for the year and paid a cash dividend of $3,000. Company P's earnings for the year were $19,000 at this time (excluding any income from its investment in Company S).

On December 31, Year 2, Company P would make the following journal entries under the equity method:

Investment in S (10,000 × 80%)	8,000	
Investment income		8,000
80% of Company S, Year 2, net income		
Cash (3,000 × 80%)	2,400	
Investment in S		2,400
Dividends received from Company S		
Investment income (80 × 80%)	64	
Investment in S		64
Acquisition-differential amortization and impairment — Year 2		

The investment account captures all adjustments since the date of acquisition whereas investment income captures adjustments for the current period.

After these journal entries are posted, the investment in S account and the investment income account in the records of P Company will show the following changes and balances:

	Investment in S	Investment income
December 31, Year 1	$17,400	$ nil
December 31, Year 2		
Income from S	8,000	8,000
Dividends from S	(2,400)	
Acquisition-differential amortization and impairment	(64)	(64)
Balance, December 31, Year 2	$22,936	$7,936

Company P combines its Year 2 investment income ($7,936) with the earnings from its own operations ($19,000) and reports a final net income of $26,936. Once again, it is not a coincidence that P's net income is now equal to P's share of consolidated net income.

The parent's use of the equity method should always produce the following results:

- Consolidated net income attributable to the shareholders of the parent in any one year will always be equal to the parent's net income reported in its internal records for that year.

- Consolidated retained earnings are always equal to the parent's retained earnings in its internal records.

The parent's retained earnings under the equity method should be equal to consolidated retained earnings.

The equity method captures the parent's share of the net effect of any adjustments made on consolidation. When the cost method is used, the consolidated net income attributable to the parent and consolidated retained earnings *do not* equal the parent's net income and retained earnings recorded in its internal records. However, one of the consolidation procedures involved when using the working paper approach is to adjust the parent's accounts from the cost method to the balances that would have resulted if the equity method had been used instead. A thorough understanding of the equity method and the financial statement numbers that it produces will help you to understand the consolidated statement preparation process. The appendix to this chapter illustrates the working paper approach for the same examples used in this chapter.

GAAP for Private Enterprises

- As mentioned in Chapter 3, private companies can either consolidate their subsidiaries or report their investments in subsidiaries under the cost method or the equity method.

- All intangible assets and goodwill should be tested for impairment whenever events or changes in circumstances indicate that the carrying amount may exceed the fair value.

Recoverable amount is defined differently under PE GAAP.

- An impairment loss should be recognized for intangible assets with definite useful lives when both of these two conditions are met: (1) the carrying amount of a long-lived asset exceeds its recoverable amount (i.e., the sum of the undiscounted cash flows expected to result from its use and eventual disposition) and (2) the carrying amount exceeds its fair value.

- For intangible assets with indefinite useful lives and goodwill, an impairment loss should be recognized when the carrying amount exceeds its fair value.

- In all cases, the impairment loss is equal to the excess of carrying amount over the fair value, and impairment losses cannot be reversed.

U.S. GAAP Differences

U.S. GAAP and IFRSs for consolidated statements subsequent to the date of acquisition have many similarities. The significant differences are summarized as follows:

1. Whereas goodwill is allocated to cash-generating units under IFRSs, it is allocated to reporting units under U.S. GAAP. A reporting unit is defined as an operating segment or one level below an operating segment.

2. Under IFRSs, goodwill is impaired when the recoverable amount is less than the carrying amount; the recoverable amount is the higher of fair value less costs to sell and discounted future cash flows. Under U.S. GAAP, impairment testing is a two-stage approach. If the carrying value is greater than the undiscounted future cash flows in step 1, then the carrying value is compared to the fair value in step 2.

SUMMARY

While a parent company can account for its investment by either the equity method or the cost method, the consolidated statements are the same regardless of the method used. The method of presentation is quite different between the separate-entity financial statements and the consolidated financial statements.

When the parent uses the equity method on its separate-entity financial statements, the parent's share of the subsidiary's income and net assets is typically shown on one line on the income statement (investment income) and one line on the balance sheet (investment in subsidiary). Accordingly, the equity method is sometimes referred to as the one-line consolidation. The income and retained earnings reported by the parent on its separate-entity financial statements will be equal to the consolidated net income attributable to shareholders of the parent and consolidated retained earnings, respectively.

This chapter has illustrated the preparation of consolidated financial statements covering a two-year period after the date of acquisition when the parent has used the cost method to account for its investment. Additional calculations were performed to convert the income and retained earnings from the amounts shown on the separate-entity financial statements to the consolidated financial statements.

The basic steps in the consolidation process when the parent has used the equity and cost methods are outlined in Exhibit 5.16. It is important to have a good grasp of the procedures under both methods because these procedures are the foundation for the consolidation issues we will introduce in the chapters that follow.

Exhibit 5.16

PREPARATION OF CONSOLIDATED FINANCIAL STATEMENTS
Basic Steps

	Parent company uses	
	Cost method	Equity method
1. Calculate and allocate the acquisition differential on the date of acquisition.	Yes	Yes
2. Prepare an acquisition-differential amortization and impairment schedule (date of acquisition to present date).	Yes	Yes
3. Calculate consolidated net income — current year.	Yes	No*
4. Prepare the consolidated income statement.	Yes	Yes
5. Calculate the start-of-year balance of consolidated retained earnings.**	Yes	No*
6. Prepare the consolidated retained earnings statement.***	Yes	Yes
7. Calculate the end-of-year balance of consolidated retained earnings.	Yes	No*
8. Calculate non-controlling interest at the end of the year (for the consolidated balance sheet).	Yes	Yes
9. Prepare a statement of changes in non-controlling interest (optional).	Yes	Yes
10. Prepare a consolidated balance sheet.	Yes	Yes

* If the parent company uses the equity method of accounting, the parent's net income equals consolidated net income attributable to the shareholders of the parent, and the parent's retained earnings always equal consolidated retained earnings. Therefore, the calculations in steps 3, 5, and 7 are not necessary.

** Only do so if preparing a statement of retained earnings.

*** Not required in all problems.

Significant Changes in the Last Two Years

1. For publicly accountable enterprises, IFRSs have replaced the former sections of the *CICA Handbook*. The following table shows the IFRSs covered in this chapter along with their counterparts from the former sections of the *CICA Handbook*:

IFRSs	CICA Handbook *Counterparts*
IAS 36: Impairment of Assets	Section 3063: Impairment of Long-lived Assets Section 3064: Goodwill and Intangible Assets
IAS 27: Consolidated and Separate Financial Statements	Section 1601: Consolidated Financial Statements Section 1602: Non-controlling Interests
IAS 28: Investments in Associates	3051: Investments

2. When an impairment loss occurs, the asset is written down to the higher of fair value less costs of disposal and value in use, which is the present value of future cash flows. It used to be written down to fair value.

3. Impairment losses relating to intangible assets other than goodwill can be reversed in certain situations.

4. Consolidated net income is now the total income of the combined entity, whereas it used to be the parent's share of the net income of the combined entity. Consolidated net income is segregated between the portion attributed to the shareholders of the parent company and the non-controlling interest on the bottom part of the income statement.

5. IAS 1 requires a statement of changes in equity, which incorporates the changes in retained earnings.

Changes Expected in the Next Three Years

No major changes are expected in the next three years.

SELF-STUDY PROBLEM

On January 1, Year 1, Allen Company acquired 7,000 (70 percent) of the outstanding common shares of Bell Company for $87,500 in cash. On that date Bell had common shares of $50,000 and retained earnings of $45,000. The Bell shares were trading for $11 per share just after the date of acquisition. At acquisition the identifiable assets and liabilities of Bell had fair values that were equal to book values except for plant assets, which had a fair value $30,000 greater than book value; inventory, which had a fair value $8,000 less than book value; and bonds payable, which had a fair value $12,420 greater than book value. The plant assets had a remaining useful life of eight years on January 1, Year 1, and are amortized on a straight-line basis. The bonds payable mature on December 31, Year 8; pay interest annually; and are amortized using the effective interest method. The market rate of interest for similar bonds is 6 percent.

Financial statements for the Year 6 fiscal year are as follows:

	Allen	Bell
Income statements		
Sales	$ 400,000	$100,000
Rent revenue	15,000	—
Dividend revenue	3,500	—
	418,500	100,000
Cost of sales	200,000	45,000
Depreciation	55,000	20,000
Interest expense	32,000	8,000
Other expenses	28,000	17,000
	315,000	90,000
Profit	$ 103,500	$ 10,000
Retained earnings statements		
Balance, January 1	$ 400,000	$135,000
Profit	103,500	10,000
	503,500	145,000
Dividends	30,000	5,000
Balance, December 31	$ 473,500	$140,000
Statement of financial position		
Plant and equipment	$1,200,000	$470,000
Accumulated depreciation	(300,000)	(220,000)
Investment in Bell — cost method	87,500	—
Inventory	200,000	40,000
Accounts receivable	60,000	25,000
Cash	12,500	10,000
	$1,260,000	$325,000
Common shares	$ 300,000	$ 50,000
Retained earnings	473,500	140,000
Bonds payable, 8%	400,000	100,000
Accounts payable	86,500	35,000
	$1,260,000	$325,000

Additional Information

In Year 2, a goodwill impairment loss of $7,000 was recorded ($6,300 pertained to Allen's 70 percent interest). Subsequent goodwill testing yielded no further evidence of impairment until Year 6, when a decline in the recoverable amount of Bell Company occurred and management decided to reflect an impairment loss of $6,000 in the year's consolidated statements ($5,400 pertained to Allen's 70 percent interest).

On December 31, Year 6, Bell Company owes Allen Company $9,000.

Required:

(a) Using the direct approach, prepare the following Year 6 consolidated financial statements:
   (i) Income statement.
   (ii) Retained earnings statement.
   (iii) Statement of financial position.
(b) Prepare a schedule of the Year 6 changes in non-controlling interest.

Solution to Self-study Problem

	Parent's 70%	Non-controlling interest's 30%	Total 100%
Cost of 70% of Bell	$87,500		
Value of 30% of Bell (3,000 × 11)		$33,000	
Imputed value of 100% of Bell			$120,500
Book value of Bell's net assets = Book value of shareholders' equity			
Common shares	50,000		
Retained earnings	45,000		
	95,000		
	95,000	66,500	28,500	95,000
Acquisition differential		21,000	4,500	25,500
Allocated:	FV − BV			
Plant assets	30,000 **(a)**			
Inventory	− 8,000 **(b)**			
Bonds payable	−12,420 **(c)**			
	9,580	6,706	2,874	9,580
Goodwill (approximately 90% of total)		$14,294 **(d)**		
Goodwill (approximately 10% of total)			$ 1,626 **(e)**	
Total goodwill				$ 15,920

BOND AMORTIZATION SCHEDULE

Date	Cash paid	Interest expense	Bond premium amortization	Amortized cost of bonds
Jan 1/ Year 1				$112,420
Dec 31/ Year 1	$ 8,000	$ 6,745	$ 1,255	111,165
Dec 31/ Year 2	8,000	6,670	1,330	109,835
Dec 31/ Year 3	8,000	6,590	1,410	108,425
Dec 31/ Year 4	8,000	6,506	1,494	106,931
Dec 31/ Year 5	8,000	6,416	1,584	105,347
	40,000	32,927	7,073	
Dec 31/ Year 6	8,000	6,321	1,679	103,668 **(f)**
Dec 31/ Year 7	8,000	6,220	1,780	101,888
Dec 31/ Year 8	8,000	6,112	1,888	100,000
	$64,000	$51,580	$12,420	

ACQUISITION-DIFFERENTIAL AMORTIZATION AND IMPAIRMENT

	Balance Jan. 1/Year 1	Amortization and Impairment To end of Year 5	Year 6	Balance Dec. 31/Year 6
Plant assets **(a)**	$ 30,000	$ 18,750	$ 3,750	$ 7,500 **(g)**
Inventory **(b)**	− 8,000	− 8,000	—	— **(h)**
Bonds payable **(c)**	−12,420	− 7,073	−1,679	−3,668 **(i)**
	9,580	3,677	2,071	3,832 **(j)**
Goodwill — parent **(d)**	14,294	6,300	5,400	2,594 **(k)**
Goodwill — NCI **(e)**	1,626	700	600	326 **(l)**
Goodwill — total	15,920	7,000	6,000	2,920 **(m)**
	$ 25,500	$10,677	$ 8,071	$ 6,752

CALCULATION OF CONSOLIDATED NET INCOME
ATTRIBUTABLE TO PARENT
Year 6

Profit — Allen		$103,500
Less dividend from Bell		3,500 **(n)**
		100,000
Profit — Bell	10,000 **(o)**	
Allen's ownership	70%	7,000
Parent's share of acquisition-differential amortization and impairment		
(70% × **(j)** 2,071 + **(k)** 5,400)		−6,850 **(p)**
		$100,150 **(q)**

CALCULATION OF CONSOLIDATED NET INCOME ATTRIBUTABLE TO NCI

Net income — Bell	$10,000
NCI's ownership	30%
	3,000
NCI's share of acquisition-differential amortization and impairment	
(30% × **(j)** 2,071 + **(l)** 600)	−1,221
	$ 1,779 **(r)**

CALCULATION OF CONSOLIDATED RETAINED EARNINGS
January 1, Year 6

Retained earnings — Allen		$400,000
Retained earnings — Bell	135,000	
Retained earnings — Bell, acquisition date	45,000	
Increase since acquisition	90,000	
Allen's ownership	70%	
		63,000
Parent's share of acquisition-differential amortization and impairment		
(70% × **(j)** 3,677 + **(k)** 6,300)		−8,874
		$454,126 **(s)**

CALCULATION OF CONSOLIDATED RETAINED EARNINGS
December 31, Year 6

Retained earnings — Allen		$473,500
Retained earnings — Bell	140,000	
Retained earnings — Bell, acquisition date	45,000	
Increase since acquisition	95,000	
Allen's ownership	70%	66,500
Parent's share of acquisition-differential amortization and impairment		
(**(p)** 6,850 + **(s)** 8,874)		−15,724 **(t)**
		$524,276 **(u)**

CALCULATION OF NON-CONTROLLING INTEREST
at December 31, Year 6

Common shares — Bell	$ 50,000
Retained earnings — Bell	140,000
	190,000
NCI's ownership	30%
	57,000
NCI's share of unamortized acquisition differential	
(30% × **(j)** 3,832 + **(l)** 326)	1,476
	$ 58,476 **(v)**

(a) (i)

ALLEN COMPANY
CONSOLIDATED INCOME STATEMENT
for the Year Ended December 31, Year 6

Sales (400,000 + 100,000)	$500,000
Rent revenue	15,000
Dividend revenue (3,500 + 0 − **(n) 3,500**)	—
	515,000
Cost of sales (200,000 + 45,000)	245,000
Depreciation (55,000 + 20,000 + **(g) 3,750**)	78,750
Interest expense (32,000 + 8,000 − **(i) 1,679**)	38,321
Other expenses (28,000 + 17,000)	45,000
Goodwill impairment loss **(m)**	6,000
	413,071
Profit	$101,929
Attributable to	
Shareholders of Allen **(q)**	$100,150
Non-controlling interest **(r)**	1,779

(ii)

ALLEN COMPANY
CONSOLIDATED RETAINED EARNINGS STATEMENT
for the Year Ended December 31, Year 6

Balance, January 1 **(s)**	$454,126
Profit	100,150
	554,276
Dividends	30,000
Balance, December 31 **(u)**	$524,276

(iii)

ALLEN COMPANY
CONSOLIDATED STATEMENT OF FINANCIAL POSITION
December 31, Year 6

Plant and equipment (1,200,000 + 470,000 + **(a) 30,000**)	$1,700,000
Accumulated depreciation	
(300,000 + 220,000 + **(g) 18,750** + **(g) 3,750**)	(542,500)
Goodwill **(m)**	2,920
Inventory (200,000 + 40,000)	240,000
Accounts receivable (60,000 + 25,000 − ***9,000**)	76,000
Cash (12,500 + 10,000)	22,500
	$1,498,920
Common shares	$ 300,000
Retained earnings **(u)**	524,276
Non-controlling interest **(v)**	58,476
	882,752
Bonds payable (400,000 + 100,000 + **(i) 3,668**)	503,668
Accounts payable (86,500 + 35,000 − ***9,000**)	112,500
	$1,498,920

* Intercompany receivable/payable

(b)   **YEAR 6 CHANGES IN NON-CONTROLLING INTEREST**

Balance, January 1*		$58,197
Allocation of entity net income **(r)**		1,779
		59,976
Dividends (30% × 5,000)		1,500
Balance, December 31 **(v)**		$58,476

* Common shares	$50,000	
Retained earnings, January 1	135,000	
	185,000	
NCI's ownership	30%	
	55,500	
NCI's share of unamortized acquisition differential		
(30% × **(j)** [9,580 − 3,677] + **(l)** [1,626 − 700])	2,697	
	$58,197	

APPENDIX 5A

Preparing Consolidated Financial Statements Using the Working Paper Approach

In this chapter, we have illustrated the direct approach for preparing consolidated financial statements when the parent has used the cost method to account for its investment. In the examples used, we first examined the situation where the subsidiary was 100 percent owned, and then the situation where the parent's ownership was 80 percent. We will now illustrate the working paper approach using the same examples.

Year 1 Consolidated Financial Statement Working Paper

There are many different ways of using a working paper to support the preparation of consolidated financial statements.

A number of methods can be used to prepare consolidated financial statement working papers when the parent has used the cost method. All methods used must result in identical consolidated amounts. The approach that we will illustrate adjusts the parent's accounts on the working paper to what they would have been if the equity method had been used to account for the investment. This requires the same additional calculations used in the direct approach. Then, we make "adjustments and eliminations" similar to Chapters 3 and 4. In this chapter, we have shortened the description to "eliminations." Exhibit 5A.1 on page 212 shows the preparation of the consolidated financial statements for Year 1 using a working paper, assuming Company S is a 100-percent-owned subsidiary of Company P. To compare it with the direct approach, see Exhibit 5.5 on page 186. Before explaining the various entries, a few comments about the overall format would be useful.[6]

1. In observing the effect of the elimination entries, the reader must take into account the debit and credit balances of the financial statement items. Revenues, net income, retained earnings, liabilities, and share capital accounts have credit balances, while expenses, dividends, and assets have debit balances. The debit and credit elimination entries are either increasing or decreasing these financial statement items depending on their nature.

2. Some elimination entries affect two or more of the financial statements, but the total debits and credits for each entry are equal.

---

[6] It should be emphasized again that the elimination entries shown in the working paper are not recorded in the accounting records of either the parent or the subsidiary.

Exhibit 5A.1

CONSOLIDATED FINANCIAL STATEMENT WORKING PAPER
December 31, Year 1 (cost method)

	P	S	Eliminations Dr.		Eliminations Cr.		Consolidated
Sales	$ 50,000	$30,000					$ 80,000
Dividend income	2,500		**(a)**	$ 2,500			
Investment income			**(1)**	5,250	**(a)**	$ 5,250	
	52,500	30,000					80,000
Cost of sales	26,500	14,700	**(3)**	2,000			43,200
Goodwill impair. loss			**(3)**	50			50
Misc. expenses	5,200	8,000					13,200
	31,700	22,700					56,450
Net income[1]	$ 20,800	$ 7,300		$ 9,800		$ 5,250	$ 23,550
Retained earnings, Jan. 1	$ 85,000	$ 6,000	**(2)**	$ 6,000			$ 85,000
Net income	20,800	7,300		9,800		$ 5,250	23,550
	105,800	13,300					108,550
Dividends	6,000	2,500			**(1)**	2,500	6,000
Retained earnings, Dec. 31	$ 99,800	$10,800		$15,800		$ 7,750	$102,550
Assets, misc.	$147,800	$18,300					$166,100
Inventory	30,000	14,000					44,000
Investment in S	19,000		**(a)**	$ 2,750	**(1)**	$ 2,750	
					(2)	19,000	
Acquisition differential			**(2)**	3,000	**(3)**	3,000	
Goodwill			**(3)**	950			950
	$196,800	$32,300					$211,050
Liabilities	$ 47,000	$11,500					$ 58,500
Common shares	50,000	10,000	**(2)**	10,000			50,000
Retained earnings	99,800	10,800		15,800		7,750	102,550
	$196,800	$32,300		$32,500		$32,500	$211,050

[1] Attributable to shareholders of Company P.

3. The totals from the net income line from the income statement, including the totals of the elimination entries made there, are carried down to the net income line in the retained earnings statement. In a similar manner, the end-of-year retained earnings totals are carried down to the retained earnings on the balance sheet. Because the cumulative effect of the elimination entries from each statement has been carried down to the balance sheet, the total elimination debits and credits on that statement are equal.

Entry **(a)** adjusts the accounts of Company P as at December 31, Year 1, to what they would have been under the equity method. The information for this entry is contained in the calculation of consolidated net income for Year 1 on page 185.

(a) Dividend income — Company P	2,500	
Investment in S — Company P	2,750	
Investment income — Company P		5,250

All relevant items in the financial statements of Company P except the December 31, Year 1, retained earnings contain balances arrived at using the equity method.

The working paper elimination entries are reproduced below, with an explanation of each.

Investment income is eliminated since it will be replaced by the subsidiary's revenues and expenses plus the amortization of the acquisition differential.

(1) Investment income — Company P	5,250	
Dividends — Company S		2,500
Investment in S — Company P		2,750

The parent's equity method investment income does not appear in the consolidated income statement, and the subsidiary's dividends do not appear in the consolidated retained earnings statement. Therefore, these accounts need to be eliminated.Through an elimination of the investment income and the parent's share of the subsidiary's dividends against the investment account, this account has been adjusted to its start-of-year balance ($19,000).

The investment account is eliminated since it will be replaced by the carrying value of the subsidiary's assets and liabilities plus the unamortized acquisition differential.

(2) Retained earnings Jan. 1 — Company S	6,000	
Common shares — Company S	10,000	
Acquisition differential	3,000	
Investment in S — Company P		19,000

This entry eliminates the parent's share of the start-of-year retained earnings and common shares of Company S, and the investment in S account of Company P, and establishes the acquisition differential at the beginning of the year. (In Year 1 this is the acquisition differential on acquisition date.)

(3) Cost of sales — Company S	2,000	
Goodwill impairment loss	50	
Goodwill	950	
Acquisition differential		3,000

This entry eliminates the acquisition differential established by entry (2) and allocates it in accordance with the acquisition-differential amortization schedule by (a) adjusting the expenses of Company S and (b) reflecting the unamortized balance at the end of the year on the consolidated balance sheet.

At this point it is useful to discuss a further relationship that results from the use of the equity method of accounting. The balance in the investment account at any point in time can be broken down into two components — the book value of the subsidiary's net assets and the unamortized acquisition differential. The following illustrates this point at December 31, Year 1:

At any point, the investment account under the equity method can be reconciled to the subsidiary's net assets plus the unamortized acquisition differential.

Net assets, Company S (Dec. 31, Year 1)		
Assets	$32,300	
Liabilities	11,500	
	20,800	
Parent's ownership	100%	
Book value component		$20,800
Unamortized acquisition differential		950
Balance in investment account, Dec. 31, Year 1		$21,750

www.mcgrawhillconnect.ca

Year 2 Consolidated Financial Statement Working Paper

The working papers for the preparation of the Year 2 consolidated financial statements are presented in Exhibit 5A.2. See Exhibit 5.8 on page 190 to compare the direct approach.

The elimination entries **(a)** and **(b)** adjust the accounts of Company P to equity method balances. These entries are reproduced below.

(a)	Investment in S — Company P	2,750	
	Retained earnings, Jan. 1 — Company P		2,750

Exhibit 5A.2

CONSOLIDATED FINANCIAL STATEMENT WORKING PAPER
December 31, Year 2 (cost method)

		P	S	Eliminations Dr.	Cr.	Consolidated
The entries on the income statement are adjustments for one period to bring the accounts to the desired balance for one period of time, i.e., for one year.	Sales	$ 60,000	$40,000			$100,000
	Dividend income	3,000		**(b)** $ 3,000		
	Investment income			**(1)** 9,920	**(b)** $ 9,920	
		63,000	40,000			100,000
	Cost of sales	32,000	18,000			50,000
	Goodwill impair. loss			**(3)** 80		80
	Expenses, misc.	9,000	12,000			21,000
		41,000	30,000			71,080
	Net income[1]	$ 22,000	$10,000	$13,000	$ 9,920	$ 28,920
	Retained earnings, Jan. 1	$ 99,800	$10,800	**(2)** $10,800	**(a)** $ 2,750	$102,550
	Net income	22,000	10,000	13,000	9,920	28,920
		121,800	20,800			131,470
	Dividends	8,000	3,000		**(1)** 3,000	8,000
	Retained earnings, Dec. 31	$113,800	$17,800	$23,800	$15,670	$123,470
	Assets, misc.	$131,800	$21,000			$152,800
	Inventory	35,000	16,000			51,000
	Investment in S	19,000		**(a)** $ 2,750 **(b)** 6,920	**(1)** $ 6,920 **(2)** 21,750	
The entries on the balance sheet are cumulative adjustments to bring the accounts to the desired balance at the end of the period, i.e., at a point in time.	Acquisition differential			**(2)** 950	**(3)** 950	
	Goodwill			**(3)** 870		870
		$185,800	$37,000			$204,670
	Liabilities	$ 22,000	$ 9,200			$ 31,200
	Common shares	50,000	10,000	**(2)** 10,000		50,000
	Retained earnings	113,800	17,800	23,800	15,670	123,470
		$185,800	$37,000	$45,290	$45,290	$204,670

[1] Attributable to shareholders of Company P.

First, convert the parent's income statement and beginning retained earnings from the cost method to the equity method.

This entry adjusts the investment in S account and the January 1 retained earnings of Company P to the equity method balances at the beginning of the year. The amount used is readily apparent in the calculation of consolidated retained earnings as at January 1, Year 2.

(b)	Dividend income — Company P	3,000	
	Investment in S — Company P	6,920	
	Investment income — Company P		9,920

Entry **(b)** adjusts the accounts of Company P to the equity method balances at the end of Year 2. The calculation of consolidated net income for Year 2 on page 187 provides the amounts for this entry.

The working paper elimination entries are reproduced below, with an explanation of each.

(1)	Investment income — Company P	9,920	
	Dividends — Company S		3,000
	Investment in S — Company P		6,920

This entry eliminates Company P's investment income account and the dividend account of Company S against the investment in S account of Company P. This leaves the investment account with a December 31, Year 1, balance of $21,750.

(2)	Retained earnings Jan. 1 — Company S	10,800	
	Common shares — Company S	10,000	
	Acquisition differential	950	
	Investment in S		21,750

These entries bring the consolidated account balances to the desired amounts.

This entry eliminates the common shares and retained earnings of Company S on December 31, Year 1, against the December 31, Year 1, balance of Company P's investment account; it also establishes the difference as the *unamortized* acquisition differential on that date. This relationship was illustrated on page 213.

(3)	Goodwill impairment loss	80	
	Goodwill	870	
	Acquisition differential		950

This entry eliminates the unamortized acquisition differential at the end of Year 1 and allocates it in accordance with the Year 2 acquisition-differential amortization schedule.

80-Percent-Owned Subsidiary — Year 1

Exhibit 5A.3 on page 216 shows the preparation of the consolidated financial statements as at December 31, Year 1, using a working paper. See Exhibit 5.12 on page 194 to compare the direct approach.

Working paper elimination entry **(a)** adjusts the accounts of Company P as at December 31, Year 1, to what they would have been under the equity method. The dividend income under the cost method is replaced by investment income under the equity method. See page 202 for the calculation of investment income under the equity method.

Exhibit 5A.3

CONSOLIDATED FINANCIAL STATEMENT WORKING PAPER
December 31, Year 1 (cost method)

	P	S	Eliminations Dr.	Eliminations Cr.	Consolidated
Sales	$ 50,000	$30,000			$ 80,000
Dividend income	2,000		(a) $ 2,000		
Investment income			(1) 4,200	(a) $ 4,200	
	52,000	30,000			80,000
Cost of sales	26,500	14,700	(3) 2,000		43,200
Goodwill impair. loss			(3) 50		50
Misc. expenses	5,200	8,000			13,200
	31,700	22,700			56,450
Net income attributable to					23,550
Non-controlling interest			(4) 1,050		1,050
Company P's shareholders	$ 20,300	$ 7,300	$ 9,300	$ 4,200	$ 22,500
Retained earnings, Jan. 1	$ 85,000	$ 6,000	(2) $ 6,000		$ 85,000
Net income	20,300	7,300	9,300	$ 4,200	22,500
	105,300	13,300			107,500
Dividends	6,000	2,500		(1) 2,000	6,000
				(5) 500	
Retained earnings, Dec. 31	$ 99,300	$10,800	$15,300	$ 6,700	$101,500
Assets, misc.	$151,100	$18,300			$169,400
Equipment (net)	30,000	14,000			44,000
Investment in S	15,200		(a) $ 2,200	(1) $ 2,200	
				(2) 15,200	
Acquisition differential			(2) 3,000	(3) 3,000	
Goodwill			(3) 950		950
	$196,300	$32,300			$214,350
Liabilities	$ 47,000	$11,500			$ 58,500
Common shares	50,000	10,000	(2) 10,000		50,000
Retained earnings	99,300	10,800	15,300	6,700	101,500
Non-controlling interest				(2) 3,800	
			(5) 500	(4) 1,050	4,350
	$196,300	$32,300	$31,950	$31,950	$214,350

Sidebar notes (left margin):

The entries on the worksheet are recorded only on the worksheet and are not recorded in the separate-entity books of the parent or the subsidiary.

Non-controlling interest appears both on the income statement (for a period of time) and on the balance sheet (at a point in time).

These entries convert the parent's income statement and beginning retained earnings from the cost method to the equity method.

(a) Dividend income — Company P 2,000
    Investment in S — Company P 2,200
        Investment income — Company P 4,200

After this entry has been entered in the working paper, all relevant items in the financial statements of Company P, except retained earnings as of December 31, Year 1, contain balances arrived at under the equity method.

Investment income is eliminated since it will be replaced by the subsidiary's revenues and expenses, amortization of the acquisition differential, and non-controlling interest.

The other working paper entries are produced and explained below. The only new items here are the entries required to establish the non-controlling interest.

(1) Investment income — Company P   4,200
     Dividends — Company S   2,000
     Investment in S — Company P   2,200

This entry eliminates the investment income and Company P's share of the dividends of Company S against the investment account. The investment account has now been adjusted to the balance at the beginning of the year ($15,200).

The investment account is eliminated since it will be replaced by the carrying value of the subsidiary's assets and liabilities, the unamortized acquisition differential, and non-controlling interest.

(2) Retained earnings, Jan. 1 — Company S   6,000
Common shares — Company S   10,000
Acquisition differential   3,000
     Investment in S — Company P   15,200
     Non-controlling interest   3,800

This entry eliminates 100 percent of the start-of-year shareholders' equity of Company S and the investment account, and establishes the acquisition differential and the non-controlling interest as at the beginning of the year. Notice that there is not a separate section of the working paper for changes in non-controlling interest. Instead, the establishment of non-controlling interest at the beginning of the year is recorded directly to non-controlling interest in the balance sheet section of the working paper. Entries **(4)** and **(5)**, which appear later on this page, record the changes to non-controlling interest during the year. They are also recorded directly to non-controlling interest in the balance sheet section of the working paper. These entries to non-controlling interest will be needed to prepare the non-controlling interest column in the statement of changes in equity during the year.

(3) Cost of sales — Company S   2,000
Goodwill impairment loss   50
Goodwill   950
     Acquisition differential   3,000

In accordance with the schedule, this entry reflects the acquisition-differential amortization on the consolidated income statement and the unamortized balance of the acquisition differential on the consolidated balance sheet.

(4) Non-controlling interest (income statement)   1,050
     Non-controlling interest (balance sheet)   1,050

This entry allocates the net income attributable to the non-controlling interest to the non-controlling interest on the consolidated balance sheet.

(5) Non-controlling interest (balance sheet)   500
     Dividends — Company S   500

This final entry eliminates 20 percent of the dividends of Company S that were paid to the non-controlling interest shareholders and reduces the equity of that group on the consolidated balance sheet.

80-Percent-Owned Subsidiary — Year 2

Exhibit 5A.4 shows the working paper approach to the preparation of the Year 2 consolidated financial statements. See Exhibit 5.15 on page 197 to compare the direct approach.

The elimination entries (a) and (b) adjust the accounts of Company P to equity method balances. These entries are reproduced below.

(a)	Investment in S — Company P	2,200	
	Retained earnings, Jan. 1 — Company P		2,200

Exhibit 5A.4

CONSOLIDATED FINANCIAL STATEMENT WORKING PAPER
December 31, Year 2 (cost method)

	P	S	Eliminations Dr.	Eliminations Cr.	Consolidated
Sales	$ 60,000	$40,000			$100,000
Dividend income	2,400		**(b)** $ 2,400		
Investment income			**(1)** 7,936	**(b)** $ 7,936	
	62,400	40,000			100,000
Cost of sales	32,000	18,000			50,000
Goodwill impair. loss			**(3)** 80		80
Expenses, misc.	9,000	12,000			21,000
	41,000	30,000			71,080
Net income attributable to					28,920
Non-controlling interest			**(4)** 1,984		1,984
Company P's shareholders	$ 21,400	$10,000	$12,400	$ 7,936	$ 26,936
Retained earnings, Jan. 1	$ 99,300	$10,800	**(2)** $10,800	**(a)** $ 2,200	$101,500
Net income	21,400	10,000	12,400	7,936	26,936
	120,700	20,800			128,436
Dividends	8,000	3,000		**(1)** 2,400	8,000
				(5) 600	
Retained earnings, Dec. 31	$112,700	$17,800	$23,200	$13,136	$120,436
Assets, misc.	$134,500	$21,000			$155,500
Inventory	35,000	16,000			51,000
Investment in S	15,200		**(a)** $ 2,200	**(1)** $ 5,536	
			(b) 5,536	**(2)** 17,400	
Acquisition differential			**(2)** 950	**(3)** 950	
Goodwill			**(3)** 870		870
	$184,700	$37,000			$207,370
Liabilities	$ 22,000	$ 9,200			$ 31,200
Common shares	50,000	10,000	**(2)** 10,000		50,000
Retained earnings	112,700	17,800	23,200	13,136	120,436
Non-controlling interest				**(2)** 4,350	5,734
			(5) 600	**(4)** 1,984	
	$184,700	$37,000	$43,356	$43,356	$207,370

Consolidated net income attributable to parent's shareholders is equal to the parent's separate-entity income under the equity method.

Consolidated retained earnings is equal to the parent's separate-entity retained earnings under the equity method.

Entries *(a)* and *(b)* convert the parent's figures on the consolidated working paper from the cost method to the equity method.

This entry adjusts the investment account and the January 1 retained earnings of Company P to the equity method balances at the beginning of the year. The amount used is readily apparent in the calculation of consolidated retained earnings as at January 1, Year 2, as indicated on page 197.

(b)	Dividend income — Company P	2,400	
	Investment in S — Company P	5,536	
	Investment income — Company P		7,936

Entry **(b)** adjusts the accounts of Company P to the equity method balances at the end of Year 2. See page 203 for the calculation of investment income under the equity method.

After these entries have been made in the working paper, all of the accounts of Company P contain balances arrived at using the equity method. The remaining elimination entries are produced and explained below.

(1)	Investment income — Company P	7,936	
	Dividends — Company S		2,400
	Investment in S — Company P		5,536

This entry eliminates Company P's investment income account and 80 percent of the dividends of Company S against Company P's investment account. The investment account now has a December 31, Year 1, balance of $17,400. The remaining 20 percent of the dividends of Company S are eliminated in entry **(5)**.

(2)	Retained earnings, January 1 — Company S	10,800	
	Common shares — Company S	10,000	
	Acquisition differential	950	
	Investment in S — Company P		17,400
	Non-controlling interest		4,350

This entry eliminates 100 percent of the start-of-year retained earnings and common share accounts of Company S against the start-of-year balance in Company P's investment account, and establishes both the unamortized acquisition differential and the non-controlling interest at the beginning of Year 2. The amount for non-controlling interest ($4,350) is 20 percent of the start-of-year common shares and retained earnings accounts of Company S plus 20 percent of the unamortized acquisition differential.

(3)	Goodwill impairment loss	80	
	Goodwill	870	
	Acquisition differential		950

Entry **(3)** allocates the unamortized acquisition differential in accordance with the Year 2 amortization schedule.

These journal entries appear only on the consolidated worksheet and are not posted to the separate-entity accounting records.

(4)	Non-controlling interest (income statement)	1,984	
	Non-controlling interest (balance sheet)		1,984

Entry **(4)** allocates the net income attributable to the non-controlling interest for Year 2 to the equity of the non-controlling interest on the balance sheet.

| **(5)** Non-controlling interest (income statement) | 600 | |
| Dividends — Company S | | 600 |

The final entry eliminates the remaining 20 percent of the dividends of Company S and reduces the equity of the non-controlling interest on the balance sheet by this amount.

In this appendix, we have illustrated the working paper approach. This approach allows the reader to see where all of the eliminations end up. However, as we proceed with some of the more difficult aspects of consolidated statement preparation, the number of elimination entries used becomes overwhelming. Not only that, there is no set standard working paper approach. This appendix presented elimination entries associated with a financial statement working paper. Other approaches could use a different set of entries and still arrive at the same consolidated amounts. If a trial balance working paper approach had been used instead, the entries would have been different. In practice, a computerized spreadsheet or a specialized software program would probably be used in the majority of cases. The working paper entries required by these programs would no doubt be different from those illustrated here.

As you will see, working papers are not used in the chapters that follow. The reason for this is that the major focus of this text is the direct approach, which stresses understanding of relationships rather than memorization of working paper entries. If a thorough understanding of the consolidation process is present, it can then be applied to any computerized working paper program that may be seen in practice. When consolidation questions appear on professional accounting examinations in Canada, a direct approach is invariably expected to be used when formulating an answer.

REVIEW QUESTIONS

Questions, cases, and problems that deal with the appendix material are denoted with an asterisk.

1. Briefly outline the process for determining if goodwill is impaired.

2. Is the impairment test for intangibles other than goodwill the same as the one used for goodwill? Briefly explain.

3. When the parent has used the equity method, the parent's net income equals consolidated net income attributable to the parent's shareholders, and the parent's retained earnings equal consolidated retained earnings. However, the parent's financial statements are not the same as consolidated statements. On consolidated statements, which assets and income are replaced from the parent's statements, and what are they replaced with?

4. A parent company's 75-percent-owned subsidiary declared and paid a dividend totalling $10,000. How would the parent company record this dividend under the equity method? Under the cost method?

5. By which method — cost or equity — do IFRSs require a parent company to record its investment in a subsidiary? Why?

6. The retained earnings column in the statement of changes in equity shows dividends declared during the year. Do these dividends consist of the parent's, or the subsidiary's, or both? Explain.

7. "An acquisition differential allocated to revalue the land of a subsidiary on acquisition date will always appear on subsequent consolidated balance sheets." Do you agree? Explain.

8. "Under the equity method, the investment account is adjusted for the investor's share of post-acquisition earnings computed by the consolidation method." Explain this statement.

9. At the end of the year, the parent's investment account had an equity method balance of $120,000. At this time its 75-percent-owned subsidiary had shareholders' equity totalling $125,000. How much was the unamortized acquisition differential at the end of the year?

10. On the consolidated balance sheet, what effect does the elimination of intercompany receivables and payables have on shareholders' equity and non-controlling interest?

11. Explain how the matching principle is applied when amortizing the acquisition differential.

12. What accounts in the financial statements of the parent company have balances that differ depending on whether the cost or the equity method has been used?

13. Why does adding the parent's share of the increase in retained earnings of the subsidiary and the parent's retained earnings under the cost method result in consolidated retained earnings? Assume that there is no acquisition differential.

*14. What are the initial entries on the working paper when the parent has used the cost method to account for its investment?

15. A subsidiary was acquired in the middle of the fiscal year of the parent. Describe the preparation of the consolidated income statement for the year.

*16. When the parent company uses the cost method, an adjustment must be made to the parent's retained earnings on consolidation in every year after the year of acquisition. Why is this entry necessary? Why is a similar entry not required when the parent utilized the equity method?

17. How would the consolidation of a parent-founded subsidiary differ from the consolidation of a purchased subsidiary?

MULTIPLE-CHOICE QUESTIONS

1. On January 1, Year 3, CD Corp. acquired 70 percent of the common shares of XY Inc. for $980,000. In allocating the purchase price, $120,000 was assigned to goodwill. CD did not have any goodwill recorded on its separate-entity financial statements on January 1, Year 3. A goodwill impairment loss of $36,000 was recorded in Year 5. On December 31, Year 6, the recoverable amount for goodwill was determined to be $70,000. What value would be reported for goodwill on the consolidated balance sheet at December 31, Year 6?
   a. $58,800
   b. $70,000
   c. $84,000
   d. $120,000

2. Parent Inc. purchased all of the outstanding shares of Sub Ltd. on January 1, Year 1, for $214,000. Amortization of the acquisition differential amounted to

$16,000 in each of Years 1 and 2. Parent Inc. reported net income of $100,000 in Year 1 and $110,000 in Year 2, and paid $40,000 in dividends each year. Sub Ltd. reported net income of $33,000 in Year 1 and $39,000 in Year 2, and paid $8,000 in dividends each year. What is the Investment in Sub Ltd. balance on Parent's books as at December 31, Year 2, if the equity method has been used?

  a. $238,000
  b. $246,000
  c. $278,000
  d. $286,000

3. Which of the following *best* describes accounting for intangible assets (other than goodwill) that have an indefinite useful life?

  a. They should be amortized in a systematic and rational manner.
  b. They should be tested annually for impairment, with any impairment amortized to expense in a systematic and rational manner.
  c. They should be carried at fair value on the balance sheet.
  d. They should be tested annually for impairment, with any impairment recorded as a loss.

(CGA-Canada adapted)

4. OP Corporation acquired 60 percent of KD Corporation on March 31, Year 6. Because OP controls KD, it uses the consolidation method for *reporting* its investment. OP should use which of the following for *recording* its investment in KD for internal record-keeping?

  a. The cost method must be used.
  b. The equity method must be used.
  c. The cost method or the equity method may be used.
  d. The consolidation method must be used.

(CGA-Canada adapted)

5. Jonston Ltd. owns 75 percent of the outstanding shares of Saxon Corp. Saxon currently owes Jonston $400,000 for inventory acquired during the last month. In preparing consolidated financial statements, what amount of this debt should be eliminated?

  a. $0
  b. $100,000
  c. $300,000
  d. $400,000

6. AG acquired 80 percent of the shares of its subsidiary LM on January 1, Year 4. On this date the fair value of the land of LM was greater than its carrying value. Which of the combinations of LM's net book value (NBV) and fair value increments (FVI) would be included in its consolidated asset values for land on December 31, Year 6?

  a. 80 percent of NBV and 80 percent of FVI.
  b. 100 percent of NBV and 80 percent of FVI.
  c. 100 percent of NBV and 100 percent of FVI.
  d. 80 percent of NBV and 100 percent of FVI.

Use the following data for Questions 7 to 12.

On January 1, Year 4, Place Inc. acquired an 80 percent interest in Setting Co. for $800,000 cash. At that time, Setting's assets and liabilities had book values equal to fair values, except for the following:

Inventory	Undervalued by $75,000	Turns over 6 times a year
Plant and equipment	Undervalued by $50,000	Remaining useful life: 10 years
Bonds payable	Overvalued by $40,000	Maturity date: December 31, Year 8

The premium/discount on bonds payable is amortized on a straight-line basis.

At January 1, Year 4, Setting had 100,000 common shares outstanding with a book value of $550,000 and retained earnings of $50,000.

The abbreviated financial statements of Place and Setting on December 31, Year 6, are as follows:

STATEMENTS OF FINANCIAL POSITION

	Place	Setting
Plant and equipment (net)	$1,250,000	$1,555,000
Investment in Setting	800,000	—
Current assets	950,000	800,000
	$3,000,000	$2,355,000
Common shares	$1,000,000	$ 550,000
Retained earnings	1,500,000	725,000
10% bonds payable	—	800,000
Current liabilities	500,000	280,000
	$3,000,000	$2,355,000

COMBINED INCOME AND RETAINED EARNINGS STATEMENTS

	Place	Setting
Sales	$2,500,000	$900,000
Cost of goods sold	1,200,000	330,000
Expenses	400,000	220,000
	1,600,000	550,000
Net operating income	900,000	350,000
Dividends received from Setting	100,000	—
Profit	1,000,000	350,000
Retained earnings, Jan. 1, Year 6	800,000	500,000
	1,800,000	850,000
Dividends declared and paid	300,000	125,000
Retained earnings, Dec. 31, Year 6	$1,500,000	$725,000

7. Which of the following is the amount of the inventory fair value increment that will be recognized on Place's consolidated income statement for the year ended December 31, Year 4?
   a. $0
   b. $56,250
   c. $60,000
   d. $75,000

8. Which of the following is the amount of the fair value increment relating to plant and equipment (net) that will be recognized as an increase to

depreciation expense on Place's consolidated income statement for the year ended December 31, Year 5?
a. $4,000
b. $5,000
c. $8,000
d. $32,000

9. Which of the following is the correct adjustment to interest expense for the amortization of the bond fair value increment on Place's consolidated income statement for the year ended December 31, Year 4?
a. $6,400 increase.
b. $8,000 increase.
c. $6,400 decrease.
d. $8,000 decrease.

10. How many years' worth of fair value increment amortizations must be used to calculate consolidated retained earnings at January 1, Year 6, from Place's cost-basis accounting records?
a. 0
b. 1
c. 2
d. 3

11. At December 31, Year 4, Place's consolidated statement of financial position reported a non-controlling interest of $260,000. Setting did not declare any dividends during Year 4. What did Place's consolidated income statement for the year ended December 31, Year 4, report as the non-controlling interest's share of consolidated net income?
a. $60,000
b. $70,000
c. $140,000
d. $180,000

*12. Under the working paper approach to consolidation, which of the following will be included in the elimination journal entry to remove dividends paid by subsidiary during Year 6?
a. Debit non-controlling interest $25,000.
b. Credit non-controlling interest $25,000.
c. Debit dividends declared and paid $100,000.
d. Credit dividends declared and paid $100,000.

Use the following information for Questions 13 to 15.

On January 1, Year 6, AB Inc. purchased 80 percent of the common shares of CD Corp. for $1,400,000. On the date of acquisition, CD's shareholders' equity was as follows:

Common shares	$600,000
Retained earnings	608,000

Any acquisition differential was allocated to goodwill. During Year 6, CD earned a net income of $400,000 and paid dividends of $300,000. On December 31, Year 6, a goodwill impairment loss of $30,000 was recorded.

13. What is the amount of non-controlling interest on the consolidated balance sheet as at December 31, Year 6?
   a. $241,600
   b. $255,600
   c. $261,600
   d. $364,000

14. What is consolidated net income attributable to the non-controlling interest on the consolidated income statement for the year ended December 31, Year 6?
   a. $20,000
   b. $60,000
   c. $74,000
   d. $80,000

15. What is the amount of goodwill on the consolidated balance sheet as at December 31, Year 6?
   a. $403,600
   b. $409,600
   c. $433,600
   d. $512,000

16. On January 1, Year 2, Law Corporation acquired 90 percent of the common shares of Yer Ltd. On that date, Yer's equipment had a book value of $300,000 and a fair value of $400,000. How would the account balance for equipment on the consolidated balance sheet at the end of Year 4 differ if Law had used the cost method rather than the equity method in accounting for its investment in Yer?
   a. There would be no difference.
   b. The consolidated equipment account would be higher when Law used the cost method.
   c. The consolidated equipment account would be lower when Law used the cost method.
   d. Further information is needed to determine the difference.

Use the following data for Questions 17 and 18.

On January 1, Year 1, CFL Company acquired 70 percent of the common shares of NFL Company for $700,000 in cash. The acquisition differential of $100,000 was allocated to a patent with an estimated remaining useful life of 5 years. CFL used the entity theory when preparing the consolidated financial statements for Year 1.

17. What would be the impact on the ratio of amortization expense to total revenue on the Year 1 consolidated income statement if CFL had used the parent company extension theory instead of the entity theory?
   a. It would increase.
   b. It would decrease.
   c. It would not change.
   d. The impact cannot be determined based on the information provided.

18. What would be the impact on the return on shareholders' equity for the Year 1 consolidated financial statements if the acquisition differential had been

allocated to inventory instead of patents? Assume that NFL's inventory turnover is six times per year.

a. It would increase.
b. It would decrease.
c. It would not change.
d. The impact cannot be determined based on the information provided.

CASES

Case 1 BIO Company is a private company. It employs 30 engineers and scientists who are involved with research and development of various biomedical devices. All of the engineers and scientists are highly paid and regarded in the field of biomedical research. BIO is 50 percent owned by Rod Smart, who started the company in Year 3, and 50 percent owned by a group of venture capitalists who contributed $10 million of equity capital in Year 4 to fund the R & D activity of the group.

On January 1, Year 6, REX Ltd., a public company listed on the TSX Venture Exchange, acquired 100 percent of the shares of BIO by issuing 5 million of its own shares. Its shares were trading at $4 per share on the date of this transaction.

The balance sheet for BIO on January 1, Year 6, was as follows:

Cash and marketable securities	$ 2,500,000
Tangible capital assets — net	800,000
Development costs	3,000,000
	$ 6,300,000
Liabilities	$ 900,000
Common shares	10,100,000
Deficit	(4,700,000)
	$ 6,300,000

The cash, marketable securities, tangible capital assets and liabilities have fair values equal to carrying values. Prior to Year 5, all of the research and development costs were expensed. Starting in Year 5, the developments costs were capitalized because the management of BIO felt that they were getting close to patenting some of their products.

The management of REX is aware that BIO will need to be included in REX's consolidated financial statements. Management has the following questions related to these consolidated financial statements.

Required:

(a) Will any of the purchase price be allocated to BIO's skilled workers? If so, how will this asset be valued and how will it be amortized or checked for impairment on an annual basis?

(b) Will any of the purchase price be allocated to identifiable intangible assets? If so, how will this asset be valued and how will it be amortized or checked for impairment on an annual basis?

(c) How much of the purchase price will be allocated to goodwill and how will goodwill be evaluated for impairment on an annual basis?

Case 2 When Valero Energy Corp. acquired Ultramar Diamond Shamrock Corp. (UDS) for US$6 billion, it created the second-largest refiner of petroleum products in North

America, with over 23,000 employees in the United States and Canada, total assets of $10 billion, and combined revenues of $32 billion. Combined, it had 13 refineries with a total throughput capacity of just under 2 million barrels per day (BPD); it also became one of the continent's largest retailers, with more than 5,000 retail outlets in the United States and Canada. The Canadian operations of UDS continued to operate under the Ultramar brand.

It was announced that the combination of Valero's complex refining system and an extensive UDS refining, logistics, and retail network created synergies and strategic benefits that would result in cost savings of approximately $200 million per year and the enhanced ability to compete effectively in a rapidly consolidating industry.

The retail assets included in the acquisition included the brands Ultramar, Diamond Shamrock, Beacon, and Total. UDS had more than 2,500 company-owned sites in the United States and Canada, and also supplied 2,500 dealer, truck-stop, and cardlock sites. The company-owned stores had extensive brand support programs such as proprietary consumer and fleet credit cards, radio and television brand support, and strong in-store marketing programs, to which Valero was able to add its 350-store retail network in California. In addition, UDS operated one of the largest home heating oil businesses in North America, selling heating oil to approximately 250,000 households.

The acquisition clearly included more than the physical assets of Ultramar Diamond Shamrock. A variety of unrecorded intangible assets were represented in the portfolio of assets held by UDS, and these are the matters that require your attention at this time.

Required:

With reference to IFRS 3, prepare a memorandum to the chief financial officer of Valero. In this memo,

- discuss the valuation of the various intangible assets included in this acquisition,
- indicate which items should be included in the amount assigned to goodwill in the acquisition,
- indicate which items should be separately identified and valued as intangible assets, and
- discuss how you would assign values to the various items identified and what amortization policy (if any) is appropriate.

(*case prepared by Peter Secord, St. Mary's University*)

Case 3   Gerry's Fabrics Ltd. (GFL), a private company, manufactures a variety of clothing for women and children and sells it to retailers across Canada. Until recently, the company has operated from the same plant since its incorporation under federal legislation 40 years ago. Over the years, the profits of the company have varied widely, and there have been periods of losses.

In the year ended March 31, Year 1, the company entered into an arrangement whereby it issued common shares from treasury to a group of new shareholders. At the same time, the existing shareholders were given the option of exchanging their common shares for preferred shares, which are redeemable at the option of the company and retractable at the option of the shareholder. One shareholder, who had held 25 percent of the common shares, elected to accept the preferred shares, while the other shareholders elected to retain their common shares.

A "Preferred Share Agreement" (the Agreement), was signed by the shareholder who had accepted the preferred shares (the "preferred shareholder"). Under the Agreement, the preferred shareholder can require GFL to redeem all of his shares in any year, after giving at least 90 days' notice prior to the fiscal year-end. The Agreement does not provide for partial redemptions. The total redemption price for all shares is 1.25 times "income before taxes" for that year. The term *income before taxes* is defined in the Agreement as follows:

1. Income before taxes for the year of redemption must be calculated
    *   in accordance with the accounting policies set forth in this Agreement, or
    *   where no accounting policy has been clearly specified, in accordance with policies consistent in intent with the policies contained in this Agreement.
2. Income before taxes for the year of redemption need not, for the purposes of the Agreement, be the same as that which is reported to shareholders or that which is used for calculating income taxes payable.

The Agreement specifies the applicable accounting policies as follows:

A. Revenue recognition:
    1. In cases where a deposit of 10 percent or more of the sales price has been received from the customer, revenue shall be recognized on completion of the manufacturing of the goods ordered.
    2. In all other cases, revenue shall be recognized upon shipment to the customer, and no allowance shall be made for returned merchandise or adjustments.
B. Cost of goods sold and inventory:
    1. All inventory on hand at the end of a fiscal year (excluding raw materials) shall be costed at actual production costs, including its full share of all overhead expenditures.
    2. Raw materials inventory shall include all expenditures that were needed to make the inventory available for use, including unpacking and storing costs.
C. Amortization:
    1. All applicable amortization shall be computed on a straight-line basis using realistic residual values.
    2. Amortization shall be recorded over the physical life of the assets, regardless of their useful life to the company.
    3. No amortization shall be recorded on assets that are increasing in value.
D. Capitalization:
    1. All expenditures shall be capitalized as assets unless their life is limited to the current financial period. All maintenance and repair costs that extend an asset's useful life shall be capitalized.
    2. Assets shall be recorded at cost and amortized in accordance with C above.
E. Liabilities:
    1. Each liability shall be recorded at the amount required to settle the obligation. A debt-to-equity ratio of 1:1 is assumed to exist. Interest incurred on debt in excess of this ratio will not be deductible in computing income before taxes.
F. Errors and adjustments:
    1. All errors, adjustments, and changes in value shall be attributed to the year to which the error or adjustment or change relates.

G. Compensation and related transactions:
   1. Average compensation per employee shall be in accordance with levels used in fiscal Year 1 adjusted by the Consumer Price Index.
   2. All related-party transactions must be measured at fair value or values established in the marketplace for transactions between GFL and unrelated third parties.

The Agreement also contains a separate clause that deals with "arbitration procedures." These procedures allow an independent arbitrator to calculate the share redemption price after having obtained full access to the books and records of GFL.

The preferred shareholder has advised GFL of his intention to have GFL redeem his preferred shares and has provided GFL with the required 90 days' notice. The redemption price, calculated by GFL, was based on the March 31, Year 5, financial statements. However, the preferred shareholder disagrees with GFL's figure for income before taxes.

Since the price is being disputed, the matter is to be resolved by an independent arbitrator. Both parties have agreed to engage Cook & Co., Chartered Accountants, to make a binding decision. You, CA, are employed by Cook & Co. The engagement partner has asked you to prepare a memo providing complete analyses required for and recommendations to be considered in the calculation of the share-redemption price. Your notes from your investigations are contained in Exhibit I.

Required:

Prepare the memo to the partner.

(*CICA adapted*)

Exhibit I

NOTES FROM INVESTIGATION OF GFL

1. The disputed share-redemption price calculation was prepared by the vice-president of finance of GFL and is 1.25 times the company's unaudited income before taxes of $895,420 for the year ended March 31, Year 5.

2. The unaudited financial statements for the year ended March 31, Year 5, reflect the following transactions and accounting policies:
    *   During fiscal Year 4, GFL acquired all the shares of a competing company (J Ltd.) for $8 million. Most of the amount by which the purchase price exceeded the book value of the assets and liabilities acquired was recorded as goodwill and is being amortized over 10 years. The purchase was financed almost entirely by debt at 10 percent interest for five years.
    *   On January 1, Year 5, a volume discount policy was introduced. At March 31, Year 5, an estimated liability of $95,500 was provided for volume discounts that may become due.
    *   In fiscal Year 4, the manufacturing processes were altered to introduce more mechanization, and standard costing was adopted. All variances from standard costs are being expensed.
    *   In order to reduce taxable income and save cash, all employee incentives are being accrued at year-end and paid five months later.
    *   In Year 3, GFL decided to account for one of its successful investments on the equity basis. During fiscal Year 5, the directors of GFL chose to revert to the cost basis for the investment.
    *   In fiscal Year 5, GFL commenced construction of another manufacturing facility at a cost of $1.8 million, including equipment. Some manufacturing occurred in a part of the new facility before the whole facility was ready for use. To be conservative, any costs that were incurred after manufacturing had commenced were expensed, except for new equipment installations.

(*continued*)

- Land that has been held for several years for future expansion of the company was recorded at cost plus carrying costs (property taxes, maintenance, and similar) until fiscal Year 5. The land was reclassified in late fiscal Year 5 as inventory and was written down to the lower of cost and net realizable value.
- In March Year 5, GFL sold some of its capital assets under a deferred payment arrangement. Gains on disposal will be recorded as payment is received, on a proportional basis.
- In April Year 5, an enhanced executive pension plan was introduced. The March 31, Year 5, financial statements include pension expenses that reflect the additional costs resulting from the new pension plan enhancements.

3. Notes to the financial statements for fiscal Year 5 disclose the following:
   - During the year, GFL sold $4 million worth of goods to DGR Ltd. DGR is owned by several of the common shareholders of GFL. DGR paid a special price for goods that was about $380,000 lower than the price paid by other retailers.
   - A $200,000 liability has been recorded for legal costs pertaining to a patent infringement case that is before the courts.

Case 4   Total Protection Limited (TPL) was recently incorporated by five homebuilders in central Canada to provide warranty protection for new-home buyers. Each shareholder owns a 20 percent interest in TPL. While most homebuilders provide one-year warranties, TPL offers ten-year warranties and includes protection for a number of items not usually covered. For example, if a problem arose as a result of faulty construction or construction materials, TPL would protect its customers against any resulting decline in the market value of their property and would provide for the costs of restoring the property. TPL does not, however, cover general declines in market value.

The five shareholders believe TPL will increase their home sales and at the same time minimize their individual risks. The idea for TPL originated with Safe-Way Builders and, therefore, this shareholder will receive a royalty payment of 5 percent of income before income taxes. The shareholders have engaged your firm to prepare a report that will assist them in managing TPL in order to maximize its long-term profitability. In addition, as a separate report, the shareholders would like your firm to recommend appropriate financial accounting policies for TPL.

You, CA, and the partner on the engagement, meet with Gina Filmore, president of Safe-Way Builders. Filmore is currently operating TPL from the offices of Safe-Way Builders, for which TPL will be charged rent. Filmore provides you with the following information on TPL's operations.

"TPL's revenues consist of an initial fee paid at the time of purchase of the warranty and an annual maintenance fee paid over the term of the warranty. Currently, the initial fee and annual maintenance fee depend on a number of factors, including the cost of the home, reputation of the builder, construction design of the home (e.g., brick versus aluminum siding), and the home's location. The warranties are sold through each builder, who can adjust the initial fee and the annual maintenance fee if an adjustment is considered necessary to make the sale. The builder receives a commission of 10 percent of the total warranty revenue, which should ensure that the builder would try to maximize the initial fee and the annual maintenance fee. Typically, a buyer of a brick house worth $250,000 that was constructed by a good-quality builder should expect to pay an initial fee of $2,000 plus an annual maintenance fee of $250.

"To date, TPL has been doing very well, primarily as a result of two factors: central Canada has been experiencing a boom in the residential construction industry, and TPL has expanded to offer coverage for homes built by builders other than the shareholders. Quite frankly, an increasing share of our business is from these outside builders, many of which have entered the industry just to try to capitalize on the demand. We don't think that permitting these homebuilders to sell coverage will hurt our home sales since most of them are in the low-price segment of the market, keeping costs down by employing new, less expensive construction methods and materials. We require that their initial fee be at least $1,500 per home to ensure that they don't lower the price just to make a sale.

"Our real problem is keeping up with the paperwork. I have my own business to run and cannot devote much time to TPL. We haven't even had time to get organized or set up any system for TPL. Lately, I must admit that I've lost track of what's going on. All I know is that we're making money. In just 11 months, TPL has collected about $1.6 million while paying out only $224,000 in repair costs. Keep in mind, however, that I've been able to keep these repair costs down by having Safe-Way Builders do the repairs. Business will only get better when we expand within the next month to offer coverage in western Canada and the southwestern United States.

"Since we have accumulated a lot of cash, we recently decided, in a 3-to-2 vote among the shareholders, to buy 100 percent of the shares of Gainery Construction Ltd., a local construction company. Mr. Gainery, the owner of the company, had a heart attack about six months ago and wanted to get out of the business. Details of the purchase agreement are provided in Exhibit I."

Just before you leave the client's premises, you manage to collect some additional information on the operations of TPL (see Exhibit II on page 232).

Exhibit I

INFORMATION GATHERED FROM PURCHASE AGREEMENT

1. Closing date will be September 1, Year 1.
2. TPL will purchase 100 percent of the shares of Gainery Construction Ltd. for $500,000 in cash on closing, plus $500,000 per year for the next two years.
3. Mr. Gainery will provide without additional consideration a minimum of 300 hours of consulting services in the first year and a minimum of 150 hours in the second year to ensure a smooth transition of the business.
4. The carrying value and estimated fair value of identifiable assets and liabilities were as follows on the date of acquisition:

	Carrying value	Fair value
Cash	$ 100,000	$ 100,000
Accounts receivable	200,000	200,000
Homes under construction	1,300,000	1,500,000
Undeveloped land	1,000,000	1,600,000
Equipment, net	700,000	650,000
Other assets	70,000	70,000
	$3,370,000	$4,120,000
Liabilities	$2,470,000	$2,470,000
Common shares	100,000	
Retained earnings	800,000	
	$3,370,000	

Exhibit II

INFORMATION GATHERED FROM CLIENT'S RECORDS
TPL Shareholders

	Larkview Estates	Towne Homes	Granite Homes	Kings Road	Safe-Way Builders	Other Builders	Total
Number of warranties sold	50	85	190	250	175	465	1,215
Warranty revenue ($000s)	$120	$165	$395	$90	$160	$705	$1,635
Repair costs incurred ($000s)	$ 6	$ 9	$ 21	$42	$ 39	$107	$ 224

When you return to the office, the partner reminds you that he will be meeting with TPL shareholders in one week and asks you to prepare the reports requested by the shareholders.

Required:

Prepare the reports requested by the partner.

(CICA adapted)

Case 5   In the course of the audit of King Limited (King), you, CA, while reviewing the draft financial statements for the year ended August 31, Year 17, noticed that King's investment in Queen Limited (Queen) was valued on the cost basis. In Year 16, it had been valued on the equity basis. Representing a 22 percent interest in Queen, this investment had been made 10 years ago to infuse fresh equity, with a view to protecting King's source of supply for drugs.

King's controller informed CA that Queen had suffered a large loss in Year 17, as shown by the May interim financial statements. King's representative on Queen's board of directors had resigned because King's purchases from Queen now constitute less than 5 percent of its total purchases. In addition, Queen had been uncooperative in providing profit data in time to make the year-end equity adjustment. Consequently, King's controller had revised the method of accounting for the investment in Queen.

You then found out that King's managers are planning a share issue in Year 18 and do not want their earnings impaired by Queen's poor performance. However, they are reluctant to divest themselves of Queen in case the rumoured development by Queen of a vaccine for a serious viral disease materializes.

When you approached Queen's managers, they refused to disclose any information on Queen's operations. You then learned from a stockbroker friend that Queen's poor results were due to its market being undercut by generic drug manufacturers. The loss had been increased when Queen's management wrote off most of Queen's intangible assets. You summarized the relevant information on the treatment of the investment for your audit file (Exhibit I).

Required:

Discuss how King should report its investment in Queen and describe what should be disclosed in the notes to the Year 17 financial statements. Assume that King and Queen are public companies.

(CICA-adapted)

Exhibit I

YOUR (THE CA'S) NOTES ON KING'S INVESTMENT IN QUEEN'S SHARES

Extracts from King's draft financial statements for the year ended August 31, Year 17, in thousands of dollars, follow:

	Year 17	Year 16
Investment in Queen (Note 1)	$25,000	$27,400
Retained Earnings:		
Opening balance	$ 6,500	$ 2,350
plus: net earnings	4,500	7,300
	11,000	9,650
less: prior-period adjustment (Note 2)	2,400	—
dividends	2,250	3,150
Closing balance	$ 6,350	$ 6,500

Note 1:

The investment in Queen originally cost $25 million. The carrying value under the equity method at the end of Year 16 was $27.4 million. The equity adjustment for Year 16 involved the elimination of King's share of the $5 million unrealized profit included in ending inventory, on sales from Queen to King.

Note 2:

In the nine months ended May 31, Year 17, Queen reported a net loss of $140 million after writing off development and patent costs as unusual items. At the end of Year 17, King changed its method of accounting for the investment from the equity method to the cost method and reduced the investment account from $27.4 million back to its original cost of $25 million. The unrealized profit in King's ending inventory for Year 17 amounts to $1 million. King has not made any adjustment for its share of this unrealized profit in the investment account.

   Stock market trading in Queen's common shares has been heavy in the last year. Prices were as follows:

August 31, Year 16	$20
February 28, Year 17	5
August 31, Year 17	13

   King owns 2,000,000 common shares of Queen. Queen did not pay any dividends in Year 16 or Year 17.

PROBLEMS

Problem 1   When Pill Ltd. acquired 85 percent of Sill Corporation on January 1, Year 1, for $238,000, the imputed acquisition differential of $60,000 was allocated entirely to goodwill. On December 31, Year 1, a goodwill impairment loss of $1,500 was recognized. Pill uses the cost method for internal purposes to account for its investment. Pill reported a separate-entity Year 1 net income of $25,000 and declared no dividends. Sill reported a separate-entity net income of $40,000 and paid dividends of $9,000 in Year 1.

Required:

Compute the following:
(a) Consolidated net income attributable to Pill's shareholders for Year 1.
(b) Consolidated net income attributable to non-controlling interest that would appear on the Year 1 consolidated income statement.
(c) Investment in Sill at December 31, Year 1 (equity method).

Problem 2   Large Ltd. purchased 75 percent of Small Company on January 1, Year 1, for $600,000, when the statement of financial position for Small showed common shares of $400,000 and retained earnings of $100,000. On that date, the inventory of Small was undervalued by $40,000, and a patent with an estimated remaining life of 5 years was overvalued by $70,000.

Small reported the following subsequent to January 1, Year 1:

	Profit	Dividends
Year 1	$ 80,000	$25,000
Year 2 (loss)	(35,000)	10,000
Year 3	90,000	40,000

A test for goodwill impairment on December 31, Year 3, indicated a loss of $19,300 being recorded for Year 3 on the consolidated income statement. Large uses the cost method to account for its investment in Small and reported the following for Year 3 for its separate-entity statement of changes in equity:

Retained earnings, beginning	$500,000
Profit	200,000
Dividends	(70,000)
Retained earnings, end	$630,000

Required:

(a) Prepare the cost method journal entries of Large for each year.
(b) Compute the following on the consolidated financial statements for the year ended December 31, Year 3:
   (i)   Goodwill.
   (ii) Non-controlling interest on the statement of financial position.
   (iii) Retained earnings, beginning of year.
   (iv) Profit attributable to Large's shareholders.
   (v)   Profit attributable to non-controlling interest.
(c) Now assume that Large uses the equity method to record its investment in Small.
   (i)   Prepare Large's journal entries for each year related to its investment in Small.
   (ii) Determine the investment in Small at December 31, Year 3.

Problem 3   On January 1, Year 2, Gros Corporation acquired 70 percent of the outstanding common shares of Petite Company for a total cost of $84,000. On that date, Petite had $35,000 of common shares and $25,000 of retained earnings. The book values of each of Petite's identifiable assets and liabilities were equal to their fair values except for the following:

	Book value	Fair value
Inventory	$ 45,000	$ 55,000
Equipment	70,000	90,000

The equipment had an estimated useful life of 10 years as at January 1, Year 2, and the entire inventory was sold during Year 2.

Selected account balances from the records of Gros and Petite for the year ended December 31, Year 6, were as follows:

	Gros	Petite
Inventory	$150,000	$ 80,000
Equipment, net	326,000	160,000
Goodwill		
Non-controlling interest on balance sheet		
Retained earnings, end of year	270,000	50,000
Cost of goods purchased	500,000	450,000
Change in inventory	20,000	12,000
Amortization expense	35,000	20,000
Non-controlling interest on income statement		
Net income	90,000	48,000
Dividends paid	30,000	10,000

Additional Information

- Gros uses the cost method to account for its investment in Petite.
- An independent valuator has estimated that the goodwill associated with Gros's acquisition of Petite had a recoverable amount of $28,000 as of December 31, Year 6. (Note: No impairment losses have been recognized in all years prior to Year 6.)

Required:

(a) Determine the amounts on the Year 6 consolidated financial statements for the above-noted accounts.

(b) If the independent appraisal of the recoverable amount for goodwill as at December 31, Year 6, showed an amount of $8,000 instead of the $28,000 indicated above, what would be the impact on the following?

   (i) Consolidated net income attributable to Gros's shareholders.

   (ii) Consolidated retained earnings.

   (iii) Consolidated net income attributable to non-controlling interest.

Problem 4 Summarized balance sheets of Corner Company and its subsidiary Brook Corporation on December 31, Year 4, were as follows:

	Corner	Brook	Consolidated
Current assets	$ 160,000	$ 700,000	$ 860,000
Investment in Brook (cost)	640,000		
Other assets	600,000	900,000	1,500,000
	$1,400,000	$1,600,000	$2,360,000
Liabilities	$ 800,000	$ 200,000	$1,000,000
Common shares	900,000	600,000	900,000
Retained earnings	(300,000)	800,000	180,000
Non-controlling interest	—	—	280,000
	$1,400,000	$1,600,000	$2,360,000

On the date that Corner acquired its interest in Brook, there was no acquisition differential and the book values of Brook's net assets were equal to fair values. During Year 4, Corner reported a net loss of $60,000 while Brook reported a net income of

$140,000. No dividends were declared by either company during Year 4. Corner uses the cost method to account for its investment.

Required:

Compute the following:
(a) The percentage of Brook's shares owned by Corner.
(b) Consolidated net income attributable to Corner's shareholders for Year 4.
(c) Corner's December 31, Year 3, retained earnings if it had used the equity method to account for its investment.
(d) The retained earnings of Brook on the date that Corner acquired its interest in Brook.

Problem 5 Pen Ltd. acquired an 85-percent interest in Silk Corp. on December 31, Year 1, for $646,000. On that date Silk had common shares of $500,000 and retained earnings of $100,000. The imputed acquisition differential was allocated $70,000 to inventory, with the balance to patents being amortized over 10 years. Silk reported profit of $30,000 in Year 2 and $52,000 in Year 3. While no dividends were declared in Year 2, Silk declared a dividend of $15,000 in Year 3.

Pen, which uses the cost method, reported a profit of $28,000 in Year 2 and a *loss* of $45,000 in Year 3. Pen's retained earnings on December 31, Year 3, were $91,000.

Required:

Compute the following:
(a) Non-controlling interest in profit for Year 2 and Year 3.
(b) Consolidated profit attributable to Pen's shareholders for Year 2 and Year 3.
(c) Consolidated retained earnings at December 31, Year 3.
(d) Non-controlling interest at December 31, Year 3.
(e) Investment in Silk at December 31, Year 3, if Pen had used the equity method.
(f) Consolidated patents at December 31, Year 3.

Problem 6 Peach Ltd. acquired 70 percent of the common shares of Cherry Company on January 1, Year 4. On that date, Cherry had common shares of $600,000 and retained earnings of $300,000.

The following is a summary of the changes in Peach's investment account from January 1, Year 4, to December 31, Year 6:

INVESTMENT IN CHERRY

January 1, Year 4	Cost	$651,000
December 31, Year 4	Investment income	51,800
	Dividends	(28,000)
December 31, Year 5	Investment income	63,700
	Dividends	(35,000)
December 31, Year 6	Investment income	78,400
	Dividends	(42,000)
	Balance	$739,900

Additional Information
- Dividends declared by Cherry each year were equal to 50 percent of Cherry's reported profit each year.
- On January 1, Year 4, the book values of the identifiable net assets of Cherry were equal to fair values.

Required:

Calculate the following:

(a) The amount of dividends declared by Cherry in Year 4.

(b) The reported profit of Cherry for Year 5.

(c) The amount for non-controlling interest that would appear in the Year 6 consolidated income statement and statement of financial position.

(d) The amount of goodwill that would appear on the December 31, Year 6, consolidated statement of financial position.

Problem 7 On January 1, Year 3, Grant Corporation bought 8,000 (80 percent) of the outstanding common shares of Lee Company for $70,000 cash. Lee's shares were trading for $7 per share on the date of acquisition. On that date, Lee had $25,000 of common shares outstanding and $30,000 retained earnings. Also on that date, the book value of each of Lee's identifiable assets and liabilities was equal to its fair value except for the following:

	Book value	Fair value
Inventory	$50,000	$55,000
Patent	10,000	20,000

The patent had an estimated useful life of 5 years at January 1, Year 3, and all of the inventory was sold during Year 3. Grant uses the cost method to account for its investment.

Additional Information

- The recoverable amount for goodwill was determined to be $10,000 on December 31, Year 6. The goodwill impairment loss occured in Year 6.
- Grant's accounts receivable contain $30,000 owing from Lee.
- Amortization expense is grouped with distribution expenses and impairment losses are grouped with other expenses.

The following are the separate-entity financial statements of Grant and Lee as at December 31, Year 6.

BALANCE SHEETS
December 31, Year 6

	Grant	Lee
Assets		
Cash	$ 5,000	$ 18,000
Accounts receivable	185,000	82,000
Inventory	310,000	100,000
Investment in Lee	70,000	—
Equipment, net	230,000	205,000
Patent, net	—	2,000
	$800,000	$407,000
Liabilities and Shareholders' Equity		
Accounts payable	$190,000	$195,000
Other accrued liabilities	60,000	50,000
Income taxes payable	80,000	72,000
Common shares	170,000	25,000
Retained earnings	300,000	65,000
	$800,000	$407,000

INCOME STATEMENT
Year ended December 31, Year 6

	Grant	Lee
Sales	$900,000	$360,000
Cost of goods sold	(340,000)	(240,000)
Gross margin	560,000	120,000
Distribution expense	(30,000)	(25,000)
Other expenses	(180,000)	(56,000)
Income tax expense	(120,000)	(16,000)
Net income	$230,000	$ 23,000

Required:

(a) Calculate consolidated retained earnings at December 31, Year 6.

(b) Prepare consolidated financial statements for Year 6.

Problem 8   The following statements of income and retained earnings were prepared by Paris Corporation and Slater Company on December 31 of the current year:

	Paris	Slater
Sales	$900,000	$500,000
Dividend income	60,000	—
	960,000	500,000
Cost of sales	600,000	300,000
Operating expenses	200,000	80,000
	800,000	380,000
Net income	160,000	120,000
Retained earnings, January 1	301,000	584,000
	461,000	704,000
Dividends	150,000	75,000
Retained earnings, December 31	$311,000	$629,000

Paris obtained its 80 percent interest in Slater eight years ago when Slater had retained earnings of $53,000. The $100,000 acquisition differential on acquisition date was allocated entirely to intangible assets with an estimated remaining useful life of 10 years. Paris uses the cost method to account for its investment.

Required:

Prepare the following statements for the current year:

(a) Consolidated income statement.

(b) Consolidated retained earnings statement.

Problem 9   On July 1, Year 5, Big purchased 80 percent of the outstanding common shares of Little for $82,080. On that date Little's equipment had a fair value that was $21,600 less than book value. The equipment had an estimated remaining useful life of 8 years. All other assets and liabilities had book values equal to fair values. On June 30, Year 6, goodwill had a recoverable amount of $20,000.

On June 30, Year 6, the following financial statements were prepared. Big uses the cost method to account for its investment.

INCOME STATEMENTS

	Big	Little
Sales	$270,000	$162,000
Investment income	10,800	—
	280,800	162,000
Cost of sales	140,100	94,380
Expenses (misc.)	31,080	28,200
	171,180	122,580
Net income	$109,620	$ 39,420

RETAINED EARNINGS STATEMENTS

	Big	Little
Balance, July 1	$459,000	$ 32,400
Net income	109,620	39,420
	568,620	71,820
Dividends	32,400	13,500
Balance, June 30	$536,220	$ 58,320

BALANCE SHEETS — June 30, Year 6

	Big	Little
Miscellaneous assets	$ 875,940	$128,820
Equipment (net)	102,000	45,600
Investment in Little	82,080	—
	$1,060,020	$174,420
Liabilities	$ 253,800	$ 62,100
Common shares	270,000	54,000
Retained earnings	536,220	58,320
	$1,060,020	$174,420

Required:

(a) Prepare the consolidated financial statements of Big as at June 30, Year 6.

(b) Prepare a schedule showing the changes in non-controlling interest during the year.

Problem 10 On December 31, Year 2, Palm Inc. purchased 80 percent of the outstanding common shares of Storm Company for $310,000. At that date, Storm had common shares of $200,000 and retained earnings of $60,000. In negotiating the purchase price, it was agreed that the assets on Storm's statement of financial position were fairly valued except for plant assets, which had a $40,000 excess of fair value over net book value. It was also agreed that Storm had unrecognized intangible assets consisting of customer lists that had an estimated value of $24,000. The plant assets had a remaining useful life of 8 years at the acquisition date and the customer lists would be amortized over a 12-year period. Any goodwill arising from this business combination would be tested periodically for impairment. Palm accounts for its investment using the cost method.

Additional Information

- Impairment tests performed at the end of Year 6 indicated that the goodwill had a recoverable amount of $50,000 and the customer lists had a recoverable amount of $13,750. The impairment loss on these assets occurred entirely in Year 6.

- On December 26, Year 6, Palm declared dividends of $36,000 while Storm declared dividends of $20,000.
- Amortization expense is reported in selling expenses while impairment losses are reported in other expenses.

Financial statements for Palm and Storm for the year ended December 31, Year 6, were as follows:

STATEMENTS OF FINANCIAL POSITION
December 31, Year 6

	Palm	Storm
Assets		
Plant assets — net	$230,000	$160,000
Investment in Storm Company	310,000	—
Other investments	82,000	22,000
Notes receivable	—	10,000
Inventory	100,000	180,000
Accounts receivable	88,000	160,000
Cash	20,000	30,000
	$830,000	$562,000
Shareholders' Equity and Liabilities		
Common shares	$500,000	$200,000
Retained earnings	110,000	150,000
Notes payable	130,000	100,000
Other current liabilities	10,000	50,000
Accounts payable	80,000	62,000
	$830,000	$562,000

INCOME STATEMENTS
Year ended December 31, Year 6

	Palm	Storm
Sales	$870,000	$515,000
Cost of goods sold	(638,000)	(360,000)
Gross profit	232,000	155,000
Selling expenses	(22,000)	(35,000)
Other expenses	(148,000)	(72,000)
Interest and dividend income	34,000	2,000
Profit	$ 96,000	$ 50,000

Required:

(a) Prepare consolidated financial statements.
(b) If none of the acquisition differential had been allocated to customer lists at the date of acquisition, how would this affect
  (i) the return on total shareholders' equity for Year 6?
  (ii) the debt-to-equity ratio at the end of Year 6?

Problem 11 On July 1, Year 4, Aaron Co. purchased 80 percent of the voting shares of Bondi Ltd. for $543,840. The statement of financial position of Bondi on that date appears on the following page.

The accounts receivable of Bondi were collected in October Year 4, and the inventory was completely sold by May Year 5. Bondi's fixed assets had a remaining life of 15 years on July 1, Year 4, and the bonds payable mature on June 30, Year 8. The bonds were issued on July 1, Year 1. The stated rate of interest on the bonds is 6 percent payable semi-annually. The market rate of interest was 8 percent on July 1, Year 4. Tests for impairment of goodwill indicated a loss of $8,329 in Year 5 and $5,553 in Year 6.

BONDI LTD.
STATEMENT OF FINANCIAL POSITION
as at July 1, Year 4

	Net book value	Fair value
Plant assets (net)	$540,000	$450,000
Inventory	180,000	228,000
Accounts receivable	120,000	144,004
Cash	96,000	96,000
	$936,000	
Common shares	$120,000	
Retained earnings	508,800	
Bonds payable	200,000	186,534
Current liabilities	107,200	107,200
	$936,000	

The financial statements for Aaron and Bondi at December 31, Year 6, are presented below. Aaron has used the cost method to account for its investment in Bondi.

STATEMENTS OF FINANCIAL POSITION

	Aaron	Bondi
Plant assets (net)	$ 720,000	$ 540,000
Investment in Bondi	543,840	—
Other investments	250,666	—
Inventory	300,000	276,000
Accounts receivable	180,000	114,000
Cash	120,000	84,000
	$2,114,506	$1,014,000
Common shares	$ 300,600	$ 120,000
Retained earnings	1,318,706	558,200
Bonds payable	315,000	200,000
Current liabilities	180,200	135,800
	$2,114,506	$1,014,000

INCOME STATEMENTS

Sales	$1,261,000	$1,200,000
Dividend income from Bondi	4,000	—
Income from other investments	25,000	—
	1,290,000	1,200,000
Raw materials used	880,000	1,005,000
Change in inventory	(40,000)	15,000
Depreciation	60,000	54,000
Interest expense	37,000	26,400
Other expenses	227,000	91,200
	1,164,000	1,191,600
Profit	$ 126,000	$ 8,400

Required:

(a) Prepare the consolidated financial statements for the year ended December 31, Year 6.

(b) Calculate goodwill impairment loss and non-controlling interest on the consolidated income statement for the year ended December 31, Year 6, under the parent company extension theory.

(c) Calculate goodwill and non-controlling interest on the consolidated statement of financial position at December 31, Year 6, under the parent company extension theory.

Problem 12 Foxx Corp. purchased 75 percent of the outstanding shares of Rabb Ltd. on January 1, Year 3, at a cost of $117,000. On that date, Rabb had common shares of $50,000 and retained earnings of $30,000. Fair values were equal to carrying values for all the net assets except the following:

	Carrying value	Fair value
Inventory	$30,000	$19,000
Equipment	45,000	69,000
Software	—	15,000

The equipment had an estimated remaining useful life of 6 years on January 1, Year 3, and the software was to be amortized over 10 years. Foxx uses the cost method to account for its investment. The testing for impairment at December 31, Year 6, yielded the following fair values:

Software	$ 8,000
Goodwill	20,000

The impairment loss on these assets occurred entirely in Year 6. Amortization expense is grouped with administrative expenses and impairment losses are grouped with miscellaneous expenses.

The following are the financial statements of Foxx Corp. and its subsidiary Rabb Ltd. as at December 31, Year 6:

BALANCE SHEETS
December 31, Year 6

	Foxx Corp.	Rabb Ltd.
Cash	$ —	$ 10,000
Accounts receivable	40,000	30,000
Note receivable	—	40,000
Inventory	66,000	44,000
Equipment, net	220,000	76,000
Land	150,000	30,000
Investment in Rabb	117,000	—
	$593,000	$230,000
Bank indebtedness	$ 90,000	$ —
Accounts payable	70,000	60,000
Notes payable	40,000	—
Common shares	150,000	50,000
Retained earnings	243,000	120,000
	$593,000	$230,000

STATEMENTS OF RETAINED EARNINGS
Year ended December 31, Year 6

	Foxx Corp.	Rabb Ltd.
Retained earnings, January 1, Year 6	$153,000	$ 92,000
Net income	120,000	48,000
Dividends	(30,000)	(20,000)
Retained earnings, December 31, Year 6	$243,000	$120,000

INCOME STATEMENTS
Year ended December 31, Year 6

	Foxx Corp.	Rabb Ltd.
Sales	$821,000	$320,000
Investment income	15,000	3,600
	836,000	323,600
Cost of sales	480,000	200,000
Administrative expenses	40,000	12,000
Miscellaneous expenses	116,000	31,600
Income taxes	80,000	32,000
	716,000	275,600
Net income	$120,000	$ 48,000

Additional Information

The notes payable are intercompany.

Required:
(a) Prepare the Year 6 consolidated financial statements.
(b) Calculate goodwill impairment loss and non-controlling interest on the consolidated income statement for the year ended December 31, Year 6, under the parent company extension theory.
(c) If Foxx used the parent company extension theory rather than the entity theory, how would this affect the debt-to-equity ratio at the end of Year 6?

Problem 13 The following financial statements were prepared on December 31, Year 6.

BALANCE SHEET

	Pearl	Silver
Cash	$ 300,000	$ 100,000
Accounts receivable	200,000	—
Inventory	2,000,000	420,000
Plant and equipment	3,000,000	2,690,000
Accumulated depreciation	(750,000)	(310,000)
Investment in Silver Company — at cost	2,400,000	—
	$7,150,000	$2,900,000
Liabilities	$ 900,000	$ 300,000
Common shares	2,850,000	1,600,000
Retained earnings	3,400,000	1,000,000
	$7,150,000	$2,900,000

INCOME STATEMENT

Sales	$4,000,000	$1,000,000
Dividend income	150,000	—
	4,150,000	1,000,000
Cost of sales	2,500,000	400,000
Miscellaneous expenses	320,000	70,000
Administrative expense	80,000	10,000
Income tax expense	250,000	120,000
	3,150,000	600,000
Net income	$1,000,000	$ 400,000

RETAINED EARNINGS STATEMENT

Balance, January 1	$2,900,000	$ 800,000
Net income	1,000,000	400,000
	3,900,000	1,200,000
Dividends	500,000	200,000
Balance, December 31	$3,400,000	$1,000,000

Additional Information

Pearl purchased 75 percent of the outstanding voting shares of Silver for $2,400,000 on July 1, Year 2, at which time Silver's retained earnings were $400,000. The acquisition differential on this date was allocated as follows:

- 30 percent to undervalued inventory.
- 40 percent to equipment — remaining useful life 8 years.
- Balance to goodwill.

During Year 3, a goodwill impairment loss of $70,000 was recognized, and an impairment test conducted as at December 31, Year 6, indicated that a further loss of $20,000 had occurred.

Amortization expense is grouped with cost of goods sold and impairment losses are grouped with administrative expenses.

Silver owes Pearl $75,000 on December 31, Year 6.

Required:

(a) Prepare consolidated financial statements on December 31, Year 6.
(b) Calculate goodwill impairment loss and non-controlling interest on the consolidated income statement for the year ended December 31, Year 6, under the parent company extension theory.
(c) Calculate goodwill and non-controlling interest on the consolidated balance sheet at December 31, Year 6, under the parent company extension theory.

Problem 14   Balance sheet and income statement data for two affiliated companies for the current year appear below.

Additional Information

- Albeniz acquired an 80 percent interest in Bach on January 1, Year 1, for $272,000. On that date the following information was noted about specific net assets of Bach:

	Book value	Fair value
Inventory	$20,000	$50,000
Land	25,000	45,000
Equipment (estimated useful life 15 years)	60,000	78,000
Misc. intangibles (estimated useful life 20 years)	—	42,000

Amortization expense is grouped with distribution expenses.

- On January 1, Year 1, Bach had a retained earnings balance of $30,000.
- Albeniz carries its investment at cost.

BALANCE SHEET
as at December 31, Year 4

	Albeniz	Bach
Cash	$ 40,000	$ 21,000
Receivables	92,000	84,000
Inventories	56,000	45,000
Land	20,000	60,000
Plant and equipment	200,000	700,000
Accumulated depreciation	(80,000)	(350,000)
Investment in Bach Company (cost)	272,000	—
Advances to Bach Company	100,000	—
Total assets	$700,000	$560,000
Accounts payable	$130,000	$ 96,500
Advances payable	—	100,000
Common shares	400,000	200,000
Retained earnings	170,000	163,500
Total liabilities and shareholders' equity	$700,000	$560,000

INCOME STATEMENT
Year Ended December 31, Year 4

	Albeniz	Bach
Sales revenues	$600,000	$400,000
Interest income	6,700	—
Dividend income from Bach	6,400	—
Total revenues	613,100	400,000
Cost of goods sold	334,000	225,000
Distribution expense	20,000	70,000
Selling and administrative expense	207,000	74,000
Financing expense	1,700	6,000
Income taxes expense	20,700	7,500
Total expenses	583,400	382,500
Net income	$ 29,700	$ 17,500

Required:

Prepare the following:
(a) Consolidated income statement.
(b) Consolidated balance sheet.

Problem 15 On January 2, Year 1, Brady Ltd. purchased 80 percent of the outstanding shares of Partridge Ltd. for $4,120,000. Partridge's statement of financial position and the fair values of its identifiable assets and liabilities for that date appear on the following page.

The patents had a remaining useful life of 10 years on the acquisition date. The bonds were issued on January 1, Year 1, and mature on December 31, Year 10. Goodwill impairment losses were recorded as follows:

- Year 1: $25,000.
- Year 3: $12,500.

	Book value	Fair value
Plant and equipment (net)	$4,500,000	$4,500,000
Patents (net)	1,000,000	1,500,000
Inventory	2,000,000	2,200,000
Accounts receivable	1,500,000	1,500,000
Cash	500,000	500,000
	$9,500,000	
Common shares	$2,000,000	
Retained earnings	2,500,000	
10% bonds payable	3,000,000	3,300,000
Accounts payable	2,000,000	2,000,000
	$9,500,000	

On December 31, Year 3, the financial statements of the two companies are as follows:

STATEMENT OF FINANCIAL POSITION

	Brady	Partridge
Plant and equipment (net)	$ 8,000,000	$5,000,000
Patents (net)	—	700,000
Investment in Partridge Ltd. (cost)	4,120,000	—
Inventory	4,600,000	1,900,000
Accounts receivable	1,000,000	1,300,000
Cash	400,000	600,000
	$18,120,000	$9,500,000
Common shares	$ 5,000,000	$2,000,000
Retained earnings	6,120,000	3,100,000
Bonds payable	4,000,000	3,000,000
Accounts payable	3,000,000	1,400,000
	$18,120,000	$9,500,000

INCOME STATEMENTS

	Brady	Partridge
Sales	$10,000,000	$5,000,000
Dividend revenue from Partridge	80,000	—
	10,080,000	5,000,000
Cost of goods purchased	6,930,000	2,890,000
Change in inventory	70,000	110,000
Depreciation expense	900,000	400,000
Patent amortization expense	—	100,000
Interest expense	480,000	300,000
Other expenses	680,000	850,000
Income taxes	600,000	150,000
	9,660,000	4,800,000
Profit	$ 420,000	$ 200,000

Required:
(a) Prepare consolidated financial statements on December 31, Year 3.
(b) If Brady had used the equity method, which items on Brady's separate-entity financial statements would have amounts different from those shown? Compute the equity method balances of these items.

WEB-BASED PROBLEMS

Problem 1 When accounting for the acquisition of a non-wholly-owned subsidiary, the parent can use the entity theory or the parent company extension theory to account for the business combination. Access the most recent consolidated financial statements for Vodafone, a British company. (Go to the investor relations section at www.vodafone. com.) Answer the questions below. For each question, indicate where in the financial statements you found the answer and/or provide a brief explanation.

(a) Which theory of consolidation did the parent use to account for the business combination?

(b) What percentage of net income for the year is represented by non-controlling interest (sometimes referred to as minority interest)?

(c) What portion of the additions to other intangible assets during the year came from business combinations and what portion came from direct purchases?

(d) What was the goodwill impairment loss for the year? Describe the two main factors contributing to the goodwill impairment.

(e) Assume that performance bonuses for the company's top executives are based, in part, on net income. How will the goodwill impairment loss for the year affect the bonuses for the executives in the current year? In future years?

(f) Explain why different discount rates are used for different geographical areas and explain how a change in discount rate can negatively affect the value of goodwill.

(g) Assume that the company used the other acceptable theory of accounting for its business combinations. How would this change in theory affect the return on shareholders' equity for the current year?

Problem 2 Access the most recent consolidated financial statements for Siemens, a German company. (Go to the investor relations section at www.siemens.com.) Answer the same questions as in Problem 1. For each question, indicate where in the financial statements you found the answer and/or provide a brief explanation. (Some questions may not be applicable.)

Chapter 6 Intercompany Inventory and Land Profits

LEARNING OBJECTIVES

After studying this chapter, you should be able to do the following:

1. Describe the effect on consolidated profit of the elimination of both intercompany revenues (and expenses) and intercompany asset profits.
2. Prepare consolidated financial statements that reflect the elimination of upstream and downstream intercompany profits in inventory and land.
3. Prepare consolidated financial statements that reflect the realization of upstream and downstream intercompany profits in inventory and land that were held back in previous periods.
4. Explain how the revenue recognition and matching principles are used to support adjustments for intercompany transactions when preparing consolidated financial statements.
5. Prepare the journal entries under the equity method to reflect the elimination and subsequent realization of intercompany profits in inventory and land.

INTRODUCTION

Consolidated financial statements should reflect only transactions with entities outside of the consolidated entity.

In previous discussions we stressed that consolidated financial statements report the activities of a group of affiliated companies as if they constitute a single company. While these companies may transact business with one another as well as with nonaffiliated companies, all intercompany transactions are eliminated so that the final consolidated statements reflect only transactions with entities outside the group. The elimination of intercompany transactions and unrealized profit is one of the most significant problems encountered in the consolidation process. The volume of transfers within most large enterprises can be quite large. For example, Vodaphone Group, a world leader in wireless communication, reported intersegment revenue of €572 million in 2008. Such transactions are especially common in companies that have been constructed as a vertically integrated chain of organizations. These entities reduce their costs by developing affiliations in which one operation furnishes products to another.

Intercompany transactions are also used to shift income from one jurisdiction to another to minimize or avoid paying income taxes. As a result, Canadian legislation prevents Canadian companies from trying to avoid paying income tax by using offshore tax havens such as non-resident trusts and foreign investment entities. The legislation was enacted because the government felt that multinational companies operating in Canada had avoided "hundreds of millions" of dollars in taxes over the previous decade through the use of tax havens.

Chapter 5 illustrated the elimination of intercompany receivables and payables. The next two chapters focus on the elimination of all other transactions that occur between a parent and its subsidiaries or between two or more subsidiaries that have a common parent.

Intercompany Revenue and Expenses

Intercompany Sales and Purchases

The following simple example will be used to illustrate the basic idea behind the elimination of intercompany sales and purchases in the preparation of a consolidated income statement.

The transaction with the dealer is an arm's-length transaction (i.e., with an outsider).

Let your imagination stray a bit and suppose that when you went shopping for groceries, the change you received from the cashier included some dollar coins. When you got home you noticed that the loon on one of these coins was upside down. You took the coin to a dealer and learned that some coins with this flaw had been accidentally released into circulation by the Royal Canadian Mint and as a result were worth substantially more than their face value. The dealer offered you $41 for this dollar coin, which you accepted. It is obvious that you made a profit of $40 on this transaction. An income statement showing only this transaction would appear as follows:

INCOME STATEMENT — COIN TRANSACTION

Revenue is recognized when it is earned in a transaction with an outsider in accordance with the revenue recognition principle.

Sales	$41
Cost of sales	1
Net income	$40

Now let your imagination stray even further and assume that the following events took place between the time you received the coin from the supermarket and the time you sold it to the coin dealer. Your pants have four pockets. Let's call them pocket 1, pocket 2, pocket 3, and pocket 4. Pocket 1 received the coin from the supermarket and sold it to pocket 2 for $10. Pocket 2 sold the coin to pocket 3 for $15. Pocket 3 sold the coin to pocket 4 for $25, and then pocket 4 sold the coin to the dealer for $41. Has any part of the transaction changed as far as you (as an entity) are concerned? The answer of course is no. You still had sales of $41, cost of goods sold of $1, and a net income of $40. But assume that each of your pockets recorded its part in the transaction and prepared an income statement:

The cost of the coin is expensed in the same period as the revenue in accordance with the matching principle.

Income was recorded when the coin was moved from one pocket to another.

INCOME STATEMENTS OF FOUR POCKETS

	Pocket 1	Pocket 2	Pocket 3	Pocket 4
Sales	$10	$15	$25	$41
Cost of goods sold	1	10	15	25
Net income	$ 9	$ 5	$10	$16

The arrows indicate the interpocket transactions that took place. Also, the sum of the net incomes of your four pockets is equal to your net income of $40. We should therefore be able to prepare an income statement for you (as an entity) by combining the components of the income statements of your four pockets as follows:

COMBINED INCOME STATEMENT

Sales (10 + 15 + 25 + 41)	$91
Cost of goods sold (1 + 10 + 15 + 25)	51
Net income	$40

Income should be recognized only when it is earned in a transaction with an outsider.

However, sales and cost of goods sold are not the correct amounts because they contain the interpocket sales and purchases. Both items should reflect only sales to and purchases from *outside* the entity. If we eliminate the interpocket sales and purchases, we will have an income statement that reflects only transactions that you as an entity incurred with others outside the entity. This statement can be prepared as follows:

COMBINED INCOME STATEMENT — ENTITY

	Total of four pockets	Interpocket sales & purchases	Total
Sales	$91	$50	$41
Cost of goods sold	51	50	1
Net income	$40	$ 0	$40

Notice that if we eliminate an equal amount of revenue and expense from an income statement, the resultant net income remains unchanged.

Your four pockets in this example are similar in all respects to a parent company and its subsidiary companies. Let us assume that a parent company (P) has holdings in three subsidiaries as follows: P owns 80 percent of S1, 90 percent of S2, and 75 percent of S3. The coin transactions previously illustrated were carried out by P and its three subsidiaries. These were the only transactions that took place during the current year. At year-end, the parent and its subsidiaries prepared the following income statements:

Only S3 had a transaction with an outsider.

INCOME STATEMENTS — PARENT AND SUBSIDIARIES

	P	S1	S2	S3
Sales	$10	$15	$25	$41
Cost of goods sold	1	10	15	25
Net income	$ 9	$ 5	$10	$16

We are assuming that P uses the equity method but has made no entries during the current year and that all acquisition differentials have been fully amortized in prior years.

Before preparing a consolidated income statement, we can calculate consolidated net income attributable to P as follows:

P's net income					$ 9
	S1	S2	S3	Total	
Subsidiary net income	$ 5	$ 10	$ 16	$31	
P's ownership	80%	90%	75%		
Share of subsidiary's net income	$ 4	$ 9	$ 12		25
Consolidated net income attributable to P					$34

Suppose we prepare a consolidated income statement without eliminating intercompany sales and purchases, in the following manner:

P AND SUBSIDIARIES
CONSOLIDATED INCOME STATEMENT
for Current Year

Sales (10 + 15 + 25 + 41)	$91
Cost of goods sold (1 + 10 + 15 + 25)	51
Net income	$40
Attributable to	
Shareholders of parent	$34
Non-controlling interest	6

Sales and cost of sales are overstated because intercompany sales and purchases have not yet been eliminated.

CALCULATION OF NET INCOME
ATTRIBUTABLE TO NON-CONTROLLING INTEREST

S1 (20% × 5)	$1
S2 (10% × 10)	1
S3 (25% × 16)	4
	$6

Note that the net income of the consolidated entity is made up of the net incomes of the parent and its three subsidiaries. But we have not eliminated the intercompany sales and purchases that took place during the year. If we eliminate these intercompany transactions, the bottom-line net income earned by the consolidated entity will not change. Non-controlling interest and consolidated net income are only *allocations* of the entity's net income, so they also will not be affected by the elimination of these intercompany sales and purchases. The consolidated income statement after the elimination of intercompany sales and purchases is as follows:

CONSOLIDATED INCOME STATEMENT
(after elimination of intercompany items)

Sales (91 − 50)	$41
Cost of goods sold (51 − 50)	1
Net income	$40
Attributable to	
Shareholders of parent	$34
Non-controlling interest	6

The consolidated income statement now reflects only the transactions with outsiders.

Other Examples of Intercompany Revenue and Expenses

Suppose the parent company lends $100,000 to the subsidiary company and receives a note payable on demand with interest at 10 percent paid annually. The transactions would be recorded as follows:

These transactions are recorded on the separate-entity books of the parent and the subsidiary.

Parent Company			*Subsidiary Company*		
Note receivable	100,000		Cash	100,000	
Cash		100,000	Note payable		100,000

To record intercompany borrowings on January 1 of the current year

Cash	10,000		Interest expense	10,000	
Interest revenue		10,000	Cash		10,000

To record the intercompany payment of interest on December 31 of the current year

Consolidated net income does not change when we eliminate an equal amount of revenue and expense.

From the consolidated entity's point of view, all that has happened is that cash has been transferred from one bank account to another. No revenue has been earned, no expense has been incurred, and there are no receivables or payables with parties outside the consolidated entity. The elimination of $10,000 interest revenue and interest expense on the consolidated income statement does not change the net income of the consolidated entity. If total net income is not affected, then the amount allocated to the non-controlling and controlling interest is also not affected. On the consolidated balance sheet, we eliminate $100,000 from notes receivable and notes payable. An equal elimination of assets and liabilities on a balance sheet leaves the amounts of the two equities (non-controlling interest and controlling interest) unchanged.

Note also that if the roles are reversed and the *subsidiary* lends $100,000 to the *parent*, the eliminations on the consolidated income statement and balance sheet are the same and have no effect on the amount of the non-controlling interest appearing on each statement.

Intercompany Management Fees   Often the parent will charge its subsidiary companies a yearly management fee as a means of allocating head office costs to all the companies within the group. (We will not discuss the pros and cons of this procedure here. Readers who are interested in the reasons for, and effectiveness of, allocations of this nature are advised to consult a management accounting textbook.) From an external reporting point of view, we have intercompany revenues and expenses that must be eliminated on the consolidated income statement.

Intercompany Rentals   Occasionally buildings or equipment owned by one company are used by another company within the group. Rather than transfer legal title, the companies agree on a yearly rental to be charged. In such cases, intercompany rental revenues and expenses must be eliminated from the consolidated income statement.

The elimination entries are recorded on the consolidated working papers and not in the separate-entity books of the parent and the subsidiary.

The four examples mentioned above and any other intercompany revenues and expenses are eliminated to ensure that revenue is recognized only when it is earned with a party outside of the consolidated entity and to stop the double-counting of revenues and expenses. This has no effect on the calculation of the non-controlling interest in the net income of the subsidiary companies since there is no change to consolidated net income.

Intercompany Profits in Assets

The consolidated financial statements should reflect only the results of transactions with outsiders.

When one affiliated company sells assets to another affiliated company, it is possible that the profit or loss recorded on the transaction has not been realized from the point of view of the consolidated entity. If the purchasing affiliate has sold these assets outside the group, all profits (losses) recorded are realized. If, however, all or a portion of these assets have not been sold outside the group, we must eliminate the remaining intercompany profit and may need to eliminate the intercompany loss[1] from the consolidated statements. The intercompany profit (loss) will be realized for consolidation purposes during the accounting period in which the particular asset is

---

[1]   Intercompany losses are not eliminated when the assets are impaired. This situation will be discussed later in this chapter.

sold to outsiders. The sale to outsiders may also result in an additional profit (loss) that is not adjusted in the consolidation process. Three types of unrealized intercompany profits (losses) are eliminated:

- Profits in inventory;
- Profits in nondepreciable assets; and
- Profits in depreciable assets.

The first two of these will be discussed in this chapter; the last one will be discussed in Chapter 7.

The examples that follow illustrate the holdback of unrealized intercompany profits in one accounting period and the realization of the profit in a subsequent period.

Downstream and upstream are defined by who the seller is.

When the parent sells to the subsidiary, the transaction is referred to as a downstream transaction. When the subsidiary sells to the parent or another subsidiary, the transaction is referred to as an upstream transaction.

As a means of illustrating the concepts involved in the elimination of intercompany profits, we will use as a simple example the financial statements of a parent and its 90-percent-owned subsidiary one year after the acquisition date.

On January 1, Year 1, Parent Company acquired 90 percent of the common shares of Sub Incorporated for $11,250. On that date Sub had common shares of $8,000 and retained earnings of $4,500, and there were no differences between the fair values and the book values of its identifiable net assets. The acquisition differential was calculated as follows:

Cost of 90% of Sub		$11,250
Implied value of 100% of Sub		$12,500
Book value of Sub's net assets (equals Sub's shareholders' equity)		
Common shares	8,000	
Retained earnings	4,500	
		12,500
Acquisition differential		$ 0

The financial statements of Parent and Sub as at December 31, Year 1, are presented in Exhibit 6.1 on page 254. Parent accounts for its investment using the cost method, and because there were no dividends declared by Sub, no entry was made on December 31, Year 1.

Intercompany Inventory Profits: Subsidiary Selling (Upstream Transactions)

The following intercompany transactions occurred during Year 1:

From Sub's separate-entity perspective, it earned the income on the sale to the Parent.

1. During Year 1, Sub made sales to Parent amounting to $5,000 at a gross profit rate of 30 percent.

2. At the end of Year 1, Parent's inventory contained items purchased from Sub for $1,000.

3. Sub paid (or accrued) income tax on its taxable income at a rate of 40 percent.

Holdback of Inventory Profits — Year 1   It should be noted that the subsidiary recorded a gross profit of $1,500 (30% × $5,000) on its sales to the parent during the year and paid income tax of $600 (40% × $1,500) on this profit. If the parent had sold

Exhibit 6.1

YEAR 1 INCOME STATEMENTS

	Parent	Sub
Sales	$20,000	$ 8,000
Cost of sales	13,000	4,300
Miscellaneous expenses	1,400	900
Income tax expense	2,200	1,100
	16,600	6,300
Net income	$ 3,400	$ 1,700

These are the separate-entity statements of the parent and the subsidiary.

BALANCE SHEETS — December 31, Year 1

	Parent	Sub
Inventory	$ 7,500	$ 4,000
Assets (miscellaneous)	21,650	19,200
Investment in Sub Inc.	11,250	—
	$40,400	$23,200
Liabilities	$12,000	$ 9,000
Common shares	15,000	8,000
Retained earnings	13,400	6,200
	$40,400	$23,200

The parent uses the cost method in its separate-entity records.

all of its intercompany purchases to customers outside the entity, this $1,500 gross profit would be considered realized from the point of view of this consolidated single entity. But the parent's inventory contains items purchased from the subsidiary for $1,000. There is an unrealized intercompany profit of $300 (30% × $1,000) in this inventory, which must be held back from consolidated income in Year 1 and realized in the period in which it is sold to outsiders. In addition, the $120 tax expense relating to this profit must also be held back from the Year 1 consolidated income statement. When this $300 gross profit is realized on a future consolidated income statement, the income tax expense will be matched on that statement with the profit realized.

From the consolidated perspective, some of Sub's income was not realized with an outsider.

Income tax should be expensed in the same period as revenue.

Not only do we have to hold back an unrealized profit for consolidation purposes, but also we must make an adjustment for the income taxes relating to that profit. Since income taxes are computed at the individual company level rather than at the consolidated entity level, the company that recorded the profit also paid (or accrued) income taxes on that profit, and the income tax expense on its income statement reflects this. The matching of expenses with revenues is a basic accounting concept; the adjustment made for income taxes on intercompany profits is a perfect example of this matching process.

The difference between the buyer's tax basis and the cost of transferred assets as reported in the consolidated financial statements meets the definition of a temporary difference and will give rise to deferred income taxes. While IAS 27 explicitly states that profits and losses resulting from intragroup transactions should be eliminated in full, it does not explicitly state how the eliminated amount should be allocated between the controlling and non-controlling interests. Because the amount

From a consolidated perspective, some of the tax paid by the subsidiary was prepaid since the income was not yet earned.

attributed to non-controlling interest will affect the amount attributed to the shareholders of the parent, the handling of this issue can affect the reported profitability of a business combination.

Non-controlling interest is not affected by intercompany profits made on downstream transactions.

To determine an appropriate allocation, the relationship between an intercompany transaction and the non-controlling shareholders must be analyzed. If a transfer were downstream, a logical view would be that the unrealized gross profit belongs to the parent company. The parent made the original sale; therefore, the gross profit is included in its financial records. Since the non-controlling shareholders do not have any interest in the parent company, it seems appropriate that they should not be affected by the elimination of the profit on downstream transactions.

Non-controlling interest is affected and will share in intercompany profits made on upstream transactions.

In contrast, if the subsidiary sells inventory to the parent, the subsidiary's financial records recognizes the gross profit. If this profit is eliminated when preparing the consolidated financial statements, the parties having an interest in the subsidiary's profit are affected by the elimination of the profit. Since the non-controlling shareholders do have an interest in the subsidiary, it seems appropriate that they should be affected by the elimination of the profit on upstream transactions. Throughout this textbook, the non-controlling interest's share of profit and retained earnings will be computed based on the reported profit and the retained earnings of the subsidiary after they have been adjusted for any unrealized profits on upstream transactions.

Using the direct approach, we will now prepare the Year 1 consolidated statements after making the consolidation adjustments shown in Exhibit 6.2 on page 256.

Remember that the purpose of the calculation of consolidated net income is to adjust the parent's cost method net income to what it would have been under the equity method. Notice that the after-tax profit is deducted from the net income of Sub, because the subsidiary was the selling company and its net income contains this profit being held back for consolidation purposes. Note also that the non-controlling interest's share of the Year 1 income is based on the *adjusted income* of Sub.

Exhibit 6.3 on page 257 illustrates the preparation of the Year 1 consolidated financial statements.

The first two numbers in brackets are from the statements of Parent and Sub. Any additional numbers, which are in boldface and labelled, are adjustments made to eliminate the intercompany transactions. The eliminations made on the income statement require further elaboration:

1. The eliminations of intercompany sales and purchases are equal reductions of revenues and expenses that do not change the net income of the consolidated entity or the amount allocated to the non-controlling and controlling equities.

2. To hold back the gross profit of $300 from the consolidated entity's net income, we increase cost of goods sold by $300. The reasoning is as follows:

   (a) Cost of goods sold is made up of opening inventory, plus purchases, less ending inventory.

   (b) The ending inventory contains the $300 gross profit.

When ending inventory is overstated, cost of sales is understated.

   (c) If we subtract the $300 profit from the ending inventory on the balance sheet, the ending inventory is now stated at cost to the consolidated entity.

Exhibit 6.2

INTERCOMPANY TRANSACTIONS

Intercompany sales and purchases	$ 5,000	**(a)**
Intercompany inventory profits:		
Ending inventory — Sub Inc. selling	$ 300	**(b)**
Income tax (40%)	120	**(c)**
After-tax profit	$ 180	**(d)**

CALCULATION OF CONSOLIDATED NET INCOME — Year 1

The unrealized profit is always deducted from the selling company's income

Net income — Parent Co.		$ 3,400
Net income — Sub Inc.	1,700	
Less after-tax profit in ending inventory **(2d)**	180	
Adjusted net income — Sub Inc.		1,520
Net income		$ 4,920
Attributable to		
Shareholders of parent		$ 4,768 **(e)**
Non-controlling interest (10% × 1,520)		152 **(f)**

CALCULATION OF CONSOLIDATED RETAINED EARNINGS
at December 31, Year 1

The unrealized profit at the end of Year 1 must be eliminated when calculating consolidated retained earnings at the end of Year 1.

Retained earnings — Parent Co.		$13,400
Retained earnings — Sub Inc.	6,200	
Acquisition retained earnings	4,500	
Increase since acquisition	1,700	
Less profit in opening inventory **(2d)**	180	
Adjusted increase since acquisition	1,520	
Parent Co.'s share	90%	1,368
Consolidated retained earnings		$14,768 **(g)**

CALCULATION OF NON-CONTROLLING INTEREST
at December 31, Year 1

Non-controlling interest is affected when there are unrealized profits on upstream transactions.

Shareholders' equity — Sub Inc.	
Common shares	$ 8,000
Retained earnings	6,200
	14,200
Less after-tax profit in ending inventory	180
Adjusted shareholders' equity	14,020
Non-controlling interest's share	10%
	$ 1,402 **(h)**

(d) A reduction of $300 from ending inventory in the cost of goods sold calculation increases cost of goods sold by $300.

(e) This increase to cost of goods sold reduces the before-tax net income earned by the entity by $300.

The $300 adjustment to inventory and cost of goods sold is similar to the adjustment we studied in Intermediate Accounting to correct errors in inventory.

Exhibit 6.3	**Year 1 Consolidated Statements**

Elimination of Intercompany Profits in Inventory
(direct approach)

PARENT COMPANY
CONSOLIDATED INCOME STATEMENT
for the Year Ended December 31, Year 1

The unrealized profits are eliminated on the consolidated financial statements.	

Sales (20,000 + 8,000 − **(2a) 5,000**)	$23,000
Cost of sales (13,000 + 4,300 − **(2a) 5,000** + **(2b) 300**)	12,600
Miscellaneous expenses (1,400 + 900)	2,300
Income tax expense (2,200 + 1,100 − **(2c) 120**)	3,180
	18,080
Net income	$ 4,920
Attributable to	
Shareholders of parent **(2e)**	$ 4,768
Non-controlling interest **(2f)**	152

PARENT COMPANY
CONSOLIDATED BALANCE SHEET
at December 31, Year 1

By eliminating the unrealized profit, inventory is now stated at cost to the consolidated entity.	

Inventory (7,500 + 4,000 − **(2b) 300**)	$11,200
Assets — miscellaneous (21,650 + 19,200)	40,850
Deferred income taxes (0 + 0 + **(2c) 120**)	120
	$52,170
Liabilities (12,000 + 9,000)	$21,000
Common shares	15,000
Retained earnings **(2g)**	14,768
Non-controlling interest **(2h)**	1,402
	$52,170

If you have difficulty understanding the adjustments for unrealized profits in inventory, you may want to go back to your intermediate accounting text to review the adjustment for errors in inventory.

When cost of sales is increased, income decreases and income tax expense should decrease.

3. Because the entity's before-tax net income has been reduced by $300, it is necessary to reduce the income tax expense (the tax paid on the profit held back) by $120.

4. A reduction of income tax expense increases the net income of the consolidated entity.

5. A $300 increase in cost of goods sold, together with a $120 reduction in income tax expense, results in the after-tax profit of $180 being removed from consolidated net income.

The unrealized profits are not eliminated on the separate-entity financial statements.

It is important to realize that all of the above adjustments are being made on the consolidated working papers and not on the separate-entity financial statements. What was recorded on the subsidiary's own books was legitimate from its own perspective. But from the consolidated perspective, some of the profit was not yet realized. It must be held back from the consolidated financial statements.

Again it is important to note the following components of the entity's net income:

Net Income — Parent Co.	$3,400
Adjusted net income — Sub Inc.	1,520
Consolidated net income	$4,920

The only new concepts relating to the preparation of the consolidated balance sheet involve the adjustments made on the asset side (a) to eliminate the unrealized profit in inventory and (b) to set up the deferred income taxes on this profit. These adjustments are shown in boldface in Exhibit 6.3 on page 257 and are labelled to correspond with the calculations in Exhibit 6.2 on page 256. The reasons for these adjustments can be further explained as follows:

The unrealized profit is deducted from the inventory to bring inventory back to its original cost in accordance with the historical cost principle.

1. The holdback of the $300 gross profit on the consolidated income statement was accomplished by reducing the amount of ending inventory in calculating the cost of goods sold. (A reduction in ending inventory increases cost of goods sold.) The ending inventory in the cost of goods sold calculation is the inventory balance on the consolidated balance sheet. Removing the $300 gross profit from the asset results in the consolidated inventory being reflected at cost to the entity.

Income tax will be expensed when the profit is realized in accordance with the matching principle.

2. On the consolidated income statement, we reduced income tax expense by $120, representing the tax paid on the gross profit. As far as the consolidated entity is concerned, this tax of $120 was paid prematurely because the income was not yet earned. The tax will become an expense when the inventory is sold to outsiders. This results in a temporary difference for the consolidated entity. The resultant deferred income taxes are "added into" the assets on the consolidated balance sheet. (The illustration assumes that neither the parent nor the subsidiary had deferred income taxes on their individual balance sheets.)

3. A reduction of $300 from inventory and a $120 increase in deferred income taxes results in a net reduction to consolidated assets of $180, which equals the $180 reduction that has been made on the equity side.

Equity Method Journal Entries   While our example has assumed that Parent uses the cost method to account for its investment, it is useful to see where the differences would lie if the equity method were used. If Parent was using the equity method, the following journal entries would be made on December 31, Year 1:

The equity method captures the net effect of all consolidation entries.

Investment in Sub Inc.	1,530	
Investment income		1,530
90% of the net income of Sub Inc.		
(90% × 1,700 = 1,530)		

Investment income	162	
Investment in Sub Inc.		162
To hold back 90% of the after-tax inventory profit recorded		
by Sub Inc. (90% × 180 = 162)		

After these entries were posted, the two related equity method accounts of Parent would show the following changes and balances:

	Investment in Sub Inc.	Investment income
January 1, Year 1	$11,250	$ —
December 31, Year 1		
Income from Sub Inc.	1,530	1,530
After-tax inventory profit (held back)	(162)	(162)
Balance, December 31, Year 1	$12,618	$1,368

The parent's income under the equity method should be equal to consolidated net income.

Parent's total income under the equity method would be $4,768, consisting of $3,400 from its own operations as reported in Exhibit 6.1 on page 254. plus investment income of $1,368, as reported above. This income of $4,768 should be and is equal to consolidated net income attributable to Parent's shareholders.

In Year 2, the parent sold its Year 1 inventory to outsiders.

Realization of Inventory Profits — Year 2 The previous example illustrated the holdback of an unrealized intercompany inventory profit in Year 1. We will continue our example of Parent Company and Sub Inc. by looking at the events of Year 2. On December 31, Year 2, Parent reported earnings from its own operations of $4,050 and declared dividends of $2,500. Sub reported a net income of $3,100 and again did not declare a dividend. Using the cost method, Parent made no journal entries with respect to the operations of Sub. During Year 2, there were no intercompany transactions, and at year-end, the inventory of Parent contained no items purchased from Sub. In other words, the December 31, Year 1, inventory of Parent was sold during Year 2, and the unrealized profit that was held back for consolidated purposes in Year 1 will have to be released into income in Year 2.

The financial statements of Parent and Sub are presented in Exhibit 6.4.

Exhibit 6.4

YEAR 2 INCOME STATEMENTS

	Parent	Sub
Sales	$25,000	$12,000
Cost of sales	16,000	5,500
Miscellaneous expenses	2,350	1,400
Income tax expense	2,600	2,000
	20,950	8,900
Net income	$ 4,050	$ 3,100

Cost of sales for the parent includes the inflated inventory value at the beginning of the year.

BALANCE SHEETS — December 31, Year 2

	Parent	Sub
Inventory	$ 9,900	$ 7,500
Assets (miscellaneous)	22,800	20,800
Investment in Sub Inc.	11,250	—
	$43,950	$28,300
Liabilities	$14,000	$11,000
Common shares	15,000	8,000
Retained earnings	14,950	9,300
	$43,950	$28,300

Inventory at the end of Year 2 does not include any unrealized profit.

Exhibit 6.5

INTERCOMPANY INVENTORY PROFITS — Year 2

Intercompany inventory profits:		
Opening inventory — Sub Inc. selling	$ 300	**(a)**
Income tax (40%)	120	**(b)**
After-tax profit	$ 180	**(c)**

CALCULATION OF CONSOLIDATED NET INCOME — Year 2

When the profits are realized, they are credited to the income of the original seller.

Net income — Parent Co.		$ 4,050
Net income — Sub Inc.	3,100	
Add after-tax profit in opening inventory **(5c)**	180	
Adjusted net income — Sub Inc.		3,280
Net income		$ 7,330
Attributable to		
Shareholders of parent		$ 7,002 **(d)**
Non-controlling interest (10% × 3,280)		328 **(e)**

CALCULATION OF CONSOLIDATED RETAINED EARNINGS
December 31, Year 2

Retained earnings — Parent Co.		$14,950
Retained earnings — Sub Inc.	9,300	
Acquisition retained earnings	4,500	
Increase since acquisition	4,800	
Parent Co.'s share	90%	4,320
Consolidated retained earnings		$19,270 **(f)**

CALCULATION OF NON-CONTROLLING INTEREST
December 31, Year 2

All of subsidiary's shareholders' equity is legitimate from a consolidated perspective at the end of Year 2.

Common shares — Sub Inc.	$ 8,000
Retained earnings — Sub Inc.	9,300
	17,300
	10%
	$ 1,730 **(g)**

Before we prepare the Year 2 consolidated income statement, we must carry out the calculations shown in Exhibit 6.5.

The after-tax inventory profit of $180 that was held back in Year 1 is being realized in Year 2 and is added to the net income of Sub, because the subsidiary was the company that originally recorded the profit. Note that the non-controlling interest's share of the Year 2 net income of Sub is based on the *adjusted net income* of that company.

The calculation of consolidated retained earnings at December 31, Year 2, does not require any adjustments for unrealized profits because there are no unrealized profits at the end of Year 2. The subsidiary had reported profits in Year 1 on an intercompany sale to the parent. The unrealized profits were eliminated when calculating consolidated retained earnings at the end of Year 1. When the parent sold the inventory to outsiders, the previous unrealized profit was realized from a consolidated perspective. Since neither the parent nor the subsidiary had any inventory at the end of Year 2 that had been purchased through an intercompany sale, there was no unrealized profit in ending inventory. Consequently, there is no unrealized profit in retained earnings at the end of Year 2.

Exhibit 6.6		

Year 2 Consolidated Statements
(direct approach)

**PARENT COMPANY
CONSOLIDATED INCOME STATEMENT**
for the Year Ended December 31, Year 2

The unrealized profits from the end of Year 1 are released into consolidated income in Year 2.	

Sales (25,000 + 12,000)	$37,000
Cost of sales (16,000 + 5,500 − **(5a) 300**)	21,200
Miscellaneous expenses (2,350 + 1,400)	3,750
Income tax expense (2,600 + 2,000 + **(5b) 120**)	4,720
	29,670
Net income	$ 7,330
Attributable to	
Shareholders of parent **(5d)**	$ 7,002
Non-controlling interest **(5e)**	328

**PARENT COMPANY
CONSOLIDATED BALANCE SHEET**
December 31, Year 2

Inventory (9,900 + 7,500)	$17,400
Assets — miscellaneous (22,800 + 20,800)	43,600
	$61,000
Liabilities (14,000 + 11,000)	$25,000
Common shares	15,000
Retained earnings **(5f)**	19,270
Non-controlling interest **(5g)**	1,730
	$61,000

There are no unrealized profits at the end of Year 2.

Exhibit 6.6 illustrates the preparation of the Year 2 consolidated financial statements using the *direct* approach.

In preparing the Year 2 consolidated income statement, we make consolidation adjustments that bring the original before-tax profit into the income statement and increase income tax expense for the tax on this profit. The eliminations (i.e., adjustments) made are shown in boldface and are labelled. The elimination entries are explained as follows:

1. There were no intercompany sales or purchases in Year 2, and therefore no elimination is required on the income statement.
2. To realize the gross profit of $300 in Year 2, we decrease cost of goods sold by $300. The reasoning behind this is as follows:
   (a) Cost of goods sold is made up of opening inventory, plus purchases, less ending inventory.
   (b) The opening inventory contains the $300 gross profit. After we reduce it by $300, the opening inventory is at cost to the entity.
   (c) A reduction of $300 from opening inventory decreases cost of goods sold by $300.
   (d) This decrease in cost of goods sold increases the before-tax net income earned by the entity by $300.

Since beginning inventory was inflated, cost of sales for Year 2 was inflated.

When cost of sales is decreased, income increases and tax expense should increase.

3. Using the concepts of matching, we increase income tax expense by $120 in order to match it with the $300 gross profit being realized. Note that the deferred income tax on the December 31, Year 1, consolidated balance sheet (see Exhibit 6.3 on page 257.) becomes an expense on the Year 2 consolidated income statement, because the December 31, Year 1, inventory was sold in Year 2.

4. A $300 decrease in cost of goods sold, together with a $120 increase in income tax expense, results in the after-tax intercompany Year 1 profit of $180 being realized for consolidation purposes in Year 2.

Before the consolidated balance sheet is prepared, we must calculate non-controlling interest at December 31, Year 2. This calculation was shown in Exhibit 6.5 on page 260.

The preparation of the consolidated balance sheet on December 31, Year 2, is straightforward because no inventory profit eliminations are required. The inventory of Parent does not contain any unrealized profit, and there are no related deferred income taxes on the balance sheet. All previous unrealized inventory profits have now been realized for consolidation purposes.

When you view the adjustments that were made to prepare the Year 2 consolidated statements (see Exhibit 6.6 on page 261), it may strike you that the adjustments made on the income statement have not been reflected in the rest of the consolidated statements, and that as a result the statements should not balance. But they *do* balance, so the $180 increase in the after-tax net income of the entity must have been offset by a $180 change in the retained earnings statement and balance sheet.

To see where this $180 difference ended up, it is useful to prepare a calculation that shows the changes in non-controlling interest during Year 2. This calculation is shown below:

CHANGES IN NON-CONTROLLING INTEREST — Year 2

Non-controlling interest is based on Sub's shareholders' equity after it has been adjusted for unrealized profit on upstream transactions.

Sub Inc.

Common shares	8,000	
Retained earnings — January 1	6,200	
	14,200	
Less unrealized inventory profit	180	
Adjusted	14,020	
	10%	
Non-controlling interest, January 1		$1,402
Allocation of Year 2 consolidated net income		328
Non-controlling interest, December 31		$1,730

The intercompany profit of $180 was recorded in Sub's separate-entity income in Year 1 but reported in consolidated income in Year 2.

In examining this calculation and the calculation of consolidated retained earnings on December 31, Year 1, in Exhibit 6.2 on page 256, we see that the $180 increase in the entity's Year 2 consolidated net income was offset by a $180 *decrease* in the December 31, Year 1, balances of non-controlling interest and retained earnings, allocated as follows:

To non-controlling interest (10% × 180)	$ 18
To controlling interest (90% × 180)	162
	$180

Equity Method Journal Entries   If Parent had used the equity method, the following journal entries would have been made on December 31, Year 2:

Investment in Sub Inc.	2,790	
Investment income		2,790
To record 90% of the reported income of Sub Inc. (90% × 3,100)		

Investment in Sub Inc.	162	
Investment income		162
To release in Year 2 the after-tax inventory profit held back in Year 1 (90% × 180)		

The equity method captures the net effect of all consolidation entries including the adjustment for realized profits.

After these entries are posted, the two related equity method accounts of Parent show the following changes and balances:

	Investment in Sub Inc.	Investment income
January 1, Year 2	$12,618	$ —
December 31, Year 2		
Income from Sub Inc.	2,790	2,790
After-tax inventory profit (realized)	162	162
Balance, Dec. 31, Year 2	$15,570	$2,952

Note that the January 1 balance ($12,618) included the $162 holdback, and that this amount was realized during the year with a journal entry. It should be obvious that the December 31 balance ($15,570) does not contain any holdback.

Intercompany Inventory Profits: Parent Selling (Downstream Transactions)

In our previous example, the subsidiary was the selling company in the intercompany profit transaction (an upstream transaction). This resulted in the $180 after-tax profit elimination being allocated to the controlling and non-controlling equities.

Suppose we had assumed that it was the parent company that sold the inventory to the subsidiary (a downstream transaction). The calculation of consolidated net income for each of the two years should indicate where the differences lie.

CALCULATION OF CONSOLIDATED NET INCOME — Year 1

Unrealized profits on downstream transactions are deducted from the parent's separate-entity income.

Net income — Parent Co.	$3,400
Less after-tax profit in ending inventory	180
Adjusted net income — Parent Co.	3,220
Net income — Sub Inc.	1,700
Consolidated net income	$4,920
Attributable to	
Shareholders of parent	$4,750
Non-controlling interest (10% × 1,700)	170

Notice that the after-tax profit is deducted from the net income of Parent because it was the selling company, and that Parent's net income contains this profit being held back for consolidation purposes.

The eliminations on the consolidated income statement for intercompany sales and purchases and for unrealized profit in inventory, and the related adjustment to income tax expense would not change. But the split of the consolidated net income between the shareholders of the parent and the non-controlling interest is different,

Non-controlling interest is not affected by the elimination of unrealized profits on downstream transactions.

as indicated in the previous calculation. Because Parent was the selling company, all of the $180 holdback was allocated to the parent and none was allocated to the non-controlling interest.

On the December 31, Year 1, consolidated balance sheet, the elimination entries to adjust inventory and deferred income taxes would be the same as before. However, the non-controlling interest on the consolidated balance sheet is based on the December 31, Year 1, balances of the common shares and retained earnings of Sub. The after-tax inventory holdback is *not* allocated to non-controlling interest; because Parent was the selling company, it has been allocated entirely to consolidated retained earnings.

Year 2 consolidated net income is calculated as follows:

When unrealized profits on downstream transactions are realized, they are added to the parent's separate-entity income.

Net income — Parent Co.	$4,050
Add after-tax profit in opening inventory	180
Adjusted net income — Parent Co.	4,230
Net income — Sub Inc.	3,100
Consolidated net income	$7,330
Attributable to	
Shareholders of parent	$7,020
Non-controlling interest (10% × 3,100)	310

The elimination entries on the Year 2 consolidated income statement would be the same as in the previous illustration (see Exhibit 6.6 on page 261), but because the amount for non-controlling interest is $310, the consolidated net income attributable to Parent's shareholders is a higher amount, as indicated in the previous calculations.

To summarize, the holdback and subsequent realization of intercompany profits in assets is allocated to the non-controlling and controlling equities *only if* the subsidiary was the original seller in the intercompany transaction. If the parent was the original seller, the allocation is entirely to the controlling equity.

Equity Method Journal Entries   If Parent used the equity method to account for its investment, it would make the following entries as at December 31, Year 1:

Investment in Sub Inc.	1,530	
Investment income		1,530
To record 90% of the reported Year 1 net		
income of Sub Inc. (90% × 1,700)		

The parent absorbs the full charge for unrealized profits on downstream transactions in Year 1.

Investment income	180	
Investment in Sub Inc.		180
To hold back the after-tax inventory profit recorded by		
Parent Co. in Year 1		

An astute reader will notice that because the parent was the selling company, the second entry is removing the profit from accounts that did not contain it in the first place. This is of course quite true. However, it is the investment income account that establishes the equality between Parent's net income (under the equity method) and consolidated net income attributable to Parent's shareholders. In the same manner, the investment in Sub on the balance sheet of Parent establishes the equality between Parent's retained earnings (under the equity method) and consolidated retained

The equity method is referred to as the one-line consolidation.

earnings. This means that all adjustments that affect consolidated net income are reflected in these two accounts.

On December 31, Year 2, Parent would make the following journal entries if it used the equity method:

Investment in Sub Inc.	2,790	
Investment income		2,790
To record 90% of the reported net income of Sub Inc.		

Investment in Sub Inc.	180	
Investment income		180
To release in Year 2 the after-tax inventory profit held		
back in Year 1		

The parent receives the full benefit when unrealized profits on downstream transactions are realized in Year 2.

Unrealized Profits with Associates When the investor only has significant influence in an associate, it cannot control the decisions made by the associate. As such, transactions with the associate are similar to transactions with outsiders. Therefore, the accounting for unrealized profits on downstream transactions is a bit different for an investment in an associate. Rather than eliminating all of the profit, only the investor's percentage ownership of the associate times the profit earned on the transaction with the associate is eliminated. For example, if X Co. had a 40 percent interest in Y Co. and made a profit of $100 on a transaction with Y Co., only $40 (40% × 100) of the profit would be eliminated as part of the entries under the equity method. The $100 of profit would be recorded in the sales and cost of sales account and the $40 would be eliminated through the investment account. That leaves $60 of profit remaining in income. This $60 is deemed to be a transaction with outsiders.

Only the investor's share of profit on intercompany transactions with associates is eliminated.

Income Statement with Expenses Classified by Nature The previous illustrations in this chapter presented cost of goods sold as a separate line on the income statement. This would typically occur under two scenarios:

1. When expenses are classified according to their function and cost of goods sold represents the expenses of the production function.
2. When expenses are classified by nature and the reporting entity is a merchandising company, i.e., it buys and sells finished goods.

When a manufacturing company presents its expenses according to their nature, a cost of goods sold line typically does not exist. Instead, raw materials consumed, labour costs, depreciation of factory equipment, and other conversion costs are shown separately. In addition, there is a separate line for changes in inventories of work in progress and finished goods.

The adjustments on consolidation to eliminate the intercompany transactions and any unrealized profits are slightly different when expenses are classified according to their nature. If the intercompany transaction involves raw materials, all consolidation adjustments are put through the raw materials account on the balance sheet and the raw materials consumed account on the income statement. If the intercompany transaction involves work in progress or finished goods, the intercompany purchase is eliminated from the purchases of work in progress and finished goods account on the income statement; the unrealized profits are

Consolidation adjustments for unrealized profits in inventory will likely be made to the changes in inventory account rather than cost of goods sold.

eliminated from work in progress and finished goods inventory on the balance sheet and the changes in inventories of work in progress and finished goods account on the income statement.

Losses on Intercompany Transactions

When one affiliated company sells inventory to another affiliated company at a loss, the intercompany transaction and any unrealized losses should be eliminated on consolidation in a similar fashion to the previous discussion for unrealized profits. However, selling inventory at a loss raises a red flag that it may be impaired. If the inventory is impaired, it should be written down to its net realizable value. Ideally, the impairment should be reported on the separate-entity statements. If not, the impairment will have to be reported on the consolidated statements. The following example illustrates these issues.

Sub has inventory with an original cost of $5,500 and a net realizable value of $4,800. If Sub were to value its inventory at net realizable value at this point, it would recognize a loss of $700.

In Year 1, Sub sells this inventory to Parent for $5,000. It had not written down the inventory to its net realizable value prior to the sale to Parent. Before the end of Year 1, Parent sells 80 percent of these goods to outsiders for $3,840, which equals their net realizable value. It has the remaining inventory purchased from Sub on its books at $1,000 at the end of Year 1. The net realizable value of this inventory is $960, which is the same net realizable value prior to the sale by Sub.

Based solely on the above information, selected accounts from the financial statements for Parent and Sub for Year 1 are as follows:

	Parent	Sub
Inventory on balance sheet	$1,000	
Sales	3,840	$5,000
Cost of sales	4,000	5,500
Gross profit	$-160	$-500

The following adjustments would normally be made on consolidation:

(a) Sales and cost of goods sold should be reduced by $5,000, being the amount of the intercompany sale.

(b) Unrealized loss in ending inventory of $100 (10% × 1,000) should be eliminated.

The consolidated financial statements show the following amounts for the selected accounts:

Inventory on balance sheet (1,000 + 0 + **(b) 100**)	$1,100
Sales (3,840 + 5,000 − **(a) 5,000**)	3,840
Cost of sales (4,000 + 5,500 − **(a) 5,000** − **(b) 100**)	4,400
Gross profit	$-560

By eliminating the unrealized loss and not making any adjustment for impairment of the inventory, the inventory is valued at $1,100, which is 20 percent of the original cost to Sub. This is consistent with the historical cost principle. However, this inventory is stated above its net realizable value of $960. It should be written down from $1,100 to $960, a write-down of $140. If the write-down were made as

Impairment tests for inventory are usually performed at the end of the fiscal period.

When intercompany losses are eliminated, the inventory is brought back to the original cost to the selling entity.

adjustment (c) on consolidation, the consolidated financial statements would show the following amounts for the selected accounts:

Inventory on the consolidated balance sheet should be reported at the lower of cost and net realizable value.

Inventory on balance sheet (1,000 + 0 + **(b) 100** − **(c) 140**)	$ 960
Sales (3,840 + 5,000 − **(a) 5,000**)	3,840
Cost of sales (4,000 + 5,500 − **(a) 5,000** − **(b) 100**)	4,400
Gross profit	−560
Loss in value of inventory (0 + 0 + **(c) 140**)	−140
Profit before tax on the above items	$−700

Now, the consolidated balance sheet reports inventory at the lower of cost and net realizable value and the consolidated income statement reports a loss of $700, being the total impairment loss on the inventory. This more faithfully represents the situation for the consolidated entity.

It may appear strange to adjust the inventory upward by $100 in (b) and then to adjust it downward by $140 in (c). The same result could have been achieved by not eliminating the unrealized loss in (b) and then writing down the inventory from $1,000 to $960 for a $40 adjustment in (c). For this reason, some people believe that unrealized losses should not be eliminated on consolidation, but the losses should be a warning sign for potential impairment.

If the subsidiary had not sold any of the inventory to the parent or to outsiders, it should have tested the inventory for impairment at the end of Year 1. In so doing, it would have determined that inventory was impaired and that an impairment loss of $700 would need to be reported.

Intercompany transactions are not always consummated at market value.

In some cases, the exchange price on intercompany transactions between the parent and the subsidiary does not reflect the true value of the inventory. Even though the net realizable value of the inventory in the above example was $4,800, the subsidiary could have sold the inventory to the parent for $4,000. If so, the inventory would be reported by the parent at less than net realizable value on its separate-entity balance sheet. If the unrealized loss is not eliminated, the inventory and net income of the consolidated entity will be understated. For this reason, IFRSs suggest that the intercompany loss be eliminated on consolidation. Then, the reporting entity should perform an impairment test to determine if the inventory is impaired from the perspective of the consolidated entity.

Intercompany Land Profit Holdback

The holdback and realization of an intercompany profit in land is accomplished in a more straightforward manner on the consolidated income statement. Suppose that in Year 1 there was an intercompany sale of land for $2,300 on which a before-tax profit of $300 was recorded, that $120 tax was accrued, and that on December 31, Year 1, the land was still held by the purchasing company. (Throughout the text and end-of-chapter material, we assume that these gains are not capital gains.)

The selling company would make the following entry to record the intercompany transaction:

The purchasing company's cost is $300 higher than the selling company's cost.

Cash	2,300	
Land		2,000
Gain on sale of land		300

The purchasing company would record the intercompany transaction as follows:

Land	2,300	
Cash		2,300

When consolidated financial statements are prepared, the profit elimination and the related income tax adjustment will take place as follows:

PARENT COMPANY
CONSOLIDATED INCOME STATEMENT
Year 1

Gain on sale of land (300 − **300**)	$ 0
Income tax expense (P + S − **120**)	XXX
Net income	$XXX
Attributable to	
Shareholders of parent	$XXX
Non-controlling interest	XXX

The after-tax profit is deducted from the selling company's separate-entity income.

It should be obvious that the holdback of the gain, along with the reduction of the income tax expense, has reduced the entity's net income by $180. If the subsidiary is the selling company, the $180 after-tax profit held back will be used to calculate non-controlling interest in the consolidated income statement; in this manner it will be allocated to the two equities. If the parent is the selling company, non-controlling interest will not be affected and the entire after-tax holdback will be allocated to the controlling entity.

The following shows the eliminations required in the preparation of the assets section of the Year 1 balance sheet:

After eliminating the profit, the land is stated at the original cost to the consolidated entity.

PARENT COMPANY
CONSOLIDATED BALANCE SHEET
December 31, Year 1

Land (2,600 − **300**)	$2,300
Deferred income taxes (+ **120**)	120
Total assets	$ XXX

The balance sheet eliminations for a land profit are very similar to those for an inventory profit. The before-tax profit is deducted from land rather than inventory. The tax asset is added into the consolidated balance sheet. We will refer to this tax asset as deferred income taxes.

The equity side of the balance sheet is not presented. If the subsidiary is the selling company, the calculation of non-controlling interest on December 31, Year 1, will have to reflect this fact. If the parent is the selling company, the entire $180 after-tax profit holdback is attributed to the parent company's shareholders and is reflected in the retained earnings shown on the balance sheet.

Realization of Intercompany Land Profits

An unrealized intercompany inventory profit held back for consolidated purposes in Year 1 is considered realized in Year 2 because any inventory on hand at the beginning of a year has usually been sold by the end of that year.

The unrealized profits will be eliminated from retained earnings of the selling company on the consolidated working papers each year until the land is sold to outsiders.

When are intercompany land profits considered realized for consolidation purposes? The answer is this: when the land is sold to outsiders, which may be many years later. At the end of each successive year prior to the sale to outsiders, the preparation of the consolidated balance sheet requires the same adjustments as those of Year 1. Consolidated income statements require no adjustment until the year of the sale to outsiders because, in each year prior to that event, the income statements of both affiliates will not contain any transactions with regard to the land.

However, assuming that Parent Company uses the cost method, the calculation of beginning consolidated retained earnings each year will have to include an adjustment to hold back the $180 unrealized land profit. The calculation would be identical to that shown in Exhibit 6.5 on page 260 except that it would be described as land profit rather than profit in opening inventory. (This particular calculation is based on the assumption that Sub Inc. was the selling company.) Each successive year would require the same adjustment until the land is sold to outsiders.

In this case, let us assume that the land was sold to outsiders during Year 8 at a profit of $1,300. The company making the sale in Year 8 would record the following journal entry:

The gain on the separate-entity income statement is $1,300.

Cash	3,600	
Land		2,300
Gain on sale of land		1,300

While the selling company recorded a gain of $1,300, the gain to the entity is $1,600 (1,300 + 300). On the Year 8 consolidated income statement, the gain held back in Year 1 is realized and the income tax expense is adjusted as follows:

PARENT COMPANY
CONSOLIDATED INCOME STATEMENT
Year 8

Gain on sale of land (1,300 + **300**)	$1,600
Income tax expense (P + S + **120**)	XXX
Net income	$ XXX
Attributable to	
Shareholders of parent	$ XXX
Non-controlling interest	XXX

The gain on the consolidated income statement is $1,600 ($1,300 + $300 previously held back).

The entity's net income is increased by $180 ($300 − $120). If the subsidiary was the original selling company, the net income of the non-controlling interest is affected in Year 8; the entire $180 is attributed to the controlling interest if the parent was the original seller.

Equity Method Journal Entries   Parent Co.'s equity journal entries for the land gain in Years 1 and 8 would be identical to the entries illustrated previously for inventory in Years 1 and 2, depending of course on which company was the original seller in the intercompany profit transaction.

Revaluation Model   In the previous example, the companies used the cost model to account for land. We will use the same figures from the previous example to illustrate the accounting when the companies periodically revalue land to fair value under the revaluation model.

At the end of Year 0, selected account balances from the separate-entity balance sheet for the company holding the land were as follows:

An entity can report its property, plant, and equipment at fair value on an annual basis.

Land at cost	$2,000
Fair value excess for land	250
Deferred income tax liability (40% × 250)	100
Accumulated revaluation surplus, net of tax (250 − 100)	150

The fair value excess for land is a contra account[2] to the land account. When added to the land account, land will be reported at fair value. The accumulated revaluation surplus account is a component of shareholders' equity. It is also referred to as accumulated other comprehensive income.

The selling company would make the following entries pertaining to the sale of the land in Year 1:

Cash	2,300	
Land		2,000
Fair value excess for land		250
Gain on sale of land		50
To record sale of land		

The revaluation surplus is transferred to retained earnings when the property is sold.

Accumulated revaluation surplus	150	
Retained earnings		150
To transfer revaluation surplus to retained earnings on sale of land		

Income tax expense	20	
Deferred income tax liability	100	
Income tax payable		120
To record tax on sale and transfer deferred income tax liability to current income taxes payable		

Assuming that the fair value of the land is $2,325 at the end of Year 1, the purchasing company would make the following entries pertaining to the land in Year 1:

Land	2,300	
Cash		2,300
To record purchase of land		

Fair value excess for land	25	
Other comprehensive income — revaluation surplus for land		25
To revalue land to fair value		

The revaluation surplus is reported through other comprehensive income on an after-tax basis.

Other comprehensive income — income tax on revaluation surplus for land	10	
Deferred income tax liability		10
To record income tax on revaluation surplus		

---

[2] The use of a contra account is optional. Companies could record the adjustment to fair value directly in the land account. If so, they would lose track of the original cost.

The following summarizes what would be reported on the separate-entity statements and what should be reported on the consolidated statements for Year 1:

The consolidated statements should report amounts that would have existed had the intercompany transaction not occurred.

	Selling Co.	Buying Co.	Consolidated
Land		$2,300	$2,000
Fair value excess		25	325
Income tax payable	$120		
Deferred income tax liability		10	130
Accumulated revaluation surplus		15	195
Gain on sale of land	50		
Income tax expense	20		
Other comprehensive income — revaluation surplus for land, net of tax		15	45

The consolidated statements present what would have been reported on the selling company's statements had the intercompany transaction not taken place.

Intercompany Transfer Pricing

In our coin example at the beginning of this chapter, we saw a loonie sold for a gross profit of $40, which was allocated to the four related companies as follows:

Parent	$ 9
Sub 1	5
Sub 2	10
Sub 3	16
Total	$40

Intercompany transactions are sometimes undertaken to transfer profit from high-tax to low-tax jurisdictions.

From a financial reporting point of view we are not concerned with the amount of profit earned by each company, but only with eliminating intercompany transactions and profits that are unrealized because they have not been sold outside the consolidated "single entity." From a Canadian taxation point of view, the consolidated entity is not subject to tax; rather each company pays tax on its taxable income. It should seem obvious that the management of the parent company would be interested in maximizing the after-tax profit of this single entity if possible. If all of the companies are in one taxation jurisdiction, there is nothing that management can do to increase the after-tax profit. However, if some of the companies are in jurisdictions with low rates of corporate income tax while others are in high-tax-rate jurisdictions, management may try to structure each company's transfer price so that the majority (or all) of the $40 profit is earned in low-tax-rate jurisdictions. This will often bring companies into conflict with the governments of the high-tax-rate jurisdictions.

The examples in this chapter regarding the elimination of unrealized intercompany profits follow the dictates of entity theory. The entity theory is also required when valuing the subsidiary's assets and liabilities at fair value at the date of acquisition, as we learned in Chapter 4. Therefore, the CICA standard-setters are consistent in requiring the use of the entity theory in many different aspects of preparing consolidated financial statements.

Disclosure Requirements The disclosure requirements for consolidated financial statements were summarized in Chapters 3 and 4. In addition to those requirements, the entity would normally indicate that intercompany transactions have been

Exhibit 6.7

Extracts from Aviva's 2008 Financial Statements

(D) CONSOLIDATION PRINCIPLES

Subsidiaries are those entities (including special purpose entities) in which the Group, directly or indirectly, has power to exercise control over financial and operating policies in order to gain economic benefits. Subsidiaries are consolidated from the date on which effective control is transferred to the Group and are excluded from consolidation from the date of disposal. All intercompany transactions, balances and unrealized surpluses and deficits on transactions between Group companies have been eliminated.

Source: Reproduced with permission from Aviva Canada Inc., https://avivacanada.com/.

eliminated. The excerpt in Exhibit 6.7 is taken from the 2008 financial statements of Aviva, a U.K. company. Aviva is the world's fifth largest insurance group, serving 50 million customers across Europe, North America, and Asia Pacific.

GAAP for Private Enterprises

As mentioned in Chapter 3, private companies can either consolidate their subsidiaries or report their investments in subsidiaries under the cost method or the equity method.

U.S. GAAP Differences

U.S. GAAP and IFRSs for intercompany transactions have many similarities. The significant differences are summarized as follows:

1. Whereas IFRSs do not allow the use of LIFO for reporting inventory, LIFO is allowed under U.S. GAAP.

2. Whereas IFRSs require the use of net realizable value to determine whether inventory is impaired, U.S. GAAP uses the midpoint of net realizable value, replacement cost, and net realizable value less normal gross margin.

SUMMARY

To ensure that consolidated financial statements reflect only transactions between the single entity and those outside the entity, all intercompany transactions are eliminated. The elimination of intercompany revenues and expenses does not affect the net income of this entity; therefore, it cannot affect the amounts allocated to the two equities in the balance sheet.

Intercompany profits in assets are not recognized in the consolidated financial statements until the assets have been sold outside the group or consumed. (The concept of realization as a result of consumption is discussed in the next chapter.)

The elimination of unrealized intercompany profits in assets reduces the net income of the consolidated entity. Also, it will affect the amount allocated to non-controlling interest only if the subsidiary was the selling company. The income tax recorded on the unrealized profit is also removed from the consolidated income statement and is shown as deferred income taxes until a sale to outsiders takes place.

When the assets that contain the intercompany profit are sold outside (or consumed), the profit is considered realized and is reflected in the consolidated income statement. The appropriate income tax is removed from the consolidated balance sheet and reflected as an expense in the income statement. The adjustments for income tax ensure that income tax expense is properly matched to income recognized on the consolidated income statement.

Significant Changes in the Last Two Years

1. For publicly accountable enterprises, IFRSs have replaced the former sections of the *CICA Handbook*. The following table shows the IFRSs covered in this chapter along with their counterparts from the former sections of the *CICA Handbook*:

IFRSs	CICA Handbook *Counterparts*
IAS 27: Consolidated and Separate Financial Statements	Section 1601: Consolidated Financial Statements Section 1602: Non-controlling Interests

2. The bottom portion of the consolidated income statement segregates consolidated profit into two components: attributable to shareholders of parent company and attributable to non-controlling interest.

3. When the income statement classifies expenses by their nature, the elimination of intercompany sales, purchases, and unrealized profit in inventory could affect many different accounts including raw materials consumed, labour costs, depreciation of factory equipment, other conversion costs, and changes in inventories of work in progress and finished goods.

4. When losses are recognized on intercompany transactions, the intercompany transactions should be eliminated on consolidation. Then, the assets involved in the intercompany transaction should be checked for impairment.

5. The consolidation adjustments to eliminate intercompany transactions and unrealized profits will differ depending on whether the reporting entity uses the cost model or the revaluation model for accounting for their property, plant, and equipment. The consolidated statements should present the property, plant, and equipment at the values that would have been reported on the selling company's statements had the intercompany transaction not taken place.

Changes Expected in the Next Three Years

No major changes are expected in the next three years for the topics presented in this chapter.

SELF-STUDY PROBLEM

The following are the Year 5 financial statements of Peter Corporation and its subsidiary, Salt Company:

	Peter	Salt
Year 5 income statements		
Sales	$900,000	$250,000
Management fees	25,000	—
Interest	—	3,600
Gain on land sale	—	20,000
Dividends	12,000	—
	937,000	273,600
Cost of sales	540,000	162,000
Interest expense	3,600	—
Other expenses	196,400	71,600
Income tax expense	80,000	16,000
	820,000	249,600
Profit	$117,000	$ 24,000
Year 5 retained earnings statements		
Balance, January 1	$153,000	$ 72,000
Profit	117,000	24,000
	270,000	96,000
Dividends	50,000	15,000
Balance, December 31	$220,000	$ 81,000
Statements of financial position — December 31, Year 5		
Land	$175,000	$ 19,000
Plant and equipment (net)	238,000	47,000
Investment in Salt Co.	65,000	—
Inventory	32,000	27,000
Notes receivable	—	60,000
Accounts receivable	70,000	10,000
Cash	12,000	8,000
	$592,000	$171,000
Common shares	$100,000	$ 50,000
Retained earnings	220,000	81,000
Notes payable	60,000	—
Other liabilities	212,000	40,000
	$592,000	$171,000

Additional Information

- On January 1, Year 3, Peter purchased 80 percent of the common shares of Salt for $65,000. On that date, Salt had retained earnings of $10,000, and the book values of its identifiable net assets were equal to fair values.

- The companies sell merchandise to each other. Peter sells to Salt at a gross profit rate of 35 percent; Salt earns a gross profit of 40 percent from its sales to Peter.

- The December 31, Year 4, inventory of Peter contained purchases made from Salt amounting to $7,000. There were no intercompany purchases in the inventory of Salt on this date.

- During Year 5 the following intercompany transactions took place:
  - (a) Salt made a $25,000 payment to Peter for management fees, which was recorded as "other expense."
  - (b) Salt made sales of $75,000 to Peter. The December 31, Year 5, inventory of Peter contained merchandise purchased from Salt amounting to $16,500.
  - (c) Peter made sales of $100,000 to Salt. The December 31, Year 5, inventory of Salt contained merchandise purchased from Peter amounting to $15,000.
  - (d) On July 1, Year 5, Peter borrowed $60,000 from Salt and signed a note bearing interest at 12 percent per annum. Interest on this note was paid on December 31, Year 5.
  - (e) In Year 5, Salt sold land to Peter, recording a gain of $20,000. This land is being held by Peter on December 31, Year 5.
- Goodwill impairment tests have been conducted yearly since the date of acquisition. Losses due to impairment were as follows: Year 3, $2,600; Year 4, $800; Year 5, $1,700.
- Peter accounts for its investment using the cost method.
- Both companies pay income tax at a rate of 40 percent.

Required:

(a) Prepare the Year 5 consolidated financial statements.
(b) Prepare the following:
  (i) A calculation of consolidated retained earnings as at December 31, Year 5.
  (ii) A statement of changes in non-controlling interest for Year 5.
  (iii) A statement of changes in deferred income taxes for Year 5.
(c) Assume that Peter uses the equity method for its internal records.
  (i) Calculate the balance in the investment account as at December 31, Year 4.
  (ii) Prepare Peter's equity method journal entries for Year 5.

Solution to Self-study Problem

(a) Supporting Schedules

CALCULATION AND IMPAIRMENT OF THE ACQUISITION DIFFERENTIAL

Cost of 80% of Salt, Jan. 1, Year 3		$65,000
Implied value of 100% of Salt		$81,250
Book value of Salt, Jan. 1, Year 3		
Common shares	50,000	
Retained earnings	10,000	
		60,000
Acquisition differential		21,250
Allocated to revalue the net assets of Salt		–0–
Goodwill, Jan. 1, Year 3		21,250
Impairment losses		
Year 3–Year 4	3,400 **(a)**	
Year 5	1,700 **(b)**	5,100
Goodwill, Dec. 31, Year 5		$16,150 **(c)**

INTERCOMPANY ITEMS

Notes receivable and payable	$ 60,000 **(d)**
Management fee revenue and expense	$ 25,000 **(e)**
Sales and purchases (100,000 + 75,000)	$175,000 **(f)**
Interest revenue and expense (12% × 60,000 × ½ year)	$ 3,600 **(g)**
Dividend from Salt (80% × 15,000)	$ 12,000 **(h)**

UNREALIZED PROFITS

	Before tax	40% tax	After tax
Inventory			
Opening (7,000 × 40%) — Salt selling	$ 2,800	$1,120	$ 1,680 **(i)**
Ending			
Salt selling (16,500 × 40%)	$ 6,600	$2,640	$ 3,960 **(j)**
Peter selling (15,000 × 35%)	5,250	2,100	3,150 **(k)**
	$11,850	$4,740	$ 7,110 **(l)**
Land — Salt selling	$20,000	$8,000	$12,000 **(m)**

CALCULATION OF CONSOLIDATED PROFIT — Year 5

Profit of Peter			$117,000
Less: Dividends from Salt **(h)**		12,000	
Ending inventory profit **(k)**		3,150	15,150
Adjusted profit			101,850
Profit of Salt		24,000	
Less: Ending inventory profit **(j)**	3,960		
Land gain **(m)**	12,000		
Impairment of acquisition differential **(b)**	1,700	17,660	
		6,340	
Add opening inventory profit **(i)**		1,680	
Adjusted profit			8,020
Profit			$109,870
Attributable to			
Shareholders of parent			$108,266 **(n)**
Non-controlling interest (20% × 8,020)			1,604 **(o)**

CALCULATION OF CONSOLIDATED RETAINED EARNINGS
January 1, Year 5

Retained earnings — Peter		$153,000
Retained earnings — Salt	72,000	
Acquisition retained earnings	10,000	
Increase	62,000	
Less opening inventory profit **(i)**	1,680	
Less acquisition-differential impairment Year 3–Year 4 **(a)**	3,400	
Adjusted increase	56,920	
Peter's share	80%	45,536 **(p)**
Consolidated retained earnings, Jan. 1, Year 5		$198,536 **(q)**

CALCULATION OF DEFERRED INCOME TAXES — December 31, Year 5

Ending inventory **(l)**	$ 4,740
Land **(m)**	8,000
	$12,740 **(r)**

CALCULATION OF NON-CONTROLLING INTEREST — December 31, Year 5

Common shares — Salt		$50,000
Retained earnings — Salt		81,000
		131,000
Add: Unamortized acquisition differential **(c)**		16,150
Less: Ending inventory profit **(j)**	3,960	
Land gain **(m)**	12,000	(15,960)
Adjusted		131,190
Non-controlling interest's share		20%
		$26,238 **(s)**

PETER CORPORATION
CONSOLIDATED INCOME STATEMENT — Year 5

Sales (900,000 + 250,000 – **(f) 175,000**)	$975,000*
Cost of sales (540,000 + 162,000 – **(f) 175,000** – **(i) 2,800** + **(l) 11,850**)	536,050**
Other expenses (196,400 + 71,600 + **(b) 1,700** – **(e) 25,000**)	244,700
Income tax (80,000 + 16,000 – **(m) 8,000** + **(i) 1,120** – **(l) 4,740**)	84,380
Total expense	865,130
Net income	$109,870
Attributable to	
Shareholders of parent **(n)**	$108,266
Non-controlling interest **(o)**	1,604

* Revenue items completely eliminated from statement:	
Management fees	$25,000
Interest	3,600
Land gain	20,000
Dividends	12,000
** Expense items completely eliminated from statement:	
Interest	$ 3,600

PETER CORPORATION
CONSOLIDATED RETAINED EARNINGS STATEMENT — Year 5

Balance, January 1 **(q)**	$198,536
Profit	108,266
	306,802
Dividends	50,000
Balance, Dec. 31	$256,802

PETER CORPORATION
CONSOLIDATED STATEMENT OF FINANCIAL POSITION
— December 31, Year 5

Land (175,000 + 19,000 − **(m) 20,000**)	$174,000
Plant and equipment (net) (238,000 + 47,000)	285,000
Goodwill **(c)**	16,150
Deferred income taxes **(r)**	12,740
Inventory (32,000 + 27,000 − **(l) 11,850**)	47,150
Accounts receivable (70,000 + 10,000)	80,000
Cash (12,000 + 8,000)	20,000
	$635,040
Common shares	$100,000
Retained earnings	256,802
Non-controlling interest **(s)**	26,238
Other liabilities (212,000 + 40,000)	252,000
	$635,040

(b)(i)
CALCULATION OF CONSOLIDATED RETAINED EARNINGS
— December 31, Year 5

Retained earnings, Dec. 31, Year 5 — Peter			$220,000
Less: Ending inventory profit **(k)**			3,150
Adjusted			216,850
Retained earnings, Dec. 31, Year 5 — Salt		81,000	
Acquisition retained earnings		10,000	
Increase		71,000	
Less: Acquisition-differential impairment **(a)** + **(b)**	5,100		
Ending inventory profit **(j)**	3,960		
Land gain **(m)**	12,000	21,060	
Adjusted increase		49,940	
Peter's share		80%	39,952
Consolidated retained earnings,			
December 31, Year 5			$256,802

(ii)
CHANGES IN NON-CONTROLLING INTEREST — Year 5

Common shares — Salt	$50,000
Retained earnings, Jan. 1, Year 5 — Salt	72,000
	122,000
Add: Unamortized acquisition differential (21,250 − **(a) 3,400**)	17,850
Less: profit in beginning inventory **(i)**	(1,680)
	138,170
Non-controlling interest's share	20%
Non-controlling interest, Jan. 1, Year 5	27,634
Allocation of entity income, Year 5 **(o)**	1,604
	29,238
Dividends (20% × 15,000)	3,000
Non-controlling interest, December 31, Year 5	$26,238

(iii)

CHANGES IN DEFERRED INCOME TAXES — Year 5

Balance, Jan. 1, Year 5 (inventory) **(i)**		$ 1,120
Taxes paid in Year 5 but deferred		
Inventory **(l)**	4,740	
Land **(m)**	8,000	12,740
		13,860
Expensed Year 5 **(i)**		1,120
Balance, Dec. 31, Year 5		$ 12,740

(c)(i)

Investment in Salt, Dec. 31, Year 4 (cost method)			$ 65,000
Retained earnings, Dec. 31, Year 4 — Salt		72,000	
Acquisition retained earnings		10,000	
Increase		62,000	
Less inventory profit **(i)**	1,680		
Amort. of acquisition differential **(a)**	3,400	5,080	
Adjusted increase		56,920	
Peter's share		80%	45,536
Investment in Salt, December 31, Year 4			
(equity method)			$110,536

(ii)

EQUITY METHOD JOURNAL ENTRIES — Year 5
(See Calculation of Consolidated Profit)

Investment in Salt Co.	6,416	
Investment income		6,416
80% of adjusted profit of Salt Co. (80% × 8,020)		
Cash	12,000	
Investment in Salt Co.		12,000
Dividends from Salt Co. **(h)**		
Investment income	3,150	
Investment in Salt Co.		3,150
Ending inventory profit — Peter selling **(k)**		

REVIEW QUESTIONS

1. In what way are an individual's pants with four pockets similar to a parent company with three subsidiaries? Explain, with reference to intercompany revenues and expenses.

2. List the types of intercompany revenue and expenses that are eliminated in the preparation of a consolidated income statement, and indicate the effect that each elimination has on the amount of net income attributable to non-controlling interest.

3. "From a consolidated-entity point of view, intercompany revenue and expenses and intercompany borrowings do nothing more than transfer cash from one bank account to another." Explain.

4. If an intercompany profit is recorded on the sale of an asset to an affiliate within the consolidated entity in Period 1, when should this profit be considered realized? Explain.

5. Explain how the revenue recognition principle supports the elimination of intercompany transactions when preparing consolidated financial statements.

6. "The reduction of a $1,000 intercompany gross profit from ending inventory should be accompanied by a $400 increase to deferred income taxes in consolidated assets." Do you agree? Explain.

7. Explain how the matching principle supports adjustments to income tax expense when eliminating intercompany profits from consolidated financial statements.

8. A parent company rents a sales office to its wholly owned subsidiary under an operating lease requiring rent of $2,000 a month. What adjustments to income tax expense should accompany the elimination of the parent's $24,000 rent revenue and the subsidiary's $24,000 rent expense when a consolidated income statement is being prepared? Explain.

9. "Intercompany losses recorded on the sale of assets to an affiliate within the consolidated entity should always be eliminated when consolidated financial statements are prepared." Do you agree with this statement? Explain.

10. Describe the effects that the elimination of intercompany sales and intercompany profits in ending inventory will have on the various elements of the consolidated financial statements.

11. What difference does it make on the consolidated financial statements if there are unrealized profits in land resulting from a downstream transaction as compared to an upstream transaction?

12. When there are unrealized profits in inventory at the end of Year 1, consolidated profit would normally be affected for Years 1 and 2. Explain.

13. An intercompany gain on the sale of land is eliminated in the preparation of the consolidated statements in the year that the gain was recorded. Will this gain be eliminated in the preparation of subsequent consolidated statements? Explain.

14. A subsidiary periodically revalues its land to fair value under the revaluation option for property, plant, and equipment. Explain the adjustments required to the consolidated financial statements if the subsidiary sells this land to the parent at an amount in excess of its carrying value.

MULTIPLE-CHOICE QUESTIONS

Use the following data for Questions 1 to 6.

The financial statements of Post Company and Stamp Company on December 31, Year 5, were as follows:

BALANCE SHEETS

	Post	Stamp
Assets		
Cash	$ 50,000	$ 10,000
Accounts receivable	250,000	100,000
Inventories	3,000,000	520,000
Equipment (net)	6,150,000	2,500,000
Buildings (net)	2,600,000	500,000
Investment in Stamp (at cost)	850,000	—
	$12,900,000	$3,630,000
Liabilities and Shareholders' Equity		
Current liabilities	$ 300,000	$ 170,000
Long-term liabilities	4,000,000	1,100,000
Common shares	3,000,000	500,000
Retained earnings	5,600,000	1,860,000
	$12,900,000	$3,630,000

STATEMENTS OF INCOME AND RETAINED EARNINGS

	Post	Stamp
Sales revenue	$ 3,500,000	$ 900,000
Other revenues	300,000	30,000
	3,800,000	930,000
Cost of goods sold	1,700,000	330,000
Selling and administrative expenses	300,000	100,000
Other expenses	200,000	150,000
Income tax expense	300,000	70,000
	2,500,000	650,000
Net income	1,300,000	280,000
Retained earnings, beginning balance	4,500,000	1,600,000
	5,800,000	1,880,000
Dividends declared	200,000	20,000
Retained earnings, ending balance	$ 5,600,000	$1,860,000

Additional Information

- Post owns 70 percent of Stamp and carries its investment in Stamp on its books by the cost method.
- During Year 4, Post sold Stamp $100,000 worth of merchandise, of which $60,000 was resold by Stamp in the year. During Year 5, Post had sales of $200,000 to Stamp, of which 40 percent was resold by Stamp. Intercompany sales are priced to provide Post with a gross profit of 30 percent of the sales price.
- On December 31, Year 4, Post had in its inventories $150,000 of merchandise purchased from Stamp during Year 4. On December 31, Year 5, Post had in its ending inventories $100,000 of merchandise that had resulted from purchases of $350,000 from Stamp during Year 5. Intercompany sales are priced to provide Stamp with a gross profit of 60 percent of the sale price.
- Both companies are taxed at 25 percent.

1. What amount of sales revenue would appear on Post's consolidated income statement for the year ended December 31, Year 5?
   a. $3,850,000
   b. $4,050,000
   c. $4,200,000
   d. $4,400,000

2. To calculate Post's consolidated cost of goods sold, the first step is to add together the unadjusted totals from Post's and Stamp's separate-entity financial statements. What is the adjustment to this figure for unrealized profits in beginning inventory for the year ended December 31, Year 5?
   a. −$102,000
   b. −$96,000
   c. −$76,500
   d. −$6,000

3. Refer to Question 2. What is the total adjustment to consolidated cost of goods sold for intercompany sales for Year 5 and unrealized profits in ending inventory at December 31, Year 5?
   a. −$448,000
   b. −$454,000
   c. −$478,000
   d. −$556,000

4. To calculate Post's consolidated income tax expense, first add together the unadjusted totals from Post's and Stamp's separate-entity financial statements. What is the adjustment to this figure related to the unrealized profit in beginning inventory for the year ended December 31, Year 5?
   a. $22,500
   b. $24,000
   c. $25,500
   d. $28,000

5. Which of the following would appear on Post's consolidated income statement for the year ended December 31, Year 5, for the net income attributable to non-controlling interest?
   a. $77,250
   b. $84,000
   c. $90,750
   d. $99,000

6. Which of the following would appear on Post's consolidated balance sheet at December 31, Year 5, for non-controlling interest?
   a. $694,500
   b. $708,000
   c. $714,750
   d. $721,500

7. Pedro Company owns 80 percent of Sunita Ltd. During Year 2, Pedro sold raw materials inventory with a 10 percent gross margin to Sunita. Sunita sold all of these goods in Year 2. How should the Year 2 consolidated income statement be adjusted?
   a. Profit attributable to Pedro's shareholders should be reduced by 80 percent of the gross profit of the intercompany sales.

b. Profit attributable to Pedro's shareholders should be reduced by 100 percent of the gross profit on the intercompany sales.

c. Sales and raw materials consumed should be reduced by the intercompany sales.

d. Sales and raw materials consumed should be reduced by 80 percent of the intercompany sales.

8. In Year 2, an 80-percent-owned subsidiary sold land to the parent at a gain of $50,000. The parent still owns this land at the end of Year 5. Which of the following consolidation adjustments is appropriate for the Year 5 consolidated financial statements?

a. Decrease gain on sale of land by $50,000.

b. Decrease the non-controlling interest's share of consolidated profit by $10,000.

c. Increase non-controlling interest on the balance sheet by $10,000.

d. Decrease land by $50,000.

9. If unrealized inventory profits have occurred, what is the impact on consolidated financial statements of upstream and downstream transfers?

a. Downstream transfers may be ignored since they are made by the parent company.

b. Downstream transfers affect the computation of the non-controlling interest's share of consolidated net income but upstream transfers do not.

c. No difference exists in consolidated financial statements between upstream and downstream transfers.

d. Upstream transfers affect the computation of the non-controlling interest's share of consolidated net income but downstream transfers do not.

10. Castle Corp. owns 75 percent of the outstanding shares of Moat Ltd. During Year 5, Moat sold merchandise to Castle for $200,000. At December 31, Year 5, 50 percent of this merchandise remains in Castle's inventory. For Year 5, gross profit percentages were 40 percent for Castle and 30 percent for Moat. How much unrealized profit should be eliminated from ending inventory in the consolidation process at December 31, Year 5?

a. $30,000

b. $40,000

c. $45,000

d. $60,000

11. Bell Co. owns 90 percent of Tower Inc. During Year 4, Tower sold finished goods inventory costing $75,000 to Bell for $100,000. A total of 16 percent of this inventory was not sold to outsiders until Year 5. During Year 5, Bell sold finished goods inventory which cost $96,000 to Tower for $120,000. Thirty-five percent of this inventory was not sold to outsiders until Year 6. Bell reported an increase in finished goods inventory of $380,000 in Year 5, while Tower reported an amount of $210,000. What amount should be reported as changes in finished goods inventory on the Year 5 consolidated income statement?

a. $577,600

b. $585,600

c. $594,400

d. $602,400

Use the following data for Questions 12 and 13.

Hardwood Ltd. owns 90 percent of the common shares of Softwood Corp. Both companies use the revaluation method to account for capital assets and pay income tax at the rate of 40 percent. Softwood Corp. purchased land in Year 3 for $100,000. The land had a fair value of $110,000 on December 31, Year 4, and $115,000 on December 31, Year 5. On June 30, Year 5, Softwood sold the land to Hardwood for $112,000.

12. At what amount should the land be reported on the consolidated balance sheet at December 31, Year 5?
    a. $100,000
    b. $110,000
    c. $112,000
    d. $115,000

13. What is the revaluation surplus pertaining to the land in the shareholders' equity section of the consolidated balance sheet at December 31, Year 5?
    a. $1,800
    b. $3,000
    c. $9,000
    d. $15,000

14. When preparing the consolidated balance sheet, any unrealized profit is removed from ending inventory. Which of the following financial statement concepts best supports this accounting practice?
    a. Recognition criteria.
    b. Timeliness.
    c. Historical cost measurement assumption.
    d. Full disclosure principle.

(*CGA-Canada adapted*)

15. You are preparing the consolidated financial statements for PALE Corp. and its 80-percent-owned subsidiary, SALE Inc., for the year ended July 31, Year 5. Which of the following transactions would give rise to a deferred income tax asset being recorded on the consolidated balance sheet?
    a. PALE sells inventory to SALE at a markup of 30 percent, and SALE resells all of this inventory prior to year-end.
    b. PALE sells inventory to SALE at a markup of 30 percent, and SALE resells 60 percent of this inventory prior to year-end.
    c. SALE sells inventory that it had acquired from PALE in the previous year to an unrelated party at a markup of 30 percent.
    d. SALE sells inventory that it had acquired from PALE in the previous year to an unrelated party at a loss of $1,000.

(*CGA-Canada adapted*)

Use the following data for Questions 16 and 17.

On January 1, Year 1, VEN Company acquired 70 percent of the common shares of TOR Company. During Year 2, VEN sold inventory to TOR for $100,000 and earned a gross margin of 30 percent. At the end of Year 2, TOR still had the goods purchased from VEN in its inventory. Both companies turn over their inventory at least five times a year.

16. What would be the impact on inventory turnover for the Year 2 consolidated financial statements if no consolidation adjustments were made with respect to the intercompany sale and unrealized profit?
    a. It would be overstated.
    b. It would be understated.
    c. It would not be affected.
    d. The impact cannot be determined based on the information provided.

17. What would be the impact on the Year 2 consolidated net income attributable to the shareholders of VEN if the intercompany sale had been by TOR to VEN rather than by VEN to TOR?
    a. It would increase.
    b. It would decrease.
    c. It would not change.
    d. The impact cannot be determined based on the information provided.

CASES

Case 1   You, the controller, recently had the following discussion with the president:

President: I just don't understand why we can't recognize the revenue from the intercompany sale of inventory on the consolidated financial statements. The subsidiary company sold the goods to the parent at fair value and received the cash for the sale. We need to record the profit on this sale in order to maintain a steady earnings growth for our company. Otherwise, the bank will be concerned about our ability to repay the loan.

Controller: You are right that the sub has received the cash, but that is not the main criterion for determining when to recognize the revenue. Furthermore, you need to understand that the consolidated financial statements are different from the individual financial statements for the parent and the subsidiary.

President: I have never understood why we need to prepare consolidated financial statements. It is just extra work. Who uses these statements? Furthermore, the profit on the intercompany transaction should be reported on the income statement because tax had to be paid on this profit. Surely, if tax is paid, the profit is legitimate.

Controller: Once again, cash payments do not determine when we report income tax expense on the income statement. How about we get together for lunch tomorrow? I will prepare a brief presentation to illustrate the difference between the income for the parent and subsidiary and the income for the consolidated entity and will explain how all of these statements properly apply generally accepted accounting principles for revenue and expense recognition.

As part of the presentation, you decided to prepare monthly income statements for the parent, subsidiary, and consolidated entity for the following situation:
- Parent owns 100 percent of the subsidiary.
- Subsidiary buys goods for $100 in July and sells them to the parent in August at a markup of 20 percent of cost.
- In September, Parent sells these goods to an outsider at a markup of 20 percent of selling price.
- Both companies pay income tax at the rate of 40 percent.

Required:

Prepare notes for your presentation to the president.

Case 2   Beaver Ridge Oilers' Players Association and Mr. Slim, the CEO of the Beaver Ridge Oilers Hockey Club (Club), ask for your help in resolving a salary dispute. Mr. Slim presents the following income statement to the player representatives:

BEAVER RIDGE OILERS HOCKEY CLUB
INCOME STATEMENT

Ticket revenues		$3,000,000
Player salaries	$ 600,000	
Stadium rent	2,100,000	
Staff salaries	500,000	
Advertising	100,000	3,300,000
Net income (loss)		$ (300,000)

Mr. Slim argues that the Club loses money and cannot afford a salary increase. After further investigation, you determine that the Club owns 90 percent of the voting shares of Oilers Stadium Inc. (Stadium), which is used primarily by the Oilers. The Club accounts for its investment in the Stadium under the cost method. The Stadium has not declared any dividends since its inception three years ago. As such, the Club has never reported any income on its investment in the Stadium.

Mr. Slim insists that the income for the Stadium should not be a factor in the negotiation of the players' salaries since the Stadium is a separate legal entity and is taxed as a separate legal entity. The income statement for the Stadium is as follows:

OILERS STADIUM INC.
INCOME STATEMENT

Stadium rent revenue	$2,100,000	
Concession revenue	1,200,000	
Parking revenue	100,000	$3,400,000
Cost of concessions	400,000	
Depreciation of stadium	500,000	
Staff salaries	700,000	1,600,000
Net income		$1,800,000

Required:

(a) What advice would you give the negotiating parties regarding the issue of whether to consider the Stadium's income in the salary negotiations? Give supporting arguments. Indicate what other pertinent information you would need to provide specific recommendations.

(b) How would your advice change if the Stadium were 90 percent owned by Mr. Slim directly rather than the Club? Explain.

Case 3   Metal Caissons Limited (MCL) was incorporated on December 15, Year 8, to build metal caissons, which are large containers used for transporting military equipment. John Ladd (president) and Paul Finch (vice-president) each own 50 percent of MCL's shares. Until September 30, Year 9, MCL's first fiscal year-end, they applied their energy to planning and organizing the business. John and Paul developed the product, sought government assistance, designed the plant, and negotiated a sales contract.

In October Year 9, MCL signed a $7.5 million contract with the Canadian Department of National Defence (DND). The contract stipulates that MCL must deliver one caisson to DND on the first business day of each month over a period of five years, commencing on April 1, Year 10. Any delay in delivery entails a $2,000 penalty per day, per caisson delivered late, up to a maximum of $50,000 per caisson. DND has the right to cancel its contract with MCL at any time if the company is unable to meet its commitments. The caissons must be manufactured according to DND's detailed plans and specifications. Any caisson not meeting the specifications will be rejected, thereby causing a delay in delivery.

During November Year 9, MCL obtained two government grants. Details of the grant agreements are as follows:

1. A $1 million grant for the construction of a manufacturing plant. The plant must be located in a designated area of the country and must be constructed primarily of Canadian-made components, failing which MCL must repay the grant in full.
2. A $500,000 grant for job creation. As a condition of the grant, MCL must employ at least 85 percent of its total workforce in the plant for a period of three years. If employment at the plant falls below this minimum level, MCL will have to repay the grant in full.

On December 1, Year 9, MCL borrowed $1 million from the bank to construct the plant in northern Quebec, one of the designated areas. Construction was scheduled to start immediately and to be completed by the end of February Year 10. Unfortunately, construction was delayed, and the manufacturing section of the plant was not fully operational until the beginning of May. As a result, the April, May, and June caissons were delivered 25, 18, and 12 days late, respectively. The inexperienced employees had to work quickly but met the delivery deadlines for the July and August caissons. The administrative section of the plant (supervisors' office, etc., representing 5 percent of the total area) is still under construction.

As a condition of a bank loan and the DND contract, the company must issue audited financial statements commencing with the year ending September 30, Year 10.

It is now mid-September, Year 10. Linda Presner, a partner with Presner & Wolf, Chartered Accountants, and you, the CA in charge of the audit, have just met with MCL's senior management to discuss MCL's accounting policies. During the meeting, you obtained the condensed internal financial statements of MCL as at August 31, Year 10 (Exhibit I on page 288), and other information on MCL (Exhibit II on pages 288–289). After the meeting, Linda asks you to prepare a memo for her dealing with the accounting issues connected with this engagement.

Required:

Prepare the memo requested by the partner.

(*CICA adapted*)

Exhibit I

METAL CAISSONS LIMITED CONDENSED BALANCE SHEET
(in thousands of dollars, unaudited)

	Aug. 31 Year 10	Sept. 30 Year 9
Current assets	$2,388	$242
Property, plant, and equipment — net of amortization (Note 1)	2,154	
Capitalized expenditures — net of amortization (Note 1)	109	120
Investment in MSI, at cost	240	
	$4,891	$362
Current liabilities	$2,489	$120
Long-term liabilities	1,000	
Shareholders' equity	1,402	242
	$4,891	$362

METAL CAISSONS LIMITED CONDENSED INCOME STATEMENT
For the 11 months ended August 31, Year 10
(in thousands of dollars)

Revenues	$2,125
Cost of sales	375
Gross margin	1,750
Administrative expenses	590
Net income	$1,160

METAL CAISSONS LIMITED
EXTRACTS FROM NOTES TO CONDENSED FINANCIAL STATEMENTS
For the 11 months ended August 31, Year 10

1. Accounting policies

Inventories. Inventories are valued at the lower of cost and net realizable value. Cost is determined on a first-in, first-out basis.

Property, plant, and equipment. Property, plant, and equipment are recorded at cost. Depreciation is calculated on a straight-line basis over the following periods:

Plant	50 years
Production equipment	15 years
Office equipment	20 years
Computer equipment	10 years

Capitalized expenditures. Capitalized expenditures consist of costs incurred during the start-up of the company. Amortization is calculated on a straight-line basis over a 10-year period.

Capitalized interest. The company is capitalizing 100 percent of the interest on the long-term debt until construction of the plant is complete. This interest is included in the cost of the plant.

Exhibit II

INFORMATION GATHERED BY CA

The bank loan bears interest at 8 percent and is secured by a mortgage on the plant. The loan is repayable over 10 years, with monthly payments of interest and principal of $12,133.

The head office of MCL, located in Montreal, is strictly an administrative unit. Twenty-four people, including the president and the vice-president, work at head office. A bookkeeper who joined MCL in February Year 10 supervises the preparation of the various financial and administrative reports. The plant employs 90 people.

As at September 30, Year 9, capitalized expenditures included the following items:

Incorporation costs	$ 5,000
Office equipment	24,000
Travel costs related to search for plant site	16,000
Costs of calls for tenders for manufacturing plant	12,000
Product development costs	22,000
Grant negotiation costs	13,000
Costs related to contract negotiations with DND	10,000
Miscellaneous administrative costs	11,000
Miscellaneous legal fees	7,000
	$120,000

The capitalized legal fees of $7,000 as at September 30, Year 9, include $2,000 in fees related to a $2.5 million lawsuit filed by Deutsch Production (a German company) against MCL for patent infringements. As at September 15, Year 10, John Ladd is unable to determine the outcome of the suit. In fiscal Year 10, $12,000 in legal fees has been incurred and expensed.

MCL had no income or expenses in its Year 9 fiscal year.

DND did not take any action following the delays in delivery.

On October 1, Year 9, MCL purchased 60 percent of the shares of Metal Supply Inc. (MSI) for $180,000. There was no acquisition differential on this acquisition. During fiscal Year 10, MSI sold parts to MCL for $300,000 and earned a gross margin of 30 percent. At August 31, Year 10, there was $100,000 of these intercompany purchases in MCL's inventory. MSI reported a profit of $30,000 but paid no dividends for the 11 months ended August 31, Year 10.

Case 4   In early September Year 1, your firm's audit client, D Ltd. (D) acquired in separate transactions an 80 percent interest in N Ltd. (N) and a 40 percent interest in K Ltd. (K). All three companies are federally incorporated Canadian companies and have August 31 year-ends. They all manufacture small appliances, but they do not compete with each other.

You are the senior on the audit of D. The partner has just received the preliminary consolidated financial statements from the controller of D along with unconsolidated statements for the three separate companies. Extracts from these statements are summarized in Exhibit I on page 290. The partner has requested that you provide him with a memorandum discussing the important financial accounting issues of D. Account balances for the consolidated financial statements should be recalculated to the extent that information is available.

D acquired the 80 percent interest in N for $4,000,000 paid as follows:

(1) $2,000,000 in cash and
(2) 160,000 common shares of D recorded in the books of D at $2,000,000.

D acquired its 40 percent interest in K at a cost of $2,100,000 paid as follows:

(1) $100,000 in cash and
(2) 160,000 common shares of D recorded in the books of D at $2,000,000.

Exhibit I

EXTRACTS FROM FINANCIAL STATEMENTS
At August 31, Year 2
(in 000s)

| | Unconsolidated | | | Consolidated |
	D	N	K	D
Investment in N Ltd., at cost	$4,000			
Investment in K Ltd., at cost	2,100			$2,100
Deferred development costs		$ 90		
Goodwill		60		
Non-controlling interest				590
Common shares	6,000	1,000	$2,000	6,000
Retained earnings, beginning	618	1,850	1,760	618
Profit	600	300	100	660
Dividends	(400)	(200)	(150)	(400)
Retained earnings, end of year	$ 818	$1,950	$1,710	$ 878

During the course of the audit, the following information was obtained:

1. The book value of 80 percent of N's net assets at the date of acquisition was $2,280,000. The acquisition differential consisted of the following:

The excess of fair value of land over book value	$ 800,000
The excess of fair value of plant and equipment over book value	700,000
20% non-controlling interest's share of excess of fair value over book value	(300,000)
Goodwill of N written off	(48,000)
Deferred research and development expenditures written off	(72,000)
Unallocated excess	640,000
	$1,720,000

The plant and equipment had a remaining useful life of 10 years when D acquired N.

2. The price paid by D for its investment in K was 10 percent lower than 40 percent of the fair value of K's identifiable net assets.

3. During August Year 2, K sold goods to D as follows:

Cost to K	$1,000,000
Normal selling price	1,250,000
Price paid by D	1,200,000

D had not sold these goods as of August 31, Year 2.
N also sold goods to D in August Year 2 and D had not sold them by August 31, Year 2.

Cost to N	$600,000
Normal selling price	750,000
Price paid by D	850,000

4. For the year ended August 31, Year 2, D's sales were $8,423,300 and N's sales were $6,144,500.

Required:

Prepare the memorandum requested by the partner.

(CICA adapted)

Case 5   Good Quality Auto Parts Limited (GQ) is a medium-sized, privately owned producer of auto parts, which are sold to car manufacturers, repair shops, and retail outlets. In March Year 10, the union negotiated a new three-year contract with the company for the 200 shop-floor employees. At the time, GQ was in financial difficulty and management felt unable to meet the contract demands of the union. Management also believed that a strike of any length would force the company into bankruptcy.

The company proposed that, in exchange for wage concessions, the company would implement a profit-sharing plan whereby the shop floor employees would receive 10 percent of the company's annual after-tax profit as a bonus in each year of the contract. Although the union generally finds this type of contract undesirable, it believed that insisting on the prevailing industry settlement would jeopardize GQ's survival. As a result, the contract terms were accepted.

The contract specifies that no major changes in accounting policies may be made without the change being approved by GQ's auditor. Another clause in the contract allows the union to engage a chartered accountant to examine the books of the company and meet with GQ's management and auditor to discuss any issues. Under the terms of the contract, any controversial accounting issues are to be negotiated by the union and management to arrive at a mutual agreement. If the parties cannot agree, the positions of the parties are to be presented to an independent arbitrator for resolution.

GQ presented to the union its annual financial statements and the unqualified audit report, for the year ended February 28, Year 11, the first year during which the profit-sharing plan was in effect. The union engaged you, CA, to analyze these financial statements and determine whether there are any controversial accounting issues. As a result of your examination, you identified a number of issues that are of concern to you. You met with the controller of the company and obtained the following information:

1. GQ wrote off $250,000 of inventory manufactured between Year 4 and Year 7. There have been no sales from this inventory in over two years. The controller explained that up until this year she had some hope that the inventory could be sold as replacement parts. However, she now believes that the parts cannot be sold.

2. The contracts GQ has with the large auto manufacturers allow the purchaser to return items for any reason. The company has increased the allowance for returned items by 10 percent in the year just ended. The controller contends that, because of the weak economy and stiff competition faced by the auto manufacturers with whom GQ does business, there will likely be a significant increase in the parts returned.

3. In April Year 10, GQ purchased $500,000 of new manufacturing equipment. To reduce the financial strain of the acquisition, the company negotiated a six-year payment schedule. Management believed that the company would be at a serious competitive disadvantage if it did not emerge from the current downturn with updated equipment. GQ decided to use accelerated depreciation at a rate of 40 percent for the new equipment. The controller argued that because of the rapid technological changes occurring in the industry, equipment purchased now is more likely to become technologically, rather than operationally, obsolete. The straight-line depreciation method applied to the existing equipment has not been changed.

www.mcgrawhillconnect.ca

4. In Year 5, GQ purchased a small auto parts manufacturer and merged it into its own operation. At the time of acquisition, $35,000 of goodwill was recorded and was being amortized over 35 years. The company has written off the goodwill in the year just ended. The controller explained that the poor performance of the auto parts industry, and of GQ in particular, has made the goodwill worthless.

5. In February Year 11, the president and the chairman of the board, who between them own 75 percent of the voting shares of the company, received bonuses of $250,000 each. GQ did not pay any dividends during the current year. In the prior year, dividends amounting to $650,000 were paid. The controller said that the board of directors justified the bonuses as a reward for keeping the company afloat despite extremely difficult economic times.

6. Until this year, GQ used the taxes-payable method for accounting purposes. In all previous years the company received a qualified audit opinion from the auditors due to this deviation from GAAP. This year, the company has used the liability method of accounting for income taxes. The change has been made retroactively. The effect of the change has been to reduce net income for fiscal Year 11. The controller argued that, because the company is likely to need significant external financing from new sources in the upcoming year, a clean audit opinion would reduce any fears prospective lenders might have about the company. The controller also believed that, in light of the contract with the union, the financial statements should be prepared in accordance with GAAP.

The union has asked you to prepare a report on the position it should take on the issues identified when discussing them with management. The union also wants to know what additional information you require in order to support this position.

Required:

Prepare the report.

(CICA adapted)

PROBLEMS

Problem 1   On January 1, Year 2, PAT Ltd. acquired 90 percent of SAT Inc. when SAT's retained earnings were $900,000. There was no acquisition differential. PAT accounts for its investment under the cost method. SAT sells inventory to PAT on a regular basis at a markup of 30 percent of selling price. The intercompany sales were $150,000 in Year 2 and $180,000 in Year 3. The total amount owing by PAT related to these intercompany sales was $50,000 at the end of Year 2 and $40,000 at the end of Year 3. On January 1, Year 3, the inventory of PAT contained goods purchased from SAT amounting to $60,000, while the December 31, Year 3, inventory contained goods purchased from SAT amounting to $70,000. Both companies pay income tax at the rate of 40 percent.

Selected account balances from the records of PAT and SAT for the year ended December 31, Year 3, were as follows:

Inventory	$ 500,000	$ 300,000
Accounts payable	600,000	320,000
Retained earnings, beginning of year	2,400,000	1,100,000
Sales	4,000,000	2,500,000
Cost of sales	3,100,000	1,700,000
Income tax expense	80,000	50,000

Required:

(a) Determine the amount to report on the Year 3 consolidated financial statements for the above noted accounts.

(b) Indicate how non-controlling interest on the Year 3 consolidated income statement and Year 3 consolidated balance sheet will be affected by the intercompany transactions noted above.

Problem 2 The consolidated income statement of a parent and its 90-percent-owned subsidiary appears below. It was prepared by an accounting student before reading this chapter.

CONSOLIDATED INCOME STATEMENT

Sales	$500,000
Rental revenue	24,000
Interest revenue	50,000
Total revenue	574,000
Cost of goods sold	350,000
Rent expense	24,000
Interest expense	35,000
Administration expenses	45,000
Income tax expense	42,000
Non-controlling interest in profit	9,000
Total costs and expenses	505,000
Profit	$ 69,000

The following items were overlooked when the statement was prepared:

- The opening inventory of the parent contained an intercompany profit of $5,000. This inventory was sold by the parent during the current year.
- During the year, intercompany sales (at a 30 percent gross profit rate) were made as follows:

By the parent	$100,000
By the subsidiary	80,000

- At the end of the year, half of the items purchased from the parent remained in the inventory of the subsidiary and none of the inventory purchased from the subsidiary remained in the parent's inventory.
- All of the rental revenue and 70 percent of the interest revenue were intercompany and appeared on the income statement of the parent.
- Assume a 40 percent rate for income tax.

Required:

Prepare a correct consolidated income statement.

Problem 3 On January 1, Year 1, Spike Ltd. purchased land for $100,000. On December 31, Year 1, Pike Co. acquired all of the common shares of Spike. The fair value of Spike's land on this date was $115,000.

On December 31, Year 2, Spike sold its land to Pike for $125,000. On December 31, Year 3, Pike sold the land to an arm's-length party for $128,000.

Both companies use the cost model for valuing their land and pay income tax at the rate of 40 percent. Assume that any gain on sale of land is fully taxable. The only land owned by these two companies is the land purchased by Spike in Year 1.

Required:

Determine the account balances for land, gain on sale of land, and income tax on gain for Years 1, 2, and 3 for three sets of financial statements (i.e., separate-entity statements for Pike and Spike and consolidated statements) by completing the following table:

	Land	Gain on Sale	Income Tax on Gain
December 31, Year 1 Pike Spike Consolidated			
December 31, Year 2 Pike Spike Consolidated			
December 31, Year 3 Pike Spike Consolidated			

Problem 4 The income statements for Paste Company and its subsidiaries, Waste Company and Baste Company, were prepared for the year ended December 31, Year 6, and are shown below:

	Paste	Waste	Baste
Income			
Sales	$450,000	$270,000	$190,000
Dividend	43,750	—	—
Rent	—	130,000	—
Interest	10,000	—	—
	503,750	400,000	190,000
Expenses			
Cost of sales	300,000	163,000	145,000
General and administrative	93,000	48,000	29,000
Interest	—	10,000	—
Income tax	27,000	75,000	7,000
	420,000	296,000	181,000
Profit	$ 83,750	$104,000	$ 9,000

Additional Information

- Paste purchased its 80 percent interest in Waste on January 1, Year 1. On this date, Waste had a retained earnings balance of $40,000, and the acquisition differential amounting to $15,000 was allocated entirely to plant with an estimated remaining life of eight years. The plant is used exclusively for manufacturing goods for resale.
- Paste purchased its 75 percent interest in Baste on December 31, Year 3. On this date, Baste had a retained earnings balance of $80,000. The acquisition differential amounting to $19,000 was allocated to goodwill; however, because Baste had failed to report adequate profits, the goodwill was entirely written off for consolidated purposes by the end of Year 5.

- Paste has established a policy that any intercompany sales will be made at a gross profit rate of 30 percent.
- On January 1, Year 6, the inventory of Paste contained goods purchased from Waste for $15,000.
- During Year 6, the following intercompany sales took place:

Paste to Waste	$ 90,000
Waste to Baste	170,000
Baste to Paste	150,000

- On December 31, Year 6, the inventories of each of the three companies contained items purchased on an intercompany basis in the following amounts:

Inventory of	
Paste	$90,000
Waste	22,000
Baste	60,000

- In addition to its merchandising activities, Waste is in the office equipment rental business. Both Paste and Baste rent office equipment from Waste. General and administrative expenses for Paste and Baste include rent expense of $25,000 and $14,000 respectively.
- During Year 6, Waste paid $10,000 interest to Paste for intercompany advances.
- All of Paste's dividend revenue pertains to its investments in Waste and Baste.
- Retained earnings at December 31, Year 6, for Paste, Waste, and Baste were $703,750, $146,000, and $79,000, respectively.
- Paste Company uses the cost method to account for its investments, and uses tax allocation at a rate of 40 percent when it prepares consolidated financial statements.

Required:

(a) Prepare a consolidated income statement for Year 6.
(b) Calculate consolidated retained earnings at December 31, Year 6.
(c) Use the criteria for revenue recognition to explain the adjustments for unrealized profits on intercompany sales when preparing consolidated financial statements.
(d) Now assume that Paste uses the equity method. Calculate its income from investments for Year 6.

Problem 5   X Co. acquired 75 percent of Y Co. on January 1, Year 1, when Y Co. had common shares worth $100,000 and retained earnings of $70,000. The acquisition differential was allocated as follows on this date:

Inventory	$ 60,000
Equipment (15-year life)	45,000
Total acquisition differential	$105,000

Since this date the following events have occurred:

Year 1

- Y Co. reported a net income of $130,000 and paid dividends of $25,000.
- On July 1, X Co. sold land to Y Co. for $102,000. This land was carried in the records of X Co. at $75,000.
- On December 31, Year 1, the inventory of X Co. contained an intercompany profit of $30,000.
- X Co. reported a net income of $400,000 from its own operations.

Year 2

- Y Co. reported a net loss of $16,000 and paid dividends of $5,000.
- Y Co. sold the land that it purchased from X Co. to an unrelated company for $130,000.
- On December 31, Year 2, the inventory of Y Co. contained an intercompany profit of $12,000.
- X Co. reported a net income from its own operations of $72,000.

Required:

Assume a 40 percent tax rate.

(a) Prepare X Co.'s equity method journal entries for each of Years 1 and 2.
(b) Calculate consolidated net income attributable to X Co.'s shareholders for each of Years 1 and 2.
(c) Prepare a statement showing the changes in non-controlling interest in each of Years 1 and 2.
(d) Calculate the balance in X Co.'s "Investment in Y Co. (equity method)" account as at December 31, Year 2.

Problem 6   L Co. owns a controlling interest in M Co. and Q Co. L Co. purchased an 80 percent interest in M Co. at a time when M Co. reported retained earnings of $500,000. L Co. purchased a 70 percent interest in Q Co. at a time when Q Co. reported retained earnings of $50,000. There was no acquisition differential for either of these acquisitions.

An analysis of the changes in retained earnings of the three companies during the current year appears below:

	L Co.	M Co.	Q Co.
Retained earnings balance, beginning of current year	$ 976,000	$ 843,000	$ 682,000
Profit	580,000	360,000	240,000
Dividends paid or declared	(250,000)	(200,000)	(150,000)
Retained earnings balance, end of current year	$1,306,000	$1,003,000	$ 772,000

Q Co. sells parts to L Co., which after further processing and assembly are sold by L Co. to M Co., where they become a part of the finished product sold by M Co. Intercompany profits included in raw materials inventories at the beginning and end of the current year are estimated as follows:

	Beginning inventory	Ending inventory
Intercompany profit in raw materials inventory		
On sales from Q to L	$90,000	$ 35,000
On sales from L to M	52,000	118,000

L Co. uses the cost method to account for its investments, and income tax allocation at a 40 percent rate when it prepares consolidated financial statements.

Required:

(a) Calculate consolidated profit attributable to M Co's shareholders for the current year.
(b) Calculate consolidated retained earnings at the beginning of the current year.

Problem 7   On January 1, Year 3, the Most Company purchased 80 percent of the outstanding voting shares of the Least Company for $1.6 million in cash. On that date, Least's balance sheet and the fair values of its identifiable assets and liabilities were as follows:

	Carrying value	Fair value
Cash	$ 25,000	$ 25,000
Accounts receivable	310,000	290,000
Inventories	650,000	600,000
Plant and equipment (net)	2,015,000	2,050,000
Total assets	$3,000,000	
Current liabilities	$ 300,000	300,000
Long-term liabilities	1,200,000	1,100,000
Common shares	500,000	
Retained earnings	1,000,000	
Total liabilities and shareholders' equity	$3,000,000	

On January 1, Year 3, Least's plant and equipment had a remaining useful life of eight years. Its long-term liabilities matured on January 1, Year 7. Goodwill, if any, is to be tested yearly for impairment.

The balance sheets as at December 31, Year 9, for the two companies were as follows:

BALANCE SHEETS
December 31, Year 9

	Most	Least
Cash	$ 500,000	$ 40,000
Accounts receivable	1,700,000	500,000
Inventories	2,300,000	1,200,000
Plant and equipment (net)	8,200,000	4,000,000
Investment in Least (at cost)	1,600,000	—
Land	700,000	260,000
Total assets	$15,000,000	$6,000,000
Current liabilities	$ 600,000	$ 200,000
Long-term liabilities	3,000,000	3,000,000
Common shares	1,000,000	500,000
Retained earnings	10,400,000	2,300,000
Total liabilities and shareholders' equity	$15,000,000	$6,000,000

Additional Information

- The inventories of both companies have a maximum turnover period of one year. Receivables have a maximum turnover period of 62 days.
- On July 1, Year 7, Most sold a parcel of land to Least for $100,000. Most had purchased this land in Year 4 for $150,000. On September 30, Year 9, Least sold the property to another company for $190,000.
- During Year 9, $2 million of Most's sales were to Least. Of these sales, $500,000 remain in the December 31, Year 9, inventories of Least. The December 31, Year 8, inventories of Least contained $312,500 of merchandise purchased from Most. Most's sales to Least are priced to provide it with a gross profit of 20 percent.
- Most and Least reported net income of $1,000,000 and $400,000, respectively, for Year 9.

- During Year 9, $1.5 million of Least's sales were to Most. Of these sales, $714,280 remain in the December 31, Year 9, inventories of Most. The December 31, Year 8, inventories of Most contained $857,140 of merchandise purchased from Least. Least's sales to Most are priced to provide it with a gross profit of 30 percent.
- Dividends declared on December 31, Year 9, were as follows:

Most	$350,000
Least	100,000

- Goodwill impairment tests resulted in losses of $52,200 in Year 4 and $8,700 in Year 9.
- Assume a 40 percent tax rate for both companies.

Required:
(a) Prepare the consolidated statement of changes in equity for Year 9.
(b) Prepare the consolidated balance sheet.
(c) Explain how the matching principle supports the adjustments to cost of goods sold when eliminating intercompany sales from the consolidated financial statements.
(d) If Most had used the parent company extension theory rather than the entity theory, how would this affect the debt-to-equity ratio at the end of Year 9?

Problem 8   H Co. has controlling interests in three subsidiaries, as shown in the data below:

		Subsidiaries		
	H Co.	L Co.	J Co.	K Co.
Retained earnings at acquisition		$30,000	$40,000	$25,000
Percent of ownership		95%	90%	85%
Retained earnings, Jan. 1, Year 5	$12,000	50,000	43,000	30,000
Profit (loss), Year 5		20,000	(5,000)	30,000
Dividends paid, Year 5	10,000	5,000	3,000	15,000
Intercompany sales		50,000	70,000	

K Co. had items in its inventory on January 1, Year 5, on which L Co. had made a profit of $5,000.

J Co. had items in its inventory on December 31, Year 5, on which K Co. had made a profit of $10,000.

J Co. rents premises from L Co. at an annual rental of $8,500.

The parent company has no income (other than from its investments) and no expenses. It uses the equity method of recording its investments but has made no entries during Year 5. Assume a 40 percent tax rate.

Required:
Prepare the following related to its investments:
(a) Entries that H Co. would make in Year 5.
(b) A calculation of consolidated retained earnings, January 1, Year 5.
(c) A calculation of consolidated profit attributable to shareholders of H Co. for Year 5.

Problem 9   Purple Company purchased a 70 percent interest in Sand Company several years ago in order to obtain retail outlets for its major products. Since that time Purple has sold to Sand a substantial portion of its merchandise requirements. At the beginning of the current year, Sand's inventory of $690,000 was composed 60 percent of goods purchased from Purple at markups averaging 30 percent on Purple's cost. Sales from Purple to Sand during the current year were $5,600,000. The estimated intercompany profit in Sand's ending inventory was $194,000.

Purple owns buildings and land used in Sand's retail operations and rented to Sand. Rentals paid by Sand to Purple during the current year amounted to $743,000. At the end of the current year, Purple sold to Sand for $250,000 land to be used in the development of a shopping centre that had cost Purple $203,500. The gain was included in Purple's net income for the current year. Purple also holds a one-year, 6 percent note of Sand on which it has accrued interest revenues of $22,500 during the current year.

During the current year, Purple reported net income of $568,100 and Sand reported net income of $248,670. Purple uses the cost method to account for its investment.

Required:

Calculate the current year's consolidated net income attributable to Purple's shareholders. Assume a 40 percent tax rate.

Problem 10 The income statements of Evans Company and Falcon Company for the current year are shown below:

	Evans	Falcon
Sales revenues	$450,000	$600,000
Dividend revenues	32,000	—
Rental revenues	33,600	—
Interest revenues	—	18,000
	515,600	618,000
Raw materials and finished goods purchased	268,000	328,000
Changes in inventory	20,000	25,000
Other expenses	104,000	146,000
Interest expense	30,000	—
Income taxes	31,700	43,500
	453,700	542,500
Profit	$ 61,900	$ 75,500

The following amounts were taken from the statement of changes in equity for the two companies:

	Evans	Falcon
Retained earnings, beginning of year	$632,000	$348,000
Dividends declared	30,000	40,000

Evans owns 80 percent of the outstanding common shares of Falcon, purchased at the time the latter company was organized.

Evans sells parts to Falcon at a price that is 25 percent above cost. Total sales from Evans to Falcon during the year were $85,000. Included in Falcon's inventories were parts purchased from Evans amounting to $21,250 in beginning inventories and $28,750 in the ending inventory.

Falcon sells back to Evans certain finished goods, at a price that gives Falcon an average gross profit of 30 percent on these intercompany sales. Total sales from

Falcon to Evans during the year were $177,000. Included in the inventories of Evans were finished goods acquired from Falcon amounting to $11,000 in beginning inventories and $3,000 in ending inventories.

Falcon rents an office building from Evans, and pays $2,800 per month in rent. Evans has borrowed $600,000 through a series of 5 percent notes, of which Falcon holds $360,000 as notes receivable. Use income tax allocation at a 40 percent rate.

Required:

(a) Prepare a consolidated income statement with expenses classified by nature.
(b) Calculate retained earnings, beginning of year, and dividends declared for the consolidated statement of changes in equity for the current year.

Problem 11   The partial trial balances of P Co. and S Co. at December 31, Year 5, were as follows:

	P Co.		S Co.	
	Dr.	Cr.	Dr.	Cr.
Investment in S. Co.	90,000			
Common shares		150,000		60,000
Retained earnings (charged with dividends, no other changes during the year)		101,000		34,000

Additional Information

- The investment in the shares of S Co. (a 90 percent interest) was acquired January 2, Year 1, for $90,000. At that time, the shareholders' equity of this company was as follows: common shares, $60,000; retained earnings, $20,000.
- Net incomes of the two companies for the year were as follows:

P Co.	$60,000
S Co.	48,000

- During Year 5, sales of P Co. to S Co. were $10,000, and sales of S Co. to P Co. were $50,000. Rates of gross profit on intercompany sales in Years 4 and 5 were 40 percent of sales.
- On December 31, Year 4, the inventory of P Co. included $7,000 of merchandise purchased from S Co., and the inventory of S Co. included $3,000 of merchandise purchased from P Co. On December 31, Year 5, the inventory of P Co. included $20,000 of merchandise purchased from S Co. and the inventory of S Co. included $5,000 of merchandise purchased from P Co.
- During the year ended December 31, Year 5, P Co. paid dividends of $12,000 and S Co. paid dividends of $10,000.
- At the time that P Co. purchased the shares of S Co., the acquisition differential was allocated to patents of S Co. These patents are being amortized for consolidation purposes over a period of five years.
- In Year 3, land that originally cost $45,000 was sold by S Co. to P Co. for $50,000. The land is still owned by P Co.
- Assume a corporate tax rate of 40 percent.

Required:

Prepare a consolidated statement of changes in equity for the year ended December 31, Year 5.

Problem 12   On January 2, Year 1, Road Ltd. acquired 70 percent of the outstanding voting shares of Runner Ltd. The acquisition differential of $280,000 on that date was allocated in the following manner:

Inventory	$100,000	
Land	50,000	
Plant and equipment	60,000	estimated life 5 years
Patent	40,000	estimated life 8 years
Goodwill	30,000	
	$280,000	

The Year 5 income statements for the two companies were as follows:

	Road	Runner
Sales	$4,000,000	$2,100,000
Intercompany investment income	210,700	—
Rental revenue	—	70,000
Total income	4,210,700	2,170,000
Materials used in manufacturing	2,000,000	800,000
Changes in work-in-progress and finished goods inventory	45,000	(20,000)
Employee benefits	550,000	480,000
Interest expense	250,000	140,000
Depreciation	405,000	245,000
Patent amortization	—	25,000
Rental expense	35,000	—
Income tax	300,000	200,000
Total expenses	3,585,000	1,870,000
Profit	$ 625,700	$ 300,000

Additional Information

- Runner regularly sells raw materials to Road. Intercompany sales in Year 5 totalled $420,000.
- Intercompany profits in the inventories of Road were as follows:

January 1, Year 5	$75,000
December 31, Year 5	40,000

- Road's entire rental expense relates to equipment rented from Runner.
- A goodwill impairment loss of $3,000 occurred in Year 5.
- Retained earnings at December 31, Year 5, for Road and Runner were $2,525,700 and $1,150,000, respectively.
- Road uses the equity method to account for its investment, and uses income tax allocation at the rate of 40 percent when it prepares consolidated statements.

Required:

(a) Prepare a consolidated income statement for Year 5 with expenses classified by nature.

(b) Calculate consolidated retained earnings at December 31, Year 5.

(c) If Road had used the parent company extension theory rather than the entity theory, how would this affect the return on equity attributable to shareholders of Road for Year 5?

Problem 13 The following are the financial statements of Post Corporation and its subsidiary, Sage Company, as at December 31, Year 3:

STATEMENTS OF FINANCIAL POSITION
December 31, Year 3

	Post	Sage
Land	$175,000	$ 19,000
Plant and equipment	520,000	65,000
Accumulated depreciation	(229,400)	(17,000)
Investment in Sage, at cost	63,000	—
Inventory	34,000	27,000
Notes receivable	—	55,000
Accounts receivable	17,200	9,100
Cash	12,200	12,900
	$592,000	$171,000
Common shares	$100,000	$ 50,000
Retained earnings	225,000	81,000
Notes payable	55,000	—
Accounts payable	212,000	40,000
	$592,000	$171,000

STATEMENTS OF PROFIT — Year 3

	Post	Sage
Sales	$900,000	$240,000
Management fee revenue	26,500	—
Interest revenue	—	6,800
Gain on sale of land	—	30,000
Dividend revenue	10,500	—
	937,000	276,800
Cost of goods sold	540,000	162,000
Interest expense	20,000	—
Other expenses	180,000	74,800
Income tax expense	80,000	16,000
	820,000	252,800
Profit	$117,000	$ 24,000

Additional Information

- Post purchased 70 percent of the outstanding shares of Sage on January 1, Year 1, at a cost of $63,000, and has used the cost method to account for its investment. On that date Sage had retained earnings of $15,000, and fair values were equal to carrying values for all its net assets except inventory (overvalued by $12,000) and office equipment (undervalued by $18,000). The equipment had an estimated remaining life of five years.
- The companies sell merchandise to each other at a gross profit rate of 25 percent.
- The December 31, Year 2, inventory of Post contained purchases made from Sage amounting to $14,000. There were no intercompany purchases in the inventory of Sage on this date.
- During Year 3 the following intercompany transactions took place:
  — Sage made a payment of $26,500 to Post for management fees, which was recorded under the category "other expenses."

— Sage made sales of $90,000 to Post. The December 31, Year 3, inventory of Post contained goods purchased from Sage amounting to $28,000.

— Post made sales of $125,000 to Sage. The December 31, Year 3, inventory of Sage contained goods purchased from Post amounting to $18,000.

— On July 1, Year 3, Post borrowed $55,000 from Sage and signed a note bearing interest at 12 percent per annum. The interest on this note was paid on December 31, Year 3.

— During the year, Sage sold land to Post and recorded a gain of $30,000 on the transaction. This land is being held by Post on December 31, Year 3.

• Goodwill impairment losses occurred as follows: Year 1, $2,600; Year 2, $460; Year 3, $1,530.

• Both companies pay income tax at 40 percent on their taxable incomes.

Required:

(a) Prepare the following consolidated financial statements for Year 3:
  (i) Income statement.
  (ii) Statement of financial position.

(b) Calculate goodwill impairment loss and profit attributable to non-controlling interest for the year ended December 31, Year 3, under the parent company extension theory.

(c) Calculate goodwill and non-controlling interest on the consolidated statement of financial position at December 31, Year 3, under the parent company extension theory.

Problem 14 On January 1, Year 1, the Vine Company purchased 60,000 of the 80,000 common shares of the Devine Company for $80 per share. On that date, Devine had common shares of $3,500,000, and retained earnings of $2,100,000. When acquired, Devine had inventories with fair values $100,000 less than carrying value, a parcel of land with a fair value $200,000 greater than the carrying value, and equipment with a fair value $200,000 less than carrying value. There were also internally generated patents with an estimated market value of $400,000 and a five-year remaining life. A long-term liability had a market value $100,000 greater than book value; this liability was paid off December 31, Year 4. All other identifiable assets and liabilities of Devine had fair values equal to their carrying values.

At the acquisition date, the equipment had an expected remaining useful life of 10 years. The equipment and patents are used in manufacturing. Both companies use the straight-line method for all depreciation and amortization calculations and the FIFO inventory cost flow assumption. Assume a 40 percent income tax rate on all applicable items.

On September 1, Year 5, Devine sold a parcel of land to Vine and recorded a total nonoperating gain of $400,000.

Sales of finished goods from Vine to Devine totalled $1,000,000 in Year 4 and $2,000,000 in Year 5. These sales were priced to provide a gross profit margin on selling price of 33¹/3 percent to the Vine Company. Devine's December 31, Year 4, inventory contained $300,000 of these sales; December 31, Year 5, inventory contained $600,000.

Sales of finished goods from Devine to Vine were $800,000 in Year 4 and $1,200,000 in Year 5. These sales were priced to provide a gross profit margin on selling price of 40 percent to the Devine Company. Vine's December 31, Year 4, inventory contained $100,000 of these sales; the December 31, Year 5, inventory contained $500,000.

Vine's investment in Devine's account is carried in accordance with the cost method and includes advances to Devine of $200,000.

There are no intercompany amounts other than those noted, except for the dividends of $500,000 (total amount) declared and paid by Devine.

INCOME STATEMENTS
for Year Ending December 31, Year 5
(in $000s)

	Vine	Devine
Sales	$11,600	$3,000
Dividends, investment income, and gains	400	1,000
Total income	12,000	4,000
Cost of goods sold	8,000	1,500
Other expenses	500	300
Income taxes	500	200
Total expenses	9,000	2,000
Profit	$ 3,000	$2,000

STATEMENTS OF FINANCIAL POSITION
December 31, Year 5
(in $000s)

	Vine	Devine
Land	$ 6,000	$ 2,500
Plant and equipment	13,000	6,800
Investment in Devine (cost)	5,000	
Inventories	4,600	2,400
Cash and current receivables	900	300
Total assets	$29,500	$12,000
Common shares	$10,000	$ 3,500
Retained earnings	12,000	7,000
Long-term liabilities	6,600	1,100
Deferred income taxes	200	100
Current liabilities	700	300
Total equity and liabilities	$29,500	$12,000

Required:

(a) Show the allocation of the purchase price at acquisition and the related amortization schedule. Show and label all calculations.

(b) Compute the investment income under the equity method that would be reported if Vine had been permitted to use the equity method, rather than consolidate, in Year 5.

(c) Prepare a consolidated income statement with expenses classified by function.

(d) Calculate consolidated retained earnings at December 31, Year 5.

(e) Prepare a consolidated statement of financial position for Vine Company at December 31, Year 5.

(adapted from a problem prepared by Peter Secord, St. Mary's University)

Problem 15 Paper Corp. purchased 70 percent of the outstanding shares of Sand Ltd. on January 1, Year 2, at a cost of $84,000. Paper has always used the cost method to account for its investments. On January 1, Year 2, Sand had common shares of $50,000 and retained earnings of $30,000, and fair values were equal to carrying values for all its net assets except inventory (fair value was $9,000 less than book value) and equipment (fair value was $24,000 greater than book value). The equipment, which is used for research, had an estimated remaining life of six years on January 1, Year 2.

The following are the financial statements of Paper Corp. and its subsidiary Sand Ltd. as at December 31, Year 5:

BALANCE SHEETS
December 31, Year 5

	Paper	Sand
Cash	$ —	$ 10,000
Accounts receivable	36,000	30,000
Note receivable	—	40,000
Inventory	66,000	44,000
Equipment, net	220,000	76,000
Land	150,000	30,000
Investment in Sand	84,000	—
	$556,000	$230,000
Bank indebtedness	$ 90,000	$ —
Accounts payable	50,000	60,000
Notes payable	40,000	—
Common shares	150,000	50,000
Retained earnings	226,000	120,000
	$556,000	$230,000

INCOME STATEMENTS
for the year ended December 31, Year 5

	Paper	Sand
Sales	$798,000	$300,000
Management fee revenue	24,000	—
Investment income	14,000	3,600
Gain on sale of land	—	20,000
	836,000	323,600
Cost of sales	480,000	200,000
Research and development expenses	40,000	12,000
Interest expense	10,000	—
Miscellaneous expenses	106,000	31,600
Income taxes	80,000	32,000
	716,000	275,600
Net income	$120,000	$ 48,000

Additional Information

- During Year 5, Sand made a cash payment of $2,000 per month to Paper for management fees, which is included in Sand's "Miscellaneous expenses."
- During Year 5, Paper made intercompany sales of $100,000 to Sand. The December 31, Year 5, inventory of Sand contained goods purchased from Paper amounting to $30,000. These sales had a gross profit of 35 percent.

- On April 1, Year 5, Paper acquired land from Sand for $40,000. This land had been recorded on Sand's books at a net book value of $20,000. Paper paid for the land by signing a $40,000 note payable to Sand, bearing yearly interest at 8 percent. Interest for Year 5 was paid by Paper in cash on December 31, Year 5. This land was still being held by Paper on December 31, Year 5.
- The fair value of consolidated goodwill remained unchanged from January 1, Year 5, to July Year 5. On July 1, Year 5, a valuation was performed, indicating that the recoverable amount of consolidated goodwill was $3,500.
- Retained earnings at December 31, Year 5, for Paper and Sand were $226,000 and $120,000, respectively.
- Sand and Paper pay taxes at a 40 percent rate. Assume that none of the gains or losses were capital gains or losses.

Required:

(a) Prepare, in good form, a calculation of goodwill and any unamortized acquisition differential as of December 31, Year 5.
(b) Prepare Paper's consolidated income statement for the year ended December 31, Year 5, with expenses classified by function.
(c) Calculate the following balances that would appear on Paper's consolidated balance sheet as at December 31, Year 5.
  (i) Inventory.
  (ii) Land.
  (iii) Notes payable.
  (iv) Non-controlling interest.
  (v) Common shares.
(d) Now assume that Paper switches to the equity method. Calculate the balance in the Investment in Sand account as at December 31, Year 5.

(*CGA–Canada adapted*)

WEB-BASED PROBLEMS

Problem 1 Access the most recent consolidated financial statements for Vodafone, a British company. (Go to the investor relations section at www.vodafone.com.) Answer the questions below. For each question, indicate where in the financial statements you found the answer and/or provide a brief explanation.

(a) What inventory costing method does the company use?
(b) What portion of the companies' assets is inventory? Has the portion increased or decreased from last year?
(c) Does the company eliminate intercompany transactions and unrealized profits when preparing consolidated financial statements?
(d) Ignore your answer to part (c) and assume the following: (1) 25 percent of the companies' inventory had been sold by the parent to a wholly owned subsidiary during the year; (2) the gross margin on the sale was the same as the average gross margin for the consolidated entity as a whole; and (3) the intercompany sale and unrealized profit were not eliminated when preparing the consolidated financial statements. What is the impact of these errors on inventory turnover and earnings per share for the year?

(e) Does the company value its land at cost or fair value?

(f) Now assume that the company changes its policy to report its land at fair value (or to cost if it was using fair value). Also, assume that the fair value of land has increased steadily since it was acquired. What impact would this change in policy have on the debt-to-equity ratio at the end of the year and on return on average equity for the year?

Problem 2   Access the most recent financial statements for Siemens, a German company. (Go to the investor relations section at www.siemens.com.) Answer the same questions as in Problem 1. For each question, indicate where in the financial statements you found the answer and/or provide a brief explanation. (Some questions may not be applicable.)

Chapter 7 (A) Intercompany Profits in Depreciable Assets (B) Intercompany Bondholdings

LEARNING OBJECTIVES

After studying this chapter, you should be able to do the following:

1. Prepare consolidated financial statements that reflect the elimination and subsequent realization of upstream and downstream intercompany profits in depreciable assets.

2. Explain how the historical cost principle supports the elimination of unrealized profits resulting from intercompany transactions when preparing consolidated financial statements.

3. Prepare the journal entries under the equity method to reflect the elimination and subsequent realization of intercompany profits in depreciable assets.

4. Calculate the gain or loss that results from the elimination of intercompany bondholdings and the allocation of such gain or loss to the equities of the controlling and non-controlling interests.

5. Explain how the recognition of gains on the elimination of intercompany bondholdings is consistent with the principle of recording gains only when they are realized.

6. Prepare consolidated financial statements that reflect the gains or losses that are the result of intercompany bondholdings.

INTRODUCTION

The elimination of intercompany transactions and unrealized profit is one of the most significant problems encountered in the consolidation process. The volume of transfers within most large enterprises can be quite large. For example, Petro-Canada, one of Canada's largest oil and gas companies, reported intersegment revenue of $2,747[1] million in 2008, which represented almost 9 percent of total revenues.

In this chapter, we complete our examination of intercompany profits in assets; we also examine the consolidation issues that arise from intercompany bondholdings. Because these transactions are so distinctly different in their impact on the consolidated statements, this chapter is divided into two parts.

Part (A) looks at the elimination and realization of intercompany profits (losses) in depreciable assets. The concepts involved in the holdback of profits

---

[1] www.suncor.com/pdf/consolidated_financial_statements_notes_2008-e.pdf, accessed November 10, 2009.

(losses) are similar to those examined previously with regard to intercompany land profits (losses), but the realization concepts are different because they are based on consumption rather than a sale.

Part (B) examines the gains (losses) that are created in the consolidated financial statements when intercompany bondholdings are eliminated.

(A) Intercompany Profits in Depreciable Assets
Holdback and Realization — Year 1

Profit is recognized when the goods are sold to outsiders.

In Chapter 6, we illustrated the holdback of an intercompany profit in inventory and land. In both cases, the before-tax profit of $300 and the corresponding income tax of $120 were held back in the year of the intercompany transaction and realized in the year that the asset was sold to outsiders. In both cases, the profit was eventually recognized in both the financial statements of the individual companies and the consolidated financial statements. Only the timing of the recognition was different. We will now examine the holdback and the realization in the consolidated statements of an intercompany profit in a depreciable asset.

We return to the Chapter 6 example of Parent Company and its 90-percent-owned subsidiary, Sub Inc. The Year 1 financial statements of the two companies are shown in Exhibit 7.1 on page 310. Parent has used the cost method to account for its investment.

Notice that although the net incomes and total assets of the two companies are unchanged, the details on each statement have been changed so that we can focus on the following intercompany transaction involving equipment that occurred during the year. On July 1, Year 1, Sub sold highly specialized equipment with a very short useful life to Parent and recorded a profit of $300 on the transaction. We are assuming that Sub purchased this equipment for $1,500 on this date with the intention of using it, but instead immediately sold it to Parent for $1,800. This intercompany transaction was recorded in the following manner by the two companies:

Parent Company			Sub Inc.		
Equipment	1,800		Cash	1,800	
Cash		1,800	Equipment		1,500
			Gain on sale of		
			equipment		300

It is also assumed that this transaction was not a capital gain for tax purposes, and that Sub's tax rate is 40 percent. This means that Sub paid $120 (40% × 300) income tax on this profit. We further assume that this is the only depreciable asset held by either company and that the equipment is expected to be obsolete in one-and-a-half years. On December 31, Year 1, Parent recorded depreciation expense on this equipment in the following manner:

The parent's depreciation expense is based on the parent's cost.

Depreciation expense	600	
Accumulated depreciation		600
To record depreciation for half a year		
(1,800 ÷ 1½ = 1,200; 1,200 × ½ = 600)		

Exhibit 7.1

The gain on sale is recorded on the separate-entity books of Sub.

INCOME STATEMENTS — for Year 1

	Parent	Sub
Sales	$20,000	$ 7,700
Gain on sale of equipment	—	300
	20,000	8,000
Depreciation expense	600	—
Miscellaneous expenses	13,800	5,200
Income tax expense	2,200	1,100
	16,600	6,300
Net income	$ 3,400	$ 1,700

RETAINED EARNINGS STATEMENTS — for Year 1

	Parent	Sub
Balance, January 1	$12,000	$ 4,500
Net income	3,400	1,700
	15,400	6,200
Dividends	2,000	—
Balance, December 31	$13,400	$ 6,200

BALANCE SHEETS — at December 31, Year 1

The equipment is recorded at the parent's cost on the separate-entity books of Parent.

	Parent	Sub
Assets (miscellaneous)	$27,950	$ 23,200
Equipment	1,800	—
Accumulated depreciation	(600)	—
Investment in Sub Inc.	11,250	—
	$40,400	$ 23,200
Liabilities	$12,000	$ 9,000
Common shares	15,000	8,000
Retained earnings	13,400	6,200
	$40,400	$ 23,200

The cost of the equipment to the single entity was $1,500.

It should be noted that if Sub had sold the equipment at its cost, Parent's Year 1 depreciation expense would have been $500 (1,500 ÷ 1½ × ½ = 500). This is the amount of depreciation expense that should appear in the income statement of the entity (i.e., in the consolidated income statement) for Year 1, in that it represents depreciation based on the historical cost of the equipment to the entity.

When we examine the separate income statements of the two companies (Exhibit 7.1), it should be obvious that the $300 gain is not a gain from a single-entity point of view, and that the $600 depreciation expense does not represent historical cost depreciation to the entity. Two adjustments need to be made when the Year 1 consolidated income statement is prepared; these have opposite effects on the before-tax income of the entity. The first adjustment eliminates the gain on sale of equipment recorded on July 1, Year 1, because as of that date the gain is unrealized from the single-entity point of view. This adjustment reduces before-tax income by $300 and holds back this profit for consolidation purposes. A corresponding reduction of $120 should be made to income tax expense so that a net after-tax gain of

$180 is held back. This concept is similar in all respects to the holdback of the land gain that was illustrated in Chapter 6.

The depreciation expense for the single entity was $500.

The second adjustment reduces depreciation expense by $100 ($300 ÷ 1½ × ½). The amount of the reduction represents the depreciation taken in Year 1 on this $300 gain and results in a consolidated depreciation expense of $500 based on historical cost, as required. This reduction of depreciation expense increases the before-tax income of the entity by $100. In other words, the parent uses the equipment to carry out its business of selling goods or providing services to its customers. Even though the equipment is not sold to outsiders, the products or services are sold to outsiders. Therefore, the gain from the intercompany sale of the equipment is realized over the life of the equipment as the parent uses the equipment to produce goods or provide services for outsiders. This concept bases the realization of the gain on the consumption (by depreciation) of the asset that contains the unrealized gain. A corresponding increase of $40 should be made to income tax expense to match the tax with the portion of the gain realized. The result will be a net after-tax realization of $60 for consolidation purposes.

The net effect of the two after-tax adjustments results in the entity's Year 1 net income being reduced by $120 ($180 − 60). Because Sub was the selling company, this $120 reduction is allocated to the non-controlling and controlling interests in the same manner as was illustrated in Chapter 6.

The preceding paragraphs have briefly outlined the concepts involved in the holdback and realization of an intercompany gain in a depreciable fixed asset. We will now apply these concepts by preparing the Year 1 consolidated financial statements of Parent using the direct approach. It is useful to start by preparing the three calculations shown in Exhibit 7.2

It should be noted that the calculation of consolidated net income attributable to the parent is made to adjust the net income of the parent from the cost method to the equity method. If the parent had used the equity method, we would still have to adjust for unrealized profits from intercompany transactions.

Exhibit 7.2

EQUIPMENT GAIN — SUB INC. SELLING

This is an upstream transaction since Sub sold to Parent.

	Before tax	40% tax	After tax
Gain, July 1, Year 1	$300	$120	$ 180 **(a)**
Less realized by depreciation for Year 1	100	40	60 **(b)**
Balance, unrealized at Dec. 31, Year 1	$200	$ 80	$ 120 **(c)**

CALCULATION OF CONSOLIDATED NET INCOME — for Year 1

Sub's income is adjusted for both the unrealized gain and the realization of the gain through depreciation by Parent.

Net income — Parent Co.		$ 3,400
Net income — Sub Inc.	1,700	
Less after-tax gain on sale of equipment **(2a)**	180	
	1,520	
Add after-tax gain realized by depreciation **(2b)**	60	
Adjusted net income — Sub Inc.		1,580
Consolidated net income		$ 4,980
Attributable to		
Shareholders of Parent		$ 4,822 **(d)**
Non-controlling interest (10% × 1,580)		158 **(e)**

(continued)

CALCULATION OF NON-CONTROLLING INTEREST
at December 31, Year 1

Non-controlling interest is affected by unrealized profits on upstream transactions.

Shareholders' equity — Sub Inc.		
Common shares		$ 8,000
Retained earnings		6,200
		14,200
Less net unrealized equipment gain after tax **(2c)**		120
Adjusted shareholders' equity		14,080
Non-controlling interest's share		10%
		$ 1,408 **(f)**

Exhibit 7.3 illustrates the preparation of the consolidated financial statements using the direct approach.

The consolidated income statement was prepared by combining, line by line, the revenues and expenses of the two companies. The amount for non-controlling interest is based on the *adjusted income* of Sub. The intercompany eliminations are shown in Exhibit 7.3 in boldface and are summarized as follows:

(i) The $300 gain on the equipment and the income tax expense for the tax on this gain are eliminated. The net effect is to reduce the after-tax income of the entity by $180.

(ii) The excess depreciation to the single entity in Year 1 is eliminated. Consolidated depreciation is now based on historical cost. Because this elimination results in a realization of $100 of the original gain, income tax expense is increased by $40 to match the tax with the gain realized. The net result is an after-tax realization of $60.

The two eliminations decreased the entity's net income by $120, which was allocated to the two equities as follows:

To non-controlling interest (10% × 120)	$ 12
To controlling interest (90% × 120)	108
	$120

The consolidated retained earnings statement has been prepared in the normal manner. Because we are consolidating one year after acquisition, the parent's retained earnings at the beginning of the year are equal to consolidated retained earnings on that date.

The consolidated balance sheet was prepared by combining the assets and liabilities of the two companies and by making the following adjustments (shown in Exhibit 7.3 in boldface) for the equipment gain:

The tax paid on the unrealized profits represents a prepayment from a consolidated viewpoint.

(i) When the before-tax gain of $300 is removed from the equipment, the resulting balance of $1,500 represents the original cost to the entity. The $120 increase to deferred income taxes represents the tax on this gain and corresponds to the reduction of tax expense in the income statement.

Accumulated depreciation is based on the original cost to the consolidated entity.

(ii) The amount of the gain contained in accumulated depreciation is removed. The resulting amount ($500) is the accumulated depreciation on the original cost. The $40 decrease to deferred income taxes corresponds to the increase in income tax expense made in the income statement.

Exhibit 7.3

Year 1 Consolidated Statements
Adjusted for Intercompany Equipment Profit
(direct approach)

PARENT COMPANY
CONSOLIDATED INCOME STATEMENT
for the Year Ended December 31, Year 1

Sales (20,000 + 7,700)	$27,700
Gain on sale of equipment (0 + 300 − **(2a) 300**)	–0–
	27,700
Depreciation expense (600 + 0 − **(2b) 100**)	500
Miscellaneous expenses (13,800 + 5,200)	19,000
Income tax expense (2,200 + 1,100 − **(2a) 120** + **(2b) 40**)	3,220
	22,720
Net income	$ 4,980
Attributable to	
Shareholders of Parent **(4d)**	$ 4,822
Non-controlling interest **(4e)**	158

Income tax expense is matched to the income of the consolidated entity.

PARENT COMPANY
CONSOLIDATED RETAINED EARNINGS STATEMENT
for the Year Ended December 31, Year 1

Balance, January 1	$12,000
Net income	4,822
	16,822
Dividends	2,000
Balance, December 31	$14,822

PARENT COMPANY
CONSOLIDATED BALANCE SHEET
at December 31, Year 1

Assets — miscellaneous (27,950 + 23,200)	$51,150
Equipment (1,800 + 0 − **(2a) 300**)	1,500
Accumulated depreciation (600 + 0 − **(2b) 100**)	(500)
Deferred income taxes (0 + 0 + **(2a) 120** − **(2b) 40**)	80
	$52,230
Liabilities (12,000 + 9,000)	$21,000
Common shares	15,000
Retained earnings	14,822
Non-controlling interest	1,408
	$52,230

The equipment is reported at the cost when it was purchased from outsiders.

Note that the $200 reduction of the net book value of the equipment ($300 − $100), together with an increase in deferred income taxes of $80 (40% × $200), results in total consolidated assets being reduced by $120, which corresponds to the reduction made to the entity's net income in the consolidated income statement. The fact that this reduction was allocated to the two equities was noted on page 312.

Equity Method Journal Entries Our example has assumed that Parent uses the cost method to account for its investment. If Parent was using the equity method, the following journal entries would be made on December 31, Year 1:

The equity method captures the net effect of all consolidation entries.

Investment in Sub Inc.	1,530	
Investment income		1,530
90% of the net income of Sub Inc. (90% × 1,700 = 1,530)		
Investment income	162	
Investment in Sub Inc.		162
To hold back 90% of the after-tax equipment profit recorded by Sub (90% × 180 = 162)		
Investment in Sub Inc.	54	
Investment income		54
To realize 90% of the after-tax profit realized by depreciation (90% × 60 = 54)		

After these entries are posted, the two related equity method accounts of Parent will show the following changes and balances:

The investment account is a balance sheet account at the end of the year, whereas investment income is an income statement account for one period of time.

	Investment in Sub Inc.	Investment income
Balance, January 1, Year 1	$11,250	
Income from Sub Inc.	1,530	$1,530
Equipment profit (held back)	(162)	(162)
Equipment profit realized	54	54
Balance, December 31, Year 1	$12,672	$1,422

The parent's income under the equity method should be equal to consolidated net income attributable to the parent.

Parent's total income under the equity method would be $4,822, consisting of $3,400 from its own operations as reported on page 310 plus investment income of $1,422 as reported above. This income of $4,822 should be and is equal to consolidated net income attributable to the parent.

Realization of Remaining Gain — Year 2

The equipment sold to the parent on July 1, Year 1, had a remaining life of 1½ years on that date. When the Year 1 consolidated income statement was prepared, both the holdback of the total gain and the realization of one-third of the gain took place. When the Year 2 consolidated income statement is prepared, adjustments will be made to realize the remaining two-thirds of the gain. This intercompany gain will be fully realized for consolidation purposes at the end of Year 2, only because the equipment had an unusually short remaining life of 1½ years on the date of the intercompany sale.

The Year 2 financial statements for the two companies are shown in Exhibit 7.4.

Before the consolidated financial statements are prepared, we must make the four calculations shown in Exhibit 7.5 on page 316.

In the first table in Exhibit 7.5, you should note that the $300 gain on sale in Year 1 is fully realized from a consolidated perspective by the end of Year 2. From a consolidated perspective, the $300 gain was eliminated in Year 1 but was realized by adjusting depreciation expense over the remaining life of the equipment. Since the remaining life of the equipment was only 1½ years at the date of the intercompany sale, the $300 gain was brought into consolidated income over 1½ years. If the remaining useful life were five years, the $300 gain would be brought into consolidated income over five years.

Exhibit 7.4

INCOME STATEMENTS — for Year 2

	Parent	Sub
Sales	$25,000	$12,000
Depreciation expense	1,200	—
Miscellaneous expenses	17,150	6,900
Income tax expense	2,600	2,000
	20,950	8,900
Net income	$ 4,050	$ 3,100

The parent reports depreciation expense for one full year on its separate-entity income statement.

RETAINED EARNINGS STATEMENTS — for Year 2

	Parent	Sub
Balance, January 1	$13,400	$ 6,200
Net income	4,050	3,100
	17,450	9,300
Dividends	2,500	—
Balance, December 31	$14,950	$ 9,300

BALANCE SHEETS — at December 31, Year 2

	Parent	Sub
Assets (miscellaneous)	$32,700	$28,300
Equipment	1,800	—
Accumulated depreciation	(1,800)	—
Investment in Sub Inc.	11,250	—
	$43,950	$28,300
Liabilities	$14,000	$11,000
Common shares	15,000	8,000
Retained earnings	14,950	9,300
	$43,950	$28,300

The parent reports accumulated depreciation for 1½ years on its separate-entity balance sheet.

At the end of Year 2, the equipment's net book value is zero on Parent's separate-entity balance sheet and on the consolidated balance sheet.

The Year 2 consolidated financial statements prepared using the direct approach are shown in Exhibit 7.6 on page 317. (Eliminations required for the intercompany equipment gain are shown in boldface.)

When the consolidated income statement is prepared, the depreciation expense is reduced by $200. The result is a consolidated depreciation expense of $1,000 based on the entity's cost. This adjustment realizes $200 of the equipment gain for consolidation purposes. Income tax expense is increased by $80 to match expense with the gain realized. The net effect of the two adjustments in the income statement is to increase the entity's net income by an after-tax realization amounting to $120.

The Year 2 consolidated retained earnings statement is prepared using the calculated January 1 balance, consolidated net income attributable to the parent, and the dividends of Parent Company.

Two adjustments are required in the preparation of the consolidated balance sheet. A reduction of $300 in equipment removes the gain and restates the equipment to the $1,500 historical cost to the entity. This equipment is fully depreciated on December 31, Year 2; therefore, accumulated depreciation should be equal to the historical cost of $1,500. When the accumulated depreciation is reduced by $300, the resulting balance ($1,500) is equal to the entity's historical cost.

Exhibit 7.5

EQUIPMENT GAIN — SUB INC. SELLING

	Before tax	40% tax	After tax
Gain, July 1, Year 1	$300	$120	$180 **(a)**
Less realized by depreciation for Year 1	100	40	60 **(b)**
Balance unrealized, at Dec. 31, Year 1	200	80	120 **(c)**
Less realized by depreciation for Year 2	200	80	120 **(d)**
Balance unrealized, at Dec. 31, Year 2	$ –0–	$ –0–	$ –0–

Differentiate between adjustments for a period of time (i.e., for Year 2) versus a point in time (i.e., at the end of Year 1).

CALCULATION OF CONSOLIDATED NET INCOME — for Year 2

This schedule shows the calculation for a period of time, i.e., for Year 2.

Net income — Parent Co.		$4,050
Net Income — Sub Inc.	3,100	
Add after-tax equipment gain realized by depreciation **(5d)**	120	
Adjusted net income — Sub Inc.		3,220
Consolidated net income		$7,270
Attributable to		
Shareholders of Parent		$6,948 **(e)**
Non-controlling interest (10% × 3,220)		322 **(f)**

CALCULATION OF CONSOLIDATED RETAINED EARNINGS
at January 1, Year 2

This schedule shows the calculation at a point in time, i.e., at the beginning of Year 2, which is the same as the end of Year 1.

Retained earnings — Parent Co.		$13,400
Retained earnings — Sub Inc.	6,200	
Acquisition retained earnings	4,500	
Increase since acquisition	1,700	
Less unrealized after-tax equipment gain, Jan. 1 **(5c)**	120	
Adjusted increase since acquisition	1,580	
Parent Co.'s share	90%	1,422
Consolidated retained earnings		$14,822 **(g)**

CALCULATION OF NON-CONTROLLING INTEREST
at December 31, Year 2

At the end of Year 2, the intercompany gain has been fully realized and no adjustment is necessary from a consolidated viewpoint.

Common shares — Sub Inc.	$ 8,000
Retained earnings — Sub Inc.	9,300
	17,300
Non-controlling interest's share	10%
	$ 1,730 **(h)**

Note that when both the equipment and the accumulated depreciation are reduced by $300, total consolidated assets are not changed. The net gain held back on the Year 1 consolidated balance sheet has been realized as at the end of Year 2. If no unrealized gains are being held back, there will be no deferred income tax adjustments made in the consolidated balance sheet. The deferred charge of $80 that appeared in the December 31, Year 1, consolidated balance sheet became an expense in the Year 2 consolidated income statement.

The unrealized profit at the end of Year 1 was realized in income for Year 2.

As discussed above, the adjustments made in the consolidated income statement increased the entity's net income by $120, while the adjustments made in the asset side of the consolidated balance sheet did not change total assets. In order for this

Exhibit 7.6

**Year 2 Consolidated Statements
Adjusted for Intercompany Equipment Profit**
(direct approach)

**PARENT COMPANY
CONSOLIDATED INCOME STATEMENT**
for the Year Ended December 31, Year 2

Sales (25,000 + 12,000)	$37,000
Depreciation expense (1,200 + 0 − **(5d) 200**)	1,000
Miscellaneous expenses (17,150 + 6,900)	24,050
Income tax expense (2,600 + 2,000 + **(5d) 80**)	4,680
	29,730
Net income	$ 7,270
Attributable to	
Shareholders of Parent **(5e)**	$ 6,948
Non-controlling interest **(5f)**	322

Depreciation expense for one year is based on the original cost to the consolidated entity.

**PARENT COMPANY
CONSOLIDATED RETAINED EARNINGS STATEMENT**
for the Year Ended December 31, Year 2

Balance, January 1	$14,822
Net income	6,948
	21,770
Dividends	2,500
Balance, December 31	$19,270

**PARENT COMPANY
CONSOLIDATED BALANCE SHEET**
at December 31, Year 2

Assets — miscellaneous (32,700 + 28,300)	$61,000
Equipment (1,800 + 0 − **(5a) 300**)	1,500
Accumulated depreciation (1,800 + 0 − **(5b + 5d) 300**)	(1,500)
	$61,000
Liabilities (14,000 + 11,000)	$25,000
Common shares	15,000
Retained earnings	19,270
Non-controlling interest **(5h)**	1,730
	$61,000

Accumulated depreciation is total depreciation taken to the end of Year 2 based on the original cost to the consolidated entity.

to balance out, there must have been both an increase and a decrease of $120 on the liability side of the consolidated balance sheet. The $120 increase occurred in the income statement and was allocated to the two equities in the balance sheet. The $120 decrease occurred in Sub's retained earnings at the beginning of the year and was allocated to the two equities. In the calculation of consolidated retained earnings on page 316, Parent absorbs $108 (90% × 120). In the schedule on page 318, which shows the changes in non-controlling interest for the year, it is obvious where the remaining $12 (10% × 120) decrease went.

CHANGES IN NON-CONTROLLING INTEREST — for Year 2

Sub Inc.:	
Common shares	$8,000
Retained earnings, Jan. 1	6,200
	14,200
Less after-tax equipment profit **(5c)**	120
Adjusted	14,080
	10%
Non-controlling interest Jan. 1	1,408
Year 2 entity net income allocated **(5f)**	322
Non-controlling interest, Dec. 31 **(5h)**	$1,730

NCI is affected by the realization of the gain in Year 2 even though Parent recorded the excess depreciation.

Equity Method Journal Entries   If Parent had been using the equity method, the following journal entries would have been made on December 31, Year 2:

Investment in Sub Inc.	2,790	
Investment income		2,790
90% of Sub Inc.'s Year 2 net income (90% × 3,100 = 2,790)		
Investment in Sub Inc.	108	
Investment income		108
90% of the portion of the after-tax equipment gain realized by depreciation in Year 2 (90% × 120 = 108)		

After these entries are posted, the two related equity method accounts of Parent show the following changes and balances:

The investment account contains all adjustments to the end of the period, whereas the investment income account contains adjustments for only one period.

	Investment in Sub Inc.	Investment income
Balance, January 1, Year 2	$12,672	
Income from Sub Inc.	2,790	$2,790
Equipment gain realized	108	108
Balance, December 31, Year 2	$15,570	$2,898

Intercompany Sale of a Used Depreciable Asset   In the preceding illustration, the equipment sold by Sub was a new asset. As such, Sub had not yet recorded any accumulated depreciation, and the cost to Sub was the same as the net book value on the date of the intercompany sale. Let's now consider the sale of a used depreciable asset, i.e., an asset with accumulated depreciation.

Assume that Sub had acquired the equipment for $5,000 3½ years prior to the intercompany sale and had been depreciating it over an estimated useful life of five years. The accumulated depreciation on July 1, Year 1, would have been $3,500 and the net book value would have been $1,500. Sub would have made the following entry when it sold the equipment to Parent for $1,800:

Cash	1,800	
Accumulated depreciation	3,500	
Equipment		5,000
Gain on sale of equipment		300

All of the previous calculations of unrealized gains and excess depreciation would be the same for this situation. However, the consolidated balance sheet at the end of Year 1 should reflect the equipment at $5,000, the original cost to the consolidated entity, and accumulated depreciation at $4,000, the amount that would have appeared on Sub's books had the intercompany transaction not occurred. Therefore, the following journal entry should be made in the consolidation working papers at the end of Year 1 to gross up the equipment and accumulated depreciation:

Equipment and accumulated depreciation need to be grossed up to the original cost to the consolidated entity.

Equipment	3,500	
Accumulated depreciation		3,500

This entry does not change the net book value of the equipment but does change the cost and accumulated depreciation on the consolidated balance sheet. This entry should be made on the consolidation working papers year after year as long as Parent has this equipment on its separate-entity books.

Appendix 7A of this chapter illustrates the consolidation adjustments relating to an intercompany sale of a depreciable asset when the parent company periodically revalues its equipment to fair value under IAS 16.

Comparison of Realization of Inventory and Equipment Profits over a Two-year Period

In Chapter 6, the holdback and realization of an intercompany profit in inventory was illustrated. In this chapter, we have illustrated the holdback and realization of an intercompany gain in equipment. In both cases, the after-tax profit (gain) was $180 (60% × 300), and the subsidiary was the selling company. The following summarizes the effect on the entity's net income over a two-year period.

INTERCOMPANY INVENTORY PROFIT

	Year 1	Year 2	Total
Parent Co., net income	$3,400	$4,050	$ 7,450
Sub Inc., net income	1,700	3,100	4,800
	5,100	7,150	12,250
After-tax profit (held back) realized	(180)	180	–0–
Net income — consolidated entity	$4,920	$7,330	$12,250
Allocated to the two equities:			
Non-controlling interest	$ 152	$ 328	$ 480
Shareholders of parent	4,768	7,002	11,770
	$4,920	$7,330	$12,250

The intercompany profits are eventually realized from a consolidated viewpoint.

INTERCOMPANY EQUIPMENT GAIN

	Year 1	Year 2	Total
Parent Co., net income	$3,400	$4,050	$ 7,450
Sub Inc., net income	1,700	3,100	4,800
	5,100	7,150	12,250
After-tax gain (held back)	(180)	–0–	(180)
After-tax gain realized	60	120	180
Net income — consolidated entity	$4,980	$7,270	$12,250
Allocated as follows:			
Non-controlling interest	$ 158	$ 322	$ 480
Shareholders of parent	4,822	6,948	11,770
	$4,980	$7,270	$12,250

Intercompany profits on depreciable assets are realized as the assets are used over their useful lives.

The two-year summaries shown on the previous page help illustrate a number of significant points in relation to consolidated financial statements:

Differentiate between point-in-time (balance sheet) versus period-of-time (income statement) adjustments.

1. The consolidated entity's net income is measured for periods of time that are usually one year in length.

2. During this measurement process, the holdback and subsequent realization of profits (losses) resulting from intercompany transactions takes place.

3. The realization of previously held back profits (losses) occurs during the period in which the acquiring company either sells the asset containing the profit (loss) to outsiders or depreciates the asset, therefore consuming the asset while it produces other products or services for outsiders.

4. If we examine a time period longer than one year, and if, at the end of that period, the assets of the constituent companies do not contain intercompany profits, the following becomes evident:

   The consolidated entity's net income for this longer period consists of

   (a) the reported net income of the parent company, exclusive of intercompany investment or dividend income,

   (b) *plus* the reported net income of the subsidiary company (or companies),

   (c) *minus* the acquisition-differential amortization.

   In the illustration on page 319, we assumed that the acquisition differential was zero.

5. The entity's net income measurement for this longer time period is not affected by the fact that assets were sold at intercompany profits (losses) during the period. (See the two-year total column.) The same is true of the allocation to the two equities.

6. When consolidated statements are prepared at the end of an intervening time period (e.g., Year 1, Year 2) we have to determine whether there were profits (losses) recorded by any of the constituent companies that were not realized by the end of the period.

Adjustments for unrealized and realized profits from intercompany transactions are always charged/credited to the original seller.

7. The profit holdbacks and realizations are used in the measurement of the entity's net income and are adjustments to the reported net income of the selling constituent in the allocation of that net income.

In Chapter 6, we also illustrated the holdback and realization of a $180 after-tax intercompany gain in land. In that case, the realization process took place in Year 8; however, the overall concepts discussed above remain the same.

(B) Intercompany Bondholdings

Our discussions so far have focused on gains (losses) resulting from the intercompany sale of inventory, land, and depreciable assets. The treatment of these gains (losses) in the preparation of consolidated financial statements can be summarized as follows: gains (losses) resulting from the intercompany sale of assets are realized subsequent to the recording of the intercompany transaction by the selling affiliate.

Occasionally, one affiliate will purchase all or a portion of the bonds issued by another affiliate. When consolidated financial statements are being prepared, the elimination of the intercompany accounts (investment in bonds and bonds

Gains/losses on
intercompany bondholdings
are reported on consolidated
statements prior to recording
them on the separate-entity
statements.

payable; interest revenue and interest expense) may result in a gain (loss) being reflected in those statements. The treatment of this type of gain (loss) can be summarized in the following manner: gains (losses) arising because of the elimination of intercompany bondholding accounts are realized prior to the recording of these gains (losses) by the affiliates on their separate-entity statements. Before we examine how these gains and losses occur in the elimination of the intercompany accounts, let us look at intercompany bondholding situations that do not result in gains or losses.

Intercompany Bondholdings — No Gain or Loss

Not all intercompany bondholdings result in gains or losses being reflected in the consolidated statements. For example, let us assume that one affiliate issued $10,000 in bonds and that another affiliate acquired the whole issue.

(The amounts used are unrealistically low for a bond issue but are realistic in relation to the size of Parent Company and Sub Inc., the two companies that we have been using in our illustrations. In any case, the concepts are the same regardless of the amounts used.)

Immediately after the issue, the records of the two companies would show the following accounts:

The asset and liability appear on the separate-entity financial statements.

Acquiring Affiliate's Records		Issuing Affiliate's Records	
Investment in bonds	10,000	Bonds payable	10,000

From the entity's point of view, the two accounts are similar to intercompany receivables and payables and would be eliminated by the following working paper entry when the consolidated balance sheet is being prepared:

This entry is made on the consolidation working papers.

Bonds payable	10,000	
Investment in bonds		10,000

It is important to note that the eliminations are equal, and because of this, there is no gain or loss resulting from the working paper elimination of these two intercompany accounts. At the end of each succeeding year, this working paper elimination is repeated until the bonds mature. After that date, the two accounts no longer exist in the affiliates' records and further working paper eliminations are not required.

The consolidated balance sheet is not the only statement requiring working paper eliminations. If we assume that the bonds pay interest at the rate of 10 percent, the income statement of the issuing affiliate will show interest expense of $1,000, while the income statement of the acquiring affiliate will show interest revenue of $1,000. These intercompany revenue and expense accounts are eliminated by the following working paper entry when the consolidated income statement is being prepared:

This entry does not change the net income of the consolidated entity.

Interest revenue	1,000	
Interest expense		1,000

Again, it is important to note that the amounts are equal, and that because of this there is no gain or loss resulting from this working paper elimination. The consolidated income statement working paper elimination is repeated each year until the bonds mature.

Our example has assumed that the bonds were issued at par. Suppose, now, that the bonds were issued to the purchasing affiliate at a premium or a discount. Provided that both affiliates use the same methods to amortize the issue premium or discount, and the purchase premium or discount, the amounts in the intercompany accounts on all successive balance sheets and income statements will be equal. The important concept of equal eliminations on both statements would still be true.

Intercompany Bondholdings — With Gain or Loss

The market price of bonds moves inversely with changes in interest rates.

When the market rate is different from the coupon rate on the date of a bond issue, the bonds will be issued at a price that is different from the par or face value. If the interest rates are higher (lower) than the coupon rate, the bonds will be issued at a discount (premium). Subsequent to the issue, bond market prices will rise (fall) if the market interest rate falls (rises). It is the market price differential on the date of an intercompany purchase, combined with any unamortized issue discount or premium, that causes the consolidated gains or losses that result from the elimination of intercompany bondholdings. Let us change our example slightly to illustrate this.

Parent Co. has a $10,000 bond issue outstanding that pays 10 percent interest annually on December 31. The bonds were originally issued at a premium, which is being amortized by the company on a straight-line basis at the rate of $25 per year.[2] On December 31, Year 1, the unamortized issue premium amounts to $100. The bonds mature on December 31, Year 5.

Sub purchased the bonds in the market for $9,800, which is $300 less than the net book value of these bonds on Parent's books.

On December 31, Year 1, Sub purchases all of the outstanding bonds of Parent on the open market at a cost of $9,800. Immediately after Sub acquires these bonds, the records of the two companies would show the following accounts.

Sub Inc.'s Records		*Parent Co.'s Records*	
Investment in bonds of		Bonds payable	$10,000
Parent Co.	$10,000	Add unamortized issue	
Less discount on purchase	200	premium	100
Net	$ 9,800	Net	$10,100

The net amounts reflect how the asset and the liability would be presented on the respective balance sheets of the two companies on December 31, Year 1. The preparation of the consolidated balance sheet on this date would require the elimination of the two intercompany amounts by the following working paper entry:

A gain of $300 is recorded on the consolidation working papers.

Bonds Payable — Parent Co.	10,100	
Investment in bonds of Parent Co. — Sub. Inc.		9,800
Gain on bond retirement		300

To eliminate the intercompany bond accounts and recognize the resulting gain on the retirement of bonds

---

[2] We will use the straight-line method in the first few illustrations because it is easier to understand. Later in the chapter, we will illustrate the effective-interest method, which is required by GAAP.

From the consolidated perspective, Parent's bonds have been retired; Parent no longer has a bond payable to outsiders.

The eliminations of the asset and the liability would appear in the consolidated balance sheet working paper. The balancing amount of the elimination entry "Gain on bond retirement" appears in the consolidated income statement working paper. From the consolidated entity's point of view, the bonds of the entity have been purchased on the open market and retired. The retirement gain can be calculated in the following manner:

Carrying amount of the bond liability	$10,100
Cost of purchasing bonds in the open market	9,800
Gain on bond retirement	$ 300

The gain on bond retirement was realized on a transaction with outsiders.

The gain should be recognized because the benefits and risks of the consolidated entity have substantially changed in a transaction with outsiders. From a consolidated perspective, the entity has retired a liability of $10,100 by paying $9,800. Its financial position has improved; the gain has been realized and should be recognized.

The gain is reported on the consolidated statements, not on the single-entity statements.

Note that if Parent had acquired and retired its own bonds in the same manner, it would have recorded a gain on bond retirement of the same amount. This gain would appear on Parent's income statement and would also appear on the consolidated income statement. The actual event was different (Sub purchased the bonds), but because the two companies are a single economic entity, the gain will still appear on the consolidated income statement. The only difference is that the gain on the consolidated income statement does not appear on the income statement of the parent. Instead, it appears on the consolidated income statement as a result of the unequal elimination of the intercompany asset and liability accounts in the preparation of the consolidated balance sheet.

An examination of the make-up of the asset and liability accounts will indicate why there is a gain of $300. If the bonds had originally been issued at par (face value), and if the bonds had been acquired on the open market at a price equal to par, there would be no gain on retirement. It is the unamortized issue premium and the discount on the bond purchase that cause the gain. This premium and discount will be amortized by the two companies in Years 2 to 5 and thus will be reflected in the individual income statements of the two companies in those future periods. This will become clearer when we examine the consolidation procedures in Year 2. The important point to note at this stage is that the constituent companies will pay tax on this gain in future periods when the actual recording of the gain takes place. The consolidated entity is realizing the gain in Year 1; therefore, this timing difference requires income tax allocation if a proper matching is to take place. Assuming a 40 percent tax rate, the following additional working paper elimination entry is required:

Income tax expense is reported on the consolidated statements in accordance with the matching principle.

Income tax expense	120	
Deferred income tax liability		120
To record the deferred income tax liability and expense on the Year 1 intercompany bond gain (40% × 300 = 120)		

The effect the two eliminating entries on the Year 1 consolidated income is to increase the net income of the entity by $180 (300 − 120). The entity's net income consists of the net income of the parent, plus the net income of the subsidiary; therefore, the after-tax increase must affect one or the other, or perhaps both.

Four possible approaches could be taken:

There are various approaches to allocate the gain between the two companies.

1. Allocate the gain to the issuing company, because the company purchasing the bonds is acting as an agent for the issuing company.

2. Allocate the gain to the purchasing company, because its investment led to the retirement of the bonds for consolidation purposes.

3. Allocate the gain to the parent company, because its management controls the actions of all the affiliated companies in the group. This would only be a separate alternative if both parties to the transaction were subsidiaries of that parent.

4. Allocate the gain between the issuing and purchasing companies, because each will record its portion of the gain in future periods.

An allocation of the gain would not be required in the case of 100-percent-owned subsidiaries because there would be no non-controlling interest in the consolidated financial statements. The approach adopted is very important when the subsidiaries are less than 100 percent owned, because approaches 1, 2, and 4 could result in all or a portion of the gain being allocated to the subsidiary company, and this would affect non-controlling interest. IFRS is silent regarding the approach to be taken. In the illustrations that follow, any gains (losses) from the elimination of intercompany bondholding will be allocated to the purchasing and issuing affiliates (approach 4), because it reflects how each company will actually record the transaction in future years. The agency approach is briefly discussed on page 337.

We will use approach 4 because it is consistent with the income measurement by the separate entities in future years.

Calculation of the Portion of the Gain Allocated to the Affiliates

From the point of view of the purchasing affiliate, the cost of the acquisition is compared with the par value of the bonds acquired, the difference being a gain or loss. From the point of view of the issuing affiliate, the cost to retire the bonds is compared to the par value of the bonds; the difference between the par value and the carrying value is the gain or loss.

The gain and its allocation can be calculated in the following manner:

Par (face) value of bond liability	$10,000
Cost of investment in bonds	9,800
Gain allocated to purchasing affiliate — before tax	$ 200
Carrying amount of bond liability	$10,100
Par (face) value of bond liability	10,000
Gain allocated to issuing affiliate — before tax	$ 100

The $300 gain is allocated to the affiliates based on the premium or discount on their separate-entity books.

Notice that the gain to the consolidated entity of $300 is made up of the two gains allocated to the affiliates (200 + 100). The gain allocated to the purchasing affiliate is equal to the discount on the purchase affiliate's books, and the gain allocated to the issuing affiliate is equal to the premium on the issuing affiliate's books. Both the entity's gain and the amounts allocated are expressed in before-tax dollars. The chart in Exhibit 7.7 is useful in calculating the after-tax amounts required when the entity's after-tax net income is being allocated to the two equities.

The Year 1 financial statements of the two companies are shown in Exhibit 7.8. Parent Co. has used the cost method to account for its investment.

Exhibit 7.7

This chart shows how the after-tax gains are allocated for consolidation purposes.

ALLOCATION OF GAIN ON BOND

	Entity			Parent Co.			Sub Inc.		
	Before tax	40% tax	After tax	Before tax	40% tax	After tax	Before tax	40% tax	After tax
Gain on bond retirement — Dec. 31, Year 1	$300	$120	$180	$100	$40	$60	$200	$80	$120
	(a)	(b)	(c)	(d)	(e)	(f)	(g)	(h)	(i)

Exhibit 7.8

Sub has no interest revenue because it purchased the bonds on the last day of the year.

INCOME STATEMENTS — for Year 1

	Parent	Sub
Sales	$20,000	$8,000
Interest expense	975	—
Miscellaneous expenses	13,425	5,200
Income tax expense	2,200	1,100
	16,600	6,300
Net income	$ 3,400	$1,700

RETAINED EARNINGS STATEMENTS — for Year 1

	Parent	Sub
Balance, January 1	$12,000	$ 4,500
Net income	3,400	1,700
	15,400	6,200
Dividends	2,000	—
Balance, December 31	$13,400	$ 6,200

BALANCE SHEETS — at December 31, Year 1

The investment in bonds and bonds payable are reported on the separate-entity balance sheets.

	Parent	Sub
Assets (miscellaneous)	$29,150	$13,400
Investment in Parent Co. bonds	—	9,800
Investment in Sub Inc.	11,250	—
	$40,400	$23,200
Miscellaneous liabilities	$ 1,900	$ 9,000
Bonds payable	10,100	—
Common shares	15,000	8,000
Retained earnings	13,400	6,200
	$40,400	$23,200

The net incomes and total assets of the two companies are unchanged from previous examples. However, the details on each statement have been changed to reflect the intercompany bond transaction that occurred on December 31, Year 1.

Parent has interest expense of $975 on its separate-entity books.

Remember that the intercompany bond purchase occurred on that date, and that the interest expense of Parent for Year 1 related to bonds held by bondholders outside the consolidated entity. The amount of expense ($975) is made up of the $1,000 interest paid less the $25 amortization of the issue premium.

Before the Year 1 consolidated financial statements are prepared, the three calculations in Exhibit 7.9 are made.

Exhibit 7.10 illustrates the direct approach to the preparation of the Year 1 consolidated financial statements.

Exhibit 7.9

CALCULATION OF CONSOLIDATED NET INCOME — for Year 1

The gain on bond retirement is allocated to the two affiliates as a consolidation adjustment.

Net income — Parent Co.		$ 3,400
Add after-tax bond gain allocated **(7f)**		60
Adjusted		3,460
Net income — Sub Inc.	1,700	
Add after-tax bond gain allocated **(7i)**	120	
Adjusted		1,820
Consolidated net income		$ 5,280
Attributable to		
Shareholders of Parent		$ 5,098 **(a)**
Non-controlling interest (10% × 1,820)		182 **(b)**

CALCULATION OF NON-CONTROLLING INTEREST
at December 31, Year 1

The gain allocated to Sub affects non-controlling interest at the end of the year.

Sub Inc.	
Common shares	$ 8,000
Retained earnings	6,200
	14,200
Add after-tax bond gain allocated **(7i)**	120
Adjusted	14,320
Non-controlling interest's ownership	10%
	$ 1,432 **(c)**

CALCULATION OF CONSOLIDATED RETAINED EARNINGS
at December 31, Year 1

This schedule shows the calculation at a point in time, i.e., at the end of Year 1.

Retained earnings — Parent Co.		$13,400
Add after-tax bond gain allocated **(7f)**		60
Adjusted		13,460
Retained earnings — Sub Inc.	6,200	
Acquisition retained earnings	4,500	
Increase since acquisition	1,700	
Add after-tax bond gain allocated **(7i)**	120	
Adjusted	1,820	
Parent's ownership	90%	1,638
		$15,098 **(d)**

Exhibit 7.10

Year 1 Consolidated Statements
Adjusted for Intercompany Bondholdings
(direct approach)
PARENT COMPANY
CONSOLIDATED INCOME STATEMENT
for the Year Ended December 31, Year 1

The gain on bond retirement appears on the consolidated income statement because the gain was realized with a transaction with outsiders.

Sales (20,000 + 8,000)	$28,000
Gain on bond retirement (0 + 0 + **(7a) 300**)	300
	28,300
Interest expense (975 + 0)	975
Miscellaneous expenses (13,425 + 5,200)	18,625
Income tax expense (2,200 + 1,100 + **(7b) 120**)	3,420
	23,020
Net income	$ 5,280
Attributable to	
Shareholders of Parent **(9a)**	$ 5,098
Non-controlling interest **(9b)**	182

PARENT COMPANY
CONSOLIDATED RETAINED EARNINGS STATEMENT
for the Year Ended December 31, Year 1

Balance, January 1	$12,000
Net income	5,098
	17,098
Dividends	2,000
Balance, December 31	$15,098

PARENT COMPANY
CONSOLIDATED BALANCE SHEET
at December 31, Year 1

The bonds payable are zero on the consolidated balance sheet because outsiders no longer hold them.

Assets — miscellaneous (29,150 + 13,400)	$42,550
Investment in Parent Co. bonds (0 + 9,800 − **9800**)	–0–
	$42,550
Miscellaneous liabilities (1,900 + 9,000)	$10,900
Bonds payable (10,100 + 0 − **10,100**)	–0–
Deferred income tax liability (0 + 0 + **(7b) 120**)	120
Total liabilities	11,020
Common shares	15,000
Retained earnings	15,098
Non-controlling interest **(9c)**	1,432
	$42,550

Exhibit 7.7 on page 325, which was prepared to allocate the gain in both before-tax and after-tax dollars, was used in preparing the consolidated income statement and in calculating consolidated net income and retained earnings, as follows:

1. The entity column reflects the amounts used in preparing the consolidated income statement. Note that the after-tax column is not used.

2. Both of the allocation columns (Parent Co. and Sub Inc.) were used to calculate consolidated net income attributable to the parent and non-controlling interest for the year, and to calculate non-controlling interest and consolidated retained earnings at the end of the year, but only in after-tax amounts. This is because they are used to adjust the after-tax net incomes and equities of the two companies. The before-tax and tax columns are presented only to show that the columns cross-add.

In summary, the eliminations made for the intercompany bondholdings had the following effect on the consolidated statements:

Income tax is accrued on the consolidated financial statements to match the gain on bond retirement.

1. The elimination of $9,800 in assets and $10,100 in liabilities resulted in a $300 before-tax gain, which was reflected in the income statement.

2. An increase of $120 (40% × 300) to income tax expense and to a deferred tax liability reflected the tax effects of the gain.

3. The two adjustments in the income statement increased the net income of the entity by $180; this was allocated to the two equities in the balance sheet, as follows:

	Total	Non-controlling interest	Controlling interest
The after-tax gain is allocated to non-controlling and controlling interests. Gain allocated to Parent Co.	$ 60	$ —	$ 60
Gain allocated to Sub Inc.	120	12	108
	$180	$12	$168

4. The adjustments made in preparing the consolidated balance sheet can be summarized conceptually as follows:

Asset side:
Investment in bonds   − 9,800

Liability side:
Bonds payable   −10,100
Deferred income tax liability   +   120
Non-controlling interest   +   12
Consolidated retained earnings   +   168
                                                       − 9,800

Equity Method Journal Entries

If Parent used the equity method, the following entries would be made on December 31, Year 1:

These entries capture the net effect of all consolidation adjustments.

Investment in Sub Inc.	1,530	
Investment income		1,530

90% of the Year 1 net income of Sub Inc.
(90% × 1,700 = 1,530)

Investment in Sub Inc.	60	
Investment income		60

Bond gain allocated to Parent Co.

Investment in Sub Inc.	108	
Investment income		108

90% of bond gain allocated to Sub Inc.
(90% × 120 = 108)

The related equity method accounts of Parent will show the following changes and balances in Year 1:

<table>
<tr><td></td><td></td><td>Investment
in Sub Inc.</td><td>Investment
income</td></tr>
<tr><td colspan="2">January 1, Year 1</td><td>$11,250</td><td></td></tr>
<tr><td colspan="2">December 31, Year 1</td><td></td><td></td></tr>
<tr><td></td><td>Income from Sub Inc.</td><td>1,530</td><td>$1,530</td></tr>
<tr><td></td><td>Bond gain to parent</td><td>60</td><td>60</td></tr>
<tr><td></td><td>90 percent of bond gain to subsidiary</td><td>108</td><td>108</td></tr>
<tr><td></td><td>Balance, December 31, Year 1</td><td>$12,948</td><td>$1,698</td></tr>
</table>

The investment account contains cumulative adjustments to the end of the period, whereas the investment income account contains adjustments for only one period.

Accounting for Gain in Subsequent Years

We will now focus on Year 2 so that we can illustrate the consolidation eliminations that must be made in years subsequent to the original intercompany bond purchase.

At the end of Year 2, the two companies prepared the financial statements shown in Exhibit 7.11.

Exhibit 7.11

INCOME STATEMENTS — for Year 2

	Parent	Sub
The separate-entity income statements show interest revenue and expense for bonds that were retired from a consolidated viewpoint.		
Sales	$25,000	$10,950
Interest revenue	—	1,050
	25,000	12,000
Interest expense	975	—
Miscellaneous expenses	17,375	6,900
Income tax expense	2,600	2,000
	20,950	8,900
Net income	$ 4,050	$ 3,100

RETAINED EARNINGS STATEMENTS — for Year 2

	Parent	Sub
Balance, January 1	$13,400	$ 6,200
Net income	4,050	3,100
	17,450	9,300
Dividends	2,500	—
Balance, December 31	$14,950	$ 9,300

BALANCE SHEETS — at December 31, Year 2

	Parent	Sub
Assets (miscellaneous)	$32,700	$18,450
Investment in Parent Co. bonds	—	9,850
Investment in Sub Inc.	11,250	—
	$43,950	$28,300
Miscellaneous liabilities	$ 3,925	$11,000
Bonds payable	10,075	—
Common shares	15,000	8,000
Retained earnings	14,950	9,300
	$43,950	$28,300

The separate-entity balance sheets show investment and bonds payable for bonds that were retired from a consolidated viewpoint.

Focus initially on the items "interest revenue"[3] and "interest expense," which each company recorded in the following manner:

Parent Company			*Sub Inc.*		

These entries are made on the separate-entity books of Parent and Sub.

Parent Company			*Sub Inc.*		
Interest expense	1,000		Cash	1,000	
Cash		1,000	Interest revenue		1,000
To record payment of Year 2 interest			To record receipt of Year 2 interest		
Bonds payable	25		Investment in bonds of		
Interest expense		25	Parent Co.	50	
To amortize issue premium			Interest revenue		50
(100 ÷ 4 = 25)			To amortize discount on the purchase		
			of bonds (200 ÷ 4 = 50)		

The income being reported by the separate entities has already been reported on the consolidated financial statements.

Notice that the entry recording the amortization of the issue premium and the purchase discount increased the respective net incomes of the two companies. Thus, in Year 2, Parent recorded one-quarter of the original gain allocated to it in Year 1 $(100 \times \frac{1}{4} = 25)$; in the same manner, Sub also recorded one-quarter of the original gain allocated to it in Year 1 $(200 \times \frac{1}{4} = 50)$. Because the bonds mature four years after the date of the intercompany purchase, and because the original gain on bond retirement was created because of the existence of the unamortized issue premium and the discount on the intercompany purchase of bonds $(100 + 200 = 300)$, the concept that the gain is realized on the consolidated financial statements before it is recorded by the constituent companies becomes evident.

Both Sub's interest revenue of $1,050 $(1,000 + 50)$ and Parent's interest expense of $975 $(1,000 - 25)$ represent intercompany revenues and expenses that are eliminated on the Year 2 consolidated income statement with the following *incomplete* working paper entry:

The difference between interest revenue and interest expense is due to the difference in amortization of the bond premium and discount.

Interest revenue	1,050	
Interest expense		975
To eliminate Year 2 intercompany interest revenue and expense		

The intercompany interest must be eliminated on consolidation to avoid double-counting of the gain on bond retirement.

In past examples, the elimination of intercompany revenues and expenses (sales and purchases, rental revenue and expense, etc.) had no effect on the net income of the entity, because the amounts eliminated were always equal. Referring back to the journal entries made by both companies, you will see that this equal component is still present. We are still eliminating $1,000 in interest revenue and expense in the working paper elimination. However, we are also eliminating the portions of the gain on bond retirement that were recorded by both companies as a result of the amortization of the premium and discount in Year 2. Failure to do this would result in the gain on bond retirement being recorded twice over the life of the bonds. It is because we do not allow this portion of the gain to be reflected in the Year 2 consolidated income statement that we have an unequal elimination of intercompany revenue and expense on the working paper elimination entry. The elimination of $1,050 intercompany interest revenue and $975 intercompany interest expense decreases the before-tax net income of the entity by $75. We will describe this reduction of the entity's before-tax net income as the "interest elimination loss."

---

[3] The entry for interest revenue or interest expense is usually one entry that incorporates the amortization of the premium or discount on the bonds. In this example, we are showing two separate entries so it is easier to see that the cash amounts are equal and offsetting.

The realization of a gain on bond retirement on the consolidated income statement in the year of acquisition of intercompany bonds will always result in an "interest elimination loss" affecting the entity's before-tax net income in all subsequent consolidated income statements until the bonds mature. This "interest elimination loss" does not appear as such in the consolidated income statement because it results from eliminating an amount of intercompany interest revenue that is larger than the amount of intercompany interest expense eliminated. Conversely, the realization of a loss on bond retirement in the year of acquisition of intercompany bonds will always result in an "interest elimination gain" in all subsequent consolidated income statements because the amount of interest expense eliminated will always be larger than the amount of interest revenue eliminated.

Income tax expense must be eliminated on consolidation to match with the elimination of the interest revenue and interest expense.

As stated previously, the entity's Year 2 before-tax net income has been decreased by $75. This results from eliminating the portion of the gain on bond retirement recorded by the constituent companies in Year 2. Recall that the entire before-tax gain was realized for consolidated purposes in Year 1; also recall that to satisfy the matching principle an income tax expense was recorded and a deferred tax liability was set up on the consolidated balance sheet. Both companies paid (or accrued) income tax on a portion of this gain in Year 2 — a total of $30 (75 × 40%). These companies also recorded the income tax paid (or accrued) as an expense, but from a consolidated point of view, the payment was a reduction of the deferred tax liability previously set up. We must therefore decrease income tax expense when preparing the consolidated income statement[4] because it is not a consolidated expense. The *incomplete* income statement working paper elimination entry is as follows:

Interest revenue	1,050	
Interest expense		975
Income tax expense		30

To eliminate Year 2 intercompany interest revenue and expense and to adjust for the income tax effect of the elimination

The addition of the income tax expense entry still leaves us with an unequal elimination on the consolidated income statement. However, this interest elimination loss is now in after-tax dollars and amounts to $45 (1,050 − 975 − 30). A reconstruction of the intercompany bond chart for the life of the bonds as shown in Exhibit 7.12 on page 332 will illustrate how this loss is allocated to the two constituents each year.

To further illustrate this, examine the interest accounts of the two companies from the date of the intercompany purchase to the date of maturity of the bonds.

By the end of Year 5, the cumulative income recorded on the separate-entity books of Parent and Sub is equal to the $300 gain on bond retirement that was reported in the Year 1 consolidated income statement.

Year ended Dec. 31	Parent's interest expense	Sub's interest revenue	Difference
Year 2	$ 975	$1,050	$ 75
Year 3	975	1,050	75
Year 4	975	1,050	75
Year 5	975	1,050	75
	$3,900	$4,200	$300

---

[4] We must also reduce the amount of the deferred tax liability that was set up in Year 1 by $30.

Exhibit 7.12

ALLOCATION OF GAIN ON BOND

	Entity			Parent Co.			Sub Inc.		
	Before tax	40% tax	After tax	Before tax	40% tax	After tax	Before tax	40% tax	After tax
Gain on bond, Dec. 31, Year 1	$300	$120	$180	$100	$40	$60	$200	$80	$120 **(a)**
Interest elimination loss — Year 2	75	30	45	25	10	15	50	20	30 **(b)**
Balance — gain — Dec. 31, Year 2	225	90	135	75	30	45	150	60	90 **(c)**
Interest elimination loss — Year 3	75	30	45	25	10	15	50	20	30
Balance — gain — Dec. 31, Year 3	150	60	90	50	20	30	100	40	60
Interest elimination loss — Year 4	75	30	45	25	10	15	50	20	30
Balance — gain — Dec. 31, Year 4	75	30	45	25	10	15	50	20	30
Interest elimination loss — Year 5	75	30	45	25	10	15	50	20	30
Balance, Dec. 31, Year 5	$ –0–	$ –0–	$ –0–	$ –0–	$–0–	$–0–	$ –0–	$–0–	$ –0–

The interest elimination loss for each year is equal to the amortization of the bond premium and bond discount on the separate-entity books.

The preparation of a bond chart would be the first step in the preparation of the Year 2 consolidated statements. This chart would have the same format as the one shown above but would comprise only the first three lines from that particular chart. Before the Year 2 consolidated financial statements are prepared, the three calculations in Exhibit 7.13 are made.

The Year 2 consolidated financial statements prepared using the direct approach are shown in Exhibit 7.14 on page 334.

The unequal elimination of the intercompany interest revenue and expense, and the income tax adjustment made in the preparation of the consolidated income statement, were explained on the previous page. This created the "hidden" after-tax interest elimination loss of $45 in this statement. This loss is depicted and allocated in the chart above.

The eliminations made in the preparation of the Year 2 consolidated balance sheet require elaboration. The item "Investment in Parent Co. bonds" in the balance sheet of Sub has a balance of $9,850 after the Year 2 amortization of the discount on purchase (9,800 + 50). Bonds payable in the balance sheet of Parent Co. has a balance of $10,075 after the Year 2 amortization on the issue premium (10,100 − 25). When the consolidated balance sheet is being prepared, these two intercompany accounts are eliminated by the following *incomplete* entry:

This entry eliminates the bonds payable and investment in bonds but is not yet complete.

Bonds payable	10,075	
Investment in Parent Co. bonds		9,850

To eliminate the intercompany bonds on December 31, Year 2

Exhibit 7.13

CALCULATION OF CONSOLIDATED NET INCOME — Year 2

The interest elimination loss is allocated to Parent and Sub based on Exhibit 7.12.

Net income — Parent Co.		$4,050
Less after-tax interest elimination loss allocated **(12b)**		15
Adjusted		4,035
Net income — Sub Inc.	3,100	
Less after-tax interest elimination loss allocated **(12b)**	30	
Adjusted		3,070
Consolidated net income		$7,105
Attributable to		
Shareholders of Parent		$6,798 **(a)**
Non-controlling interest (10% × 3,070)		307 **(b)**

CALCULATION OF CONSOLIDATED RETAINED EARNINGS
at January 1, Year 2

This schedule shows the calculation at a point in time, i.e., at the beginning of Year 2, which is the same as at the end of Year 1.

Retained earnings — Parent Co.		$13,400
Add after-tax bond gain allocated (Dec. 31, Year 1) **(12a)**		60
Adjusted		13,460
Retained earnings — Sub Inc.	6,200	
Acquisition retained earnings	4,500	
Increase since acquisition	1,700	
Add after-tax bond gain allocated (Dec. 31, Year 1) **(12a)**	120	
Adjusted	1,820	
Parent Co. ownership	90%	1,638
Consolidated retained earnings		$15,098 **(c)**

CALCULATION OF NON-CONTROLLING INTEREST
at December 31, Year 2

Only the portion of the gain on bond retirement allocated to Sub affects non-controlling interest.

Sub Inc.	
Common shares	$ 8,000
Retained earnings	9,300
	17,300
Add after-tax bond gain allocated as at Dec. 31, Year 2 **(12c)**	90
Adjusted shareholders' equity	17,390
Non-controlling interest's ownership	10%
	$ 1,739 **(d)**

At the end of Year 2, the deferred tax liability is the 40 percent tax on the difference between income recognized for consolidation purposes ($300) and income recognized by the separate entities ($75).

This entry is somewhat similar to the entry made on December 31, Year 1 (see page 322), except that the before-tax amount needed to balance at this time is a gain of $225 instead of the $300 gain that was required a year ago. Furthermore, the $225 gain does not appear as such in the consolidated income statement in Year 2. Recall that the $300 gain appeared on the Year 1 consolidated income statement. A gain on bond retirement appears as such only once in the year of the intercompany purchase. Recall also that a portion of the gain was recorded in Year 2 by Parent and Sub, was eliminated in preparing the Year 2 consolidated income

Exhibit 7.14

Year 2 Consolidated Statements
Adjusted for Intercompany Bondholdings
(direct approach)

PARENT COMPANY
CONSOLIDATED INCOME STATEMENT
for the Year Ended December 31, Year 2

There was no interest revenue earned from outsiders and no interest expense paid to outsiders *during the year.*

Sales (25,000 + 10,950)	$35,950
Interest revenue (0 + 1,050 − **1,050**)	–0–
	35,950
Interest expense (975 + 0 − **975**)	–0–
Miscellaneous expenses (17,375 + 6,900)	24,275
Income tax expense (2,600 + 2,000 − **(12b) 30**)	4,570
	28,845
Net income	$ 7,105
Attributable to	
Shareholders of Parent **(13a)**	$ 6,798
Non-controlling interest **(13b)**	307

PARENT COMPANY
CONSOLIDATED RETAINED EARNINGS STATEMENT
for the Year Ended December 31, Year 2

Balance, January 1 **(13c)**	$15,098
Net income	6,798
	21,896
Dividends	2,500
Balance, December 31	$19,396

PARENT COMPANY
CONSOLIDATED BALANCE SHEET
at December 31, Year 2

There is no bond payable to outsiders and no investment in bonds of outsiders *at the end of the year.*

Assets — miscellaneous (32,700 + 18,450)	$51,150
Investment in Parent Co. bonds (0 + 9,850 − **9,850**)	–0–
	$51,150
Miscellaneous liabilities (3,925 + 11,000)	$14,925
Bonds payable (10,075 + 0 − **10,075**)	–0–
Deferred income tax liability (0 + 0 + **(12c) 90**)	90
Total liabilities	15,015
Shareholders' equity	
Common shares	15,000
Retained earnings	19,396
Non-controlling interest **(13d)**	1,739
	$51,150

statement, and is not reflected again. The $225 needed to balance is a before-tax gain as at December 31, Year 2. A referral to the bond chart (see Exhibit 7.12 on page 332) indicates that the entity's deferred income tax liability with respect to this gain is $90 as at this date. We can now extend the working paper entry by including the deferred tax component as follows:

Bonds payable	10,075	
Investment in Parent Co. bonds		9,850
Deferred income tax liability		90

To eliminate the intercompany bond accounts and set up the deferred tax liability as at December 31, Year 2

The after-tax gain needed to balance is now $135. The bond chart on page 332 shows this gain as allocated $45 to Parent and $90 to Sub.

To summarize, the Year 2 elimination entries made for the intercompany bond-holdings had the following effect on the consolidated statements:

1. The adjustments made in the income statement created an after-tax interest elimination loss of $45, which decreased the entity's net income and was allocated to the two equities as follows:

The interest elimination loss for the year is first allocated to Parent and Sub and then to non-controlling and controlling interests *for the year.*

	Total	Non-controlling interest	Controlling interest
Loss allocated to Parent Co.	$15	$—	$15
Loss allocated to Sub Inc.	30	3	27
	$45	$3	$42

2. The elimination of $9,850 in assets and $10,075 in bond liabilities, together with the adjustment to reflect the $90 deferred tax liability, resulted in an after-tax increase of $135 in the equity side of the balance sheet. This was allocated to the two equities, at December 31, Year 2, as follows:

The difference between gain on bond retirement and interest elimination loss for all years to date is first allocated to Parent and Sub and then to non-controlling and controlling interests *at the end of the year.*

	Total	Non-controlling interest	Controlling interest
Gain allocated to Parent Co.	$ 45	$ —	$ 45
Gain allocated to Sub Inc.	90	9	81
	$135	$ 9	$126

Remember that the original $300 gain in Year 1 was allocated to the two equities in the consolidated balance sheet as at December 31, Year 1 (see page 325).

3. The adjustments made in the preparation of both the December 31, Year 2, balance sheet and the Year 2 income statement can be summarized conceptually with respect to their effect on the consolidated balance sheet as follows:

This chart shows the adjustments to the consolidated balance sheet at the end of Year 2.

Asset side: Investment in bonds			− $ 9,850
Liability side:			
Bonds payable			− $10,075
Deferred income tax liability			+ 90
Non-controlling interest			
Balance, Dec. 31, Year 1	+ 12		
Year 2 entity net income	− 3	+	9
Consolidated retained earnings			
Balance, Dec. 31, Year 1	+168		
Year 2 entity net income	− 42	+	126
			$ 9,850

The $126 increase in consolidated retained earnings is automatically reflected when the consolidated income and retained earnings statements are prepared. The $9 increase in non-controlling interest is captured in the calculation of the amount of this equity (see page 335).

Equity Method Journal Entries   If Parent has used the equity method, the following entries will be made on December 31, Year 2:

> *These entries should cause Parent's separate-entity income under the equity method to be equal to consolidated net income attributable to Parent's shareholders.*

Investment in Sub Inc.	2,790	
Investment income		2,790
90% of the Year 2 net income of Sub Inc. (90% × 3,100 = 2,790)		
Investment income	15	
Investment in Sub Inc.		15
Interest elimination loss allocated to Parent Co.		
Investment income	27	
Investment in Sub Inc.		27
90% of interest elimination loss allocated to Sub Inc. (90% × 30 = 27)		

The related equity method accounts of Parent will show the following changes and balances in Year 2:

> *The investment account under the equity method ($15,696) is different than the investment account under the cost method ($11,250 as per page 329).*

	Investment in Sub Inc.	Investment income
December 31, Year 1	$12,948	
December 31, Year 2		
Income from Sub Inc.	2,790	$2,790
Interest loss to parent	(15)	(15)
90% of interest loss to subsidiary	(27)	(27)
Balance, December 31, Year 2	$15,696	$2,748

Less Than 100 Percent Purchase of Affiliate's Bonds

Our example assumed that Sub purchased 100 percent of Parent's bonds for $9,800 on December 31, Year 1. Suppose we changed the assumption so that only 40 percent of Parent's bonds were purchased, for $3,920. The elimination needed to prepare the Year 1 consolidated statements would be as follows:

> *A gain on bond retirement is recognized only on the portion of the bonds being retired from a consolidated perspective.*

Bonds payable (40% × 10,100)	4,040	
Investment in bonds of Parent Co.		3,920
Gain on bond retirement		120

If only 40 percent of the bond liability has been eliminated, the consolidated balance sheet will show bonds payable amounting to $6,060, representing the 60 percent that is not intercompany and is payable to bondholders outside the entity.

When consolidated income statements are later prepared, only 40 percent of the interest expense will be eliminated; the remaining 60 percent will be left as consolidated interest expense.

Intercompany Purchases during the Fiscal Year

Our previous example also assumed that the intercompany purchase of bonds took place on the last day of the fiscal year. If the purchase took place *during* the fiscal year, the Year 1 consolidated income statement contains both the gain on bond retirement and the hidden loss resulting from the elimination of intercompany interest revenue earned and expense incurred for the period subsequent to the acquisition.

Gains (Losses) Not Allocated to the Two Equities

The other approaches would allocate the gain on bond retirement differently to Parent and Sub, which changes the amounts allocated to non-controlling interest.

On page 324 the four approaches that can be taken to allocate bond gains (losses) were outlined. The illustrations used approach 4; the calculations for this approach are more complicated than for approaches 1 to 3. Because IFRSs are silent on this matter, any of these approaches may be used. Under approaches 1 to 3, the gain or loss is allocated to only one of the companies, and the bond chart (page 332) is much simpler, as it needs only the entity columns.

The "agency" method (#1) may well have the greatest merit: because only a company that has issued bonds can logically retire them, allocating the gain or loss to the issuing company puts the emphasis on the economic substance of the transaction rather than on its actual form. In the example used, the entire $300 gain would be allocated to Parent Co. If the example used was changed so that the bonds were originally issued by Sub. Inc., and the agency method was followed, the $300 gain would at first be allocated to the subsidiary; however, because Parent owns 90 percent of Sub, non-controlling interest would reflect 10 percent of this gain.

Gains (Losses) Allocated to Two Equities — Loss to One, Gain to the Other

Suppose that the issuing affiliate had $10,000 in bonds outstanding with a carrying value of $10,350, and the purchasing affiliate paid $10,050 to acquire all of the issue on the open market. From the entity point of view there is a before-tax gain on bond retirement of $300, calculated as follows:

The gain is equal to the difference between the cost to retire the bonds and the carrying value of the bonds when they are retired.

Carrying amount of bonds	$10,350
Cost to purchase bonds	10,050
Gain on bond retirement	$ 300

If we allocate the gain to the two affiliates (approach 4), we see that the issuing affiliate is allocated a gain of $350, while the purchasing affiliate is allocated a loss of $50. This can be verified by the following calculation:

The $300 gain is allocated to the affiliates based on the premium or discount on their separate-entity books.

Carrying amount of bond liability	$10,350
Par value of bond liability	10,000
Gain to issuing affiliate	$ 350
Cost of investment in bonds	$10,050
Par value of bond liability	10,000
Loss to purchasing affiliate	$ 50

In subsequent years the entity's interest elimination loss will be allocated as a *loss* to the issuing affiliate and a *gain* to the purchasing affiliate.

Effective-Yield Method of Amortization

Our previous examples have assumed that both companies use the straight-line method to amortize the premiums and discounts. All of the end-of-chapter problems assume the straight-line method unless stated otherwise. This method leads to fairly easy calculations because the yearly amortizations are equal. If one or both companies use the effective-interest method of amortization, the calculations become more complex, but the concepts remain the same.

The following examples illustrate the effective-interest method.

On December 31, Year 0, Subco issued $100,000 face value bonds for a price of $92,791. The bonds pay interest on December 31 each year at a stated rate of 10 percent and mature on December 31, Year 5. The market rate of interest was 12 percent on December 31, Year 0. Given that the stated rate of interest was lower than the market rate, the bonds were issued at a discount. The issue price of the bonds can be determined by taking the present value of future cash flows using a discount rate of 12 percent as follows:

The effective rate used in the present value calculations and bond amortization tables is the market rate of 12 percent.

Principal $100,000 × (P/F, 12%, 5 years) (0.56743)	$56,743
Interest 10,000 × (P/A, 12%, 5 years) (3.60478)	36,048
	$92,791

The following schedule shows how Subco would amortize the discount for its separate-entity financial statements and shows that the amortization of the bond discount increases interest expense (decreases income) each year over the term of the bonds:

The bond discount is amortized on Subco's separate-entity books over the remaining term of the bonds using the effective rate of 12 percent.

Period	Interest paid	Interest expense	Amortization of bond discount	Amortized cost of bonds
Year 0				$ 92,791
Year 1	$10,000[1]	$11,135[2]	$1,135[3]	93,926[4]
Year 2	10,000	11,271	1,271	95,197
Year 3	10,000	11,424	1,424	96,621
Year 4	10,000	11,594	1,594	98,215
Year 5	10,000	11,785	1,785	100,000

[1] $100,000 × 10% = $10,000
[2] $92,791 × 12% = $11,135
[3] $10,000 − $11,135 = −$1,135
[4] $92,791 + $1,135 = $93,926

The market value of the bonds will increase when the market rate decreases.

The market rate of interest for these bonds decreased to 8 percent, and these bonds were trading at a price of $105,154 on December 31, Year 2. If Subco redeems the bonds on this date, it will prepare the following journal entry:

Loss on bond redemption	9,957	
Bonds payable	95,197	
Cash		105,154

Now assume that Subco did not redeem its own bonds but Pubco purchased Subco's bonds in the open market on December 31, Year 2, for $105,154. The following schedule shows the amortization of this premium by Pubco using the effective-interest method and shows that the amortization of the bond premium decreases interest revenue (decreases income) each year over the remaining term of the bonds:

Period	Interest received	Interest revenue	Amortization of bond premium	Amortized cost of bonds
Year 2				$105,154
Year 3	$10,000[1]	$8,412[2]	$1,588[3]	103,566[4]
Year 4	10,000	8,285	1,715	101,851
Year 5	10,000	8,149	1,851	100,000

Pubco amortizes its bond premium on its separate-entity books using its effective rate of 8 percent.

[1] $100,000 \times 10\% = \$10,000$
[3] $\$10,000 - \$8,412 = \$1,588$

[2] $\$105,154 \times 8\% = \$8,412$
[4] $\$105,154 - \$1,588 = \$103,566$

From a separate legal entity perspective, Subco has bonds payable on its balance sheet, while Pubco has an investment in bonds on its balance sheet. From a consolidated perspective, these bonds were redeemed when Pubco purchased them on the open market. A loss on redemption of $9,957 (105,154 − 95,197) should be recorded on the consolidated income statement. In subsequent years, Subco and Pubco will amortize the bond discount and premium on their separate-entity books. From a consolidated perspective, the amortization of the bond discount and premium should be eliminated because the bonds no longer exist. The following bond chart shows how the loss on bond redemption and the elimination of bond amortization is allocated to Pubco and Subco each year over the remaining life of the bonds:

From a consolidated perspective, the bonds were redeemed at a loss of $9,957.

	Entity	Pubco	Subco
Loss on bond, Dec. 31, Yr 2	$9,957	$5,154	$4,803
Interest elimination gain — Yr 3	3,012	1,588	1,424
Balance — loss — Dec. 31, Yr 3	6,945	3,566	3,379
Interest elimination gain — Yr 4	3,309	1,715	1,594
Balance — loss — Dec. 31, Yr 4	3,636	1,851	1,785
Interest elimination gain — Yr 5	3,636	1,851	1,785
Balance — loss — Dec. 31, Yr 5	$ −0−	$ −0−	$ −0−

To further illustrate, examine the interest accounts of the two companies from the date of the intercompany purchase to the date of maturity of the bonds:

From the separate-entity perspective, Pubco and Subco continue to amortize the bond discount or premium using their effective rates.

Year ended Dec. 31	Pubco's interest revenue	Subco's interest expense	Difference
Year 3	$ 8,412	$11,424	$3,012
Year 4	8,285	11,594	3,309
Year 5	8,149	11,785	3,636
	$24,846	$34,803	$9,957

The loss on redemption was recognized in Year 2 from a consolidated perspective and over the three-year period ending in Year 5 from a single-entity perspective.

Under the effective-interest method, the difference between interest revenue and interest expense changes over time. Under the straight-line method, the difference would be $3,319 ($9,957/3) each year for three years. Under both methods, a loss on bond redemption of $9,957 is recorded on the consolidated income statement in Year 2. In turn, consolidated income is increased by a total of $9,957 over the three-year remaining term of the bonds as the amortization of the bond premium and discount is eliminated.

Disclosure Requirements The disclosure requirements for consolidated financial statements were summarized in Chapters 3 and 4. In addition to those requirements, the entity would normally indicate that intercompany transactions have been eliminated. The excerpt below is taken from the 2008 financial statements of Bell Canada Enterprises, Canada's largest telecommunications company.

> **Basis of Consolidation** We consolidate the financial statements of all of the companies we control. All transactions and balances between these companies have been eliminated on consolidation.[5]

GAAP for Private Enterprises

- As mentioned in Chapter 3, private companies can either consolidate their subsidiaries or report their investments in subsidiaries under the cost method or the equity method.

- Whereas public companies can opt to periodically revalue their property, plant, and equipment to fair value under IAS 16, private companies must value these assets at cost less accumulated amortization and accumulated impairment losses.

U.S. GAAP Differences

U.S. GAAP and IFRSs for intercompany transactions have many similarities. The significant differences are summarized as follows:

1. Whereas IFRSs require that property, plant, and equipment and intangible assets be accounted for using the cost method or the revaluation method, these assets must be reported at cost less accumulated amortization and accumulated impairment losses under U.S. GAAP.

2. Whereas impairment losses on capital assets can be reversed under IFRSs in certain circumstances, they cannot be reversed under U.S. GAAP.

SUMMARY

This chapter completed the illustrations of the holdback and realization of intercompany profits and gains in assets by examining the consolidation procedures involved when the profit is in an asset subject to amortization. The gain is held back in order to state the depreciable asset at its undepreciated historical cost from a consolidated perspective. The intercompany profit is subsequently realized as the assets are used or consumed in generating revenues over the remaining life of the assets. Because there are differences between the periods in which the tax is paid and the periods in which the gains are realized in the consolidated statements, income tax must be allocated.

The second part of the chapter examined the gains and losses that are created in the consolidated statements by the elimination of intercompany bondholdings. When the investing company purchases the bonds from outsiders, the bonds are effectively retired from a consolidated perspective. The difference between the price paid to retire the bonds and the book value of the bonds is a gain or a

---

[5] Reproduced with the permission of BCE Inc. Copyright © 2009. All rights reserved.

loss. These gains and losses can occur only if there were premiums or discounts involved in the issue or purchase of these bonds. In the case of intercompany bondholdings, the gains or losses are recognized in the consolidated statements before they are recorded by the affiliated companies, whereas intercompany asset gains are recorded by the affiliated companies before they are recognized in the consolidated statements.

When the parent company uses the revaluation model to revalue its property, plant, and equipment under IAS 16, the consolidated financial statements should reflect the fair value of these assets less accumulated amortization based on fair value. When intercompany transactions occur, the gain or loss on the intercompany transaction must be eliminated and the values reinstated as if the intercompany transaction had not occurred.

Significant Changes in the Last Two Years

1. For publicly accountable enterprises, IFRSs have replaced the former sections of the *CICA Handbook*. The following table shows the IFRSs covered in this chapter along with their counterparts from the former sections of the *CICA Handbook*:

IFRSs	CICA Handbook *Counterparts*
IAS 27: Consolidated and Separate Financial Statements	Section 1601: Consolidated Financial Statements Section 1602: Non-controlling Interests
IAS 16: Property, Plant and Equipment	Section 3061: Property, Plant and Equipment

2. Public companies can choose to periodically value property, plant, and equipment at fair value instead of cost less accumulated amortization and accumulated impairment losses.

Changes Expected in the Next Three Years

No major changes are expected in the next three years.

SELF-STUDY PROBLEM 1

The following are the Year 15 financial statements of Penn Company and its subsidiary Sill Corp.

	Penn	Sill
Year 15 income statements		
Miscellaneous revenues	$500,000	$300,000
Investment income	9,194	—
Gain on sale of equipment	14,000	—
Gain on sale of patent	—	7,500
	523,194	307,500
Miscellaneous expenses	309,600	186,500
Depreciation expense	120,000	80,000
Patent amortization expense	800	—
Income tax expense	33,000	16,000
	463,400	282,500
Profit	$ 59,794	$ 25,000

Year 15 retained earnings statements

Balance, January 1	$162,000	$154,000
Profit	59,794	25,000
	221,794	179,000
Dividends	25,000	8,000
Balance, December 31	$196,794	$171,000

Statement of financial position, December 31, Year 15

Land and buildings	$200,000	$656,000
Equipment	—	44,000*
Accumulated depreciation	(80,000)	(250,000)
Patent (net)	19,200	—
Investment in Sill Corp.	285,994	—
Miscellaneous assets	271,600	131,000
	$696,794	$581,000
Common shares	$400,000	$200,000
Retained earnings	196,794	171,000
Miscellaneous liabilities	100,000	210,000
	$696,794	$581,000

* For illustrative purposes, we are assuming that this is the only equipment owned by either company.

Additional Information

Penn owns 80 percent of Sill and has used the equity method to account for its investment. The acquisition differential on acquisition date has been fully amortized for consolidation purposes prior to Year 15, and there were no unrealized intercompany profits or losses in the assets of the companies on December 31, Year 14. During Year 15, the following intercompany transactions took place:

- On January 1, Year 15, Penn sold used equipment to Sill and recorded a $14,000 gain on the transaction as follows:

Selling price of equipment		$44,000
Book value of equipment sold		
Cost	60,000	
Accumulated depreciation — Dec. 31, Year 14	30,000	30,000
Gain on sale of equipment		$14,000

  This equipment had an estimated remaining life of eight years on this date.

- On January 1, Year 5, Sill developed a patent at a cost of $34,000. It has been amortizing this patent over 17 years. On October 1, Year 15, Sill sold the patent to Penn and recorded a $7,500 gain, calculated as follows:

Selling price of patent			$20,000
Book value of patent sold			
Cost		34,000	
Amortization:			
To December 31, Year 14 (10 × 2,000)	20,000		
Year 15 (¾ × 2,000)	1,500	21,500	12,500
Gain on sale of patent			$ 7,500

  Penn is amortizing this patent over its remaining legal life of 6¼ years.

- Both gains were assessed income tax at a rate of 40 percent.

Required:

(a) Using the reported profits of both companies, prepare a calculation that shows that Penn's separate-entity profit is equal to consolidated profit attributable to Penn's shareholders.

(b) Using Penn's investment account, prepare a calculation that shows that the acquisition differential is fully amortized.

(c) Prepare the following Year 15 consolidated financial statements:
  (i) Income statement.
  (ii) Retained earnings statement.
  (iii) Statement of financial position.

Solution to Self-study Problem 1

UNREALIZED PROFITS

	Before tax	40% tax	After tax
Equipment (Penn selling):			
Gain recorded, Jan. 1, Year 15	$14,000	$5,600	$8,400 **(a)**
Depreciation, Year 15 (14,000 ÷ 8)	1,750	700	1,050 **(b)**
Balance unrealized, Dec. 31, Year 15	$12,250	$4,900	$7,350 **(c)**
Patent (Sill selling):			
Gain recorded, Oct. 1, Year 15	$ 7,500	$3,000	$4,500 **(d)**
Amortization, Year 15 (7,500 ÷ 6¼ × ¼)	300	120	180 **(e)**
Balance unrealized Dec. 31, Year 15	$ 7,200	$2,880	$4,320 **(f)**
Deferred income tax asset — December 31, Year 15:			
Equipment profit			$4,900 **(g)**
Patent profit			2,880 **(h)**
			$7,780 **(i)**

(a)
Profit Penn Co.		$ 59,794
Less investment income		9,194
Profit Penn Co. — own operations		50,600
Less January 1 equipment gain **(a)**		8,400
		42,200
Add after-tax equipment gain realized in Year 15 **(b)**		1,050
Adjusted net income		43,250
Profit Sill Corp.	25,000	
Less October 1 patent gain **(d)**	4,500	
	20,500	
Add after-tax patent gain realized in Year 15 **(e)**	180	
Adjusted net income		20,680
Consolidated profit		$ 63,930
Attributable to		
Shareholders of Penn		$ 59,794 **(j)**
Non-controlling interest (20% × 20,680)		4,136 **(k)**

(b) Investment in Sill Corp. (equity method):

Balance, Dec. 31, Year 15		$285,994
Add unrealized after-tax equipment gain, Dec. 31, Year 15 **(c)**		7,350
		293,344
Sill Corp., Dec. 31, Year 15:		
Common shares	200,000	
Retained earnings	171,000	
	371,000	
Less unrealized after-tax patent gain, Dec. 31, Year 15 **(f)**	4,320	
Adjusted shareholders' equity	366,680	
Penn's ownership	80%	293,344
Unamortized acquisition differential		$ –0–

(c) (i)   **CONSOLIDATED INCOME STATEMENT** — for Year 15

Miscellaneous revenues (500,000 + 300,000)	$800,000
Gain on sale of equipment (14,000 + 0 − **(a) 14,000**)	–0–
Gain on sale of patents (0 + 7,500 − **(d) 7,500**)	–0–
Miscellaneous expenses (309,600 + 186,500)	496,100
Depreciation expense (120,000 + 80,000 − **(b) 1,750**)	198,250
Patent amortization expense (800 − **(e) 300**)	500
Income tax expense (33,000 + 16,000 − **(c) 4,900** − **(f) 2,880**)	41,220
	736,070
Net income	$ 63,930
Attributable to	
Shareholders of Parent **(j)**	$ 59,794
Non-controlling interest **(k)**	4,136

(ii)   **CONSOLIDATED RETAINED EARNINGS STATEMENT** — for Year 15

Balance, January 1	$162,000
Net income	59,794
	221,794
Dividends	25,000
Balance, December 31	$196,794

(iii) **CONSOLIDATED STATEMENT OF FINANCIAL POSITION** — at December 31, Year 15

Land and buildings (200,000 + 656,000)	$856,000
Equipment (0 + 44,000 − **(a) 14,000** + **30,000***)	60,000
Accumulated depreciation (80,000 + 250,000 − **(b) 1,750** + **30,000***)	(358,250)
Patent (19,200 + 0 − **(f) 7,200**)	12,000
Deferred income taxes (0 + 0 + **(i) 7,780**)	7,780
Miscellaneous assets (271,600 + 131,000)	402,600
	$980,130
Common shares	$400,000
Retained earnings	196,794
Non-controlling interest**	73,336
Miscellaneous liabilities (100,000 + 210,000)	310,000
	$980,130

* It is necessary to increase equipment and accumulated depreciation by $30,000 in order to re-establish the original historical cost of the equipment and the accumulated depreciation as at the date of the intercompany sale.

** Sill Corp. — Adjusted shareholders' equity (see part (b))	$366,680
	20%
Non-controlling interest	$ 73,336

SELF-STUDY PROBLEM 2

The financial statements of Parson Corp. and Sloan Inc. for the year ended December 31, Year 5, are as follows:

INCOME STATEMENTS — for Year 5

	Parson	Sloan
Miscellaneous revenues	$650,000	$200,000
Interest revenue	5,625	—
Dividend revenue	7,500	—
	663,125	200,000
Miscellaneous expenses	432,000	129,600
Interest expense	—	9,700
Income tax expense	92,000	24,000
	524,000	163,300
Profit	$139,125	$ 36,700

RETAINED EARNINGS STATEMENTS — for Year 5

	Parson	Sloan
Balance, January 1	$245,000	$ 90,000
Profit	139,125	36,700
	384,125	126,700
Dividends	70,000	10,000
Balance, December 31	$314,125	$116,700

STATEMENTS OF FINANCIAL POSITION — at December 31, Year 5

	Parson	Sloan
Investment in Sloan shares	$ 96,000	$ —
Investment in Sloan bonds	61,125	—
Miscellaneous assets	607,000	372,600
	$764,125	$372,600
Common shares	$150,000	$ 80,000
Retained earnings	314,125	116,700
Bonds payable	—	100,900
Miscellaneous liabilities	300,000	75,000
	$764,125	$372,600

Additional Information

- Parson acquired 75 percent of Sloan on January 1, Year 1, at a cost of $96,000. On this date Sloan's retained earnings amounted to $40,000, and the acquisition differential was allocated entirely to goodwill. Impairment tests conducted yearly since acquisition yielded a loss of $3,200 in Year 2 and a further loss of $800 in Year 5. Parson uses the cost method to account for the investment.
- Sloan has a 10 percent, $100,000 bond issue outstanding. These bonds were originally issued at a premium and mature on December 31, Year 8. On January 1, Year 5, the unamortized issue premium amounted to $1,200. Sloan uses the straight-line method to amortize the premium.
- On January 1, Year 5, Parson acquired $60,000 face value of Sloan's bonds at a cost of $61,500. The purchase premium is being amortized by Parson using the straight-line method.

- Both companies pay income tax at a rate of 40 percent.
- Gains and losses from intercompany bondholdings are to be allocated to the two companies when consolidated statements are prepared.

Required:

(a) Prepare the following Year 5 consolidated financial statements:
   (i) Income statement.
   (ii) Retained earnings statement.
   (iii)Statement of financial position.
(b) Prepare a calculation of consolidated retained earnings at December 31, Year 5.
(c) Prepare the Year 5 journal entries that would be made by Parson if the equity method was used to account for the investment in Sloan's shares.
(d) Calculate the balance in the "Investment in Sloan shares" account as at December 31, Year 5, if Parson had used the equity method.

Solution to Self-study Problem 2

Cost of 75% of Sloan		$ 96,000
Implied value of 100% of Sloan		$128,000
Book value of Sloan, January 1, Year 1		
Common shares	80,000	
Retained earnings	40,000	
		120,000
Acquisition differential — January 1, Year 1		8,000
Allocated to revalue Sloan's identifiable net assets		–0–
Balance — goodwill		8,000
Impairment losses		
Year 1 to Year 4		3,200 **(a)**
Year 5		800 **(b)**
Balance — goodwill, December 31, Year 5		$ 4,000 **(c)**
Non-controlling interest's share (25%)		$ 1,000 **(d)**

INTERCOMPANY TRANSACTIONS
YEAR 5 BEFORE-TAX BOND LOSS

Cost of 60% of Sloan's bonds acquired Jan. 1, Year 5		$61,500
Carrying amount of liability		
Bonds payable	100,000	
Bond premium	1,200	
	101,200	
Amount acquired by Parson	60%	60,720
Bond loss to be reflected in the Year 5 consolidated income statement		$ 780 **(e)**
Allocated as follows:		
Cost of bonds		$61,500
Face value of bonds (intercompany portion)		60,000
Before-tax loss — Parson		$ 1,500 **(f)**
Face value of bonds		$60,000
Carrying amount of bonds (intercompany portion)		60,720
Before-tax gain — Sloan		$ 720 **(g)**

INTERCOMPANY INTEREST REVENUE AND EXPENSE

Interest expense		
10% × 100,000	10,000	
Premium amortization (1,200 ÷ 4)	300	
Total expense	9,700	
Intercompany portion	60%	$5,820 **(h)**
Interest revenue		
10% × 60,000	6,000	
Premium amortization (1,500 ÷ 4)	375	5,625 **(i)**
Before-tax interest elimination gain to entity		$ 195 **(j)**
Allocated:		
Before-tax loss to Sloan (300 × 60%)		$ 180 **(k)**
Before-tax gain to Parson		375 **(l)**
Total gain allocated (before-tax dollars)		$ 195 **(m)**

SUMMARY

	Entity			Parson Co.			Sloan Inc.		
	Before tax	40% tax	After tax	Before tax	40% tax	After tax	Before tax	40% tax	After tax
Jan. 1/Year 5 bond loss (gain)	$780	$312	$468	$1,500	$600	$900	$(720)	$(288)	$(432) **(n)**
Int. elim. gain (loss) Year 5	195	78	117	375	150	225	(180)	(72)	(108) **(o)**
Dec. 31/ Year 5 balance loss (gain)	$585	$234	$351	$1,125	$450	$675	$(540)	$(216)	$(324) **(p)**

(a) (i)

CALCULATION OF CONSOLIDATED NET INCOME — for Year 5

Profit — Parson		$139,125
Less: Dividend from Sloan	7,500	
January 1 after-tax bond loss allocated **(n)**	900	8,400
		130,725
Add Year 5 after-tax interest elimination gain allocated **(o)**		225
Adjusted profit — Parson		130,950
Profit — Sloan	36,700	
Add January 1 after-tax bond gain allocated **(n)**	432	
Less: Year 5 after-tax interest elimination loss allocated **(o)**	(108)	
Acquisition-differential amortization **(b)**	(800)	
Adjusted profit — Sloan		36,224
Consolidated profit		$167,174
Attributable to		
Shareholders of Parson		$158,118 **(q)**
Non-controlling interest (25% × 36,224)		9,056 **(r)**

CONSOLIDATED INCOME STATEMENT — for Year 5

Miscellaneous revenues (650,000 + 200,000)	$850,000
Interest revenue (5,625 + 0 − **(i) 5,625**)	
Dividend revenue (7,500 + 0 − **7,500**)	
Miscellaneous expenses (432,000 + 129,600)	561,600
Loss on bond retirement **(n)**	780
Interest expense (9,700 − **(h) 5,820**)	3,880
Goodwill impairment loss **(b)**	800
Income tax expense (92,000 + 24,000 − **(p) 234**)	115,766
	682,826
Profit	$167,174
Attributable to	
Shareholders of Parson **(q)**	$158,118
Non-controlling interest **(r)**	9,056

(ii)

CALCULATION OF CONSOLIDATED RETAINED EARNINGS
at January 1, Year 5

Retained earnings — Parson		$245,000
Retained earnings — Sloan	90,000	
Acquisition retained earnings	40,000	
Increase since acquisition	50,000	
Less: Goodwill impairment loss **(a)**	3,200	
	46,800 **(s)**	
Parson's ownership	75%	35,100
Consolidated retained earnings, Jan. 1, Year 5		$280,100 **(t)**

CONSOLIDATED RETAINED EARNINGS STATEMENT — for Year 5

Balance, January 1 **(t)**	$280,100
Profit	158,118
	438,218
Dividends	70,000
Balance, December 31	$368,218

(iii)

CALCULATION OF NON-CONTROLLING INTEREST
at December 31, Year 5

Shareholders' equity — Sloan	
Common shares	$ 80,000
Retained earnings	116,700
	196,700
Add: net Year 5 after-tax bond gain allocated **(p)**	324
Add: Unimpaired goodwill **(c)**	4,000
Adjusted shareholders' equity	201,024
	25%
	$ 50,256 **(u)**

CONSOLIDATED STATEMENT OF FINANCIAL POSITION — at December 31, Year 5

Goodwill **(c)**	$ 4,000
Deferred income tax asset **(p)**	234
Investment in Sloan bonds (61,125 + 0 − 61,125)	
Miscellaneous assets (607,000 + 372,600)	979,600
	$983,834
Common shares	$150,000
Retained earnings	368,218
Non-controlling interest **(u)**	50,256
Bonds payable (100,900 − 60,000 − **(p) 540**)	40,360
Miscellaneous liabilities (300,000 + 75,000)	375,000
	$983,834

(b)

PROOF — CONSOLIDATED RETAINED EARNINGS
at December 31, Year 5

Retained earnings — Parson		$314,125
Less: Net Year 5 after-tax bond loss allocated **(p)**		675
Adjusted retained earnings		313,450
Retained earnings — Sloan	116,700	
Acquisition retained earnings	40,000	
Increase since acquisition	76,700	
Less: Goodwill impairment losses (**(a) 3,200** + **(b) 800**)	(4,000)	
Add net Year 5 after-tax bond gain allocated **(p)**	324	
Adjusted increase	73,024	
Parsons' ownership	75%	54,768
Consolidated retained earnings		$368,218

(c)

EQUITY METHOD JOURNAL ENTRIES

Investment in Sloan	27,525	
Investment income		27,525
75% of Sloan's Year 5 profit (75% × 36,700)		
Investment in Sloan	243	
Investment income		243
75% of the net Year 5 bond gain allocated to Sloan (75% × 324)		
Cash	7,500	
Investment in Sloan		7,500
Dividends received from Sloan		
Investment income	600	
Investment in Sloan		600
Year 5 goodwill impairment loss (75% × 800)		
Investment income	675	
Investment in Sloan		675
Year 5 net bond loss allocated to Parson		

(d)

	Investment in Sloan shares
Balance, December 31, Year 4 — cost method	$ 96,000
Increase in retained earnings to Jan. 1, Year 5 ((s) 46,800 × 75%)	35,100
Balance, December 31, Year 4 — equity method	131,100
Investment income, Year 5 (see equity method journal entries)	26,493
Dividends from Sloan	(7,500)
Balance, December 31, Year 5 — equity method	$150,093

APPENDIX 7A

Depreciable Assets under Revaluation Model

IAS 16: Property, Plant and Equipment allows a reporting entity the option to periodically revalue its property, plant, and equipment to fair value. The revaluation adjustment is reported in other comprehensive income unless it indicates an impairment loss, in which case it is reported in net income. The reversal of an impairment loss is also reported in net income. Depreciation expense is based on the revalued amount. The accumulated other comprehensive income relating to the revaluation surplus is transferred directly to retained earnings when the asset is sold.

We will use the same example from page 318 to illustrate the preparation of consolidated financial statements when there has been an intercompany sale of equipment, which had been revalued under the revaluation model allowed in IAS 16.

Sub acquired the equipment for $5,000 and was depreciating the equipment over an estimated useful life of five years. After three years, the accumulated depreciation was $3,000 and the net book value was $2,000. Let us now assume that Sub revalued its equipment to $2,300, the fair value of the equipment, and that both the original cost and the accumulated depreciation were to be grossed up for the increase in value. Sub had not revalued the equipment since it was acquired. Sub would make the following entry on its separate-entity books:

Equipment [(2,300/2,000 × 5,000) − 5,000]	750	
Accumulated depreciation [(2,300/2,000 × 3,000) − 3,000]		450
Other comprehensive income — revaluation surplus		300

Depreciation expense for the first six months of Year 1 would have been $575 (2,300/2 years × 6/12). When Sub sold the equipment to Parent for $2,100 on July 1, Year 1, it would make the following entries on its separate-entity books:

Cash	2,100	
Accumulated depreciation (3,000 + 450 + 575)	4,025	
Equipment (5,000 + 750)		5,750
Gain on sale of equipment		375
To record sale of equipment		
Accumulated other comprehensive income — revaluation surplus	300	
Retained earnings		300
To transfer revaluation surplus to retained earnings		

Given that the parent controls the subsidiary, the sale price for the equipment could have been imposed by the parent. It does not necessarily reflect the fair value of the equipment. The parent would make the following entries related to the equipment in Year 1:

Equipment	2,100	
Cash		2,100
To purchase equipment		

Depreciation expense (2,100/1½ × ½)	700	
Accumulated depreciation		700
Depreciation expense for six months		

When preparing the consolidated financial statements at the end of Year 1, the following entries would have to be made in the consolidated working papers to report the amounts that would have appeared had the intercompany transaction not occurred:

Gain on sale of equipment	375	
Equipment		375
To reverse gain on sale		

Equipment	4,025	
Accumulated amortization		4,025
To reinstate accumulated amortization at date of intercompany sale		

Accumulated depreciation	125	
Depreciation expense		125
To recognize gain through usage of equipment by reversing excess depreciation		

Retained earnings	300	
Accumulated other comprehensive income — revaluation surplus		300
To reinstate revaluation surplus		

The following table summarizes what would have appeared on the three sets of financial statements for Year 1 after processing the journal entries indicated above:

	Parent	Sub	Consolidated
Equipment	2,100		5,750
Accumulated depreciation	700		4,600
Equipment — net	1,400		1,150
Accumulated other comprehensive income			300
Gain on sale		375	
Depreciation expense	700	575	1,150

The consolidated amounts reflect what would have been on Sub's separate-entity financial statements and on the consolidated financial statements had the intercompany transaction not occurred.

REVIEW QUESTIONS

Questions, cases, and problems that deal with the appendix material are denoted with an asterisk.

1. Explain how an intercompany gain of $2,700 on the sale of a depreciable asset is held back on the consolidated income statement in the year of sale and realized on subsequent consolidated income statements. What income tax adjustments should be made in each instance?

2. "The realization of intercompany inventory and depreciable asset profits is really an adjustment made in the preparation of consolidated income statements to arrive at historical cost numbers." Explain.

3. An intercompany inventory profit is realized when the inventory is sold outside the entity. Is this also the case with respect to an intercompany profit in a depreciable asset? Explain.

4. An intercompany gain on a depreciable asset resulting from a sale by the parent company is subsequently realized by an adjustment to the subsidiary's depreciation expense in the preparation of consolidated income statements. Should this adjustment be taken into account in the calculation of net income attributable to non-controlling interest? Explain.

5. Why does an intercompany sale of a depreciable asset (such as equipment or a building) require subsequent adjustments to depreciation expense within the consolidation process?

6. If an intercompany sale of a depreciable asset has been made at a price above book value, the beginning retained earnings of the seller are reduced when preparing each subsequent consolidation. Why does the amount of the adjustment change from year to year?

7. When there has been an intercompany sale of a used depreciable asset (i.e., accumulated depreciation has been recorded for this asset), it is necessary to gross up the asset and accumulated depreciation when preparing the consolidated financial statement. Explain what is meant by grossing up the asset and accumulated depreciation and why this action is necessary.

*8. When a company sells equipment that had previously been revalued to fair value under the revaluation model of IAS 16, it transfers the revaluation surplus from accumulated other comprehensive income directly to retained earnings. What adjustments must be made to accumulated other comprehensive income when preparing consolidated financial statements if the sale is from the parent to the subsidiary?

*9. "There should never be a gain on an intercompany sale of equipment when the selling company uses the revaluation model under IAS 16 and the equipment is sold at fair value." Is this statement true or false? Explain.

10. Four approaches could be used to allocate gains (losses) on the elimination of intercompany bondholdings in the preparation of consolidated financial statements. Outline these four approaches. Which approach is conceptually superior? Explain.

11. An interest elimination gain (loss) does not appear as a distinguishable item on a consolidated income statement. Explain.

12. The adjustment for the holdback of an intercompany gain in assets requires a corresponding adjustment to a consolidated deferred tax asset. The adjustment for a gain from intercompany bondholdings requires a corresponding adjustment to a consolidated deferred tax liability. In both cases the tax adjustment is made because of a gain. Why is the tax adjustment different? Explain.

13. "Some intercompany gains (losses) are realized for consolidation purposes subsequent to their actual recording by the affiliates, while others are recorded by the affiliates subsequent to their realization for consolidation purposes." Explain, referring to the type of gains (losses) that apply in each case.

14. Explain how the recognition of gains on the elimination of intercompany bondholdings is consistent with the principle of recording gains only when they are realized.

15. Explain how the matching principle supports the recognition of deferred income tax expense when a gain is recognized on the elimination of intercompany bondholdings.

MULTIPLE-CHOICE QUESTIONS

Use the following data to answer Questions 1 to 8.

On January 1, Year 1, Present Inc. purchased 80 percent of the outstanding voting shares of Sunrise Co. for $3,000,000. On that date, Sunrise's shareholders' equity consisted of retained earnings of $1,500,000 and common shares of $1,000,000. Sunrise's identifiable assets and liabilities had fair values that were equal to their carrying values on January 1, Year 1.

Account balances for selected accounts for the Year 5 financial statements were as follows:

	Present	Sunrise
Property, plant, and equipment (net)	$2,100,000	$3,500,000
Common shares	1,500,000	1,000,000
Retained earnings, beginning of Year 5	2,600,000	2,800,000
Amortization expense	250,000	300,000
Income tax expense	300,000	350,000
Net income	450,000	525,000
Dividends paid	300,000	0

Additional Information

- Present carries its investment in Sunrise on its books by the cost method.
- At the beginning of Year 4, Sunrise sold Present a machine for its fair value of $800,000. Sunrise had purchased the machine in Year 1. The book value at the time of the sale to Present was $640,000. The machine had an estimated remaining useful life of eight years on the date of the intercompany sale.
- Any goodwill arising from the business combination is to be tested annually for impairment. Goodwill has not been impaired in any year since the date of acquisition.
- Both companies use the straight-line method for depreciation.
- Both companies are taxed at 40 percent.

1. What amount of goodwill arose from Present's acquisition of Sunrise?
   a. $400,000
   b. $500,000
   c. $1,000,000
   d. $1,250,000

2. What amount would appear on Present's consolidated balance sheet at December 31, Year 5, for property, plant, and equipment (net)?
   a. $5,440,000
   b. $5,480,000
   c. $5,504,000
   d. $5,600,000

354 CHAPTER 7 (A) INTERCOMPANY PROFITS IN DEPRECIABLE ASSETS (B) INTERCOMPANY BONDHOLDINGS

3. What is the amortization expense on the consolidated income statement for Year 5?
    a. $530,000
    b. $538,000
    c. $550,000
    d. $570,000

4. What is the income tax expense on the consolidated income statement for Year 5?
    a. $642,000
    b. $650,000
    c. $658,000
    d. $666,000

5. What is the net income attributable to non-controlling interest on the consolidated income statement for Year 5?
    a. $85,800
    b. $102,600
    c. $105,000
    d. $107,400

6. What is the non-controlling interest on the consolidated balance sheet at the end of Year 5?
    a. $850,600
    b. $995,600
    c. $1,100,600
    d. $1,148,600

7. Which of the following statements is true related to deferred income tax on the consolidated financial statements for Year 5?
    a. There will be a deferred tax expense of $48,000 on the consolidated income statement.
    b. There will be a deferred tax recovery of $48,000 on the consolidated income statement.
    c. There will be a deferred tax asset of $48,000 on the consolidated balance sheet.
    d. There will be a deferred tax liability of $48,000 on the consolidated balance sheet.

8. Which of the following is (are) the consolidation adjustment(s) to retained earnings, at the beginning of Year 5, as a result of the intercompany sale of machinery?
    a. Decrease Sunrise's retained earnings by $84,000.
    b. Decrease Sunrise's retained earnings by $140,000.
    c. Decrease Sunrise's retained earnings by $160,000.
    d. Decrease Sunrise's retained earnings by $96,000 and increase Present's retained earnings by $12,000.

9. Black Ltd. owns all of the outstanding shares of White Inc. On January 1, Year 5, White sold equipment to Black and recorded a before-tax profit of $20,000 on the transaction. (White's tax rate is 40 percent.) Black is depreciating this equipment over five years, using the straight-line method. The

net adjustments to calculate the Year 5 and Year 6 consolidated net income attributable to Black's shareholders would be an increase of how much?

	Year 5	Year 6
a.	$9,600	$2,400
b.	$20,000	$ 0
c.	$16,000	$4,000
d.	$20,000	$4,000

10. A parent company has bonds outstanding that were originally issued at a premium. At the beginning of the current year, a subsidiary purchased all of the parent's bonds on the open market at a discount. Which of the following statements is true?
    a. The interest income and expense will agree in amount and should be offset when the consolidated income statement is prepared.
    b. Whether the balances agree or not, the bond interest income and expense should be reported in the consolidated income statement.
    c. In computing net income attributable to non-controlling interest, the interest expense should be included but the interest income should not.
    d. Whether the balances agree or not, the bond interest income and expense should be eliminated when preparing the consolidated income statement.

11. A subsidiary issues bonds directly to its parent at a discount. Both use the same amortization method. Which of the following statements is true?
    a. Because of the discount, the bond interest accounts on the two sets of financial statements will not agree.
    b. Since the bond was issued by the subsidiary, the amount for non-controlling interest must be affected.
    c. Bond interest income and expense will be equal in amount and must be eliminated when preparing the consolidated income statement.
    d. Elimination is not necessary for consolidation purposes because the bond was acquired directly from the subsidiary.

12. A bond that had been issued by a subsidiary at a premium was acquired several years ago by its parent on the market at a discount. The bond issue is still outstanding. Which of the following statements is true?
    a. The bond issue has no impact on the preparation of current consolidated financial statements because the bond acquisition was made in the past.
    b. The original gain would be reported in the current year's consolidated income statement.
    c. The interest income and interest expense balances exactly offset so that no adjustment to retained earnings or income is necessary.
    d. For consolidated purposes, retained earnings must be increased at the beginning of the current year, but by an amount that is smaller than the original gain.

Use the following data to answer Questions 13 to 15.

Ravens owns 90 percent of the outstanding common shares of Gaels. On January 1, Year 2, Gaels issued $200,000 of five percent, 10-year bonds payable for $240,000.

The interest is paid annually on December 31. On December 31, Year 8, Ravens purchased 30 percent of these bonds on the open market for $56,000. Both companies use the straight-line method to amortize any bond premium or discount. The bond accounts for Ravens and Gaels on their separate-entity financial statements at December 31, Year 8 were as follows:

	Ravens	Gaels
Investment in bonds	$56,000	
Bonds payable		$200,000
Premium on bonds		12,000

13. What is the net book value of the bonds payable on the consolidated balance sheet at December 31, Year 8?
    a. $140,000
    b. $148,400
    c. $156,000
    d. $212,000

14. What is the non-controlling interest's share of the adjustment on the consolidated income statement for the year ended December 31, Year 8?
    a. $360
    b. $760
    c. $3,600
    d. $7,600

15. Assume that Gaels' bonds were the only bonds payable for the consolidated entity. Which of the following statements is true related to bond interest expense for the consolidated income statements?
    a. There will be no interest expense on the Year 8 income statement.
    b. There will be no adjustments for interest expense on consolidation for the Year 8 income statement.
    c. There will be no interest expense on the Year 9 income statement.
    d. There will be no adjustments for interest expense on consolidation for the Year 9 income statement.

Use the following data for Questions 16 to 17.

On January 1, Year 1, FOR Company acquired 70 percent of the common shares of MAT. During Year 2, MAT sold equipment to FOR for $1,000,000 and reported a gain of $50,000 on its separate-entity financial statements. This equipment had an estimated remaining useful life of five years on the date of the intercompany sale. At the end of Year 3, FOR still owned and was using this equipment. Both companies have a ratio of sales to assets of approximately 1.5.

16. What would be the impact on the asset turnover ratio for the Year 2 consolidated financial statements if no consolidation adjustments were made with respect to the intercompany sale and unrealized profit?
    a. It would be overstated.
    b. It would be understated.
    c. It would not be affected.
    d. The impact cannot be determined based on the information provided.

17. What would be the impact on the Year 4 consolidated net income attributable to the non-controlling interests if no consolidation adjustments were made with respect to the intercompany sale and unrealized profit?
    a. It would be overstated.
    b. It would be understated.
    c. It would not be affected.
    d. The impact cannot be determined based on the information provided.

CASES

Case 1   Enron Corporation's 2000 financial statements disclosed the following transaction with LIM2, a nonconsolidated special purpose entity (SPE) that was formed by Enron:

> In June 2000, LIM2 purchased dark fiber optic cable from Enron for a purchase price of $100 million. LIM2 paid Enron $30 million in cash and the balance in an interest-bearing note for $70 million. Enron recognized $67 million in pre-tax earnings in 2000 related to the asset sale.

Investigators later discovered that LIM2 was in many ways controlled by Enron. In the wake of the bankruptcy of Enron, both American and Canadian standard-setters introduced accounting standards that require the consolidation of SPEs that are essentially controlled by their sponsor firm.

By selling goods to SPEs that it controlled but did not consolidate, did Enron overstate its earnings?

Required:

Determine how this transaction should have been accounted for assuming that

(a) Enron controlled LIM2 and used consolidated financial statements to report its investment in LIM2.
(b) Enron had significant influence over LIM2 and used the equity method to report its investment.
(c) Enron did not have control or significant influence over LIM2 but LIM2 was considered a related party and Enron had to apply IAS 24: Related Party Disclosures.

Case 2   Several years ago, the Penston Company purchased 90 percent of the outstanding shares of Swansan Corporation. The acquisition was made because Swansan produced a vital component used in Penston's manufacturing process. Penston wanted to ensure an adequate supply of this item at a reasonable price. The former owner, James Swansan, who agreed to continue managing this organization, retained the remaining 10 percent of Swansan's shares. He was given responsibility over the subsidiary's daily manufacturing operations but not for any of the financial decisions.

At a recent meeting, the president of Penston and the company's chief financial officer began discussing Swansan's debt position. The subsidiary had a debt-to-equity ratio that seemed unreasonably high considering the significant amount of cash flows being generated by both companies. Payment of the interest expense, especially on the subsidiary's outstanding bonds, was a major cost, one that the corporate officials hoped to reduce. However, the bond indenture specified that Swansan could retire this debt prior to maturity only by paying 107 percent of face value.

This premium was considered prohibitive. Thus, to avoid contractual problems, Penston acquired a large portion of Swansan's liability on the open market for 101 percent of face value. Penston's purchase created an effective loss on the debt of $300,000: the excess of the price over the book value of the debt as reported on Swansan's books.

Company accountants are currently computing the non-controlling interest's share of consolidated net income to be reported for the current year. They are unsure about the impact of this $300,000 loss. The subsidiary's debt was retired, but officials of the parent company made the decision.

Required:

(a) Determine who lost the $300,000.
(b) Explain how the loss should be allocated on the consolidated financial statements.

Case 3

On January 1, Year 1, Plum purchased 100 percent of the common shares of Slum. On December 31, Year 2, Slum purchased a machine for $90,000 from an external supplier. The machine had an estimated useful life of six years with no residual value. On December 31, Year 4, Plum purchased the machine from Slum for $100,000. The estimated remaining life at the time of the intercompany sale was four years. Plum pays income tax at the rate of 40 percent, whereas Slum is taxed at a rate of 30 percent.

When preparing the consolidated statements for Year 5, the controller and manager of accounting at Plum got into a heated debate as to the proper tax rate to use when eliminating the tax on the excess depreciation being taken by Plum. The controller thought that Slum's tax rate should be used since Slum was the owner of this machine before the intercompany sale. The manager of accounting thought that Plum's tax rate should be used since Plum was the actual company saving the tax at the rate of 40 percent.

In Year 6, the Canada Revenue Agency (CRA) audited Plum. It questioned the legitimacy of the intercompany transaction for the following reasons:

1. Was the selling price of $100,000 a fair reflection of market value?
2. Was Plum trying to gain a tax advantage by saving tax at a rate of 40 percent rather than the 30 percent saving that Slum used to realize?

Plum argued that, under the terms of the sale, CRA was better off because CRA received tax in Year 4 from the gain on the intercompany sale. Had the intercompany sale not occurred, CRA would not have received this tax.

Required:

(a) Determine the economic benefits, if any, to the consolidated entity from tax savings as a result of this intercompany transaction. Was it a good financial decision to undertake this transaction? Explain.
(b) Would your answer to (a) be any different if Plum owned only 60 percent of the common shares of Slum? Explain.
(c) Indicate what amount of tax savings related to depreciation expense would be reflected on the consolidated income statement under the alternatives suggested by the controller and manager or other options you could suggest. Which method would you recommend? Explain your answer using basic accounting principles.

Case 4 Stephanie Baker is an audit senior with the public accounting firm of Wilson & Lang. It is February Year 9 and the audit of Canadian Development Limited (CDL) for the year ended December 31, Year 8, is proceeding. Stephanie has identified several transactions that occurred in the Year 8 fiscal year that have major accounting implications. The engagement partner has asked Stephanie to draft a memo to her addressing the accounting implications, financial statement disclosure issues, and any other important matters regarding these transactions.

CDL is an important player in many sectors of the economy. The company has both debt and equity securities that trade on a Canadian stock exchange. Except for a controlling interest (53 percent) owned by the Robichaud family, CDL's shares are widely held. The company has interests in the natural resources, commercial and residential real estate, construction, transportation, and technology development sectors, among others.

Changes in capital structure

During Year 8, CDL's underwriters recommended some changes to the company's capital structure. As a result, the company raised $250 million by issuing one million convertible, redeemable debentures at $250 each. Each debenture is convertible into one common share at any time. CDL's controlling shareholders acquired a sizeable block of the one million debentures issued; a few large institutional investors took up the remainder.

The company proposes to partition the balance sheet in a manner that will include a section titled "Shareholders' Equity and Convertible Debentures." The company views this classification as appropriate because the convertible debt, being much more akin to equity than debt, represents a part of the company's permanent capital. Maurice Richard, the controller of CDL, has emphasized that the interest rate on the debentures is considerably lower than on normal convertible issues and that it is expected that the majority of investors will exercise their conversion privilege. The company has the option of repaying the debt at maturity in 20 years' time, through the issuance of common shares. The option will be lost if the company is unable to meet certain solvency tests at the maturity date. The company's intention was to raise additional permanent capital, and convertible debt was chosen because of the attractive tax savings. The debentures are redeemable at $250 from January 1, Year 15, to January 1, Year 18.

At the same time as the company issued the convertible debentures, two million common shares were converted into two million preferred, redeemable shares. The net book value of the two million common shares was $20 million. The preferred shares do not bear dividends and are mandatorily redeemable in five years at $20 per share. They have been recorded at their redemption value of $40 million, and the difference between this redemption value and the net book value of the common shares ($20 million) has been charged against retained earnings.

Disposal of residential real estate segment

Intercity Real Estate Corporation (IRE) is a wholly owned subsidiary of CDL and has two operating divisions: a money-losing residential real estate division and a highly profitable commercial real estate division. The two divisions had been combined into one legal entity for tax purposes as the losses arising from the residential real estate division have more than offset the profits from the commercial real estate division.

During Year 8, CDL decided to dispose of its shares of IRE. However, CDL wished to retain the commercial real estate division and decided to transfer the division's assets to another corporation prior to selling the shares of IRE. As part of the sale agreement, just before the closing, the commercial real estate assets were transferred out of IRC to CDL, which then transferred the assets to a newly created subsidiary, Real Property Inc. (RPI). In order to maximize the asset base of RPI, the commercial real estate assets were transferred at fair values, which greatly increased their tax base and created considerable income for tax purposes.

Maurice has explained to Stephanie that, since the transfer would create income for tax purposes, it was necessary for both CDL and the purchaser to agree on the fair value of the commercial real estate assets, even though they were not part of the IRC sale. IRC's purchaser agreed to the values used, because the loss carryforwards, which would otherwise have expired, offset the income for tax purposes.

CDL is planning to take RPI public some time this year. The commercial real estate assets of RPI have been recorded at the values established in the sale of IRC because management believes that this amount represents the cost of acquiring the business from IRC. Maurice has stressed that the transfer between IRC and RPI is very different from the majority of transactions between companies under common control. He argues that the transfer of the commercial real estate assets to RPI represents a bona fide business combination since there is a change of substance and not just of form. CDL maintains a policy of granting subsidiaries a high degree of autonomy and, in substance, they do not function "under common control." Maurice indicated that the real estate assets are worth more to CDL as a result of this transaction because of the increase in the tax values of the assets. Finally, an unrelated party was involved in the transaction and in the determination of the fair value of the assets.

Stephanie noted that after the transfer, the real estate business changed. RPI has undertaken a major refurbishing program and has just bought a large chain of shopping centres that has doubled the company's asset base.

Required:

Assume the role of Stephanie Baker and prepare the memo for the partner.

(*CICA adapted*)

Case 5   Bakersfield Ball Boys Limited (BBB) operates a Canadian professional baseball club, the Bakersfield Ball Boys, that won the Canadian Baseball League title in October Year 10. BBB is 30 percent owned by Mr. Bill Griffin, Bakersfield's wealthiest citizen; 19 percent owned by Excavating Inc., a real estate development company; and 51 percent owned by Tall Bottle Ltd. (Tall Bottle), a national brewery.

Your employer, Mayer & Partners, has audited BBB's financial statements for the past several years. It is now May 3, Year 11, and you, CA, are responsible for the audit of BBB for the year ending June 30, Year 11. The club's year-end was chosen to correspond with the year-end of Tall Bottle, even though the baseball season runs from April to October.

In addition to marking BBB's first-ever Canadian championship, the year ending June 30, Year 11, will be noteworthy from an operational standpoint. You and your staff have become aware of the following:

1. BBB moved into Big Top, a newly built stadium with a retractable roof, on August 1, Year 10. Seating capacity is 70,000. The new stadium is a great

improvement over the 30,000-seat NoWay Park stadium used for the preceding seven years. On July 20, Year 10, BBB signed a 10-year lease with the new stadium's owners. However, BBB's lease on the old premises was not due to expire until January 1, Year 14. BBB therefore paid $3.6 million to terminate its lease.

2. Commencing with the Year 10 baseball season (April Year 10 to October Year 10), the league started a new revenue equalization program. In October, each baseball club in the league is required to remit to the league 50 percent of the revenues from the ticket sales for the season. The league then distributes these revenues, after deducting league costs, in equal amounts to each club. For the Year 10 baseball season, BBB contributed $11.6 million to the league and received $9.2 million, its share of net league revenues. The new equalization program was not accounted for in the June 30, Year 10, financial statements.

3. Immediately before the start of the Year 11 baseball season in April, three of the club's top players were signed to long-term contracts. As a result of these commitments, the club decided to purchase annuities on behalf of these players that would fund the amount required to cover each salary. The annuities for each player were purchased on April 2, Year 11. Amounts of the contracts and annuities are as follows:

Player	Term	Salary	Annuity purchased
Frank Ferter	3 years	$1,500,000 per year	$4,166,000
Hugh G. Blast	5 years	$ 900,000 per year	$3,950,000
Bill Board	4 years	$1,200,000 per year	$4,370,000

The contracts of Ferter and Blast specify that if they suffer a career-ending injury, their contracts will become null and void. Board's contract is guaranteed for the full term.

On April 15, Year 11, Board was injured, forcing him to retire from playing baseball. As required by his contract, he has since been moved to the front office and is performing public relations and administrative services for both BBB and Tall Bottle. Tall Bottle pays BBB $5,000 for each of Board's appearances at a Tall Bottle function. Board has made two appearances at Tall Bottle since his injury.

Ferter has a bonus clause in his contract under which he will be paid $50,000 if he is selected to play for the All Star Team. Although he is favoured to capture this honour, the selections will not be announced until after the financial statements have been issued.

Because of Ferter's exceptional ability and the fact that he is considered a "player who will increase the popularity of the sport in this city for many years to come," management proposes to amortize the cost of his contract over a 10-year period.

4. On April 2, Year 11, the club renewed its contract with Sportsplus, a local television station, for three years. Sportsplus will pay BBB $30,000 per game for the right to televise 25 regular season games and $75,000 for each playoff game. In addition, BBB received a $250,000 bonus for re-signing, and $315,000 for its high ratings over the previous contract term. Tall Bottle enjoys an exclusive advertising contract with Sportsplus as BBB's official sponsor. The contract

provides Tall Bottle with three one-minute ads for each game televised by Sportsplus. The advertising was granted to Tall Bottle by Sportsplus free of charge in exchange for BBB's local television rights.

5. BBB's contract with its management includes a bonus clause, to take effect in the year ended June 30, Year 11. Bill Griffin and Excavating Inc. had opposed the scheme, as the bonus is based on annual pre-tax income. However, they agreed to it after much pressure from management and Tall Bottle.

6. On October 3, Year 10, the day before the last playoff game, a windstorm caused the roof at Big Top to collapse, resulting in structural damage of $4,500,000 to the stadium. This unforeseen event forced BBB's last playoff game to be played at NoWay Park. Hence, the club announced that some of the 70,000 seats sold for Big Top could be used at NoWay Park and that the $35 cost of the remaining tickets could be either refunded or applied toward the cost of tickets for any of BBB's Year 11 games. Also, the 40,000 fans who could not attend the game at NoWay were given $10 gift certificates that could be used toward purchasing tickets for any future BBB game.

As a result of the roof collapse at Big Top, BBB incurred the following costs for its final playoff game at NoWay:

Groundskeepers	$ 9,000
Cleaning crew	15,250
Food vendors	19,200
Stadium rental	132,500

A separate cleaning crew had to be hired for the NoWay Park game, as the club's regular cleaning crew was required to assist in the clean-up at Big Top. BBB's lease costs of $50,000 were not waived during the reconstruction of Big Top.

Had the playoff game been played at Big Top, the following costs would have been incurred:

Groundskeepers	$16,500
Cleaning crew	25,750
Food vendors	32,900

Actual food sales at NoWay were $191,750, with food costs averaging 50 percent of sales. BBB was required to pay the stadium owners a 10 percent share of sales, whereas, at Big Top, BBB would have been required to pay a 15 percent share of sales.

BBB's management has asked your firm to prepare a statement of loss to support its claim for damages in accordance with its business-interruption insurance policy. The insurance policy covers the loss of income as well as the additional expenses that result from a disaster.

The partner in charge of the engagement has asked you, CA, to prepare the information requested by the client. In addition, the partner would like a memo presenting your analysis of the accounting issues of which you and your staff have become aware, and your recommendations.

Required:

Prepare the information requested by the client and the memo to the partner.

(*CICA adapted*)

PROBLEMS

Problem 1
X Company owns 80 percent of Y Company and uses the equity method to account for its investment. On January 1, Year 2, the investment in Y Company account had a balance of $86,900, and Y Company's common shares and retained earnings totalled $100,000. The unamortized acquisition differential had an estimated remaining life of six years at this time. The following intercompany asset transfers took place in Years 2 and 3: January 1, Year 2, sale of asset to X at a profit of $45,000, and April 30, Year 3, sale of asset to Y at a profit of $60,000. Both assets purchased are being depreciated over five years. In Year 2, Y reported a net income of $125,000 and dividends paid of $70,000, while in Year 3 its net income and dividends were $104,000 and $70,000, respectively.

Required:
Calculate the December 31, Year 3, balance in the account "Investment in Y." (Assume a 40 percent tax rate.)

Problem 2
Peggy Company owns 75 percent of Sally Inc. and uses the cost method to account for its investment. The following data were taken from the Year 4 income statements of the two companies:

	Peggy	Sally
Revenues	$580,000	$270,000
Miscellaneous expenses	110,000	85,000
Depreciation expense	162,000	97,000
Income tax expense	123,000	35,000
Total expenses	395,000	217,000
Profit	$185,000	$ 53,000

In Year 2, Sally sold equipment to Peggy at a gain of $15,000. Peggy has been depreciating this equipment over a five-year period. Use income tax allocation at a rate of 40 percent.

Required:
(a) Calculate consolidated profit attributable to Peggy's shareholders for Year 4.
(b) Prepare a consolidated income statement for Year 4.
(c) Calculate the deferred income tax asset that would appear on the Year 4 consolidated statement of financial position.

Problem 3
The comparative consolidated income statements of a parent and its 75-percent-owned subsidiary were prepared incorrectly as at December 31 and are shown on the following page. The following items were overlooked when the statements were prepared:

• The Year 5 gain on sale of assets resulted from the subsidiary selling equipment to the parent on September 30. The parent immediately leased the equipment back to the subsidiary at an annual rental of $12,000. This was the only intercompany rent transaction that occurred each year. The equipment had a remaining life of five years on the date of the intercompany sale.
• The Year 6 gain on sale of assets resulted from the January 1 sale of a building, with a remaining life of seven years, by the subsidiary to the parent.
• Both gains were taxed at a rate of 40 percent.

CONSOLIDATED INCOME STATEMENTS

	Year 5	Year 6
Miscellaneous revenues	$750,000	$825,000
Gain on sale of assets	8,000	42,000
Rental revenue	3,000	12,000
	761,000	879,000
Miscellaneous expenses	399,800	492,340
Rental expense	52,700	64,300
Depreciation expense	75,000	80,700
Income tax expense	81,000	94,500
Non-controlling interest	32,500	5,160
	641,000	737,000
Net income	$120,000	$142,000

Required:

Prepare correct consolidated income statements for Years 5 and 6.

Problem 4   On December 31, Year 2, HABS Inc. sold equipment to NORD at its fair value of $2,000,000 and recorded a gain of $500,000. This was HABS's only income (other than any investment income from NORD) during the year. NORD reported income (other than any investment income from HABS) of $200,000 for Year 2. Both companies paid dividends of $100,000 during Year 2.

Required:

(a) Calculate NORD's income before taxes for Year 2 assuming that
  (i) HABS and NORD are not related.
  (ii) NORD owns 75 percent of HABS and reports its investment in HABS on a consolidated basis.
  (iii) NORD owns 75 percent of HABS and reports its investment in HABS using the equity method.
  (iv) NORD owns 75 percent of HABS and reports its investment in HABS using the cost method.

(b) Calculate HABS's income before taxes for Year 2 assuming that
  (i) NORD and HABS are not related.
  (ii) HABS owns 75 percent of NORD and reports its investment in NORD on a consolidated basis.
  (iii) HABS owns 75 percent of NORD and reports its investment in NORD using the equity method.
  (iv) HABS owns 75 percent of NORD and reports its investment in NORD using the cost method.

(c) Compare and contrast the income reported under the reporting methods (ii), (iii), and (iv) above. Which method best reflects the economic reality of the business transaction?

Problem 5   The balance sheets of Forest Company and Garden Company are presented below as at December 31, Year 8.

BALANCE SHEETS — at December 31, Year 8

	Forest	Garden
Cash	$ 13,000	$ 48,800
Receivables	25,000	86,674
Inventories	80,000	62,000
Investment in shares of Garden	207,900	—
Plant and equipment	740,000	460,000
Accumulated depreciation	(625,900)	(348,400)
Patents	—	4,500
Investment in bonds of Forest	—	58,426
	$440,000	$372,000
Current liabilities	$ 59,154	$ 53,000
Dividends payable	6,000	30,000
Bonds payable 6%	94,846	—
Common shares	200,000	150,000
Retained earnings	80,000	139,000
	$440,000	$372,000

Additional Information

- Forest acquired 90 percent of Garden for $207,900 on July 1, Year 1, and accounts for its investment under the cost method. At that time, the shareholders' equity of Garden amounted to $175,000, and the assets of Garden were undervalued by the following amounts:

Inventory	$12,000	
Buildings	$10,000	remaining life 10 years
Patents	$16,000	remaining life 8 years

- During Year 8, Forest reported net income of $41,000 and paid dividends of $25,000, whereas Garden reported net income of $63,000 and paid dividends of $50,000.
- During Years 2 to 7, goodwill impairment losses totalled $1,950. An impairment test conducted in Year 8 indicated a further loss of $7,150.
- Forest sells goods to Garden on a regular basis at a gross profit of 30 percent. During Year 8, these sales totalled $150,000. On January 1, Year 8, the inventory of Garden contained goods purchased from Forest amounting to $18,000, while the December 31, Year 8, inventory contained goods purchased from Forest amounting to $22,000.
- On August 1, Year 6, Garden sold land to Forest at a profit of $16,000. During Year 8, Forest sold one-quarter of the land to an unrelated company.
- Forest's bonds have a par value of $100,000, pay interest annually on December 31 at a stated rate of 6 percent, and mature on December 31, Year 11. Forest incurs an effective interest cost of 8 percent on these bonds. These bonds had a carrying value of $93,376 on January 1, Year 8. On that date, Garden acquired $60,000 of these bonds on the open market at a cost of $57,968. Garden will earn an effective rate of return of 7 percent on these bonds. Both companies use the effective-interest method to account for their bonds.

The Year 8 income statements of the two companies show the following with respect to bond interest.

	Forest	Garden
Interest expense	$7,470	
Interest revenue		$4,058

- Garden owes Forest $22,000 on open account on December 31, Year 8.
- Assume a 40 percent corporate tax rate and allocate bond gains (losses) between the two companies.

Required:

(a) Prepare the following statements:
   (i) Consolidated balance sheet.
   (ii) Consolidated retained earnings statement.
(b) Prepare the Year 8 journal entries that would be made on the books of Forest if the equity method was used to account for the investment.
(c) Explain how a loss on the elimination of intercompany bondholdings is viewed as a temporary difference and gives rise to a deferrred income tax asset.
(d) If Forest had used the parent company extension theory rather than the entity theory, how would this affect the debt-to-equity ratio at the end of Year 9?

Problem 6   Income statements of M Co. and K Co. for the year ended December 31, Year 6, are presented below:

	M Co.	K Co.
Sales	$600,000	$350,000
Rent revenue	—	50,000
Interest revenue	6,700	—
Income from subsidiary	30,320	—
Gain on land sale	—	8,000
	637,020	408,000
Cost of goods sold	334,000	225,000
Distribution expense	80,000	70,000
Administrative expense	147,000	74,000
Interest expense	1,700	6,000
Income tax expense	20,700	7,500
	583,400	382,500
Profit	$ 53,620	$ 25,500

Additional Information

- M Co. uses the equity method to account for its investment in K Co.
- M Co. acquired its 80 percent interest in K Co. on January 1, Year 1. On that date the acquisition differential of $25,000 was allocated entirely to buildings; it is being amortized over a 20-year period.
- Amortization expense is grouped with distribution expenses, and impairment losses, if any, are grouped with other expenses.
- M Co. made an advance of $100,000 to K Co. on July 1, Year 6. This loan is due on demand and requires the payment of interest at 12 percent per year.
- M Co. rents marine equipment from K Co. During Year 6, $50,000 rent was paid and was charged to administrative expense.

- In Year 4, M Co. sold land to K Co. and recorded a profit of $10,000 on the sale. K Co. held the land until October, Year 6, when it was sold to an unrelated company.
- During Year 6, K Co. made sales to M Co. totalling $90,000. The December 31, Year 6, inventories of M Co. contain an unrealized profit of $5,000. The January 1, Year 6, inventories of M Co. contained an unrealized profit of $12,000.
- On January 1, Year 4, M Co. sold machinery to K Co. and recorded a profit of $13,000. The remaining useful life on that date was five years. Assume straight-line depreciation.
- Tax allocation is to be used, assuming a 40 percent average corporate tax rate for this purpose.

Required:

Prepare a consolidated income statement for Year 6.

Problem 7 The Pure Company purchased 70 percent of the common shares of the Gold Company on January 1, Year 6, for $483,000 when the latter company's common shares and retained earnings were $500,000 and $40,000, respectively. On this date, an appraisal of the assets of Gold disclosed the following differences:

	Carrying value	Fair value
Land	$150,000	$200,000
Plant and equipment	700,000	770,000
Inventory	120,000	108,000

The plant and equipment had an estimated life of 20 years on this date.

The statements of financial position of Pure and Gold, prepared on December 31, Year 11, follow:

	Pure	Gold
Land	$ 100,000	$ 150,000
Plant and equipment	625,000	940,000
Less accumulated depreciation	(183,000)	(220,000)
Patent (net of amortization)	31,500	—
Investment in Gold Co. shares (equity method)	544,710	—
Investment in Gold Co. bonds	227,000	—
Inventory	225,000	180,000
Accounts receivable	212,150	170,000
Cash	41,670	57,500
	$1,824,030	$1,277,500
Common shares	$ 750,000	$ 500,000
Retained earnings	1,018,000	200,000
Bonds payable (due Year 20)	—	477,500
Accounts payable	56,030	100,000
	$1,824,030	$1,277,500

Additional Information

- Goodwill impairment tests have resulted in impairment losses totalling $28,000.
- On January 1, Year 1, Gold issued $500,000 of 8½ percent bonds at 90, maturing in 20 years (on December 31, Year 20).

- On January 1, Year 11, Pure acquired $200,000 of Gold's bonds on the open market at a cost of $230,000.
- On July 1, Year 8, Gold sold a patent to Pure for $63,000. The patent had a carrying value on Gold's books of $42,000 on this date and an estimated remaining life of seven years.
- Pure uses tax allocation (rate 40 percent) and allocates bond gains between affiliates when it consolidates Gold.
- Pure uses the equity method to account for its investment.

Required:

Prepare a consolidated statement of financial position as at December 31, Year 11.

Problem 8 On January 2, Year 1, Poplar Ltd. purchased 80 percent of the outstanding shares of Spruce Ltd. for $2,000,000. At that date, Spruce had common shares of $500,000 and retained earnings of $1,250,000. Poplar acquired the Spruce shares to obtain control of copyrights held by Spruce. These copyrights, with a remaining life of eight years, had a fair value of $750,000 in excess of their carrying value. Except for the copyrights, the carrying values of the recorded assets and liabilities of Spruce were equal to their fair values. On December 31, Year 4, the trial balances of the two companies were as follows:

	Poplar	Spruce
Cash	$ 1,000,000	$ 500,000
Accounts receivable	2,000,000	356,000
Inventory	3,000,000	2,250,000
Plant and equipment	14,000,000	2,500,000
Copyrights (net)	—	400,000
Investment in Spruce (cost)	2,000,000	—
Investment in Poplar bonds	—	244,000
Cost of goods sold	2,400,000	850,000
Other expenses	962,000	300,000
Interest expense	38,000	—
Income tax expense	600,000	350,000
Dividends	600,000	250,000
	$26,600,000	$8,000,000
Accounts payable	$ 2,492,000	$2,478,500
Accumulated depreciation: plant and equipment	4,000,000	1,000,000
Bonds payable	500,000	—
Premium on bonds payable	8,000	—
Common shares	4,500,000	500,000
Retained earnings, January 1	10,000,000	2,000,000
Sales	4,900,000	2,000,000
Dividend revenue	200,000	—
Interest revenue	—	21,500
	$26,600,000	$8,000,000

Additional Information

- The Year 4 net incomes of the two companies are as follows:

| Poplar Ltd. | $1,100,000 |
| Spruce Ltd. | 521,500 |

- On January 2, Year 2, Spruce sold equipment to Poplar for $500,000. The equipment had a net book value of $400,000 at the time of the sale. The remaining useful life of the equipment was five years.
- The Year 4 opening inventories of Poplar contained $500,000 of merchandise purchased from Spruce during Year 3. Spruce had recorded a gross profit of $200,000 on this merchandise.
- During Year 4, Spruce's sales to Poplar totalled $1,000,000. These sales were made at a gross profit rate of 40 percent.
- Poplar's ending inventory contains $300,000 of merchandise purchased from Spruce.
- Other expenses include depreciation expense and copyright amortization expense.
- On January 2, Year 2, Poplar issued 8 percent, seven-year bonds with a face value of $500,000 for $514,000. Interest is paid annually on December 31. On January 2, Year 4, Spruce purchased one-half of this issue on the open market at a cost of $242,500. Intercompany bond gains (losses) are to be allocated between the two affiliates.
- Tax allocation will be at a rate of 40 percent.

Required:

(a) Prepare the following consolidated financial statements:
   (i) Income statement.
   (ii) Retained earnings statement.
   (iii) Balance sheet.
(b) Calculate the December 31, Year 4, balance in the account "Investment in Spruce" if Poplar had used the equity method to account for its investment.

Problem 9 On January 1, Year 1, Porter Inc. purchased 85 percent of the voting shares of Sloan Ltd. for $3,026,000 in cash. On this date, Sloan had common shares outstanding in the amount of $2,200,000 and retained earnings of $1,100,000. The identifiable assets and liabilities of Sloan had fair values that were equal to their carrying values except for the following:

- Plant and equipment (net) had a fair value $200,000 greater than its carrying value. The remaining useful life on January 1, Year 1, was 20 years with no anticipated salvage value.
- Accounts receivable had a fair value $75,000 less than carrying value.
- Long-term liabilities had a fair value $52,680 less than carrying value. These liabilities were issued at par and mature on December 31, Year 10.

Additional Information

- Between January 1, Year 1, and December 31, Year 3, Sloan earned $345,000 and paid dividends of $115,000.
- Goodwill impairment tests yielded losses as follows: Year 1, $30,300; Year 2, $6,075; Year 4, $12,125.
- On January 1, Year 2, Sloan sold a patent to Porter for $165,000. On this date, the patent had a carrying value on the books of Sloan of $185,000 and a remaining useful life of five years.
- On September 1, Year 3, Porter sold land to Sloan for $93,000. The land had a carrying value on the books of Porter of $72,000. Sloan still owned this land on December 31, Year 4.

- For the year ending December 31, Year 4, the income statements revealed the following:

	Porter	Sloan
Total revenues	$2,576,000	$973,000
Cost of goods sold	1,373,000	467,000
Amortization expense	483,000	176,000
Interest expense	115,000	44,700
Other expenses (including income tax)	237,000	108,300
Total expenses	2,208,000	796,000
Net income	$ 368,000	$177,000

Porter records its investment in Sloan using the cost method and includes dividend income from Sloan in its total revenues.

- Porter and Sloan paid dividends of $125,000 and $98,000, respectively, in Year 4.
- Sloan issued no common shares subsequent to January 1, Year 1. Selected balance sheet accounts for the two companies as at December 31, Year 4, were as follows:

	Porter	Sloan
Accounts receivable (net)	$ 987,000	$ 133,000
Inventories	1,436,000	787,000
Plant and equipment (net)	3,467,000	1,234,000
Patent (net)	263,000	–0–
Land	872,000	342,000
Long-term liabilities	1,876,000	750,000
Retained earnings	4,833,000	1,409,000

- During Year 4, Porter's merchandise sales to Sloan were $150,000. The unrealized profits in Sloan's inventory on January 1 and December 31, Year 4, were $14,000 and $10,000, respectively. At December 31, Year 4, Sloan still owed Porter $5,000 for merchandise purchases.
- During Year 4, Sloan's merchandise sales to Porter were $55,000. The unrealized profits in Porter's inventory on January 1 and December 31, Year 4, were $1,500 and $2,500, respectively. At December 31, Year 4, Porter still owed Sloan $2,000 for merchandise purchases.
- Use income tax allocation at a rate of 40 percent and straight-line amortization of property, plant, and equipment, and long-term liabilities.

Required:

(a) Compute the balances that would appear in the consolidated balance sheet of Porter and Sloan as at December 31, Year 4, for the following:
   (i) Patent (net).
   (ii) Goodwill.
   (iii) Non-controlling interest.
   (iv) Retained earnings.
   (v) Long-term liabilities.

(b) Porter has decided not to prepare consolidated financial statements and will report its investment in Sloan by the equity method. Calculate the total revenues, including investment income, that would be presented in the income statement drawn up by Porter for the year ended December 31, Year 4.

(c) Assume that Sloan pays interest annually at the rate of 6 percent on its long-term liabilities. When Porter acquired Sloan on January 1, Year 1, the fair value of Sloan's long-term liabilities would have produced an effective yield of 7 percent. Calculate long-term liabilities on the consolidated financial statements assuming that Porter and Sloan use the effective-interest method to account for their long-term liabilities.

(SMA adapted)

Problem 10 Alpha Corporation owns 90 percent of the common shares of Beta Corporation and uses the equity method to account for its investment.

On January 1, Year 4, Alpha purchased $160,000 of Beta's 10 percent bonds for $150,064. Beta's bond liability on this date consisted of $800,000 par 10 percent bonds due January 1, Year 8, and unamortized discount of $73,065. Interest payment dates are June 30 and December 31. The effective rate of interest is 6 percent every six months on Alpha's bond investment and 6.5 percent every six months for Beta's bond liability.

Both companies have a December 31 year-end and use the effective-interest method to account for bonds. Alpha uses income tax allocation at a 40 percent tax rate when it prepares its consolidated financial statements.

Beta reported a profit of $114,000 in Year 4 and declared a dividend of $30,000 on December 31.

Required:

(a) Calculate the amount of the gain or the loss that will appear as a separate item on the Year 4 consolidated income statement as a result of the bond transaction that occurred during the year.

(b) Prepare the equity method journal entries that Alpha would make on December 31, Year 4.

(c) Calculate the amount of the bond liability that will appear on the December 31, Year 4, consolidated statement of financial position.

Problem 11 Parent Co. owns 75 percent of Sub Co. and uses the cost method to account for its investment. The following are summarized income statements for the year ended December 31, Year 7. (Sub Co. did not declare or pay dividends in Year 7.)

INCOME STATEMENTS — for Year 7

	Parent	Sub
Interest revenue	$ 8,750	$ —
Other misc. revenues	900,000	500,000
	908,750	500,000
Interest expense	—	44,000
Other misc. expenses	600,000	350,000
Income tax expense	124,000	42,000
	724,000	436,000
Net income	$184,750	$ 64,000

Additional Information

On July 1, Year 7, Parent purchased 40 percent of the outstanding bonds of Sub for $152,500. On that date, Sub had $400,000 of 10 percent bonds payable outstanding, which mature in five years. The bond discount on the books of Sub on July 1, Year 7, amounted to $20,000. Interest is payable January 1 and July 1. Any gains (losses) are to be allocated to each company. Both companies use the straight-line method to account for bonds.

Required:

Prepare a consolidated income statement for Year 7 using a 40 percent tax rate.

Problem 12   Palmer Corporation owns 70 percent of the common shares of Scott Corporation and uses the equity method to account for its investment.

Scott purchased $80,000 par of Palmer's 10 percent bonds on October 1, Year 5, for $76,000. Palmer's bond liability on October 1, Year 5, consisted of $400,000 par of 10 percent bonds due on October 1, Year 9, with unamortized discount of $8,000. Interest payment dates are April 1 and October 1 of each year and straight-line amortization is used. Intercompany bond gains (losses) are to be allocated to each affiliate.

Both companies have a December 31 year-end. Scott's financial statements for Year 5 indicate that it earned profit of $70,000 and that on December 31, Year 5, it declared a dividend of $15,000.

Required:

(a) Prepare the journal entries under the equity method that Palmer would make in Year 5. (Assume a 40 percent tax rate.)
(b) Compute the amount of the bond liability that will appear on the December 31, Year 5, consolidated statement of financial position.

Problem 13   On December 31, Year 1, RAV Company purchased 60 percent of the outstanding common shares of ENS Company for $780,000. On that date, ENS had common shares of $500,000 and retained earnings of $120,000. In negotiating the purchase price, it was agreed that assets and liabilities were fairly valued except for equipment, which had a $30,000 excess of carrying value over fair value, and land, which had a $120,000 excess of fair value over carrying value. The equipment had a remaining useful life of six years at the acquisition date and no salvage value. ENS did not record the fair value deficiency on the equipment because ENS felt that it would recover the carrying value of this equipment through future cash flows.

The adjusted trial balances for RAV and ENS for the year ended December 31, Year 5, were as follows:

	RAV	ENS
Cash	$ 150,000	$ 75,000
Accounts receivable	275,000	226,000
Inventory	594,000	257,000
Land	600,000	170,000
Building — net	710,000	585,000
Equipment — net	690,000	349,000
Investment in ENS	516,000	
Cost of goods purchased	2,340,000	2,137,000
Change in inventory	60,000	(30,000)
Amortization expense	240,000	120,000
Income taxes and other expenses	960,000	432,000
Dividends paid	540,000	304,000
Total debits	$7,675,000	$4,625,000
Accounts payable	$ 465,000	$ 296,000
Long-term debt	900,000	540,000
Common shares	1,200,000	500,000
Retained earnings, beginning	600,000	279,000
Sales	4,220,000	3,010,000
Other revenues	80,000	
Investment income from ENS	210,000	
Total credits	$7,675,000	$4,625,000

Additional Information

- Each year, goodwill is evaluated to determine if there has been a loss. The recoverable impairment amount for ENS's goodwill was valued at $100,000 at the end of Year 4 and $75,000 at the end of Year 5.
- RAV's inventories contained $200,000 of merchandise purchased from ENS at December 31, Year 5, and $250,000 at December 31, Year 4. During Year 5, sales from ENS to RAV were $600,000. Merchandise was priced at the same profit margin as applicable to other customers. RAV owed $150,000 to ENS at December 31, Year 5, and $157,000 at December 31, Year 4.
- On July 1, Year 2, ENS purchased a building from RAV for $750,000. The building had an original cost of $800,000 and a net book value of $600,000 on RAV's books on July 1, Year 2. ENS estimated the remaining life of the building was 15 years at the time of the purchase from RAV.
- ENS rented another building from RAV throughout the year for $5,000 per month.
- RAV uses the equity method of accounting for its long-term investments.
- Both companies pay tax at the rate of 40 percent. Ignore deferred income taxes when allocating and amortizing the acquisition differential.

Required:

(a) Prepare a consolidated income statement for the year ended December 31, Year 5.
(b) Prepare the current assets and property, plant, and equipment sections of the consolidated balance sheet at December 31, Year 5.

(c) Calculate non-controlling interest on the consolidated balance sheet at December 31, Year 4.

(d) If RAV had used the cost method instead of the equity method of accounting for its investment in ENS, would RAV's net income for Year 5 increase, decrease, or remain the same on
   (i) its separate entity income statement?
   (ii) the consolidated income statement?
   Briefly explain.

(*CGA-Canada adapted*)

Problem 14   Shown below are selected ledger accounts from the trial balance of a parent and its subsidiary as of December 31, Year 9.

	P Co.	S Co.
Investment in bonds of P	$ —	$ 39,000
Investment in shares of S (equity method)	139,899	—
Sales	630,000	340,000
Interest income	—	1,850
Investment income	15,339	—
Gain on sale of land	7,000	—
Common shares	300,000	100,000
Retained earnings	85,000	50,000
Bonds payable 8 percent	198,000	—
Cost of sales	485,000	300,000
Interest expense	17,000	—
Selling and administrative expense	50,000	20,000
Income tax expense	34,000	8,740
Dividends	10,000	8,000

Additional Information

- P Company purchased its 90 percent interest in S Company in Year 1, on the date that S Company was incorporated, and has followed the equity method to account for its investment since that date.
- On April 1, Year 5, land that had originally cost $15,000 was sold by S Company to P Company for $21,000. P purchased the land with the intention of developing it, but in Year 9 it decided that the location was not suitable and the land was sold to a chain of drug stores.
- On January 1, Year 2, P Company issued $200,000 face value bonds due in 10 years. The proceeds from the bond issue amounted to $190,000.
- On July 1, Year 9, S Company purchased $40,000 of these bonds on the open market at a cost of $38,750. Intercompany bondholding gains (losses) are allocated between the two affiliates.
- S Company had $75,000 in sales to P Company during Year 9.
- Use income tax allocation at a 40 percent tax rate.

Required:

(a) Prepare a consolidated income statement for Year 9.
(b) Prepare a consolidated statement of retained earnings for Year 9.

Problem 15   Financial statements of Champlain Ltd. and its 80-percent-owned subsidiary Samuel Ltd. as at December 31, Year 5, are presented below.

STATEMENTS OF FINANCIAL POSITION — at December 31, Year 5

	Champlain	Samuel
Property, plant, and equipment	$198,000	$ 104,000
Accumulated depreciation	(86,000)	(30,000)
Investment in Samuel — at cost	129,200	—
Inventories	35,000	46,000
Accounts receivable	60,000	55,000
Cash	18,100	20,600
	$354,300	$195,600
Common shares	$225,000	$ 50,000
Retained earnings	68,300	70,000
Dividends payable	5,000	5,500
Accounts payable	56,000	70,100
	$354,300	$195,600

STATEMENTS OF INCOME AND RETAINED EARNINGS
for the Year Ended December 31, Year 5

	Champlain	Samuel
Sales	$535,400	$270,000
Dividend and miscellaneous income	9,900	—
	545,300	270,000
Cost of sales	364,000	206,000
Selling expense	78,400	24,100
Administrative expense (including depreciation and goodwill impairment)	46,300	20,700
Income taxes	13,800	6,200
	502,500	257,000
Profit	42,800	13,000
Retained earnings, January 1	45,500	68,000
Dividends paid	(20,000)	(11,000)
Retained earnings, December 31	$ 68,300	$ 70,000

Additional Information

- Champlain acquired 8,000 common shares of Samuel on January 1, Year 1, for $129,200. Samuel's shares were trading for $14 per share on the date of acquisition. The retained earnings of Samuel were $12,000 on that date, and there have been no subsequent changes in the common shares account. On January 1, Year 1, fair values were equal to carrying values except for the following:

	Carrying value	Fair value
Inventory	$50,000	$32,000
Patent	–0–	14,000

- The patent of Samuel had a remaining legal life of eight years on January 1, Year 1, and any goodwill was to be tested annually for impairment. As a result, impairment losses occurred as follows:

Pertaining to	Year 2	Year 4	Year 5
Champlain's purchase	$21,000	$13,800	$19,200
Non-controlling interest's share	4,000	2,600	3,600
	$25,000	$16,400	$22,800

- On January 1, Year 5, the inventories of Champlain contained items purchased from Samuel on which Samuel had made a profit of $1,900. During Year 5, Samuel sold goods to Champlain for $92,000, of which $21,000 remained unpaid at the end of the year. Samuel made a profit of $3,300 on goods remaining in Champlain's inventory at December 31, Year 5.
- On January 1, Year 3, Samuel sold equipment to Champlain at a price that was $21,000 in excess of its book value. The equipment had an estimated remaining life of six years on that date.
- Champlain sold a tract of land to Samuel in Year 2 at a profit of $7,000. This land is still held by Samuel at the end of Year 5.
- Assume a corporate tax rate of 40 percent.

Required:

(a) Prepare the following consolidated financial statements:
   (i) Income statement.
   (ii) Retained earnings statement.
   (iii)Statement of financial position.
(b) Explain how the historical cost principle supports the elimination of the profit on the sale of the equipment from Samuel to Champlain when preparing Samuel's consolidated financial statements.
(c) If Champlain had used the parent company extension theory rather than the entity theory, how would this affect the return on equity attributable to shareholders of Champlain for Year 5?
(d) Calculate goodwill and non-controlling interest on the consolidated statement of financial position at December 31, Year 5, under the parent company extension theory.

Problem 16   On December 31, Year 1, the Peach Company purchased 80 percent of the outstanding voting shares of the Orange Company for $964,000 in cash. The balance sheet of Orange on that date and the fair values of its tangible assets and liabilities were as follows:

	Book value	Fair value
Cash and accounts receivable	$ 200,000	$175,000
Inventories	300,000	300,000
Plant and equipment	600,000	800,000
Accumulated depreciation	(100,000)	
	$1,000,000	
Current liabilities	$ 100,000	100,000
Long-term liabilities	200,000	216,850
Common shares	500,000	
Retained earnings	200,000	
	$1,000,000	

The difference between the fair value and the book value of cash and accounts receivable of the subsidiary at December 31, Year 1, was adjusted by Orange in Year 2. At the acquisition date, the plant and equipment had an estimated remaining useful life of 10 years with no residual value. The long-term liabilities mature on December 31, Year 6. Any goodwill arising from the business combination will be tested for impairment. Peach uses the cost method to account for its investment in Orange. Both Peach and Orange use the straight-line method to calculate all depreciation for depreciable assets and amortization of premiums or discounts on long-term liabilities.

The statements of income and changes in retained earnings of the two companies for the year ending December 31, Year 5, were as follows:

	Peach	Orange
Sales of merchandise	$6,000,000	$1,000,000
Other revenues	200,000	20,000
Total revenues	6,200,000	1,020,000
Cost of goods purchased	2,525,000	390,000
Change in inventory	(25,000)	10,000
Depreciation expense	500,000	80,000
Interest expense	400,000	16,000
Other expenses (including income tax)	1,300,000	194,000
Total expenses	4,700,000	690,000
Net income	1,500,000	330,000
Retained earnings, 1/1/Year 5	4,200,000	300,000
Dividends	(200,000)	(50,000)
Retained earnings, 31/12/Year 5	$5,500,000	$ 580,000

Additional Information

- Goodwill impairment losses were recorded as follows: Year 2, $3,600; Year 4, $30,000; Year 5, $11,200.
- On December 31, Year 4, Orange sold a warehouse to Peach for $54,000. It had been purchased on January 1, Year 3, for $100,000 and had an estimated 20-year life on that date with no salvage value.
- During Year 4, Orange sold merchandise that it had purchased for $120,000 to Peach for $250,000. None of this merchandise had been resold by Peach by December 31, Year 4. Both companies account for inventories on the first-in, first-out basis.
- Peach had sales of $200,000 to Orange during Year 4, which gave rise to a gross profit of $125,000. This inventory was resold by Orange during Year 4 for $225,000.
- During Year 5, Orange sold merchandise that had been purchased for $160,000 to Peach for $300,000. Since the sales occurred in December of Year 5, all of this merchandise remained in the December 31, Year 5, inventories of Peach and had not been paid for by Peach.
- During September Year 5, Peach had sales of $280,000 to Orange, which increased Peach's gross profit by $160,000. By December 31, Year 5, one-half of this merchandise had been sold to the public by Orange.

- On January 1, Year 5, Peach sold to Orange for $28,000 a machine that had cost $40,000. On January 1, Year 5, it had been depreciated for six years of its estimated eight-year life.
- During Year 5, Peach charged Orange $25,000 for management fees.
- Assume a 40 percent corporate tax rate.

Required:

(a) Prepare a consolidated income statement for Peach and its subsidiary, Orange, for the year ending December 31, Year 5. Assume that the loss from sale of the warehouse will be eliminated.

(b) Prepare a consolidated statement of retained earnings for Peach and its subsidiary, Orange, for the year ending December 31, Year 5.

(c) Explain the rationale for not always eliminating losses on intercompany sales of depreciable assets when preparing consolidated financial statements.

(d) Assume that Orange pays interest annually at the rate of 8 percent on its long-term liabilities. When Peach acquired Orange on December 31, Year 1, the fair value of Sloan's long-term liabilities would have produced an effective yield of 6 percent. Calculate interest expense and non-controlling interest on the consolidated income statement assuming that Peach and Orange use the effective-interest method to account for their long-term liabilities.

(SMA *adapted*)

Problem 17 On January 1, Year 1, Handy Company (Handy) purchased 70 percent of the outstanding common shares of Dandy Limited (Dandy) for $7,000. On that date, Dandy's shareholders' equity consisted of common shares of $250 and retained earnings of $4,500.

The financial statements for Handy and Dandy for Year 6 were as follows:

BALANCE SHEETS
at December 31, Year 6

	Handy	Dandy
Cash	$ 1,340	$ 780
Accounts receivable	2,800	1,050
Inventory	3,400	2,580
Property, plant, and equipment — net	4,340	3,010
Investment in Dandy	7,000	—
Total	$18,880	$7,420
Current liabilities	$ 4,200	$ 540
Long-term liabilities	3,100	1,230
Common shares	1,000	250
Retained earnings	10,580	5,400
Total	$18,880	$7,420

STATEMENTS OF INCOME AND RETAINED EARNINGS
year ended December 31, Year 6

	Handy	Dandy
Sales	$21,900	$7,440
Cost of sales	14,800	3,280
Gross profit	7,100	4,160
Other revenue	1,620	—
Selling and administrative expense	(840)	(420)
Other expenses	(5,320)	(2,040)
Income before income taxes	2,560	1,700
Income tax expense	800	680
Net income	1,760	1,020
Retained earnings, beginning of year	10,420	5,180
Dividends paid	(1,600)	(800)
Retained earnings, end of year	$10,580	$5,400

Additional Information

- In negotiating the purchase price at the date of acquisition, it was agreed that the fair values of all of Dandy's assets and liabilities were equal to their book values, except for the following:

	Book value	Fair value
Inventory	$2,100	$2,200
Equipment	2,500	3,000

- Both companies use FIFO to account for their inventory and the straight-line method for amortizing their property, plant, and equipment. Dandy's equipment had a remaining useful life of 10 years at the acquisition date.

- Goodwill is not amortized on a systematic basis. However, each year, goodwill is evaluated to determine if there has been a permanent impairment. It was determined that goodwill on the consolidated balance sheet should be reported at its recoverable amount of $1,100 on December 31, Year 5, and $1,030 on December 31, Year 6.

- During Year 6, inventory sales from Dandy to Handy were $5,000. Handy's inventories contained merchandise purchased from Dandy for $2,000 at December 31, Year 5, and $2,500 at December 31, Year 6. Dandy earns a gross margin of 40 percent on its intercompany sales.

- On January 1, Year 2, Handy sold some equipment to Dandy for $1,000 and recorded a gain of $200 before taxes. This equipment had a remaining useful life of eight years at the time of the purchase by Dandy.

- Handy charges $50 per month to Dandy for consulting services and has been doing so throughout Years 5 and 6.

- Handy uses the cost method of accounting for its long-term investment.

- Both companies pay taxes at the rate of 40 percent.

- Amortization expense is grouped with production expenses, and impairment losses are grouped with other expenses.

Required:

(a) Prepare a consolidated statement of income for the year ended December 31, Year 6. Show supporting calculations.

(b) Calculate consolidated retained earnings at January 1, Year 6, and then prepare a consolidated statement of retained earnings for the year ended December 31, Year 6. Show supporting calculations.

(c) Explain how the historical cost principle supports the adjustments made on consolidation when there has been an intercompany sale of equipment.

(d) Calculate goodwill impairment loss and non-controlling interest on the consolidated income statement for the year ended December 31, Year 6, under the parent company extension theory.

(CGA-Canada adapted)

*Problem 18   SENS Ltd. acquired equipment on January 1, Year 1, for $500,000. The equipment was depreciated on a straight-line basis over an estimated useful life of 10 years.

On January 1, Year 3, SENS sold this equipment to MEL Corp., its parent company, for $420,000. MEL is depreciating this equipment on a straight-line basis over an estimated useful life of 8 years.

MEL and SENS revalue their property, plant, and equipment to fair value each year under IAS 16 and transfer the revaluation surplus to retained earnings over the useful life of the asset or upon sale of the asset. The fair value of this equipment was $460,000 at the end of Year 1, $415,000 at the end of Year 2, and $370,000 at the end of Year 3. When the equipment is revalued to fair value, both the original cost and accumulated depreciation are grossed up for the increase in value.

Required:

Assume that this equipment is the only equipment owned by the two companies and ignore income tax. Compute the balances that would appear in MEL's separate-entity statements, SENS's separate-entity statements, and MEL's consolidated statements for Years 1, 2, and 3 for each of the following:

(a) Equipment.

(b) Accumulated depreciation.

(c) Accumulated other comprehensive income — revaluation surplus.

(d) Gain on sale of equipment.

(e) Depreciation expense.

WEB-BASED PROBLEMS

Problem 1   Access the most recent consolidated financial statements for Vodafone, a British company. (Go to the investor relations section at www.vodafone.com.) Answer the questions below. For each question, indicate where in the financial statements you found the answer and/or provide a brief explanation.

(a) Are the expenses on the income statement presented by function or nature? Briefly explain.

(b) What is amortization on the other intangible assets during the year and why does amortization expense not appear as a separate component on the income statement?

(c) Review the useful lives of the company's intangible and tangible assets. If you had to pick one instance where you felt that the useful life was either understated or overstated, which asset would it be and why?

(d) What portion of the company's assets is property, plant, and equipment? Has the portion increased or decreased from last year?

(e) How does the company value its plant and equipment?

(f) Assume that one of the subsidiaries sold equipment to the parent two years ago and reported a substantial gain. The parent still owns and uses this equipment. Due to an oversight, the intercompany gain has never been eliminated when preparing the consolidated statements. What is the impact of this error on total asset turnover and return on assets for the current year?

*(g) Now assume that the company changes its policy to report its plant and equipment at fair value. Also, assume that the fair value of plant and equipment is greater than its carrying value. What impact would this change in policy have on return on equity for the year and the share price for the company?

Problem 2   Access the most recent financial statements for Siemens, a German company. (Go to the investor relations section at www.siemens.com.) Answer the same questions as in Problem 1. For each question, indicate where in the financial statements you found the answer and/or provide a brief explanation. (Some questions may not be applicable.)

Chapter 8 Consolidated Cash Flows and Ownership Issues

LEARNING OBJECTIVES

After studying this chapter, you should be able to do the following:

1. Prepare a consolidated cash flow statement by applying concepts learned in prior courses and unique consolidation concepts discussed here.
2. Prepare consolidated financial statements in situations where the parent's ownership has increased (step purchase).
3. Prepare consolidated financial statements after the parent's ownership has decreased.
4. Prepare consolidated financial statements in situations where the subsidiary has preferred shares in its capital structure.
5. Calculate consolidated net income attributable to the shareholders of the parent and non-controlling interest in situations where a parent has direct and indirect control over a number of subsidiary companies.

INTRODUCTION

Different classes of shares typically have different voting and/or different dividend rights.

While it is still the norm for the capital structure of a company to consist of common and/or preferred shares, some companies no longer use the terms *common shares* and *preferred shares* to describe their shares. Instead, they may use terms such as *Class A* and *Class B* shares and then describe the essential features of the shares. Celestica Inc., a world leader in the delivery of innovative electronics manufacturing services, refers to its two classes of shares as *subordinate voting shares* and *multiple voting shares*. The subordinate shares entitle the holder to one vote per share, whereas the multiple voting shares entitle the holder to 25 votes per share. The holders of the subordinate voting shares and multiple voting shares are entitled to share ratably in any dividends of the company. Onex Corporation, one of Canada's largest corporations, with global operations in the services, manufacturing, and technology industries, owns the multiple voting shares of Celestica, while the non-controlling shareholders own most of the subordinated voting shares. This share distribution gives Onex Corporation 79 percent of the votes but only 13 percent of the dividends. The non-controlling interests get 21 percent of the votes but 87 percent of the dividends.

Up to now in this text, the companies involved in the business combination had only common shares outstanding, and the parent obtained control over the subsidiary in one purchase. Later in this chapter, we will consider situations where the subsidiary also has preferred shares outstanding and situations where the parent's ownership interest changes. We commence the chapter with a discussion of certain factors that are unique to the overall consolidation process and that must be considered when the consolidated cash flow statement is prepared.

Consolidated Cash Flow Statement

Under the indirect method, we start with net income and show the adjustments to convert it to a cash basis.

In the previous chapters we illustrated the direct approach to preparing the consolidated balance sheet and the consolidated income and retained earnings statements. In this approach, the individual statements of the parent and its subsidiaries are combined. We will now focus on the preparation of the final consolidated statement — the cash flow statement. While this statement could be prepared by combining the separate cash flow statements of the parent and its subsidiaries, this would involve eliminating all intercompany transactions, including intercompany transfers of cash. It is much easier to prepare the cash flow statement using comparative consolidated balance sheets and the consolidated income statement, because these statements do not contain any intercompany transactions. In all the illustrations in this chapter, we will assume that cash flows from operations are presented using the indirect method, whereby net income is adjusted for the effects of non-cash items such as amortizations and changes in working capital items, and for gains and losses associated with investing and financing cash flows. If the direct method were used, only the items affecting cash would be presented in the first place. Therefore, we would not need to adjust for non-cash items.

The change in cash can be determined by analyzing the change in non-cash items during the period.

The preparation of the cash flow statement for a single unconsolidated company is well covered in introductory and intermediate accounting texts. The basic process used to determine the reasons for the change in cash or cash equivalents is one of analyzing the changes that have occurred in all non-cash items on the balance sheet. The procedures used to carry out this analysis (a working paper or a series of T-accounts) will not be repeated here. Instead, we will describe items that are unique to consolidated statements and that must be taken into account in the analysis. The major items that require special attention are summarized below:

The consolidated cash flow statement contains adjustments for items that are unique to consolidated financial statements such as amortization of acquisition differential.

1. Acquisition-date fair value differences are amortized in the consolidated income statement. While some of the amortizations may be obvious from their descriptions in the income statement, others may be buried in expense accounts. Because amortizations have no effect on cash flows, we must adjust the year's net income for them in order to arrive at cash flow from operations.

2. Dividends paid by subsidiaries to the parent company do not change the entity's cash. Dividends paid by the parent to its shareholders, and dividends paid by the subsidiaries to non-controlling shareholders, reduce the cash of the consolidated entity. The dividends paid to non-controlling shareholders must be disclosed or presented separately and can be presented as either an operating or a financing activity.

3. A change in the parent's ownership percentage during the year requires a careful analysis to determine its effect on consolidated assets, liabilities, and equities. This will be illustrated in a later section of this chapter (on ownership changes).

4. In the year that a subsidiary is acquired, special disclosures are required in the cash flow statement. The following example illustrates this.

The consolidated balance sheet of Parent Company and its five subsidiaries as at December 31, Year 1, is shown below.

PARENT COMPANY
CONSOLIDATED BALANCE SHEET
at December 31, Year 1

Cash	$ 500,000
Other assets	900,000
Goodwill	120,000
	$1,520,000
Liabilities	$ 500,000
Common shares	200,000
Retained earnings	720,000
Non-controlling interest	100,000
	$1,520,000

On January 2, Year 2, Parent acquired 80 percent of the outstanding common shares of its sixth subsidiary, Sable Ltd., for a total cost of $140,000. The shareholders of Sable received cash of $90,000 and common shares of Parent with a market value of $50,000 in this transaction. The management of Parent determined that the other assets of Sable had a fair value of $205,000 on this date. The balance sheet of Sable on December 31, Year 1, is shown below:

SABLE LTD.
BALANCE SHEET
at December 31, Year 1

This is the separate-entity balance sheet of Sable.

Cash	$ 30,000
Other assets	200,000
	$230,000
Liabilities	$ 70,000
Common shares	100,000
Retained earnings	60,000
	$230,000

Parent's journal entry to record the acquisition of 80 percent of the common shares of Sable would be as follows on January 2, Year 2:

This entry is recorded on the separate-entity records for Parent.

Investment in Sable Ltd.	140,000	
Common shares		50,000
Cash		90,000

We will now prepare the consolidated balance sheet of Parent on January 2, Year 2, incorporating the latest acquisition.

The calculation and allocation of the acquisition differential for the Sable investment is shown on the following page:

The components of the acquisition differential are reported on the consolidated balance sheet.

Cost of 80% investment in Sable	$140,000
Implied value of 100% of Sable	$175,000
Book value of Sable	160,000
Acquisition differential	15,000
Allocated:	
Other assets	5,000
Goodwill	$ 10,000
Non-controlling interest (175,000 × 20%)	$ 35,000

The consolidated balance sheet appears below:

PARENT COMPANY
CONSOLIDATED BALANCE SHEET
at January 2, Year 2

The assets and liabilities of the subsidiary are added to the consolidated balance sheet.

Cash (500,000 + 30,000 − **90,000**)	$ 440,000
Other assets (900,000 + 200,000 + **5,000**)	1,105,000
Goodwill (120,000 + **10,000**)	130,000
	$1,675,000
Liabilities (500,000 + 70,000)	$ 570,000
Common shares (200,000 + **50,000**)	250,000
Retained earnings	720,000
Non-controlling interest (100,000 + **35,000**)	135,000
	$1,675,000

Preparing the Consolidated Cash Flow Statement

We can now prepare the consolidated cash flow statement for the two-day period that has elapsed by analyzing the changes in the two consolidated balance sheets. We know that the only transaction that has taken place is Parent's acquisition of 80 percent of Sable. The journal entry of Parent to record the acquisition was illustrated earlier. If we were preparing the cash flow statement of the parent company, we would use our knowledge of this entry in our analysis. But we are preparing the consolidated cash flow statement, and the account "Investment in Sable" does not appear in the consolidated balance sheet. In order to do the proper analysis we need to visualize the effect of this new acquisition on the consolidated balance sheet. We can depict this effect in the form of a "consolidating entry" in the following manner:

This entry shows the incremental effect of purchasing the subsidiary.

Cash	**30,000**	
Other assets (200,000 + 5,000)	**205,000**	
Goodwill	**10,000**	
Liabilities		**70,000**
Non-controlling interest		**35,000**
Cash		90,000
Common shares		50,000

Notice that the portion of the entry shown in boldface is the amount of the account "Investment in Sable" that made up the parent's acquisition journal entry. Using this analysis, we would normally show the purchase of other assets and goodwill as cash outflows from investing activities and the increase in liabilities,

The investment account is replaced by the underlying assets and liabilities in the consolidation process.

non-controlling interest, and common shares as cash inflows from financing activities. However, IAS 7 requires that only the net cash outflow from a business combination be presented on the cash flow statement and the details of the changes in non-cash accounts arising from the business combination be disclosed in the notes to financial statements.[1] Therefore, the consolidated cash flow statement for Parent Company would be presented as follows:

PARENT COMPANY
CONSOLIDATED CASH FLOW STATEMENT
for the Two-day Period Ended January 2, Year 2

Only the net change in cash is presented on the consolidated cash flow statement.

Operating cash flow:	$ nil
Investing cash flow:	
Acquisition of Sable, less cash acquired in acquisition $30,000 (note 1)	(60,000)
Financing cash flow:	nil
Net change in cash for the two-day period	(60,000)
Cash, December 31, Year 1	500,000
Cash, January 2, Year 2	$440,000

Note 1: Effective January 2, Year 2, the company acquired 80% of the common shares of Sable for a total consideration of $140,000. The acquisition, which was accounted for by the acquisition method, is summarized as follows:

The details of the changes in non-cash items are disclosed in the notes to the consolidated cash flow statement.

Net assets acquired:	
Other assets	$205,000
Goodwill	10,000
Liabilities	(70,000)
Non-controlling interest	(35,000)
	$110,000
Consideration given:	
Common shares	$ 50,000
Cash	90,000
	140,000
Less cash acquired on acquisition	30,000
	$110,000

Notice that the only item appearing on the cash flow statement is a $60,000 cash outflow under investing activities. The $60,000 is the difference between the cash paid for the shares of the subsidiary ($90,000) and the cash held by the subsidiary on the date of acquisition ($30,000). The other assets acquired and liabilities assumed in the business acquisition are not shown on the face of the cash flow statement as investing and financing activities but are disclosed in the notes to the financial statements. So, when we prepare a cash flow statement, we must differentiate between those changes in non-cash items arising from a business combination and those changes arising from other activities. Those changes arising from the business combination are netted and given one line on the cash flow statement, with the details disclosed in the notes to the financial statements. The other changes are presented on the face of the cash flow statement according to normal practices.

In our discussion of the consolidated cash flow statement, we have focused entirely on items unique to consolidated statements, on the assumption that the overall

---

[1] IAS 7, paragraphs 39 and 40.

process for preparing such statements has been covered in earlier financial accounting courses. The next major topic in this chapter, *ownership change*, also presents items that require analysis as to their effects on consolidated cash flows. The cash flow effects for these ownership changes will be discussed in the appropriate sections.

Changes in Parent's Ownership Interest

The parent's percentage of ownership can change when the parent buys or sells shares of the subsidiary or when the subsidiary issues or repurchases shares.

A parent's ownership interest will change if

(a) the parent purchases additional holdings in its subsidiary (block acquisitions); or

(b) the parent sells some of its holdings in its subsidiary; or

(c) the subsidiary issues additional common shares to the public, and the parent does not maintain its previous ownership percentage; or

(d) the subsidiary repurchases some of its common shares from the non-controlling interest.

Any time the parent's percentage of ownership increases, we will account for the transaction as a purchase. Any time the parent's percentage decreases, we will account for the transaction as a sale.

When the parent's ownership changes, the percentage of subsidiary common shares held by the non-controlling interest also changes. The major consolidation problem involved with ownership change is the effect such changes have on the valuation of subsidiary net assets and non-controlling interest in the consolidated statements. When the parent's ownership percentage *increases*, a portion of the unamortized acquisition differential will be transferred from the non-controlling interest to the parent. When the parent's ownership *decreases*, a portion of the unamortized acquisition differential will be transferred from the parent to the non-controlling interest. We will use a comprehensive example to illustrate various changes in a parent's ownership interest. We will begin with step-by-step acquisitions.

Block Acquisitions of Subsidiary (Step Purchases)

The subsidiary is valued at fair value on the consolidated balance on the date the parent obtains control.

The consolidation illustrations that we have used in previous chapters have assumed that the parent company achieved its control in a subsidiary by making a single purchase of the subsidiary's common shares. On the date of acquisition, the fair values of the subsidiary's assets (including goodwill) and liabilities were determined and then brought onto the consolidated balance sheet along with the book values of the parent's assets and liabilities. The non-controlling interest at the date of acquisition was also valued at fair value. In periods subsequent to the date of acquisition, the subsidiary's net assets were accounted for based on the values determined at the date of acquisition. They were not revalued to fair value at each reporting date.

We will now consider a situation where the parent achieves its control position through a series of block acquisitions (sometimes described as step purchases).

Purchase of First Block of Shares   On January 1, Year 1, Par Company acquires 1,000 common shares (10 percent of the outstanding shares) of Star Company for $20,000. The 10 percent voting interest does not give Par control or significant influence. The investment is classified as fair value through profit or loss. On this date, the shareholders' equity of Star consists of common shares of $100,000 and retained earnings of $70,000. During Year 1, Star reported net income of $10,000 and did not declare any dividends. At the end of Year 1, the fair value of Star's shares was $22 per share.

Par's journal entries for Year 1 for the FVTPL investment are shown on the following page:

FVTPL investments are reported at fair value at each reporting date.

Investment in Star	20,000	
Cash		20,000
To record purchase of 1,000 shares of Star for $20 per share		

Investment in Star	2,000	
Gain on Star		2,000
To record unrealized gain on FVTPL investment in Star		

The acquisition differential at the date of acquisition is ignored. Par's share of Star's income for the year is also ignored because the investment is reported at its fair value of $22,000 at the end of Year 1.

Purchase of Second Block of Shares   On January 1, Year 2, Par acquires another 2,000 common shares of Star for $44,000. The book values of Star's net assets are equal to fair values except for specialized equipment, which is undervalued by $10,000. The equipment has an estimated remaining useful life of five years. During Year 2, Star reported a net income of $30,000 and paid dividends of $20,000. At December 31, Year 2, the fair value of Star's shares was $25 per share.

The equity method is used once the investor obtains significant influence.

Par now owns 30 percent of Star and has obtained significant influence in the key decisions for Star. As a result, Star is now an associate and Par will now adopt the equity method of accounting for its 30 percent interest. The change in reporting method will be accounted for prospectively as a change in estimate because the circumstances changed from not having significant influence to having significant influence.[2] In our current example, the investment in Star will reflect the fair value of Star's share at January 1, Year 2. Par paid fair value for the 2,000 shares it just purchased. The carrying amount of the previous investment also reflects its fair value because as a FVTPL investment it must be reported at fair value.

If the previous investment had been reported at cost, it would not have been revalued when the equity method was first adopted. The carrying amount of the investment in Star after the new investment would be the sum of the previous carrying amount (i.e., cost of previous investment) and the cost of the new investment.

Under the equity method, an acquisition differential is calculated and subsequently amortized, similar to the process used for consolidation. The acquisition differential is first calculated when the equity method first becomes applicable and is calculated as if the entire 30 percent were purchased on this date. The purchase price incorporates the cost of the current purchase plus the carrying value of prior purchases.

The calculation and allocation of the acquisition differential as at January 1, Year 2, is as follows:

The acquisition differential must be allocated and amortized under the equity method.

Amount paid for 30% of Star (20,000 + 2,000 + 44,000)		$66,000
Book value of Star's net assets:		
Common shares	100,000	
Retained earnings (70,000 + 10,000)	80,000	
Total shareholders' equity	180,000	
Par's ownership interest	30%	54,000
Acquisition differential		12,000
Allocated:		
Equipment (10,000 × 30%)		3,000
Goodwill		$ 9,000

---

[2] See page 52 for a further discussion of changes to and from the equity method.

Since the fair value of Star's shares went up during Year 2, there appears to be no impairment in Star's goodwill. The fair value excess attributed to the equipment must be amortized over its useful life of five years. Par's journal entries for Year 2 for the significant-influence investment would be as follows:

Investment in Star	44,000	
Cash		44,000
To record purchase of 2,000 shares of Star for $22 per share		

Investment in Star	9,000	
Investment income		9,000
To record 30% of reported income for the year (30% × 30,000)		

Investment income	600	
Investment in Star		600
To record amortization of acquisition differential related to equipment (3,000/5 years)		

Cash	6,000	
Investment in Star		6,000
To record dividends received during the year (30% × 20,000)		

The investment is not reported at fair value under the equity method.

The balance in the investment account at the end of Year 2 is $68,400 (22,000 + 44,000 + 9,000 − 600 − 6,000). The fair value of the investment is $75,000 (3,000 shares × $25 per share) but is ignored under the equity method.

Purchase of Third Block of Shares On January 1, Year 3, Par acquires another 1,000 common shares of Star for $25,000. The book values of Star's net assets are equal to fair values except for specialized equipment, which is undervalued by $8,000. The equipment has an estimated remaining useful life of four years. During Year 3, Star reported a net income of $40,000 and paid dividends of $20,000. At December 31, Year 3, the fair value of Star's shares was $29 per share.

Par now owns 40 percent of Star, still has significant influence in the key decisions for Star, and will continue using the equity method. An acquisition differential for this 10 percent step is calculated and allocated as follows:

A separate allocation of the acquisition differential should be prepared for each incremental investment.

Cost of 10% of Star		$25,000
Book value of Star's net assets:		
Common shares	100,000	
Retained earnings (80,000 + 30,000 − 20,000)	90,000	
Total shareholders' equity	190,000	
Par's ownership interest	10%	19,000
Acquisition differential		6,000
Allocated:		
Equipment (8,000 × 10%)		800
Goodwill		$ 5,200

There are now two separate and incremental calculations and allocations of acquisition differential based on the purchase price for each step. The allocation for the 30 percent step is carried forward with its previous values and is not revalued to fair value on the date of the third step. The following acquisition-differential amortization schedule is prepared to keep track of the allocation and amortization of the acquisition differentials for each step:

ACQUISITION-DIFFERENTIAL AMORTIZATION SCHEDULE

	Second Step		Third Step		
	Equip.	Goodwill	Equip.	Goodwill	Total
Jan 1, Year 2, purchase	$3,000	$9,000			$12,000
Amortization for Year 2	(600)				(600)
Balance, December 31, Year 2	2,400	9,000			11,400
Jan 1, Year 3, purchase			$800	$5,200	6,000
Amortization for Year 3	(600)		(200)		(800)
Balance, December 31, Year 3	$1,800	$9,000	$600	$5,200	$16,600

The previous block acquisitions are not normally revalued when there is a new acquisition.

Since the fair value of Star's shares went up during Year 3, there appears to be no impairment in Star's goodwill. The fair value excess attributed to the equipment is being amortized over its useful life.

Par's journal entries for Year 3 for the investment in Star, an associate, would be as follows:

Investment in Star	25,000	
Cash		25,000
To record purchase of 1,000 shares of Star for $25 per share		
Investment in Star	16,000	
Investment income		16,000
To record 40% of reported income for the year (40% × 40,000)		
Investment income	800	
Investment in Star		800
To record amortization of acquisition differential related to equipment		
Cash	8,000	
Investment in Star		8,000
To record dividends received during the year (40% × 20,000)		

The amortization of the acquisition differential is recorded in the investment account under the equity method.

The balance in the investment account at the end of Year 3 is $100,600 (68,400 + 25,000 + 16,000 − 800 − 8,000). The fair value of the investment is $116,000 (4,000 shares × $29 per share) but is ignored under the equity method.

Purchase of Fourth Block of Shares

On January 1, Year 4, Par acquires another 3,000 common shares of Star for $87,000. The book values of Star's net assets are equal to fair values except for specialized equipment, which is undervalued by $7,500. The equipment has an estimated remaining useful life of three years. During Year 4, Star reported a net income of $50,000 and paid dividends of $20,000. At December 31, Year 4, the fair value of Star's shares was $34 per share.

The investment account is adjusted to fair value when the investor first obtains control of the investee.

Par now owns 70 percent of Star and has control over Star. The business combination should be reported on a consolidated basis. The change in reporting method will be accounted for prospectively as a change in estimate because the circumstances changed from not having control to having control. IFRS 3 states that the subsidiary should be valued at fair value as of the acquisition date, and any gains or losses resulting from adjusting the investment to fair value should be recognized in income. If, before the business combination, the acquirer recognized changes in the value of its non-controlling equity investment in other comprehensive income, the amount that was recognized in other comprehensive income is reclassified and included in the calculation of any gain or loss as of the acquisition date. Therefore, Par will make the following entries on January 1, Year 4:

Investment in Star	15,400	
Unrealized gain on investment		15,400
To adjust investment in Star to fair value (116,000 − 100,600)		

Investment in Star	87,000	
Cash		87,000
To record purchase of 3,000 shares at $29 per share		

Any previous purchase price allocations are replaced by a new purchase price allocation on the date of a business combination.

The investment in Star now contains a balance of $203,000 (100,600 + 15,400 + 87,000), which is equal to the fair value of the 7,000 shares. When the parent first obtains control of the subsidiary, we must prepare a new calculation and allocation of the acquisition differential for the percentage ownership at the time of the purchase to reflect the revaluation of the entire subsidiary to fair value. In so doing, we will ignore the acquisition differentials and amortizations from the previous steps. The acquisition-differential calculation and amortization for the 70 percent interest as at January 1, Year 4 is as follows:

The acquisition differential is calculated and allocated to value the subsidiary at 100 percent of its fair value.

Value of 70% of Star		$203,000
Implied value of 100% of Star		$290,000
Book value of Star's net assets:		
Common shares	100,000	
Retained earnings (90,000 + 40,000 − 20,000)	110,000	
Total shareholders' equity		210,000
Acquisition differential		80,000
Allocated:		
Equipment		7,500
Goodwill		$ 72,500

Since the fair value of Star's shares went up during Year 4, there appears to be no impairment in Star's goodwill. The fair value excess attributed to the equipment must be amortized over its useful life of three years. The following acquisition-differential amortization schedule is prepared to keep track of the allocation and amortization of the acquisition differential.

ACQUISITION-DIFFERENTIAL AMORTIZATION SCHEDULE

	Balance Jan. 1, Year 4	Amortization Year 4	Balance Dec. 31, Year 4
Equipment	$ 7,500	$2,500	$ 5,000
Goodwill	72,500		72,500
	$80,000	$2,500	$77,500

Assuming that Par continues to use the equity method on its separate-entity books, the journal entries for Year 4 would be as follows:

Investment in Star	35,000	
Investment income		35,000
To record 70% of reported income for the year (70% × 50,000)		

Only the parent's share of the amortization of the acquisition differential is recorded in the parent's books.

Investment income	1,750	
Investment in Star		1,750
To record Par's share of amortization of acquisition differential related to equipment (70% × 2,500)		

Cash	14,000	
Investment in Star		14,000
To record dividends received during the year (70% × 20,000)		

The investment account is not adjusted to fair value subsequent to the date of acquisition.

The balance in the investment account at the end of Year 4 is $222,250 (203,000 + 35,000 − 1,750 −14,000). The fair value of the investment is $238,000 (7,000 shares × $34 per share) but is ignored under the equity method and under consolidation.

Purchase of Fifth Block of Shares   On January 1, Year 5, Par acquires another 2,000 common shares of Star for $68,000. The book values of Star's net assets are equal to fair values except for specialized equipment, which is undervalued by $6,000. The equipment has an estimated remaining useful life of two years. During Year 5, Star reported a net income of $60,000 and paid dividends of $20,000. At December 31, Year 5, the fair value of Star's shares was $38 per share.

Par now owns 90 percent of Star, continues to have control over Star, and continues to report its investment on a consolidated basis. However, it does not treat this additional purchase like the other step purchases; i.e., it does not calculate an acquisition differential for this purchase and does not revalue the existing acquisition differential. The transaction is treated as an equity transaction, i.e., a transaction with owners in their capacity as owners. Simply put, the parent is acquiring an additional 20 percent of Star from the non-controlling interests. In such circumstances, the carrying amount of the portion of the non-controlling interests sold to the parent will be allocated to the parent. Any difference between the amount by which the non-controlling interests are adjusted and the fair value of the consideration paid or received by the parent must be recognized as a direct charge or credit to owners' equity and attributed to the owners of the parent.

The subsidiary's net assets are not revalued on the consolidated financial statements when the parent's percentage ownership increases.

The carrying amount of the non-controlling interests sold to the parent was $63,500, calculated as follows:

Star's common shares	$100,000
Star's retained earnings (110,000 + 50,000 − 20,000)	140,000
	240,000
Unamortized acquisition differential	77,500
	317,500
Non-controlling interests' percentage ownership	30%
Non-controlling interests at December 31, Year 4	$ 95,250
Portion sold to controlling interest (20,000/30,000)	$ 63,500

Any difference between the amount paid and the carrying amount of net assets being purchased from the non-controlling interest is recognized as a direct charge or credit to owner's equity.

Since Par paid $68,000 for the shares, it paid $4,500 more than the carrying amount previously attributed to these shares on the consolidated balance sheet. This

$4,500 would be recognized as a direct charge to consolidated retained earnings on the date of the purchase.

Since the fair value of Star's shares went up during the year, there appears to be no impairment in Star's goodwill. The acquisition-differential amortization schedule for Year 5 is as follows:

	Balance Jan. 1, Year 5	Amortization Year 5	Balance Dec. 31, Year 5
Equipment	$ 5,000	$2,500	$ 2,500
Goodwill	72,500		72,500
	$77,500	$2,500	$75,000

Assuming that Par continues to use the equity method on its separate-entity books, the journal entries for Year 5 would be as follows:

These entries are recorded on the separate-entity books of the parent.

Investment in Star	63,500	
Retained earnings	4,500	
Cash		68,000

To record purchase of 2,000 shares at $34 per share

Investment in Star	54,000	
Investment income		54,000

To record 90% of reported income for the year (90% × 60,000)

Investment income	2,250	
Investment in Star		2,250

To record Par's share of amortization of acquisition differential related to equipment (90% × 2,500)

Cash	18,000	
Investment in Star		18,000

To record dividends received during the year (90% × 20,000)

The balance in the investment account at the end of Year 5 is $319,500 (222,250 + 63,500 + 54,000 − 2,250 − 18,000). The investment account can be segregated as follows:

The investment account can be reconciled to the subsidiary's equity at any point in time when the parent uses the equity method.

Book value of Star's net assets:	
Common shares	$100,000
Retained earnings (140,000 + 60,000 − 20,000)	180,000
Total shareholders' equity	280,000
Unamortized acquisition differential	75,000
	355,000
Par's ownership interest	90%
Total	$319,500

Similarly, the non-controlling interest can be calculated using these same components as follows:

Non-controlling interest on the balance sheet comprises the non-controlling interest's share of the subsidiary's equity and the unamortized acquisition differential at the balance sheet date.

Book value of Star's net assets:		
Unamortized acquisition differential	$280,000	
	75,000	
	355,000	
Non-controlling interest's ownership interest	10%	$35,500

We will now illustrate the consolidation process by using the following condensed balance sheets for Par and Star at the end of Year 5:

	Par	Star
Investment in Star (equity method)	$ 319,500	
Equipment — net	500,000	$140,000
Other assets	700,000	490,000
	$1,519,500	$630,000
Liabilities	$ 450,000	$350,000
Common shares	500,000	100,000
Retained earnings	569,500	180,000
	$1,519,500	$630,000

The parent's retained earnings under the equity method are equal to consolidated retained earnings.

The consolidated balance sheet at December 31, Year 5, is as follows:

PAR COMPANY
CONSOLIDATED BALANCE SHEET
at December 31, Year 5

Both the parent's and the non-controlling interest's shares of the unamortized acquisition differential appear on the consolidated balance sheet.

Equipment — net (500,000 + 140,000 + **2,500**)	$ 642,500
Other assets (700,000 + 490,000)	1,190,000
Goodwill (0 + 0 + **72,500**)	72,500
	$1,905,000
Liabilities (450,000 + 350,000)	$ 800,000
Common shares	500,000
Retained earnings	569,500
Non-controlling interest	35,500
	$1,905,000

Numerous small purchases can be grouped into one block purchase when calculating and allocating the acquisition differential.

Numerous Small Purchases   Assume that Par attempts to purchase the remaining outstanding shares of Star by making daily open-market purchases of the subsidiary's shares. At the end of two months it abandons the idea. During this period it has made 35 separate share purchases that in total represent 4 percent of the subsidiary's outstanding shares. Since it would be impractical to calculate 35 acquisition differentials, these purchases can be combined and treated as a single block purchase of 4 percent.

Repurchase of Shares by Subsidiary   When the subsidiary repurchases and cancels some or all of the common shares being held by the non-controlling shareholders, the parent's percentage ownership in the common shares will increase. The increase in ownership will be accounted for as an equity transaction similar to the purchase of the fifth block of shares.

Consolidated Retained Earnings — Cost Method   The examples used to illustrate block purchases have assumed that the parent company uses the equity method to account for its investment. When the parent has used the cost method, a calculation adjusting to the equity method is required when consolidated statements are prepared. This calculation has been extensively illustrated in earlier chapters and requires only slight modification when block acquisitions have been made.

In our comprehensive example, Par used the equity method during the period it had control of Star. If Par had used the cost method for internal record keeping, it would have adopted the cost method when it first obtained control of Star on January 1, Year 4. It would simply have added the $87,000 cost of the purchase to the carrying amount of the investment at that point. It would not likely have made any adjustment to value the investment at fair value as required for consolidation purposes. If so, the balance in the investment account at December 31, Year 5, would have been $271,000 and retained earnings would have been $521,000. Consolidated retained earnings would be calculated as follows:

CALCULATION OF CONSOLIDATED RETAINED EARNINGS
at December 31, Year 5

Retained earnings of parent — cost method		$505,600
Adjust investment account to fair value at date of business combination		15,400
Adjusted retained earnings of parent at date of business combination, Jan. 1, Year 4		521,000
Less: Parent's share of acquisition-differential amortizations		
Year 4 purchase	1,750	
Year 5 purchase	2,250	(4,000)
Retained earnings of subsidiary at the time of		
Year 5 purchase	140,000	
Retained earnings of subsidiary at the time of		
Year 4 purchase	110,000	
Increase since Year 4 purchase	30,000	
Parent's ownership percentage	70%	21,000
Retained earnings of subsidiary — Dec. 31, Year 5	180,000	
Retained earnings of subsidiary at the time		
of Year 5 purchase	140,000	
Increase since Year 5 purchase	40,000	
Parent's ownership percentage	90%	36,000
Loss on purchase of shares from non-controlling interest, Jan. 1, Year 5		(4,500)
Consolidated retained earnings		$569,500

Consolidated retained earnings should recognize the parent's percentage ownership for each step of the step-by-step acquisitions.

Consolidated Cash Flow Analysis   Par Company's fifth block purchase of shares (on January 1, Year 5, for $68,000) requires further analysis to determine the effect on the Year 5 consolidated balance sheet. This cash has left the consolidated entity, so the effect of the transaction must appear on the Year 5 consolidated cash flow statement. We can depict the effect of the fifth purchase on the consolidated balance sheet with the following entry:

Retained earnings	4,500	
Non-controlling interest	63,500	
Cash		68,000

The cost of purchasing additional shares in the subsidiary should be reported in financing activities on the consolidated cash flow statement.

This transaction simply reallocated shareholders' equity between the controlling and non-controlling interests. The $68,000 cash outflow should appear in the financing activities section of the cash flow statement and would be described as "Purchase of additional shares in subsidiary from non-controlling interests."

Disclosure Requirements   The disclosure requirements for a business combination were listed on page 90. Deloitte has developed Model Financial Statements under IFRSs. Excerpts to illustrate the disposal of a subsidiary and the disposal of a portion of a subsidiary from Deloitte's 2009 model financial statements are presented in Exhibit 8.1 on page 396.

Exhibit 8.1

**EXTRACTS (IN PART) FROM DELOITTE'S 2009 MODEL
FINANCIAL STATEMENTS**

**Notes to the consolidated
financial statements**

3.3 Basis of consolidation

Subsidiaries are consolidated from the date of control to the date control is lost.

The results of subsidiaries acquired or disposed of during the year are included in the consolidated statement of comprehensive income from the effective date of acquisition and up to the effective date of disposal, as appropriate.

Changes in the Group's interests in subsidiaries that do not result in a loss of control are accounted for as equity transactions. The carrying amounts of the Group's interests and the non-controlling interests are adjusted to reflect the changes in their relative interests in the subsidiaries. Any difference between the amount by which the non-controlling interests are adjusted and the fair value of the consideration paid or received is recognised directly in equity and attributed to owners of the Company.

When the Group loses control of a subsidiary, the profit or loss on disposal is calculated as the difference between (i) the aggregate of the fair value of the consideration received and the fair value of any retained interest and (ii) the previous carrying amount of the assets (including goodwill), and liabilities of the subsidiary and any non-controlling interests. Amounts previously recognised in other comprehensive income in relation to the subsidiary are accounted for (i.e. reclassified to profit or loss or transferred directly to retained earnings) in the same manner as would be required if the relevant assets or liabilities were disposed of. The fair value of any investment retained in the former subsidiary at the date when control is lost is regarded as the fair value on initial recognition for subsequent accounting under IAS 39 *Financial Instruments: Recognition and Measurement* or, when applicable, the cost on initial recognition of an investment in an associate or jointly controlled entity.

3.4 Business combinations

The subsidiary is valued at fair value at the acquisition date.

Where a business combination is achieved in stages, the Group's previously held interests in the acquired entity are remeasured to fair value at the acquisition date (i.e. the date the Group attains control) and the resulting gain or loss, if any, is recognised in profit or loss. Amounts arising from interests in the acquiree prior to the acquisition date that have previously been recognised in other comprehensive income are reclassified to profit or loss, where such treatment would be appropriate if that interest were disposed of.

19. Subsidiaries

Details of the Company's subsidiaries at 31 December 2009 are as follows.

Name of subsidiary	Principal activity	Place of incorporation and operation	Proportion of ownership interest and voting power held	
			31/12/09	31/12/08
Subzero Limited	Manufacture of toys	A Land	Nil	100%
Subone Limited	Manufacture of electronic equipment	A Land	90%	100%

During the period, the Group disposed of 10% of its interest in Subone Limited, reducing its continuing interest to 90%. The proceeds on disposal of CU213,000 were received in cash.

An amount of CU179,000 (being the proportionate share of the carrying amount of the net assets of Subone Limited) has been transferred to non-controlling interests (see note 31). The difference of CU34,000 between that amount and the consideration received has been credited to retained earnings.

31. Non-Controlling Interests

	2009 CU'000	2008 CU'000
Balance at beginning of year	20,005	17,242
Share of profit for the year	4,000	2,763
Non-controlling interests arising on the acquisition of Subsix Limited	132	—
Additional non-controlling interests arising on disposal of interest in Subone Limited (see note 19)	179	—
Balance at end of year	24,316	20,005

NCI increases when the parent sells a portion of its shares in the subsidiary.

45. Disposal of Subsidiary

On 30 November 2009, the Group disposed of Subzero Limited which carried out all of its toy manufacturing operations.

45.1 Consideration received

	Year ended 31/12/09 CU'000	Year ended 31/12/08 CU'000
Consideration received in cash and cash equivalents	7,854	—
Deferred sales proceeds	960	—
Total consideration received	8,814	—

45.2 Analysis of asset and liabilities over which control was lost

Companies must disclose details of the change in assets and liabilities due to the loss of control of the subsidiary.

	Year ended 31/12/09 CU'000	Year ended 31/12/08 CU'000
Current assets		
Cash and cash equivalents	288	—
Trade receivables	1,034	—
Inventories	2,716	—
Non-current assets		—
Property, plant and equipment	5,662	—
Goodwill	3,080	—
Current liabilities		
Payables	(973)	—
Non-current liabilities		
Borrowings	(4,342)	—
Deferred tax liabilities	(471)	—
Net assets disposed of	6,994	—

45.3 Gain on disposal of subsidiary

	Year ended 31/12/09 CU'000	Year ended 31/12/08 CU'000
Consideration received	8,814	—
Net assets disposed of	(6,994)	—
Non-controlling interests	—	—
Cumulative gain/loss on available-for-sale financial assets reclassified from equity on loss of control of subsidiary	—	—
Cumulative exchange differences in respect of the net assets of the subsidiary and related hedging instruments reclassified from equity on loss of control of subsidiary	120	—
Gain on disposal	1,940	—

The gain on disposal is included in the profit for the year from discontinued operations in the [statement of comprehensive income/income statement]. *(continued)*

45.4 Net cash inflow on disposal of subsidiary

	Year ended 31/12/09 CU'000	Year ended 31/12/08 CU'000
Consideration received in cash and cash equivalents	7,854	—
Less: cash and cash equivalent balances disposed of	(288)	—
	7,566	—

Source: Deloitte Touche Tohmatsu, www.iasplus.com/fs/fs.htm#2009ifrsmod.

Parent Sells Some of Its Holdings in Subsidiary

Let's continue with the previous illustration involving Par and Star. Assume that on January 1, Year 6, Par sold 900 shares in Star Company on the open market for $34,200.

Note that after the sale, Par's ownership percentage is 81 percent (8,100 ÷ 10,000). Note also that Par has disposed of 10 percent of its investment in Star (900 ÷ 9,000). Another way of calculating the percentage of investment disposed is as follows:

Ownership before sale	90%
Ownership after sale	81%
Change	9%

Percentage of investment sold: 9 ÷ 90 = 10%

Gains (losses) on transactions with shareholders are credited (charged) directly to shareholders' equity.

Since Par still has control of Star, consolidated financial statements will continue to be prepared. This transaction is, once again, treated as an equity transaction, i.e., a transaction between shareholders of the consolidated entity. The parent is selling part of its interest in Star to the non-controlling interest. The carrying amount of the portion sold is $31,950 (10% × 319,500); it will be allocated from the parent to the non-controlling interest. Since the amount received was $34,200, the owners of the parent are better off by $2,250 as a result of this transaction. This benefit is not reported in net income since it is a transaction between owners. The gain will be recognized as a direct increase to consolidated contributed surplus.

Since the equity method should produce the same results as the consolidated financial statements, Par would make the following entry to record the sale of 900 shares:

Cash	34,200	
Investment in Star (10% × $319,500)		31,950
Contributed surplus		2,250

Non-controlling interest is increased by the carrying value of the shares sold by the parent.

The total unamortized acquisition differential to be reported on the consolidated financial statements would remain the same in total. However, the portion belonging to the non-controlling interest would increase because the non-controlling interest now owns 19 percent of the subsidiary. The portion belonging to the controlling interest would decrease because the parent has sold 10 percent of its interest.

The following schedule shows the change in values for the controlling and non-controlling interests as a result of Par's sale of 900 shares:

	Controlling Interest			Non-controlling Interest		
	Before	Sold	After	Before	Bought	After
Percentage ownership	90%	9%	81%	10%	9%	19%
Share of Star's shareholders' equity	$252,000	$25,200	$226,800	$28,000	$25,200	$53,200
Unamortized acquisition differential						
Equipment	2,250	225	2,025	250	225	475
Goodwill	65,250	6,525	58,725	7,250	6,525	13,775
Total	$319,500	$31,950	$287,550	$35,500	$31,950	$67,450

We will now illustrate the consolidation process by using the following condensed balance sheets for Par and Star at January 1, Year 6. The previous balance sheets have been updated for the entry to record the sale of 900 shares by Par.

	Par	Star
Investment in Star (319,500 − 31,950)	$ 287,550	
Equipment — net	500,000	$140,000
Other assets (700,000 + 34,200)	734,200	490,000
	$1,521,750	$630,000
Liabilities	$ 450,000	$350,000
Common shares	500,000	100,000
Retained earnings	569,500	180,000
Contributed surplus	2,250	
	$1,521,750	$630,000

The consolidated balance sheet at January 1, Year 6, is as follows:

PAR COMPANY
CONSOLIDATED BALANCE SHEET
At January 1, Year 6

The subsidiary's net assets are not revalued when the parent sells a portion of its investment in the subsidiary.

Equipment — net (500,000 + 140,000 + **2,025 + 475**)	$ 642,500
Other assets (734,200 + 490,000)	1,224,200
Goodwill (**58,725 + 13,775**)	72,500
	$1,939,200
Liabilities (450,000 + 350,000)	$ 800,000
Common shares	500,000
Retained earnings	569,500
Contributed surplus	2,250
Non-controlling interest	67,450
	$1,939,200

The sale of the shares to the non-controlling interest increased the entity's cash by $34,200. This cash inflow must appear on the consolidated cash flow statement. We can depict the effect of the sale on the consolidated balance sheet with the following entry:

Cash	34,200	
Non-controlling interest		31,950
Contributed surplus		2,250

The proceeds from selling shares in the subsidiary should be reported in financing activities on the consolidated cash flow statement.

This transaction simply reallocated shareholders' equity between the controlling and non-controlling interests. The $34,200 cash inflow should appear in the financing activities section of the cash flow statement and would be described as "Sale of shares in subsidiary to non-controlling interest."

Income Statement Analysis

On December 31, Year 6, Star reported a net income of $40,000 and paid dividends amounting to $15,000. A goodwill impairment test conducted on December 31, Year 6, indicated that an impairment loss of $6,000 had occurred. The following acquisition-differential amortization schedule would be made on December 31, Year 6:

ACQUISITION-DIFFERENTIAL AMORTIZATION AND IMPAIRMENT SCHEDULE

	Balance Jan. 1, Year 6	Amortization/Impairment Year 6	Balance Dec. 31, Year 6
Equipment	$ 2,500	$2,500	$ 0
Goodwill	72,500	6,000	66,500
	$75,000	$8,500	$66,500

Note that the Year 6 amortization completely eliminates the acquisition differential related to the equipment because this is the last year of the equipment's useful life.

Par's equity method journal entries for Year 6 would be as follows:

Investment in Star	32,400	
Investment income		32,400
To record 81% of Star's net income for Year 6 (40,000 × 81%)		

Cash	12,150	
Investment in Star		12,150
To record dividends received from Star in Year 6 (15,000 × 81%)		

Investment income	6,885	
Investment in Star		6,885
To record Par's share of amortization of the acquisition differential for Year 6 (8,500 × 81%)		

Dividends received from the subsidiary are recorded as a reduction in the investment account under the equity method.

The following are the Year 6 income statements of Par and Star:

	Par	Star
Miscellaneous revenue	$200,000	$150,000
Investment income	25,515	—
	225,515	150,000
Miscellaneous expenses	130,000	90,000
Equipment depreciation expense	—	20,000
	130,000	110,000
Net income	$ 95,515	$ 40,000

Investment income is replaced with the revenues and expenses of Star, the amortization of the acquisition differentials, and the non-controlling interest. The Year 6 consolidated income statement prepared using the direct approach appears below:

PAR COMPANY
CONSOLIDATED INCOME STATEMENT
Year Ended December 31, Year 6

Miscellaneous revenues (200,000 + 150,000)	$350,000
Miscellaneous expenses (130,000 + 90,000)	220,000
Equipment depreciation (0 + 20,000 + **2,500**)	22,500
Goodwill impairment loss (0 + 0 + **6,000**)	6,000
	248,500
Net income	$101,500
Attributable to	
Shareholders of Par Company	$ 95,515
Non-controlling interest [19% × (40,000 − 8,500)]	5,985

The non-controlling interest is charged with its share of the amortization of the acquisition differential.

Subsidiary Issues Additional Shares to Public

Let us assume that Par did not sell 900 shares on January 1, Year 6, and that, instead, Star Company issued an additional 2,500 shares for $95,000 on January 1, Year 6. Star would record this transaction as follows:

Cash	95,000	
Common shares		95,000
To record the issuance of 2,500 shares		

The parent's percentage interest decreases when the subsidiary issues additional shares and the parent does not purchase any of the additional shares.

Star now has 12,500 common shares issued. Because Par did not buy any of the new issue, its holdings have remained constant (9,000 shares), but its ownership interest has declined to 72 percent (9,000 ÷ 12,500). This represents a 20 percent reduction in its investment, calculated as follows:

Ownership before share issue	90%
Ownership after share issue	72%
Change	18%
Percentage of investment reduced: 18 ÷ 90 = 20%	

The effect of this reduction on the unamortized acquisition differential is the same as if the parent had sold a portion of its holding in the subsidiary to the non-controlling interest. In this case, 20 percent of the parent's share of the unamortized acquisition differential has been "disposed of" as a result of the share issue. However, at this point the only entry made to record the transaction is the entry made by Star. Parent must also adjust its investment account to record the effect of this transaction on its investment. The following analysis indicates the amount of the adjustment:

The parent gave up 20 percent of its old investment and received 72 percent of the increase in the subsidiary's equity.

Loss due to reduction of investment account — 20% × 319,500	$63,900
Gain due to ownership of new assets resulting from subsidiary	
share issue — 72% × 95,000	68,400
Net benefit to parent due to share issue	$ 4,500

In our previous example, we explained the reasoning for removing 20 percent from the investment account. The unamortized acquisition differential is included in the $319,500 amount, and if this discrepancy has been reduced by 20 percent, a logical extension is to remove 20 percent from the total investment balance. If the subsidiary had issued the 2,500 shares for no consideration, the investment account would have to be reduced by $63,900, and a loss equal to that amount would be recorded by Par as a direct charge to owner's equity. But Star received $95,000 for its new share issue, and Par now owns 72 percent of the net assets of its subsidiary, including the additional cash received as a result of the new share issue. Par has gained by the 72 percent ownership interest in the assets received by Star. It should be obvious that the net charge or credit to owners' equity resulting from the transaction depends on the amount that the subsidiary received from its new share issue.

Gains (losses) on transactions with shareholders are not reported in net income.

This gain is not reported in net income since it is a transaction between owners. The gain will be recognized as a direct increase to consolidated contributed surplus and to the parent's separate-entity contributed surplus under the equity method. Given the facts of this particular example, Par would make the following journal entry under the equity method on January 1, Year 6:

Investment in Star	4,500	
Contributed surplus		4,500
To record the effect of subsidiary's issue of 2,500 shares on parent's investment		

As in our previous example, we assume that in Year 6, Star reported a net income of $40,000 and paid $15,000 in dividends. Par's equity method journal entries for Year 6 would be as follows:

Investment in Star	28,800	
Investment income		28,800
To record 72% of Star's net income for Year 6 (40,000 × 72%)		
Cash	10,800	
Investment in Star		10,800
To record dividends received from Star in Year 6 (15,000 × 72%)		

The parent absorbs 72 percent of the amortization of the acquisition differential.

Investment income	6,120	
Investment in Star		6,120
To record Par's share of the amortization of the acquisition differential for Year 6 (8,500 × 72%)		

The elimination of the parent's interest in the subsidiary's shareholders' equity against the parent's investment account leaves a balance equal to the unamortized acquisition differential. This will now be illustrated.

The investment account comprises the parent's share of the subsidiary's equity plus the unamortized acquisition differential.

Investment in Star		
Balance, December 31, Year 5		$319,500
Increase due to subsidiary share issue		4,500
Star net income (40,000 × 72%)		28,800
Star dividends (15,000 × 72%)		(10,800)
Acquisition-differential amortization		(6,120)
Balance, December 31, Year 6		335,880
Shareholders' equity of Star		
Common shares — December 31, Year 5	100,000	
Share issue — Year 6	95,000	
Common shares, December 31, Year 6	195,000	
Retained earnings, December 31, Year 6		
(180,000 + 40,000 − 15,000)	205,000	
Total, December 31, Year 6	400,000	
Par's ownership interest	72%	288,000
Balance — unamortized acquisition differential		$ 47,880

The unamortized acquisition differential is not revalued when the parent's percentage ownership changes as long as the parent still has control.

The amortization schedule on page 400 shows how the unamortized acquisition differential would be allocated to equipment and goodwill in the preparation of the consolidated balance sheet on December 31, Year 6. Non-controlling interest would appear in the amount of $130,620 (28% × [400,000 + 66,500]).

The Year 6 income statements of Par and Star are shown below, followed by the consolidated income statement.

	Par	Star
Miscellaneous revenue	$200,000	$150,000
Investment income	22,680	—
	222,680	150,000
Miscellaneous expenses	130,000	90,000
Equipment depreciation expense	—	20,000
	130,000	110,000
Net income	$ 92,680	$ 40,000

PAR COMPANY
CONSOLIDATED INCOME STATEMENT
Year Ended December 31, Year 6

Miscellaneous revenues (200,000 + 150,000)	$350,000
Miscellaneous expenses (130,000 + 90,000)	220,000
Equipment depreciation (0 + 20,000 + **2,500**)	22,500
Goodwill impairment loss (0 + 0 + **6,000**)	6,000
	248,500
Net income	$101,500
Attributable to	
Shareholders of Par Company	$ 92,680
Non-controlling interest [28% × (40,000 − 8,500)]	8,820

Consolidated Cash Flow Analysis   To recap, the issue of 2,500 shares on January 1, Year 6, was recorded by Star Company with the following journal entry:

Cash	95,000	
Common shares		95,000

Also, in order to record the effect of the reduction on its investment, Par made the following journal entry on this date:

Investment in Star	4,500	
Contributed surplus		4,500

The effect of this transaction on the consolidated financial statements can be depicted as follows and as shown in the calculation on the next page:

The consolidated entity received cash from the non-controlling interest.

Cash	95,000	
Non-controlling interest		90,500
Contributed surplus		4,500

CHANGES IN NON-CONTROLLING INTEREST

Non-controlling interest can be reconciled to the subsidiary's shareholders' equity and the unamortized acquisition differential at any point in time.

NCI after subsidiary share issue		
Shareholders' equity before issue	$280,000	
New share issue	95,000	
Shareholders' equity after issue	375,000	
Unamortized acquisition differential	75,000	
	450,000	
NCI's share	28%	
		126,000
NCI before subsidiary share issue (see page 394)		35,500
Increase in non-controlling interest		$ 90,500

This transaction increased the equity of both the controlling and the non-controlling interests. The $95,000 cash inflow should appear in the financing activities section of the cash flow statement and would be described as "Issuance of shares by subsidiary to non-controlling interest."

Subsidiary with Preferred Shares Outstanding

All of the consolidation examples that we have used up to this point have assumed that the subsidiary companies have only one class of shares — common shares — in their capital structures. We now examine situations where the subsidiary also has preferred shares. The basic concepts of consolidation do not change, but when there is more than one class of shares outstanding, there is an additional problem involved in determining the amount of non-controlling interest in the net assets and net income of the subsidiary. The following example will illustrate the approach that is used.

Illustration — Preferred Shareholdings

On December 31, Year 1, the shareholders' equity of Sonco Inc. was as follows:

If the subsidiary were wound up today, how much of its equity would go to the preferred shareholders?

Preferred shares, $10 dividend, cumulative, redeemable at $105 per share Issued and outstanding 1,000 shares	$100,000
Common shares Issued and outstanding 30,000 shares	360,000
Total share capital	460,000
Retained earnings (note 1)	140,000
	$600,000

Note 1: On December 31, Year 1, dividends on preferred shares were one year in arrears.

On January 1, Year 2, Parco Ltd. purchased 27,000 common shares of Sonco for $450,000. The acquisition differential was allocated entirely to franchise agreements, to be amortized over a 10-year period.

Because the parent company acquired control by purchasing 90 percent of the voting common shares, the non-controlling interest consists of the shareholdings represented by 10 percent of the common shares and 100 percent of the preferred shares. In order to calculate any acquisition differential associated with the common share purchase, and the amount of the non-controlling interest in both classes of shares, it is necessary to split the shareholders' equity of Sonco into its preferred and common share capital components in the following manner:

The preferred shareholders would get the first $115,000 and the common shareholders would get the rest.

	Total	Preferred	Common
Preferred shares	$100,000	$100,000	$ —
Redemption premium on preferred	—	5,000	(5,000)
Common shares	360,000	—	360,000
Total share capital	460,000	105,000	355,000
Retained earnings	140,000	10,000	130,000
	$600,000	$115,000	$485,000

The $115,000 allocated to preferred share capital represents the total amount that the company would have to pay to the preferred shareholders if the preferred shares were redeemed on this date. It is made up of the redemption price on 1,000 shares ($105,000) and the one year's dividends in arrears ($10,000) on these shares.

By using the two components of shareholders' equity, both the acquisition differential and the non-controlling interest on the date of acquisition can be calculated, as follows:

Cost of 90% of common shares	$ 450,000
Implied value of 100% of Sonco's common shares	$ 500,000
Book value of common shares of Sonco	485,000
Acquisition differential	15,000
Allocated: franchise agreement	15,000
Balance	$ —0—
Non-controlling interest, January 1, Year 2	
Preferred shares (115,000 × 100%)	$ 115,000
Common shares (500,000 × 10%)	50,000
	$ 165,000

The acquisition differential on the common shares is calculated in the same way as before.

The preparation of the consolidated balance sheet on January 1, Year 2, will not be illustrated, but it should be obvious that the only difference from previous examples lies in how the non-controlling interest is calculated on this date.

The financial statements of Parco and Sonco on December 31, Year 2, are shown in Exhibit 8.2. Parco uses the cost method to account for its investment.

Exhibit 8.2

YEAR 2 INCOME STATEMENTS

	Parco	Sonco
Revenues — miscellaneous	$750,000	$420,000
Dividends from Sonco	27,000	—
	777,000	420,000
Expenses — miscellaneous	688,000	360,000
Net income	$ 89,000	$ 60,000

The parent received 90 percent of the dividends paid to common shareholders.

YEAR 2 RETAINED EARNINGS STATEMENTS

	Parco	Sonco
Balance, January 1	$381,000	$140,000
Net income	89,000	60,000
	470,000	200,000
Dividends	90,000	50,000
Balance, December 31	$380,000	$150,000

BALANCE SHEETS — December 31, Year 2

	Parco	Sonco
Assets — miscellaneous	$510,000	$810,000
Investment in Sonco — at cost	450,000	—
	$960,000	$810,000
Liabilities	$180,000	$200,000
Preferred shares	—	100,000
Common shares	400,000	360,000
Retained earnings	380,000	150,000
	$960,000	$810,000

The parent has an investment in the common shares of the subsidiary but no investment in the preferred shares.

In order to prepare the Year 2 consolidated financial statements, it is again necessary to split the shareholders' equity of Sonco into its preferred and common share components. Because there has been no change in total share capital, the allocation of this component is identical to the one made as at January 1 (see above). But retained earnings *has* changed, and so we will allocate the retained earnings statement in the following manner:

Any calculations involving the subsidiary's equity must be split between common and preferred shareholders.

	Total	Preferred	Common
Balance, January 1, Year 2	$140,000	$ 10,000	$130,000
Net income (see point 2)	60,000	10,000	50,000
	200,000	20,000	180,000
Dividends (see point 1)	50,000	20,000	30,000
Balance, December 31, Year 2	$150,000	$ —0—	$150,000

It is important to note the following regarding the allocation process:

1. All dividends in arrears plus the current year's dividends must be paid to preferred shareholders before any dividends are paid to common shareholders. In this situation the dividends paid by Sonco were as follows:

Preferred ($10 × 1,000 × 2 years)	$ 20,000
Common	30,000
	$ 50,000

The preferred shareholders' claim on income is one year's worth of dividends in any given year, whether or not dividends are declared in that year.

2. When preferred shares are cumulative, the preferred shareholders are entitled to income equal to the yearly dividend even when the company has no income or has suffered a loss for the year. This means that the net income (or loss) for a particular year must be allocated to its preferred and common shareholders. In the situation we are examining, the Year 2 net income is allocated as follows:

To preferred shareholders	$ 10,000
To common shareholders	50,000
Total net income	$ 60,000

The allocation of total shareholders' equity as at December 31, Year 2, can now be prepared as shown below:

	Total	Preferred	Common
Share capital	$460,000	$105,000	$355,000
Retained earnings	150,000	—0—	150,000
	$610,000	$105,000	$505,000

Because Parco has used the cost method to account for its investment, we must make the two calculations shown in Exhibit 8.3 before preparing the Year 2 consolidated financial statements:

The Year 2 consolidated financial statements are shown in Exhibit 8.4 on page 408.

Other Types of Preferred Shares

The amount of income, dividends, and equity belonging to the preferred shareholders depends on the rights of the preferred shareholders.

In the example above, the preferred shares are cumulative. If the shares were non-cumulative, net income would be allocated to the preferred shares only if preferred dividends were declared during the year, and of course dividends are never in arrears with this type of preferred share. If dividends are not declared in a particular year, no income would be allocated to the preferred shares because the preferred shareholders

Exhibit 8.3

The preferred shareholders' claim on income is one year's worth of dividends.

CALCULATION OF CONSOLIDATED NET INCOME, YEAR 2

Net income, Parco		$ 89,000
Less common dividends from Sonco (90% × 30,000)		27,000
		62,000
Net income, Sonco	60,000	
Less allocated to preferred shares	10,000	
Net income, common shares	50,000	
Less acquisition-differential amortization (15,000 ÷ 10)	1,500 **(a)**	
Adjusted income for common shares		48,500
Income for preferred shares		10,000
Consolidated net income		$120,500
Attributable to		
Shareholders of Parent (62,000 + 90% × 48,500)		$105,650 **(b)**
Non-controlling interest		
Preferred net income (100% × 10,000)	10,000	
Common net income (10% × 48,500)	4,850	
		14,850 **(c)**

The non-controlling interest owns all of the preferred shares and 10 percent of the common shares of the subsidiary.

CALCULATION OF NON-CONTROLLING INTEREST
at December 31, Year 2

Preferred equity	105,000 × 100%	$105,000
Common equity	(505,000 + 15,000 − **(a) 1,500**) × 10%	51,850
		$156,850 **(d)**

would never get a dividend for that year. If the preferred shares are participating, the allocation of net income will follow the participation provisions.

Subsidiary Preferred Shares Owned by Parent

Any acquisition differential related to the preferred shares should be treated similar to a retirement of the preferred shares by the subsidiary itself.

A parent company may own all or a portion of its subsidiary's preferred shares in addition to its common share investment. When the cost of the investment in preferred shares is different from the book value of the stock acquired, a problem arises as to how to treat the preferred share acquisition differential in the consolidated financial statements. Since preferred shares do not share in the value changes that take place in the subsidiary (the exception is fully participating shares), market price changes in preferreds result from changes in interest rates. Because of this, the acquisition differential should not be used to revalue the subsidiary's identifiable net assets or goodwill. Instead, the purchase of the preferred shares should be treated as a retirement of the preferred shares, which is a capital transaction. Consequently, the acquisition differential should be adjusted to consolidated contributed surplus or retained earnings. For example, assume that in addition to its common share investment in its subsidiary, a parent owns 30 percent of the subsidiary's non-cumulative preferred shares. The parent uses the equity method to account for both investments, and on December 31, Year 9, had retained earnings amounting to $136,500 and no contributed surplus. On this date, the acquisition differential from the 30 percent interest in preferred shares amounted to $11,865. Instead of presenting this amount among the assets on

Exhibit 8.4

Year 2 Consolidated Statements
(when subsidiary has preferred shares)

PARCO LTD.
CONSOLIDATED INCOME STATEMENT
for the Year Ended December 31, Year 2

The non-controlling interest includes all of the income pertaining to the preferred shares and 10 percent of the income pertaining to the common shares.

Revenues (750,000 + 420,000)	$1,170,000
Expenses (688,000 + 360,000 + **(3a) 1,500**)	1,049,500
Net income	$ 120,500
Attributable to	
Shareholders of Parent **(3b)**	$ 105,650
Non-controlling interest **(3c)**	14,850

PARCO LTD.
CONSOLIDATED RETAINED EARNINGS STATEMENT
for the Year Ended December 31, Year 2

Balance, January 1	$ 381,000
Net income	105,650
	486,650
Dividends	90,000
Balance, December 31	$ 396,650

PARCO LTD.
CONSOLIDATED BALANCE SHEET
at December 31, Year 2

Assets — miscellaneous (510,000 + 810,000)	$1,320,000
Franchise agreements (15,000 − **(3a) 1,500**)	13,500
	$1,333,500

The subsidiary's common and preferred shares do not appear on the consolidated balance sheet.

Liabilities (180,000 + 200,000)	$ 380,000
Common shares	400,000
Retained earnings	396,650
Non-controlling interest **(3d)**	156,850
	$1,333,500

the consolidated balance sheet, we should treat it as a premium to retire the preferred shares and deduct it from retained earnings so that consolidated retained earnings on December 31, Year 9, will be reported at $124,635 (136,500 − 11,865).

Indirect Shareholdings

When one company has control over another company, financial reporting by means of consolidated financial statements is required. In all examples that we have used up to this point, the parent has had a direct ownership of over 50 percent of the common shares of the subsidiary. We continue to assume that over 50 percent ownership of the voting shares is necessary for control, but we now modify the assumption to allow this percentage to be achieved by both direct and indirect ownership.

The following diagrams illustrate both direct and indirect holdings. In this first diagram, B and C are subsidiaries of A through direct control:

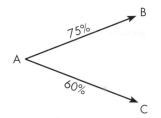

Both F and G are considered to be subsidiaries of E and therefore should be consolidated with E.

The second example, below, illustrates indirect control. G is a subsidiary of F, but F in turn is a subsidiary of E. Because E can control the voting shares of G through its control of F, G is also a subsidiary of E.

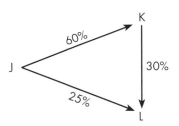

J can control L because it has control of 55 percent of the votes at L's shareholders' meetings.

In the third example, K is a subsidiary of J through direct control. L is also a subsidiary of J through indirect control, because 55 percent of its voting shares are controlled directly or indirectly by J, even though only 43 percent [25% + (60% × 30%)] of L's net income will flow to J under the equity method of accounting.

While many Canadian companies have intercorporate structures that are far more complex than those illustrated, the consolidation procedures for indirect holdings are not as complicated as the diagrams might indicate. Remember that if a parent company has 50 subsidiaries, the amount of cash appearing on the consolidated balance sheet is the sum of the cash from 51 separate balance sheets. This basic concept applies to most items appearing in the consolidated statements. In addition, we emphasized in past chapters the following statements that describe the fundamental relationships resulting from the parent's use of the equity method to account for its investment:

The parent's separate-entity net income under the equity method should be equal to consolidated net income attributable to the parent's shareholders.

1. The parent's net income equals consolidated net income attributable to the parent.
2. The parent's retained earnings equal consolidated retained earnings.
3. The elimination of the parent's share of the shareholders' equity of the subsidiary against the investment account leaves a balance consisting of the parent's share of the unamortized acquisition differential. This balance is used to revalue the net assets of the subsidiary when the consolidated balance sheet is prepared.
4. The portion of the shareholders' equity of the subsidiary that is not eliminated and the non-controlling interest's share of the unamortized acquisition differential appear on the consolidated balance sheet as non-controlling interest.

The principles applied when consolidating directly controlled subsidiaries apply equally well when consolidating indirectly controlled subsidiaries.

Since these fundamental relationships also apply when we have indirect holdings, the key to the preparation of consolidated statements when control is achieved by a mixture of direct and indirect investments is the use of the equity method of accounting for each investment for internal record-keeping purposes. (If the cost method has been used, adjustments to the equity method must be made.) The following example will illustrate these concepts.

Parent Inc. owns 80 percent of the common shares of Subone Ltd. (which is sufficient for control) and 45 percent of the common shares of Subtwo Ltd. (which we assume is not sufficient for control). However, Subone owns 25 percent of the common shares of Subtwo. This investment combined with the parent's 45 percent investment gives the parent control of 70 percent of the voting shares; therefore, Subtwo is considered to be a subsidiary of Parent.

Each investment is accounted for using the equity method for internal record-keeping purposes. In order to simplify the illustration, we assume that on acquisition date the fair values of the identifiable net assets of the investee corporations were equal to their book values, with the acquisition differentials from each investment being allocated to unrecorded computer databases.

We will illustrate the preparation of consolidated financial statements for Year 6, during which Parent had a net income from its own operations amounting to $135,000. Subone had a net income from its own operations amounting to $75,000, while the net income of Subtwo was $40,000. Exhibit 8.5, which shows the calculation of the Year 6 consolidated net income, is useful because it illustrates the use of the equity method of accounting by both Subone and Parent.

The amortization of the acquisition differential is allocated to the subsidiary to which it pertains.

Regarding the preparation and interpretation of Exhibit 8.5, the following should be noted:

1. Acquisition-differential amortizations are recorded by each company owned by another company in the group. This is the first adjustment shown. The amounts

---

Exhibit 8.5

CALCULATION OF CONSOLIDATED NET INCOME — Year 6

Subone accrues its share of Subtwo's income before Parent accrues its share of Subone's income.

	Parent	Subone	Subtwo	Total
Net income before investment income	$135,000	$75,000	$40,000	$250,000
Less database amortization — Subtwo			(300)	(300) **(a)**
			39,700	
Allocate Subtwo				
25% to Subone		9,925	(9,925)	
45% to Parent	17,865		(17,865)	
Less database amortization — Subone		(200)		(200) **(b)**
Consolidated net income	152,865	84,725	11,910	249,500
Allocate Subone				
80% to Parent	67,780	(67,780)		
Non-controlling interest		$16,945	$11,910	28,855 **(c)**
Parent net income — equity method	$220,645			
Consolidated net income attributable to parent				$220,645 **(d)**

have been assumed. Any adjustments required for intercompany gains and losses are also made here (as would the deduction for intercompany dividends if the cost method had been used by Parent and Subone).

2. Because Parent cannot record its 80 percent share of Subone's net income until Subone has recorded its 25 percent share of Subtwo's net income, Subtwo's net income is allocated first.

3. Subone's net income using the equity method can now be determined.

4. After Subone's net income has been allocated, Parent's net income using the equity method is determined. This amount, of course, equals consolidated net income.

5. The portion of the net income of Subtwo and Subone that was not allocated is the non-controlling interest in that net income.

6. The "Total" column shows amounts that appear in the consolidated income statement. Consolidated net income attributable to the parent is $220,645, while non-controlling interest is $28,855.

Exhibit 8.6 shows the Year 6 financial statements of the three companies.

The allocation of income to investors must start at the lowest level of the corporate hierarchy and work its way up.

Exhibit 8.6

INCOME STATEMENTS — Year 6

	Parent	Subone	Subtwo
Miscellaneous revenues	$475,000	$285,000	$90,000
Investment income — Subone	67,780	—	—
Investment income — Subtwo	17,865	9,925	—
	560,645	294,925	90,000
Miscellaneous expenses	340,000	210,000	50,000
Net income	$220,645	$ 84,925	$40,000

For these separate-entity statements, the investor has used the equity method to account for its investment.

RETAINED EARNINGS STATEMENTS — Year 6

	Parent	Subone	Subtwo
Balance, January 1	$279,120	$116,400	$ 80,000
Net income	220,645	84,925	40,000
	499,765	201,325	120,000
Dividends	45,000	30,000	10,000
Balance, December 31	$454,765	$171,325	$110,000

BALANCE SHEETS — December 31, Year 6

	Parent	Subone	Subtwo
Other assets	$608,500	$402,925	$460,000
Investment in Subone	281,900	—	—
Investment in Subtwo	104,365	53,400	—
	$994,765	$456,325	$460,000
Liabilities	$300,000	$110,000	$250,000
Common shares	240,000	175,000	100,000
Retained earnings	454,765	171,325	110,000
	$994,765	$456,325	$460,000

In preparing the Year 6 consolidated income statement, we eliminate the three investment income accounts and replace them with the revenues and expenses of the two subsidiaries, the database amortization expense, and the non-controlling interest in the net incomes of the subsidiaries. The consolidated retained earnings statement is identical to that of Parent and requires no preparation.

In preparing the consolidated balance sheet, we eliminate the investors' portion of the shareholders' equity of the investee companies against the investment accounts; this leaves a balance consisting of the unamortized acquisition differentials. The amount of shareholders' equity not eliminated represents non-controlling interest. The following calculations illustrate this:

The unamortized acquisition differential can be derived by backing out the parent's share of the subsidiary's equity from the investment account.

Parent:		
Investment in Subone		$281,900
Shareholders' equity, Subone		
Common shares	175,000	
Retained earnings	171,325	
	346,325	
Parent ownership	80%	277,060
Balance — Parent's share of unamortized databases		4,840
Non-controlling interest's share of unamortized databases (assumed)		1,210
Total unamortized databases from Subone		$ 6,050
Investment in Subtwo		$104,365
Shareholders' equity, Subtwo		
Common shares	100,000	
Retained earnings	110,000	
	210,000	
Parent's ownership	45%	94,500
Balance — Parent's share of unamortized databases		9,865

The unamortized acquisition differential relating to the non-controlling interest is an assumed figure, which must be incorporated in the consolidated financial statements.

Subone:		
Investment in Subtwo		53,400
Shareholders' equity, Subtwo (above)	210,000	
Subone ownership	25%	52,500
Balance — Investor's share of unamortized databases		900
Parent's total share of unamortized databases		10,765
Non-controlling interest's share of unamortized databases (assumed)		4,615
Total unamortized databases from Subtwo		$ 15,380

CALCULATION OF NON-CONTROLLING INTEREST
at December 31, Year 6

Shareholders' equity, Subone (346,325 × 20% + 1,210)	$ 70,475
Shareholders' equity, Subtwo (210,000 × 30% + 4,615)	67,615
	$138,090

Exhibit 8.7 shows the preparation of the Year 6 consolidated financial statements using the direct approach.

GAAP for Private Enterprises

- As mentioned in Chapter 3, private companies can either consolidate their subsidiaries or report their investments in subsidiaries under the cost or equity method.

Exhibit 8.7

PARENT INC.
CONSOLIDATED FINANCIAL STATEMENTS
December 31, Year 6

CONSOLIDATED INCOME STATEMENT

The consolidated income statement includes the amortization of the acquisition differential for a period of time for the directly controlled and indirectly controlled subsidiaries.

Miscellaneous revenues (475,000 + 285,000 + 90,000)	$850,000
Miscellaneous expense (340,000 + 210,000 + 50,000)	600,000
Database amortization ((**5a**) 300 + (**5b**) 200)	500
	600,500
Net income	$249,500
Attributable to	
Shareholders of Parent (**5d**)	$220,645
Non-controlling interest (**5c**)	28,855

CONSOLIDATED RETAINED EARNINGS STATEMENT

Balance, January 1	$279,120
Net income	220,645
	499,765
Dividends	45,000
Balance, December 31	$454,765

CONSOLIDATED BALANCE SHEET

The consolidated balance sheet includes the unamortized acquisition differential at a point in time for the directly controlled and indirectly controlled subsidiaries.

Other assets (608,500 + 402,925 + 460,000)	$1,471,425
Databases (**6,050 + 15,380**)	21,430
	$1,492,855
Liabilities (300,000 + 110,000 + 250,000)	$ 660,000
Common shares	240,000
Retained earnings	454,765
Non-controlling interest	138,090
	$1,492,855

- When consolidated statements are not prepared, any investment in preferred shares that are quoted in an active market should be reported at fair value, with any adjustments to fair value reported in net income. These are the rules normally applied to held-for-trading investments. Investments in preferred shares that are not quoted in an active market should be reported at cost less impairment and the impairment losses reported in net income.

U.S. GAAP Differences

U.S. GAAP and IFRSs for topics in this chapter are virtually the same.

SUMMARY

In this chapter we examined four topics that present special problems in consolidated financial statement preparation. While the consolidated balance sheet and income statement are prepared by combining the statements of the parent and its subsidiaries, the consolidated cash flow statement is best prepared by analyzing the changes in successive consolidated balance sheets.

The next topic was concerned with changes in the parent's percentage ownership and the effect that such changes have on the non-controlling interest and particularly on unamortized acquisition differentials. These ownership changes also require special attention when the consolidated cash flow statement is prepared.

Preferred shares in the capital structure of subsidiary companies present unique problems in calculating non-controlling interest if the parent's ownership of the preferred shares is not the same as its ownership of the common shares. The problem is solved by allocating shareholders' equity and any changes therein to preferred and common share components.

Control by a parent company can be achieved through direct ownership of the subsidiary's voting shares or through indirect ownership by other subsidiaries or investees. If the equity method is used for all of the investment accounts, the consolidation process is fairly easy, because the major problem involved with indirect holdings is how to determine the amount for non-controlling interest. If the cost method is used to account for the investments, we apply the basic procedure of adjusting from cost to equity, and then continue preparing the consolidated statements in the normal manner. This adjustment from cost to equity can be very involved when the affiliation structure is complex.

Significant Changes in the Last Two Years

1. For publicly accountable enterprises, IFRSs have replaced the former sections of the *CICA Handbook*. The following table shows the IFRSs covered in this chapter along with their counterparts from the former sections of the *CICA Handbook*:

IFRSs	CICA Handbook *Counterparts*
IFRS 3: Business Combinations	Section 1582: Business Combinations
IAS 27: Consolidated and Separate Financial Statements	Section 1601: Consolidated Financial Statements Section 1602: Non-controlling Interests
IAS 7: Statement of Cash Flows	Section 1540: Cash Flow Statements

2. Once the parent has control, any change in percentage ownerships without a loss of control is accounted for as an equity transaction. The unamortized acquisition differential is redistributed between the controlling and non-controlling interests. Any difference between the amount paid or received by the parent and the carrying value of the parent's investment is reported as a direct charge or credit to shareholders' equity.

Changes Expected in the Next Three Years

The direct method may be required for the cash flow statement. The notes to the financial statements would require a reconciliation of cash flows (starting point) to net income (ending point).

SELF-STUDY PROBLEM

On January 1, Year 1, X Company acquired 800 common shares of Y Company for $24,000 and 180 $5 cumulative, nonparticipating preferred shares for $19,800. On this date, the shareholders' equity accounts of Y Company were as follows:

Common shares (1,000 no par value shares issued)	$10,000
Preferred shares (200 no par value shares issued)	20,000
Retained earnings (note 1)	12,000

Note 1: Preferred dividends were two years in arrears on January 1, Year 1.

The income statements for the two companies for the year ended December 31, Year 5, are presented on the next page.

Additional Information

- Any acquisition differential is allocated to patents, to be amortized over 10 years.
- In Year 5, Y paid dividends totalling $9,000. Preferred dividends were two years in arrears on December 31, Year 4.
- X uses the cost method to account for its investment in Y.
- Y purchases merchandise for resale from X. In Year 5, Y purchased $33,000 in merchandise from X and had items in inventory on December 31, Year 5, on which X had made a profit of $2,500. The January 1, Year 5, inventory contained an intercompany profit of $1,400.
- X rents equipment from Y and in Year 5 paid a rental charge of $3,000 and recorded an account payable to Y of $2,000 for the balance of the rentals.
- On July 1, Year 3, Y sold a building to X at a profit of $13,000. X is depreciating this building on a straight-line basis over a 10-year useful life.
- Amortization and rent of tangible capital assets are included in distribution expense, whereas amortization of intangible assets is included in selling and administrative expense.
- Y paid $20,000 to X for management fees in Year 5.
- Assume a corporate tax rate of 40 percent.

	X Company	Y Company
Sales	$600,000	$400,000
Dividend and management fees	27,500	—
Rental revenue	—	11,200
	627,500	411,200
Cost of sales	343,900	234,700
Distribution expense	25,000	70,000
Selling and administrative expense	207,000	74,000
Interest expense	1,700	6,000
Income tax expense	20,000	9,000
	597,600	393,700
Profit	$ 29,900	$ 17,500

Required:

Prepare a consolidated income statement for Year 5.

Solution to Self-study Problem

Calculation of acquisition differential

Cost of 90% of preferred shares (180/200)		$19,800
Book value of preferred:		
Preferred shares	$20,000	
Dividends in arrears (200 × 5 × 2)	2,000	
	22,000	
	90%	19,800
Acquisition differential		$ -0-
Cost of 80% of common shares (800/1,000)		$24,000
Implied value of 100% of common shares		$30,000
Book value of common:		
Common shares	10,000	
Retained earnings	12,000	
Less preferred dividend arrears	(2,000)	
		20,000
Acquisition differential — patents		$10,000

Intercompany revenues and expenses

Dividends — preferred (90% × 1,000 × 3)		$ 2,700
— common (80% × [9,000 − 3,000])		4,800
		$ 7,500 **(a)**
Management fees		$20,000 **(b)**
Rent (3,000 + 2,000)		$ 5,000 **(c)**
Sales		$33,000 **(d)**

Intercompany profits

	Before tax	Tax 40%	After tax	
Opening inventory — X selling	$1,400	$ 560	$ 840	**(e)**
Closing inventory — X selling	$2,500	$1,000	$1,500	**(f)**
Building realized — Y selling	$1,300	$ 520	$ 780	**(g)**

Calculation of consolidated net income — for Year 5

X net income		$29,900
Less: Dividends from Y **(a)**	7,500	
Closing inventory profit **(f)**	1,500	9,000
		20,900
Add: opening inventory profit **(e)**		840
		21,740

	Total	Preferred	Common		
Y net income	17,500	1,000	16,500		
Less: Patent amortization (10,000 ÷ 10)			(1,000)	**(h)**	
Add: building profit **(g)**			780		
		1,000	16,280	**(i)**	17,280

Consolidated net income	$39,020
Attributable to	
Shareholders of Parent	
(21,740 + 90% × 1,000 + 80% × 16,280)	$35,664 **(j)**
Non-controlling interest	
(10% × 1,000 + 20% × 16,280)	3,356 **(k)**

CONSOLIDATED INCOME STATEMENT — for Year 5

Sales (600,000 + 400,000 − **(d) 33,000**)	$967,000
Dividend and management fees (27,500 + 0 − **(a) 7,500** − **(b) 20,000**)	0
Rental revenue (0 + 11,200 − **(c) 5,000**)	6,200
	973,200
Cost of sales (343,900 + 234,700 − **(d) 33,000** − **(e) 1,400** + **(f) 2,500**)	546,700
Distribution (25,000 + 70,000 − **(c) 5,000** − **(g) 1,300**)	88,700
Selling and administrative (207,000 + 74,000 − **(b) 20,000**) + **(h)1,000**)	262,000
Interest (1,700 + 6,000)	7,700
Income tax (20,000 + 9,000 + **(e) 560** + **(g) 520** − **(f) 1,000**)	29,080
	934,180
Net income	$ 39,020
Attributable to	
Shareholders of Parent **(i)**	$ 35,664
Non-controlling interest **(k)**	3,356

REVIEW QUESTIONS

1. Is the consolidated cash flow statement prepared in the same manner as the consolidated balance sheet and income statement? Explain.

2. A parent company acquired a 75 percent interest in a subsidiary company in Year 4. The acquisition price was $1,000,000, made up of cash of $700,000 and the parent's common shares with a current market value of $300,000. Explain how this acquisition should be reflected in the Year 4 consolidated cash flow statement.

3. Why is the amortization of the acquisition differential added back to consolidated net income to compute net cash flow from operating activities in the consolidated cash flow statement?

4. Why are dividend payments to non-controlling shareholders treated as an outflow of cash in the consolidated cash flow statement but not included as dividends paid in the consolidated retained earnings statement?

5. When should the change in accounting for a long-term investment from the cost method to the equity method be accounted for retroactively and when should it be accounted for prospectively?

6. When a parent increases its investment in a subsidiary from 60 to 75 percent, should the acquisition differential from the 60 percent purchase be revalued to fair value? Explain.

7. When a parent decreases its investment in a subsidiary from 76 to 60 percent, should the non-controlling interest be revalued to fair value? Explain.

8. A parent company will realize a loss or a gain when its subsidiary issues common shares at a price per share that differs from the carrying amount per share of the parent's investment, and the parent's ownership percentage declines. Explain why this is so. Also explain how the gain or loss is recognized in the financial statements.

9. If a gain or a loss is realized by a parent company as a result of the sale of a portion of the investment in a subsidiary, should the gain or loss be eliminated in the preparation of the consolidated income statement? Explain.

10. The shareholders' equity of a subsidiary company contains preferred and common shares. The parent company owns 100 percent of the subsidiary's common shares. Will the consolidated financial statements show non-controlling interest? Explain.

11. A company's net income for the year was $17,000. During the year, the company paid dividends on its non-cumulative preferred shares amounting to $12,000. Calculate the amount of the year's net income that "belongs to" the common shares.

12. Explain how an acquisition differential from an investment in preferred shares should be reflected in the consolidated financial statements.

13. Explain how the non-controlling interest in the net assets and net income of a subsidiary is reported when the parent owns 90 percent of the subsidiary's common shares and 30 percent of the subsidiary's cumulative preferred shares.

14. Explain the difference in the calculation of consolidated net income attributable to shareholders of parent and consolidated retained earnings depending on whether the preferred shares of a subsidiary are cumulative or non-cumulative.

15. What is the major consolidation problem associated with indirect shareholdings?

MULTIPLE-CHOICE QUESTIONS

Use the following information to answer Questions 1 to 4.

The abbreviated consolidated financial statements of Print Inc. and its subsidiary, Set Inc., for the two years ended December 31, Year 5 and Year 6, are presented below.

BALANCE SHEETS

	Year 6	Year 5	Increase (decrease)
Cash	$ 150,000	$ 290,000	$(140,000)
Accounts receivable	1,415,000	1,350,000	65,000
Inventory	380,000	400,000	(20,000)
Investment in Run Inc.	185,000	160,000	25,000
Plant and equipment (net)	1,270,000	900,000	370,000
	$3,400,000	$3,100,000	$ 300,000
Current liabilities	$ 520,000	$ 750,000	$(230,000)
10% debentures	800,000	600,000	200,000
Common shares	1,000,000	900,000	100,000
Retained earnings	900,000	700,000	200,000
Non-controlling interest	180,000	150,000	30,000
	$3,400,000	$3,100,000	$ 300,000

CONSOLIDATED INCOME AND RETAINED EARNINGS STATEMENT
for the Year Ended December 31, Year 6

Sales	$2,500,000
Cost of goods sold	1,140,000
Research and development expense	460,000
Administration expenses	355,000
	1,955,000
Net operating income	545,000
Investment income from Run	35,000
Net income	580,000
Less: non-controlling interest	80,000
Net income attributed to Print's shareholders	500,000
Retained earnings at January 1, Year 6	700,000
	1,200,000
Dividends declared and paid	300,000
Retained earnings at December 31, Year 6	$ 900,000

Additional Information

- Set is a 75-percent-owned subsidiary of Print.
- Print owns a 25 percent interest in Run that is accounted for using the equity method.
- During Year 6, Set declared and paid $200,000 in dividends and Run declared and paid $40,000 in dividends.
- Depreciation of $440,000 is included in the cost of goods sold and research and development expenses.

The questions are based on the preparation of Print's consolidated cash flow statement under the indirect method for the year ended December 31, Year 6.

1. Which of the following would be shown as an adjustment to Print's consolidated net income for investment income from Run?
   a. $0
   b. +$25,000
   c. +$35,000
   d. −$35,000

2. Which of the following is the correct presentation for the change in property, plant, and equipment in the investing section of Print's consolidated cash flow statement for the year ended December 31, Year 6?
   a. Purchase of property, plant, and equipment, −$370,000.
   b. Purchase of property, plant, and equipment, −$810,000.
   c. Proceeds from sale of property, plant, and equipment, +$370,000.
   d. Proceeds from sale of property, plant, and equipment, +$810,000.

3. Print classifies all dividend payments to and received from affiliated corporations as financing activities, along with its own dividend payments. Which of the following is the correct amount that must be presented for dividends paid to non-controlling interests on Print's consolidated cash flow statement for the year ended December 31, Year 6?
   a. $10,000
   b. $50,000
   c. $60,000
   d. $240,000

4. Which of the following is the correct amount that must be presented for dividends received from Run on Print's consolidated cash flow statement for the year ended December 31, Year 6?
   a. $0
   b. +$10,000
   c. +$30,000
   d. +$40,000

5. Which of the following best describes the disclosure required on the cash flow statement in the year a parent corporation acquires a controlling interest in a subsidiary corporation?
   a. The net investment should be presented as an operating activity.
   b. The net assets acquired, other than cash and cash equivalents, should be presented as an investing activity, and the method of financing the acquisition should be presented separately.
   c. The working capital assets acquired, other than cash and cash equivalents, should be presented as an operating activity; the long-term assets acquired should be presented as an investing activity; and the financing acquired should be presented as a financing activity.
   d. The net increase in the investment account should be presented as an investing activity, and no other presentation is required.

6. For which of the following situations would it be appropriate to prepare a consolidated statement for VAN, COU, and VER?
   a. VAN owns 60 percent of COU, and COU owns 40 percent of VER.
   b. VAN owns 40 percent of COU, and COU owns 60 percent of VER.
   c. VAN owns 20 percent of COU and 40 percent of VER, and COU owns 60 percent of VER.
   d. VAN owns 60 percent of COU, COU owns 40 percent of VER, and VER owns 60 percent of VAN.

(CGA-Canada adapted)

7. For which of the following situations would the subsidiary's identifiable assets and liabilities be valued at 100 percent of their fair value on the consolidated balance sheet?
   a. When the parent purchased additional shares of the subsidiary to increase its percentage ownership from 40 to 60 percent.
   b. When the parent purchased additional shares of the subsidiary to increase its percentage ownership from 60 to 80 percent.
   c. When the parent sold shares of the subsidiary to decrease its percentage ownership from 90 to 60 percent.
   d. When the parent sold shares of the subsidiary to decrease its percentage from 60 to 40 percent.

Use the following information to answer Questions 8 to 12.

Pot Inc. acquired an 80 percent interest in the common shares of Shot Inc. on July 1, Year 5, for $264,000. The equity sections of the statements of financial position for Pot and Shot at December 31, Year 4, were as follows:

	Pot	Shot
Common shares	$400,000	$200,000
Preferred shares (10,000 8% shares redeemable at $13 each)	—	100,000
Retained earnings	70,000	60,000
	$470,000	$360,000

Additional Information

- The after-tax profit of Shot for Year 5 amounted to $60,000 and was earned evenly throughout the year.
- The preferred shares are cumulative and nonvoting.
- Dividends on the preferred shares are payable on June 30 and December 31 each year. Dividends were two years in arrears at December 31, Year 4, and were not paid on June 30, Year 5.

For Questions 8 to 11, assume Pot did not purchase any of Shot's preferred shares on July 1, Year 5.

8. When Pot Inc. calculates goodwill arising from its purchase of Shot Inc., which of the following represents the claim of the preferred shareholders on Shot's net asset position for dividends in arrears?
   a. $0
   b. $4,000
   c. $16,000
   d. $20,000

9. When Pot Inc. calculates goodwill arising from its purchase of Shot Inc., which of the following represents the claim of the preferred shareholders at redemption (other than dividends in arrears) on Shot's net asset position?
   a. $80,000
   b. $100,000
   c. $108,000
   d. $130,000

10. When Pot Inc. consolidates Shot Inc. immediately after acquisition, what amount will be presented as non-controlling interest related to common shares?
    a. $48,000
    b. $52,000
    c. $58,000
    d. $66,000

11. When Pot Inc. consolidates Shot Inc. immediately after acquisition, what amount will be presented as non-controlling interest related to preferred shares?
    a. $100,000
    b. $120,000
    c. $150,000
    d. $160,000

12. Assume that on July 1, Year 5, Pot purchases 40 percent of Shot's preferred shares in addition to the 80 percent of common shares. Pot pays an additional $40,000 for these shares.

    On December 31, Year 5, Shot pays $24,000 in dividends to preferred shareholders. What amount will Pot present as dividend revenue from preferred shares on its consolidated income statement for the year ended December 31, Year 5?
    a. $0
    b. $1,600
    c. $3,200
    d. $9,600

Use the following information to answer Questions 13 to 16.

On August 31, Year 6, Plow Inc. purchased 75 percent of the outstanding common shares of Share Inc. for $750,000. At January 1, Year 6, Share had common shares of $500,000 and retained earnings of $240,000. At the date of acquisition, plant and equipment on Share's books was undervalued by $40,000. This plant had a remaining useful life of five years. The balance of the acquisition differential was allocated to unrecorded trademarks of Share to be amortized over a 10-year period. Share's net income for Year 6 was $90,000, earned evenly throughout the year. On December 15, Year 6, Share declared and paid dividends of $10,000.

On December 31, Year 6, Plow sold 20 percent of its 75 percent interest in Share for $160,000.

13. Which one of the following is the correct amount of trademarks that should appear on Plow's consolidated statements at December 31, Year 6 (assuming Share is Plow's only subsidiary)?
    a. $92,800
    b. $108,000
    c. $123,733
    d. $154,667

14. What is the amount of the gain or the loss that will arise from Plow's disposition of Share at December 31, Year 6?
    a. $8,200
    b. $8,700
    c. $10,000
    d. $46,150

15. What percentage of Share does Plow own after the disposition?
    a. 55 percent
    b. 60 percent
    c. 67.5 percent
    d. 85 percent

16. How will the gain or loss from partial disposition of ownership in Share be presented on Plow's consolidated financial statements at December 31, Year 6?
    a. It will not appear on the consolidated financial statements.
    b. It will appear in the notes only.
    c. It will appear as a direct charge or credit to owners' equity on the consolidated balance sheet.
    d. It will appear on the consolidated income statement.

17. On January 1, Year 3, PEAL Corporation acquired 60 percent of the common shares of SEAL Inc. for $1,000,000. On that date, the fair value of land owned by SEAL was $200,000 greater than its carrying value. On December 31, Year 5, the fair value of the land was $300,000 greater than its carrying value. Which of the following transactions on December 31, Year 5, would cause an increase in non-controlling interests on the consolidated balance sheet?
   a. SEAL sells the land to PEAL at its fair value.
   b. SEAL sells the land to one of PEAL's other subsidiaries at its fair value.
   c. SEAL sells the land to an unrelated party at its fair value.
   d. PEAL repurchases an additional 20 percent of SEAL's shares.

Use the following data for Questions 18 and 19.

On January 1, Year 3, PEN Ltd. purchased 80 percent of the common shares of NUM Corp. for $1,200,000. On the date of acquisition, NUM's shareholders' equity was as follows:

Preferred shares, 8%, non-cumulative, callable at $102, 1,000 shares outstanding	$ 100,000
Common shares, no par value, 20,000 shares outstanding	500,000
Retained earnings	604,000
Total	$1,204,000

Any acquisition differential is allocated to a patent that had a remaining useful life of five years at the date of acquisition. During Year 3, NUM earned a net income of $200,000 and paid dividends of $110,000.

18. Which of the following Year 3 consolidated financial statement accounts would increase if the preferred shares were callable at $100 instead of $102?
   a. Patents.
   b. Patent amortization expense.
   c. Non-controlling interests at December 31, Year 3.
   d. Net income attributable to non-controlling interests.

19. What would be the impact on the debt-to-equity ratio for the consolidated balance sheet at the date of acquisition if PEN had acquired all of NUM's outstanding preferred shares for an amount greater than the book value attributable to these preferred shares in addition to its 80 percent interest in the common shares?
   a. It would increase.
   b. It would decrease.
   c. It would not be affected.
   d. The impact cannot be determined based on the information provided.

CASES

Case 1 On December 31, Year 7, Pepper Company, a public company, agreed to a business combination with Salt Limited, an unrelated private company. Pepper issued 72 of its common shares for all (50) of the outstanding common shares of Salt. This transaction increased the number of outstanding Pepper shares from 100 to 172. Pepper's shares were trading at around $10 per share in days leading up to the business combination. The condensed balance sheets for the two companies on this date were as follows (in 000s):

| | Pepper | | Salt | |
	Book value	Fair value	Book value	Fair value
Tangible assets	$500	$600	$100	$120
Intangible assets (excluding goodwill)	200	500	250	350
	$700		$350	
Liabilities	$400	410	$170	200
Shareholders' equity	300		180	
	$700		$350	

On January 1, Year 8, Pepper sold 40 percent of its investment in Salt to an unrelated third party for $500 in cash. The CFO at Pepper stated that Salt must have been worth $1,250 if the unrelated third party was willing to pay $500 for a 40 percent interest in Salt. If so, Pepper saved $530 by buying Salt for only $720. Accordingly, the CFO wants to recognize a gain of $530 in the Year 7 income statement to reflect the true value of the Salt shares.

You have been asked by the CFO to prepare a presentation to senior management on the accounting implications for the business combination and subsequent sale of 40 percent of the investment. She would like you to consider two alternative methods of valuing Salt on the consolidated balance at the date of acquisition — one based on cost of purchase and one based on the implied value of the subsidiary based on the sales price on January 1, Year 8.

Required:

Prepare this presentation, answering the following questions:
(a) How would Pepper's consolidated balance sheet differ at the date of acquisition under the two different valuation alternatives? Which method best reflects economic reality? Which method is required by GAAP?
(b) How would Pepper's consolidated balance sheet look after the sale of the 40 percent interest in Salt to the unrelated third party under the two alternatives?

Case 2   For the past 10 years, Prince Company (Prince) has owned 75,000 or 75 percent of the common shares of Stiff Inc. (Stiff). Elizabeth Winer owns another 20 percent and the other 5 percent are widely held. Although Prince has the controlling interest, you would never know it during the annual shareholders' meetings. Winer keeps the board of directors on its toes by asking a lot of tough questions and continually threatening legal action if her rights as a minority shareholder are not protected.

Rick Impatient owns 100 percent of the shares of Prince. After Prince's latest shareholders' meeting, he decided that Prince would offer to purchase Winer's shares in Stiff or Prince would sell its interest in Stiff as Impatient was tired of all of the heckling from Winer. The shares of Stiff were recently trading for $100 per share.

On November 13, Year 13, Prince offered to pay $110 per share to Winer for her 20 percent interest in Stiff. To Impatient's surprise, Winer accepted the offer and the transaction was consummated on December 31, Year 13. At December 31, Year 13, the unamortized acquisition differential relating to prior purchases by Prince was $500,000, which pertained solely to goodwill. On the closing date, the shares of Stiff had a book value of $70 per share and all identifiable net assets had a fair value equal to book value except for unrecognized patents, which had a fair value of $1.3 million and an estimated useful life of four years.

The CFO of Prince wants to recognize the entire acquisition differential related to the new purchase from Winer as goodwill in order to minimize the impact on earnings for Years 13 and 14. The controller, on the other hand, believes that some of the acquisition differential should be charged to income in Year 13 as a loss because of the excessive price paid for the shares.

Required:

How would you resolve the dispute? Provide the arguments to support your position and indicate the impact of your decision on consolidated profit attributable to Prince's shareholders for Years 13 and 14. State your assumptions.

Case 3 Traveller Bus Lines Inc. (TBL) is a wholly owned subsidiary of Canada Transport Enterprises Inc. (CTE). CTE is a publicly traded transportation and communications conglomerate. TBL is primarily in the business of operating buses over short- and long-distance routes in central and western Canada and the United States. TBL also has a school bus division operating in Eastern Canada. CTE and its subsidiaries are audited by DeBoy Shoot, which issued an unqualified audit opinion on CTE's June 30 year-end consolidated financial statements. This was the only audit opinion issued on the CTE group of companies. TBL has a July 31 year-end. It is now September 8, Year 7. CTE has been reporting operating losses for several years and has put TBL up for sale as part of a strategy to change its focus. This is the first of several planned divestitures, designed to restore CTE's lacklustre share price.

Currently, the only interested party is an employee group led by TBL's president, Dan Williams. Williams's management buyout team consists of the vice-president of operations and the CFO. Handling the negotiations at CTE's corporate office is Eva Joel, vice-president of strategic divestitures.

The buyout team has submitted the first draft agreement of purchase and sale for review. Exhibit I on page 426 contains extracts from the draft agreement; notes made by CTE's lawyer are shown in italics. You, a CA at Heatley Dan LLP, have gathered some additional background information (Exhibit II on page 426).

Andrew wants to maximize the total selling price. He asked the partner in charge of the advisory services at Heatley Dan LLP to review the information given and provide recommendations on how CTE can maximize the total selling price and how the agreement should be changed to minimize possible disputes in the future. In addition, he would like a summary of the accounting issues of significance to CTE that will arise on the sale of TBL. The partner has asked you to prepare the draft report to Joel.

Required:
Prepare the draft report.

(CICA adapted)

Exhibit I

EXTRACTS OF DRAFT PURCHASE AND SALE AGREEMENT

Agreement of purchase and sale between the employee group (hereinafter the Purchaser) and Canada Transport Enterprises Inc. (hereinafter CTE) for the assets and liabilities of the business known as Traveller Bus Lines Inc. (TBL)

1. The assets and liabilities of TBL are those included in its draft July 31, Year 7, financial statements.

2. Excluded from the liabilities to be assumed by the purchaser are all environmental liabilities, including, but not limited to, gasoline and diesel fuel spills and tank leakage, pesticide residues, and all other chemical contamination.

3. The purchase price is determined by the sum of (A) the book value of the net assets at July 31, Year 7, which is twelve million dollars ($12 million), plus (B) 55 percent of the net reported income after taxes, for the 12-month period ending July 31, Year 8 (the contingent consideration). *Lawyer's Note — The contingent consideration should be worth at least $3.6 million since the division's earnings computed on this basis have averaged more than $6.6 million for the last four years before deducting head office charges.*

4. This agreement is conditional on the Purchaser obtaining adequate financing and, after inspection, finding TBL's records satisfactory.

5. CTE agrees not to compete with the Purchaser for 10 years.

6. CTE will provide a loan guarantee for up to 25 percent of the purchase price for the Purchaser.

7. The Purchaser agrees to provide full maintenance services to the truck and trailer fleet of one of CTE's other subsidiaries for five years. Charges will be based on cost plus 10 percent.

8. The central bus station will be restored by CTE to its original condition by December 31, Year 7.

9. CTE will provide free advertising to the Purchaser, on request, for one year following the closing date. The Purchaser will create all the advertising material, including TV commercials.

10. All bus route rights will be assigned to the Purchaser.

11. The purchase price will be allocated based on book values.

12. The sale will close on October 1, Year 7, at 12:01 A.M., and the entire consideration with the exception of the contingent consideration will be due and payable one (1) month after closing. The contingent consideration is due one (1) month after the July 31, Year 8, financial statements are finalized.

13. Overdue amounts will be charged interest at a rate of 11 percent per annum.

14. CTE will act in a consulting capacity to advise the Purchaser for a fee of $25,000 per annum.

Exhibit II

INFORMATION GATHERED

1. Exclusive rights to most bus routes were obtained almost 40 years ago when the provincial governments were handing out the routes at no cost to the local bus lines. They had no competition at that time. Other similar bus routes were subsequently purchased for significant amounts.

2. TBL's summary draft financial statements for July 31, Year 7, are as follows (in thousands of dollars):

Revenue	$48,123
Expenses (including $2,403 of head office charges)	40,239
Income before income taxes	7,884
Current taxes	2,995
Deferred taxes	567
Net income	$ 4,322

Current assets	$14,133
Long-term assets	25,131
Liabilities	(21,264)
Deferred taxes	(6,000)
Equity	$12,000

3. The TBL Maintenance Department has recently completed a study that demonstrated that the school buses would last 15 years rather than the 10 years on which the straight-line depreciation rates have always been based.

4. All school boards pay a non-refundable deposit, three months before the beginning of the school year in September, to guarantee bus service for the coming school year.

5. TBL ran a "Travel the Country" promotion in June Year 7. Sales of the three-month passes for unlimited travel, costing $400, were brisk. The driver punches the pass each time the holder takes a trip. To compensate travellers who use their passes fewer than 10 times in the three-month period, TBL permits them to trade in their passes for either a pair of skis or a pair of in-line skates or the cash value of these items ($150).

6. CTE's consolidation entries for Year 7 related to TBL are a fair value increment of $432,300 for property, plant, and equipment and $2,332,000 for goodwill, which is checked for impairment on an annual basis.

7. Included in TBL's long-term assets is a note receivable for $3.1 million, secured by the real property of a chain of four gas stations. Because of fierce competition from stations owned by the large oil companies, the value of the properties has declined from $4.2 million, the amount stated in the May Year 6 appraisal, to $2.4 million, according to the May Year 7 appraisal released on July 22, Year 7. The payments on the note are being made on schedule.

8. On August 18, Year 7, the Panamee School District announced the cancellation of all school bus services previously contracted for Year 7/8 in the school district.

9. The management buyout team plans to spend $500,000 on TV advertisements that promote bus travel in a national advertising campaign starting in early Year 8. The team also plans to retrofit all long-distance buses at substantial cost.

10. TBL moved all maintenance operations to a new facility in June Year 7. The building was purchased for $3.4 million, and the company had to vacate a leased facility 18 months before the end of the lease. The prospects of subletting the facility do not look good.

Case 4   Capilano Forest Company Ltd. (CFCL) has been owned and managed by an experienced forester, Don Strom, for 20 years. The company has performed well in the last few years, but the industry is cyclical. In the interior of British Columbia, CFCL manufactures lumber of all grades from raw logs. A small lumberyard and sales office are located in Vancouver.

Your firm has been re-appointed auditor for CFCL, and you, CA, the senior on this engagement, have been going over some issues with the recently hired controller of the company, Everett Green. CFCL had been searching for a controller for several months. Green agreed to accept the position with the condition that his compensation package include a bonus based on net income. Strom finally agreed to this form of remuneration, despite initial resistance.

A large Japanese lumber importer has recently expressed an interest in purchasing CFCL. Therefore, Green proposes to make changes to CFCL's accounting policies, which he believes will maximize the value of the company.

During the year, CFCL was granted, by the Ministry of Forests, the right to log a large area of standing timber on Crown land. Although CFCL does not own the land, it does have the right to log all the timber on it subject to an allowable annual limit. This right was granted to the company at no initial cost. However, a fee is paid to the Ministry based on the number of logs removed from the forest. Shortly after CFCL received this right, the Ministry announced that all holders of logging rights over Crown land are responsible for reforesting the lands at their own cost; the ruling applies to all rights granted in the last five years. After eight months of logging, CFCL has still not carried out any reforestation. The controller is proposing that CFCL record receipt of this right at fair value. In addition, he would like to include in the financial statements the fair value of rights received from the Ministry two years ago. These rights do not currently appear on the company's balance sheet.

CFCL recently purchased the right to log the standing timber on a mine site. As part of the purchase contract, CFCL agreed that it would cease logging in five years when mining commenced. Although CFCL would probably be unable to log all the timber in this period, the five-year rights were considered to be worth considerably more than the purchase price. Since logging operations began, however, it has become apparent that many of the trees are infested with insects and are therefore worthless. Green does not think that this presents a valuation problem for financial reporting. "These rotten trees are part of the cost of the good ones and will be expensed as the good trees are sold. The purchase price will be allocated to all the good trees on the mine site."

With respect to the costing of trees on land that CFCL owns, Green contends that these trees really have no cost. "We paid for the land, which produces the trees. The trees themselves do not have any cost. If anything, replanting and pesticide expenses are the only costs we have. The situation is similar to owning land on which we have a building and machinery producing widgets. When we sell the widgets, we don't expense the land, do we?"

Last year, the company acquired 100 percent of the common shares of NAN Limited, a forestry company operating out of Nanaimo, British Columbia, for $3 million. The acquisition differential of $500,000 was assigned to the timber. NAN owned a large tract of land and timber along the Pacific Coast. This year, 20 percent of this tract, along the shoreline, was sold to a resort developer. CFCL has assigned a cost of $25,000 to this parcel. At the date of original purchase, CFCL considered this parcel to be worthless from a logging standpoint. The rest of this land is abundant in timber. CFCL paid a premium for NAN because its land had rich soil and a moist, coastal climate ideal for tree growth. Lately, however, the company has been having problems logging the area. Environmentalists have vowed that no one will be allowed to destroy its natural beauty. Roadways have been blocked on several occasions by these protesters. In addition, they have campaigned aggressively against the company and its products. In response, CFCL has spent large amounts on public relations advertising and on legal costs in order to obtain injunctions. These amounts, as well as the estimated costs of idle time related to the protests, will be capitalized as goodwill.

On December 1, CFCL signed an agreement to sell 25 percent of its interest in NAN for $800,000. It wants to report a gain of $50,000 on the sale.

Green intends to include in goodwill costs relating to forest fires burning in areas surrounding CFCL's land. Although none of CFCL's timber has been damaged by the fires, the company did pay for resources to help control the disaster. As the controller explained, "It was in our best interests to help combat fires because they were headed toward our timber." The fires continue to burn, and CFCL has promised an additional $300,000 in aid.

CFCL has gained a reputation among Japanese companies as a good source of clear pine. CFCL can sell the Japanese as much pine as it can cut. Orders currently outstanding will take the company at least six months to fill. Under the terms of the contracts, the purchase price, denominated in yen, may be increased or decreased by a maximum of 5 percent, depending on the grade as determined by inspection at a Japanese harbour. The company would like to record the revenue on these contracts as soon as the lumber is cut.

The company sells wood chips as a by-product of its sawmill operations. It entered into a three-year contract with a large pulp mill, Remul Ltd., under which Remul can purchase all the chips produced by CFCL. CFCL would have plenty of willing customers, given the current market demand, for any chips that Remul did not take. CFCL transports the chips by truck and rail car. The truck drivers have been on strike for the last two weeks. Green does not see this strike lasting much longer, and he would, therefore, like to recognize the revenue on the chips as they are produced.

The partner on this engagement has asked you to prepare a memo discussing the accounting alternatives and to make recommendations for the issues raised with the controller.

Required:

Prepare the requested memo.

PROBLEMS

Problem 1 The following Year 1 consolidated cash flow statement was prepared for Standard Manufacturing Corp. and its 60-percent-owned subsidiary, Pritchard Windows Inc.:

STANDARD MANUFACTURING CORP.

CONSOLIDATED CASH FLOW STATEMENT

for the Year Ended December 31, Year 1

Cash flows from operating activities:		
Consolidated net income*	$129,800	
Non-cash items included in income		
Depreciation	45,200	
Goodwill impairment loss	1,000	
Bond premium amortization	(2,000)	
Loss on sale of equipment	23,000	
Decrease in inventory	20,000	
Increase in accounts receivable	(12,000)	
Net cash provided by operating activities		$205,000
Cash flows from investing activities		
Purchase of buildings	(150,000)	
Sale of equipment	60,000	
Net cash used in investing activities		(90,000)
Cash flows from financing activities		

* Consolidated net income was $120,000 attributable to Standard's shareholders and $9,800 attributable to non-controlling interests.

(continued)

Dividends paid		
To Standard shareholders	(50,000)	
To non-controlling shareholders	(6,000)	
Bond issue	100,000	
Preferred share redemption	(120,000)	
Net cash used in financing activities		(76,000)
Net increase in cash		39,000
Cash balance, January 1		50,000
Cash balance, December 31		$ 89,000

Required:

(a) Did the loss on the sale of equipment shown above result from a sale to an affiliate or a non-affiliate? Explain.

(b) Explain why the amortization of bond premium is treated as a deduction from net income in arriving at net cash flow from operations.

(c) Determine the net income of Pritchard Windows for Year 1 (assume no inter-company transactions or unrealized profits and that the only change in the unamortized acquisition differential during the year was the goodwill impairment loss).

(d) Explain why dividends to non-controlling shareholders are not shown as a dividend in the consolidated retained earnings statement but are shown as a distribution of cash in the consolidated cash flow statement.

(e) Determine the amount of dividends paid by Pritchard Windows in Year 1.

Problem 2 Financial statements of Par Corp. and its subsidiary Star Inc. on December 31, Year 12, are shown below:

BALANCE SHEETS
at December 31, Year 12

	Par	Star
Cash	$ 40,000	$ 1,000
Accounts receivable	100,000	85,000
Inventories	55,000	48,000
Land	30,000	70,000
Plant and equipment	400,000	700,000
Accumulated depreciation	(180,000)	(300,000)
Investment in Star common shares	280,000	—
	$725,000	$604,000
Accounts payable	$ 92,000	$180,000
Accrued liabilities	8,000	10,000
Preferred shares	—	50,000
Common shares	450,000	200,000
Retained earnings	175,000	164,000
	$725,000	$604,000

RETAINED EARNINGS STATEMENTS
for the Year Ended December 31, Year 12

	Par	Star
Balance, January 1	$180,000	$208,000
Net income (loss)	30,000	(24,000)
	210,000	184,000
Dividends	35,000	20,000
Balance, December 31	$175,000	$164,000

Other Information

- On January 1, Year 5, the balance sheet of Star showed the following shareholders' equity:

$8 cumulative preferred shares, 500 shares issued	$ 50,000
Common shares, 2,000 shares issued	200,000
Deficit (note 1)	(80,000)
	$170,000

Note 1: Dividends on preferred shares are two years in arrears.

On this date, Par acquired 1,400 common shares of Star for a cash payment of $280,000.

The fair values of Star's identifiable net assets differed from carrying values only with respect to the following:

	Carrying amount	Fair value
Accounts receivable	$ 42,000	$ 40,000
Inventory	65,000	72,000
Plant	600,000	650,000
Long-term liabilities	400,000	420,000

The plant had an estimated remaining useful life of five years on this date, and the long-term liabilities had a maturity date of December 30, Year 12. Any goodwill is to be tested annually for impairment.

- Both Par and Star make substantial sales to each other at an intercompany selling price that yields the same gross profit as the sales they make to unrelated customers. Intercompany sales in Year 12 were as follows:

Par to Star	$400,000
Star to Par	330,000

- During Year 12, Par billed Star $2,000 per month in management fees. At year-end, Star had paid for all months except for December.
- The January 1, Year 12, inventories of the two companies contained unrealized intercompany profits as follows:

Inventory of Par	$30,000
Inventory of Star	21,000

- The December 31, Year 12, inventories of the two companies contained unrealized intercompany profits as follows:

Inventory of Par	$35,000
Inventory of Star	37,000

- On July 1, Year 7, Star sold equipment to Par for $82,000. The equipment had a carrying value in the records of Star of $60,000 on this date and an estimated remaining useful life of five years.
- Goodwill impairment losses were recorded as follows: Year 7, $92,500; Year 9, $46,470; and Year 12, $19,710.
- Assume a 40 percent corporate tax rate.
- Par has accounted for its investment in Star by the cost method.
- All dividends in arrears were paid by December 31, Year 11.

Required:

(a) Prepare, with all necessary calculations, the following:
  (i) The Year 12 consolidated retained earnings statement.
  (ii) The consolidated balance sheet as at December 31, Year 12.
(b) How would the return on equity attributable to Par's shareholders for Year 12 change if Star's preferred shares were non-cumulative instead of cumulative?
(c) On January 1, Year 13, Star issued common shares for $100,000 in cash. Because Par did not purchase any of these shares, Par's ownership percentage declined from 70 to 56 percent.

   Calculate the gain or loss that would be charged or credited to consolidated shareholders' equity as a result of this transaction.

Problem 3   On December 31, Year 5, the accountant of Regent Corporation prepared a reconciliation (see below), which was used in the preparation of the consolidated financial statements on that date.

Investment in Argyle Ltd. — equity method balance		$315,000
Shareholders' equity of Argyle		
8,000 common shares	50,000	
Retained earnings	175,000	
	225,000	
Regent's ownership	90%	202,500
Regent's share of unamortized acquisition differential		112,500
Non-controlling interest's share of unamortized acquisition differential		12,500
Total unamortized acquisition differential		$125,000
Allocated: Land		$ 28,333
Equipment — remaining useful life 8 years		44,444
Trademarks — remaining useful life 10 years		52,223
		$125,000

Additional Information
- On December 31, Year 6, Argyle reported a net income of $50,000 (earned evenly throughout the year) and declared dividends of $20,000.

- On April 1, Year 6, Argyle issued an additional 2,000 common shares at a price of $75 each. Regent did not acquire any of these shares.
- On October 1, Year 6, because the market price of Argyle's common shares had fallen, Regent purchased 1,300 shares of Argyle on the open market at $60 per share. The decline in value is not believed to be permanent. Any acquisition differential was allocated 20 percent to land, 35 percent to equipment, and 45 percent to trademark.

Required:

(a) Prepare an acquisition-differential amortization schedule for Year 6 while showing the controlling and non-controlling interests' share of the changes occurring throughout the year.

(b) Calculate the equity method balance in the investment in Argyle account as at December 31, Year 6, and reconcile this balance to Argyle's shareholders' equity and to the unamortized acquisition differential.

Problem 4 The comparative consolidated statement of financial position at December 31, Year 2, and the consolidated income statement for Year 2, of Parent Ltd. and its 70-percent-owned subsidiary are shown below.

	Year 2	Year 1
Plant and equipment	$5,350,000	$5,100,000
Accumulated depreciation	(2,350,000)	(1,980,000)
Goodwill	530,000	565,000
Inventory	989,500	490,000
Accounts receivable	600,000	710,000
Cash	810,000	335,000
	$5,929,500	$5,220,000
Common shares	$ 800,000	$ 800,000
Retained earnings	916,000	520,000
Non-controlling interest	515,000	—
Long-term liabilities	3,100,000	2,600,000
Current liabilities	598,500	1,300,000
	$5,929,500	$5,220,000
Revenues	$8,500,000	
Cost of purchases and other expenses	8,179,600	
Change in inventory	(499,500)	
Depreciation	370,000	
Goodwill impairment loss	35,000	
	8,085,100	
Profit	$ 414,900	
Attributable to		
Shareholders of Parent	$ 376,500	
Non-controlling interest	38,400	

Additional Information

- On December 31, Year 1, Parent owned 100 percent of Sub. On this date, the shareholders' equity of Sub amounted to $1,120,000 and the parent's unamortized acquisition differential of $565,000 was allocated entirely to the goodwill of Sub.

- On January 1, Year 2, Parent sold 30 percent of its shares of Sub for $629,000 cash and recorded an increase to retained earnings of $123,500 on the transaction. Parent uses the equity method to account for its investment.
- Parent paid $104,000 in dividends during Year 2.

Required:

Prepare, in good form, a consolidated cash flow statement for Year 2 in accordance with the requirements of IAS 7.

Problem 5 On April 1, Year 7, Princeton Corp. purchased 70 percent of the common shares of Simon Ltd. for $910,000. On this same date, Simon purchased 60 percent of the common shares of Fraser Inc. for $600,000. On April 1, Year 7, the acquisition differentials from the two investments were allocated entirely to broadcast rights to be amortized over 10 years. The cost method is being used to account for both investments.

During Year 7, the three companies sold merchandise to each other. On December 31, Year 7, the inventory of Princeton contained merchandise on which Simon recorded a gross margin of $32,000. On the same date, the inventory of Fraser contained merchandise on which Princeton recorded a gross margin of $18,000. Assume a 40 percent tax rate.

The following information is available:

	Princeton	Simon	Fraser
Common shares	$600,000	$550,000	$300,000
Retained earnings — Jan. 1, Year 7	650,000	400,000	300,000
Profit — Year 7*	100,000	200,000	150,000
Dividends declared — Dec. 31	25,000	30,000	70,000

* Earned evenly throughout the year.

Required:

Calculate the following:
(a) Consolidated profit attributable to Princeton's shareholders — Year 7.
(b) Non-controlling interest as at December 31, Year 7.
(c) Consolidated broadcast rights as at December 31, Year 7.

Problem 6 On January 1, Year 5, PET Company acquired 800 common shares of SET Company for $56,000. On this date, the shareholders' equity accounts of SET Company were as follows:

Common shares (1,000 no par value shares issued)	$20,000
Preferred shares (4,000 no par value shares issued) (note 1)	40,000
Retained earnings	30,000
	$90,000

Note 1: The preferred shares are $1, cumulative, nonparticipating with a liquidation value of 1.05. They were two years in arrears on January 1, Year 5.

The following are the statements of retained earnings for the two companies for Year 5:

	PET	SET
Retained earnings, beginning of year	$50,000	$30,000
Profit	30,000	20,000
Dividends	(25,000)	(15,000)
Retained earnings, end of year	$55,000	$35,000

Additional Information

- PET uses the cost method to account for its investment in SET.
- Any acquisition differential is allocated to patents with an estimated useful life of six years as at January 1, Year 5. Neither company has any patents recorded on their separate-entity records.

Required:

(a) Prepare a consolidated statement of retained earnings for Year 5.
(b) Prepare an independent calculation of consolidated retained earnings at the end of Year 5 using a format similar to the schedule on page 278.
(c) Calculate non-controlling interest for the consolidated income statement for Year 5 and non-controlling interest for the consolidated statement of financial position at the end of Year 5.

Problem 7 On January 1, Year 8, Summer Company's shareholders' equity was as follows:

Common shares	$20,000
Retained earnings	70,000
	$90,000

Plumber Company held 90 percent of the 4,000 outstanding shares of Summer on January 1, Year 8, and its investment in Summer Company account had a balance of $126,000 on that date. Plumber accounts for its investment by the equity method. Any acquisition differential was allocated to unrecorded trademarks with a remaining useful life on January 1, Year 8, of 10 years.

The following events took place subsequent to January 1, Year 8:

- On July 1, Year 8, Plumber sold 720 of the Summer Company shares it held at a price of $30 per share.
- During Year 8, Summer reported a net income of $20,000 (earned equally throughout the year) and declared dividends of $5,000 on December 31.
- During Year 9, Summer reported a net income of $28,000 and paid dividends of $8,000 on November 15.
- On December 29, Year 9, Summer issued an additional 500 shares to third parties at a price of $46 per share.

Required:

(a) Calculate the gain or loss in Year 8 and Year 9 as a result of the ownership change that took place each year.
(b) Would the gain or loss appear on the consolidated income statement each year? Explain.
(c) Calculate the consolidated trademarks as at December 31, Year 9.
(d) Does the value for the trademarks on the consolidated balance sheet as calculated in part (c) comply with the historical cost principle? Explain.

Problem 8 The accountant of Kara Enterprises has just finished preparing the consolidated balance sheet, income statement, and retained earnings statement for Year 2, and has asked you for assistance in preparing the consolidated cash flow statement. Kara has only one subsidiary, which is 80 percent owned, and in addition has a long-term investment of 45 percent in the outstanding shares of Pacific Finance Co.

The following items have been prepared from the analysis of the Year 2 consolidated statements:

Decrease in accounts receivable	$ 23,000
Increase in accounts payable	5,000
Increase in inventory	15,000
Equity earnings from Pacific Finance	90,000
Increase in bonds payable	120,000
Building purchased for cash	580,000
Depreciation reported for current period	73,000
Gain recorded on sale of equipment	8,000
Carrying value of equipment sold	37,000
Goodwill impairment loss	3,000
Dividends received from Pacific Finance	25,000
Net income attributable to Kara's shareholders	450,000
Net income attributable to non-controlling interest	14,000
Dividends paid by parent company	60,000
Dividends paid by subsidiary company	30,000
Cash balance, January 1, Year 2	42,000

Required:

Prepare the consolidated cash flow statement.

Problem 9 Parent Co. owns 9,500 shares of Sub Co. and accounts for its investment by the equity method. On December 31, Year 5, the shareholders' equity of Sub was as follows:

Common shares (10,000 shares issued)	$100,000
Retained earnings	170,000

On January 1, Year 6, Parent sold 1,900 shares from its holdings in Sub for $66,500. On this date and prior to the sale, the balance in the investment in Sub account was $320,000, and the unamortized acquisition differential was allocated in the following manner:

35 percent to land
40 percent to equipment (remaining useful life 4 years)
25 percent to patents (remaining useful life 10 years)

During Year 6, Sub reported a net income of $150,000 and paid dividends totalling $70,000.

Required:

(a) (i) Prepare the journal entry that Parent would make on January 1, Year 6, to record the sale of the 1,900 shares.

(ii) Calculate the amount of the unamortized acquisition differential that would be allocated to land, equipment, and patents on December 31, Year 6.

(iii) Prepare an independent proof of the unamortized acquisition differential on December 31, Year 6.

(b) The accountant of Parent must prepare a consolidated cash flow statement for Year 6 by analyzing the changes in the consolidated balance sheets from December 31, Year 5, to December 31, Year 6. She needs some assistance in determining what effect Parent's sale of 1,900 shares had on the consolidated financial statements.

Prepare a journal entry to record the effect that the January 1, Year 6, sale of shares had on the consolidated entity.

Problem 10   On January 1, Year 5, Pic Company acquired 7,500 common shares of Sic Company for $600,000. On January 1, Year 6, Pic Company acquired an additional 2,000 common shares of Sic Company for $166,000. On January 1, Year 5, the shareholders' equity of Sic was as follows:

Common shares (10,000 no par value shares issued)	$200,000
Retained earnings	300,000
	$500,000

The following are the statements of retained earnings for the two companies for Years 5 and 6:

	Pic		Sic	
	Year 5	Year 6	Year 5	Year 6
Retained earnings, beginning of year	$500,000	$530,000	$300,000	$310,000
Profit	130,000	140,000	100,000	110,000
Dividends	(100,000)	(120,000)	(90,000)	(90,000)
Retained earnings, end of year	$530,000	$550,000	$310,000	$330,000

Additional Information
- Pic uses the cost method to account for its investment in Sic.
- Any acquisition differential is allocated to patents with a life expectancy until December 31, Year 9. Neither company has any patents recorded on their separate-entity records.
- There were no unrealized profits from intercompany transactions since the date of acquisition.

Required:

(a) Calculate consolidated profit attributable to Pic's shareholders for Year 6.
(b) Calculate the following account balances for the consolidated statement of financial position at December 31, Year 6:
   (i)   Patents.
   (ii) Non-controlling interest.
   (iii) Retained earnings.

Problem 11   Intercompany shareholdings of an affiliated group during the year ended December 31, Year 2, were as follows:

York Ltd.	Queen's Company	McGill Company
90% of Queen's Company	70% of Carleton Ltd.	60% of Trent Ltd.
80% of McGill Company	10% of McGill Company	

The equity method is being used for intercompany investments, but no entries have been made in Year 2. The profits before equity method earnings for Year 2 were as follows:

	Profit
York Ltd.	$54,000
Queen's Company	22,000
McGill Company	26,700
Carleton Ltd.	15,400
Trent Ltd.	11,600

Intercompany profits before taxes in the December 31, Year 2, inventories and the selling companies were as follows:

Selling corporation	*Profit made by selling corporation*
York Ltd.	$10,000
McGill Company	1,000
Carleton Ltd.	2,400

Use income tax allocation at a 40 percent rate. Assume that there is no acquisition differential for any of the intercompany shareholdings.

Required:

(a) Calculate consolidated profit attributable to York's shareholders for Year 2.
(b) Calculate the amount of consolidated profit attributable to non-controlling interest that would appear on the Year 2 consolidated income statement.
(c) Will the consolidation adjustment for unrealized profits be any different if McGill Company sells inventory to Carleton Ltd. or York Ltd.? Use the revenue recognition principle to explain your answer.

Problem 12   Craft Ltd. held 80 percent of the outstanding common shares of Delta Corp. as at December 31, Year 12. In order to establish a closer relationship with Nonaffiliated Corporation, a major supplier to both Craft and Delta, all three companies agreed that Nonaffiliated would take an equity position in Delta. Accordingly, for a cash payment of $15 per share, Delta issued 12,250 additional common shares to Nonaffiliated on December 31, Year 12. This was the last transaction that occurred on this date. Statements of financial position for the two companies just prior to this transaction were as follows.

CRAFT LTD.
STATEMENT OF FINANCIAL POSITION
At December 31, Year 12

Buildings and equipment (net)	$ 600,000
Investment in Delta	490,000
Inventory	180,000
Accounts receivable	90,000
Cash	50,000
	$1,410,000
Common shares	$ 480,000
Retained earnings	610,000
Mortgage payable	250,000
Accounts payable	70,000
	$1,410,000

DELTA CORP.
STATEMENT OF FINANCIAL POSITION
at December 31, Year 12

Buildings and equipment (net)	$400,000
Inventory	200,000
Accounts receivable	120,000
Cash	65,000
	$785,000
Common shares (note)	$250,000
Retained earnings	350,000
Accrued liabilities	85,000
Accounts payable	100,000
	$785,000

Note: 49,000 common shares outstanding on December 31, Year 12.

Additional Information
- Craft has used the equity method of accounting for its investment in Delta since it acquired its 80 percent interest in Delta in Year 2. At that time, the acquisition differential was entirely allocated to inventory and patent, which still exists but is not recorded on Delta's separate-entity books.
- There were no unrealized intercompany asset profits as at December 31, Year 12.

Required:

Prepare a consolidated statement of financial position as at December 31, Year 12 (show calculations for all items on the balance sheet).

Problem 13 A Company owns 75 percent of B Company and 40 percent of C Company. B Company owns 40 percent of C Company. The following information was assembled at December 31, Year 7.

	A Company	B Company	C Company
Cash	$ 117,800	$ 49,300	$ 20,000
Accounts receivable	200,000	100,000	44,000
Inventory	277,000	206,000	58,000
Investment in C	85,000	92,000	—
Investment in B	409,250	—	—
Property, plant, and equipment	2,800,000	1,500,000	220,000
Accumulated depreciation	(1,120,000)	(593,000)	(90,000)
	$2,769,050	$1,354,300	$252,000
Accounts payable	$ 206,000	$ 88,000	$ 2,000
Bonds payable	1,000,000	700,000	—
Preferred shares	—	50,000	—
Common shares	1,200,000	400,000	200,000
Retained earnings, January 1	314,250	61,000	30,000
Net income	118,800	55,300	20,000
Dividends	(70,000)	—	—
	$2,769,050	$1,354,300	$252,000

Additional Information

- A Company purchased its 40 percent interest in C Company on January 1, Year 4. On that date, the negative acquisition differential of $10,000 on the 40 percent investment was allocated to equipment with an estimated useful life of 10 years.
- A Company purchased its 75 percent of B Company's common shares on January 1, Year 6. On that date, the 100 percent implied acquisition differential was allocated $40,000 to buildings with an estimated useful life of 20 years, and $53,333 to patents to be amortized over 8 years. The preferred shares of B Company are non-cumulative.
- On January 1, Year 7, B Company purchased its 40 percent interest in C Company for $92,000. The book value of C Company's identifiable net assets approximated fair value on this date.
- The inventory of B Company contains a profit of $2,400 on merchandise purchased from A Company. The inventory of A Company contains a profit of $3,000 on merchandise purchased from C Company.
- On December 31, Year 7, A Company owes $20,000 to C Company and B Company owes $2,000 to A Company.
- Both A Company and B Company use the equity method to account for their investments but have made no equity method adjustments in Year 7.
- An income tax rate of 40 percent is used for consolidation purposes.

Required:

(a) Calculate non-controlling interest's share of consolidated net income for Year 7.
(b) Prepare a consolidated statement of retained earnings for Year 7.
(c) Prepare a consolidated balance sheet as at December 31, Year 7. Show all calculations.

Problem 14 Parento Inc. owns 80 percent of Santana Corp. The consolidated financial statements of Parento are shown below and on the next page:

PARENTO INC.
CONSOLIDATED BALANCE SHEET
At December 31, Year 4

	Year 4	Year 3
Cash	$118,600	$ 49,800
Accounts receivable	115,000	126,000
Inventory	232,000	192,000
Land	86,000	114,000
Buildings and equipment	598,000	510,000
Accumulated depreciation	(205,000)	(168,000)
Databases	16,800	19,200
	$961,400	$843,000
Accounts payable	$ 54,400	$ 31,200
Accrued liabilities	7,200	27,000
Bonds payable	320,000	240,000
Bond premium	9,600	10,800
Common shares	180,000	180,000
Retained earnings	363,480	330,000
Non-controlling interest	26,720	24,000
	$961,400	$843,000

PARENTO INC.
CONSOLIDATED INCOME STATEMENT
For the Year Ended December 31, Year 4

Sales		$960,000
Cost of sales	535,000	
Selling expense	144,600	
Administrative expense	159,800	
Interest expense	31,400	
Income tax	37,000	907,800
Net income		$ 52,200
Attributable to		
Parent's shareholders		$ 47,880
Non-controlling interest		4,320

Parento Inc. purchased its 80 percent interest in Santana Corp. on January 1, Year 2, for $114,000 when Santana had net assets of $90,000. The acquisition differential was allocated $24,000 to databases (10-year life), with the balance allocated to equipment (20-year life).

Parento issued $80,000 in bonds on December 31, Year 4. Santana reported a net income of $24,000 for Year 4 and paid dividends of $8,000.

Selling and administrative expense includes the following:

Depreciation of buildings and equipment	$37,000
Database amortization	2,400
Loss on land sale	2,000

Parento reported a Year 4 equity method income of $47,880 and paid dividends of $14,400.

Required:

(a) Prepare a consolidated cash flow statement for Year 4.
(b) Why are 100 percent of the dividends paid by Santana not shown as a cash outflow on the cash flow statement?

Problem 15 On January 1, Year 5, Wellington Inc. owned 90 percent of the outstanding common shares of Sussex Corp. Wellington accounts for its investment using the equity method. The balance in the investment account on January 1, Year 5, amounted to $235,800. The unamortized acquisition differential on this date was allocated entirely to vacant land held by Sussex.

The shareholders' equity of Sussex on January 1, Year 5, was as follows:

Common shares (7,200 shares outstanding)	$ 28,000
Retained earnings	134,000
	$162,000

The following events occurred in Year 5:

- The net income of Sussex for Year 5 amounted to $36,000, earned equally throughout the year.
- On April 1, Year 5, Sussex issued 1,800 shares at a price of $25 per share. Wellington did not acquire any of these shares.

www.mcgrawhillconnect.ca

- On June 30, Year 5, Sussex paid dividends amounting to $12,000.
- On September 15, Year 5, Sussex sold 30 percent of its vacant land at its carrying amount.
- On December 31, Year 5, Wellington sold 648 shares of its investment in Sussex for $22,000.

Required:

Calculate the following as at December 31, Year 5:

(a) The acquisition differential allocated to vacant land and the split in value between the parent and the non-controlling interest.
(b) The balance in the investment account using the equity method.
(c) The amount of non-controlling interest on the consolidated balance sheet.

Problem 16   On January 1, Year 8, Panet Company acquired 40,000 common shares of Saffer Corporation for $500,000. This purchase represented 8 percent of the outstanding shares of Saffer. It was the intention of Panet to acquire more shares in the future in order to eventually gain control of Saffer.

On January 1, Year 10, Panet purchased an additional 135,000 common shares of Saffer for $1,890,000. Saffer's shareholders' equity section was as follows:

10% non-cumulative preferred shares	$ 500,000
Common shares, no par value,	
500,000 shares outstanding	3,000,000
Retained earnings	2,700,000

On this date, the fair values of Saffer's assets were equal to book values, except for inventory, which was undervalued by $120,000, and land, which was undervalued by $1,000,000.

On January 1, Year 11, Panet purchased an additional 225,000 common shares of Saffer for $3,600,000. Saffer's shares were trading on the open market for $15 per share on the date of acquisition. The shareholders' equity section for Saffer was as follows:

10% non-cumulative preferred shares	$ 500,000
Common shares, no par value,	
500,000 shares outstanding	3,000,000
Retained earnings	3,200,000

On January 1, Year 11, the fair values of Saffer's assets were equal to book values except for the following:

	Book value	Fair value
Accounts receivable	$ 200,000	$ 140,000
Plant and equipment (net)	10,000,000	10,900,000
Long-term liabilities	2,000,000	2,200,000

The plant and equipment had a remaining useful life of 20 years. The long-term liabilities mature on December 31, Year 20.

The balance sheets as at December 31, Year 12, and the income statements for the year ending December 31, Year 12, for the two companies are as follows:

BALANCE SHEET

	Panet	Saffer
Assets:		
Cash	$ 500,000	$ 200,000
Accounts receivable	2,400,000	300,000
Inventories	500,000	400,000
Plant and equipment (net)	10,610,000	9,000,000
Investment in Saffer (at cost)	5,990,000	—
Land	5,500,000	1,000,000
Total assets	$25,500,000	$10,900,000
Liabilities:		
Current liabilities	$ 3,000,000	$ 500,000
Long-term liabilities	4,000,000	2,000,000
	7,000,000	2,500,000
Shareholders' equity:		
10% non-cumulative preferred shares	—	500,000
Common shares	9,000,000	3,000,000
Retained earnings	9,500,000	4,900,000
	18,500,000	8,400,000
Total liabilities and shareholders' equity	$25,500,000	$10,900,000

INCOME STATEMENT

	Panet	Saffer
Sales	$15,000,000	$ 9,000,000
Dividend revenue	120,000	—
	15,120,000	9,000,000
Cost of goods sold	9,500,000	6,200,000
Selling and administrative expense	2,500,000	530,000
Income tax	1,032,000	730,000
Other expenses	468,000	440,000
	13,500,000	7,900,000
Net Income	$ 1,620,000	$ 1,100,000

Additional Information

- Dividends declared and paid during Year 12:

Panet	$500,000
Saffer	200,000

- On January 1, Year 12, the inventory of Panet contained an $85,000 inter-company profit, and the inventory of Saffer contained an intercompany profit amounting to $190,000.
- During Year 12, Saffer sold inventory to Panet for $2,600,000 at a gross profit margin of 35 percent. Sales of $400,000 remained in Panet's inventory at December 31, Year 12.
- During Year 12, Panet sold inventory to Saffer for $3,900,000 at a gross profit margin of 45 percent. Sales of $250,000 remained in Saffer's inventory at December 31, Year 12.

- Saffer sold a piece of equipment to Panet on July 1, Year 12, for $450,000. At that time, the carrying value of the equipment in Saffer's books was $240,000, and it had a remaining useful life of 10.5 years. Panet still owes Saffer for 30 percent of the purchase price of the equipment. The gain on sale has been netted against other expenses in Saffer's Year 12 income statement.
- Both companies follow the straight-line method for depreciating plant and equipment and premiums or discounts on long-term liabilities.
- A goodwill impairment loss of $92,000 was recorded in Year 11, and a further loss of $58,000 occurred in Year 12. The impairment losses are to be applied at 80 percent to Panet's shareholders and 20 percent to non-controlling interest.
- Depreciation expense is included with selling and administrative expenses, whereas goodwill impairment losses are included in other expenses.
- Assume a 40 percent tax rate.

Required:

(a) Prepare the following Year 12 consolidated financial statements:
  (i) Income statement.
  (ii) Balance sheet.
(b) Calculate goodwill impairment loss and non-controlling interest on the consolidated income statement for the year ended December 31, Year 12, under the parent company extension theory.
(c) If Panet had used the parent company extension theory rather than the entity theory, how would this affect the debt-to-equity ratio at the end of Year 12?

Problem 17 On December 31, Year 6, Ultra Software Limited purchased 70,000 common shares (70 percent) of a major competitor, Personal Program Corporation (PPC), at $30 per share. The remaining common shares and the preferred shares were owned by several shareholders who were unwilling to sell at that time.

The preferred shares, which are non-cumulative, are entitled to a $12 dividend. Each is convertible into two common shares. Immediate conversion of these preferred shares has been, and will continue to be, highly unlikely due to the current market conditions for the shares. Management is concerned, however, about the effect that any future conversion would have.

At December 31, Year 6, PPC's net assets had a book value of $1,525,000. The identifiable assets and liabilities had book values equal to fair values, with the following exceptions:

- Land, with a book value of $200,000, had a fair value of $295,000.
- Software patents and copyrights had a total market value estimated as $300,000 above book value. These were expected to have a five-year useful life.
- Inventories of packaged software had a cost to PPC of $20,000 and an estimated selling price of $140,000. Estimated future selling expenses for these items were $15,000.
- An unrecorded brand name had an estimated fair value of $2,375,000. This will be amortized over 40 years.

The trial balances at December 31, Year 8, for these two companies are provided as Exhibit I.

Exhibit I

TRIAL BALANCES
December 31, Year 8 ($000s)

	Ultra		PPC	
Cash	$ 320		$ 150	
Accounts receivable	300		280	
Inventory	350		380	
Patents and copyrights	350		450	
Furniture and equipment (net)	540		675	
Building (net)	800		925	
Land	450		200	
Investment in PPC	2,100		—	
Accounts payable		$ 340		$ 138
Mortgage payable		350		
Bank loan payable				320
Preferred shares (12,500 outstanding)				1,400
Common shares (300,000 outstanding)		3,000		
Common shares (100,000 outstanding)				100
Retained earnings		1,300		117
Sales		6,200		4,530
Other income		120		7
Gain on sale of patent				50
Loss on sale of computer	1,080			
Cost of purchases	4,035		2,590	
Change in inventory	15		10	
Other expenses (incl. tax)	850		675	
Depreciation	75		142	
Interest	45		35	
Dividends			150	
	$11,310	$11,310	$6,662	$6,662

In Year 7, PPC sold packaged software costing $30,000 to Ultra at a price of $45,000. Of this software, 60 percent was still in Ultra's inventory at December 31, Year 7. During Year 8, packaged software costing $42,000 was sold by PPC to Ultra for $60,000. Ultra's inventory at December 31, Year 8, included $22,000 of goods purchased in this sale. Neither of these packaged software inventories sold to Ultra had a fair value difference at acquisition.

Included in the Year 8 income of PPC was a gain of $50,000 on the sale of patents to another company. This sale took place on June 30, Year 8. These patents had a fair value difference of $20,000 at acquisition.

On September 30, Year 8, Ultra sold surplus computer hardware to PPC. This equipment had a cost of $6,000,000, was one-half depreciated, and was sold for its fair value of $2,000,000. Disassembly and shipping costs of $80,000 were paid by Ultra. There was estimated to be a nine-year remaining useful life in its new use.

Preferred dividends were paid in all years, and no new shares have been issued since the acquisition date.

Assume a 40 percent tax rate.

Required:

(a) In accordance with GAAP, prepare the following:

   (i) A consolidated income statement for the year ended December 31, Year 8.

   (ii) A consolidated statement of retained earnings for the year ended December 31, Year 8.

   (iii) A schedule showing the values of the following consolidated balance sheet accounts as at December 31, Year 8:

     1. Software patents and copyrights.

     2. Packaged software inventory.

     3. Non-controlling interest.

(b) Write a brief note to the management of Ultra in which you outline the financial reporting implications in the event that the preferred shareholders of PPC exercise their conversion privilege.

(problem prepared by Peter Secord, St. Mary's University)

Problem 18 The summarized trial balances of Phase Limited and Step Limited as of December 31, Year 5, are as follows (amounts in thousands):

	Phase	*Step*
Property, plant, and equipment	$ 540	$298
Investment in Step	257	—
Current assets	173	89
Dividends declared	80	40
Cost of goods sold	610	260
Other expenses	190	55
	$1,850	$742
Common shares	$ 400	$200
Retained earnings, beginning	360	104
Liabilities	88	38
Sales, gains, and other revenue	1,002	400
	$1,850	$742

Phase had acquired the investment in Step in three stages:

Date	Shares	Cost	Step's retained earnings
Jan 1/Year 2	4,000	$ 50,700	$ 28,000
Jan 1/Year 4	6,000	98,300	69,000
Jan 1/Year 5	6,000	108,000	104,000

The January 1, Year 2, acquisition enabled Phase to elect 3 members to the 10-member board of directors of Step. The January 1, Year 4, acquisition did not give Phase control over Step. Any difference between cost and the underlying book value for each acquisition is attributable equally to land and to patents, which are expected to produce benefits until December 31, Year 11. Step had issued 20,000 shares on July 1, Year 1, the date of incorporation, and has neither issued nor retired shares since that date. Other information follows:

- Sale of depreciable assets (six-year remaining useful life), from Phase to Step, on June 30, Year 5, at a gain of $60,000.
- Intercompany sales:

Year 4	Phase to Step	$50,000
	Step to Phase	20,000
Year 5	Phase to Step	80,000
	Step to Phase	10,000

- Opening inventory of Phase contained merchandise purchased from Step for $10,000. Company policy was for a 20 percent gross margin on intercompany sales. Ending inventory of Phase contained merchandise purchased from Step for $5,000. One-half of the goods sold intercompany during Year 5 had not been paid for by year-end.
- Assume a 40 percent tax rate.

Required:

Compute the following consolidated amounts as of December 31, Year 5:
(a) Patents.
(b) Property, plant, and equipment.
(c) Current assets (ignore deferred income taxes).
(d) Non-controlling interest on statement of financial position.
(e) Retained earnings, beginning.
(f) Cost of goods sold.
(g) Profit attributable to Phase's shareholder's (statement not required).

(adapted from a problem prepared by Peter Secord, St. Mary's University)

WEB-BASED PROBLEMS

Problem 1   Access the most recent consolidated financial statements for Vodafone, a British company. (Go to the investor relations section at www.vodafone.com.) Answer the questions below. For each question, indicate where in the financial statements you found the answer and/or provide a brief explanation.

(a) Does the company employ the direct or indirect method of accounting for operating cash flows?
(b) What was the biggest cash outflow during the year?
(c) Describe the reporting for cash paid for business acquisitions in the statement of cash flows.
(d) Were there any transactions between the company and non-controlling shareholders that resulted in a loss of control of a subsidiary? If so, indicate how these transactions affected goodwill and indicate how any gains or losses on these transactions were reported.
(e) Were there any transactions between the company and non-controlling shareholders that did not result in gaining or losing control? If so, describe how the transactions were reported.

(f) If the company had reported gains or losses on sale of subsidiaries in income from continuing operations rather than in income from discontinued operations, what impact would this have had on the company's share price? Briefly explain.

Problem 2   Access the most recent financial statements for Siemens, a German company. (Go to the investor relations section at www.siemens.com.) Answer the same questions as in Problem 1. For each question, indicate where in the financial statements you found the answer and/or provide a brief explanation. (Some questions may not be applicable.)

Chapter 9

Other Consolidation Reporting Issues

After studying this chapter, you should be able to do the following:
1. Identify when a special-purpose entity should be consolidated and prepare consolidated statements for a sponsor and its controlled special-purpose entities.
2. Explain how the definitions of assets and liabilities can be used to support the consolidation of special-purpose entities.
3. Describe and apply the current accounting standards that govern the reporting of interests in joint arrangements.
4. Explain how the gain recognition principle supports the recognition of a portion of gains occurring on transactions between the venturer and the joint venture.
5. Understand the deferred tax implications of the accounting for a business combination.
6. Describe the IFRS requirements for segment disclosures and apply the quantitative thresholds to determine reportable segments.

INTRODUCTION

In the previous chapters, the parent controlled the subsidiary through voting rights. However, there are other means of controlling the operating and financial policies of the subsidiary. Enron Corp. controlled a number of special-purpose entities by signing contracts with other investors in the entity. Shoppers Drug Mart, the leading player in Canada's retail drugstore marketplace and the number one provider of pharmacy products and services, controls associate-owned stores through franchise and operating agreements. As we will see in this chapter, the entities that are controlled by contracts and operating agreements must be consolidated in a fashion similar to what we used in previous chapters.

Many Canadian companies participate in arrangements whereby they jointly control the operations of another entity. For example, ATCO Group, an Alberta-based utilities and power generation company, has significant investments in power-generating plants, which are jointly controlled with other entities. ATCO's income before taxes in 2008 in these joint ventures represented almost 40 percent of the company's total income. Later in this chapter, we will consider various types of joint arrangements. After that, we look at how IAS 12 on deferred income taxes affects the accounting for a business combination. This chapter concludes with the disclosure requirements associated with a company's operating segments.

Special-purpose Entities

Special-purpose entities (SPEs) have long been used by businesses as a vehicle to carry out specific activities. Until recently the only financial reporting involvement for a company establishing an SPE was the disclosure requirements regarding related party transactions. Now GAAP requires that some types of SPEs are subject to consolidation in the same manner as is a subsidiary.

An SPE is an entity created to accomplish a very specific business activity.

An SPE is a proprietorship, partnership, corporation, or trust set up to accomplish a very specific and limited business activity. Over the past decade, SPEs have been used to lease manufacturing assets, hedge financial instruments, borrow against high-quality receivables, conduct research and development activities, and carry out a variety of other specified functions.

SPEs are often able to obtain debt financing at very favourable interest rates.

Low-cost financing of asset purchases is often a major benefit of establishing an SPE. Rather than engaging in the business transaction directly, the sponsoring business sets up an SPE to purchase and finance the asset acquisition. The SPE then leases the asset to the sponsor. This strategy saves the business money because the SPE is often eligible for a lower interest rate. This advantage is achieved for several reasons. First, the SPE typically operates with a very limited set of assets — in many cases just one asset. By isolating an asset in an SPE, the risk of the asset is isolated from the overall risk of the sponsoring firm. Thus, the SPE's creditors remain protected by the specific collateral in the asset. Second, the business activities of an SPE can be strictly limited by its governing documents. These limits further protect lenders by preventing the SPE from engaging in any activities not specified in its agreements.

Before GAAP were changed, many companies used SPEs as a vehicle for "off-balance-sheet financing."

Another apparent reason for establishing an SPE was to avoid the consolidation of the SPE with the sponsoring enterprise and thereby avoid having to show additional debt on the consolidated balance sheet. Because governing agreements limited the activities and decision-making in most SPEs, the sponsoring enterprise was able to control the activities of the SPEs through the governing agreements. They did not have to own a majority of the voting shares to maintain control. In fact, a sponsoring enterprise usually owned very little, if any, of the voting shares of the SPE. Therefore, the sponsoring enterprise did not control the SPE through a voting interest and did not, until the late 1990s, have to consolidate the SPE. Like all business entities, SPEs generally have assets, liabilities, and investors with equity interests. Unlike most businesses, the role of the equity investors can be fairly minor. They may serve simply as a technical requirement to allow the SPE to function as a legal entity. Because they bear relatively low economic risk, equity investors are typically provided only a small rate of return.

The risks and rewards may not be distributed in accordance with equity ownership but rather with some other variable interest attaching to a sponsoring firm as a result of contractual arrangements.

Small equity investments are normally insufficient to induce lenders to provide a low-risk interest rate for an SPE. As a result, another party (often the sponsoring firm that benefits from the SPE's activities) must be prepared to contribute substantial resources to enable the SPE to secure the additional financing needed to accomplish its purpose. For example, the sponsoring firm may guarantee the debt of the SPE. Other contractual arrangements may limit returns to equity holders, while participation rights provide increased profit potential and risks to the sponsoring firm. Risks and rewards such as these cause the sponsor's economic interest to vary depending on the success of the created entity — hence the term *variable-interest entity* (VIE). In contrast to a traditional entity, an SPE's risks and rewards may not be distributed according to share ownership but according to other variable interests. Exhibit 9.1 provides several examples of variable interests in SPEs.

Exhibit 9.1

VARIABLE INTERESTS IN SPEs

The following are some examples of variable interests in SPEs and the related potential for losses or returns accruing to the sponsor:

Variable interests	*Potential losses or returns*
• Guarantees of debt	• If an SPE cannot repay liabilities, sponsor will pay and incur a loss.
• Subordinated debt instruments	• If an SPE cannot repay its senior debt, the sponsor as subordinated debt holder may be required to absorb the loss.
• Variable-rate liability	• Sponsor as holder of debt may participate in returns of SPE.
• Lease residual guarantee	• If leased asset declines below the residual value, sponsor as lessee will make up the shortfall.
• Non-voting equity instruments	• Sponsor as holder of debt or equity may participate in residual profits.
• Services	• Sponsor as service provider receives portion of residual profits.

A firm with variable interests in an SPE increases its risk with the level (or potential level in the case of a guarantee) of resources provided. With increased risks come increased incentives to exert greater influence over the decision-making of the SPE. In fact, the primary sponsor of the SPE will regularly limit the decision-making power of the equity investors through the governance documents that establish the SPE. Although, technically, the equity investors are the owners of the SPE, in reality they may retain little of the traditional responsibilities, risks, and benefits of ownership. In fact, the equity investors often cede financial control of the SPE to the primary sponsor in exchange for a guaranteed rate of return.

> The equity investors of an SPE typically receive a guaranteed rate of return as a reward for ceding control to the SPE's sponsor.

Consolidation of SPEs In 1998, the IASB issued SIC 12 Consolidation — Special Purpose Entities. It required that an SPE should be consolidated when the substance of the relationship between an entity and the SPE indicates that the SPE is controlled by that entity. Canada and the United States did not adopt any special rules related to an SPE until 2003, after the collapse of Enron.

Enron Corp. provided what was undoubtedly the most famous example in recent memory of the improper use of SPEs. In the investigation of its bankruptcy, in which its creditors and employees lost an estimated $60 billion, the following questionable accounting practices came to light:

> The collapse of Enron shed light on many questionable accounting practices.

- Not consolidating SPEs and thereby keeping billions of dollars of debt off its balance sheet;
- Recognizing inflated profits on sales to the nonconsolidated SPEs;
- Recognizing revenue from sales of forward contracts that were, in effect, disguised loans;
- Inflating the fair value of investments;
- Not adequately disclosing related party transactions.

In the wake of the Enron collapse, the American and Canadian accounting standards boards adopted accounting standards for the consolidation of SPEs that were controlled by means other than voting interests. These standards have been commonly referred to as the "Enron standards."

Although Canada did not have any special rules for consolidating SPEs at the time of Enron's collapse, Canadian GAAP did require a Canadian company to prepare consolidated statements when one company controlled another entity regardless of the form of control, i.e., voting control or control through other means. In the United States, consolidation was required when one entity owned the majority of the voting shares. Therefore, SPEs would typically not have been consolidated in the United States prior to 2004.

In June 2003, the CICA issued Accounting Guideline 15 (AcG-15): Consolidation of Variable Interest Entities. This guideline was effective for fiscal periods beginning on or after November 1, 2004. A variable interest entity (VIE) is a special-purpose entity that is not subject to control through voting ownership interests, but is nonetheless controlled by another enterprise. Each enterprise involved with a VIE must determine whether the financial support provided by that enterprise makes it the primary beneficiary of the VIE's activities. The primary beneficiary of the VIE is then required to include the assets, liabilities, and results of the VIE in its consolidated financial statements.

In December 2008, the IASB issued an exposure draft to revise IAS 27 to provide a broader and more encompassing definition of control, including control of a structured entity, which is defined as an entity whose activities are restricted (i.e., an SPE) and whose activities are not directed by entities with voting rights. The revised IAS 27 does not use the terms *primary beneficiary* or *variable interest entity*. It uses the more generic terms of *parent* and *subsidiary*. In this chapter, we will continue to use the terms *primary beneficiary* and *variable interest entity* to distinguish between control achieved through contractual agreements and control achieved through voting shares.

When assessing control of a structured entity, it is necessary to identify how returns from the entity's activities are shared and how decisions, if any, are made about the activities that affect those returns. A reporting entity must consider all relevant facts and circumstances in making the judgment as to whether it has control, including the items discussed below.

Understanding the purpose and design of a structured entity helps us assess how the activities of that entity are directed and how returns are shared among its participants. For example, a reporting entity is likely to control a structured entity that has been created to undertake activities that are part of the reporting entity's ongoing activities (e.g., the entity might have been created to hold legal title to an asset that the reporting entity uses in its own activities, providing a source of financing for the reporting entity).

Generally, the more a reporting entity is exposed to the variability of returns from its involvement with an entity, the more power the reporting entity is likely to have to direct the activities of that entity that cause the returns to vary. A reporting entity is likely to have the power to direct the activities of a structured entity if it is exposed to a variability of returns that is potentially significant to the structured entity and if the reporting entity's exposure is more than that of any other party.

In order to determine if consolidation is required, it is first necessary to determine if there is a primary beneficiary of the VIE.

Many SPEs are created to conduct activities that are part of the primary beneficiary's ongoing activities.

The more risks taken on by the sponsor, the greater the returns received by the sponsor.

Control of an SPE is usually based on who directs the key activities of the SPE.

Control of an entity that has a limited range of activities, such as an entity that manages an asset securitization, is determined on the basis of how that limited range of activities is directed and how the returns it receives from its involvement with the entity are shared. A reporting entity identifies what activities cause the returns to vary and assesses whether it has the power to direct those activities. A reporting entity's ability to act when circumstances arise constitutes power if that ability relates to the activities that cause the reporting entity's returns to vary. A reporting entity does not have to exercise its power in order to have power to direct the activities of a structured entity.

For example, if the only assets of an entity are receivables, then managing any defaulting receivables is the only activity that causes the returns to vary and, thus, affects the returns of the structured entity's participants. In this example, the party with the power to direct how any defaulting receivables are managed, and in having that power can affect its returns from its involvement with the entity, controls that entity.

A reporting entity can control a structured entity by means of related arrangements. For example, a reporting entity could establish a structured entity whose founding documents restrict its activities to purchasing fixed-rate receivables of the reporting entity for cash, collecting payments from those receivables, and passing those payments to the investors in the structured entity. Receivables that are overdue by more than a specified period are put back to the reporting entity.

A reporting entity can have the power to direct the activities of a structured entity if the reporting entity can change the restrictions or predetermined strategic operating and financing policies according to which the structured entity operates. For example, a reporting entity can have the power to direct the activities of a structured entity by having the right to dissolve the entity or to change (or veto any changes to) the entity's charter or by-laws. A reporting entity can have the right to dissolve an entity by holding liquidation, redemption, or other rights.

The definitions of assets and liabilities can be used to support the inclusion of the SPE's assets and liabilities on the consolidated balance sheet.

Since the primary beneficiary controls the resources of the VIE and will obtain the future returns from these resources, these resources meet the definition of an asset and should be included on the consolidated balance sheet of the primary beneficiary. Similarly, since the primary beneficiary usually bears the risk of absorbing the bulk of any expected loss of the VIE, it is effectively assuming responsibility for the liabilities of the VIE. Accordingly, these liabilities should be included on the consolidated balance sheet of the primary beneficiary. The fact that the primary beneficiary may own no voting shares whatsoever becomes inconsequential because such shares do not effectively allow the equity investors to exercise control. Thus, in assessing control, a careful examination of the VIE's governing documents and the contractual arrangements among the parties involved is necessary to determine who bears the majority of the risks and has the greatest participation in the potential upside in the value of the net assets of the VIE.

The following scenario provides an example of a structured entity and its primary beneficiary.

Example Fleur Co. is a Quebec-based utility company. It is negotiating to acquire a power-generating plant from Rouyn Inc. for $105 million. If Fleur purchased the plant directly, it would finance the acquisition with a 5 percent bank loan for $100 million and $5 million in cash. Alternatively, it could set up a separate legal entity whose sole purpose would be to own the power-generating plant and lease it back to Fleur. Because the separate entity would isolate the plant from Fleur's other risky assets and liabilities and provide specific collateral, the interest rate of the financing would be 4 percent, which would save the company $1 million per year. To obtain the lower interest rate, Fleur must guarantee the separate entity's debt and must also maintain certain predefined debt-to-equity ratios on its own balance sheet.

To take advantage of the lower interest rate, on January 1, Year 1, Fleur establishes Energy Co. for the sole purpose of owning and leasing the power plant to Fleur. An outside investor will provide $5 million in cash in exchange for 100 percent of the common shares of Energy Co. Fleur and Energy sign an agreement with the following terms:

- Energy's sole purpose is to purchase and own a power-generating plant. The purchase price will be financed by a $100 million loan and a $5 million equity investment.
- Fleur has veto power on all key operating, investing, and financing decisions.

The equity investors will earn a 10 percent return and bear very little risk.

- Fleur will lease the power plant for five years for annual payments of $4.5 million to cover the cost of the interest and provide a 10 percent return on the $5 million investment by the outside investor.
- At the end of five years (or any extension), Fleur can renew the lease for a further five years, purchase the power plant for $105 million, or pay $5 million to buy the common shares from the outside investor.

It appears that Energy is a structured entity controlled by Fleur for the following three reasons:

1. Energy was established to provide power solely to Fleur and the power is essential to Fleur's ongoing activities.

2. The outside investor will earn a 10 percent return and has very little risk. Fleur bears most of the risk of a change in utility rates and will receive any profit from the sale of power or the sale of the plant at the end of the lease term after the investor has received the guaranteed return.

3. The activities of Energy are restricted to owning and operating a power-generating plant. Fleur has the power to direct these activities through its veto power on all key operating, investing, and financing decisions.

The primary beneficiary bears most of the risks and receives the residual returns.

Fleur is the primary beneficiary. It has control over Energy and is exposed to the major risks, even though it has invested no assets in Energy. Accordingly, Energy should be consolidated with Fleur.

To summarize the preceding discussion, a VIE is a corporation, partnership, trust, or any other legal structure used for business purposes that, by design, either (a) does not have equity investors with voting rights to control the entity or (b) has equity investors that do not provide sufficient resources to support its intended purposes.

With two exceptions, the initial consolidation records the assets and liabilities of a VIE at fair values.

Initial Measurement Issues The financial reporting principles for consolidating VIEs require assets, liabilities, and non-controlling interests (NCIs) to be initially recorded at fair values, with two notable exceptions. First, if any of the SPE's assets have been transferred from the primary beneficiary, these assets will be measured at the carrying value before the transfer. Second, the asset valuation procedures in IAS 27 also rely on the allocation principles described in IFRS 3, which identifies some instances where assets and liabilities are not reported at fair value at the date of acquisition. Also, recall that IFRS 3 requires an allocation of the cost of an acquisition based on the underlying fair values of its assets and liabilities. In a VIE, control is not obtained by incurring a cost but through governance agreements and contractual arrangements. Therefore, an implied value substitutes for the acquisition cost in determining the valuation of a VIE. The implied value for what is viewed as a 100 percent purchase of the VIE is the sum of

An implied value of the VIE has to be determined in order to perform the initial consolidation.

- consideration paid by the primary beneficiary (plus the reported values of any previously held interests), and
- the fair value of the NCIs of the VIE.

The implied value is compared to the value of consideration received, which is the sum of

- the carrying value of the amount invested by the primary beneficiary, and
- the fair value of the VIE's own net assets excluding goodwill prior to investment by the primary beneficiary.

The amounts of the implied value and the consideration received are compared to determine the amount of any goodwill or negative goodwill.

If the implied value is less than the value of consideration received (which we will refer to as the assessed value), then there is negative goodwill. All fair values used for NCIs and assets and liabilities of the structured entity must be carefully reviewed to ensure that they are accurate. Once the values are confirmed, the excess of the assessed value (i.e., consideration received) over the implied value (i.e., consideration given) is reported as a gain on purchase. If the implied value is greater than the assessed value, the difference is reported as goodwill when the SPE is a business or as a reduction in the amounts assigned to the assets acquired when the SPE is not a business. A business is defined in IFRS 3 as an integrated set of activities and assets that is capable of being conducted and managed for the purpose of providing a return in the form of dividends, lower costs, or other economic benefits directly to investors or other owners, members, or participants.

The following example will illustrate the consolidation process for an SPE.

Example   XYZ Co. invests $5 million in cash in VAR Inc. on January 1, Year 3. VAR is deemed to be a VIE, and XYZ is the primary beneficiary. The balance sheet of VAR at the date of acquisition after XYZ's investment is as follows (in millions):

	Book value	Fair value
Cash	$ 5	$ 5
Capital assets	60	80
Total assets	$65	
Liabilities	40	40
Owners' equity		
XYZ	5	5
NCI	20	??
Total liabilities and equity	$65	

The allocations to be used in the consolidation of XYZ and VAR depend on the value assigned to NCI. We will demonstrate these valuation principles using the following fair values for NCI:

In this example, the fair value of NCI is varied for illustrative purposes.

Situation	Fair value of NCI
A	$40
B	37
C	44

	A	B	C
Implied Value of VAR's net assets			
Fair value of amount invested by XYZ	5	5	5
Fair value of NCI in VAR	40	37	44
Total implied value	45	42	49
Assessed Value of VAR's net assets			
Carrying value of amount invested by XYZ	5	5	5
Fair value of VAR's own assets	80	80	80
Less: Fair value of VAR's liabilities	(40)	(40)	(40)
Total assessed value	45	45	45
Difference between implied and assessed values	0	(3)	4
Assigned on consolidation to			
Goodwill			4
Gain on purchase		(3)	
Balance to assign	0	0	0

Note that the value assigned to the NCI is used to determine the value of VAR Inc. as a whole. This amount becomes the equivalent of the acquisition cost for XYZ Co. In situation A, the value of the entity equals the sum of the fair values of the entity's assets and liabilities. In situation B, the value of VAR as a whole is less than the sum of VAR's net assets, resulting in a "negative goodwill" situation, which is accounted for as prescribed in IFRS 3. In situation C, the value of VAR as a whole is greater than the sum of VAR's net assets and the difference is reflected as goodwill. The following journal entries summarize the values for VAR to be consolidated with XYZ under the three different scenarios:

If VAR meets the definition of a business, positive goodwill can be reported on the consolidated balance sheet.

	A	B	C
Goodwill			4
Cash	5	5	5
Capital assets	80	80	80
Liabilities	(40)	(40)	(40)
NCI	(40)	(37)	(44)
Owners' equity re XYZ	(5)	(5)	(5)
Gain on purchase		(3)	

The credit to owners' equity of $5 million will be eliminated against the debit balance for the investment in VAR on XYZ's books when preparing the consolidated balance sheet.

In subsequent years the normal consolidation procedures are followed.

Consolidation Issues Subsequent to Initial Measurement   After the initial measurement, consolidations of VIEs with their primary beneficiary should follow the same process as if the entity were consolidated based on voting interests. The implied acquisition differential must be amortized. All intercompany transactions must be eliminated. The income of the VIE must be allocated among the parties involved (i.e., equity-holders and the primary beneficiary). For a VIE, contractual arrangements, as opposed to ownership percentages, typically specify the distribution of its income.

Disclosure Requirements   The IASB's Exposure Draft on Consolidated Financial Statements proposes that a reporting entity must disclose information that enables users of its financial statements to evaluate

The primary beneficiary must disclose its basis of control and the nature and extent of risks resulting from its involvement with the SPE.

(a)   the basis of control and the related accounting consequences;
(b)   the interest that the NCIs have in the group's activities;
(c)   the nature and financial effect of restrictions that are a consequence of assets and liabilities being held by subsidiaries; and
(d)   the nature and extent of, and changes in, the market risk (interest rate, prepayment, currency, and other price risk), credit risk, and liquidity risk from the reporting entity's involvement with structured entities that the reporting entity does not control.

The disclosure requirements for a SPE are very extensive.

To meet objective (d) for a VIE, the exposure draft has very extensive disclosure requirements including the following:

- Summary information about the nature, purpose, and activities of the structured entities;
- Income from and the value of assets transferred to those structured entities;
- Categories and credit rating, weighted-average life of assets of the structured entities, and whether any assets have been written down or downgraded by rating agencies;
- The forms of structured entities' funding (e.g., commercial paper, medium-term notes) and their weighted-average life;
- Estimated exposure to loss or range of outcomes of that loss; and
- The nature and terms of any obligation of the reporting entity to provide liquidity support to structured entities and the extent of support provided.

Barclays Bank, a British financial services company, consolidated a number of SPEs, which it controlled. Relevant excerpts from Barclays Bank's 2008 financial statements are presented in Exhibit 9.2.

Exhibit 9.2

EXTRACTS (IN PART) FROM BARCLAYS BANK'S 2008 FINANCIAL STATEMENTS

4. Consolidation

Subsidiaries

The consolidated financial statements combine the financial statements of Barclays Bank PLC and all its subsidiaries, including certain special purpose entities (SPEs) where appropriate, made up to 31st December. Entities qualify as subsidiaries where the Group has the power to govern the financial and operating policies of the entity so as to obtain benefits from its activities, generally accompanying a shareholding of more than one half of the voting rights. The existence and effect of potential voting rights that are currently exercisable or convertible are considered in assessing whether the Group controls another entity. Details of the principal subsidiaries are given in Note 42.

SPEs are consolidated when the substance of the relationship between the Group and that entity indicates control. Potential indicators of control include, amongst others, an assessment of the Group's exposure to the risks and benefits of the SPE.

(continued)

29 Securitisations

Barclays packaged various loans, transferred them to SPEs, and used the loans as security to issue debt to third-party investors.

The Group was party to securitisation transactions involving Barclays residential mortgage loans, business loans and credit card balances. In addition, the Group acts as a conduit for commercial paper, whereby it acquires static pools of residential mortgage loans from other lending institutions for securitisation transactions.

In these transactions, the assets, or interests in the assets, or beneficial interests in the cash flows arising from the assets, are transferred to a special purpose entity, or to a trust which then transfers its beneficial interests to a special purpose entity, which then issues floating rate debt securities to third-party investors.

Securitisations may, depending on the individual arrangement result in continued recognition of the securitised assets and the recognition of the debt securities issued in the transaction; lead to partial continued recognition of the assets to the extent of the Group's continuing involvement in those assets or to derecognition of the assets and the separate recognition, as assets or liabilities, of any rights and obligations created or retained in the transfer. Full derecognition only occurs when the Group transfers both its contractual right to receive cash flows from the financial assets, or retains the contractual right to receive the cash flows, but assumes a contractual obligation to pay the cash flows to another party without material delay or reinvestment, and also transfers substantially all the risks and rewards of ownership, including credit risk, prepayment risk and interest rate risk.

The assets and liabilities of the SPEs were often included on Barclays' consolidated financial statements.

The following table shows the carrying amount of securitised assets, stated at the amount of the Group's continuing involvement where appropriate, together with the associated liabilities, for each category of asset in the balance sheet:

| | **The Group** | | | |
| | **2008** | | 2007 | |
	Carrying amount of assets £m	**Contractual amount of associated liabilities £m**	Carrying amount of assets £m	Contractual amount of associated liabilities £m
Loans and advances to customers				
Residential mortgage loans	**12,754**	**(13,172)**	16,000	(16,786)
Credit card receivables	**1,888**	**(2,109)**	4,217	(3,895)
Other personal lending	**212**	**(256)**	422	(485)
Wholesale and corporate loans and advances	**7,702**	**(8,937)**	8,493	(8,070)
Total	**22,556**	**(24,474)**	29,132	(29,236)
Assets designated at fair value through profit or loss				
Retained interest in residential mortgage loans	**316**	**—**	895	—

| | **The Bank** | | | |
| | **2008** | | 2007 | |
	Carrying amount of assets £m	**Contractual amount of associated liabilities £m**	Carrying amount of assets £m	Contractual amount of associated liabilities £m
Loans and advances to customers				
Residential mortgage loans	**8,073**	**(8,491)**	11,569	(12,219)
Credit card receivables	**1,888**	**(2,109)**	4,217	(3,895)
Other personal lending	**—**	**—**	—	—
Wholesale and corporate loans and advances	**7,702**	**(8,937)**	8,493	(8,070)
Total	**17,663**	**(19,537)**	24,279	(24,184)
Assets designated at fair value through profit or loss				
Retained interest in residential mortgage loans	**316**	**—**	895	—

Retained interests in residential mortgage loans are securities which represent a continuing exposure to the prepayment and credit risk in the underlying securitised assets. The total amount of the loans was £31,734m (2007: £23,097m) for the Group and £31,734m (2007: £23,097m) for the Bank. The retained interest is initially recorded as an allocation of the original carrying amount based on the relative fair values of the portion derecognised and the portion retained.

43 Other entities

There are a number of entities that do not qualify as subsidiaries under UK Law but which are consolidated when the substance of the relationship between the Group and the entity (usually a Special Purpose Entity (SPE)) indicates that the entity is controlled by the Group. Such entities are deemed to be controlled by the Group when relationships with such entities gives rise to benefits that are in substance no different from those that would arise were the entity a subsidiary.

Barclays disclosed its basis of control in the SPEs.

The consolidation of such entities may be appropriate in a number of situations, but primarily when:

—the operating and financial policies of the entity are closely defined from the outset (i.e. it operates on an 'autopilot' basis) with such policies being largely determined by the Group;
—the Group has rights to obtain the majority of the benefits of the entity and/or retains the majority of the residual or ownership risks related to the entity; or
—the activities of the entity are being conducted largely on behalf of the Group according to its specific business objectives.

Such entities are created for a variety of purposes including securitisation, structuring, asset realisation, intermediation and management.

Entities may have a different reporting date from that of the parent of 31st December. Dates may differ for a variety of reasons including local reporting regulations or tax laws. In accordance with our accounting policies, for the purpose of inclusion in the consolidated financial statements of Barclays PLC, entities with different reporting dates are made up until 31st December.

Entities may have restrictions placed on their ability to transfer funds, including payment of dividends and repayment of loans, to their parent entity. Reasons for the restrictions include:

—Central bank restrictions relating to local exchange control laws.
—Central bank capital adequacy requirements.
—Company law restrictions relating to treatment of the entities as going concerns.

Barclays disclosed when it did not control an entity even though it owned greater than 50 percent of the voting rights.

Although the Group's interest in the equity voting rights in certain entities exceeds 50%, or it may have the power to appoint a majority of their Boards of Directors, they are excluded from consolidation because the Group either does not direct the financial and operating policies of these entities, or on the grounds that another entity has a superior economic interest in them. Consequently, these entities are not deemed to be controlled by Barclays.

The table below includes information in relation to such entities as required by the Companies Act 1985, Section 231(5).

Country of registration or incorporation	Name	Percentage of ordinary share capital held %	Equity share-holders' funds £m	Retained loss for the year £m
UK	Oak Dedicated Limited	100	(4)	(1)
UK	Oak Dedicated Two Limited	100	(4)	—
UK	Oak Dedicated Three Limited	100	1	—
UK	Fitzroy Finance Limited	100	—	—
Cayman Islands	St James Fleet Investments Two Limited	100	2	—
Cayman Islands	BNY BT NewCo Limited	—	—	—

Clearly, the IASB wishes to enhance disclosures for all SPEs. Given that in the past, SPEs were often created in part to keep debt off a sponsoring firm's balance sheet, these enhanced disclosures are a significant improvement in financial reporting transparency.

The 2007 edition of *Financial Reporting in Canada* reported that of the 200 companies surveyed, 89 referred to VIEs in their disclosures, but only 46 indicated that they were primary beneficiaries and that the consolidation had a material effect on their financial statements.

Some examples of VIEs in Canada are described below.

Air Canada uses SPEs for leasing aircraft and engines and for the fueling of aircraft.

1. Air Canada has aircraft and engine leasing transactions with a number of SPEs that are VIEs. As at December 31, 2008, Air Canada was the primary beneficiary of a number of VIEs covering 44 aircraft. Air Canada also participates in fuel facilities arrangements operated through fuel facility corporations along with other airlines to contract for fuel services at various major Canadian airports. The fuel facility corporations are organizations incorporated under federal or provincial business corporations acts in order to acquire, finance, and lease assets used in connection with the fuelling of aircraft and ground support equipment. As at December 31, 2008, Air Canada was the primary beneficiary of three of the fuel facility corporations in Canada. Air Canada's involvement with five other fuel facility corporations was not consolidated because Air Canada felt that its risk of loss was remote.

Empire consolidates many of its franchise affiliate stores even though it does not own a majority interest in these stores.

2. Empire Company Limited, which owns 100 percent of Sobeys, consolidates many of its franchise affiliate stores because franchise agreements result in the company being deemed the primary beneficiary of the stores. The company also consolidates an independent entity that provides warehouse and distribution services for one of its distribution centres.

3. CanWest Global Communications Corp. is an international media company with interests in conventional television, specialty television channels, out-of-home advertising, publishing, and Web sites in Canada, Australia, Turkey, and the United States. The company provided interest-free loans to a third party to acquire the shares of companies that hold licences for various radio stations. The company, through wholly owned subsidiaries, also entered into agreements to provide operational, sales, and advisory services to each station on a fee-for-service basis. As a result of the company's financing of the purchase and operational agreements, the company determined that it was the primary beneficiary and accordingly consolidated these radio stations.

In an interesting departure from the examples above, Gildan Activewear Inc. determined that its joint venture company, CanAm Yarns LLC, met the criteria of being a VIE, requiring full consolidation instead of proportionate consolidation as was used in previous years. The consolidation of joint arrangements is discussed in the next section of this chapter.

Joint Arrangements

In a joint arrangement, participants contribute resources to carry out a specific undertaking.

A joint arrangement is a contractual arrangement whereby two or more parties undertake an activity together and jointly control that activity. IFRS 10: Joint Arrangements requires that parties to a joint arrangement recognize their contractual rights and obligations arising from that arrangement. A common example of a joint arrangement is where one venturer provides the technical expertise and the other provides marketing and/or financial expertise. Joint arrangements are often formed for expensive and risky projects. They are fairly common in the oil-and-gas exploration sector and in large real estate developments. Also, a Canadian company will often form a joint arrangement with a foreign company or the government of a foreign country as a means of expanding into international markets. For example, Bombardier produces trains for China by operating under a joint agreement with a Chinese car manufacturer.

In many joint operations, the venturers contribute the use of assets but retain title to the assets.

Joint arrangements are typically classified into two types — joint operations and joint ventures. The type of joint arrangement an entity is a party to depends on the rights and obligations that arise from the contractual arrangement. Under a jointly controlled operation, each venturer contributes the use of assets or resources to the joint venture activity but maintains individual title to and control of these assets and resources. An example would be a case in which one venturer manufactures part of a product, a second venturer completes the manufacturing process, and a third venturer handles the marketing of the product. Revenue and expenses are shared in accordance with the joint arrangement agreement. In some joint operations, the venturers may jointly control some of the assets used in the joint arrangement. These joint arrangements do not involve the establishment of a corporation, partnership, or other entity, or a financial structure that is separate from the venturers themselves. An example of this type of arrangement is an oil pipeline. The venturers may contribute assets to the construction of the pipeline. Once the pipeline is completed, it is jointly owned and used by the venturers, who share the costs in accordance with an agreement. An entity is a party to a joint venture if it has rights only to a share of the outcome generated by a separate entity, which has its own assets and liabilities. The separate entity may be a corporation, partnership, or other entity, or a financial structure that is separate from the venturers themselves.

In most joint ventures, the venturers contribute assets to a separate legal entity, which has title to the assets.

Of the 200 companies that made up the sample used in the 2007 edition of *Financial Reporting in Canada*, 86 reported investments in joint ventures. We will illustrate the accounting for both types of joint arrangements.

The accounting principles involved with reporting a joint arrangement are contained in IFRS 10. It deals with the financial reporting of an interest in a joint arrangement; it does not cover the accounting for the joint arrangement itself. IFRS 10 presents the following definitions relevant to our discussions:

> **Joint control** is the contractually agreed sharing of control by all parties to undertake an activity together.

> A **venturer** is a party to a joint arrangement, has joint control over that joint arrangement, has the right and ability to obtain future returns from the resources of the joint arrangement, and is exposed to the related risks.

According to GAAP, joint control is the key feature in a joint arrangement, which means no one venturer can unilaterally control the venture regardless of the size of its equity contribution.

A distinctive feature of these descriptions is the concept of *joint control*, which must be present for a joint arrangement to exist. Joint control is established by an agreement between the venturers (usually in writing), whereby no one venturer can unilaterally control the joint arrangement regardless of the number of assets it contributes. For example, a single venturer (Company L) could own more than 50 percent of the voting shares of Company M. This would normally indicate that Company M is a subsidiary; however, if there was an agreement establishing joint control, Company M would be a joint arrangement and not a subsidiary, and Company L would be a venturer and not a parent.

Accounting for Joint Operations

A venturer's interest in a joint operation is reported in a fashion similar to activities carried out by any entity. It applies relevant IFRSs as it recognizes the following:

(a) The assets it controls and the liabilities it incurs;
(b) The expenses it incurs; and
(c) Its share of the revenue and expenses from the sale of goods or services by the joint arrangement.

Example 1   APP Inc., BIB Ltd., and COT Inc. sign an agreement to produce fridges for sale to wholesalers. APP will produce the motors and condensers for use in the fridges. BIB will receive the motors and condensers from APP, purchase all other parts, and assemble the fridges. COT will market, sell, and distribute the fridges to wholesalers. The three companies must agree to all major operating and financing decisions. The proceeds from sale of the fridges will be distributed 25 percent to APP, 45 percent to BIB, and 30 percent to COT.

APP will account for the assets, liabilities, and expenses involved with producing the motors and condensers for the joint operations in the same manner as it would if it were producing these items for its own operations. The cost of the motors and condensers would be included in inventory. When the inventory is shipped to BIB, it is similar to inventory on consignment. No revenue is recognized until the inventory is eventually sold by COT. At that time, APP would recognize its 25 percent share of the sales revenue related to the sale of the fridges.

APP reports the assets contributed to the joint operations on its own books until the final product is sold to the end customer.

In this example, each of the three companies used their own assets to fulfill their contribution to the joint arrangement. They shared in the revenues only from the sale of the fridges.

When the venturers jointly own certain assets, the accounting becomes a bit more complicated. In addition to accounting for their own assets and liabilities used in the joint operation, they would have to account for their share of the costs and expenses involved with the jointly owned assets. This is a form of proportionate consolidation but on a very limited basis.

Example 2   DOC Inc., EGG Ltd., and FRY Inc. sign an agreement to collectively purchase an oil pipeline and to hire a company to manage and operate the pipeline on their behalf. The costs involved in running the pipeline and the revenue earned from the pipeline are shared by the three parties based on their ownership percentage. All major operating and financing decisions related to the pipeline must be agreed to by the three companies. The cost of purchasing the pipeline was $10,000,000. The pipeline has an estimated 20-year useful life with no residual value. The management fee for operating the pipeline for Year 1 was $2,000,000. Revenue earned from the pipeline in Year 1 was $3,300,000. DOC invested $3,000,000 for a 30 percent interest in the pipeline.

DOC reports its proportionate share of the assets, liabilities, revenues, and expenses of the joint operation.

DOC would prepare the following entries for Year 1 to capture its share of the activities related to the pipeline:

Pipeline	3,000,000	
Cash		3,000,000
Pipeline operating expenses (30% × 2,000,000)	600,000	
Cash		600,000
Cash (30% × 3,300,000)	990,000	
Revenue from pipeline		990,000
Amortization expense — pipeline (3,000,000/20 years)	150,000	
Accumulated amortization — pipeline		150,000

Example 3   Instead of contributing cash for a 30 percent interest in the pipeline, DOC contributed steel pipes to be used by the company constructing the pipeline. DOC had manufactured the pipes at a cost of $2,200,000. All parties to the contract agreed that the fair value of these pipes was $3,000,000 and the fair value of the pipeline once it was completed was $10,000,000. All other facts are the same as in Example 2.

IFRS 10 indicates the following:

A portion of the gain can be recognized on the contribution of assets to a joint operation under certain circumstances.

> When a venturer contributes an asset to a jointly controlled operation, recognition of any portion of a gain or loss from the transaction shall reflect the substance of the transaction. While the assets are retained by the joint operation and provided the venturer has transferred the significant risks and rewards of ownership, the venturer shall recognize only that portion of the gain or loss that is attributable to the interests of the other venturers. However, the venturer shall recognize the full amount of any loss when the contribution or sale provides evidence of a reduction in the net realizable value of current assets or an impairment loss.

In our illustration, the other venturers have a 70 percent interest in the joint operation. If the significant benefits and risks are transferred, DOC could recognize a gain of $560,000 (70% × [3,000,000 − 2,200,000]).

A gain can be recognized when the significant risks and rewards have been transferred.

When the item transferred is a non-monetary asset, SIC 13 provides guidance in determining whether the benefits and risks are transferred. It states that the gain can be recognized except when

(a) the significant risks and rewards of ownership of the contributed non-monetary asset(s) have not been transferred to the jointly controlled entity; or

(b) the gain or loss on the non-monetary contribution cannot be measured reliably; or

(c) the contribution transaction lacks commercial substance, as that term is described in IAS 16.

A gain can be recognized when the commercial substance test is met.

IAS 16 states that an exchange transaction has commercial substance if

(a) the amount, timing and risk of the future cash flows of the asset received differ from those of the asset(s) transferred out; or

(b) the after-tax cash flows of the part of the business affected by the transaction (entity-specific value) have changed as a result of the exchange; and

(c) the difference in (a) or (b) is significant relative to the fair values of the assets exchanged.

IAS 18: Revenue provides guidance to assess when the significant risks and rewards of ownership are transferred. SIC 13 states that unrealized gains or losses on non-monetary assets contributed to jointly controlled operations must be eliminated against the underlying assets. Such unrealized gains or losses must not be presented as deferred gains or losses in the venturer's consolidated statement of financial position.

The following journal entries would be recorded, assuming that the significant risks and rewards of ownership have been transferred:

Pipeline	3,000,000	
Steel pipes		2,200,000
Gain on steel pipes (70% of gain)		560,000
Unrealized gain — contra account (30% of gain)		240,000
Amortization expense (3,000,000/20)	150,000	
Accumulated amortization		150,000
Unrealized gain — contra account (240,000/20)	12,000	
Amortization expense		12,000

The venturer's own interest in the gain is recognized over the life of the asset.

The unrealized gain is a contra account to the pipeline account; it should not be reported as a deferred gain on the liability side of the balance sheet. When DOC prepares a balance sheet, the unrealized gain will be offset against the pipeline such that the pipeline's net cost is $2,760,000 ($3,000,000 − $240,000). As the net cost of the pipeline is being amortized, the unrealized gain account is also being amortized. In effect, the unrealized gain is being brought into income over the life of the pipeline. As the pipeline is being used to generate revenue on transactions with outsiders, the venturer's own share of the unrealized gain is being recognized in income. This is similar to what happened in Chapter 7, when the unrealized profits from an intercompany sale of a depreciable asset were realized over the life of the depreciable asset.

Accounting for an Interest in a Joint Venture

Proportionate consolidation was required for reporting joint ventures in Canada prior to 2011.

When parties to an agreement to establish or purchase a corporation, partnership, or other entity, or a financial structure that is separate from the venturers themselves, and this entity is jointly controlled by two or more venturers, this entity is called a joint venture. Until the implementation of IFRSs in 2011, Canadian GAAP requires that proportional consolidation be used when reporting an interest in a joint venture. Proportionate consolidation is a method of accounting whereby a venturer's share of each of the assets, liabilities, income, and expenses of a jointly controlled entity is combined line by line with similar items in the venturer's financial statements or reported as separate line items in the venturer's financial statements. Proportional consolidation is an application of the proprietary theory, which was illustrated in Chapter 4.

The equity method is required for reporting joint ventures under IFRS 10.

Under IFRS 10, the venturer must use the equity method to report its investment in a joint venture. Under the equity method, the venturer recognizes its share of the income earned by the joint venture through one line on the income statement, income from joint venture, and through one line on the balance sheet, investment account. In addition, the venturer needs to make adjustments through these same accounts for its share of the following items, which are illustrated below:

- Allocation and amortization of acquisition differentials,
- Unrealized profits from intercompany transactions, and
- Contributions to the joint venture.

Acquisition Differentials   The formation of a joint venture by its venturers cannot result in acquisition differentials in the investment accounts of the venturers. However, if a venturer purchased an interest in an existing entity, it could pay an amount different from its interest in the carrying value of the joint venture's net assets, resulting in an acquisition differential. This acquisition differential would be allocated and amortized in the same manner illustrated previously for parent–subsidiary affiliations.

Intercompany Transactions   You will recall from our discussions in past chapters that intercompany profits in assets are fully eliminated from the consolidated statements of a parent and its subsidiaries. If the subsidiary was the selling company, 100 percent of the profit, net of income tax, is eliminated and allocated to both the NCI and the controlling interest. If the parent was the selling company, the entire net-of-tax profit is eliminated and allocated to the shareholders of the parent.

For a joint venture, the venturer's share of any intercompany asset profits are eliminated regardless of whether the sale was upstream or downstream.

For intercompany transactions between a venturer and the joint venture, only the venturer's share of the unrealized profit is eliminated. The other venturers' share of the profit from the intercompany transaction is considered realized if the other venturers are not related to each other. Since none of the venturers can individually control the entity, any transaction carried out by the joint venture should be viewed as an arm's-length transaction to the extent of the other venturers' interest in the joint venture. The venturer's own interest in the profit from the intercompany transaction is not realized because the venturer cannot make a profit by selling to or buying from itself.

The same treatment is prescribed for the sale of assets at a loss, except in situations where the transaction provides evidence of a reduction in the net realizable value of the asset, in which case the full amount of the loss is immediately recognized.

Example 4 below illustrates the use of the equity method to report an interest in a joint venture. Appendix 9A repeats Example 4 using proportionate consolidation rather than the equity method. The method of presentation is quite different. However, the net income attributable to and the retained earnings of the investor in the joint venture are the same under both methods.

Example 4 Explor Ltd., a Calgary-based oil exploration company, is a joint venture in which A Company has a 45 percent ownership interest. A Company, an original founder of Explor, uses the equity method to account for its investment but has made no entries to its investment account for Year 4. The following are the financial statements of the two companies on December 31, Year 4:

INCOME STATEMENTS — Year 4

	A Company	Explor
Sales	$900,000	$300,000
Cost of sales	630,000	180,000
Miscellaneous expenses	100,000	40,000
	730,000	220,000
Net income	$170,000	$ 80,000

BALANCE SHEETS — December 31, Year 4

	A Company	Explor
Miscellaneous assets	$654,500	$277,000
Inventory	110,000	90,000
Investment in Explor	85,500	—
	$850,000	$367,000
Miscellaneous liabilities	$130,000	$ 97,000
Common shares	300,000	100,000
Retained earnings, January 1	250,000	90,000
Net income — Year 4	170,000	80,000
	$850,000	$367,000

Financial statements of a venturer and a joint venture.

During Year 4, A Company sold merchandise totalling $110,000 to Explor and recorded a gross profit of 30 percent on these sales. On December 31, Year 4, the inventory of Explor contained items purchased from A Company for $22,000, and Explor had a payable of $5,000 to A Company on this date.

The unrealized after-tax profit to be eliminated at the end of Year 4 is $1,782, calculated as follows:

Intercompany profits in inventory:	
Total at end of year (22,000 × 30%)	$6,600
Before-tax profit considered realized — 55 percent	3,630
Unrealized before-tax profit — 45 percent	2,970
Tax on profit (40%)	1,188
After-tax unrealized profit	$1,782

The following entries would be made by Company A in Year 4 under the equity method:

Invest in Explor (45% × 80,000)	36,000	
Income from joint venture		36,000

Only the venturer's share of profits is eliminated.

Income from joint venture	1,782	
Invest in Explor		1,782
To eliminate unrealized profits		

These entries will increase Company A's net income to $204,218, calculated as follows:

Income of A Company		$170,000
Less after-tax unrealized inventory profit		1,782
Adjusted net income		168,218
Income of Explor	$80,000	
A's ownership interest	45%	36,000
Net income		$204,218

Since A Company used the equity method prior to this year, no adjustments are necessary for its retained earnings at the beginning of the year.

Contributions to the Joint Venture

Suppose that on the date of formation of a joint venture, instead of contributing cash, a venturer contributes non-monetary assets and receives an interest in the joint venture, and that the assets contributed have a fair value that is greater than their carrying value in the records of the venturer. Would it be appropriate for the venturer to record a gain from investing in the joint venture? And if so, how much, and when should it be recognized? The requirements set out in IFRS 10 regarding this matter are as follows:

1. The investment should be recorded at the fair value of the non-monetary assets transferred to the joint venture.

2. Only the gain represented by interests of the other nonrelated venturers should be recognized on the date of the contribution and only if the significant risks and rewards of ownership of the contributed non-monetary asset have been transferred to the joint venture. This same principle was applied in Example 3 on a transfer of an asset to a joint operation.

The unrealized gain is recognized as the asset is used to generate a profit on transactions with outsiders.

3. The portion of the gain represented by the venturer's own interest should be unrealized until the asset has been sold to unrelated outsiders by the joint venture. Alternatively, the unrealized gain can be recognized over the life of the asset if the asset is being used to generate a positive net income for the joint venture. In effect, the product or service being sold by the joint venture to an outsider is allowing the venturer to recognize a portion of the unrealized gain. It

is similar to selling a portion of the asset to outsiders. The unrealized gains are contra accounts to the investment in joint venture account. They will be offset in the investment account on the balance sheet.

4. If a loss results from the recording of the investment, the portion of the loss represented by the interest of the other unrelated venturers is recognized immediately into income. When it is evident that the loss is permanent, the entire loss is immediately recognized.

5. When the venturer transfers assets to the joint venture and receives cash in addition to an interest in the joint venture, the cash received can be considered the proceeds from the partial sale of the assets to the other unrelated venturers, provided that the cash came from the investment of the other venturers or from the other venturers' share of joint venture borrowings.

> **When cash is indirectly received from the other venturers, the cash is considered to be proceeds of a partial sale to the other venturers.**

The following examples will illustrate these concepts.

Example 1   A Co. and B Inc. formed JV Ltd. on January 1, Year 1. A Co. invested equipment with a book value of $200,000 and a fair value of $700,000 for a 40 percent interest in JV Ltd., while B Inc. contributed equipment with a total fair value of $1,050,000, for a 60 percent interest in JV Ltd. We will concern ourselves only with the recording by A Co. of its 40 percent interest in JV Ltd., and we will assume that the equipment has an estimated useful life of 10 years. On December 31, Year 1, JV Ltd. reported a net income of $204,000. We will assume that the significant risks and rewards of ownership have not transferred in this situation because A Co. owned equipment both before and after the contribution to the joint venture. The gains are calculated as follows:

Fair value of equipment transferred to JV Ltd.	$700,000
Carrying value of equipment on A Co.'s books	200,000
Unrealized gain on transfer to JV Ltd. to be netted against investment account	$500,000

A Co.'s journal entry to record the initial investment on January 1, Year 1, is as follows:

> **A Co.'s $500,000 gain from investing equipment is unrealized.**

Investment in JV Ltd.	700,000	
Equipment		200,000
Unrealized gain — contra account		500,000

Using the equity method of accounting, A Co. will record its 40 percent share of the yearly net incomes or losses reported by JV Ltd.; in addition, it will recognize the unrealized gains in income over the life of the equipment.

The December 31, Year 1, entries are as follows:

Investment in JV Ltd.	81,600	
Equity earnings from JV Ltd. (40% × 204,000)		81,600

> **A portion of the unrealized gain is taken into income each year.**

Unrealized gain — contra account	50,000	
Gain on transfer of equipment to JV Ltd. (500,000 ÷ 10 years)		50,000

This method of recognizing the gain from investing will be repeated over the next nine years, unless JV Ltd. sells this equipment before that period expires. If it does, A Co. will immediately take the balance in the unrealized gains account into income.

Example 2   The facts from this example are identical in all respects to those from Example 1 except that we assume that A Co. receives a 40 percent interest in JV Ltd. plus $130,000 in cash in return for investing equipment with a fair value of

$700,000 while B Inc. contributed equipment with a fair value of $725,000 plus cash of $130,000 for a total contribution of $855,000.

The original gain on the transfer ($500,000) is the same as in Example 1. However, because the $130,000 in cash received by A Co. came entirely from the cash invested by B Inc., it is considered to be the sale proceeds of the portion of the equipment deemed to have been sold. In other words, A Co. is considered to have sold a portion of the equipment to B Inc. (through the joint venture) and will immediately record a gain from selling, computed as follows:

A gain is recognized for the portion (130 ÷ 700) of the equipment deemed to be sold.

Sale proceeds	$130,000
Carrying value of equipment sold (130 ÷ 700 × 200,000)	37,143
Immediate gain from selling equipment to B Inc.	$ 92,857

A Co.'s January 1, Year 1, journal entry to record the investment of equipment and the receipt of cash would be as follows:

Cash	130,000	
Investment in JV Ltd.	570,000	
Equipment		200,000
Gain on transfer of equipment to JV Ltd.		92,857
Unrealized gain — contra account		407,143

The December 31, Year 1, entries are as follows:

Investment in JV Ltd.	81,600	
Equity earnings from JV Ltd. (40% × 204,000)		81,600
Unrealized gain — contra account	40,714	
Gain on transfer of equipment to JV Ltd. (407,143 ÷ 10 years)		40,714

Assuming a December 31 year-end, the $133,571 (92,857 + 40,714) gain on transfer of equipment to JV Ltd. will appear in A Co's Year 1 income statement. The unamortized balance of the unrealized gain of $366,429 (407,143 − 40,714) will be offset against the investment account. The gross and net amounts of the investment account will be $651,600 (570,000 + 81,600) and $285,171 (651,600 − 366,429), respectively.

Example 3 In this last example, we will increase the amount of cash that A Co. received when it invested equipment for a 40 percent interest in JV Ltd. Let us assume that the cash received was $150,000 instead of the $130,000 that we used in Example 2. Because B Inc. invested only $130,000 cash in the joint venture, the additional $20,000 was borrowed by JV Ltd. In this situation, the $150,000 cash received is considered to be partly sale proceeds and partly a return of equity to A Co. The allocation of the cash between sale proceeds and return of equity is made as follows:

When some of the cash received by A Co. comes from joint venture borrowings, only B Co.'s share of the cash borrowed is considered proceeds from the sale of land.

Sale proceeds:		
From B Inc.'s investment in JV Ltd.		$130,000
From borrowings of JV Ltd.	20,000	
B Inc.'s proportion	60%	12,000
		142,000
Return of equity to A Co.:		
A Co.'s proportion of JV borrowings	40%	8,000
Total cash received		$150,000

The gain from selling is computed as follows:

Sale proceeds	$142,000
Carrying value of assets sold (142/700 × 200,000)	40,571
Immediate gain from selling equipment to B Inc.	$101,429

A Co.'s January 1, Year 1, journal entry would be as follows:

The gain of $500,000 is allocated to A Co. and B Co., with a portion of B Co.'s gain recognized as a result of the cash proceeds.

Cash	150,000	
Investment in JV Ltd.	550,000	
Equipment		200,000
Gain from transfer of equipment to JV Ltd.		101,429
Unrealized gain — contra account		398,571

On December 31, Year 1, A Co.'s journal entries would be as follows:

Investment in JV Ltd.	81,600	
Equity earnings from JV Ltd. (40% × 204,000)		81,600
Unrealized gain — contra account	39,857	
Gain from transfer of equipment to JV Ltd. (398,571 ÷ 10 years)		39,857

In the preceding examples, A Co. used the equity method to report its interest in the joint venture. If A Co. had used proportionate consolidation, the unrealized gain — contra account becomes a contra account to the assets originally contributed to the joint venture. It will be deducted from the venturer's share of the related assets. These assets on the proportionately consolidated balance sheet will be reported at an amount equal to the venturer's share of what would remain of the carrying amount of the assets had they not been contributed to the joint venture. In effect, the contra account brings these assets back to the historical cost amounts on the consolidated balance sheet.

Disclosure Requirements An entity must provide a description of the nature and extent of its operations conducted through each of the different types of joint arrangement. An entity should disclose information about commitments and contingent liabilities relating to its interest in joint arrangements. A venturer must disclose information that enables users of its financial statements to evaluate its activities conducted through joint ventures. To meet this objective, the more substantial items required to be disclosed are as follows:

An entity must disclose the nature and extent of its operations conducted through joint arrangements.

- A list and description of interests in significant joint ventures and the proportion of ownership interest held;
- The venturer's interest in each of current assets, non-current assets, current liabilities, non-current liabilities, revenues, and profit or loss from joint ventures; and
- The nature and extent of any significant restrictions on the ability of the joint ventures to transfer funds to the venturer.

Exhibit 9.3 on page 470 provides an example of the type of disclosure required by IFRS 10: Joint Arrangements.

Exhibit 9.3

ILLUSTRATIVE DISCLOSURE EXAMPLE — JOINT ARRANGEMENTS

Joint ventures

SampleCo uses the equity method to account for its investments in joint ventures.

A joint venture is a contractual arrangement whereby two or more parties undertake an economic activity that is subject to joint control. A jointly controlled entity is a joint venture that involves the establishment of a separate entity in which each venturer has an interest. SampleCo recognizes its interest in joint ventures using the equity method. Under the equity method, the investment in the joint venture is carried in the balance sheet at cost plus post-acquisition changes in SampleCo's share of net assets of the joint venture. The income statement reflects the share of the results of operations of the joint venture. Periodically SampleCo determines whether it is necessary to recognize an impairment loss with respect to SampleCo's net investment in the joint venture. The reporting dates of the joint ventures are the same as those of SampleCo and the accounting policies of the joint ventures conform to those used by SampleCo.

5.9.2 Joint ventures
MSCure, United States

In September 2008, ABC Products Inc., and SampleCo established a joint venture, MSCure, to operate the MSCure MS7 Development Center in San Francisco, California. Each company holds 50% of the shares. The initial contribution amounts to $500. The joint venture further develops the PER.C6 cell line and provides a unique solution for the production of pharmaceutical proteins to licensees utilizing the PER.C6 human cell line in the biotech industry. MSCure recharges the costs incurred to the venturers. No additional fundings are planned.

Summary financial information of this joint venture, not adjusted for the percentage ownership held by SampleCo is as follows:

In thousands of Euro

SampleCo discloses details of the assets, liabilities, revenues, and expenses for the joint venture.

	2009	2008
Joint Venture's balance sheet (MSCure)		
Current assets	**12,060**	11,131
Non-current assets	**11,360**	1,981
Current liabilities	**(11,440)**	(1,965)
Non-current liabilities	—	—
Net assets	**11,980**	11,147
Joint Venture's revenues and expenses		
Revenues	**18,721**	18,081
Expenses	**(17,972)**	(17,348)
Profit for the period	**749**	733

The tax charge for MSCure MS7 Development Center is accounted for in the financial statements of the venturers. The tax charge recognized in the financial statements relating to the percentage owned by SampleCo amounts to € 151 in 2009 (2008: € 146).

Investor in Joint Arrangement   An investor in a joint arrangement is a party to a joint arrangement and does not have joint control over that joint arrangement. The investor wants to receive a return on investment without being actively involved in the operating and financing decisions of the joint arrangement. He or she must account for the investment in accordance with IAS 39 or by using the equity method if it has significant influence in the joint arrangement.

Deferred Income Taxes and Business Combinations

Up to this point, we have ignored the income tax implications associated with business combinations. Corporate tax law in this area is quite complex and can be fully understood only by readers who have been exposed to the topic through in-depth tax courses. There is always the danger that essential accounting concepts associated with business combinations and consolidated financial statements could be overshadowed if an attempt is made to combine basic accounting issues with complex tax allocation procedures. Attentive readers will now have achieved a reasonable understanding of the broad accounting concepts behind consolidated statements. To complete our coverage of this financial reporting process, we now turn our attention to the additional effects that income tax allocation can have on the accounting for a business combination. But before we do this, we provide the following useful background material.

Deferred Income Tax Concepts

A temporary difference occurs when the carrying amount of an asset or a liability does not equal its tax base.

IAS 12: Income Taxes uses the balance sheet (or liability) approach. This approach requires that the differences between the carrying value of an asset or a liability in the balance sheet and its tax base be accounted for. These differences are called *temporary differences.* The tax base of an asset is the amount that will be deductible for tax purposes against any taxable economic benefits that will flow to an entity when it recovers the carrying amount of the asset. If those economic benefits will not be taxable, the tax base of the asset is equal to its carrying amount. The tax base of a liability is its carrying amount, less any amount that will be deductible for tax purposes in respect of that liability in future periods. In the case of revenue received in advance, the tax base of the resulting liability is its carrying amount, less any amount of the revenue that will not be taxable in future periods.

Under IAS 12, there are two basic types of temporary differences: deductible and taxable. A *deductible temporary difference* is one that can be deducted in determining taxable income in the future when the asset or liability is recovered or settled for its carrying amount. These differences exist when (a) the carrying amount of an asset is less than its tax base, or (b) an amount related to a liability can be deducted for tax purposes. Accounting for these differences results in *deferred income tax assets*.

When the carrying amount of an asset is greater than its tax base, the result is a deferred tax liability.

A *taxable temporary difference* is one that will result in future taxable amounts when the carrying amount of the asset or the liability is recovered or settled. Such differences, which result in *deferred income tax liabilities*, occur mainly when the carrying amount of an asset is greater than its tax base.

A few examples will illustrate some of these concepts. We assume a 40 percent tax rate in each case.

Example 1   A company has an account payable of $3,000 on its balance sheet at the end of Year 1 for unpaid expenses that were deducted for tax purposes during Year 1. The carrying amount is $3,000. The tax base of the liability is as follows:

Carrying amount	$3,000
Less: amount deductible for tax in future periods	–0–
Tax base	$3,000

Because the carrying amount and the tax base are equal, a temporary difference does not exist.

Example 2   At the end of Year 1, a company has an account receivable of $1,000 from sales made during the year. This receivable is expected to be collected through a series of instalments during Years 2 and 3. For tax purposes, the revenue is taxable in the year of collection. The carrying amount at the end of Year 1 is $1,000, while the tax base is zero. This creates a taxable temporary difference of $1,000, requiring a deferred tax liability of $400.

A deductible temporary difference gives rise to a deferred tax asset.

Example 3   At the end of Year 1, a company has a warranty liability of $1,500. Warranty costs are deductible for tax purposes only when they have been paid. The carrying value is $1,500, while the tax base is zero. We have a deductible temporary difference of $1,500, requiring a deferred tax asset of $600.

Example 4   An asset is purchased at a cost of $2,000. For financial statement purposes, it will be depreciated using the straight-line method over a five-year life, with no estimated residual value. For tax purposes, capital cost allowance (CCA) will be taken at a 30 percent rate, subject to the half-year rule in the first year. The following illustrates the yearly depreciation and CCA over the first three years:

When the amount of CCA taken exceeds book depreciation, the result is a deferred tax liability.

	Carrying value	Tax base
Year 1 cost	$2,000	$2,000
Year 1: Depreciation	400	—
CCA	—	300
Balance, end of Year 1	1,600	1,700
Year 2: Depreciation	400	—
CCA	—	510
Balance, end of Year 2	1,200	1,190
Year 3: Depreciation	400	—
CCA	—	357
Balance, end of Year 3	$ 800	$ 833

Note that at the end of Year 1, there is a deductible temporary difference of $100, requiring a deferred tax asset of $40. At the end of Year 2, we have a taxable temporary difference of $10, requiring a deferred tax liability of $4. By the end of Year 3, we are back to a deductible temporary difference of $33, requiring a deferred tax asset of approximately $13. Note also that while the carrying value of this asset becomes zero at the end of Year 5, it will have a positive tax base for an infinite number of future years. In other words, the reversing that inevitably must occur is often a very long time happening.

These examples have focused on some of the basics behind the balance sheet approach, and will be useful in understanding some of the business combination illustrations that follow. However, before we examine the deferred income tax effects associated with a business combination, there is one other interesting provision of IAS 21 that needs to be examined.

The Acquisition of an Asset at a Price Different from the Tax Base (other than in a business combination)   Because the balance sheet approach requires the recording of a deferred tax asset or liability whenever the carrying value of an asset or liability

differs from its tax base, a unique situation exists when a single asset is purchased and its tax base is different from its cost on the date that it was acquired. IAS 12 states that when an asset is acquired other than in a business combination, and the transaction does not affect accounting profit or taxable profit, the entity does not recognize any deferred tax liability or asset either on initial recognition or subsequently. For example, an entity purchases an asset for $1,000 with an estimated useful life of five years and an estimated residual value of zero. However, the tax base is zero because depreciation of the asset is not deductible for tax purposes. On disposal, any capital gain would not be taxable and any capital loss would not be deductible. Although there is a taxable temporary difference on the date the asset was acquired, IAS 12 states that a deferred tax liability should not be recognized in this situation. If the liability were recorded, the carrying value of the asset would have to be increased by this amount. Then, the reported amount would be different than the amount paid, which may be confusing or less transparent to the users of the financial statements.

> **Deferred taxes are not recorded when acquiring a single asset for which there is a temporary difference.**

Business Combination Illustrations

IAS 12 not only requires application of the balance sheet approach, but also requires that deferred income taxes associated with the acquisition differential be accounted for.

We use the following simple illustrations to convey the basic concepts involved and the reasoning behind them.

Example Sub Co. has a single productive asset. The balance sheet of this company is shown below:

SUB CO. — BALANCE SHEET
December 31, Year 3

> **There is a deferred tax asset on the separate entity books of the subsidiary.**

Asset	$800
Deferred income taxes	12
	$812
Liabilities	$300
Shareholders' equity	512
	$812

The tax base of the single asset and the liabilities is as follows:

Asset	$830
Liabilities	300
Net	$530

Using a 40 percent tax rate, Sub Co. has correctly applied the provisions of IAS 12 by setting up in its separate-entity statements a deferred tax asset of $12 for the deductible temporary difference of $30.

On January 1, Year 4, Parent Inc. purchased 100 percent of Sub Co. for $1,000 cash. Parent determines that the fair value of Sub's single asset is $950 and that the fair value of its liabilities is $300. The calculation of the acquisition differential is made in the following manner:

When a business combination occurs, the acquirer records the net assets acquired at fair values, and when the tax base of these net assets are a different amount, a deferred tax asset or liability becomes part of the allocation of the acquisition cost.

Cost of 100 percent of Sub Co.		$1,000
Net assets of Sub Co.	512	
Parent's ownership	100%	512
Acquisition differential		488
Allocated:		
Asset (950 − 800)	150	
Deferred income tax asset (liability) (see calculation below)	(60)	90
Balance, goodwill		$ 398

The calculation of the deferred tax liability to be used for consolidation purposes is as follows:

In this example, a subsidiary's deferred tax asset is replaced by a deferred tax liability upon consolidation.

Asset fair value used in consolidation	$950
Tax base of the asset	830
Taxable temporary difference	120
Tax rate of Sub Co.	40%
Deferred tax liability — as recalculated for consolidation	48
Deferred tax asset — as previously stated by Sub	12
Fair value adjustment required on consolidation	$ 60

Because the fair value and the tax base of Sub's liabilities are both $300, no deferred income tax implications are associated with these liabilities. Note that in applying these concepts, we are replacing a $12 deferred tax asset on the balance sheet of Sub Co. with a deferred tax liability of $48 on the consolidated balance sheet with respect to the same asset. Note also that no deferred taxes are recorded in relation to the goodwill of $398. Goodwill is measured as a residual. Therefore, it would be inappropriate to recognize a deferred tax liability on the temporary difference related to the goodwill because it would increase the carrying amount of goodwill and it would no longer be a residual amount. Also, goodwill is usually not deductible for tax purposes. Any difference between the carrying amount for goodwill and the tax base would be a permanent difference.

Let us assume that Parent Inc. was formed on December 31, Year 3, by the issuance of common shares for $1,000 in cash. The nonconsolidated balance sheet of Parent is shown below, followed by the consolidated balance sheet (with bracketed amounts indicating its preparation using the direct approach):

PARENT INC. — BALANCE SHEET
January 1, Year 4

Investment in Sub Co.	$1,000
Common shares	$1,000

PARENT INC. — CONSOLIDATED BALANCE SHEET
January 1, Year 4

Assets (800 + 150)	$ 950
Goodwill	398
	$1,348
Liabilities	$ 300
Deferred income taxes	48
Common shares	1,000
	$1,348

The deferred income tax liability that appears on the consolidated balance sheet can be verified as follows:

Carrying value of assets above (excluding goodwill)	$950
Tax base of assets	830
Taxable temporary difference	120
Tax rate	40%
Deferred income tax liability	$ 48

In preparing consolidated financial statements in subsequent periods, the values used for each subsidiary's net assets have to be compared to their tax base in order to determine new values for deferred tax assets and liabilities.

The allocation of the purchase price at the date of acquisition is fairly complicated in situations involving deferred income taxes. In subsequent periods, we must compare the carrying value of an asset or liability to its tax base on each date that a balance sheet is prepared, and make an adjustment to previously recorded deferred income tax balances. When we prepare a consolidated balance sheet subsequent to acquisition, we will have to compare the values used in the consolidation for a subsidiary's net assets with the tax base of these assets in the records of the subsidiary.

Operating Loss Carry-forwards

Under IAS 12, accounting recognition can be given to the carry-forward of unused tax losses to the extent that it is probable that taxable profit will be available against which the deductible temporary difference can be utilized. If the acquired company has already recognized a deferred tax asset due to the potential carry-forward of unused tax losses, this deferred tax asset will be allowed to stand on the date of the business combination. The combining of the two companies does not ordinarily change this status. However, if the acquired company was not able to recognize unused tax losses, the fact that it is combining with the acquiring company may provide the additional impetus to satisfy the "probability" criterion. This could result because the two companies combined will do business with each other or will be able to reduce future costs, all of which could result in greater possibilities of having future taxable incomes than was the case before the combination. The deferred income tax asset would be included on the consolidated financial statements when the cost of the purchase is allocated. Note that recognizing such a deferred tax asset at the date of acquisition as part of the allocation of the acquisition cost reduces the amount that otherwise would have been allocated to goodwill. This concept must also be taken into account in situations where a deferred tax asset was *not* recognized as an allocation of the acquisition cost, but subsequently becomes recognizable. An entity shall recognize acquired deferred tax benefits that it realizes after the business combination as follows:

The tax benefits of operating loss carry-forwards, that were not previously recognizable by either party to the business combination, form part of the allocation of the purchase cost.

(a) Acquired deferred tax benefits recognized within the measurement period (maximum of one year from acquisition date) that result from new information about facts and circumstances that existed at the acquisition date must be applied to reduce the carrying amount of any goodwill related to that acquisition. If the carrying amount of that goodwill is zero, any remaining deferred tax benefits must be recognized in profit or loss.

(b) All other acquired deferred tax benefits realized must be recognized in profit or loss.

The acquiring company could also benefit from a business combination in that the probability of realizing a pre-acquisition deferred tax asset of the acquirer could change. An acquirer may consider it probable that it will recover its own deferred tax asset that was not recognized before the business combination. For example, the acquirer may be able to utilize the benefit of its unused tax losses against the future taxable profit of the acquiree. In such cases, the acquirer recognizes a change in the deferred tax asset in the period of the business combination but does not include it as part of the accounting for the business combination. Therefore, the acquirer does not take it into account in measuring the goodwill or bargain purchase gain it recognizes in the business combination.

Disclosure Requirements The following summarizes the more substantial items required to be disclosed pertaining to deferred income tax arising from a business combination:

The entity must disclose the amount and reason for changes in deferred tax assets pertaining to a business combination.

- The amount of the change if a business combination in which the entity is the acquirer causes a change in the amount recognized for its pre-acquisition deferred tax asset, and
- A description of the event or change in circumstances that caused the deferred tax benefits to be recognized if the deferred tax benefits acquired in a business combination are not recognized at the acquisition date but are recognized after the acquisition date.

Segment Disclosures

For simplicity, most of the examples used in previous chapters were unrealistic, in that they consisted of a parent company and a single subsidiary. When you consider all companies that trade on the Toronto Stock Exchange, very few are made up of only two companies, and many of the larger ones consist of the parent and a substantial number of subsidiaries. The consolidation process treats these separate legal entities as a single economic entity by aggregating the components of their financial statements. In past years, all companies comprising a given consolidated group were often in a single line of business and were located in Canada, so this aggregation of statements provided useful information to the users of the consolidated statements. However, the tremendous corporate expansion that started in the 1970s created companies engaged in diversified activities in many parts of the world, and it became obvious that the basic consolidated financial statements were not providing adequate information. Financial statement users needed information about a company that would allow them to assess all of its different components, which have different growth potentials, profitability characteristics, and inherent risks, which all vary with the products and services being provided and the markets being entered. Consolidated financial statements do not provide this information.

Corporate expansion has created multinational companies engaged in diversified activities.

In 1979, the first *Handbook* section on segmented information was issued as a response to this user need. This section required footnote disclosures that disaggregated the consolidated financial statements into industry segments and geographic segments. It also required that information be provided about the company's export sales.

IFRS 8: Operating Segments

In 2011, IFRS 8: Operating Segments will have to be applied for the separate and consolidated financial statements of an entity whose debt or equity instruments are traded in a public market or of an entity that files, or is in the process of filing, the financial statements with a securities commission or other regulatory organization for the purpose of issuing any class of instruments in a public market. The entity must disclose information about its operating segments and, in addition, information about its products and services, the countries in which it operates, and its major customers. It is expected that such information will provide users with a better understanding of a company's performance and its prospects for future cash flows.

Operating segments are identified based on the way that a company's management organizes its components internally for assessing performance and making strategic decisions. This identification focuses on the financial information that the company's decision-makers use for that purpose. Each component is called an operating segment and is defined as one

(a) that engages in business activities from which it may earn revenues[1] and incur expenses (including revenues and expenses relating to transactions with other components of the same enterprise),

(b) whose operating results are regularly reviewed by the entity's chief operating decision-maker to make decisions about resources to be allocated to the segment and assess its performance, and

(c) for which discrete financial information is available.

Identification of Reportable Operating Segments

IFRS 8 requires information to be disclosed about all operating segments that meet certain *quantitative thresholds*. This requirement is described as follows.

An enterprise should disclose separately information about an operating segment that meets *any* of the following quantitative thresholds:

(a) Its reported revenue, including both sales to external customers and intersegment sales or transfers, is 10 percent or more of the combined revenue, internal and external, of all operating segments.

(b) The absolute amount of its reported profit or loss is 10 percent or more of the greater, in absolute amount, of

(i) the combined reported profit of all operating segments that did not report a loss, and

(ii) the combined reported loss of all operating segments that did report a loss.

(c) Its assets are 10 percent or more of the combined assets of all operating segments.

These quantitative thresholds establish which reportable operating segments require separate disclosures. Any segments falling outside these guidelines may be combined under the category "Other," provided that at least 75 percent of a company's total external revenue is included in reportable segments. If it is not, additional

---

Public companies are required to disclose information about their lines of business, products and services, countries where they operate, and major customers.

Three tests (revenue, profit, and assets) are used to determine whether or not a particular operating segment is reportable. Each test applies a 10 percent rule.

At least 75 percent of a company's total external revenue must be reported in a segment other than the "other" segment.

---

[1] Start-up operations may also be operating segments before earning revenues.

operating segments must be disclosed. IFRS 8 also suggests that from a practical point of view, the total number of operating segments reported will probably not exceed 10 segments.

Example The following illustrates an application of quantitative thresholds. For internal evaluation purposes, JK Enterprises Inc. generates information from its six divisions. In terms of IFRS 8, these divisions are operating segments. The following amounts (stated in millions) have been assembled to determine which of these operating segments are reportable in accordance with the standard's quantitative thresholds.

Operating segments	Revenues	Operating profit (loss)	Assets
Auto parts	$53.9	$18.1	$10.9
Office furnishings	8.6	1.3	1.2
Publishing	6.5	(2.1)	1.4
Retail	5.0	(2.8)	3.2
Finance	11.8	3.7	14.0
Software	7.9	3.9	0.9
	$93.7	$22.1	$31.6

Revenue Test

$$10\% \times \$93.7 = \$9.37$$

From this test, auto parts and finance are identified.

Operating Profit (Loss) Test

The operating profit test considers the larger of the absolute amount of total profits and total losses.

To apply this test, first compute separate totals for all profits and all losses. Then choose the largest of the absolute amount of the two totals, as follows:

Total of all operating profits	$27.0
Total of all operating losses	4.9

$$10\% \times \$27.0 = \$2.7$$

Auto parts, retail, finance, and software are identified.

Asset Test

$$10\% \times \$31.6 = \$3.16$$

Auto parts, retail, and finance are identified.

Following is a summary of all three quantitative tests for JK Enterprises:

Separate disclosure is required if a segment satisfies any one test.

Operating segments	Revenues	Operating profit (loss)	Assets
Auto parts	X	X	X
Office furnishings			
Publishing			
Retail		X	X
Finance	X	X	X
Software		X	

Thus, separate disclosures are required for auto parts, retail, finance, and software, as each satisfies at least one of the tests. Office furnishings and publishing can be combined and reported under the heading "Other."

Disclosure Requirements   The following disclosures are required for *each reportable segment* that has been identified by the quantitative thresholds:

IFRS 8 outlines extensive disclosures required for each reportable segment.

1. Factors used by management to identify segments.

2. The types of products and services that generate revenues.

3. A measure of profit (loss).

4. Total assets.

5. Liabilities for each reportable segment if such amounts are regularly provided to the chief operating decision-maker.

6. Each of the following *if* the specific amounts are included in the measure of profit (loss) regularly reviewed by the chief operating decision-maker:
   (a) Revenues from external customers.
   (b) Intersegment revenues.
   (c) Interest revenue and expense. (This may be netted for a particular segment only if that segment receives a majority of its revenues from interest *and* if the chief operating decision-maker uses the net number to assess performance.)
   (d) Amortization.
   (e) Unusual revenues, expenses, and gains (losses).
   (f) Equity income from significant-influence investments and joint ventures.
   (g) Income taxes.
   (h) Significant non-cash items other than amortization above.

7. The amount of investment in associates and joint ventures accounted for by the equity method.

8. The amounts of additions to non-current assets other than financial instruments, deferred tax assets, and post-employment benefits assets.

9. An explanation of how a segment's profit (loss) and assets have been measured, and how common costs and jointly used assets have been allocated, and of the accounting policies that have been used.

Reconciliations of the segments' total revenues, profits, assets, and liabilities to the entity's overall revenues, profits, assets, and liabilities must be provided.

10. Reconciliations of the following:
    (a) The total of the reportable segments' revenues to the entity's revenue.
    (b) The total of the reportable segments' measures of profit or loss to the entity's profit or loss.
    (c) The total of the reportable segments' assets to the entity's assets.
    (d) The total of the reportable segments' liabilities to the entity's liabilities if segment liabilities are reported separately.
    (e) The total of the reportable segments' amounts for every other material item of information disclosed to the corresponding amount for the entity.

The following information must also be disclosed, unless such information has already been clearly provided as part of the segment disclosures. This additional information is also required in situations where the company has only a single reportable segment:

Revenue must be segregated by product or service and by geographical area.

1. The revenue from external customers for each product or service, or for each group of similar products and services, whenever practical.

2. The revenue from external customers broken down between those from the company's country of domicile (i.e., Canada) and those from all foreign countries. Where revenue from an individual country is material, it must be separately disclosed.

3. Goodwill and capital assets broken down between those located in Canada and those located in foreign countries. Where assets located in an individual country are material, they must be separately disclosed.

4. When a company's sales to a single external customer are 10 percent or more of total revenues, the company must disclose this fact, as well as the total amount of revenues from each customer and which operating segment reported such revenues. The identity of the customer does not have to be disclosed.

As with all financial reporting, comparative amounts for at least the last fiscal year must also be presented.

The disclosures required by IFRS 8 provide external users with the information that top management uses to assess performance. The presentation of a measure of profit, revenue, and assets for each reportable segment allows a statement user to calculate a measure of return on assets, margin, and turnover, so that the relative contribution of each segment to the overall profitability of the company can be assessed and compared with that of the previous year.

Daimler AG, a Germany company, produces Mercedes cars and trucks. Relevant excerpts from its 2008 financial statements pertaining to its different operating segments are presented in Exhibit 9.4.

Exhibit 9.4

EXTRACTS (IN PART) FROM DAIMLER AG'S 2008 FINANCIAL STATEMENTS

31. Segment Reporting

Daimler has determined four reportable segments that are largely organized and managed separately according to nature of products and services provided, brands, distribution channels and profile of customers.

The segment information presented below does not include amounts relating to discontinued operations and only reflects the activities of continuing segments. The segment assets and liabilities as well as capital expenditures, depreciation and amortization of the discontinued operations are included in the reconciliation to the consolidated amounts in 2007 and 2006.

Mercedes-Benz Cars. This segment includes activities primarily related to the development, design, manufacture, assembly and sale of passenger cars and off-road vehicles under the brand names Mercedes-Benz, Smart and Maybach, as well as related parts and accessories.

Daimler AG has four reportable segments.

Daimler Trucks. This segment includes activities primarily related to the development, design, manufacture, assembly and sale of trucks under the brand names Mercedes-Benz, Freightliner, Western Star and Mitsubishi Fuso, as well as related parts and accessories.

Daimler Financial Services. The activities in this segment primarily comprise the marketing of financial services in the area of retail and lease financing for vehicles, dealer financing, and insurance brokerage. This segment also includes the Group's equity method investment in Toll Collect.

Vans, Buses, Other. Vans, Buses, Other comprises all other operations of the Group. It primarily includes the Group's Mercedes-Benz Vans segment (vans sold under the brand names Mercedes-Benz, Freightliner and Dodge) and the bus operating unit (buses sold under the brand names Mercedes-Benz, Setra and Orion). In addition, Vans, Buses, Other includes the real estate activities and the equity method investments in Chrysler, EADS and Tognum. Prior to its sale, the Off-Highway business formed part of Vans, Buses, Other.

Management reporting and controlling systems. The Group's management reporting and controlling systems use accounting policies that are the same as those described in Note 1 in the summary of significant accounting policies under IFRS.

The Group measures the performance of its operating segments through a measure of segment profit or loss which is referred to as "EBIT" in our management and reporting system.

EBIT is the measure of segment profit (loss) used in segment reporting and comprises gross profit, selling and general administrative expenses, research and non-capitalized development costs, other operating income (expense), net, and our share of profit (loss) from companies accounted for using the equity method, net, as well as other financial income (expense), net.

Intersegment revenue is generally recorded at values that approximate third-party selling prices.

Segment assets principally comprise all assets. The industrial business segments' assets exclude income tax assets, assets from defined benefit plans and certain financial assets (including liquidity).

Segment liabilities principally comprise all liabilities. The industrial business segments' liabilities exclude income tax liabilities, liabilities from defined benefit plans and certain financial liabilities (including financing liabilities).

Pursuant to risk sharing agreements between Daimler Financial Services and the respective vehicle segment the residual value risk associated with the Group's operating leases and its finance lease receivables is primarily borne by the vehicle segment or unit that manufactured the leased equipment. The terms of the risk sharing arrangement vary by segment and geographic region.

Information in the table below about capital expenditures and depreciation/amortization comprises intangible assets (excluding goodwill) as well as property, plant and equipment (excluding finance leases).

With respect to information about geographical regions, revenue is allocated to countries based on the location of the customer; non-current assets are disclosed according to the physical location of these assets.

Segment information as of and for the years ended December 31, 2008:

> **Segmented information is provided for revenue, profit (loss), assets, liabilities, capital expenditures, and depreciation.**

(in millions of €) 2008	Mercedes-Benz Cars	Daimler Trucks	Daimler Financial Services	Vans, Buses, Other	*thereof Mercedes-Benz Vans*	Total Segments	Recon-ciliation	Consolidated
Revenue	46,480	26,018	8,778	14,597	*9,157*	95,873	—	95,873
Intersegment revenue	1,292	2,554	504	373	*322*	4,723	(4,723)	—
Total revenue	47,772	28,572	9,282	14,970	*9,479*	100,596	(4,723)	95,873
Segment profit (loss) (EBIT)	2,117	1,607	677	(1,239)	*818*	3,162	(432)	2,730
Segment assets	33,956	16,930	67,708	12,521	*5,243*	131,115	1,104	132,219
Segment liabilities	20,611	9,651	63,076	5,483	*3,351*	98,821	674	99,495
Capital expenditures	3,379	1,366	61	285	*160*	5,091	11	5,102
Thereof investments in property, plant and equipment	2,246	991	41	270	*150*	3,548	11	3,559
Depreciation and amortization	1,960	646	35	382	*314*	3,023	—	3,023

Mercedes-Benz Cars. In 2008, as a result of the reassessment of residual values of leased vehicles, the Group recorded impairment charges of €465 million. In addition, an amendment of a defined benefit plan resulted in past service income of €84 million, which is included in the segment's 2008 EBIT.

(continued)

Daimler Trucks. In 2008, the segment's EBIT includes expenses of €233 million associated with the decision to optimize and reposition the business operations of Daimler Trucks North America. From this amount, €32 million relate to non-cash impairment charges and write downs. In addition, an amendment of a defined benefit plan resulted in past service income of €29 million in 2008.

In December 2008, Daimler acquired a 10% stake in the Russian commercial vehicle manufacturer Kamaz. The Group accounts for its equity interest in Kamaz using the equity method and allocates the proportionate share in the results to the Daimler Trucks segment. The equity investment amounted to €168 million as of December 31, 2008.

Daimler Financial Services. In 2008, capital expenditure for non-inventory related equipment on operating leases amounts to €5,390 million (2007: €6,093 million; 2006: €6,955 million) and related depreciation charges amount to €2,465 million (2007: €2,283 million; 2006: €2,453 million).

Vans, Buses, Other. EBIT of Vans, Buses, Other includes the Group's share in the net profit (loss) of EADS of €177 million (2007: €13 million; 2006: €(193) million). In addition, EBIT comprises gains related to the transfer of portions of the Group's equity interest in EADS (2008: €130 million; 2007: €1,573 million; 2006: €519 million). The equity investment in EADS included in segment assets amounts to €2,886 million in 2008 (2007: €3,442 million; 2006: €4,371 million).

In addition, EBIT of Vans, Buses, Other includes the Group's share in the net loss of Chrysler Holding LLC of €1,390 million in 2008 (2007: €377 million). These losses reduced the carrying amount of the Group's equity investment to zero (carrying amount included in segment assets at December 31, 2007: €916 million).

In 2008, the Group acquired an aggregate 28.4% stake in Tognum. The Group accounts for its equity interest in Tognum using the equity method and allocates the proportionate results to Vans, Buses, Other. The equity investment in Tognum amounted to €706 million as of December 31, 2008. The proportionate share in the profit (loss) of Tognum was insignificant in 2008.

Reconciliations. Reconciliations of the total segment measures to respective items included in financial statements are as follows:

(in millions of €)	2008
Total segments' profit (EBIT)	3,162
Corporate items	(442)
Eliminations	10
Group EBIT	2,730
Interest income (expense), net	65
Profit before income taxes	2,795
Total segments' assets	131,115
Assets of Chrysler activities	—
Income tax assets	3,110
Unallocated financial assets (including liquidity) and assets from defined benefit plans	7,975
Other corporate items and eliminations	(9,981)
Group assets	132,219
Total segments' liabilities	98,821
Liabilities of Chrysler activities	—
Income tax liabilities	(81)
Unallocated financial liabilities and liabilities from defined benefit plans	9,998
Other corporate items and eliminations	(9,243)
Group liabilities	99,495

Information by segment is provided for unusual items and significant non-cash items.

Reconciliations to corporate totals are provided for profit (loss), assets, and liabilities.

The reconciliation includes items that by definition are not part of the segments. In addition, the reconciliation includes corporate items that are not allocated, for example items for which headquarters are responsible. Transactions between the segments are eliminated in the context of consolidation and the eliminated amounts are included in the reconciliation.

The assets and liabilities of the Chrysler activities are derived under the same definitions as for the segments.

Revenue and non-current assets by region. Revenue from external customers is as follows:

(in millions of €)	Germany	Western Europe[1]	United States	Other American countries	Asia	Other countries	Consolidated
2008	21,817	24,099	17,922	7,652	13,771	10,612	95,873

[1] *Excluding Germany.*

Germany accounts for €21,252 million of non-current assets, which include intangible assets, property, plant and equipment as well as equipment on operating leases (2007: €19,542 million; 2006: €19,628 million), the United States for €10,759 million (2007: €11,819 million; 2006: €43,184 million) and other countries for €8,687 million (2007: €8,129 million; 2006: €14,498).

Source: Daimler AG 2008 Annual Report, http://www.sec.gov/Archives/edgar/data/1067318/000104746909001917/a2190793z20-f.htm.

GAAP for Private Enterprises

Private enterprises

- can report their association with VIEs using full consolidation, the cost method, or the equity method;
- can report their interest in joint ventures using proportionate consolidation, the cost method, or the equity method;
- can use the taxes payable method or the future income tax payable method, which is similar to the deferred income taxes method under IFRSs, to account for income tax;
- are not required to disclose any information about their operating segments.

Private enterprises can use proportionate consolidation to report their investments in joint ventures.

For the third point above, deferred income taxes need not be recognized; however, the entity must prepare and disclose a reconciliation between the statutory rate and the effective tax rate.

U.S. GAAP Differences

U.S. GAAP and IFRSs have many similarities for the topics presented in this chapter. The significant differences are summarized as follows:

U.S. GAAP considers benefits and risks rather than control when determining whether or not an SPE should be consolidated.

1. IFRSs require that an interest in an SPE be consolidated when the parent controls the SPE. The same definition of control is used for assessing control based on voting interest versus contractual arrangements. U.S. GAAP assess control of an SPE by determining whether the reporting entity receives the majority of benefits from and is exposed to the majority of the risks of loss for the SPE.

2. Under IFRSs, an interest in a joint venture must be accounted for using either proportionate consolidation or the equity method. Under U.S. GAAP, the equity method is generally required. However, proportionate consolidation is permitted in certain limited circumstances for unincorporated entities in certain industries.

3. Under IFRSs, a gain can be recognized when a venturer contributes a group of non-monetary assets to a joint venture but only if the benefits and risks have been transferred to other parties. Under U.S. GAAP, except under limited circumstances, the investor measures its interest in the joint venture at the carrying value of the assets transferred, and no gain or loss is recognized.

4. Under IFRSs, there is an exemption from recognizing a deferred tax liability (asset) for the initial recognition of an asset or a liability in a transaction that is not a business combination and at the time of the transaction affects neither accounting profit nor taxable profit. Under U.S. GAAP, there is no such exemption.

5. Whereas IFRSs require the disclosure of liabilities of operating segments when this information is provided to the chief operating decision-maker, U.S. GAAP do not require this disclosure even if this information is provided to the chief operating decision-maker.

SUMMARY

In this chapter, we have examined four different topics, which almost wind up our study of business combinations and the preparation of consolidated financial statements. Consolidation is required for a VIE, which is controlled by a primary beneficiary on a basis of control other than through ownership of a voting interest. For an interest in a joint operation, the venturer should recognize the assets it controls and the liabilities it incurs, the expenses it incurs, and its share of the revenue and expenses from the sale of goods or services by the joint arrangement.

The consolidated expenses resulting from the allocation of the acquisition differential are not deductible for tax purposes, but under the balance sheet approach the reflection of deferred tax assets and liabilities is required for the differences between the carrying values and the tax bases of subsidiary company's net assets shown on consolidated balance sheets.

Consolidation hides information about the lines of business conducted by multinational conglomerates. Required segment disclosures are designed to provide financial statement users with relevant information that will aid them in assessing company results.

Significant Changes in the Last Two Years

1. For publicly accountable enterprises, IFRSs have replaced the former sections of the *CICA Handbook*. The table on the next page shows the IFRSs covered in this chapter along with their counterparts from the former sections of the *CICA Handbook*:

www.mcgrawhillconnect.ca

IFRSs	CICA Handbook *Counterparts*
IFRS 3: Business Combinations IAS 27: Consolidated and Separate Financial Statements SIC 12: Consolidation — Special Purpose Entities	Section 1582: Business Combinations Section 1601: Consolidated Financial Statements Section 1602: Non-controlling Interests AcG15: Consolidation of Variable Interest Entities
IFRS 10: Joint Arrangements SIC 13: Jointly Controlled Entities — Non-monetary Contributions by Venturers	Section 3055: Interests in Joint Ventures
IAS 12: Income Taxes	Section 3465: Income Taxes
IFRS 8: Operating Segments	Section 1701: Segment Disclosures

2. Definition of control has changed to provide a broader definition so as to include control through voting rights and control through contracts or operating agreements.

3. Interests in joint ventures are reported using the equity method rather than proportional consolidation.

4. A venturer can recognize the portion of a gain that is attributable to the interests of the other venturers on contribution of a non-monetary asset to a joint venture if the significant risks and benefits are transferred to the joint venture.

5. When disclosing information by operating segments, the entity must disclose the liabilities for each reportable segment if such amounts are regularly provided to the chief operating decision-maker.

Changes Expected in the Next Three Years

The definition of control may change again since IASB and FASB are working on a joint project related to consolidated financial statements.

SELF-STUDY PROBLEM

The following are the Year 5 financial statements of MAR Corporation and OTT Company, a joint venture in which MAR has a 35 percent ownership interest:

	MAR	OTT
Year 5 income statements		
Sales	$906,750	$250,000
Management fees	25,000	—
Interest	—	3,600
Gain on land sale	—	20,000
Dividends	5,250	—
	937,000	273,600
Cost of sales	540,000	162,000
Interest expense	3,600	—
Other expenses	196,400	71,600
Income tax expense	80,000	16,000
	820,000	249,600
Profit	$117,000	$ 24,000

Year 5 retained earnings statements

Balance, January 1	$153,000	$ 72,000
Profit	117,000	24,000
	270,000	96,000
Dividends	50,000	15,000
Balance, December 31	$220,000	$ 81,000

Statements of Financial Position — At December 31, Year 5

Cash	$ 12,000	$ 15,000
Accounts and notes receivable	70,000	63,000
Inventory	32,000	27,000
Property, plant, and equipment (net)	448,000	66,000
Investment in OTT Company	30,000	—
	$592,000	$171,000
Notes payable	$ 60,000	$ —
Other liabilities	212,000	40,000
Common shares	100,000	50,000
Retained earnings	220,000	81,000
	$592,000	$171,000

Additional Information

- On January 1, Year 3, MAR purchased 35 percent of the common shares of OTT for $30,000 and signed a joint venture agreement with the other two parties in the joint venture. On that date, OTT had retained earnings of $10,000, and the book values of its identifiable net assets were equal to fair values.

- The companies sell merchandise to each other. MAR sells to OTT at a gross profit rate of 38 percent; OTT earns a gross profit of 40 percent from its sales to MAR.

- The December 31, Year 4, inventory of MAR contained purchases made from OTT amounting to $7,000. There were no intercompany purchases in the inventory of OTT on this date.

- During Year 5 the following intercompany transactions took place:
  (a) OTT made a $25,000 payment to MAR for management fees, which was recorded as "other expense."
  (b) OTT made sales of $75,000 to MAR. The December 31, Year 5, inventory of MAR contained merchandise purchased from OTT amounting to $16,500.
  (c) MAR made sales of $100,000 to OTT. The December 31, Year 5, inventory of OTT contained merchandise purchased from MAR amounting to $15,000.
  (d) On July 1, Year 5, MAR borrowed $60,000 from OTT and signed a note bearing interest at 12 percent per annum. Interest on this note was paid on December 31, Year 5.
  (e) In Year 5, OTT sold land to MAR, recording a gain of $20,000. This land is being held by MAR on December 31, Year 5.

- Goodwill impairment tests have been conducted yearly by MAR since the date of acquisition. MAR's 35 percent share of the losses due to impairment was as follows: Year 3, $1,040; Year 4, $320; Year 5, $680.

- MAR has accounted for its investment using the cost method for internal record-keeping.

- Both companies pay income tax at a rate of 40 percent. Ignore income tax on the acquisition differential.

Required:

(a) Calculate the following account balances to be reported by MAR under the equity method:
  (i) Retained earnings as at December 31, Year 4.
  (ii) Net income for Year 5.
  (iii)Investment in OTT as at December 31, Year 5.
(b) Prepare MAR's journal entries under the equity method for Year 5.
(c) Prepare consolidated financial statements for MAR for Year 5.

Solution to Self-study Problem

Supporting Schedules

CALCULATION AND AMORTIZATION OF THE ACQUISITION DIFFERENTIAL

Cost of 35% of OTT, Jan. 1, Year 3		$ 30,000
Book value of OTT, Jan. 1, Year 3		
Common shares	50,000	
Retained earnings	10,000	
	60,000	
MAR's shares (35%)		21,000
Acquisition differential		9,000
Allocated to revalue the net assets of OTT		–0–
Goodwill, Jan. 1, Year 3		9,000
Amortized (impairment losses):		
Year 3–Year 4	1,360 **(a)**	
Year 5	680 **(b)**	2,040
Goodwill, Dec. 31, Year 5		$ 6,960 **(c)**

INTERCOMPANY ITEMS

Notes receivable and payable (35% × 60,000)	$ 21,000 **(d)**
Management fee revenue and expense (35% × 25,000)	8,750 **(e)**
Sales and purchases (35% × [75,000 + 100,000])	61,250 **(f)**
Interest revenue and expense (35% × [12% × 60,000 × 1/2 yr])	1,260 **(g)**
Dividend from OTT (35% × 15,000)	5,250 **(h)**

UNREALIZED PROFITS

	After tax	Before tax	40% tax	
Inventory				
Opening (7,000 × 40% × 35%) — OTT selling	$ 980	$ 392	$ 588	**(i)**
Ending				
OTT selling (16,500 × 40% × 35%)	$ 2,310	$ 924	$ 1,386	**(j)**
MAR selling (15,000 × 38% × 35%)	1,995	798	1,197	**(k)**
	$ 4,305	$1,722	$ 2,583	**(l)**
Land — OTT selling (20,000 × 35%)	$ 7,000	$2,800	$ 4,200	**(m)**

(a) (i)

CALCULATION OF RETAINED EARNINGS
December 31, Year 4

Retained earnings — MAR		$153,000
Less: Amortization of acquisition differential **(a)**		1,360
		151,640
Retained earnings — OTT	72,000	
Acquisition retained earnings	10,000	
Increase	62,000	
MAR's interest (35%)	21,700	
Less opening inventory profit **(i)**	588	
Adjusted increase		21,112 **(n)**
Consolidated retained earnings, Jan. 1, Year 5		$172,752 **(o)**

(a) (ii)

CALCULATION OF NET INCOME — Year 5

Income of MAR			$117,000
Less: Dividends from OTT **(h)**		5,250	
Ending inventory profit **(k)**		1,197	
Amortization of acquisition differential **(b)**		680	7,127
Adjusted net income			109,873
Income of OTT		24,000	
MAR's interest (35%)		8,400	
Less: Ending inventory profit **(j)**	1,386		
Land gain **(m)**	4,200	5,586	
		2,814	
Add: Opening inventory profit **(i)**		588	
Adjusted net income			3,402
Net income under equity method			$113,275 **(p)**

(a) (iii)

BALANCE IN INVESTMENT ACCOUNT
At December 31, Year 5

Balance in investment account under cost method			$ 30,000
Less: Ending inventory profit **(k)**		1,197	
Amortization of acquisition differential **(a & b)**		2,040	3,237
Adjusted			26,763
Retained earnings, Dec. 31, Year 5 — OTT		81,000	
Acquisition retained earnings		10,000	
Increase		71,000	
MAR's interest (35%)		24,850	
Less: Ending inventory profit **(j)**	1,386		
Land gain **(m)**	4,200	5,586	
Adjusted increase			19,264
Balance in investment account under equity method			$ 46,027

(b)
YEAR 5 EQUITY METHOD JOURNAL ENTRIES
(See Calculation of Net Income)

Investment in OTT Co.	3,402	
Investment income		3,402
35% of adjusted net income of OTT Co.		
Cash	5,250	
Investment in OTT Co.		5,250
Dividends from OTT Co.		
Investment income	1,197	
Investment in OTT Co.		1,197
Ending inventory profit — MAR selling		
Investment income	680	
Investment in OTT Co.		680
Amortization of acquisition differential		

(c)
MAR CORPORATION
Consolidated Income Statement

Sales (906,750 + 35% × 250,000 − **(f) 61,250**)	$933,000
Management fees (25,000 + 35% × 0 − **(e) 8,750**)	16,250
Interest (0 + 35% × 3,600 − **(g) 1,260**)	
Gain on land sale (0 + 35% × 20,000 − **(m) 7,000**)	
Dividends (5,250 + 35% × 0 − **(h) 5,250**)	
	949,250
Cost of sales (540,000 + 35% × 162,000 − **(f) 61,250** − **(i) 980** + **(j) 2,310** + **(k) 1,995**)	538,775
Interest expense (3,600 + 35% × 0 − **(g) 1,260**)	2,340
Other expenses (196,400 + 35% × 71,600 − **(e) 8,750**)	212,710
Goodwill impairment loss (0 + 35% × 0 + **(b) 680**)	680
Income tax expense (80,000 + 35% × 16,000 + **(i) 392** − **(j) 924** − **(k) 798** − **(m) 2,800**)	81,470
	835,975
Profit	$113,275

Retained Earnings Statement

Balance, January 1	$172,752
Profit	113,275
	286,027
Dividends	50,000
Balance, December 31	$236,027

Statement of Financial Position

Cash (12,000 + 35% × 15,000)	$ 17,250
Accounts and notes receivable (70,000 + 35% × 63,000 − **(d) 21,000**)	71,050
Inventory (32,000 + 35% × 27,000 − **(j) 2,310** − **(k) 1,995**)	37,145
Property, plant, and equipment (net) (448,000 + 35% × 66,000 − **(m) 7,000**)	464,100
Deferred income taxes (0 + 35% × 0 + **(j) 924** + **(k) 798** + **(m) 2,800**)	4,522
Goodwill **(c)**	6,960
	$601,027
Notes payable (60,000 + 35% × 0 − **(d) 21,000**)	$ 39,000
Other liabilities (212,000 + 35% × 40,000)	226,000
Common shares	100,000
Retained earnings	236,027
	$601,027

APPENDIX 9A

Reporting an Interest in a Joint Venture Using Proportionate Consolidation

Example   Explor Ltd., a Calgary-based oil exploration company, is a joint venture in which A Company has a 45 percent ownership interest. A Company, an original founder of Explor, uses the equity method to account for its investment but has made no entries to its investment account for Year 4. The following are the financial statements of the two companies on December 31, Year 4:

INCOME STATEMENTS — Year 4

	A Company	Explor
Sales	$900,000	$300,000
Cost of sales	630,000	180,000
Miscellaneous expenses	100,000	40,000
	730,000	220,000
Net income	$170,000	$ 80,000

BALANCE SHEETS — December 31, Year 4

	A Company	Explor
Miscellaneous assets	$654,500	$277,000
Inventory	110,000	90,000
Investment in Explor	85,500	—
	$850,000	$367,000
Miscellaneous liabilities	$130,000	$ 97,000
Common shares	300,000	100,000
Retained earnings, January 1	250,000	90,000
Net income — Year 4	170,000	80,000
	$850,000	$367,000

Financial statements of a venturer and a joint venture.

During Year 4, A Company sold merchandise totalling $110,000 to Explor and recorded a gross profit of 30 percent on these sales. On December 31, Year 4, the inventory of Explor contained items purchased from A Company for $22,000, and Explor had a payable of $5,000 to A Company on this date. A Company will use the proportionate consolidation method when it reports its investment in Explor for Year 4.

The following are the calculations of the amounts that are used in the elimination of intercompany transactions in the preparation of the consolidated financial statements:

The other venturer's share of the intercompany transactions are considered realized from a consolidated viewpoint.

Intercompany sales and purchases:
Total for the year $110,000
A Company's ownership interest 45%
Amount eliminated $ 49,500 **(a)**

Intercompany receivables and payables:
Total at end of year $ 5,000
A Company's ownership interest 45%
Amount eliminated $ 2,250 **(b)**

Intercompany profits in inventory:
Total at end of year (22,000 × 30%) $ 6,600
Profit considered realized — 55% 3,630
Unrealized — 45% $ 2,970 **(c)**

The following explanations will clarify the calculations made:

Only the venturer's share of intercompany transactions are eliminated when consolidation takes place.

1. Because the proportionate consolidation method will use 45 percent of Explor's financial statement items, we eliminate only 45 percent of the intercompany revenues, expenses, receivables, and payables. If we eliminated 100 percent of these items, we would be eliminating more than we are using in the consolidation process.

2. The inventory of Explor contains an intercompany profit of $6,600 recorded by A Company. Because there is joint control, A Company has realized $3,630 of this profit by selling to the other unaffiliated venturers, and therefore only A Company's 45 percent ownership interest is considered unrealized.

3. Income tax allocation is required when timing differences occur. Assuming that A Company pays income tax at a rate of 40 percent, the income tax effects of the inventory profit elimination can be calculated as follows:

	Before tax	40% tax	After tax
Inventory — A selling	$2,970	$1,188	$1,782 **(d)**

Because A Company has not recorded this year's equity method journal entries, we must calculate consolidated net income for Year 4 as follows:

Unrealized profit is always eliminated from the selling company's income.

Income of A Company		$170,000
Less after-tax unrealized inventory profit **(d)**		1,782
Adjusted net income		168,218
Income of Explor	$80,000	
A's ownership interest	45%	36,000
Consolidated net income		$204,218

A Company has used the equity method prior to this year, and therefore its retained earnings at the beginning of the year are equal to consolidated retained earnings. We can prepare the consolidated retained earnings statement for Year 4 as follows:

A COMPANY
CONSOLIDATED STATEMENT OF RETAINED EARNINGS
for the Year Ended December 31, Year 4

Balance, January 1	$250,000
Net income	204,218
Balance, December 31	$454,218

The preparation of the remaining Year 4 consolidated statements without the use of a working paper is illustrated on the following page.

A COMPANY
CONSOLIDATED INCOME STATEMENT
for the Year Ended December 31, Year 4

Sales (900,000 + [45% × 300,000] − **(a) 49,500**)	$985,500
Cost of sales	
(630,000 + [45% × 180,000] − **(a) 49,500** + **(c) 2,970**)	664,470
Miscellaneous expenses	
(100,000 + [45% × 40,000] − **(d) 1,188**)	116,812
	781,282
Net income	$204,218

A COMPANY
CONSOLIDATED BALANCE SHEET
December 31, Year 4

Intercompany revenues and expenses, receivables and payables, and unrealized profits in assets are eliminated in the preparation of the consolidated financial statements.

Miscellaneous assets		
(654,500 + [45% × 277,000] − **(b) 2,250**)		$776,900
Inventory (110,000 + [45% × 90,000] − **(c) 2,970**)		147,530
Deferred charge — income taxes **(d)**		1,188
Total assets		$925,618
Miscellaneous liabilities		
(130,000 + [45% × 97,000] − **(b) 2,250**)		$171,400
Shareholders' equity		
Common shares	300,000	
Retained earnings	454,218	754,218
Total liabilities and shareholders' equity		$925,618

The amounts used in the preparation are explained as follows:

Under the proportionate consolidation process, only the venturer's share of the joint venture's financial statement items are used.

1. With the exception of shareholders' equity and deferred income tax, the first two amounts used come from the individual financial statements and consist of 100 percent of A Company plus 45 percent of Explor.

2. The adjustments labelled (a) through (d) eliminate the intercompany revenues and expenses, receivables and payables, unrealized inventory profit, and income tax on the unrealized inventory profit. It is assumed that miscellaneous expenses include income tax expense.

3. The investment account and shareholders' equity of Explor were eliminated in the following manner:

Investment in Explor		$85,500
Shareholders' equity of Explor		
Common shares	$100,000	
Retained earnings, January 1	90,000	
	190,000	
A Company's ownership interest	45%	85,500
Acquisition differential		$ −0−

4. Consolidated shareholders' equity consists of the common shares of A Company plus consolidated retained earnings.

REVIEW QUESTIONS

Questions, cases, and problems that deal with the appendix material are denoted with an asterisk.

1. Explain the similarities and differences between a subsidiary and a variable interest entity and between a majority shareholder for a subsidiary and a primary beneficiary for a variable interest entity.

2. Explain how the definitions of assets and liabilities can be used to support the consolidation of variable interest entities.

3. Explain how to account for an interest in a joint operation.

4. Y Company has a 62 percent interest in Z Company. Are there circumstances where this would not result in Z Company being a subsidiary of Y Company? Explain.

5. The treatment of an unrealized intercompany inventory profit differs between a parent–subsidiary affiliation and a venturer–joint venture affiliation. Explain where the differences lie.

6. A venturer invested non-monetary assets in the formation of a new joint venture and did not receive any monetary consideration. The fair value of the assets invested was greater than the book value in the accounting records of the venturer. Explain how the venturer should account for the investment.

7. Explain how the gain recognition principle supports the recognition of a portion of gains occurring on transactions between the venturer and the joint venture.

8. X Company recently acquired control over Y Company. On the date of acquisition the fair values of Y Company's assets exceeded their tax bases. How does this difference affect the consolidated balance sheet?

9. A parent company has recently acquired a subsidiary. On the date of acquisition, both the parent and the subsidiary had unused income tax losses that were unrecognized in their financial statements. How would this affect the consolidation figures on the date of acquisition?

10. What is the difference between a *deductible* temporary difference and a *taxable* temporary difference?

11. Explain how it is possible to have a deferred tax liability with regard to the presentation of a subsidiary's assets in a consolidated balance sheet, whereas on the subsidiary's balance sheet the same assets produce a deferred tax asset.

12. Explain how the definition of a liability supports the recognition of a deferred income tax liability when the fair value of an asset acquired in a business combination is greater than the tax base of this asset.

13. Describe the three tests for identifying reportable operating segments.

14. For each of its operating segments that require separate disclosure, what information must an enterprise disclose?

15. In accordance with IFRS 8: Operating Segments:
    (a) What information must be disclosed about business carried out in other countries?
    (b) What information must be disclosed about a company's products or services?
    (c) What information must be provided about a company's customers?

16. What sort of reconciliations are required for segmented reporting?

17. Explain how the use of the information provided in segment disclosures can aid in the assessment of the overall profitability of a company.

MULTIPLE-CHOICE QUESTIONS

1. Which of the following is not a characteristic of a primary beneficiary of a variable interest entity?
   a. Its equity at risk in the variable interest entity is a substantial portion of the total financing of the entity.
   b. It has the direct or indirect ability to make the key decisions about the entity's operating activities.
   c. It will absorb a substantial portion of the expected losses of the entity if they occur.
   d. It has the right to receive a substantial portion of the expected residual returns of the entity if they occur.

2. Which of the following could not be considered a variable interest entity and would not be consolidated by the primary beneficiary?
   a. A single asset jointly owned by two people.
   b. A business owned by one individual.
   c. A corporation that operates a business.
   d. A trust that owns a number of assets and carries out an integrated series of activities.

3. Which of the following is not reported at fair value on the statement of financial position on the date a primary beneficiary obtains control of a variable-interest entity?
   a. Identifiable assets owned by the variable interest entity prior to the investment by the primary beneficiary.
   b. Liabilities of the variable interest entity prior to the primary beneficiary obtaining control over the variable-interest entity.
   c. Assets contributed by the primary beneficiary upon taking control over the variable interest entity.
   d. Non-controlling interests in the variable interest entity.

Use the following data for Questions 4 and 5.

On January 1, Year 1, PAR Ltd. invested $10 in cash for a 10 percent interest in VIC Inc. An analysis has been performed, and it has been determined that VIC is a variable interest entity and PAR is the primary beneficiary of VIC. The book values and fair values of both companies immediately prior to the investment by PAR were as follows:

	PAR Ltd.		VIC Inc.	
	Book value	Fair value	Book value	Fair value
Identifiable assets	$200	$240	$130	$150
Identifiable liabilities	110	110	70	70
Shareholders' equity	90	145	60	90

4. What amount would PAR report on its consolidated balance sheet for identifiable assets on the date it obtained control of VIC?
   a. $330
   b. $350
   c. $370
   d. $390

5. What amount would PAR report on its consolidated balance sheet for goodwill on the date it obtained control of VIC?
   a. $0
   b. $10
   c. $15
   d. $25

6. PRI has a 40 percent interest in NCE, a joint venture. During Year 5, NCE reported net income of $100,000 and paid a dividend of $60,000. NCE's inventory includes goods purchased from PRI on which PRI had made a profit of $10,000. What amount of income should PRI report on its investment in NCE for Year 5 under the equity method? (Ignore income taxes.)
   a. $24,000
   b. $30,000
   c. $36,000
   d. $40,000

(CGA-Canada adapted)

Use the following data for Questions 7 and 8.

Golden Company has assembled the following data regarding its operating segments (000s omitted):

Segment	Revenues	Operating profit	Assets
A Prepackaged food	$ 77,000	$ 4,500	$ 180,000
B Canned food	465,000	29,000	235,000
C Frozen food	156,000	12,400	900,000
D Frozen beverages	820,000	(35,000)	750,000
E Canned beverages	1,200,000	305,000	350,000
	$2,718,000	$315,900	$2,415,000

7. Using only the operating profit test, which of the operating segments would be reportable?
   a. B, E
   b. D, E
   c. E
   d. B, D, E

8. Using all of the tests for operating segments in IFRS 8, which of the above would be reportable?
   a. A, B, C, D, E
   b. B, C, D, E
   c. B, D, E
   d. D, E

*9. On January 1, Year 6, REK Ltd. contributed equipment to a joint venture and received a 40 percent interest in the joint venture. The equipment had a net book value of $200,000 and a fair value of $240,000 on the date of the transfer. What amount of the gain related to the transfer of the equipment would be reported by REK on the consolidated financial statements on the date of the transfer?

   a. No gain will be recognized regardless of whether the substantial benefits and risks have transferred.

   b. 40 percent will be recognized regardless of whether the substantial benefits and risks have transferred.

   c. 40 percent will be recognized if the substantial benefits and risks have transferred.

   d. 60 percent will be recognized if the substantial benefits and risks have transferred.

Use the following data for Questions 10 and 11.

On January 1, Year 1, ANT Ltd. invested $400,000 in cash for a 30 percent interest in TAM Inc. As a part of the investment, ANT and the other shareholder in TAM signed an agreement under which the two shareholders had joint control over TAM. The acquisition differential on ANT's 30 percent investment was $50,000. It pertained entirely to one of TAM's patents, which had a remaining useful life of five years at the date of the investment by ANT. During Year 1, TAM reported net income of $170,000 and paid dividends of $100,000. ANT reports its investment in TAM using the equity method.

10. How much will ANT report as investment income from TAM for the year ended December 31, Year 1?

   a. $21,000
   b. $30,000
   c. $41,000
   d. $51,000

11. What amount would ANT report on its statement of financial position for investment in TAM at December 31, Year 1?

   a. $411,000
   b. $421,000
   c. $441,000
   d. $451,000

12. On January 1, Year 3, Gaspe Ltd. purchased an asset for $500,000. The company amortizes the capital asset on a straight-line basis over its useful life of five years. The residual value is expected to be $150,000. The capital cost allowance rate is 30 percent, and the tax rate for Year 3 is 30 percent. Which one of the following statements best describes the items and amounts that would be shown on the balance sheet of Gaspe Ltd. as at December 31, Year 3, if the asset acquired was the company's only capital asset and the company uses the half-year rule?

   a. A capital asset with a net carrying amount of $280,000 and a deferred tax liability of $1,500.

   b. A capital asset with a net carrying amount of $350,000 and a deferred tax liability of $1,500.

    c.   A capital asset with a net carrying amount of $430,000 and a deferred tax asset of $1,500.

    d.   A capital asset with a net carrying amount of $430,000 and a deferred tax liability of $1,500.

(CICA adapted)

13.   Which of the following would not be a criterion for identifying a reportable operating segment for segmented reporting purposes?

    a.   Discrete financial information is available for the segment, which is reviewed by the company's chief operating decision-maker.

    b.   The activities of the segment fall into a different Statistics Canada industry classification than other company operations.

    c.   The segment incurs both revenues and expenses.

    d.   Revenue of the segment is 10 percent or more of the total revenues from all segments.

14.   Robertson Inc. purchased all of Gaddy Corp. for $420,000. On that date, Gaddy had net assets with a $400,000 fair value and a carrying value of $300,000. The tax base of the net assets was $270,000. Assuming a 30 percent tax rate, what amount of goodwill should be recognized for this acquisition?

    a. $20,000

    b. $59,000

    c. $120,000

    d. $129,000

15.   On January 1, Year 5, Holiday Corporation purchased a 100 percent interest in the common shares of Card Ltd. for $270,000. At this date, Card Ltd.'s balance sheet included the following:

	Book value	Fair value	Tax base
Assets	$560,000	$600,000	$375,000
Current liabilities	360,000	360,000	360,000
Deferred tax liability	74,000		
Common shares	50,000		
Retained earnings	72,000		

    Assume that Holiday has a deferred tax liability of $98,000 on its January 1, Year 5, balance sheet. Both companies are subject to 40 percent income tax rates. If a consolidated balance sheet were prepared for Holiday immediately following the acquisition of Card Ltd., what would be reported for a deferred tax liability?

    a. $90,000

    b. $172,000

    c. $176,000

    d. $188,000

Use the following data for Questions 16 and 17.

On January 1, Year 1, BAT Company acquired 60 percent of the common shares of STIC Company and obtained control over STIC. Of the $300,000 acquisition differential, $200,000 was allocated to land and $100,000 was allocated to goodwill.

Deferred income tax implications related to the acquisition differential were not recognized. During Year 2, BAT sold inventory to STIC for $100,000 and earned a gross margin of 30 percent. At the end of Year 2, STIC still had the goods purchased from BAT in its inventory.

16. What would be the impact on the debt-to-equity ratio if deferred income taxes related to the acquisition differential were recognized on the consolidated balance sheet at the date of acquisition?
    a. It would increase.
    b. It would decrease.
    c. It would not be affected.
    d. The impact cannot be determined based on the information provided.

17. What would be the impact on the return on shareholders' equity attributable to BAT's shareholders for the Year 2 consolidated financial statements if BAT had joint control rather than control over STIC?
    a. It would increase.
    b. It would decrease.
    c. It would not be affected.
    d. The impact cannot be determined based on the information provided.

18. Which of the following is true with respect to GAAP for Private Enterprises as per Part 2 of the *CICA Handbook?*
    a. It applies only if all owners unanimously consent to its use.
    b. The entity can apply some sections from Part 2 for private enterprises and some sections from Part 1 for publicly accountable enterprises.
    c. The entity must consolidate an interest in a variable interest entity.
    d. The entity could choose the cost method or the equity method to report an investment in a joint venture.

CASES

Case 1 Mr. Landman has spent the last 10 years developing small commercial strip malls and has been very successful. He buys a residential property in a high traffic area, rezones the property, and then sells the property to a contractor who builds the plaza and sells it to investors. Mr. Landman has often been hired to manage the commercial plazas for a fee.

Mr. Landman now wants to become a real estate baron. Rather than just developing the plazas for resale, he wants to form partnerships with builders and/or investors to build commercial properties and keep them as long-term investments.

He has found two properties suitable for development and has made offers to the current owners to purchase these properties on January 1, Year 2. The offers are conditional upon arranging suitable financing for the acquisition of these properties.

Mr. Landman intends to set up two separate companies to buy, develop, and hold the properties. Elgin Company will purchase the property on Elgin Street for $1,200,000 and build a small office building at an expected cost of $2,800,000. Mr. Landman's holding company, Holdco, will invest $1,200,000 in Elgin for 30 percent of its common shares. Ms. Richer, a private investor, will invest $2,800,000 for a 70 percent interest in Elgin. According to the terms of the shareholders' agreement, Mr. Landman and Ms. Richer must agree on all major operating and financing decisions. Otherwise, the property will be sold in the open market and the company will be wound up.

The second company, Metcalfe Inc., will buy a recently developed strip mall on Metcalfe Street for $2,000,000. The purchase will be financed with a first mortgage of $1,500,000 and $500,000 of equity. Mr. Landman's holding company will invest $200,000 in Metcalfe for 40 percent of its common shares and will manage the property. Ms. Richer will invest $300,000 for a 60 percent interest in Metcalfe. The shareholders' agreement contains the following terms:

- Ms. Richer will be guaranteed a return of her investment of $300,000 plus cumulative dividends of $24,000 a year.
- Mr. Landman will be responsible for making all key operating, investing, and financing decisions.
- Mr. Landman's holding company will guarantee the payment of dividends to Ms. Richer on an annual basis. After both shareholders have received cumulative dividends equal to 8 percent of their initial investments, Ms. Richer will receive 10 percent and Mr. Landman's holding company will receive 90 percent of the undistributed profits.

Required:

How should these two investments be reported on the financial statements of Holdco? Provide arguments to support your recommendations.

Case 2 P Co. is looking for some additional financing in order to renovate one of the company's manufacturing plants. It is having difficulty getting new debt financing because its debt-to-equity ratio is higher than the 3:1 limit stated in its bank covenant. It is unable to attract an equity partner because the sole owner of P Co. has set conditions for an equity partner that make it practically impossible to find a new equity investor.

Part of the problem results from the use of historical cost accounting. If the company's assets were recorded at fair value, the debt-to-equity ratio would be much lower. In order to get around the rules for historical cost accounting, the CFO for P Co. came up with the following plan.

On September 2, Year 5, P Co. will sell its manufacturing facility to SPE for $600,000 in the form of a non-interest-bearing note receivable. SPE will be set up for the sole purpose of renovating the manufacturing facility. No other activities may be carried out by SPE without the approval of P Co. Mr. Renovator, an unrelated party, will invest $400,000 in cash to cover the estimated cost of the renovation and will be the sole owner of SPE. On January 1, Year 6, after the renovation is complete and one day after P Co.'s year-end, SPE will sell the manufacturing facility back to P Co. at $1,040,000 and will be wound up. P will finance the repurchase with a $440,000 bank loan and by offsetting the remaining $600,000 against the note receivable from SPE from the original sale of the manufacturing facility to SPE. By selling the unrenovated facility and repurchasing the renovated facility, P Co. hopes to reflect the facility at its fair value, borrow the money to finance the renovation, and improve its debt-to-equity position.

The existing and pro forma balance sheets (in 000s) and debt-to-equity ratios for P Co. and SPE are presented below in condensed form:

	P Co. Sep. 1/5	P Co. Dec. 31/5	P Co. Jan. 1/6	SPE Dec. 31/5
Note receivable from SPE		$ 600		
Manufacturing facility	$ 100		$1,040	$1,000
Other assets	900	900	900	0
	$1,000	$1,500	$1,940	$1,000
Note payable to P Co.				$600
Other liabilities	$ 800	$ 800	$1,240	
Common shares	10	10	10	400
Retained earnings	190	690	690	0
	$1,000	$1,500	$1,940	$1,000
Debt-to-equity ratio	4:1	1.14:1	1:77:1	1:5:1

The CFO would like you to prepare a memo in which you discuss the accounting issues related to these proposed transactions.

Required:

Prepare the memo requested by the CFO. Ignore income taxes.

Case 3   IAS 27 affects many Canadian business enterprises that are involved with variable-interest entities (VIEs). Retrieve the annual reports of any two of the following companies:

- Tim Hortons Inc.
- Air Canada
- George Weston Limited
- Empire Company Limited
- Canadian Tire Corporation Limited
- CanWest Global Communications Corp.

Required:

Write a brief report on each company that describes

1. the extent of its involvement with VIEs.
2. the effect of the requirements of IAS 27 on its financial statements.

Case 4   Tropical Juices Limited (Tropical) was incorporated under Canadian federal legislation two years ago as a 50:50 joint venture of Citrus Growers Cooperative (Citrus) of the United States and Bottle Juices Corporation (Bottle) of Canada to sell Citrus's juices in Canada. Excerpts from the joint venture agreement are provided in Exhibit I. Both Citrus and Bottle produce and sell juices separately as well as through Tropical.

One year ago the owners of Bottle sold all their shares in Bottle to Douglas Investments Limited (DIL). The contract of sale between DIL and the former shareholders of Bottle included representations and warranties with respect to Tropical. Excerpts from the sale contract are provided in Exhibit II.

Exhibit I

TROPICAL JUICES LIMITED
EXCERPTS FROM THE JOINT VENTURE AGREEMENT

Citrus shall provide the following to Tropical:

- the blending formula and drink recipes,
- its brand names,
- an ongoing supply of juice concentrates, and
- advertising in Canada.

Bottle shall provide the following to Tropical on an ongoing basis:

- the capital equipment and personnel needed to process the juice at their existing premises,
- a supply of returnable bottles, and
- the processing and distribution of the juice.

Citrus and Bottle shall share equally in the net income of Tropical, after specific charges are made to Tropical for services provided by Citrus and Bottle. The specific charges are as follows:

1. Bottle is allowed to charge Tropical 16 percent per year on the capital investment in assets needed to process, bottle, and distribute the juices.
2. Both Bottle and Citrus are permitted to charge Tropical for
   a. disbursements they make on behalf of Tropical, and
   b. reasonable charges for administrative and other allocations of joint costs incurred on behalf of Tropical juices and their own juices.
3. Citrus is permitted to charge fair value for all juice concentrates provided to Tropical.

Citrus and Bottle shall help market Tropical juices, although Tropical shall have primary responsibility for selling its own juices. Citrus and Bottle shall allocate to Tropical its proportionate share of any revenue from sales that consist of both Tropical juices and their own juices.

Exhibit II

BOTTLE JUICES CORPORATION EXCERPTS FROM THE SALE CONTRACT

The following terms, representations, and warranties are made with respect to Tropical:

1. DIL is entitled to one-half of the net income of Tropical commencing with the second year of operations, which ends on June 30, Year 2. One-half of the net income of Tropical for the first year of operations shall be paid to the former shareholders of Bottle.
2. Bottle warrants that the total revenue will not be less than $3 million for each of the years ended June 30, Year 2 and Year 3.
3. Bottle warrants that operating expenses excluding depreciation, interest, and imputed charges shall not exceed $1.6 million for each of the years ended June 30, Year 2 and Year 3.
4. Bottle warrants that depreciation, interest, and imputed charges shall not exceed, for each of the years ended June 30, the following amounts:

Year 2	$550,000
Year 3	500,000

5. All computations are to be in accordance with generally accepted accounting principles for private enterprises.
6. If the representations and warranties are not fulfilled, then DIL shall be fully compensated for its portion of the amount of the deficiency.

DIL required that representations and warranties about Tropical be written into the sale contract because Citrus and Bottle were still negotiating the accounting policies to be used by Tropical. The selection of accounting policies is still not resolved, and the two parties cannot come to an agreement.

Draft financial statements for Tropical for the years ended June 30, Year 1, and June 30, Year 2, were prepared, based on the accounting policies selected by Bottle's controller. For the second year, the results were as follows:

Revenue	$2,690,000
Operating expenses, excluding depreciation, interest, and imputed charges	1,935,000
Depreciation, interest, and imputed charges	585,000

The joint venture agreement between Citrus and Bottle permits the appointment of an arbitrator to resolve disputes over accounting policies. Your firm has been appointed arbitrator and has been asked by all three parties (owners of Citrus, and present and previous owners of Bottle) to submit a report containing binding decisions on all matters of contention. Each decision in this arbitration report must be supported by sound reasoning so that each party can fully understand the decisions.

You, CA, have been asked to prepare the arbitration report. You interview each of the parties and are told the following:

Comments of Citrus

1. "We disagree with Bottle's charge for the cost of returnable bottles. It charged the entire cost of the bottles (which it owns) to the first year in Tropical even though the bottles have a life of 20 to 25 months."
2. "Bottle had to purchase new machinery for bottling Tropical juices because a different shape of bottle is used for Tropical juices. It borrowed the necessary funds and charged the interest to Tropical. We reject this charge."
3. "Bottle spent $328,000 training its employees to manufacture and sell Tropical juices. We disagree with this sum being expensed and charged to Tropical in the first year."
4. "Bottle charged Tropical 16 percent on the capital investment being used to produce Tropical juices. We agree with the 16 percent, but we do not agree with the 16 percent being applied from the date that the first Tropical juices were produced."
5. "Bottle charged Tropical fair value for the computer services it provided. We believe that Bottle should have charged Tropical for these services at cost."
6. "Bottle had a three-week strike. When the strike was over, Bottle produced its own juices to replenish its own inventory, and did not produce Tropical juices for almost one month after the strike ended. We believe that Tropical should be credited in the first year for imputed gross profits during the months after the strike."

Comments of Previous Owners of Bottle

7. "Tropical has benefitted from Citrus's advertising of the Citrus brand names in the United States. Citrus has charged Tropical for this advertising using the ratio

of the Canadian population reached by the U.S. television-advertising signal to the combined Canadian and U.S. populations reached by the signal. In our opinion, this does not make sense."

8. "We understand that Citrus is complaining that we were charging proportionate repair costs for the machinery and equipment being used to produce Tropical juices and our own juices. We consider this to be an appropriate charge."

9. "We charged Tropical on the basis of our costs of producing Tropical juices. Citrus objects to our use of full absorption costing even though this was the method we used for our financial statements."

Comments of DIL

10. "After completing the purchase of Bottle, we discovered that Bottle's management had been manipulating the profits between years."

11. "Tropical sells large quantities of juices to distributors who pay Tropical only when the juices are resold. However, Tropical has recorded revenue when the juices are shipped to the distributors. We disagree with this practice."

12. "Citrus bought a new refrigerated tanker truck in the second year to deliver bulk concentrates to Tropical. It is charging the cost to Tropical at one-third per year, commencing in the second year. We disagree with this approach."

13. "Citrus charges interest to Tropical on the account receivable from Tropical. We disagree."

Required:

Prepare the report.

Case 5   Segment reporting can provide useful information for investors and competitors. Segment disclosures can result in competitive harm for the company making the disclosures. By analyzing segment information, potential competitors can identify and concentrate on the more successful areas of a disclosing company's business. Indeed, the IASB recognizes that competitive harm is an issue of concern for companies disclosing segment information. In developing IFRS 8, the IASB considered giving but ultimately decided not to give companies an exemption from providing segment information if they believed that doing so would result in competitive harm. The IASB believed that such an exemption would be inappropriate because it would provide a means for broad non-compliance with the new standard.

IFRS 8 requires disclosures to be provided by country when revenues or long-lived assets in an individual country are material. However, IFRS 8 does not specify what is material for this purpose but leaves this to management judgment. Some commentators have expressed a concern that firms might use high materiality thresholds to avoid making individual country disclosures, perhaps to avoid potential competitive harm.

Required:

What factors might a company consider in determining whether an individual foreign country is material to its operations? Should the IASB establish a percentage test to determine when an individual country is material?

PROBLEMS

Problem 1   Pharma Company (Pharma) is a pharmaceutical company operating in Winnipeg. It is developing a new drug for treating multiple sclerosis (MS). On January 1, Year 3, Benefit Ltd. (Benefit) signed an agreement to guarantee the debt of Pharma and guarantee a specified rate of return to the common shareholders. In return, Benefit will obtain the residual profits of Pharma. After extensive analysis, it has been determined that Pharma is a variable interest entity and Benefit is its primary beneficiary.

The balance sheets (in 000,000s) of Benefit and Pharma on January 1, Year 3, were as follows:

	Benefit *book value*	*Pharma* *book value*	*Pharma* *fair value*
Current assets	$250	$ 50	$ 50
Property, plant, and equipment	400	80	90
Intangible assets	50	20	70
	$700	$150	$210
Current liabilities	$145	$ 60	$ 60
Long-term debt	325	120	125
Common shares	10	1	
Retained earnings	220	(31)	
	$700	$150	

An independent appraiser determined the fair values of Pharma's non-current assets. The appraiser was quite confident with the appraised value for the property, plant, and equipment but had some reservations in putting a specific value on the intangible assets.

Required:

Prepare a consolidated balance sheet at January 1, Year 3, assuming that the agreement between Benefit and Pharma established the following fair values for the common shares of Pharma:

(a) $25
(b) $15
(c) $30

Problem 2   Leighton Corp. has just acquired 100 percent of the voting shares of Knightbridge Inc. and is now preparing the financial data needed to consolidate this new subsidiary. Leighton paid $700,000 for its investment. Details of all of Knightbridge's assets and liabilities on acquisition date were as follows:

	Fair value	*Tax base*
Land	$100,000	$100,000
Buildings	180,000	110,000
Equipment	200,000	130,000
Inventory	150,000	150,000
Instalment accounts receivable	120,000	–0–
Trade liabilities	240,000	240,000

Required:

Determine the amounts that will be used to prepare a consolidated statement of financial position on the date of acquisition, assuming that Knightbridge's tax rate is 45 percent. Knightbridge has not set up deferred tax amounts for any of its assets or liabilities.

Problem 3   On December 31, Year 4, Russell Inc. invested $20,000 in Charger Corp. Prior to this Russell had no interest in Charger. Upon review of the documentation related to Russell's investment, the controller of Russell determined that Charger is a variable interest entity and Russell is its primary beneficiary. Immediately after Russell's investment, Charger Corp. prepared the following balance sheet:

Cash	$ 20,000	Long-term debt	$120,000
Marketing software	140,000	Russell equity interest	20,000
Computer equipment	40,000	Non-controlling interest	60,000
	$200,000		$200,000

Each of the above amounts represents the fair value at December 31, Year 4, except for marketing software. Charger Corp. is carrying on a business.

Required:

(a) If the marketing software was undervalued by $20,000, what reported amounts for Charger's financial statement items would appear in Russell's December 31, Year 4, financial statements?

(b) If the marketing software was overvalued by $20,000, what reported amounts for Charger's financial statement items would appear in Russell's December 31, Year 4, financial statements?

Problem 4   On January 1, Year 5, AB Company (AB) purchased 80 percent of the outstanding common shares of Dandy Limited (Dandy) for $8,000. On that date, Dandy's shareholders' equity consisted of common shares of $1,000 and retained earnings of $6,000.

In negotiating the purchase price at the date of acquisition, it was agreed that the fair values of all of Dandy's assets and liabilities were equal to their book values and tax base except for the following:

	Fair value	Carrying value	Tax base
Equipment	$950	$700	$600

Dandy has recorded deferred income taxes on its separate-entity balance sheet on all temporary differences. Dandy had a loss carry-forward of $800 as at December 31, Year 4. This carry-forward can be applied against taxable income in the future. Dandy did not previously recognize the benefit of the carry-forward because it was not sure whether it would earn $800 in taxable income in the future. Now that AB controls Dandy, AB is sure that Dandy will be able to utilize the loss carry-forwards because AB will transfer income-earning assets to Dandy if necessary to generate taxable income in Dandy. AB plans to utilize these loss carry-forwards as soon as possible.

Both companies use the straight-line method for amortizing their capital assets and pay taxes at a rate of 40 percent. Dandy's equipment had a remaining useful life of 10 years at the date of acquisition.

Dandy reported income before application of any loss carry-forwards as follows for the first three years after being acquired by AB:

Year	Net income
Year 5	$ 0
Year 6	100
Year 7	200

Required:

(a) Calculate goodwill at the date of acquisition. Be sure to consider the deferred tax implications on the acquisition differential.
(b) Calculate non-controlling interest at the date of acquisition.
(c) Prepare a schedule to show the amortization of the acquisition differential for the three-year period ending December 31, Year 7. Assume that the goodwill impairment loss was $300 in Year 6, the deferred income tax liability is amortized at the same rate as the equipment, and the loss carry-forwards are applied against income as the income is earned.
(d) Explain why the acquisition differential related to the equipment gives rise to a deferred income tax liability.

Problem 5 On January 1, Year 1, Green Inc. purchased 100 percent of the common shares of Mansford Corp. for $335,000. Green's balance sheet data on this date just prior to this acquisition were as follows:

	Book value	Tax base
Cash	$ 340,000	$ 340,000
Accounts receivable	167,200	–0–
Inventory	274,120	274,120
Land	325,000	325,000
Buildings (net)	250,000	150,000
Equipment (net)	79,000	46,200
	$1,435,320	$1,135,320
Current liabilities	$ 133,000	$ 133,000
Deferred tax liability	120,000	—
Non-current liabilities	—	
Common shares	380,000	
Retained earnings	802,320	
	$1,435,320	

The balance sheet and other related data for Mansford are as follows:

MANSFORD CORP. — BALANCE SHEET
January 1, Year 1

	Book value	Fair value	Tax base
Cash	$ 52,500	$ 52,500	$ 52,500
Accounts receivable	61,450	61,450	61,450
Inventory	110,000	134,000	110,000
Land	75,000	210,000	75,000
Buildings (net)	21,000	24,000	15,000
Equipment (net)	17,000	16,000	12,000
	$336,950	$497,950	$325,950
Current liabilities	$ 41,115	$ 41,115	$ 41,115
Non-current liabilities	150,000	155,000	150,000
Deferred tax liability	4,400		—
Common shares	100,000		
Retained earnings	41,435		
	$336,950		

For both companies, the income tax rate is 40 percent.

Required:

Prepare a consolidated balance sheet at January 1, Year 1.

Problem 6 Assume that all of the facts in Problem 5 remain unchanged except that Green paid $201,000 for 60 percent of the voting shares of Mansford.

Required:

(a) Prepare a consolidated balance sheet at January 1, Year 1.
(b) Explain how the definition of a liability supports the recognition of a deferred income tax liability when a parent purchases shares in a subsidiary and the fair values of the subsidiary's identifiable net assets are greater than their net book values.

Problem 7 The statements of financial position of Prime Inc. and Variable Ltd. on December 31, Year 11, were as follows:

	Prime	Variable Ltd.	
	Book value	Book value	Fair value
Land	$ 400,000	$ 80,000	$200,000
Manufacturing facility	750,000	320,000	300,000
Accounts receivable	250,000	50,000	50,000
Cash	200,000		
	$1,600,000	$450,000	$550,000
Common shares	$ 50,000	$ 10,000	
Retained earnings	750,000	90,000	
Long-term debt	525,000	290,000	$280,000
Current liabilities	275,000	60,000	60,000
	$1,600,000	$450,000	

Variable's manufacturing facility is old and very costly to operate. For the year ended December 31, Year 11, the company lost money for the first time in its history. Variable does not have the financial ability to refurbish the plant. It must either cease operations or find a partner to carry on operations.

On January 1, Year 12, Prime agreed to provide an interest-free loan of $200,000 to Variable on the following terms and conditions:

- Prime Inc. would be hired by Variable to refurbish the manufacturing facility at a fixed cost of $200,000 and would be retained to manage the business.
- Prime Inc. would have full authority to make all major operating, investing, and financing decisions related to Variable.
- The common shares of Variable were valued at $208,000 as at January 1, Year 12. Prime has the option to buy the shares of Variable at any time after January 1, Year 17, at $208,000 plus any dividends in arrears.
- The existing shareholders of Variable would be guaranteed a cumulative dividend of 8 percent a year on the value of their shares. Prime would receive the residual profits after the dividends were paid to the common shareholders.

Variable earned income of $200,000 and paid dividends of $50,000 over the five-year period ended December 31, Year 16. The statements of financial position of Prime Inc. and Variable Ltd. on December 31, Year 16 were as follows:

	Prime	Variable
Land	$ 400,000	$ 80,000
Manufacturing facility	650,000	260,000
Accounts receivable	275,000	70,000
Cash	20,000	180,000
	$1,345,000	$590,000
Common shares	$ 50,000	$ 10,000
Retained earnings	660,000	240,000
Long-term debt	450,000	290,000
Current liabilities	185,000	50,000
	$1,345,000	$590,000

Assume that Variable is a variable interest entity and Prime is the primary beneficiary. The manufacturing facility had an estimated remaining useful life of 10 years as at January 1, Year 12. The long-term debt matures on December 31, Year 21. Prior to Year 12, Prime had no business relations with Variable.

Required:
(a) Calculate consolidated retained earnings at December 31, Year 16.
(b) Prepare a consolidated statement of financial position for Prime at December 31, Year 16.
(c) Use the definition of a liability to explain the rationale for including the liabilities of the variable interest entity on the consolidated statement of financial position for the primary beneficiary.

Problem 8 The following information has been assembled about Casbar Corp. as at December 31, Year 5 (amounts are in thousands):

Operating segment	Revenues	Profit	Assets
A	$12,000	$3,100	$24,000
B	9,600	2,680	21,000
C	7,200	(1,440)	15,000
D	3,600	660	9,000
E	5,100	810	8,400
F	1,800	(270)	3,600

Required:

Determine which operating segments require separate disclosures.

Problem 9 The following are the December 31, Year 9, balance sheets of three related companies:

	Pro Ltd.	Forma Corp.	Apex Inc.
Cash	$ 70,000	$ 1,500	$200,000
Accounts receivable	210,000	90,000	110,000
Inventory	100,000	62,500	70,000
Investment in Forma Corp. — at cost	416,000	—	—
Investment in Apex Inc. — at cost	150,000	—	—
Land	100,000	110,000	60,000
Plant and equipment	636,000	550,000	290,000
Accumulated depreciation	(185,000)	(329,000)	(60,000)
	$1,497,000	$485,000	$670,000
Accounts payable	$ 175,000	$ 90,000	$130,000
Bonds payable	312,000	—	—
Common shares	800,000	100,000	500,000
$12 preferred shares	—	200,000	—
Retained earnings	210,000	95,000	40,000
	$1,497,000	$485,000	$670,000

Additional Information

- On January 1, Year 5, Pro purchased 40 percent of Forma for $116,000. On that date, Forma's shareholders' equity was as follows:

Common shares	$100,000
Retained earnings	80,000
	$180,000

  All of the identifiable net assets of Forma had fair values equal to carrying values except for the following, for which fair values exceeded carrying values as follows:

Inventory	$20,000
Land	40,000
Plant and equipment	50,000

- On September 30, Year 7, Pro purchased the remaining 60 percent of Forma for $300,000. On that date, Forma's shareholders' equity was as follows:

Common shares	$100,000
Retained earnings	110,000
	$210,000

On this date, the following net assets of Forma were undervalued by the amounts shown:

Inventory	$10,000
Land	60,000
Plant and equipment	70,000

- For consolidation purposes, any acquisition differential allocated to plant and equipment is amortized over 20 years from each date of aquisition. A goodwill impairment loss amounting to $2,025 was recorded in Year 8.
- During Year 8, Forma issued 2,000 cumulative, $12, no-par-value preferred shares. Pro did not acquire any of these shares.
- The inventories of Pro contained intercompany profits from items purchased from Forma in the following amounts:

December 31, Year 8	$40,000
December 31, Year 9	45,000

- During Year 9, Pro and two other unrelated companies formed Apex, which is a joint venture. Pro invested $150,000 cash for its 30 percent interest in Apex.
- The year-end inventories of Apex contained a $12,000 intercompany profit from items purchased from Pro since its formation in Year 9.
- Forma paid dividends in all years prior to Year 9.
- On December 31, Year 9, the accounts receivable of Pro contained the following:

Receivable from Forma	$13,000
Receivable from Apex	$40,000

- Use income tax allocation at a 40 percent rate as it applies to unrealized profits only. Ignore deferred income taxes on the acquisition differential.

Required:

Prepare the Year 9 consolidated balance sheet assuming that Pro reports its investment in Apex using
(a) the equity method.
*(b) proportionate consolidation.

Problem 10   The following are the Year 9 income statements of Kent Corp. and Laurier Ltd.

INCOME STATEMENTS
for the Year Ended December 31, Year 9

	Kent	Laurier
Sales	$3,000,000	$1,200,000
Other income	200,000	70,000
Gain on sale of land	—	100,000
	3,200,000	1,370,000
Cost of sales	1,400,000	560,000
Selling and administrative expenses	500,000	300,000
Other expenses	100,000	130,000
Income tax	400,000	150,000
	2,400,000	1,140,000
Net income	$ 800,000	$ 230,000

Additional Information
- Kent acquired its 40 percent interest in the common shares of Laurier in Year 3 at a cost of $825,000 and uses the cost method to account for its investment for internal record-keeping.
- The acquisition-differential amortization schedule pertaining to Kent's 40 percent interest showed the following write-off for Year 9:

Buildings	$ 9,000
Goodwill impairment loss	13,000
	22,000
Long-term liabilities	12,500
Acquisition-differential amortization — Year 9	$ 9,500

- Depreciation expense and goodwill impairment loss are included with selling and administrative expenses.
- In Year 9, rent amounting to $125,000 was paid by Laurier to Kent. Kent has recorded this as other income.
- In Year 6, Kent sold land to Laurier and recorded a profit of $75,000 on the transaction. During Year 9, Laurier sold 30 percent of the land to an unrelated land development company.
- During Year 9, Laurier paid dividends totalling $80,000.
- It has been established that Kent's 40 percent interest would *not* be considered control in accordance with IFRSs.
- Assume a 40 percent tax rate.

Required:

*(a) Assume that Laurier is a joint venture that is owned by Kent and two other unrelated venturers. Also assume that Kent acquired its interest after Laurier's initial formation, and that the acquisition differentials are therefore valid. Prepare Kent's consolidated income statement for Year 9 using proportionate consolidation (show all calculations).

(b) Assume that Laurier is a joint venture. Prepare the income statement of Kent for Year 9 using the equity method (show all calculations).

Problem 11   Albert Company has an investment in the voting shares of Prince Ltd. On December 31, Year 5, Prince reported a net income of $860,000 and declared dividends of $200,000.

During Year 5, Albert had sales to Prince of $915,000, and Prince had sales to Albert of $500,000. On December 31, Year 5, the inventory of Albert contained an after-tax intercompany profit of $40,000, and the inventory of Prince contained an after-tax intercompany profit of $72,000.

On January 1, Year 4, Albert sold equipment to Prince and recorded an after-tax profit of $120,000 on the transaction. The equipment had a remaining useful life of five years on this date. Albert uses the equity method to account for its investment in Prince.

Required:

Prepare Albert's Year 5 equity method journal entries under each of the following two assumptions:

(a) Albert owns 64 percent of Prince.

(b) Albert owns 30 percent of Prince, and Prince is a joint venture.

Problem 12   On January 1, Year 1, Amco Ltd. and Newstar Inc. formed Bearcat Resources, a joint venture. Newstar contributed miscellaneous assets with a fair value of $750,000 for a 60 percent interest in the venture. Amco contributed plant and equipment with a book value of $300,000 and a fair value of $1,000,000 and received a 40 percent interest in the venture plus $450,000 in cash. On December 31, Year 1, Bearcat reported a profit of $180,000 and declared a dividend of $75,000. Amco has a December 31 year-end and will account for its 40 percent interest using the equity method. (Assume a 20-year useful life for the plant and equipment.)

Required:

(a) Assume that the miscellaneous assets contributed by Newstar included cash of $450,000. Also, assume that the significant benefits and risks were transferred when Amco transferred the plant and equipment to the joint venture.

Prepare Amco's Year 1 journal entries.

(b) Assume that there was no cash in the assets contributed by Newstar and that the cash received by Amco had been borrowed by Bearcat. Also, assume that the significant benefits and risks were not transferred when Amco transferred the plant and equipment to the joint venture.

Prepare Amco's Year 1 journal entries.

Problem 13   The following are the Year 9 income statements of Poker Inc. and Joker Company:

INCOME STATEMENTS
Year ended December 31, Year 9

	Poker	Joker
Sales	$1,000,000	$800,000
Other income	200,000	110,000
Gain on sale of trademark	—	40,000
	1,200,000	950,000
Cost of goods sold	600,000	550,000
Selling and administrative expenses	200,000	150,000
Other expenses	50,000	40,000
Income before income taxes	350,000	210,000
Income taxes	105,000	63,000
Profit	$ 245,000	$147,000

Additional Information

- Poker acquired a 60 percent interest in the common shares of Joker on January 1, Year 4, at a cost of $420,000 and uses the cost method to account for its investment. At that time, Joker's net book value of shareholders' equity was $600,000 and the fair value of each of its assets and liabilities equalled book value except for equipment, which had a fair value of $100,000 in excess of carrying value and an estimated remaining useful life of 10 years.
- In Year 9, Joker paid a management fee of $50,000 to Poker. Poker recorded this as other income.
- In Year 5, Poker sold two trademarks with an indefinite life to Joker and recorded a total gain on sale of $60,000 ($30,000 for each trademark). During Year 9, Joker sold one of these trademarks to an unrelated company for a gain of $40,000.
- Depreciation expense is included with selling and administrative expenses.
- During Year 9, Joker declared and paid dividends totalling $200,000.
- The income tax rate is 30 percent for both companies.

Required:

(a) Assume that Joker is a joint venture that is jointly owned by Poker and several unrelated venturers and that Poker uses the equity method to report its investment. Prepare Poker's income statement for the year ended December 31, Year 9.
(b) Assume that Joker is not a joint venture and, furthermore, that Poker's long-term investment provides it with control over Joker. Prepare Poker's consolidated income statement for the year ended December 31, Year 9.

Problem 14   Jager Ltd., a joint venture, was formed on January 1, Year 3. Cliffcord Corp., one of the three founding venturers, invested equipment for a 40 percent interest in the joint venture. The other two venturers invested land and cash for their 60 percent equity in Jager. All of the venturers agreed that the equipment had a fair value of $2,000,000, and a remaining useful life of approximately eight years. This equipment had been acquired by Cliffcord two years ago, and the carrying value on Cliffcord's records on January 1 was $1,800,000. Cliffcord recorded its investment in the joint venture at $2,000,000. On December 31, Year 3, Jager recorded a net loss of $100,000.

Cliffcord uses the equity method to record its investment.

Required:

(a) Assume that the significant benefits and risks were not transferred when Clifford transferred the equipment to the joint venture. Prepare Cliffcord's Year 3 journal entries.
(b) Assume Cliffcord had received a 40 percent interest and $1,000,000 in cash in return for investing this equipment in the venture. Also assume that the other venturers contributed cash in excess of $1,000,000 for their ownership interests and that the significant benefits and risks were transferred when Clifford transferred the equipment to the joint venture. Prepare Clifford's Year 3 journal entries.

Problem 15   The following balance sheets have been prepared as at December 31, Year 5, for Kay
Corp. and Adams Co. Ltd.:

	Kay	Adams
Cash	$ 60,000	$ 30,000
Accounts receivable	80,000	170,000
Inventory	600,000	400,000
Property and plant	1,400,000	900,000
Investment in Adams	360,000	—
	$2,500,000	$1,500,000
Current liabilities	$ 400,000	$ 150,000
Bonds payable	500,000	600,000
Common shares	900,000	450,000
Retained earnings	700,000	300,000
	$2,500,000	$1,500,000

Additional Information

- Kay acquired its 40 percent interest in Adams for $360,000 in Year 1, when
  Adams's retained earnings amounted to $170,000. The acquisition differential
  on that date was fully amortized by the end of Year 5.
- In Year 4, Kay sold land to Adams and recorded a gain of $60,000 on the
  transaction. This land is still being used by Adams.
- The December 31, Year 5, inventory of Kay contained a profit recorded by
  Adams amounting to $35,000.
- On December 31, Year 5, Adams owes Kay $29,000.
- Kay has used the cost method to account for its investment in Adams.
- Use income tax allocation at a rate of 40 percent but ignore income tax on
  the acquisition differential.

Required:

(a) Prepare *three* separate balance sheets for Kay as at December 31, Year 5, assuming that the investment in Adams is a
   (i) Control investment.
   (ii) Joint venture investment and is reported using proportionate consolidation.
   (iii) Significant influence investment.
(b) Calculate the debt-to-equity ratio for each of the balance sheets in part (a).
Which reporting method presents the strongest position from a solvency point
of view? Briefly explain.

WEB-BASED PROBLEMS

Problem 1   Access the most recent consolidated financial statements for Vodafone, a British
company. (Go to the investor relations section at www.vodafone.com.) Answer the
questions below. For each question, indicate where in the financial statements you
found the answer and/or provide a brief explanation.
(a) How does the company report its interest in companies it controls through
means other than majority share ownership?
(b) What impact does the consolidation of special-purpose entities have on the
company's debt-to-equity ratio?

(c) What portion of the company's net income is derived from investments in joint ventures?

(d) Until 2011, under IFRSs, joint ventures can be reported using proportionate consolidation or the equity method. What method of reporting did the company use in the current year? If it had used the other method, what would the impact on the debt-to-equity ratio and the return on equity ratio have been?

(e) What were the statutory and effective tax rates on income from continuing operations? Identify the two biggest factors that caused these two rates to be different.

(f) What amount of deferred income tax was recorded as part of the accounting for the main business acquisition during the year, and how did this affect the amount allocated to goodwill?

Problem 2 Access the most recent financial statements for Siemens, a German company. (Go to the investor relations section at www.siemens.com.) Answer the same questions as in Problem 1. For each question, indicate where in the financial statements you found the answer and/or provide a brief explanation. (Some questions may not be applicable.)

Problem 3 Access the most recent consolidated financial statements for Vodafone, a British company. (Go to the investor relations section at www.vodafone.com.) Answer the questions below. For each question, indicate where in the financial statements you found the answer and/or provide a brief explanation.

(a) Are the company's operating segments based on product lines, geographic areas, or some other factor?

(b) Does the company provide disclosures about major customers? If so, what is the nature of the disclosure?

(c) Which of the operating segments is the biggest in terms of revenues?

(d) Which of the operating segments reported the highest growth in revenues from the previous year?

(e) Which of the operating segments is the biggest in terms of profit?

(f) Which of the operating segments reported the most improvement in profit margin from the previous year?

(g) Which of the operating segments is the biggest in terms of assets?

(h) Which of the operating segments reported the most improvement in return on assets from the previous year?

Problem 4 Access the most recent financial statements for Siemens, a German company. (Go to the investor relations section at www.siemens.com.) Answer the same questions as in Problem 3. For each question, indicate where in the financial statements you found the answer and/or provide a brief explanation. (Some questions may not be applicable.)

Chapter ⑩ Foreign-currency Transactions

LEARNING OBJECTIVES

After studying this chapter, you should be able to do the following:

1. Translate foreign-currency transactions and balances into the presentation currency.
2. Describe when to use the closing rate and when to use the historical rate when translating assets and liabilities denominated in a foreign currency. Evaluate whether this practice produces results consistent with the normal measurement and valuation of assets and liabilities for domestic transactions and operations.
3. Describe the concept of hedging, and prepare a list of items that could be used as a hedge.
4. Prepare journal entries and subsequent financial statement presentation for forward exchange contracts that hedge existing monetary positions, firm commitments, or are entered into for speculative purposes.
5. Apply the concept of hedge accounting to long-term debt acting as a hedge of a future revenue stream.
6. Differentiate between the accounting for a fair value hedge and a cash flow hedge.

INTRODUCTION

Many Canadian companies conduct business in foreign countries as well as in Canada. For some companies, foreign business simply means purchasing products and services from foreign suppliers, or selling products and services to foreign customers. Other companies go far beyond importing and exporting; they borrow and lend money in foreign markets and conduct business in foreign countries through sales offices, branches, subsidiaries, and joint ventures. Of 200 Canadian public companies recently sampled, 139 made disclosures about geographic areas.[1] These companies are generating revenues, incurring costs, and employing assets in countries other than Canada. Bombardier Inc., a Canadian transportation company, in its 2009 annual report, reported export revenues of $18.9 billion, representing 96 percent of total sales.[2]

---

[1] *Financial Reporting in Canada 2007*, 32nd edition. Toronto: CICA, chapter 13.
[2] http://www2.bombardier.com/en/6_0/pdf/Annual_report_2009_en.pdf.

Many Canadian companies enter into foreign-currency-denominated transactions.

No specific accounting issues arise when the parties involved in an import or export transaction agree that the settlement will be in Canadian dollars. Because it is a *Canadian-dollar-denominated transaction*, the company will record the foreign purchase or sale in exactly the same manner as any domestic purchase or sale. In many situations, however, the agreement calls for the transaction to be settled in a foreign currency. This means one of two things: (a) the Canadian company will have to acquire foreign currency in order to discharge the obligations resulting from its imports, or (b) the Canadian company will receive foreign currency as a result of its exports and will have to sell the foreign currency in order to receive Canadian dollars. Transactions such as these are called *foreign-currency-denominated transactions*.

As the foreign currency exchange rate fluctuates, so does the Canadian dollar value of these foreign transactions. Companies often find it necessary to engage in some form of hedging activity to reduce losses arising from fluctuating exchange rates. The Bank of Nova Scotia uses derivative financial instruments to accommodate the risk management needs of its customers, for proprietary trading and asset/liability management purposes. Derivative instruments designated as "asset/liability management" are those used to manage the bank's interest rate, foreign currency, and other exposures, which include instruments designated as hedges. At the end of fiscal year 2008, The Bank of Nova Scotia, Canada's third-largest bank, reported foreign-exchange and gold derivative financial instruments with a notional value of $1,562 billion.[3]

Many tools and techniques are available to hedge against different kinds of risks.

Aside from foreign-currency risk, there are many other types of risk a company is exposed to and many different ways of hedging this risk. Bombardier used an innovative contract to increase sales by 38 percent. It offered buyers a $1,000 rebate on its snowmobiles if a pre-set amount of snow did not fall that season. The company was able to make such a guarantee by buying a weather derivative based on a snowfall index. When the season ended the level of snowfall had been such that no payment was received on the weather derivative. However, Bombardier did not have to pay any rebates to its customers either. Furthermore, the buyers purchased the snowmobiles earlier in the season because they did not wait for the snow to fall before making their purchase. This change led to a reduction in working-capital requirements (due to lower inventory-holding costs) and less strain on production capabilities. The company therefore benefited from lower costs as well as increased earnings.

This chapter covers accounting issues related to foreign-currency transactions and foreign-currency hedging activities. Chapter 11 deals with the translation of the financial statements of a foreign operation. To provide background for subsequent discussions, this chapter begins with a brief look at exchange rates.

Currency Exchange Rates

An exchange rate is the price to change one currency into another currency.

Both the recording of foreign-currency-denominated transactions and the translation of foreign-currency financial statements require the use of currency exchange rates. An exchange rate is simply the price of one currency in terms of another currency. Exchange rates fluctuate on a daily basis. Historically, governments have tried to stabilize rates between their currencies. Shortly after World War II, a group of the world's major trading nations agreed to "peg" the rates at which their currencies would be

---

[3] www.scotiabank.com/images/en/filesaboutscotia/19578.pdf.

exchanged in terms of U.S. dollars. Since these pegged rates stayed reasonably steady, the accounting for foreign transactions was fairly simple. Differences in inflation rates and major changes in the balance of payments among the participating nations were contributing factors to the eventual demise of this agreement in the early 1970s.

The end of pegged rates led to the present system, in which exchange rates are determined by market forces. This system of floating exchange rates is not totally market driven in the short term, because governments often intervene in the marketplace to lessen the swings in the value of their currencies. It is not uncommon to hear that the Canadian dollar has weakened in relation to the U.S. dollar, and that the Bank of Canada has made massive purchases of Canadian dollars in order to soften the decline, or that the U.S. Federal Reserve Bank and the central banks of other countries have intervened in the foreign-currency markets by purchasing U.S. dollars because the U.S. dollar was declining in relation to other major currencies. Sometimes interventions of this nature are fruitless, as was the case in 1994, when Mexico's central bank abandoned its attempt to prop up the peso and allowed a substantial devaluation to take place.

Reasons for Fluctuating Exchange Rates   Currencies trade in markets in such major cities as New York, London, Paris, and Tokyo, and transfers of enormous amounts of currency between countries can take place in a matter of seconds. The price of a currency will fluctuate in much the same manner as the price of any other commodity. There are many reasons why a country's currency price changes, of which the major ones are the following:

Exchange rates fluctuate over time due primarily to differences in inflation rates, interest rates, and trading practices between the two countries.

- *Inflation rates.* As a general rule, if country A has a higher rate of inflation than country B, the price of A's currency will weaken relative to B's. In a period of inflation, the purchasing power of a country's currency declines. If this currency will not buy as much in goods as it did before, then neither will it buy as much currency of another country as it did before.

- *Interest rates.* Higher interest rates attract foreign investment to a country and in so doing drive up the price of the currency of the country with the higher interest rates.

- *Trade surpluses and deficits.* As a country exports more than it imports, its currency strengthens and becomes worth more.

Exchange rates can be quoted directly or indirectly.

The direct method is the reciprocal of the indirect method.

Exchange Rate Quotations   Exchange rates showing the value of the Canadian dollar in terms of other foreign currencies are quoted daily in many Canadian business newspapers. The amounts that usually appear are called *direct quotations*, which means that the amount represents the cost in Canadian dollars to purchase one unit of foreign currency. For example, a quotation of 1 euro = CDN$1.47865 means that it costs 1.47865 Canadian dollars to purchase 1 euro. An *indirect quotation* would state the cost in a foreign currency to purchase 1 Canadian dollar. For example, a quotation of 1 dollar = 0.67629 euro indicates that it costs 0.67629 euros to purchase 1 Canadian dollar. An indirect quotation can be obtained by computing the reciprocal of the *direct* quotation. Conversely, a direct quotation can be obtained by computing the reciprocal of the *indirect* quotation ($1 \div 1.47865 = 0.67629$, and $1 \div 0.67629 = 1.47865$).

Direct quotations are the most useful ones for recording transactions denominated in foreign currencies. Using the exchange rates quoted above, a Canadian company would record the purchase of £10,000 of inventory from a European supplier as $14,786.

Examples of foreign-exchange quotations on a particular day for three countries' currencies are shown in Exhibit 10.1. These rates represent the amount in Canadian dollars that a commercial bank would charge if it sold one unit of foreign currency to a major customer. The first rate quoted is called the *spot rate*. If a customer wanted to purchase 5,000 euros on the date that these rates were quoted, the cost would be $7,402 (5,000 × 1.4805). Note that if the bank were to purchase euros from the customer, the amount that it would pay the customer would be slightly less than the amount quoted per euro. The bank's selling rate has to be greater than its purchasing rate if it is to make a profit dealing in foreign currencies. The forward rates quoted (one month forward, two months forward, etc.) are the rates for forward exchange contracts. A *forward exchange contract* is an agreement between a bank and a customer to exchange currencies on a specified future date at a specified rate. For example, when a bank enters into a forward exchange contract with a customer to purchase 5,000 euros six months forward, the bank is committing itself to take delivery of this quantity of euros six months from this date, and to pay the customer $7,400 (5,000 × 1.4799) at that time. Of course, there is also a commitment on the part of the customer to sell 5,000 euros to the bank in six months' time. The use of forward exchange contracts in hedging transactions will be illustrated later in this chapter.

> The spot rate is the rate to exchange currency today, whereas the forward rate is the rate agreed to today for exchanging currency at a future date.

Accounting for Foreign-currency Transactions

Before we deal with the detailed accounting rules for foreign transactions, it is important to note that currency issues can be discussed and analyzed from many different

---

Exhibit 10.1

FOREIGN-EXCHANGE DIRECT QUOTATIONS

Country	Currency	CDN$ per unit
United States	Dollar	1.0296
1 month forward		1.0296
2 months forward		1.0297
3 months forward		1.0297
6 months forward		1.0298
12 months forward		1.0315
European Union	Euro	1.4805
1 month forward		1.4803
3 months forward		1.4802
6 months forward		1.4799
12 months forward		1.4802
Japan	Yen	0.011335
1 month forward		0.011337
3 months forward		0.011341
6 months forward		0.011351
12 months forward		0.011405

> Notice that the Canadian dollar is expected to decrease in value relative to the U.S. dollar but increase in value relative to the euro over the next 12 months.

perspectives. For Chapters 10 and 11, we need to differentiate among the following perspectives:

We need to differentiate between the denominated, recording, functional, and presentation currencies.

- Currency in which the transaction is denominated (denominated currency);
- Currency in which the transaction is recorded in the internal accounting records (recording currency or internal record-keeping currency);
- Currency of the primary economic environment in which the entity operates (functional currency);
- Currency in which the financial statements are presented by the reporting entity (presentation currency, which is commonly referred to as reporting currency).

Exhibit 10.2 shows examples of how these different currency perspectives could exist for individual companies. The last line indicates the method used to translate from one currency to another in the order in which the currencies are translated. Company E will need to translate three different times.

Up until now in this book, we have been dealing with Company A, where the Canadian dollar was the currency used for the four perspectives listed above. The transactions were denominated in Canadian dollars, i.e., the invoices, agreements, cheques, etc., were written in Canadian dollars; the general ledger was maintained in Canadian dollars; the company operated in Canada; and the financial statements were presented in Canadian dollars. In this chapter, we deal with transactions that are denominated in different currencies. We are then faced with deciding which currency should be used to record the transaction and which currency should be used when presenting the financial statements to external users.

All transactions must be translated to the functional currency of the reporting entity.

IAS 21 requires that individual transactions be *translated into* the *functional currency* of the reporting entity. In turn, IAS 21 states that an entity can *present* or *report* its financial statements in any currency it wants to use. Presumably, the entity will present its financial statements in the currency most useful to its users. Most Canadian companies will present their financial statements in Canadian dollars. However, some Canadian companies may present their financial statements in U.S. dollars because many of the users of the financial statements will be American investors or creditors or will be international investors or creditors who understand and monitor the U.S. dollar more easily and readily than the Canadian dollar.

IAS 21 defines *functional currency* as the currency of the primary economic environment in which the entity operates and *foreign currency* as any currency other

---

Exhibit 10.2

EXAMPLES OF CURRENCY PERSPECTIVES

Currency perspective	Company A	Company B	Company C	Company D	Company E
Incorporated in	Canada	Canada	Germany	Japan	Argentina
Denominated	Canadian $	Various	Various	Various	Various
Recording	Canadian $	Canadian $ (1)	Euro (1)	Yen (1)	Peso (1)
Functional	Canadian $	Canadian $	Canadian $ (2)	Yen	Canadian $ (2)
Presentation	Canadian $	Canadian $	Canadian $	Canadian $ (2)	US $ (3)
Method used for translation	N/A N/A	(1) Temporal (2) N/A	(1) Temporal (2) Temporal	(1) Temporal (2) Current rate	(1) Temporal (2) Temporal (3) Current rate

Company E must translate from one currency to another currency three different times.

Exhibit 10.3

INDICATORS FOR CHOOSING FUNCTIONAL CURRENCY

Indicator	Functional currency	
	Canadian dollar	Not Canadian dollar
1. Sales prices	Sales occur in Canada and are denominated in Canadian dollars.	Sales occur in foreign countries and are not denominated in Canadian dollars.
2. Operating costs	Labour and materials are obtained in Canada and denominated in Canadian dollars.	Labour and materials are obtained from foreign countries and are not denominated in Canadian dollars.
3. Competition and regulation	Competitors are Canadian or company is listed on a Canadian exchange.	Competition comes from foreign entities or companies listed on a foreign exchange.
4. Financing	Debt and equity instruments are issued in Canadian dollars.	Debt and equity instruments are not issued in Canadian dollars.
5. Operating surpluses	Excess cash is retained in Canadian dollars.	Excess cash is not retained in Canadian dollars.

The functional currency is the currency of the primary economic environment in which the entity operates.

than the functional currency of the entity. The primary economic environment is normally the one in which the entity primarily generates and expends cash. Exhibit 10.3 lists the indicators that should be considered when determining the functional currency and gives an example of a condition that would indicate that the Canadian dollar is or is not the functional currency.

When the above indicators are mixed and the functional currency is not obvious, management uses its judgment to determine the functional currency that most faithfully represents the economic effects of the underlying transactions, events, and conditions. As part of this approach, management gives priority to indicators 1 and 2 before considering the other indicators, which are designed to provide additional supporting evidence to determine an entity's functional currency.

In this chapter, the Canadian dollar is the recording, functional, and presentation currency.

Professional judgment must be exercised in identifying the functional currency. In this chapter, we will assume, unless otherwise noted, that we are dealing with Company B, where the Canadian dollar is the recording currency, the functional currency, and the presentation currency.

In Chapter 12, we will deal with Companies C, D, and E, where the recording currency is different from the functional and/or the presentation currency.

We will now focus on the issues associated with import/export transactions and foreign-currency-denominated debt. Accounting problems arise when there are exchange rate changes between the date of a transaction and the eventual settlement in foreign currency. During this period, the company holds foreign-currency-denominated monetary assets and liabilities, and questions arise as to how to measure these items if financial statements need to be prepared in the intervening period, and what to do with any gains or losses that may result from such measure-

A monetary item is converted into cash at a fixed and predetermined amount of currency.

ments. Monetary items are units of currency held and assets and liabilities to be received or paid in a fixed or determinable number of units of currency. Accounts receivable and investments in bonds are some obvious examples of monetary assets; accounts payable and bond liabilities are monetary liabilities. A foreign-currency-denominated monetary position is a net asset position if monetary assets exceed monetary liabilities, or a net liability position if monetary liabilities exceed monetary assets.

Some not so obvious examples of monetary items are pensions and other employee benefits to be paid in cash, provisions that are to be settled in cash, and cash dividends that are recognized as a liability. Similarly, a contract to receive (or deliver) a variable number of the entity's own equity instruments or a variable amount of assets in which the fair value to be received (or delivered) equals a fixed or determinable number of units of currency is a monetary item. Conversely, the essential feature of a non-monetary item is the absence of a right to receive (or an obligation to deliver) a fixed or determinable number of units of currency. Examples are amounts prepaid for goods and services (e.g., prepaid rent); goodwill; intangible assets; inventories; property, plant, and equipment; and provisions that are to be settled by the delivery of a non-monetary asset.[4]

For accounting purposes, there are basically three rates used in translating foreign currency into the reporting currency: the closing rate, the historical rate, and the forward rate. The spot rate at the end of the reporting period of the financial statements is called the closing rate. The spot rate on the date of a transaction is called the historical rate for that transaction. The agreed rate for exchange of currencies at a future date is called the forward rate. To illustrate the use of these terms, consider the following example.

> *The historical rate is the rate on the date of the transaction, and the closing rate is the rate at the end of the reporting period.*

Example   ABC Co. has a year-end of December 31. On November 13, Year 1, ABC purchased inventory from a French supplier when the spot rate for one euro (€) was €1 = $1.50. On November 14, Year 1, ABC entered into a contract with a bank to purchase euros in 60 days at a rate of €1 = $1.48. The spot rate on December 31, Year 1, was €1 = $1.49. The financial statements for Year 1 were finalized on March 14, Year 2, and released to users on March 15, Year 2. In this example, the closing rate is $1.49, the historical rate for the purchase of the inventory is $1.50, and the forward rate for the planned purchase of euros is $1.48.

If inventory was purchased every day throughout the year, the historical rate for each purchase should technically be used to translate the purchase for each day. This procedure is very costly and usually not worth the cost–benefit trade-off. From a practical point of view, it is usually sufficient to use an average rate to approximate the actual rates for the period. The average rate represents the average of the historical rates throughout the period. However, if exchange rates fluctuate significantly, the use of the average rate for a period is inappropriate.

> *The average rate is the weighted average of the historical rates for the period.*
>
> *Individual transactions must be translated into the functional currency at the historical rate.*

According to IAS 21, a foreign-currency transaction must be recorded, on initial recognition in the functional currency, by applying to the foreign-currency amount the spot exchange rate between the functional currency and the foreign currency at the date of the transaction. At the end of each reporting period,

(a) foreign-currency monetary items must be translated using the closing rate;

(b) non-monetary items that are measured in terms of historical cost in a foreign currency must be translated using the historical rate; and

(c) non-monetary items that are measured at fair value in a foreign currency must be translated using the exchange rates at the date when the fair value was determined.

---

[4] See IAS 27, paragraph 16.

For ease of identification, we will refer to this method of translation as the temporal method.

Any exchange adjustments arising on the settlement of monetary items or on the translation of monetary items at rates different from those at which they were translated on initial recognition during the period or in previous financial statements must be recognized in profit or loss in the period in which they arise, with two exceptions. First, when a gain or loss on a non-monetary item is recognized in other comprehensive income, any exchange adjustment pertaining to that item must also be recognized in other comprehensive income. For example, IAS 16 requires some gains and losses arising on a revaluation of property, plant, and equipment to be recognized in other comprehensive income. When such an asset is measured in a foreign currency, any exchange difference resulting from the translation of the revalued amount into the functional currency should also be recognized in other comprehensive income. Second, a monetary available-for-sale financial asset (such as an investment in bonds) is treated as if it were carried at amortized cost in the foreign currency. Exchange differences resulting from changes in the amortized cost of this asset are recognized in profit or loss, and other changes in carrying amount are recognized in other comprehensive income.

This translation process should produce results consistent with the valuation practices for domestic operations. For a financial statement item to be reported at historical cost, the historical cost of the item in foreign currency multiplied by the historical rate will derive the historical cost in Canadian dollars. For a financial statement item to be reported at fair value at the end of the year, the fair value of the item in foreign currency multiplied by the spot rate on the date when fair value was determined will derive the fair value in Canadian dollars. If historical cost in foreign currency is multiplied by the closing rate or if the fair value in foreign currency is multiplied by the historical rate, the Canadian dollar figure is neither historical cost nor fair value.

When an item is reported at fair value, the fair value is usually determined at the end of the reporting period. If so, the exchange rate at the end of the period (i.e., the closing rate) is used to translate this item into Canadian dollars. Unless otherwise specified, the examples in the text always assume that fair values were determined at the end of the reporting period.

According to Canadian GAAP, monetary assets and monetary liabilities are typically valued at fair value, non-monetary assets are usually valued at the lower of historical cost and market value, and non-monetary liabilities and shareholders' equity are usually valued at historical amounts. Revenues and expenses are usually measured at historical amounts. As we study the different translation methods in this chapter and the next chapter, we should evaluate whether the translation methods preserve the normal measurement rules under Canadian GAAP.

Import/Export Transactions Denominated in Foreign Currency

When a Canadian company purchases goods from a foreign supplier, it is usually billed in the currency of the foreign country. However, the transaction is recorded in the company's accounting records in the functional currency, which is assumed to be the Canadian dollar. The following example illustrates the accounting for an import transaction.

An Import Example   On June 1, Year 1, Maritime Importers Inc. purchased merchandise from a supplier in Australia at a cost of 10,000 Australian dollars (A$), with payment in full to be made in 60 days. The exchange rate on the date of purchase was

A\$1 = CDN\$0.941 and A\$1 = CDN\$0.949 on June 30, Year 1, the company's year-end. Maritime paid its supplier on July 30, Year 1, when the exchange rate was A\$1 = CDN\$0.953. The following journal entries, recorded in Canadian dollars, illustrate the company's purchase of merchandise, year-end adjustments, and subsequent payment.

June 1, Year 1

Inventory	9,410	
Accounts payable (10,000 × 0.941)		9,410

The cost of the purchase is finalized when the item is purchased.

The purchase of the inventory at a cost of 10,000 Australian dollars and the related liability are translated at the spot rate on the date of purchase. The value of the inventory has been fixed at its historical cost and is not exposed to exchange fluctuations, except in the situation where the market price in Australian dollars declines and the lower of cost and market rule is applied. In such a case, the lower of cost and market rule would be applied by comparing the Canadian dollar historical cost of the inventory with the market price in Australian dollars translated at the closing rate.[5]

On the other hand, Maritime now has a monetary position that is exposed to exchange fluctuations. The Canadian dollar amount required to pay the 10,000 Australian dollars will change as the exchange rate changes. To better reflect the cost of settling this obligation, this monetary liability should be revalued to current value at each reporting date.

On the company's year-end, the account payable of 10,000 Australian dollars must be translated at the closing rate. The previously recorded amount (\$9,410) is increased by \$80 to reflect a translated liability of \$9,490 (10,000 × 0.949).

June 30, Year 1

Exchange loss	80	
Accounts payable		80
To adjust the account payable to the current rate		

The resulting foreign-exchange loss would appear on the income statement for the year ended June 30, Year 1.

Foreign-exchange adjustments are included in profit in the period in which they occur.

On the settlement date, the exchange rate has increased from CDN\$0.949 to CDN\$0.953. The A\$10,000 account payable is increased by \$40 to reflect its translation at the spot rate at this date (10,000 × 0.953 = 9,530). The company purchases 10,000 Australian dollars from its bank at a cost of \$9,530 and remits the dollars to its Australian supplier. The foreign-exchange loss of \$40 will appear on the income statement for the year ended June 30, Year 2. The following journal entries record the transactions:

July 30, Year 1

Exchange loss	40	
Accounts payable		40
To adjust the account payable to the spot rate		
Accounts payable	9,530	
Cash (10,000 × 0.953)		9,530
Payment to supplier		

---

[5] For example, if the market price of the inventory purchased had declined to A\$9,950 on June 30 (assuming that none of the inventory purchased had been sold by year-end), the market price in Canadian dollars would be \$9,443 (A\$9,950 × 0.949). Because the translated market price is greater than the previous translated historical cost of \$9,410, a write-down would not be required.

An Export Example   We will now consider an example of the export of goods by a Canadian company.

On November 15, Year 1, Regina Malt Producers Ltd. shipped a carload of malt to a brewery in the United States, with full payment to be received on January 31, Year 2. The selling price of the malt was US$26,000. Regina Malt has a December 31 year-end. The following exchange rates existed on the dates significant for accounting purposes:

Transaction date — Nov. 15, Year 1
   Selling price US$26,000
   Exchange rate US$1 = CDN$1.125
Year-end — Dec. 31, Year 1
   Exchange rate US$1 = CDN$1.129
Settlement date — Jan. 31, Year 2
   Exchange rate US$1 = CDN$1.119

The journal entries required on the dates noted above are as follows:

Nov. 15, Year 1

Accounts receivable	29,250	
Sales		29,250

The accounts receivable and the sales are recorded at the November 15 spot rate (US$26,000 × 1.125 = CDN$29,250). The sales amount has been established at historical value and is unaffected by future exchange rate fluctuations. The accounts receivable (a monetary item) is at risk to exchange rate fluctuations. Note that while accounts receivable has been recorded at CDN$29,250, it is in fact a receivable of US$26,000.

At the company's year-end, the exchange rate has changed to US$1 = CDN$1.129, and the receivable must appear in the financial statements at $29,354 (US$26,000 × 1.129). The following journal entry adjusts the accounts receivable to the closing rate:

Dec. 31, Year 1

Accounts receivable	104	
Exchange gain		104

This exchange gain will appear in the company's Year 1 income statement.

By January 31, Year 2, which is the settlement date, the value of the U.S. dollar has declined relative to the Canadian dollar. When Regina Malt collects US$26,000 from its customer and delivers the U.S. dollars to its bank, it receives only CDN$29,094 (26,000 × 1.119). The journal entry to record the receipt of US$26,000, and its conversion to Canadian dollars and the resultant loss, is as follows:

Jan. 31, Year 2

Cash	29,094	
Exchange loss	260	
Accounts receivable		29,354
Payment from U.S. customer		

The exchange loss of $260 will appear in the Year 2 income statement. Note that the actual exchange loss between the transaction date and the settlement date was $156 (29,250 − 29,094). Because the company's year-end occurred between

The sale is translated at the historical rate to produce a historical price in Canadian dollars. This is consistent with normal measurement rules to record sales at historical values.

The accounts receivable is translated at the closing rate to produce a current value in Canadian dollars. This is consistent with normal measurement rules to record monetary items at current values.

these two dates, the exchange loss will appear in the two income statements in the following manner:

Year 1 income statement	
Exchange gain	$104
Year 2 income statement	
Exchange loss	260
Total exchange loss on the transaction	$156

Exchange gains are reported in profit even though they are unrealized.

The previous examples have illustrated the concept that exchange gains and losses resulting from the translation of a *monetary position* (i.e., a receivable or payable) are reflected in income in the year in which they occur. Note that these exchange gains and losses are actually unrealized in the sense that they result from the translation of a liability or a receivable. This practice places representational faithfulness as a higher priority than prudence. The actual exchange gain or loss results from the settlement of the position, as was illustrated above.

Transaction Gains and Losses from Non-current Monetary Items

Many Canadian companies borrow money in foreign markets, mainly because the capital markets in Canada are relatively small. The following example illustrates the accounting for foreign-currency-denominated debt.

Example   Sable Company has a calendar year-end. On January 1, Year 1, the company borrowed 2,000,000 Swiss francs from a Swiss bank. The loan is to be repaid on December 31, Year 4, and requires interest at 8 percent to be paid each December 31. Both the annual interest payments and the loan repayment are to be made in Swiss francs.

During the term of the loan, the following exchange rates necessary for our analysis were in effect:

Jan. 1, Year 1	SF1 = $1.076
Average, Year 1	SF1 = $1.073
Dec. 31, Year 1	SF1 = $1.069
Dec. 31, Year 2	SF1 = $1.070
Dec. 31, Year 3	SF1 = $1.071
Dec. 31, Year 4	SF1 = $1.069

Sable Company would record the transactions as follows:

Jan. 1, Year 1

Cash	2,152,000	
Loan payable (2,000,000 × 1.076)		2,152,000

Interest expense is translated at the average of the historical rates to produce a historical price in Canadian dollars. This is consistent with normal measurement rules to record interest expense at historical values.

This entry records the incurrence of a four-year loan of SF2,000,000 translated at the spot rate. On December 31, the company purchases 160,000 Swiss francs (2,000,000 × 8 percent) from its bank to make the interest payment, at a cost of 171,040 (160,000 × 1.069). A question arises as to whether the amount paid should be reflected as the interest expense for the past year. Remember that interest expense was SF160,000, which accrued throughout the year. It seems logical, therefore, to translate the interest expense using the average of the Year 1 exchange rates, or better still to translate the monthly interest at the average rate for each month. In either case, when the interest is actually paid at the end of the year, an exchange gain or loss will have to be recorded. Using the average exchange rate for Year 1, the journal entry to record the interest expense and payment is as follows:

Dec. 31, Year 1

Interest expense	171,680	
Exchange gain		640
Cash		171,040

To record interest expense at the average Year 1 rate of SF1 = $1.073, and the payment of interest at the year-end rate of SF1 = $1.069

The loan payable is translated at the closing rate to produce a current value in Canadian dollars. This is consistent with normal measurement rules to record monetary items at current values.

On December 31, the loan is translated for financial statement purposes at $2,138,000 (2,000,000 × 1.069). The next entry adjusts the loan payable to the amount required on that date:

Dec. 31, Year 1

Loan payable	14,000	
Exchange gain		14,000

The $14,640 total exchange gain resulting from the interest payment and the translation of the loan will appear in the Year 1 income statement.

Exchange gains and losses occur on items translated at the closing rate but not on items translated at historical rates.

Journal entries for Years 2 through 4 will not be illustrated; however, the following summarizes the yearly exchange gains and losses from translating this loan liability.

	Total	Year 1	Year 2	Year 3	Year 4
Exchange gain (loss)	$16,000	$14,000	$(2,000)	$(2,000)	$6,000

Speculative Forward Exchange Contracts

In a forward exchange contract, two parties agree to exchange currencies at a future date at a specified exchange rate.

A forward exchange contract is one in which an exchange broker (usually a bank) and its customer agree to exchange currencies at a set price on a future date. Forward contracts can be either fixed dated or option dated. A fixed-dated contract specifies a fixed date such as June 18, for example. An option-dated contract specifies a certain period such as the month of June. A company may enter into a forward exchange contract purely to speculate on future exchange movements. For example, a company might enter into a contract to purchase foreign currency at a 60-day forward rate in anticipation that the spot rate in 60 days' time will be greater than the original forward rate. If its projection turns out to be accurate, it will purchase the foreign currency from the bank at the contracted price and immediately sell the currency to the bank at the higher spot rate. The following example deals with a speculative forward exchange contract.

Example On December 1, Year 1, Raven Company enters into a forward contract to sell 1 million Philippines pesos (PP) to its bank on March 1, Year 2, at the market rate for a 90-day forward contract of PP1 = $0.0227. On December 31, Year 1, Raven's year-end, the 60-day forward rate to sell Philippines pesos on March 1 has changed to PP1 = $0.0222. On March 1, Year 2, the currencies are exchanged when the spot rate is PP1 = $0.0220.

According to IAS 39, this forward contract is considered to be a financial instrument. It must be recorded at fair value on the date the contract is entered into and be revalued at fair value throughout its life, with any gains or losses reflected in income as they occur. There are two methods of recording this forward contract: the gross method and the net method. Under the gross method, the receivable from the bank and the payable to the bank are each recorded separately at fair value. Under the net method, the receivable and payable are netted against each other and only the net receivable or net payable is recorded. The entries for this contract under the gross and net methods are shown in Exhibit 10.4. Either method is acceptable for internal recording-keeping purposes. However, when the financial statements are prepared, the receivable from the bank and the payable to the bank will be netted against each other and only the net amount shown as either an asset or a liability on the balance sheet. We will use the gross method for all subsequent illustrations in this chapter.

Under the gross method, the receivable and payable under the forward contract will be offset against each other and only the net amount will be reported on the balance sheet at each reporting date.

Exhibit 10.4

JOURNAL ENTRIES FOR SPECULATIVE FORWARD CONTRACT

	Gross method		Net method	
December 1, Year 1				
Receivable from bank ($)	22,700			
Payable to bank (PP)		22,700		
Record forward contract at forward rate (PP1,000,000 × 0.0227 = $22,700)				
December 31, Year 1				
Forward contract			500	
Payable to bank (PP)	500			
Exchange gain		500		500
Revalue forward contract at fair value (PP1,000,000 × (0.0227 − 0.0222) = $500)				
March 1, Year 2				
Forward contract			200	
Payable to bank (PP)	200			
Exchange gain		200		200
Revalue forward contract at fair value (PP1,000,000 × (0.0222 − 0.0220) = $200)				
Payable to bank (PP)	22,000			
Cash (PP)		22,000		
Deliver PP1,000,000 to bank to pay off liability (PP1,000,000 × 0.0220 = $22,000)				
Cash ($)	22,700			
Receivable from bank ($)		22,700		
Receive $22,700 from bank				
Cash ($)			700	
Forward contract				700
Settle forward contract on net basis by receiving $700 (22,700 − 22,000)				

A forward contract is a financial instrument which must be valued at fair value throughout its life.

When the forward rate changes, the fair value of the forward contract changes.

The $ symbol behind receivable from bank in the first entry indicates that the account receivable is denominated in Canadian dollars, whereas the PP behind the payable to bank indicates that the accounts payable is denominated in Philippines pesos. In other words, Raven will receive Canadian dollars and will pay Philippines pesos to settle this forward contract.

The fair value of the forward contract on December 1, Year 1, is zero because the two parties have just entered into a contract at the market rate for forward contracts. Under the gross method, the receivable and payable are both recorded at the future rate. Since the receivable and payable are equal and offsetting, there is no entry under the net method.

Some accountants may object to recording the forward contract on December 1 because forward exchange contracts are "executory" in nature. An *executory contract* is one in which neither party has performed its obligation to the other. Most contracts trigger accounting recognition only when one of the parties fulfills the obligation as agreed. For example, when a company places an order with a manufacturer for the purchase of machinery, neither party makes an accounting entry. The delivery of the machinery, or a down payment prior to delivery, results in accounting recognition by both parties because of the performance by one.

Forward contracts must be recorded according to IFRSs.

While forward exchange contracts are certainly executory, they are also firm commitments, and once entered cannot be cancelled. For this reason, IFRSs require that the forward contract be recorded.

The forward contract is worth more when the Phillipines peso declines in value, i.e., the Canadian dollar increases in value.

On December 31, the forward contract is remeasured at fair value. We use the market rate for forward contracts maturing on March 1 to determine the fair value of Raven's contract. On this date, the 60-day forward rate to sell Philippines pesos on March 1 is PP1 = $0.0222, whereas Raven's contract is locked in at PP1 = $0.0227. Raven's contract will generate $22,700 on March 1, whereas contracts executed on December 31 will generate only $22,200 on March 1 for 1 million Philippines pesos. Therefore, Raven's contract is worth an extra $500 as of March 1. Theoretically, we should discount this $500 for two months. Practically speaking, the amount would usually not be discounted because the difference between the nominal amount of $500 and the present value of $500 for two months is not material and is not worth the effort to calculate.

In the appendix to this chapter, we illustrate how this forward contract would be accounted for with discounting. Unless otherwise noted, no examples in the text will use discounting. The forward contract will simply be valued at the forward rate for the term to maturity.

Notice that the gain of $500 is recorded under both the gross and net methods. When financial statements are prepared at December 31 under the gross method, the due from bank of $22,700 and the due to bank of $22,200 will be offset against each other and only the net receivable of $500 will be presented on the balance sheet and will likely be called forward contract. Therefore, the financial statement presentation will be the same under both the gross and net methods even though the underlying accounts have different balances.

On March 1, Year 2, the forward contract is once again revalued to fair value. Since the contract is being settled on this date, the market value of this forward contract is based on the spot rate for this date, i.e., PP1 = $0.0220. The contract is worth $700 because Raven will get $22,700 from the bank, whereas PP1,000,000 is worth only $22,000 in the market on March 1. Therefore, Raven has gained $700 on this contract in total and $200 since December 31. The first entry on March 1 records this $200 gain. The other entries record the exchange of pesos for dollars.

If we combine all of the journal entries under both the gross and net methods, we end up with the following entry:

Cash ($)	700	
Exchange gain — Year 1		500
Exchange gain — Year 2		200

The gross and net methods produce the same overall result in the end.

In the end, Raven gained $700 by speculating on rate changes. If the exchange rates had changed in the other direction, i.e., if the Canadian dollar had decreased in value rather than increased, Raven would have lost money on this speculative contract.

In the next few sections, we will illustrate how forward contracts can be used to hedge existing and anticipated exposure to foreign-currency risk. Throughout the remainder of this chapter and in the end-of-chapter material, we will use the gross method of accounting for forward contracts. This makes it easier to see how the forward contract is effective in hedging against the currency risk under different situations.

Hedges

The previous examples illustrated the accounting for the foreign-exchange gains and losses that result from holding a foreign-currency-denominated monetary position during a period of exchange rate changes. There are many possible ways for an enterprise to protect itself from the economic (and accounting) effects that result from such a position. This type of protection is generally referred to as "hedging," which can be defined as a means of transferring risk arising from foreign-exchange (or interest rate, or price) fluctuations from those who wish to avoid it to those who are willing to assume it.[6] In order to hedge the risk of exchange rate fluctuations, a company takes a foreign-currency position opposite to the position that it wishes to protect. The item with the risk exposure that the entity wishes to hedge and has taken steps to hedge is called the hedged item. The item used to offset the risk is called the hedging instrument. In the ideal case, the hedged item is perfectly hedged by the hedging instrument and there is no longer any overall exposure to currency fluctuations. The entity has eliminated the overall risk of further exchange losses but also loses any possibility of gains from currency fluctuations.

A hedge is a means of reducing or eliminating exchange losses on an overall basis by entering into a position to offset the risk exposure.

IAS 39 suggests that the following hedging instruments could be used to hedge against the risk of exchange fluctuations:

- *A derivative financial instrument.* For example, a forward exchange contract, a foreign-currency option contract, or a foreign-currency futures contract could be used to hedge a monetary asset or liability, firm commitment, or an anticipated future transaction.

A hedging instrument is the item used to offset the risk exposure. The hedged item is the item with the risk exposure that the entity has taken steps to modify.

- *A non-derivative financial instrument.* For example, an existing non-derivative financial asset or liability could be used to hedge a commitment or an anticipated future transaction.

IAS 39 also states that an anticipated future transaction can be a hedged instrument but it cannot be a hedging instrument. Therefore, it is not possible to designate

---

[6] See John E. Stewart. "The Challenges of Hedge Accounting." *Journal of Accountancy* (November 1989), pp. 48–56.

a future revenue stream as a hedge of an existing monetary liability for accounting purposes. A derivative can be a hedging instrument but would not typically be a hedged item.

When accounting for the hedge, we want to properly reflect whether the hedge has been effective. If the hedge is truly effective, there should be no overall exchange gain or loss hitting the income statement other than the cost of establishing the hedge. The exchange gains or losses on the hedged item will be offset by exchange losses or gains on the hedging instrument. But what happens when the hedging instrument is purchased in advance of the hedged item? For example, a forward contract may be purchased in Year 1 to hedge a transaction expected to occur in Year 2. How can the Year 1 gains or losses on the forward contract be offset against the Year 2 losses or gains on the anticipated transaction when the anticipated transaction has not yet occurred?

The solution is hedge accounting as defined and described in IAS 39. Under hedge accounting, the exchange gains or losses on the hedging instrument will be recognized in profit in the same period as the exchange gains or losses on the hedged item when they would otherwise be recognized in different periods. To qualify for hedge accounting, the following four conditions must be met:

> **Under hedge accounting, the exchange gains or losses on the hedging instrument will be reported in income in the same period as the exchange gains or losses on the hedged item.**

1. At the inception of the hedge, there is formal designation and documentation of the hedging relationship and the entity's risk management objective and strategy for undertaking the hedge. That documentation must include identification of the hedging instrument, the hedged item or transaction, the nature of the risk being hedged, and how the entity will assess the hedging instrument's effectiveness in offsetting the exposure to changes in the hedged item's fair value or cash flows attributable to the hedged risk. Only instruments with external counter parties can be designated as hedging instruments.

2. The hedge is expected to be highly effective in achieving offsetting changes in fair value or cash flows attributable to the hedged risk, consistently with the originally documented risk management strategy for that particular hedging relationship.

3. The effectiveness of the hedge can be reliably measured; i.e., the fair value or cash flows of the hedged item that are attributable to the hedged risk and the fair value of the hedging instrument can be reliably measured.

4. The hedge is assessed on an ongoing basis and determined actually to have been highly effective throughout the financial reporting periods for which the hedge was designated.

First of all, note that hedge accounting is optional. The entity can choose to apply hedge accounting and thereby ensure that gains and losses on the hedged item are reported in income in the same period as the gains and losses on the hedging instrument. Alternatively, it could choose to not apply hedge accounting and account for the hedged item and the hedging instrument in isolation of each other.

> **The entity chooses whether to designate the hedge as a fair value hedge or a cash flow hedge.**

Secondly, hedges can be designated for accounting purposes as fair value hedges, cash flow hedges, or hedges of a net investment in a foreign operation.[7] In a fair

---

[7] Accounting for a net investment in a foreign operation will be discussed in Chapter 11.

value hedge, the entity uses a hedging instrument to hedge against the fluctuation in the fair value of the hedged item. This method will be used when the hedged item (such as long-term debt) will be valued at fair value. The gain or loss in the fair values of the hedging instrument and hedged items are both recognized in profit in the period of the change in exchange rates.

In a cash flow hedge, the entity uses a hedging instrument (such as a derivative) to hedge against the fluctuation in the Canadian dollar value of future cash flows (such as future sales). The gain or loss on the hedging instrument is initially reported in other comprehensive income and subsequently reclassified to profit when the hedged item affects profit. Although there are many different types of hedging instruments, we will use forward exchange contracts to illustrate hedge accounting.

Hedging a Recognized Monetary Item

Vulcan Corporation of Toronto, Ontario, has a December 31 year-end. On November 1, Year 1, when the Bulgarian lev (BL) was worth $0.870, Vulcan sold merchandise to a Bulgarian customer for BL200,000. The terms of the sale required payment in full on February 15, Year 2. On November 15, Year 1, the spot rate was BL1 = $0.865 and the three-month forward rate was BL1 = $0.842. In order to protect the account receivable from further exchange losses, Vulcan entered into a contract with its bank on this date, to deliver BL200,000 in three months' time. At year-end, the spot rate was BL1 = $0.869 and the 45-day forward rate was $0.852. On February 15, Year 2, Vulcan received BL200,000 from the customer and settled the forward contract with the bank when the spot and forward rates were $0.860.

Before preparing the journal entries, try to understand the rationale for entering into the hedge and the expected results. From November 1 to November 14, the Canadian dollar value of the receivable declined in value from $174,000 (200,000 × 0.870) to $173,000 (200,000 × 0.865) because of the strengthening of the Canadian dollar relative to the Bulgarian lev. Vulcan is concerned about a further slide in the value of the lev and further erosion in the value of the receivable. To minimize the loss from a further decline, Vulcan entered into a forward exchange contract to fix the amount it will receive in Canadian dollars when the receivable is collected and that is $168,400 (200,000 × 0.842). In effect, Vulcan was prepared to pay $4,600 ($173,000 − $168,400) in order to avoid bigger losses. This differential of $4,600 is called a discount on the forward contract. It will be expensed as a foreign-exchange loss over the term of the forward exchange contract.

Although the forward contract is a hedge of the accounts receivable, we will not have to use hedge accounting in this situation. Both the accounts receivable and the forward contract are valued at fair value at each reporting date with the exchange adjustments reported in profit. Since the exchange adjustments on both items are already being reported in profit in the same period, it is not necessary to use hedge accounting. We will account for each item separately as we did for the previous examples in this chapter. If the company wanted to use hedge accounting and designated the forward contract as a fair value hedge, the accounting would look exactly the same as accounting for each item separately. So, there is no point in using hedge accounting in this particular situation. Hedge accounting is necessary only when the exchange adjustments would otherwise be reported in profit in different periods.

The forward contract is used to offset the risk of decline in value of the accounts receivable from the customer.

Hedge accounting is optional and will not be applied in this situation.

A timeline for the transactions follows:

Nov 1	Nov 15	Dec 31	Feb 15
Sell goods on account	Hedge receivable	Year-end	Collect receivable and settle forward exchange contract

Vulcan will record the sale and the receivable at the spot rate on the transaction date with the following journal entry:

The BL indicates that the accounts receivable is denominated in Bulgarian levs. The $ indicates that the sale is being measured in dollars and will not be adjusted for exchange rate changes.

Nov. 1, Year 1

Accounts receivable (BL)	174,000	
Sales ($)		174,000

BL200,000 × 0.870 = 174,000

On November 15, the receivable is hedged when the spot rate is BL1 = $0.865. The exchange loss that occurred during the period when the account receivable was *not* hedged is recorded next, followed by the entry to record the forward contract.

Nov. 15, Year 1

Exchange gains and losses	1,000	
Accounts receivable (BL)		1,000

Exchange loss prior to the date of hedge, BL200,000 × (0.870 − 0.865)

Receivable from bank ($)	168,400	
Payable to bank (BL)		168,400

To record forward contract at forward rate — BL 200,000 × 0.842

The receivable from the bank represents the amount of Canadian dollars that Vulcan will receive when it delivers BL200,000 to the bank in three months. As this is denominated in Canadian dollars, it will not be affected by subsequent changes in the spot rate. The payable to bank represents an obligation of Vulcan to deliver BL200,000 to the bank in three months' time and is denominated in Bulgarian levs. It should be reported at fair value throughout the term of the contract. The fair value is determined by multiplying BL200,000 by the forward rate for the remaining term of the contract. At year-end, the accounts receivable and payable to the bank are adjusted to fair value as follows:

The closing rate is used when the item can be settled at any time, whereas the forward rate is used when the item must be settled at a future date.

Dec. 31, Year 1

Accounts receivable (BL)	800	
Exchange gains and losses		800

To adjust the account receivable to the December 31 spot rate
— BL200,000 × (0.869 − 0.865)

Exchange gains and losses	2,000	
Payable to bank (BL)		2,000

To adjust the forward contract to the December 31 forward rate
— BL200,000 × (0.852 − 0.842)

The $2,000 adjustment can be broken down as follows:

- An $800 loss on forward contract, the hedging instrument offsets the $800 gain on the accounts receivable, the hedged item.
- The other $1,200 is the portion of the $4,600 discount on the forward contract being expensed in this period.

Financial statements are prepared as at December 31. The following partial trial balance is presented to show only the accounts used to record these particular transactions.

PARTIAL TRIAL BALANCE
December 31, Year 1

	Dr.	Cr.
Accounts receivable	$173,800	
Exchange gains and losses	2,200	
Sales		$174,000
Receivable from bank ($)	168,400	
Payable to bank (BL)		170,400
	$344,400	$344,400

The accounts associated with the hedge have been segregated in the trial balance to emphasize their nature. These executory contract items should be shown at their net amount in the balance sheet because they will be settled simultaneously and on a net basis. The presentation of the items shown on the trial balance in the year-end financial statements is shown next.

VULCAN CORP.
PARTIAL BALANCE SHEET
December 31, Year 1

Assets	
Accounts receivable	$173,800
Other items	XXX
	$ XXX

The receivable from and payable to the bank are offset against each other and only the net difference of a $2,000 liability is reported.

Liabilities and Shareholders' Equity	
Forward contract (170,400 − 168,400)	$ 2,000
Other items	XXX
	$ XXX

VULCAN CORP.
PARTIAL INCOME STATEMENT
for the Year Ended December 31, Year 1

Sales		$174,000
Expenses:		
Foreign-exchange loss	$2,200	
Other	XXX	XXX
Profit		$ XXX

The $2,200 foreign-exchange loss consists of the $1,000 loss before the hedge was put in place and $1,200 expense pertaining to the $4,600 discount on the forward contract.

On the February 15 settlement date, the receivable from the Bulgarian customer and the payable to bank are adjusted to current value as follows:

Only the foreign-denominated receivables and payables must be revalued. The receivable from the bank is denominated in Canadian dollars and is not affected by changes in exchange rates.

Feb. 15, Year 2

Exchange gains and losses	1,800	
Accounts receivable (BL)		1,800

To adjust the account receivable to the spot rate —
BL200,000 × (0.869 − 0.860)

Exchange gains and losses	1,600	
Payable to bank (BL)		1,600

To adjust the forward contract to the forward rate —
BL200,000 × (0.860 − 0.852)

The total of the exchange losses recognized in Year 2 is $3,400, which is the remaining amount of the discount on the forward contract. This brings the total exchange loss on the forward contract to $4,600 ($1,200 from Year 1 and $3,400 for Year 2), which is equal to the discount on the forward contract.

The Bulgarian customer sends BL200,000 to Vulcan, which is deposited in a Bulgarian lev cash account. Vulcan delivers the BL200,000 to the bank to discharge its forward contract obligation and receives $168,400 as agreed. The following journal entries record these events:

Feb. 15, Year 2

Cash (BL)	172,000	
Accounts receivable (BL)		172,000
Collection from Bulgarian customer		
Payable to bank (BL)	172,000	
Cash (BL)		172,000
Delivery of levs to bank		
Cash	168,400	
Receivable from bank		168,400
Receipt of Canadian dollars from bank		

You may be overwhelmed with the number of entries above and may not appreciate the overall effect. To see the big picture, all of the above entries for Year 1 and Year 2 can be condensed into one entry as follows:

Cash ($)	168,400	
Foreign-exchange loss before hedge	1,000	
Foreign-exchange loss (= discount on forward contract)	4,600	
Sales		174,000

The net impact on profit is equal to the amount of cash received. This is a typical result in accounting. Sales were recorded at the historical rate, which is consistent with our measurement model. The exchange losses occurred for two reasons. First, the company lost $1,000 in the value of the accounts receivable due to the increase in value of the Canadian dollar relative to the Bulgarian lev before the hedge was put into place. Then, the company incurred a loss of $4,600 to put the hedge into place. In the end, the accounting for the hedge reflects the objective of the hedge in the first place.

Hedging an Unrecognized Firm Commitment

On June 2, Year 2, when the spot rate was US$1 = CDN$1.26, Manning Inc. of Vancouver ordered merchandise from an American supplier for US$350,000. Delivery was scheduled for August 1 with payment to be made in full on delivery. Upon placing the order, Manning immediately entered into a 60-day forward contract with its bank to purchase US$350,000 on August 1 at the forward rate of US$1 = CDN$1.28. Manning's year-end is June 30. On August 1, the merchandise was received, and Manning purchased the U.S. dollars from the bank and paid its supplier.

In this example, the purpose of the forward contract is to fix the amount to be paid for the inventory. The hedged item is the commitment and the hedging instrument is the forward contract. The commitment to purchase the inventory is not recognized for accounting purposes because there is no asset or liability at the time of the commitment. The inventory and related accounts payable will be recorded only when the inventory is actually received. Since we must report the forward contract when the contract is signed, we will have a mismatch in the current year because the hedging instrument is recognized but the hedged item is not. Without hedge accounting, the exchange gains or losses on the forward contract would be reported in the current year, whereas no exchange gain or losses would be reported on the accounts payable because it does not legally exist in the current year. Therefore, hedge accounting is necessary to report the exchange gains or losses on the hedged item and the hedging instrument in the same period. We can designate the forward contract as a cash flow hedge and defer the recognition in profit of the exchange gains or losses on the forward contract. Alternatively, we could designate the forward contract as a fair value hedge and advance the recognition in profit of the exchange gains or losses on the commitment.

Cash Flow Hedge   With a cash flow hedge, the gain or loss on the hedging instrument is initially reported in other comprehensive income (OCI). The exchanges gains/losses will be taken out of OCI and reported in profit when the hedged item affects profit. In our example, the hedged item is the commitment that will be included in profit when the inventory is sold.

The premium on the forward contract is a cost of fixing the purchase price of the inventory.

The premium on the forward contract is $7,000 [US$350,000 × (1.28 − 1.26)]. It is the amount that Manning is prepared to pay to fix the amount of the cash flows required to purchase the inventory. Since the forward contract was intended to fix the cost of the inventory, the $7,000 will be reported as a cost of the inventory and will be reflected in income when the inventory is sold.

The relevant exchange rates for this example are as follows:

Date	Spot Rate	Forward Rate
June 2	US$1 = CDN$1.260	US$1 = CDN$1.280
June 30	US$1 = CDN$1.268	US$1 = CDN$1.275
August 1	US$1 = CDN$1.272	US$1 = CDN$1.272

A timeline for the transactions follows:

June 2	June 30	August 1
Order goods and hedge order	Year-end	Receive goods, settle forward contract, and pay supplier

The order does not meet the definition of an asset or a liability.

Manning would not make a journal entry to record the merchandise ordered. However, the hedging of the commitment by entering into a forward contract to purchase U.S. dollars would be recorded with the following entry:

June 2, Year 2		
Receivable from bank (US$)	448,000	
Payable to bank (CDN$)		448,000
To record forward contract at forward rate — 350,000 × 1.280		

Payable to bank represents the amount in Canadian dollars that Manning will pay the bank in August when it receives US$350,000. The amount recorded will not be affected by future exchange rate fluctuations. *Receivable from bank* is the hedge of the expected future liability. It is denominated in U.S. dollars and represents Manning's right to receive U.S. dollars from the bank in August. It should be reported at fair value and is accordingly translated at the forward exchange rate.

Note that the net balance of this executory contract is zero, and if a balance sheet were prepared at this time the accounts would not be shown.

At year-end, the receivable from the bank is adjusted to its fair value as follows:

<table>
<tr><td colspan="3">*June 30, Year 2*</td></tr>
<tr><td>OCI — cash flow hedge</td><td>1,750</td><td></td></tr>
<tr><td>   Receivable from bank (US$)</td><td></td><td>1,750</td></tr>
<tr><td colspan="3">To adjust forward contract to June 30 forward rate —</td></tr>
<tr><td colspan="3">350,000 × (1.280 − 1.275)</td></tr>
</table>

> **The exchange gains or losses on the hedging instrument are reported in other comprehensive income for now and will be reported in profit when the exchange gains or losses on the hedged items are reported in profit.**

Notice that the exchange adjustment is reported in other comprehensive income and not in profit. On the June 30, Year 2, balance sheet, the $1,750 difference between the receivable from the bank ($446,250) and the payable to the bank ($448,000) would be reported as forward contract under current liabilities. The OCI for cash flow hedges is reported on the statement of changes in equity in a separate column for cash flow hedges. In turn, the balance at the end of the year for accumulated OCI for cash flow hedges is reported as a separate component of shareholders' equity.

On August 1, the receivable from the bank is adjusted to its fair value, the forward contract is settled, and the delivery of inventory is recorded as follows:

<table>
<tr><td colspan="3">*August 1, Year 2*</td></tr>
<tr><td>OCI — cash flow hedge</td><td>1,050</td><td></td></tr>
<tr><td>   Receivable from bank (US$)</td><td></td><td>1,050</td></tr>
<tr><td colspan="3">To adjust forward contract to August 1 forward rate —</td></tr>
<tr><td colspan="3">350,000 × (1.275 − 1.272)</td></tr>
<tr><td colspan="3"> </td></tr>
<tr><td>Payable to bank (CDN$)</td><td>448,000</td><td></td></tr>
<tr><td>   Cash</td><td></td><td>448,000</td></tr>
<tr><td colspan="3">Payment to bank</td></tr>
<tr><td colspan="3"> </td></tr>
<tr><td>Cash (US$)</td><td>445,200</td><td></td></tr>
<tr><td>   Receivable from bank (US$)</td><td></td><td>445,200</td></tr>
<tr><td colspan="3">Receipt of US$350,000 from bank, translated at the</td></tr>
<tr><td colspan="3">August 1 spot rate (350,000 × 1.272)</td></tr>
<tr><td colspan="3"> </td></tr>
<tr><td>Inventory</td><td>445,200</td><td></td></tr>
<tr><td>   Cash (US$)</td><td></td><td>445,200</td></tr>
<tr><td colspan="3">To record the inventory purchase and payment at the</td></tr>
<tr><td colspan="3">August 1 spot rate (350,000 × 1.272)</td></tr>
</table>

There are two options for removing the accumulated exchange adjustment of $2,800 from other comprehensive income. Option one is to remove the $2,800 when the inventory is delivered and report it as an adjustment of the inventory. In turn, this amount will affect the amount reported as cost of goods sold when the inventory is sold. The second option is to remove the $2,800 when the inventory is sold and show it as other income on the income statement. In both cases, the $2,800 will be reflected in the income statement when the inventory is sold. Since the objective of the hedge was to fix the price of the inventory, the first option will be used and is accounted for as follows:

> **The exchange losses incurred on the hedging instrument to this point increase the cost of the inventory and will be reported in profit when the inventory is sold.**

<table>
<tr><td colspan="3">*August 1, Year 2*</td></tr>
<tr><td>Inventory</td><td>2,800</td><td></td></tr>
<tr><td>   OCI — cash flow hedge</td><td></td><td>2,800</td></tr>
<tr><td colspan="3">To remove exchange adjustments from other comprehensive income</td></tr>
</table>

All of the August entries can be condensed into one entry as follows:

Inventory	448,000	
Cash (CDN$)		448,000

The inventory will eventually become part of cost of goods sold. Therefore, the impact on profit will once again be equal to the amount of cash paid. This is a typical result in accounting. At the beginning of this problem, we determined that the company was willing to pay a premium of $7,000 to fix the amount of the inventory. In the end, the inventory was recorded at $448,000, the amount fixed by the forward contract. Furthermore, no exchange gains or losses were reported in profit because the commitment to purchase inventory was effectively hedged by the forward contract.

In the above example, the inventory was paid for on delivery. If Manning had purchased the inventory on credit, it would have been exposed to foreign-currency risk on the accounts payable. It could have entered into a forward contract to hedge both the commitment to buy inventory and the amount required to settle the account payable. In this case, the $7,000 premium would have to be split between the two objectives. Part of the $7,000 would be reported as a cost of the inventory and reflected in profit when the inventory is sold. The other part would be recognized in profit over the period of time between the origination and settlement of the accounts payable.

Fair Value Hedge   If Manning designated the forward contract as a fair value hedge, the gain or loss on the firm commitment would have to be reported in profit in the current year to match the gain or loss on the forward contract. Both the forward contract and the firm commitment will be measured at fair value using the forward rate. As such, the exchange loss on the forward contract will be offset by the exchange gain on the firm commitment. The $7,000 premium on the forward contract will be incorporated in the cost of purchasing the inventory.

When Manning enters into the forward contract on June 2, Year 2, the following journal entry will be recorded:

June 2, Year 2

Receivable from bank (US$)	448,000	
Payable to bank (CDN$)		448,000
To record forward contract at forward rate — 350,000 × 1.280		

At year-end, the receivable from the bank and the commitment are adjusted to fair value as follows:

June 30, Year 2

Exchange gains and losses	1,750	
Receivable from bank (US$)		1,750
To adjust forward contract to June 30 forward rate — 350,000 × (1.280 − 1.275)		

Commitment asset	1,750	
Exchange gains and losses		1,750
To adjust value of upcoming accounts receivable to June 30 forward rate — 350,000 × (1.280 − 1.275)		

On the June 30, Year 2, balance sheet, the $1,750 difference between the receivable from bank ($446,250) and the payable to bank ($448,000) would be reported as forward contract under current liabilities. In addition, the commitment asset would be reported as a current asset. The exchange gains and losses offset each other and have no impact on profit.

On August 1, the receivable from the bank and the commitment asset are adjusted to their fair values as follows:

The receivable from bank and the payable to bank are offset against each other and reported in the balance sheet on a net basis.

```
August 1, Year 2
Exchange gains and losses                                    1,050
    Receivable from bank (US$)                                       1,050
To adjust forward contract to August 1 forward rate —
350,000 × (1.275 − 1.272)


Commitment asset                                             1,050
    Exchange gains and losses                                        1,050
To adjust value of upcoming accounts receivable to August 1 forward rate —
350,000 × (1.275 − 1.272)
```

Manning settles the forward contract by paying CDN$448,000 to the bank and by receiving US$350,000, and records the following journal entries:

```
Payable to bank (CDN$)                                      448,000
    Cash (CDN$)                                                     448,000
Payment to bank


Cash (US$)                                                 445,200
    Receivable from bank (US$)                                      445,200
Receipt of US$350,000 from bank at August 1 spot rate —
350,000 × 1.272
```

Manning then pays the supplier US$350,000 and records the following entry:

```
Inventory                                                  448,000
    Commitment asset                                                  2,800
    Cash (US$)                                                      445,200
To record the inventory purchase, clear commitment asset, and pay cash
    at the August 1 spot rate — 350,000 × 1.272
```

All of the above entries can be condensed into one entry as follows:

```
Inventory                                                  448,000
    Cash (CDN$)                                                     448,000
```

The inventory will eventually become part of cost of goods sold. Therefore, the impact on profit will once again be equal to the amount of cash paid. This is a typical result in accounting.

In the end, the hedge fixed the purchase price of the inventory at the forward rate on the date of the hedge.

At the beginning of this problem, we determined that the company was willing to pay a premium of $7,000 as a cost of financing the purchase of the inventory. In the end, this $7,000 was incorporated in the cost of the inventory. The final balance in the inventory account is $448,000, the amount fixed by the forward contract.

Hedging a Forecasted Transaction

The following example illustrates the accounting when long-term debt is used as a hedge of a future revenue stream and will be accounted for as a cash flow hedge.

The loan payable is the hedging instrument, and the future revenue stream is the hedged item.

Alana Enterprises, a Canadian company that has carried out business activities in Singapore for a number of years, has decided to protect itself against foreign currency fluctuations over the next three years, during which it expects a revenue stream of at least 200,000 Singapore dollars (SD) per year. On January 1, Year 1, the company borrows SD600,000, payable in full at the end of three years, and designates the loan as a hedge against the future three-year revenue stream. In order to simplify the illustration, we will omit the payment of yearly interest and assume that there is no difference between the exchange rate at the end of each year and the average exchange rate for that year. Furthermore, we will assume that the cash received in Singapore dollars will be immediately used to pay operating expenses.

Relevant exchange rates for the Singapore dollar are as follows:

Jan. 1, Year 1	SD1 = $0.852
Dec. 31, Year 1	SD1 = $0.849
Dec. 31, Year 2	SD1 = $0.835
Dec. 31, Year 3	SD1 = $0.840

Applying the concepts of hedge accounting, Alana will make the following journal entries:

Jan. 1, Year 1

Cash	511,200	
Loan payable (SD)		511,200
(600,000 × 0.852)		

During Year 1, the revenue stream is recorded at the average exchange rate for the year. Thus, the following entry is recorded:

Cash	169,800	
Sales revenue		169,800
(200,000 × 0.849)		

In Year 1, the entire loan is needed to hedge three years of forecasted revenues, and the entire exchange gain on the loan should be reported in other comprehensive income to be eventually offset against the future revenue stream.

On December 31, Year 1, the loan payable has to be reflected in the financial statements at fair value using the closing rate. The entry to record the exchange gain on the loan payable resulting from a decrease in the exchange rate from $0.852 to $0.849 is as follows:

Dec. 31, Year 1

Loan payable (SD)	1,800	
OCI — cash flow hedge (Year 1)		1,800
(600,000 × [0.852 − 0.849])		

One-third of the hedged revenue stream has been received, and so the following adjusting entry is made to match one-third of the gain from the hedge against the revenue received:

Since one-third of the revenue stream has been realized, one-third of the other comprehensive income should be brought into income.

Dec. 31, Year 1

OCI — cash flow hedge (Year 1)	600	
Sales revenue		600
(200/600 × 1,800)		

Two-thirds of the exchange gain is deferred in other comprehensive income to be matched against the foreign-currency revenues when they are received in the following two years. The company has *lost* because it has received less revenue in Canadian dollars than would be the case if the exchange rate had not changed, but it has also *gained* due to the fact that its liability (measured in Canadian dollars) has decreased. The liability hedges the revenue stream; consequently, the gain in one offsets the loss in the other. The total revenue for the year is $170,400, which is made up of the translated revenue of $169,800 plus the recognized exchange gain on the hedge of $600. Note that this is the same amount as would have been received in translated revenue if the exchange rates had not changed since January 1, Year 1 (200,000 × 0.852). If the exchange rates do not change over the next two years, the total translated revenue *plus* the recognized revenue from the hedge will be $170,400 each year.

Note also that while the loan is still SD600,000, one-third of the foreign revenue stream has been received; therefore, one-third of this loan balance no longer qualifies as a hedge and is exposed to foreign-currency risk. Because of this, any future exchange gains and losses on this portion must be reflected immediately in income.

During Year 2, revenue in Singapore dollars is received and translated at the average rate. This results in the following entry:

Cash	167,000	
Sales revenue		167,000
(200,000 × 0.835)		

On December 31, Year 2, the loan payable is reduced by $8,400 (600,000 × [0.849 − 0.835]) to reflect its translation at the closing rate; also, the gain on the one-third portion that no longer qualifies as a hedge is immediately reflected in profit, and the balance of the gain from the hedge portion is initially deferred with the following entry:

In Year 2, only two-thirds of the loan is a hedging instrument. The other one-third of the loan is exposed to foreign-currency risk; the related exchange gain is reported in profit.

Dec. 31, Year 2		
Loan payable (SD)	8,400	
Exchange gain (⅓ × 8,400)		2,800
OCI — cash flow hedge (Year 2)		5,600

The other comprehensive income hedges the foreign-currency revenues of Years 2 and 3. Year 2 revenue has been received and translated at the average exchange rate for the year. Therefore, the Year 2 portion (one-half) of the deferred gain is matched against this revenue with the following entry:

Dec. 31, Year 2		
OCI — cash flow hedge (Year 2)	2,800	
Sales revenue (½ × 5,600)		2,800

In addition, the portion of the deferred Year 1 exchange gain must be matched against Year 2 revenues with the following entry:

Dec. 31, Year 2		
OCI — cash flow hedge (Year 1)	600	
Sales revenue		600

The final revenue figure of $170,400 is the equivalent Canadian dollar value of the anticipated sale when the hedge was first put into place.

Remember that the purpose of the hedge was to ensure that the foreign-currency revenue in Year 2 was at least $170,400 (200,000 × 0.852). The actual foreign revenue adjusted for the hedge gains was equal to this amount, as the following calculation indicates:

Foreign-currency revenue (200,000 × 0.835)	$167,000
Exchange gain on Year 1 hedge	600
Exchange gain on Year 2 hedge	2,800
	$170,400

In addition, the Year 2 income statement will reflect the additional exchange gain ($2,800) that came from the portion of the loan that no longer qualifies as a hedge.

The balance of the accumulated other comprehensive income (AOCI) that will appear on the December 31, Year 2, balance sheet is shown on the following page:

OCI, Year 1		1,800	
Less reflected in income:			
Year 1	600		
Year 2	600	1,200	$ 600
OCI, Year 2		5,600	
Less reflected in income Year 2		2,800	2,800
AOCI, December 31, Year 2			$3,400

Because SD400,000 from the total revenue of SD600,000 has been received at the end of Year 2, the loan balance that still qualifies as a hedge is only SD200,000.

The Year 3 entries to record the foreign-currency revenues and to adjust the loan to the current rate are as follows:

In Year 3, only one-third of the loan is a hedging instrument. The other two-thirds of the loan is exposed to foreign-currency risk; the related exchange gain is reported in profit.

Cash	168,000	
Sales revenue		168,000
(200,000 × 0.840)		

Dec. 31, Year 3		
OCI — cash flow hedge (Year 3) (¹/₃ × 3,000)	1,000	
Exchange loss (²/₃ × 3,000)	2,000	
Loan payable (SD)		3,000
(600,000 × 0.005)		

The foreign-currency revenue has all been received, so none of the Year 3 loss pertaining to the hedge ($1,000) needs to be deferred. The remaining loss from the portion of the loan that is not a hedge ($2,000) is also expensed in the year.

By the end of Year 3, all of the other comprehensive income has been transferred to profit to match the timing of the income recognition on the hedged item, being the revenue stream.

A final entry is made to match the balance of the other comprehensive income from prior years against the Year 3 foreign-currency revenue:

OCI — cash flow hedge (Year 1)	600	
OCI — cash flow hedge (Year 2)	2,800	
OCI — cash flow hedge (Year 3)		1,000
Sales revenue		2,400

An entry would also be made to pay off the loan that is due on this date. The following calculation summarizes the amount reflected in profit in Year 3 from the foreign-currency revenue, the hedge gains and losses, and the exchange loss from the non-hedge portion of the loan:

The hedging instrument was used to fix the final revenue figure at $170,400, the equivalent Canadian dollar value of the anticipated sale when the hedge was first put into place.

Foreign-currency revenue (200,000 × 0.840)		$168,000
Year 1 and 2 exchange gains on hedge	3,400	
Year 3 exchange loss on hedge	1,000	2,400
Hedged foreign-currency revenue		170,400
Remainder of Year 3 loan exchange loss		2,000
Effect on Year 3 profit		$168,400

This simplified example has illustrated a possible use of hedge accounting. In a more realistic situation, differences would occur because the average rates used to translate the revenue stream are different from the year-end rates used to translate the foreign-currency loan, and the actual revenues would probably turn out to be different from those expected when the hedge was designated. However, the broad concepts illustrated would still apply, and because an increasing portion of the foreign-currency-denominated debt ceases to be eligible for a hedge each year, the resultant income recognition pattern is similar to the defer-and-amortize pattern that used to occur for foreign-currency debt.

Disclosure Requirements The following summarizes the main disclosures required in IAS 21 for the effects of changes in foreign-exchange rates:

(a) the amount of exchange differences recognized in profit or loss; and

(b) net exchange differences recognized in other comprehensive income.

The following summarizes the main disclosures required in IAS 39 related to hedges:

The entity must disclose the type of hedge and the risks being hedged.

1. For each type of hedge, the entity must disclose
   (a) a description of each type of hedge;
   (b) a description of the hedging instruments and their fair values at the end of the reporting period; and
   (c) the nature of the risks being hedged.

The entity must disclose the flow into and out of other comprehensive income during the year relating to cash flow hedges.

2. For cash flow hedges, the entity must disclose
   (a) the periods when the cash flows are expected to occur and when they are expected to affect profit or loss;
   (b) the amount that was recognized in other comprehensive income during the period;
   (c) the amount that was reclassified from equity to profit or loss for the period; and
   (d) the amount that was removed from equity during the period and included in the initial cost or other carrying amount of a non-financial asset or non-financial liability.

3. An entity must disclose separately
   (a) gains or losses attributable to fair value hedges;
   (b) the ineffectiveness recognized in profit or loss that arises from cash flow hedges; and
   (c) the ineffectiveness recognized in profit or loss that arises from hedges of net investments in foreign operations.

Alcatel-Lucent is a French company that develops and integrates technologies, applications, and services to offer innovative global communications solutions. It has transactions in numerous countries around the world. Exhibit 10.5 contains excerpts from Alcatel's 2008 financial statements pertaining to foreign-currency transactions and hedges.

Exhibit 10.5

EXTRACTS (IN PART) FROM ALCATEL-LUCENT'S 2008 FINANCIAL STATEMENTS

Translation of foreign currency transactions

Foreign currency transactions are translated at the rate of exchange applicable on the transaction date. At period-end, foreign currency monetary assets and liabilities are translated at the rate of exchange prevailing on that date. The resulting exchange gains or losses are recorded in the income statement in "other financial income (loss)".

In order for a currency derivative to be eligible for hedge accounting treatment (cash flow hedge or fair value hedge), its hedging role must be defined and documented and it must be seen to be effective for the entirety of its period of use. Fair value hedges allow companies to protect themselves against exposure to changes in fair value of their assets, liabilities or firm

(continued)

commitments. Cash flow hedges allow companies to protect themselves against exposure to changes in future cash flows (for example, revenues generated by the company's assets).

The value used for derivatives is their fair value. Changes in the fair value of derivatives are accounted for as follows:

Alcatel-Lucent has both cash flow and fair value hedges.

- for derivatives treated as cash flow hedges, changes in their fair value are accounted for in shareholders' equity and then transferred from equity to the income statement (cost of sales) when the hedged revenue is accounted for. The ineffective portion is recorded in "other financial income (loss)";
- for derivatives treated as fair value hedges, changes in their fair value are recorded in the income statement where they offset the changes in fair value of the hedged asset, liability or firm commitment.

In addition to derivatives used to hedge firm commitments documented as fair value hedges, from April 1, 2005 onwards, Alcatel-Lucent has designated and documented highly probable future streams of revenue and has entered into hedge transactions with respect to such revenue. The corresponding derivatives are accounted for in accordance with the requirements governing cash flow hedge accounting.

Certain foreign exchange derivatives are not considered eligible for hedge accounting treatment, as the derivatives are not designated as such for cost/benefit reasons.

Derivatives related to commercial bids are not considered eligible for hedge accounting treatment and are accounted for as trading financial instruments. Changes in fair values of such instruments are included in the income statement in cost of sales (in the segment "other").

Once a commercial contract is effective, the corresponding firm commitment is hedged with a derivative treated as a fair value hedge. Revenues made pursuant to such a contract are then accounted for, throughout the duration of the contract, using the spot rate prevailing on the date on which the contract was effective, insofar as the exchange rate hedging is effective.

NOTE 28 MARKET-RELATED EXPOSURES

The Group has a centralized treasury management in order to minimize the Group's exposure to market risks, including interest rate risk, foreign exchange risk, and counterparty risk. The Group uses derivative financial instruments to manage and reduce its exposure to fluctuations in interest rates and foreign exchange rates. These instruments are not complex and the determination of their fair values does not represent any particular difficulties.

Alcatel-Lucent had derivatives of more than 15 billion euros to manage its foreign currency risk.

Estimated future cash flows (for example firm commercial contracts or commercial bids) are hedged by forward foreign exchange transactions or currency options.

Currency risk
i. Outstanding currency derivatives at December 31
ANALYSIS BY TYPE AND CURRENCY

(in millions of euros)	U.S. dollar	British pound	Other	Total	2008 Market value	Total	2007 Market value	Total	2006 Market value
Buy/Lend foreign currency									
Forward exchange contracts	2,151	145	390	2,686	(77)	2,735	(52)	1,604	(18)
Short-term exchange swaps	347	281	53	681	(61)	500	(5)	-	-
Cross currency swaps	-	-	-	-	-	-	-	1,063	(19)
Currency option contracts:									
Buy call	-	82	135	217	16	1,697	29	1,120	5
Sell put	304	-	3,682	3,986	38	3,081	(34)	3,339	(35)
Total	**2,802**	**508**	**4,260**	**7,570**	**(84)**	**8,013**	**(62)**	**7,126**	**(67)**

(in millions of euros)	U.S. dollar	British pound	Other	Total	2008 Market value	2007 Total	2007 Market value	2006 Total	2006 Market value
Sell/Borrow foreign currency									
Forward exchange contracts	1,218	76	305	1,599	(11)	2,466	74	2,644	30
Short-term exchange swaps	1,496	131	138	1,765	(6)	915	15	1,283	20
Cross currency swaps	-	-	-	-	-	-	-	-	-
Currency option contracts:									
Sell call	-	82	190	272	(17)	1,553	(23)	911	(4)
Buy put	304	-	3,347	3,651	(36)	3,870	71	4,223	52
Total	**3,018**	**289**	**3,980**	**7,287**	**(70)**	**8,804**	**137**	**9,061**	**98**
Total market value					(154)		75		31

ANALYSIS BY ACCOUNTING CATEGORY

(in millions of euros)	Market value 2008	Market value 2007	Market value 2006
Fair value hedges	(117)	34	18
Cash flow hedges	(6)	(10)	3
Instruments not qualifying for hedge accounting	(31)	51	10
TOTAL	**(154)**	**75**	**31**

ii. Exchange rate sensitivity

The most used cross currencies in the Group are U.S.D against EUR, GBP against U.S.D and U.S.D against CNY. The sensitivity is calculated by increasing or decreasing U.S.D by 6% against other currencies.

The company discloses the impact on net income and shareholders' equity of a 6 percent change in exchanges rates.

An increase of foreign currency exchange rates versus euro of 6%, applied to foreign exchange derivatives, would have a negative impact of € 42 million in 2008 (against € 50 million in 2007 and € 92 million in 2006). This impact would affect the income statement only for foreign exchange derivatives, which do not qualify for hedge accounting.

For foreign exchange derivatives qualified as a fair value hedge, an increase of 6% in foreign currency exchange rate would have a negative impact of € 39 million in 2008 (against € 37 million in 2007 and € 73 million in 2006). However, this negative effect would be offset by a positive impact due to the re-evaluation of the underlying items. The impact on income statement would therefore be zero.

For foreign exchange derivatives qualified as a cash flow hedge, a 6% increase in foreign currency exchange rate would have a positive impact of € 12 million on shareholders' equity in 2008 (against a positive impact of € 17 million in 2007 and a negative impact of € 3 million in 2006).

(in millions of euros)	2008 Fair value	2008 Fair value variation if U.S.D falls by 6%	2008 Fair value variation if U.S.D rises by 6%	2007 Fair value	2007 Fair value variation if U.S.D falls by 6%	2007 Fair value variation if U.S.D rises by 6%	2006 Fair value	2006 Fair value variation if U.S.D falls by 6%	2006 Fair value variation if U.S.D rises by 6%
Outstanding foreign exchange derivatives									
Fair value hedges	(117)	34	(39)	34	37	(37)	18	76	(73)
Cash flow hedges	(6)	(12)	12	(10)	(16)	17	3	(4)	3
Derivatives not qualifying for hedge accounting	(31)	17	(15)	51	47	(30)	10	36	(22)
TOTAL OUTSTANDING DERIVATIVES	**(154)**	**39**	**(42)**	**75**	**68**	**(50)**	**31**	**108**	**(92)**

(continued)

Impact of outstanding derivatives on financial result	(10)	16	(14)	10	8	(7)	(1)	14	(13)
Impact of outstanding derivatives on income (loss) from operating activities	(21)	1	(1)	41	39	(23)	11	22	(9)
Impact of outstanding derivatives on shareholders' equity	(6)	(12)	12	(10)	(16)	17	3	(4)	3

iii. Reclassification to income statement of gains or losses on hedging transactions that were originally recognized in equity

(in millions of euros)

Cash flow hedges accounted for in shareholders' equity at December 31, 2007	**(10)**
Changes in fair value	(9)
Reclassification of gains or losses to income statement	19

CASH FLOW HEDGES ACCOUNTED FOR IN SHAREHOLDERS' EQUITY AT DECEMBER 31, 2008 **0**

The amounts recognized directly in the shareholders' equity indicated in this schedule differ from the one disclosed in the Statement Of Recognized Income and Expense (SORIE) in page 5, due to the amounts related to discontinued activities and commodities derivatives, which are excluded in the above schedule.

Source: Reprinted with permission of Alcatel-Lucent USA Inc.

GAAP for Private Enterprises

- Hedge accounting is permitted only when the critical terms of the hedging instrument match those of the hedge item. Enterprises are not required to assess hedge effectiveness. An enterprise is required to determine only that the critical terms of the two components of the hedging arrangement continue to match.

- An entity may designate only the following hedging relationships:
  - an anticipated purchase or sale of a commodity hedged with a forward contract to mitigate the effect of future price changes of the commodity;
  - an anticipated transaction denominated in a foreign currency hedged with a forward contract to mitigate the effect of changes in future foreign-currency exchange rates;
  - a foreign-currency-denominated interest-bearing asset or liability hedged with a cross-currency interest rate swap to mitigate the effect of changes in interest rates and foreign-currency exchange rates;
  - the net investment in a self-sustaining foreign operation hedged with a derivative or a non-derivative financial instrument to mitigate the effect of changes in foreign-currency exchange rates.

Hedge accounting is much simpler for private enterprises.

- Hedge accounting for private companies follows an accrual-based model and is much simpler than hedge accounting for public companies. For example, an entity accounts for a qualifying hedge of an anticipated transaction as follows:
  - When the anticipated transaction occurs, it is recognized initially at the amount of consideration paid or received.

- When the forward contract matures, the gain or loss on the contract is recorded as an adjustment of the carrying amount of the hedged item. When the hedged item is recognized directly in net income, the gain or loss on the forward contract is included in the same category of net income.

• Disclosure is minimal compared to the disclosure required for public companies.

U.S. GAAP Differences

U.S. GAAP and IFRSs for foreign-currency transactions have many similarities. The significant differences are summarized as follows:

1. Whereas IFRSs give priority to certain indicators when determining the functional currency, U.S. GAAP do not give priority to any of the indicators.

2. Whereas IFRSs report foreign-currency gains or losses on available-for-sale debt securities in net income, U.S. GAAP report these exchange gains or losses in other comprehensive income.

SUMMARY

Transactions denominated in foreign-currency are recorded in Canadian dollars at the spot rate in effect on the date of the transaction. At the date of the balance sheet, foreign-currency assets and liabilities are translated into Canadian dollars to preserve the normal measurement at either historical cost or current value. Any gains or losses arising from changes in exchange rates on the exposed items are reflected in profit for the period.

The use of hedging instruments, such as forward exchange contracts, removes the risks associated with exchange rate changes. If all risks are removed, the hedge is "perfect." It also is possible to have a situation in which only a portion of a position is hedged and the balance is at risk, or in which, as was illustrated, a portion of the hedging instrument ceases to act as a hedge and becomes exposed to foreign-currency risk.

In a fair value hedge and in a speculative forward exchange contract, exchange gains and losses are recognized in profit in the period of the change in exchange rates. In a cash flow hedge, the exchange gains and losses on the hedging instrument are initially reported in other comprehensive income and subsequently reclassified to profit when the hedged item affects profit.

Significant Changes in the Last Two Years

1. For publicly accountable enterprises, IFRSs have replaced the former sections of the *CICA Handbook*. The following table shows the IFRSs covered in this chapter along with their counterpart from the former sections of the *CICA Handbook*:

IFRSs	CICA Handbook *Counterparts*
IAS 21: The Effects of Changes in Foreign Exchange Rates	Section 1651: Foreign Currency Translation
IFRS 7: Financial Instruments: Disclosure	Section 3862: Financial Investments — Disclosures
IAS 39: Financial Instruments — Recognition and Measurement	Section 3865: Hedges

2. The term *closing rate* replaces the term *current rate* when referring to the spot rate at the end of the reporting period.

3. The reporting entity must identify its functional currency and record all transactions in its accounting records using the functional currency. The entity is free to use a presentation currency that is different from the functional currency.

4. When a foreign currency item is valued at fair value, it is translated using the spot rate on the date when fair value was determined rather than using the closing rate.

5. Unrealized foreign exchange gains and losses on the amortized cost portion of available-for-sale monetary financial assets are recognized immediately in profit.

Changes Expected in the Next Three Years

1. IAS 39 on financial instruments may be simplified. The concept of other comprehensive income may be eliminated for cash flow hedges.

2. Hedge accounting may also be simplified or eliminated.

SELF-STUDY PROBLEM 1

Hedging an Existing Monetary Position

On November 15, Year 1, Domco Ltd. of Montreal bought merchandise from a supplier located in Brunei for 100,000 Brunei dollars (BD). The Brunei dollar was trading at $0.81 on that date, and the terms of the purchase required Domco to pay the account on January 30, Year 2. On December 1, when the spot rate was BD1 = $0.813, Domco entered into a forward contract with its bank to receive BD100,000 at the 60-day forward rate of BD1 = $0.82. On December 31, Year 1, Domco's year-end, the spot rate was BD1 = $0.825 and the 30-day forward rate was BD1 = $0.831. On January 30, Year 2, when the spot rate was BD1 = $0.838, Domco settled the forward contract with its bank and paid BD100,000 to the Swiss supplier.

Required:

(a) Prepare the journal entries required in Year 1 and Year 2 assuming that hedge accounting is not applied.

(b) Prepare a partial statement of financial position as at December 31, Year 1, that shows the accounts payable and the presentation of the hedge accounts.

(c) Prepare one journal entry to summarize the combined effect of all entries in part (a).

Solution to Self-Study Problem 1

(a) *Nov. 15, Year 1*
Inventory ($) 81,000
   Accounts payable (BD) (BD100,000 × 0.81) 81,000

Dec. 1, Year 1
Exchange gains/losses 300
    Accounts payable (BD) 300
To adjust the accounts payable to the Dec. 1
  spot rate of BD1 = $0.813 (BD100,000 × [0.813 − 0.810])

Receivable from bank (BD) 82,000
    Payable to bank ($) 82,000
To record the forward contract at 82,000 (BD100,000 × 0.82)

Dec. 31, Year 1
Exchange gains/losses 1,200
    Accounts payable (BD) 1,200
To adjust the accounts payable to the Dec. 31
  spot rate of BD1 = $0.825 (BD100,000 × [0.825 − 0.813])

Receivable from bank (BD) 1,100
    Exchange gains/losses 1,100
To adjust the forward contract to the Dec. 31
  forward rate of BD1 = $0.831 (BD100,000 × [0.831 − 0.820])

Jan. 30, Year 2
Exchange gains/losses 1,300
    Accounts payable (BD) 1,300
To adjust the accounts payable to the Jan. 30
  spot rate of BD1 = $0.838 (BD100,000 × [0.838 − 0.825])

Receivable from bank (BD) 700
    Exchange gains/losses 700
To adjust the forward contract to the Jan. 30
  forward rate of BD1 = $0.838 (BD100,000 × [0.838 − 0.831])

Payable to bank ($) 82,000
    Cash ($) 82,000
Deliver Canadian dollars to bank

Cash (BD) 83,800
    Receivable from bank (BD) 83,800
Receive BD100,000 from bank (BD100,000 × 0.838)

Accounts payable (BD) 83,800
    Cash (BD) 83,800
Pay BD100,000 to supplier (BD100,000 × 0.838)

(b)

DOMCO LTD.
STATEMENT OF FINANCIAL POSITION
at December 31, Year 1

Assets
Forward contract* .... $ 1,100

Liabilities
Accounts payable 82,500

*Receivable from bank 83,100
 Payable to bank 82,000
    Net amount of forward contract .... $ 1,100

(c)	Inventory	81,000	
	Exchange loss (before hedge)	300	
	Exchange loss (= premium on contract)	700	
	Cash		82,000

SELF-STUDY PROBLEM 2

Hedging an Unrecognized Firm Commitment

On October 15, Year 2, Sellcompany Ltd., located in Canada, signed a contract to sell equipment to Buycompany, which is located in a country whose currency is the foreign currency unit (FC). The selling price of the equipment was FC200,000 and the terms of the sale called for delivery to be made on January 30, Year 3, with payment in full due on delivery.

Having signed the sales order, Sellcompany immediately entered into a forward contract with its bank to sell FC200,000 on January 30, Year 3, at the forward rate of FC1 = $1.22. The spot rate on October 15 was FC1 = $1.20. On December 31, the year-end of Sellcompany, the spot rate was FC1 = $1.222 and the 30-day forward rate was FC1 = $1.231. On January 30, Year 3, when the spot rate was FC1 = $1.24, Sellcompany delivered the equipment, received FC200,000 from Buycompany, and settled the forward contract with the bank.

Required:

(a) Prepare the journal entries required in Year 2 and Year 3 for Sellcompany assuming that the forward contract is designated as a cash flow hedge.

(b) Prepare a partial statement of financial position as at December 31, Year 2, that shows the presentation of the hedge accounts.

(c) Prepare one journal entry to summarize the combined effect of all entries in part (a).

Solution to Self-study Problem 2

(a)   *Oct. 15, Year 2*

Receivable from bank ($)	244,000	
Payable to bank (FC)		244,000
To record the forward contract at 244,000		
(FC200,000 × 1.22)		

Dec. 31, Year 2

OCI — cash flow hedge	2,200	
Payable to bank (FC)		2,200
To adjust the forward contract to the forward rate		
FC200,000 × (1.231 − 1.220)		

Jan. 30, Year 3

OCI — cash flow hedge	1,800	
Payable to bank (FC)		1,800
To adjust the forward contract to the Jan. 30 forward rate		
FC200,000 × (1.240 − 1.231)		

Cash (FC)	248,000	
Sales		248,000
To record equipment sale at FC200,000 × 1.24		

Payable to bank (FC)	248,000	
Cash (FC)		248,000
Deliver FC to bank		

Cash ($)	244,000	
Receivable from bank ($)		244,000
Receive Canadian dollars from bank		

Sales	4,000	
OCI — cash flow hedge		4,000
To reclassify other comprehensive income as an adjustment of sales		

(b)

SELLCOMPANY LTD.
STATEMENT OF FINANCIAL POSITION
at December 31, Year 2

Liabilities	
Forward contract*	$ 2,200
*Payable to bank	246,200
Receivable from bank	244,000
Net amount of forward contract	$ 2,200

(c)

Cash	244,000	
Sales		244,000

In the end, the sales were recorded at $244,000, the amount fixed by the forward contract. Furthermore, no exchange gains or losses were reported in income because the commitment to sell the equipment was effectively hedged by the forward contract.

APPENDIX 10A

Determining the Fair Value of Forward Exchange Contracts

The fair value of a forward contract is based on its relative merits compared to other contracts in the market and the time value of money.

The fair value of a forward exchange contract is based on the relative merits of the contract compared to other contracts in the market and the time value of money. If the contract states that the company must sell foreign currency at a rate that is better than what is currently available in the market, the contract has a positive value. On the other hand, if the contract states that the company must sell foreign currency at a rate that is worse than what is currently offered in the market, the contract has a negative value. Therefore, the following factors are usually considered to determine the fair value of a forward contract at any point in time:

1. The forward rate when the forward contract was entered into.

2. The current forward rate for a contract that matures on the same date as the forward contract entered into.

3. A discount rate, typically the company's incremental borrowing rate.

On page 524, we considered the first two factors above when we valued the forward contract at $500 at December 31, Year 1. Since the $500 value will be realized only on March 1, Year 2, it should be discounted to derive its present value at December 31, Year 1. Assuming that Raven's incremental borrowing rate is

12 percent per annum or 1 percent per month, the fair value of the forward contract at December 31 is $490.15 ($500 × 0.9803).[8]

The journal entries to record the fair value of the forward contract for the example on page 527 under the gross and net methods when discounting is applied are shown in Exhibit 10A.1. Only the first three entries are shown here because the remaining entries would be the same as in Exhibit 10.4 on page 528.

Exhibit 10A.1

JOURNAL ENTRIES FOR SPECULATIVE FORWARD CONTRACT

	Gross method		Net method	
December 1, Year 1				
Receivable from bank ($)	22,700			
Payable to bank (PP)		22,700		
Record forward contract at forward rate				
(PP1,000,000 × 0.0227 = $22,700)				
December 31, Year 1				
Forward contract			490	
Payable to bank (PP)	490			
Exchange gain		490		490
Revalue forward contract at fair value				
(PP1,000,000 × (0.0227 − 0.0222) × 0.9803 = $490)				
March 1, Year 2				
Forward contract			210	
Payable to bank (PP)	210			
Exchange gain		210		210
Revalue forward contract at fair value				
([22,700 − 490] − PP1,000,000 × 0.0220 = $210)				

The value of a forward contract should be recorded in present value terms.

REVIEW QUESTIONS

1. Briefly summarize the accounting issues arising from foreign-currency-denominated transactions.
2. What is the difference between pegged and floating exchange rates?
3. You read in the newspaper, "One U.S. dollar can be exchanged for 1.15 Canadian dollars." Is this a direct or an indirect quotation? If your answer is *indirect*, what is the direct quotation? If your answer is *direct*, what is the indirect quotation?
4. Differentiate between a spot rate and a forward rate.
5. How are foreign-currency-denominated assets and liabilities measured on the transaction date? How are they measured on a subsequent balance sheet date?
6. Describe when to use the closing rate and when to use the historical rate when translating assets and liabilities denominated in a foreign currency.

---

[8] The present value factor for two months at 1 percent per month is calculated as $1/1.01^2$ or 0.9803.

Explain whether or not this practice is consistent with the way we normally measure assets and liabilities.

7. Differentiate between a spot rate and a closing rate.

8. Differentiate between the accounting for a fair value hedge and a cash flow hedge.

9. List some ways that a Canadian company could hedge against foreign-currency exchange rate fluctuations.

10. What are some typical reasons for acquiring a forward exchange contract?

11. If a foreign-currency-denominated payable has been hedged, why is it necessary to adjust the liability for balance sheet purposes?

12. Explain the application of lower of cost and market to inventory that was purchased from a foreign supplier.

13. How does the accounting for a fair value hedge differ from the accounting for a cash flow hedge of an unrecognized firm commitment?

14. What is the suggested financial statement presentation of hedge accounts recorded under the gross method? Why?

15. What is meant by *hedge accounting*?

16. Would hedge accounting be used in a situation where the hedged item and the hedging instrument were both monetary items on a company's statement of financial position? Explain.

17. When long-term debt hedges a revenue stream, a portion of the long-term debt becomes exposed to the risk of changes in exchange rates. Why is this?

18. When will the premium paid on a forward contract to hedge a firm commitment to purchase inventory be reported in income under a cash flow hedge? Explain.

MULTIPLE-CHOICE QUESTIONS

Use the following data for Questions 1 to 3.

On April 15, Year 5, Bailey Inc. negotiated a large sale of their premium maple syrup to Sweet Co. for US$3,000,000. The contract required payment in three years from the date of delivery of the goods. Bailey delivered the goods on July 15, Year 5. The company has a December 31 year-end.

The exchange rates at various dates are given below.

	Spot rates	Forward rates
April 15, Year 5	US$1 = CDN$1.28	US$1 = CDN$1.22
July 15, Year 5	US$1 = CDN$1.30	US$1 = CDN$1.20
December 31, Year 5	US$1 = CDN$1.42	US$1 = CDN$1.25

1. Assuming the transaction is *not* hedged, which of the following amounts will be used to record the receivable in Bailey's books at July 15, Year 5?
   a. $3,000,000
   b. $3,840,000
   c. $3,900,000
   d. $4,260,000

2. Assuming the transaction is *not* hedged, which of the following amounts will be reported on Bailey's December 31, Year 5, income statement as an exchange gain from this transaction?
   a. $0
   b. $300,000
   c. $360,000
   d. $420,000

3. Assuming the transaction *is* hedged with a forward contract on April 15, Year 5, and hedge accounting is not applied, which of the following amounts will be used to report the receivable on Bailey's December 31, Year 5, balance sheet?
   a. $3,600,000
   b. $3,660,000
   c. $3,840,000
   d. $4,260,000

   (CGA-Canada adapted)

4. In November, Roy Incorporated purchased inventory for US$200,000 when the exchange rate was US$1 = CDN$1.25. At year-end, the inventory had a net realizable value of US$210,000 and the exchange rate was US$1 = CDN$1.18. What will be the total gain (loss) on this inventory for the current year?
   a. Zero.
   b. $2,200 loss.
   c. $14,000 loss.
   d. $12,500 gain.

   (CICA adapted)

5. At December 31, Year 3, Post Inc. had a Swiss franc receivable resulting from export sales to Switzerland and a Mexican peso payable resulting from imports from Mexico. Post recorded foreign-exchange gains related to both its franc receivable and peso payable. Did the foreign currencies increase or decrease in value from the date of the transaction to the year-end?

	Franc	Peso
a.	Increase	Increase
b.	Increase	Decrease
c.	Decrease	Increase
d.	Decrease	Decrease

6. A company purchases a piece of equipment from a Brunei supplier for BND100,000, payable one month later. On the date when the equipment is received, the company enters into a foreign-exchange forward contract whereby it agrees to purchase Brunei dollars on the payment date of the equipment. Assuming that hedge accounting is not adopted and considering the following exchange rates, what will the carrying value of the equipment be after the equipment has been paid for?

Spot rate when the order was placed:	BNDI = CDN$0.83
Spot rate when the equipment was received:	BNDI = CDN$0.84
Spot rate when the payment was made:	BNDI = CDN$0.86
Forward rate when the equipment was received:	BNDI = CDN$0.85

   a. $83,000
   b. $84,000
   c. $85,000
   d. $86,000

   (CICA adapted)

7. On October 12, Year 5, Jiambalvo International, a clothing manufacturer, ordered bolts of fabric from an Asian supplier. The agreed upon price for the goods was FC400,000. The fabric was received by Jiambalvo on December 1, Year 5. The invoice was paid on December 28, Year 5. All fabric from this order was in the company's inventory at their December 31 year-end. Spot rates during the period were as follows:

October 12	FC1 = $0.36
December 1	FC1 = $0.33
December 28	FC1 = $0.32
December 31	FC1 = $0.31

   For inventory valuation purposes, what would be the cost of the purchased fabric?
   a. $124,000
   b. $128,000
   c. $132,000
   d. $144,000

8. If a company hedges an expected foreign-currency-denominated purchase of equipment for cash and accounts for the hedge as a cash flow hedge, how will the premium on the forward contract be treated?
   a. It will be charged to income when the equipment is purchased.
   b. It will be charged to income over the life of the equipment.
   c. It will be charged to other comprehensive income when the equipment is purchased.
   d. It will be charged to other comprehensive income over the life of the equipment.

Use the following data for Questions 9 to 11.
PL Corporation has a December 31, Year 5, year-end. It submitted a purchase order for US$30,000 of equipment on July 1, Year 5, when the exchange rate was CDN$1 = US$0.6500. It received the equipment on September 30, Year 5, when the exchange rate was US$0.6667; it paid US$20,000 to the supplier on December 1, Year 5, when the exchange rate was US$0.6900. On December 31, Year 5, the exchange rate was US$0.7000. The company uses straight-line amortization commencing in the month following acquisition. The equipment is expected to last five years and has no residual value.

9. What would be the net book value of PL's equipment on its December 31, Year 5, statement of financial position?
   a. $40,715
   b. $42,748
   c. $43,850
   d. $45,000

10. On PL's December 31, Year 5, financial statements, what amount would the accounts payable relating to the equipment purchase be recorded at?
    a. $6,500
    b. $7,000
    c. $14,286
    d. $15,385

11. Assume PL entered into a forward contract with the bank for the remaining $10,000 accounts payable on December 1, Year 5, to provide US$10,000 on January 31, Year 6 — the expected date of payment to the equipment

manufacturer. Assume the forward rate was CDN$1 = US$0.6750 on December 1, Year 5, and CDN$1 = US$0.6755 on December 31, Year 5. Assuming that hedge accounting is not adopted, how much exchange gain/loss would PL record on the forward contract for the year ended December 31, Year 5?

   a. CDN$11
   b. CDN$161
   c. CDN$311
   d. CDN$322   *(CGA-Canada adapted)*

Use the following data for Questions 12 and 13.

On November 2, Year 5, a company purchased a machine for 200,000 Swiss francs with payment required on March 1, Year 6. To eliminate the risk of foreign-exchange losses on this payable, the company entered into a forward exchange contract on December 1, Year 5, to receive SF200,000 at a forward rate of SF1 = $1.10 on March 1, Year 6. Hedge accounting is not applied. The spot rate was SF1 = $1.05 on November 2, Year 5, and SF1 = $1.07 on December 1, Year 5.

12. What is the amount of the premium or discount on the forward exchange contract?

   a. Discount of $6,000.
   b. Discount of $10,000.
   c. Premium of $6,000.
   d. Premium of $10,000.   *(CICA adapted)*

13. How should the premium or discount on the forward exchange contract be accounted for?

   a. It should be expensed on the inception date of the forward exchange contract.
   b. It should be expensed on the maturity date of the forward exchange contract.
   c. It should be expensed over the three-month term of the forward exchange contract.
   d. It should be added to the cost of the machine.

                                                     (CGA-Canada adapted)

14. On October 1, Year 1, CAR Ltd. issued a 6 percent, 10-year debenture denominated in euros. What rate should be used to translate interest expense for this 10-year debenture for the year ended December 31, Year 1?

   a. The rate on October 1, Year 1.
   b. The average rate for the year ended December 31, Year 1.
   c. The average rate for the quarter ended December 31, Year 1.
   d. The rate on December 31, Year 1.

15. LET Inc. enters into a forward contract with Scotiabank at a three-month forward rate of FC1 = CDN$1.20. One month later, the rate for a two-month forward contract is FC1 = CDN$1.22. Which of the following would result in a credit to other comprehensive income for the first month of the forward contract?

   a. The forward contract is designated as a cash flow hedge of an anticipated sale.
   b. The forward contract is designated as a cash flow hedge of an anticipated purchase.

    c.   The forward contract is designated as a fair value hedge of an anticipated sale.

    d.   The forward contract is designated as a fair value hedge of an anticipated purchase.

16.   On January 1, Year 4, PAC Limited purchased land in a foreign country for FC100,000. At December 31, Year 4, this land was worth FC110,000. The increase in the value of the land occurred evenly throughout the year. The Canadian dollar is PAC's functional and presentation currency. Under which of the following situations would PAC report an exchange gain pertaining to the land for Year 4?

    a.   The land is reported at historical cost, and the Canadian dollar has increased in value relative to the FC during the year.

    b.   The land is reported at historical cost, and the Canadian dollar has decreased in value relative to the FC during the year.

    c.   The land is reported at fair value under the revaluation model, and the Canadian dollar has increased in value relative to the FC during the year.

    d.   The land is reported at fair value under the revaluation model, and the Canadian dollar has decreased in value relative to the FC during the year.

CASES

Case 1   Interfast Corporation, a fastener manufacturer, has recently been expanding its sales through exports to foreign markets. Earlier this year, the company negotiated the sale of several thousand cases of fasteners to a wholesaler in the country of Loznia. The customer is unwilling to assume the risk of having to make payment in Canadian dollars. Desperate to enter the Loznian market, the vice-president for international sales agrees to denominate the sale in lrubles (LR), the national currency of Loznia. The current exchange rate for the lruble is $2.00. In addition, the customer indicates that he cannot make payment until all of the fasteners have been sold. Payment of LR100,000 is scheduled for six months from the date of sale.

    Fearful that the lruble might depreciate in value over the next six months, the head of the risk management department at Interfast Corporation enters into a forward contract to sell lrubles in six months at a forward rate of $1.80. The forward contract is designated as a fair value hedge of the lruble receivable. Six months later, when payment is received from the Loznian customer, the exchange rate for the lruble is $1.70. The corporate treasurer calls the head of the risk management department into her office.

Treasurer: I see that your decision to hedge our foreign-currency position on that sale to Loznia was a bad one.

Department Head: What do you mean? We have a gain on that forward contract. We're $10,000 better off from having entered into that hedge.

Treasurer: That's not what the books say. The accountants have recorded a net loss of $20,000 on that particular deal. I'm afraid I'm not going to be able to pay you a bonus this year. Another bad deal like this one and I'm going to have to demote you back to the interest rate swap department.

www.mcgrawhillconnect.ca

Department Head: Those bean counters have messed up again. I told those guys in international sales that selling to customers in Loznia was risky, but at least by hedging our exposure, we managed to receive a reasonable amount of cash on that deal. In fact, we ended up with a gain of $10,000 on the h edge. Tell the accountants to check their debits and credits again. I'm sure they just put a debit in the wrong place or some accounting thing like that.

Required:

Have the accountants made a mistake? Does the company have a loss, a gain, or both from this forward contract? Explain.

Case 2   Long Life Enterprises was a long-established, Toronto-based company engaged in the importation and wholesale marketing of specialty grocery items originating in various countries of the western Pacific Rim. They had recently also entered the high-risk business of exportation, to several of these same countries, of fresh Atlantic lobster and crab.

Although Canada has extensive trading relationships with several countries in the Pacific Rim, these transactions were not normally priced or settled in terms of the Canadian dollar. Both the U.S. dollar and the Japanese yen were somewhat more common in these transactions. Further, various local currencies were involved, especially for small transactions involving specialty items, and a wide variety of credit terms were in use for both imports and exports. The entire situation was complicated by the perishable nature of some of the imports and the high mortality risk for both lobster and crab. Both situations led to uncertainty as to the face amount of the associated receivable or payable and hindered the ability of the firm to adopt the policy of specific hedging of each of the receivable or payable contracts.

Most recently, the Canadian dollar had risen against other major currencies, leading to major losses on the large receivables outstanding because of the seasonal lobster harvest. More generally, management was concerned about losses that might arise from both export and import transactions. For the most recent fiscal year, foreign-currency losses had exceeded gains by some $40,000 — an amount more than the company could afford during the present stage of rapid growth.

Required:

What steps would you propose to the management of Long Life Enterprises to reduce the foreign-exchange costs associated with their receivables and payables? As a part of this process, suggest a way of structuring transactions or affairs that would reduce the impact of fluctuations in the relative values of currencies.

(*case prepared by Peter Secord, St. Mary's University*)

Case 3   Canada Cola Inc. (CCI) is a public company engaged in the manufacture and distribution of soft drinks across Canada. Its primary product is Canada Cola ("Fresh as a Canadian stream"), which is a top seller in Canada and generates large export sales.

You met with Jane MacNamara, the partner in charge of the CCI audit engagement, to commence planning for the upcoming audit of CCI. During this meeting MacNamara informed you that early this year CCI entered into an agreement

Exhibit I

SUMMARY OF AGREEMENT

1. The Russian government will provide the land and the building for the plant. It will make no further investment.
2. CCI will install bottling machinery costing $5 million in the Russian plant. Once installed, this machinery may not be removed from Russia.
3. CCI will be required to provide the funds for the initial working capital. CCI will sell US dollars to the Russian government in exchange for local currency (rubles).
4. CCI will be wholly responsible for the management and daily operations of the plant. Canadian managers will be transferred to Russia.
5. CCI will be permitted to export its cola syrup to Russia at CCI's Canadian cost.
6. CCI and the Russian government will share equally in the profits from the sale of Canada Cola in Russia.
7. Although foreign currency can be converted into rubles, rubles cannot be converted back into any foreign currency. Therefore, the Russian government will sell vodka to CCI (at the prevailing export market price in Russia) in exchange for the rubles CCI earns in profits. CCI will be permitted to export this vodka to Canada, where it may be sold in the Canadian domestic market only.

---

with the government of Russia and has commenced the manufacture and sale of Canada Cola in Russia. A short summary of this agreement is contained in Exhibit I. MacNamara would like you to prepare a detailed report that discusses the accounting implications of this new division of CCI for this engagement.

Required:

Prepare the report.

(CICA adapted)

Case 4   International Manufacturing Company (IMC) is a large, Canadian-based corporation with worldwide operations. IMC has issued debt instruments in Swiss francs, euros, and U.S. dollars to take advantage of low interest rates. All these financing arrangements were completed on a fixed-interest-rate basis.

The Canadian dollar has weakened considerably in the past few years, and as a result IMC has accrued substantial foreign-exchange losses on the debt instruments. These losses have seriously impaired IMC's ability to report increased earnings during the last few years, in spite of its successful operations.

IMC's investment banker has recommended the following alternatives to management:

1. IMC considers using the currency-swap market to minimize losses on its debt. IMC would enter into an agreement with a third party whereby IMC agreed to pay the obligation of the third party's debt in Canadian dollars in exchange for the third party agreeing to pay the obligation of IMC's foreign debt. Pursuing this option would entail an additional cost if the investment banker were required to guarantee the payment of the foreign debt.

2. IMC considers buying back the Swiss franc, euro, and U.S. dollar bonds on the bond market and refinancing them now. Interest rates for all currencies are much higher at present than at the time that these bonds were issued.

Management has asked you, CA, to prepare a report that discusses the accounting and financial reporting implications of each of the investment banker's recommendations. Management is considering a third option as well: using the existing debt to hedge IMC's new operations in foreign countries. Management also wants to know the accounting and financial reporting implications of this option.

Required:

Prepare the report.

(*CICA adapted*)

PROBLEMS

Note: Some problems use direct exchange rate quotations; others use indirect quotations.

Problem 1 Manitoba Exporters Inc. (MEI) sells Inuit carvings to countries throughout the world. On December 1, Year 5, MEI sold 10,000 carvings to a wholesaler in a foreign country at a total cost of 600,000 foreign currency units (FCs) when the spot rate was FC1 = $0.741. The invoice required the foreign wholesaler to remit by April 1, Year 6. On December 3, Year 5, MEI entered into a forward contract with the Royal Bank at the 120-day forward rate of FC1 = $0.781. Hedge accounting is not applied.

The fiscal year-end of MEI is December 31, and on this date the spot rate was FC1 = $0.757 and the forward rate was FC1 = $0.791. The payment from the foreign customer was received on April 1, Year 6, when the spot rate was FC1 = $0.802.

Required:

(a) Prepare the journal entries to record
   (i) the sale and the forward contract.
   (ii) any adjustments required on December 31.
   (iii) the cash received in Year 6.
(b) Prepare a partial balance sheet of MEI on December 31, Year 5, that shows the presentation of the receivable and the accounts associated with the forward contract.

Problem 2 Moose Utilities Ltd. (MUL) borrowed $50,000,000 in U.S. funds on January 1, Year 1, at an annual interest rate of 12 percent. The loan is due on December 31, Year 4, and interest is paid annually on December 31. The Canadian exchange rates for U.S. dollars over the life of the loan were as follows:

January 1, Year 1	CDN$1.159
December 31, Year 1	CDN$1.168
December 31, Year 2	CDN$1.160
December 31, Year 3	CDN$1.152
December 31, Year 4	CDN$1.155

Exchange rates changed evenly throughout the year.

Required:

(a) Prepare journal entries for MUL for Year 1.
(b) Calculate the exchange gains or losses that would be reported in the profit of the company each year over the life of the loan.

Problem 3 Grammy Ltd., a Canadian company, is dealing with a supplier in a foreign country. On May 1, Year 4, the company made purchases totalling FF2,270,000; this amount is payable in six months. Grammy did not hedge the transaction in any way.

On the due date, Grammy found itself in financial difficulty. The supplier agreed to accept a non-interest-bearing note payable for FF2,000,000 and FF270,000 in cash. The note payable is due July 1, Year 6. Grammy did not hedge the note.
Grammy has a December 31 fiscal year-end.

May 1, Year 4	$1 = FF2
November 1, Year 4	$1 = FF2.6
December 31, Year 4	$1 = FF3.8

Required:

Prepare the journal entries for Year 4 for the accounts payable and the note payable.

(*CGA-Canada adapted*)

Problem 4   On January 1, Year 5, Ornate Company Ltd. purchased US$1,000,000 of the bonds of the Gem Corporation. The bonds were trading at par on this date, pay interest at 9 percent each December 31, and mature on December 31, Year 7. The following Canadian exchange rates were quoted during Year 5:

January 1, Year 5	US$1 = CDN$1.372
December 31, Year 5	US$1 = CDN$1.321

Exchange rates changed evenly throughout the year. These bonds were trading at 102 at December 31, Year 5.

Required:

Prepare the journal entries for Year 5 assuming that the investment in bonds is
(a) held to maturity.
(b) held for trading.
(c) available for sale.

Problem 5   On October 1, Year 6, Versatile Company contracted to sell merchandise to a customer in Switzerland at a selling price of SF400,000. The contract called for the merchandise to be delivered to the customer on January 31, Year 7, with payment due on delivery. On October 1, Year 6, Versatile arranged a forward contract to deliver SF400,000 on January 31, Year 7, at a rate of SF1 = $1.20. Versatile's year-end is December 31.

The merchandise was delivered on January 31, Year 7, and SF400,000 were received and delivered to the bank.

Exchange rates were as follows:

	Spot rates	Forward rates
October 1, Year 6	SF1 = $1.18	SF1 = $1.20
December 31, Year 6	SF1 = $1.21	SF1 = $1.22
January 31, Year 7	SF1 = $1.19	SF1 = $1.19

Required:

(a) Prepare the journal entries that Versatile should make to record the events described assuming that the forward contract is designated as a cash flow hedge.
(b) Prepare a partial trial balance of the accounts used as at December 31, Year 6, and indicate how each would appear on the company's financial statements.
(c) Prepare the journal entries that Versatile should make to record the events described assuming that the forward contract is designated as a fair value hedge.

(d) Prepare a partial trial balance of the accounts used as at December 31, Year 6, and indicate how each would appear on the company's financial statements.

(e) Describe how the accounting for the hedge affects the current ratio and indicate which accounting treatment for the hedge would show the strongest liquidity position.

Problem 6   Hamilton Importing Corp. (HIC) imports goods from countries around the world for sale in Canada. On December 1, Year 3, HIC purchased 10,000 watches from a foreign wholesaler for DM600,000 when the spot rate was DM1 = $0.741. The invoice called for payment to be made on April 1, Year 4. On December 3, Year 3, HIC entered into a forward contract with the Royal Bank at the 120-day forward rate of DM1 = $0.781. Hedge accounting is not applied.

The fiscal year-end of HIC is December 31. On this date, the spot rate was DM1 = $0.757 and the 90-day forward rate was DM1 = $0.786. The payment to the foreign supplier was made on April 1, Year 4, when the spot rate was DM1 = $0.802.

Required:

(a) Prepare the journal entries to record
   (i) the purchase and the forward contract.
   (ii) any adjustments required on December 31.
   (iii) the payment in Year 4.

(b) Prepare a partial statement of financial position for HIC on December 31, Year 3, that presents the liability to the foreign supplier and the accounts associated with the forward contract.

Problem 7   On August 1, Year 3, Carleton Ltd. ordered machinery from a supplier in Hong Kong for HK$500,000. The machinery was delivered on October 1, Year 3, with terms requiring payment in full by December 31, Year 3. On August 2, Year 3, Carleton entered a forward contract to purchase HK$500,000 on December 31, Year 3, at a rate of $0.165. On December 31, Year 3, Carleton settled the forward contract and paid the supplier.

Exchange rates were as follows:

	Spot rates	Forward rates
August 1 and 2, Year 3	HK$1 = C$0.160	HK$1 = C$0.165
October 1, Year 3	HK$1 = C$0.164	HK$1 = C$0.168
December 31, Year 3	HK$1 = C$0.169	HK$1 = C$0.169

Required:

(a) Assume that the forward contract was designated as a cash flow hedge of the anticipated transaction to purchase the machinery and that the entire balance in accumulated other comprehensive income on October 1 was transferred to the machinery account when the machinery was delivered. Calculate the following amounts for the financial statements for the year ended December 31, Year 3:
   (i)   Machinery.
   (ii) Exchange gains/losses.
   (iii) Cash flows for the period.

(b) Assume that the forward contract was designated as a cash flow hedge of both the purchase of the machinery and the payment of the accounts payable. Fifty percent of the balance in accumulated other comprehensive income on

October 1 was transferred to the machinery account when the machinery was delivered and the other 50 percent was reclassified into net income when the supplier was paid. Calculate the following amounts for the financial statements for the year ended December 31, Year 3:

(i) Machinery.

(ii) Exchange gains/losses.

(iii) Cash flows for the period.

(c) Explain the similarities and differences between the account balances under the two scenarios above. Which scenario would present the higher return on equity for Carleton for Year 3?

Problem 8   EnDur Corp (EDC) is a Canadian company that exports computer software. On February 1, Year 2, EDC contracted to sell software to a customer in Denmark at a selling price of 600,000 Danish krona (DK) with payment due 60 days after installation was complete. On February 2, Year 2, EDC entered into a forward contract with the Royal Bank at the five-month forward rate of CDN$1 = DK5.20. The installation was completed on April 30, Year 2. On June 30, Year 2, the payment from the Danish customer was received and the forward contract was settled.

Exchange rates were as follows:

	Spot rates	Forward rates
February 1 and 2, Year 2	$1 = DK5.06	$1 = DK5.20
April 30, Year 2	$1 = DK5.09	$1 = DK5.18
June 30, Year 2	$1 = DK5.14	$1 = DK5.14

Required:

(a) Assume that the forward contract was designated as a cash flow hedge of the anticipated sale and that the entire balance in accumulated other comprehensive income (AOCI) on April 30 was transferred to sales when the installation was completed. Calculate the following amounts for the financial statements for the year ended June 30, Year 2:

(i) Sales.

(ii) Exchange gains/losses.

(iii) Cash flows for the period.

(b) Assume that EDC could have entered into a three-month forward contract on February 2, Year 2, to hedge the sale of the software with a forward rate of $1 = DK5.15. If so, this forward contract would have fixed the sales price for the software. Also, assume that the amount transferred from AOCI to the sales account on April 30 is the amount required to fix the sales price at the three-month forward rate and the balance of the AOCI is reclassified into net income when EDC received payment from the customer. Calculate the following amounts for the financial statements for the year ended June 30, Year 2:

(i) Sales.

(ii) Exchange gains/losses.

(iii) Cash flows for the period.

(c) Explain the similarities and differences between the account balances under the two scenarios above.

Problem 9   Winn Ltd. conducted two foreign-currency transactions on September 1, Year 4.

In the first transaction, it sold DM750,000 in merchandise to a foreign company. Since this sale was so special, Winn agreed to collect the note receivable on September 1, Year 8. There is no risk of default on the receivable, since the customer is a very large and prosperous company. The note has an interest rate of 10 percent per year, payable at the end of December each year. Both the interest and the note will be paid in DMs. This receivable was not hedged in any way.

In the second transaction, Winn purchased FF1,200,000 worth of inventory from a company in another foreign country. This amount will be payable on November 1, Year 5. There is no interest on this liability, and it is not hedged.

EXCHANGE RATES

September 1, Year 4	Spot rate	$1 = DM2.5	$1 = FF3.9
December 31, Year 4	Spot rate	$1 = DM2.8	$1 = FF3.4
Year 4	Average rate	$1 = DM2.3	$1 = FF4.1
Sept.–Dec., Year 4	Average rate	$1 = DM2.6	$1 = FF3.6
November 1, Year 5	Spot rate		$1 = FF3.1
December 31, Year 5	Spot rate	$1 = DM3.6	
Year 5	Average rate	$1 = DM3.0	

Required:

Prepare all the journal entries for Years 4 and 5 for the two transactions. Assume a December 31 year-end.

(CGA-Canada adapted)

Problem 10   On August 1, Year 1, Zip Ltd. purchased some merchandise from a foreign company for DM450,000. The liability was not due until March 1, Year 2. Zip was quite confident that the exchange rate fluctuations were not a problem and took no action to hedge the liability. On November 1, Year 1, Zip looked at the exchange rates and decided that they had better hedge the liability with a 120-day forward contract. Assume a December 31 year-end, assume all months have 30 days, and assume hedge accounting is not adopted.

EXCHANGE RATES

August 1, Year 1	Spot rate	$1 = DM2.5
November 1, Year 1	Spot rate	$1 = DM2.1
November 1, Year 1	120-day forward rate	$1 = DM1.9
December 31, Year 1	Spot rate	$1 = DM1.7
December 31, Year 1	60-day forward rate	$1 = DM1.8
March 1, Year 2	Spot rate	$1 = DM2.7
December 31, Year 2	Spot rate	$1 = DM2.9
March 1, Year 3	Spot rate	$1 = DM2.4

Required:

(a) Prepare all the journal entries for Years 1 and 2 for Zip for these transactions.

(b) Assume that the liability was a note due on March 1, Year 3 (instead of Year 2, as given above), and that Zip does not hedge in any way. Prepare all the journal entries for Year 1.

(c) Explain why some of the financial statement items in this problem are translated at historical rates whereas other items are translated at closing rates.

(CGA-Canada adapted)

Problem 11   On February 1, Year 3, Harrier Ltd., a Canadian company, sold goods to a company in a foreign country and took a note receivable for FF6,200,000. The note matures on February 1, Year 5, and bears interest at the market rate of 6 percent, payable annually. There was no danger of default on the note, but Harrier decided to hedge the cash receivable from the note with a forward contract. The contract was for one year and matured on February 1, Year 4. On that date, Harrier settled the forward contract and decided to leave the note in an unhedged position for the remainder of its life. Hedge accounting is not applied.

Harrier has a December 31 year-end.

	Spot rates	Forward rates
February 1, Year 3	$1 = FF3.9	$1 = FF3.3
December 31, Year 3	$1 = FF3.1	$1 = FF3.0
February 1, Year 4	$1 = FF4.2	$1 = FF4.2
December 31, Year 4	$1 = FF3.4	
February 1, Year 5	$1 = FF3.3	

Required:

Prepare all the journal entries related to the note receivable for Years 3 and 4.

(CGA-Canada adapted)

Problem 12   On June 1, Year 3, Forever Young Corp. (FYC) ordered merchandise from a supplier in Turkey for Turkish lira (TL) 200,000. The goods were delivered on September 30 with terms requiring cash on delivery. On June 2, Year 3, FYC entered a forward contract as a cash flow hedge to purchase TL200,000 on September 30, Year 3, at a rate of $0.73. FYC's year-end is June 30.

On September 30, Year 3, FYC paid the foreign supplier in full and settled the forward contract.

Exchange rates were as follows:

	Spot rates	Forward rates
June 1 and 2, Year 3	TL1 = $0.70	TL1 = $0.730
June 30, Year 3	TL1 = $0.69	TL1 = $0.725
September 30, Year 3	TL1 = $0.74	TL1 = $0.740

Required:

(a) (i) Prepare all journal entries required to record the transactions described above.

(ii) Prepare a June 30, Year 3, partial trial balance of the accounts used in (i), and indicate how each account would appear in the year-end financial statements.

(b) Prepare all necessary journal entries under the assumption that no forward contract was entered.

(c) Prepare all necessary journal entries to record the transactions described above assuming that the forward contract was designated as a fair value hedge.

Problem 13   Hull Manufacturing Corp. (HMC), a Canadian company, manufactures instruments used to measure the moisture content of barley and wheat. The company sells primarily to the domestic market, but in Year 3 it developed a small market in Argentina. In Year 4, HMC began purchasing semifinished components from a supplier in Romania. The management of HMC is concerned about the possible adverse effects of foreign-exchange fluctuations. To deal with this matter, all of HMC's foreign-currency-denominated receivables and payables are hedged with contracts with the company's bank. The year-end of HMC is December 31.

The following transactions occurred late in Year 4:

- On October 15, Year 4, HMC purchased components from its Romanian supplier for 800,000 Romanian leus (RL). On the same day, HMC entered into a forward contract for (RL800,000 at the 60-day forward rate of RL1 = $0.408. The Romanian supplier was paid in full on December 15, Year 4.
- On December 1, Year 4, HMC made a shipment to a customer in Argentina. The selling price was 2,500,000 Argentinean pesos (AP), with payment to be received on January 31, Year 5. HMC immediately entered into a forward contract for AP2,500,000 at the two-month forward rate of AP1 = $0.226. During this period, the exchange rates were as follows:

	Spot rates	Forward rates
October 15, Year 4	RL1 = $0.395	
December 1, Year 4	AP1 = $0.249	
December 15, Year 4	RL1 = $0.387	
December 31, Year 4	AP1 = $0.233	AP1 = $0.222

Hedge accounting is not adopted.

Required:

(a) Prepare the Year 4 journal entries to record the transactions described above and any adjusting entries necessary.
(b) Prepare the December 31, Year 4, balance sheet presentation of the receivable from the Argentinian customer and the accounts associated with the forward contract.

Problem 14   As a result of its export sales to customers in Switzerland, the Lenox Company has had Swiss franc–denominated revenues over the past number of years. In order to gain protection from future exchange rate fluctuations, the company decides to borrow its current financing requirements in Swiss francs. Accordingly, on January 1, Year 1, it borrows SF1,400,000 at 12 percent interest, to be repaid in full on December 31, Year 3. Interest is paid annually on December 31. The management designates this loan as a cash flow hedge of future SF revenues, which are expected to be received as follows:

Year 1	SF 560,000
Year 2	490,000
Year 3	350,000
	SF1,400,000

Actual revenues turned out to be exactly as expected each year and were received in cash. Exchange rates for the Swiss franc during the period were as follows:

January 1, Year 1	$1.05
Average, Year 1	$1.10
December 31, Year 1	$1.15
Average, Year 2	$1.20
December 31, Year 2	$1.25
Average, Year 3	$1.27
December 31, Year 3	$1.30

Required:

Prepare the journal entries required each year.

Problem 15 On January 1, Year 4, a Canadian firm, Canuck Enterprises Ltd., borrowed US$200,000 from a bank in Seattle, Washington. Interest of 7 percent per annum is to be paid on December 31 of each year during the four-year term of the loan. Principal is to be repaid on the maturity date of December 31, Year 7. The foreign-exchange rates for the first two years were as follows:

January 1, Year 4	US$1.00 = CDN$1.38
December 31, Year 4	US$1.00 = CDN$1.41
December 31, Year 5	US$1.00 = CDN$1.35

Exchange rates changed evenly throughout the year.

Required:

Determine the exchange gain (loss) on the loan to be reported in the financial statements of Canuck Enterprises for the years ended December 31, Year 4 and Year 5.

(CGA-Canada adapted)

WEB-BASED PROBLEMS

Problem 1 Access the most recent consolidated financial statements for Vodafone, a British company. (Go to the investor relations section at www.vodafone.com.) Answer the questions below. For each question, indicate where in the financial statements you found the answer and/or provide a brief explanation.
(a) What currency is used in presenting the financial statements?
(b) What percentage of net income is represented by foreign-exchange gains or losses?
(c) Identify the location(s) in the annual report where the company provides disclosures related to its management of foreign-exchange risk.
(d) Indicate if and how the company describes the significance of foreign-currency issues to the overall success/profitability of the company and sensitivity of its income to a change in foreign-exchange rates.
(e) Describe the types of hedging instruments the company uses to hedge foreign-exchange risk.
(f) Describe the manner in which the company discloses the fact that its hedges are effective in offsetting gains and losses on the underlying items being hedged.
(g) Does the company apply hedge accounting to accounting for its hedging instruments? If so, what portion of its hedging instruments are fair value hedges and what portion are cash flow hedges?
(h) What was the amount of foreign-exchange gains or losses for the year on cash flow hedges? Describe how these gains or losses are reported.

Problem 2 Access the most recent financial statements for Siemens, a German company. (Go to the investor relations section at www.siemens.com.) Answer the same questions as in Problem 1. For each question, indicate where in the financial statements you found the answer and/or provide a brief explanation. (Some questions may not be applicable.)

Chapter **11** **Translation and Consolidation of the Financial Statements of Foreign Operations**

LEARNING OBJECTIVES

After studying this chapter, you should be able to do the following:

1. Contrast an enterprise's foreign-currency accounting exposure with its economic exposure to exchange rate changes.

2. Differentiate between an integrated and a self-sustaining foreign operation, and describe the translation method and functional currency that is used in the translation of each type.

3. Prepare translated financial statements for each type of foreign operation.

4. Explain how the temporal method produces results consistent with the normal measurement and valuation of assets and liabilities for domestic transactions and operations.

5. Explain why the reporting enterprise's exposure to exchange rate changes is limited to its net investment if the investment is in a self-sustaining foreign operation.

6. Use translated financial statements to prepare consolidated financial statements, particularly in situations where there is an acquisition differential and a non-controlling interest.

INTRODUCTION

Consolidated financial statements are required when one entity has control over another entity or when a venturer has joint control over a joint venture. With the ever-expanding global economy, it is now very common for a subsidiary to be in a foreign country as indicated by the following:

Most Canadian public companies have subsidiaries in foreign countries.

- Magna International Inc., a leading global supplier of technologically advanced automotive systems, components, and complete modules, directly or indirectly owned 15 or more wholly owned foreign subsidiaries in 4 countries at December 31, 2008.

- Potash Corporation of Saskatchewan, the world's largest producer of potash, directly or indirectly owned 51 or more foreign subsidiaries in 7 countries at December 31, 2008.

- Royal Bank of Canada, Canada's largest bank and one of the world's most highly rated financial institutions, directly or indirectly owned 56 foreign subsidiaries in 14 countries at October 31, 2009.

Foreign-currency-denominated financial statements must be translated to the presentation currency of the reporting entity.

Companies establish operations in foreign countries for a variety of reasons, including developing new markets for their products, taking advantage of lower production costs, or gaining access to raw materials. Some multinational companies have reached a stage in their development in which domestic operations are no longer considered to be of higher priority than international operations.

Prior to preparing consolidated financial statements or accounting for an investment under the equity method, the financial statements of the foreign subsidiary or investee company must be translated into the investor company's presentation currency. IAS 27 requires that consolidated financial statements be prepared using uniform accounting policies for like transactions and other events in similar circumstances. This means that the financial statements of the foreign operations should be adjusted to reflect the accounting policies of the parent company. Unless otherwise noted, we will assume the reporting entity is a Canadian company and its functional currency is the Canadian dollar. This chapter deals with the issue of translating the foreign entity's financial statements into the parent's presentation currency prior to consolidation.

Three major issues are related to the translation process: (1) what is the functional currency of the foreign operation, (2) what is the presentation currency (also known as the reporting currency) of the parent company, and (3) where should the resulting translation adjustment be reported in the consolidated financial statements. These issues are examined first from a conceptual perspective and second by the manner in which they have been resolved by the IASB. We will start by discussing the difference between accounting exposure and economic exposure.

Accounting Exposure versus Economic Exposure

Exposure is the risk that something could go wrong. Foreign-currency exposure is the risk that a loss could occur if foreign-exchange rates changed. Foreign-currency risk can be viewed as having three components: translation exposure (accounting exposure), transaction exposure, and economic exposure.[1] Readers must keep these in mind as they interpret financial statements that contain foreign-currency gains and losses.

Accounting exposure exists when financial statement items are translated at the closing rate or the forward rate.

Translation (Accounting) Exposure This exposure results from the translation of foreign-currency-denominated financial statements into dollars. Only those financial statement items translated at the closing rate or the forward rate create an accounting exposure. If an item is translated at the historical rate, the Canadian dollar amount is fixed at historical cost and will not be affected by rate changes. However, if an item is translated at the closing rate or the forward rate, the Canadian dollar amount will change every time the exchange rate changes. Each item translated at the closing rate is exposed to translation adjustment. A separate translation adjustment exists for each of the exposed items. Positive translation adjustments increase shareholders' equity, whereas negative translation adjustments decrease shareholders' equity. Positive translation adjustments on assets can be offset by negative translation adjustments on liabilities. If total exposed assets are equal to total exposed liabilities

---

[1] See "Foreign Currency Risk Management." Management Accounting Guideline #6. Hamilton: Society of Management Accountants of Canada, 1987.

throughout the year, the translation adjustments (although perhaps significant on an individual basis) net to a zero balance. The *net* translation adjustment needed to keep the consolidated balance sheet in balance is based solely on the *net asset* or *net liability* exposure.

Net asset exposure means that more assets than liabilities are exposed.

A foreign operation has a net asset exposure when assets translated at the closing or forward exchange rate are larger in amount than liabilities translated at the closing or forward exchange rate. A net liability exposure exists when liabilities translated at the closing or forward exchange rate are larger than assets translated at the closing or forward exchange rate. The relationship among exposure, exchange rate fluctuations, and effect on shareholders' equity (S/E) is summarized as follows:

	Foreign currency	
Balance sheet exposure	Appreciates	Depreciates
Net asset	Increases S/E	Decreases S/E
Net liability	Decreases S/E	Increases S/E

The gains and losses that result from the translation are usually unrealized in the sense that they do not represent actual cash flows. Because these accounting gains and losses are reflected in the financial statements, they may have an impact on the enterprise's dividend policies, share prices, and so on. It is important to assess the extent to which they represent transaction and/or economic exposure.

Transaction exposure exists when there is a lapse in time between the origination of a receivable or payable and the settlement of the receivable or payable.

Transaction Exposure   This exposure exists between the time of entering a transaction involving a receivable or payable and the time of settling the receivable or payable with cash. It affects the current cash flows of the enterprise. The resulting cash gains and losses are realized and affect the enterprise's working capital and earnings. The concept of transaction exposure was discussed in Chapter 10.

Economic exposure exists when the present value of future cash flows would change as a result of changes in exchange rates.

Economic Exposure   Economic exposure takes a longer-term view of the situation than either of the others. It arises because of "the possible reduction, in terms of the domestic reporting currency, of the discounted future cash flows generated from foreign investments or operations due to real changes (inflation adjusted) in exchange rates."[2] It represents a long-term potential threat or benefit to a company carrying out business in foreign countries.

Economic exposure is not easy to measure.

For example, a Canadian assembly plant that purchases components from a company in Japan will suffer economically if the dollar weakens in relation to the Japanese yen and the Canadian competition is such that the cost increase cannot be passed on to the company's customers. The situation is no different if the Japanese supplier is related to, or is a subsidiary of, the Canadian assembler, because it measures its results in yen and expects to be paid in that currency. Economically, there is a potential loss in this situation when the Canadian dollar weakens in relation to the yen. However, if the Canadian parent does *not* purchase the output of its Japanese subsidiary, the economic exposure is quite different. If this were a stand-alone foreign operation with no intercompany transactions, the Canadian parent would benefit by receiving more dollars from its subsidiary's dividends. Therefore, the economic exposure is dependent on whether the foreign subsidiary is closely linked to the activities of the parent or operating independently of the parent. IAS 21: The Effects

---
[2]   Ibid.

of Changes in Foreign Exchange Rates tries to capture the economic effects by establishing a situational approach to determining the translation method to be used for certain foreign operations.

Translation Methods

The translated statements should reflect the reporting enterprise's exposure to exchange rate changes.

Until the adoption of IFRSs in 2011, two major methods for translating foreign operations will be used under Canadian GAAP: (1) the temporal method and (2) the current rate method. IAS 21 uses a similar approach for translating foreign operations but does not refer to the approaches by a particular name. For ease of identification, we will continue to refer to these methods using the same names, i.e., temporal method and current rate method. Where differences exist between the IFRS rules and the old Canadian rules, the IFRS rules will be used.

The objective of translation is to express financial statements of the foreign operation in Canadian dollars (or other presentation currency) in the manner that best reflects the reporting enterprise's exposure to exchange rate changes as determined by the economic facts and circumstances. We will discuss these methods from the perspective of a Canadian-based multinational company translating foreign-currency financial statements into Canadian dollars. The same principles could be applied if the Canadian company decided to use a reporting currency other than the Canadian dollar. For example, the Canadian company may choose to use the U.S. dollar as its reporting currency in order to satisfy the external users of the financial statements. We will discuss this option later in this chapter.

The Temporal Method

The temporal method gives the same results as if the transactions had occurred in Canada.

The basic objective underlying the temporal method is to produce a set of translated financial statements as if the transactions had occurred in Canada in the first place. In other words, use the same process we used in Chapter 10 to translate individual transactions and account balances into Canadian dollars. Use the Canadian dollar as the unit of measure and value financial statement items according to the normal measurement practices for Canadian domestic transactions and operations.

Under normal measurement practices, certain financial statement items are reported at historical cost, whereas other items are reported at fair value. The temporal method is designed to maintain this reporting practice when translating the foreign-currency statements into Canadian dollars.

If the financial statement item is supposed to be reported at fair value, when translating the item into Canadian dollars we need to take the fair value of the item in foreign currency and apply the rate of the date that the fair value was determined.

Use historical exchange rates to translate revenues and expenses.

To obtain historical values, revenues and expenses should be translated in a manner that produces substantially the same reporting currency amounts that would have resulted had the underlying transactions been translated on the dates they occurred. To translate revenues of a foreign subsidiary, use the exchange rate on the date that the transaction giving rise to the revenue occurred. The following examples illustrate this concept. In all of these examples, assume the following exchange rates:

January 1	FC1 = $1.50
January 31	FC1 = $1.60
Average for January	FC1 = $1.56

Example A On January 1, Subco sold goods for cash of FC100. The revenue is earned and determined on this date. The revenue of FC100 would be translated into $150, its historical value.

Example B On January 1, Subco sold goods for FC100 with payment due within 30 days. On January 31, FC100 was received from the customer. The revenue is earned and determined on January 1. The revenue of FC100 would be translated into $150. Receiving the cash on January 31 does not change the historical value of the sale. It does result in an exchange gain on the accounts receivable of $10 [FC100 × ($1.60 − $1.50)].

Example C On January 1, Subco received FC100 as a prepayment for goods to be delivered within 30 days. On January 31, Subco delivered the goods and earned the sale. Although the revenue was earned on January 31, the amount of the revenue in Canadian dollars was determined on January 1 when the cash was received. The revenue of FC100 would be translated into $150.

Use average rates to approximate exchange rates throughout the period.

Example D On each day in January, Subco sold goods for cash of FC100. Rather than using 31 different exchange rates for the 31 days of the month, the average rate for the month, $1.56, can be applied to the total revenue for the month, FC100 × 31 × $1.56 = $4,836.

The same concept can be applied in translating expenses. Use the exchange rate on the date that the transaction giving rise to the expense occurred. Since depreciation expense is directly related to the purchase of a depreciable asset, depreciation expense should be translated using the exchange rate on the date that the depreciable asset was purchased. Similarly, cost of goods sold is based on the cost of the inventory. Therefore, use the exchange rate on the date when the inventory was purchased when translating the cost of goods sold.

Use historical rates to measure expenses based on the historical cost of the related balance sheet items.

The Current Rate Method

The current rate method preserves the relationship of balance sheet items.

Under the current rate method, all of the assets and liabilities of a foreign entity are translated at the closing rate on the date of the balance sheet; this preserves the relationship in dollars between all balance sheet items that formerly existed in the foreign currency. Share capital is translated at historical rates. All revenues and expenses are translated using the exchange rate in effect on the dates on which such items are recognized in income during the period. If the revenues or expenses were recognized in income evenly throughout the period, the average rate for the period is used to translate these items. Under the current rate method, the net assets of the foreign entity (and therefore the Canadian parent's investment) are exposed to foreign-exchange fluctuations. A peculiarity resulting from this method is that a property carried at historical cost in the foreign entity's statements will be translated into differing Canadian dollar values if exchange rates fluctuate over some time frame. The following example will illustrate this.

Example A German entity has land in its balance sheet with a historical cost of 100,000 euros. On five successive balance sheets, denominated in euros, the land appears as €100,000. If the value of the euro changes with respect to the Canadian dollar each year during the five-year period and the current rate method of translation is used, the translated amount will be different each year. A reader of the German financial statements would observe the same amount reflected each year. A

Using historical cost in foreign currency and the current rate does not provide historical cost or fair value in Canadian dollars.

reader of the translated financial statements would see a different amount each year and may improperly conclude that land sales or purchases have taken place. Despite this particular shortcoming, this method is one of the two methods currently sanctioned under IFRSs. The IASB recognizes that the exchange adjustments under the current rate method have little or no direct effect on the present and future cash flows from operations. Accordingly, the exchange adjustments are not recognized in profit or loss; they are included in other comprehensive income.

Both of the translation methods that have been discussed will produce different amounts for balance sheet and income statement items and different amounts for the translation gain or loss[3] because the total amount of the balance sheet items at risk to exchange rate changes is different under each.

Translation under IAS 21

IAS 21 establishes accounting standards for the translation of the financial statements of a foreign operation (a subsidiary, joint venture, associate, or branch) for use by a reporting enterprise (a Canadian investor). A foreign operation is viewed as either *integrated* or *self-sustaining* for translation purposes depending on whether the functional currency of the foreign entity is the same as or different from the functional currency of the Canadian reporting entity.

The functional currency is the primary currency of the entity's operating environment.

To determine whether a specific foreign operation is integrated with its parent or self-sustaining, IAS 21 created the concept of the functional currency. As discussed in Chapter 10, the functional currency is the primary currency of the entity's operating environment. The foreign entity's functional currency can be either the parent's functional currency (usually the Canadian dollar) or a foreign currency (usually the local currency of the foreign entity). The interrelationship of the functional currency, the classification of the foreign entity, and the translation method can be depicted as follows:

Functional currency of foreign entity	Classification of foreign entity	Translation method	Translation adjustment reported in
Same as parent's	Integrated	Temporal method	Net income
Different from parent's	Self-sustaining	Current rate method	Other comprehensive income

In addition to introducing the concept of functional currency, IAS 21 introduced some new terminology. The *presentation currency* is the currency in which the entity presents its financial statements. For Canadian-based corporations, this is typically the Canadian dollar. The presentation currency of a foreign operation is typically the currency of the country in which its main operations are located.

The foreign operation is integrated with the parent if it has the same functional currency as the parent.

The financial statements of the foreign operation must be translated in order to prepare consolidated financial statements. If the foreign operation's presentation currency is a foreign currency, but its functional currency is the same as the parent's functional currency (i.e., the Canadian dollar), the foreign entity's financial statements must be translated to Canadian dollars using the temporal method; any translation adjustments

---

[3] It is not inconceivable to have an exchange gain from the use of one method and an exchange loss from the use of the other method.

The foreign operation is self-sustaining if it has a different functional currency than the parent.

must be reported as exchange gains or losses in net income. (This is an example of a Company C from Exhibit 10.2 on page 520 in Chapter 10.) If the foreign operation's functional currency is the not the same as the parent's functional currency, the foreign entity's financial statements must be translated to Canadian dollars using the current rate method; any translation adjustments must be reported as exchange gains or losses in other comprehensive income. (This is an example of a Company D from Exhibit 10.2.)

Foreign exchange adjustments are reported in other comprehensive income for self-sustaining foreign operations.

The exchange adjustments for the self-sustaining subsidiary are not recognized in net income because the changes in exchange rates have little or no direct effect on the present and future cash flows from operations. They merely serve to keep the balance sheet in equilibrium and are a mechanical by-product of the translation process. The cumulative amount of the exchange differences is presented in a separate component of equity until disposal of the foreign operation. When the exchange differences relate to a foreign operation that is consolidated but not wholly owned, they must be allocated to the shareholders of the parent company and the non-controlling interest in the consolidated statement of comprehensive income and, in turn, in the consolidated statement of changes in equity.

When the parent sells all or part of its self-sustaining foreign operations, or receives a liquidating dividend, a proportionate portion of the accumulated exchange gains and losses is taken out of other comprehensive income, and the realized exchange gains or losses are reported in net income. We will illustrate the presentation of other comprehensive income and a separate component of equity for accumulated other comprehensive income later in this chapter. If the parent hedges its investment in a self-sustaining foreign operation with a forward exchange contract, the exchange gains or losses on the forward contract are also reported in other comprehensive income to offset the unrealized losses or gains on the investment.

Exhibit 11.1 lists the indicators that should be considered when determining the functional currency for a foreign operation and gives an example of a condition

---

Exhibit 11.1

INDICATORS FOR EVALUATING A FOREIGN OPERATION

In effect, the indicators determine whether the foreign operation is integrated or self-sustaining.

Indicator	Functional Currency	
	Canadian dollar	Not Canadian dollar
1. to 5.	See Exhibit 10.3 on page 521.	See Exhibit 10.3 on page 521.
6. Extension of parent	Only goods imported from the parent are sold.	The foreign operation generates income, incurs expenses, and accumulates cash in its local currency.
7. Autonomy	The parent dictates the operating procedures.	The foreign entity has a significant degree of autonomy.
8. Intercompany transactions	Intercompany transactions are a high proportion of overall activities.	Intercompany transactions are a low proportion of overall activities.
9. Cash flows	Cash flows of the foreign operation directly affect cash flows of the parent.	Cash flows of the foreign operation have little effect on cash flows of the parent.
10. Financing cash flows	The parent provides cash to pay obligations.	Cash from local operations is sufficient to pay obligations.

that would indicate whether the Canadian dollar is the functional currency. The first five indicators were explained in Chapter 10; they apply to domestic and foreign operations.

When the above indicators are mixed and the functional currency is not obvious, management uses its professional judgment to determine the functional currency that most faithfully represents the economic effects of the underlying transactions, events, and conditions. As part of this approach, management gives priority to indicators 1 to 3 before considering the other indicators, which are designed to provide additional supporting evidence to determine an entity's functional currency.

The temporal method should be used to translate an integrated foreign operation.

The *temporal method* of translation is used for integrated operations because it produces essentially the same results that would have occurred had the reporting enterprise itself undertaken all of the transactions that were incurred by the foreign operation.

If a foreign operation is considered to be integrated, the relationship between the two entities is such that the activities of the reporting enterprise are or will be directly affected by the cash flows of the foreign operation.

A self-sustaining foreign operation is one that is financially and operationally independent of the reporting enterprise such that the exposure to exchange rate changes is limited to the reporting enterprise's net investment in the foreign operation.

The current rate method should be used to translate a self-sustaining foreign operation.

The current rate method was chosen to translate the foreign-currency financial statements of a self-sustaining operation, with *one* exception, discussed next.

Highly Inflationary Economies   While Canada has had fairly low rates of inflation in the past 25 years, this has not been the case in other parts of the world. Argentina, Brazil, Chile, Mexico, Turkey, and Israel have all had inflation rates higher than Canada's during this period. Between 1985 and 1993, Argentina experienced yearly rates of between 120 percent and 3,000 percent.

If the self-sustaining foreign operation operates in a highly inflationary environment relative to that of the reporting enterprise, translation using the current rate method could produce distorted and meaningless results. IAS 29 does not establish an absolute rate at which hyper-inflation is deemed to arise. Hyper-inflation is indicated by characteristics of the economic environment of a country that include, but are not limited to, the following:

Hyper-inflation causes the population to measure wealth and value using a currency of a more stable country.

(a) The general population prefers to keep its wealth in non-monetary assets or in a relatively stable foreign currency.

(b) The general population regards monetary amounts not in terms of the local currency but in terms of a relatively stable foreign currency. Prices may be quoted in that currency.

(c) Sales and purchases on credit take place at prices that compensate for the expected loss of purchasing power during the credit period, even if the period is short.

(d) Interest rates, wages, and prices are linked to a price index.

(e) The cumulative inflation rate over three years is approaching, or exceeds, 100 percent.

The following example illustrates the kind of distortion that can occur when the current rate method is used during a period of very high inflation.

Example   In Year 1, a Canadian company purchases a self-sustaining foreign subsidiary located in Chile. The exchange rate at this time is 1 peso = $1.00, and it remains constant during the year. The subsidiary has land carried at a historical cost of Ps1,000,000. On December 31, Year 1, the land is translated into dollars for consolidation purposes as follows:

$$Ps1,000,000 \times 1.00 = \$1,000,000$$

There is usually an inverse relationship between the strength of a country's currency and the level of inflation in that country.

During Year 2, Chile experiences an inflation rate of 500 percent. Because the inflation rate in Canada is minuscule during this period, this large inflation differential is fully reflected in the foreign-exchange market. The result is a weakening of the peso relative to the Canadian dollar.

On December 31, Year 2, the exchange rate is Ps1 = $0.20. If the land were translated at the closing rate on this date, the result would be as follows:

$$Ps1,000,000 \times 0.20 = \$200,000$$

While it is easy to see in this example that the $800,000 difference is due to the exchange rate change, large differences such as this are difficult to interpret without all the facts.

If the Chilean subsidiary prepared price-level-adjusted historical cost statements, the land would appear on the subsidiary's balance sheet at Ps5,000,000. Translation using the current rate method on December 31, Year 2, would *not* produce distorted results, as the following illustrates:

$$Ps5,000,000 \times 0.20 = \$1,000,000$$

Price-level-adjusted financial statements are useful for countries experiencing high inflation.

When a self-sustaining foreign operation operates in a hyper-inflationary economy, its financial statements must be translated into Canadian dollars using the following procedures:

(a) All amounts (i.e., assets, liabilities, equity items, income, and expenses for the current year) must be translated at the closing rate.

(b) Comparative amounts must be those that were presented as current-year amounts in the relevant prior-year financial statements (i.e., they are not adjusted for subsequent changes in exchange rates).

The foreign entity must restate its financial statements in accordance with IAS 29 before applying the translation method set out above. When the economy ceases to be hyper-inflationary and the entity no longer restates its financial statements in accordance with IAS 29, it must use as the historical costs for translation the amounts restated to the price level at the date the entity ceased restating its financial statements.

Under IAS 29, both the current year's figures and last year's comparatives must be stated in terms of the measuring unit current at the end of the reporting period. Using the example of the Chilean subsidiary above, the measuring unit is the peso, which experienced 500 percent inflation during the year. Non-monetary items that were carried at historical costs are restated by applying a general price index. Monetary and non-monetary items that were carried at fair value or recoverable amount are not restated because they are already expressed in terms of the monetary unit current at the end of the reporting period. After the restatement, all assets and liabilities are stated at fair value or at a price-level-adjusted value, which may approximate fair value. When these items are translated to the Canadian dollar at the closing rate, the translated values will approximate the fair value in terms of Canadian dollars.

Unit of Measure

The two methods of translation actually use different currencies as the underlying unit of measure. The temporal method uses the Canadian dollar as the functional currency and the measuring unit, while the current rate method uses the foreign currency as the functional currency and the measuring unit. Under both methods, the presentation currency for the Canadian reporting entity is the Canadian dollar.

The temporal method uses the Canadian dollar as the underlying unit of measure.

Because it produces results that are identical to those that would have been produced had the Canadian parent itself entered into all of the transactions incurred by the foreign operation, the temporal method of translation essentially takes all of the transactions that have been measured in a foreign currency and re-measures them in Canadian dollars using the exchange rate in effect on the date of the transaction. Financial statement ratios computed using the foreign currency as the original measuring unit will change when the statements are re-measured using the Canadian dollar.

The current rate method uses the foreign currency as the underlying unit of measure.

Under the current rate method, the unit of measure is the foreign currency. Each transaction of the foreign operation is measured in foreign currency. In order for the consolidation to take place by adding dollars to dollars, the foreign-currency financial statements are translated to Canadian dollars, the presentation currency. Balance sheet ratios (e.g., the current ratio) remain unchanged. Income statement ratios (e.g., net income to sales) will remain the same if revenues and expenses occurred evenly throughout the period and the average rate is used for all income statement items. Income statement ratios will change if revenues and expenses occurred at different times during the period and a number of different exchange rates were used in translating the revenues and expenses. Ratios of income statement items to balance sheet items (e.g., return on investment) will be different after the translation because the rates used to translate the balance sheet are different from the rates used for the income statement.

Illustration of Translation and Consolidation

The translation and preparation of consolidated financial statements will now be illustrated under the two translation methods required by IAS 21.

Example   On December 31, Year 1, Starmont Inc., a Canadian company, acquired 100 percent of the common shares of Controlada S.A., located in Estonia, at a cost of 2,000,000 kroons. The exchange rate was K1 = $0.128 on this date. Starmont's journal entry (in Canadian dollars) to record the share acquisition is as follows:

Dec. 31, Year 1
Investment in Controlada ... 256,000
   Cash ... 256,000
(K2,000,000 × 0.128)

When the parent acquires the subsidiary, the parent indirectly buys all of the net assets of the subsidiary.

This example assumes that the carrying values of the subsidiary's net assets were equal to fair values and that there is no goodwill on consolidation. Because this is an "acquisition" business combination, the exchange rate on the date of acquisition is used to translate all accounts of the subsidiary on acquisition date and becomes the historical rate to be used in subsequent years, where appropriate.

The translation of the balance sheet of Controlada from kroons into Canadian dollars at December 31, Year 1, is shown in Exhibit 11.2. Note that the translation of a subsidiary on the date of acquisition is the same regardless of whether the entity is integrated or self-sustaining.

With no acquisition differential and the subsidiary wholly owned, the investment account is equal to the subsidiary's shareholders' equity.

The preparation of the acquisition-date consolidated balance sheet appears in Exhibit 11.3. Note that the translated shareholders' equity of the subsidiary is equal to the parent's investment account, so the consolidating procedure is simply to eliminate one against the other.

Exhibit 11.2

CONTROLADA S.A.
TRANSLATION OF BALANCE SHEET TO CANADIAN DOLLARS
at December 31, Year 1

		Estonian kroons	Exchange rate	Canadian dollars
For consolidation purposes, we never use an exchange rate older than the rate at the date of acquisition.	Cash	K 40,000	0.128	$ 5,120
	Accounts receivable	360,000	0.128	46,080
	Inventories	1,200,000	0.128	153,600
	Plant and equipment (net)	900,000	0.128	115,200
		K2,500,000		$320,000
	Current liabilities	K 50,000	0.128	$ 6,400
	Bonds payable	450,000	0.128	57,600
	Common shares	1,500,000	0.128	192,000
	Retained earnings	500,000	0.128	64,000
		K2,500,000		$320,000

Exhibit 11.3

PREPARATION OF CONSOLIDATED BALANCE SHEET
at December 31, Year 1

		Starmont	Controlada	Starmont Consolidated
Controlada has to be translated into dollars in order to consolidate with Starmont's Canadian dollar financial statements.	Cash	$ 70,000	$ 5,120	$ 75,120
	Accounts receivable	90,000	46,080	136,080
	Inventories	200,000	153,600	353,600
	Plant and equipment	300,000	115,200	415,200
	Investment in Controlada	256,000	—	—
		$916,000	$320,000	$980,000
	Current liabilities	$ 80,000	$ 6,400	$ 86,400
	Bonds payable	300,000	57,600	357,600
	Common shares	200,000	192,000	200,000
	Retained earnings	336,000	64,000	336,000
		$916,000	$320,000	$980,000

Translation and Consolidation Subsequent to Acquisition

On December 31, Year 2, Controlada forwarded the financial statements shown in Exhibit 11.4 to the Canadian parent. Sales, purchases, bond interest, and other expenses occurred evenly throughout the year.

The translation process will now be illustrated under these two assumptions:

(a) the subsidiary is self-sustaining because its functional currency is not the Canadian dollar, and

(b) the subsidiary is integrated because its functional currency is the Canadian dollar.

The exchange rates for the year were as follows:

December 31, Year 1	K1 = $0.128
December 31, Year 2	K1 = $0.104
Average for Year 2	K1 = $0.115
Date of purchase for inventory on hand at end of Year 2	K1 = $0.110
Date dividends declared	K1 = $0.104

Exhibit 11.4

CONTROLADA S.A.
FINANCIAL STATEMENTS
December 31, Year 2
(in kroons)

INCOME STATEMENT

The subsidiary uses its local currency, kroon, in its own financial records and for reporting in its own country.

Sales	K9,000,000
Cost of goods purchased	7,400,000
Change in inventory	(400,000)
Depreciation expense	100,000
Bond interest expense	45,000
Other expenses	1,555,000
	8,700,000
Net income	K 300,000

STATEMENT OF RETAINED EARNINGS

Balance, beginning of year	K 500,000
Net income	300,000
	800,000
Dividends	100,000
Balance, end of year	K 700,000

BALANCE SHEET

Cash	K 100,000
Accounts receivable	400,000
Inventory	1,600,000
Plant and equipment (net)	800,000
	K2,900,000
Current liabilities	K 250,000
Bonds payable	450,000
Common shares	1,500,000
Retained earnings	700,000
	K2,900,000

Exhibit 11.5

Exchange Rates

Financial statement items	Self-sustaining	Integrated
Monetary	closing	closing
Non-monetary — at cost	closing	historical
Non-monetary — at fair values	closing	closing
Deferred revenues	closing	historical
Common shares	historical	historical
Dividends	historical	historical
Revenues	historical	historical
Depreciation and amortization	historical	historical
Cost of sales	historical	—
Opening inventory	—	historical
Purchases	—	historical
Ending inventory	—	historical

Exhibit 11.5 illustrates the rates to be used for self-sustaining operations (the current rate method) and integrated operations (the temporal method). Translation of the numerous revenues, expenses, gains, and losses at the historical rates is generally impractical. A weighted-average exchange rate for the period would normally be used to translate such items.

Self-sustaining Foreign Operation   If the subsidiary is considered self-sustaining, the translation of its Year 2 financial statements will be as shown in Exhibit 11.6.

The procedure used in Exhibit 11.6 was to translate the income statement first, then the retained earnings statement, and then the balance sheet. The following features of the current rate translation process are emphasized:

The average rate is used when the revenues and expenses occur evenly throughout the year.

* The average rate for Year 2 is used for all revenues and expenses in the income statement.

* All assets and liabilities are translated at the closing rate.

All items within shareholders' equity are translated using the historical rate applicable for each item.

* Common shares and beginning retained earnings are translated at the acquisition date historical rate, thus establishing the translated amount on that date. In future periods, the amount for the translated beginning retained earnings will have to be calculated. In practice, the accountant will look at last year's translated financial statements for this amount. Dividends are translated at the historical rate on the date of declaration. In situations where the dividends were not paid by year-end, the dividends payable will be translated at the closing rate, and a hidden exchange gain or loss will result from the translation of these items. (In this example, the dividends were declared and paid on December 31.)

Differentiate between other comprehensive income for the year that is reported in comprehensive income and accumulated other comprehensive income that is reported in shareholders' equity.

* The amount required to balance the balance sheet is the unrealized exchange loss from the translation of the subsidiary's financial statements using the current rate method. The unrealized exchange losses for the year must be presented in other comprehensive income on the statement of other comprehensive income. The accumulated exchange losses for all years to date are presented as a separate component of shareholders' equity. Since Year 2 is the first year in which Controlada is reporting unrealized exchange losses, the cumulative losses on the balance sheet are equal to the loss reported in comprehensive

Exhibit 11.6

CONTROLADA S.A.
TRANSLATION OF FINANCIAL STATEMENTS TO CANADIAN DOLLARS
December 31, Year 2
(self-sustaining foreign operation)

INCOME STATEMENT

	Kroons	Exchange rate	Canadian dollars
Sales	K9,000,000	0.115	$1,035,000
Cost of goods purchased	7,400,000	0.115	851,000
Change in inventory	(400,000)	0.115	(46,000)
Depreciation expense	100,000	0.115	11,500
Bond interest expense	45,000	0.115	5,175
Other expenses	1,555,000	0.115	178,825
	8,700,000		1,000,500
Net income	K 300,000	0.115	$ 34,500

All revenues and expenses are assumed to have occurred evenly throughout the year.

STATEMENT OF COMPREHENSIVE INCOME

	Kroons	Exchange rate	Canadian dollars
Net income	K 300,000	0.115	$ 34,500
Other comprehensive income			
Foreign-currency translation adjustments			(51,300)
Comprehensive income	K 300,000		$(16,800)

STATEMENT OF RETAINED EARNINGS

	Kroons	Exchange rate	Canadian dollars
Balance, beginning of year	K 500,000	0.128	$ 64,000
Net income	300,000	0.115	34,500
	800,000		98,500
Dividends	100,000	0.104	10,400
Balance, end of year	K 700,000		$ 88,100

Only the net income from the regular income statement is carried forward to the statement of retained earnings.

BALANCE SHEET

	Kroons	Exchange rate	Canadian dollars
Cash	K 100,000	0.104	$ 10,400
Accounts receivable	400,000	0.104	41,600
Inventory	1,600,000	0.104	166,400
Plant and equipment (net)	800,000	0.104	83,200
	K2,900,000		$ 301,600
Current liabilities	K 250,000	0.104	$ 26,000
Bonds payable	450,000	0.104	46,800
Common shares	1,500,000	0.128	192,000
Retained earnings	700,000		88,100
Accumulated translation adjustments			(51,300)
	K2,900,000		$ 301,600

All assets and liabilities are translated at the current rate.

Other comprehensive income is carried forward to accumulated other comprehensive income.

income for the year. In this example, comprehensive income is presented as a separate statement. It includes net income from the income statement and other comprehensive income.

In this illustration, the financial statements were translated sequentially, with the foreign-exchange loss being the "plug" needed to complete the balance sheet. In reality, the gain or loss can be calculated before attempting the translation process. Exhibit 11.7 illustrates this process. In a self-sustaining operation such as this one, it is the net assets (assets less liabilities) that are at risk and are exposed to currency fluctuations. Net assets equal shareholders' equity, and if the common shares remain unchanged, the only changes that usually occur are the net income and dividend changes to retained earnings. The process involves translating the opening position, using the historical rates at that time, and translating the changes at the rates at which they occurred. The result is a calculated position. The actual end-of-year net asset position is translated at closing rates, with the difference between the two numbers representing the exchange gain or loss from translation. Notice that if the exchange rate had remained constant throughout Year 2, all items in Exhibit 11.7 would have been translated at $0.128 with no exchange gain or loss occurring.

Stormont uses the equity method for internal record keeping purposes. It would make the following journal entries on December 31, Year 2:

> **Exchange gains and losses occur only on those items translated at the closing rate and only if the rates change during the period.**

> **Starmont's journal entries are recorded in Canadian dollars.**

Investment in Controlada	34,500	
Equity earnings		34,500
100% of translated net income		
Cash	10,400	
Investment in Controlada		10,400
Dividend received		
Other comprehensive income	51,300	
Investment in Controlada		51,300
To record 100% of the change in the unrealized exchange loss from translation for Year 2		

Exhibit 11.7

INDEPENDENT CALCULATION OF YEAR 2 TRANSLATION LOSS
(self-sustaining foreign operation)

> **Assets minus liabilities are called net assets and are equal in amount to shareholders' equity.**

	Kroons		Exchange rate	Canadian dollars
Net assets, December 31, Year 1	K2,000,000	×	0.128	$256,000
Changes in net assets, Year 2				
Net income	300,000	×	0.115	34,500
Dividends	(100,000)	×	0.104	(10,400)
Calculated net assets				280,100
Actual net assets	K2,200,000	×	0.104	228,800
Exchange loss from translation				$ 51,300

Net equity earnings should be equal to the subsidiary's net income when there is no acquisition differential or non-controlling interest.

Exhibit 11.8 illustrates the preparation of the consolidated financial statements. Notice that equity earnings are equal to the subsidiary's net income ($34,500) and are therefore eliminated and replaced with the subsidiary's revenue and expenses.

Exhibit 11.8

PREPARATION OF CONSOLIDATED FINANCIAL STATEMENTS
YEAR 2
(self-sustaining foreign operation)
STATEMENT OF NET INCOME AND COMPREHENSIVE INCOME

	Starmont	Controlada	Starmont Consolidated
Sales	$3,000,000	$1,035,000	$4,035,000
Equity earnings	34,500	—	—
	3,034,500	1,035,000	4,035,000
Cost of goods purchased	2,520,000	851,000	3,371,000
Change in inventory	(20,000)	(46,000)	(66,000)
Depreciation	20,000	11,500	31,500
Bond interest	30,000	5,175	35,175
Other expenses	200,000	178,825	378,825
	2,750,000	1,000,500	3,750,500
Net income	284,500	34,500	284,500
Other comprehensive income Foreign-currency translation adjustments	(51,300)	(51,300)	(51,300)
Comprehensive income	$ 233,200	$ (16,800)	$ 233,200

Other comprehensive income is reported separately from net income.

RETAINED EARNINGS

Balance — beginning	$ 336,000	$ 64,000	$ 336,000
Net income	284,500	34,500	284,500
	620,500	98,500	620,500
Dividends	50,000	10,400	50,000
Balance — end	$ 570,500	$ 88,100	$ 570,500

Consolidated retained earnings are the same as the parent's retained earnings under the equity method.

BALANCE SHEETS

Cash	$ 100,000	$ 10,400	$ 110,400
Accounts receivable	290,400	41,600	332,000
Inventories	220,000	166,400	386,400
Plant and equipment (net)	280,000	83,200	363,200
Investment in Controlada (equity method)	228,800	—	—
	$1,119,200	$ 301,600	$1,192,000
Current liabilities	$ 100,000	$ 26,000	$ 126,000
Bonds payable	300,000	46,800	346,800
Common shares	200,000	192,000	200,000
Retained earnings	570,500	88,100	570,500
Accumulated translation adjustments	(51,300)	(51,300)	(51,300)
	$1,119,200	$ 301,600	$1,192,000

Accumulated translation adjustments are reported separately from retained earnings.

The parent's investment account is eliminated against the shareholders' equity of the subsidiary in the following manner:

The investment account under the equity method should be equal to the subsidiary's shareholders' equity when there is no acquisition differential or non-controlling interest.

Investment in Controlada		$228,800
Shareholders' equity — Controlada		
Common shares	192,000	
Retained earnings	88,100	
Accumulated translation adjustments	(51,300)	228,800
Acquisition differential		$ –0–

With no acquisition differential or non-controlling interest, the investment account is replaced with the assets and the liabilities of the subsidiary. Notice that the parent's share (in this case 100 percent) of the subsidiary's accumulated translation adjustments appears as a separate component of consolidated shareholders' equity. The parent's equity method journal entries made the consolidation process straightforward.

The consolidated statement of changes in equity for the year ended December 31, Year 2, is presented in Exhibit 11.9. Note that net income is added to retained earnings, whereas other comprehensive income is added to accumulated translation adjustments.

Integrated Foreign Operation Assuming that Controlada is an integrated foreign operation, the statements would be translated using the temporal method. Exhibit 11.10 illustrates this process. The following discussion regarding the exchange rates used and the disposition of the translation gain should be noted:

- Monetary items are translated at the current rate, while non-monetary items are translated at appropriate historical rates.

Shareholders' equity accounts are translated at historical rates.

- Common shares and beginning-of-year retained earnings are translated at the historical rate on the date of acquisition. In future years, the translated amount for retained earnings will have to be calculated.

- Revenue and expenses, with the exception of depreciation and cost of goods sold, are translated at the average rate for the year. Depreciation is translated at the historical rates used to translate the related assets.

Exhibit 11.9

CONSOLIDATED STATEMENT OF CHANGES IN EQUITY
(self-sustaining foreign operation)

	Common shares	Retained earnings	ATA*	Total
Balance — beginning	$200,000	$336,000	$ 0	$536,000
Net income		284,500		284,500
Other comprehensive income			(51,300)	(51,300)
Dividends		(50,000)		(50,000)
Balance — end	$200,000	$570,500	$(51,300)	$719,200

* ATA = Accumulated translation adjustments

Exhibit 11.10

CONTROLADA S.A.
TRANSLATION OF FINANCIAL STATEMENTS TO CANADIAN DOLLARS
December 31, Year 2
(integrated foreign operation)

INCOME STATEMENT

		Kroons	Exchange rate	Canadian dollars
Cost of goods sold and depreciation expense are translated using the historical rates of the related balance sheet accounts.	Sales	K9,000,000	0.115	$1,035,000
	Cost of goods purchased	7,400,000	0.115	851,000
	Change in inventory	(400,000)	calculated	(22,400)
	Depreciation expense	100,000	0.128	12,800
	Bond interest expense	45,000	0.115	5,175
	Other expenses	1,555,000	0.115	178,825
	Total expenses	8,700,000		1,025,400
	Net income (before translation loss — note 1)	K 300,000		$ 9,600

RETAINED EARNINGS

	Kroons	Exchange rate	Canadian dollars
Balance — beginning	K 500,000	0.128	$ 64,000
Net income (note 1)	300,000		9,600
	800,000		73,600
Dividends	100,000	0.104	10,400
Balance — end	K 700,000		$ 63,200

BALANCE SHEET

		Kroons	Exchange rate	Canadian dollars
Assets to be reported at fair value are translated at the closing rate and assets to be reported at cost are translated at the historical rates.	Cash	K 100,000	0.104	$ 10,400
	Accounts receivable	400,000	0.104	41,600
	Inventory	1,600,000	0.110	176,000
	Plant and equipment (net)	800,000	0.128	102,400
		K2,900,000		$ 330,400
	Current liabilities	K 250,000	0.104	$ 26,000
	Bonds payable	450,000	0.104	46,800
	Common shares	1,500,000	0.128	192,000
	Retained earnings (note 1)	700,000		63,200
				328,000
	Balancing translation adjustment (note 1)	—		2,400
		K2,900,000		$ 330,400

Note 1: Because this translation adjustment is a preliminary balancing amount, the net income and retained earnings are not the final translated amounts.

- Because the components of cost of goods sold are translated using different rates, the translated amount for this item is calculated as follows:

Beginning inventory	K 1,200,000	×	0.128	$ 153,600
Less: ending inventory	1,600,000	×	0.110	176,000
Change in inventory	(400,000)			(22,400)
Purchases	7,400,000	×	0.115	851,000
Cost of goods sold	K 7,000,000			$ 828,600

The three components of cost of goods sold are each translated at the rate when these goods were purchased.

Purchases are translated at the average rate for the year. Inventories are translated at historical rates.

The exchange gain or loss is reported in net income under the temporal method.

- The balance sheet item "Balancing translation adjustment" is the "plug" needed to balance the statements after translation. It represents the foreign-exchange gain due to changes in the exposed position during the year. IAS 21 requires that this amount be reflected in the Year 2 income statement. In Exhibit 11.12, the financial statements of Controlada have been adjusted accordingly. The sequential translation illustrated in Exhibit 11.10 on page 585 is cumbersome, because the translated net income does not contain the year's exchange gain or loss. A better method would be to first calculate the exchange gain or loss resulting from the monetary position, and then translate the financial statements and include the gain or loss in the income statement. Exhibit 11.11 shows how the gain or loss can be calculated before the actual financial statement translation takes place.

After the translation adjustment is reflected in Controlada's income statement (see Exhibit 11.12), the translated statements are ready for the consolidation process. They become the basis for the following equity method journal entries by Starmont on December 31, Year 2:

The translated income is quite different under the temporal method than under the current rate method.

Investment in Controlada	12,000	
Equity earnings (9,600 + 2,400 from Exhibit 11.10)		12,000
To record 100% of the Year 2 net income of Controlada Company		
Cash	10,400	
Investment in Controlada		10,400
Dividend received from Controlada Company		

Exhibit 11.12 shows the Year 2 financial statements of Starmont, the translated statements of Controlada using the temporal method, and the consolidated financial statements. Note that the investment account equals the shareholders' equity of the subsidiary, and that there is no non-controlling interest or acquisition differential. The investment account is replaced with the assets and the liabilities of Controlada, and equity earnings are replaced with revenues and expenses.

The exchange gains or losses are based on the accounting exposure, which is based on the translation method.

In both illustrations (self-sustaining and integrated), the financial statements were translated first with the foreign-exchange gain or loss determined as a "plug" to balance. Then, as a proof, the foreign-exchange gain or loss was verified by translating the changes that had occurred in either the net asset position or the net monetary position. It should be obvious that in both situations the exchange gains and losses can be determined prior to the translation of the financial statements.

Exhibit 11.11

CALCULATION OF YEAR 2 TRANSLATION ADJUSTMENT
(integrated foreign operation)

This schedule reconciles the change in accounting exposure during the year and calculates the gains or losses due to the change in exchange rates.

	Kroons	Exchange rates	Canadian dollars
Net monetary position			
Dec. 31, Year 1*	K (100,000) ×	0.128	$ (12,800)
Changes during Year 2			
Sales	9,000,000 ×	0.115	1,035,000
Purchases	(7,400,000) ×	0.115	(851,000)
Bond interest expense	(45,000) ×	0.115	(5,175)
Other expenses	(1,555,000) ×	0.115	(178,825)
Dividends	(100,000) ×	0.104	(10,400)
Net changes	(100,000)		(10,400)
Calculated net monetary position			
Dec. 31, Year 2			(23,200)
Actual net monetary position			
Dec. 31, Year 2*	K (200,000) ×	0.104	(20,800)
Exchange gain, Year 2			$ 2,400

*NET MONETARY POSITION, KROONS

Only monetary items are exposed to exchange rate changes in this illustration.

	December 31	
	Year 2	Year 1
Cash	K 100,000	K 40,000
Accounts receivable	400,000	360,000
Current liabilities	(250,000)	(50,000)
Bonds payable	(450,000)	(450,000)
Net monetary position	K(200,000)	K(100,000)

Exhibit 11.12

PREPARATION OF CONSOLIDATED FINANCIAL STATEMENTS YEAR 2
(integrated foreign operation)

INCOME STATEMENT

The exchange gain is reported in net income.

	Starmont	Controlada	Starmont Consolidated
Sales	$3,000,000	$1,035,000	$4,035,000
Equity earnings	12,000	—	—
	3,012,000	1,035,000	4,035,000
Cost of goods purchased	2,520,000	851,000	3,371,000
Change in inventory	(20,000)	(22,400)	(42,400)
Depreciation	20,000	12,800	32,800
Bond interest	30,000	5,175	35,175
Other expenses	200,000	178,825	378,825
Foreign-exchange gain	—	(2,400)	(2,400)
	2,750,000	1,023,000	3,773,000
Net income	$ 262,000	$ 12,000	$ 262,000

(continued)

RETAINED EARNINGS

		Starmont	Controlada	Starmont Consolidated
The parent's income under the equity method is equal to consolidated net income.	Balance — beginning	$ 336,000	$ 64,000	$ 336,000
	Net income	262,000	12,000	262,000
		598,000	76,000	598,000
	Dividends	50,000	10,400	50,000
	Balance — end	$ 548,000	$ 65,600	$ 548,000

BALANCE SHEETS

		Starmont	Controlada	Starmont Consolidated
The subsidiary's assets and liabilities replace the investment account.	Cash	$ 100,000	$ 10,400	$ 110,400
	Accounts receivable	290,400	41,600	332,000
	Inventories	220,000	176,000	396,000
	Plant and equipment (net)	280,000	102,400	382,400
	Investment in Controlada (equity)	257,600	—	—
		$1,148,000	$ 330,400	$1,220,800
	Current liabilities	$ 100,000	$ 26,000	$ 126,000
	Bonds payable	300,000	46,800	346,800
	Common shares	200,000	192,000	200,000
	Retained earnings	548,000	65,600	548,000
		$1,148,000	$ 330,400	$1,220,800

Comparative Observations of the Two Translation Methods

Integrated subsidiaries usually have a net liability exposure, whereas self-sustaining subsidiaries usually have a net asset exposure.

Under the current rate method, the net assets position of the foreign entity is at risk from currency fluctuations, while under the temporal method it is the monetary position that is at risk. For most companies, monetary liabilities are greater than monetary assets, so they are usually in a net monetary liability position. This is the case with Controlada S.A. If the foreign currency weakens with respect to the Canadian dollar, a self-sustaining operation will show a foreign-exchange loss while an integrated foreign operation will show a foreign-exchange gain. This can be seen in Exhibit 11.7 on page 582, where a self-sustaining operation produced a loss of $51,300, and Exhibit 11.11 on page 587, where an integrated operation produced a gain of $2,400. If the Canadian dollar weakens with respect to the foreign currency (i.e., the foreign currency strengthens) a self-sustaining operation will reflect an exchange gain and an integrated operation will reflect an exchange loss. These observations are only true when monetary liabilities are greater than monetary assets.

Complications with an Acquisition Differential

The previous example assumed a 100-percent-controlled subsidiary and no acquisition differential. The existence of an acquisition differential presents complications in the consolidation process when the current rate method is used and the subsidiary is less than 100 percent owned. We will change some of the facts from the previous example in order to illustrate this.

Example Assume that Starmont purchased 90 percent of Controlada on December 31, Year 1, at a cost of K2,340,000. The carrying values of Controlada's net assets were equal to fair values on this date except for a patent, which had a fair value of K600,000 in excess of carrying amount. The patent had a remaining useful life of 10 years and no residual value at the date of acquisition. The same exchange rates are assumed; thus, the financial statements of Controlada and their translation will not change from the previous example. However, the change in the acquisition cost and the percentage purchased creates an acquisition differential and a non-controlling interest. Starmont's journal entry to record the acquisition on December 31, Year 1, is as follows:

Investment in Controlada	299,520	
Cash		299,520

To record the acquisition of 90% of Controlada for $299,520
(2,340,000 × 0.128)

The following calculation of the acquisition differential in kroons and Canadian dollars on December 31, Year 1, is made to prepare the acquisition-date consolidated balance sheet:

> **The acquisition differential is translated at the exchange rate on the date of acquisition.**

Cost of 90% investment	K2,340,000	×	0.128	=	$299,520
Implied value of 100%	K2,600,000	×	0.128	=	$332,800
Book value of subsidiary's net assets					
Assets	2,500,000	×	0.128	=	320,000
Liabilities	(500,000)	×	0.128	=	(64,000)
Net assets	2,000,000				256,000
Acquisition differential	600,000	×	0.128	=	76,800
Patent	600,000	×	0.128	=	76,800
Balance — goodwill	K —0—				$ —0—

Exhibit 11.13 shows the December 31, Year 1, balance sheets of the parent and the subsidiary and the consolidated balance sheet.

Exhibit 11.13

PREPARATION OF CONSOLIDATED BALANCE SHEET
At December 31, Year 1

> **Patent and non-controlling interest appear on the consolidated balance sheet.**

	Starmont	Controlada	Starmont Consolidated
Cash	$ 26,480	$ 5,120	$ 31,600
Accounts receivable	90,000	46,080	136,080
Inventories	200,000	153,600	353,600
Plant and equipment	300,000	115,200	415,200
Investment in Controlada	299,520	—	—
Patent	—	—	76,800
	$916,000	$320,000	$1,013,280
Current liabilities	$ 80,000	$ 6,400	$ 86,400
Bonds payable	300,000	57,600	357,600
Common shares	200,000	192,000	200,000
Retained earnings	336,000	64,000	336,000
Non-controlling interest*	—	—	33,280
	$916,000	$320,000	$1,013,280

* 10% × $332,800

The subsidiary's separate-entity financial statements are the same regardless of the parent's percentage ownership in the subsidiary.

Consolidation — Self-sustaining   Assuming that Controlada is a self-sustaining operation, we will now illustrate the preparation of the Year 2 consolidated financial statements. The translated financial statements are the same as were shown in the previous example, and are reproduced again as part of Exhibit 11.14 on page 592. Included in the subsidiary's shareholders' equity is the accumulated unrealized loss of $51,300. The non-controlling interest in the consolidated balance sheet includes 10 percent of the subsidiary's shareholders' equity and therefore includes 10 percent of this accumulated loss. Consolidated shareholders' equity attributable to the parent will show the other 90 percent of this translation adjustment. A further exchange loss arises in the consolidation process because of the manner in which the acquisition-differential amortization schedule is translated. Assume that the amortization expense related to the patent occurred evenly throughout the year. The acquisition-differential amortization schedule is translated as follows:

TRANSLATION OF ACQUISITION-DIFFERENTIAL AMORTIZATION SCHEDULE

A patent for a self-sustaining subsidiary is translated at the closing rate.

Patent — December 31, Year 1	K600,000	× 0.128	=	$76,800
Patent amortization — Year 2	60,000	× 0.115	=	6,900
Calculated patent — December 31, Year 2				69,900
Actual patent — December 31, Year 2	K540,000	× 0.104	=	56,160
Exchange loss — unrealized				$13,740

The following points should be noted:

- The acquisition differential (in this case patent) on December 31, Year 1, is translated at the historical rate on that date.

Amortization expense is translated at the average rate.

- The Year 2 amortization expense is translated at the average rate for Year 2 because the expense was incurred evenly throughout the year.

- The unamortized balance on December 31, Year 2, is translated at the closing rate.

An exchange adjustment occurs because the patent is restated when it is translated at the closing rate at the end of the year.

When different exchange rates are used to translate the schedule, an exchange gain or loss will always result. In this case, there is a loss of $13,740, which appears as part of the accumulated translation adjustments in the shareholders' equity of the parent company. The allocation of the two exchange losses resulting from the translation of the financial statements and the acquisition differential to controlling and non-controlling interest is illustrated next.

DISPOSITION OF ACCUMULATED UNREALIZED LOSSES

	Total	90% control	10% non-control
Accumulated unrealized loss — subsidiary statements	$51,300	$46,170	$5,130
Accumulated unrealized loss — acquisition differential	13,740	12,366	1,374
	$65,040	$58,536	$6,504

Using the translated financial statements of Controlada (see Exhibit 11.14 on page 592) and the translated acquisition-differential amortization schedule, Starmont would make the following equity method journal entries on December 31, Year 2:

The equity method records the parent's share of the exchange adjustment reported by the subsidiary and relating to the acquisition differential.	Cash (90% × 10,400)	9,360	
	Other comprehensive income (90% × 51,300)	46,170	
	Equity earnings (90% × 34,500)		31,050
	Investment in Controlada		24,480
	To record the parent's share of dividends, net income, and		
	loss on translation of statement		
	Equity earnings (90% × 6,900)	6,210	
	Other comprehensive income (90% × 13,740)	12,366	
	Investment in Controlada		18,576
	To record the amortization and exchange adjustment on		
	the acquisition differential		

The preparation of the Year 2 consolidated financial statements is illustrated in Exhibit 11.14 on page 592.

The following explanations regarding the preparation of the consolidated statements should be noted:

1. Consolidated statement of comprehensive income:

Non-controlling interest on the income statement is based on the income recorded by the subsidiary plus the consolidation adjustments for patent amortization loss and exchange loss.

(a) Equity earnings are eliminated and replaced with the revenues and expenses of the subsidiary, the patent amortization expense, and the non-controlling interest.

(b) Non-controlling interest in net income is 10 percent of subsidiary net income less 10 percent of the patent amortization expense.

(c) This statement takes the net income and deducts the unrealized foreign-exchange loss to determine comprehensive income.

(d) Non-controlling interest absorbs 10 percent of the unrealized exchange loss reported in other comprehensive income.

2. Consolidated retained earnings:

Because the parent has used the equity method, all items are identical to the parent's retained earnings.

3. Consolidated balance sheet:

(a) The investment account is eliminated and replaced with the assets and the liabilities of the subsidiary, the unamortized acquisition differential, and the non-controlling interest.

Non-controlling interest on the balance sheet is based on the subsidiary's shareholders' equity plus the consolidation adjustment for unamortized patent at the end of the year.

(b) The non-controlling interest is calculated as follows:

Common shares	$192,000
Retained earnings	88,100
Accumulated translation adjustments	(51,300)
Patent	56,160
	284,960
	10%
	$ 28,496

4. Consolidated accumulated translation adjustments:

This account shows the parent's share of the accumulated translation adjustments at the end of the year. Since Year 2 is the first year after acquisition, the accumulated losses are equal to the losses reported in other comprehensive income for the year.

Exhibit 11.14

PREPARATION OF CONSOLIDATED FINANCIAL STATEMENTS — YEAR 2
(self-sustaining)

STATEMENT OF NET INCOME AND COMPREHENSIVE INCOME

	Starmont	Controlada	Starmont Consolidated
Sales	$3,000,000	$1,035,000	$4,035,000
Equity earnings	24,840	—	—
	3,024,840	1,035,000	4,035,000
Cost of goods purchased	2,520,000	851,000	3,371,000
Change in inventory	(20,000)	(46,000)	(66,000)
Depreciation	20,000	11,500	31,500
Bond interest	30,000	5,175	35,175
Other	200,000	178,825	378,825
Patent amortization	—	—	6,900
	2,750,000	1,000,500	3,757,400
Individual net incomes	274,840	34,500	
Net income			277,600
Other comprehensive income			
Foreign currency translation adjustments	(58,536)	(51,300)	(65,040)
Comprehensive income	$ 216,304	$ (16,800)	$ 212,560
Net income attributable to			
Shareholders of Starmont			$ 274,840
Non-controlling interest			2,760
			$ 277,600
Comprehensive income attributable to			
Shareholders of Starmont			$ 216,304
Non-controlling interest			(3,744)
			$ 212,560

The patent amortization and non-controlling interest appear only on the consolidated income statement.

Consolidated other comprehensive income includes $51,300 from translating the subsidiary's separate-entity statements plus $13,740 from translating the acquisition differential on consolidation.

RETAINED EARNINGS

	Starmont	Controlada	Starmont Consolidated
Balance — beginning	$ 336,000	$ 64,000	$ 336,000
Net income	274,840	34,500	274,840
	610,840	98,500	610,840
Dividends	50,000	10,400	50,000
Balance — end	$ 560,840	$ 88,100	$ 560,840

BALANCE SHEETS

	Starmont	Controlada	Starmont Consolidated
Cash	$ 55,440	$ 10,400	$ 65,840
Accounts receivable	290,400	41,600	332,000
Inventories	220,000	166,400	386,400
Plant and equipment	280,000	83,200	363,200
Investment in Controlada (equity)	256,464	—	—
Patent	—	—	56,160
	$1,102,304	$ 301,600	$1,203,600
Current liabilities	$ 100,000	$ 26,000	$ 126,000
Bonds payable	300,000	46,800	346,800
Common shares	200,000	192,000	200,000
Retained earnings	560,840	88,100	560,840
Accumulated translation adjustments	(58,536)	(51,300)	(58,536)
Non-controlling interest	—	—	28,496
	$1,102,304	$ 301,600	$1,203,600

Accumulated translation adjustments is only the parent's share. The non-controlling interest's share of accumulated translation adjustments is included in the $28,496 for non-controlling interest.

The unamortized acquisition differential can be verified by the following calculation:

Investment in Controlada		$256,464
Shareholders' equity of Controlada	228,800	
	90%	205,920
Unamortized acquisition differential (patent) — parent's share		50,544
— non-controlling interest's share (10% × 56,160)		5,616
Total unamortized acquisition differential (patent)		$ 56,160

Consolidation — Integrated   We will conclude this example by assuming that 90-percent-owned Controlada is an integrated foreign operation. In this case, the existence of an acquisition differential and a non-controlling interest poses no particular consolidation problems. The acquisition-differential amortization schedule for Year 2 is shown below:

ACQUISITION-DIFFERENTIAL AMORTIZATION SCHEDULE

Sidenote						
There is no exchange adjustment because patent is translated at the historical rate under the temporal method.	Patent — December 31, Year 1	K600,000	×	0.128	=	$76,800
	Amortization — Year 2	60,000	×	0.128	=	7,680
	Patent — December 31, Year 2	K540,000	×	0.128	=	$69,120

Using the Year 2 acquisition differential amortization schedule and Controlada's translated financial statements (see Exhibit 11.15 on page 594), Starmont would make the following equity method journal entries on December 31, Year 2:

The parent accrues its share of the subsidiary's income after it has been translated into Canadian dollars.

Cash (90% × 10,400)	9,360	
Investment in Controlada	1,440	
Equity earnings (90% × 12,000)		10,800
To record parent's share of dividends and net income		
Equity earnings (90% × 7,680)	6,912	
Investment in Controlada		6,912
Amortization of acquisition differential		

The equity earnings are quite different under the temporal method than under the current rate method.

Note that Year 2 equity earnings are $3,888 in this example (integrated); in the previous example (self-sustaining), equity earnings were $24,840. The difference is due to (a) the use of different exchange rates in the translation, and (b) the fact that there is no exchange loss on the translation of the acquisition-differential amortization schedule under the temporal method.

Exhibit 11.15 on page 594 shows the preparation of the Year 2 consolidated financial statements.

The following points are worth noting in regard to the preparation of the consolidated statements:

1. Consolidated income statement:
   (a) Equity earnings are eliminated and replaced with the revenues and the expenses of the subsidiary, patent amortization, and the non-controlling interest, as follows:

Patent amortization and non-controlling interest are consolidation adjustments.

Net income, Controlada	$12,000
Patent amortization	(7,680)
Non-controlling interest	(432)
Equity earnings	$ 3,888

Exhibit 11.15

PREPARATION OF CONSOLIDATED FINANCIAL STATEMENTS — YEAR 2
(integrated foreign operation)

INCOME STATEMENT

	Starmont	Controlada	Starmont Consolidated
Sales	$3,000,000	$1,035,000	$4,035,000
Equity earnings	3,888	—	—
	3,003,888	1,035,000	4,035,000
Cost of goods purchased	2,520,000	851,000	3,371,000
Change in inventory	(20,000)	(22,400)	(42,400)
Depreciation	20,000	12,800	32,800
Bond interest	30,000	5,175	35,175
Other expenses	200,000	178,825	378,825
Patent amortization	—	—	7,680
Foreign exchange gain	—	(2,400)	(2,400)
	2,750,000	1,023,000	3,780,680
Net income	$ 253,888	$ 12,000	$ 254,320
Attributable to			
Shareholders of Starmont			$ 253,888
Non-controlling interest			432

Patent amortization and non-controlling interest appear only on the consolidated income statement.

RETAINED EARNINGS

	Starmont	Controlada	Starmont Consolidated
Balance — beginning	$ 336,000	$ 64,000	$ 336,000
Net income	253,888	12,000	253,888
	589,888	76,000	589,888
Dividends	50,000	10,400	50,000
Balance — end	$ 539,888	$ 65,600	$ 539,888

The parent's retained earnings under the equity method are equal to consolidated retained earnings.

BALANCE SHEETS

	Starmont	Controlada	Starmont Consolidated
Cash	$ 55,440	$ 10,400	$ 65,840
Accounts receivable	290,400	41,600	332,000
Inventories	220,000	176,000	396,000
Plant and equipment (net)	280,000	102,400	382,400
Investment in Controlada (equity)	294,048	—	—
Patent	—	—	69,120
	$1,139,888	$ 330,400	$1,245,360
Current liabilities	$ 100,000	$ 26,000	$ 126,000
Bonds payable	300,000	46,800	346,800
Common shares	200,000	192,000	200,000
Retained earnings	539,888	65,600	539,888
Non-controlling interest	—	—	32,672
	$1,139,888	$ 330,400	$1,245,360

There is no accumulated translation adjustment for exchange gains or losses under the temporal method.

(b) Non-controlling interest is 10 percent of the subsidiary's net income less 10 percent of the patent amortization.

2. Consolidated retained earnings:

Because the parent has used the equity method, all items are identical to the parent's retained earnings.

3. Consolidated balance sheet:

(a) The investment account is eliminated and replaced with the assets and the liabilities of the subsidiary, the unamortized acquisition differential, and the non-controlling interest.

(b) The non-controlling interest is calculated as follows:

Non-controlling interest on the balance sheet is based on the subsidiary's shareholders' equity plus the unamortized patent at the end of the year.

Common shares	$192,000
Retained earnings	65,600
Patent	69,120
	326,720
	10%
	$ 32,672

The unamortized acquisition differential can be verified by the following calculation:

Investment in Controlada		$294,048
Shareholders' equity of Controlada (192,000 + 65,600)	257,600	
	90%	231,840
Unamortized acquisition differential (patent) — parent's share		62,208
— non-controlling interest's share (10% × 69,120)		6,912
Total unamortized acquisition differential (patent)		$ 69,120

Other Considerations

The previous examples have illustrated the translation of a foreign operation's financial statements and the consolidation of these statements with those of the reporting enterprise. We will now look at some other items that must be considered when a foreign subsidiary is being consolidated.

Inventory is translated at the closing rate for a self-sustaining operation and the LCNRV principle need not be applied.

For an integrated operation, the LCNRV principle must be applied using historical cost in Canadian dollars and market value in Canadian dollars.

Lower of Cost and Net Realizable Value (LCNRV) Certain items, such as inventory, will be valued at the LCNRV. If the subsidiary is self-sustaining, the method of valuation used is of no consequence in the translation because all of the assets are translated at the closing rate regardless of whether they are carried at cost or net realizable value.

If the foreign operation is integrated, assets carried at cost are translated at historical rates, while assets carried at net realizable value are translated at the closing rate. Remember that the temporal method remeasures, in Canadian dollars, transactions that have been incurred by the foreign operation. Therefore, the translated financial statements should reflect the LCNRV in Canadian dollars as if the parent itself had carried out the inventory acquisitions of its foreign subsidiary. When assets are valued at the LCNRV, a write-down to net realizable value may be required in the translated financial statements even though no write-down is required in the foreign-currency financial statements. For example, if the net realizable value (denominated in foreign currency) is greater than historical cost (denominated in foreign currency), no write-down will have occurred in the foreign operation's statements. But if the foreign currency weakens, it is quite possible that the net realizable value translated at the closing rate will be less than historical cost translated at the historical rate. In this situation, translated net realizable value will be used in the translated financial statements.

On the other hand, it may be necessary to reverse a write-down in the foreign-currency financial statements prior to translation if the net realizable value amount translated at the closing rate exceeds historical cost translated at the historical rates. For example, if the net realizable value (denominated in foreign currency) is less than historical cost (denominated in foreign currency), a write-down would have taken place in the foreign operation's statements. If the foreign currency has strengthened so that the net realizable value translated at the closing rate is greater than historical cost translated at the historical rate, this write-down will have to be reversed prior to translation. The inventory (now carried at cost) will be translated at the historical rate.

Intercompany Profits   In the preparation of consolidated financial statements, intercompany profits in assets are eliminated. If the profits are contained in the assets of the Canadian parent, there is no particular problem eliminating them. The asset acquired was recorded by the parent at the foreign-currency-denominated price translated at the exchange rate on the date of the transaction. The profit rate can be applied for the items still on hand to determine the amount of profit to be eliminated. If the profits are contained in the assets of an integrated subsidiary, the amount of unrealized profit can still be determined in foreign currency. Because the asset itself is translated at the historical rate, using the historical rate to translate and eliminate the profit will result in a translated asset at historical cost to the consolidated entity.

> **The historical rate should be used in determining the intercompany profit to be eliminated. This eliminates the same profit that was recorded in the first place.**

When the profit is contained in the assets of a translated self-sustaining subsidiary, the asset has been translated at the closing rate. The historical exchange rate should be used to calculate the amount of the profit. This eliminates the same profit that was recorded in the first place. However, the translated assets will not be reported at historical cost to the consolidated entity.[4] This is one of the anomalies of the current rate method.

> **A cash flow statement is prepared by analyzing the change in a non-cash item on the balance sheet after it has been translated into Canadian dollars.**

Cash Flow Statement   To prepare a cash flow statement for a foreign subsidiary, we ignore the cash flow statement of the foreign subsidiary, i.e., we do not translate each item on the foreign-currency cash flow statement into Canadian dollars by applying a translation rate to each item. Rather, we use the translated balance sheet and translated income statement to determine the cash flows during the year. We analyze the changes in the translated balance sheet accounts from last year to this year using either a worksheet approach or T-account approach and then prepare the cash flow statement based on this analysis. This is a similar approach to what we used in Chapter 8 when we prepared a consolidated cash flow statement by analyzing the changes in the consolidated balance sheet from last year to this year.

Tax Effects of Exchange Adjustments   Exchange differences arising from translating the financial statements of a foreign operation into Canadian dollars are usually not taxable or deductible until the gains or losses are realized. Since these differences were recognized for accounting purposes but not for tax purposes, a temporary difference occurs and deferred income taxes should be recognized in the financial statements of the reporting entity.

---

[4] For a more detailed discussion of this, see Dr. Pierre Vezina, "Foreign Currency Translation," Toronto: CICA, 1985.

Also, as we learned in Chapter 9, a temporary difference arises on the consolidated financial statements when an acquisition differential is allocated to an asset other than goodwill. We ignored the tax impact on the acquisition differential and for the foreign-exchange adjustments in the illustrations in this chapter to avoid complicating the illustrations.

Disclosure Requirements   The following summarizes the main disclosures required in IAS 21 for the effects of changes in foreign-exchange rates related to foreign operations:

An entity must disclose the exchange adjustments reported in profit and other comprehensive income.

(a) The amount of exchange differences recognized in profit or loss.

(b) Net exchange differences recognized in other comprehensive income.

(c) When the presentation currency is different from the functional currency, that fact must be stated with disclosure of the functional currency and the reason for using a different presentation currency.

(d) When there is a change in the functional currency, that fact and the reason for the change in functional currency must be disclosed.

Alumina Limited is a leading Australian company with world-wide investments in bauxite mining, alumina refining, and selected aluminum smelting operations. Exhibit 11.16 contains excerpts from Alumina's 2008 financial statements pertaining to foreign-currency operations.

Exhibit 11.16

EXTRACTS (IN PART) FROM ALUMINA'S 2008 FINANCIAL STATEMENTS

Foreign Currency Translation

Functional and presentation currency

The Australian dollar is both the functional currency and the presentation currency.

Items included in the financial statements of each of the Group's entities are measured using the currency of the primary economic environment in which the entity operates ("the functional currency"). The consolidated financial statements are presented in Australian dollars, which is Alumina Limited's functional and presentation currency.

Controlled foreign entities

The results and financial position of all the Group entities that have a functional currency different from the presentation currency are translated into the presentation currency as follows:

The current rate method is used when the functional currency differs from the presentation currency.

— assets and liabilities for each balance sheet presented are translated at the closing rate at the date of that balance sheet;

— income and expenses for each income statement are translated at average exchange rates (unless this is not a reasonable approximation of the cumulative effect of the rates prevailing on the transaction dates, in which case income and expenses are translated at the dates of the transactions); and

— all resulting exchange differences are recognised as a separate component of equity.

On consolidation, exchange differences arising from the translation of any net investment in foreign entities, and of borrowings and other financial instruments designated as hedges of such investments, are taken to the translation reserve in shareholders' equity. When a foreign operation is sold or borrowings are repaid, a proportionate share of such exchange differences are recognised in the income statement, as part of the gain or loss on sale where applicable.

Goodwill and fair value adjustments arising on the acquisition of a foreign entity are treated as assets and liabilities of the foreign entity and translated at the closing rate.

(continued)

Net investment in a foreign operations hedge

The portion of a gain or loss on an instrument used to hedge a net investment in a foreign operation that is determined to be an effective hedge is recognised directly in equity. The ineffective portion is recognised immediately in the income statement. The gain or loss on hedging instruments relating to the effective portion of the hedge that has been recognized directly in equity shall be recognised in profit or loss on disposal of the foreign operation.

2. FINANCIAL RISK MANAGEMENT

The Group and the parent entity have exposure to the following risks from their use of financial instruments:
— Market risk
— Credit risk
— Liquidity risk

This note presents information about the Group's and parent entity's exposure to each of the above risks, their objectives, policies and processes for measuring and managing risk, and the management of capital. Further quantitative disclosures are included throughout this financial report. The exposures to these risks by the parent are similar to those of the Group. Financial risk management is carried out by a Treasury Committee which is responsible for developing and monitoring risk management policies.

Alumina identifies risks, sets risk limits, and controls and monitors adherence to the limits.

Risk management policies are established to identify and analyse the risks faced by the Group and the parent, to set appropriate risk limits and controls, and to monitor risks and adherence to limits. Risk management policies and systems are reviewed regularly to reflect changes in market conditions and the Group and parent's activities.

(a) MARKET RISK

Market risk is the risk that changes in market prices, such as foreign exchange rates, interest rates and equity prices will affect the Group's income or the value of its holdings of financial instruments. The objective of market risk management is to manage and control market risk exposures within acceptable parameters, while optimising the return.

The Group enters into derivatives, and also incurs financial liabilities, in order to manage market risks. All such transactions are carried out within the guidelines of the Treasury Committee.

(i) Foreign exchange risk

Foreign exchange risk arises when future commercial transactions and recognised assets and liabilities are denominated in a currency that is not the Group's or parent entity's functional currency. The Group operates internationally and is exposed to foreign exchange risk arising from various currencies, primarily the US dollar in which most of AWAC's sales are denominated.

Alumina uses forward contracts and call options to manage its foreign currency risk.

During 2008 the Group managed this risk partly by borrowing in US dollars to provide a hedge of its US dollar denominated assets, and by borrowing in Australian dollars for its further funding needs, however these Australian dollar borrowings have been repaid in full.

The Group generally does not hedge its other exposures except through the near-term forward purchase of currency to meet operating requirements. However, in December 2008 the Group paid US$9.3 million for BRL Call Options to reduce its exposure to movements in the BRL/USD exchange rate arising from capital expenditure on the Juruti and Alumar projects. The Group's assessed sensitivity of after tax profit to each one US cent movement in the average US dollar / Australian dollar exchange rate during 2008 was approximately $12 million. In addition, had the Australian Dollar at 31 December 2008, weakened / strengthened by 20 per cent against the US Dollar, with all other variables held constant, post-tax profit for the year would have been $4.0 million higher / $6.0 million lower (2007: $4.2 million higher / $5.1 million lower based on 10 per cent), mainly as a result of foreign exchange gains/losses on translation of Alcoa of Australia's US dollar denominated trade receivables, trade payables and the effect on the fair value of embedded derivatives in long term raw material purchase contracts. Equity would have been $4.0 million higher / $6.0 million lower (2007: $4.2 million higher / $5.1 million lower based on 10 per cent) had the Australian dollar weakened / strengthened by 20 per cent against the US dollar, arising mainly as a result of foreign exchange gains/losses on translation of US dollar denominated items as detailed in the above section relating to profit. The sensitivity factors relating to Equity are the same as detailed in the above section relating to profit.

Alumina reports translation adjustments on cash flow hedges and self-sustaining foreign operations directly in equity.

	Consolidated Entity		Parent Entity	
	2008	2007	2008	2007
Total equity at the beginning of the year	1,663.9	1,754.6	1,426.0	1,505.1
Change in the fair value of cash flow hedges, net of tax	0.5	16.7	—	—
Exchange differences on translation of foreign operations	157.8	(18.8)	—	—
Net income/(loss) recognised directly in equity	158.3	(2.1)	—	—

5. OTHER INCOME

	Consolidated Entity		Parent Entity	
	2008	2007	2008	2007
Foreign exchange gains (net)	—	—	—	66.8
Sundry income	0.4	0.2	0.4	0.2
Total other income	0.4	0.2	0.4	67.0

Source: 2008 Financial Statements © Alumina Limited.

GAAP for Private Enterprises

- As mentioned in Chapter 3, private companies can either consolidate their subsidiaries or report their investments in subsidiaries under the cost method or the equity method or at fair value if the securities are traded in an active market. Under the cost method or the fair value method, the financial statements of a foreign subsidiary do not have to be translated.

- The exchange rate at the end of the reporting period is called the current rate, not the closing rate.

- The functional currency is not used to classify foreign operations. Instead, the foreign operation is classified as either integrated or self-sustaining using similar, but not exactly the same, factors to those used under IFRSs to determine the functional currency.

The temporal method is used when the foreign operation is in a highly inflationary environment.

- When the foreign operations are located in a highly inflationary environment, the temporal method is used regardless of whether the operation is integrated or self-sustaining. No adjustments are made for inflation prior to translation.

U.S. GAAP Differences

U.S. GAAP and IFRSs for foreign operations have many similarities. The only significant difference is summarized as follows:

Under IFRSs, the financial statements of a foreign operation whose functional currency is highly inflationary are adjusted for inflation prior to being translated to the presentation currency. Under U.S. GAAP, no adjustments are made for inflation. Instead, the financial statements are translated as if the parent's reporting currency were the functional currency.

SUMMARY

Before the equity method or consolidation reporting can be used, the financial statements of foreign entities must be translated into the parent company's presentation currency. If the entity is considered to be an integrated foreign operation, the temporal method of translation is used. This method produces results that are consistent with the normal measurement and valuation of assets and liabilities for domestic transactions and operations. Exchange gains or losses are included in net income.

The current rate method is used when the foreign operation is self-sustaining. This method results in some assets and liabilities being reported in the presentation currency at values other than historical cost or current value. Exchange gains and losses from the translation are not reflected in net income but rather are shown in other comprehensive income, which ends up being reported on a cumulative basis as a separate component of shareholders' equity. The consolidation of the translated financial statements of a self-sustaining subsidiary creates additional exchange gains and losses from the translation of the acquisition differential.

Significant Changes in the Last Two Years

1. For publicly accountable enterprises, IFRSs have replaced the former sections of the *CICA Handbook*. The following table shows the IFRSs covered in this chapter along with their counterparts from the former sections of the *CICA Handbook:*

IFRSs	CICA Handbook *Counterparts*
IAS 21: The Effects of Changes in Foreign Exchange Rates	Section 1651: Foreign Currency Translation
IAS 29: Financial Reporting in Hyperinflationary Economies	No equivalent standard
IAS 1: Presentation of Financial Statements	Section 1530: Comprehensive Income Section 3251: Equity

2. The term *closing rate* replaces the term *current rate* when referring to the spot rate at the end of the reporting period.
3. The reporting entity must identify its functional currency and record all transactions in its accounting records using the functional currency. The entity is free to use a presentation currency that is different from the functional currency.
4. When a foreign-currency item is valued at fair value, it is translated using the spot rate on the date when fair value was determined rather than using the closing rate.
5. IAS 21 takes a functional currency approach rather than classifying subsidiaries as integrated or self-sustaining. Each entity determines its functional currency and prepares its separate-entity financial statements in its functional currency. Then, the separate-entity financial statements are translated into the parent's presentation currency for inclusion in the consolidated financial statements.
6. IAS 29 requires a company with high inflation to adjust its financial statements for inflation prior to translation.

Changes Expected in the Next Three Years

IAS 21 on financial instruments may be simplified. The concept of other comprehensive income may be eliminated for self-sustaining foreign operations.

SELF-STUDY PROBLEM

Barros Corp., located in Brazil, is a 90-percent-owned subsidiary of a Canadian parent. The company was incorporated on January 1, Year 1, and issued its no-par common shares for 5.0 million Brazilian reals (R). The Canadian parent acquired 90 percent of these shares at this time for $2.25 million when the exchange rate was CDN$1 = R2. The financial statements for Barros on December 31, Year 2, are shown below:

STATEMENT OF FINANCIAL POSITION
at December 31, Year 2

	Year 2	Year 1
Plant assets	R6,000,000	R6,000,000
Accumulated depreciation	(1,000,000)	(500,000)
Inventory	1,050,000	1,155,000
Accounts receivable	2,710,000	2,550,000
Cash	1,000,000	500,000
	R9,760,000	R9,705,000
Common shares	R5,000,000	R5,000,000
Retained earnings	2,160,000	1,005,000
Bonds payable — due Jan. 3, Year 11	2,500,000	2,500,000
Accrued liabilities	40,000	350,000
Accounts payable	60,000	850,000
	R9,760,000	R9,705,000

INCOME STATEMENT
for the Year Ended December 31, Year 2

Sales	R35,000,000
Cost of sales	28,150,000
Interest	200,000
Selling and administrative	2,440,000
Miscellaneous expenses	800,000
Income tax	1,045,000
	32,635,000
Profit	R 2,365,000

STATEMENT OF RETAINED EARNINGS
for the Year Ended December 31, Year 2

Balance, January 1	R1,005,000
Profit	2,365,000
	3,370,000
Dividends	1,210,000
Balance, December 31	R2,160,000

Additional Information
- On January 3, Year 1, Barros issued bonds for R2.5 million.
- Barros acquired the plant assets on February 1, Year 1, for R6.0 million. The plant assets are being depreciated on a straight-line basis over a 10-year life.
- Barros uses the FIFO basis to value inventory. The December 31, Year 1, inventory was acquired on October 1, Year 1. The inventory on hand on December 31, Year 2, was acquired on December 15, Year 2.
- Selling and administrative expense includes depreciation expense of R500,000.
- Barros did not pay dividends in Year 1, and the Year 2 dividends were declared and paid on December 31, Year 2.
- Under the temporal method, Barros's December 31, Year 1, retained earnings were translated as $561,169.

- Exchange rate information:

January 3, Year 1	CDN$1 = R1.98
February 1, Year 1	CDN$1 = R1.96
October 1, Year 1	CDN$1 = R1.94
Average, Year 1	CDN$1 = R1.95
December 31, Year 1	CDN$1 = R1.91
December 15, Year 2	CDN$1 = R1.80
Average, Year 2	CDN$1 = R1.86
December 31, Year 2	CDN$1 = R1.82

Required:
(a) Translate Barros's Year 2 financial statements into dollars, assuming that Barros's functional currency is the Canadian dollar.
(b) Assume that Barros's functional currency is the Brazilian real:
  (i) Translate the Year 2 financial statements.
  (ii) Prepare the Year 2 equity method journal entries that would be made by the Canadian parent.

Solution to Self-study Problem

(a) **Canadian dollar is functional currency**

	Reals	Rate	Dollars
Year 2			
Inventory Jan. 1	1,155,000	/ 1.94	595,361
Purchases	28,045,000	/ 1.86	15,077,956
	29,200,000		15,673,317
Inventory Dec. 31	1,050,000	/ 1.80	583,333
Cost of sales	28,150,000		15,089,984
Depreciation expense	500,000	/ 1.96	255,102
Other selling and administrative	1,940,000	/ 1.86	1,043,011
Total selling and administrative	2,440,000		1,298,113
Net monetary position			
Dec. 31, Year 1*	(650,000)	/ 1.91	(340,314)
Changes Year 2			
Sales	35,000,000	/ 1.86	18,817,204
Purchases	(28,045,000)	/ 1.86	(15,077,956)
Interest	(200,000)	/ 1.86	(107,527)
Selling and administrative	(1,940,000)**	/ 1.86	(1,043,011)
Miscellaneous expenses	(800,000)	/ 1.86	(430,108)
Income tax	(1,045,000)	/ 1.86	(561,828)
Dividends	(1,210,000)	/ 1.82	(664,835)
	1,760,000		931,939
Calculated Dec. 31, Year 2			591,625
Actual Dec. 31, Year 2***	1,110,000	/ 1.82	609,890
Exchange gain Year 2			18,265

* 500 + 2,550 − 850 − 350 − 2,500
** excluding R500,000 of depreciation expense
*** 1,000 + 2,710 − 40 − 60 − 2,500

	Reals	Rate	Dollars
Translation of Year 2 income statement			
Sales	35,000,000	/ 1.86	18,817,204
Cost of sales	28,150,000	Calc.	15,089,984
Interest	200,000	/ 1.86	107,527
Selling and administrative	2,440,000	Calc.	1,298,113
Miscellaneous expenses	800,000	/ 1.86	430,108
Income tax	1,045,000	/ 1.86	561,828
	32,635,000		17,487,560
Net income before exchange gain	2,365,000		1,329,644
Exchange gain	—		18,265
Profit	2,365,000		1,347,909
Translation of Year 2 retained earnings			
Balance Jan. 1	1,005,000	given	561,169
Profit	2,365,000	above	1,347,909
	3,370,000		1,909,078
Dividends	1,210,000	/ 1.82	664,835
Balance Dec. 31	2,160,000		1,244,243
Translation of Year 2 balance sheet			
Plant assets	6,000,000	/ 1.96	3,061,224
Accumulated depreciation	(1,000,000)	/ 1.96	(510,204)
Inventory	1,050,000	/ 1.80	583,333
Accounts receivable	2,710,000	/ 1.82	1,489,011
Cash	1,000,000	/ 1.82	549,451
	9,760,000		5,172,815
Common shares	5,000,000	/ 2.00	2,500,000
Retained earnings	2,160,000		1,244,243
Bonds payable	2,500,000	/ 1.82	1,373,627
Accrued liabilities	40,000	/ 1.82	21,978
Accounts payable	60,000	/ 1.82	32,967
	9,760,000		5,172,815

(b)(i) Brazilian real is functional currency

	Reals	Rate	Dollars
Year 1			
Net assets Jan. 1 Year 1	5,000,000	given	2,500,000
Profit — Year 1	1,005,000	/ 1.95	515,385
Calculated Dec. 31, Year 1			3,015,385
Actual net assets Dec. 31, Year 1	6,005,000	/ 1.91	3,143,979
Exchange gain Year 1 (to be reported in other comprehensive income)			128,594
Year 2			
Net assets Jan. 1, Year 2	6,005,000	/ 1.91	3,143,979
Profit — Year 2	2,365,000	/ 1.86	1,271,505
	8,370,000		4,415,484
Dividends	1,210,000	/ 1.82	664,835
Calculated Dec. 31, Year 2			3,750,649
Actual net assets Dec. 31, Year 2	7,160,000	/ 1.82	3,934,066
Exchange gain Year 2 (to be reported in other comprehensive income)			183,417

	Reals	Rate	Dollars
Cumulative translation adjustment			
Balance Dec. 31, Year 1			128,594
Exchange gain — Year 2			183,417
Balance Dec. 31, Year 2			312,011
Translation of Year 2 income statement			
Sales	35,000,000	/ 1.86	18,817,204
Cost of sales	28,150,000	/ 1.86	15,134,408
Interest	200,000	/ 1.86	107,527
Selling and administrative	2,440,000	/ 1.86	1,311,828
Miscellaneous expenses	800,000	/ 1.86	430,108
Income tax	1,045,000	/ 1.86	561,828
	32,635,000		17,545,699
Profit	2,365,000		1,271,505
Other comprehensive income —			
unrealized exchange gain			183,417
Comprehensive income			1,454,922
Translation of Year 2 retained earnings			
Balance Jan. 1	1,005,000	/ 1.95	515,384
Profit	2,365,000	/ 1.86	1,271,505
	3,370,000		1,786,889
Dividends	1,210,000	/ 1.82	664,835
Balance Dec. 31	2,160,000		1,122,054
Translation of Year 2 balance sheet			
Plant assets	6,000,000	/ 1.82	3,296,703
Accumulated depreciation	(1,000,000)	/ 1.82	(549,451)
Inventory	1,050,000	/ 1.82	576,923
Accounts receivable	2,710,000	/ 1.82	1,489,011
Cash	1,000,000	/ 1.82	549,451
	9,760,000		5,362,637
Common shares	5,000,000	/ 2.00	2,500,000
Retained earnings	2,160,000		1,122,054
Accumulated translation adjustment			312,011
Bonds payable	2,500,000	/ 1.82	1,373,627
Accrued liabilities	40,000	/ 1.82	21,978
Accounts payable	60,000	/ 1.82	32,967
	9,760,000		5,362,637

(ii) Equity method journal entries of Canadian parent — Year 2

Investment in Barros Corp.	1,144,354	
Investment income		1,144,354
90% of Year 2 translated net income (90% × 1,271,505)		
Cash	598,352	
Investment in Barros Corp.		598,352
90% of Year 2 dividends (90% × 664,835)		
Investment in Barros Corp.	165,075	
Other comprehensive income		165,075
90% of Year 2 exchange gain (90% × 183,417)		

REVIEW QUESTIONS

1. The temporal and current rate methods each produce different amounts for translation gains and losses due to the items at risk. Explain.

2. What are the three major issues related to the translation of foreign-currency financial statements?

3. Why might a company want to hedge its balance sheet exposure? What is the paradox associated with hedging balance sheet exposure?

4. How are gains and losses on financial instruments used to hedge the net investment in a self-sustaining foreign operation reported in the consolidated financial statements?

5. What is the major objective to be achieved in the translation of foreign-currency-denominated financial statements?

6. What should happen if a foreign subsidiary's financial statements have been prepared using accounting principles different from those used in Canada?

7. What is the difference between a self-sustaining and an integrated foreign operation? What method of translation should be used for each?

8. What translation method should be used for a self-sustaining subsidiary that operates in a highly inflationary environment? Why?

9. How are translation exchange gains and losses reflected in financial statements if the foreign operation's functional currency is the Canadian dollar? Would the treatment be different if the foreign operation's functional currency were not the Canadian dollar? Explain.

10. Does the temporal method use the same unit of measure as the current rate method? Explain.

11. The amount of the accumulated foreign exchange adjustments appearing in the translated financial statements of a subsidiary could be different from the amount appearing in the consolidated financial statements. Explain how.

12. The application of the lower of cost and net realizable value rule to the translated financial statements requires different treatment with regard to the two classifications of foreign operations described in IAS 21. Explain fully.

13. If the translation of an integrated foreign operation produced a gain, the translation of the same company could produce a loss if the operation were instead considered to be self-sustaining. Do you agree with this statement? Explain.

14. Explain how the temporal method produces results that are consistent with the normal measurement and valuation of assets and liabilities for domestic transactions and operations.

15. When translating the financial statements of the subsidiary at the date of acquisition by the parent, the exchange rate on the date of acquisition is used to translate plant assets rather than the exchange rate on the date when the subsidiary acquired the plant assets. Explain the rationale for this practice.

16. If the sales of a foreign subsidiary all occurred on one day during the year, would the sales be translated at the average rate for the year or the rate on the date of the sales? Explain.

MULTIPLE-CHOICE QUESTIONS

1. What happens when the temporal method of foreign-currency translation is used?
   a. Monetary assets and liabilities are translated at the historical rate.
   b. The lower of cost and net realizable value rule to determine the need for a write-down of inventory is applied after translation.
   c. Translation gains and losses are shown as a separate component of shareholders' equity.
   d. Deferred revenue is translated at the closing rate.

2. The temporal and current rate methods are being compared. Which of the following statements is true?
   a. The amount reported for inventory is normally the same under both methods.
   b. The amount reported for equipment is normally the same under both methods.
   c. The amount reported for sales is normally the same under both methods.
   d. The amount reported for depreciation expense is normally the same under both methods.

3. What rates should be used to translate the following balance sheet accounts of a self-sustaining foreign operation?

	Equipment	*Accumulated amortization — equipment*
a.	closing	closing
b.	historical	historical
c.	average for the year	closing
d.	closing	historical

4. On January 1, Year 5, REV Limited purchased 60 percent of the common shares of LON Inc. for 3 million Swiss francs (SF). Of the SF500,000 acquisition differential, SF200,000 was allocated to land and SF300,000 was allocated to bonds payable, which mature on December 31, Year 9. Lon's functional currency is the Swiss franc. During Year 5, the Swiss franc appreciated relative to the Canadian dollar. What would be the impact on return on shareholders' equity (where return is based on comprehensive income) for the Year 5 consolidated financial statements relating to the acquisition differential, if LON's functional currency were the Canadian dollar rather than the Swiss franc?
   a. It would increase.
   b. It would decrease.
   c. It would not be affected.
   d. The impact cannot be determined based on the information provided.

5. At what point in the process should a Canadian parent company adjust its foreign subsidiary's accounts to bring them into accordance with IFRSs?
   a. Prior to the beginning of the translation process.
   b. After translation, but prior to consolidation.
   c. After consolidation, but prior to reporting.
   d. No adjustments are necessary, since foreign countries already use IFRSs.

6. What rates should be used to translate the following statement of financial position accounts of an integrated foreign operation?

Equipment	*Accumulated amortization — equipment*
a. closing	closing
b. closing	average for the year
c. closing	historical
d. historical	historical

Use the following data for Questions 7 and 8.

The following balance sheet accounts of a foreign entity have been translated into Canadian dollars at the following amounts under two different methods:

	Closing	*Historical*
Accounts receivable	$264,000	$240,000
Investment in held-to-maturity bonds	132,000	120,000
Land	66,000	60,000
Patents	102,000	96,000

7. The foreign entity is considered to be integrated. What total should appear on the balance sheet of this entity's Canadian parent for these items?
    a. $516,000
    b. $540,000
    c. $552,000
    d. $564,000

8. The foreign entity is considered to be self-sustaining. What total should appear on the balance sheet of its Canadian parent for these items?
    a. $516,000
    b. $540,000
    c. $552,000
    d. $564,000

9. A Canadian company owns a self-sustaining subsidiary in Spain, where the currency is the euro (€). On January 1, Year 5, the subsidiary had €500,000 in cash and no other assets or liabilities. On January 1, the subsidiary used €100,000 to purchase equipment. On April 1, the subsidiary used cash to purchase merchandise inventory costing €80,000. This merchandise was sold on May 29 for €120,000 in cash. On November 29, the subsidiary paid cash dividends in the amount of €15,000, and on December 31 it recorded depreciation on the equipment for the year of €20,000. The appropriate exchange rates were as follows:

January 1, Year 5	€1 = $1.48
April 1, Year 5	€1 = $1.51
May 29, Year 5	€1 = $1.53
November 29, Year 5	€1 = $1.54
December 31, Year 5	€1 = $1.56
Average for Year 5	€1 = $1.52

What is the amount of the Year 5 translation adjustment to be included in accumulated foreign exchange adjustments in the shareholders' equity section of the translated statement of financial position?

a. $40,100 loss.
b. $40,100 gain.
c. $40,500 loss.
d. $40,500 gain.

Use the following data for Questions 10 and 11.

A subsidiary of a Canadian company purchased government bonds and inventory on March 1, Year 5, for 80,000 pesos (Ps) each. Both of these items were paid for on May 1, Year 5, and were still on hand at year-end. The government bonds are classified as fair value through profit or loss and are reported at their market value of Ps85,000. Inventory is carried at cost under the lower of cost and net realizable value rule. Currency exchange rates are as follows:

March 1, Year 5	Ps1 = $0.20
May 1, Year 5	Ps1 = $0.22
December 31, Year 5	Ps1 = $0.24

10. Assuming that the subsidiary is integrated, what balances are reported on the December 31, Year 5, consolidated balance sheet?
a. Government bonds = $17,000, inventory = $16,000.
b. Government bonds = $20,400, inventory = $16,000.
c. Government bonds = $17,000, inventory = $17,600.
d. Government bonds = $20,400, inventory = $17,600.

11. Assuming the subsidiary is self-sustaining, what balances are reported on the December 31, Year 4, consolidated balance sheet?
a. Government bonds = $17,000, inventory = $16,000.
b. Government bonds = $20,400, inventory = $16,000.
c. Government bonds = $17,000, inventory = $19,200.
d. Government bonds = $20,400, inventory = $19,200.

Use the following data for Questions 12 to 16.

On January 1, Year 4, Pizza purchased 100 percent of the outstanding common shares of Saza for 50,000 foreign currency units (FC). Saza is located in Zania. On January 1, Year 4, it had common shares of FC30,000 and retained earnings of FC10,000. At the date of acquisition, the acquisition differential was allocated entirely to buildings, with a remaining useful life of 20 years.

Saza's financial statements at December 31, Year 5, are shown below in the FC of its native country:

INCOME STATEMENT
for the Year Ended December 31, Year 5

Sales	FC130,000
Beginning inventory	12,000
Purchases	72,000
Ending inventory	(15,000)
Cost of goods sold	69,000
Gross profit	61,000
Operating expenses	32,000
Amortization expense	11,000
Profit	FC 18,000

STATEMENT OF FINANCIAL POSITION

Plant and equipment (net)	FC34,000
Inventory	15,000
Current monetary assets	43,000
	FC92,000
Common shares	FC30,000
Retained earnings	15,000
10% bonds payable	20,000
Current monetary liabilities	27,000
	FC92,000

Sales, purchases, and operating expenses were made evenly throughout the year. Year-end inventory was purchased at the year-end rate. Equipment additions of FC5,000 with a useful life of five years were purchased on January 1, Year 5. There were no other purchases or sales of capital assets in Year 4 or Year 5. In Year 4, Saza earned FC20,000 and paid dividends of FC18,000. In Year 5, Saza paid dividends of FC15,000. Dividends were declared and paid on December 31 of each year. The bonds payable were issued on January 1, Year 4, and mature on January 1, Year 9.

Saza's net current monetary position at December 31, Year 4, was FC10,000. Saza's retained earnings at December 31, Year 4, were FC12,000.

Exchange rates at various dates are given below.

January 1, Year 4	FC1 = $2.10
Average, Year 4	FC1 = $2.15
January 1, Year 5	FC1 = $2.20
Average, Year 5	FC1 = $2.25
December 31, Year 5	FC1 = $2.30

12. Which of the following amounts would be reported as cost of goods sold on Saza's translated financial statements at December 31, Year 5, assuming it is an integrated subsidiary?
    a. $153,900
    b. $154,500
    c. $155,250
    d. $158,700

13. Which of the following amounts would be reported as amortization expense on Saza's translated financial statements at December 31, Year 5, assuming it is an integrated subsidiary?
    a. $23,100
    b. $23,200
    c. $24,200
    d. $24,750

14. Which of the following amounts would be reported in other comprehensive income as the unrealized foreign-currency gain for the year ended December 31, Year 5, assuming Saza is a self-sustaining subsidiary?
    a. $2,100
    b. $4,100
    c. $5,100
    d. $10,100

15. Which of the following amounts would be reported as the accumulated foreign exchange adjustments on Saza's translated financial statements at December 31, Year 5, assuming it is a self-sustaining subsidiary?
    a. $5,000
    b. $5,100
    c. $6,000
    d. $10,100

16. Which of the following amounts is the translation gain that would arise from the translation of the acquisition differential on Pizza's consolidated financial statements at December 31, Year 4, and reported in other comprehensive income, assuming it is a self-sustaining operation?
    a. $0
    b. $900
    c. $950
    d. $975

(CGA-Canada adapted)

17. Brass Ltd. has a wholly owned, self-sustaining subsidiary in Eastern Asia. For the past six years, the country in which the East Asian subsidiary is located experienced a very low level of inflation. Beginning in Year 5, the country experienced hyper-inflation. What method should be used to translate the inflation-adjusted financial statements of the East Asian subsidiary for the year ended December 31, Year 5?
    a. The closing rate should be used for all financial statement items in place of the temporal method, and the change should be accounted for retroactively.
    b. The closing rate should be used for all financial statement items in place of the temporal method, and the change should be accounted for prospectively.
    c. The closing rate should be used for all financial statement items in place of the current rate method, and the change should be accounted for retroactively.
    d. The closing rate should be used for all financial statement items in place of the current rate method, and the change should be accounted for prospectively.

18. On January 1, Year 5, CAN acquired a 70 percent interest in SEN, a Swiss company, for SF500,000. On that date, the exchange rate was SF1 = C$1.07. SEN is an integrated foreign operation. In translating the financial statements of SEN at December 31, Year 5, which of the following statements on accounting exposure is true?
    a. SEN will recognize an exchange loss on translation pertaining to its investment in land if the exchange rate changes to SF1 = C$1.08.
    b. SEN will recognize an exchange loss on translation pertaining to its investment in land if the exchange rate changes to SF1 = C$1.06.
    c. SEN will recognize an exchange loss on translation pertaining to its accounts receivable if the exchange rate changes to SF1 = C$1.08.
    d. SEN will recognize an exchange loss on translation pertaining to its accounts receivable if the exchange rate changes to SF1 = C$1.06.

(CGA-Canada adapted)

19. Which of the following will result in an exchange gain being reported in profit for an integrated foreign operation?
    a. Translating notes receivable when the Canadian dollar has appreciated relative to the foreign currency.
    b. Translating notes receivable when the Canadian dollar has depreciated relative to the foreign currency.
    c. Translating land when the Canadian dollar has appreciated relative to the foreign currency.
    d. Translating land when the Canadian dollar has depreciated relative to the foreign currency.

CASES

Case 1   The Rider Corporation operates throughout Canada buying and selling widgets. In hopes of expanding into more profitable markets, the company recently decided to open a small subsidiary in California. On October 1, Year 2, Rider invested CDN$928,000 in Riderville USA Ltd. Its investment was immediately converted into US$800,000. One-half of this money was used to purchase land to be held for the possible construction of a plant and one-half was invested in equity securities.

Nothing further happened at Riderville throughout the remainder of Year 2. However, the U.S. dollar strengthened relative to the Canadian dollar and the exchange rate at December 31, Year 2, was US$1 = CDN$1.20. Fortunately, the value of the land purchased by Riderville increased to US$420,000 and the securities were worth US$425,000 at the end of the year.

The accountant for Rider realized that the investments of the U.S. subsidiary had increased in value but did not plan to report this unrealized gain in the consolidated financial statements. However, the CEO wants to report the true economic value of these investments.

Required:

(a) What is the true economic value of the assets owned by Riderville USA at the end of Year 2?

(b) Can Rider report the economic value of these assets in the consolidated balance sheet under IFRSs? If not, how should Rider report each of these assets on its consolidated balance sheet and how should the related gains be reported? Assume that the securities are classified as fair value through profit or loss.

Case 2   Summarized below are the balances in the accumulated unrealized exchange accounts in the consolidated balance sheets of four companies at the end of two successive years. Each company reported in footnote disclosures that its foreign subsidiaries were self-sustaining and that the financial statements of the subsidiaries had been translated into Canadian dollars using the current rate method. Assume that the balance sheets of each of the companies' foreign subsidiaries have not changed significantly during Year 6.

	Accumulated unrealized exchange gains (losses) (millions of dollars)	
	Year 6	Year 5
A Company	201	30
B Company	52	(75)
C Company	(170)	(100)
D Company	(18)	(164)

Required:

For each company, give a logical explanation for the change that has occurred in the accumulated unrealized exchange accounts during the year. For each company, indicate whether the Canadian dollar is stronger or weaker in Year 6, compared with Year 5.

Case 3   Nova Mine Engineering is a junior Canadian company with a variety of operating subsidiaries and other undertakings that provide mine engineering and management services in Canada and in several less developed countries. One of these subsidiaries is active in Zimbabwe, which is rich in mineral resources and has an active mining industry. This company, Zimbabwe Platinum Management (ZPM), is under review prior to year-end translation and consolidation. The staff of ZPM consists primarily of junior and intermediate Nova staff who have been seconded to the operation on one- to three-year terms. Between the companies there is information flow but no product movement. Capital investment in Zimbabwe is restricted to movable equipment and working capital with a value of about CDN$3,000,000.

Management of Nova has long been concerned about its inability to hedge against fluctuations in the Zimbabwean dollar. All payments to ZPM from the state Mineral Marketing Corporation have recently been made in this currency, rather than in U.S. dollars as specified in earlier contracts. It is this inability to hedge that has increased Nova's concern about the long-run fit of ZPM within the portfolio of Nova companies, and about current financial statement presentation. The currency has declined in value by 65 percent during the year. Other concerns include Zimbabwe's persistent high inflation, recently about 35 percent, which is expected to increase even further. Political uncertainty is also a concern, as a result of recent nationalizations in the agricultural sector and growing unrest among the poor.

Required:

In a briefing note, advise senior management of Nova how the investment in the subsidiary ZPM should be measured and reported, and what disclosures should be made with respect to this investment in the annual report of the parent company.
(case prepared by Peter Secord, St. Mary's University)

Case 4   Vulcan Manufacturing Limited (VML) is a Canadian-based multinational plastics firm, with subsidiaries in several foreign countries and worldwide consolidated total assets of $500 million. VML's shares are listed on a Canadian stock exchange.

VML is attracted by the growing demand for its products in developing countries. In recognition of trade barriers designed to encourage domestic production in those countries and in order to service local demand, VML incorporated a foreign subsidiary in a South American country on September 1, Year 4. The subsidiary, South American Plastics Inc. (SAPI), manufactures patented sheet plastic and sells virtually all of its output locally. Also, almost all labour and raw materials are provided locally. SAPI finances its day-to-day activities from its own operations and local borrowing.

During Year 4 and Year 5, the South American country suffered an inflation rate of more than 100 percent, accompanied by substantial devaluation of the local currency and a drastic increase in interest rates. The government is expected to impose wage and price controls in Year 6. The inflation rate is expected to stabilize at more moderate levels sometime in Year 6 or Year 7.

The CFO of VML has recently received SAPI's draft balance sheet as at August 31, Year 5 (Exhibit I), together with some comments prepared by SAPI's controller (Exhibit II on page 614). He is somewhat surprised by the return on investment of nearly 12 percent. This figure is well above the target rate agreed upon for bonus purposes, which was set at 3 percent in recognition of start-up costs associated with the first year of operations. The apparently favourable performance will result in large bonuses having to be paid to SAPI's management.

Increases in SAPI's domestic selling price have kept pace with the general rate of inflation and with increases in input prices and borrowing costs in the South American country. The CFO is satisfied that the inflation and devaluation the country has experienced has not seriously affected SAPI's cash flows from operations.

In the annual report to Canadian shareholders for the year ended August 31, Year 5, the CFO wants to communicate to shareholders the economic impact that inflation and devaluation in the South American country have had on VML's investment in SAPI. He is concerned that gains or losses arising from translation of the statements in accordance with IAS 21 will mislead shareholders. The CFO believes that the exchange gains and losses will obscure the true impact of foreign inflation and devaluation on SAPI's economic value in Canadian dollar terms. He has called the audit partner and you, Senior, into his office. The following conversation ensues:

CFO: We have to issue our financial statements soon, and we have to apply IAS 21 to our South American subsidiary. I must confess that I don't know

---

Exhibit I

SOUTH AMERICAN PLASTICS INC.
Extracts from draft balance sheet
as at August 31, Year 5
(in 000s)

Assets

Cash	FC* 10,020
Held-to-maturity investments	3,120
Accounts receivable	93,000
Inventory (at cost)	67,200
Prepaid expenses	8,040
	181,380
Plant assets	143,111
Less accumulated depreciation	14,311
	128,800
	FC 310,180

Liabilities and Shareholders' Equity

Current monetary liabilities	FC 65,140
Long-term debt	157,200
	222,340
Common shares	51,000
Retained earnings	36,840
	87,840
	FC 310,180

* An FC is a unit of the currency used in the South American country in which SAPI is located.

Exhibit II

SOUTH AMERICAN PLASTICS INC.
Controller's comments on financial statements

1. Opening Balances
    SAPI's balance sheet on September 1, Year 4, consisted of cash of FC208,200,000, long-term debt of FC157,200,000, and common shares of FC51,000,000.

2. Held-to-maturity Investments
    The held-to-maturity investments were purchased when 1FC = $0.30. The aggregate market value for the investments at August 31, Year 5, was FC3,000,000 due to an increase in interest rates in the market.

3. Inventories
    Inventories were purchased when 1FC = $0.30. VML values inventory at the lower of cost and net realizable value. The aggregate net realizable value of the inventory was FC100,000,000 at August 31, Year 5.

4. Prepaid Expenses
    The amounts, representing prepaid rent and property taxes, were paid when 1FC = $0.25.

5. Plant Assets
    Plant assets were purchased shortly after the date of SAPI's formation at a time when 1FC = $0.40. The recoverable amount of the fixed assets (in their current condition) was FC200,000,000 at August 31, Year 5.

6. Current Liabilities
    All current liabilities were incurred at a time when 1FC = $0.25.

7. Long-term Debt
    The debt represents a floating interest rate loan, which will be repaid in foreign currency units on August 31, Year 8.

8. Retained Earnings
    No dividends were paid during the Year 5 fiscal year.

9. Exchange Rates

September 1, Year 4	1 FCU = $0.40
August 31, Year 5	1 FCU = $0.20
Average rate for year	1 FCU = $0.30

IAS 21 as well as you two do. My staff tells me that we must use a special method this year, due to the local hyper-inflation, although I confess that I don't see why. Apparently we will have a choice between the temporal method and the current rate method once the inflation rate stabilizes, which I expect to happen in Year 6 or Year 7. I am very reluctant to use a special method on this year's statements. It forces me to include fictitious gains and losses in our consolidated income statement.

Partner: Your staff is correct in stating that IAS 21 requires the use of a special method for the year just ended. However, shareholders should not be misled by exchange gains or losses in comprehensive income provided that they are fully disclosed as such.

CFO: I guess I just do not understand IAS 21. For example, how might the adoption of the current rate method in Year 6 or Year 7 improve matters? It seems to me that an overall exchange loss will arise if the rate keeps on going down. What does the loss mean? As long as our subsidiary's cash flows keep pace with local inflation, it will be able to maintain its expected rate of profitability and therefore its ability to pay dividends to us. Yet shareholders will see an exchange loss!

Partner: I will have Senior prepare a report that explains to you how the exchange gains or losses under either translation method tie in with the notion of risk underlying IAS 21. We will also explain how this notion alleviates your concern about communicating the true economic risk to shareholders. Senior will recommend ways to tell the whole story to shareholders.

CFO: Sounds great. I would also like Senior to provide advice on any other important issues related to SAPI. For starters, I have some concerns about the way our bonus plan for SAPI's management is working. One possibility I am considering is to evaluate SAPI's performance in Canadian dollar terms.

Required:

Prepare the report to the CFO.

(*CICA adapted*)

Case 5 RAD Communications Ltd. (RAD), a Canadian public company, recently purchased the shares of TOP Systems Inc. (TOP), a Canadian-controlled private corporation. Both companies are in the communications industry and own television, radio, and magazine and newspaper businesses. Both companies have subsidiaries operating worldwide.

After it purchased TOP, RAD decided to divest itself of some of the TOP subsidiaries (the Group).

BritCo is a private British company that is in the process of acquiring from TOP the shares of the Group. The purchase price for the Group being sold has been determined, in general terms, to be a fixed price adjusted for the working capital balance of the Group at RAD's year-end date of March 31, Year 9. March 31, Year 9, was also the closing date of the purchase-and-sale transaction. The parties have 90 days after the closing date of the transaction to agree on the calculation of the working capital balance.

Janis Marczynski, the chief negotiator for BritCo, has approached Paul Bouchard, a partner at Bouchard and Beatrix, Chartered Accountants (B&B), to provide her with advice on the purchase transaction. Specifically, Marczynski wants B&B to review the agreement and relevant facts to determine whether RAD has appropriately determined the amount of the closing working capital. Furthermore, if any matters come to B&B's attention that suggest the financial statements of the Group may have misled BritCo, then B&B should bring these items to her attention.

Marczynski has stated that BritCo now thinks that the purchase price for the Group may be too high and is looking for ways to reduce the price. Thus, she wants to be made aware of any possible points that she can use in her final negotiations.

BritCo has provided B&B with a copy of the purchase-and-sale agreement, excerpts of which are presented in Exhibit I on page 616.

It is now May 15, Year 9, and BritCo has received the unaudited consolidated working capital statement of the Group prepared by RAD (see Exhibit II on page 616). Marczynski is concerned about the dramatic increase in the working capital compared to that reflected in previous financial statements.

Exhibit I

TOP SYSTEMS INC. (VENDOR) AND BRITCO (PURCHASER) EXCERPTS FROM PURCHASE-AND-SALE AGREEMENT

5.1. The share purchase price shall be adjusted by an amount equal to the "consolidated working capital." This amount is hereafter referred to as the "price adjustment," as defined in clause 5.2.

5.2. The price adjustment shall be determined as follows:

    a. Combine the working capital of the Group (aggregated current assets of the Group less aggregated current liabilities of the Group), less the non-controlling interest as at March 31, Year 9, adjusted for any sums payable to or receivable from other members of the Group.

    b. Include accounts for each of the companies of the Group and, in the case of those companies with subsidiaries, on a consolidated basis, in accordance with International Financial Reporting Standards ("IFRSs").

5.3. The vendor shall prepare a draft consolidated working capital statement as soon as practicable after the agreement date.

5.4. For the purpose of review, the vendor agrees to instruct JR to permit the purchaser to examine all final working papers, schedules, and other documents used or prepared by JR.

5.5. If the purchaser objects to the calculation of the price adjustment, the purchaser shall give notice in writing to the vendor. The purchaser shall set out in reasonable detail the nature of any such objections and the amount by which the purchase price will be reduced if the purchaser's objections are accepted. The vendor shall have the right to recover from the purchaser any costs associated with reviewing and analyzing objections of the purchaser that are of a frivolous and unsupportable nature.

Exhibit II

CONSOLIDATED WORKING CAPITAL STATEMENT OF THE GROUP (NOTE 1)
At March 31, Year 9
(in millions of Canadian dollars)

Current assets	
Cash	$ 215
Receivables	19,763
Inventory	4,225
Prepaids	7,655
Other	2,917
	34,775
Current liabilities	
Bank indebtedness	7,000
Accounts payable	1,191
Deferred revenue	6,332
Other	1,345
	15,868
Consolidated working capital (price adjustment)	$18,907

Note 1: Comprises the accounts of the companies being sold, i.e., GermanyCo., FranceCo., U.K.Co., SwitzerlandCo., and a Canadian subsidiary, CanadaCo.

RAD has arranged for Jeanette Riley, Chartered Accountant (JR), the auditor of TOP's financial statements for the year in question, to supply the necessary working papers to assist B&B in its review. JR will provide B&B with her working papers once they have completed their audit for Year 9. RAD has already provided

B&B with excerpts of JR's working papers for Year 8, reproduced in Exhibit III, copies of which TOP had obtained informally from the audit staff during the course of the audit.

You, CA, work for B&B. Bouchard asks you to draft a memo addressing the concerns and requirements of Marczynski.

Required:

Prepare the memo.

(CICA adapted)

Exhibit III

EXCERPTS FROM THE WORKING PAPERS OF JR
RELATING TO THE AUDIT OF TOP SYSTEMS INC. AND ITS SUBSIDIARIES
FOR THE YEAR 8 FISCAL PERIOD

1. Only selected subsidiaries of TOP were audited. Those companies were audited on a limited basis only, owing to the consolidated materiality level.
2. Included in the "Receivables" balance of FranceCo. is an intercompany note receivable from a Canadian company that is not part of the Group. The note bears interest at the prime rate in Canada plus 3 percent. The rate charged on the note was generally about 4 percent below interest rates on French notes of similar terms and risks at the time that the note was issued. The Canadian company has recorded the note as a long-term obligation.
3. "Other current assets" include an amount reflecting the refundable dividend tax on hand (RDTOH). The amount of the RDTOH was immaterial; thus, no audit work in this area was warranted.
4. Included in the "Receivables" balance are certain income tax refunds that GermanyCo. will receive when dividends are paid to its shareholders. No accruals are made for foreign withholding taxes that may be payable when dividends are paid by GermanyCo.
5. "Other current assets" include an amount for goodwill. This goodwill relates to the acquisition of a subsidiary by CanadaCo.
6. "Deferred revenues" include payments made by advertisers for long-term contracts. Some of these contracts can be for up to five years. Some advertisers pay up-front signing fees, which are taken into income when received. Some advertisers who sign up for long-term contracts may receive one additional year of free advertising. Advertisers can elect to take this free year at the beginning or at the end of the contract term.
7. "Prepaids" include costs for various broadcasting licences. The accounts include the initial costs of obtaining the licences, such as various regulatory fees, legal and accounting fees, other consulting fees, etc., and various fees for limited-term licences, ranging from one- to ten-year periods.
8. Certain printing presses of SwitzerlandCo. were leased instead of being purchased. The future lease payments were not disclosed in the consolidated financial statements. The lease was immaterial and thus did not warrant any further audit work.
9. A Belgian company that is not being acquired effectively hedged certain current debts payable by CanadaCo. The financial statements did not record any gain or loss because of the fluctuations in the value of the Canadian dollar.
10. Foreign-exchange losses on transactions were included as part of "Deferred revenue," while gains were taken into income in the current period.

PROBLEMS

Note: Some problems use direct exchange rate quotations, while others use indirect quotations. For direct quotations, the foreign currency is multiplied by the exchange rate to arrive at Canadian dollars; for indirect quotations, division is used.

Problem 1   On December 31, Year 1, Precision Manufacturing Inc. (PMI) of Edmonton purchased 100 percent of the outstanding common shares of Sandora Corp. of Flint, Michigan.

Sandora's comparative statement of financial position and Year 2 income statement are as follows:

STATEMENT OF FINANCIAL POSITION
at December 31

	Year 2	Year 1
Plant and equipment (net)	US$ 6,600,000	US$ 7,300,000
Inventory	5,700,000	6,300,000
Accounts receivable	6,100,000	4,700,000
Cash	780,000	900,000
	US$19,180,000	US$19,200,000
Common shares	US$ 5,000,000	US$ 5,000,000
Retained earnings	7,480,000	7,000,000
Bonds payable — due Dec. 31, Year 6	4,800,000	4,800,000
Current liabilities	1,900,000	2,400,000
	US$19,180,000	US$19,200,000

INCOME STATEMENT
for the Year Ended December 31, Year 2

Sales	US$30,000,000
Cost of purchases	23,400,000
Change in inventory	600,000
Depreciation expense	700,000
Other expenses	3,800,000
	28,500,000
Profit	US$ 1,500,000

Additional Information
- Exchange rates

December 31, Year 1	US$1 = CDN$1.10
September 30, Year 2	US$1 = CDN$1.07
December 31, Year 2	US$1 = CDN$1.05
Average for Year 2	US$1 = CDN$1.08

- Sandora declared and paid dividends on September 30, Year 2.
- The inventories on hand on December 31, Year 2, were purchased when the exchange rate was US$1 = CDN$1.06.

Required:

(a) Assume that Sandora's functional currency is the Canadian dollar.
  (i) Calculate the Year 2 exchange gain (loss) that would result from the translation of Sandora's financial statements.
  (ii) Translate the Year 2 financial statements into Canadian dollars.
(b) Assume that Sandora's functional currency is the U.S. dollar.
  (i) Calculate the Year 2 exchange gain (loss) that would result from the translation of Sandora's financial statements and would be reported in other comprehensive income.
  (ii) Translate the Year 2 financial statements into Canadian dollars.
(c) Which functional currency would Sandora prefer to use if it wants to show
  (i) the strongest solvency position for the company?
  (ii) the best return on shareholders' equity?
  Briefly explain your answers.

Problem 2 On December 31, Year 1, Kelly Corporation of Toronto paid 13 million Libyan dinars (LD) for 100 percent of the outstanding common shares of Arkenu Company of Libya. On this date, the fair values of Arkenu's identifiable assets and liabilities were equal to their carrying values. Arkenu's comparative balance sheets and Year 2 income statement are as follows:

BALANCE SHEET
at December 31

	Year 2	Year 1
Current monetary assets	LD10,780,000	LD 9,600,000
Inventory	1,800,000	2,400,000
Plant and equipment (net)	6,600,000	7,200,000
	LD19,180,000	LD19,200,000
Current monetary liabilities	LD 1,900,000	LD 2,400,000
Bonds payable, due Dec. 31, Year 6	4,800,000	4,800,000
Common shares	5,000,000	5,000,000
Retained earnings	7,480,000	7,000,000
	LD19,180,000	LD19,200,000

INCOME STATEMENT
for the Year Ended December 31, Year 2

Sales	LD16,000,000
Inventory, January 1	2,400,000
Purchases	10,840,000
Inventory, December 31	(1,800,000)
Depreciation expense	600,000
Other expenses	2,360,000
	14,400,000
Net income	LD 1,600,000

Additional Information

- Exchange rates

December 31, Year 1	LD1 = $0.52
September 30, Year 2	LD1 = $0.62
December 31, Year 2	LD1 = $0.65
Average for Year 2	LD1 = $0.58

- Arkenu Company declared and paid dividends on September 30, Year 2.
- The inventories on hand on December 31, Year 2, were purchased when the exchange rate was LD1 = $0.63.

Required:

(a) Assume that Arkenu's functional currency is the Canadian dollar.
   (i) Calculate the Year 2 exchange gain or loss that would result from the translation of Arkenu's financial statements.
   (ii) Prepare translated financial statements for Year 2.

(b) Assume that Arkenu's functional currency is the Libyan dinar.
   (i) Calculate the Year 2 exchange gain or loss that would result from the translation of Arkenu's financial statements.
   (ii) Prepare translated financial statements for Year 2.
   (iii) Calculate the amount of goodwill that would appear on the December 31, Year 2, consolidated balance sheet if there was an impairment loss of LD50,000 during the year.
   (iv) Calculate the amount, description, and location of the exchange gain or loss that would appear in Kelly's Year 2 consolidated financial statements.

(c) Which functional currency would Arkenu prefer to use if it wants to show
   (i) the strongest solvency position for the company?
   (ii) the best return on shareholders' equity?
   Briefly explain your answers.

Problem 3 On January 1, Year 3, Jets Ltd., a Winnipeg-based company, purchased 80 percent of the shares of Buenos Inc. for 1,900,000 argentine pesos (AP) — an amount which, at that date, translated to $655,172.

The Year 3 financial statements for Buenos are as follows:

BALANCE SHEET
at December 31, Year 3

Cash	AP 820,000
Accounts receivable	317,500
Inventory	730,000
Plant assets, net	1,722,500
	AP3,590,000
Current monetary liabilities	AP 380,000
Notes payable	700,000
Common shares	900,000
Retained earnings	1,610,000
	AP3,590,000

INCOME STATEMENT
for the Year Ended December 31, Year 3

Sales	AP10,350,000
Cost of sales	6,400,000
Gross profit	3,950,000
Other expenses	3,490,000
Net income	AP 460,000

Additional Information

- The FIFO inventory method is used. The opening inventory, which was purchased before December 31, Year 2, cost AP600,000. The exchange rate at the time of inventory purchase was $1 = AP2.71.
  The purchases during the year were:

	AP	Exchange rate
Purchase Number 1	2,000,000	$1 = AP3.0
Purchase Number 2	4,530,000	$1 = AP3.12

- The plant assets were purchased when the company was formed (January 1, Year 1). The common shares were issued at the same time. The exchange rate at that date was $1 = AP1.5. The cost of the plant assets is AP2,450,000, and the accumulated depreciation is AP727,500 at December 31, Year 3. Depreciation expense of AP122,500 is included with other expenses.
- The notes payable are due on January 1, Year 7, and were issued on December 31, Year 2. There is no interest on these notes.
- The "sales" and "other expenses" on the income statement were incurred evenly throughout the year.
- The dividends of AP200,000 were paid on December 31, Year 3.
- The balances in pesos at December 31, Year 2, were as follows:

Cash	AP 350,000
Accounts receivable	AP 405,000
Current monetary liabilities	AP(250,000)
Notes payable	AP(700,000)

- Exchange rates:

December 31, Year 2	$1 = AP2.9
January 1, Year 3	$1 = AP2.9
Year 3 average	$1 = AP3.25
December 31, Year 3	$1 = AP3.6

Required:

(a) There will be a foreign-exchange gain or loss on the translated income statement prepared in part (b). Prepare a schedule to calculate the foreign-exchange gain or loss under the temporal method.

(b) Prepare the Canadian dollar income statement for Buenos for Year 3, using the temporal method and assuming that the income statement will be used to consolidate with Jets Ltd.

(CGA-Canada adapted)

Problem 4   On January 1, Year 1, P Company (a Canadian company) purchased 90 percent of S Company (located in a foreign country) at a cost of 14,400 foreign currency units (FC).

The book values of S Company's net assets were equal to fair values on this date except for plant and equipment, which had a fair value of FC22,000, with a remaining useful life of 10 years. A goodwill impairment loss of FC100 occurred evenly throughout Year 1.

The following exchange rates were in effect during Year 1:

January 1	FC1 = $1.10
Average for year	FC1 = $1.16
When ending inventory purchased	FC1 = $1.19
December 31	FC1 = $1.22

The statement of financial position of S Company on January 1, Year 1, is as follows:

	S Company (FC)
Plant and equipment (net)	20,000
Inventory	8,000
Monetary assets (current)	10,000
	38,000
Common shares	10,000
Retained earnings	3,000
Bonds payable (mature in eight years)	16,000
Current liabilities	9,000
	38,000

The December 31, Year 1, financial statements of P Company (in $) and S Company (in FC) are shown below:

STATEMENT OF FINANCIAL POSITION

	P Company $	S Company FC
Plant and equipment (net)	60,000	18,000
Investment in S Company (at cost)	15,840	—
Inventory	30,000	11,000
Monetary assets (current)	31,552	17,000
	137,392	46,000
Common shares	30,000	10,000
Retained earnings	41,392	8,000
Bonds payable	40,000	16,000
Current monetary liabilities	26,000	12,000
	137,392	46,000

INCOME STATEMENT

	P Company $	S Company FC
Sales	360,000	100,000
Dividend income	4,392	—
Cost of sales	(180,000)	(59,000)
Other expenses (including depreciation)	(155,000)	(32,000)
Profit	29,392	9,000

Dividends were declared on December 31, Year 1, in the amount of $22,000 by P Company and FC4,000 by S Company.

Required:

Prepare the December 31, Year 1, consolidated financial statements, assuming that S Company's functional currency is

(a) the Canadian dollar.

(b) the foreign-currency unit.

Problem 5   Mex Ltd. is an integrated foreign subsidiary. At the end of the current year, the inventory of the company was as follows:

Cost	14,862,000 pesos
Net realizable value	12,100,000 pesos

Applying the lower of cost and net realizable value, the company wrote the inventory down by Ps2,762,000 for presentation in its financial statements. When these financial statements were received by the parent company in Canada for translation, it was determined that the year-end spot rate was $1 = Ps392. The closing inventory at cost is composed of the following:

Purchase	Amount in pesos	Historical exchange rate
1	3,200,000	$1 = Ps341
2	6,132,000	$1 = Ps360
3	5,530,000	$1 = Ps375

Required:

(a) At what amount would the inventory be shown on the translated balance sheet of Mex? And what amount of loss from write-down would appear on the translated income statement?

(b) If the year-end spot rate was $1 = Ps281, at what amount would the inventory be shown on the translated balance sheet? And what amount of loss from write-down would appear on the translated income statement?

(CGA-Canada adapted)

Problem 6   Maple Limited (Maple) was incorporated on January 2, Year 1, and commenced active operations immediately in Greece. Common shares were issued on the date of incorporation for 100,000 euros (€), and no more common shares have been issued since then.

On December 31, Year 4, the Oak Company (Oak) purchased 100 percent of the outstanding common shares of Maple.

The balance sheet for Maple at December 31, Year 10, was as follows:

Cash	€ 100,000
Accounts receivable (Note 1)	200,000
Inventory (Note 2)	300,000
Equipment — net (Note 3)	1,100,000
	€1,700,000
Accounts payable	€ 250,000
Bonds payable (Note 4)	700,000
Common shares	100,000
Retained earnings	650,000
	€1,700,000

Additional Information

- The accounts receivable relate to sales occurring evenly throughout the month of December, Year 10.
- Maple uses the FIFO method to account for its inventory. The inventory available for sale during the year was purchased as follows:

Date of purchase	Cost of purchase	Exchange rate
December 31, Year 9	€100,000	€1 = $1.56
March 1, Year 10	1,000,000	€1 = $1.60
November 1, Year 10	180,000	€1 = $1.63

- The equipment was purchased on May 26, Year 4.
- The bonds were issued on May 26, Year 4, to finance the purchase of the equipment.
- Maple reported net income of €200,000, which was earned evenly throughout the year and paid dividends of €160,000 on July 1, Year 10.
- Foreign-exchange rates were as follows:

January 2, Year 1	€1 = $1.30
May 26, Year 4	€1 = $1.40
December 31, Year 4	€1 = $1.42
December 31, Year 9	€1 = $1.56
July 1, Year 10	€1 = $1.61
Average for Year 10	€1 = $1.59
Average for December Year 10	€1 = $1.64
December 31, Year 10	€1 = $1.65

Required:

(a) Translate the balance sheet of Maple at December 31, Year 10, into Canadian dollars assuming that Maple's functional currency is the Canadian dollar. Assume that the translated balance sheet will be consolidated with Oak's balance sheet. For retained earnings, simply use the amount required to balance your balance sheet.

(b) Calculate the foreign-exchange gain or loss on the bonds payable for the year ended December 31, Year 10, and state how it would be reported on the year-end financial statements.

(c) Prepare an independent calculation of the unrealized exchange gains or losses that would be reported in other comprehensive income for Year 10 assuming that Maple's functional currency is the euro.

(d) Since the current rate method uses the closing rate to translate equipment, the translated amount should represent the fair value of the equipment in Canadian dollars. Do you agree or disagree? Briefly explain.

(CGA-Canada adapted)

Problem 7 In preparation for translating the financial statements of a foreign subsidiary that is highly integrated with its Canadian parent, you have the following information:

	FC
Inventory (FIFO cost, net realizable value of FC1,300,000)	1,150,000

An examination of the working papers of the foreign subsidiary's auditor shows the following information:

Opening inventory	FC 350,000
Purchases	
February 15, Year 3	205,000
April 15, Year 3	588,000
August 1, Year 3	410,000
October 12, Year 3	362,000
November 15, Year 3	547,000
Cost of goods sold for the year	1,312,000

Exchange rates:

January 1, Year 3 (opening inventory)	$1 = FC2.5
February 15, Year 3	$1 = FC3.1
April 15, Year 3	$1 = FC3.4
August 1, Year 3	$1 = FC4.3
October 12, Year 3	$1 = FC4.8
November 15, Year 3	$1 = FC5.5
December 31, Year 3	$1 = FC6.1
Year 3 average	$1 = FC4.0

Note: This is not considered excessive or high inflation in terms of the temporal method.

Required:

(a) Calculate the Canadian dollar amount of the inventory at the fiscal year-end (December 31), and the Canadian dollar amount of any item(s) that would appear on the income statement.

(b) If the foreign subsidiary were self-sustaining, what would your answer to part (a) be?

(c) Define accounting exposure and describe its impact on the translation of financial statement items in this problem.

(CGA-Canada adapted)

Problem 8 On December 31, Year 2, PAT Inc. of Halifax, Nova Scotia, acquired 90 percent of the voting shares of Gioco Limited of Italy, for 690,000 euros (€). On the acquisition date, the fair values equalled the carrying values for all of Gioco's identifiable assets and liabilities.

Selected account balances from Gioco's general ledger on December 31, Year 2, were as follows:

Equipment	€ 250,000
Building	1,350,000
Accumulated amortization	195,000
Common shares	600,000
Retained earnings	96,000

Gioco purchased the building and equipment on January 1, Year 1.

The condensed trial balance of Gioco for the year ending December 31, Year 5, was as follows:

Accounts receivable	€ 197,000
Inventory	255,000
Building	1,350,000
Equipment	350,000
Cost of goods purchased	1,080,000
Change in inventory	120,000
Amortization expense	130,000
Other expenses	470,000
Dividends paid	300,000
Total debits	€4,252,000
Current monetary liabilities	€ 682,000
Common shares	600,000
Retained earnings, beginning	300,000
Sales	2,250,000
Accumulated amortization	420,000
Total credits	€4,252,000

Additional Information

- Gioco's sales, inventory purchases, and other expenses occurred uniformly over the year.
- Gioco's inventory on hand at the end of each year was purchased uniformly over the last quarter of the year. On December 31, Year 4, the inventories totalled €375,000, and on December 31, Year 5, they totalled €255,000.
- On January 1, Year 5, Gioco purchased equipment for €100,000. The equipment has an estimated useful life of eight years and a residual value of €5,000. Gioco uses the double-declining-balance method to calculate amortization expense. There were no other purchases of property, plant, and equipment between Year 2 and Year 5.
- The dividends were declared and paid on January 1, Year 5.
- The exchange rates for the euro and the Canadian dollar were as follows:

January 1, Year 1	$1 = €0.50
December 31, Year 2	$1 = €0.60
Average for the Year 4 fourth quarter	$1 = €0.68
December 31, Year 4/January 1, Year 5	$1 = €0.70
December 31, Year 5	$1 = €0.80
Average for Year 5	$1 = €0.76
Average for the Year 5 fourth quarter	$1 = €0.79

Required:

(a) Translate into Canadian dollars the following items on Gioco's financial statements for the year ended December 31, Year 5, assuming that Gioco's functional currency is the Canadian dollar.
  (i)   Accounts receivable.
  (ii) Inventory.
  (iii) Equipment.
  (iv) Accumulated amortization.
  (v)   Common shares.

CHAPTER 11 TRANSLATION AND CONSOLIDATION OF THE FINANCIAL STATEMENTS OF FOREIGN OPERATIONS **627**

(b) Translate into Canadian dollars the following items on Gioco's financial statements for the year ended December 31, Year 5, assuming that Gioco's functional currency is the euro.
  (i) Cost of goods purchased.
  (ii) Amortization expense.
  (iii) Inventory.
  (iv) Common shares.
(c) Prepare an independent calculation of the unrealized exchange gains or losses to be included in other comprehensive income for Year 5, assuming that Gioco's functional currency is the euro.
(d) For integrated foreign operations, the reporting enterprise's exposure to exchange rate changes is similar to the exposure that would exist had the transactions and activities of the foreign operation been undertaken by the reporting enterprise. Therefore, the financial statements of the foreign operation should be expressed in a manner that is consistent with the measurement of domestic transactions and operations.

Explain how the temporal method used in translating foreign operations is consistent with the measurement of assets and liabilities for domestic transactions and operations.

(CGA-Canada adapted)

Problem 9   Dom Ltd. has a subsidiary, Tarzan Inc., in a country that uses the tar (Tz) as its currency. Before this 100-percent-owned subsidiary can be consolidated, the financial statements must be translated from tars to Canadian dollars. However, the person responsible for the translation has quit suddenly and left you with a half-finished job. Certain information is available but the rest you must determine.

TARZAN INC.
FINANCIAL STATEMENTS (IN TZ)
December 31, Year 4

Land	Tz 500,000
Buildings (Note 1)	800,000
Accumulated depreciation	(300,000)
Inventory (Note 2)	400,000
Accounts receivable	200,000
Cash	100,000
	Tz1,700,000
Common shares	Tz 300,000
Retained earnings	750,000
Note payable (Note 3)	400,000
Accounts payable	250,000
	Tz1,700,000
Sales	Tz5,200,000
Cost of goods sold	3,100,000
	2,100,000
Other expenses (including depreciation of 80,000)	(1,950,000)
Profit	Tz 150,000

Additional Information

1. There were two buildings and one piece of land. The land and building 1 (Tz300,000) were acquired when Tarzan was formed by Dom. The exchange rate at that time was $1 = Tz2. Building 2 was acquired when the exchange rate was $1 = Tz3.2. The depreciation expense is proportional to the purchase prices. The accumulated depreciation relating to Building 2 is Tz200,000.
2. The opening inventory was Tz500,000, and the purchases during the period were Tz3,000,000. Tarzan uses a periodic FIFO inventory system. The opening inventory had an exchange rate of $1 = Tz3.5, and the purchases were made 30 percent from the parent and 70 percent from the local area. The local area purchases were made evenly throughout the year; the purchases from the parent were recorded by the parent at $232,558. The ending inventory was purchased when the exchange rate was $1 = Tz4.0.
3. The note payable, which is due on January 1, Year 8, was created on July 1, Year 4.
4. The retained earnings at January 1, Year 4, translated into $181,818.
5. The other expenses were incurred evenly throughout the year.
6. No dividends were declared during the year:
7. Exchange rates:

January 1, Year 4	$1 = Tz3.7
2004 average, July 1, Year 4	$1 = Tz3.9
December 31, Year 4	$1 = Tz4.1

Required:

(a) Assume that Tarzan's functional currency is the Canadian dollar. Prepare the financial statements of Tarzan in Canadian dollars. Show your calculations *in good form*.

(b) If the net realizable value of the ending inventory was Tz350,000, what would the Canadian dollar value of the inventory be? Assume all the other information given in the question remains constant.

(CGA-Canada adapted)

Problem 10 In Year 1, Victoria Textiles Limited decided that its Asian operations had expanded such that an Asian office should be established. The office would be involved in selling Victoria's current product lines; it was also expected to establish supplier contacts. In the Asian market, there were a number of small manufacturers of top-quality fabrics, particularly silk and lace, but from Victoria's home office in Ontario it was difficult to find and maintain these suppliers. To assist in doing so, a wholly owned company, Victoria Textiles (India) Limited, was created, and a facility was established in India in January Year 2. The new company, VTIL, was given the mandate from head office to buy and sell with other Victoria divisions and offices across Canada, as if it were an autonomous, independent unit. To establish the company, an investment of 10,000,000 Indian rupees (IR) was made on January 1, Year 2.

VTIL proved to be quite successful, as shown in the following financial statements at December 31, Year 4. After one year of operations, VTIL had borrowed funds and expanded facilities substantially, as the initial market estimates had turned out to be quite conservative. However, during this time the rupee had fallen in value relative to the Canadian dollar. As a result, Victoria's management was somewhat confused about how to evaluate VTIL's success, given the changing currency values.

FINANCIAL STATEMENTS
(000s, Indian rupees)

BALANCE SHEETS

	Year 4	Year 3
Cash	4,100	3,900
Accounts receivable	2,900	2,100
Inventories	4,800	3,500
Prepaid expenses	1,900	1,700
Plant assets (net)	7,900	8,900
	21,600	20,100
Current monetary liabilities	2,400	900
Unearned revenue	800	500
Long-term debt	6,000	6,000
	9,200	7,400
Common shares	10,000	10,000
Retained earnings	2,400	2,700
	21,600	20,100

INCOME STATEMENTS

	Year 4	Year 3
Sales	20,200	12,000
Cost of sales	11,300	6,300
Gross profit	8,900	5,700
Operating expenses	4,400	2,800
Interest	700	400
Taxes	600	400
Net income	3,200	2,100

Additional Information
- The exchange rate at January 1, Year 2, when VTIL was originally established, was $0.075 per rupee.
- Of the original investment of IR10 million, IR4 million was used to acquire plant and equipment, which is being depreciated on a straight-line basis over 10 years.
- At June 30, Year 3, an expansion was completed at a cost of IR6 million, which was financed entirely by a six-year note obtained from an Indian bank. Interest is to be paid semiannually. The exchange rate at July 1, Year 3, was $0.062 per rupee. The new expansion is also to be depreciated on a straight-line basis over 10 years. (A half-year's depreciation was recorded in Year 3.) Depreciation expense of IR1,000 in Year 4 and IR700 in Year 3 is included in operating expenses.
- Inventory is accounted for on the FIFO basis. The inventory at the end of Year 3 and Year 4 was acquired when the exchange rates were $0.045 and $0.027 per rupee, respectively.
- Sales, purchases, and operating expenses were incurred evenly throughout the year, and the average exchange rate for the year was $0.031.
- The prepaid expenses and unearned revenue at December 31, Year 4, arose when the exchange rates were $0.03 and $0.028 per rupee, respectively.
- Income taxes were paid in equal monthly instalments throughout the year.
- Dividends of 3,500 in Year 4 and 500 in Year 3 were declared and paid each year on December 31.

- The foreign-exchange rates per rupee at each of the following dates were as follows:

December 31, Year 3	$0.041
June 30, Year 4	$0.036
December 31, Year 4	$0.025

Required:

(a) Prepare a Canadian dollar balance sheet at December 31, Year 4, and an income statement for the year then ended, assuming that VTIL's functional currency is
  (i) the Canadian dollar.
  (ii) the Indian rupee.

  (Note: There is insufficient information to translate retained earnings and accumulated foreign exchange adjustments. Plug these two items with the amount required to balance the balance sheet.)

(b) Which method should Victoria Textiles Limited apply to its investment in this subsidiary? Explain.

(adapted from a problem prepared by Peter Secord, St. Mary's University)

Problem 11 The financial statements of Malkin Inc., of Russia, as at December 31, Year 11, follow the Other Information section.

Additional Information

- On January 1, Year 11, Crichton Corporation of Toronto acquired a controlling interest in Malkin.
- Relevant exchange rates for the Russian ruble (RR) were as follows:

January 1, Year 11	$1 = RR28.00
December 31, Year 11	$1 = RR28.20
Average for Year 11	$1 = RR28.11

- The land and buildings were purchased in Year 5 when the exchange rate was RR26.50.
- During Year 11, equipment costing RR125,000 was purchased for cash. Depreciation totalling RR25,000 has been recorded on this equipment. The exchange rate on the date of the equipment purchase was RR28.18.

  The remaining equipment was purchased on the date the subsidiary was acquired, and no other changes have taken place since that date. Depreciation on the buildings of RR105,00 and depreciation of RR63,000 on all the equipment are included in other expenses.
- The December 31, Year 11, inventory was acquired during the last quarter of the year, when the average exchange rate was RR28.04.
- On January 1, Year 11, the inventory was RR525,000 and was acquired when the average exchange rate was RR28.27.
- The bonds mature on December 31, Year 16.
- Other operating expenses were incurred equally throughout the year.
- Dividends were declared and paid on December 31, Year 11.
- On January 1, Year 11, liabilities were greater than monetary assets by the amount of RR1,033,000.
- The common shares were issued in Year 1 when the exchange rate was RR25.00.

FINANCIAL STATEMENTS
December 31, Year 11

BALANCE SHEET

Cash		RR 105,000
Accounts receivable		168,000
Inventories — at cost		357,000
Land		430,000
Buildings	1,460,000	
Accumulated depreciation	420,000	1,040,000
Equipment	483,000	
Accumulated depreciation	168,000	315,000
		RR2,415,000
Accounts payable		RR 210,000
Miscellaneous payables		105,000
Bonds payable		600,000
Common shares		850,000
Retained earnings		650,000
		RR2,415,000

RETAINED EARNINGS STATEMENT

Balance, January 1	RR 470,000
Net income	630,000
	1,100,000
Dividends	450,000
Balance, December 31	RR 650,000

INCOME STATEMENT

Sales	RR3,150,000
Cost of sales	1,680,000
Other expenses	840,000
	2,520,000
Net Income	RR 630,000

Required:

(a) Assume that Malkin's functional currency is the Canadian dollar. Translate the financial statements into Canadian dollars for consolidation purposes.

(b) Assume that Malkin's functional currency is the Russian ruble. Translate the balance sheet only into Canadian dollars for consolidation purposes.

(c) Explain whether the current rate method produces results that are consistent with the normal measurement and valuation of assets and liabilities for domestic transactions and operations.

Problem 12 SPEC Co. is a Canadian investment company. It acquires real estate properties in foreign countries for speculative purposes. On January 1, Year 5, SPEC incorporated a wholly owned subsidiary, CHIN Limited. CHIN immediately purchased a property in Shanghai, China, for 70 million Chinese yuan (Y). At that time, the land and building were valued at Y30 million and Y40 million, respectively. The previous owner had purchased the property in Year 1 for Y36 million when the exchange rate was $1 = Y5.13. The building had an estimated useful life of 20 years with no residual value on January 1, Year 5.

The draft financial statements for CHIN as at and for the year ended December 31, Year 5, follow:

CHIN LIMITED
Statement of Financial Position
at December 31, Year 5

Land	Y30,000,000
Building	40,000,000
Accumulated amortization	(2,000,000)
	Y68,000,000
Common shares	Y20,000,000
Retained earnings (deficit)	(2,000,000)
Mortgage payable	50,000,000
	Y68,000,000

CHIN LIMITED
Income Statement
for the year ended December 31, Year 5

Rent revenue	Y 6,000,000
Interest expense	(5,000,000)
Amortization expense	(2,000,000)
Other expenses	(1,000,000)
Profit (loss)	Y(2,000,000)

Additional Information

- The purchase of the property was financed with Y20 million of equity provided by SPEC and a Y50 million mortgage from a Chinese investor. The mortgage payable has a term of 10 years and requires interest-only payments of Y5 million on December 31 each year and a final payment of Y50 million on December 31, Year 14. The market rate of interest on the mortgage was equal to the stated rate throughout Year 5.
- The property is rented for Y0.5 million per month, which is consistent with rent being charged by other property owners in the area. The rent is due on the last day of each month. CHIN hires local workers and buys all of its materials and supplies from local suppliers. CHIN incurred the other expenses evenly throughout the year.
- The exchange rates were as follows:

January 1, Year 5	$1 = Y6.92
Average for Year 5	$1 = Y7.20
Average for 12 days when rent payments were received	$1 = Y7.25
December 31, Year 5	$1 = Y7.50

Required:

(a) Should CHIN be classified as a self-sustaining or an integrated subsidiary? Explain.

(b) Ignore your answer to part (a). Calculate the foreign-exchange adjustment for Year 5 assuming that CHIN's functional currency is the Chinese yuan, and indicate how this adjustment will be reported in CHIN's Canadian dollar financial statements. Show supporting calculations.

(c) Ignore your answers to parts (a) and (b). Translate CHIN's Year 5 income statement into Canadian dollars assuming that CHIN's functional currency is the Canadian dollar. Ignore foreign-exchange gains and losses.

(d) Assume that SPEC does not own any shares of CHIN. Instead, SPEC acquired the property in Shanghai directly. SPEC financed the acquisition with Y20 million of its own funds and a Y50 million mortgage. If SPEC argued that the mortgage payable is a hedge of the anticipated sale of the land, what difference would it make for reporting purposes whether or not the mortgage payable is deemed to be an effective hedge of the anticipated sale of the land? Briefly explain.

(CGA-Canada adapted)

Problem 13   White Company was incorporated on January 2, Year 1, and commenced active operations immediately. Common shares were issued on the date of incorporation and no new common shares have been issued since then. On December 31, Year 5, Black Company purchased 70 percent of the outstanding common shares of White for 1.4 million foreign pesos (FP). On this date, the fair values of White's identifiable net assets were equal to their book values except for a building, which had a fair value of FP100,000 in excess of book value. The remaining useful life of the building was 10 years at the date of acquisition.

The following information was extracted from the financial records of the two companies for the year ended December 31, Year 6:

	Black	White
Building — net	$3,000,000	FP2,700,000
Common shares	100,000	200,000
Retained earnings, beginning of year	800,000	900,000
Depreciation expense — buildings	200,000	300,000
Income before foreign exchange	150,000	160,000
Dividends paid	80,000	100,000

Additional Information

- Black uses the cost method to account for its investment in White.
- White purchased its building on December 31, Year 3.
- The recoverable amount for goodwill at the end of Year 6 was FP720,000.
- Dividends were declared and paid on July 1.
- Foreign-exchange rates were as follows:

January 2, Year 1	FP1 = $0.30
December 31, Year 3	FP1 = $0.24
December 31, Year 5	FP1 = $0.20
Average for Year 6	FP1 = $0.18
July 1, Year 6	FP1 = $0.17
December 31, Year 6	FP1 = $0.15

Required:

(a) Compute the balances that would appear in the Year 6 consolidated financial statements for the following items assuming that White's functional currency is the Canadian dollar. White's income before foreign exchange gains is

$30,000 and the exchange gains from translating White's separate-entity financial statements to Canadian dollars is $50,000.

    (i)   Building — net.

    (ii)   Goodwill.

    (iii) Depreciation expense — building.

    (iv) Net income (excluding other comprehensive income).

    (v)   Other comprehensive income.

    (vi) Non-controlling interest on the income statement.

    (vii) Non-controlling interest on the balance sheet.

(b) Compute the balances that would appear in the Year 6 consolidated financial statements for the same accounts as in part (a) assuming that White's functional currency is the foreign peso.

WEB-BASED PROBLEMS

Problem 1   Access the most recent annual report for Vodafone, a British company. (Go to the investor relations section at www.vodafone.com.) Answer the questions below. For each question, indicate where in the financial statements you found the answer and/or provide a brief explanation.

(a) What is the functional currency of the parent company and what currency is used in presenting the financial statements?

(b) What is the predominant currency of the company's foreign operations and what other currencies are functional currencies of entities within the consolidated group?

(c) What were the foreign-exchange gains or losses reported in net income during the year? Are the foreign-exchange gains or losses segregated between foreign transactions and foreign operations?

(d) Explain if and how the company hedges its net investments in foreign operations and how it reports exchange gains or losses on these hedges.

(e) If the reporting currency appreciates by 10 percent relative to the U.S. dollar in the next year, will the company likely report foreign-exchange gains or foreign-exchange losses in operating income?

(f) If the company had used the U.S. dollar as its presentation currency this past year, would it likely have reported exchange gains or exchange losses? Briefly explain.

Problem 2   Access the most recent annual report for Siemens, a German company. (Go to the investor relations section at www.siemens.com.) Answer the same questions as in Problem 1. For each question, indicate where in the financial statements you found the answer and/or provide a brief explanation. (Some questions may not be applicable.)

Chapter 12 Accounting for Not-for-profit Organizations and Governments

LEARNING OBJECTIVES

After studying this chapter, you should be able to do the following:

1. Describe the not-for-profit accounting practices currently mandated in the *CICA Handbook*.
2. Explain the use and the workings of a budgetary control system that uses encumbrances.
3. Prepare journal entries and financial statements using the deferral method of recording contributions.
4. Prepare journal entries and financial statements using the restricted fund method of recording contributions.
5. Explain the purpose behind fund accounting.
6. Outline the basics of government financial reporting.

INTRODUCTION

Over 180,000 NFPOs in Canada receive more than $112 billion each year from government grants and private donations.

A substantial portion of Canada's economic activity is conducted by organizations whose purpose is to provide services (or products) on a non-profit basis. The size of the portion becomes clear when one considers that included in this *non-business area* is the *government sector* encompassing the federal, provincial, and local governments, as well as the *not-for-profit sector*. This latter sector encompasses a wide variety of organizations such as charities, hospitals, universities, professional and fraternal organizations, and community clubs. While our major concern in this chapter is the accounting and financial reporting for Canadian not-for-profit organizations (NFPOs), the reporting requirements for governments are summarized in Appendix 12B. The NFPO sector is a very large one in our economy and consists of over 90,000 registered charities and an additional 70,000 voluntary organizations. It has been estimated that the charity sector alone receives over $112 billion a year from governments, private individuals, and corporations.

Not-for-profit organizations are defined in the *CICA Handbook* as

... entities, normally without transferable ownership interests, organized and operated exclusively for social, educational, professional, religious, health, charitable or any other not-for-profit purpose. A not-for-profit organization's members, contributors and other resource providers do not, in such capacity, receive any financial return directly from the organization. [4400.02]

There are a number of ways in which NFPOs differ from profit-orientated organizations.

NFPOs differ from profit-oriented organizations in the following ways:

- They typically provide services or goods to identifiable segments of society without the expectation of profit. They accomplish this by raising resources and subsequently spending or distributing these resources in a manner that fulfills the organization's objectives.

- The resources are provided by contributors without the expectation of gain or repayment. Most of these resources consist of donations from the general public and grants from governments and other NFPOs. Often a portion of the resources received have restrictions attached that govern the manner in which they can be spent.

- As the definition cited above indicates, there is no readily defined ownership interest that can be sold, transferred, or redeemed in any way by the organization.

- While many NFPOs have paid employees, they are governed by volunteers who receive little or no remuneration or gain for the time and effort they provide. In some small organizations there are no paid employees and all effort is provided entirely by volunteers.

Well-defined GAAP for NFPOs have existed in Canada only since 1997.

While financial reporting for NFPOs in Canada is well defined today, this has been the case only since April 1997, when seven very detailed *Handbook* sections became operational. Prior to this date, accounting in this area was in a state of flux, moving from a situation where there were no real authoritative pronouncements at all, to one where there was only a single *Handbook* section that gave only broad guidance for some issues and left many other important ones unresolved. A few large organizations, such as hospitals and universities, published detailed manuals in an attempt to establish consistent reporting practices for all members of a given association. Unfortunately, the practices set out for hospitals were different from those recommended for universities, and in both situations members did not have to follow their organization's recommendations. Smaller NFPOs followed a wide range of diverse practices, such as using the cash basis only, or a mixture of cash and accrual accounting. Many did not capitalize capital asset acquisitions, and of the few that did capitalize, many did not provide for subsequent periodic amortization. A wide range of practices was also followed for donated materials, services, and capital assets, ranging from no recording to a full recording of all items. A large number of NFPOs used fund accounting in their end-of-year financial statement presentations, and many organizations still do. Later in this chapter we fully explore the concepts involved in fund accounting and fund presentations in accordance with current *Handbook* requirements. First, though, it is useful to examine the basic idea behind fund accounting and to give a brief illustration of how various funds are presented in an organization's financial statements.

The Basics of Fund Accounting

NFPOs often have unrestricted and restricted resources.

The resources that an NFPO receives can be broadly categorized as *unrestricted* or *restricted*. *Unrestricted resources* can be used for any purposes that are consistent with the goals and objectives of the organization. *Restricted resources* can be used only in accordance with the wishes of the contributor. For example, a donation may be received with the proviso that it be spent in some specified manner. In some situations the original donation must be invested, and only the interest earned on the funds invested can be spent by the organization. A donation of this type is called an *endowment*.

There are many examples of endowments. University scholarships are often funded by the interest earned on endowment contributions made by donors in prior years. Some well-known private universities, such as Harvard and Stanford, have hundreds of millions of dollars in endowment funds, and use the earnings as their major source of revenue, since they do not receive government funding. The Toronto Symphony Orchestra has established an endowment fund as a device to help fund its daily operations. And finally, the Winnipeg Foundation operates with substantial endowment funds.

Quite often, restrictions are also placed on how the endowment interest can be spent. In other words, interest revenue can be restricted or unrestricted. NFPOs sometimes conduct special campaigns to raise money for major acquisitions of buildings and equipment, and any moneys raised are restricted to this particular purpose. In some cases, the board of directors of an NFPO may pass a resolution designating a portion of unrestricted resources as restricted for a certain purpose, or to be held indefinitely, with only the interest earned to be spent. The restrictions imposed by the board or management are referred to as internal restrictions. They are reported differently than the restrictions imposed by external parties mainly because future boards could reverse the designation. In accordance with the *Handbook*'s definition, restricted contributions are those that may be spent only in accordance with the wishes of the donor (or, in the case of endowments, may never be spent).

Fund accounting has been used very successfully to keep track of restricted resources and to convey information through the financial statements about the restrictions placed on the organization's resources. The concepts involved can be summarized as follows:

> Fund accounting comprises the collective accounting procedures resulting in a self-balancing set of accounts for each fund established by legal, contractual or voluntary actions of an organization. Elements of a fund can include assets, liabilities, net assets, revenues and expenses (and gains and losses where appropriate). Fund accounting involves an accounting segregation, although not necessarily a physical segregation, of resources. [4400.02]

The following simple example illustrates the use of fund accounting as a means of reporting this form of stewardship.

Example The financial statements of the Helpful Society (HS) at the end of Year 1 are presented in Exhibit 12.1 on page 638.

HS presents two funds in its year-end financial statements. The resources in the *general* fund can be used to carry out the normal activities of the organization, while the resources in the *building* fund, which was established during the current year, are restricted. Each year the organization raises money through donations and spends the funds raised on programs A, B, and C. During the current year, the general fund's revenues were $7,100 greater than its expenses; as a result, its equity (described as fund balance) increased by this amount. Note that revenues and expenses are measured under the accrual method, so the statement does not show cash inflows and outflows. The assets on hand at the end of the year can be viewed as resources that are

Exhibit 12.1

This exhibit illustrates fund accounting. When combined with a policy of non-capitalization of capital assets it becomes a resources in and out form of stewardship reporting.

HELPFUL SOCIETY
STATEMENT OF FINANCIAL POSITION
December 31, Year 1

	General fund	Building fund	Total
Assets			
Cash	$ 17,500	$ 6,000	$ 23,500
Pledges receivable	50,000		50,000
Investments in debt securities	25,000	88,635	113,635
Total	$ 92,500	$ 94,635	$ 187,135
Liabilities and Fund Balance			
Accounts payable and accrued liabilities	$ 60,300		$ 60,300
Fund balance	32,200	$ 94,635	126,835
Total	$ 92,500	$ 94,635	$ 187,135

STATEMENT OF REVENUE AND EXPENSES
AND CHANGES IN FUND BALANCE
for the Year Ended December 31, Current Year

	General fund	Building fund	Total
Revenues			
Contributions	$923,000	$102,000	$1,025,000
Interest	2,700		2,700
Total	925,700	102,000	1,027,700
Expenses			
Program A	625,000		625,000
Program B	190,000		190,000
Program C	100,000		100,000
Fundraising	3,600	6,410	10,010
Miscellaneous		955	955
Total	918,600	7,365	925,965
Excess of revenue over expenses	7,100	94,635	101,735
Fund balance, January 1	25,100	0	25,100
Fund balance, December 31	$ 32,200	$ 94,635	$ 126,835

spendable. The liabilities at this date are a claim against these resources; therefore, the fund balance at the end of the current year represents net resources amounting to $32,200 that are available for spending next year.

During the current year a special fundraising campaign was initiated to raise the money necessary to purchase and furnish a building. The building fund's resources on hand at the end of the year, amounting to $94,635, were the result of $102,000 that was collected during the year less the fundraising costs and miscellaneous expenses incurred, which amounted to $7,365. The campaign will continue until its goal is reached. At that time the purchase of the building and furnishings will be recorded as an asset of this fund.

NFPO accounting has shifted from reporting the cost of resources spent to provide services, to reporting the cost of services provided.

This example was presented to illustrate the basic idea behind financial reporting on a fund basis. In our example, the columnar approach was used to present the two funds. An alternative that gained some prior acceptance was the layered approach, which presented funds one after another, so that the first page would show the operating fund statements, the second page would show the building fund, and so on. Under the provisions of the new *Handbook* sections, the columnal approach is preferred because of a requirement to show totals for each financial statement item for all funds presented.

Not-for-profit Reporting Today

Many sections of the *Handbook* that previously applied only to profit-orientated organizations now apply to NFPOs as well.

In 1997, seven new sections specifically dedicated to NFPOs were added to the *CICA Handbook*. In 2008, the NFPO *Handbook* sections underwent a major review. As a result, one new NFPO section was added, many changes were made to other NFPO sections, and the list of other *Handbook* sections of general applicability to NFPOs from Part V of the *CICA Handbook* was increased. As of January 1, 2009, 11 of these other *Handbook* sections are generally applicable to NFPOs, 27 are applicable to an NFPO with relevant transactions, and 24 have limited or no applicability to NFPOs.

Cautionary Note In December 2008, the AcSB and the PSAB jointly issued an Invitation to Comment, *Financial Reporting by Not-for-Profit Organizations.* The Invitation to Comment sets out options for the direction of accounting standards for both private- and public-sector NFPOs. Private-sector NFPOs would likely have to choose between IFRSs and GAAP for private enterprises, supplemented by standards specific to NFPOs, i.e., the 4400 series. Public-sector NFPOs would likely have to choose between IFRSs and the *Public Sector Accounting Handbook,* supplemented by standards specific to NFPOs, i.e., the 4400 series. In choosing between the two options, the organization would consider the needs of the users of their financial statements and the comparability of their financial reporting with counterparts in either the private sector or the public sector.

The CICA expects to make a decision on this issue in 2010. Until a decision is made and new standards become effective, NFPOs must continue to apply the existing *Handbook* sections. This chapter was written on the basis of standards in the *CICA Handbook* as of December 2009. The authors will use Connect (at www.mcgrawhillconnect.ca) to provide updates as decisions are made by the CICA.

All *Handbook* sections referred to in this chapter are contained in Part V of the *CICA Handbook.* Part V will remain in effect until Part III of the *CICA Handbook* (i.e., the new standards for not-for-profit organizations) becomes effective, which is expected to be for fiscal years beginning on or after January 1, 2011.

The *Handbook* sections applicable to NFPOs only are as follows:

The non-profit area of the *Handbook* contains eight sections that deal with issues that are unique to NFPOs.

- Section 4400: Financial Statement Presentation by Not-for-Profit Organizations
- Section 4410: Contributions — Revenue Recognition
- Section 4420: Contributions Receivable
- Section 4430: Capital Assets Held by Not-for-Profit Organizations
- Section 4440: Collections Held by Not-for-Profit Organizations
- Section 4450: Reporting Controlled and Related Entities by Not-for-Profit Organizations
- Section 4460: Disclosure of Related Party Transactions by Not-for-Profit Organizations
- Section 4470: Disclosure of Allocated Expenses by Not-for-Profit Organizations

The eight NFPO sections deal with accounting issues that either are unique to NFPOs or are dealt with in the other *Handbook* sections in a manner that is not appropriate for NFPOs. For example, Section 3061: Property, Plant and Equipment, would apply to both not-for-profit and profit organizations if it were not for the existence of Section 4430: Capital Assets Held by Not-for-Profit Organizations.

In the material that follows, the pronouncements of each section will be discussed and in some instances illustrated. Sections 4400 and 4410 will be discussed and illustrated last because they are closely related and involve fund accounting.

Section 4420: Contributions Receivable

A contribution is a type of revenue that is unique to NFPOs. It is defined as "a non-reciprocal transfer to a not-for-profit organization of cash or other assets or a non-reciprocal settlement or cancellation of its liabilities" (paragraph 4420.02). Non-reciprocal means that the contributor does not directly receive anything for the contribution. Included here are donations of cash, property or services, government grants, pledges, and bequests. Besides receiving contribution revenue, NFPOs may also receive other types of revenue, such as from investments or from the sale of goods and services. These other types of revenue are accounted for in accordance with the regular *Handbook* Section 3400: Revenue. Government funding to an NFPO is typically classified as a contribution because the government itself does not receive anything from the contribution. When the government is the direct recipient of the good or the service, the receipt from the government is recognized as revenue earned rather than contribution revenue. In the same fashion, payments received from members of an NFPO are classified as either revenues earned or contributions, depending on whether the member does or does not receive goods or services for the amount paid.

> **Contribution revenue is a type of revenue that is unique to NFPOs, because it is non-reciprocal.**

Section 4420 provides guidance on how to apply accrual accounting concepts to contributions. It states the following:

A contribution receivable should be recognized as an asset when it meets the following criteria:

(a) the amount to be received can be reasonably estimated; and

(b) ultimate collection is reasonably assured. [4420.03]

Normally a contribution receivable represents a future inflow of cash, but it could also represent the future receipt of other assets or services valued at fair value. The credit side of the journal entry could be to revenue, using the restricted fund method, or if the deferral method of recording is being used, to deferred revenue for a restricted contribution, or to increase net assets of endowments for an endowment contribution. (The restricted fund and deferral methods are discussed later in this chapter). The section provides additional guidelines for the recording of receivables associated with pledges and bequests.

> **Pledges are promises to donate cash or other assets to an NFPO, but they are legally unenforceable.**

Because pledges cannot be legally enforced, collectibility is out of the control of the organization. If the organization has the ability to estimate the collectibility based on historical results, it should recognize the pledged amounts as a receivable offset with an allowance for estimated uncollectible amounts. Otherwise, the recognition of pledges should be delayed until the time cash is received. It should be noted that when an allowance for pledges is established, the debit is typically made to contribution revenue rather than to bad debt expense. Since the pledge is not legally binding, it is inappropriate to call the non-payment of a pledge a bad debt expense.

> **Bequests are normally not recorded until a will has been probated.**

Bequests also pose a problem of uncertainty relating both to the timing of receipt and to the amount to be collected. Wills must be probated and at times are subject to legal challenges. Because of this extreme uncertainty, bequests are generally not accrued until probation has been completed and the time for appeal has passed.

Section 4450: Reporting Controlled and Related Entities by Not-for-Profit Organizations

This section outlines the financial statement presentation and disclosures required when an NFPO has a control, significant influence, joint venture, or economic interest type of relationship with both profit-oriented and not-for-profit organizations. The breakdown used is quite similar to that for profit-oriented organizations, but the required financial reporting has some differences.

A control investment is one that gives an NFPO control over both profit-orientated organizations and other NFPOs.

Control Investments An NFPO can have an investment or relationship that gives it the continuing power to determine the strategic operating, investing, and financing policies of another entity without the cooperation of others. The other entity can be profit-oriented or an NFPO. Control of a profit-oriented organization is normally evidenced by the right to appoint the majority of the board of directors because of ownership of voting shares. Because an NFPO does not issue shares, control of such an entity is normally evidenced by the right to appoint the majority of the board of directors as allowed by that entity's by-laws or articles of incorporation.

Control over NFPOs An example of a not-for-profit control situation is a national organization with local chapters. A large portion of funds raised by the local chapters goes to the national body, and any projects carried out by the local bodies must be approved (and perhaps funded) by the national organization.

The *Handbook*'s reporting requirements are as follows:

Consolidation of an NFPO is one of three alternatives allowed.

An organization should report each controlled not-for-profit organization in one of the following ways:

(a) by consolidating the controlled organization in its financial statements;

(b) by providing the disclosure set out in Paragraph 4450.22; or

(c) if the controlled organization is one of a large number of individually immaterial organizations, by providing the disclosure set out in Paragraph 4450.26 [4450.14].

Because there is no investment account in one statement of financial position and no shareholders' equity in the others, consolidation is achieved by simply combining the financial statements on a line-by-line basis and at the same time eliminating any transactions that occurred between the organizations.

The alternatives apply to each controlled NFPO.

Since three alternatives are allowed, the management of the organization has to determine the accounting policy to be used. Note that the alternatives listed above are for each controlled entity. This means that if an organization has control over three NFPOs, all of which are material, it could choose to consolidate only one, and provide the required disclosure for the other two, provided that it reports consistently on a year-to-year basis. Later paragraphs further clarify the overall meaning by suggesting that if an NFPO has control over a large number of NFPOs, the decision to consolidate or not should be applied on a group basis. For example, it could establish a policy to consolidate all organizations in Groups A and B and not consolidate the organizations in Group C.

Paragraph 22 requires the disclosure of the totals of all of the assets, liabilities, net assets, revenues, expenses, and cash flows of any controlled NFPOs that are not consolidated. Paragraph 26 requires the disclosure of the reasons that the controlled organizations have been neither consolidated nor included in the disclosure set out in paragraph 4450.22. Possible reasons could include cost/benefit considerations and the decision not to exercise financial control.

Consolidation was a controversial topic when it was proposed in the earlier exposure drafts. The following arguments were presented in its favour:

- The statements present the economic substance of the situation.
- All controlled economic resources are reflected in a single set of financial statements.
- Users of the financial statements get a much better picture than would be the case if unconsolidated statements were presented.

The following are some of the arguments presented against consolidation:

- Consolidation of entities that have different activities may be confusing to users.
- The consolidation of a research centre (with substantial endowments) with a hospital that struggles to break even on a yearly basis may present a misleading financial picture at first glance. Footnote disclosures should clarify the situation.
- The yearly cost of financial reporting will increase.

Control over Profit-oriented Companies

The *Handbook* states an NFPO should report each controlled profit-oriented enterprise in either of the following ways:

A controlled profit-orientated organization can either be consolidated or reported using the equity method.

(a) by consolidating the controlled enterprise in its financial statements; or

(b) by accounting for its investment in the controlled enterprise using the equity method and disclosing total assets, liabilities, and shareholders' equity at the reporting date and revenues, expenses, net income and cash flows for the period.

It should be noted that the requirements here are also applicable to each controlled entity, which could result in some subsidiaries being reported under the equity method and others being consolidated. Consolidation of profit-oriented enterprises was also controversial, with similar arguments for and against as those presented above. The final result was also a compromise.

Joint Control

This is the contractual right to jointly control an organization with at least one other entity. An interest in a joint venture would be reported by either

A jointly controlled organization can be either proportionately consolidated or reported using the equity method.

- proportionately consolidating the joint venture, or
- reporting the interest using the equity method.

Consistent with the requirements for controlled entities, the alternatives here apply to each joint venture, so that some may be proportionately consolidated and others may not, depending on the accounting policy determined by management. The arguments for and against using the proportionate consolidation method are basically the same as those presented previously for controlled investments. The section also states that if the NFPO's proportionate interest in the joint venture cannot be determined, it should not be considered to be a joint venture in accordance with this section, but might be either a significant influence or a control type of relationship. This seems to indicate that the joint venture would have to be one that issued shares, and thus probably a profit-oriented organization. However, if two or three NFPOs created another NFPO as a joint venture to carry out certain activities, and agreed to the percentage owned by each of the non-profit venturers, then the reporting alternatives outlined here would apply.

Significant Influence When control is not present, the NFPO may still be able to exercise significant influence over the strategic operating, investing, and financing activities of the other entity. Factors suggesting the presence of significant influence include the ability to place members on the board of directors, the ability to participate in policy-making, substantial transactions between the entities, and the sharing of senior personnel. If the significant-influence investment is in a profit-oriented enterprise, it must be accounted for using the equity method. If the significant-influence relationship is with another NFPO, the equity method is not used; instead, full disclosure of the relationship is required. This provision makes sense when one considers that applying the equity method requires using a percentage based on the number of shares held. Because an NFPO does not issue shares, it would be virtually impossible to determine the percentage needed to apply the method.

Economic Interest An economic interest in another NFPO exists if that organization holds resources for the reporting organization or if the reporting organization is responsible for the other organization's debts. There are varying degrees of economic interest, ranging from control or significant influence to neither of the two. When an organization has an economic interest in another NFPO over which it does not have control or significant influence, the nature and extent of this interest should be disclosed.

An investment in a profit-oriented organization that is not subject to control, significant influence, or joint control, is reported at fair value or using the cost method as per the rules in the *Handbook* sections for financial instruments.

This concludes the discussion of Section 4450. A summary of the various types of investment that an NFPO can have and the reporting requirements for each follows:

Investment	*Required reporting*
Control of NFPO	Consolidate or disclose
Control of profit entity	Consolidate or equity method
Joint venture	Proportionately consolidate or equity method
Significant Influence	
NFPO	Full disclosure
Profit entity	Equity method
Economic interest	Full disclosure
Other investment	
Profit entity	Fair value method or cost method

Section 4460: Disclosure of Related Party Transactions by Not-for-Profit Organizations

Related parties exist where one party is able to exercise control, joint control, or significant influence over another party. The other party may be either another NFPO or a profit-oriented enterprise. If one NFPO has an economic interest in another NFPO, the two parties are related. A related-party transaction has occurred when there has been a transfer of economic resources or obligations or services between the parties. Unlike *Handbook* Section 3840, which prescribes both measurements and disclosures, this not-for-profit section prescribes only disclosures for related-party transactions. The disclosures required here are virtually identical to those required in Section 3840.

There was strong opposition to the proposal that all NFPOs be required to capitalize and amortize acquisitions of capital assets.

Section 4430: Capital Assets Held by Not-for-Profit Organizations

Prior to the introduction of this section into the *Handbook*, NFPOs followed a variety of practices with regard to the financial reporting of their capital assets. Some organizations capitalized all acquisitions and amortized them over their estimated useful lives in the operating statement. Others capitalized them but did not provide amortization. A fairly large number wrote them off in their operating statements in the year of acquisition. In this latter situation, the operating statement showed revenues and expenditures and from a user perspective reflected the inflow and outflow of spendable resources.

When the AcSB proposed the requirement of capitalization and amortization of all acquisitions, respondents to the exposure drafts voiced strong opposition. The arguments against capitalization were as follows:

- It would change the nature of the operating statement from one that reflects resources spent to one that reflects the cost of resources used.

- Users would not understand the new accounting, having become used to seeing capital asset acquisitions as expenditures.

- As most other assets appearing in a statement of financial position represent spendable resources, the addition of non-spendable resources such as unamortized capital assets would confuse readers.

- Capitalization and amortization would be costly to apply, especially on a retroactive basis.

- Small NFPO financial statement users are interested in seeing only what money has been spent and what money is left over.

The counter-arguments in favour of capitalization were as follows:

- Readers of the financial statements of profit-oriented entities are quite used to seeing capital assets in the statement of financial position and amortization in the operating statement. They are confused when they do not see it in the financial statements of an NFPO.

- The cash flow statement adequately shows resources spent. The operating statement should reflect resources used.

GAAP require large NFPOs to capitalize and amortize all of their capital assets.

Section 4430 requires an NFPO to capitalize all capital assets in the statement of financial position and to amortize them as appropriate in the statement of operations. The cost of a purchased capital asset includes all costs incurred to make the asset ready for use. When a capital asset is donated, it is recorded at fair value (if known), and the resultant credit is recorded based on the rules for contributions, which will be discussed later in this chapter. If the entity paid below fair value, the asset is recorded at fair value and the difference between fair value and cost is recorded as a contribution. Capital assets of limited useful life are to be amortized on a rational basis over their estimated useful lives. No maximum period of amortization is specified. When an NFPO enters into a lease agreement that would be treated as a capital lease in accordance with *Handbook* Section 3065, the asset is capitalized in accordance with the provisions of that section. When an asset no longer contributes to the organization's ability to provide services, it should be written down to estimated residual value, with the resulting loss reported as an expense in the statement of operations. Note that this section does not provide a quantitative impairment test in the same manner as prescribed by *Handbook* Section 3061.

When Section 4430 was first issued, it required that yearly provisions be made for future asset removal and site restoration costs. In January 2003, Section 3110: Asset Retirement Obligations became operative and Section 4430 was revised to say that the new section's provisions should be used by all NFPOs where applicable. For example, if leasehold improvements must be removed at the end of a lease, provision for that future cost should be added to the cost of the asset and amortized over the asset's useful life.

Asset retirement obligations must be recognized by NFPOs.

Small NFPOs Section 4430 contains a compromise provision applicable to NFPOs whose two-year average annual revenues in the statement of operations are less than $500,000. Organizations such as these are encouraged to follow the section's recommendations but are exempted from doing so if they disclose

An exemption from the requirement to capitalize is granted to small NFPOs (those whose two-year average revenues are less than $500,000).

- their accounting policy for capital assets,
- information about capital assets not shown in the statement of financial position and
- the amount expensed in the current period if their policy is to expense capital assets when acquired.

This leaves a small NFPO the choice of

- expensing when acquired,
- capitalizing but not amortizing, or
- capitalizing and amortizing.

If an NFPO has revenues above $500,000, it is required to capitalize and amortize. If its revenues subsequently fall below $500,000, it is not allowed to change its policy.

If an NFPO has revenues below $500,000, chooses not to capitalize and amortize, and subsequently has revenues above $500,000, then it ceases to be a small NFPO and must capitalize and amortize retroactively. This requirement should be recognized by all small NFPOs that decide to exempt themselves from the section's recommendations, because retroactive restatement can be costly.

When an NFPO no longer meets the exemption test, it must capitalize and amortize its capital assets and apply the new policy on a retroactive basis.

Capitalization of capital assets was a contentious issue when the not-for-profit exposure drafts were being discussed. The small-organization exemption and the special provisions for collections (discussed next) were introduced to satisfy some of the objections that were raised.

Section 4440: Collections Held by Not-for-Profit Organizations
Collections are works of art and historical treasures that have been excluded from the definition of capital assets because they meet all of the following criteria:

- They are held for public exhibition, education, or research;
- They are protected, cared for, and preserved;
- They are subject to organizational policies that require any proceeds from their sale to be used to acquire other items for the collection, or for the direct care of the existing collection.

Collections have been excluded from the definition of capital assets, and NFPOs are allowed three alternative reporting options.

The requirements of Section 4440 allow an NFPO to choose an accounting policy from the following:

- Expense when acquired.
- Capitalize but do not amortize.
- Capitalize and amortize.

NFPOs that have collections are required to include in their disclosures a description of the accounting policies followed with regard to collections, a description of the collection, any significant changes made to the collection during the period, the amount spent on the collection during the period, the proceeds from any sales of collection items, and a statement of how the proceeds were used.

Section 4470: Disclosure of Allocated Expenses by Not-for-Profit Organizations When an organization classifies its expenses by function on the statement of operations, it may need or want to allocate certain expenses to a number of functions to which the expenses relate. For example, fundraising expenses and general support expenses usually contribute to, or produce, the output of more than one function and are often considered to be directly related to the output of each of those functions. Since aggregate amounts reported for fundraising and general support functions are often of particular significance to financial statement users, the *Handbook* requires that the following be disclosed when these two types of expenses are allocated to other functions:

An NFPO must disclose details related to any allocation of fundraising and general support costs to different functions.

- The accounting policy for the allocation of expenses among functions, the nature of the expenses being allocated, and the basis on which such allocations have been made; and
- The amounts allocated from each of these two functions, and the amounts and the functions to which they have been allocated.

However, this section does not require organizations to classify their expenses by function or to undertake any allocations. Only if it does so is the above disclosure necessary.

Sections 4400 and 4410 Section 4400: Financial Statement Presentation by Not-for-Profit Organizations and Section 4410: Contributions — Revenue Recognition are so directly related to each other that we will discuss their requirements as a single topic. There are two very key points embodied in these two sections:

Under the matching concept for NFPOs, expenses are recognized first and then revenues are matched to expenses under the deferral method.

- Restrictions on an organization's resources should be clearly stated in the financial statements.
- The matching concept as it applies to NFPOs must be applied in the measurement of yearly results under the deferral method.

For an NFPO that has restricted revenues, the concept of revenue and expense matching is the exact opposite to that for a profit-oriented enterprise. With the latter, revenues are recognized and then expenses are matched with those revenues. With an NFPO, restricted revenues are matched to expenses. This means that if contributions have been collected to fund certain expenses, and those expenses have yet to be incurred, the contributions are deferred until a later period, when they can be matched with the expenses. When the restricted fund method of accounting is used to account for restricted resources, this matching is not necessary; when this method is not used, this form of matching for restricted resources is imperative.

As outlined earlier, an NFPO can have two basic types of revenues:

- Contributions, and
- Other types (from investments, or from the sale of goods and services).

Contributions are a type of revenue unique to NFPOs. They are specifically described in order to apply recognition and presentation principles. The *Handbook* defines three different types of contributions:

Handbook **Section 4410 describes three different types of contributions: restricted, endowment, and unrestricted.**

- Restricted contributions,
- Endowment contributions, and
- Unrestricted contributions.

Restricted contributions are subject to *externally imposed* stipulations as to how the funds are to be spent or used. The organization must use the resources in the manner specified by the donor. There may be times when the directors of an organization decide to use certain contributions for certain purposes, but these are considered to be *internally imposed* restrictions and do not fall within the definition of restricted contributions.

Endowment contributions are a special type of restricted contribution. The donor has specified that the contribution cannot be spent, but must be maintained permanently. Endowment contributions are often invested in high-grade securities.

Unrestricted contributions are those that are not restricted or endowment contributions.

As we shall see in the next section, financial statement presentations for NFPOs are based in part on these three types of contributions.

Financial Statements

An NFPO must present the following financial statements for external reporting purposes:

An NFPO must present four financial statements.

- A statement of financial position,
- A statement of operations,
- A statement of changes in net assets, and
- A statement of cash flows.

The names provided here are for descriptive purposes only; an organization can choose the titles it wishes to use. For example, the statement of financial position could be called a balance sheet, the statement of operations is sometimes called the statement of revenues and expenses, and net assets is sometimes referred to as fund balances or accumulated surplus. The statement of operations can be combined with the statement of changes in net assets.

A fund basis can be used, but it is not necessary to prepare all statements using this method. For example, the operating statement could be presented on a fund basis while the rest of the statements could be presented on a non-fund basis.

The statement of financial position should show classifications for current assets, non-current assets, current liabilities, and non-current liabilities. Net assets (total assets less total liabilities) must be broken down into the following categories (if applicable):

- Net assets maintained permanently in endowments.
- Internally restricted and other externally restricted net assets.
- Unrestricted net assets.

Prior to 2009, net assets invested in capital assets had to be shown as a separate component of net assets. Starting in 2009, a reporting entity has three options for reporting this item:

- Continue to show it as a separate component of net assets.
- Disclose it in the notes to the statements.
- Do not present or disclose it separately.

Many organizations will likely present or disclose this item separately because it indicates that this portion of net assets is not available for current use. However, some organizations will not present or disclose the item separately because their users may not fully understand its nature.

The statement of operations will show the revenues and the expenses for the period. Expenses may be classified by object (e.g., salaries, rent, utilities); by function (e.g., administrative, research, ancillary operations); or by program. An organization should use the method that results in the most meaningful presentation under the circumstances. When an organization has expenses and revenues from the provision of goods or services and acted as a principal in the transactions involved, it recognizes the expenses and the revenues on a gross basis. When an organization is not acting as a principal in the transactions, it earns the equivalent of a commission or fee or receives the equivalent of a contribution and recognizes revenue for only the net amount received.

The following two examples provide guidance in determining whether to recognize revenues and expenses on the gross basis or the net basis.

Example 1   An NFPO engages in a number of fundraising activities, which include a fundraising telethon, a telephone campaign, a direct mail campaign, special events, and a lottery. The organization uses an outside fundraising consultant to conduct the telethon and uses the organization's own staff and volunteers in the telethon and the telephone campaign. Funds solicited in each of the activities are raised in the name of the organization.

Even though the organization uses an outside fundraising consultant to conduct the telethon, the organization is the principal in the relationship with the donors as the funds are raised in its name and using its staff and volunteers. The organization has discretion in selecting the outside fundraiser, in establishing the fees to be paid, and in determining the specifications of the telethon. The organization also has the credit risk if donors to the telethon do not pay according to their pledge. Thus, the organization recognizes the gross fundraising amounts raised in each of the activities as revenue of the organization, and the total expenses of each activity, including the fees charged by any outside party, as expenses of the organization.

Example 2   An NFPO is given the net proceeds from an event held by others to benefit the organization without having any control over, or responsibility for, the gross

---

The equity section of the statement of financial position is called "net assets" and must be broken down into three categories (if applicable).

Revenues and expenses should be reported on a gross basis when the entity acts as a principal in the transactions.

amounts of revenues or expenses involved. In this situation, the organization is not the principal in the fundraising event as it was not involved in organizing the event and did not bear any risks in connection with it. The amount received by the organization is a donation from the organizers of the event. Neither the gross revenues nor the gross expenses of the event are recognized in the organization's financial statements. The net proceeds received are recognized as a contribution. Disclosure of gross revenues and expenses is not required.

Other comprehensive income does not exist as a separate category on the statement of operations.

The statement of operations does not have a section for other comprehensive income. Similar to a private for-profit entity, the adjustments to fair value for available-for-sale investments, the foreign-exchange adjustments for a self-sustaining foreign operation, and the exchange adjustments for a cash flow hedge are given special treatment. For an NFPO, these adjustments are recognized directly and accumulated separately in the net assets section of the statement of financial position.

The statement of changes in net assets must show changes in each of the three net asset categories required to be shown on the statement of financial position. The cash flow statement must segregate changes in cash between operating, investing, and financing activities. Cash flows from operations can be presented using either the direct method or the indirect method.

The 2008 financial statements (excluding footnotes) of the United Way of Ottawa-Carleton presented in Appendix 12A provide an example of an NFPO's financial statements.

Accounting for Contributions

An NFPO can choose either the deferral method or the restricted fund method to account for contributions.

The *Handbook* has defined two methods of accounting for contributions: the *deferral* method and the *restricted fund* method. The deferral method can be used with or without fund accounting. The restricted fund method has to be used in combination with fund accounting.

If the organization wants to present an overall picture of the organization, i.e., a set of statements with only one column for each year, it must use the deferral method. If it wants to report on a fund accounting basis, i.e., separate columns for different funds, it can choose the deferral method for all funds or the restricted fund method.

With fund accounting, it is easier to present and report on the different restrictions placed on contributions. However, as we will see, the deferral method does a better job of matching revenues to expenses, which makes it easier to see what portion of expenses is financed by contributions and what portion is financed by other sources.

The Deferral Method

The deferral method requires that contribution revenue be matched to expenses.

The deferral method matches contribution revenues with related expenses. Unrestricted contributions are reported as revenue in the period received or receivable because there are no particular related expenses associated with them.

Endowment contributions are not shown in the operating statement; rather, they are reflected in the statement of changes in net assets. This is because endowment contributions, by definition, will never have related expenses.

Restricted contributions must be matched against related expenses. This matching principle has different implications for different kinds of restricted contributions, as follows:

- Restricted contributions for expenses of future periods are deferred and recognized as revenue in the same periods as the related expenses are incurred.

Contributions for a depreciable asset are recognized as revenue as the asset is being amortized.

- The handling of restricted contributions for the acquisition of capital assets depends on whether related expenses are associated with them. If the capital asset is subject to amortization, the related expense is the yearly amortization. The restricted contribution is deferred and recognized as revenue on the same basis as the asset is being amortized. If the capital asset is not subject to amortization (e.g., land), there will be no expenses to match against. In the same manner as for endowment contributions, the restricted capital asset contributions of this type are reflected in the statement of changes in net assets.

- Restricted contributions for expenses of the current period are recognized as revenue in the current period. Matching is achieved, and there is no need for deferral.

Investment income can be either unrestricted or restricted. Unrestricted investment income is recognized as revenue when it is earned. Restricted investment income has to be recognized in the same manner as restricted contributions. For example, if an endowment contribution states that the purchasing power of the contribution must be preserved, some portion of the interest earned must be used to increase the endowment. This portion is treated in exactly the same manner as an endowment contribution, and is reflected in the statement of changes in net assets. Other types of restricted investment income must be deferred and matched against expense in the manner previously discussed. If all investment income is restricted, it is quite possible that all investment income earned in a period will be deferred.

The Restricted Fund Method

This method requires an NFPO to report a general fund; at least one restricted fund; and if it has endowments or receives endowment contributions, an endowment fund. The restricted funds will be used to record externally restricted revenue. Specific requirements are outlined as follows:

Contributions are reported as revenue when received/ receivable if a separate restricted or endowment fund has been established for these contributions.

- Endowment contributions will be reported as revenue in the endowment fund, and because there are no related expenses associated with endowment contributions, no expenses will appear in the statement of operations of the endowment fund.

- The general fund records all unrestricted contributions and investment income, including unrestricted income from endowment fund investments.

- If some of the endowment fund income is restricted, it is reflected as revenue in the particular restricted fund involved.

- If some of the endowment fund income is permanently restricted, because the purchasing power of the endowment is required to be maintained, it is recorded as revenue of the endowment fund.

- Externally restricted contributions for which there is a corresponding restricted fund are recorded as revenue of the restricted fund.

The provisions of the deferral method might have to be applied when the restricted fund method is used.

- If an externally restricted contribution or externally restricted investment income is received for which there is no corresponding restricted fund, the amounts are recorded in the general fund in accordance with the deferral method. In other words, they are recorded as deferred revenue in the general fund and matched with the related expenses in that fund when these expenses are incurred.

- If management decides to impose internal restrictions on general fund unrestricted contributions, the contributions are initially reported as revenue in the general fund. The transfers are reported in the statement of changes in fund balances below the line "excess of revenue over expenses." Note disclosure should clearly indicate the amount of resources shown in restricted funds that have been designated as such by management, because these amounts do not satisfy the *Handbook*'s definition of a contribution.

The excess of revenues over expenses in the general fund represents the increase in unrestricted resources during the period. The fund balance in the general fund shows the unrestricted net assets at the end of the period.

A restricted fund shows no deferred revenue. The fund balance of a restricted fund represents the amount of net assets that are restricted for that particular fund's purpose.

The fund balance in the endowment fund represents the net assets that have permanent restrictions on them.

Under the restricted fund method, instead of presenting a statement of changes in net assets (as is required under the deferral method of recording contributions), a statement of changes in fund balances is prepared. Because of the requirement to capitalize long-lived assets, capital assets must appear on the statement of financial position of either the general fund or one of the restricted funds (excluding the endowment fund).

This has been a summary of the two methods of accounting for contributions. Before we show these concepts in an extensive illustration, some additional topics must be addressed.

Fund balances for the restricted and endowment funds represent the amount of net assets restricted for that fund's purpose.

Net Assets Invested in Capital Assets

An NFPO can report "net assets invested in capital assets" as a separate component of net assets.

The *Handbook* provides an option to report "net assets invested in capital assets" as a separate component of net assets. This amount represents resources spent on and tied up in capital assets and therefore not available for future spending. The amount shown depends on the method used to account for contributions. If the restricted fund method is used, the amount represents the unamortized portion of *all* capital assets less associated debt, regardless of whether they were purchased from restricted or unrestricted resources. If the deferral method is used, the amount presented represents the unamortized portion of capital assets (net of associated debt) that were purchased with *unrestricted* resources. The following example will illustrate the differences.

Example At the beginning of the current period, an NFPO purchases equipment costing $5,000 with a useful life of two years. We will assume first that the equipment is acquired from restricted resources, and then from unrestricted resources. We will focus on the equipment transaction only and the effect of the transaction on the financial statements of the NFPO. In order to do this, we also assume that the organization was formed at the beginning of the period and that the equipment acquisition is the only transaction that has occurred.

The Restricted Fund Method

Purchase from Restricted Resources

Assume that the equipment is purchased from a restricted fund contribution of $5,100. The capital fund records contributions of this nature, as well as the acquisition of capital assets and their subsequent amortization. The journal entries are as follows:

The restricted contribution is reported as revenue when received.

Capital fund

Cash	5,100	
Contribution revenue		5,100
Equipment	5,000	
Cash		5,000
Amortization expense	2,500	
Accumulated amortization		2,500

Because the capital fund did not exist before the start of the period, the financial statements at the end of the period appear as follows:

CAPITAL FUND
OPERATING STATEMENT AND CHANGES IN FUND BALANCE

Contribution revenue	$5,100
Amortization expense	2,500
Excess of revenue over expense	2,600
Fund balance — start of period	0
Fund balance — end of period	$2,600

STATEMENT OF FINANCIAL POSITION

Cash		$ 100
Equipment	$5,000	
Accumulated amortization	2,500	2,500
Total assets		$2,600

The unamortized balance of equipment purchased with restricted resources is reflected in the amount of fund balance invested in capital assets.

Fund balance	
Invested in capital assets	$2,500
Externally restricted funds	100
Total fund balance	$2,600

Note that the fund balance section shows two classifications:

- The $2,500 invested in capital assets represents the unamortized balance of spent resources that have not yet been reflected in the statement of operations as an expense.

- Externally restricted funds of $100 represent resources that can be spent only to acquire capital assets.

As the equipment is amortized on the operating statement, the fund balance itself is reduced, and it is the statement of financial position category "invested in capital assets" that reflects the reduction.

Purchase from Unrestricted Resources

Now assume that the equipment is purchased from unrestricted resources. The general fund receives an unrestricted contribution of $5,000 and uses it to acquire equipment.

The journal entries in the general fund and the capital fund are as follows:

General fund

Cash	5,000	
Contribution revenue		5,000
Transfer to capital fund	5,000	
Cash		5,000

The general fund's operating statement after the transaction shows the following:

GENERAL FUND
STATEMENT OF OPERATIONS AND CHANGES IN FUND BALANCE

Transfers between funds are reported in changes in fund balances, not as revenues and expenses.

Revenues	$5,000
Expenses	0
Excess of revenue over expense	5,000
Fund balance — start of period	0
Transfer to capital fund	(5,000)
Fund balance — end of period	$ 0

It should be obvious that the general fund's statement of financial position at the end of the period contains no elements.

The capital fund records the acquisition of the equipment and its amortization with the following entries:

Capital fund

Equipment	5,000	
Transfer from general fund		5,000
Amortization expense	2,500	
Accumulated amortization		2,500

The end-of-period financial statements show the following:

CAPITAL FUND
STATEMENT OF OPERATIONS AND CHANGES IN FUND BALANCE

Amortization expense	$2,500
Excess of revenue over expense	(2,500)
Fund balance — start of period	0
Transfer from general fund	5,000
Fund balance — end of period	$2,500

STATEMENT OF FINANCIAL POSITION

The unamortized balance of equipment purchased with unrestricted resources is also reflected in the amount of fund balance invested in capital assets.

Equipment	$5,000
Accumulated amortization	2,500
Total assets	$2,500
Fund balance	
Invested in capital assets	$2,500
Total fund balance	$2,500

Note that regardless of the source of resources used to acquire the equipment (restricted or unrestricted), the unamortized balance appears as an asset on the statement of financial position of the capital fund, and the fund balance shows a classification "invested in capital assets" in an amount equal to the asset balance. This is not the case when the deferral method with no fund accounting is used.

The Deferral Method

Purchase from Restricted Resources

Assume that the equipment is purchased from a restricted fund contribution of $5,100. The journal entries to record the contribution, the acquisition, and the first year's amortization are as follows:

Deferred contributions includes unspent resources restricted to purchase capital assets in the future.

Cash	5,100	
Deferred contributions — capital assets		5,100
Equipment	5,000	
Cash		5,000
Amortization expense	2,500	
Accumulated amortization		2,500
Deferred contributions — capital assets	2,500	
Contribution revenue		2,500

Financial statements that reflect these transactions are as follows:

STATEMENT OF OPERATIONS AND CHANGES IN FUND BALANCE

Contribution revenue	$2,500
Amortization expense	2,500
Excess of revenue over expenses	0
Net assets — start of period	0
Net assets — end of period	$ 0

STATEMENT OF FINANCIAL POSITION

Cash		$ 100
Equipment	$5,000	
Accumulated amortization	2,500	2,500
Total assets		$2,600
Deferred contributions — capital assets		$2,600
Net Assets		
Unrestricted		0
Total		$2,600

Deferred contributions includes restricted resources that have been spent to acquire capital assets, but that have not yet been matched to amortization expense.

Deferred contributions of $2,600 includes two components: $100 in unspent resources restricted to future spending on capital assets and $2,500 in restricted resources that has been spent acquiring capital assets, but has not yet been reflected as revenue on the operating statement because there has yet to be an expense to match it against. When amortization occurs, an equal amount is recognized as revenue. Because there is no effect on the "excess of revenue over expense" amount, there is no effect on the equity section "net assets." As the equipment decreases on the asset side due to amortization, the amount "deferred contributions" decreases by the same amount on the liability side. Because this equipment was purchased from restricted resources, there can be no amount shown under "invested in capital assets" in the "net assets" section.

Purchase from Unrestricted Resources   Assume now that the equipment was purchased from an unrestricted contribution of $5,000. The journal entries to record the events are as follows:

<table>
<tr><td>**Unrestricted contributions are reported as revenue when received.**</td><td>Cash</td><td>5,000</td><td></td></tr>
</table>

	Cash	5,000	
	Contribution revenue		5,000
	Equipment	5,000	
	Cash		5,000
	Amortization expense	2,500	
	Accumulated amortization		2,500

The financial statements that reflect these transactions are as follows:

STATEMENT OF OPERATIONS

Contribution revenue	$5,000
Amortization expense	2,500
Excess of revenue over expenses	$2,500

STATEMENT OF FINANCIAL POSITION

Equipment	$5,000
Accumulated amortization	2,500
Total assets	$2,500
Net Assets	
Invested in capital assets	$2,500
Unrestricted	0
Total	$2,500

Net assets invested in capital assets represents the unamortized balance of equipment purchased with unrestricted resources.

Note that the statement of operations does not include a reconciliation of opening and ending net assets. A separate statement is usually presented. Because "net assets" represents total equity, the changes in the classifications of this equity must be shown in the statement as follows:

STATEMENT OF CHANGES IN NET ASSETS

	Invested in capital assets	Unrestricted	Total
Balance — start of period	$ 0	$ 0	$ 0
Excess of revenue over expenses	(2,500)	5,000	2,500
Investment in capital assets	5,000	(5,000)	0
Balance — end of period	$2,500	$ 0	$2,500

Under the deferral method, a statement of changes in net assets is prepared.

The "unrestricted" column represents resources that can be spent for any purpose. The organization received an unrestricted contribution of $5,000 and spent it on equipment. At the end of the period it has no resources left to spend. The transfer of $5,000 to the category "invested in capital assets" depicts the acquisition of capital assets from unrestricted resources. The operating statement shows an excess of revenue over expenses of $2,500. A $2,500 deduction for the amortization of assets purchased with unrestricted resources was used to arrive at these operating results. Note that this does not represent resources spent, but rather the cost of services provided by the equipment. By transferring this deduction to "invested in capital assets," the amount of the operating results allocated to unrestricted resources becomes $5,000, which represents the actual inflow of spendable resources, and the amount shown for "invested in capital assets" is equal to the unamortized balance of the equipment purchased from unrestricted resources.

Donated Capital Assets, Materials, and Services

Donated capital assets must be recorded at fair value or, if fair value cannot be determined, at a nominal value.

Donated Capital Assets   An NFPO is required to record the donation of capital assets at fair value. If fair value cannot be determined, a nominal value will be used. A nominal value could be in the range of $1 to $100 for small NFPOs, and $1,000 and higher for large NFPOs. If an organization receives an unsolicited donation of a capital asset that it has no intention of using, it should be reflected in its financial statements as "other assets" instead of "capital assets," and a loss or gain should be reflected in the statement of operations when disposal of the asset occurs. The following illustrates the recording of donated capital assets.

Example   A capital asset with a fair value of $10,000 is donated to an NFPO. The initial treatment depends on which of the two methods of recording contributions is being used.

If the deferral method is being used, and the capital asset is subject to amortization (e.g., equipment), the journal entry is as follows:

A donated depreciable asset is reported as deferred contributions under the deferral method.

Equipment	10,000	
Deferred contributions — capital assets		10,000

Assuming a five-year useful life, in each succeeding year the following entry will be made as the equipment is amortized:

Amortization expense	2,000	
Accumulated amortization		2,000
Deferred contributions — capital assets	2,000	
Contribution revenue		2,000

If the deferral method is being used and the asset is not subject to amortization (e.g., land), the following entry is made:

Land	10,000	
Net assets invested in capital assets		10,000

Because no future expense will be associated with the asset, deferral is not required and the donation of land is reflected in the statement of net assets.

If the restricted fund method is being used, the fair value of the donated capital asset is recorded as revenue in the capital fund as follows:

A donated depreciable asset is reported as contribution revenue under the restricted fund method.

Capital fund		
Equipment	10,000	
Contribution revenue — donated equipment		10,000

Donated land will be treated in the same manner, except that the debit will be to land instead of equipment. Small NFPOs that have adopted a policy of non-capitalization of acquisitions of capital assets will still be required to record donated capital assets at fair value. For example, the donation of equipment with a fair value of $10,000 is recorded in the following manner:

Equipment expense	10,000	
Contribution revenue — donated equipment		10,000

Regardless of whether the organization uses the deferral method or the restricted fund method, the entry is the same because the required matching automatically occurs with the entry.

Donated materials and services can be reported if they are needed by the organization.

Donated Materials and Services   The requirements for the reporting of donated materials and services are different from those for donated capital assets. An NFPO has the option of reporting or not reporting donated material and services; however, it should do so only if fair value can be determined, and if the materials and services would normally be used in the organization's operations and would have been purchased if they had not been donated.

The *Handbook* section also makes it clear that the fair value of the services of volunteers is normally not recognized due to the difficulty in determining such values. Furthermore, an organization would probably not record donated materials if it acts as an intermediary for immediate distribution. For example, due to the difficulty of determining fair values and the large number of transactions, a food bank would not normally record the donation of food that it distributes to its clients.

Example   A radio station donated free airtime to help a charity publicize its fund-raising campaign. The fair value of the airtime is $5,200, and the policy of the organization is to record the value of donated materials and services. The journal entry is as follows:

Advertising expense	5,200	
Revenue — donated airtime		5,200

If the restricted fund method was being used, this entry would be made in the general fund.

If the donation consisted of office supplies rather than airtime, the entry to record the donation under the deferral method would be as follows:

Office supplies (asset)	5,200	
Deferred contribution		5,200

If half of the supplies were used, the entries would be as follows:

Donated materials and services should be reported as contribution revenue when the materials and services are expensed.

Supplies expense	2,600	
Office supplies		2,600
Deferred contribution	2,600	
Contribution revenue		2,600

In order to achieve proper matching, the same entries would be used under the restricted fund method. Due to the nature of the items donated, the transaction would normally be recorded in the general fund.

Budgetary Control and Encumbrances

The actual recording of the budget in the records, along with the use of an encumbrance system, is a device used by NFPOs and governments to control spending.

Governments and many NFPOs often use a *formal budget recording system* together with an *encumbrance system* as a device to help control spending. Prior to the commencement of a fiscal year, a formal budget is drawn up that shows the budgeted revenues and expenses for the coming year. The usual starting point in the process is a preliminary expense budget based on how the managers of the organization would like to see spending take place. Then a revenue budget is prepared based on the expected results from the revenue-raising activities of the coming year. If this revenue budget is realistic, the next step is to scale down the controllable expenses so that the organization does not plan to have expenses greater than its expected revenues. NFPOs and local governments do not (and in the case of many local governments, are not allowed to) budget for a deficit in any one year unless they have a surplus from prior years. Because both types of organizations raise money each year and then spend it, any deficit spending in a particular year eventually must be offset by surplus spending in later years. Once the budget has been formally passed by the board of directors (or the local government legislative body), the spending for applicable budgeted expenses commences. Often an NFPO's actual expenses turn out to be equal to the amount budgeted, and problems arise when actual revenues are less than budget. Government grants are sometimes reduced, or do not increase as much as was budgeted for, or some fundraising activity is not as successful as was forecast. If this happens over a series of years, the accumulated deficit problem will have to be addressed and the NFPO will have to organize special deficit-reduction fundraising activities in addition to the normal, annual fundraising for operations.

Budgetary Control   If deficits are to be avoided, the managers of NFPOs must have timely information regarding actual results compared with amounts budgeted. This can be accomplished by formally recording the budget in the accounting system.

Example   The following is the summarized budget that was approved by the board of directors of an NFPO:

Budgeted revenues (in detail)	$900,000
Budgeted expenses (in detail)	890,000
Budgeted surplus	$ 10,000

If the organization records the budget in its accounting records, the following journal entry is made at the start of the fiscal year:

Estimated revenues (control account)	900,000	
Appropriations (control account)		890,000
Budgetary fund balance		10,000

Budget accounts are used as a control device, and the amounts are not reflected in an NFPO's external financial statements.

While it may appear strange to debit an account for budgeted revenues and to credit an account for budgeted expenses, the logic becomes clearer when one considers that budgeted revenues represent *expected* resource inflows and that budgeted expenses (with the exception of amortization) represent *expected* resource outflows. The general ledger accounts used are control accounts to the very detailed subsidiary ledger accounts needed to keep track of actual versus budgeted amounts, particularly in relation to expenses. Spending is often a continuous process, while revenues are received at various times throughout the year. If during the year it appears that actual revenues will be less than budget, it is a difficult task to reduce the budgeted expenses remaining in order to avoid a deficit. It is, however, possible with a system such as this to ensure that actual expenses do not exceed budget. The overall concept of "spending" in this context is based on an accrual system of measurement, not on a cash basis. At the end of the fiscal year the budget accounts are reversed as part of the closing journal entries, and these amounts are not reflected in the organization's external financial statements.

Encumbrance Accounting This involves making entries in the accounting records to record the issuance of purchase orders for the acquisition of goods and services from outside suppliers. The amounts recorded are estimates of the actual costs. It is not the normal practice to use encumbrance accounting for employee wage costs because this particular type of expenditure can be controlled by other means; nor is it normal to use encumbrances for amortization. When the goods and services ordered are actually received, the original encumbrance entry is reversed and the invoiced cost of the goods or services acquired is recorded.

Example Purchase order #3056A is issued for the acquisition of office supplies expected to cost $950. The journal entry to record the purchase order is as follows:

Encumbrances	950	
Estimated commitments[1]		950

When the supplies ordered under purchase order #3056A are received at an invoiced cost of $954, the following journal entries are required:

Estimated commitments	950	
Encumbrances		950
Supplies expense	954	
Accounts payable		954

Control over expenditures is achieved by mandating that the spending of a budgeted amount has occurred when the purchase order is issued, not when the goods are received or paid for. In this example, if the budgeted amount for supplies is $3,000, there is an unspent budget amount of $2,050 after the purchase order is issued, and an unspent amount of $2,046 after the receipt of the actual supplies. The use of encumbrance accounting along with a system of budgetary control prevents the issuing of purchase orders when there are no uncommitted budgeted amounts.

The only accounting problem involved is the financial statement presentation of outstanding purchase orders at the end of a fiscal period. Should the encumbrances be reflected in the operations statement as similar to expenses, and the estimated commitments appear in the statement of financial position as liabilities? In the past, NFPOs have presented these accounts in this manner. The *Handbook* sections do not mention the concept of encumbrances; however, a purchase order is an executory contract under which neither party has performed. It follows that outstanding encumbrances should not be reflected as elements of financial statements, but rather should be disclosed in the footnotes to the statements if the amounts are material.[2]

Encumbrance accounting involves the actual recording of purchase orders at the time of issuance. From a control standpoint, a budget item has been spent at this moment.

Amounts for outstanding encumbrances are considered to be executory contracts and therefore are not recorded in an NFPO's external financial statements.

---

[1] An alternative term often used is *reserve for encumbrances.*

[2] A similar conclusion was made in a CICA research study. See "Financial Reporting for Nonprofit Organizations" (Toronto: CICA, 1980), p. 52.

Illustration of the Restricted Fund Method

The following example (with 000s omitted) will be used to illustrate the journal entries made for various funds and the annual general-purpose financial statements prepared using the restricted fund method of accounting for contributions.

The Blue Shield Agency is a charitable organization located in a mid-sized Canadian city. The major goal of the organization is to provide food and shelter for the homeless. It operates out of its own premises, and while it has some permanent employees, it also relies heavily on volunteers.

The agency's funds have four sources:

- Government grants are received annually to fund the regular food and shelter operating activities. When the need arises, special government grants are solicited to fund capital asset additions and major renovations.

- Donations are received as a result of public campaigns held each March to raise funds for the current year's operating costs.

- A United Way grant is received each November to help fund the next year's operations.

- Interest is received from an endowment fund and other investments.

The agency maintains its records in accordance with the restricted fund method of accounting for contributions and prepares its annual financial statements on this basis. The three funds being used are described below.

The general fund captures the agency's operating activities.

General Fund   This fund is used to record the agency's operating activities. Revenues consist of government operating grants, the proceeds from the annual fundraising campaign, the United Way grant, interest from the endowment fund, and term deposit interest. Each year the grant from the United Way is recorded as deferred revenue to be matched against the operating expenses of the year following. Expenses are for the food and shelter programs and for administration costs. An encumbrance system is used to ensure that costs do not exceed budgeted amounts, but the budget itself is not formally recorded in the accounting records. While some donated materials and services are received each year, no record of these donations is made in the ledger accounts. Small-equipment purchases made from this fund are capitalized in the capital fund.

Capital Fund   This fund is used to account for restricted funds raised for building and equipment acquisitions. The capital fund also records the capitalization of buildings and equipment and the amortization taken. Equipment acquisitions made from the general fund are also capitalized in this fund.

Because the agency's policy, prior to the issuance of the current *Handbook*, was non-capitalization of capital asset purchases, a retroactive catch-up entry was required.

Approximately 20 years ago the city donated a building to the agency. While the city retained title to the land on which the building is situated, the agency will not be required to move, and the building will not be torn down, as long as the agency continues with its programs. The value of the donated building was *not* recorded at the time of the donation because it was the organization's policy not to capitalize buildings and equipment. When the current *Handbook* sections became operative several years ago, the organization spent considerable time and money searching past records to determine the cost of capital assets purchased from both restricted and non-restricted contributions and the fair values of capital assets donated. The new *Handbook* sections had to be applied retroactively, and the following journal entry was made at that time to accomplish this:

The previously unreported capital assets were recorded in the capital fund with an accompanying increase in net assets.

Equipment and furniture	1,100	
Buildings	2,000	
Accumulated amortization		1,200
Net assets (capital fund balance)		1,900

Endowment Fund   The $500 in this fund was bequeathed to the agency by its founder five years ago. Interest earned is to be used for operating purposes and is recorded in the general fund.

The statements of financial position of the funds of Blue Shield as at January 1, Year 6 (the start of the next fiscal year), are presented in Exhibit 12.2.

Exhibit 12.2

BLUE SHIELD AGENCY
STATEMENT OF FINANCIAL POSITION
January 1, Year 6
(in thousands of dollars)

When reporting on a fund basis, the total for each financial statement item must be shown.

	General fund	Capital fund	Endowment fund	Total
Current Assets				
Cash and term deposits	$417	$ 62		$ 479
Pledges receivable	490			490
	907	62		969
Investments			$500	500
Capital assets				
Equipment and furniture		1,482		1,482
Buildings		2,095		2,095
Accumulated amortization		(1,517)		(1,517)
		2,060		2,060
Total assets	$907	$2,122	$500	$3,529
Current Liabilities				
Accounts payable	$613	$ 50		$ 663
Wages payable	70			70
Accrued liabilities	82			82
Deferred revenue	40			40
	805	50		855
Fund Balances				
Investment in capital assets		2,060		2,060
Externally restricted		12	$500	512
Unrestricted	102			102
	102	2,072	500	2,674
Total liabilities and fund balances	$907	$2,122	$500	$3,529

This form of presentation of fund financial statements is called the *multicolumn approach* because each of the fund's financial statements is presented in its own separate column. If fund accounting is used, the *Handbook* requires that totals be shown for each item presented in the statement of financial position and statement of changes in fund balances, so that the "big picture" for the entire organization can be seen. This approach can become very cumbersome if an organization has a large number of funds that need to be presented separately because of all of the restrictions involved. An alternative is to combine the funds into a single set of statements (the deferral method of accounting for contributions), with extensive footnote disclosure of resource restrictions. For the statement of operations, a total column must be presented for general funds, endowment funds, and restricted funds. Although it is desirable to show a total for all funds, it is not necessary under the restricted fund method.

Year 6 Events The year's events are summarized as follows (all dollar amounts are in thousands unless stated otherwise):

(a) The accounts and wages payable and the accrued liabilities at the beginning of the year were paid.

(b) The deferred revenue from Year 5 consisted of the grant from the United Way. An entry was made to recognize this as revenue in Year 6.

(c) The pledges receivable at the beginning of the year were collected in full.

(d) The Year 6 fundraising campaign was held in March. Cash of $1,187 was collected, and pledges expected to realize $800 were received. Total fundraising costs were $516, of which $453 was paid in cash, $50 is owed to suppliers, and $13 has been accrued.

(e) During Year 6, the agency announced a plan to construct an addition to its building at an estimated cost of $1,500. The budget includes equipment acquisitions. The addition will be built in two phases, with completion expected in Year 8. At the end of Year 6 the first phase was out for tender, with construction to commence early in Year 7.

   The government announced a grant of $600 in Year 6 to cover the first phase and has remitted $450 of this, with the balance promised in Year 7. The agency spent $103 on equipment near the end of Year 6, of which $91 has been paid and $12 is still owing. At the beginning of the year the agency had $62 on hand from a previous building campaign and an unpaid liability of $50 for capital asset purchases. A public campaign will be conducted next year to raise the balance of the funds needed to complete the project.

(f) Government grants for operating purposes totalled $1,200 in Year 6, of which $910 was received during the year, with the balance expected in January, Year 7.

(g) The agency uses an encumbrance system as a means of controlling expenditures. (Note: Wages of agency employees are not subject to encumbrance because purchase orders are not issued for this type of expenditure.) During the year, orders estimated to total $1,964 were issued for the purchase of goods and services.

(h) Invoices totalling $1,866 were received on purchase orders originally recorded at an estimated cost of $1,870. Suppliers were paid $1,446 on account for these invoices, and the balance owing is still outstanding. The costs were allocated as follows:

Shelter program	$650
Food program	960
Administration	256

(i) The total wage costs, of which $357 was paid and $183 is payable at year-end, were as follows:

Shelter program	$ 90
Food program	150
Administration	300

(j) The United Way grant amounting to $65 was received in December.

(k) Late in the year a prominent supporter donated $50 to be held in endowment, with the interest earned to be unrestricted.

(l) The investments in the endowment fund earned interest of $40; a further $14 in interest was received from the term deposits held in the general fund.

(m) Refrigeration equipment costing $3 was purchased with general fund cash.

(n) The Year 6 amortization charges amounted to $150.

(o) At the end of the year the balances in the encumbrance accounts were closed.

The journal entries required to record these events in each of the three funds are presented next in the order listed:

Accounting records are maintained for each individual fund. Journal entries show the fund being adjusted.

(a) *General fund*

Accounts payable	613	
Wages payable	70	
Accrued liabilities	82	
Cash		765

Capital fund

Accounts payable	50	
Cash		50

(b) *General fund*

Deferred revenue	40	
Revenue — United Way grant		40

(c) *General fund*

Cash	490	
Pledges receivable		490

Contributions and pledges for the current year are reported as revenue in the current year.

(d) *General fund*

Cash	1,187	
Pledges receivable	800	
Revenue — donations		1,987
Expenses — fundraising	516	
Cash		453
Accounts payable		50
Accrued liabilities		13

Contributions and pledges for a restricted fund are reported as revenue when received/ receivable.

(e) *Capital fund*

Cash	450	
Government grant receivable	150	
Revenue — government grant		600
Equipment	103	
Cash		91
Accounts payable		12

(f) *General fund*

Cash	910	
Government grant receivable	290	
Revenue — government grant		1,200

(g) *General fund*

Encumbrances	1,964	
Estimated commitments		1,964

Encumbrances are reversed when the goods and services are received.

(h) *General fund*

Estimated commitments	1,870	
Encumbrances		1,870
Expenses — shelter program	650	
Expenses — food program	960	
Expenses — administration	256	
Cash		1,446
Accounts payable		420

(i) *General fund*

Expenses — shelter program	90	
Expenses — food program	150	
Expenses — administration	300	
Cash		357
Wages payable		183

Contributions for next year's activities are deferred when a separate restricted fund is not established for the contributions.

(j) *General fund*

Cash	65	
Deferred revenue — United Way		65

(k) *Endowment fund*

Cash	50	
Revenue — contribution		50

(l) *General fund*

Cash	54	
Revenue — investment income		54

(m) *General fund*

Transfer to capital fund	3	
Cash		3

Capital fund

Equipment	3	
Transfer from general fund		3

(n) *Capital fund*

Expenses — amortization	150	
Accumulated amortization		150

(o) *General fund*

Estimated commitments	94	
Encumbrances		94

After these journal entries are posted, financial statements as at December 31, Year 6, can be prepared as shown in Exhibit 12.3.

Note that while a fund type of cash flow statement could be prepared, the one in this illustration has been prepared on a non-fund basis, which is in accordance with the *Handbook*'s pronouncements. Letters shown in parentheses represent the journal entries affecting the cash account.

Exhibit 12.3

BLUE SHIELD AGENCY
STATEMENT OF FINANCIAL POSITION
December 31, Year 6
(in thousands of dollars)

	General fund	Capital fund	Endowment fund	Total
The deferral method is used to account for contributions reported in the general fund.				
Current Assets				
Cash and term deposits	$ 99	$ 371	$ 50	$ 520
Pledges receivable	800			800
Government grants receivable	290	150		440
	1,189	521	50	1,760
Investments			500	500
Capital assets				
Equipment and furniture		1,588		1,588
Buildings		2,095		2,095
Accumulated depreciation		(1,667)		(1,667)
		2,016		2,016
Total assets	$1,189	$2,537	$550	$4,276
Current Liabilities				
Accounts payable	$ 470	$ 12		$ 482
Wages payable	183			183
Accrued liabilities	13			13
Deferred revenue	65			65
	731	12		743
Fund Balances				
Investment in capital assets[3]		2,016		2,016
Externally restricted funds		509	550	1,059
Unrestricted funds	458			458
	458	2,525	550	3,533
Total liabilities and fund balances	$1,189	$2,537	$550	$4,276

Fund balances show the restrictions on the net assets of the organization.

(continued)

---

[3] If the entity chooses to not present this account separately, the $2,016 would be included in the other two components of net assets based on whether the capital assets were purchased with restricted or unrestricted resources.

BLUE SHIELD AGENCY
STATEMENT OF REVENUES, EXPENSES, AND
CHANGES IN FUND BALANCES
for the Year Ended December 31, Year 6
(in thousands of dollars)

	General fund	Capital fund	Endowment fund	Total
Revenues				
Government grants	$1,200	$ 600		$1,800
United Way grant	40			40
Contributions	1,987		$ 50	2,037
Investment income	54			54
	3,281	600	50	3,931
Expenses				
Shelter program	740			740
Food program	1,110			1,110
Administration	556			556
Fundraising	516			516
Amortization		150		150
	2,922	150		3,072
Excess of revenue over expenses	359	450	50	859
Interfund transfers	(3)	3		
Fund balances, January 1	102	2,072	500	2,674
Fund balances, December 31	$ 458	$2,525	$550	$3,533

Expenses are classified by function. (margin note)

BLUE SHIELD AGENCY
CASH FLOW STATEMENT
for the Year Ended December 31, Year 6
(in thousands of dollars)

It is not required to present a cash flow statement on a fund basis. (margin note)

Cash Flows from Operating Activities	
Cash received from government operating grants **(f)**	$ 910
Cash received from United Way grant **(j)**	65
Cash received from general contributions **(c)**, **(d)**	1,677
Cash received from investment income **(l)**	54
Cash paid to suppliers **(a)**, **(h)**	(2,141)
Cash paid to employees **(a)**, **(i)**	(427)
Cash paid for fundraising **(d)**	(453)
Net cash used in operating activities	(315)
Cash Flows from Investing Activities	
Cash paid for capital asset acquisitions **(a)**, **(e)**, **(m)**	(144)
Net cash used in investing activities	(144)
Cash Flows from Financing Activities	
Contributions of cash for endowment **(k)**	50
Cash received from government grant **(e)**	450
Net cash generated through financing activities	500
Net increase in cash and term deposits	41
Cash and term deposits — January 1	479
Cash and term deposits — December 31	$ 520

The closing entries for each fund are prepared as follows:

Revenues, expenses, and fund transfers are closed to fund balances.

General fund

Revenue — government grant	1,200	
Revenue — United Way grant	40	
Revenue — contributions	1,987	
Revenue — investment income	54	
Expenses — shelter program		740
Expenses — food program		1,110
Expenses — administration		556
Expenses — fundraising		516
Fund balance		359
Fund balance	3	
Transfer to capital fund		3

Capital fund

Revenue — government grant	600	
Expenses — amortization		150
Fund balance		450
Transfer from general fund	3	
Fund balance		3

Endowment fund

Revenue contributions	50	
Fund balance		50

This comprehensive example has illustrated the accounts used and the resulting financial statements under the restricted fund method. The extensive footnote disclosures required by the *Handbook* have not been illustrated.

Illustration of the Deferral Method

To illustrate the journal entries made and the annual general-purpose financial statements prepared using the deferral method of accounting for contributions, we will use the same basic information as was used in the previous example (with 000s omitted). Although not required, Blue Shield will show "net assets invested in capital assets" as a separate component of net assets.

When the *Handbook*'s current NFPO sections became operative several years ago, the organization spent considerable time and money searching past records to determine the cost of capital assets purchased from both restricted and non-restricted contributions, as well as the fair values of capital assets donated. Because the new *Handbook* had to be applied retroactively, the following journal entries were made at that time to accomplish this:

Net assets invested in capital assets represent the portion of unrestricted net assets that is tied up in capital assets and is not available for future spending.

Equipment and furniture	1,100	
Accumulated amortization		300
Net assets invested in capital assets		800

This entry recognized the cost of equipment acquired in past years using unrestricted contributions and the accumulated amortization to date.

Buildings	2,000	
Accumulated amortization		900
Deferred contributions related to capital assets		1,100

Deferred contributions represent the unamortized amount of capital assets either donated or acquired with restricted contributions.

This entry recorded the fair value of the building donated by the city and the accumulated amortization taken to date. A capital asset donation is treated in the same manner as a contribution restricted for the purchase of a capital asset. As the asset is amortized, a portion of the deferred contribution is recognized as a match against this expense.

The statement of financial position of Blue Shield as at January 1, Year 6 (the start of the next fiscal year), is presented in Exhibit 12.4.

Exhibit 12.4

BLUE SHIELD AGENCY
STATEMENT OF FINANCIAL POSITION
January 1, Year 6
(in thousands of dollars)

It is quite common to not present separate funds when the entity uses the deferral method.

Current Assets	
Cash and term deposits	$ 479
Pledges receivable	490
	969
Investments	500
Capital assets	
Equipment and furniture	1,482
Buildings	2,095
Accumulated amortization	(1,517)
	2,060
Total assets	$3,529
Current Liabilities	
Accounts payable	$ 663
Wages payable	70
Accrued liabilities	82
Deferred revenue	40
	855
Long-term Liabilities	
Deferred contributions related to capital assets	550
Deferred building campaign contributions	12
	562

Net assets invested in capital assets represents the unamortized amount of capital assets purchased from unrestricted contributions.

Net Assets	
Net assets invested in capital assets[4]	1,510
Net assets restricted for endowment purposes	500
Unrestricted net assets	102
	2,112
Total liabilities and net assets	$3,529

---

[4] If the entity chooses to not present this account separately, the $1,510 would be included in the unrestricted net assets component of net assets.

When this statement of financial position is compared to the statement of financial position under the restricted fund method (see Exhibit 12.2 on page 661), the amounts used on the asset side are fairly obvious. The liability side needs further clarification. The amount in *deferred revenue* is the United Way grant. The *deferred building campaign contributions* balance is the externally restricted fund balance from the capital fund, and represents restricted funds received but not spent on capital assets. When this money is spent, an amount will be transferred from this deferred contribution account to the *deferred contributions related to capital assets* account. The *deferred contributions related to capital assets* balance represents that portion of the unamortized balance of capital assets that was either donated or purchased from contributions restricted for capital asset purchases. This will be transferred to revenue in future periods as these assets are amortized. The balance of $550 was not shown in the capital fund in the previous statement of financial position.

The differences in presentation are as follows:

Restricted fund method:

Fund balances — investment in capital assets	$2,060
Fund balances — externally restricted	12
	$2,072

Deferral method:

Liability — deferred contributions related to capital assets	$ 550
Liability — deferred building campaign contributions	12
	562
Net assets — net assets invested in capital assets	1,510
	$2,072

The $500 *net assets restricted for endowment purposes* is the fund balance from the endowment fund and originated from the founder's bequest. Interest earned is not restricted.

The *unrestricted net asset balance* comes from the general fund balance.

Year 6 Events   The year's events for all transactions are the same as were used in the previous example. The journal entries required to record these events are presented next in the order listed.

(a)	Accounts payable	663
	Wages payable	70
	Accrued liabilities	82
	Cash	815
(b)	Deferred revenue	40
	Revenue — United Way grant	40
(c)	Cash	490
	Pledges receivable	490

The deferred contributions distinguish between unspent contributions and the unamortized portion of contributions being matched to amortization expense.

The financial statement presentation for contributions is substantially different under the two different reporting methods.

Fund accounting is not applied and journal entries are not segregated by fund.

Contributions and pledges for the current year are reported as revenue in the current year.

(d)	Cash	1,187	
	Pledges receivable	800	
	Revenue — donations		1,987
	Expenses — fundraising	516	
	Cash		453
	Accounts payable		50
	Accrued liabilities		13

Contributions restricted for depreciable capital assets are reported as deferred contributions.

(e)	Cash	450	
	Government grant receivable	150	
	Deferred building campaign contributions		600
	Equipment	103	
	Cash		91
	Accounts payable		12
	Deferred building campaign contributions	103	
	Deferred contributions — capital assets		103
(f)	Cash	910	
	Government grant receivable	290	
	Revenue — government grant		1,200
(g)	Encumbrances	1,964	
	Estimated commitments		1,964
(h)	Estimated commitments	1,870	
	Encumbrances		1,870
	Expenses — shelter program	650	
	Expenses — food program	960	
	Expenses — administration	256	
	Cash		1,446
	Accounts payable		420
(i)	Expenses — shelter program	90	
	Expenses — food program	150	
	Expenses — administration	300	
	Cash		357
	Wages payable		183

Contributions for next year's activities are deferred until related expenses are recognized.

Endowment contributions are reported directly in net assets.

(j)	Cash	65	
	Deferred revenue — United Way		65
(k)	Cash	50	
	Net assets — endowment		50
(l)	Cash	54	
	Revenue — investment income		54
(m)	Equipment	3	
	Cash		3

(n) Expenses — amortization	150	
Accumulated amortization		150
Deferred contributions — capital assets	90	
Amortization of deferred contributions		90
(o) Estimated commitments	94	
Encumbrances		94

Deferred contributions are brought into income as the capital assets are amortized over their useful lives.

After these journal entries are posted, financial statements as at December 31, Year 6, can be prepared as shown in Exhibit 12.5 on page 672.

The statement of revenue and expenses shows not only unrestricted revenues and expenses, but also the restricted revenues recognized during the year as a match to the expenses associated with them (amortization in this case). The $299 excess of revenues over expenses is transferred to the "total" column in the statement of changes in net assets.

The excess of revenues over expenses is split between invested in capital assets and unrestricted in the statement of changes in net assets.

The portion of the amortization expense from assets acquired with unrestricted resources is transferred so that it is deducted in the *invested in capital assets* column, leaving $359 as the amount of operating results allocated to unrestricted resources. Because a portion of amortization has been removed ($60), and the remainder ($90) has been offset with an equal amount of revenue, this amount represents the increase in resources that can be spent in future periods. The unrestricted resources that were spent on equipment during the period ($3) are shown as a transfer from the unrestricted column to the invested in capital assets column.

An examination of the statement of financial position shows the following equality regarding capital assets purchased from restricted and unrestricted resources:

Deferred contributions — capital assets (restricted)	$ 563
Net assets invested in capital assets (unrestricted)	1,453
Total capital assets (from both sources)	$2,016

If the entity chooses to not present the "net assets invested in capital assets" account separately, the balance from this account would be included in unrestricted net assets. There would not be a separate column for invested in capital assets in the statement of changes in net assets. There would be no need to allocate amounts between the unrestricted column and invested in capital assets column as described above. The accounting would be simpler but the information value of this account would be lost.

The endowment contribution received during the year does not appear on the operating statement because no expenses will ever appear for the required matching process to occur. Instead, this special restricted resource is shown on the statement of changes in *net assets* as an increase in the column net assets restricted for endowment. Extensive footnote disclosure is required when statements are prepared using the deferral method, in order to clearly define the amount and nature of restricted and unrestricted resources.

Exhibit 12.5

BLUE SHIELD AGENCY
STATEMENT OF FINANCIAL POSITION
December 31, Year 6
(in thousands of dollars)

Current Assets	
Cash and term deposits	$ 520
Pledges receivable	800
Government grants receivable	440
	1,760
Investments	500
Capital Assets	
Equipment and furniture	1,588
Buildings	2,095
Accumulated amortization	(1,667)
	2,016
Total assets	$4,276
Current Liabilities	
Accounts payable	$ 482
Wages payable	183
Accrued liabilities	13
Deferred revenue	65
	743
Long-term Liabilities	
Deferred contributions related to capital assets	563
Deferred building campaign contributions	509
	1,072
Net Assets	
Net assets invested in capital assets	1,453
Net assets restricted for endowment purposes	550
Unrestricted net assets	458
	2,461
Total liabilities and net assets	$4,276

The unamortized portion of spent restricted contributions is segregated from the unspent restricted contributions.

The net assets invested in capital assets account does not have to be reported separately; it could be combined with unrestricted net assets.

BLUE SHIELD AGENCY
STATEMENT OF REVENUES AND EXPENSES
for the Year Ended December 31, Year 6
(in thousands of dollars)

Revenues	
Government grants	$1,200
United Way grant	40
Contributions	1,987
Investment income	54
Amortization of deferred contributions	90
	3,371

Expenses

Shelter program	740
Food program	1,110
Administration	556
Fundraising	516
Amortization of capital assets	150
	3,072
Excess of revenues over expenses	$ 299

BLUE SHIELD AGENCY
STATEMENT OF CHANGES IN NET ASSETS
for the Year Ended December 31, Year 6
(in thousands of dollars)

	Invested in capital assets	Restricted for endowment purposes	Unrestricted	Total
Balance, Jan. 1	$1,510	$500	$102	$2,112
Excess of revenues over expenses	(60)		359	299
Endowment contributions		50		50
Investment in capital assets	3		(3)	
Balance, Dec. 31	$1,453	$550	$458	$2,461

The net assets invested in capital assets captures the portion of the unrestricted net assets that is not available for future spending.

BLUE SHIELD AGENCY
CASH FLOW STATEMENT
for the Year Ended December 31, Year 6
(in thousands of dollars)

Cash Flows from Operating Activities

Cash received from government operating grants **(f)**	$ 910
Cash received from United Way grant **(j)**	65
Cash received from general contributions **(c)**, **(d)**	1,677
Cash received from investment income **(l)**	54
Cash paid to suppliers **(a)**, **(h)**	(2,141)
Cash paid to employees **(a)**, **(i)**	(427)
Cash paid for fundraising **(d)**	(453)
Net cash used in operating activities	(315)

The cash flow statement segregates cash flows by operating, investing, and financing activities.

Cash Flows from Investing Activities

Cash paid for capital asset acquisitions **(a)**, **(e)**, **(m)**	(144)
Net cash used in investing activities	(144)

Cash Flows from Financing Activities

Contributions of cash for endowment **(k)**	50
Cash received from government grant **(e)**	450
Net cash generated through financing activities	500
Net increase in cash and term deposits	41
Cash and term deposits, Jan. 1	479
Cash and term deposits, Dec. 31	$ 520

Closing entries as at December 31, Year 6, are presented next.

Revenues and expenses are closed to fund balances.

Revenue — government grant	1,200	
Revenue — United Way grant	40	
Revenue — contributions	1,987	
Revenue — investment income	54	
Expenses — shelter program		740
Expenses — food program		1,110
Expenses — administration		556
Expenses — fundraising		516
Unrestricted net assets		359
To close the unrestricted revenues and expenses		

Unrestricted net assets	3	
Net assets invested in capital assets		3

Net assets invested in capital assets is updated for changes in capital assets financed by unrestricted resources.

To transfer the amount of capital assets acquired from unrestricted resources[5]

Net assets invested in capital assets	60	
Amortization of deferred contributions	90	
Expenses — amortization		150

To close restricted revenues and the expenses related to capital assets[6]

Disclosure Requirements   The disclosure requirements for NFPOs are quite extensive. Some of those requirements were briefly described throughout the chapter. The following summarizes the main disclosures required in Section 4410 related to revenue from contributions:

The major sources of and accounting policies for contributions must be disclosed.

- Its contributions by major sources including the nature and amount of contributed materials and services recognized in the financial statements;

- The policies followed in accounting for endowment contributions, restricted contributions, and contributed materials and services;

- The nature and amount of changes in deferred contribution balances for the period;

- How and where net investment income earned on resources held for endowment is recognized in the financial statements.

United Way/Centraide Ottawa is a non-profit Ontario corporation and a registered charity. Excerpts from United Way/Centraide Ottawa's 2008 financial statements are provided in Exhibit 12.6.

Exhibit 12.6

EXTRACTS (IN PART) FROM UNITED WAY/CENTRAIDE OTTAWA'S 2008 FINANCIAL STATEMENTS

Significant accounting policies:

(a)   Revenue recognition:

United Way/Centraide Ottawa follows the deferral method of accounting for contributions and expenditures. Support from the general public consists of pledges and contributions

---

[5]   This entry would not be necessary if the entity chose not to present net assets invested in capital assets separately.

[6]   These two accounts would be closed to unrestricted net assets if the entity chose not to present net assets invested in capital assets separately.

relating to the prior year's campaign. Pledges receivable from individuals and organizations are recorded at an estimated realizable value at the time of pledge commitment. Funds raised during a campaign, net of related campaign expenses and provisions, are used to provide funds for funded programs, other Canadian registered charities and operations in the following fiscal year. Accordingly, they are deferred at the end of the campaign year and are recorded in the statement of operations in the following year.

Investment revenue earned on endowments is recognized as revenue when the related expenditure is incurred.

Contributions to endowments are recorded as direct increases to the endowment net asset balance.

(b)   Deferred revenue:

Restricted contributions are recognized as revenue in the year in which the related expenses are incurred.

(c)   Donated services:

Donated services are not recognized because the value of the services is not objectively measurable.

No amounts have been reflected in the financial statements for donated services, since no objective basis is available to measure the value of such services. Nevertheless, a substantial number of volunteers have donated significant amounts of their time in United Way/Centraide Ottawa programs, services and fundraising campaigns.

Source: Reproduced with permission from United Way/Centraide Ottawa.

SUMMARY

Eight *Handbook* sections are specifically dedicated to NFPOs, along with 38 others, which are applicable to all or many NFPOs. These *Handbook* sections have dramatically changed the financial reporting of NFPOs over the past 15 years. We have moved from a situation where virtually no authoritative standards existed to one where full and proportionate consolidation of controlled and jointly controlled entities is allowed, and asset capitalization and amortization are required for all but "small" organizations. Rather than mandating a single reporting model, the new standard gives NFPOs the choice between the deferral and restricted fund methods of financial statement presentation and allows them the flexibility to use a mix of both methods if they feel that it will result in a better presentation. While these changes have moved not-for-profit more toward a business approach of reporting and away from the stewardship-of-resources approach that was previously used, not-for-profit reporting is still very distinct, and certainly far more complex than it was before.

Significant Changes in the Last Two Years

1.   Although IFRSs have been adopted for publicly accountable enterprises, no decision has been made as to the applicability of IFRSs for NFPOs. IFRSs do not currently contain any standards specifically tailored for NFPOs.

2.   Net assets invested in capital assets are no longer required to be shown separately in the net assets section of the statement of financial position. This amount can be shown as an internal restriction and grouped with other restricted net assets, disclosed in the notes, or not dealt with as a separate component.

3.   NFPOs are now required to present a cash flow statement showing the three categories of cash flows from operating, investing, and financing activities.

4. When an NFPO acts as a principal in a transaction, revenues and expenses are to be reported at their gross amounts.

5. A new *Handbook* section was added that provides guidance on the allocation of fundraising and general support costs to other functions if such an allocation is chosen by an NFPO.

Changes Expected in the Next Three Years

The CICA will decide on the reporting options available to NFPOs. It will decide whether an NFPO can or must use IFRSs, can or must use GAAP for private enterprises, and can or must use the 4400 series of *Handbook* sections. This decision could have major reporting implications for NFPOs.

SELF-STUDY PROBLEM

Watrous Housing Corporation (WHC) is a community-sponsored not-for-profit housing organization that was incorporated on September 1, Year 5. Its purpose is to provide residential accommodation for physically disabled adults in the town of Watrous. The nature of WHC's operations and its source of funding are described in Exhibit I. The executive director of WHC has asked for your assistance in establishing accounting policies for WHC for its general-purpose year-end financial statements. The accounting policies should be consistent with GAAP.

Exhibit I

NATURE OF OPERATIONS

- In October Year 5, WHC purchased a 15-unit apartment building in downtown Watrous for $750,000. It then spent $250,000 in renovations to upgrade the building to make it accessible for physically disabled adults.

- WHC offers 24-hour non-medical attendant care. Support care services are provided through a combination of staff members and volunteers. The staff members receive a monthly salary. As an inducement to recruit and retain qualified support care workers, each staff member is allowed 15 sick days per year. The employee can bank the sick days not used in any one year. Upon termination or retirement, the employee is paid for banked sick days at the wage rate in effect at that time.

- Rental payments are due the first day of each month and are geared to each tenant's income. Most of the tenants are very good about making their rent payments on time. Some rental payments are received late. On August 31, Year 6, there was $13,000 of unpaid rent.

- WHC plans to install central air conditioning in the building in April Year 7 at an expected cost of $50,000. This expenditure is being financed by a special fundraising drive. By August 31, Year 6, this fundraising drive had raised $20,000 in cash and $15,000 in pledges from citizens in the local community.

SOURCES OF FUNDING

- The cost of acquiring and renovating the apartment building was financed by a $1,000,000 cash donation received from the estate of Mr. Smith.

- The provincial government funds approximately 70 percent of non-medical care and support costs. Claims are made monthly for the previous month's eligible costs.
- WHC depends on outside fundraising efforts, primarily door-to-door canvassing and sponsored bingos, to cover the remaining non-medical care and support costs.

Required:

Identify the major accounting issues, and provide recommendations on the accounting treatment of these issues in WHC's financial statements for the year ended August 31, Year 6. Assume that WHC wants to use fund accounting with two funds, a general fund and a capital fund, and wants to use the deferral method to account for contributions. Also assume that annual revenues exceed $700,000.

Solution to Self-study Problem

WHC should adopt the following recommendations for the related accounting issues for its year-end financial statements:

- The accrual basis of accounting should be used in order to properly match revenues to expenses.
- The cost of acquiring and renovating the apartment building should be capitalized as an asset in the capital fund.
- The building should be amortized over its useful life. Amortization expense should be reported as an expense of the capital fund.
- The $1,000,000 cash donation from Mr. Smith and the cash received for the planned expenditures on air-conditioning equipment should be recorded as deferred contributions in the capital fund. The deferred contributions should be amortized into revenue over the life of the related assets to match to the amortization expense on these assets.
- Salary costs should be expensed as incurred in the general fund.
- The estimated costs of unpaid sick leave should be set up as a liability and as an expense of the general fund on an annual basis.
- The value of the volunteers' time provided for support care services can be set up as revenue and an expense of the general fund, if the amount is measurable and such services would be purchased had the volunteers not provided them.
- The contributions from the provincial government should be accrued as a receivable and revenue of the general fund at the end of each month based on actual costs incurred during the month.
- The rent from the tenants should be recognized as revenue of the general fund in the month in which it is due. At the end of the year, an allowance should be set up for any doubtful accounts.
- Donations from door-to-door canvassing and proceeds received from bingos should be recognized as revenue of the general fund as the cash is received.
- The pledges received for the planned expenditure on air-conditioning equipment should be recorded as pledges receivable and deferred contributions of the capital fund to the extent that the amount to be received can be reasonably estimated and the ultimate collection is reasonably assured.

APPENDIX 12A

Sample Financial Statements for Not-for-Profit Organizations

This appendix contains the 2008 statement of financial position, statement of operations, statement of changes in net assets, and cash flow statement for United Way/ Centraide Ottawa.[7] This organization brings people together from all parts of its community to identify, develop, and provide solutions for community needs, helping to ensure that the donations received will go where they are needed most and where they will have the greatest impact. The deferral method of accounting has been used for contributions, and expenses have been recorded using the accrual basis.

UNITED WAY/CENTRAIDE OTTAWA
Statement of Financial Position
December 31, 2008, with comparative figures for 2007

	2008	2007
Assets		
Current assets:		
Cash	$ 3,947,196	$ 5,902,801
Pledges receivable	23,818,948	21,447,373
Accounts receivable	1,990,510	2,101,224
Prepaid expenses	53,930	159,991
	29,810,584	29,611,389
Long-term assets:		
Investments:		
Restricted funds (endowment)	2,443,948	2,410,423
Unrestricted	351,516	466,575
	2,795,464	2,876,998
Capital assets	825,100	801,715
	3,620,564	3,678,713
	$ 33,431,148	$ 33,290,102
Liabilities and Fund Balances		
Current liabilities:		
Accounts payable and accrued liabilities	$ 2,547,359	$ 2,766,957
Deferred revenue	1,550,170	1,477,030
Designations payable	13,504,452	12,195,424
Deferred campaign funds	11,394,570	11,878,868
	28,996,551	28,318,279
Long-term liabilities:		
Deferred lease inducement	36,222	39,240
Net assets:		
Unrestricted	977,476	1,443,031
Internally restricted for community services	151,851	277,414
Internally restricted for capital assets	825,100	801,715
Endowment	2,443,948	2,410,423
	4,398,375	4,932,583
Lease commitments		
Contingency and guarantee		
	$ 33,431,148	$ 33,290,102

[7] For a complete copy of United Way/Centraide Ottawa's financial statements, go to www.unitedwayottawa.ca.

UNITED WAY/CENTRAIDE OTTAWA
Statement of Operations
Year ended December 31, 2008, with comparative figures for 2007

	2008	2007
Revenue:		
Donations	$ 29,520,331	$ 27,559,581
Funds transferred from/to other United Ways/Centraides	319,826	653,551
Gross campaign revenue	29,840,157	28,213,132
Less: provision for uncollectible pledges	(1,715,800)	(1,623,000)
Recovery of uncollectible pledges	396,067	62,686
Net campaign revenue	28,520,424	26,652,818
Other revenue	1,687,680	1,772,627
	30,208,104	28,425,445
Expenses:		
Fundraising	4,503,400	4,168,377
Net revenue available for programs	25,704,704	24,257,068
Programs:		
Allocations and designations	20,421,884	19,345,555
United Way/Centraide Ottawa programs	5,815,737	4,653,597
	26,237,621	23,999,152
Capacity development expenses	34,816	—
Excess (deficiency) of revenue over expenses	$ (567,733)	$ 257,916

UNITED WAY/CENTRAIDE OTTAWA
Statement of Changes in Net Assets
Year ended December 31, 2008, with comparative figures for 2007

	2008	2007
Unrestricted:		
Balance, beginning of year	$ 1,443,031	$ 1,203,967
Excess (deficiency) of revenue over expenses	(567,733)	257,916
Adjustment for adoption of new accounting standards	—	14,963
	875,298	1,476,846
Transfer from internally restricted for community services	125,563	112,514
Transfer to internally restricted for capital assets	(23,385)	(146,329)
Balance, end of year	$ 977,476	$ 1,443,031
Internally restricted for community services:		
Balance, beginning of year	$ 277,414	$ 389,928
Transfer to unrestricted	(125,563)	(112,514)
Balance, end of year	$ 151,851	$ 277,414
Internally restricted for capital assets:		
Balance, beginning of year	$ 801,715	$ 655,386
Transfer from unrestricted	23,385	146,329
Balance, end of year	$ 825,100	$ 801,715
Endowment:		
Balance, beginning of year	$ 2,410,423	$ 2,289,196
Contributions	33,525	121,227
Balance, end of year	$ 2,443,948	$ 2,410,423
Total net assets	$ 4,398,375	$ 4,932,583

UNITED WAY/CENTRAIDE OTTAWA
Statement of Cash Flows
Year ended December 31, 2008, with comparative figures for 2007

	2008	2007
Cash provided by (used in):		
Operations:		
Excess (deficiency) of revenue over expenses	$ (567,733)	$ 257,916
Items not involving cash		
Amortization of capital assets	191,744	173,464
Amortization of deferred lease inducement	(3,018)	(3,019)
Unrealized loss on unrestricted investments	18,163	22,030
Change in non-cash operating working capital:		
Pledges receivable	(2,371,575)	(1,142,196)
Accounts receivable	110,714	(437,965)
Prepaid expenses	106,061	(70,218)
Accounts payable and accrued liabilities	(219,598)	483,249
Deferred revenue	199,420	716,510
Designations payable	1,309,028	1,155,102
Deferred campaign funds	(484,298)	(191,983)
	(1,711,092)	962,890
Investing:		
Acquisition of capital assets	(215,129)	(319,793)
Net acquisitions of investment	(62,909)	(183,811)
Contributions to endowment	33,525	121,227
Opening adjustment for unrealized gain on endowed investments	—	14,963
	(244,513)	(367,414)
Increase (decrease) in cash	(1,955,605)	595,476
Cash, beginning of year	5,902,801	5,307,325
Cash, end of year	$ 3,947,196	$ 5,902,801

Source: Reproduced with permission from United Way/Centraide Ottawa.

APPENDIX 12B

Accounting for Governments

Governments differ from business organizations in a number of ways.

Governments differ from business organizations in many ways, some of which can be summarized as follows:

- Governments do not exist to make a profit but rather to provide services.

- While the major source of business revenue comes from the sale of goods or services or both, most of a government's revenue comes from taxation.

- Businesses have to compete, while governments operate in essentially a non-competitive environment.

- Often a major goal of government is the redistribution of wealth. A major goal of a business is the maximization of the wealth of its owners.

- The federal and provincial governments have virtually an unlimited capacity to borrow, constrained only by their ability to raise taxes in order to repay. A business's earning capacity is a major constraining factor in its ability to issue debt.

- While a business purchases capital assets in order to earn a return, a government's capital asset acquisitions are made to provide services.

www.mcgrawhillconnect.ca

- A government's budget plan, approved by a legislative process at the start of a fiscal period, attracts considerable attention in the press, as does the eventual comparison of actual results with those budgeted for originally. Businesses do not normally report their budgets, and their annual results are usually compared with results of prior periods with no mention of the year's budget.

With such differences it is not surprising that government reporting models have been quite different from those used by businesses. This was certainly the case 10 or 15 years ago, but lately, changes have been made that have brought government accounting rules much closer to those required for business, although many differences still exist. This will be more evident when government accounting standards are summarized later in this appendix.

Prior to 1980, there was much diversity in reporting by government organizations.

Prior to the 1980s, a comprehensive body of accounting principles for governments did not exist. The CICA was involved only with setting the financial reporting standards for business organizations; no other body had established authoritative standards for governments. The desperate financial condition of some large American cities, which, it was argued, was not adequately reported in their financial statements, became the focus of attention of standard-setting bodies in the United States, soon followed by the CICA in Canada. Before plunging into this area, the CICA created a committee with a mandate to determine what practices were being followed by the federal, provincial, and territorial governments[8] and to recommend needed changes. As a result of the findings and recommendations of this committee, the CICA established the Public Sector Accounting and Auditing Committee (PSAAC) in 1981 and charged it with the development of accounting principles for governments. Before proceeding, PSAAC created a second study group, with a similar mandate to that of the first one, to report on the financial reporting practices of cities, municipalities, towns, and villages.[9] This study group made reference to a previous research study commissioned by the Certified General Accountants Association of Canada[10] and concluded that it would use the CGA study's findings and recommendations as a starting point for its own study. All three research studies came to similar conclusions about government financial reporting practices in general. These conclusions can be summarized by saying *that there was such a diversity of terminology, measurements, and reporting practices being used that comparability among similar government organizations*[11] *was virtually impossible and that this situation should not be allowed to continue.*

The CICA has created a new *Public Sector Accounting Handbook*, which contains the GAAP applicable to federal, provincial, territorial, and local governments.

At first the standard-setting process proceeded slowly and only a few statements on accounting and auditing were issued by PSAAC. Then in 1998 the CICA formed the Public Sector Accounting Board (PSAB) and proceeded with the reorganization of the *CICA Handbook* by transferring the auditing recommendations to the Assurance section of the *Handbook*, and the creation of a new *Public Sector Accounting Handbook*. Previously issued accounting statements were revised and amended as *Public Sector Accounting Handbook* sections.

---

[8] "Financial Reporting by Governments," a research study, Toronto: CICA, 1980.

[9] "Local Government Financial Reporting," a research study, Toronto: CICA, 1985.

[10] A. Beedle, "Accounting for Local Government in Canada: The State of the Art," Vancouver: Canadian Certified General Accountants' Research Foundation, 1981.

[11] For example, the provinces of Manitoba and Nova Scotia, and the cities of Vancouver and Montreal.

Compliance with PSAB Reporting Standards

If a business organization does not follow the *CICA Handbook* in its financial reporting it can suffer substantial penalties because legislation and security regulations require GAAP to be used. When a new accounting standard is issued, businesses (especially public companies) tend to adopt the new standard immediately. NFPOs also tend to follow the *Handbook* in their financial reporting. Failure to do so could result in a reduction of support, especially in the area of grants from governments amendment and from other NFPOs. Governments, though, are different. They often exhibit tardiness in adopting new standards, and sometimes refuse to adopt certain standards. The reasons for this are as follows:

Some governments in Canada have failed to adopt new government accounting standards for a number of reasons.

- The federal government and each of the provincial and territorial governments prepare their financial reports in accordance with the legislation enacted by each body. The adoption of a new reporting standard often requires an amendment to an act.

- Local governments are created by an act of the legislature of the province or territory in which they are located. Changes in local government reporting often require changes in legislation.

- Legislative changes necessary to adopt new accounting standards do not rank high in the priorities of many governments.

- When auditors report that a government is not following proper accounting practices in its financial statements (an event that often occurs), the press notes the outrage of the opposition parties and the government's denial of any impropriety, and then the matter is forgotten. The general public, which by and large does not understand accounting at all, does not seem to be particularly interested.

- The adoption of certain new standards may be perceived by a government as having the potential to make its financial condition look worse than the government is currently reporting. If so, a change in reporting would not be a high priority.

GAAP for Governments

Prior to February 2007, the *Public Sector Accounting Handbook* contained four sections that applied only to federal, provincial, and territorial governments; two sections that applied only to local governments; and a number of specific item sections that applied to all governments. In 2005, a new model for senior governments was introduced that involved some drastic changes from previous practices. While the old model focused mainly on government spending (the operating statement showed revenues and expenditures), the new model presents a government-cost approach, although it still contains the reporting of government spending. One major change that took place was the requirement that senior governments capitalize their tangible asset acquisitions and amortize them in the statement of operations. In February 2007, an amendment withdrew both the local government sections and any references to federal, provincial, and territorial governments. Now the *Public Sector Accounting Handbook* contains thirty sections and seven accounting guidelines that apply to all governments in Canada. The following briefly summarizes the reporting requirement of the PSAB standards.

Governments are required to present four financial statements.

Under the new model, four financial statements are required: a consolidated statement of financial position, a consolidated statement of operations, a consolidated statement of change in net debt, and a consolidated cash flow statement.

Consolidated statement of financial position   This statement presents financial assets and then deducts liabilities, with the resultant difference presented as "net debt." Then non-financial assets are added or subtracted to arrive at a final line called "accumulated surplus/deficit."

Financial assets include cash and equivalents, receivables, inventories for resale, loans to other governments, available-for-sale investments, and investments in government enterprises.

Liabilities include accounts payable and accrued liabilities, pension and employee future-benefit liabilities, deferred revenue, borrowings, and loans from other governments.

The net debt position indicates the extent to which the government will have to raise revenues in the future to cover its past spending.

Non-financial assets are tangible capital assets, inventories held for consumption or use, and prepaid expenses. Tangible capital assets are assets used by the government to provide services and include land, buildings, equipment, roads, and so on. They *do not* include intangible assets, natural resources, and Crown lands.

The accumulated surplus/deficit represents the net recognized economic resources (net assets) of the government, and provides an indicator of the government's ability to provide future services at the end of a fiscal year.

Consolidated statement of operations   This statement reports the government's revenues and expenses for the year, with the difference described as the year's surplus or deficit. This result is added to the accumulated surplus/deficit at the beginning of the year to arrive at the last line, which is called the accumulated surplus/deficit at the end of the year.

Revenues include taxes, non-tax sources (including gains), and transfers from other governments. Revenue for the period should be accrued unless it is impractical to measure. If this is the case the cash basis should be used.

Expenses are to be reported by function or major program. Note disclosure should report the breakdown between the major types of expenses such as salaries, debt servicing costs, amortization of the costs of tangible capital assets, and transfer payments to other governments. A comparison must be made between the actual results for the year and results of the prior year and also with expectations (the budget) at the beginning of the year.

Consolidated statement of change in net debt   This statement reconciles the net surplus/deficit for the year with the change in net debt for the year, by adding back amortization expense for the year (and other items) and deducting the cost of tangible capital assets and other non-financial assets acquired during the year. The change in net debt is then added to the net debt at the beginning of the year to arrive at the net debt at the end of the year.

This statement is designed to provide information about the extent to which expenditures for the year have been met by the year's revenues. An increase in net debt indicates that revenues of future periods will have to be raised to pay for this year's spending. This statement also has to be prepared in comparative form to the budget and the prior year's results.

Consolidated cash flow statement   This statement reconciles cash and cash equivalents at the beginning of the year with cash and cash equivalents at the end of the

The statement of financial position must show financial assets, liabilities, net debt, non-financial assets, and accumulated surplus/deficit.

The operating statement must show revenues, expenses, and the year's surplus or deficit. Comparative amounts for the previous year are required to be shown as well as the current year's budget.

A statement showing the year's changes in net debt is required in comparative form with both the budget and the previous year.

The cash flow statement shows operating, capital, investing, and financing transactions.

year by providing details of receipts and payments in the four categories of operating transactions, capital transactions, investing transactions, and financing transactions. Either the direct or the indirect method can be used to arrive at cash from operations, but the direct method is strongly encouraged because it provides details of cash receipts from a number of categories and therefore is much more informative than the indirect method. This statement is similar to the statement used by business organizations except that the latter would report capital asset acquisitions as an investing activity, while this one reports such acquisitions as a separate category.

PS 1300 requires the consolidation of the financial statements of all organizations controlled by the government. Controlled business organizations are not consolidated but rather are reported using the modified equity method.

Section PS 1300 — The Financial Reporting Entity

Section PS 1300, issued in June 1996 and amended in January 2003, states the following:

- The government reporting entity comprises all organizations controlled by the government. An organization is controlled if the government has power over its financial and operating policies and benefits from or is exposed to the results of its operating activities.
- The government statements are prepared by consolidating the statements of the organizations making up the government entity.
- An exception is that government business enterprises are not consolidated but rather reported using the modified equity method. This will reflect the business enterprise's profit or loss in the government's operating results but will not include its assets and liabilities on the government's statement of financial position.
- The modified equity method is exactly the same as the equity method described in Chapter 2 except that the business enterprise's accounting principles are not adjusted to conform to the accounting principles used by the government.

SUMMARY

The PSAB has exerted considerable effort on the establishment of a new financial reporting model covering federal, provincial, territorial, and local governments. The resultant standards exhibit significant differences from those required for businesses and NFPOs. Differences will always exist because the operations and user needs of governments, NFPOs, and business organizations are different. While separate standards previously existed for local governments, recent amendments have eliminated any differences so that no one set of standards applies to all government organizations.

REVIEW QUESTIONS

Questions, cases, and problems that deal with the appendix material are denoted with an asterisk.

1. Briefly outline how NFPOs differ from profit-oriented organizations.
2. The *Handbook* describes revenue that is unique to NFPOs. What is this revenue called, and what characteristic does it have that makes it unique?
3. Distinguish between unrestricted and restricted contributions of a charitable organization.
4. Briefly explain the concept of fund accounting.

5. It is common for an NFPO to receive donated supplies, equipment, and services. Do current accounting standards require the recording of donations of this kind? Explain.

6. Outline the *Handbook*'s requirements with regard to accounting for the capital assets of NFPOs.

7. What guidelines does the *Handbook* provide for pledges received by an NFPO?

8. The net assets section of an NFPO's statement of financial position should be divided into three main sections. List the sections, and explain the reasons for each.

9. How should transfers of resources between funds be presented in fund financial statements? How should they be presented in a single set of non-fund financial statements?

10. What is the major difference between the capital asset impairment tests used by profit-oriented and not-for-profit organizations?

11. Contrast the revenue recognition and matching concepts that apply to profit-oriented organizations with those that apply to NFPOs.

12. Outline the financial reporting requirements for an NFPO's investments in other organizations.

13. Explain the use of budgetary accounting and encumbrances by NFPOs.

14. Name the two methods of accounting for contributions, and explain how the methods differ from each other.

15. Is it possible that an organization would be required to use certain aspects of the deferral method even though it reports using the restricted fund method? Explain.

16. An organization raises funds for purchasing capital assets. Briefly outline how the accounting for such funds raised would differ under the two methods of accounting for contributions.

*17. Governments are different from business organizations and NFPOs in many respects and yet in some respect they are similar. Explain.

*18. Distinguish between a government's financial assets and any other assets a government might have. Explain.

*19. Briefly outline how the presentation of assets and liabilities on the statement of financial position of a government differs from the presentation shown on the balance sheet of a typical business enterprise.

MULTIPLE-CHOICE QUESTIONS

1. NP is an NFPO that has held its annual fundraising drive every May for the past five years. Based on previous fundraising drives, it estimated that 95 percent of pledges received will be collected. During May, NP received $100,000 of pledges. NP recorded two journal entries for the pledges. The first was as follows:

Contribution receivable	100,000	
Contribution revenue		100,000

Which of the following is the second journal entry?

a.	Bad debt expense	5,000	
	Allowance for doubtful accounts		5,000
b.	Bad debt expense	5,000	
	Contributions receivable		5,000
c.	Contributions revenue	5,000	
	Contributions receivable		5,000
d.	Contributions revenue	5,000	
	Allowance for doubtful accounts		5,000

(*CGA-Canada adapted*)

2. An individual contributed $100,000 of cash and pledged another $50,000 to an NFPO to cover the $50,000 salary of its executive director for the current year and the next two years. How should the contributions be reported, assuming that the organization uses the deferral method of accounting for contributions?

   a. $50,000 should be reported as contribution revenue in the current year and $100,000 should be reported as deferred contribution revenue at the end of the current year, assuming that the pledge receivable is likely to be collected.

   b. $100,000 should be reported as contribution revenue in the current year and $50,000 should be reported as contribution revenue when the individual remits the other $50,000.

   c. $100,000 should be reported as contribution revenue in the current year and $50,000 should be reported as deferred contribution revenue at the end of the current year, assuming that the pledge receivable is likely to be collected.

   d. $150,000 should be reported as contribution revenue in the current year.

3. Which of the following treatments is *not* in accordance with GAAP for an NFPO?

   a. An NFPO with revenue of $480,000 in the current year and $450,000 in the preceding year recorded the purchase of capital assets as an expense in the current year.

   b. An NFPO with revenue in excess of $1 million recorded the donation of a collection of artwork at fair value but does not intend to amortize the artwork.

   c. An NFPO recorded at fair value the donation of the services of volunteer fundraising canvassers.

   d. An NFPO received a collection of historical treasures but did not record the contribution because a fair value of the treasures could not be reasonably estimated.

(*CGA-Canada adapted*)

4. Mercy Hospital, an NFPO, has an investment in a joint venture. How should the hospital report its interest in the joint venture?

   a. It is required to use proportionate consolidation.

   b. It is required to use the equity method.

   c. It can choose between using the equity method and proportionate consolidation.

   d. Instead of using the equity method or proportionate consolidation, it can choose to disclose details of the joint venture in its notes to financial statements.

5. Which of the following is an acceptable way for an NFPO to account for a donation of $50,000 that is restricted for the purchase of office equipment, assuming the restricted fund method of accounting for contributions is used?
   a. Revenues in the operating fund.
   b. Deferred revenues in the capital fund.
   c. Revenues in the capital fund.
   d. Direct increase in net assets in the capital fund.

   (CGA-Canada adapted)

6. Under the deferral method, how should endowment contributions be recognized?
   a. As revenue in the year they are received.
   b. As revenue in the endowment fund.
   c. According to the terms of the endowment agreement.
   d. As direct increases in net assets in the period they are received.

   (CGA-Canada adapted)

The following scenario applies to Questions 7 and 8, although each question should be considered independently.

First Harvest (FH) collects food for distribution to people in need. During its first month of operations, the organization collected a substantial amount of food and also $26,000 in cash from a donor. The donor specified that the money was to be used to pay down a loan that the organization had with the local bank. The loan had been taken out to buy land, on which the organization plans to build a warehouse facility. A warehouse is needed since, although the organization does not plan to keep a lot of food in stock, sorting and distribution facilities are crucial. FH has also received $100,000, which, according to the donor, is to be deposited, with any income earned to be used as FH sees fit.

7. In which of the following ways should the food donation and the $26,000 be reflected in the financial statements? Assume that fair values are available and that FH uses the deferral method and does not maintain separate funds.

	Food donations	$26,000 cash donation
a.	Deferred revenues	Increase in net assets
b.	Revenues	Increase in net assets
c.	Revenues	Deferred revenues
d.	Not recorded	Deferred revenues

   (CICA adapted)

8. In which of the following ways should the $100,000 contribution be accounted for under the following revenue recognition methods?

	Deferral method	Restricted fund method
a.	Direct increase in net assets	Revenue of the general fund
b.	Revenue	Revenue of the endowment fund
c.	Revenue	Revenue of the general fund
d.	Direct increase in net assets	Revenue of the endowment fund

   (CICA adapted)

9. Wilson Centre, an NFPO, owns a collection of works of art estimated to be worth about $85,000. These were donated to the centre many years ago and have not been reflected in past financial statements. However, this year, the centre's new auditors wish to include them. If the *CICA Handbook*'s minimum requirements for collections are followed, how should the works of art be accounted for?
   a. Capitalization at fair value.
   b. They should not be reported at all.
   c. Amortization over a maximum of 40 years.
   d. Disclosure of a description of the collection.

(*CGA-Canada adapted*)

The following scenario applies to Questions 10, 11, and 12, although each question should be considered independently.

In the fall of Year 5, the city of Westra approved its budget of $10,000,000 for the construction of a new water treatment plant. Construction began in Year 6. The building was completed on November 30, Year 6, but none of the water treatment equipment had yet been installed. The city uses a fund accounting system and maintains separate funds for general operations and capital projects. It uses an encumbrance system to control operating and capital costs.

The following table summarizes the financial activities related to the water treatment plant for the year ended December 31, Year 6:

Nature of costs	Budget	Value of purchase orders issued	Value of purchase orders outstanding	Actual cost of work completed	Amount paid on work completed
Engineering	$ 2,000,000	$ 2,100,000	$ 200,000	$1,800,000	$1,500,000
Building	5,000,000	5,200,000	—	5,350,000	4,815,000
Equipment	3,000,000	2,860,000	2,860,000	—	—
Total	$10,000,000	$10,160,000	$3,060,000	$7,150,000	$6,315,000

Purchase orders have been issued to cover all work required to complete the facility. The work has not yet commenced on the activities for which purchase orders are currently outstanding but work has been completed on all of the other purchase orders. All of the engineering work completed to date relates to the building. The outstanding engineering work relates to the water treatment equipment. The building and equipment will be capitalized and amortized on a straight-line basis over 20 years for the building and 10 years for the equipment.

10. What amount should be used to report the water treatment building at the end of December Year 6?
    a. $4,815,000
    b. $5,350,000
    c. $6,315,000
    d. $7,150,000

(*CGA-Canada adapted*)

11. How should the outstanding purchase order of $2,860,000 for the equipment be presented on the financial statements for the year ended December 31, Year 6?
    a. Offset the $2,860,000 encumbrance against the $2,860,000 estimated commitment and show no impact on the financial statements.

    b. $2,860,000 should be added to the cost of equipment.

    c. $2,860,000 should be added as a current liability.

    d. $2,860,000 should be reported as an encumbrance expense on the income statement.

(CGA-Canada adapted)

12. Based on information available at the time, how much is the water treatment plant expected to cost once the equipment is installed and the plant is operational?
    a. $7,150,000
    b. $9,375,000
    c. $10,160,000
    d. $10,210,000

(CGA-Canada adapted)

13. John is an avid supporter of the Environmental Cleanup Organization (ECO), an NFPO. In Year 4, he donated land and buildings with a total fair value of $150,000 to ECO. The land and buildings originally cost him $100,000. In Year 4, he also donated $10,000 of paper supplies that would not otherwise have been purchased by ECO. At what amount should John's donation be recorded on ECO's books in Year 4?
    a. $100,000
    b. $110,000
    c. $150,000
    d. $160,000

14. TK is an NFPO that runs camps for needy children. It recently received a donation of land with a fair value of $100,000. To record this donation, it used the deferral method and debited its land account. Which account should be credited, and for what amount?
    a.   Credit contributions revenue for the nominal amount of $1.
    b.   Credit net assets invested in capital assets for the nominal amount of $1.
    c.   Credit deferred contribution revenue for $100,000.
    d.   Credit net assets invested in capital assets for $100,000.

(CGA-Canada adapted)

15. How should a transfer of $50,000 from the operating fund to the capital fund be accounted for by an NFPO?
    a.   As an expense of the operating fund and a revenue of the capital fund.
    b.   As an expense of the capital fund and a revenue of the operating fund.
    c.   As a decrease in the fund balance for the operating fund and an increase in the fund balance for the capital fund in the statement of changes in fund balances.
    d.   As an increase in the fund balance for the operating fund and a decrease in the fund balance for the capital fund in the statement of changes in fund balances.

(CGA-Canada adapted)

16. FarmSafe is an NFPO involved in teaching farmers how to cope with crop disease outbreaks. During the past year, it received $500,000 of unrestricted donations plus pledges of $100,000, of which 70 percent is expected to be

collected. Which of the following should be reported on FarmSafe's financial statement for the year?

a. $500,000 donation revenue.
b. $570,000 donation revenue.
c. $600,000 donation revenue.
d. $600,000 donation revenue and $30,000 bad debt expense.

(CGA-Canada adapted)

17. The board of directors for the Ivory Rehabilitation Centre approved the following budget:

Revenues	$700,000
Expenses	680,000
Budgeted surplus	$ 20,000

Which of the following is the correct journal entry to record the budget?

a.	Estimated revenues	700,000	
	Appropriations		680,000
	Budgetary fund balance		20,000
b.	Encumbrances	700,000	
	Estimated commitments		680,000
	Budgetary fund balance		20,000
c.	Estimated expenses	680,000	
	Budgetary fund balance	20,000	
	Estimated revenues		700,000
d.	Encumbrances	680,000	
	Budgetary fund balance	20,000	
	Estimated commitments		700,000

18. GOLD College is an NFPO. It uses the deferral method to account for contributions. Although it receives contributions in many forms, it recognizes only cash contributions in its financial statements. The users of the financial statements are very concerned about costs of running the college. If the college were to recognize non-cash donations in its financial statements, which of the following non-cash contributions would cause the largest increase in expense in the statement of operations in the year of the contribution?

a. $50,000 of time donated by teaching assistants.
b. $50,000 van donated by former student.
c. $50,000 piece of land to be used for new gymnasium.
d. $50,000 investment portfolio to be held as endowment fund; income from fund to be used for awarding scholarships.

19. Silver Home Care is an NFPO. It uses the restricted fund method to account for contributions and sets up a restricted fund for any restricted contribution. The users of the financial statements are very concerned about fund balances/surpluses. If Silver were to switch to the deferral method of accounting for contributions, which of the following cash contributions would cause the largest decrease in fund balances/surplus?

a. $50,000 for use as the board sees fit.
b. $50,000 to supplement the executive director's salary for the next three years.
c. $50,000 to purchase a new van with an estimated useful life of five years.
d. $50,000 to purchase artwork with an indefinite useful life.

CASES

Case 1   Beaucoup Hospital is located near Montreal. A religious organization created the not-for-profit hospital more than 70 years ago to meet the needs of area residents who could not otherwise afford adequate health care. Although the hospital is open to the public in general, its primary mission has always been to provide medical services for the poor.

On December 23, Year 2, a gentleman told the hospital's chief administrative officer the following story: "My mother has been in your hospital since October 30. The doctors have just told me that she will soon be well and can go home. I cannot tell you how relieved I am. The doctors, the nurses, and your entire staff have been just wonderful; my mother could not have gotten better care. She owes her life to your hospital.

I am from Alberta. Now that my mother is on the road to recovery, I must return immediately to my business. I am in the process of attempting to sell an enormous tract of land. When this acreage is sold, I will receive $15 million in cash. Because of the services that Beaucoup Hospital has provided for my mother, I want to donate $5 million of this money." The gentlemen proceeded to write this promise on a piece of paper that he dated and signed.

Obviously, all of the hospital's officials were overwhelmed by this individual's generosity. This $5 million gift was 50 times as large as any other gift ever received. However, the controller was concerned about preparing the financial statements for Year 2. "I have a lot of problems with recording this type of donation as an asset. At present, we are having serious cash flow problems; but if we show $5 million in this manner, our normal donors are going to think we have become rich and don't need their support."

Required:

What problems are involved in accounting for the $5 million pledge? How should Beaucoup Hospital report the amount?

Case 2   You have just completed an interview with the newly formed audit committee of the Andrews Street Youth Centre (ASYC). This organization was created to keep neighbourhood youth off the streets by providing recreational facilities where they can meet, exercise, play indoor sports, and hold dances. Since its inception, the organization has managed to survive on the basis of user fees charged to parents whose children use the program. This year the centre received support from a new provincial government program, in the form of an operating grant along with subsidy fees for those parents whose income is considered insufficient to pay the user fee. A local foundation, with a long history in the community and a reputation for honouring its commitments, has also come to the aid of the centre. This outside financial support came with the provision that the centre now present audited financial statements annually.

Your firm is attempting to obtain the audit, as it is a November year-end, and the audit would be completed at a traditionally slow time of year. Many questions were posed during the interview, and the ASYC audit committee has requested a written response to the issues raised. Excerpts from the interview follow:

- "We are looking for financial statements that are understandable to the board. For example, we have heard that we might have to capitalize and depreciate leasehold improvements. We have just completed $20,000 in expenditures to set up a weight room. We don't understand this amortization idea. Will it make us look like we exceeded our operating budget since this budget is based on all expenditures, capital and operating? The government might consider reducing our next operating grant because of this accounting. If you were selected as our auditor, would you have any problem if we simply expensed capital assets as incurred?"

- "The Parent Advisory Group has organized several fundraising events, and the net receipts have been deposited in a separate 'Computer Fund' bank account to allow for the purchase of some PCs. Last year, our financial statements did not reflect this fund. Is that okay with you?"

- "The manager of Sports Supplies Ltd. is a good friend of the centre's. This year his company gave us a variety of items, such as exercise and bodybuilding apparatus and some basketball equipment. This is pretty neat stuff and must be worth at least $12,000 to $15,000. The audit committee does not want to record this because they are concerned that if it ends up in revenue our operating grants might be reduced."

- "Certain of the parents have donated goods or their time and would like to receive a tax receipt for the value of these donations. We are not certain whether we will have to reflect these in our financial statements this year. For example,
    1. Jane Barnes provided valuable advice on improved management efficiency. She is a professional consultant and although these consulting fees were not budgeted for, the centre made several changes that resulted in a reduction of administrative costs. Ms. Barnes estimates that her full-rate fee would have been $7,500.
    2. Rick James, who is a qualified Phys. Ed. instructor, has been substituting one day a week at no charge, which reduced our budgeted expenditures by $4,500 this year.
    3. Parents have donated an awful lot of their time to operate fundraising activities (in addition to those involved with the Computer Fund). This time must be worth thousands of dollars."

- "Some of the staff have not been able to take their vacation this year, due to scheduling problems. As a result, we will have to pay them vacation pay. These funds will be paid out after the year-end and will likely be covered by next year's operating grant. To keep revenues and expenses matched, we want to record the vacation pay on a cash basis. Would that be okay? Otherwise, we'll record a portion of next year's grant as receivable this year."

- "The local foundation has provided the centre with a $30,000 grant to cover the expenses of a volunteer coordinator for two years. We received an instalment of $12,000, but we haven't hired a coordinator yet. The coordinator will be paid on an hourly basis, and the number of hours each month will fluctuate over the next two years depending on the monthly activities."

Required:

Prepare a draft of the response that will be sent to the audit committee.

Case 3 You have been recently elected to the position of treasurer on the board of directors for Canoes Are Us, a community-based service and NFPO that provides canoeing lessons and canoe rentals to various community groups.

Canoes Are Us is a large NFPO with annual donations and grants in excess of $2 million. For the past several years, the canoe program has been funded through lesson fees, member contributions, and donations from the community. Canoes Are Us also relies on a large number of volunteers, including volunteers for the solicitation of donations and the performance of routine bookkeeping. Volunteer instructors are allowed to borrow canoes for their personal use for a nominal rental fee of $25 per month, as long as there are spare canoes available.

The board has recently set up a program in conjunction with the local community centre to provide lessons and rentals to various groups of children from low-income families. The municipal government and the lottery commission have announced that they will provide, in total, a one-time grant of $250,000 this year to Canoes Are Us for this initiative. The grant has a number of conditions:

1. $50,000 is to be used to purchase a new truck and trailer to transport the canoes.
2. $150,000 is to be used for the purchase of new canoes and safety equipment.
3. $50,000 is restricted to covering operating costs, such as salaries, advertising, and campaign costs.
4. An external audit by independent auditors must be conducted at the end of the year and the report must be submitted to the municipal government. The books and records of Canoes Are Us were not previously audited.

During a recent fundraising campaign, Canoes Are Us raised $45,000 in cash and received an additional $20,000 in pledges. The pledges are expected to be received by the middle of the next fiscal year. In addition, a local manufacturer has donated a new canoe valued at $2,500 to the program.

When you review the financial information for Canoes Are Us, you discover that the books and records have been kept on a modified accrual basis, whereby the cash basis is used for inflows but payables are accrued for outflows. Capital expenditures have been expensed in the year of purchase. There is no master list of existing canoes, and, in fact, some of the canoes appear to be in the possession of volunteer instructors on a semi-permanent basis even though the organization has full storage facilities available. The secretary to the board of directors is one of the volunteer instructors who has a canoe in her possession. You have also been advised that several instructors have unpaid rental accounts ranging from $50 to $400 each, and it appears that no serious efforts have been made to collect these accounts.

In discussions with the previous treasurer about how the new grant and other funds are to be used and accounted for, you discover that she is very opposed to any changes in the way that the accounting records are kept and the financial statements are prepared. She says that changes would make it difficult to compare the programs and to understand how the funds are being used. She was very active in setting up the organization and was one of the driving forces behind obtaining the grant for the new program.

Required:

Prepare a memorandum to the board of directors recommending, with supporting explanations, what changes in accounting and reporting are required in order to comply with GAAP and to fulfill the stewardship reporting objective. Assume that the deferral method is used to account for contributions.

(CGA-Canada adapted)

Case 4   The Sassawinni First Nation is located adjacent to a town in northern Saskatchewan. The Nation is under the jurisdiction of the federal government's Department of Indian Affairs and Northern Development, and for years has received substantial funding from that department. The money has been used mainly to fund housing construction on the reserve and to provide maintenance payments to families that do not have a source of income. The houses are the property of the Sassawinni First Nation, and the band council allocates them to families on the basis of need. In addition to the housing, the band has been able to build a recreational centre, which also contains the band's council chamber and administrative offices.

A few years ago some council members with an entrepreneurial flair persuaded the Nation's members to build a shopping centre containing a large grocery store and several small specialty stores. The shopping centre is located on reserve land, and the band provided approximately 20 percent of the financing, with the balance coming from a provincially guaranteed bank loan. The shopping centre operates under the name Great Northern Centre, Inc., and the Sassawinni First Nation owns 100 percent of its outstanding common shares. The centre has been a financial success, drawing a large proportion of its business from the adjoining town and surrounding agricultural area. Not only has it been a source of employment for First Nation families, but it has also generated enough cash to keep its loan payments current and has recently been able to declare and pay a dividend.

Flushed with its success, the Sassawinni First Nation has submitted to the provincial government a business plan to construct a gambling casino on band property. It will be an incorporated entity and will be under the complete control of the Nation, subject only to provincial government gambling regulations.

Up to the present time, the band has provided stewardship reports to the Department of Indian Affairs and Northern Development that outline the funds received from the federal government and the manner in which they have been spent. Government auditors have verified these statements, but no formal audit reports have been considered necessary. Now, with all of this new business activity taking place, proper audited financial statements will be required for the next fiscal year. You are employed by Fox, Fox, and Jameson, the public accounting firm that is the auditor of Great Northern Centre, Inc. Your firm has just been appointed auditor of Sassawinni First Nation, and this will be the firm's first audit of an organization of this nature. Jane Fox, the managing partner in charge of this audit, has asked you to provide her with a written report outlining the specific accounting principles that will be applicable in this case. "I am going to have to catch up quickly," she said. "I am aware that there have been some changes in GAAP recently, but because our firm has not been involved with audits of this nature I have not paid much attention to what has been going on. One of the benefits of hiring new university grads like yourself is that you provide us with up-to-date technical knowledge."

You have just returned from interviewing the band chief, Joe Sullivan. "I am absolutely certain that we are going to get this casino," he said. "The announcement will be made by the premier within two weeks, and I have received information from a knowledgeable insider that we will be on the list of First Nations to be granted casino licences. It will be a financial godsend to our people, employing well over 100 band members and providing us with substantial profits, a portion of which will have to be devoted entirely to accommodations in accordance with the licensing agreement. This will allow us to build more housing for our members, but with all the jobs that we now have, we will probably start charging rent for housing provided to those with jobs. Not only that, but we have three permanent employees who have been with us for a while, and council has instructed me to investigate the possibility of providing a pension plan for them as well as for the permanent employees in our business enterprises."

When asked about the band's accounting records, Sullivan responded, "We have a very good bookkeeper, and the government auditor has always complimented her on the accuracy of her records. She provides timely statements showing us how much we have to spend. Our records are all here and go back at least 20 years. I would just as soon carry on the way we have been doing things, but with this new casino we'll have to provide audited financial statements to the two governments — and, of course, to our members."

Required:

Prepare the report requested by your firm's managing partner.

Case 5 Confidence Private is a high school in the historic city of Jeanville. It engages students in a dynamic learning environment and inspires them to become intellectually vibrant, compassionate, and responsible citizens. The private school has been run as an NFPO since its inception 20 years ago.

In an effort to attract sports-minded students from a variety of economic backgrounds, Confidence initiated a fundraising program in July Year 8, to raise $5 million to build a new gymnasium, swimming pool, and fitness centre, and to create an endowment fund for scholarships. The fundraising campaign was a huge success. By May 31, Year 9, the school had received the following contributions:

1. $2.0 million in cash contributions specifically designated for construction and maintenance of the facilities.
2. $3.1 million in cash contributions specifically designated for the scholarship fund.
3. Fitness equipment valued at $0.2 million.

On June 15, Year 9, at the graduation ceremony, the headmaster thanked the parents, students, alumni, and staff for all their support, and officially closed the capital campaign. He provided the following details of the campaign:

- The construction of the facility was nearing completion and would be ready for classes in September Year 9. The final cost for the facility would be approximately $1.9 million.
- The contribution of fitness equipment would more than adequately equip the fitness centre.
- $3.1 million in cash would be invested and managed by a professional investment adviser.

The income earned on the endowment fund would be used to provide scholarships to students. Five students would receive full or partial scholarships in the fall of Year 10. Each year thereafter, it was expected that 25 to 30 students would receive full or partial scholarships to offset the annual tuition fee of $15,000.

You are proud to be an alumnus of Confidence. You attended the graduation ceremony. At the garden reception after the ceremony, you accepted the headmaster's request to help out with the accounting for the capital campaign and related events. He was unsure of whether the school should use the restricted fund or deferral method of accounting for contributions. You agreed to provide a memo in which you would provide recommendations for accounting policies to be applied for the year ended June 30, Year 9, and for future years when the facilities are being used and when the scholarships are disbursed.

Required:

Prepare a memo for the headmaster. Explain the rationale for your recommendations and state your assumptions.

(CGA-Canada adapted)

*Case 6   Access Records Limited (ARL), which commenced operations on April 1, Year 1, is owned by the provincial government (50 percent) and three private companies (16 percent each). The provincial government currently maintains, on a manual basis, all descriptive information on land in the province, such as information on ownership, legal descriptions, etc. ARL's mandate is to computerize this information and to provide additional data not available from the manual system. The conversion of the manual system for several geographical regions of the province commenced on May 1, Year 1, with a targeted completion of all regions by September Year 3. The manual systems for each region will be maintained by ARL until each regional computerized system is operational.

The computer files are to be available to online users; others not online must obtain the information they need by going to designated government offices for hard copies. The prime users are market research firms, publishers of databases, real estate companies, and a variety of individuals and corporations. ARL charges the users a fee based on the information obtained. Computerization will permit additional descriptive information to be added to the database. As a result, user fees will increase as a region is computerized. No other organization provides this information.

In calculating the pre-tax income of ARL, the following items must be taken into account:

- In return for providing the original information, the provincial government receives a royalty for revenue generated from information that was previously available from the manual system. Two of the private companies receive a royalty for revenue generated from any new information that they gather and enter into the database. The computer system automatically identifies charges for previously available information and charges for the new information.
- The three private companies are to receive, for 10 years, a 20 percent rate of return on the original cost of the computer equipment and technology they were required to provide to ARL. At the end of 10 years, the computer equipment and technology will become the property of ARL.
- One of the three private companies entered into a 10-year agreement to provide the land and building from which ARL operates. It receives a 12 percent rate of return per year on its investment in the land and building. All operating costs, including repairs and maintenance, property taxes, and necessary improvements, are to be paid by ARL.
- The shareholders of ARL are to receive interest at the rate of prime plus one percent on any funds lent to ARL.

If the private owners, in operating ARL, do not meet certain specified performance standards, the provincial government can acquire their shares at cost.

It is now September Year 1. Your employer, Martin and Partners, Chartered Accountants, has been engaged by ARL as consultant for the fiscal year ending March 31, Year 2. Martin and Partners has been asked to submit a detailed report addressing significant accounting matters.

You obtain the following information:

1. The cash contribution of the four owners totals $40 million. Another $30 million to $50 million will be needed to complete the computerization. ARL will borrow the additional cash from a chartered bank, using ARL's assets as collateral.
2. Most of the total conversion cost of $70 million to $90 million is for the costs of mapping, aerial photography, and computer graphics.
3. At the end of 10 years, the government is entitled to acquire, at fair value, the 50 percent of the shares that it does not own. The private companies are entitled to a reduced royalty if the provincial government acquires their shares.
4. The user-fee schedule is set by the provincial government.
5. Discounts are offered to volume users.
6. ARL intends to sell its technology to other provinces.
7. The province's auditor is permitted access to ARL's financial records.

Required:

Prepare the report.

PROBLEMS

Problem 1   The OPI Care Centre is an NFPO funded by government grants and private donations. It prepares its annual financial statements using the deferral method of accounting for contributions, and it uses only the operations fund to account for all activities. It uses an encumbrance system as a means of controlling expenditures.

The following summarizes some of the transactions made in Year 6.

1. The founding member of OPI contributed $100,000 on the conditions that the principal amount be invested in marketable securities and that only the income earned from the investment be spent on operations.
2. During the year, purchase orders were issued to cover the budgeted cost of $1,400,000 for goods and contracted services.
3. During the year, a public campaign was held to raise funds for daily operations for the current year. Cash of $800,000 was collected, and pledges for an additional $100,000 were received by the end of the year. It is estimated that approximately 95 percent of these pledges will be collected early in the new year.
4. The provincial government pledged $600,000 for the year to cover operating costs and an additional $1,000,000 to purchase equipment and furniture. All of the grant money was received by the end of the year, except for the last $50,000 to cover operating costs for December.
5. OPI used the $1,000,000 received from the provincial government to purchase equipment and furniture for the care facility. The amortization of these assets amounted to $100,000 for the year. A purchase order had not been issued for this purchase.

6. Invoices totalling $1,450,000 were received for goods and contracted services. Of these invoices, 90 percent were paid by the end of the fiscal year. Purchase orders in the amount of $1,375,000 had been issued for these services.

Required:

In accordance with the requirements of the *CICA Handbook*, prepare the journal entries necessary to reflect the transactions.

(CGA-Canada adapted)

Problem 2 The Perch Falls Minor Hockey Association was established in Perch Falls in January Year 5. Its mandate is to promote recreational hockey in the small community of Perch Falls. With the support of the provincial government, local business people, and many individuals, the association raised sufficient funds to build an indoor hockey arena and it also established an endowment fund for paying travel costs to tournaments on an annual basis.

The following schedule summarizes the cash flows for the year ended December 31, Year 5.

PERCH FALLS MINOR HOCKEY ASSOCIATION
($000s)

	Operating fund	Capital fund	Endowment fund
Cash inflows			
Government grant for operating costs	$ 90		
Government grant for hockey arena		$500	
Corporate donations for hockey arena		460	
Registration fees	50		
Contribution for tournaments			$50
Rental of hockey arena	70		
Interest received			3
	210	960	53
Cash outflows			
Operating expenses	205		
Construction of hockey arena		960	
Purchase of marketable securities			50
Travel costs for tournament			3
	205	960	53
Cash, end of year	$ 5	$ 0	$ 0

Additional Information

- The new hockey arena was completed in late August Year 5. The official opening was held on August 30 with a game between the Perch Falls Old-Timers and the local firefighters. The arena is expected to have a 40-year useful life and no residual value.
- A long-time resident of Perch Falls donated the land on which the arena was built. The land was valued at $100,000. The association gave a donation receipt to the donor.
- A former resident of Perch Falls donated ice-making and ice-cleaning equipment to the association. A receipt for $60,000 was issued for the donation. The equipment has a useful life of 10 years and no residual value.

- The donation for tournaments was contributed on January 1, Year 5, with the condition that the principal amount of $50,000 be invested in 6 percent corporate bonds. The interest earned on the investment can be used only for travel costs for out-of-town tournaments. All investments in bonds will be held to their maturity date.
- The provincial government pledged $100,000 a year for operating costs. Ninety percent of the grant is advanced throughout the year. Upon receipt of the association's annual report, the government will issue the last 10 percent of the annual grant to the association.
- Registration fees and rental fees for the hockey arena are received at the beginning of the hockey season and cover the entire season, from September 1, Year 5, to April 30, Year 6.
- At the end of the year, the association owed $7,000 for services received in the month of December.
- The assocation wants to use the restricted fund method of accounting for contributions and to use three separate funds — operating fund, capital fund, and endowment fund. All capital assets are to be capitalized and amortized, as applicable, over their estimated useful lives.

Required:

Prepare a statement of financial position and statement of operations for each of the three funds as at and for the year ended December 31, Year 5.

(CGA-Canada adapted)

Problem 3   Zak Organization is an NFPO set up for famine relief. It uses the restricted fund method of accounting and has three funds: a general fund, a capital fund (through which it is raising cash to support the purchase of a new administrative building), and an endowment fund. Zak has been operating for 25 years and has a December 31 year-end. Zak's policy with respect to capital assets is to capitalize and amortize the capital assets over their expected useful lives.

On June 30, Year 5, Zak received three donations from a former director:

- $30,000 cash for general famine relief efforts.
- $50,000 to be used solely for construction of the new administrative building. Of the $50,000, 70 percent was received in cash, with the remainder promised in February Year 6. (Construction is expected to commence in October Year 6.)
- $600,000 cash, which was invested on July 1, Year 5, in long-term Government of Canada bonds, with 10 percent interest to be paid semi-annually on December 31 and June 30. The $600,000 donation was given with the stipulation that it be invested in interest-bearing securities with the principal to be maintained by Zak, although interest earned on the securities is not restricted.

Required:

(a) Briefly explain how each of the three donations should be accounted for using the restricted fund method of accounting. In particular, should each of the donations be recognized as revenue for the year ended December 31, Year 5?

If yes, in which fund(s) would the revenue be recognized (including interest earned in fiscal Year 5 on the bonds purchased with the $600,000 donation)? Note: Do not prepare journal entries.

(b) If Zak used the deferral method of accounting instead of the restricted fund method, how would this change the requirements for accounting for the $50,000 and $600,000 donations?

(c) Despite the recent donations from its former director, Zak is increasingly faced with severe budgetary constraints. Zak is considering implementing encumbrance accounting in the coming year.

(i) Briefly describe the process of encumbrance accounting.

(ii) Briefly describe how encumbrance accounting might serve as a device to help control spending when it is used in conjunction with a formal budgeting system.

(CGA-Canada adapted)

Problem 4   You have been recruited to act as the treasurer on the board of directors of an NFPO that has had difficulty in recent years controlling its expenditures. The board of directors has very limited accounting experience. The organization, Protect Purple Plants (PPP), is considering implementing an encumbrance accounting system to assist in expenditure control. PPP receives an estimated $800,000 per year in regular contributions from the federal government.

Required:

(a) State *two* advantages and *two* disadvantages of implementing an encumbrance accounting system.

(b) PPP uses the deferral method of accounting for contributions and has no separate fund for restricted contributions. On January 1, Year 6, PPP received its first restricted cash contribution — $100,000 for the purchase and maintenance of land and a greenhouse building for its rare purple plant collection.

On July 1, Year 6, PPP acquired land and a building for $22,000 and $60,000 cash, respectively. The building has an estimated useful life of 20 years and zero residual value. On December 31, Year 6, the remaining $18,000 cash was paid to KJ Maintenance Ltd. for a three-year maintenance contract that requires KJ personnel to provide maintenance services four days per month until December 31, Year 9. Assuming that encumbrance accounting will *not* be implemented until Year 7, prepare the journal entries for the following dates:

(i) January 1, Year 6.

(ii) July 1, Year 6.

(iii) December 31, Year 6.   *(CGA-Canada adapted)*

Problem 5   The Fara Littlebear Society is an NFPO funded by government grants and private donations. It was established in Year 5 by the friends of Fara Littlebear to encourage and promote the work of Native Canadian artists. Fara achieved international recognition for her art depicting images of journey and exploration.

The society leased a small building in January Year 5. The building contains a small art gallery on the first floor and office space on the second floor. The society spent $83,850 for leasehold improvements. The art gallery opened for public viewing on April 1, Year 5.

The unadjusted trial balance for the year ended December 31, Year 5, was as follows:

	Debit	Credit
Cash	$ 5,000	
Investment in bonds (Note 1)	80,000	
Artwork (Note 2)	300,000	
Leasehold improvements (Note 3)	83,850	
Government grant — operating costs (Note 6)		$ 90,000
Government grant — restricted for purchase of artwork		150,000
Corporate donations — restricted for purchase of artwork		150,000
Corporate donations — restricted for leasehold improvements		78,000
Individual donations restricted for scholarships (Note 1)		80,000
Interest income		4,000
Revenue from admission fees to art gallery		67,000
Rent expense (Note 3)	26,000	
Salaries expense (Note 4)	66,000	
Other expenses	53,150	
Scholarship awarded	5,000	
	$619,000	$619,000

Additional Information

- A wealthy individual donated $80,000 with the condition that the principal be invested in low-risk investments. The principal was invested in long-term bonds, which are expected to be held to maturity. The interest on the bonds is to be used to provide scholarships to aspiring Native artists who wish to study art at a Canadian university or college. The first scholarship of $5,000 was awarded in September Year 5.
- The artwork consists of 20 paintings from a number of Canadian artists. These paintings are expected to be held for at least 10 years. The paintings will likely appreciate in value over the time they are owned by the art gallery.
- The society signed a five-year lease on the building with an option to renew for one further term of five years. The term of the lease commenced on January 1, Year 5. The total rent paid for the year included a deposit of $2,000 for the last month's rent. The leasehold improvements were completed on March 31, Year 5. The office space was occupied by the staff of the society, and the art gallery was opened for business on April 1, Year 5.
- Salaries earned but not yet paid amounted to $3,000 at December 31, Year 5.
- The society received office equipment from a local business person on January 1, Year 5. A donation receipt for $10,000 was given for this contribution. The office equipment has a useful life of five years with no residual value.
- The provincial government provided an operating grant of $100,000 for Year 5, of which $90,000 was received by the end of the year. The remaining $10,000 will be received once the society provides financial statements prepared in accordance with GAAP.
- The society wishes to use the deferral method of accounting for contributions.

Required:

(a) Explain how the matching principle is applied when the deferral method is used to account for restricted contributions.

(b) Prepare a statement of financial position for the society at December 31, Year 5. Show your supporting calculations and state your assumptions. (You can use an assumed number for excess of revenue over expenses to balance your statement of financial position.)

(*CGA-Canada adapted*)

Problem 6   The Brown Training Centre is a charitable organization dedicated to providing computer training to unemployed people. Individuals must apply to the centre and indicate why they would like to take the three-month training session. If their application is accepted, they must pay a $100 deposit. The deposit is refunded upon successful completion of the course or is forfeited as a processing fee if the individual does not complete the course.

During the first year of operations in Year 3, 90 individuals were accepted into the course. Of these 90 individuals, 50 completed the course, 10 dropped out, and 30 were still taking the course at the end of the fiscal year.

The centre receives most of its funding from the provincial government. During the year, the government advanced $500,000 to cover operating costs. Within two months of the year-end, the centre must provide financial statements prepared in accordance with GAAP. The government will cover all operating costs. The excess of amounts advanced over the amount expended must be carried over and applied to operating costs of the next year. Operating costs to be reimbursed are defined to exclude purchases of capital assets and are to be reduced by the amount of application fees forfeited.

A private company donated computers and office equipment with a fair value of $160,000. The centre was fortunate to receive this donation. Otherwise, it would have had to raise money through other means to purchase these items. The capital assets were put into use as of April 1, Year 3, and have an estimated useful life of three years. The centre uses the straight-line method to amortize its capital assets.

The part-time bookkeeper for the centre prepared the following cash flow statement for the year ended December 31, Year 3:

Cash receipts	
Government grant	$500,000
Deposits from course participants	9,000
Total cash receipts	509,000
Cash expenditures	
Salaries and benefits	310,000
Administration and supplies	110,000
Rent and utilities	80,000
Refund of deposits	5,000
Total cash disbursements	505,000
Cash balance at end of year	$ 4,000

At the end of the year the following costs had been incurred but not yet paid:

Salaries and benefits	$ 4,000
Utilities	3,000

The executive director of the centre has asked you for assistance in preparing the financial statements for the centre for the first year of operations. The deferral method should be used in accounting for the contributions.

Required:

(a) Briefly explain how the accrual basis of accounting is applied when accounting for capital assets for an NFPO.
(b) Prepare the statement of revenues and expenses for the centre for the year ended December 31, Year 3.
(c) Compute the following liabilities on the statement of financial position for the centre at December 31, Year 3:
  (i) Accrued liabilities.
  (ii) Deposits from course participants.
  (iii) Deferred contributions.

(CGA-Canada adapted)

Problem 7   The Ford Historical Society is an NFPO funded by government grants and private donations. It uses both an operating fund and a capital fund. The capital fund accounts for moneys received and restricted for major capital asset acquisitions. The operating fund is used for all other activities.

The society uses the deferral method for the operating fund and the restricted fund method for the capital fund. An encumbrance system is used within the operating fund to ensure that expenditures made in any one year do not exceed the amounts budgeted. Donated materials and services are recorded if such items would have been purchased had they not been received as donations.

The following are some selected activities that took place during the current year:

- Purchase orders in the amount of $500,000 for goods and services were issued during the year.
- Pledges totalling $350,000 were made to the society, of which $150,000 applies to the operations of the following year. It is estimated that 3 percent of all pledges will be uncollectible.
- Pledges of $310,000 were collected, and pledges totalling $5,000 were written off.
- A government grant of $500,000 for acquisition and renovation of an office building for the society was approved by the government. All of the grant money was received except for the last 10 percent, which is expected to be received in the first month of the next fiscal year.
- Invoices for all of the goods and services ordered during the year were received. The total cost was $510,000, of which $480,000 was paid for by the end of the year.
- An old office building was acquired and renovated for a cost of $500,000. Amortization expense on the office building was $10,000.
- A local radio station donated free airtime to the society. The society saved the $5,000 it would normally have paid for this airtime.

Required:

Prepare the journal entries required to record these activities, and indicate which fund each journal entry will be recorded in.

(CGA-Canada adapted)

Problem 8   Fairchild Centre is an NFPO funded by government grants and private donations. It was established on January 1, Year 5, to provide counselling services and a drop-in centre for single parents.

On January 1, Year 5, the centre leased an old warehouse in the central part of Smallville for $2,000 per month. It carried out minor renovations in the warehouse to create a large open area for use as a play area for children and three offices for use by the executive director and counsellors. The lease runs from January 1, Year 5, to June 30, Year 7. By that time, the centre hopes to move into new quarters that are more suitable for the activities carried out by the centre.

The following schedule summarizes the cash flows for the year ended December 31, Year 5:

Cash inflows

Government grant for operating costs (Note 1)	$ 50,000
Donations from individuals with no restrictions	63,000
Donations from individuals for rent of warehouse for 2½ years	60,000
Donations from individuals for purchase of land (Note 3)	28,000
	201,000

Cash outflows

Renovations of warehouse	25,000
Salary of executive director (Note 4)	33,000
Fees paid to counsellors (Note 4)	20,000
Rent paid for 2½ years	60,000
Other operating expenses	34,000
	172,000
Cash, end of year	$ 29,000

Additional Information

- The provincial government agreed to provide an operating grant of $50,000 per year. In addition, the government has pledged to match contributions collected by the centre for the purchase of land for constuction of a new complex for the centre. The maximum contribution by the government toward the purchase of land is $100,000.
- The centre has signed an agreement to purchase a property in the downtown area of Smallville for $225,000. There is an old house on the property, which is currently used as a rooming house. The closing date is any time between July 1, Year 6, and December 31, Year 6. The centre plans to demolish the existing house and build a new complex.
- The centre has recently commenced a fundraising program to raise funds to purchase the land and construct a new building. So far, $28,000 has been raised from individuals toward the purchase of the land. In the new year, the centre will focus its efforts to solicit donations from businesses in the area. The provincial government will advance the funds promised under its pledge on the closing date for the purchase of the property.

- All the people working for the centre are volunteers except for the executive director and the counsellors. The executive director receives a salary of $36,000 a year, while the counsellors bill the centre for professional services rendered based on the number of hours they work at the centre. The director has not yet received her salary for the month of December. One of the counsellors received an advance of $1,000 in December Year 5, for work to be performed in January Year 6.
- The centre wishes to use the deferral method of accounting for contributions and to segregate its net assets between restricted and unrestricted. It capitalizes the cost of capital assets and amortizes the capital assets over their useful lives.

Required:

(a) State the assumptions necessary to recognize the pledge contributions from the provincial government, and prepare the journal entry to record the pledge, if applicable.
(b) Prepare a statement of revenues and expenses for the centre for the year ended December 31, Year 5. Show your supporting calculations and state your assumptions.
(c) Prepare a statement of changes in net assets for the centre for the year ended December 31, Year 5.

(*CGA-Canada adapted*)

Problem 9   The Far North Centre is an anti-poverty organization funded by contributions from governments and the general public. For a number of years it has been run by a small group of permanent employees with the help of part-timers and dedicated volunteers. It owns its premises, which are in the process of being renovated. The funds for this were obtained through a special capital fund campaign carried out last year. Its main program is the daily provision of meals to the needy. It also distributes clothing, most of which is donated. Operating funds come from government grants, interest earned from endowment investments, and a public campaign held in the latter part of each year to raise funds for the needs of the next fiscal year. The organization maintains its records in accordance with the restricted fund method of accounting for contributions, and prepares its financial statements using an operating fund, a capital fund (for all activities related to capital assets), and an endowment fund.

The following are the fund trial balances as at January 1, Year 6:

	Debit	Credit
Operating Fund		
Cash	$ 570,500	
Pledges receivable	705,000	
Allowance for uncollectible pledges		$ 30,000
Grants receivable	217,500	
Accounts payable		427,500
Wages payable		137,250
Accrued liabilities		9,750
Deferred revenue		800,000
Fund balance		88,500
	$1,493,000	$1,493,000

(continued)

Capital Fund

Cash	$ 287,500	
Grants receivable	112,500	
Land and building	810,250	
Furniture and equipment	491,000	
Accumulated amortization		$ 648,200
Accounts payable		9,000
Investment in capital assets		653,050
Fund balance		391,000
	$1,701,250	$1,701,250

Endowment Fund

Cash	$ 37,500	
Investments	375,000	
Fund balance		$ 412,500
	$ 412,500	$ 412,500

The following transactions took place in Year 6.

1. The Year 6 budget, the totals of which are summarized below, was recorded.

Budgeted revenues	$2,200,000
Budgeted expenses	2,150,000
Budgeted surplus	$ 50,000

2. The agency uses an encumbrance system in the operating fund as a means of controlling expenditures. During the year, purchase orders for goods and services at an estimated amount of $1,450,000 were issued.
3. $35,000 from endowment fund cash was invested in marketable securities.
4. Office equipment costing $2,500 was purchased with operating fund cash.
5. Invoices totalling $1,375,000 were received on purchase orders originally recorded at an estimated cost of $1,392,000. These invoices were recorded as accounts payable and were allocated 55 percent to food program, 20 percent to clothing program, and 25 percent to administration.
6. The capital fund grants receivable were collected in full, and the $9,000 in accounts payable was paid. During Year 6, building renovations costing $300,000 and equipment purchases of $85,000 were made. Of this cost, 90 percent was paid, with the balance held back and still owing at year-end.
7. Operating fund accounts payable amounting to $1,560,000 and the wages payable and accrued liabilities at the beginning of the year were all paid.
8. All of the operating fund pledges and grants receivable at the beginning of the year were collected in full.
9. The deferred revenue from the Year 5 fundraising campaign was made up of the following:

Contributions	$1,200,000
Less: campaign expense	400,000
	$ 800,000

An entry was made to recognize these items as Year 6 revenues and expenses.
10. Government grants for operating purposes totalled $900,000, of which $850,000 was received during the year, with the balance expected early in Year 7.

11. The total wage costs for the year amounted to $400,000, of which $325,000 was paid and $75,000 is payable at year-end. These costs are to be allocated 40 percent each to the food and clothing programs, with the balance to administration.
12. The campaign to raise funds for next year's operations was held in December. Cash of $500,000 was collected and pledges of $700,000 were received. It is expected that 5 percent of these pledges will be uncollectible. Total fundraising costs were $322,000, of which $75,000 is still owed to suppliers.
13. An endowment contribution of $8,000 cash was received. In addition, the investments in the endowment fund earned $31,200 in interest.
14. The annual depreciation on the buildings and equipment amounted to $92,000.
15. At the end of the year, the balances in the encumbrance accounts and the budget accounts were closed.

Required:

(a) Prepare the journal entries necessary to reflect the Year 6 events.
(b) For each fund, prepare a Year 6 statement of financial position and statement of operations and changes in fund balance.
(c) Prepare a cash flow statement on a non-fund basis.
(d) Prepare closing entries.

Problem 10   All facts about this NFPO are identical to those described in Problem 9, except that the deferral method of recording contributions is used for accounting and for external financial reporting. Fund accounting is not used. The Year 6 transactions are also identical to those described in Problem 9.

The organization's statement of financial position on January 1, Year 6, is shown below.

FAR NORTH CENTRE
STATEMENT OF FINANCIAL POSITION
January 1, Year 6

Current Assets	
Cash	$ 895,500
Pledges receivable	705,000
Allowance for uncollectible pledges	(30,000)
Grants receivable	330,000
	1,900,500
Investments	375,000
Capital Assets	
Land and buildings	810,250
Furniture and equipment	491,000
Accumulated depreciation	(648,200)
	653,050
	$2,928,550

Current Liabilities

Accounts payable	$ 436,500
Wages payable	137,250
Accrued liabilities	9,750
	583,500

Deferred Revenue

Deferred contributions	800,000
Deferred building campaign contributions	391,000
Deferred contributions related to capital assets	240,500
	1,431,500

Net Assets

Net assets invested in capital assets	412,550
Net assets restricted for endowment purposes	412,500
Unrestricted net assets	88,500
	913,550
	$2,928,550

Required:

(a) Prepare the journal entries necessary to reflect the Year 6 events.

(b) Prepare a Year 6 statement of financial position, a statement of revenues and expenses, and a statement of changes in net assets for the year.

(c) Prepare a cash flow statement for the year.

(d) Prepare closing entries.

Problem 11   The William Robertson Society is a charitable organization funded by government grants and private donations. It prepares its annual financial statements using the restricted fund method in accordance with the *CICA Handbook*, and uses both an operating fund and a capital fund.

The operating fund records the regular operating activities of the society. An encumbrance system is used within the fund to ensure that expenditures made in any one year do not exceed the amounts budgeted. It is the policy of the society to record donated materials and services received during the year, if such items would have been purchased had they not been received as donations.

The capital fund accounts for moneys received from special fundraising campaigns conducted when there is a need for major fixed assets acquisitions.

The following are *some* selected events that took place during the current year:

- Pledges for current year's operating costs amounting to $125,000 were received, of which $90,000 was collected in cash.

- Purchase orders were issued during the year as follows:

For office equipment	$ 15,000
For goods and services	100,000

- A grant of $70,000 for this year's operations was announced by the government, of which $55,000 had been received by the society at year-end.

- Employee wages totalled $60,000 for the year. Wages amounting to $2,000 were unpaid at year-end.

- Invoices for all of the goods and services ordered during the year were received. Of the invoiced amounts, 80 percent was paid. The invoiced amounts were equal to those on the purchase orders.

- The office equipment that was ordered arrived. The invoiced amount of $15,030 was paid in cash, using operating funds.

- A local radio station donated free airtime to the society. The station would normally bill a customer $3,000 for this airtime.
- A prominent citizen made a pledge of $35,000 to help fund the operating expenditures of the next fiscal year.

Required:

Prepare the journal entries required to record these events, and indicate in which fund each journal entry will be recorded.

WEB-BASED PROBLEMS

Problem 1   Go to the Web site of the Salvation Army (www.salvationarmy.ca). Download the most recent Canadian financial statements and answer the following questions.
  (a) Read the auditor's report. There is a paragraph there that is unique to NFPOs. Explain what message it is conveying.
  (b) Approximately how much of the organization's net assets are restricted? What can they be spent on?
  (c) How many funds are reported?
  (d) Approximately what percentage of the year's revenues was spent on fundraising?
  (e) What is its largest single source of revenue?
  (f) Has the organization's cash increased or decreased over the past two years? What was a major factor in the change?
  (g) Outline what is included in the accounting entity.
  (h) Briefly explain the army's amortization policy.
  (i) Which method of revenue recognition for contributions is being used?
  (j) What is their policy with respect to donated materials and services?

Problem 2   Download the latest financial statements of the Canadian Cancer Society (www.cancer.ca) and answer as many of the questions from Problem 1 as you can. (Some questions may not be applicable.)

Problem 3   Go to the Web site of the University of Saskatchewan (www.usask.ca). Search for the most recent financial statements and answer the following questions and document where in the report you located the relevant information.
  (a) What accounting policy was used for reporting contributions?
  (b) What percentage of total revenue came from government grants? Tuition fees? Donations?
  (c) What was the ratio of scholarship expense to tuition fee revenue?
  (d) Did the university report any pledges receivable and, if so, for how much? What amount is not expected to be collected within one year?
  (e) What percentage of total expenses was spent on educating the students, and what was spent on research during the period? List the items you include for each category.
  (f) What was the total value of endowment funds at the end of the year? What portion of the endowment funds is designated for scholarships? For research?
  (g) What method of reporting was used for investments in the various funds? What was the unrealized gain or loss from these investments during the year and how were these gains or losses reported?
  (h) What was the average cost for the university to graduate a student?

Credits

Page	Description	Source
27	Review Question 15	CICA (adapted)
28	Multiple Choice 8, 10, 11	CGA-Canada (adapted)
33	Case 5	CICA (adapted)
61	Multiple Choice 6, 7	CGA-Canada (adapted)
62	Multiple Choice 11	CGA-Canada (adapted)
69	Problem 6	CGA-Canada (adapted)
101	Multiple Choice 5	CICA (adapted)
101	Multiple Choice 6	CGA-Canada (adapted)
103	Multiple Choice 15	CGA-Canada (adapted)
105	Case 3	Adapted from a case prepared by J.C. Thatcher, Lakehead University, and Margaret Forbes, University of Saskatchewan
106	Case 4	Case prepared by Peter Secord, St. Mary's University
108	Case 6	Adapted from a case prepared by Peter Second, St. Mary's University
118	Problem 14	CICA (adapted)
150	Multiple Choice 6, 7	CICA (adapted)
151	Multiple Choice 9, 12	CGA-Canada (adapted)
153	Case 2	CICA (adapted)
155	Case 3	Adapted from a case prepared by J.C. Thatcher, Lakehead University, and Margaret Forbes, University of Saskatchewan
156	Case 5	CGA-Canada (adapted)
222	Multiple Choice 3, 4	CGA-Canada (adapted)
226	Case 2	Case prepared by Peter Secord, St. Mary's University
227–232	Cases 3, 4, 5	CICA (adapted)
284	Multiple Choice 14, 15	CGA-Canada (adapted)
286–292	Cases 3, 4, 5	CICA (adapted)
303	Problem 14	Adapted from a problem prepared by Peter Secord, St. Mary's University
305	Problem 15	CGA-Canada (adapted)
359–362	Cases 4, 5	CICA (adapted)
369	Problem 9	SMA (adapted)
372	Problem 13	CGA-Canada (adapted)
376	Problem 16	SMA (adapted)
378	Problem 17	CGA-Canada (adapted)
420	Multiple Choice 6	CGA-Canada (adapted)
423	Case 3	CICA (adapted)
444	Problem 17	Problem prepared by Peter Secord, St. Mary's University
446	Problem 18	Adapted from a problem prepared by Peter Secord, St. Mary's University
495	Multiple Choice 6	CGA-Canada (adapted)
496	Multiple Choice 12	CICA (adapted)
554	Multiple Choice 3	CGA-Canada (adapted)
554	Multiple Choice 4, 6	CICA (adapted)
555	Multiple Choice 11	CGA-Canada (adapted)
555	Multiple Choice 12	CICA (adapted)

555	Multiple Choice 13	CGA-Canada (adapted)
558	Case 2	Case prepared by Peter Secord, St. Mary's University
559–560	Cases 3, 4	CICA (adapted)
560	Problem 3	CGA-Canada (adapted)
564–565	Problem 9, 10, 11	CGA-Canada (adapted)
567	Problem 15	CGA-Canada (adapted)
610	Multiple Choice 16, 18	CGA-Canada (adapted)
612	Case 3	Case prepared by Peter Secord, St. Mary's University
612	Case 4	CICA (adapted)
615	Case 5	CICA (adapted)
620	Problem 3	CGA-Canada (adapted)
623–627	Problems 5, 6, 7, 8, 9	CGA-Canada (adapted)
628	Problem 10	Adapted from a case prepared by Peter Secord, St. Mary's University
631	Problem 12	CGA-Canada (adapted)
685	Multiple Choice 1	CGA-Canada (adapted)
686	Multiple Choice 3	CGA-Canada (adapted)
687	Multiple Choice 5, 6	CGA-Canada (adapted)
687	Multiple Choice 7, 8	CICA (adapted)
688–689	Multiple Choice 9, 10, 11, 12, 14, 15, 16	CGA-Canada (adapted)
692	Case 3	CGA-Canada (adapted)
695	Case 5	CGA-Canada (adapted)
697–704	Problems 1, 2, 3, 4, 5, 6, 7, 8	CGA-Canada (adapted)

Index

A

accounting changes
  convergence, 12
  equity method, changes to and from, 52
accounting exposure, 569–570
Accounting Guideline 15 (AcG-15), 452
accounting income, and taxation, 4
Accounting Standards Board (AcSB)
  adoption of IFRSs, 19
  Financial Reporting by Not-For-Profit Organizations, 20
accounts receivable, 521, 525, 532–533
accrual method, 49, 535
accumulated depreciation, 312, 315f, 319
accumulated other comprehensive income, 580
acquired deferred tax benefits, 475–476
acquisition. *See* business combinations
acquisition costs
  allocation, 77–78
  business combinations, 77
  carrying amount on date of change, 52
  goodwill, 133
  greater than acquirer's interest, 78
  greater than book values, 50–51
  reverse takeovers, 96–97, 99
acquisition date
  consolidated financial statements on acquisition date. *See* consolidated statements on acquisition date
  consolidated financial statements subsequent to acquisition date. *See* consolidated statements subsequent to acquisition date
  fair value differences, 383
acquisition differential
  allocation, 87, 87f, 90, 388, 389–390, 391
  amortization. *See* amortization of acquisition differential
  bonds, 199–200
  calculation, 87, 87f, 90
  and consolidated balance sheet, 89
  deferred income taxes, 473–475
  80-percent-owned subsidiary, 191f
  end of year 1, 184, 185f, 193f
  end of year 2, 188f, 196f
  entity theory, 137
  foreign operations, 588–589
  impairment schedule, 185f, 193f, 196f
  inventory, 184
  joint ventures, 464
  liabilities, 198–200
  long-term assets with definite useful lives, 174
  negative acquisition differential, 128
  negative goodwill, 126f
  preferred shares, 407
  purchase price, 183

push-down accounting, 125
and shareholders' equity, 404–405
subsidiary with goodwill, 128–129, 129f
translated financial statements, 588–589
unamortized acquisition differential, 174, 394f, 402, 412, 595
wholly owned subsidiaries, on acquisition date, 122, 122f
wholly owned subsidiaries, subsequent to acquisition date, 183f
writing off, 174
acquisition method, 74, 75, 79–82, 121
acquisition-differential amortization schedule
  consolidation, integrated foreign operations, 593f
  consolidation, self-sustaining foreign operations, 590f
  consolidation subsequent to acquisition, 185f, 188f, 193f, 196f
  ownership interest, changes in, 399–400
  parent's sale of portion of subsidiary holdings, 399–400
  step purchases, 390f, 391f
additional payments. *See* contingent consideration
adjustments
  acquisition differential. *See* acquisition differential
  consolidated financial statements, 383
  cumulative effect of adjustments, 189
  exchange adjustments, 523, 524, 537, 574, 596–597
  to fair value, 533
  investment account, 203, 390
  point-in-time *vs.* period-of-time, 320
  realized profits from intercompany transactions, 320
  of retained earnings under cost method, 189
  retrospective adjustments of prior-period results, 49
  revaluation adjustment, 350
  translation adjustment, 573, 587f, 591
  unrealized profits from intercompany transactions, 320
agency method, 337
Air Canada, 460
Akzo-Nobel N.V., 91–92f, 180, 181–182f
Alcatel-Lucent, 543–546f
Alumina Limited, 597–599f
amalgamation. *See* business combinations
American Accounting Association, 133–134
amortization
  acquisition differential. *See* amortization of acquisition differential
  acquisition-date fair value differences, 383

bond investment, 198–199
bond premium and discount, 330
capital assets, by NFPOs, 644–645
effective interest method, 199, 338–340
expense, 671
and intangibles, 175
straight-line method, 199, 200, 322n
amortization of acquisition differential
  consolidation subsequent to acquisition, 184, 186, 193
  described, 174
  indirect shareholdings, 410–411
  step purchases, 388, 390
anticipated future transaction, 530–531
arm's length transaction, 249
Arthur Andersen, 86
asset exchanges, 12
asset revaluations, 2
asset test, 477, 478
assets
  acquisition, at price different from tax base, 472–473
  asset purchase form of business combination, 73, 80–82
  capital assets, and NFPOs, 644–645, 651–657
  collections, 645–646
  current assets, 45
  definition of, and control, 83
  depreciable assets. *See* intercompany profits in depreciable assets
  identifiable assets, 77–78
  impairment. *See* impairment of assets
  intangible assets. *See* intangible assets
  intercompany profits in assets. *See* intercompany profits (losses)
  net asset exposure, 570
  net assets, 51n, 75, 648, 651–656, 671
  noncurrent assets, 45
  special-purpose entities, 453
  used depreciable asset, 318–319
associates
  see also significant influence
  defined, 47
  IAS 28 - Investments in Associates (Equity Method), 47–48
  investment in, 42
  long-term interests, and losses, 53
  other equity changes, 49–50
  private enterprises, 54–56
  unrealized profits with associates, 265
ATCO Group, 449
Australia
  adoption of IFRS, 11
  recent initiatives, 10–11
available-for-sale investments, 40–41, 45–46
Aviva, 272, 272f

B

balance sheet
 consolidated balance sheet. *See*
  consolidated balance sheet
 net assets, 648
 use of term, 44
balance sheet approach, 472
Bank of Nova Scotia, 517
Barclays Bank, 457, 457f
bargain purchase, 126
Beedle, A., 681n
Bell Canada Enterprises, 340
bequests, 640–641
Big Four accounting firms, 15
Big GAAP/Little GAAP concept, 18
block acquisitions of subsidiary, 387–395
Bombardier Inc., 461, 516, 517
bond chart, 332, 334–335
bonds
 acquisition differential, 199–200
 amortization, 330
 amortization tables, 338
 intercompany bondholdings. *See*
  intercompany bondholdings
 investments, amortization of, 198–199
 market price and interest rates, 322
 market value, 338
 premium, 199
book value
 acquisition costs greater than, 50–51
 and fair value excess, 88
 net book value, 315, 319
budgetary control, 658–659
business combinations
 see also consolidated financial
  statements; consolidation
 accounting methods, 74–78
 acquisition cost, 77
 acquisition differential, 87, 87f, 90
 acquisition method, 74, 75, 79–82, 121
 allocation of acquisition cost, 77–78
 asset purchase form, 73, 80–82
 conglomerate business combination, 71
 contingent consideration, 140–144
 control, determination of, 84–86
 control and consolidated financial
  statements, 82–92
 convergence, 12
 deferred income taxes, 471–476
 disclosure requirements, 90–91
 expected changes, 94
 financial reporting after combination, 78
 forms of business combinations, 73–74
 friendly business combinations, 72
 horizontal business combination, 71
 identification of acquirer, 76–*77
 IFRS 3 - Business Combinations, 43, 44,
  74, 76–78, 136–137, 144, 455
 illustrations of business combination
  accounting, 79–82
 negative goodwill, 126
 new entity method, 74, 76
 pooling-of-interests method, 74, 75
 private enterprises, GAAP for, 92

 purchase method, 74–75
 requirements for, 71–72
 reverse takeovers, 95–99
 share purchase form, 73–74, 87
 significant changes in last two years,
  93–94
 special-purpose entities, 86–87
 statutory amalgamation, 74
 substance of relationship, 82
 takeover defences, 72–73
 types of, 71
 unfriendly business combinations,
  72–73
 U.S. GAAP differences, 93
 variations in form of, 74
 vertical business combination, 71

C

Canada
 see also CICA Handbook
 acquisitions of foreign companies, 72
 capital resources, 1
 inflation levels, 5
 and international standards, 8
 net income, 3
 variable-interest entities, 460
Canadian dollar, 518
Canadian GAAP
 see also CICA Handbook
 Big GAAP/Little GAAP concept, 18
 expected changes. *See* significant changes
  in last two years
 GAAP for public companies, 15–18
 governments, 682–684
 vs. IFRSs, 21
 monetary assets and liabilities, 523
 non-monetary assets and liabilities, 523
 not-for-profit organizations, 20
 private enterprises, 18–20
 push-down accounting, 125
 significant changes. *See* significant
  changes in last two years
 vs. U.S. GAAP, 11
Canadian Institute of Chartered Accountants
 (CICA)
 Accounting Guideline 15 (AcG-15), 452
 Canadian Standards in Transition, 17–18
 CICA Handbook. See CICA Handbook
 exposure drafts, 41
 Public Sector Accounting Handbook, 681
Canadian-dollar-denominated transaction,
 517
CanAm Yarns LLC, 460
CanWest Global Communications Corp.,
 460
capital assets
 donated capital assets, 656–657
 net assets invested in, 651–656, 671
 and NFPOs, 644–645, 651–657
capital cost allowance, 472
capital fund, 660–661
capital markets, 4
capital structure, 382
 see also ownership interest; shares

"carve-out for IAS 39," 13
cash flow hedge, 532, 536–538
cash flow statement (foreign subsidiary), 596
cash-generating units, 177–179
Celestica Inc., 382
central banks, 518
changes. *See* accounting changes; expected
 changes; significant changes in last
 two years
China, and international standards, 8
CICA. *See* Canadian Institute of Chartered
 Accountants (CICA)
CICA Handbook
 see also Canadian GAAP
 bond investment, amortization of,
  198–199
 changeover date, 18
 control, 84
 differential reporting options, 18–19
 expected changes. *See* significant changes
  in last two years
 harmonization with IFRSs, 15–17
 and IFRSs. *See* International Financial
  Reporting Standards (IFRSs)
 not-for-profit organizations (NFPOs),
  635, 636, 639–649
 Part I. *See* International Financial
  Reporting Standards (IFRSs)
 private enterprises, GAAP for, 19
 proprietary theory, 133
 reorganization, 20–21
 role of, 4
 Section 1590 - Subsidiaries, 92
 Section 1625, Comprehensive
  Revaluation of Assets and Liabilities,
  125
 Section 3051 - Significant Influence
  Investments, 54–55
 Section 3110 - Asset Retirement
  Obligations, 645
 Section 3400 - Revenue, 640
 Section 3856 - Financial Instruments, 56
 Section 4400 - Financial Statement
  Presentation by Not-for-Profit
  Organizations, 646–647
 Section 4410 - Contributions, Revenue
  Recognition, 646–647
 Section 4420 - Contributions Receivable,
  640–641
 Section 4430 - Capital Assets Held
  by Not-for-Profit Organizations,
  644–645
 Section 4440 - Collections Held by Not-
  for-Profit Organizations, 645–646
 Section 4450 - Reporting Controlled and
  Related Entities by Not-for-Profit
  Organizations, 641–643
 Section 4460 - Disclosure of Related
  Party Transactions by Not-for-Profit
  Organizations, 643
 Section 4470 - Disclosure of Allocated
  Expenses by Not-for-Profit
  Organizations, 646
 separate section for IFRSs, 17

significant changes. *See* significant changes in last two years
"CICA's Guide to IFRS in Canada," 17–18
Cisco Systems, Inc., 120
closing rate, 522, 527, 533
Coca-Cola Company, 145
Coca-Cola Enterprises Inc., 145
code law systems, 4, 5
Cognos Inc., 72
collections, 645–646
columnar approach, 638
Commerce Bancorp, 72
commercial substance test, 463
common law systems, 4
common shares, 382, 584
conglomerate business combination, 71
consolidated balance sheet
    accounts, 186f
    acquisition differential, 89
    acquisition method, 89
    adjustments, 320
    direct approach, 124f, 128, 131f
    80-percent-owned subsidiary, 192
    elimination entries, 130–131
    entity theory, 138f
    foreign operations, acquisition date, 578, 578f
    immediately after business combination, 89
    intercompany inventory profits, elimination of, 258
    inventory, 267
    non-controlling interest (NCI), 393
    point-in-time adjustments, 320
    preparation of, 89
    reverse takeovers, 97–98, 97f
    wholly owned subsidiaries, on acquisition date, 122–123, 127f
    wholly owned subsidiaries, subsequent to acquisition date, 184
consolidated cash flow analysis, 395, 403
consolidated cash flow statement, 383–387
    adjustments, 383
    disclosures in year of acquisition, 384
    governments, 683–684
    IAS 7 - Statement of Cash Flows, 386
    incremental effect of purchasing subsidiary, 385
    indirect method, 383
    net change in cash, 386f
    non-cash items, change in, 383, 386f
    preparation of, 385–387
    private enterprises, 412–413
consolidated financial statements
    see also business combinations; consolidation
    on acquisition date. *See* consolidated statements on acquisition date
    acquisition differential. *See* acquisition differential
    basic preparation steps, 205f
    business combinations, 82–92
    consolidated balance sheet. *See* consolidated balance sheet

consolidated cash flow statement, 383–387
consolidated income statement. *See* consolidated income statement
consolidation theories, 132–140
contingent consideration, 140–144
and control, 82–92
defined, 83
described, 120
direct approach, 123–124, 124f, 128f, 131f
disclosure requirements, 90–91
elimination entries, 89
foreign subsidiaries. *See* foreign operations
IAS 27 - Consolidated and Separate Financial Statements, 42, 82–83, 84, 144, 455
intercompany transactions, elimination of, 83
limitations, 83–84
non-controlling interest (NCI), 131–132
non-wholly owned subsidiaries, 131–132
private enterprises, 144
reverse takeovers, 97–98, 97f, 99, 99f
subsequent to acquisition date. *See* consolidated statements subsequent to acquisition date
transactions with outsiders, 51
use of, 83
wholly owned subsidiaries, 121–131
working papers, 88–89, 89f, 211–220
consolidated income statement
    adjustments, 320
    consolidation adjustments, 193
    intercompany inventory profits, parent selling, 265–266
    intercompany sales and purchases, elimination of, 251, 251f
    parent's sale of portion of subsidiary holdings, 399–400
    period-of-time adjustments, 320
    pro formal consolidated income statement, 201
    subsequent to acquisition date, 173–174
consolidated net income
    bond retirement, 326
    consolidation subsequent to acquisition, 185f, 186f, 189
    elimination of revenue and expense, 252
    equity method, 173
    indirect shareholdings, 410f
    intercompany inventory profits, parent selling, 263
    intercompany inventory profits, subsidiary selling, 256
    preferred shares outstanding, 407
consolidated retained earnings, 174, 189, 260, 393
consolidated statement of change in net debt, 683
consolidated statement of financial position, 683
consolidated statement of operations, 683

consolidated statements on acquisition date
    consolidation theories, 132–140
    contingent consideration, 140–144
    direct approach, 123–124, 124f, 128f, 131f
    foreign operations, 578, 578f
    non-controlling interest (NCI), 131–132
    non-wholly owned subsidiaries, 131–132
    private enterprises, 144
    U.S. GAAP differences, 144–145
consolidated statements subsequent to acquisition date
    accounting methods, 171–173
    acquisitional differential assigned to liabilities, 198–200
    amortization of acquisition differential, 174
    consolidated income statement, 173–174
    consolidated retained earnings statement, 173–174
    cost method, 171, 173, 184, 187
    80-percent-owned subsidiary, 191–198, 215–220
    elimination entries, 211
    end of year 1, 184–187, 186f, 192–195, 192f, 193f, 194f, 211–214, 215–217
    end of year 2, 187–190, 190f, 195–198, 196–198f, 214–215, 218–220
    equity method, 171–173, 202–204
    foreign operations, 579–586
    impairment testing, 175–182
    intercompany receivables and payables, 201
    private enterprises, 204
    subsequent-year comparisons, 201
    subsidiary acquired during the year, 201
    U.S. GAAP differences, 204
    wholly-owned subsidiary, 183–190
    working paper approach, 211–220
consolidation
    see also business combinations; consolidated financial statements
    joint arrangements, 460–470
    not-for-profit organizations (NFPOs), 641
    prepaid taxes, 254, 312
    procedures, 50
    process, 173
    proportionate consolidation, 43, 133, 490–492
    requirements, 85–86
    and special-purpose entities, 86–87, 450–460
    variable-interest entity, 450–460
    wholly owned subsidiaries, 121–131
consolidation theories, 132–140
    entity theory, 132, 133–138
    parent company extension theory, 132, 140
    parent company theory, 132, 139
    proprietary theory, 132, 133
contingent consideration, 140–144
    disclosure, 141–142, 143–144
    equity, classification as, 143

fair value, 140–141
liability, classification as, 142–143
contingent liability, 78
contra account, 270n, 464
contributions, 640–641, 646–647, 649–651
control
    see also jointly controlled entities
    assets, 83
    and consolidated financial statements,
      82–92
    and consolidation, 85
    defined, 42, 83, 84, 652
    determination of, 84–86
    indirect holdings, 410
    joint control, 461, 642
    with less than 50 percent, 85
    by not-for-profit organizations (NFPOs),
      641–642
    other means of control, 449
    and protective rights, 85–86
    special-purpose entities, 453
    temporary control, 85
control investments, and NFPOs, 641
convergence
    organizations working toward, 5–9
    Short Term Convergence Project, 12
cost method
    consolidated retained earnings, 394–395
    described, 171
    dividend income, 184, 187, 195
    nonstrategic investments, 46–47
    use of, 173
cost model, 269
cost of goods sold, 586
cost of sales, 255–257, 262
costs
    acquisition costs. *See* acquisition costs
    fair value, estimate of, 41
creditors, and separate-entity financial
    statements, 83–84
Crucell N.V., 469, 470f
cumulative preferred shares, 406
currency exchange rates. *See* exchange rates
currency perspectives, 520–521, 520f
current rate method, 572–573, 577, 586

D

Daimler AG, 480–483f
deductible temporary difference, 471
deferral method, 649–650, 654–656,
    667–674
deferred contributions, 654, 668, 669
deferred income taxes
    acquired deferred tax benefits,
      475–476
    acquisition differential, 473–475
    acquisition of asset at price different
      from tax base, 472–473
    assets, 78
    balance sheet approach, 472
    and business combinations, 471–476
    concepts, 471–472
    disclosure, 476
    illustrations, 473–475

operating loss carry-forwards, 475–476
temporary differences, 471
U.S. GAAP differences, 484
definite useful lives, 176
Deloitte, 15, 144, 145f, 395, 396f
Denmark, 6
denominated currency, 520
depreciable assets. *See* intercompany profits
    in depreciable assets
depreciation expense, 309–311, 315f
derivative instruments, 517, 530
differential reporting options, 18–19
direct approach, 123–124
    consolidated balance sheet, 124f
    80-percent-owned subsidiary, 194f, 197f
    entity theory, 137f
    goodwill, 131f
    intercompany bondholdings, 327f, 334f
    intercompany inventory profits,
      257f, 261f
    intercompany profits in depreciable
      assets, 317
    negative goodwill, 128f
    parent company extension theory, 141f
    parent company theory, 139f
    wholly-owned subsidiary, on acquisition
      date, 123–124, 124f, 128, 128f, 131f
    wholly-owned subsidiary, subsequent to
      acquisition date, 183
direct quotation, 518–519, 519f
disclosure
    allocated expenses, and NFPOs, 646
    business combinations, 90–91
    consolidated cash flow statement, 384
    consolidated financial statements,
      90–91
    contingent consideration, 141–142,
      143–144
    deferred income taxes, 476
    disposal of subsidiary or portion of
      subsidiary, 395, 396f
    equity method, 54
    exchange rate changes, and foreign
      operations, 597
    footnote disclosure, 83
    geographic areas, 516
    hedges, 543
    IAS 27 - Consolidated and Separate
      Financial Statements, 144
    IFRS 3 - Business Combinations, 144
    impairment losses, 180–182, 181–182f
    intercompany eliminations, 271–272,
      340
    international accounting, 2
    joint arrangements, 469, 470f
    long-term investments, accounting
      policies for, 143
    note disclosure, 54
    not-for-profit organizations (NFPOs),
      674
    related-party transactions, by NFPOs, 643
    reportable segments, 479–480
    required by IAS 28 - Investments in
      Associates (Equity Method), 54

retrospective adjustments of prior-period
    results, 49
reverse takeovers, 97–98
segment disclosures, 43, 476–483, 484
special-purpose entities, 457
dividend
    on consolidated retained earnings
      statement, 186f
    income, recording of, 45, 184, 192
    liquidating dividend, 46–47, 574
    paid by subsidiary to parent company,
      383
donated capital assets, 656–657
donated materials and services, 657
downstream transactions, 263–266
Duvernay Oil Corp., 72

E

earnings
    Canadian *vs.* U.S. GAAP, 11
    retained earnings. *See* retained earnings
economic exposure, 570–571
economic ties between countries, 5
effective interest method, 199, 338–340
80-percent-owned subsidiary, 191–198,
    215–220
elimination entries, 89, 211
elimination of intercompany transactions.
    See intercompany eliminations
Emera Inc., 39
Empire Company Limited, 460
EnCana, 11
encumbrance accounting, 659
endowment contributions, 647
endowment fund, 661–662
endowment interest, 637
endowments, 637
Enron Corporation, 86, 357, 449,
    451–452
"Enron standards," 452
entity theory, 132, 133–138
"The Entity Theory of Consolidated
    Statements" (Moonitz), 134
equity, contingent consideration as, 143
equity investments
    available-for-sale investments, 40–41,
      45–46
    business combinations. *See* business
      combinations
    cost method, 46–47
    directly related IFRSs, 42–43
    equity method, 47–54
    expected changes, 57
    fair value, investments not valued at,
      46–54
    fair value, investments valued at, 45–46
    fair value changes, 41
    fair value through profit or loss (FVTPL),
      45–46, 52
    long-term investments, 143
    nonstrategic investments, 40, 43
    other related IFRSs, 43–45
    overview, 40–41
    private enterprises, GAAP for, 54–56

reporting methods, summary of, 40f
significant changes in last two years, 57
strategic investments, 40
types of share investments, 40
U.S. GAAP differences, 56
equity method, 47–54
  accrual method, 49
  acquisition costs greater than book
    values, 50–51
  additional features, 49–54
  changes to and from equity method, 52
  consolidated net income, 186f
  and consolidated net income, 173
  consolidated retained earnings
    statement, 173
  consolidated statements on acquisition
    date, 128
  consolidated statements subsequent to
    acquisition date, 171–173, 202–204
  defined, 171
  disclosure requirements, 54
  and fair value of investment, 389
  future cash flow potential, 49
  IAS 28 - Investments in Associates
    (Equity Method), 47–48, 171–172
  illustration of basics, 48–49
  impairment losses, 53
  intercompany bondholdings, 328–329,
    336
  intercompany inventory profits, parent
    selling, 264–265
  intercompany inventory profits,
    subsidiary selling, 258–259, 263
  intercompany land profits, 269
  intercompany profits in depreciable
    assets, 314, 318
  investor's investment account, changes
    in, 49
  losses exceeding balance in investment
    account, 52–53
  net effect of consolidation entries, 258
  other changes in associate's equity,
    49–50
  parent's income, 259, 314, 409
  retained earnings, 394
  sale of investments, gains and losses
    on, 53
  significant influence, 42, 388
  translated financial statements, 582,
    590–591
  unrealized profits, 51
  use of, 42, 43
  wholly owned subsidiaries, 128
Ernst and Young, 10
euro, 6
European Commission, 15
European Union
  adoption of IFRS, 11
  "carve-out for IAS 39," 13
  directives, 6
  effect on accounting standards, 5
  foreign companies listed on E.U.
    markets, 15
  formation of, 3

goal of, 6
harmonization and convergence, 5–6
recent initiatives, 10–11
Evraz Group SA, 72
exchange adjustments, 523, 524, 537, 574,
  596–597
exchange gains (losses), 526, 527, 531,
  573n, 586
exchange rates, 517–519
  average rates, 572, 580
  closing rate, 522, 527, 533
  direct quotation, 518–519, 519f
  disclosure, 597
  fluctuations in, 518
  forward exchange rate, 570
  forward rate, 522
  historical rate, 522, 525, 572
  historical rates, 571
  IAS 21 - Foreign Exchange Rates, 44,
    520–521, 522, 543, 570–571,
    573–577, 597
  IAS 21 (Foreign Exchange Rates), 44
  indirect quotation, 518
  and inflation rates, 518
  and interest rates, 518
  quotations, 518–519
  spot rate, 519
  and trade surpluses and deficits, 518
executory contract, 529, 659
expected changes
  business combinations, 94
  consolidated cash flow statements, 414
  consolidated statements on acquisition
    date, 146
  consolidated statements subsequent to
    acquisition date, 206
  control, 485
  equity investments, 57
  foreign operations, 600
  foreign-currency transactions, 547–548
  intercompany profits (losses), 273, 341
  not-for-profit organizations (NFPOs),
    676
expenses
  allocated expenses, and NFPOs, 646
  amortization expense, 671
  depreciation expense, 309–311, 315f
  gross basis, 648
  income tax expense, 254, 258, 323
  intercompany revenue and expenses,
    249–252
  interest expense, 326, 330, 330n, 527
  recognition, gross vs. net basis, 648–649
  translation of, 584
export transactions, 523–526
exposure drafts, 41
external financial statements, 172

F
fair value
  acquisition-date fair value differences,
    383
  adjustment of investment account, 390
  changes, 41

contingent consideration, 140–141
cost as appropriate estimate, 41
defined, 175
excess, 88
fair value through profit or loss (FVTPL),
  45–46, 52, 388
forward contracts, 529, 551–552
investments not valued at, 46–54
investments valued at, 45–46
non-controlling interest (NCI), 134–136
property, plant and equipment, 270
of subsidiary, 134–135
fair value hedge, 531–532, 538–539
FASB. See Financial Accounting Standards
  Board (FASB)
federal government. See government sector
Financial Accounting Standards Board
  (FASB)
  Interpretation No. 46 - Consolidation of
    Variable Interest Entities, 86
  memorandum of understanding (MOU),
    12, 14
  Norwalk Agreement, 11–12
  role of, 4
  rule-based pronouncements, 11
financial instruments
  CICA Handbook, Section 3856, 56
  convergence, 12
  derivative financial instruments,
    517, 530
  forward exchange contract, 527–530
  hedging instruments, 530
  IAS 39 - Financial Instruments, 40, 43,
    45, 84, 543
  non-derivative financial instrument, 530
  private enterprises, 56
Financial Reporting by Not-For-Profit
  Organizations, 20
Financial Reporting in Canada, 460, 461
financial statements
  balance sheet. See balance sheet
  cash flow statement (foreign subsidiary),
    596
  consolidated financial statements. See
    consolidated financial statements
  external financial statements, 172
  external users, 172
  Framework for the Preparation and
    Presentation of Financial Statements
    (IASB), 78, 83
  fund basis, 647
  governments, 682–684
  IAS 1 - Presentation of Financial
    Statements, 43–44, 173n
  income statement. See income statement
  joint ventures, 465f, 490f
  not-for-profit organizations (NFPOs),
    646–647, 647–649
  separate financial statements, 83–84
  titles and formats, 44
  translated financial statements. See
    translated financial statements
  variations in descriptions and
    presentations, 2

first in, first out (FIFO), 53, 184*n*
footnotes. *See* disclosure
Fording Canadian Coal Trust, 72
forecasted transaction, 539–541
foreign exchange rates. *See* exchange rates
foreign operations
    acquisition differential, 588–589
    acquisition-date consolidated balance
        sheet, 578, 578*f*
    acquisition-differential foreign
        operations, 590*f*, 593*f*
    cash flow statement, 596
    consolidated accumulated translation
        adjustments, 591
    consolidation, financial statement
        preparation, 583–584, 583*f*
    consolidation, illustration of, 577–597
    consolidation, integrated foreign
        operations, 593–595
    consolidation, self-sustaining, 590–593
    consolidation, subsequent to
        acquisition, 579–586
    current rate method, 572–573
    disclosure, 597
    disposition of accumulated unrealized
        losses, 590*f*
    economic exposure, 570–571
    exchange adjustments, 574, 596–597
    foreign-currency risk, 569–571
    functional currency, 573, 574–575
    highly inflationary economies, 575–576
    IAS 27 - Consolidated and Separate
        Financial Statements, 569
    IAS 29 - Financial Reporting in
        Hyperinflationary Economies,
        575, 576
    indicators for evaluation of, 574–575,
        574*f*
    integrated foreign operation, 584–587,
        593–595
    intercompany profits, 596
    lower of cost and net realizable value
        (LCNRV), 595–596
    presentation currency, 573
    private enterprises, 599
    sale of, 574
    self-sustaining foreign operation, 575,
        580–584, 590–593
    tax effects of exchange adjustments,
        596–597
    transaction exposure, 570
    translated financial statements. *See*
        translated financial statements
    translation, illustration of, 577–597
    translation, subsequent to acquisition,
        579–586
    translation (accounting) exposure,
        569–570
    translation adjustment, 587*f*, 591
    translation methods, 571–573
    translation under IAS 21, 573–577
    unamortized acquisition differential, 595
    units of measure, 577
    U.S. GAAP differences, 599

foreign subsidiaries. *See* foreign operations
foreign-currency exposure, 569
foreign-currency risk, 569–571
foreign-currency transactions
    accounting for, 519–527
    closing rate, 522, 527, 533
    currency perspectives, 520–521, 520*f*
    denominated currency, 520
    described, 517
    exchange adjustments, 523
    exchange gains, 526
    exchange rates. *See* exchange rates
    foreign currency, 520–521
    foreign-exchange adjustments, 523, 524
    forward rate, 522
    functional currency, 520–521, 521*f*
    hedges, 530–546
    historical rate, 522, 525
    import/export transactions denominated
        in foreign currency, 523–526
    interest expense, 527
    internal record-keeping currency, 520
    monetary items, 521–522, 525
    non-current monetary items, gains and
        losses from, 526–527
    presentation currency, 520
    recording currency, 520
    recording of, 522–523
    reporting currency, 520
    risks, 517
    speculative forward exchange contract,
        527–530
    translation method, 522–523
    U.S. GAAP differences, 547
foreign-exchange adjustments, 523,
    524, 537
forward exchange contract
    defined, 519
    fair value, 529, 551–552
    hedging an unrecognized firm
        commitment, 535–536
    premium, 536
    and risk, 532
    speculative forward exchange contract,
        527–530, 552*f*
forward exchange rate, 570
forward rate, 522
*Framework for the Preparation and Presentation
    of Financial Statements* (IASB), 78, 83
France
    accounting standards, and legislation, 10
    standard setting, 5
friendly business combinations, 72
Frito-Lay, 120
functional currency, 520–521, 521*f*, 573,
    574–575
fund accounting, 636–639, 662
fund basis, 647

G

GAAP. *See* generally accepted accounting
    principles (GAAP)
gains
    see also profit

equipment, 310, 311*f*
    exchange gains, 526, 527, 531, 573*n*, 586
    intercompany bondholdings. *See*
        intercompany bondholdings
    intercompany gains. *See* intercompany
        profits (losses)
    joint operations, 463–464
    joint ventures, and unrealized gains,
        466–468
    non-current monetary items, 526–527
    on sale of investments, 53
    transactions with shareholders, 398, 401
general fund, 660
generally accepted accounting principles
    (GAAP)
    see also Canadian GAAP; U.S. GAAP
    interperiod tax allocation, 3
    variations in, 2
Germany
    accounting standards, and legislation, 10
    standard setting, 5
    taxation, role of, 4
Gildan Activewear Inc., 460
goodwill
    and acquisition cost, 133
    allocation, 178
    calculation of, 88
    cash-generating units, 177–179
    defined, 78
    determination of value, 136
    impairment testing, 175–182
    internally generated goodwill, 180
    negative goodwill, 126–128, 128*f*
    reverse takeovers, 97
    wholly owned subsidiaries, 128–131
government sector, 635, 680–684
gross method, 529, 530
group, 83
guarantee of obligations, 52–53

H

harmonization
    choice of, 17
    of *CICA Handbook* with IFRSs, 15–17
    organizations working toward, 5–9
Harvard, 637
hedges, 530–546
    accounts receivable, 532–533
    anticipated future transaction, 530–531
    cash flow hedge, 532, 536–538
    conditions, 531
    defined, 530
    derivative financial instruments, 530
    designation, 531–532
    disclosure, 543
    effectiveness of, 531
    exchange gains or losses, 531
    fair value hedge, 531–532, 538–539
    fixing purchase price, 539
    forecasted transaction, 539–541
    hedging instruments, 530
    long-term debt, 539–541
    net investment in a foreign operation
        (IFRIC 16), 45

net investment in foreign operation, 531
non-derivative financial instrument, 530
private enterprises, 546–547
recognized monetary item, 532–535
trial balance, 534
unrecognized firm commitment, 535–539
highly inflationary economies, 575–576
historical cost principle
in foreign currency and current rate, 573
and inflation, 5
inventory, and unrealized profit, 258
historical rate, 522, 525, 571, 572
holdback
intercompany inventory profit, 253–258
intercompany land profit, 267–268
Homburg Invest Inc., 21
horizontal business combination, 71
hyper-inflation, 575

I

IASB. *See* International Accounting
Standards Board (IASB)
IASs. *See* International Accounting
Standards (IASs)
IBM Corp., 72
IFRIC. *See* International Financial Reporting
Interpretations Committee (IFRIC)
IFRS. *See* International Financial Reporting
Standards (IFRSs)
IFRS for SMEs, 20
IFRSs and U.S. GAAP - A Pocket Comparison
(Deloitte), 15
impairment losses
see also impairment testing
application, 179
described, 53
disclosure, 180–182, 181–182*f*
reversal, 179–180
impairment of assets
see also impairment losses; impairment
testing
acquisition differential, 188*f*, 193*f*, 196*f*
cost method, 46
described, 44
fair value, 175
IAS 36 - Impairment of Assets, 44, 175,
176, 177
intercompany losses, 252*n*
recoverable amount, 175, 178, 181
value in use, 175
impairment testing, 175–182
see also impairment losses
annual testing, 177
at business unit level, 181
cash-generating units, 177–179
consolidated *vs.* subsidiary level, 176
external factors, 176
goodwill, 177–179
intangible assets with definite useful
lives, 176
intangible assets with indefinite useful
lives, 177
internal factors, 176
professional judgment, 179

implied value, 455
import transactions, 523–526
income
accounting income, 4
net income. *See* net income
recognition, 250
temporal method *vs.* current rate
method, 586
income statement
consolidated income statement. *See*
consolidated income statement
investor's income statement, 49
profit, 44
use of term, 44
in year of acquisition, 124–125
income tax. *See* taxation
income tax expense, 254, 258, 323
independent business valuation, 136
indirect method, 383
indirect quotation, 518
indirect shareholdings, 408–412
inflation
highly inflationary economies, 575–576
hyper-inflation, 575
IAS 29 - Financial Reporting in
Hyperinflationary Economies,
575, 576
inflation levels, 5
inflation rates, and exchange rates, 518
South America, 5
intangible assets
business combinations, 77–78
with definite useful lives, 176
goodwill. *See* goodwill
IAS 38 - Intangible Assets, 44–45,
77–78, 180
impairment testing, 175–182
with indefinite useful lives, 177
negative goodwill, 78
integrated foreign operation, 584–587,
593–595
intercompany bondholdings, 320–340
after-tax gain, 328, 335
agency method, 337
allocation of gain, 324–329,
325*f*, 332*f*
approaches for allocation of gain, 324
bond chart, 334–335
bond chart, preparation of, 332
consolidated statements, effect on, 328,
335–336
direct approach, 327*f*, 334*f*
effective interest method, 338–340
equity method journal entries, 328–329,
336
gain in subsequent years, 329–336
with gain or loss, 322–324
gains (losses) allocated to two
equities, 337
gains (losses) not allocated to two
equities, 337
gains/losses, 321
intercompany purchases during fiscal
year, 336–337

interest elimination loss, 331, 333*f*
less than 100 percent purchase of
affiliate's bonds, 336
loss on redemption, 339
no gain or loss, 321–322
intercompany eliminations
disclosure, 271–272, 340
intercompany bondholdings, 320–340
intercompany inventory profits,
253–267
intercompany land profits, 267–271
intercompany management fees, 252
intercompany profits in depreciable
assets, 309–320
intercompany receivables and payables,
201
intercompany rentals, 252
intercompany revenue and expenses,
249–252
intercompany sales and purchases,
249–251
joint ventures, 465
intercompany interest, 330
intercompany inventory profits, 253–267
consolidated net income, 263
consolidation adjustments, 261–262, 265
downstream transactions, 263–266
elimination of unrealized profits, 257,
257*f*
equity method journal entries, parent
selling, 264–265
equity method journal entries, subsidiary
selling, 258–259, 263, 264
holdback of inventory profits, year 1,
253–258
income statement, 265–266
losses, 266–267
non-controlling interest (NCI), 262
parent selling, 263–266
vs. realization of equipment profits,
319–320
realization of inventory profits, year 2,
259–263
subsidiary selling, 253–263
unrealized profits with associates, 265
upstream transactions, 253–263
intercompany land profits, 267–271
contra account, 270*n*
cost model, 269
equity method journal entries, 269
holdback, 267–268
realization of intercompany land profits,
268–269
revaluation model, 269–271
intercompany management fees, 252
intercompany profits in depreciable assets,
309–320
direct approach, 317
equity method journal entries, 314, 318
holdback and recognition, year 1,
309–314
net book value, 315, 319
vs. realization of inventory profits,
319–320

realization of remaining gain, year 2, 314–319
revaluation model, 350–351
used depreciable asset, intercompany sale of, 318–319
intercompany profits (losses)
depreciable assets, 309–320
foreign operations, 596
impairment and losses, 252n
intercompany bondholdings, 320–340
intercompany inventory profits, 253–267
intercompany land profits, 267–271
intercompany transfer pricing, 271–272
private enterprises, 272, 340
types of unrealized intercompany profits (losses), 253
unrealized profits (losses), 252–253
U.S. GAAP differences, 272, 340
intercompany rentals, 252
intercompany revenue and expenses, 249–252
intercompany sales and purchases, 249–251
other examples, 251–252
intercompany sales and purchases, 249–251
intercompany transactions
see also intercompany eliminations
and consolidated statements, 83
downstream transactions, 263–266
exchange price, 267
joint ventures, 464–466
and market value, 267
profits from, 51
transfer pricing, 271–272
upstream transactions, 253–263
use of, 248
intercompany transfer pricing, 271–272
interest elimination loss, 331, 333f
interest expense, 326, 330, 330n, 527
interest rates, and exchange rates, 518
interest revenue, 330, 330n
internal record-keeping currency, 520
internal records, 172
international accounting standards
see also International Accounting Standards (IASs); International Financial Reporting Standards (IFRSs)
accounting harmonization and convergence, 5–9
asset revaluations, 2
capital markets, level of development, 4
disclosure, 2
financial statement elements, variations in, 2
IFRSs *vs.* U.S. GAAP, 11–15
inflation levels, 5
influencing factors, 3–5
legal systems, 4–5
recent initiatives, 10–11
taxation, role of, 3–4

ties between countries, 5
variations in GAAP, 2
International Accounting Standards (IASs)
alternative accounting treatments, 7
"carve-out for IAS 39," 13
IAS 1 - Presentation of Financial Statements, 43–44, 173n
IAS 7 - Statement of Cash Flows, 386
IAS 12 - Income Taxes, 449, 471, 473, 475
IAS 16 - Property, Plant and Equipment, 180, 350, 463
IAS 18 - Revenue, 463
IAS 21 - Foreign Exchange Rates, 44, 520–521, 522, 543, 570–571, 573–577, 597
IAS 27 - Consolidated and Separate Financial Statements, 42, 47, 82–83, 84, 144, 455, 569, 652
IAS 28 - Investments in Associates (Equity Method), 47–48, 53, 54, 171–172
IAS 29 - Financial Reporting in Hyperinflationary Economies, 42, 575, 576
IAS 31 - Joint Arrangements, 42–43
IAS 36 - Impairment of Assets, 44, 175, 176, 177
IAS 38 - Intangible Assets, 44–45, 77–78, 180
IAS 39 - Financial Instruments, 40, 43, 45, 84, 199, 527–529, 530, 543
International Accounting Standards Board (IASB)
see also International Financial Reporting Standards (IFRSs)
Exposure Draft on Consolidated Financial Statements, 457
exposure drafts, 41
Framework for the Preparation and Presentation of Financial Statements, 78, 83
harmonization and convergence, 6–8
IFRS for SMEs, 20
major restructuring, 7
memorandum of understanding (MOU), 12, 14
Norwalk Agreement, 11–12
International Accounting Standards Committee (IASC), 6–7
International Financial Reporting Interpretations Committee (IFRIC), 45
International Financial Reporting Standards (IFRSs)
adoption of, 8
vs. Canadian GAAP, 21
complexity of, 10–11
equity investments, 42–45
foreign registrants in United States, 12–13
harmonization with *CICA Handbook,* 15–17
IFRS 3 - Business Combinations, 43, 44, 74–75, 76–78, 136–137, 144, 455

IFRS 8 - Operating Segments, 43, 477, 480
IFRS 9 - Financial Instruments, 14, 40–41, 43
IFRS 10 - Joint Arrangements, 461, 464, 466
IFRS 12 - Income Taxes, 44
list of current standards, 8f
net income, 13–14
push-down accounting, 125
and reconciliation with U.S. GAAP, 3, 3n
vs. U.S. GAAP, 11–15, 16f
use of IFRS by country, 9f
use of term, 7
interperiod tax allocation, 3
inventory
on consolidated balance sheet, 267
convergence, 12
first in, first out (FIFO), 53, 184n
intercompany inventory profits. *See* intercompany inventory profits
last in, last out (LIFO), 53, 184n, 272
overstatement of ending inventory, 255–256
investment account
adjustments, 203, 318
and consolidated balance sheet, 187
fair value, adjustment to, 390
guarantee of obligations, 52–53
vs. investment income, 314, 329
losses exceeding balance in, 52–53
in parent's separate-entity balance sheet, 185f
reconciliation, 203
reconciliation to subsidiary's equity, 393
replacement, 386
subsidiary's shareholders' equity, 584
investments
in bonds, 521
control investments, and NFPOs, 641
economic interest in another NFPO, 643
equity investments. *See* equity investments
investment income, 314, 329, 650
net investment in foreign operation, 531
IPSCO Inc., 72

J
Japan
standard setting, 5
taxation, role of, 4
joint arrangements, 42–43, 460–470
defined, 460
disclosure, 469, 470f
example, 461
IFRS 10 - Joint Arrangements, 461, 464, 466
joint control, 461
joint operations, 461, 462–464
joint ventures, 461, 464–469
proportionate consolidation, 490–492

types of, 461
U.S. GAAP differences, 484
venturer, 461
joint control, 461, 642
joint operations, 461, 462–464
joint ventures, 461, 464–469
    acquisition differentials, 464
    contributions to, 466–469
    financial statements, 465f, 490f
    intercompany transactions, 464–466
    unrealized gain, recognition of, 466–468
jointly controlled entities
    see also control
    equity method, 43
    SIC 13 (Jointly Controlled Entities -
      Non-monetary Contributions by
      Venturers), 45

K

KPMG, 72

L

last in, last out (LIFO), 53, 184n, 272
layered approach, 638–639
legal systems, 4–5
liabilities
    acquisition differential, 198–200
    contingent consideration, 142–143
    contingent liability, 78
    net liability exposure, 570
    special-purpose entities, 453
liquidating dividend, 46–47, 574
local government. *See* government sector
long-term debt, as hedge, 539–541
long-term investments, 143
losses
    exceeding investment account balance,
      52–53
    exchange losses, 526, 527, 531, 573n,
      586
    impairment losses, 53, 179–180
    intercompany bondholdings. *See*
      intercompany bondholdings
    intercompany losses. *See* intercompany
      profits (losses)
    interest elimination loss, 331
    and long-term interests in associate, 53
    non-current monetary items, 526–527
    on sale of investments, 53
    transactions with shareholders, 398, 401
lower of cost and net realizable value
    (LCNRV), 595–596

M

Magna International Inc., 568
market value, 267, 338
matching principle, 249, 258, 331
memorandum of understanding (MOU),
    12, 14
merger. *See* business combinations
Mexico
    central bank, 518
    price level accounting, 5

minority shareholders, and separate-entity
    financial statements, 83–84
Model Financial Statements (Deloitte),
    395, 396f
monetary items, 521–522, 525
    non-current monetary items, 526–527
    recognized monetary item, hedging,
      532–535
    translated financial statements, 584
Moonitz, Maurice, 134
multicolumn approach, 662

N

negative acquisition differential, 128
negative goodwill, 78, 126–128, 128f
net asset or net liability exposure, 570
net assets, 51n, 75, 648, 651–656, 671
net book value, 315, 319
net income
    adjusted net income, 260
    in Canada, 3
    components of, 258
    consolidated net income. *See*
      consolidated net income
    cumulative net income, 189
    under IFRSs, 13–14
    reconciliation of, and U.S. GAAP, 3,
      13–14
    and retained earnings, 46
    reverse takeovers, and consolidated net
      income, 98
    of subsidiary after acquisition date, 124n
    in United States, 3
net investment in foreign operation, 531
net method, 530
net realizable value, 595–596
new entity method, 74, 76
New Zealand
    adoption of IFRS, 11
    recent initiatives, 10–11
NFPOs. *See* not-for-profit organizations
    (NFPOs)
non-arm's length transactions. *See*
    intercompany transactions
non-cash items, 383, 386f
non-controlling interest (NCI), 131–132
    changes in, 195
    consolidated balance sheet, 393
    and consolidation theories, 133–137,
      133f
    disclosure, 144, 145f
    80-percent-owned subsidiary, 191f
    gain on bond retirement, 326f, 333f
    indirect shareholdings, 412f
    intercompany inventory profits, 262, 264
    intercompany profits, downstream
      transactions, 255
    intercompany profits, upstream
      transactions, 255
    parent's sale of portion of subsidiary
      holdings, 398
    realization of year 2 gain, 318
    and shareholders' equity, 404–405

special-purpose entities, 455–456
subsidiary issues additional shares to
    public, 403
unrealized profits on upstream
    transactions, 312
valuation issues, 132
noncumulative preferred shares, 406–407
noncurrent assets, 45
non-current monetary items, 526–527
non-derivative financial instrument, 530
non-monetary items, 584
non-profit sector. *See* not-for-profit
    organizations (NFPOs)
non-reciprocal transfer, 640
nonstrategic investments, 40, 43
non-wholly owned subsidiaries, 131–132
Nortel Networks Corporation, 170–171
North American Free Trade Agreement, 3
Norwalk Agreement, 11–12
note disclosure, 54
not-for-profit organizations (NFPOs)
    bequests, 640–641
    budgetary control, 658–659
    capital fund, 660–661
    CICA Handbook provisions, 636,
      639–649
    CICA Handbook Section 4400 - Financial
      Statement Presentation, 646–647
    CICA Handbook Section 4410 -
      Contributions, Revenue Recognition,
      646–647
    CICA Handbook Section 4420 -
      Contributions Receivable, 640–641
    CICA Handbook Section 4430 - Capital
      Assets Held by Not-for-Profit
      Organizations, 644–645
    CICA Handbook Section 4440 -
      Collections Held by Not-for-Profit
      Organizations, 645–646
    CICA Handbook Section 4450 - Reporting
      Controlled and Related Entities,
      641–643
    CICA Handbook Section 4460 - Disclosure
      of Related Party Transactions, 643
    CICA Handbook Section 4470 - Disclosure
      of Allocated Expenses, 646
    columnar approach, 638
    consolidation, 641
    contributions, 640–641, 646–647,
      649–651
    control investments, 641
    control over NFPOs, 641–642
    control over profit-oriented companies,
      642
    deferral method, 649–650, 654–656,
      667–674
    deferred contributions, 654, 668, 669
    defined, 635
    disclosure requirements, 674
    donated capital assets, 656–657
    donated materials and services, 657
    economic interest in another NFPO, 643
    encumbrance accounting, 659

endowment contributions, 647
endowment fund, 661–662
endowment interest, 637
endowments, 637
Financial Reporting by Not-For-Profit Organizations, 20
financial statements, 646–647, 647–649
fund accounting, 636–639
fund balances, 651
fund basis, 647
GAAP, 20
general fund, 660
government funding, 640
investment income, 650
joint control, 642
large NFPOs, 644–645
layered approach, 638–639
multicolumn approach, 662
net assets invested in capital assets, 651–656, 671
not-for-profit sector, 635
pledges, 640
vs. profit-oriented organizations, 636
recognition of revenues and expenses, 648–649
reporting, 639–649
restricted contributions, 647
restricted fund method, 650–651, 652–654, 660–667
restricted resources, 636–637, 652, 654–655
significant influence, 643
size of sector, 635
small NFPOs, 645
statement of financial position, 648
statement of operations, 649
unrestricted contributions, 647
unrestricted net asset balance, 669
unrestricted resources, 636, 652–654, 655–656
not-for-profit sector, 635
numerous small purchases, 394

O

"Observations on the Implementation of IFRS" (Ernst and Young), 10
off-balance-sheet financing, 86, 450
offshore tax havens, 248–249
oil pipelines, 461
one-line consolidation. *See* equity method
Onex Corporation, 382
operating loss carry-forwards, 475–476
operating profit (loss) test, 477, 478
operating segments, 43, 476–483, 484
other comprehensive income (OCI)
    vs. accumulated other comprehensive income, 580
    exchange adjustment, 537
    fair value changes on equity investments, 41
    profit, 44

reporting options, 46
revaluation surplus, 270
and shareholders' equity, 46
ownership interest
    see also shares
    block acquisitions of subsidiary, 387–395
    change in ownership interest, 383, 387–400
    consolidated cash flow analysis, 395, 403
    consolidated retained earnings, cost method, 394–395
    decrease in, 387
    income statement analysis, 399–400
    increase in, 387
    indirect shareholdings, 408–412
    numerous small purchases, 394
    private enterprises, 412–413
    repurchase of shares by subsidiary, 394
    sale of portion of holdings in subsidiary, 398–399
    step purchases, 387–395
    subsidiary issues additional shares to public, 401–403
    subsidiary preferred shares owned by parent, 407–408
    subsidiary with preferred shares outstanding, 404–408
    U.S. GAAP differences, 413
    and valuation of subsidiary's net assets, 392
    when ownership interest changes, 387

P

Pac-man defence, 73
parent company
    accumulated depreciation, 315*f*
    bonds, after consolidation, 323
    consolidation procedures, 50
    control with less than 50 percent, 85
    cost method, 189, 198
    defined, 71, 83
    depreciation expense, 309–311, 315*f*
    dividend payments from subsidiary company, 383
    equity method, 204, 314, 409
    income, under equity method, 259
    intercompany inventory profits, 263–266
    ownership changes. *See* ownership interest
    parent company extension theory, 132, 140
    parent company theory, 132, 139
    retained earnings, 174
    reverse takeovers, 96
    subsidiary formed by parent, 125, 125*n*
    subsidiary preferred shares, ownership of, 407–408
    as wholly owned subsidiary, 84
parent company extension theory, 132, 140

parent company theory, 132, 139
Part I of *CICA Handbook. See* International Financial Reporting Standards (IFRSs)
payables, intercompany, 201
PE GAAP. *See* private enterprises
pegged rates, 517–518
PepsiCo, Inc., 120
Pepsi-Cola Company, 120
period-of-time adjustments, 320
peso, 518
Petro-Canada, 308
pledges, 640
point-in-time adjustments, 320
poison pill, 72
political ties between countries, 5
pooling-of-interests method, 74, 75
Potash Corporation of Saskatchewan, 568
preferred shares, 382, 404–408
presentation currency, 520, 573
price level accounting, 5
PrimeWest Energy Trust, 72
private enterprises
    business combinations, 92
    consolidated cash flow statements, 412–413
    consolidated statements on date of acquisition, 144
    consolidated statements subsequent to acquisition date, 204
    deferred income taxes, 483
    equity investments, 54–56
    financial instruments, 56
    foreign operations, 599
    GAAP, 18–20
    hedges, 546–547
    intercompany profits, 272, 340
    joint arrangements, 483
    nonstrategic investments in, 40
    operating segments, 483
    ownership interest, 412–413
    reverse takeovers, 95
    small and medium-sized entities (SMEs), 19–20
    variable-interest entities, 483
private universities, 637
probability criterion, 475
profit
    income statement, 44
    intercompany profits. *See* intercompany profits (losses)
    intercompany transactions, 51
    other comprehensive income, 44
    recognition of, 309
    unrealized profits, 51
profit test, 477, 478
property, plant and equipment
    fair value, 270
    IAS 16 - Property, Plant and Equipment, 180, 350
    intercompany land profits. *See* intercompany land profits

intercompany profits in depreciable assets. *See* intercompany profits in depreciable assets
proportionate consolidation, 43, 133, 490–492
proprietary theory, 132, 133
protective rights, 85–86
provincial government. *See* government sector
public companies
  differential reporting options, 18–19
  GAAP, 15–18
  mergers and acquisitions, 72
  publicly accountable enterprise (PAE), 17
Public Sector Accounting Board (PSAB), 20, 681, 682
Public Sector Accounting Handbook, 681
publicly accountable enterprise (PAE), 17
purchase differential, 51
purchase method, 74–75
purchase price, 183
push-down accounting, 73n, 125

Q
Quaker Foods, 120
quantitative threshold, 477

R
receivables, intercompany, 201
recording currency, 520
recoverable amount, 175, 176, 178, 181
related-party transactions, 643
replacement cost accounting (case), 31
reportable operating segments, 477–480
reporting currency, 520
repurchase of shares by subsidiary, 394
research and development (R&D) expenditures (case), 30–31
reserve for encumbrances, 659n
restricted contributions, 647
restricted fund method, 650–651, 652–654, 660–667
restricted resources, 636–637, 652, 654–655
retained earnings
  beginning-of-year, translation of, 584
  consolidated retained earnings, 174, 189, 260, 393, 394–395
  consolidated retained earnings statement, 173–174
  cost method, 189
  cumulative effect of adjustments, 189
  and cumulative net income, 189
  equity method, 394
  and net income, 46
  parent company, 174
revaluation adjustment, 350
revaluation model, 180, 269–271, 350–351
revaluation surplus, 270
revenue
  contributions, 646–647

gross basis, 648
IAS 18 - Revenue, 463
interest revenue, 330, 330n
recognition, gross *vs.* net basis, 648–649
reportable operating segments, 477
revenue recognition principle, 249
segregation, 480
translation of, 584
revenue test, 477, 478
reverse takeovers, 95–99
risk
  economic exposure, 570–571
  foreign-currency exposure, 569
  foreign-currency risk, 569–571
  foreign-currency transactions, 517
  and forward contracts, 532
  transaction exposure, 570
  translation (accounting) exposure, 569–570
Royal Bank of Canada, 568

S
sale of investments, gains and losses on, 53
scholarships, 637
Section PS 1300, 684
Securities and Exchange Commission (SEC)
  reconciliations of net income, 3
  requirements for foreign registrants, 12–13
  U.S. issuers, and IFRS financial statements, 14–15
  use of IFRSs, 12–13
segment disclosures, 43, 476–483, 484
self-sustaining foreign operation, 575, 580–584, 590–593
selling the crown jewels, 73
separate financial statements, 83–84
share capital, translation of, 572
share investments. *See* equity investments
shareholders, transactions with, 398, 401
shareholders' equity
  accumulated other comprehensive income, 580
  acquisition differential, calculation of, 404–405
  investment account, 584
  and net assets, 51n
  non-controlling interest, calculation of, 404–405
  and other comprehensive income (OCI), 46
  reverse takeovers, 97
  subsidiary company, 260f
  translation of items, 580, 584
shares
  see also ownership interest
  block acquisitions of subsidiary, 387–395
  capital structure. *See* capital structure
  common shares, 382, 584
  cumulative preferred shares, 406
  investments. *See* equity investments
  noncumulative preferred shares, 406–407

numerous small purchases, 394
preferred shares, 382, 404–408
repurchase of shares by subsidiary, 394
share purchase form of business combination, 73–74, 87
step purchases, 387–395
Shell Canada, 72
Shoppers Drug Mart, 449
Short Term Convergence Project, 12
SIC. *See* Standing Interpretations Committee (SIC)
Siemens AG, 143–144
significant changes in last two years
  business combinations, 93–94
  consolidated cash flow statements, 414
  consolidated statements on acquisition date, 146
  consolidated statements subsequent to acquisition date, 206
  equity investments, 57
  foreign operations, 600
  foreign-currency transactions, 547–548
  intercompany profits (losses), 273, 341
  joint arrangements, 485
  not-for-profit organizations (NFPOs), 675–676
  ownership interests, 414
  segment disclosure, 485
  special purpose entities, 484–485
significant influence
  see also associates
  associates, investments in, 42, 47
  CICA Handbook, Section 3051, 54–55
  equity method, 42, 388
  guideline for determination, 47
  IAS 28 - Investments in Associates (Equity Method), 47–48
  loss of, 52
  and not-for-profit organizations (NFPOs), 643
  voting shares, 47–48
small and medium-sized entities (SMEs), 19–20
small purchases, numerous, 394
Sobeys, 460
South America, inflation in, 5
special-purpose entities
  Accounting Guideline 15 (AcG-15), 452
  assets, recording of, 454–455
  assets and liabilities, definition of, 453
  and consolidation, 86–87, 450–460
  control, 453
  debt financing, 450
  defined, 450
  disclosure, 457
  "Enron standards," 452
  example, 453–454
  FASB Interpretation No. 46 - Consolidation of Variable Interest Entities, 86
  guaranteed rate of return, 451

implied value, 455
improper use of, 451–452
initial measurement issues, 454–456
liabilities, recording of, 454–455
non-controlling interest (NCI), 455–456
off-balance-sheet financing, 86, 450
private enterprises, 483
purpose and design, 452
risks and rewards, distribution of, 450
SIC 12 - Consolidation, Special-Purpose Entities, 45, 86–87
subsequent consolidation issues, 456
U.S. GAAP differences, 483
variability of returns, 452
variable-interest entity, 450, 451f, 452
speculative forward exchange contract, 527–530, 552f
spot rate, 519, 522
Standing Interpretations Committee (SIC)
SIC 12 - Consolidation, Special-Purpose Entities, 45, 86–87
SIC 13 - Jointly Controlled Entities, Non-monetary Contributions by Venturers, 45, 463
Stanford, 637
start-up operations, 477n
statement of financial position, 44, 648
see also balance sheet
statement of operations, 649
statement of profit or loss, 44
see also income statement
statutory amalgamation, 74
step purchases, 387–395
Stewart, John E., 530n
straight-line method, 199, 200, 322n
strategic investments, 40
subsequent events, 12
subsequent-year comparisons, 201
subsidiary company
see also business combinations; consolidated financial statements; ownership interest
acquired during the year, 201
allocation of acquisition cost, 44
block acquisitions of subsidiary, 387–395
CICA Handbook, Section 1590, 92
consolidation procedures, 50
defined, 71, 83
disposal of subsidiary or portion of subsidiary, 395, 396f
dividend payments to parent company, 383
80-percent-owned subsidiary, 191–198, 215–220
foreign subsidiaries. *See* foreign operations
intercompany inventory profits, 253–263
issue of additional shares to public, 401–403
net assets, purchase of, 577

net assets, revaluation of, 392
non-wholly owned subsidiaries, 131–132
preferred shares outstanding, 404–408
repurchase of shares by subsidiary, 394
reverse takeovers, 96
shareholders' equity, 260f
step purchases, 387–395
total value, 88
trading value of shares, 135–136
wholly owned subsidiaries, 121–131
Sweden, 6

T
takeover. *See* business combinations
takeover defences, 72–73
TAQA, 72
taxable temporary difference, 471
taxation
accounting income, 4
acquisition of asset at price different from tax base, 472–473
capital cost allowance, 472
deferred income tax assets, 78
deferred income taxes, 471–476
and exchange adjustments, 596–597
IAS 12 - Income Taxes, 449, 471, 473, 475
IFRS 12 (Income Taxes), 44
income tax expense, 254, 258, 323, 331
net income, 3
non-consolidated statements, 172
offshore tax havens, 248–249
prepaid taxes, 254, 312
role of, 3–4
temporary differences, 471
technological improvements, 3
Teck Cominco Ltd., 72
temporal method, 571–572, 575, 577, 586
temporary control, 85
temporary differences, 471
10 percent rule, 477
territorial government. *See* government sector
Toronto Symphony Orchestra, 637
Toronto-Dominion Bank, 72
trade surpluses and deficits, 518
transaction exposure, 570
transfer pricing, intercompany, 271–272
translated financial statements
see also foreign operations
on acquisition date, 578, 578f
acquisition differential, 588–589
beginning-of-year retained earnings, 584
common shares, 584
comparative observations of translation methods, 588
consolidated financial statements, preparation of, 583–584, 583f
cost of goods sold, 586
current rate method, 572–573, 577, 586
equity method, 582, 590–591
exchange gains or losses, 586
expenses, 584
IAS 21 - Foreign Exchange Rates, 573–577

illustration, 577–597
monetary items, 584
non-monetary items, 584
purchases, 586
revenue, 584
shareholders' equity items, 580
subsequent to acquisition, 579–586
temporal method, 571–572, 575, 577, 586
translation adjustment, 587f, 591
translation methods, 571–573, 588
units of measure, 577
translation (accounting) exposure, 569–570
translation adjustment, 573, 587f, 591
translation method, 522–523
translation methods, 571–573, 588

U
unamortized acquisition differential, 174, 394f, 402, 412
unfriendly business combinations, 72–73
unit of measure, 577
United Kingdom
euro, 6
inflation levels, 5
private standard-setting body, 4
United States
see also Financial Accounting Standards Board (FASB); Securities and Exchange Commission (SEC)
inflation levels, 5
and international standards, 8
inventory costs, and taxation, 4
net income, 3
United Way/Centraide Ottawa, 674–675f
unrealized losses, 266–267
see also intercompany profits (losses)
unrealized profits, 51
see also intercompany profits (losses)
unrealized profits with associates, 265
unrecognized firm commitment, 535–539
unrestricted contributions, 647
unrestricted net asset balance, 669
unrestricted resources, 636, 652–654, 655–656
upstream transactions, 253–263
U.S. dollar, 518
U.S. Federal Reserve Bank, 518
U.S. GAAP
business combinations, 93
vs. Canadian GAAP, 11
consolidated statements on date of acquisition, 144–145
consolidated statements subsequent to acquisition date, 204
deferred income taxes, 484
equity investments, 56
foreign operations, 599
foreign-currency transactions, 547
vs. IFRSs, 11–15, 16f
intercompany profits (losses), 272, 340
joint arrangements, 484
ownership interests, 413

reconciliation of net income, 3
segment disclosures, 484
special-purpose entities, 483
used depreciable asset, 318–319

V
value in use, 175
variable-interest entity, 450–460
    see also special-purpose entities
venturer, 461, 490*f*
vertical business combination, 71
Vezina, Pierre, 596*n*
Vodaphone Group, 248

W
West Fraser Timber Co. Ltd., 143
white knight, 73
wholly owned subsidiaries
    acquisition differential, 122*f*, 125, 126*f*
    acquisition method, 121
    consolidated statements on acquisition
        date, 121–131
    consolidated statements subsequent to
        acquisition date, 183–190
    direct approach, 123–124, 124*f*, 128,
        128*f*, 131*f*
    elimination entries, 130–131

end of year 1, 184–187, 186*f*
end of year 2, 187–190
equity method, 128
goodwill, 128–131
income statement in year of acquisition,
    124–125
negative acquisition differential, 128
negative goodwill, 126–128, 128*f*
push-down accounting, 125
subsidiary formed by parent, 125, 125*n*
Winnipeg Foundation, 637
working paper approach, 211–220